HUMAN RESOURCE MANAGEMENT

HUMAN RESOURCE MANAGEMENT

ELEVENTH EDITION

Gary Dessler

Florida International University

Upper Saddle River, NJ 07458

Library of Congress Cataloging-in-Publication Data

Dessler, Gary
   Human resource management / Gary Dessler. — 11th ed.
      p. cm.
   Includes bibliographical references and index.
   ISBN 0-13-174617-0 (alk. paper)
   1. Personnel management. I. Title.
   HF5549.D4379 2008
   658.3—dc22

                                     2007034147

Executive Editor: *Bob Horan*
Editor-in-Chief: *David Parker*
Product Development Manager: *Ashley Santora*
Assistant Editor, Media: *Kristen Varina*
Assistant Editor: *Denise Vaughn*
Senior Marketing Manager: *Jodi Bassett*
Marketing Assistant: *Ian Gold*
Senior Managing Editor: *Judy Leale*
Associate Managing Editor: *Renata Butera*
Project Manager: *Kelly Warsak*
Manager, Rights & Permissions: *Charles Morris*
Senior Operations Supervisor: *Arnold Vila*
Senior Art Director: *Pat Smythe*
Interior Design: *Brian Salisbury*

Cover Design: *Brian Salisbury*
Cover Image: *Andrew Stanton/Stock Illustration
      Source, Inc.—Images.com*
Illustration (Interior): *ICC Macmillan Inc.*
Director, Image Resource Center: *Melinda Patelli*
Manager, Rights and Permissions: *Zina Arabia*
Manager, Visual Research: *Beth Brenzel*
Manager, Cover Visual Research & Permissions: *Karen Sanatar*
Image Permission Coordinator: *Angelique Sharps*
Composition: *ICC Macmillan Inc.*
Full-Service Project Management: *ICC Macmillan Inc.*
Printer/Binder: *R. R. Donnelly & Sons Company*
Cover Printer: *Phoenix Color Corp.*
Typeface: 10/12 Times

Credits and acknowledgments borrowed from other sources and reproduced, with permission, in this textbook appear on appropriate page within text.

Microsoft® and Windows® are registered trademarks of the Microsoft Corporation in the U.S.A. and other countries. Screen shots and icons reprinted with permission from the Microsoft Corporation. This book is not sponsored or endorsed by or affiliated with the Microsoft Corporation.

Pearson Education Ltd.
Pearson Education Singapore, Pte. Ltd.
Pearson Education, Canada, Ltd.
Pearson Education–Japan

Pearson Education Australia PTY, Limited
Pearson Education North Asia Ltd.
Pearson Educación de Mexico, S.A. de C.V.
Pearson Education Malaysia, Pte. Ltd.

10 9 8 7 6 5 4 3 2
ISBN-13: 978-0-13-174617-6
ISBN-10: 0-13-174617-0

Dedicated to My Mother

BRIEF CONTENTS

Appendices

CONTENTS

Part 3   Training and Development   291

Chapter 8 Training and Developing Employees   291

Appendices

PREFACE

Human Resource Management provides students in human resource management courses and practicing managers with a complete, comprehensive review of essential personnel management concepts and techniques in a highly readable and understandable form. As this new edition goes to press, I feel even more strongly than I did when I wrote the first that all managers—not just HR managers—need a strong foundation in HR/personnel management concepts and techniques to do their jobs. Because all managers do have personnel-related responsibilities, I again wrote *Human Resource Management,* 11th edition, for all students of management, not just those who will someday carry the title Human Resource Manager. This edition thus continues to focus on practical applications that all managers need to deal with their HR-related responsibilities. This publication is designed to provide accurate and authoritative information in regard to the subject matter covered, but it is not intended to be a source of legal or other professional advice for any purpose.

Everyone involved in creating this book—not just I as the author, but also the many people on the Pearson Prentice Hall editorial, sales, and production teams—is very proud of what we've achieved. *Human Resource Management* is now the number one or one of the top selling books in this market, and as you read this students around the world are using it in many languages, including French, Spanish, Indonesian, Russian, and both traditional and simplified Chinese.

KEY ELEVENTH EDITION FEATURES

We've retained and/or modified several of the popular in-text features from the 10th edition.

When You're on Your Own: HR for Line Managers and Entrepreneurs

Aimed especially at line and small-business managers, the *When You're on Your Own* features show managers how, for instance, to recruit and train new employees when their HR department is too busy to help, how to avoid committing management malpractice, how to develop a workable pay plan and testing program, and how to create a simple training program.

Improving Productivity Through HRIS

HR managers increasingly rely on information technology to help support their companies' strategic aims. Special integrated *Improving Productivity Through HRIS* sections throughout the chapters illustrate how managers use technology to improve the productivity of HR. For example, one Chapter 6 section explains how managers use applicant-tracking systems to compile web-based resumes, to test and prescreen applicants online, and to discover candidates' hidden talents.

Know Your Employment Law

Today, virtually every HR-related decision managers make has legal implications, a fact underscored by the Human Resource Certification Institute's emphasis, in its exams, on candidates for certification having a solid knowledge of employment law. Most of this edition's chapters therefore contain one or more *Know Your Employment Law* features. For example, in Chapter 6 this feature explains what line managers should know about the federal and state laws governing how employers acquire and use applicants' and employees' background information. This includes, for instance, disclosure and authorization, certification, providing copies of reports, and notice of adverse action.

The New Workforce

Because globalization and diversity are central HR issues today, these new *The New Workforce* features focus on the special issues involved in managing a diverse workforce. For example, the one in Chapter 6 (selection) explains gender issues in employee testing. These features replace the 10th edition's broader *The New Workplace* features.

Integrated Strategic HR

The intensely competitive nature of business today means human resource managers must be able to defend their plans and contributions in strategic and measurable terms. This textbook is the first to provide specific, actionable explanations and illustrations showing how to use devices such as the HR Scorecard process (explained fully in Chapter 3) to measure HR's effectiveness in achieving the company's strategic aims. A continuing "Hotel Paris" case after each chapter gives readers practice in applying strategic human resource management in action. I cover the core concepts of strategic HR in Chapter 1, for adopters who choose not to cover Chapter 3.

WHAT'S NEW IN THE ELEVENTH EDITION?

The user feedback, reviews, and experience with the 10th edition were very favorable, so I have kept the same chapter outline for the 11th edition; moving from the 10th to the 11th edition should therefore be seamless, and I'll be posting on the book's Web site information for professors regarding specific chapter-by-chapter additions and deletions. There are however several important improvements to this 11th edition. We redesigned the book. We've spread out the text and features to make the pages more readable; that added about 60 pages to the 11th edition. However, the number of words in each chapter is about the same as in the previous edition. The previous edition had Hotel Paris strategy examples within the body of each chapter. I rewrote these examples as cases and they now appear as end-of-chapter cases, after each chapter. Three other improvements follow.

Completely Updated

First, I completely updated the material throughout. You'll find hundreds of *new examples and research references and topics*. I also updated for this edition many of the book's *figures and tables*.

New Video and Comprehensive Cases

Second, to provide faculty members with a richer and more flexible textbook, I've added 11 new video cases, two (or more) each at the end of each of the book's five Parts, and five new, longer, comprehensive cases in an appendix at the end of the book. The *in-book video cases* provide a basis for in-class discussion of 11 videos available to adopters. I wrote the five new *comprehensive cases* to provide students and faculty with an opportunity to discuss and apply the book's concepts and techniques by addressing more comprehensive and realistic case-based issues. You'll find them at the end of the book, in Appendix B.

New SHRM Guidelines In-Book Study Guide

Third, SHRM, the Society for Human Resource Management, recently published its new HR curriculum guidelines. In a nutshell, they contain SHRM's recommended curriculum objectives and guidelines regarding the human resource management curriculum—relevant content, personal competencies, and business knowledge. To enable faculty members who may want to address one or more of these new guidelines to do so, I've created a new and unique brief in-textbook SHRM study guide for this edition. It contains, among other things, SHRM guidelines. It contains discussion and case questions you can use to help cover the new SHRM guidelines' relevant topics and behavioral objectives. It is after Chapter 17, in a separate Appendix A.

Note that this new SHRM study guide is in addition to the SHRM Certification material we included in the 10th edition (and include again here in Chapter 17). The profession of HR management is becoming increasingly demanding. Responding to these new demands, thousands of HR managers have successfully passed the certification exams offered by the Human Resource Certification Institute (HRCI), thus earning the designations Professional in HR (PHR) and Senior Professional in HR (SPHR). This edition again contains, in each chapter, an *HRCI-related exercise* students can use to apply their knowledge of that chapter's material within the HRCI exam context, as well as a comprehensive listing of the topics that these exams address, also in this SHRM guidelines appendix.

SUPPLEMENTS

Instructor's Manual: This comprehensive supplement provides extensive instructional support. The instructor's manual includes a course planning guide and chapter guides for each chapter in the text. The chapter guides include a chapter outline, lecture notes, answers to discussion questions, definitions to key terms, and references to the figures, tables, cases, and PPTs in the text. The IM also includes a Video Guide.

Test Item File: The test item file contains approximately 110 questions per chapter including multiple choice, true/false, and short-answer/essay-type questions. Suggested answers, difficulty ratings, AACSB call-outs, and page number references are included for all questions.

Instructor's Resource Center (IRC) on CD: This supplement gives instructors access to the Instructor's Manual, Test Item File, and PowerPoints in downloadable format. Useful student and instructor links are also found on the IRC on CD. If you ever need assistance, our dedicated technical support team is ready to help with the media supplements that accompany this text. Visit www.247.prenhall.com for answers to frequently asked questions and toll-free user support phone numbers.

Videos on DVD: The DVD Video features video clips which bring HR issues covered in *Human Resource Management,* 11th edition to students' attention and draw them into the text materials. Clips include, for example, "Recruitment and Placement" and "Ernst and Young."

Companion Website: This text's Companion Website at www.prenhall.com/dessler contains valuable resources for both students and professors, including access to a student version of the PowerPoint package and an online Study Guide.

VangoNotes in MP3 Format

Students can study on the go with VangoNotes, chapter reviews in downloadable MP3 format that offer brief audio segments for each chapter:

Big Ideas: The vital ideas in each chapter

Practice Test: Lets students know if they need to keep studying

Key Terms: Audio "flashcards" that review key concepts and terms

Rapid Review: A quick drill session—helpful right before tests

Students can learn more at www.vangonotes.com

ACKNOWLEDGMENTS

While I am of course solely responsible for the content in *Human Resource Management*, I want to thank several people for their assistance. This includes first, the faculty who reviewed this and the 10th edition:

Scott Boyar, *University of South Alabama*
Cynthia F. Cohen, *University of South Florida*
Larry Dionne, *Robert Morris College*
Kim Gower, *Virginia Commonwealth University*
Gundars Kaupins, *Boise State University*
P.C. Smith, *University of Tulsa*

At Pearson/Prentice Hall, I am again grateful for the support and dedicated assistance of a great publishing team. David Parker, Editor-in-Chief, Bob Horan, Executive Editor, Denise Vaughn, Assistant Editor, Judy Leale, Senior Managing Editor, and Kelly Warsak, Project Manager, along with Winifred Sanchez at ICC Macmillan Inc. worked hard to make this a book that we're all very proud of. Thanks to Jodi Bassett, Senior Marketing Manager, and the Pearson sales staff, without whose efforts this book would no doubt languish on the shelf. I want to thank Jenny Sang and David Zhang and their colleagues in Pearson International for all their efforts and effectiveness in managing the internationalization of this book in Asia.

At home, I want to acknowledge the support of my wife Claudia during the many hours I spent working on this edition. My son Derek, certainly still the best people manager I know and a source of enormous pride, and my daughter-in-law Lisa were always in my thoughts as I worked on these pages. My mother Laura was always a great source of support and encouragement and would have been very proud to see this book.

1 Introduction to Human Resource Management

Several years ago, Shanghai's Portman Hotel was good but not exceptional. Employee and guest satisfaction ratings averaged 70% to 80%. Finances were average.[1] When it took over the hotel recently, the Ritz-Carlton company and the hotel's new general manager Mark DeCocinis set out to make the Portman a premier property. Their strategy for doing so was to dramatically improve customer service. Mr. DeCocinis knew the hotel's employees were crucial to such an effort: "We're a service business, and service comes only from people." He introduced the Ritz-Carlton company's human resource system. Their efforts paid off. In the past few years, the Portman Ritz-Carlton was named the "Best Employer in Asia." The hotel now scores 98% in employee satisfaction. •

After studying this chapter, you should be able to:

1 Explain what human resource management is and how it relates to the management process.
2 Give at least eight examples of how all managers can use human resource management concepts and techniques.
3 Illustrate the human resources responsibilities of line and staff (HR) managers.
4 Provide a good example that illustrates HR's role in formulating and executing company strategy.
5 Write a short essay that addresses the topic: Why metrics and measurement are crucial to today's HR managers.
6 Outline the plan of this book.

The main purpose of this chapter is to provide you with an introductory overview of what human resource management is, and of why it is important to all managers. We'll see that human resource management activities such as hiring, training, compensating, appraising, and developing employees are part of every manager's job. And we'll see that human resource management is also a separate business function, usually with its own human resource or "HR" manager. The main topics we'll cover include the manager's human resource management jobs, global and competitive trends affecting human resource management, and how managers use modern human resource management methods to create high-performance companies and work systems.

HUMAN RESOURCE MANAGEMENT AT WORK

❶ Explain what human resource management is and how it relates to the management process.

What Is Human Resource Management?

Most experts agree that there are five basic functions all managers perform: planning, organizing, staffing, leading, and controlling. In total, these functions represent the **management process**. Some of the specific activities involved in each function include:

management process
The five basic functions of planning, organizing, staffing, leading, and controlling.

- *Planning.* Establishing goals and standards; developing rules and procedures; developing plans and forecasting.
- *Organizing.* Giving each subordinate a specific task; establishing departments; delegating authority to subordinates; establishing channels of authority and communication; coordinating the work of subordinates.
- *Staffing.* Determining what type of people should be hired; recruiting prospective employees; selecting employees; setting performance standards; compensating employees; evaluating performance; counseling employees; training and developing employees.
- *Leading.* Getting others to get the job done; maintaining morale; motivating subordinates.
- *Controlling.* Setting standards such as sales quotas, quality standards, or production levels; checking to see how actual performance compares with these standards; taking corrective action as needed.

In this book, we are going to focus on one of these functions—the staffing, personnel management, or *human resource management (HRM)* function. **Human resource management** is the process of acquiring, training, appraising, and compensating employees, and of attending to their labor relations, health and safety, and fairness concerns. The topics we'll discuss should therefore provide you with the concepts and techniques you need to perform the "people" or personnel aspects of your management job. These include:

human resource management (HRM)
The policies and practices involved in carrying out the "people" or human resource aspects of a management position, including recruiting, screening, training, rewarding, and appraising.

- *Conducting job analyses* (determining the nature of each employee's job)
- *Planning labor needs* and *recruiting* job candidates
- *Selecting* job candidates
- *Orienting and training* new employees
- *Managing wages and salaries* (compensating employees)
- *Providing incentives and benefits*
- *Appraising performance*
- *Communicating* (interviewing, counseling, disciplining)
- *Training and developing* managers
- *Building employee commitment*

And what a manager should know about:

- Equal opportunity and affirmative action
- Employee health and safety
- Handling grievances and labor relations

Why Is Human Resource Management Important to All Managers?

Why are these concepts and techniques important to all managers? Perhaps it's easier to answer this by listing some of the personnel mistakes you *don't* want to make while managing. For example, you don't want to:

- Hire the wrong person for the job
- Experience high turnover
- Have your people not doing their best
- Waste time with useless interviews
- Have your company taken to court because of discriminatory actions
- Have your company cited under federal occupational safety laws for unsafe practices
- Have some employees think their salaries are unfair and inequitable relative to others in the organization
- Allow a lack of training to undermine your department's effectiveness
- Commit any unfair labor practices

Carefully studying this book will help you avoid mistakes like these. And, more important, it can help ensure that you get results—through people. Remember that you can do everything else right as a manager—lay brilliant plans, draw clear organization charts, set up modern assembly lines, and use sophisticated accounting controls—but still fail, by hiring the wrong people or by not motivating subordinates. On the other hand, many managers—presidents, generals, governors, supervisors—have been successful even with inadequate plans, organizations, or controls. They were successful because they had the knack of hiring the right people for the right jobs and motivating, appraising, and developing them. Remember as you read this book that *getting results* is the bottom line of managing, and that, as a manager, you will have to get those results through people. As one company president summed up:

> For many years it has been said that capital is the bottleneck for a developing industry. I don't think this any longer holds true. I think it's the work force and the company's inability to recruit and maintain a good work force that does constitute the bottleneck for production. I don't know of any major project backed by good ideas, vigor, and enthusiasm that has been stopped by a shortage of cash. I do know of industries whose growth has been partly stopped or hampered because they can't maintain an efficient and enthusiastic labor force, and I think this will hold true even more in the future.[2]

We'll see in a moment that intensified global competition, technological advances, and the changing nature of work mean that at no time in our history has that president's statement been truer than it is today.

Line and Staff Aspects of Human Resource Management

> 2 Give at least eight examples of how all managers can use human resource management concepts and techniques.

All managers are, in a sense, human resource managers, since they all get involved in activities like recruiting, interviewing, selecting, and training. Yet most firms also have human resource departments with their own top managers. How do the duties of this human resource manager and his or her staff relate to "line" managers' human resource duties? Let's answer this question, starting with a short definition of line versus staff authority.

authority
The right to make decisions, direct others' work, and give orders.

Authority is the right to make decisions, to direct the work of others, and to give orders. In management, we usually distinguish between line authority and staff authority.

Line authority gives the manager the right to issue orders.

Line authority gives managers the right (or authority) to *issue orders* to other managers or employees. It creates a superior–subordinate relationship. **Staff authority** gives the manager the right (authority) to *advise* other managers or employees. It creates an advisory relationship. **Line managers** have line authority. **Staff managers** have staff authority. The latter generally cannot issue orders down the chain of command (except in their own departments).

In popular usage, managers associate line managers with managing functions (like sales or production) that the company needs to exist. Staff managers generally run departments that are advisory or supportive, like purchasing, human resource management, and quality control. This distinction makes sense as long as the "staff" department is, in fact, advisory. However, strictly speaking, it is not the type of department the person is in charge of or its name that determines if the manager in charge is line or staff. It is the nature of the relationship. The line manager can issue orders. The staff manager can advise.

Human resource managers are staff managers. They assist and advise line managers in areas like recruiting, hiring, and compensation. However, line managers still have human resource duties.

line authority
The authority exerted by an HR manager by directing the activities of the people in his or her own department and in service areas (like the plant cafeteria).

staff authority
Staff authority gives the manager the right (authority) to advise other managers or employees.

line manager
A manager who is authorized to direct the work of subordinates and is responsible for accomplishing the organization's tasks.

staff manager
A manager who assists and advises line managers.

Line Managers' Human Resource Duties

The direct handling of people has always been an integral part of every line manager's duties, from president down to first-line supervisor. For example, one major company outlines its line supervisors' responsibilities for effective human resource management under these general headings:

1. Placing the right person on the right job
2. Starting new employees in the organization (orientation)
3. Training employees for jobs that are new to them
4. Improving the job performance of each person
5. Gaining creative cooperation and developing smooth working relationships
6. Interpreting the company's policies and procedures
7. Controlling labor costs
8. Developing the abilities of each person
9. Creating and maintaining department morale
10. Protecting employees' health and physical condition

In small organizations, line managers may carry out all these personnel duties unassisted. But as the organization grows, they need the assistance, specialized knowledge, and advice of a separate human resource staff. The human resource department provides this specialized assistance.

Human Resource Manager's Duties

In providing this specialized assistance, the human resource manager carries out three distinct functions:

1. *A line function.* The human resource manager directs the activities of the people in his or her own department and in related service areas (like the plant cafeteria). In other words, he or she exerts line authority within the HR department. While they generally

implied authority
The authority exerted by an HR manager by virtue of others' knowledge that he or she has access to top management (in areas like testing and affirmative action).

functional control
The authority exerted by an HR manager as coordinator of personnel activities.

employee advocacy
HR must take responsibility for clearly defining how management should be treating employees, make sure employees have the mechanisms required to contest unfair practices, and represent the interests of employees within the framework of its primary obligation to senior management.

can't wield line authority outside, they are likely to exert **implied authority**. This is because line managers know the human resource manager has top management's ear in areas like testing and affirmative action.

2. *A coordinative function.* Human resource managers also coordinate personnel activities, a duty often referred to as **functional authority** (or functional control). Here he or she acts as the "right arm of the top executive" to ensure that line managers are implementing the firm's human resource policies and practices (for example, adhering to its sexual harassment policies).

3. *Staff (assist and advise) functions.* Assisting and advising line managers is the heart of the human resource manager's job. He or she *advises* the CEO to better understand the personnel aspects of the company's strategic options. HR *assists* in hiring, training, evaluating, rewarding, counseling, promoting, and firing employees. It administers the various benefit programs (health and accident insurance, retirement, vacation, and so on). It helps line managers comply with equal employment and occupational safety laws, and plays an important role in handling grievances and labor relations. It carries out an *innovator* role, by providing up-to-date information on current trends and new methods for better utilizing the company's employees, or human resources. It plays an **employee advocacy** role, by helping to define how management should be treating employees.

The size of the human resource department reflects the size of the company. For a very large company, an organization chart like the one in Figure 1-1 would be typical, containing a full complement of specialists for each HR function. At the other extreme, the human resource team for a small manufacturer may contain just five or six staff, and have an organization similar to that in Figure 1-2. There is *generally* about one human resource employee per 100 company employees.

Examples of human resource management specialties include:

• *Recruiters.* Search for qualified job applicants.
• *Equal employment opportunity (EEO) coordinators.* Investigate and resolve EEO grievances, examine organizational practices for potential violations, and compile and submit EEO reports.
• *Job analysts.* Collect and examine information about jobs to prepare job descriptions.
• *Compensation managers.* Develop compensation plans and handle the employee benefits program.
• *Training specialists.* Plan, organize, and direct training activities.
• *Labor relations specialists.* Advise management on all aspects of union–management relations.

❸ Illustrate the human resources responsibilities of line and staff (HR) managers.

Cooperative Line and Staff HR Management: An Example

Because both line managers and human resource managers have human resource management duties, it is useful to ask, "Exactly which HR duties are carried out by line managers, and by staff managers?" There is no single division of responsibilities we could apply across the board in all organizations, but we can make some generalizations.

The most important generalization is that the relationship is generally cooperative. For example, in recruiting and hiring, the line manager describes the qualifications employees need to fill specific positions. Then the human resource team takes over. They develop sources of qualified applicants, and conduct initial screening interviews. They administer the appropriate tests. Then they refer the best applicants to the line manager, who interviews and selects the ones he or she wants. In training, the line manager again describes what he or she expects the employee to be able to do. Then the human resource team devises a training program, which the line manager then (usually) administers.

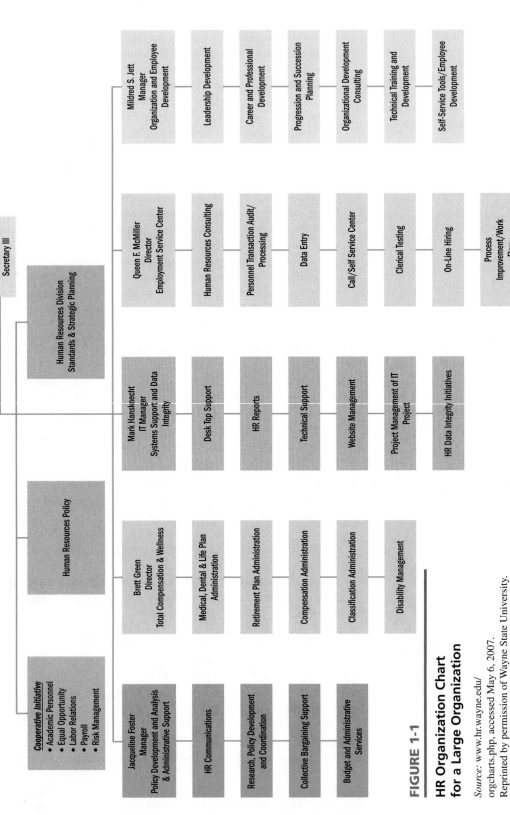

FIGURE 1-1

HR Organization Chart
for a Large Organization

Source: www.hr.wayne.edu/
orgcharts.php, accessed May 6, 2007.
Reprinted by permission of Wayne State University.

FIGURE 1-2

HR Organizational Chart (Small Company)

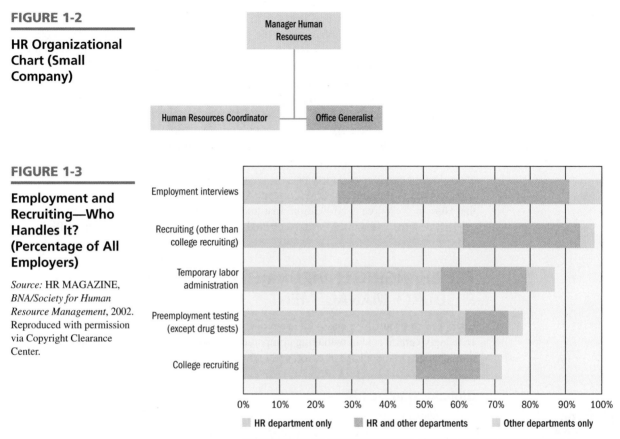

FIGURE 1-3

Employment and Recruiting—Who Handles It? (Percentage of All Employers)

Source: HR MAGAZINE, *BNA/Society for Human Resource Management,* 2002. Reproduced with permission via Copyright Clearance Center.

Note: Length of bars represents prevalence of activity among all surveyed employers.

Some activities are usually HR's alone. For example, 60% of firms assign to human resources the exclusive responsibility for preemployment testing, 75% assign it college recruiting, and 80% assign it insurance benefits administration. But employers split most activities, such as employment interviews, performance appraisal, skills training, job descriptions, and disciplinary procedures, between HR and line managers.[3]

Figure 1-3 illustrates the typical HR–line management partnership. For example, HR alone typically handles interviewing in about 25% of firms, but in about 60% of firms, HR and the other hiring departments both get involved in interviewing.

In summary, human resource management is part of every manager's job. Whether you're a first-line supervisor, middle manager, or president; or whether you're a production manager or county manager (or HR manager), getting results through committed people is the name of the game. And to do this, you will need a good working knowledge of the human resource management concepts and techniques in this book.

From Line Manager to HR Manager

Another reason to be familiar with this book's contents is that you may well make a planned (or unplanned) stopover some day as a human resource manager. A survey by the Center for Effective Organizations at the University of Southern California found that about one-fourth of large U.S. businesses appointed managers with no HR experience as their top human resource management executives. Reasons given include the fact that these people may find it easier to give the firms' human resource management efforts a more strategic emphasis, and the possibility that they may sometimes be better equipped to integrate the firm's HR efforts with the rest of the business.[4] It's not unusual at all for companies to promote their line executives through HR on their way up the corporate ladder. For example, after spending about a year and a half as Wal-Mart's chief human resource officer, the company promoted Lawrence Jackson to run its global procurement division.[5]

However, most top HR executives do have previous human resources experience. About 80% of those in one survey worked their way up within HR.[6] About 37% of those were in employment/recruitment, and so were mostly involved in activities like recruiting and selecting employees. Thirty percent were in labor relations (union–management), and 27% worked in training and development. About 17% of these HR executives had earned the Human Resource Certification Institute's senior professional in human resources (SPHR) designation, and 13% were certified professionals in human resources (PHR).

THE CHANGING ENVIRONMENT OF HUMAN RESOURCE MANAGEMENT

Changes are occurring today that are requiring human resource managers to play an increasingly central role in managing companies. These changes or trends include globalization, changes in the nature of work, and technology.

Globalization Trends

globalization
The tendency of firms to extend their sales, ownership, and/or manufacturing to new markets abroad.

Globalization is the tendency of firms to extend their sales, ownership, and/or manufacturing to new markets abroad. Sony, Apple, Zara, Nike, and Mercedes Benz are some firms that market all over the world. Toyota produces Camrys in Georgetown, Kentucky. Dell produces computers in China. In turn, globalized markets and production mean that globalized *ownership* makes more sense. In early 2006 a Dubai-based firm tried unsuccessfully to buy ownership of the company that manages several U.S. ports, but gave up after Congress resisted.

Companies expand abroad for several reasons. *Sales expansion* is one. Thus, Google recently expanded its China presence by initiating its Google China instant messaging service there. Wal-Mart is opening stores in South America. Dell, knowing that China will soon be the world's second biggest market for PCs, is aggressively building plants and selling there.

Firms also go abroad for other reasons. Some manufacturers seek *new foreign products* and services to sell, and to *cut labor costs*. Thus, Florida apparel manufacturers design and cut fabrics in Miami, and then have the actual products assembled in Central America, where labor costs are relatively low. Sometimes, it's the prospect of *forming partnerships* that drive firms to do business with firms from abroad. Several years ago, IBM sold its PC division to the Chinese firm Lenovo, in part to cement firmer ties with the booming China market. Whatever the reason, doing business internationally is big business today. For example, the total value of U.S. imports rose from $799 million in 1994 to $135 *billion* recently; exports rose from $702 million to $88 billion in the same period.

Globalization's Implications   For business people, globalization's essential characteristic is this: More globalization means more competition, and more competition means more pressure to be "world-class"—to lower costs, to make employees more productive, and to do things better and less expensively. As one expert puts it, "the bottom line is that

Many products like these Dell computers are produced worldwide.

the growing integration of the world economy into a single, huge marketplace is increasing the intensity of competition in a wide range of manufacturing and service industries."[7]

Because of this, globalization brings both benefits and threats. For consumers it means lower prices and higher quality on practically everything from computers to cars to air travel, but also the prospect of working harder, and perhaps having less secure jobs. (*Job outsourcing*—having employees abroad do jobs that, say, Americans formerly did—is one such threat. For example, IBM shifted several hundred systems analysis jobs abroad. Figure 1-4 shows that between 2005 and 2015, about three million U.S. jobs, ranging from office support and computer jobs to management, sales, and even legal jobs, will likely move offshore.)[8] For business owners globalizing means benefits like reaching millions of new consumers, but also the considerable threat of facing new and powerful global competitors at home.

Both workers and companies therefore have to work harder and smarter than they did without globalization.[9] We'll see later in this chapter, and in this book, how human resource management helps workers and companies do this.

FIGURE 1-4

Employment Exodus: Projected Loss of Jobs and Wages

Source: Michael Schroeder, "States Fight Exodus of Jobs," *Wall Street Journal*, June 3, 2003, p. 84. Reproduced with permission of Dow Jones & Co. Inc. via Copyright Clearance Center.

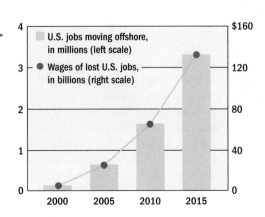

Technological Trends

The Spanish retailer Zara doesn't need the expensive inventories that burden competitors like The Gap. Zara operates its own Internet-based worldwide distribution network, linked to the checkout registers at its stores around the world. This lets it continuously monitor store sales. When its headquarters in Spain sees a garment "flying" out of a store, Zara's computerized manufacturing system swings into action. It dyes the required fabric, cuts and manufactures the item, and speeds it to that store within days.

Like Zara, few people or businesses do business today like they did even three or four years ago. We use PDAs to communicate with the office, and plan trips, manage money, and custom-build and order new computers online. Companies use virtual online communities to improve efficiency. For example, to win a $300 million navy ship deal, Lockheed-Martin established a virtual design environment with about 200 global suppliers, via a private internet existing entirely outside the firewalls of the individual companies.

Trends in the Nature of Work

One implication is that technology has also had a huge impact on how people work, and on the skills and training today's workers need.

High-Tech Jobs For example, skilled machinist Chad Toulouse illustrates the modern blue-collar worker. After an 18-week training course, this former college student now works as a team leader in a plant where about 40% of the machines are automated. In older plants, machinists would manually control machines that cut chunks of metal into things like engine parts. Today, Chad and his team spend much of their time typing commands into computerized machines that create precision parts for products including water pumps. Like other modern machinists, he earns about $45,000 per year (including overtime).[10] More and more traditional factory jobs are going high-tech. As the U.S. government's Occupational Outlook Quarterly put it, "knowledge-intensive high tech manufacturing in such industries as aerospace, computers, telecommunications, home electronics, pharmaceuticals, and medical instruments" are replacing factory jobs in steel, auto, rubber, and textiles.[11]

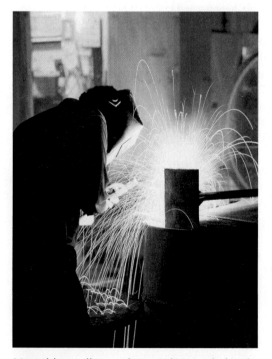

Many blue-collar workers no longer do hard physical labor with dangerous machinery like this: Instead, Chad Toulouse spends most of his time as a team leader typing commands into computerized machines.

Service Jobs Technology is not the only trend driving the change from "brawn to brains." Today over two-thirds of the U.S. workforce is employed in producing and delivering services, not products. Between 2004 and 2014, almost all the 19 million new jobs added in the U.S. will be in services, not in goods-producing industries.[12]

Several things account for this.[13] With global competition, more manufacturing jobs are shifting to low-wage countries. For example, Levi Strauss, one of the last major clothing manufacturers in the United States, closed the last of its American plants a few years ago. There has also been a dramatic increase in productivity that lets manufacturers produce more with fewer workers. Just-in-time manufacturing techniques link daily manufacturing schedules more precisely to customer demand, thus squeezing waste out of the system and reducing inventory needs. As manufacturers integrate Internet-based customer ordering with just-in-time manufacturing systems, scheduling becomes even more precise. More manufacturers are partnering with their suppliers to create integrated supply chains. For example, when a customer orders a Dell computer, the same Internet message that informs Dell's assembly line to produce the order also signals the video screen and keyboard manufacturers to prepare for UPS to pick up their parts at a particular time. The net effect is that manufacturers have been squeezing slack and inefficiencies out of the entire production system, allowing companies to produce more products with fewer employees. So, in America and much of Europe, manufacturing jobs are down, and service jobs up.

Knowledge Work and Human Capital In general, the best jobs that remain require more education and more skills. For example, we saw that automation and just-in-time manufacturing systems mean that even manufacturing jobs require more reading, mathematics, and communication skills than before.[14]

human capital
The knowledge, education, training, skills, and expertise of a firm's workers.

For managers, this means a growing emphasis on knowledge workers like skilled machinist Chad Toulouse, and therefore on *human capital*.[15] **Human capital** refers to the knowledge, education, training, skills, and expertise of a firm's workers.[16] Today, as management guru Peter Drucker predicted several years ago, "the center of gravity in employment is moving fast from manual and clerical workers to knowledge workers. . . ."[17]

Nature of Work: Implications for HR Because it is the human resource function that traditionally recruits, selects, trains, and compensates employees, changes like these make employers highly reliant on effective human resource management. For example, the key to effectively utilizing all that new technology is usually not the technology but the people. One bank installed special software that made it easier for customer service representatives to handle customers' inquiries. Seeking to capitalize on the new software, the bank upgraded the customer service representatives' jobs. The bank gave them new training, taught them how to sell more of the bank's services, gave them more authority to make decisions, and raised their wages. Here, the new computer system dramatically improved profitability.

A second bank installed a similar system, but did not change the workers' jobs. Here, the system helped the service reps handle a few more calls. But this bank saw none of the big performance gains the first bank had gotten by turning its reps into motivated, highly trained sales people.[18] The moral is that today's employers need more sophisticated human resource management selection, training, pay, and employee fairness practices than did their predecessors, ones that focus on improving performance through motivated, committed employees.[19]

Workforce Demographic Trends

At the same time, workforce demographic trends are making finding and hiring good employees more of a challenge. Labor force growth is not expected to keep pace with job growth, with an estimated shortfall of about 14 million college educated workers by 2020.[20]

Most notably, the labor force is getting older. As the baby boomers born between 1946 and 1960 start leaving the labor force in the next few years, employers will face what one study calls a "severe" labor shortage, and will have to "rethink attitudes toward older workers and reexamine a range of established practices, from retirement rules to employee benefits."[21]

The problem is that about 11% fewer Americans were born between 1966 and 1985 than were born in the 20 years after World War II. There are thus fewer people to replace the retiring baby boomers. Furthermore, over the past 50 or so years, the proportion of women in the workforce has risen dramatically, but has now stopped growing. America thus can't depend on the entry of women into the labor force to counterbalance the exiting baby boomers.

Overall, the U.S. workforce's demographics are becoming older and more multi-ethnic.[22] In the years 2004–2014, the white labor force will grow by 7%, as compared with blacks (17%), Asians (32%), and others (30%). The labor force participation rate of women, having increased from about 40% 50 years ago to about 60% today, will remain at about 60% through 2014. As the baby-boom generation ages, the number of people in the labor force age 55 to 64 will increase by about 7 million through 2014.

Employers are particularly focusing on the aging of the workforce, the growing numbers of workers with eldercare responsibilities, and high rates of immigration.[23] With the aging of its workers, "America is facing a demographic shift as significant as the massive entry of women into the workforce that began the 1960s."[24] From the 1970s through the 1990s, many employers improved their competitive positions with policies (such as more flexible work hours) that attracted more women to the workforce. Employers will now have to take similar steps to fill the openings left by retiring employees—probably by encouraging them to stay, or rehiring them.[25]

> ④ Provide a good example that illustrates HR's role in formulating and executing company strategy.

THE CHANGING ROLE OF HUMAN RESOURCE MANAGEMENT

With these trends, the human resource manager's job has grown broader and more strategic over time. In the earliest firms, "personnel" first took over hiring and firing from supervisors, ran the payroll department, and administered benefit plans. As technology in areas like testing and interviewing began to emerge, the personnel department began to play an expanded role in employee selection, training, and promotion.[26] The emergence of union legislation in the 1930s added "protecting the firm in its interaction with unions" to the personnel department's responsibilities. Then, as new equal employment legislation created the potential for discrimination-related lawsuits and penalties, personnel's advice and oversight became even more indispensable.[27] Today, globalization, technological, and nature of work trends mean that human resource managers have taken on several new responsibilities. The first is that employers expect their human resource functions to be more strategic.

Strategic Human Resource Management

Several years ago, Wisconsin-based Signicast Corp.'s president, Terry Lutz, and his board decided to build a new, computerized plant. Signicast produces metal parts from a casting process. The basic process is ancient, although Signicast has improved it dramatically. To compete, the firm needed the new, automated plant. Mr. Lutz and his team understood that "in the real world, new automation technology requires a new kind of employee." They knew the computerized plant was useless without employees who could work in teams, manage their own work, and run the plant's computerized equipment. Lutz and his management team relied on Signicast's human resource management unit to select, train, and organize the tech-friendly people the new plant required.[28] By formulating and executing the hiring and other personnel practices Signicast needed to make the plant a success, the human resources team was supporting Signicast's new strategy. It was thus engaging in strategic human resource management.

strategic plan
A strategic plan is the company's plan for how it will match its internal strengths and weaknesses with external opportunities and threats in order to maintain a competitive advantage.

What Is Strategic Planning?   Strategic human resource management is part of strategic planning. As we'll discuss in more detail in chapter 3, a **strategic plan** is the company's

strategy
The company's long-term plan for how it will balance its internal strengths and weaknesses with its external opportunities and threats to maintain a competitive advantage.

plan for how it will match its internal strengths and weaknesses with external opportunities and threats in order to maintain a competitive advantage. The essence of **strategic planning** is to ask, "Where are we now as a business, where do we want to be, and how should we get there?" The manager then formulates specific (human resources and other) strategies to take the company from where it is now to where he or she wants it to be. A **strategy** is a course of action. Signicast's strategies included closing the old plant and replacing it with a new, highly automated one.

strategic human resource management
Strategic human resource management means formulating and executing human resource policies and practices that produce the employee competencies and behaviors the company needs to achieve its strategic aims.

What Is Strategic Human Resource Management? **Strategic human resource management** means formulating and executing human resource policies and practices that produce the employee competencies and behaviors the company needs to achieve its strategic aims. Signicast's new strategy required employees with the knowledge, skills, and motivation to run the new automated plant. Signicast's strategic human resource plan included detailed guidelines regarding what skills and knowledge the workers would need, as well as exactly how to recruit, test, select, and train these sorts of workers. Signicast's management knew that without the necessary employee knowledge, training, and skills—"human capital"—in place, the new plant could not function. Its strategic human resource plans enabled the company to hire the employees who could exhibit the behaviors the company needed to accomplish its goals (in this case, make the plant succeed).

In practice, human resource management's strategic role means several things.[29] For example, as at companies like Ritz-Carlton and Signicast, human resource managers today are involved *in partnering with their top managers in both designing and executing their companies' strategies.* Today's focus on competitiveness and operational improvements also means that human resource managers must *express their departmental plans and accomplishments in measurable terms.* Top management wants to see, precisely, how the human resource manager's plans will make the company more valuable, for instance by boosting factory skill levels, and, thereby, improving performance.

Creating High-Performance Work Systems

The emphasis on strategic human resource management is one change in what human resource managers do; a focus on *productivity and performance* is another. As we noted above, more globalization means more competition, and more competition means more pressure to lower costs and to make employees more productive. Most human resource professionals recognize the need to focus on performance. When asked to rate the importance of various business issues in one survey, their top five choices were competition for market share, price competition/price control, governmental regulations, need for sales growth, and need to increase productivity.[30]

We'll see in this book that effective human resource management practices can improve performance in three main ways, in particular through the use of *technology*, through effective *human resource practices* (such as testing and training), and by instituting *high-performance work systems.* Lets look at each.

Managing with Technology Technological applications like those in Table 1-1 improve HR's performance in four main ways: self-service, call centers, productivity improvement, and outsourcing.[31] For example, using Dell's human resources intranet, the firm's employees can *self-service* many of their personnel transactions, such as updating personal information and changing benefits allocations. Technology also enabled Dell to create a centralized human resources *call center.* Here Dell human resource specialists answer questions from all Dell's far-flung employees, reducing the need for human resource departments at each Dell location.

TABLE 1-1 Technological Applications for HR

Technology	How Used by HR
Application Service Providers (ASPs) and technology outsourcing	ASPs provide software applications, for instance, for processing employment applications. The ASPs host and manage the services for the employer from their own remote computers
Web portals	Employers use these, for instance, to enable employees to sign up for and manage their own benefits packages and to update their personal information
PCs and high-speed access	Make it easier for employees to take advantage of the employers Web-assisted HR activities
Streaming desktop video	Used, for instance, to facilitate distance learning and training or to provide corporate information to employees quickly and inexpensively
The mobile Web and wireless net access	Used to facilitate employees' access to the company's Web-based HR activities
E-procurement	Used for ordering work materials more efficiently online
Internet- and network-monitoring software	Used to track employees' Internet and e-mail activities or to monitor their performance
Bluetooth	A special wireless technology used to synchronize various electronic tools like cellular phones and PCs, and thus facilitate employees' access to the employer's online HR services
Electronic signatures	Legally valid e-signatures that the employer can use to more expeditiously obtain signatures for applications and record keeping
Electronic bill presentment and payment	Used, for instance, to eliminate paper checks and to facilitate payments to employees and suppliers
Data warehouses and computerized analytical programs	Help HR managers monitor their HR systems. For example, they make it easier to assess things like cost per hire, and to compare current employees' skills with the firm's projected strategic needs

More firms are installing Internet and computer-based systems for *improving HR productivity*. For example, International Paper Corp.'s "Viking" human resource information system aimed to move the company's HR staff-to-employee ratio from about one to 100, to one to 150.[32]

outsourcing
Letting outside vendors provide services.

Technology also makes it easier to **outsource** HR activities to specialist service providers, by giving service providers real-time, Internet-based access to the employer's human resource information database.[33] Among the human resource tasks employers are outsourcing are payroll, benefits, applicant testing and screening, reference checks, exit interviews, wellness programs, and employee training.[34] About 84% of firms outsource the administration of 401(k) pension plans, and about 68% of employers outsource background checks to specialist firms.

Effective HR Practices   We'll also see in this book how human resource practices can improve performance. For example, a recent review of personality testing's effectiveness concluded that screening applicants through personality testing can produce employees who perform better.[35] (In other words, people with the right traits for the job did the job better, a finding that makes sense to anyone who's ever had a bad experience with a surly customer service clerk, or a similar.) Similarly, well-trained employees perform better than untrained ones, and safe workplaces produce fewer lost-time accidents and accident costs than do unsafe ones. The most productive and highest performing world-class companies, like Toyota, have long had world-class training and plant safety programs.

High-Performance Work Systems In fact, a growing body of evidence shows that the best-performing companies in a wide range of industries perform so well in part because of their *high-performance work systems*. A **high-performance work system** is an integrated set of human resource management policies and practices that together produce superior employee performance.

high-performance work system
A high-performance work system is an integrated set of human resource management policies and practices that together produce superior employee performance.

While there's no hard and fast rule about what comprises high-performance work systems, most organizational psychologists would agree they include these practices:

- employment security
- selective hiring
- extensive training
- self-managed teams and decentralized decision making
- reduced status distinctions between managers and workers
- information sharing
- contingent (pay-for-performance) rewards
- transformational leadership (for instance, in terms of inspirational motivation)
- measurement of management practices
- emphasis on high-quality work[36]

In terms of measurable outcomes, high-performance work systems produce, for instance, more qualified applicants per position, more employees hired based on validated selection tests, more hours of training for new employees, and a higher percentage of employees receiving regular performance appraisals. Systems like these produce many benefits for employers, some surprising.[37] One study found, for instance, that high-performance work systems produced fewer occupational injuries.[38]

Another study focused on 17 manufacturing plants, some of which used high-performance work system practices. For example, they paid more (median wages of $16 per hour compared with $13 per hour for all plants); trained more (83% offered more than 20 hours of training per year, compared with 32% for all plants); used more sophisticated recruitment and hiring practices (tests and validated interviews, for instance); and used more self-managing work teams. These plants also had the best overall performance, in terms of higher profits, lower operating costs, and lower turnover.[39] We look more closely at high-performance work systems in Chapter 3.

Measuring the Human Resource Management Team's Performance

⑤ Write a short essay that addresses the topic: Why metrics and measurement are crucial to today's HR managers.

In today's performance-based environment, employers naturally expect their human resource management teams to provide measurable evidence of their efficiency and effectiveness, and for that of their proposed programs. For example, "How much will that new testing program save us in reduced employee turnover?" "How much more productive will our employees be if we institute that new training program?" And, "How productive is our human resource team, in terms of HR staff per employee, compared to our competitors?"

metrics
A set of quantitative performance measures HR managers use to assess their operations.

The fundamental requirement for such measurability is that the human resource manager needs the numbers. Specifically, he or she needs quantitative performance measures (**metrics**). For example, median HR expenses as a proportion of companies' total operating costs average about 0.8%. There tends to be between 0.9 and 1.0 human resource staff persons per 100 employees (the ratio tends to be lower in retailing and distribution firms, and higher in public, state organizations).[40] Both manufacturing and non-manufacturing firms spend about $1,000 per employee for HR. Figure 1-5 provides a sample of several

HR Metric*	How to Calculate It	What It Measures and How to Use It**
Absence rate	[(# Days absent in month) ÷ (Average # of employees during mo.) × (# of workdays)] × 100	Measures absenteeism. See *BNA Job Absence Report* for benchmark and survey data. Determine if your company has an absenteeism problem. Analyze why and how to address issue. Analyze further for effectiveness of attendance policy and effectiveness of management in applying policy.
Cost per hire	(Advertising + agency fees + employee referrals + travel cost of applicants and staff + relocation costs + recruiter pay and benefits) ÷ number of hires	Costs involved with a new hire. Use *BNA/Cost per Hire Staffing Metrics Survey* as a benchmark for your organization. Can be used as a measurement to show any substantial improvements to savings in recruitment/retention costs. Determine what your recruiting function can do to increase savings/ reduce costs, and so on.
HR expense factor	HR expense ÷ total operating expense	HR expenses in relation to the total operating expenses of organization. Determine if expenditures exceeded, met, or fell below budget. Analyze HR practices that contributed to savings, if any. See *SHRM-BNA Survey No. 66: Human Resource Activities, Budgets & Staffs.*
Time to fill	Total days elapsed to fill requisitions ÷ number hired	Number of days from which job requisition was approved to new hire start date. How efficient/ productive is recruiting function? This is also a process measurement. See *BNA/Cost per Hire Staffing Metrics Survey* for more information.
Turnover rate	[# of separations during mo. ÷ average # of employees during mo.] × 100	This measures the rate for which employees leave a company. Calculate and compare metric to national average using Bureau of National Affairs *BNA Turnover Report* or www.bls.gov/jlt/home.htm. Is there a trend? Has metric increased/decreased? Analyze what has caused increase/decrease to metric. Determine what organization can do to improve retention efforts.

*This table shows five HR metrics employers use. Other metrics include, for example, health care costs per employee, human capital Return on Investment, turnover costs, and workers' compensation cost per employee, among many others. See sources below for more metrics.

**Compare your metrics against other organizations' metrics, survey data, and so on, to evaluate your performance. Metrics can show the benefit of your HR practices and their contribution to your organization's profits and strategic aims.

FIGURE 1-5

Five Sample HR Metrics

Sources: Robert Grossman, "Measuring Up," *HR Magazine*, January 2000, pp. 29–35; Peter V. Le Blanc, Paul Mulvey, and Jude T. Rich, "Improving the Return on Human Capital: New Metrics," *Compensation and Benefits Review*, January/February 2000, pp. 13–20; Thomas E. Murphy and Sourushe Zandvakili, "Data and Metrics-Driven Approach to Human Resource Practices: Using Customers, Employees, and Financial Metrics," *Human Resource Management* 39, no. 1 (Spring 2000), pp. 93–105; [*HR Planning*, Commerce Clearing House Incorporated, July 17, 1996;] *SHRM/BNA 2000 Cost Per Hire and Staffing Metrics Survey*; www.shrm.org. See also, SHRM Research "2006 Strategic HR Management Survey Report," Society for Human Resource Management.

other human resource–related metrics, as provided by the Society for Human Resource Management (SHRM).

Managing with the HR Scorecard Process

Managers can link such metrics or measurements together to provide a more meaningful picture. For example, (for Signicast): testing 100% of applicants using new selection test >>> improved average employee performance on automated machines >>> higher plant productivity >>> Signicast achieving its strategic profitability goals.

For most human resource management activities, one can similarly map out the cause-and-effect links, from the human resource activity, to the employee behavior, to the company performance. For example, (for a hotel): increased use of incentive plans >>> improved hotel employee customer service ratings >>> more satisfied hotel guests >>> improved hotel profits. Managers often use an *HR Scorecard Process* to consolidate linked metrics like these and present them on a "digital dashboard" computer screen, to easily visualize and measure the HR function's effectiveness in producing the employee behaviors required to achieve the company's goals. The **HR Scorecard** is a concise measurement system. It shows the metrics the firm uses to measure HR activities (such as testing, training, compensation, and safety), and to measure the employee behaviors resulting from these activities, and to measure the strategically relevant organizational outcomes of those employee behaviors (such as higher plant performance, and company profits). The dashboard-based scorecard shows the causal links between the HR activities, the emergent employee behaviors, and the resulting firm-wide strategic outcomes and performance. Chapter 3 shows how to create and use an HR Scorecard.

HR Scorecard
Measures the HR function's effectiveness and efficiency in producing employee behaviors needed to achieve the company's strategic goals.

THE HUMAN RESOURCE MANAGER'S PROFICIENCIES

As you can see, being a human resource manager today is challenging, and requires several proficiencies.

Four Proficiencies

One study found four categories of proficiencies: HR proficiencies, business proficiencies, leadership proficiencies, and learning proficiencies.

- *HR proficiencies* represent traditional knowledge and skills in areas such as employee selection, training, and compensation.
- *Business proficiencies* reflect human resource professionals' new strategic role. For example, to assist the top management team in formulating strategies, the human resource manager needs to be familiar with strategic planning, marketing, production, and finance.[41] They must also be able to "speak the CFO's language," by explaining human resource activities in financially measurable terms, such as return on investment, payback period, and cost per unit of service.[42] (A recent SHRM symposium on the future of strategic HR concluded that many human resource professionals lack such business knowledge and literacy.)[43]
- HR managers also require *leadership proficiencies*. For example, they need the ability to work with and lead management groups, and to drive the changes required—for instance, to implement new world-class employee screening and training systems.
- Finally, because the competitive landscape is changing so quickly and new technologies are being continually introduced, the human resource manager needs *learning proficiencies*. He or she must have the ability to stay abreast of and apply all the new technologies and practices affecting the profession.

FIGURE 1-6

Effects CFOs Believe Human Capital Has on Business Outcomes

Source: Steven H. Bates, "Business Partners," *HR Magazine*, September 2003, p. 49. Reproduced with permission of the Society for Human Resource Management via Copyright Clearance Center.

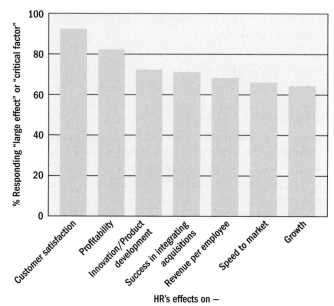

Studies show that top management and chief financial officers recognize the critical role human resource management can play in achieving a company's strategic goals.[44] Figure 1-6 summarizes some results. It shows they know that human capital—the employees' knowledge, skills, and experiences—can have a big effect on important organizational outcomes such as customer satisfaction and profitability. Partly as a result, human resource executives are increasingly well-paid. For example, average total direct compensation for top HR executives was recently just over $1.4 million per year.[45]

HR Certification

As the human resource manager's tasks grow more complex, human resource management is becoming more professionalized. Over 60,000 HR professionals have already passed one or both of the Society for Human Resource Management's (SHRM) HR professional certification exams. SHRM's Human Resource Certification Institute offers these exams. Two levels of exams test the professional's knowledge of all aspects of human resource management, including management practices, staffing, development, compensation, labor relations, and health and safety. Those who successfully complete all requirements earn the SPHR (Senior Professional in HR), or PHR (Professional in HR) certificate. Figure 1-7 summarizes the body of knowledge in the SHRM certification program. You will find certification-related exercises in the end-of-chapter exercises throughout this book. The test specifications for the HRCI exams, as well as new SHRM learning guidelines for human resource management courses, are in the SHRM appendix at the end of this book. Managers can take an online HRCI assessment exam at www.HRCI.org (or by calling 866-898-HRCI).

Managing within the Law

Human resource managers (and, in fact, anyone managing people day-to-day) must be proficient in applying employment law to employment decisions. For example, *equal employment laws* set guidelines regarding how the company writes its recruiting ads, what questions its job interviewers ask, and how it selects candidates for training programs or evaluates its managers. *Occupational safety and health laws* mandate strict guidelines regarding safety practices at work. *Labor laws* lay out, among other things, what the supervisor can and cannot

FIGURE 1-7

**2004 SHRM®
Learning System
Module
Descriptions**

Source: Reprinted by
permission of Society for
Human Resource
Management via Copyright
Clearance Center.

Module 1: Strategic Management
- The Role of Human Resources in Organizations
- The Strategic Planning Process
- Scanning the External Environment

Organizational Structure and Internal HR Partners
- Measuring Human Resource Effectiveness
- Ethical Issues Affecting Human Resources
- Human Resources and the Legislative Environment

Module 2: Workforce Planning and Employment
- Key Legislation Affecting Employee Rights
- Key Legislation Affecting Privacy and Consumer Protection
- Equal Employment Opportunity/Affirmative Action
- Gender Discrimination and Harassment in the Workplace
- Organizational Staffing Requirements
- Job Analysis and Documentation
- Recruitment
- Flexible Staffing
- Selection
- Employment Practices
- Organizational Exit
- Employee Records Management

Module 3: Human Resource Development
- Key Legislation
- Human Resource Development and the Organization
- Adult Learning and Motivation
- Assessment of HRD Needs
- HRD Program Design and Development
- HRD Program Implementation
- Evaluating HRD Effectiveness
- Career Development
- Developing Leaders
- Organizational Development Initiatives
- Performance Management

Module 4: Compensation and Benefits
- Key Legislation
- Total Compensation and the Strategic Focus of the Organization
- Pay Administration
- Compensation Systems
- Introduction to Benefit Programs
- Government-Mandated Benefits
- Voluntary Benefits
- Compensation and Benefit Programs for Employees
- Evaluating the Total Compensation System and Communicating It to Employees

Module 5: Employee and Labor Relations
- Key Legislation Affecting Employee and Labor Relations
- Employee Relations and Organizational Culture
- Employee Involvement Strategies
- Positive Employee Relations
- Work Rules
- Effective Communication of Laws, Regulations, and Organizational Policies
- Discipline and Formal Complaint Resolution
- Union Organizing
- Unfair Labor Practices
- Collective Bargaining
- Strikes and Secondary Boycotts
- Public-Sector Labor Relations
- International Employee and Labor Relations

Module 6: Occupational Health, Safety, and Security
- Key Legislation
- Safety
- Health
- Security

say and do when the union comes calling to organize the company's employees. As one employment lawyer sums up, "the use of such terms as probationary period, permanent employee, merit increases, white-collar [or] annual salary in a job offer, now causes serious exposure to a lawsuit."[46]

Consider some examples. You discharge a worker for excessive absenteeism, but a work-related injury caused her excessive absenteeism. The employee sues the company, saying that you actually fired her for filing a Workers' Compensation claim. Your company may have to show in court that you did not fire the employee in retaliation for filing the claim, but for absenteeism. As another example, your company's vice president of marketing dated one of his female marketing managers for several months. He subsequently tells her that if she doesn't start dating him again, she won't get a promotion. She refuses, but he promotes her anyway. However, she still sues for sexual harassment. The law says she has a legitimate case, even though she got her promotion. The vice president created a sexually hostile environment by suggesting she may have to return the favor if he promoted her.

Because legal issues are so central to all managers' employee-related activities, we will discuss equal employment law in the next chapter. Then, in each chapter, "Know Your Employment Law" features will address legal aspects of that chapter's topics.

Managing Ethics

There is one proficiency that is so important that it was best to cover it after the above, because if the manager fails to apply this proficiency, then everything else he or she does will have been for nought. Several years ago, MCI-WorldCom's CFO pleaded guilty to helping hide the company's true financial condition. The government accused him of having subordinates make fraudulent accounting entries, and of filing false statements with the SEC. Why would a star CFO do this? Because, he said, he thought he was helping MCI. Managers can learn some lessons from MCI-Worldcom. Even gifted managers fail if they make the wrong ethical choices. And even honest managers find it easy to convince themselves that what they're doing is not really wrong. Managing ethically is our last, but in some respects most crucial, HR manager proficiency.

ethics

Ethics refers to the standards someone uses to decide what his or her conduct should be.

Ethics refers to the standards someone uses to decide what his or her conduct should be. Ethical decisions always involve *morality*, matters of serious consequence to society's well-being, such as murder, lying, and stealing. Newspaper headlines regarding ethical lapses at Enron and MCI and questionably timed stock option grants at Apple Computer seem to never end. Given that some of these firms, such as the accounting firm Arthur Andersen, were literally put out of business by ethical lapses, one has to wonder what the managers were thinking.

Congress passed the Sarbanes-Oxley Act in 2003. To help ensure that managers take their ethics responsibilities seriously, Sarbanes-Oxley (SOX) is intended to curb erroneous corporate financial reporting. Among other things, Sarbanes-Oxley requires CEOs and CFOs to certify their companies' periodic financial reports, prohibits personal loans to executive officers and directors, and requires CEOs and CFOs to reimburse their firms for bonuses and stock option profits if corporate financial statements subsequently require restating.[47]

SOX does not just involve the firm's CEO and CFO. For example, every publicly listed company now needs a code of ethics, more often than not promulgated by human resources.

The human resource manager's responsibilities for implementing Sarbanes-Oxley are just the tip of the iceberg when it comes to human resource–related ethical practices. One survey found that six of the ten most serious ethical issues—workplace safety, security of employee records, employee theft, affirmative action, comparable work, and employee privacy rights—were human resource management related.[48] We will explain ethics in human resource management more fully in Chapter 14.

🜕 Outline the plan of this book.

THE PLAN OF THIS BOOK

The Basic Themes and Features

In this book, we use several themes and features to emphasize particularly important issues, and to provide continuity from chapter to chapter.

First, HR management is the *responsibility of every manager*—not just those in human resources. Throughout this book, you'll therefore find an emphasis on practical material that you as a manager will need to perform your day-to-day management responsibilities. In fact, even if you're a supervisor in a Fortune 500 company faced with some personnel task (like interviewing a job candidate), you may find you need more support than your HR department provides. We have therefore included, in each chapter, special "When You're on Your Own" boxed features. These show you in practical terms how the manager or small business owner who is "on his or her own" can accomplish some of the chapter's key employee-related tasks.

Second, the intensely competitive nature of business today means human resource managers must defend their plans and contributions in measurable terms. You'll therefore find frequent references throughout the book to *measuring HR's performance*. Chapter 3 explains how to use the *HR Scorecard* in this regard. Each chapter includes a metrics oriented case example.

Third, all managers need to keep the strategic reasons for and implications of their personnel actions in mind. This book therefore discusses *strategic human resource planning* fully in Chapter 3, and in end-of-chapter Hotel Paris strategy cases.

Fourth, all managers rely on information technology. "Improving Productivity Through HRIS" sections in each chapter illustrate how managers use technology to improve the productivity of the human resource function.

Fifth, we'll see in the following chapter that virtually every personnel-related decision managers make has legal implications. Each chapter therefore contains one or more relevant "Know Your Employment Law" features.

CHAPTER CONTENTS OVERVIEW

Following is a brief overview of the chapters and their content.

Part 1: Introduction

Chapter 1: Introduction to Human Resource Management. The manager's human resource management jobs, crucial global and competitive trends, how managers use technology and modern HR measurement systems to create high-performance work systems.

Chapter 2: Equal Opportunity and the Law. What you'll need to know about equal opportunity laws as they relate to human resource management activities such as interviewing, selecting employees, and evaluating performance.

Chapter 3: Strategic Human Resource Management and the HR Scorecard. What is strategic planning; high-performance work systems; strategic HR; the HR Scorecard.

Part 2: Recruitment and Placement

Chapter 4: Job Analysis. How to analyze a job; how to determine the human resource requirements of the job, as well as its specific duties and responsibilities.

Chapter 5: Personnel Planning and Recruiting. Human resource planning and planning systems; determining what sorts of people need to be hired; recruiting them.

Chapter 6: Employee Testing and Selection. Techniques you can use to ensure that you're hiring the right people.

Chapter 7: Interviewing Candidates. How to interview candidates to help ensure that you hire the right person for the right job.

Part 3: Training and Development

Chapter 8: Training and Developing Employees. Providing the training necessary to ensure that your employees have the knowledge and skills needed to accomplish their tasks; concepts and techniques for developing more capable employees, managers, and organizations.

Chapter 9: Performance Management and Appraisal. Techniques for appraising performance and for linking performance with the organization's goals.

Chapter 10: Managing Careers. Techniques such as career planning and promotion from within that firms use to help ensure employees can achieve their potential.

Part 4: Compensation

Chapter 11: Establishing Strategic Pay Plans. How to develop equitable pay plans for your employees.

Chapter 12: Pay-for-Performance and Financial Incentives. Pay-for-performance plans such as financial incentives, merit pay, and incentives that help tie performance to pay.

Chapter 13: Benefits and Services. Providing benefits that make it clear the firm views its employees as long-term investments and is concerned with their welfare.

Part 5: Employee Relations

Chapter 14: Ethics, Justice, and Fair Treatment in HR Management. Ensuring ethical and fair treatment through discipline, grievance, and career management processes.

Chapter 15: Labor Relations and Collective Bargaining. Concepts and techniques concerning the relations between unions and management, including the union organizing campaign; negotiating and agreeing upon a collective bargaining agreement between unions and management; and managing the agreement via the grievance process.

Chapter 16: Employee Safety and Health. The causes of accidents, how to make the workplace safe, and laws governing your responsibilities for employee safety and health.

Chapter 17: Managing Global Human Resources. The growing importance of international business, and HR's role in managing the personnel side of multinational operations.

The Topics Are Interrelated

In practice, managers should not think of this book's 17 chapters and topics as independent of and unrelated to the others. Each topic interacts with and affects the others, and all should fit with the employer's strategic plan. For example, hiring people who don't have the potential to learn the job will doom their performance regardless of how much training they get.

Figure 1-8 summarizes this idea. For example, how you test and interview job candidates (Chapters 6 and 7) and train and appraise job incumbents (Chapters 8 and 9) depends on the job's specific duties and responsibilities (Chapter 4). How good a job you do selecting (Chapter 6) and training (Chapter 8) employees will affect how safely they do their jobs (Chapter 16). An employee's performance and thus his or her appraisal (Chapter 9) depends not just on the person's motivation, but on how well you identified the job's duties (Chapter 4), and screened and trained the employee (Chapters 6 and 7). Furthermore, we saw that each of the employer's human resource strategies—for instance, how you recruit, select, train, appraise, and compensate employees—should make sense in terms of producing the employee behaviors required to support the company's strategic plan.

FIGURE 1-8

**Strategy and the
Basic Human
Resource
Management
Process**

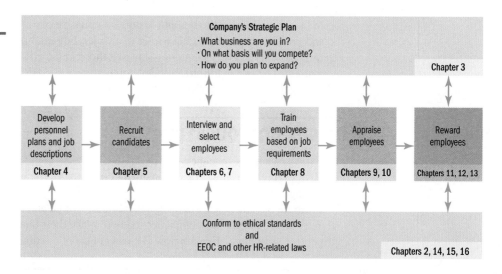

SUMMARY

1. All managers perform certain basic functions—planning, organizing, staffing, leading, and controlling. These represent the management process.
2. Staffing, personnel management, or human resource management includes activities like recruiting, selecting, training, compensating, appraising, and developing employees.
3. HR management is a part of every manager's responsibilities. These responsibilities include placing the right person in the right job, and then orienting, training, and compensating to improve his or her job performance.
4. The HR department carries out three main functions. The HR manager exerts line authority in his or her unit and implied authority elsewhere in the organization. He or she ensures that the organization's HR objectives and policies are coordinated and implemented. And he or she provides various staff services to line management, such as partnering with the CEO in designing the company's strategy, and assisting in the hiring, training, evaluating, rewarding, promoting, and disciplining of employees at all levels.
5. Trends such as globalization, technological advances, and deregulation mean that companies must be more competitive today. Other important trends include growing workforce diversity and changes in the nature of work, such as the movement toward a service society and a growing emphasis on human capital.
6. For the HR manager, the focus on competitiveness and productivity demands measurability. Management expects HR to provide measurable, benchmark-based evidence regarding HR's current efficiency and effectiveness, and regarding the expected efficiency and effectiveness of its new or proposed programs.
7. HR managers often use *HR Scorecards* to facilitate the measurement process. The HR Scorecard is a visual and/or computerized model that enables managers to demonstrate how HR contributes to the company's financial success. It shows the measurable, cause-and-effect links between three things: (1) HR activities (such as improving the firm's incentive plan), (2) intermediate employee results (such as improved morale), and (3) end-result company metrics (such as improved customer service and higher profits).

8. In this book, several themes and features emphasize particularly important issues, and provide continuity from chapter to chapter. For example, HR management is the *responsibility of every manager*—not just those in the HR department. HR is a *strategic partner* in the strategy development process. HR works with other top managers to formulate the company's strategy as well as to execute it.

DISCUSSION QUESTIONS

1. Explain what HR management is and how it relates to the management process.
2. Give examples of how HR management concepts and techniques can be of use to all managers.
3. Illustrate the HR management responsibilities of line and staff managers.
4. Why is it important for companies today to make their human resources into a competitive advantage? Explain how HR can contribute to doing this.

INDIVIDUAL AND GROUP ACTIVITIES

1. Working individually or in groups, develop outlines showing how trends like workforce diversity, technological innovation, globalization, and changes in the nature of work have affected the college or university you are attending now. Present in class.
2. Working individually or in groups, contact the HR manager of a local bank. Ask the HR manager how he or she is working as a strategic partner to manage human resources, given the bank's strategic goals and objectives. Back in class, discuss the responses of the different HR managers.
3. Working individually or in groups, interview an HR manager. Based on that interview, write a short presentation regarding HR's role today in building more competitive organizations.
4. Working individually or in groups, bring several business publications such as *BusinessWeek* and the *Wall Street Journal* to class. Based on their contents, compile a list entitled "What HR Managers and Departments Do Today."
5. Based on your personal experiences, list 10 examples showing how you did use (or could have used) human resource management techniques at work or school.
6. Laurie Siegel, senior vice president of human resources for Tyco International, took over her job just after numerous charges forced the company's previous board of directors and top executives to leave the firm. Hired by new CEO Edward Breen, Siegel had to tackle numerous difficult problems starting the moment she assumed office. For example, she had to help hire a new management team. She had to do something about what the outside world viewed as a culture of questionable ethics at her company. And she had to do something about the company's top management compensation plan, which many felt contributed to the allegations by some that some former company officers had used the company as a sort of private ATM.

   Siegel came to Tyco after a very impressive career. For example, she had been head of executive compensation at Allied Signal, and was a graduate of the Harvard Business School. But, as strong as her background was, she obviously had her work cut out for her when she took the senior vice president of HR position at Tyco.

   Working individually or in groups, conduct an Internet search and library research to answer the following questions: What human resource management-related steps did Siegel take to help get Tyco back on the right track? Do you think she took the appropriate steps? Why or why not? What, if anything, do you suggest she do now?

EXPERIENTIAL EXERCISE

Helping "The Donald"

Purpose: The purpose of this exercise is to provide practice in identifying and applying the basic concepts of human resource management by illustrating how managers use these techniques in their day-to-day jobs.

Required Understanding: Be thoroughly familiar with the material in this chapter, and with at least several episodes of *The Apprentice*, the TV show in which developer Donald Trump starred.

How to Set Up the Exercise/Instructions:

1. Divide the class into teams of three to four students.
2. Read this: As you may know by watching "the Donald" as he organizes his business teams for *The Apprentice*, human resource management plays an important role in what Donald Trump, and in what the participants on his separate teams need to do to be successful. For example, Donald Trump needs to be able to appraise each of the participants. And, for their part, the leaders of each of his teams need to be able to staff his or her teams with the right participants, and then provide the sorts of training, incentives, and evaluations that help their companies succeed and that therefore make the participants themselves (and especially the team leaders) look like "winners" to Mr. Trump.
3. Watch several of these shows (or reruns of the shows), and then meet with your team and answer the following questions:
   a. What specific HR functions (recruiting, interviewing, and so on) can you identify Donald Trump using on this show? Make sure to give specific examples based on the show.
   b. What specific HR functions (recruiting, selecting, training, etc.) can you identify one or more of the team leaders using to help manage their teams on the show? Again, please give specific answers.
   c. Provide a specific example of how HR functions (such as recruiting, selection, interviewing, compensating, appraising, and so on) contributed to one of the participants coming across as particularly successful to Mr. Trump. Can you provide examples of how one or more of these functions contributed to a participant being told by Mr. Trump, "You're fired"?
   d. Present your team's conclusions to the class.

APPLICATION CASE

Jack Nelson's Problem

As a new member of the board of directors for a local bank, Jack Nelson was being introduced to all the employees in the home office. When he was introduced to Ruth Johnson, he was curious about her work and asked her what the machine she was using did. Johnson replied that she really did not know what the machine was called or what it did. She explained that she had only been working there for two months. She did, however, know precisely how to operate the machine. According to her supervisor, she was an excellent employee.

At one of the branch offices, the supervisor in charge spoke to Nelson confidentially, telling him that "something was wrong," but she didn't know what. For one thing, she explained, employee turnover was too high, and no sooner had one employee been put on the job than another one resigned. With customers to see and loans to be made, she continued, she had little time to work with the new employees as they came and went.

All branch supervisors hired their own employees without communication with the home office or other branches. When an opening developed, the supervisor tried to find a suitable employee to replace the worker who had quit.

After touring the 22 branches and finding similar problems in many of them, Nelson wondered what the home office should do or what action he should take. The banking firm was generally regarded as a well-run institution that had grown from 27 to 191 employees during the past eight years. The more he thought about the matter, the more puzzled Nelson became. He couldn't quite put his finger on the problem, and he didn't know whether to report his findings to the president.

Questions

1. What do you think is causing some of the problems in the bank's home office and branches?
2. Do you think setting up an HR unit in the main office would help?
3. What specific functions should an HR unit carry out? What HR functions would then be carried out by supervisors and other line managers? What role should the Internet play in the new HR organization?

Source: From Claude S. George, *Supervision in Action*, 4th ed., 1985. Adapted by permission of Prentice Hall, Inc., Upper Saddle River, NJ.

CONTINUING CASE

Carter Cleaning Company

Introduction

A main theme of this book is that HR management—activities like recruiting, selecting, training, and rewarding employees—is not just the job of a central HR group but rather a job in which every manager must engage. Perhaps nowhere is this more apparent than in the typical small service business. Here the owner/manager usually has no HR staff to rely on. However, the success of his or her enterprise (not to mention his or her family's peace of mind) often depends largely on the effectiveness through which workers are recruited, hired, trained, evaluated, and rewarded. Therefore, to help illustrate and emphasize the front-line manager's HR role, throughout this book we will use a continuing case based on an actual small business in the southeastern United States. Each chapter's segment of the case will illustrate how the case's main player—owner/manager Jennifer Carter—confronts and solves personnel problems each day at work by applying the concepts and techniques of that particular chapter. Here is background information you will need to answer questions that arise in subsequent chapters. (We also present a second, unrelated "application case" case incident in each chapter.)

Carter Cleaning Centers

Jennifer Carter graduated from State University in June 2005, and, after considering several job offers, decided to do what she really always planned to do—go into business with her father, Jack Carter.

Jack Carter opened his first laundromat in 1995 and his second in 1998. The main attraction of these coin laundry businesses for him was that they were capital-rather than labor-intensive. Thus, once the investment in machinery was made, the stores could be run with just one unskilled attendant and none of the labor problems one normally expects from being in the retail service business.

The attractiveness of operating with virtually no skilled labor notwithstanding, Jack had decided by 1999 to expand the services in each of his stores to include the dry cleaning and pressing of clothes. He embarked, in other words, on a strategy of "related diversification," by adding new services that were related to and consistent with his existing coin laundry activities. He added these in part because he wanted to better utilize the unused space in the rather large stores he currently had under lease, and partly because he was, as he put it, "tired of sending out the dry cleaning and pressing work that came in from our coin laundry clients to a dry cleaner five miles away, who then took most of what should have been our profits." To reflect the new, expanded line of services he renamed each of his two stores Carter Cleaning Centers and was sufficiently satisfied with their performance to open four more of the same type of stores over the next five years. Each store had its own on-site manager and, on average, about seven employees and annual revenues of about $500,000. It was this six-store chain of cleaning centers that Jennifer joined upon graduating from State University.

Her understanding with her father was that she would serve as a troubleshooter/consultant to the elder Carter with the aim of both learning the business and bringing to it modern management concepts and techniques for solving the business's problems and facilitating its growth.

Questions

1. Make a list of five specific HR problems you think Carter Cleaning will have to grapple with.
2. What would you do first if you were Jennifer?

KEY TERMS

management process, 2
human resource management (HRM), 2
authority, 3
line manager, 4
staff manager, 4
line authority, 4
staff authority, 4
implied authority, 5
functional control, 5
employee advocacy, 5

globalization, 8
human capital, 11
strategic plan, 12
strategy, 13
strategic human resource management, 13
outsourcing, 14
high-performance work system, 15
metrics, 15
HR Scorecard, 17
ethics, 20

ENDNOTES

1. Arthur Yeung, "Setting Up for Success: How the Portman Ritz-Carlton Hotel Gets the Best from Its People," *Human Resource Management*, Summer 2006, 45, no. 2, pp. 67–75.
2. Quoted in Fred K. Foulkes, "The Expanding Role of the Personnel Function," *Harvard Business Review*, March–April, 1975, pp. 71–84. See also Michael Losey, "HR Comes of Age," *HR Magazine* 9 (1998), pp. 40–53.
3. "Human Resource Activities, Budgets and Staffs, 1999–2000," *BNA Bulletin to Management*, June 20, 2000.
4. Steve Bates, "No Experience Necessary? Many Companies Are Putting non-HR Executives in Charge of HR with Mixed Results," *HR Magazine* 46, no. 11 (November 2001), pp. 34–41.

5. "Wal-Mart HR Chief Makes Early Splash," *Workforce Management*, April 24, 2006, p. 11.

6. "A Profile of Human Resource Executives," *BNA Bulletin to Management*, June 21, 2001, p. S5.

7. Ibid., p. 9. See also "The Impact of Globalization on HR," *Workplace Visions* 5 (Society for Human Resource Management, 2000), pp. 1–8.

8. Michael Schroeder, "States Fight Exodus of Jobs," *Wall Street Journal*, June 3, 2003, p. 84. Some estimates are much higher. Consultants McKinsey & Co. estimates that by 2008 about 4.1 million service jobs will have been outsourced. "Study predicts 4.1 million service jobs offshored by 2008" *BNA Bulletin to Management*, August 2, 2005, p. 247.

9. See for example, "Promoting Productivity," *Workplace Visions*, Society for Human Resource Management, no. 1, 2006, pp. 1–8.

10. Timothy Appel, "Better Off a Blue-Collar," *Wall Street Journal*, July 1, 2003, p. B-1.

11. Roger Moncarz and Azure Reasor, "The 2000-10 Job Outlook in Brief," *Occupational Outlook Quarterly*, Spring 2002, pp. 9–44.

12. See "Charting the Projections: 2004–2014," *Occupational Outlook Quarterly*, Winter 2005–06.

13. Ibid.

14. See for example, "Engine of Change," *Workforce Management*, July 17, 2006, pp. 20–30.

15. Moncarz and Reasor, "The 2000-10 Job Outlook in Brief."

16. Richard Crawford, *In the Era of Human Capital*, New York: Harper Business, 1991, p. 26.

17. Peter Drucker, "The Coming of the New Organization," *Harvard Business Review*, January–February 1998, p. 45. See also James Guthime et al., "Correlates and Consequences of High Involvement Work Practices: The Role of Competitive Strategy," *International Journal of Human Resource Management*, February 2002, pp. 183–197.

18. www.knowledge.wharton.upe.edu, "Human Resources Wharton," downloaded January 8, 2006.

19. See for example, Anthea Zacharatos et al., "High-Performance Work Systems and Occupational Safety," *Journal of Applied Psychology* 90, no. 1, 2005, pp. 77–93.

20. Tony Carneval, "The Coming Labor and Skills Shortage," *Training & Development*, January 2005, p. 39.

21. See Diane Piktialis and Hal Morgan, "The Aging of the U.S. Workforce and Its Implications for Employers," *Compensation and Benefits Review*, January/February 2003, p. 57.

22. "Charting the Projections: 2004–2014," *Occupational Outlook Quarterly*, Winter 2005–2006, pp. 48–50.

23. Society for Human Resource Management, "Workplace Forecast: A Strategic Outlook," pp. 6–8. See also, "Aging Looms as Global Budget Buster, Speaker Says," *BNA Bulletin to Management*, April 8, 2004, p. 119 and Jennifer Schramm, "Top Trends Facing HR," *HR Magazine*, October 2004, p. 152.

24. Ibid., p. 61.

25. See for example "As Labor Shortage Looms, Phased Retirement Emerges as Retention Tool for Older Workers," *BNA Bulletin to Management*, April 12, 2005, p. 113.

26. "Immigrants in the Workplace," *BNA Bulletin to Management Datagraph*, March 15, 1996, pp. 260–261. See also Tanuja Agarwala, "Human Resource Management: The Emerging Trends," *Indian Journal of Industrial Relations*, January 2002, pp. 315–331; and Shari Caudron et al., "80 People, Events and Trends that Shaped HR," *Workforce*, January 2002, pp. 26–56.

27. "Human Capital Critical to Success," *Management Review*, November 1998, p. 9.

28. Ben Nagler, "Recasting Employees into Teams," *Workforce*, January 1998, pp. 101–106.

29. See for example, "2006 Strategic HR Management," Survey Report, Shawn Fegley, Society for Human Resource Management, October 2006. See also, "SHRM Survey Report, 2006 Strategic HR Management," p. 14, *Society for Human Resource Management*, www.SHRM.org, accessed May 6, 2007, and James Werbel and Samuel deMarie, "Aligning Strategic Human Resource Management and Person–Environment Fit," *Human Resource Management Review* 15, no. 4, December 2004, pp. 247–262.

30. Philip Way, "HR/IR Professionals' Educational Needs and Masters Program Curricula," *Human Resource Management Review*, 2002, p. 478.

31. "The Future of HR," *Workplace Visions* 6, Society for Human Resource Management, 2001, pp. 3–4.

32. Bill Roberts, "Process First, Technology Second," *HR Magazine*, June 2002, pp. 40–46.

33. Many firms are outsourcing almost all their HR activities, "end-to-end." See for example "Top End-to-End HR Outsourcing Providers," *Workforce Management*, January 16, 2006, p. 14.

34. Monica Belcourt, "Outsourcing—the Benefits and the Risks," *Human Resource Management Review* 16, 2006, pp. 69–279.

35. Mitchell Rothstein and Richard Goffin, "The Use of Personality Measures in Personnel Selection: What Does Current Research Support?," *Human Resource Management Review* 16, 2006, pp. 155–180. Helen Shipton et al., "HRM as a Predictor of Innovation," *Human Resource Management Journal* 16, no. 1, 2006, pp. 3–27. Luc Sels, et al., "Unraveling the HRM—Performance Link: Value Creating and Cost-Increasing Effects of Small-Business HRM," *Journal of Management Studies* 43, no. 2, March 2006, pp. 319–342, and Jaap Paauwe and Paul Boselie, "HRM and Performance: What's Next?" *Human Resource Management Journal* 15, no. 4, 2005, pp. 68–82.

36. Anthea Zacharatos et al., "High-Performance Work Systems and Occupational Safety," *Journal of Applied Psychology* 90, no. 1, 2005, pp. 77–93.

37. See for example, James Combs et al., "How Much Do High-Performance Work Practices Matter? A Meta-Analysis of Their Effects on Organizational Performance," *Personal Psychology* 59, 2006, pp. 501–528.

38. Zacharatos, et al., op. cit., p. 89.

39. "Super Human Resources Practices Result in Better Overall Performance, Report Says," *BNA Bulletin to Management*, August 26, 2004, pp. 273–274. See also Wendy Boswell, "Aligning Employees with the Organization's Strategic Objectives: Out of Line of Sight, Out of Mind." *International Journal of Human Resource Management* 17, no. 9, September 2006, pp. 1014–1041.

40. Chris Brewster, et al., "What Determines the Size of the HR Function? A Cross National Analysis," *Human Resource Management*, Spring 2006 45, no. 1, pp. 3–21. See also, "SHRM Survey Report, 2006 Strategic HR Management," pp. 18–19, *Society for Human Resource Management*.

41. See for example, "Employers Seek HR Executives with Global Experience, SOX Knowledge, Business Sense," *BNA Bulletin to Management*, September 19, 2006, pp. 297–298; and Robert Rodriguez, "HR's New Breed," *HR Magazine*, January 2006, pp. 67–71.

42. Susan Wells, "From HR to the Top," *HR Magazine*, June 2003, p. 49.

43. "The SHRM Symposium on the Future of Strategic HR," Society for Human Resource Management, 2005, p. 6.

44. See also James Hayton, et al., "Conversations on What the Market Wants from HR Graduates, and How Can We Institutionalize Innovation in Teaching," *Human Resource Management Review* 15, 2005, pp. 38–245.

45. Joe Vocino, "High Pay for High-Level HR," *HR Magazine*, June 2006, p. 83.

46. Kenneth Sovereign, *Personnel Law*, Upper Saddle River, NJ: Pearson, 2001, p. 6.

47. Jonathan Seggal, "The Joy of Cooking," *HR Magazine*, November 2002, pp. 52–58.

48. Kevin Wooten, "Ethical Dilemmas in Human Resource Management," *Human Resource Management Review* 11 (2001), p. 161. See also Ann Pomeroy, "The Ethics Squeeze," *HR Magazine* 51, no. 3, March 2006, pp. 48–55.

2 Equal Opportunity and the Law

A jury in New York recently ordered Wal-Mart to pay Patrick Brady $7.5 million for violating the Americans with Disabilities Act. Wal-Mart hired Brady, who has cerebral palsy, to work as a pharmacist's assistant. According to the complaint, he worked as an assistant for just one day, before the store reassigned him to collect carts and pick up trash. The complaint claims that the pharmacist didn't think the disabled man was "fit for the pharmacy job."[1] Morgan Stanley settled a similar suit for $54 million months later.[2]

The purpose of this chapter is to provide you with the knowledge to deal effectively with equal employment questions on the job. The main topics we cover are equal opportunity laws from 1964 to 1991, the laws from 1991 to the present, defenses against discrimination allegations, illustrative discriminatory employment practices, and the EEOC enforcement process. •

After studying this chapter, you should be able to:

1   Cite the main features of at least five employment discrimination laws.
2   Define *adverse impact* and explain how it is proved and what its significance is.
3   Explain and illustrate two defenses you can use in the event of discriminatory practice allegations.
4   Avoid employment discrimination problems.
5   Cite specific discriminatory personnel management practices in recruitment, selection, promotion, transfer, layoffs, and benefits.
6   Define and discuss *diversity management*.

🛈 Cite the main features
of at least five employment
discrimination laws.

EQUAL EMPLOYMENT OPPORTUNITY 1964–1991

Legislation barring discrimination against members of minority groups in the United States is nothing new. For example, the Fifth Amendment to the U.S. Constitution (ratified in 1791) states, "no person shall be deprived of life, liberty, or property, without due process of the law." The Thirteenth Amendment (1865) outlawed slavery, and courts have held it bars racial discrimination. The Fourteenth Amendment (1868) makes it illegal for any state to "make or enforce any law which shall abridge the privileges and immunities of citizens of the United States," and the courts have generally viewed it as barring discrimination based on sex, national origin, or race. The Civil Rights Act of 1866 gives all persons the same right to make and enforce contracts and to benefit from the laws of the land. Other laws as well as various court decisions similarly made discrimination against minorities illegal by the early 1900s, at least in theory.[3]

But as a practical matter, Congress and presidents avoided dramatic action on equal employment until the early 1960s. At that point, civil unrest among minorities and women and changing mores prompted them to act.

Title VII of the 1964 Civil Rights Act

Title VII of the 1964 Civil Rights Act

The section of the act that says an employer cannot discriminate on the basis of race, color, religion, sex, or national origin with respect to employment.

Title VII of the 1964 Civil Rights Act was one of the first of these 1960s-era laws. As amended by the 1972 Equal Employment Opportunity Act, Title VII states that an employer cannot discriminate based on race, color, religion, sex, or national origin. Specifically, it states that it shall be an unlawful employment practice for an employer:

(1) To fail or refuse to hire or to discharge an individual or otherwise to discriminate against any individual with respect to his/her compensation, terms, conditions, or privileges of employment, because of such individual's race, color, religion, sex, or national origin.

(2) To limit, segregate, or classify his/her employees or applicants for employment in any way that would deprive or tend to deprive any individual of employment opportunities or otherwise adversely affect his/her status as an employee, because of such individual's race, color, religion, sex, or national origin.

Who Does Title VII Cover?   Title VII bars discrimination on the part of most employers, including all public or private employers of 15 or more persons. In addition, it covers all private and public educational institutions, the federal government, and state and local governments. It bars public and private employment agencies from failing or refusing to refer for employment any individual because of race, color, religion, sex, or national origin. And it bars labor unions with 15 or more members from excluding, expelling, or classifying their membership based on race, color, religion, sex, or national origin. Joint labor–management committees established for selecting workers for apprenticeships and training similarly cannot discriminate against individuals.

Equal Employment Opportunity Commission (EEOC)

The commission, created by Title VII, is empowered to investigate job discrimination complaints and sue on behalf of complainants.

The EEOC   Title VII established the **Equal Employment Opportunity Commission (EEOC)** to administer and enforce the Civil Rights law in employment settings. Strictly speaking, it consists of five members appointed by the president with the advice and consent of the Senate. Each member serves a five-year term. In popular usage, the EEOC also includes the thousands of staff members the EEOC has in offices around the country. They receive and investigate job discrimination complaints from aggrieved individuals. When the EEOC finds reasonable cause that the charges are justified, it attempts (through conciliation) to reach an agreement eliminating the discrimination. If this fails, it can go to court. Under the Equal Employment Opportunity Act of 1972, the EEOC may file discrimination charges on behalf of aggrieved individuals, or the individuals may file themselves. We'll discuss the EEOC procedure later in this chapter.

Executive Orders

affirmative action
Steps that are taken for the purpose of eliminating the present effects of past discrimination.

Office of Federal Contract Compliance Programs (OFCCP)
This office is responsible for implementing the executive orders and ensuring compliance of federal contractors.

Various U.S. presidents have issued executive orders expanding equal employment in federal agencies. For example, Executive Orders 11246 and 11375, issued by the Johnson administration (1963–1969), didn't just ban discrimination. They also required that contractors take **affirmative action** to ensure employment opportunity for those who may have suffered discrimination in the past. All federal contractors with contracts over $50,000 and 50 or more employees must develop and implement such programs. These orders also established the **Office of Federal Contract Compliance Programs (OFCCP)**. It implements the orders and ensures compliance. For example, it reached a settlement with an aviation contractor to pay over $240,000 to settle claims that women and blacks were subjected to a "perversely hostile work environment."

Equal Pay Act of 1963

Equal Pay Act of 1963
The act requiring equal pay for equal work, regardless of sex.

The **Equal Pay Act of 1963** (amended in 1972) made it unlawful to discriminate in pay on the basis of sex when jobs involve equal work; require equivalent skills, effort, and responsibility; and are performed under similar working conditions. Differences based on a seniority system, a merit system, a system that measures earnings by quantity or quality of production, or based on any factor other than sex do not violate the act.

Age Discrimination in Employment Act of 1967

Age Discrimination in Employment Act of 1967 (ADEA)
The act prohibiting arbitrary age discrimination and specifically protecting individuals over 40 years old.

The **Age Discrimination in Employment Act of 1967 (ADEA)** made it unlawful to discriminate against employees or applicants who are between 40 and 65 years of age. Subsequent amendments eliminated the age cap, effectively ending most mandatory retirement at age 65. Most states and local agencies, when acting in the role of employer, must also adhere to provisions of the act that protect workers from age discrimination.

In *O'Connor v. Consolidated Coin Caterers Corp.*, the Supreme Court held that an employee who is over 40 may sue for discrimination if he or she is replaced by a "significantly younger" employee, even if the replacement is also over 40. The Court didn't specify what "significantly younger" meant, but O'Connor had been replaced by someone 16 years younger. In 2004, the U.S. Supreme Court (in *General Dynamics Land Systems Inc. v. Cline*) held that the ADEA does not protect workers under 40 from being treated worse than older ones.[4] The ADEA is a "favored statute" among lawyers, since it allows jury trials and double damages to those proving "willful" discrimination.[5]

Vocational Rehabilitation Act of 1973

Vocational Rehabilitation Act of 1973
The act requiring certain federal contractors to take affirmative action for disabled persons.

The **Vocational Rehabilitation Act of 1973** requires employers with federal contracts over $2,500 to take affirmative action in employing handicapped persons. It does not require hiring an unqualified person. It does require an employer to take steps to accommodate a handicapped worker unless doing so imposes an undue hardship on the employer.

Pregnancy Discrimination Act of 1978

Pregnancy Discrimination Act (PDA)
An amendment to Title VII of the Civil Rights Act that prohibits sex discrimination based on "pregnancy, childbirth, or related medical conditions."

Congress passed the **Pregnancy Discrimination Act (PDA)** in 1978 as an amendment to Title VII. It prohibits using pregnancy, childbirth, or related medical conditions to discriminate in hiring, promotion, suspension, or discharge, or any term or condition of employment. Also, if an employer offers its employees disability coverage, then it must treat pregnancy and childbirth like any other disability, and include it in the plan as a covered condition. The U.S. Supreme Court ruled in *California Federal Savings and Loan Association v. Guerra* that if an employer offers no disability leave to any of its employees, it can (but need not) grant pregnancy leave to a woman disabled for pregnancy, childbirth, or a related medical condition.

Pregnancy discrimination claims to the EEOC rose about 39% in the past 10 years, and plaintive victories rose 66%.[6] (Progressive human resources notwithstanding, one firm, an auto dealership, recently fired an employee after she said she was pregnant. The reason? Allegedly "in case I ended up throwing up or cramping in one of their vehicles. They said pregnant women do that sometimes, and I could cause an accident, which might mean a lawsuit against them.")[7]

Federal Agency Guidelines

The federal agencies charged with ensuring compliance with these laws and executive orders issue their own implementing guidelines. These spell out recommended procedures to follow in complying with the law.

The EEOC, Civil Service Commission, Department of Labor, and Department of Justice together issued **uniform guidelines**. They set forth "highly recommended" procedures regarding matters like employee selection, record keeping, preemployment inquiries, and affirmative action programs. As an example, they specify that employers must validate any employment selection devices (including but not limited to written tests) that screen out disproportionate numbers of women or minorities. They also explain how to validate a selection device. (We explain this procedure in Chapter 6.) The OFCCP has its own guidelines. The EEOC and other agencies also periodically issue updated guidelines clarifying and revising their positions on matters such as national origin discrimination and sexual harassment. The American Psychological Association has its own (non-legally binding) Standards for Educational and Psychological Testing.

uniform guidelines
Guidelines issued by federal agencies charged with ensuring compliance with equal employment federal legislation explaining recommended employer procedures in detail.

Early Court Decisions Regarding Equal Employment Opportunity

Several court decisions between 1964 and 1991 helped create the interpretive foundation for EEO laws such as Title VII.

Griggs v. Duke Power Company   *Griggs* was a landmark case, since the Supreme Court used it to define unfair discrimination. Lawyers sued the Duke Power Company on behalf of Willie Griggs, an applicant for a job as a coal handler. The company required its coal handlers to be high school graduates. Griggs claimed this requirement was illegally discriminatory because it wasn't related to success on the job and because it resulted in more blacks than whites being rejected for these jobs. Griggs won the case. The decision of the Court was unanimous, and in his written opinion, Chief Justice Burger laid out three crucial guidelines affecting equal employment legislation.

First, the Court ruled *discrimination by the employer need not be overt*. In other words, the employer does not have to be shown to have intentionally discriminated against the employee or applicant; it need only be shown that discrimination did take place. Second, the Court held that an employment practice (in this case requiring the high school degree) *must be job related* if it has an unequal impact on members of a **protected class**. (For example, if verbal ability is not required to perform the job's main functions, one should not test for it.) Third, Chief Justice Burger's opinion placed the *burden of proof on the employer* to show that the hiring practice is job related. Thus, the employer must show that the employment practice (in this case, requiring a high school degree) is necessary for satisfactory job performance if the practice discriminates against members of a protected class. In the words of Justice Burger,

protected class
Persons such as minorities and women protected by equal opportunity laws, including Title VII.

> The act proscribes not only overt discrimination, but also practices that are fair in form, but discriminatory in operation. The touchstone is business necessity. If an employment practice which operates to exclude Negroes cannot be shown to be related to job performance, the practice is prohibited.[8]

Griggs established the following principles:

1. A test or other selection practice must be job related, and the burden of proof is on the employer.
2. An employer's intent not to discriminate is irrelevant.[9]
3. If a practice is "fair in form but discriminatory in operation," the courts will not uphold it.
4. *Business necessity* is the defense for any existing program that has adverse impact. The court did not define business necessity.
5. Title VII does not forbid testing. However, the test must be job related or valid, in that performance on the test must be related to performance on the job.

Albemarle Paper Company v. Moody   The *Albemarle* case is important because here the Court provided more details regarding how an employer should validate its screening tools. It helped clarify how employers could prove that the test or other screening tools are related to or predict performance on the job.[10] For example, the Court said that if an employer is to use a test to screen candidates for a job, then the nature of that job—its specific duties and responsibilities—must first be carefully analyzed and documented. Furthermore, the performance standards for employees on the job in question should be clear and unambiguous, so the employer can identify which employees are performing better than others. The Court's ruling also had the effect of establishing the EEOC (now Federal) Guidelines on validation as the procedures for validating employment practices.

EQUAL EMPLOYMENT OPPORTUNITY 1990–91–PRESENT

The Civil Rights Act of 1991

Several subsequent Supreme Court rulings in the 1980s had the effect of limiting the protection of women and minority groups under equal employment laws. For example, they ratcheted up the plaintiff's burden of proving that the employer's acts were in fact discriminatory. This soon prompted Congress to pass a new Civil Rights Act. President George H. W. Bush signed the **Civil Rights Act of 1991 (CRA 1991)** into law in November 1991. The effect of CRA 1991 was to roll back equal employment law to where it stood before the 1980s decisions, and in some respects to place even more responsibility on employers.

Civil Rights Act of 1991 (CRA 1991)
It places burden of proof back on employers and permits compensatory and punitive damages.

Burden of Proof   First, CRA 1991 addressed the issue of *burden of proof*. Burden of proof—in this case, what the plaintiff must show to establish possible illegal discrimination, and what the employer must show to defend its actions—plays a central role in equal employment cases. Today, the heaviest burden is again on the employer. In particular, the process of filing a discrimination charge goes something like this. The plaintiff (say, a rejected applicant) demonstrates that an employment practice (such as a test) has a disparate (or "adverse") impact on a particular group. *Disparate impact* "means that an employer engages in an employment practice or policy that has a greater adverse impact [effect] on the members of a protected group under Title VII than on other employees, regardless of intent."[11] (Requiring a college degree for a job would have an adverse impact on some minority groups, for instance.) Disparate impact claims do *not* require proof of discriminatory intent. Instead, the plaintiff's burden is to show two things. First, he or she must show that a significant disparity exists between the proportion of (say) women in the available labor pool and the proportion hired. Second, he or she must show that an apparently neutral employment practice, such as word-of-mouth advertising or a requirement that the jobholder "be able to lift 100 pounds," is causing the disparity.[12]

Then, once the plaintiff fulfills his or her burden of showing such disparate impact, the *employer* has the heavier burden of proving that the challenged practice is job related. For example, the employer has to show that lifting 100 pounds is actually required for effectively performing the position in question, and that the business could not run efficiently without the requirement—that it is a business necessity.

Money Damages   CRA 1991 also makes it easier to sue for *money damages* in some cases. It provides that an employee who is claiming *intentional* discrimination (called *disparate treatment*) can ask for (1) compensatory damages and (2) punitive damages, if it can be shown the employer engaged in discrimination "with malice or reckless indifference to the federally protected rights of an aggrieved individual."[13] Before CRA 1991, victims of intentional discrimination who had not suffered financial loss and who sued under Title VII could not then sue for compensatory or punitive damages. All they could expect was to have their jobs reinstated (or be awarded a particular job). They were also eligible for back pay, attorneys' fees, and court costs.

Mixed Motives   Finally, CRA 1991 also states:

> An unlawful employment practice is established when the complaining party demonstrates that race, color, religion, sex, or national origin was a motivating factor for any employment practice, even though other factors also motivated the practice.[14]

The last phrase is pivotal. Now, an employer cannot avoid liability by proving it would have taken the same action—such as terminating someone—even without the discriminatory motive.[15] If there is any such motive, the practice may be unlawful. Plaintiffs in such so-called **"mixed motive"** cases then gained further advantage from the Supreme Court decision in *Desert Palace Inc. v. Costa*. Here the Court decided that the plaintiff, a warehouse worker, did not have to provide evidence of explicitly discriminatory conduct (such as discriminatory employer statements), but could provide circumstantial evidence (such as lowered performance evaluations) to prove the mixed motive case.[16]

The Americans with Disabilities Act

The **Americans with Disabilities Act (ADA)** of 1990 prohibits employment discrimination against qualified disabled individuals.[17] It prohibits employers with 15 or more workers from discriminating against qualified individuals with disabilities, with regard to applications, hiring, discharge, compensation, advancement, training, or other terms, conditions, or privileges of employment.[18] It also says employers must make "reasonable accommodations" for physical or mental limitations unless doing so imposes an "undue hardship" on the business.

ADA does not list specific disabilities. Instead, EEOC guidelines say someone is disabled when he or she has a physical or mental impairment that substantially limits one or more major life activities. Impairments include any physiological disorder or condition, cosmetic disfigurement, or anatomical loss affecting one or more of several body systems, or any mental or psychological disorder.[19] The act specifies conditions that are not to be regarded as disabilities, including homosexuality, bisexuality, voyeurism, compulsive gambling, pyromania, and certain disorders resulting from the current illegal use of drugs.[20]

AIDS   The EEOC's position is that the ADA prohibits discriminating against people with HIV/AIDS, and numerous state laws also shield such people. Similarly, the Labor Department's Office of Federal Contract Compliance Programs requires treating AIDS-type diseases under the Vocational Rehabilitation Act. The bottom line for most employers is that discriminating against people with AIDS is generally unlawful.

---

mixed motive case
A discrimination allegation case in which the employer argues that the employment action taken was motivated, not by discrimination, but by some non-discriminatory reason such as ineffective performance.

Americans with Disabilities Act (ADA)
The act requiring employers to make reasonable accommodations for disabled employees; it prohibits discrimination against disabled persons.

The corollary is that employers should encourage managers to persuade employees to work with HIV/AIDS-infected employees, and perhaps discipline those who will not. But in reality, many managers are reluctant to do so. One study surveyed 194 managers in various organizations. In many cases, the managers would not discipline employees for refusing to work with the AIDS-infected co-workers. This was usually because of a fear of AIDS, or because of the possibility that the employee would share health information about the infected co-worker with other employees. Efforts to get employees to work with infected co-workers would therefore likely benefit from education and support.[21]

qualified individuals
Under ADA, those who can carry out the essential functions of the job.

Qualified Individual   Simply being disabled doesn't qualify someone for a job, of course. Instead, the act prohibits discrimination against **qualified individuals**—those who, with (or without) a reasonable accommodation, can carry out the *essential functions* of the job. The individual must have the requisite skills, educational background, and experience to do the job. A job function is essential when, for instance, it is the reason the position exists, or it is so highly specialized that the person is hired for his or her expertise or ability to perform that particular function.

Reasonable Accommodation   If the individual can't perform the job as currently structured, the employer must make a "reasonable accommodation" unless doing so would present an "undue hardship." Reasonable accommodation might include redesigning the job, modifying work schedules, or modifying or acquiring equipment or other devices (such as voice recognition software) to assist the person.

Attorneys, employers, and the courts are still working through the question of what "reasonable accommodation" means. An employee with a bad back who worked as a door greeter in a Wal-Mart store asked Wal-Mart if she could sit on a stool while on duty. The store said no. She sued. The federal district court agreed with Wal-Mart that door greeters must act in an "aggressively hospitable manner," which can't be done sitting on a stool.[22] Standing was an essential job function.

Employer Defenses   Many employers have successfully defended themselves. In one case, a social worker threatened to throw her co-worker out a window and to "kick her [butt]," and continued her tirade after returning from a 10-day suspension. After transfer to another job, she was diagnosed as paranoid. After telling her supervisor several times she was "ready to kill her," she was fired. She sued under ADA. The court dismissed her case because, although she had a debilitating mental illness, ADA does not require retention of employees who make threats.[23] In another case, the Court held that the employer did not discriminate against a blind bartender by requiring her to transfer to another job because she was unable to spot underage or intoxicated customers.[24] On the other hand, one U.S. circuit court held that punctuality was not an essential job function of a laboratory assistant who was habitually late due to medical treatments. The court decided he could perform seven and a half hours of data entry even if he arrived late.[25] The employer could have made reasonable accommodations.

Technology and Accommodation   Today, technological innovations make it easier for employers to accommodate disabled employees. For example, many employees with *mobility impairments* benefit from voice recognition software that allows them to input information into their computers and interactively communicate (for instance, via e-mail) without touching a keyboard. Special typing aids, including word prediction software, suggest words based on context with just one or two letters typed.

Employees with *hearing and/or speech impairments* also benefit from e-mail and from transcription software that converts one's typed messages into audible speech. Real-time

Technology enables employers to accommodate disabled employees.

translation captioning enables them to participate in lectures and meetings. Vibrating text pagers let them know when messages arrive. Employees with *vision impairments* also benefit from voice recognition devices and from computer devices that, among other things, allow adjustments in font size, display color, and screen magnification for specific portions of the computer screen.[26] Arizona had IBM Global Services create a disability-friendly Web site, "Arizona@YourService," to help link prospective employees and others to various agencies.[27] The new Firefox Web browser incorporates special IBM software enabling people to use keyboard arrows rather than the mouse to access pull-down menus, aiding some disabled people.[28]

Mental Impairments and the ADA   The types of disabilities alleged in ADA charges usually haven't been conditions commonly associated with disability, like vision, hearing, or mobility impairments. Mental disabilities account for the greatest number of claims brought under the ADA.[29]

Under EEOC guidelines, "mental impairment" includes "any mental or psychological disorder, such as . . . emotional or mental illness." Examples include major depression, anxiety disorders, panic disorders, obsessive-compulsive disorder, and personality disorders. The guidelines basically say employers should be alert to the possibility that traits normally regarded as undesirable (such as chronic lateness, hostility to co-workers, or poor judgment) may reflect mental impairments covered by the ADA. Reasonable accommodation, says the EEOC, might then include providing room dividers, partitions, or other barriers between work spaces to accommodate individuals who have disability-related limitations.

The ADA in Practice   ADA complaints are flooding the EEOC and the courts. However, employers prevailed in almost all—96%—of federal circuit court decisions in one recent year. A main reason for these lopsided results is that employees are failing to show that they are disabled and qualified to do the job.[30] Unlike Title VII of the Civil Rights Act, there's a heavy burden on the employee to establish that he or she is protected under the ADA. The employee must establish that he or she has a disability that fits under the ADA's definition. Doing so is more complicated than proving that one is a particular age or race.

A U.S. Supreme Court decision typifies what plaintiffs face. An assembly-line worker sued Toyota, arguing that carpal tunnel syndrome and tendonitis prevented her from doing her job (*Toyota Motor Manufacturing of Kentucky, Inc. v. Williams*). The U.S. Supreme Court ruled that the ADA covers carpal tunnel syndrome and tendonitis only if her impairments affect not just her job performance, but her daily living activities too. The employee admitted that she could perform personal tasks and chores such as washing her face, brushing her teeth, tending her flower garden, and fixing breakfast and doing laundry. The Court said the disability must be central to the employee's daily living (not just job) to qualify under the ADA. The Court will therefore look at each case individually.[31]

10 ADA Employer Guidelines   The ADA imposes certain legal obligations on employers, and from this we can derive 10 employer guidelines:[32]

1. An employer should not deny a job to a disabled individual if the person is qualified and able to perform the essential functions of the job. If the person is otherwise qualified but unable to perform an essential function, the employer must make a reasonable accommodation unless doing so would result in undue hardship.[33]

2. Employers are not required to lower existing performance standards or stop using tests for a job. However, those standards or tests must be job related and uniformly applied to all employees and job candidates.

3. Employers may *not* make pre-employment inquiries about a person's disability, although employers *may* ask questions about the person's ability to perform essential job functions. The timing of any medical test is important: In the event the hiring employer rescinds an offer after the medical exam, the applicant must be able to unambiguously identify the reason for the rejection as being medical. In one case, the courts found that American Airlines had not made a "real" offer to three candidates before requiring them to take their medical exams, because (even if they passed the medical exam) the offer was still contingent on American checking their references. The medical exams showed the candidates had HIV, and American rescinded their offers. This left open the question of whether it was the exams or the reference checks that torpedoed the offer, and American lost the case.[34] Table 2-1 summarizes the inquiries employers can and cannot make regarding the applicant's disabilities.

4. Similar limitations apply to medical exams for *current* employees. In one case, superiors ordered a Chicago police officer to take a blood test to determine if the level of Prozac his physician prescribed would seriously impair his ability to do his job. At the time, the officer had not engaged in any behavior that suggested any performance problems. The court said the blood test was therefore not job related and violated the ADA's prohibition against inquiries into the nature or severity of an individual's disability.[35]

5. Employers should review job application forms, interview procedures, and job descriptions for illegal questions and statements. For example, check for questions about health, disabilities, medical histories, or previous workers' compensation claims.[36]

6. The ADA does not require employers to have job descriptions, but it is advisable to have them. In virtually any ADA legal action, a central question will be, what are the essential functions of the job? Not having a job description will hamper the employer's case.

7. Courts will tend to define "disabilities" quite narrowly.[37] Employers may therefore require that the employee provide documentation of the disorder, and assess what effect that disorder has on the employee's job performance. Employers should

TABLE 2-1 What Inquiries Can Be Made About Disabilities?

Type	External Applicants (Pre-offer Stage)	External Applicants (Post-conditional Offer Stage)	Employees
Physical exam	No	Yes (C, D)	Yes (B, E)
Psychological exam	No	Yes (C, D)	Yes (B, E)
Health questionnaire	No	Yes (C, D)	Yes (B, E)
Workers' Compensation history	No	Yes (C, D)	Yes (B, E)
Physical agility test	Yes (A, C)	Yes (A, C)	Yes (A, C)
Drug test	Yes	Yes	Yes
Alcohol test	No	Yes (B, D)	Yes (B, E)
Specific questions (oral and written):			
About existence of a disability, its nature or severity, medical condition, physical or mental limitations	No	Yes (A, C)	Yes (B, E)
About ability to perform job-related functions (essential and nonessential)	Yes	Yes	Yes
About smoking (but not allergic to it)	Yes	Yes	Yes
About history of illegal drug use	No	Yes (B, D)	Yes (B, E)
Specific requests:			
Describe how you would perform job-related functions (essential and nonessential) with or without reasonable accommodation	Yes (D, F)	Yes (C, D)	Yes (B, E)
Provide evidence of not currently using drugs	Yes	Yes	Yes

A. If given to all similarly situated applicants/employees.

B. If job related and consistent with business necessity.

C. If only job-related criteria consistent with business necessity are used afterwards to screen out/exclude the applicant, at which point reasonable accommodation must be considered.

D. If all entering employees in same job category are subjected to it and subjected to same qualification standard.

E. But only for following purposes:

—To determine fitness for duty (still qualified or still able to perform essential functions)

—To determine reasonable accommodation

—To meet requirements imposed by federal, state, or local law (DOT, OSHA, EPA, etc.)

—To determine direct threat

F. Can be requested of a particular individual if the disability is known and may interfere with or prevent performance of a job-related function.

Source: Sue Willman, "Tips for Minimizing Abuses of the Americans with Disabilities Act," *Society for Human Resource Management Legal Report*, January–February 2003, p. 8. Copyright 2003 by Society for Human Resource Management. Reproduced with permission via Copyright Clearance Center.

therefore ask questions such as: Does the employee have a disability that substantially limits a major life activity? Is the employee qualified to do the job? Can the employee perform the essential functions of the job? Can any reasonable accommodation be provided without creating an undue hardship on the employer?[38]

8. Employers "do not need to allow misconduct or erratic performance (including absences and tardiness), even if that behavior is linked to the disability."[39]

9. The employer does not have to create a new job for the disabled worker nor reassign that person to a light-duty position for an indefinite period, unless such a position exists.[40]

10. Finally, one expert advises, "don't treat employees as if they are disabled." If they can control their conditions (for instance, through medication), courts usually won't consider them disabled. However, if their employers treat them as disabled (for instance, with respect to the jobs they're assigned), they'll normally be "regarded as" disabled and protected under the ADA.[41]

State and Local Equal Employment Opportunity Laws

In addition to federal laws, all states and many local governments prohibit employment discrimination.

The effect of the state or local laws is usually to cover many employers who might otherwise come in under the EEOC's radar. Many cover employers (like those with less than 15 employees) not covered by federal legislation.[42] In Arizona, for instance, plaintiffs can bring sexual harassment claims against employers with as few as one employee. Some extend the protection of age discrimination laws to young people, barring discrimination against not only those over 40, but those under 17 (here, for instance, it would be illegal to advertise for "mature" applicants, because that might discourage some teenagers from applying). New York and New Jersey now generally bar genetic testing, as well as discrimination based on genetic information.[43]

State and local equal employment opportunity agencies (often called Human Resources Commissions, Commissions on Human Relations, or Fair Employment Commissions) also play a role in the equal employment compliance process. When the EEOC receives a discrimination charge, it usually defers it for a limited time to the state and local agencies that have comparable jurisdiction. If that doesn't achieve satisfactory remedies, the charges go back to the EEOC for resolution.

Table 2-2 summarizes selected equal employment opportunity laws, actions, executive orders, and agency guidelines.

Sexual Harassment

sexual harassment
Harassment on the basis of sex that has the purpose or effect of substantially interfering with a person's work performance or creating an intimidating, hostile, or offensive work environment.

Under Title VII, **sexual harassment** generally refers to harassment on the basis of sex when such conduct has the purpose or effect of substantially interfering with a person's work performance or creating an intimidating, hostile, or offensive work environment. Sexual harassment violates Title VII. EEOC guidelines further assert that employers have an affirmative duty to maintain workplaces free of sexual harassment and intimidation. The CRA 1991 permits victims of intentional discrimination, including sexual harassment, to have jury trials and to collect compensatory damages for pain and suffering and punitive damages in cases in which the employer acted with "malice or reckless indifference" to the individual's rights.[44] In 1998 the U.S. Supreme Court held (in *Oncale v. Sundowner Offshore Services Inc.*) that same-sex sexual harassment is also actionable under Title VII.[45]

TABLE 2-2 Summary of Important Equal Employment Opportunity Actions

Action	What It Does
Title VII of 1964 Civil Rights Act, as amended	Bars discrimination because of race, color, religion, sex, or national origin; instituted EEOC.
Executive orders	Prohibit employment discrimination by employers with federal contracts of more than $10,000 (and their subcontractors); establish office of federal compliance; require affirmative action programs.
Federal agency guidelines	Indicate guidelines covering discrimination based on sex, national origin, and religion, as well as employee selection procedures; for example, require validation of tests.
Supreme Court decisions: *Griggs v. Duke Power Co., Albemarle v. Moody*	Rule that job requirements must be related to job success; that discrimination need not be overt to be proved; that the burden of proof is on the employer to prove the qualification is valid.
Equal Pay Act of 1963	Requires equal pay for men and women for performing similar work.
Age Discrimination in Employment Act of 1967	Prohibits discriminating against a person 40 or over in any area of employment because of age.
State and local laws	Often cover organizations too small to be covered by federal laws.
Vocational Rehabilitation Act of 1973	Requires affirmative action to employ and promote qualified handicapped persons and prohibits discrimination against handicapped persons.
Pregnancy Discrimination Act of 1978	Prohibits discrimination in employment against pregnant women, or related conditions.
Vietnam Era Veterans' Readjustment Assistance Act of 1974	Requires affirmative action in employment for veterans of the Vietnam war era.
Ward Cove v. Atonio	Made it more difficult to prove a case of unlawful discrimination against an employer.
Price Waterhouse v. Hopkins	Unlawful actions may not be discriminatory if lawful actions would have resulted in the same personnel decision.
Americans with Disabilities Act of 1990	Strengthens the need for most employers to make reasonable accommodations for disabled employees at work; prohibits discrimination.
Civil Rights Act of 1991	Reverses *Ward Cove, Price Waterhouse*, and other decisions; places burden of proof back on employer and permits compensatory and punitive money damages for discrimination.

Note: The actual laws (and others) can be accessed at: http://www.usa.gov/Topics/Reference_Shelf.shtml#Laws. Accessed August 24, 2007

Federal Violence Against Women Act of 1994
Provides that a person who commits a crime of violence motivated by gender shall be liable to the party injured.

The EEOC's Web site (eeoc.gov) says that in fiscal year 2006, EEOC received 12,025 sexual harassment charges, 15.4% of which were filed by males.

The **Federal Violence Against Women Act of 1994** provides another path women can use to seek relief for violent sexual harassment. It provides that a person "who commits a crime of violence motivated by gender and thus deprives another" of her rights shall be liable to the party injured.

The EEOC guidelines define sexual harassment as unwelcome sexual advances, requests for sexual favors, and other verbal or physical conduct of a sexual nature that takes place under any of the following conditions:

1. Submission to such conduct is made either explicitly or implicitly a term or condition of an individual's employment.
2. Submission to or rejection of such conduct by an individual is used as the basis for employment decisions affecting such individual.
3. Such conduct has the purpose or effect of unreasonably interfering with an individual's work performance or creating an intimidating, hostile, or offensive work environment.

Proving Sexual Harassment   There are three main ways an employee can prove sexual harassment.

1. **Quid Pro Quo.** The most direct way is to prove that rejecting a supervisor's advances adversely affected what the EEOC calls a "tangible employment action" such as hiring, firing, promotion, demotion, undesirable assignment, benefits, compensation, and/or work assignment. Thus in one case the employee showed that continued job success and advancement were dependent on her agreeing to the sexual demands of her supervisors.
2. **Hostile Environment Created by Supervisors.** One need not show that the harassment had tangible consequences such as a demotion. For example, in one case the court found that a male supervisor's sexual harassment had substantially affected a female employee's emotional and psychological ability to the point that she felt she had to quit her job. Therefore, even though no direct threats or promises were made in exchange for sexual advances, the fact that the advances interfered with the woman's performance and created an offensive work environment were enough to prove sexual harassment. However, courts generally don't interpret as sexual harassment sexual relationships that arise during the course of employment but that do not have a substantial effect on that employment.[46] For example, the U.S. Supreme Court held that sexual harassment law doesn't cover ordinary "intersexual flirtation." In his ruling, Justice Antonin Scalia said courts must carefully distinguish between "simple teasing" and truly abusive behavior.[47]
3. **Hostile Environment Created by Co-Workers or Nonemployees.** The questionable behavior doesn't have to come from the person's supervisor. Actions of an employee's co-workers or even the employer's customers can cause the employer to be held responsible for sexual harassment. For example, one court held that a sexually provocative uniform the employer required led to lewd comments by customers. When the employee complained that she would no longer wear the uniform, they fired her. Because the employer could not show that there was a job-related necessity for requiring such a uniform and because it was required only for female employees, the court ruled that the employer, in effect, was responsible for the sexually harassing behavior. EEOC guidelines also state that an employer is liable for the sexually harassing acts of its nonsupervisor employees if the employer knew or should have known of the harassing conduct.

Various court decisions provide some insights into how courts may judge what is or is not harassment. For example, "hostile environment" sexual harassment generally means that the discriminatory intimidation, insults, and ridicule that permeated the workplace were sufficiently severe or pervasive to alter the conditions of employment. Here courts look at several things. These include whether the discriminatory conduct is frequent or severe; whether it is physically threatening or humiliating, or a mere offensive utterance; and whether it unreasonably interferes with an employee's work performance.[48] Courts may judge whether an employee subjectively perceives the work environment as abusive based for instance on whether the employee welcomed the conduct or immediately made it clear that the conduct was unwelcome, undesirable, or offensive.[49]

Supreme Court Decisions   The U.S. Supreme Court used a case called *Meritor Savings Bank, FSB v. Vinson* to broadly endorse the EEOC's guidelines on sexual harassment. Two more recent U.S. Supreme Court decisions further clarified sexual harassment law.

In the first, *Burlington Industries v. Ellerth*, the employee accused her supervisor of *quid pro quo* harassment. She said her boss propositioned and threatened her with demotion if she did not respond. The threats were not carried out, and she was in fact promoted. In the second case, *Faragher v. City of Boca Raton*, the employee accused the employer of condoning a hostile work environment. She said she quit her lifeguard job after repeated taunts from other lifeguards. The Court ruled in favor of the employees in both cases.

Implications   The Court's decisions have two implications for employers. First, they make it clear that in *quid pro quo* cases it is *not* necessary for the employee to suffer a tangible job action (such as a demotion) to win the case. Second, the Court spelled out an important defense against harassment suits. It said the employer must show that it took "reasonable care" to prevent and promptly correct any sexually harassing behavior and that the employee unreasonably failed to take advantage of the employer's policy. Therefore, an employer can defend itself against sexual harassment liability by showing two things:

- First, it must show "that the employer exercised reasonable care to prevent and correct promptly any sexually harassing behavior."
- Second, it must demonstrate that the plaintiff "unreasonably failed to take advantage of any preventive or corrective opportunities provided by the employer." The Supreme Court said that the employee's failure to use formal reporting systems would satisfy the second component.

What the Manager/Employer Should Do   Many employers promptly took steps to show they did take reasonable care. For example, they promulgated strong sexual harassment policies, trained managers and employees regarding their responsibilities for complying with these policies, instituted reporting processes, investigated charges promptly, and then took corrective actions promptly, as required.[50] In general, employers should (1) take steps to ensure that harassment does not take place, and (2) take immediate corrective action, even if the offending party is a nonemployee, once it knows (or should know) of harassing conduct. Figure 2-1 summarizes steps to take (such as issuing a strong policy statement). A form such as the one in Figure 2-2 can facilitate this process.[51]

Unfortunately legalistic steps like these are usually not, by themselves, enough. First, studies show that there are significant gender differences in perceptions of sexual harassment. Specifically, "women perceive a broader range of sociosexual behaviors as harassing," particularly when those behaviors involve "hostile work environment harassment, derogatory attitudes toward women, dating pressure, or physical sexual contact."[52]

A second reason why even apparently "reasonable" precautions may not suffice is that employees may be reluctant to use them. In one study, researchers surveyed about 6,000 employees in the U.S. military. Their findings showed that reporting harassment often triggered retaliation, and could harm the victim "in terms of lower job satisfaction and greater psychological distress." Under such conditions, the most "reasonable" thing to do was to avoid reporting.

FIGURE 2-1

HR in Practice: What Employers Should Do to Minimize Liability in Sexual Harassment Claims

Sources: Adapted from www.eeoc.gov/types/ sexual_harrasment.html, accessed May 6, 2007, and *Sexual Harassment Manual for Managers and Supervisors*, published in 1991, by CCH Incorporated, a WoltersKluwer Company.

1. Take all complaints about harassment seriously. The best reaction is to address the complaint or stop the conduct. If complaints are not taken seriously, or it's risky or futile to complain, then the firm's employees are likely to experience considerably higher levels of harassment.
2. It is helpful for the victim to inform the harasser directly that the conduct is unwelcome and must stop. The victim should use any employer complaint mechanism or grievance system available.
3. Remember that when investigating allegations of sexual harassment, the EEOC looks at the whole record: the circumstances, such as the nature of the sexual advances, and the context in which the alleged incidents occurred.
4. Issue a strong policy statement condemning such behavior. The antiharassment policy should contain a clear explanation of the prohibited conduct; assurance of protection against retaliation for employees who make complaints or provide information related to such complaints; a clearly described complaint process that provides confidentiality and accessible avenues of complaint as well as prompt, thorough, and impartial investigations; and clear assurance that the employer will take immediate and appropriate corrective action where harassment has occurred.
5. Inform all employees about the policy prohibiting sexual harassment and of their rights under the policy.
6. The EEOC encourages employers to take steps necessary to prevent sexual harassment from occurring. They should clearly communicate to employees that sexual harassment will not be tolerated. They can do so by providing sexual harassment training and policy statements to their employees and by establishing effective complaint or grievance processes, and taking immediate action when an employee complains.
7. Establish a management response system that includes an immediate reaction and investigation by senior management. The likelihood of employer liability is lessened considerably when the employer's response is "adequate" and "reasonably calculated to prevent future harassment."
8. Begin management training sessions with supervisors and managers to increase their awareness of the issues.
9. Discipline managers and employees involved in sexual harassment.
10. Keep thorough records of complaints, investigations, and actions taken.
11. Conduct exit interviews that uncover any complaints and that acknowledge by signature the reasons for leaving.
12. Re-publish the sexual harassment policy periodically.
13. Encourage upward communication through periodic written attitude surveys, hotlines, suggestion boxes, and other feedback procedures to discover employees' feelings concerning any evidence of sexual harassment and to keep management informed.
14. It is unlawful to retaliate against an individual for opposing employment practices that discriminate based on sex or for filing a discrimination charge, testifying, or participating in any way in an investigation, proceeding, or litigation under Title VII.

Evidence suggests that most sexual harassment victims don't sue or complain. Instead, they quit or try to avoid their harassers. "The few women who do formally complain do so only after encountering frequent, severe sexual harassment; at that point, considerable damage may have already occurred."[53]

Harassers sometimes don't even realize that their abominable behavior is offending others. Sexual harassment training and policies can reduce this problem.[54] Managers who take preventing sexual harassment seriously should also ensure that the firm's culture (including management's real willingness to eradicate harassment) and not just its written rules and procedures, support employees who feel harassed.[55] Minority women are particularly at risk. One study found, "women experienced more sexual harassment than men,

Completion of this form is not required to initiate a complaint; however, completing this form will assist the investigatory process. When completed please return this form to the Director of Human Resources. You will be contacted as soon as possible.

1. Today's date: _____

2. Your name:_____   **3.** Date of birth: _____

4. Signature:_____

5. Status: Student-☐   Faculty-☐   Staff-☐   Administrator-☐

6. Department:_____

7. Contact Information:

Home address:_____

Office phone: _____   Home phone:_____

Cell or pager:_____   Email: _____

8. Person(s) against whom complaint is being made:_____

      Your Status: Student-☐   Faculty-☐   Staff-☐   Manager-☐

9. The incidents which lead me to believe I have been harassed or discriminated against are as follows:

_____

_____

_____

_____

_____

_____

_____

10. Has anyone been notified of this incident? Who and when?_____

_____

11. Are there any other witnesses to the incident(s)? Who?_____

_____

Revised: 6/26/07

FIGURE 2-2

Sample Complaint Form for Filing a Complaint of Harassment or Discrimination

Employees who believe they are victims of harassment should have a mechanism for filing a complaint.

minorities experienced more ethnic harassment than whites, and minority women experience more harassment overall than majority men, minority men, and majority women."[56]

What the Employee Can Do   Keeping in mind that courts generally look to whether the harassed employee used the employer's reporting procedures to file a complaint, the steps an employee can take include:

1. File a verbal contemporaneous complaint or protest with the harasser and the harasser's boss stating that the unwanted overtures should cease because the conduct is unwelcome.
2. Write a letter to the accused. This may be a polite, low-key letter that does three things: provides a detailed statement of the facts as the writer sees them; describes his or her feelings and what damage the writer thinks has been done; and states that he or she would like to request that the future relationship be on a purely professional basis. Deliver this letter in person, with a witness, if necessary.
3. If the unwelcome conduct does not cease, file verbal and written reports regarding the unwelcome conduct and unsuccessful efforts to get it to stop with the harasser's manager and/or the human resource director.
4. If the letters and appeals to the employer do not suffice, the accuser should turn to the local office of the EEOC to file the necessary claim.
5. If the harassment is of a serious nature, the employee can also consult an attorney about suing the harasser for assault and battery, intentional infliction of emotional distress, injunctive relief, and to recover compensatory and punitive damages.

Globalization complicates the task of applying equal employment laws, as The New Workforce feature shows.

The NEW Workforce   Enforcing Equal Employment Laws with International Employees

For most employers today, their workforces are increasingly international, and this complicates the task of applying equal employment laws. For example, Dell recently announced additions to its workforce in India. Are U.S. citizens working for Dell abroad covered by U.S. equal opportunity laws? Are non-U.S. citizens covered? Are non-U.S. citizens working for Dell in the U.S. covered?

In practice, the answers depend on the interplay of U.S. laws, international treaties, and the laws of the countries in which the U.S. firms are doing business. For example, CRA 1991 specifically covers U.S. employees of U.S. firms working abroad. But in practice, the laws of the country in which the U.S. citizen is working may take precedence. (For instance, some foreign countries have statutes prohibiting the employment of women in management positions.) There is also the practical difficulty of enforcing laws like CRA 1991 abroad. For example, the EEOC investigator's first duty in such a case is to analyze the finances and organizational structure of the overseas employer, but in practice few investigators are trained for this duty and no precise standards exist for such investigations. Similarly, one expert says U.S. courts are "little help in overseas investigations, because few foreign nations cooperate with the intrusive enforcement of U.S. civil law."[57] Table 2-3 provides guidelines for applying EEO laws in an international context.[58]

TABLE 2-3 Guidelines That Specify When U.S. Employment Discrimination Laws (Title VII, ADEA, ADA) Apply to International Employers

No.	Guidelines
1.	U.S. employment discrimination laws apply to jobs located inside the United States when the employer is a U.S. entity and the employee is authorized to work in the United States.
2.	U.S. employment discrimination laws apply to jobs located inside the United States when the employer is a U.S. entity and the employee is *not* a U.S. citizen but is legally authorized to work in the United States. Depending on the jurisdiction, U.S. laws may apply to workers who are *not* authorized to work in the United States, although the remedies they receive may be limited.
3.	U.S. employment discrimination laws *do not* apply to jobs located inside the United States when the employer is a foreign entity exempted by a treaty, even though the employee is authorized to work in the United States.
4.	U.S. employment discrimination laws apply to jobs located inside the United States when the employer is a foreign entity *not* exempted by a treaty and the employee is authorized to work in the United States.
5.	U.S. employment discrimination laws *do not* apply to jobs located outside the United States when the employer is a foreign entity, even though the employee is a U.S. citizen.
6.	U.S. employment discrimination laws *do not* apply to jobs located outside the United States even if the employer is a U.S. entity, if the employees are foreign citizens.
7.	U.S. employment discrimination laws apply to jobs located outside the United States when the employer is a U.S. entity and the employee is a U.S. citizen, if compliance with U.S. laws would *not* violate foreign laws.
8.	U.S. employment discrimination laws *do not* apply to jobs located outside the United States when the employer is a U.S. entity and the employee is a U.S. citizen, if compliance with U.S. laws would violate foreign laws.

Source: Richard Posthuma et al., "Applying U.S. Employment Discrimination Laws to International Employees: Advice for Scientists and Practitioners," *Personnel Psychology*, 2006 (59) p. 710. Reprinted by permission of Wiley Blackwell.

DEFENSES AGAINST DISCRIMINATION ALLEGATIONS

2️⃣ Define *adverse impact* and explain how it is proved and what its significance is.

To understand how employers defend themselves against employment discrimination claims, we should first briefly review some basic legal terminology.

Discrimination law distinguishes between disparate *treatment* and disparate *impact*. *Disparate treatment* means intentional discrimination. It "requires no more than a finding that women (or protected minority group members) were intentionally treated differently because of their gender" (or minority status). Disparate treatment "exists where an employer treats an individual differently because that individual is a member of a particular race, religion, gender, or ethnic group.[59] Having a rule that says "we do not hire bus drivers over 60 years of age" exemplifies this.

Disparate impact means that "an employer engages in an employment practice or policy that has a greater adverse impact (effect) on the members of a protected group under Title VII than on other employees, regardless of intent."[60] A rule that says "employees must have college degrees to do this particular job" exemplifies this (because more white males than some minorities earn college degrees).

Disparate impact claims do not require proof of discriminatory intent. Instead, the plaintiff must show that the apparently neutral employment practice (such as requiring a college degree) creates an **adverse impact**—a significant disparity—between the proportion of (say) minorities who are in the available labor pool and the proportion you hire. So, the

adverse impact
The overall impact of employer practices that result in significantly higher percentages of members of minorities and other protected groups being rejected for employment, placement, or promotion.

key here is to show that the employment practice caused an adverse impact. If it has, then the employer will probably have to defend itself (for instance, by arguing that there is a business necessity for the practice).

Adverse Impact

Showing adverse impact therefore plays a central role in discriminatory practice allegations. Under Title VII and CRA 1991, a person who believes he or she was unintentionally discriminated against as a result of an employer's practices need only establish a *prima facie* case of discrimination. This means showing that the employer's selection procedures (like requiring a college degree for the job) did have an adverse impact on a protected minority group. Adverse impact "refers to the total employment process that results in a significantly higher percentage of a protected group in the candidate population being rejected for employment, placement, or promotion.[61] Employers may not institute an employment practice that causes a disparate impact on a particular class of people unless they can show that the practice is job related and necessary.[62]

What does this mean? If a protected group applicant feels he or she was a victim of discrimination, the person need only show that the employer's selection process resulted in an adverse impact on his or her group. (For example, if 80% of the white applicants passed the test, but only 20% of the black applicants passed, a black applicant has a *prima facie* case proving adverse impact.) Then, once the employee has proved his or her point, the burden of proof shifts to the employer: It becomes the employer's task to prove that its test, application blank, interview, or the like is a valid predictor of performance on the job (and that it was applied fairly and equitably to both minorities and nonminorities).

How Can Someone Show Adverse Impact? It is actually not too difficult for an applicant to show that one of an employer's procedures (such as a selection test) has an adverse impact on a protected group. There are four basic approaches:

disparate rejection rates
A test for adverse impact in which it can be demonstrated that there is a discrepancy between rates of rejection of members of a protected group and of others.

4/5ths rule
Federal agency rule that minority selection rate less than 80% (4/5ths) that of group with highest rate evidences adverse impact.

restricted policy
Another test for adverse impact, involving demonstration that an employer's hiring practices exclude a protected group, whether intentionally or not.

1. **Disparate Rejection Rates.** This means comparing the rejection rates for a minority group and another group (usually the remaining nonminority applicants).

    Federal agencies use a "**4/5ths rule**" to determine disparate rejection rates: "A selection rate for any racial, ethnic, or sex group which is less than four fifths or 80% of the rate for the group with the highest rate will generally be regarded as evidence of adverse impact, while a greater than four-fifths rate will generally not be regarded as evidence of adverse impact." For example, suppose 80% of male applicants are hired, but only 50% of female applicants. Since 50% is less than four-fifths of 80%, adverse impact exists as far as these federal agencies are concerned.[63]

2. **Restricted Policy.** The **restricted policy** approach means demonstrating that the employer's policy intentionally or unintentionally excluded members of a protected group. Here the problem is usually obvious—such as policies against hiring bartenders under six feet tall. Evidence of restricted policies such as these is enough to prove adverse impact and to expose an employer to litigation.

3. **Population Comparisons.** This approach compares (1) the percentage of Hispanic (or black or other minority/protected group) and white workers in the organization with (2) the percentage of the corresponding groups in the labor market, where labor market is usually defined as the U.S. Census data for that Standard Metropolitan Statistical Area.

    For some jobs, such as laborer or secretary, it makes sense to compare the percentage of minority employees with the percentage of minorities in the surrounding community, since these employees will come from that community. However, for other jobs, such as engineer, the surrounding community may not be the relevant labor market, since recruiting may be nationwide or even global. Determining whether an employer has enough black engineers might thus involve determining the number of black engineers available nationwide rather than just in the surrounding community. Defining the relevant labor market is therefore crucial.

4. **McDonnell-Douglas Test.** Lawyers in disparate impact cases use approaches 1 through 3 above to test if an employer's policies or actions have the effect of unintentionally screening out disproportionate numbers of women or minorities (an adverse impact, in other words). Lawyers use the McDonnell-Douglas test for showing (intentional) disparate treatment, rather than (unintentional) disparate impact.

This test grew out of a case at the former McDonnell-Douglas Corporation. The applicant was qualified but the employer rejected the person and continued seeking applicants. Does this show that the hiring company intentionally discriminated against the female or minority candidate? The U.S. Supreme Court set four rules for applying the McDonnell-Douglas test:

a. that the person belongs to a protected class;
b. that he or she applied and was qualified for a job for which the employer was seeking applicants;
c. that, despite this qualification, he or she was rejected; and
d. that, after his or her rejection, the position remained open and the employer continued seeking applications from persons with the complainant's qualifications.

If the plaintiff meets all these conditions, then a *prima facie* case of disparate treatment is established. At that point, the employer must articulate a legitimate nondiscriminatory reason for its action, and produce evidence but not prove that it acted on the basis of such a reason. If it meets this relatively easy standard, the plaintiff then has the burden of proving that the employer's articulated reason is merely a pretext for engaging in unlawful discrimination.

Adverse Impact: Example   Assume you turn down a member of a protected group for a job with your firm. You do this based on a test score (although it could have been interview questions, application-blank responses, or something else). Further assume that this person feels he or she was discriminated against due to being in a protected class, and decides to sue your company.

Basically, all he or she must do is show that your human resources procedure (such as the selection test) had an adverse impact on members of his or her minority group. There are three main approaches that he or she can apply here: disparate rejection rates, restricted policy, or population comparisons. Once the person proves adverse impact to the court's satisfaction, the burden of proof shifts to the employer to defend against the discrimination charges.

Note that there is nothing in the law that says that because one of your procedures has an adverse impact on a protected group, you cannot use the procedure. In fact, it could (and does) happen that some tests screen out disproportionately higher numbers of, say, blacks than whites. What the law does say is that once your applicant has made his or her case (showing adverse impact), the burden of proof shifts to you. Now you (or your company) must defend use of the procedure.

There are then basically two defenses employers use to justify an employment practice that has an adverse impact on members of a minority group: the bona fide occupational qualification (BFOQ) defense and the business necessity defense.

Bona Fide Occupational Qualification

An employer can claim that the employment practice is a **bona fide occupational qualification (BFOQ)** for performing the job. This is prescribed in the law. Title VII provides that "it should not be an unlawful employment practice for an employer to hire an

---

bona fide occupational qualification (BFOQ)
Requirement that an employee be of a certain religion, sex, or national origin where that is reasonably necessary to the organization's normal operation. Specified by the 1964 Civil Rights Act.

3 Explain and illustrate two defenses you can use in the event of discriminatory practice allegations.

employee . . . on the basis of religion, sex, or national origin *in those certain instances where religion, sex, or national origin is a bona fide occupational qualification* reasonably necessary to the normal operation of that particular business or enterprise."

However, courts usually interpret the BFOQ exception narrowly. It is almost always a defense to a disparate treatment case based upon direct evidence of *intentional* discrimination, and not to disparate impact (unintentional) discrimination. As a practical matter, employers use it mostly as a defense against charges of intentional discrimination based on age.

Age as a BFOQ   The Age Discrimination in Employment Act (ADEA) permits disparate treatment in those instances when age is a BFOQ.[64] For example, age is a BFOQ when federal requirements impose a compulsory age limit, such as when the Federal Aviation Agency sets a ceiling of age 65 for pilots.[65] Actors required for youthful or elderly roles or persons used to advertise or promote the sales of products designed for youthful or elderly consumers suggest other instances when age may be a BFOQ. However, courts set the bar high: The reason for the age limit must go to the essence of the business. A court said a bus line's maximum-age hiring policy for bus drivers was a BFOQ. The court said the essence of the business was safe transportation of passengers, and given that, the employer could strive to employ the most qualified persons available.[66]

Employers using the BFOQ defense admit they base their personnel decisions on age, but seek to justify them by showing that the decisions were reasonably necessary to normal business operations (for instance, the bus line arguing its maximum-age driver requirement is necessary for safety). Alternatively, an employer may raise the FOA (factors other than age) defense. Here one argues that its actions were "reasonable" based on some factor other than age, such as the terminated person's poor performance.

Religion as a BFOQ   Religion may be a BFOQ in the case of religious organizations or societies that require employees to share their particular religion. For example, religion may be a BFOQ when hiring persons to teach in a denominational school. However, remember courts construe the BFOQ defense very narrowly.

Gender as a BFOQ   Gender may be a BFOQ for positions like actor, model, and rest room attendant requiring physical characteristics necessarily possessed by one sex. However, for most jobs today, it's difficult to claim that gender is a BFOQ. For example, gender is not a BFOQ for parole and probation officers.[67] It is not a BFOQ for positions just because the positions require lifting heavy objects.

National Origin as a BFOQ   A person's country of national origin may be a BFOQ. For example, an employer who is running the Chinese pavilion at a fair might claim that Chinese heritage is a BFOQ for persons to deal with the public.

Business Necessity

"Business necessity" is a defense created by the courts. It requires showing that there is an overriding business purpose for the discriminatory practice and that the practice is therefore acceptable.

It's not easy to prove business necessity.[68] The Supreme Court has made it clear that business necessity does not encompass such matters as avoiding an inconvenience, annoyance, or expense to the employer. For example, an employer can't generally discharge employees whose wages have been garnished merely because garnishment (requiring the employer to divert part of the person's wages to pay his or her debts) creates an inconvenience. The Second Circuit Court of Appeals held that business necessity means an "irresistible demand," and that to be used the practice "must not only directly foster safety and efficiency" but also be essential to these goals.[69] Furthermore, "the business purpose must be sufficiently compelling to override any racial impact . . ."[70]

However, many employers have used the business necessity defense successfully. In *Spurlock v. United Airlines*, a minority candidate sued United Airlines, stating that its requirements that pilot candidates have 500 flight hours and college degrees were unfairly discriminatory. The court agreed that the requirements did have an adverse impact on members of the person's minority group. But it held that in light of the cost of the training program and the tremendous human and economic risks involved in hiring unqualified candidates, the selection standards were a business necessity and were job related.[71]

In general, when a job requires a small amount of skill and training, the courts closely scrutinize any pre-employment standards or criteria that discriminate against minorities. The employer in such instances has a heavy burden to demonstrate that the practices are job related. There is a correspondingly lighter burden when the job requires a high degree of skill, and when the economic and human risks of hiring an unqualified applicant are great.[72]

Attempts by employers to show that their selection tests or other employment practices are *valid* are an example of the business necessity defense. Here the employer must show that the test or other practice is job related—in other words, that it is a valid predictor of performance on the job. Where the employer can establish such validity, the courts have generally supported the use of the test or other employment practice as a business necessity. In this context, *validity* means the degree to which the test or other employment practice is related to or predicts performance on the job; Chapter 6 explains validation.

Other Considerations in Discriminatory Practice Defenses

There are three other points to remember about discrimination charges:

1. First, good intentions are no excuse. As the Supreme Court held in the *Griggs* case,

   > Good intent or absence of discriminatory intent does not redeem procedures or testing mechanisms that operate as built-in headwinds for minority groups and are unrelated to measuring job capability.

2. Second, one cannot hide behind collective bargaining agreements (for instance, by claiming that the discriminatory practice is required by a union agreement). Courts have often held that equal employment opportunity laws take precedence over the rights embodied in a labor contract.[73]

3. Third, while a strong defense is often the sensible response to a discrimination charge, it is not the only response. When confronted with the fact that one or more of its personnel practices is discriminatory, the employer can react by agreeing to eliminate the illegal practice and (when required) by compensating the people discriminated against.

4 Avoid employment discrimination problems.

ILLUSTRATIVE DISCRIMINATORY EMPLOYMENT PRACTICES

A Note on What You Can and Cannot Do

Before proceeding, we should review what federal fair employment laws allow (and do not allow) you to say and do.

Federal laws like Title VII usually don't expressly ban preemployment questions about an applicant's race, color, religion, sex, or national origin. In other words, "with the exception of personnel policies calling for outright discrimination against the members of some protected group," it's not the questions but their impact.[74] For example, it is not illegal to ask a job candidate about her marital status (although at first glance such a question might seem discriminatory). You can ask, as long as you are prepared to show either that you do not discriminate or that you can defend the practice as a BFOQ or business necessity.

But, in practice, there are two reasons to avoid such questions. First, although federal law may not bar such questions, many state and local laws do. Second, the EEOC has said that it will disapprove of such practices, so just asking the questions may draw its attention. Put another way, these are often "problem questions" because they tend to identify an applicant as a member of a protected group or to adversely affect members of a protected group. They become illegal if a complainant can show they are used to screen out a greater proportion of his or her protected group's applicants, and the employer can't prove the practice is required as a business necessity or BFOQ.

The EEOC approves using "testers"—individuals who pose as applicants to test a firm's equal employment procedures. This makes it even more important to be careful in devising selection procedures and training recruiters.[75]

Let's look now at some of the potentially discriminatory practices to avoid.[76]

Recruitment

> ⑤ Cite specific discriminatory personnel management practices in recruitment, selection, promotion, transfer, layoffs, and benefits.

Word of Mouth You cannot rely upon word-of-mouth dissemination of information about job opportunities when your workforce is all (or substantially all) white or all members of some other class such as all female, all Hispanic, and so on. Doing so reduces the likelihood that others will become aware of the jobs and thus apply for them.

Misleading Information It is unlawful to give false or misleading information to members of any group or to fail or refuse to advise them of work opportunities and the procedures for obtaining them.

Help Wanted Ads "Help wanted—male" and "help wanted—female" advertising classifications are violations unless gender is a bona fide occupational qualification for the job. The same applies to ads that suggest you discriminate based on age. For example, you cannot advertise for a "young" man or woman.

Selection Standards

Educational Requirements Courts have found educational qualifications to be illegal when (1) minority groups are less likely to possess the educational qualifications (such as a high school degree) and (2) such qualifications are also not job related. There may be jobs for which educational requirements (such as college degrees for pilot candidates) are a necessity, however.

Tests Courts deem tests unlawful if they disproportionately screen out minorities or women and are not job related. According to former Chief Justice Burger,

> Nothing in the [Title VII] act precludes the use of testing or measuring procedures; obviously they are useful. What Congress has forbidden is giving these devices and mechanisms controlling force unless they are demonstrating a reasonable measure of job performance.

Preference to Relatives Do not give preference to relatives of current employees with respect to employment opportunities if your current employees are substantially nonminority.

Height, Weight, and Physical Characteristics   Requirements for physical characteristics (such as height and weight) are unlawful unless the employer can show they're job related. For example, the Court held that a firm's requirement that a person weigh a minimum of 150 pounds for positions on its assembly lines discriminated unfairly against women. *Maximum* weight rules generally don't trigger adverse legal rulings. However, some minority groups have a higher incidence of obesity, so employers must ensure their weight rules don't adversely impact these groups. To qualify for reasonable accommodation, obese applicants must demonstrate they are 100 pounds above their ideal weight or there is a physiological cause for their disability. In practice, employers sometimes treat overweight female applicants and employees to their disadvantage, and this is a potential problem.

Arrest Records   Unless security clearance is necessary, you should not ask an applicant whether he or she has ever been arrested or spent time in jail, or use an arrest record to disqualify a person for a position automatically. There is always a presumption of innocence until proven guilty. In addition, (1) arrest records in general are not valid for predicting job performance and (2) police have arrested a higher proportion of minorities than whites. Thus, disqualifying applicants based on arrest records automatically has an adverse impact on minorities. You can ask about conviction records, and then determine on a case-by-case basis whether the facts justify refusal to employ an applicant in a particular position.

Application Forms   Employment applications generally shouldn't contain questions about applicants' disabilities, workers' compensation history, age, arrest record, or U.S. citizenship. Personal information required for legitimate tax or benefit reasons (such as who to contact in case of emergency) is best collected after you hire the person.[77] (Note that while equal employment laws discourage employers from asking for such information, no such laws prohibit the applicants themselves from offering it. One study examined 107 résumés from Australian managerial applicants. Many provided information regarding marital status, ethnicity, age, and gender.)[78]

Discharge Due to Garnishment   A disproportionate number of minorities are subjected to garnishment procedures (in which creditors make a claim to a portion of the person's wages). Therefore, firing a minority member whose salary is garnished is illegal, unless you can show some overriding business necessity.

Sample Discriminatory Promotion, Transfer, and Layoff Practices

Fair employment laws protect not just job applicants but also current employees. Any employment practices regarding pay, promotion, termination, discipline, or benefits that (1) are applied differently to different classes of persons; (2) adversely impact members of a protected group; and (3) cannot be shown to be required as a BFOQ or business necessity may be held to be illegally discriminatory. For example, the Equal Pay Act requires that equal wages be paid for substantially similar work performed by both men and women.

Personal Appearance Regulations and Title VII   Employees have filed suits against employers' dress and appearance codes under Title VII, usually claiming sex discrimination but sometimes claiming racial discrimination. A sampling of court rulings follows:[79]

- **Dress.** In general, employers do not violate Title VII's ban on sex bias by requiring all employees to dress conservatively. For example, a supervisor's suggestion that a female attorney tone down her attire was permissible when the firm consistently sought to maintain a conservative dress style and it also counseled men on dressing conservatively.

- **Hair.** Again, courts usually favor employers. For example, employer rules against facial hair do not constitute sex discrimination because they discriminate only between clean-shaven and bearded men, a type of discrimination not qualified as sex bias under Title VII. In many cases, courts also rejected arguments that grooming regulations (such as prohibitions against corn-row hair styles) are racially biased and infringe on black employees' expression of cultural identification. In one case the court decided (in favor of American Airlines) that a braided hair style is a characteristic easily changed and not worn exclusively or even predominantly by black people.
- **Uniforms.** When it comes to discriminatory uniforms and suggestive attire, however, courts have frequently sided with employees. For example, a bank's dress policy requiring female employees to wear prescribed uniforms consisting of five basic color-coordinated items but requiring male employees only to wear "appropriate business attire" is an example of a discriminatory policy. And requiring female employees (such as waitresses) to wear sexually suggestive attire as a condition of employment has also been ruled as violating Title VII in many cases.[80]

THE EEOC ENFORCEMENT PROCESS

Even prudent employers will eventually face employment discrimination claims, and have to deal with EEOC representatives. All managers should therefore have a working knowledge of the EEOC claim and enforcement process; we describe that process next. Figure 2-3 provides an overview of the process.

The process consists of these steps:

- **File Charge.** The process begins with someone filing a claim. Under CRA 1991, the discrimination claim must be filed within 300 days (when there is a similar state law) or 180 days (where there is no similar state law) after the alleged incident took place (two years for the Equal Pay Act). The filing must be in writing and under oath, by (or on behalf of) either the aggrieved person or by a member of the EEOC who has reasonable cause to believe that a violation occurred.
- **Charge Acceptance.** The EEOC's common practice is to accept a charge and orally refer it to the state or local agency on behalf of the charging party. If the agency waives jurisdiction or cannot obtain a satisfactory solution, the EEOC processes it upon the expiration of the deferral period without requiring the filing of a new charge.[81]
- **Serve Notice.** After a charge is filed (or the state or local deferral period has ended), the EEOC has 10 days to serve notice on the employer. Figure 2-4 summarizes important questions an employer should ask after receiving a bias complaint from the EEOC. They include, for example, "To what protected group does the worker belong?"
- **Investigation/Fact-Finding Conference.** The EEOC then investigates the charge to determine whether there is reasonable cause to believe it is true; it has 120 days to make this determination. Early in the investigation the EEOC holds an initial *fact finding conference*—it calls these informal meetings aimed at defining issues and determining if there's a basis for negotiation. However, the EEOC's real emphasis here is often on settlement. Its investigators use the conferences to find weak spots in each party's position to use as leverage to push for a settlement.
- **Cause/No Cause.** If in the course of the investigation no reasonable cause is found, the EEOC must dismiss the charge, and must issue the charging party a Notice of Right to Sue. The person then has 90 days to file a suit on his or her own behalf.
- **Conciliation.** If the EEOC does find cause, it has 30 days to work out a conciliation agreement. The EEOC conciliator meets with the employee to determine what

FIGURE 2-3

The EEOC Charge-Filing Process

Note: Parties may settle at any time.

Source: Based on information at www.eeoc.gov.

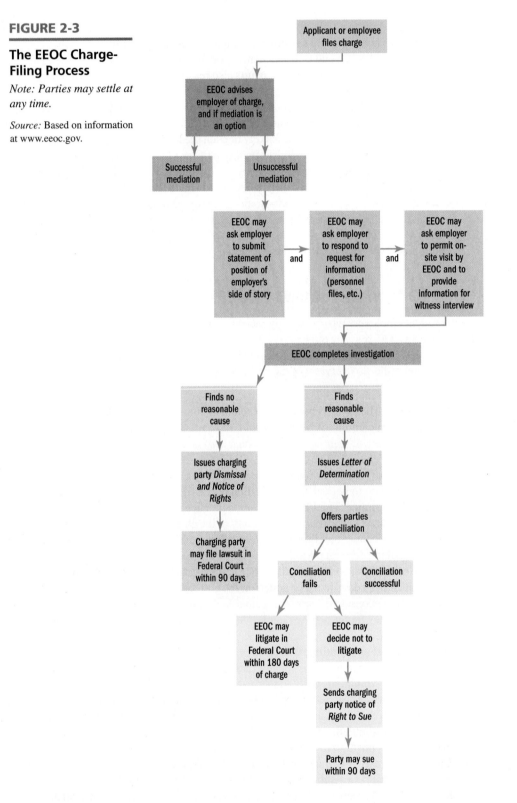

1. Exactly what is the charge and is your company covered by the relevant statutes? (For example, Title VII and the Americans with Disabilities Act generally apply only to employees with 15 or more employees; the Age Discrimination in Employment Act applies to employers with 20 or more employees; but the Equal Pay Act applies to virtually all employers with one or more employees.) Did the employee file his or her charge on time, and was it processed in a timely manner by the EEOC?
2. What protected group does the employee belong to? Is the EEOC claiming disparate impact or disparate treatment?
3. Are there any obvious bases upon which you can challenge and/or rebut the claim? For example, would the employer have taken the action if the person did not belong to a protected group? Does the person's personnel file support the action taken by the employer? Conversely, does it suggest the possibility of unjustified discriminatory treatment?
4. If it is a sexual harassment claim, are there offensive comments, calendars, posters, screensavers, and so on, on display in the company?
5. In terms of the practicality of defending your company against this claim, who are the supervisors who actually took the allegedly discriminatory actions and how effective will they be as potential witnesses? Have you received an opinion from legal counsel regarding the chances of prevailing? Even if you do prevail, what do you estimate will be the out-of-pocket costs of taking the charge through the judicial process? Would you be better off settling the case, and what are the prospects of doing so in a way that will satisfy all parties?

FIGURE 2-4

Questions to Ask When an Employer Receives Notice That EEOC Has Filed a Bias Claim

Sources: Fair Employment Practices Summary of Latest Developments, January 7, 1983, p. 3, Bureau of National Affairs, Inc. (800-372-1033); Kenneth Sovereign, *Personnel Law* (Upper Saddle River, NJ: Prentice Hall, 1999), pp. 36–37; "EEOC Investigations—What an Employer Should Know," Equal Employment Opportunity Commission (http://www.eoc.gov/employers/investigations.html), accessed May 6, 2007.

remedy would be satisfactory and then tries to negotiate a settlement with the employer. If both parties accept the remedy, they sign and submit a conciliation agreement to the EEOC for approval. If the EEOC cannot obtain an acceptable conciliation agreement, it may sue the employer in a federal district court. The EEOC is also experimenting with using outside mediators to settle claims in selected cities (more on this in a moment).

• **Notice to Sue.** If this conciliation is not satisfactory, the EEOC may bring a civil suit in a federal district court, or issue a Notice of Right to Sue to the person who filed the charge.

Voluntary Mediation

The EEOC refers about 10% of its charges to a voluntary mediation mechanism. This is "an informal process in which a neutral third party assists the opposing parties to reach a voluntary, negotiated resolution of a charge of discrimination" (www.eeoc.gov/mediate/facts). If the plaintiff agrees to mediation, the EEOC asks the employer to participate. A mediation session usually lasts up to four hours. If no agreement is reached or one of the parties rejects participation, the charge is then processed through the EEOC's usual mechanisms.[82]

The EEOC is expanding its mediation program. In the four years after the EEOC launched its mediation program a few years ago, its offices had already conducted over 44,000 mediations and settled more than 30,000 charges through the program. By then, the EEOC had also signed more than 18 nationwide agreements and 300 local agreements for mediation with participating employers. Under this latter program, the EEOC refers all eligible discrimination charges filed against these employers to the commission's mediation unit, rather than referring it to the usual charge processing system.[83]

Faced with an offer to mediate, the employer has three options: Agree to mediate the charge; make a settlement offer without mediation; or prepare a "position statement" for the EEOC. If the employer does not mediate or make an offer, the position statement is required. It should include information relating to the company's business and the charging party's position; a description of any rules or policies and procedures that are applicable; and the chronology of the offense that led to the adverse action.[84]

In one recent year, the commission obtained $385 million in awards for discrimination victims. Of this, about $116 million resulted from the mediation program, $149 million came through litigation, and the remainder resulted from negotiations among the parties at the EEOC's administrative level, including conciliation.[85]

Mandatory Arbitration of Discrimination Claims

The U.S. Supreme Court's decisions (in *Gilmer v. Interstate/Johnson Lane Corp.* and similar cases) make it clear that "employment discrimination plaintiffs [employees] may be compelled to arbitrate their claims under some circumstances."[86] Given this, the following suggestions are in order:[87]

- Employers should review all employment discrimination suits filed against them in state and federal courts to determine whether they involve an employee who is subject to some type of agreement to arbitrate. They should then decide whether to move to compel arbitration of the claim.[88]
- Employers "may wish to consider inserting a mandatory arbitration clause in their employment applications or employee handbooks."[89]
- To protect such a process against appeal, the employer should: institute steps to protect against arbitrator bias; allow the arbitrator to offer a claimant broad relief (including reinstatement); and allow for a reasonable amount of prehearing discovery (fact finding).

alternative dispute resolution or ADR program
Grievance procedure that provides for binding arbitration as the last step.

For example, after an expensive EEO lawsuit, Rockwell International implemented a grievance procedure that provides for binding arbitration as the last step. Called (as is traditional) an **alternative dispute resolution or ADR program**, Rockwell gradually extended the program to cover all nonunion employees at some locations. New hires at Rockwell must sign the agreement as a condition of employment, and current employees must sign it prior to promotion or transfer.[90] ADR plans are popular, although the EEOC generally opposes such plans for handling workplace bias claims.[91]

Management Guidelines for Addressing EEOC Claims

Here are some key things to keep in mind when dealing with a discrimination charge:

During the EEOC investigation:

- **Three Principles** If a settlement isn't reached, the EEOC will do its investigation. Here there are three principles to follow. First, ensure that there is information in the EEOC's file *demonstrating lack of merit* of the charge. Often the best way to do that is *not* by answering the EEOC's questionnaire, but by providing a detailed statement describing the firm's defense in its best and most persuasive light. Second, *limit the information supplied* to only those issues raised in the charge itself. For example, do not respond to an EEOC request for a breakdown of employees by age and sex if the charge only alleges sex discrimination.[92] Third, get as much information as possible about the *charging party's claim,* to ensure that you understand the claim and its ramifications.

- **Meet with Employee** Some experts advise meeting with the employee who made the complaint to clarify all the relevant issues. For example, ask: What happened? Who was involved? When did the incident take place? Did it affect the employee's ability to work? Were there any witnesses? Then prepare a written statement summarizing the complaints, facts, dates, and issues involved and request that the employee sign and date it.[93]

- **EEOC Authority** EEOC investigators are not judges and aren't empowered to act as courts. They cannot make findings of discrimination on their own, but they can make recommendations. If the EEOC eventually determines that an employer may be in violation of a law, its only recourse is to file a suit or issue a Notice of Right to Sue to the person who filed the charge. However, the investigator's recommendation is often the determining factor in whether the EEOC finds cause, so it is usually best to be courteous and cooperative (within limits).

- **Submitting Documents** With respect to providing documents to the EEOC, it is often in the employer's best interests to cooperate (or to appear to be cooperative). However, remember that the EEOC can only ask employers to submit documents and ask for the testimony of witnesses under oath. It cannot compel employers to comply. If an employer refuses to cooperate, the commission's only recourse is to obtain a court subpoena.

- **Position Statement** It may be useful to give the EEOC a *position statement* based on the employer's own investigation. (In the past, some EEOC offices have based their own written conclusions on these.) According to one management attorney, employers' position statements should contain words to the effect that "We understand that a charge of discrimination has been filed against this establishment and this statement is to inform the agency that the company has a policy against discrimination and would not discriminate in the manner charged in the complaint." Support the statement with some statistical analysis of the workforce, copies of any documents that support the employer's position, and/or an explanation of any legitimate business justification for the decision that is the subject of the complaint.[94]

During the Fact-Finding Conference:

As part of the investigation, there will be a fact-finding conference. If the employer wants to settle, the fact-finding conference can be a good place to negotiate, but there are four things to beware of.

- **The Records** The only official record is the notes the EEOC investigator takes, and the parties can't have access to them to rectify mistakes or clarify facts.

- **Attorney** The employer can bring an attorney, but the EEOC often "seems to go out of its way to tell employers that an attorney's presence is unnecessary."[95]

- **Information** These conferences often occur soon after a charge is filed, before the employer is fully informed of the charges and facts of the case.

- **Witnesses** The parties may use witnesses' statements as admissions against the employer's interests. Therefore, before appearing, witnesses (especially supervisors) need to be aware of the legal significance of the facts they will present and of the possible claims the charging party and other witnesses may make.

During the EEOC Determination and Attempted Conciliation:

If the fact-finding conference does not solve the matter, the EEOC will investigate and the investigator will determine whether there is reason to believe ("cause") or not to believe

When You're on Your OWN
HR for Line Managers and Entrepreneurs

Dealing with Discrimination Issues and the EEOC

In most cases, employment discrimination issues tend to grow out of actions by individual supervisors. The supervisor makes an ill-informed or foolish comment or decision, and the employee is quick to seek redress through the EEOC or the courts. Even a "nondiscriminatory" action—like losing one's temper at a protected group employee—can trigger a discrimination claim and lawsuit. The employer may prevail, but why put one's employer in the position of having to defend itself?

This has several implications for supervisors. First, in addition to the antidiscrimination training your employer may (or may not) be providing, be familiar with the concepts and tools in this chapter. For example, you should *understand the questions* you can and cannot ask when interviewing applicants, what constitutes sexual harassment, and how equal employment opportunity law affects the full range of human resources decisions, including those relating to appraisal, compensation,

promotions, disciplinary procedures, and employee dismissals.

Second, the supervisor must guard against committing *management malpractice*. In general, malpractice is conduct on the part of the manager that has serious consequences for the employee's personal or physical well-being, or which, as one court put it, "exceeds all bounds usually tolerated by society."[96] In such cases, the employee often alleges intentional infliction of emotional distress. For example, the courts have sided with the plaintiff in situations where the supervisor ridiculed, threatened, humiliated, and sexually harassed an employee. In one particularly outrageous example, the employer demoted the manager to janitor and took other steps to humiliate the person. The jury subsequently awarded the former manager $3.4 million. Supervisors who commit management malpractice may be personally liable for paying a portion of the judgment.

("no cause") that discrimination may have taken place. There are several things to keep in mind here.

- **Review Carefully** If there is a finding of cause, review it carefully, and point out inaccuracies in writing to the EEOC. Use this letter to again try to convince the EEOC, the charging party, and the charging party's attorney that the charge is without merit.
- **Conciliate Prudently** If the EEOC issues a cause finding, it has (as noted above) 30 days to work out a conciliation agreement between the parties. Some experts argue against conciliating. First, the EEOC often views conciliation not as a compromise but as complete relief to the charging party. Second, "if you have properly investigated and evaluated the case previously, there may be no real advantage in settling at this stage. It is more than likely (based on the statistics) that no suit will be filed by the EEOC."[97] Even if the EEOC or the charging party later files a suit, the employer can consider settling after receiving the complaint.

Most EEOC claims stem from the actions or inactions of first line supervisors. The "When You're On Your Own" feature explains some things that the supervisor should watch out for.

6 Define and discuss *diversity management.*

DIVERSITY MANAGEMENT AND AFFIRMATIVE ACTION PROGRAMS

To some extent demographic changes and globalization are rendering moot the motives that drove equal employment legislation. Employers, in other words, now have little choice but to willingly push for more diversity. White males no longer dominate the labor force, and women and minorities represent the lion's share of labor force growth over the foreseeable future. Furthermore, globalization increasingly requires employers to hire minority members with the cultural and language skills to deal with customers abroad. (Thus America's Central Intelligence Agency is aggressively recruiting applicants with Middle-Eastern language skills.) As the *Wall Street Journal* recently put it: "As companies do more and more business around the world, diversity isn't simply a matter of doing what is fair or good public relations. It's a business imperative."[98] So, employers are increasingly striving for racial, ethnic, and sexual workforce balance and harmony as a matter of self-interest. In this context, **diversity** generally refers to the variety or multiplicity of demographic features that characterize a company's workforce, particularly in terms of race, sex, culture, national origin, handicap, age, and religion.[99]

Managing Diversity

However, diversity is potentially a double-edged sword. **Managing diversity** means maximizing diversity's potential benefits (greater cultural awareness, and broader language skills, for instance) while minimizing the potential barriers (such as prejudices and bias) that can undermine the company's performance.

In practice, diversity management involves both compulsory and voluntary management actions. For example, we've just seen that there are many legally compulsory actions employers must take to minimize employment discrimination. But while such compulsory actions can reduce the more blatant diversity barriers, blending a diverse workforce into a close-knit and productive community also requires other steps. Any such *diversity management program* usually means starting at the top, as follows.

- *Provide strong leadership.* Companies with exemplary reputations in managing diversity typically have CEOs who champion diversity's benefits. For example, they take strong stands on advocating the need for and advantages of a diverse workforce, and act as role models for exemplifying pro-diversity behaviors, such as by promoting employees even-handedly.
- *Assess the situation.* The diversity management program itself typically starts with the company assessing the current state of affairs with respect to diversity. In particular, how diverse are we, and are there any diversity-related issues we need to address? Common tools here include equal employment hiring and retention metrics, employee attitude surveys, management and employee evaluations, and focus groups.[100]
- *Provide diversity training and education.* Assuming the assessment reveals issues the firm needs to address, some type of change program is in order. This frequently involves some type of employee training and education program, for instance having employees discuss with expert trainers the values of diversity and the types of behaviors and prejudices that may undermine it.[101] Diversity training often aims at sensitizing all employees to the need to value differences and build self-esteem, and at generally creating a more smoothly functioning and hospitable environment for the firm's diverse workforce.
- *Change culture and management systems.* To reinforce the training, management also needs to reinforce the words of the training with deeds. Ideally, combine the training programs with other concrete steps aimed at changing the organization's values, culture, and management systems. For example, change the bonus plan to incentivize managers to improve their departments' intergroup conflict employee attitude survey scores.
- *Evaluate the diversity management program.* For example, do employee attitude surveys now indicate any improvement in employees' attitudes toward diversity?

In creating diversity management programs, don't ignore obvious issues. For example, training immigrants in their native languages can facilitate learning and ensure compliance

---

diversity
Diversity generally refers to the variety or multiplicity of demographic features that characterize a company's workforce, particularly in terms of race, sex, culture, national origin, handicap, age, and religion.

Managing Diversity
maximizing diversity's potential benefits while minimizing its potential barriers.

Diversity management can blend a diverse workforce into a close-knit and productive community.

with matters such as safety rules and harassment policies, and thus ease their entry into your workforce.[102] Supervisor resistance is another issue. One study, in a large British retailer, found that typical diversity prescriptions like "recognize and respond to individual differences" conflicted with the supervisor's inclinations to treat everyone even-handedly.[103]

Workforce Diversity in Practice

In practice, employers use various means to manage diversity. Baxter Healthcare Corporation started by adopting a strong company policy: "Baxter International believes that a multi-cultural employee population is essential to the company's leadership in healthcare around the world." Baxter then publicized this philosophy throughout the company. It then took steps to foster diversity and to manage it. These steps included evaluating diversity program efforts, recruiting minority members to the board of directors, formally interacting with representative minority groups and networks, and offering diversity training programs.

Other employers facilitate the organizing of minority employees' "networks" to help them retain managerial-level minority employees. The networks' aims are to help minority employees better connect to each other and to provide mutually beneficial information, social support, and mentoring.[104] Minority employees usually organize these intra-company minority networks themselves, although management typically provides ongoing support in terms of things like meeting space and printing.

Diversity's Benefits

Does it pay to invest the employer's time and resources in broadening its diversity, and in getting its employees to work together more harmoniously? The obvious answer would seem to be "yes." IBM created several minority task forces focusing on groups such as women and Native Americans. In the ensuing 10 or so years, the task forces have expanded IBM's multicultural markets. For example, one decided to focus on expanding IBM's market amongst multicultural and women-owned businesses. They did this in part by providing ". . . much-needed sales and service support to small midsize business, a niche well populated with minority and female buyers." As a result, this market grew from $10 million to more than $300 million in revenue in just three years.[105] Longo Toyota in El Monte, California, built its competitive strategy on diversity.[106] With a 60-person salesforce that speaks more than 20 languages, Longo's staff provides a powerful competitive advantage for serving an increasingly diverse customer base. Longo's human resources department therefore has much to do with Longo's strategic success. A survey of 113 MBA job seekers concluded that women and ethnic minorities considered diversity management to be important when accepting job offers.[107] On the other hand, a recent study found "few positive or negative direct effects of diversity on performance," so having an effective diversity program seems to be key.[108]

How can one tell if the diversity initiatives are effective? There are some common-sense questions to ask:

- Are there women and minorities reporting directly to senior managers?
- Do women and minorities have a fair share of the job assignments that are the traditional stepping-stones to successful careers in the company?

- Do women and minorities have equal access to international assignments?
- Is the employer taking steps (including development-oriented performance appraisals and providing developmental opportunities) that ensure female and minority candidates will be in the company's career development pipeline?
- Are turnover rates for female and minority managers the same or lower than those for white male managers?[109]

Some employers encourage diversity through *affirmative action programs*. In this context, affirmative action means making an extra effort to hire and promote those in protected groups, particularly when those groups are under-represented.

Equal Employment Opportunity Versus Affirmative Action

Equal employment opportunity aims to ensure that anyone, regardless of race, color, disability, sex, religion, national origin, or age, has an equal opportunity based on his or her qualifications. *Affirmative action* goes beyond this by having the employer take actions (in recruitment, hiring, promotions, and compensation) to eliminate the present effects of past discrimination.

Affirmative action is still a significant workplace issue today. The incidence of major court-mandated affirmative action programs are down, but courts still use them. Furthermore, many employers must still engage in voluntary programs. For example, Executive Order 11246 (issued in 1965) requires federal contractors to take affirmative action to improve employment opportunities for groups such as women and racial minorities. EEO 11246 covers about 26 million workers—about 22% of the U.S. workforce.[110]

Steps in an Affirmative Action Program

Under EO 11246, the key aims of affirmative action programs are (1) to use numerical analysis to determine which (if any) target groups the firm is underutilizing relative to the relevant labor market, and (2) to eliminate the barriers to equal employment. When designing an affirmative action program, the **good faith effort strategy** emphasizes identifying and eliminating the obstacles to hiring and promoting women and minorities, and increasing the minority or female applicant flow. The first step is to determine that there is underrepresentation. Then, reasonable steps to take would include:

good faith effort strategy

Employment strategy aimed at changing practices that have contributed in the past to excluding or underutilizing protected groups.

1. Issue a written equal employment policy indicating that firm is an equal employment opportunity employer, as well as a statement indicating the employer's commitment to affirmative action.
2. Demonstrate top-management support for the equal employment policy—for instance, by appointing a high-ranking EEO administrator.
3. Publicize internally and externally the equal employment policy and affirmative action commitment.
4. Survey present minority and female employment by department and job classification to determine locations where affirmative action programs are especially desirable.[111]
5. Carefully analyze employer human resources practices to identify and eliminate hidden barriers.
6. Develop and implement specific programs to improve female and minority utilization. Here, review entire human resource management system (including recruitment, selection, promotion, compensation, and disciplining) to identify barriers to equal employment opportunity and to make needed changes.
7. Use focused recruitment to find qualified applicants from the target group(s).

8. Establish an internal audit and reporting system to monitor and evaluate progress in each aspect of the program.

9. Develop support for the affirmative action program, both inside the company (among supervisors, for instance by making it part of their performance appraisals) and in the community.[112]

Avoiding employee resistance to affirmative action programs is important. A review of 35 years of research suggests how employers can increase employee support. Current employees need to see that the program is fair. *Transparent selection procedures* (making it clear what selection tools and standards the company uses) help in this regard. *Communication* is also crucial. Make clear that the program doesn't involve preferential selection standards. Provide details on the qualifications of all new hires (both minority and non-minority). *Justifications* for the program should emphasize redressing past discrimination and the practical value of diversity, not underrepresentation.[113]

Improving Productivity Through HRIS: *Measuring Diversity*

The human resource manager who wants to assess the performance of his or her company's EEOC and diversity efforts has numerous metrics from which to choose. These might include, for example, the number of EEOC claims per year; the cost of HR-related litigation; percent of minority/women promotions; and various measures for analyzing the survival and loss rate among new diverse employee groups.

Even for a company with several hundred employees, keeping track of such metrics is expensive. The HR manager may therefore want to rely on various computerized solutions. One package called "Measuring Diversity Results" provides HR managers with several diversity-related software options aimed at boosting the accuracy of the information at the manager's disposal, and reducing the costs of collecting and compiling it. Among other things, vendors' diversity management packages let the manager more easily calculate: the cost per diversity hire; a workforce profile index; the numeric impact of voluntary turnover among diverse employee groups; the effectiveness of the firm's [employment] supplier diversity initiatives; current diversity measures; and such things as direct and indirect replacement cost per hire.

Recruiting Minorities Online

Talking about hiring more minorities is one thing; actually doing so is another. In practice, many minorities are less likely to be using the Internet, for instance, and less likely to hear about good jobs from their friends. One option is to direct recruiting ads to one or more of the online minority-oriented job markets. For example, Recruiting-Online lists dozens of online diversity candidate resources (www.recruiting-online.com/course55.html). Diversity candidate Web sites with job banks include the African American Network, National Action Council of Minorities in Engineering, National Urban League, Hispanic Online, Latino Web, Society of Hispanic Engineers, Gay.com, Association for Women in Science, and Minorities Job Bank.

The National Urban League's Web site is a good example (www.nul.org/). Clicking on its Career Center tab brings you to a page with five options: Job Search; Post a Job; Resume Center; Job Agents; and Career Resources. The job agents section lets job seekers create their own job profiles. It then searches for employers' listings that may match, and sends a message to the job seeker when it finds a match.

reverse discrimination
Claim that due to affirmative action quota systems, white males are discriminated against.

Reverse Discrimination

The courts have long been grappling with the use of quotas in hiring, and particularly with claims of **reverse discrimination** (discriminating against non-minority applicants and employees). Many cases addressed these issues, but no consistent answer has emerged. For example, in *Bakke v. Regents of the University of California* (1978), the University of California at Davis Medical School denied admission to white student Allen Bakke, allegedly because of the school's affirmative action quota system, which required that a specific number of openings go to minority applicants. In a 5-to-4 vote, the Court struck down the policy that made race the only factor in considering applications for a certain number of class openings and thus allowed Bakke's admission. In *Wygant v. Jackson Board of Education* (1986), the Court struck down a mechanism in a collective bargaining agreement that gave preferential treatment to minority teachers in the event of a layoff.[114] In *U.S. v. Paradise* (1987), the Court ruled that the lower courts can impose racial quotas to address the most serious cases of racial discrimination.[115] In *Johnson v. Transportation Agency, Santa Clara County* (1987), the Court held that public and private employers may voluntarily adopt hiring and promotion goals to benefit minorities and women. This ruling limited claims of reverse discrimination by white males.[116] In June 2001, the U.S. Supreme Court refused to hear Texas's challenge to a ruling that one of its law school affirmative action programs, which gives special consideration to black and Mexican-American student applicants, discriminated against whites. In 2003, the U.S. Supreme Court decided against the University of Michigan's quota-based admissions programs. In June 2007, the Court (in its Meredith case) ruled against race-based school assignment (busing) plans. In practice though, few employers now set such quotas for minority hiring, so the Court's "narrow opinion" here should have little effect in the workplace.[117]

Yet, caution is advisable. For one thing, voluntary affirmative action programs may conflict with the Civil Rights Act of 1991.[118] Read literally, it may bar employers "from giving any consideration whatsoever to an individual's status as a racial or ethnic minority or as a woman when making an employment decision."[119] Employers should therefore emphasize the external recruitment and internal development of better-qualified minority and female employees, "while basing employment decisions on legitimate criteria."[120]

Furthermore, affirmative action may influence attitudes in counterproductive ways. Non-beneficiaries may of course react negatively when they believe such programs result in their being treated unfairly.[121] But even beneficiaries may react badly. In one study, subjects who felt they'd benefited from affirmative-action-based preferential selection gave themselves unfavorable self-evaluations.[122]

REVIEW

SUMMARY

1. Legislation barring discrimination is nothing new. For example, the Fifth Amendment to the U.S. Constitution (ratified in 1791) states that no person shall be deprived of life, liberty, or property without due process of law.
2. Legislation barring employment discrimination includes Title VII of the 1964 Civil Rights Act (as amended), which bars discrimination because of race, color, religion, sex, or national origin; various executive orders; federal guidelines (covering procedures for validating employee selection tools, and more); the Equal Pay Act of 1963; and the Age Discrimination in Employment Act of 1967. In addition, various court decisions (such as *Griggs v. Duke Power Company*) and state and local laws bar discrimination.
3. Title VII of the Civil Rights Act created the EEOC. It is empowered to try conciliating discrimination complaints, but if this fails, the EEOC has the power to go to court to enforce the law.

4. The Civil Rights Act of 1991 had the effect of reversing several Supreme Court equal employment decisions. It placed the burden of proof back on employers, held that a nondiscriminatory (mixed motive) reason was insufficient to let an employer avoid liability for an action that also had a discriminatory motive, and said that Title VII applied to U.S. employees of U.S. firms overseas. It also now permits compensatory and punitive damages, as well as jury trials.

5. The Americans with Disabilities Act prohibits employment discrimination against the disabled. Specifically, qualified persons cannot be discriminated against if the firm can make reasonable accommodations without undue hardship on the business.

6. A person who feels he or she was discriminated against by a personnel procedure or decision must prove either that he or she was subjected to unlawful disparate treatment (intentional discrimination) or that the procedure in question has a disparate impact (unintentional discrimination) upon members of his or her protected class. Once a *prima facie* case of disparate treatment is established, an employer must produce evidence that its decision was based upon legitimate nondiscriminatory reasons. Once a *prima facie* case of disparate impact has been established, the employer must produce evidence that the allegedly discriminatory practice or procedure is job related and is based upon a substantial business reason.

7. There are various specific discriminatory human resource management practices that an employer should avoid in recruitment and in selection. For example, employers generally cannot advertise for "man only."

8. In practice, the EEOC often first refers a charge to a local agency. When it does proceed (and if it finds reasonable cause to believe that discrimination occurred), the EEOC has 30 days to try to work out a conciliation. Important points for the employer to remember include: (a) EEOC investigators can only make recommendations; (b) you cannot be compelled to submit documents without a court order; and (c) you may limit the information you do submit. Also, make sure to clearly document your position (as the employer).

9. An employer can use two basic defenses in the event of a discriminatory practice allegation—business necessity and bona fide occupational qualification. An employer's "good intentions" and/or a collective bargaining agreement are not defenses. (A third defense is that the decision was made on the basis of legitimate nondiscriminatory reasons—such as poor performance—having nothing to do with the prohibited discrimination alleged.)

DISCUSSION QUESTIONS

1. Explain the main features of Title VII, Equal Pay Act, Pregnancy Discrimination Act, Americans with Disabilities Act, and Civil Rights Act of 1991.
2. What important precedents were set by the *Griggs v. Duke Power Company* case? The *Albemarle v. Moody* case?
3. What is adverse impact? How can it be proved?
4. What is sexual harassment? How can an employee prove sexual harassment?
5. What are the two main defenses you can use in the event of a discriminatory practice allegation, and what exactly do they involve?
6. What is the difference between disparate treatment and disparate impact?

INDIVIDUAL AND GROUP ACTIVITIES

1. Working individually or in groups, respond to these three scenarios based on what you learned in Chapter 2. Under what conditions (if any) do you think the following constitute sexual harassment? (a) A female manager fires a male employee because he refuses her requests for sexual favors. (b) A male manager refers to female employees as "sweetie" or "baby." (c) Two male employees are overheard by a female employee exchanging sexually-oriented jokes.

2. Working individually or in groups, discuss how you would set up an affirmative action program.

3. Compare and contrast the issues presented in *Bakke* with more recent court rulings on affirmative action. Working individually or in groups, discuss the current direction of affirmative action.

4. Working individually or in groups, write a paper entitled "What the manager should know about how the EEOC handles a person's discrimination charge."

5. Explain the difference between affirmative action and equal employment opportunity.

6. Assume you are the manager in a small restaurant; you are responsible for hiring employees, supervising them, and recommending them for promotion. Working individually or in groups, compile a list of potentially discriminatory management practices you should avoid.

7. The HRCI "Test Specifications" appendix at the end of this book (pages 726–735) lists the knowledge someone studying for the HRCI certification exam needs to have in each area of human resource management (such as in Strategic Management, Workforce Planning, and Human Resource Development). In groups of four to five students, do four things: (1) review that appendix now; (2) identify the material in this chapter that relates to the required knowledge the appendix lists; (3) write four multiple-choice exam questions on this material that you believe would be suitable for inclusion in the HRCI exam; and (4) if time permits, have someone from your team post your team's questions in front of the class, so the students in other teams can take each others' exam questions.

EXPERIENTIAL EXERCISE

"Space Cadet" or Victim?

Discrimination lawsuits are rarely simple, because the employer will often argue that the person was fired due to poor performance, rather than discrimination. So, there's often a "mixed motive" element to such situations. The facts of a case illustrate this (*Burk v. California Association of Realtors*, California Court of Appeals, number 161513, unpublished, 12/12/03). The facts were as follows. The California Association of Realtors maintained a hotline service to provide legal advice to real estate agents. One of the 12 lawyers who answered this hotline on behalf of the Association was a 61-year-old California attorney who worked at the Association from 1989 to 2000. Until 1996 he received mostly good reviews and salary increases. At that time, Association members began filing complaints about his advice. His supervisor told him to be more courteous and more thorough in providing advice.

Two years later, Association members were still complaining about this individual. Among other things, Association members who called in to deal with him filed complaints referring to him as "a space cadet," "incompetent," and "a total jerk." Subsequently, his supervisor contacted six Association members whom the 61-year-old lawyer had recently counseled; five of the six said they had had bad experiences. The Association fired him for mistreating Association members and providing inadequate legal advice.

The 61-year-old lawyer sued the Association, claiming that the firing was age related. To support his claim, he noted, among other things, that one colleague had told him that he was "probably getting close to retirement" and that another colleague had told him that both he and another lawyer were "getting older." The appeals court had to decide whether the Association fired the 61-year-old lawyer because of his age, or because of his performance.

Purpose: The purpose of this exercise is to provide practice in analyzing and applying knowledge of equal opportunity legislation to a real problem.

Required Understanding: Be thoroughly familiar with the material presented in this chapter. In addition, read the preceding "space cadet" case on which this experiential exercise is based.

How to Set Up the Exercise/Instructions:

1. Divide the class into groups of three to five students.
2. Each group should develop answers to the following questions:
   a. Based on what you read in this chapter, on what legal basis could the 61-year-old California attorney claim he was a victim of discrimination?
   b. On what laws and legal concepts did the employer apparently base its termination of this 61-year-old attorney?
   c. Based on what laws or legal concepts could you take the position that it is legal to fire someone for poor performance even though there may be a discriminatory aspect to the termination (which is not to say that there necessarily was such a discriminatory aspect with this case).
   d. If you were the judge called on to make a decision on this case, what would your decision be, and why?
   e. The court's decision is below, so please do not read this until you've completed the exercise.

In this case, the California State Appeals court held that "the only reasonable inference that can be drawn from the evidence is that [plaintiff] was terminated because he failed to competently perform his job of providing thorough, accurate, and courteous legal advice to hotline callers." ("On Appeal, Hotheaded Hotline Lawyer Loses Age, Disability Discrimination Claims," *BNA Human Resources Report*, January 12, 2004, p. 17.)

APPLICATION CASE

A Case of Racial Discrimination?

John Peters (not his real name) was a 44-year-old cardiologist on the staff of a teaching hospital in a large city in the southeastern United States. Happily married with two teenage children, he had served with distinction for many years at this same hospital, and in fact had done his residency there after graduating from Columbia University's medical school.

Alana Anderson (not her real name) was an attractive African American registered nurse on the staff at the same hospital with Peters. Unmarried and without children, she lived in a hospital-owned apartment on the hospital grounds and devoted almost all her time to her work at the hospital, or to taking additional coursework to further improve her already excellent nursing skills.

The hospital's chief administrator, Gary Chapman, took enormous pride in what he called the extraordinary professionalism of the doctors, nurses, and other staff members at his hospital. Although he took a number of rudimentary steps to guard against blatant violations of equal employment opportunity laws, he believed that most of the professionals on his staff were so highly trained and committed to the highest professional standards that "they would always do the right thing," as he put it.

Chapman was therefore upset to receive a phone call from Peters, informing him that Anderson had (in Peters's eyes) "developed an unwholesome personal attraction" to him and was bombarding the doctor with Valentine's Day cards, affectionate personal notes, and phone calls—often to the doctor's home. Concerned about hospital decorum and the possibility that Peters was being sexually harassed, Chapman met privately with Anderson. He explained that Peters was very uncomfortable with the personal attention she was showing to him, and asked that she please not continue to exhibit her show of affection for the doctor.

Chapman assumed that the matter was over. Several weeks later, when Anderson resigned her position at the hospital, Chapman didn't think much of it. He was therefore shocked and dismayed to receive a registered letter from a local attorney, informing him that both the hospital and Peters and Chapman personally were being sued by Anderson for racial discrimination: Her claim was that Chapman, in their private meeting, had told her, "We don't think it's right for people of different races to pursue each other romantically at this hospital." According to the lawyer, his preliminary research had unearthed several other alleged incidents at the hospital that apparently supported the idea that racial discrimination at the hospital was widespread.

Questions
1. What do you think of the way Chapman handled the accusations from Peters and his conversation with Anderson? How would you have handled them?
2. Do you think Peters had the basis for a sexual harassment claim against Anderson? Why or why not? Do you think Anderson has a legitimate case?
3. What would you do now if you were Chapman to avoid further incidents of this type?

CONTINUING CASE

Carter Cleaning Company

A Question of Discrimination

One of the first problems Jennifer faced at her father's Carter Cleaning Centers concerned the inadequacies of the firm's current HR management practices and procedures.

One problem that particularly concerned her was the lack of attention to equal employment matters. Virtually all hiring was handled independently by each store manager, and the managers themselves had received no training regarding such fundamental matters as the types of questions that should not be asked of job applicants. It was therefore not unusual—in fact, it was routine—for female applicants to be asked questions such as, "Who's going to take care of your children while you are at work?" and for minority applicants to be asked questions about arrest records and credit histories. Nonminority applicants—three store managers were white males and three were white females, by the way—were not asked these questions, as Jennifer discerned from her interviews with the managers. Based on discussions with her father, Jennifer deduced that part of the reason for the laid-back attitude toward equal employment stemmed from (1) her father's lack of sophistication regarding the legal requirements and (2) the fact that, as Jack Carter put it,

"Virtually all our workers are women or minority members anyway, so no one can really come in here and accuse us of being discriminatory, can they?"

Jennifer decided to mull that question over, but before she could, she was faced with two serious equal rights problems. Two women in one of her stores privately confided to her that their manager was making unwelcome sexual advances toward them, and one claimed he had threatened to fire her unless she "socialized" with him after hours. And during a fact-finding trip to another store, an older gentleman—he was 73 years old—complained of the fact that although he had almost 50 years of experience in the business, he was being paid less than people half his age who were doing the very same job. Jennifer's review of the stores resulted in the following questions.

Questions

1. Is it true, as Jack Carter claims, that "we can't be accused of being discriminatory because we hire mostly women and minorities anyway"?
2. How should Jennifer and her company address the sexual harassment charges and problems?
3. How should she and her company address the possible problems of age discrimination?
4. Given the fact that each of its stores has only a handful of employees, is her company in fact covered by equal rights legislation?
5. And finally, aside from the specific problems, what other personnel management matters (application forms, training, and so on) have to be reviewed given the need to bring them into compliance with equal rights laws?

KEY TERMS

Title VII of the 1964 Civil Rights Act, 32
Equal Employment Opportunity Commission (EEOC), 32
affirmative action, 33
Office of Federal Contract Compliance Programs (OFCCP), 33
Equal Pay Act of 1963, 33
Age Discrimination in Employment Act of 1967 (ADEA), 33
Vocational Rehabilitation Act of 1973, 33
Pregnancy Discrimination Act (PDA), 33
protected class, 34
uniform guidelines, 34
Civil Rights Act of 1991 (CRA 1991), 35
mixed motive case, 36
Americans with Disabilities Act (ADA), 36

qualified individuals, 37
sexual harassment, 41
Federal Violence Against Women Act of 1994, 42
adverse impact, 48
disparate rejection rates, 49
4/5ths rule, 49
restricted policy, 49
bona fide occupational qualification (BFOQ), 50
alternative dispute resolution or ADR program, 58
diversity, 61
Managing Diversity, 61
good faith effort strategy, 63
reverse discrimination, 64

ENDNOTES

1. Lauren Weber, "Jury Awards Worker $7.5 million in Wal-Mart Disability Discrimination," Knight-Ridder/Tribune Business News, February 25, 2005 p. NA.
2. Morris, Betsey, "How Corporate America Is Betraying Women," *Fortune*, January 10, 2005, pp. 64–70.
3. Based on or quoted from *Principles of Employment Discrimination Law*, International Association of Official Human Rights Agencies, Washington, DC. See also Bruce Feldacker, *Labor*

Guide to Labor Law (Upper Saddle River, NJ: Prentice Hall, 2000); and www.eeoc.gov/. Employment discrimination law is a changing field, and the appropriateness of the rules, guidelines, and conclusions in this chapter and book may also be affected by factors unique to the employer's operation. They should be reviewed by the employer's attorney before implementation.

4. "High Court: ADEA Does Not Protect Younger Workers Treated Worse Than Their Elders," *BNA Bulletin to Management* 55, no. 10, March 4, 2004, pp. 73–80. See also D. Aaron Lacy, "You are not Quite as Old as You Think: Making the Case for Reverse Age Discrimination under the ADEA," *Berkeley Journal of Employment and Labor Law*, 26, no. 2, 2005, pp. 363–403; Nancy Ursel and Marjorie Armstrong-Stassen, "How Age Discrimination in Employment Affects Stockholders," *Journal of Labor Research* 17, no. 1, Winter 2006, pp. 89–99.

5. BNA Lawrence Kleiman and David Denton, "Downsizing: Nine Steps to ADA Compliance," *Employment Relations Today* 27, no. 3 (Fall 2000), pp. 37–45.

6. John Kohl, Milton Mayfield, and Jacqueline Mayfield, "Recent Trends in Pregnancy Discrimination Law," *Business Horizons* 48, no. 5, September 2005, pp. 421–429.

7. Nancy Woodward, "Pregnancy Discrimination Grows," *HR Magazine*, July 2005, p. 79.

8. *Griggs v. Duke Power Company*, 3FEP Cases 175.

9. This is applicable only to Title VII and CRA 91; other statutes require intent.

10. James Ledvinka, *Federal Regulation of Personnel and Human Resources Management* (Boston: Kent, 1982), p. 41.

11. Bruce Feldacker, *Labor Guide to Labor Law* (Upper Saddle River, NJ: Prentice Hall, 2000), p. 513.

12. "The Eleventh Circuit Explains Disparate Impact, Disparate Treatment," *BNA Fair Employment Practices*, August 17, 2000, p. 102. See also Kenneth York, "Disparate Results in Adverse Impact Tests: The 4/5ths Rule and the Chi Square Test," *Public Personnel Management* 31, no. 2 (Summer 2002), pp. 253–262.

13. Commerce Clearing House, "House and Senate Pass Civil Rights Compromise by Wide Margin," *Ideas and Trends in Personnel*, November 13, 1991, p. 179.

14. Ibid., p. 182.

15. Mark Kobata, "The Civil Rights Act of 1991," *Personnel Journal*, March 1992, p. 48.

16. See, for example, Margaret Clark, "Direct Discrimination Evidence not Needed in Mixed Motive Case," *HR Magazine*, July 2003, pp. 25–26.

17. Elliot H. Shaller and Dean Rosen, "A Guide to the EEOC's Final Regulations on the Americans with Disabilities Act," *Employee Relations* 17, no. 3 (Winter 1991–1992), pp. 405–430. See also Brenda Sunoo, "Accommodating Workers with Disabilities," *Workforce* 80, no. 2 (February 2001), pp. 86–93.

18. "ADA: Simple Common Sense Principles," *BNA Fair Employment Practices*, June 4, 1992, p. 63.

19. Shaller and Rosen, "A Guide to the EEOC's Final Regulations," p. 408. See also James McDonald Jr., "The Rise of Psychological Issues in Employment Law," *Employee Relations Law Journal* 25, no. 3 (Winter 1999), pp. 85–97.

20. Ibid., p. 409.

21. Michael Vest et al., "Factors Influencing a Manager's Decision to Discipline Employees for Refusal to Work with an HIV/AIDS Infected Co-worker," *Employee Responsibilities and Rights* 15, no. 1 (March 2003), pp. 31–43.

22. "No Sitting for Store Greeter," *BNA Fair Employment Practices*, December 14, 1995, p. 150.

23. *Palmer v. Circuit Court of Cook County, Illinois*, c7#95–3659–6/26/97; reviewed in "No Accommodation for Violent Employee," *BNA Fair Employment Practices*, July 10, 1997, p. 79. Also see *Miller v. Illinois Department of Corrections*, CA7, 1997, 6ad cases 678; reviewed in "Courts Define Parameters of the Americans with Disabilities Act," *BNA Fair Employment Practices*, March 20, 1997, p. 34.

24. "Blind Bartender Not Qualified for Job, Court Says in Dismissing Americans with Disabilities Act Claim," *BNA Fair Employment Practices*, February 4, 1999, p. 17.

25. "Differing Views: Punctuality as Essential Job Function," *BNA Fair Employment Practices*, April 27, 2000, p. 56.

26. Sacha Cohen, "High-Tech Tools Lower Barriers for Disabled," *HR Magazine*, October 2002, pp. 60–65.

27. Joe Mullich, "Hiring Without Limits," *Workforce Management*, June 2004, pp. 52–58.

28. Chris Reiter, "New Technology Aims to Improve Internet Access for the Impaired," the *Wall Street Journal*, September 22, 2005, p. B6.

29. James McDonald Jr., "The Americans with Difficult Personalities Act," *Employee Relations Law Journal* 25, no. 4 (Spring 2000), pp. 93–107.

30. "Odds Against Getting Even Are Long in ADA Cases," *BNA Bulletin to Management*, August 20, 2000, p. 229; "Determining Employers' Responsibilities Under ADA," *BNA Fair Employment Practices*, May 16, 1996, p. 57. See also Barbara Lee, "The Implications of ADA Litigation for Employers: A Review of Federal Appellate Court Decisions," *Human Resource Management* 40, no. 1 (Spring 2001), pp. 35–50.

31. "Supreme Court Says Manual Task Limitation Needs Both Daily Living, Workplace Impact," *BNA Fair Employment Practices*, January 17, 2002, p. 8.

32. These are adapted from Wayne Barlow and Edward Hane, "A Practical Guide to the Americans with Disabilities Act," *Personnel Journal* 72 (June 1992), p. 59.

33. "Tips for Employers with Asymptomatic HIV-Positive Employees," *BNA Fair Employment Practices*, November 27, 1997, p. 141.

34. "Airline Erred in Giving Test Before Making Formal Offer," *BNA Bulletin to Management*, March 15, 2005, p 86.

35. *Krocka v. Bransfield*, DC N111, #95C627, 6/24/97; reviewed in "Test for Prozac Violates ADA," *BNA Fair Employment Practices*, August 7, 1997, p. 91.

36. Elliot Shaller, "Reasonable Accommodation Under the Americans with Disabilities Act: What Does It Mean," *Employee Relations Law Journal* 16, no. 4 (Spring 1991), pp. 445–446.

37. Lee, "The Implications of ADA Litigation for Employers."

38. "Determining Employers' Responsibilities Under ADA," p. 57.

39. Lee, "The Implications of ADA Litigation for Employers."

40. Ibid.

41. Timothy Bland, "The Supreme Court Focuses on the ADA," *HR Magazine*, September 1999, pp. 42–46. See also James Hall and Diane Hatch, "Supreme Court Decisions Require ADA Revision," *Workforce*, August 1999, pp. 60–66.

42. James Ledvinka and Robert Gatewood, "EEO Issues with Preemployment Inquiries," *Personnel Administrator* 22, no. 2 (February 1997), pp. 22–26.

43. "1996 State Anti-Bias Laws Focus on Harassment, Genetic Testing," *BNA Fair Employment Practices*, January 9, 1997, p. 123.

44. Larry Drake and Rachel Moskowitz, "Your Rights in the Workplace," *Occupational Outlook Quarterly* (Summer 1997), pp. 19–29.

45. Richard Wiener et al., "The Fit and Implementation of Sexual Harassment Law to Workplace Evaluations," *Journal of Applied Psychology* 87, no. 4 (2002), pp. 747–764.

46. Patricia Linenberger and Timothy Keaveny, "Sexual Harassment: The Employer's Legal Obligations," *Personnel* 58 (November/December 1981), p. 64.

47. Edward Felsenthal, "Justice's Ruling Further Defines Sexual Harassment," the *Wall Street Journal*, March 5, 1998, p. B5.

48. See the discussion in "Examining Unwelcome Conduct in a Sexual Harassment Claim," *BNA Fair Employment Practices*, October 19, 1995, p. 124. See also Michael Zugelder et al., "An Affirmative Defense to Sexual Harassment by Managers and Supervisors: Analyzing Employer Liability and Protecting Employee Rights in the US," *Employee Responsibilities and Rights* 18, no. 2, 2006, pp. 111–122.

49. Ibid., "Examining Unwelcome Conduct in a Sexual Harassment Claim," p. 124.

50. See Mindy D. Bergman et al., "The (Un)reasonableness of Reporting: Antecedents and Consequences of Reporting Sexual Harassment," *Journal of Applied Psychology* 87, no. 2 (2002), pp. 230–242; see also W. Kirk Turner and Christopher Thrutchley, "Employment Law and Practices Training: No Longer the Exception—It's the Rule," *Society for Human Resource Management Legal Report* (July–August 2002), pp. 1–2.

51. See the discussion in "Examining Unwelcome Conduct in a Sexual Harassment Claim," *BNA Fair Employment Practices*, October 19, 1995, p. 124. See also Molly Bowers et al., "Just Cause in the Arbitration of Sexual Harassment Cases," *Dispute Resolution Journal* 55, no. 4 (November 2000), pp. 40–55.

52. Maria Rotundo et al., "A Meta-Analysis Review of Gender Differences in Perceptions of Sexual Harassment," *Journal of Applied Psychology* 86, no. 5 (2001), pp. 914–922.

53. Lilia Cortina and S. Arzu Wasti, "Profile to Coping: Response to Sexual Harassment across Persons, Organizations, and Cultures," *Journal of Applied Psychology* 90, no. 1, (2005), pp. 182–192.

54. Jason Janov, "Sexual Harassment and the Three Big Surprises," *HR Magazine* 46, no. 11 (November 2001), p. 123ff.

55. Bergman et al., "The (Un)reasonabless of Reporting," p. 237.

56. Jennifer Berdahl and Celia Moore, "Workplace Harassment: Double Jeopardy for Minority Women," *Journal of Applied Psychology*, 2006 91, no. 2, pp. 426–436.

57. Based on Gregory Baxter, "Over There: Enforcing the 1991 Civil Rights Act Abroad," *Employee Relations Law Journal* 1, no. 2 (Autumn 1993) pp. 257–266.

58. "Expansion of Employment Laws Abroad Impacts U.S. Employers, " *BNA Bulletin to Management*, April 11, 2006, p. 119; Richard Posthuma, Mark Roehling, and Michael Campion, "Applying U.S. Employment Discrimination Laws to International Employers: Advice for Scientists and Practitioners," *Personnel Psychology*, 2006, 59, pp. 705–739.

59. John Moran, *Employment Law* (Upper Saddle River, NJ: Prentice Hall, 1997), p. 166.

60. "The Eleventh Circuit Explains Disparate Impact, Disparate Treatment," p. 102.

61. John Klinefelter and James Thompkins, "Adverse Impact in Employment Selection," *Public Personnel Management*, May/June 1976, pp. 199–204.

62. Moran, *Employment Law*, p. 168.

63. A recent study found that using the 4/5ths rule often resulted in false-positive ratings of adverse impact, and that incorporating tests of statistical significance could improve the accuracy of applying the 4/5ths rule. See Philip Roth, Philip Bobko, and Fred Switzer, "Modeling the Behavior of the 4/5ths Rule for Determining Adverse Impact: Reasons for Caution," *Journal of Applied Psychology*, 2006 91, no. 3, pp. 507–522.

64. The ADEA does not just protect against intentional discrimination (disparate treatment). Under a recent Supreme Court decision (*Smith v. Jackson,* Miss., 2005), it also covers employer practices that seem neutral but which actually bear more heavily on older workers (disparate impact). "Employees Need Not Show Intentional Bias to Bring Claims Under ADEA, High Court Says," April 5, 2005, *BNA Bulletin to Management* 56, no. 14, p. 105.

65. "Congress Legislates to Increase Commercial Pilot Age," *Airline Industry Information*, March 15, 2001.

66. *Usery v. Tamiami Trail Tours*, 12FEP cases 1233.

67. Ledvinka, *Federal Regulation.*

68. Anderson and Levin-Epstein. Primer of Equal Employment Opportunity, pp. 13–14.

69. *U.S. v. Bethlehem Steel Company*, 3FEP cases 589.

70. *Robinson v. Lorillard Corporation*, 3FEP cases 653.

71. *Spurlock v. United Airlines*, 5FEP cases 17.

72. Anderson and Levin-Epstein, Primer of Equal Employment Opportunity, p. 14.

73. This isn't ironclad, however. For example, the U.S. Supreme Court, in *Stotts*, held that a court cannot require retention of black employees hired under a court's consent decree in preference to higher-seniority white employees who were protected by a bona fide seniority system. It's unclear whether this decision also extends to personnel decisions not governed by seniority systems. *Firefighters Local 1784 v. Stotts (BNA*, April 14, 1985).

74. Ledvinka and Gatewood, "EEO Issues with Preemployment Inquiries," pp. 22–26.

75. John Wymer III and Deborah Sudbury, "Employment Discrimination 'Testers': Will Your Hiring Practices 'Pass'?" *Employee Relations Law Journal* 17, no. 4 (Spring 1992), pp. 623–633.

76. Ledvinka and Gatewood, "EEO Issues with Preemployment Inquiries," pp. 22–26.

77. Richard Connors, "Law at Work," lawatwork.com/news/applicat.html.

78. Lynn Bennington and Ruth Wein, "Aiding and Abetting Employer Discrimination: The Job Applicant's Role," *Employer Responsibilities and Rights* 14, no. 1 (March 2002), pp. 3–16.

79. This is based on *BNA Fair Employment Practices*, April 13, 1989, pp. 45–47.

80. Eric Matusewitch, "Tailor Your Dress Codes," *Personnel Journal* 68, no. 2 (February 1989), pp. 86–91; Matthew Miklaue, "Sorting Out a Claim of Bias," *Workforce* 80, no. 6 (June 2001), pp. 102–103.

81. If the charge was filed initially with a state or local agency within 180 days after the alleged unlawful practice occurred, the charge may then be filed with the EEOC within 30 days after the practice occurred or within 30 days after the person received notice that the state or local agency has ended its proceedings.

82. "EEOC's New Nationwide Mediation Plan Offers Option of Informal Settlements," *BNA Fair Employment Practices*, February 18, 1999, p. 21.

83. "EEOC has 18 Nationwide, 300 Local Accords with Employers to Mediate Job Bias Claims Charges," *BNA Human Resources Report*, October 13, 2003, H-081.

84. Timothy Bland, "Sealed Without a Kiss," *HR Magazine*, October 2000, pp. 85–92.

85. "EEOC Reached Record of $385 Million in Benefits; Charge Filings Dropped Slightly in Fiscal 2003," *BNA Human Resources Report*, December 15, 2003, 1339.

86. Stuart Bonpey and Michael Pappas, "Is There a Better Way? Compulsory Arbitration of Employment Discrimination Claims After Gilmer," *Employee Relations Law Journal* 19, no. 3 (Winter 1993–1994), pp. 197–216.

87. These are based on ibid., pp. 210–211.

88. Ibid., p. 210.

89. Ibid.

90. David Nye, "When the Fired Fight Back," *Across-the-Board*, June 1995, pp. 31–34.

91. "EEOC Opposes Mandatory Arbitration," *BNA Fair Employment Practices*, July 24, 1997, p. 85.

92. "Tips for Employers on Dealing with EEOC Investigations," *BNA Fair Employment Practices*, October 31, 1996, p. 130.

93. "Conducting Effective Investigations of Employee Bias Complaints," *BNA Fair Employment Practices*, July 13, 1995, p. 81.

94. Based on Commerce Clearing House, *Ideas and Trends*, January 23, 1987, pp. 14–15.

95. Ibid., p. 219.

96. Kenneth Sovereign, *Personnel Law*, 4th ed. (Upper Saddle River, NJ: Prentice Hall, 1999), pp. 302–303.

97. Ibid., p. 220.

98. Carol Heimowitz, "The New Diversity," the *Wall Street Journal*, November 14, 2005, p. R1.

99. Michael Carrell and Everett Mann, "Defining Work-Force Diversity in Public Sector Organizations," *Public Personnel Management* 24, no. 1 (Spring 1995), pp. 99–111. See also Richard Koonce, "Redefining Diversity," *Training and Development Journal*, December 2001, pp. 22–33.

100. Patricia Digh, "Creating a New Balance Sheet: The Need for Better Diversity Metrics," *Mosaics* (Society for Human Resource Management, October 1999), p. 1.

101. Robert Grossman, "Is Diversity Working?" *HR Magazine*, March 2000, pp. 47–50.

102. Carol Hastings, "Tapping into Your Foreign-Born, Spanish-Speaking Workforce," *Mosaics* (Society for Human Resource Management, July/August 2002), no. 3, p. 1.

103. Carly Foster and Lynette Harris, "Easy to Say, Difficult to Do: Diversity Management in Retail," *Human Resource Management Journal* 15, no. 3, 2005, pp. 4–17.

104. Raymond Friedman and Books Holtom, "The Effects of Network Groups on Minority Employee Turnover Intentions," *Human Resource Management* 41, no. 4 (Winter 2002), pp. 405–421.

105. David Thomas, "Diversity as Strategy," *Harvard Business Review*, September 2004, pp. 98–104; see also J. T. Childs Jr., "Managing Global Diversity at IBM: A Global HR Topic that has Arrived," *Human Resource Management*, Spring 2005 44, no. 1, pp. 73–77.

106. Richard Orlando, "Racial Diversity, Business Strategy, and Firm Performance: A Resource Based View," *Public Personnel Management* 24, no. 1 (Spring 1995), pp. 99–111.

107. Eddy Ng and Ronald Burke, "Person–Organization Fit and the War for Talent: Does Diversity Management Make a Difference?" *International Journal of Human Resource Management* 16, no. 7, July 2005, pp. 1190 5–12 10.

108. Thomas Kochen et al., "The Effects of Diversity on Business Performance: Report of the Diversity Research Network," *Human Resource Management* 42, no. 1 (Spring 2003), pp. 3–21.

109. Bill Leonard, "Ways to Tell if a Diversity Program Is Measuring Up," *HR Magazine*, July 2002, p. 21.

110. David Harrison et al., "Understanding Attitudes toward Affirmative Action Programs in Employment: Summary and Meta-Analysis of 35 Years of Research," *Journal of Applied Psychology*, 2006 91, no. 5, p. 10, pp. 1013–1036.

111. Frank Jossi, "Reporting Race," *HR Magazine*, September 2000, pp. 87–94.

112. U.S. Equal Employment Opportunity Commission, *Affirmative Action and Equal Employment* (Washington, DC, January 1974); Antonio Handler Chayes, "Make Your Equal Opportunity Program Court Proof," *Harvard Business Review*, September 1974, pp. 81–89. See also David Kravitz and Steven Klineberg, "Reactions to Two Versions of Affirmative Action Among Whites, Blacks, and Hispanics," *Journal of Applied Psychology* 85, no. 4 (2000), pp. 597–611.

113. David Harrison et al., "Understanding Attitudes toward Affirmative Action Programs in Employment: Summary and Meta-Analysis of 35 Years of Research," *Journal of Applied Psychology*, 2006 91 no. 5, p. 10, p. 113, pp. 1013–1036.

114. See Michael W. Sculnick, "The Supreme Court 1985–86 EEO Decisions: A Review," *Employment Relations Today* 13, no. 3 (Fall 1986).

115. Ibid.

116. Ann McDaniel, "A Woman's Day in Court," *Newsweek*, April 6, 1987, pp. 58–59.

117. "Lawyers, Scholars Differ on Likely Impact of Affirmative Action Rulings on Workplace," *BNA Fair Employment Practices*, July 3, 2003, pp. 79–80.

118. Coil and Rice, "Managing Work-Force Diversity in the 90s," p. 548.

119. Ibid., p. 560.

120. Ibid., pp. 562–563.

121. Madeline Heilman, Winston McCullough, and David Gilbert, "The Other Side of Affirmative Action: Reactions of Nonbeneficiaries to Sex-Based Preferential Selection," *Journal of Applied Psychology* 81, no. 4 (1996), pp. 346–357.

122. Ibid., p. 346.

3 Strategic Human Resource Management and the HR Scorecard

Facing increased pressures from traditional grocers and from online firms, Albertsons, with 2,500 food and drug stores and 230,000 workers, had to improve performance and boost profitability, and fast. The firm's basic strategy for accomplishing this required aggressively controlling costs, maximizing return on invested capital, taking a customer-focused approach to growth, employing technology, and energizing associates. As in many firms today, Albertsons' top management relied on their human resource managers to help the company achieve its strategic goals. How could Albertsons' human resources team help the company control costs and hire customer-focused applicants, and then energize them? By instituting specific screening, training, pay, and other human resources policies and practices that supported top management's strategic goals.[1] •

After studying this chapter,
you should be able to:

1 Outline the steps in the strategic management process.
2 Explain and give examples of each type of companywide and competitive strategy.
3 Explain what a strategy-oriented human resource management system is and why it is important.
4 Illustrate and explain each of the ten steps in the HR Scorecard approach to creating human resource management systems.

Firms like Southwest Airlines support their strategic aims in obvious ways, such as ticketless travel, and also in less obvious ways, such as by instituting HR practices that help keep costs down.

strategic plan
A company's plan for how it will match its internal strengths and weaknesses with external opportunities and threats in order to maintain a competitive advantage.

As at Albertsons, superior managers usually shape their departments' policies and practices so they make sense in terms of (or "align with") their companies' strategic aims. The main purpose of this chapter is to show you how to develop a human resource management system that supports, and makes sense in terms of, your company's strategic aims; here we show how to translate a company's business strategy into actionable human resource policies and practices. We'll explain the strategic management process, how to develop a strategic plan, the human resource manager's role in the strategic management process, and (in the appendix) a step-by-step "HR Scorecard approach" to creating human resources policies and practices that make sense in terms of the company's strategic aims.

❶ Outline the steps in the strategic management process.

THE STRATEGIC MANAGEMENT PROCESS

Ford Motor Company, facing huge losses and hemorrhaging market share to Toyota and Nissan, knew it needed a new strategic plan. Competition was fierce, Ford's costs were higher than competitors', and Ford's unused plant capacity was draining profits. Ford's managers devised "The Way Forward." This new strategic plan entailed closing a dozen plants and terminating 20,000 employees. As at Ford, a **strategic plan** is the company's plan for how it will match its internal strengths and weaknesses with external opportunities and threats in order to maintain a competitive advantage. The essence of strategic planning is to ask, "Where are we now as a business, where do we want to be, and how should we get there?" The manager then formulates specific (human resources and other) strategies to take the company from where it is now to where he or she wants it to be. A **strategy** is a course of action. Ford's strategies included closing plants and terminating employees. We discuss various standard strategies shortly. First, we look more closely at the strategic management process.

strategy
The company's long-term plan for how it will balance its internal strengths and weaknesses with its external opportunities and threats to maintain a competitive advantage.

Steps in Strategic Management

strategic management
The process of identifying and executing the organization's mission by matching its capabilities with the demands of its environment.

Strategic planning is part of the strategic management process. **Strategic management** entails both strategic planning and implementation, and is "the process of identifying and executing the organization's strategic plan, by matching the company's capabilities with

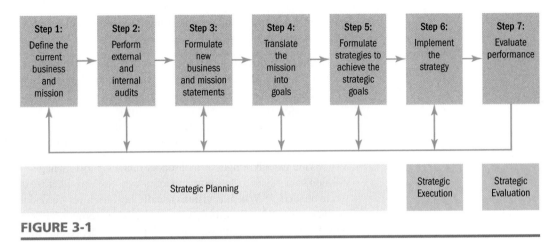

FIGURE 3-1

The Strategic Management Process

the demands of its environment." Strategic planning comprises (see Figure 3-1) the first 5 of 7 strategic management tasks: (1) defining the business and developing a mission, (2) evaluating the firm's internal and external strengths, weaknesses, opportunities, and threats, (3) formulating a new business statement, (4) translating the mission into strategic goals, and (5) formulating strategies or courses of action. In its simplest sense, however, strategic planning is remarkably simple: Decide what business you're in now and which ones you want to be in, formulate a strategy for getting there, and execute your plan. The entire 7-step strategic management process follows:

Step 1: Define the Current Business   Every company must choose the terrain on which it will compete—in particular, what products it will sell, where it will sell them, and how its products or services will differ from its competitors'. Rolex and Seiko are both in the watch business, but Rolex sells a limited product line of high-priced quality watches. Seiko sells a wide variety of relatively inexpensive but innovative specialty watches with features like compasses and altimeters.

Therefore, the most basic strategic decisions managers make involve deciding "what business" their firms should be in: For instance, in terms of the products or services they'll sell, the geographic locales in which they'll sell them, and how they'll distinguish their products or services from competitors'. They ask, "Where are we now in terms of the business we're in, and what business do we want to be in, given our company's opportunities and threats, and its strengths and weaknesses?" Managers then choose strategies—courses of action such as buying competitors or expanding overseas—to get the company from where it is today to where it wants to be tomorrow.

Managers sometimes use a *vision statement* as a sort of shorthand to summarize how they see the business down the road. The company's **vision** is a general statement of its intended direction that shows, in broad terms, "what we want to become."[2] Rupert Murdoch, chairman of News Corporation (which owns MySpace.com, the Fox network, and many newspapers and satellite TV operations), has a vision of an integrated, global satellite-based news-gathering, entertainment, and multimedia firm. WebMD launched its business based on a vision of a Web site supplying everything one might want to know about medical-related issues. One eye care company says, "our vision is caring for your vision."[3] Not surprisingly, it helps to be something of a visionary to formulate a vision statement that sums up in just a few words the manager's

vision
A general statement of its intended direction that evokes emotional feelings in organization members.

image of where the business is heading. Two management gurus, Warren Bennis and Bert Manus say,

> To choose a direction, a leader must first have developed a mental image of a possible and desirable future state for the organization. This image, which we call a vision, may be as vague as a dream or as precise as a goal or mission statement. The critical point is that a vision articulates a view of a realistic, credible, attractive future for the organization, a condition that is better in some important ways than what now exists.[4]

mission

Spells out who the company is, what it does, and where it's headed.

Visions are usually longer term, broader images; most managers also formulate mission statements to ". . . communicate 'who we are, what we do, and where we're headed.'"[5] Whereas visions usually lay out in very broad terms what the business should be, the **mission** lays out in broad terms what our main tasks are now. In the movie several years ago, "Saving Private Ryan," the team's mission was, of course, to save private Ryan. Before their more recent downturn, Ford pursued and then strayed from a remarkably successful mission, summed up by the phrase, "Where Quality is Job One." The mission of the California Energy Commission is to "to assess, advocate and act through public/private partnerships to improve energy systems that promote a strong economy and a healthy environment." (The Commission's *vision*, by way of comparison, is "for Californians to have energy choices that are affordable, reliable, diverse, safe, and environmentally acceptable.")

Step 2: Perform External and Internal Audits   Ideally, managers begin their strategic planning by methodically analyzing their external and internal situations. The strategic plan should provide a direction for the firm that makes sense, in terms of the external opportunities and threats the firm faces and the internal strengths and weaknesses it possesses. To facilitate this strategic external/internal audit, many managers use **SWOT analysis**. This involves using a SWOT chart like that in Figure 3-2 to compile and organize the process of identifying company Strengths, Weaknesses, Opportunities, and Threats.

SWOT analysis

The use of a SWOT chart to compile and organize the process of identifying company Strengths, Weaknesses, Opportunities, and Threats.

Step 3: Formulate New Business and Mission Statements   Based on the situation analysis, what should our new business be, in terms of what products it will sell, where it will sell them, and how its products or services will differ from its competitors'? What is our new mission and vision?

Step 4: Translate the Mission into Strategic Goals   Saying the mission is "to make quality job one" is one thing; operationalizing that mission for your managers is another. The firm's managers need strategic goals. What exactly does that mission mean, for each department, in terms of how we'll boost quality? As an example, WebMD's sales director needs goals regarding the number of new

FIGURE 3-2

A SWOT Chart

Strengths	**W**eaknesses
Example: strong research group	Example: aging machinery
Opportunities	**T**hreats
Example: expanding China markets	Example: merger of two competitors to form single strong one

medical-related content providers—vitamin firms, hospitals, HMOs—it must sign up per year, as well as sales revenue targets. The business development manager needs goals regarding the number of new businesses—such as using WebMD to help manage doctors' offices online—he or she is to develop and sign. Similarly, Citicorp can't function solely with a mission like, "provide integrated, comprehensive financial services worldwide." To guide managerial action, it needs goals in terms of things like building shareholder value, maintaining superior rates of return, building a strong balance sheet, and balancing the business by customer, product, and geography.[6]

Step 5: Formulate Strategies to Achieve the Strategic Goals   Again, a strategy is a course of action. It shows how the enterprise will move from the business it is in now to the business it wants to be in (as laid out by its vision, mission, and strategic goals), given the firm's opportunities, threats, strengths, and weaknesses. The strategies bridge where the company is now, with where it wants to be tomorrow. The best strategies are concise enough for the manager to express in an easily communicated phrase that resonates with employees. Figure 3-3 illustrates this principle. For example, the essence of Dell's strategy is "be direct." Wal-Mart's strategy boils down to "low prices, every day."

   Keeping the strategy clear and concise helps ensure that employees all share that strategy and so make decisions that are consistent with it. For example, the executive team's shared understanding of Nokia's strategy reportedly helps explain how the firm can make thousands of decisions each week so coherently.[7]

Step 6: Implement the Strategies   Strategy implementation means translating the strategies into actions and results—by actually hiring (or firing) people, building (or closing) plants, and adding (or eliminating) products and product lines. Strategy implementation involves drawing on and applying all the management functions: planning, organizing, staffing, leading, and controlling.

Step 7: Evaluate Performance   Strategies don't always succeed. For example, Procter & Gamble announced it was selling its remaining food businesses—Jif, Crisco, and Folger's coffee—because management wants to concentrate on household and cosmetics products.[8]

   Managing strategy is an ongoing process. Competitors introduce new products, technological innovations make production processes obsolete, and social trends reduce demand for some products or services while boosting demand for others. **Strategic control** keeps the company's strategy up to date. It is

strategic control
The process of assessing progress toward strategic goals and taking corrective action as needed.

Company	Strategic Principle
Dell	*Be direct*
eBay	*Focus on trading communities*
General Electric	*Be number one or number two in every industry in which we compete, or get out*
Southwest Airlines	*Meet customers' short-haul travel needs at fares competitive with the cost of automobile travel*
Vanguard	*Unmatchable value for the investor-owner*
Wal-Mart	*Low prices, every day*

FIGURE 3-3

Strategies in a Nutshell

Source: Arit Gadiesh and James Gilbert, "Frontline Action," *Harvard Business Review*, May 2001, p. 74. Copyright © 2001 by the Harvard Business School Publishing Corporation; all rights reserved.

the process of assessing progress toward strategic goals and taking corrective action as needed. Management monitors the extent to which the firm is meeting its strategic goals, and asks why deviations exist. Management simultaneously scans the firm's strategic situation (competitors, technical advances, customer demographics, and so on) to see if it should make any adjustments. Strategic evaluation addresses several important questions: for example, "Are all the resources of our firm contributing as planned to achieving our strategic goals?" "What is the reason for any discrepancies?" and, "Do changes in our situation suggest that we should revise our strategic plan?"

2 Explain and give examples of each type of companywide and competitive strategy.

Types of Strategies

Corporate Strategy   Managers engage in three types of strategic planning (see Figure 3-4). At the top, companywide level, many firms consist of several businesses. For example, PepsiCo runs Pepsi, Frito-Lay, and Pizza Hut. PepsiCo therefore needs a *corporate-level strategy*. A company's corporate-level strategy identifies the portfolio of businesses that, in total, comprise the company and the ways in which these businesses relate to each other. There are several generic possibilities:

- A *diversification* corporate strategy implies that the firm will expand by adding new product lines.
- A *vertical integration* strategy means the firm expands by, perhaps, producing its own raw materials, or selling its products direct.
- *Consolidation*—reducing the company's size—and
- *Geographic expansion*—for instance, taking the business abroad—are other corporate strategy possibilities.

Competitive Strategy   At the next level down, each of these businesses (such as Pizza Hut) needs a *business-level/competitive strategy*. A competitive strategy identifies how to build and strengthen the business's long-term competitive position in the marketplace.[9] It identifies, for instance, how Pizza Hut will compete with Papa John's or how Wal-Mart competes with Target. Companies try to achieve competitive advantages for each business they are in. We can define **competitive advantage** as any factors that allow a company to differentiate its product or service from those of its competitors to increase market share. Companies use several generic competitive strategies to achieve competitive advantage:

competitive advantage
Any factors that allow an organization to differentiate its product or service from those of its competitors to increase market share.

- *Cost leadership* means the enterprise aims to become the low-cost leader in an industry. Dell is a classic example. It maintains its competitive advantage through its Internet-based sales-processing and distribution system, and by selling direct.
- *Differentiation* is a second example of a competitive strategy. In a differentiation strategy, a firm seeks to be unique in its industry along dimensions that are widely

FIGURE 3-4

Relationships Among Strategies in Multiple-Business Firms

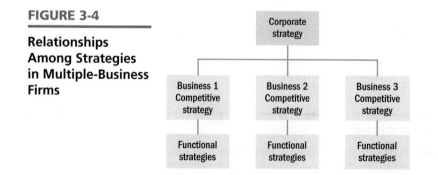

Using Computerized Business Planning Software

There are several business planning software packages available to assist the department head or small business owner in writing strategic and business plans. For example, Business Plan Pro from Palo Alto software contains all the information and planning aids you need to create a business plan. It contains 30 sample plans, step-by-step instructions (with examples) for creating each part of a plan (executive summary, market analysis, and so on), financial planning spreadsheets, easy-to-use tables (for instance, for making sales forecasts), and automatic programs for creating color 3–D charts for showing things like monthly sales and yearly profits.

Business Plan Pro's planning wizard helps the manager or small business owner develop a business plan, step-by-step. The result is an integrated plan, complete with overall strategic plan, and charts, tables, and professional formatting. For example, click "start a plan," and the planning wizard presents a series of questions, including "Does your Company sell products, services, or both?" "Would you like a detailed or basic business plan?" and, "Does your Company sell on credit?" Then, as you go to each succeeding part of the plan, the planning wizard shows you instructions with examples, making it easier to create your own executive summary (or other plan section, including the strategic plan). As you move into the quantitative part of your plan, such as making sales and financial forecasts, the planning wizard translates your numbers into tables and charts.

valued by buyers.[10] Thus, Volvo stresses the safety of its cars, Papa John's Pizza stresses fresh ingredients, Target sells somewhat more upscale brands than Wal-Mart, and Mercedes-Benz emphasizes reliability and quality. Like Mercedes-Benz, firms can usually charge a premium price if they successfully stake a claim to being substantially different from competitors in some coveted way.

- *Focusers* carve out a market niche (like Ferrari), and compete by providing a product or service customers can get in no other way.

Functional Strategy   Finally, each individual business is composed of departments, such as manufacturing, sales, and human resource management. *Functional strategies* identify the basic courses of action that each department will pursue in order to help the business attain its competitive goals. The firm's functional strategies should make sense in terms of its business/competitive strategy. Dell's human resource strategies include putting its HR activities on the Web to support Dell's low-cost competitive strategy. The "When You're on Your Own" feature illustrates a system you can use to facilitate your planning efforts.

Achieving Strategic Fit

Sometimes, managers crafting strategies face a dilemma: For example, their analysis may reveal that there are opportunities they could pursue for which they do not have the requisite corporate strengths or assets; or, there exist great competitive threats (like those facing Ford) for which the firm has seemingly overwhelming weaknesses. In such situations, should they simply "fit" their capabilities to the opportunities and threats that they see, or, should they stretch well beyond their capabilities to take advantage of an opportunity? There are two possibilities.

Fit   Strategic planning expert Michael Porter emphasizes the "fit" point of view. He says, the manager should ensure that the firm's functional strategies align with and support its corporate and competitive strategies: "It's this 'fit' that breathes life into the firm's strategy." For example, Southwest Airlines pursues a low-cost leader strategy, and then tailors its functional activities

FIGURE 3-5

The Southwest Airlines' Activity System

Note: Companies like Southwest tailor all their activities so that they fit and contribute to making their strategies a reality.

Source: Michael E. Porter, "What Is Strategy?" *Harvard Business Review* November–December 1996. Copyright © 1996 by the President and Fellows of Harvard College. All rights reserved.

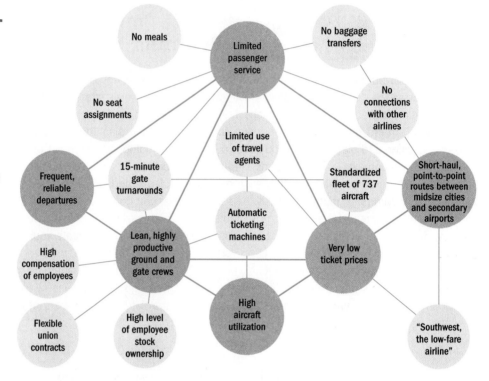

to deliver low-cost, convenient service on its short-haul routes. It gets fast, 15-minute turn-arounds at the gate, so it can keep its planes flying longer hours than rivals and have more departures with fewer aircraft. It also shuns frills like meals, assigned seats, and premium classes of service on which other full-service airlines build their competitive strategies.

Figure 3-5 illustrates this. The larger (pink) circles represent the activities at the heart of Southwest's low-cost activity system: limited passenger services; frequent, reliable departures; lean, highly productive ground and gate crews; high aircraft utilization; very low ticket prices; and short-haul, point-to-point routes. Various subactivities and decisions support each of these activities. For example, limited passenger service means things like no meals, no seat assignments, no baggage transfers, and limited use of travel agents. Highly productive ground crews mean high compensation, flexible union contracts, and a high level of employee stock ownership. Southwest's successful low-cost strategy reflects a well-managed system in which each functional component fits each other component. If Ford is concerned with fit, they'd best take steps to eliminate weaknesses (such as excess capacity) and build their design and management ranks.

Leverage   Alignment is always important, but strategy experts Hamel and Prahalad caution against being too preoccupied with strategic fit. They agree that every company "must ultimately synchronize its resources and its responsibilities." However, they argue that being too preoccupied with fit can limit growth. Basically, they say there are times when, to pursue opportunities, the manager must underplay the firm's weaknesses, and instead capitalize on some unique core company strength. Put another way, they say that **leveraging** resources—supplementing what you have and doing more with what you have—can be more important than just fitting the strategic plan to current resources. For example, "If modest resources were an insurmountable deterrent to future leadership, GM would not have found itself on the defensive with Honda." Dell—competing with giant IBM at the

leveraging
Supplementing what you have and doing more with what you have.

time—focused its relatively limited resources on building a direct sale operation and highly efficient order processing and distribution system.

HUMAN RESOURCE MANAGEMENT'S ROLE IN CREATING COMPETITIVE ADVANTAGE

To have an effective competitive strategy, the company must have one or more competitive advantages, "factors that allow an organization to differentiate its product or service."[11] Southwest Airlines achieves low-cost leader status partly through employment policies that produce the highly motivated and flexible workforce it needs to turn around its planes in 15 minutes. Larger airlines like Delta, faced with restrictive union rules, work rules, and salary structures, find it hard to compete with Southwest, whose employees eagerly rush to "turn around" an airplane in a fraction of the time it takes a Delta team.

The competitive advantage can take many forms. For a pharmaceuticals company, it may be the quality of its research team, and its patents. For a Web site like MySpace, it is a proprietary software system. At Longo Toyota ("The New Workforce") it's the diversity of the workforce and the human resource policies and practices that allow Longo to capitalize on it.

Today, most companies have easy access to the same technologies, so technology itself is rarely enough to set a firm apart. For example, Toyota doesn't have manufacturing equipment that's unavailable to Ford. Why then is Toyota so much more efficient, and its cars of such high quality? Watching Toyota's (or Saturn's) small self-managing assembly teams would reveal that at once. In most firms today, it's the employees' skills and commitment, and the management system that produces the skills and commitent, that make the difference. A production expert from Harvard University studied manufacturing firms that installed special computer-integrated manufacturing systems to boost efficiency and flexibility. Here's what he found:

> All the data in my study point to one conclusion: Operational flexibility is determined primarily by a plant's operators and the extent to which managers cultivate, measure, and communicate with them. Equipment and computer integration are secondary.[12]

The NEW Workforce   Longo Toyota

Some experts claim that diverse workforces create conflicts and rising costs. But that argument is lost on the owners of Longo Toyota in El Monte, California. Longo's human resources strategy supports its competitive strategy of serving a highly diverse customer base by hiring and developing salespeople who speak everything from Spanish and Korean to Tagalog.

By following that human resources strategy, Longo may now be one of America's top-grossing auto dealers. With a 60-person salesforce that speaks more than 20 languages, Longo's staff provides it with a powerful competitive advantage for catering to an increasingly diverse customer base. Human resource management has thereby contributed to Longo's success. While other dealerships lose half of their salespeople every year, Longo retains 90% of its staff person in part by emphasizing a promotion-from-within policy that's made more than two-thirds of its managers minorities. It has also taken steps to attract more women, for instance, by adding a sales management staff person to spend time providing the training inexperienced salespeople usually need. In a business in which competitors can easily imitate products, showrooms, and most services, Longo has built a competitive advantage based on employee diversity.

So, it wouldn't take a visitor to Toyota's Lexington, Kentucky Camry plant long to discover the secret of the Camry's quality and success. Small teams of carefully selected and highly trained assembly workers inspecting and assessing their own work, selecting their own team members, interacting with engineers and suppliers to improve components, meeting with the plant's top managers, and spending several weeks each year being trained. Costs are low and quality is high because the self-managing teams have the capacity and commitment to always do their best. Toyota's human resource strategies—a full week of employee screening and testing, three weeks per year of training, and team-based rewards that incentivize the assembly teams to self-manage their own performance, for instance— ensure they do. The preceding New Workforce feature presents another example.

Strategic Human Resource Management

Managers use the term "human resource strategies" to refer to the specific human resource management courses of action the company pursues to achieve its strategic aims.[13] For example, one of FedEx's strategic aims is to achieve superior levels of customer service and high profitability through a highly committed workforce, preferably in a nonunion environment.[14] FedEx's human resources strategies stem from this aim. They include: using various tools to build two-way communications; screening out potential managers whose values are not people-oriented; guaranteeing to the greatest extent possible fair treatment and employee security for all employees; and utilizing various promotion-from-within activities to give employees every opportunity to fully realize their potential. Figure 3-6 illustrates the interplay between human resource strategy and the company's strategic plans and results. **Strategic human resource management** means formulating and executing human resource policies and practices that produce the employee competencies and behaviors the company needs to achieve its strategic aims. Consider two examples.

strategic human resource management
Formulating and executing HR systems—HR policies and activities—that produce the employee competencies and behaviors the company needs to achieve its strategic aims.

Southwest Airlines   Most of the passengers boarding Southwest Airlines' flight 172 from Orlando to Louisville probably aren't think much about how Southwest keeps its prices low. Those who are may assume it's Southwest's young fleet of planes or fuel buying policies—but those aren't the main reasons. If they were, United and USAir could just copy Southwest.

Southwest's real secret is its human resource management strategy. Strategic human resource management means formulating and executing human resource management

FIGURE 3-6

Linking Company-Wide and HR Strategies

Source: © Gary Dessler, Ph.D., 2007.

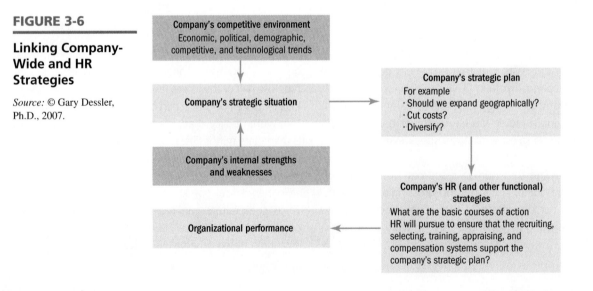

policies and practices *that produce the employee competencies and behaviors the company needs to achieve its strategic aims.* What are Southwest's aims? Its basic aim is to deliver low-cost, convenient service on short-haul routes. How does it do this? One big way is by getting fast, 15-minute turnarounds at the gate, thus keeping planes flying longer hours than rivals. What employee competencies and skills does Southwest need for these fast turnarounds? Ground crews, gate employees, and even pilots who all pitch in and do whatever it takes to get planes turned around. And what human resource management policies and practices would produce such employee competencies and behaviors? An HR strategy built on high compensation, flexible job assignments, cross training, and employee stock ownership. We can outline this as follows: (1) high compensation, flexible work assignments, and so forth, *lead to* (2) motivated flexible ground crews and employees, *who do whatever it takes to* (3) turn the planes around in 15 minutes, *so that* (4) Southwest achieves its strategic aims of delivering low-cost, convenient service.

Dell   The essence of Dell's competitive strategy has always been to be a low-cost leader. Dell's human resource managers use various HR strategies to support Dell's low-cost aims. For example, Dell delivers most of its human resources services, not through a conventional Human Resources department, but via the Web. A Manager Tools section on Dell's intranet contains about 30 automated Web applications (including executive search reports, hiring tools, and automated employee referrals). This allows managers to perform human resource tasks that previously required costly participation by human resource personnel. The intranet also lets Dell employees administer their own 401(k) plans, check job postings, and monitor their total compensation statements. This dramatically reduces the number of human resource people required to administer these activities, and thus the cost of doing so.[15] That in turn supports Dell's low cost strategy.

Strategic Human Resource Challenges

Today's human resource managers face three basic strategic challenges. One (as at Dell) is *the need to support corporate productivity and performance improvement efforts.* With the globalization of the world economy, competition has soared, and with it the need to continually improve organizational performance. Second, *employees play an expanded role in employers' performance improvement efforts.* Indeed, all the elements we associate with high-performance organizations like Toyota's—such as high-technology team-based production—are largely useless without extraordinarily high levels of employee competence and commitment.

The third challenge (stemming from the first two) is that employers see that their *human resource units must be more involved in designing—not just executing—the company's strategic plan.* It used to be just the company's operating (line) managers who had heavy input into the company's strategic plan. The president and his or her staff might decide to enter new markets, drop product lines, or embark on a five-year cost-cutting plan. Then the president would more or less entrust the personnel implications of that plan (hiring or firing new workers, hiring outplacement firms for those fired, and so on) to the human resource manager.

Today's stress on gaining competitive advantage through people renders such arrangements inadequate. Instead, top management needs the input of the human resource team in designing the strategy, since it is the team charged with hiring, training, and compensating the firm's employees. Human resource managers will therefore need "an in-depth understanding of the value creating proposition of the firm [in other words, a basic functional understanding of how the firm makes money]." What activities and processes are most critical for value creation as defined by customers and capital markets? Who in the firm executes these activities successfully?[16] Human resource professionals need to understand the basics of strategic planning and of the basic business functions such as accounting, finance, production, and sales, so they can take (as human resource advocates put it) their "seat at the table" when top management is crafting the firm's strategic plan.

HUMAN RESOURCE MANAGEMENT'S STRATEGIC ROLES

Yet, when it comes to just how involved human resource managers should be in strategic planning, there is often a disconnect between what CEOs say and do. Some do work on the assumption that human resource managers' input is crucial.[17] For example, GM CEO Rick Wagner:

> . . . organized a senior executive committee (the "Automotive Strategies Board"). It included GM's chief financial officer, chief information officer, and vice president of global human resources. As Wagner says, "I seek [the HR vice president's] counsel and perspective constantly. She has demonstrated a tremendous capacity to think and act strategically, which is essential to our HR function and what we want to achieve in making GM a globally competitive business."[18]

Some studies support the wisdom of such an approach. They show the crucial role that human resource managers can play in strategic planning. A study from the University of Michigan concluded that high-performing companies' human resource professionals should be part of the firm's strategic planning team. They help the team identify the human issues that are vital to business strategy. They help conceptualize and execute the sorts of organizational changes that companies increasingly need to execute their strategic plans. Another study, by Mercer Consulting, concluded that 39% of CEOs surveyed see human resources as more of a partner than a cost center.[19] One study, of 447 senior human resource executives, helps illustrate their strategic contribution in concrete terms. Figure 3-7 summarizes the findings. Mergers in which top management asked human resource management to apply its expertise consistently outperformed those in which human resources was less involved.[20]

On the other hand, one survey of 1,310 human resource professionals found that only about half said senior human resource managers are involved in developing their companies' business plans.[21] A similar, recent survey by the Society for Human Resource Management demonstrates the current situation regarding employers' use of strategic human resource management.[22] Overall, about 75% of the human resource managers surveyed

FIGURE 3-7

Percent of Successful Mergers in Which HR Manager Was Involved

Source: Jeffrey Schmidt, "The Correct Spelling of M & A Begins with HR," *HR Magazine,* June 2001, p. 105. Reproduced with permission of Society for Human Resource Management via Copyright Clearance Center.

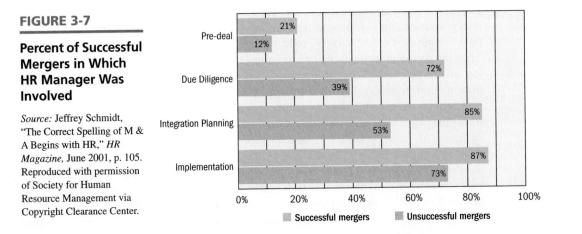

TABLE 3-1 Extent of HR's Involvement in Strategic Planning (According to HR Managers)

(n = 236)	To a Large Extent	To Some Extent	To No Extent
HR works closely with senior management in *implementing* organizational strategies	68%	29%	3%
HR works closely with senior management in *creating* organizational strategies	56%	38%	6%
HR has achieved a level of respect that is comparable with other departments in the organization	49%	45%	6%
Senior management realizes that investments in HR make financial sense	47%	47%	6%
HR *implements* strategies and processes to drive business results	46%	49%	6%
HR is involved in the communication of the business goals	46%	41%	14%
The role of HR is increasingly more focused on strategic interests	43%	49%	8%
HR is involved in the alignment of the business goals	42%	49%	10%
HR involvement is essential in all major business activities and decisions	36%	57%	7%
HR *creates* strategies and processes to drive business results	36%	54%	10%
HR is involved in the development of the business goals	31%	55%	14%
HR is involved in monitoring the achievement of business goals	30%	49%	21%

Note: Sample size is based on the actual number of respondents who answered this question using the response options provided. Percentages within each category may not total 100% due to rounding.

Source: Adapted from Society for Human Resource Management, 2006. www.shrm.org, accessed May 10, 2007.

said their companies had strategic plans in place. However, only about 56% of those in firms with strategic plans in place said their human resources departments had their own (departmental) strategic plans.

Many of these human resource managers report working closely with senior management in both formulating and implementing their firms' strategic plans. Table 3-1 summarizes these latter results. As you can see, 56% of the HR managers say "to a large extent" they work closely with senior management in creating strategic plans; 68% say they do so with respect to actually implementing the plans.

On the other hand, creating human resource management policies and practices that support the employer's strategic goals presumes that the human resource manager can measure how he or she is doing. On the whole, about 66% of large firms' have methods in place to measure the HR department's overall effectiveness; only about 31% of small firms' managers report doing so. Similarly, the use of **metrics** to measure the performance of various human resources-related activities varies widely by activity (see Table 3-2). For example, about 59% of employers use metrics to assess the firm' recruitment and selection processes; that drops off to only about 28% who use metrics for evaluating leadership development.

metrics
Statistics used to measure activities and results.

The Strategy Execution Role

In practice, human resource managers can play two basic strategic planning roles, in *strategy execution* and in *strategy formulation.*

Strategy execution is traditionally the heart of the human resource manager's strategic job. Top management formulates the company's corporate and competitive strategies. Then,

TABLE 3-2 How Often Do Human Resource Managers Measure Their Department Results?

	Frequently	Sometimes	Rarely
Recruitment and selection processes (n = 197)	59%	31%	10%
Performance management (n = 196)	52%	41%	8%
Compensation management/reward programs (n = 199)	51%	34%	15%
Benefits management (n = 192)	51%	34%	15%
Employee relations (n = 194)	49%	31%	20%
Health, safety and security programs (n = 193)	43%	39%	18%
Budgeting (n = 189)	40%	38%	23%
Retention programs (n = 191)	35%	40%	25%
Employee communication programs (n = 185)	34%	44%	23%
Diversity practices (n = 188)	32%	42%	26%
Employee engagement initiatives (n = 180)	31%	43%	27%
Analysis of trends and forecasting (n = 180)	29%	45%	26%
Leadership development (n = 187)	28%	51%	21%
Human capital measurements (n = 175)	28%	37%	35%
Retirement planning (n = 169)	27%	38%	36%
Talent management initiatives (n = 176)	26%	39%	35%
Skills development initiatives (n = 192)	21%	53%	27%
Work/life programs (n = 171)	23%	44%	33%
Succession planning (n = 174)	22%	41%	37%
Employment brand strategy/employment branding (n = 161)	21%	40%	39%
Corporate social responsibility programs (n = 156)	17%	38%	45%

Note: Percentages are row percentages and may not total 100% due to rounding.

Source: Adapted from Society for Human Resource Management, 2006. www.shrm.org, accessed May 10, 2007.

the human resource manager designs strategies, policies, and practices that make sense in terms of the company's corporate and competitive strategies. Dell's human resource strategies—the Web-based help desk, its centralized intranet service bureau—help the firm better execute Dell's low-cost strategy. FedEx's human resources strategies—supporting communication and employee development, for instance—help FedEx differentiate itself from its competitors by offering superior customer service.

Human resource management supports strategy execution in other ways. For example, it administers most firms' downsizing and restructuring efforts, outplacing employees, instituting pay-for-performance plans, reducing health care costs, and retraining employees. When Wells Fargo acquired First Interstate Bancorp, human resources played a strategic role in implementing the merger—in merging two "wildly divergent" cultures and in dealing with the uncertainty and initial shock that rippled through the workforce when the merger was announced.

The Strategy Formulation Role

We've seen that in recent years, human resource management's traditional role in executing strategy has expanded to include working with top management to formulate the company's strategic plans. Again, this expanded *strategy formulation* role reflects the reality employers face today. Globalization means more competition, more competition means more performance, and most employers (such as Dell, FedEx, and Toyota) are pursuing improved performance (in whole or part) by boosting the competence and commitment levels of their employees. That makes human resource management's knowledge and expertise (with respect to issues like: How can we boost employee productivity?) crucial to the strategy formulation process.

HR supports strategy formulation strategy in many ways. For example, formulating a strategic plan requires identifying, analyzing, and balancing the company's *external opportunities and threats*, on the one hand, and its *internal strengths and weaknesses*, on the other. Hopefully, the resulting strategic plans capitalize on the firm's strengths and opportunities, and minimize or neutralize its threats and weaknesses.

Opportunities and Threats   Externally, the human resource manager is in a unique position to supply competitive intelligence that may be useful in the strategic planning process. Details regarding competitors' incentive plans, opinion survey data from employees that elicit information about customer complaints, and information about pending legislation such as labor laws and mandatory health insurance are some examples. Furthermore:

> From public information and legitimate recruiting and interview activities, you ought to be able to construct organization charts, staffing levels, and group missions for the various organizational components of each of your major competitors. Your knowledge of how brands are sorted among sales divisions and who reports to whom can give important clues as to a competitor's strategic priorities. You may even know the track record and characteristic behavior of the executives.[23]

Strengths and Weaknesses   Human resource management also supports strategy formulation by providing input on the company's internal human strengths and weaknesses. Several years ago, Signicast Corp. decided that to compete effectively, it had to move its operations to a new highly automated plant. However, doing so required that production workers command a whole new set of competencies and skills: using computers, reading technical manuals, working in teams, and so on. Therefore, before the CEO could move far along in his strategic planning, he needed input from HR on his employees' competencies and skills. How many were computer literate? How many had the educational background to assimilate the new training? What math competencies did they have? And, could the company provide the necessary training, in time, or would they have to turn to outside vendors—or to hiring all new workers?

Some firms, thanks to such input, even build new strategies around human resource strengths. For example, in the process of automating its factories, farm equipment manufacturer John Deere developed a workforce that was exceptionally expert in factory automation. This in turn prompted the firm to establish a new-technology division to offer automation services to other companies.

3 Explain what a strategy-oriented human resource management system is and why it is important.

CREATING THE STRATEGIC HUMAN RESOURCE MANAGEMENT SYSTEM

In creating a strategically relevant human resource management system, it's useful to focus on three main components. There are the *HR professionals* who hopefully have the strategic and other skills required to build the strategy-oriented HR system. There are the HR *policies and practices* (such as how the company recruits, selects, and trains and rewards employees). And, there are the *employee behaviors and competencies* that the company's strategy requires, and that hopefully emerge from the human resource system's policies and practices (see Figure 3-8). Again, the human resource professionals should design their

The HR function	The HR system	Employee behaviors
HR professionals with strategic management competencies	High Performance Work System (HPWS) consisting of strategically aligned HR policies, practices, and activities	Employee competencies, values, motivation, and behaviors required by the company's strategic plan

FIGURE 3-8

Three Main Strategic Human Resource System Components

Source: Adapted from Brian Becker et al., *The HR Scorecard: Linking People, Strategy, and Performance* (Boston: Harvard Business School Press, 2001), p. 12. Copyright © 2001 by the Harvard Business School Publishing Corporation; all rights reserved.

policies and practices so that they produce the employee competencies and behaviors the company needs to achieve its strategic goals. It is futile for Signicast Corp. to plan a new high-tech plant, if it won't have the workers with the skills and competencies to run it.[24]

The High-Performance Work System

Every company tends to create a human resource system that's uniquely appropriate to its needs, for instance with recruitment and selection practices that make sense for it. However, there is certainly a trend toward installing HR systems that broadly share many characteristics. As noted in Chapter 1, managers call these *high-performance work systems* (HPWS). The need for such systems became apparent as global competition intensified in the 1990s. Companies needed a way to better utilize their human resources as they strove to improve quality, productivity, and responsiveness, to compete with the Toyotas of the world. In the early 1990s, the U.S. Department of Labor identified several characteristics of high-performance work organizations. These include multi-skilled work teams; empowered front-line workers; extensive training; labor management cooperation; commitment to quality; and customer satisfaction.[25] The aim of such a system is to maximize the competencies, commitment, and abilities of the firm's employees.

In a practical sense, Table 3-3 illustrates some of the human resource policies and practices that typically characterize high-performance work systems. This table shows you three things. First, as noted, it shows the sorts of things human resource systems need to do, to be high-performance systems. For example, they hire based on validated selection tests, fill more jobs from within, organize work around self-managing teams, and extensively train employees. Second, Table 3-3 helps to illustrate that high-performance work systems have a bias toward helping workers to manage themselves. Indeed, the point of such a system's recruiting, screening, training, and other human resources practices is usually to build the highly trained, empowered, self-motivated, and flexible workforce that companies today need as a competitive advantage.[26] Third, the table shows that we can measure the extent to which our human resource system is (or is not) consistent with those of a high-performance work system. Note the measurable differences between high-performance and low-performance companies' systems in the table.

Measuring HR's Effectiveness   The latter point regarding measurability bears repeating. Employers today expect their human resource managers to build a persuasive case that shows how—in specific and measurable terms—the firm's human resource activities can and do contribute to creating value for the firm, for instance in terms of higher profits and market value. Top management understandably wants its human resource professionals to create a strategy-supporting human resources system. It also wants the human resource manager to be able to build a persuasive case that shows how—in measurable terms—the human resource system is in fact supporting the employer's strategic aims.

TABLE 3-3 Comparison of HR Practices in High-Performance and Low-Performance Companies

	Low-Performance Company HR System Bottom 10% (42 firms)	High-Performance Company HR System Top 10% (43 firms)
Sample HR Practices		
Number of qualified applicants per position (*Recruiting*)	8.24	36.55
Percentage hired based on a validated *selection* test	4.26	29.67
Percentage of jobs filled from within	34.90	61.46
Percentage in a *formal HR plan* including recruitment, *development*, and succession	4.79	46.72
Number of hours of *training* for new employees (less than 1 year)	35.02	116.87
Number of hours of *training* for experienced employees	13.40	72.00
Percentage of employees receiving a regular *performance appraisal*	41.31	95.17
Percentage of workforce whose *merit increase* or *incentive pay* is tied to performance	23.36	87.27
Percentage of workforce who received *performance feedback* from multiple sources (360)	3.90	51.67
Target percentile for total compensation (market rate = 50%)	43.03	58.67
Percentage of the workforce eligible for *incentive pay*	27.83	83.56
Percentage of difference in incentive pay between a low-performing and high-performing employee	3.62	6.21
Percentage of the workforce routinely working in a self-managed, *cross-functional*, or *project team*	10.64	42.28
Percentage of HR budget spent on *outsourced activities* (e.g., recruiting, benefits, payroll)	13.46	26.24
Number of employees per HR professional	253.88	139.51
Percentage of the eligible workforce covered by a union contract	30.00	8.98
Firm Performance		
Employee turnover	34.09	20.87
Sales per employee	$158,101	$617,576
Market value to book value	3.64	11.06

Source: Adapted from Becher et al., pp. 16–17.

At a minimum, employers use broad HR effectiveness measures such as revenue per full-time employee to assess worker productivity. For example, one firm, Level 3 Communications Inc., uses revenue and income per full-time equivalent employee, average full-time employees overtime, the level of turnover and its associated costs, and overall human resource expenses. Table 3-4 summarizes median revenue and income per full-time equivalent employee for a number of industries.[27] The Bureau of National Affairs, in conjunction with the Society for Human Resource Management publishes annual human resource department benchmarks and analyses listing industrywide metrics in areas including compensation and benefits, employee relations, and staffing.[28]

TABLE 3-4 Employee-Based Benchmarks Employers Can Use as Illustrative Benchmarks

	Median Revenue per FTE	Median Income per FTE
All industries	$142,857	$10,131
Educational services	$76,896	$263
Finance	$162,712	$41,361
Government	$134,691	$0
Health care services	$103,166	$5,000
High-tech	$211,111	$16,250
Insurance	$159,150	$46,667
Manufacturing (durable goods)	$190,213	$16,463
Manufacturing (non-durable goods)	$222,222	$33,810
Retail/wholesale trade	$214,706	$41,528
Services (nonprofit)	$90,563	$1,867
Services (profit)	$113,374	$18,866
Transportation & warehousing	$192,593	*
Utilities	$374,932	$53,702
Government agency	$99,622	$725
Nonprofit organization	$107,031	$2,818
Privately owned for-profit organization	$148,148	$18,602
Publicly owned for-profit organization	$210,673	$38,751
Commercial sector	$163,848	$19,065
Defense sector	$171,004	$20,507
Government (nondefense) sector	$92,165	$155

*Data not reliable.

Source: 2006 SHRM Human Capital Benchmarking Study; Reprinted in Karen Kroll, "Repurposing Metrics for HR," *HR Magazine,* July 2006, p. 67. Reprinted by permission of Society for Human Resource Management via Copyright Clearance Center.

Based on an ongoing research program with over 2,800 corporations, firms that use high-performance policies and practices do perform at a significantly higher level than those that do not. The evidence suggests that "high-performance HR practices, [particularly] combined with new technology, produce better productivity, quality, sales, and financial performance."[29]

Translating Strategy into Human Resource Policy and Practice

As noted earlier, *strategic human resource management* means formulating and executing human resource policies and practices that produce the employee competencies and behaviors the company needs to achieve its strategic aims. The human resource manager therefore needs a practical way to translate the company's strategy into required employee competencies and behaviors, and to translate these required employee competencies and behaviors into the specific human resource policies and practices that will produce them.[30] We'll devote the remainder of this chapter to explaining how to do this.

We outline the basic process in Figure 3-9. Management formulates a *strategic plan*. That strategic plan implies certain *workforce requirements*, in terms of the employee

FIGURE 3-9

Basic Model of How to Align HR Strategy and Actions with Business Strategy

Source: Adapted from Garrett Walker and J. Randal MacDonald, "Designing and Implementing an HR Scorecard," *Human Resources Management* 40, no. 4 (2001), p. 370.

Formulate business strategy
"What are the strategic goals of the business?"

Identify workforce requirements
"What employee competencies and behaviors must HR deliver to enable the business to reach its goals?"

Formulate HR strategic policies and activities
"Which HR strategies and practices will produce these employee competencies and behaviors?"

Develop detailed HR scorecard measures
"How can HR measure whether it is executing well for the business, in terms of producing the required workforce competencies and behaviors?"

skills, attributes, and behaviors that HR must deliver to enable the business to achieve its strategic goals. (For example, must our employees dramatically improve the level of customer service?[31] Do we need more computer-literate employees to run our new machines?) Given these workforce requirements, human resource management formulates *HR strategies, policies, and practices* it believes will produce the desired workforce skills, attributes, and behaviors. (These may take the form of new selection, training, and compensation policies and practices, for instance.)[32] Finally, the human resource manager identifies scorecard measures (metrics) he or she can use to measure the extent to which its new policies and practices are actually producing the required employee compencies and skills, and thus supporting management's strategic goals.

Albertsons Example How could Albertson's human resources team help the company control costs and hire customer-focused employees? At Albertsons, reducing personnel-related costs and improving performance meant hiring employees who had a customer-focused approach and reducing turnover, improving retention, and eliminating time-consuming manual processes and procedures for store managers. Working with its information technology department, Albertsons' human resource management team chose a system from Unicru of Portland, Oregon (www.unicru.com). The system collects and analyzes the information entered by applicants online and at kiosks. It ranks applicants based on the extent to which they exhibit the customer-focused traits that predict success in retail jobs, helps track candidates throughout the screening process, and does other things, such as track reasons for departure once applicants are hired. Human resource managers were able to present a compelling business case to indicate the new system's return on investment. Working as a partner in Albertsons' strategy design and implementation process, the human resources team helped Albertsons achieve its strategic goals, by helping to control costs and hire customer-focused employees.[33]

Translating Strategy into Human Resource Policies and Practices: An Example

An organizational change effort at the Albert Einstein Healthcare Network (Einstein Medical) illustrates how companies translate strategic plans into human resource policies

At Albertson's, reducing personnel-related costs and improving performance meant hiring customer-focused employees.

and practices.[34] In the 1990s, it was apparent to Einstein's new CEO that intense competition, scientific technological changes, the growth of managed care (HMOs and PPOs), and significant cuts in Medicare and Medicaid meant that his company needed a new strategic plan. At the time, Einstein Medical was a single acute care hospital, treating the seriously ill.

New Strategy   The essence of the CEO's new strategy was to change Einstein into a comprehensive health care network of facilities providing a full range of high-quality services in various local markets.

He knew that achieving this change in strategy would require numerous changes in Einstein Medical's organization and employee behaviors. In particular, given the highly dynamic and uncertain health care environment, the new Einstein Medical would require a much more flexible, adaptable, and professional approach to delivering services. Based on that, he decided to summarize the strategic goals of his change program in three words: "initiate," "adapt," and "deliver." To achieve Einstein Medical's strategic aims, its HR and other strategies would have to help the medical center and its employees to produce new services (initiate), capitalize on opportunities (adapt), and offer consistently high-quality services (deliver).

New Employee Competencies and Behaviors   The CEO's next question was, "What sorts of employee competencies, skills, and behaviors would Einstein Medical need to produce these three outcomes?" Working with the head of human resources the CEO chose four employee skills and behaviors: Einstein employees would need to be "dedicated, accountable, generative, and resilient." They would have to be *dedicated* to Einstein's focus on initiate, adapt, and deliver. They would have to take personal *accountability* for their results. They would have to be *generative*, which means able and willing to apply new knowledge and skills in a constant search for innovative solutions. And they would have to be *resilient*, for instance, in terms of moving from job to job as the company's needs changed.

New Human Resource Policies and Practices   Given these desired employee competencies and behaviors, Einstein Medical's human resource managers could ask, "What specific HR policies and practices would help Einstein create a dedicated, accountable, generative, and resilient workforce, and thereby help it to achieve its strategic goals?" The answer was to implement several new human resource programs:

- New *training and communications programs* aimed at assuring that employees clearly understood the company's new vision and what it would require of all employees.
- *Enriching work* involved providing employees with more challenge and responsibility through flexible assignments and team-based work.
- New *training and benefits programs* promoted *personal growth*, which meant helping employees take personal responsibility for their own improvement and personal development.
- Providing *commensurate returns* involved tying employees' rewards to organization-wide results and providing nonmonetary rewards (such as more challenging jobs).
- *Improved selection, orientation, and dismissal procedures* also helped Einstein build a more dedicated, resilient, accountable, and generative workforce.

In sum, Einstein's managers translated the new strategy into specific human resource policies and practices. They knew they could not execute their new strategy without new employee competencies and behaviors. In turn, promoting these competencies and behaviors required implementing new human resource policies and practices. They could then choose measures (such as "hours of training per employee per year") to monitor the new HR strategies' actual progress.

Einstein Medical's managers used a simple, logical, and subjective process to translate strategy into required human resource policies and activities. This is perfectly acceptable. Increasingly, however, many companies are turning to a more rigorous methodology called The HR Scorecard Process. We explain that newer approach in Appendix A in this chapter, starting on page 102.

REVIEW

SUMMARY

1. In formulating their human resources strategies, HR managers must address three basic challenges: the need to support corporate productivity and performance improvement efforts; the fact that employees play an expanded role in the employer's performance improvement efforts; and the fact that HR must be more involved in designing—not just executing—the company's strategic plan.
2. There are seven basic steps in the strategic management process: Define the business and its mission; perform an external and internal audit; formulate new business and mission statements; translate the mission into strategic goals; formulate a strategy to achieve the strategic goals; implement the strategy; and evaluate performance.
3. There are three main types of strategic plans. The company's corporate-level strategy identifies the portfolio of businesses that in total comprise the company and includes diversification, vertical integration, consolidation, and geographic expansion. Each business needs a business level/competitive strategy: Differentiation and cost leadership are two examples. Finally, each individual business is composed of departments that require functional strategies. The latter identify the basic courses of action each department will pursue in order to help the business attain its strategic goals.
4. A strategy is a course of action. It shows how the enterprise will move from the business it is in now to the business it wants to be in, given its opportunities and threats and its internal strengths and weaknesses.
5. Strategic human resource management means formulating and executing HR systems that produce the employee competencies and behaviors the company requires to achieve its strategic aims.

6. The high-performance work system is designed to maximize the overall quality of human capital throughout the organization, and provides a set of benchmarks against which today's HR manager can compare the structure, content, and efficiency and effectiveness of his or her human resources system.

7. The basic process of aligning human resources strategies and actions with business strategy entails four steps: Formulate the business strategy; identify the workforce (employee) behaviors needed to produce the outcomes that will help the company achieve its strategic goals; formulate human resources strategic policies and actions to produce these employee behaviors; and develop measures (metrics) to evaluate the human resources department's performance.

8. The HR Scorecard process for creating a strategy-oriented human resources system that you may choose to read in this chapter's appendix (starting on page 102), includes ten steps: Define the business strategy; outline the company's value chain; outline a strategy map; identify the strategically required organizational outcomes; identify the required workforce competencies and behaviors; identify the strategically relevant human resources system policies and activities; create HR Scorecard; design the HR Scorecard measurement system; summarize the Scorecard measures in a digital dashboard; and periodically evaluate the measurement system.

9. The HR Scorecard is a concise measurement system that shows the quantitative standards the firm uses to measure human resources activities, to measure the employee behaviors resulting from these activities, and to measure the strategically relevant organizational outcomes of those employee behaviors.

DISCUSSION QUESTIONS

1. What is the difference between a strategy, a vision, and a mission? Please give one example of each.
2. Define and give at least two examples of the cost leadership competitive strategy and the differentiation competitive strategy.
3. Explain how human resources management can be instrumental in helping a company create a competitive advantage.
4. What is a high-performance work system? Provide several specific examples of the elements in a high-performance work system.
5. Define what an HR Scorecard is, and briefly explain each of the seven steps in the HR Scorecard approach to creating a strategy-oriented HR system.

INDIVIDUAL AND GROUP ACTIVITIES

1. With three or four other students, form a strategic management group for your college or university. Your assignment is to develop the outline of a strategic plan for the college or university. This should include such things as mission and vision statements; strategic goals; and corporate, competitive, and functional strategies. In preparing your plan, make sure to show the main strengths, weaknesses, opportunities, and threats the college faces, and which prompted you to develop your particular strategic plans.
2. Using the Internet or library resources, analyze the annual reports of five companies. Bring to class examples of how those companies say they are using their HR processes to help the company achieve its strategic goals.
3. Interview an HR manager and write a short report on the topic: "The strategic roles of the HR manager at XYZ Company."

4. Using the Internet or library resources, bring to class and discuss at least two examples of how companies are using an HR Scorecard to help create HR systems that support the company's strategic aims. Do all managers seem to mean the same thing when they refer to "HR Scorecards"? How do they differ?

5. The HRCI "Test Specifications" appendix at the end of this book (pages 726–735) lists the things someone studying for the HRCI certification exam needs to know in each area of human resource management (such as in Strategic Management, Workforce Planning, and Human Resource Development). In groups of four to five students, do four things: (1) review that appendix now; (2) identify the material in this chapter that relates to the required knowledge the appendix lists; (3) write four multiple choice exam questions on this material that you believe would be suitable for inclusion in the HRCI exam; and (4) if time permits, have someone from your team post your team's questions in front of the class, so the students in other teams can take each others' exam questions.

EXPERIENTIAL EXERCISE

Developing an HR Strategy for Starbucks

Purpose: The purpose of this exercise is to give you experience in developing an HR strategy, in this case by developing one for Starbucks.

Required Understanding: You should be thoroughly familiar with the material in this chapter, including the "Einstein Medical" HR strategy example and Figure 3.9.

How to Set the Exercise/Instructions: Set up groups of three or four students for this exercise. You are probably already quite familiar with what it's like to have a cup of coffee or tea in a Starbucks coffee shop, but if not, spend some time in one prior to this exercise. Meet in groups and develop an outline for an HR strategy for Starbucks Corp. Your outline should include four basic elements, as follows: A basic business/competitive strategy for Starbucks; identifying workforce requirements (in terms of employee competencies and behaviors) this strategy requires; specific HR policies and the activities necessary to produce fees workforce requirements; and, suggestions for metrics they could use to measure the success of the HR strategy.

APPLICATION CASE

Siemens Builds a Strategy-Oriented HR System

Siemens is a 150-year-old German company, but it's not the company it was even a few years ago. Until recently, Siemens focused on producing electrical products. Today the firm has diversified into software, engineering, and services, and is also global, with over 400,000 employees working in 190 countries. In other words, Siemens became a world leader by pursuing a corporate strategy that emphasized diversifying into high-tech products and services, and doing so on a global basis.

With a corporate strategy like that, human resource management plays a big role at Siemens. Sophisticated engineering and services require more focus on employee selection, training, and compensation than in the average firm, and globalization requires delivering these services globally. Siemens sums up the basic themes of its HR strategy in several points. These include:

1. *A living Company is a learning Company.* The high-tech nature of Siemens's business means that employees must be able to learn on a continuing basis. Siemens uses its system of combined classroom and hands-on apprenticeship training around the

world to help facilitate this. It also offers employees extensive continuing education and management development.

2. *Global teamwork is the key to developing and using all the potential of the firm's human resources.* Because it is so important for employees throughout Siemens to feel free to work together and interact, employees have to understand the whole process, not just bits and pieces. To support this, Siemens provides extensive training and development. It also ensures that all employees feel they're part of a strong, unifying corporate identity. For example, HR uses cross-border, cross-cultural experiences as prerequisites for career advances.

3. *A climate of mutual respect is the basis of all relationships—within the Company and with society.* Siemens contends that the wealth of nationalities, cultures, languages, and outlooks represented by its employees is one of its most valuable assets. It therefore engages in numerous HR activities aimed at building openness, transparency, and fairness, and supporting diversity.

Questions

1. Based on the information in this case, provide examples, for Siemens, of at least four strategically required organizational outcomes, and four required workforce competencies and behaviors.

2. Identify at least four strategically relevant HR system policies and activities that Siemens has instituted in order to help human resource management contribute to achieving Siemens' strategic goals.

3. Provide a brief illustrative outline of a strategy map (discussed in chapter appendix) for Siemens.

CONTINUING CASE

The Carter Cleaning Company: The High-Performance Work System

As a recent graduate and person who keeps up with the business press, Jennifer is familiar with the benefits of programs such as total quality management and high-performance work systems.

Jack has actually installed a total quality program of sorts at Carter, and it has been in place for about five years. This program takes the form of employee meetings. Jack holds employee meetings periodically, but particularly when there is a serious problem in a store—such as poor-quality work or machine breakdowns. When problems like these arise, instead of trying to diagnose them himself or with Jennifer, he contacts all the employees in that store and meets with them as soon as the store closes. Hourly employees get extra pay for these meetings. The meetings have been fairly useful in helping Jack to identify and rectify several problems. For example, in one store all the fine white blouses were coming out looking dingy. It turned out that the cleaner-spotter had been ignoring the company rule that required cleaning ("boiling down") the perchloroethylene cleaning fluid before washing items like these. As a result, these fine white blouses were being washed in cleaning fluid that had residue from other, earlier washes.

Jennifer now wonders whether these employee meetings should be expanded to give the employees an even bigger role in managing the Carter stores' quality. "We can't be everywhere watching everything all the time," she said to her father. "Yes, but these people only earn about $8 per hour. Will they really want to act like mini-managers?" he replied.

Questions

1. Would you recommend that the Carters expand their quality program? If so, specifically what form should it take?

2. Assume the Carters want to institute a high-performance work system as a test program in one of their stores. Write a one-page outline summarizing what such a program would consist of.

KEY TERMS

strategic plan, 78
strategy, 78
strategic management, 78
vision, 79
mission, 80
SWOT analysis, 80
strategic control, 81
competitive advantage, 82

leveraging, 84
strategic human resource management, 86
metrics, 89
HR Scorecard, 102
value chain analysis, 104
value chain, 104
strategy map, 105

ENDNOTES

1. "Automation Improves Retailer's Hiring Efficiency and Quality," *HR Focus*, 82, no. 2, (February 2005), p. 3.
2. Fred David, *Strategic Management*, (Upper Saddle River, NJ: Prentice Hall, 2007), p. 11.
3. Ibid.
4. Warren Bennis and Bert Manus, *Leaders: The Strategies for Taking Charge* (New York: Harper & Row, 1985), quoted in Andrew Campbell and Sally Yeung, "Mission, Vision and Strategic Intent," *Long-Range Planning* 24, no. 4, p. 145. See also James M. Lucas, "Anatomy of a Vision Statement," *Management Review*, February 1998, pp. 22–26.
5. See George Morrisey, *A Guide to Strategic Planning* (San Francisco: Jossey-Bass, 1996), p. 7.
6. See, for example, David, Op. Cit., p. 13.
7. David Pringle, "CEO, Marking a Decade, Faces Struggling, Quickly Changing Industry," *Wall Street Journal*, January 23, 2002, p. B70.
8. Julian Barnes, "Proctor Plans to Jettison Jif and Crisco," *New York Times*, April 26, 2001, p. C1.
9. Paul Nutt, "Making Strategic Choices," *Journal of Management Studies*, January 2002, pp. 67–96.
10. Michael Porter, *Competitive Strategy* (New York: The Free Press, 1980), p. 14.
11. David Upton, "What Really Makes Factories Flexible?" *Harvard Business Review*, July–August 1995, pp. 74–86.
12. Ibid., p. 75.
13. See for example, Catherine Truss and Lynda Gratton, "Strategic Human Resource Management: A Conceptual Approach," *International Journal of Human Resource Management* 5, no. 3 (September 1994), p. 663, and Evan Offstein, Devi Gnyawali and Anthony Cobb, "A Strategic Human Resource Perspective of Firm Competitive Behavior," *Human Resource Management Review* 15, 2005, pp. 305–318.
14. Although still largely nonunionized, FedEx's pilots did vote to join the Airline Pilots Union.
15. "Human Resource Goes High-Tech: The 1999 HR Technology Conference and Exposition," *BNA Bulletin to Management*, October 14, 1999, pp. S1–S2.
16. "The New HR Agenda: 2002 Human Resource Competencies Study, Executive Summary," University of Michigan Business School (May 2003), 6.
17. "More on What CEOs Want from HR," *HR Focus* 80, no. 4 (April 2003), p. 5.
18. Bill Leonard, "GM Drives HR to the Next Level," *HR Magazine*, March 2002, p. 48.
19. "The New HR Agenda: 2002 Human Resource Competencies Study, Executive Summary," University of Michigan Business School (May 2003).
20. Jeffrey Schmidt, "The Correct Spelling of M&A Begins with HR," *HR Magazine*, June 2001, pp. 102–108.
21. "Strategic HR Means Translating Plans into Action," *HR Magazine* 48, no. 3 (March 2003), p. 8; and, "Closer to Becoming a Strategic Partner? HR Moves Forward but Faces Obstacles," *BNA Bulletin to Management* (July 15, 2005), p. 225.
22. SHRM Research, "2006 Strategic HR Management," pp. 5–19. Society for Human Resource Management, 2006. www.SHRM.org, accessed May 10, 2007.
23. Samuel Greengard, "You're Next! There's No Escaping Merger Mania!" *Workforce*, April 1997, pp. 52–62.

24. Brian Becker, Mark Huselid, and Dave Ulrich, *The HR Scorecard: Linking People, Strategy, and Performance* (Boston: Harvard Business School Press, 2001).

25. "With High-Performance Work Organizations, Adversaries No More," *Work & Family Newsbrief*, August 2003, p. 5.

26. Robert McNabb and Keith Whitfield, "Job Evaluation and High-Performance Work Practices: Compatible or Conflictual?" *Journal of Management Studies* 38, no. 2 (March 2001), p. 294.

27. Karen Kroll, "Repurposing Metrics for HR," *HR Magazine*, July 2006, p. 66.

28. See for example "HR Department Benchmarks and Analysis 2004," BNA, Inc. 1231 25th St., Northwest Washington, DC 20037. Three writers recently pointed out that future human resource professionals will need to be more analytical: Richard Wolfe, Patrick Wright, and Dennis Smart, "Radical HRM Innovation and Competitive Advantage: The Moneyball Story," *Human Resource Management*, Spring 2006, vol. 45, no. 1, pp. 111–145.

29. Alexander Colvin et al., "How High-Performance Human Resource Practices and Workforce Unionization Affect Managerial Pay," *Personnel Psychology* 54 (2001), pp. 903–934.

30. See for example, Maria Fleurie and Lenne Fleurie, "In Search of Competence: Aligning Strategy and Competencies in the Telecommunications Industry," *International Journal of Human Resource Management* 16, no. 9, September 2005, pp. 1640–1655.

31. Garrett Walker and J. Randal MacDonald, "Designing and Implementing an HR Scorecard," *Human Resource Management* 40, no. 4 (2001), pp. 365–377.

32. See for example, James Werbel and Samuel DeMarie, "Aligning Strategic Human Resource Management and Person–Environment Fit," *Human Resource Management Review* 15, 2005, pp. 247–262.

33. "Automation Improves Retailer's Hiring Efficiency and Quality," *HR Focus*, Feb 2005 v82 i2, p. 3.

34. Richard Shafer et al., "Crafting a Human Resource Strategy to Foster Organizational Agility: A Case Study," *Human Resource Management* 40, no. 3 (Fall 2001), pp. 197–211.

APPENDIX A FOR CHAPTER 3

Using the HR Scorecard Process

Einstein Medical's managers used a simple, logical, and subjective process to translate strategy into required human resource policies and activities, and this is perfectly acceptable. Increasingly, however, many companies are turning to a more rigorous methodology called "The HR Scorecard Process." We explain that newer approach in this Appendix.

What Is an HR Scorecard?

④ Illustrate and explain each of the ten steps in the HR Scorecard approach to creating human resource management systems.

Management ultimately judges the human resource function based on whether it creates value for the company, where "value creation" means contributing in a measurable way to achieving the company's strategic goals. We've seen that human resource managers create value by engaging in activities that produce the employee behaviors the company needs to achieve these strategic goals. The question is, how does one formally outline these interrelationships, and attach measurable performance standards to each? Managers often use an HR Scorecard process to do this:

HR Scorecard

Measures the HR function's effectiveness and efficiency in producing employee behaviors needed to achieve the company's strategic goals.

The **HR Scorecard** is a concise measurement system, often summarized on a computer screen in a "digital dashboard." It shows the quantitative standards or "metrics" the firm uses to measure HR activities, and to measure the employee behaviors resulting from these activities, and to measure the strategically relevant organizational outcomes of those employee behaviors. In so doing, it highlights, in a concise but comprehensive way, the causal link between the HR activities, and the emergent employee behaviors, and the resulting firmwide strategic outcomes and performance.[1]

Three human resource experts, Becker, Huselid, and Ulrich explain the need for such a measurement system this way:

> In our view, the most potent action HR managers can take to ensure their strategic contribution is to develop a measurement system that convincingly showcases HR's impact on business performance. To design such a measurement system, HR managers must adopt a dramatically different perspective, one that focuses on how human resources can play a central role in implementing the firm's strategy.[2]

Information for Creating an HR Scorecard

To create an HR Scorecard, the manager needs three types of information. First, he or she must know what the company's *strategy* is, because (as at Einstein Medical) the strategy will determine what the important employee behaviors and strategically important organizational outcomes are, and how the firm will measure organizational performance. Second, the manager must understand the *causal links* between the HR activities, the employee behaviors, the organizational outcomes, and the organization's performance. (Figure 3-A1 summarizes, in brief, the basic sequence involved.) Third, the manager needs metrics he or she can use to measure all the activities and results involved, specifically the HR activities, the emergent employee behaviors, the strategically relevant organizational outcomes, and the organizational performance.

The 10-Step HR Scorecard Process

There are 10 steps in the HR Scorecard process.[3] They are as follows:

Step 1: Define the Business Strategy We saw that creating a strategy-oriented human resource system starts by defining what the company's strategic plans

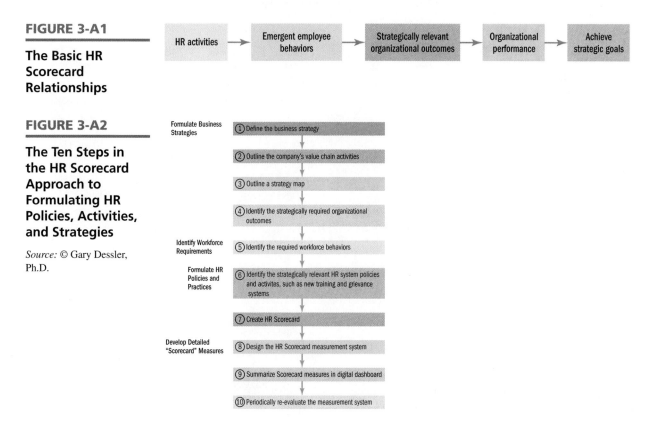

FIGURE 3-A1

The Basic HR Scorecard Relationships

FIGURE 3-A2

The Ten Steps in the HR Scorecard Approach to Formulating HR Policies, Activities, and Strategies

Source: © Gary Dessler, Ph.D.

are. For Einstein Medical, they included becoming a comprehensive health care network. Toward the end of this step, management translates its broad strategic plans into specific, actionable strategic goals.

Step 2: **Outline the Company's Value Chain**   To achieve its strategic goals, any business must engage in certain strategically required activities. For example, Einstein Medical must devise and introduce new medical services. Microsoft must write new computer programs. Each such activity requires certain employee behaviors: Einstein Medical needs employees who have the expertise to help it devise new medical services, for instance. The point is this: any manager who wants to understand what employee behaviors are vital for his or her firm's success must first understand what the firm's required activities are.

For this, **value chain analysis** can be useful. Value chain analysis means studying and analyzing the company's value chain. The company's **value chain** "identifies the primary activities that create value for customers and the related support activities." [4] Let us consider this.

As in Figure 3-A2, we can think of any business as consisting of a chain of essential activities. Each activity is part of the process of designing, producing, marketing, and delivering the company's product or service. These activities might include bringing supplies and materials into the company's warehouse; bringing these materials to the shop floor and designing the product to customers' specifications; and the various marketing, sales, and distribution activities that attract customers and get the company's product to them.

Outlining the company's value chain (in this case for a hotel, Figure 3-A3) shows the chain of essential activities. This can help managers better understand the activities that drive performance in their company. In

value chain analysis

Identifying the primary activities that create value for customers and the related support activities.

value chain

The company's value chain identifies the primary activities that create value for customers and the related support activities.

FIGURE 3-A3

Simple Value Chain for "The Hotel Paris"

Source: © Gary Dessler, Ph.D.

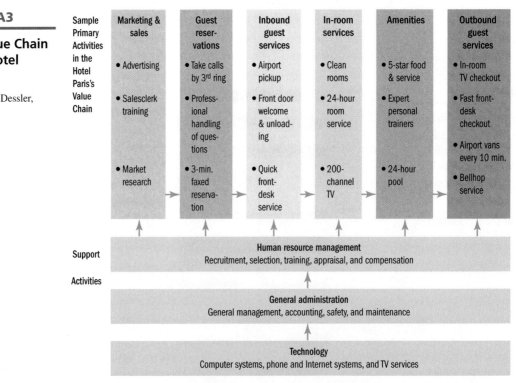

other words, it is a tool for identifying, isolating, visualizing, and analyzing the firm's most important activities and strategic costs.

Value chain analysis is more than just a tool for identifying how you do things now. It prompts questions such as: "How do our costs for this activity compare with our competitors?" "Is there some way we can gain a competitive advantage with this activity?" "Is there a more efficient way for us to deliver these services?" And, "Do we have to perform these services in-house?"

Outlining and analyzing the company's value chain can help the HR manager formulate policies and practices that make sense in terms of the firms' strategy. Consider an example. At Dell Computer, "phone technicians competently and courteously assisting Dell customers with problems" is a crucial (or "core") value chain activity; indeed, it is a big part of what Dell built its reputation on. The critical nature of this activity would be apparent from any outlining of Dell's value chain. Given this, Dell's human resources team might decide that one way for HR to add value is by improving phone technicians' performance, by installing special computerized job aids that show technicians what series of questions to ask when customers call with problems.

strategy map

A diagram that summarizes the chain of major inter-related activities that contribute to a company's success.

Step 3: Outline a Strategy Map A **strategy map** is a diagram that summarizes the chain of major inter-related activities that contribute to a company's success. It thus shows the "big picture" of how each department's or team's performance contributes to achieving the company's overall strategic goals.

Figure 3-A4 presents a strategy map for Southwest Airlines. We saw that Southwest pursues a low-cost leader competitive strategy. It therefore tailors all its activities to delivering low-cost, convenient service. The strategy map for Southwest succinctly lays out the hierarchy of big activities required for

FIGURE 3-A4

Strategy Map for Southwest Airlines

Source: Adapted from "Creating a Strategy Map," Ravi Tangri, Team@TeamCHRYSALIS.com

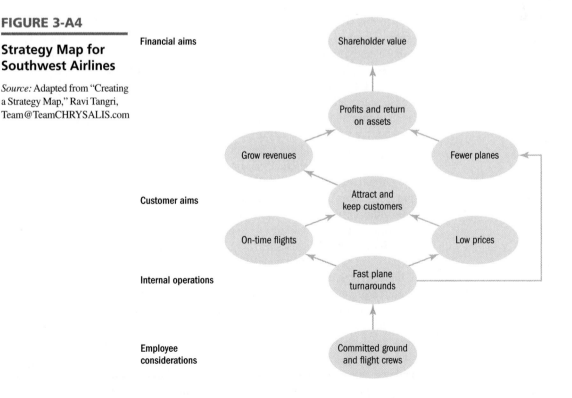

Southwest Airlines to succeed. At the top is achieving company-wide, strategic financial goals. To boost revenues and profitability, Southwest needs to fly fewer planes (to keep costs down), attract and keep customers, maintain low prices, and maintain on-time flights. In turn (further down the strategy map), on-time flights and low prices require fast turnaround. And, fast turnaround requires motivated, committed ground and flight crews. This in turn has implications for what human resource policies and practices Southwest requires.

Step 4: Identify the Strategically Required Organizational Outcomes   Every company must produce strategically relevant outcomes if it is to achieve its strategic goals. At Einstein Medical, *new services delivered* was one such required organizational outcome. At Dell, receiving *quick, competent, and courteous technical advice by phone* is one such outcome. The strategy map helps the manager recognize these core outcomes. Based on his or her understanding of how the company operates, and perhaps an analysis of the firm's value chain, the manager, in this step, identifies and specifies the firm's strategically relevant organizational outcomes.

Step 5: Identify the Required Workforce Competencies and Behaviors   Here ask, "What competencies and behaviors must our employees exhibit if our company is to produce the strategically relevant organizational outcomes, and thereby achieve its strategic goals?" At Einstein Medical, employees had to take *personal accountability* for their results, and be willing to work *proactively* (be "generative") to find new and novel solutions. Again, a strategy map can help the manager recognize what these competencies and behaviors are.

Step 6: Identify the Required HR System Policies and Activities   Once the Human Resource manager knows what the required employee competencies and behaviors are, he or she can turn to identifying the HR activities and policies that will help to produce them. For example, at Einstein Medical, these included new training and pay plans.

In this step, one should be specific. It is not enough to say, "We need new training programs, or disciplinary processes." Instead, the manager must now ask, "exactly what sorts of new training programs do we need, to produce the sorts of employee competencies and behaviors that we seek?"

Step 7: Create HR Scorecard   By expanding on the strategy map, the manager then consolidates all this information in a visual and/or computerized HR Scorecard, as in Figure 3-A5 (in this case for "The Hotel Paris"). It highlights, in a concise but comprehensive way, the causal links between the selected human resources activities, and the emergent employee behaviors, and the resulting firm-wide strategic outcomes and performance. The HR Scorecard thus helps the human resource manager demonstrate how his or her team's policies and practices contribute to the company's strategic and financial success. Several consulting firms provide Web-based services that make it easier to create HR Scorecards, based on metrics from best-practice, world-class firms.[5] Computerized Scorecard packages are available. Or, the HR Scorecard may be as simple as the strategy map from which the manager derived it.

Step 8: Choose HR Scorecard Measures   After choosing a handful of strategically required organizational outcomes, and employee competencies and behaviors, and human resource policies and activities, the question is, how shall we measure them all? For example, if we decide to "improve the disciplinary system," how precisely will the company measure such improvement? Perhaps in terms of number of grievances. HR Scorecards always contain a balance of financial and non-financial goals or measures, of short-term and long-term goals, and of external goals (for instance, what the customer thinks) and internal goals (for

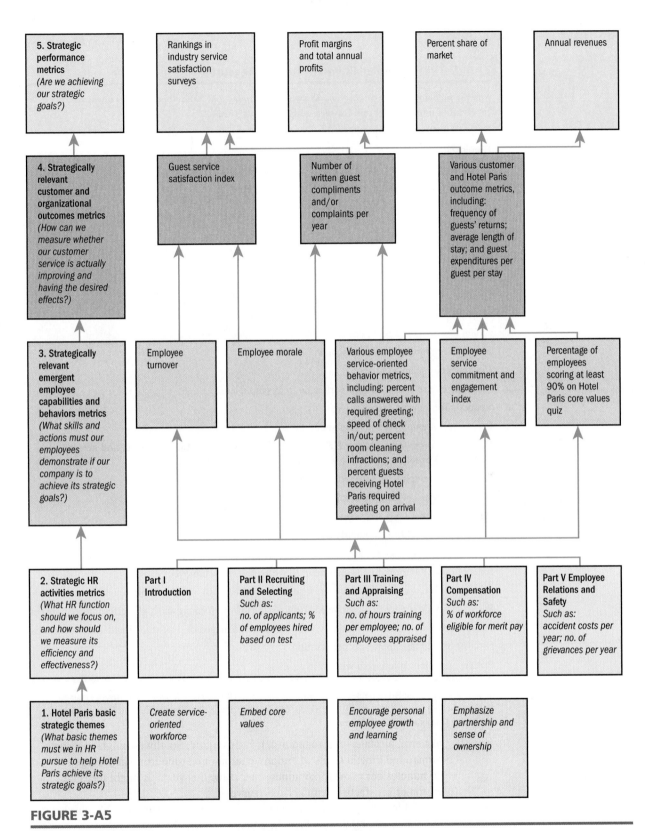

FIGURE 3-A5

HR Scorecard Process for Hotel Paris International Corporation*

*Note: An abbreviated example showing selected HR practices and outcomes aimed at implementing the competitive strategy, "To use superior guest services to differentiate the Hotel Paris properties and thus increase the length of stays and the return rate of guests, and thus boost revenues and profitability and help the firm expand geographically."

TABLE 3-A1 Sample HR Performance Measures

Sample measures for assessing employee competencies and behaviors, **such as employee motivation and morale, and for assessing HR activities.**

Employee attitude survey results

Employee turnover

Extent to which strategy is clearly articulated and well understood throughout the firm

Extent to which the average employee understands how his or her job contributes to the firm's success

Level of cross-cultural teamwork

Level of organizational learning

Extent to which employees are clear about their own goals

Percentage of employees making suggestions

Employee productivity

Requests for transfer to supervisor

Extent to which the employees can describe the company's core values

Employee commitment survey scores

Customer complaints/praise

Percentage of retention of high-performing key employees

Requests for transfer per employees

Percentage of employees making suggestions

Sample measures for assessing HR system activities **such as testing, training, and reward policies and practices**

Proportion of employees selected based on validated selection methods

Number of hours of training employees receive each year

Proportion of merit pay determined by formal performance appraisal

Percentage of workforce regularly assessed via a formal performance appraisal

Percentage of employees eligible for annual merit cash or incentive plans

Extent to which information is communicated effectively to employees

Percentage of workforce who received a performance feedback from multiple sources

Percentage of difference in incentive pay between the low-performing and high-performing employees

Percentage of the workforce routinely working in self-managed or cross-functional or project teams

Number of qualified applicants per position

Percentage of jobs filled from within

Source: Adapted from Brian Becker, Mark Huselid, and Dave Ulrich, *The HR Scorecard* (Boston: Harvard Business School Press, 2001), pp. 16–17, 63, 64, 66, 71. Copyright © 2001 by the Harvard Business School Publishing Corporation; all rights reserved.

instance, airplane turnaround time). For example, Southwest might measure turnaround time in terms of "improve turnaround time from an average of 30 minutes per plane to 26 minutes per plane this year." It might measure customer satisfaction with periodic surveys.

Table 3-A1 presents some performance measures. Measures like these serve two functions. First, they help the company assess the human resource team's performance. (Is morale up or down, for instance.) Second, they thereby help the human resource manager build a measurable and persuasive business case for how human resources contributes to achieving the company's strategic goals.

In one study, 86% of human resource professionals who responded said they expected measurement of their function to increase over the next two years, 62% said they already used metrics to assess performance, and 72% said they benchmark human resource activities (particularly compensation and rewards, and equipment and retention, and performance appraisal) by comparing their results to other firms'.[6]

Step 9: **Summarize the Scorecard Measures in a Digital Dashboard**   The saying "a picture is worth a thousand words" sums up the purpose of the digital dashboard. A digital dashboard presents the manager, via a PC-desktop screen containing graphs and charts, with a bird's eye view of how the human resource management function is doing. It summarizes how core measures from the HR Scorecard are doing. For example, a manager's dashboard for Southwest Airlines might display daily trends for activities such as fast turnaround, attracting and keeping customers, on-time flights, and employee morale.

This gives the manager time take to corrective action. For example, if ground crews are turning planes around slower today, financial results tomorrow may decline unless the manager takes action. Perhaps there's a morale problem the HR manager should attend to.

Like automobile dashboards, these digital dashboards also usually present information so it grabs the manager's attention, such as by a graph blinking red if turnaround time is trending down. For example, SAS software's Strategic Performance Management package is a web-based system that produces alerts that grab managers' attention when performance is not meeting targets.

Step 10: **Monitor, Predict, Evaluate**   A great advantage of the HR Scorecard process is that it is predictive. Financial goals such as budgets are better at telling managers how they've done than how they'll do tomorrow. Monitoring a balanced set of scorecard measures can signal problems ahead. Thus, it might prompt a Southwest Airlines manager to say, "our customer service ratings dipped, and, since customer service leads to more customers and in turn to future revenues, we should take corrective action now."

The human resource manager can't assume that the Scorecard's measures and relationships will always stay the same. Perhaps reducing grievances is not having the results the manager predicted it would on raising morale. Perhaps the company must drop some employee behavior measures (such as front-desk customer service) and add others. Perhaps the measures the HR manager chose (such as number of grievances) are proving too hard to quantify. In any case, the HR manager should periodically re-evaluate measures and links.

The Hotel Paris International: An Example

Let us examine how this Scorecard process works by considering a fictitious company, the Hotel Paris International (Hotel Paris). Starting as a single hotel in a Paris suburb in 1990, the Hotel Paris now comprises a chain of nine hotels, with two in France, one each in London and Rome, and others in New York, Miami, Washington, Chicago, and Los Angeles. As a corporate strategy, the Hotel Paris's management and owners want to continue to expand geographically. They believe doing so will let them capitalize on their reputation for good service, by providing multicity alternatives for their satisfied guests. The problem is, their reputation for good service has been deteriorating. If they cannot improve service, it would be unwise for them to expand, since their guests might actually prefer other hotels after trying the Hotel Paris.

A hotel's reputation for good service depends on choosing and training the right employees. Adi Dor, rooms control clerk at the New York Marriott, Brooklyn, personifies good service, hospitality, and a welcoming attitude as he greets a guest. It takes a well-thought out HR effort to create employee competencies and behaviors like these.

The Strategy Top management, with input from the human resources and other managers, and with the board of directors' approval, chooses a new competitive strategy and formulates new strategic goals. They decide: "The Hotel Paris International will use superior guest services to differentiate the Hotel Paris properties, and to thereby increase the length of stays and the return rate of guests, and thus boost revenues and profitability." All Hotel Paris managers—including the director of HR services—must now formulate strategies that support this competitive strategy.

The Value Chain Based on discussions with other managers, the HR director, Lisa Cruz, outlines the company's value chain (see Figure 3-A3, page 104). This should help her to identify those HR activities that are crucial in helping the hotel achieve its strategic goals. In a service business, the "product" is satisfied guests. Producing satisfied guests requires attending to all those activities along the Hotel Paris's value chain where the company has an opportunity to affect the guests' experiences. For the Hotel Paris, there are *inbound logistics activities* such as getting the guest from the airport and checked in. There are *operations activities* such as cleaning the guest's room. There are *outbound logistics activities* such as picking up baggage and getting the person checked out and to his or her plane. There are *marketing and sales activities* aimed at attracting guests to the hotel. There are *service activities* that provide post-stay services, such as travel awards to guests for multiple stays. And there are various *support activities*, such as purchasing, information systems, and human resources.

The Strategically Required Organizational Outcomes The Hotel Paris's basic strategy is to use superior guest services to expand geographically. Each step in the hotel's value chain provides opportunities for improving guest service. For HR director Lisa Cruz, reviewing the hotel's value chain activities makes it clear that achieving the hotel's strategic aims means achieving a number of required organizational outcomes. For example, Lisa and her management colleagues must take steps that produce fewer customer complaints and more written compliments, more frequent guest returns and longer stays, and higher guest expenditures per visit.

The Strategically Relevant Workforce Competencies and Behaviors The question facing Lisa, then, is this: What are the competencies and behaviors that our hotel's employees will have to exhibit, if we are to produce required organizational outcomes such as fewer customer complaints, more compliments, and more frequent guest returns? Thinking through the sorts of activities that occur at each step in the hotel's value chain helps Lisa answer that question. For example, the hotel's required employee competencies and behaviors would include, "high-quality front-desk customer service," "taking calls for reservations in a friendly manner," "greeting guests at the front door," and "processing guests' room service meals efficiently." All require motivated, high-morale employees.

The Strategically Relevant HR System Policies and Activities The HR manager's task now is to identify and specify the human resource policies and activities that will enable the hotel to produce these crucial workforce competencies and behaviors. As one example, "high-quality front-desk customer service" is one such required behavior. From this, the HR director identifies human resource activities to produce such front-desk customer service efforts. For example, she decides to *institute practices to improve the disciplinary fairness and justice in the company*, with the aim of *improving employee morale*. Her assumption is that enhanced fairness will produce higher morale and that higher morale will produce improved front-desk service.

The HR Scorecard Next, the HR director creates an HR Scorecard. This shows the cause-and-effect links among the HR activities, the workforce behaviors, and the organizational outcomes (Figure 3-A5 shows an illustrative, overall HR Scorecard for the Hotel Paris).

This scorecard and its linkages reflect certain assumptions on Lisa's part. For example, based on experience and discussions with the firm's other managers, she formulates the following *hypothesis* about how human resources affects hotel performance: Improved grievance procedures cause improved morale, which leads to improved front-desk service, which leads to increased guest returns, which leads to improved financial performance. The HR director then chooses metrics to measure each of these factors. For example, she decides to measure "improved disciplinary procedures" in terms of how many grievances employees submit each month. She measures "improved morale" in terms of "scores on our hotel's semiannual attitude survey," and measures "high-quality front-desk customer service" in terms of "customer complaints per month."

She moves on to quantifying the cause-and-effect links among these measures. For example: "Can we show top management that there is a measurable, sequential link between improved disciplinary procedures, high morale, improved front-desk service, number of guest return visits, and hotel financial performance (revenues and profits)? If she can show such links, she has a persuasive case that shows human resources' measurable contribution to the hotel's bottom-line financial performance.

In practice, the HR manager may have to rely on a largely subjective but logical argument to make the case for the cause-and-effect linkages. But ideally, she will use statistical methods such as correlation analysis to determine if links exist, and (if so) what their magnitudes are. In this way, she might find, for instance, that a 10% improvement in grievance rates is associated with an almost 20% improvement in morale. Similarly, a 20% improvement in morale is associated with a 30% reduction in customer front-desk complaints. Furthermore, a 30% reduction in complaints is associated with a 20% increase in guest return visits, and a 20% increase in return rate is associated with a 6% rise in hotel revenues. It would appear that a relatively small HR effort in reducing grievances might have a considerable effect on this hotel's bottom line!

In reality, several things complicate this measurement process. It is risky to draw cause–effect conclusions from correlation measures like these (for example do fewer grievances lead to higher morale, or vice-versa?). Furthermore, it's rare that a single factor (such as grievance rates) will have such effects alone, so we may want to measure the effects of several human resources policies and activities on morale simultaneously. And (given the huge number of things that influence hotel performance) it may not always be possible to confirm all the links in the measurement chain. If not, the HR manager must rely more on logic and common sense to make her case. The "Improving Productivity Through HRIS" discussion below shows how computerized systems can facilitate the scorecard design and management activities.

How We Will Use the Hotel Paris HR Scorecard   In reality, computerization enables the HR director for the Hotel Paris to create a more comprehensive HR Scorecard than the one in Figure 3-A5 (repeated for convenience on this book's inside back cover), one that might accommodate links among dozens of cause-and-effect metrics. For example, with computerization, the HR director need not limit herself to assessing the effects of the handful of employee behaviors (such as percentage of calls answered on time) in Figure 3-A5. Instead, she could include metrics covering dozens of activities, from recruitment and selection through training, appraisal, compensation, and labor relations. Her HR Scorecard model could also include the effects of all these activities on a wide range of workforce competencies and behaviors, and thus on organizational outcomes, and on the company's performance. In this way, her HR Scorecard would become a comprehensive model representing the value-adding effects of the full range of Hotel Paris human resource activities.

We will use a *Translating Strategy into HR Policies and Practices: The Hotel Paris Case* in the end-of-chapter material of each chapter starting with chapter 4 to show how the Hotel Paris's HR director uses the concepts and techniques from that chapter to create a human resource management system that helps the Hotel Paris achieve its strategic goals. Table 3-A2 (page 113) presents some of the metrics the director could use to measure human resource activities. For example, she could endeavor to improve workforce competencies and behaviors by instituting (as per Chapter 5) improved recruitment processes, and measure the latter in terms of "number of qualified applicants per position." Similarly, she may recommend to management that they change the firm's pay policies (see Chapter 11) so that the "target percentile for total compensation is in the top 25%," and show that doing so will have favorable effects on employee morale, employee customer service behavior, customer satisfaction, and the hotel chain's performance. In practice, all the HR functions we discuss in this book influence employee competencies and behaviors, and, thereby, organizational outcomes and performance.

Improving Productivity Through HRIS: Software Systems for Managing Scorecard Programs   Designing, executing, and managing an HR Scorecard containing dozens or hundreds of interrelated metrics can be challenging, and possibly futile. After all, what is the use of having all of these interrelated metrics (such as number of training hours per employee per year, employee morale, and guest satisfaction) if the company's top management can't monitor all the metrics on an ongoing basis, and take corrective action when something seems amiss? That is why many companies use special scorecard software systems to improve the productivity and effectiveness of their scorecard programs.

Most of this software, at the current time, aims to support companies' "balanced scorecard" programs. The *balanced scorecard* does for the company as a whole what the HR Scorecard does for the human resources function. Specifically, the balanced scorecard is a management tool, usually a computerized model, that tracks a multitude of performance measures simultaneously and shows their interactions across the company—not just

TABLE 3-A2 **Examples of HR System Activities the Hotel Paris Can Measure as Related to Each Chapter in This Book**

Chapter	Strategic Activities Metrics
2. EEOC	Number EEOC claims/year; cost of HR-related litigation; % minority/women promotions
3. Strategy	% employees who can quote company strategy/vision
4. Job Analysis	% employees with updated job descriptions
5. Recruiting	Number applicants per recruiting source; number qualified applicants/position
6. Testing	% employees hired based on validated employment test
7. Interview	% applicants receiving structured interview
8. Training	Number hours training/employee/year; number hours training new employee
9. Appraisal	Number employees getting feedback; % appraisals completed on time
10. Career Mgmt.	% employees with formal career/development plan
11. Compensation	Target percentile for total compensation (pay in top 25%)
12. Incentives	% workforce eligible for merit pay
13. Benefits	% employees 80% satisfied with benefits
14. Ethics	Number grievances/year; % employees able to quote ethics code
15. Labor Relations	% workforce in unions
16. Health and Safety	Number safety training programs/year; $ accident costs/year; hours lost time due to accidents
17. Global	% expatriates receiving predeparture screening, counseling
Overall HR Metrics	HR cost/employee; HR expense/total expenses; turnover costs

those related to human resource management. Thus, on a companywide basis, the firm's balanced scorecard would track all of the human resources, marketing, production, and finance metrics that top management believes contribute to the company's strategic success.

The company's HR scorecard is one element of the company's overall balanced scorecard. The balanced scorecard also addresses non-human-resources-related activities metrics, including those in production management, marketing, and finance.

Again, managing a scorecard program can be futile unless management computerizes the scorecard itself. Several companies provide balanced scorecard software. For example, ActiveStrategy (www.activestrategy.com) provides a software system which it calls the Balanced Scorecard Dashboard Edition. It calls it the "dashboard" because top management can monitor their scorecard metrics' real-time results in a manner similar to how you might monitor your car's dashboard. Changes in speed or fuel level might suggest to you that you need to slow down, or stop for gas. Similarly, the balanced scorecard "dashboard" provides a real-time computer screen readout that top management can use to monitor their firm's metrics and to make changes as required.

ActiveStrategy's balanced scorecard software provides a basic system that management can use to create and manage its scoreboard system. For example, it provides the basis for quickly creating a scorecard, and for measuring the metrics' trends, as well as personalized user views (so employees can monitor the sections of the scorecard that relate to their own efforts). It even provides for e-mail alert notification to draw an employee's attention to the fact that his or her metrics may be trending in the wrong way.

APPENDIX B FOR CHAPTER 3

Establishing and Computerizing Human Resource Systems

Introduction

"The devil is in the details" someone once said, and this is certainly true with respect to designing an HR system. The HR manager may talk in broad terms about the recruiting, selection, and other HR functions he or she wants to install. But, eventually, creating the HR system requires translating the HR manager's broad preferences (for "a selection program that produces more qualified candidates," for instance) into specific, "how exactly will we do this" policies, guidelines, tools, and paperwork or computerized processes. This means actually creating the infrastructure of the HR system.

Doing so is not easy. Consider the paperwork required to breathe life into a company's HR system. Just to start with, recruiting and hiring an employee might require a Notice of Available Position, a Help Wanted Advertising Listing, an Employment Application, an Interviewing Checklist, various verifications—of education, and immigration status, for instance—and a Telephone Reference Checklist. You'd then need an Employment Agreement, Confidentiality and Noncompete Agreements, and an Employer Indemnity Agreement. To process that new employee you might need a Hiring Authorization Form, an Employee Background Verification, a New Employee Checklist, and various forms for withholding tax and to obtain new employee data. And to keep track of the employee once on board, you'd need—just to start—an Employee Changes Form, Personnel Data Sheet, Daily and Weekly Time Records, an Hourly Employee's Weekly Time Sheet, an Overtime Permit, an Expense Report, a Vacation Request, an Absence Request, an Affirmative Action Summary, and an EEO Policy Statement and Analysis of Promotions. Then come the performance appraisal forms, a Critical Incidents Report, Notice of Probation, First (or Second) Warning Notice Form, a Disciplinary Notice, a New Employee Evaluation, a Performance Evaluation, and a Letter of Commendation, and (eventually) a Retirement Checklist, Notice of Dismissal, Reduction in Workforce Notice, Employee Checkout Record, Separation Notice, and Employment Reference Response.

In this Appendix, we'll see that the preceding list barely scratches the surface of the policies, procedures, and paperwork you'll need to run the HR system part of your business. This has several implications. First, you obviously can't wing it. Perhaps with just one or two employees you could keep track of everything in your head, or just write a separate memo for each HR action, and place it in a manila folder for each worker. But with more than a few employees you'll need to create a human resource system comprised of standardized forms.

Very small firms can handle all or most of this sort of HR record keeping through manual paper and pencil forms and systems. But as the company grows, various parts of the HR system—payroll, or appraising, for instance—will have to be computerized if the firm is to remain competitive. (After all, you probably don't want to spend twice as much money and time on HR as do your competitors.) We'll cover manual and computerized HR systems in this Appendix.

Basic Components of Manual HR Systems

Very small employers (say, with 10 employees or less) will probably start with a manual HR system. From a practical point of view, this generally means obtaining and organizing a set of standardized personnel forms covering each important aspect of the HR—recruitment, selection, training, appraisal, compensation, safety process—as well as some means for organizing all this information for each of your employees.

The number of forms you could conceivably need even for a small firm is quite large. This is illustrated by the menu of forms shown in Table 3-B1, which is adapted from

TABLE 3-B1 Personnel Forms

Section 1

Recruiting and Selecting

Notice of Available Position	Employment Application Disclaimer and Acknowledgement	Request for Reference
Help Wanted Advertising Listing		Request for Transcript
Bonus for Employee Referral	Applicant Waiver	Verification of Education
Employee Referral Request	Authorization to Release Information	Verification of Employment
Prospective Employee Referral	Medical Testing Authorization	Verification of Licensure
Applicant Referral Program	Applicant Interview Schedule	Verification of Military Status
Job Bid	Rescheduled Appointment	Unsuccessful Candidate Letter
Resume Acknowledgement	Interviewing Checklist	Applicant Rejection Letter 1
Applicant Acknowledgement	Applicant Rating	Applicant Rejection Letter 2
Acknowledgement of Reference	Clerical Applicant Rating	Applicant Notification
Applicant Interview Confirmation	Applicant Interview Summary	Applicant Reply
Preliminary Employment Application	Applicant Comparison Summary	No Decision on Hiring
Veteran/Handicapped Status	Telephone Reference Checklist	Employment Confirmation
Employment Application	Medical Records Request	

Section 2

Employment Agreements

Independent Contractor's Agreement	Polygraph Examination Consent Form	General Non-Compete Agreement
Employment Agreement	Agreement to Accept Night Work	Non-Compete Agreement (Accounts)
Addendum to Employment Agreement	Expense Recovery Agreement	Non-Compete Agreement (Area)
Agreement with Sales Representative	Agreement on Inventions and Patents	Non-Disclosure of Trade Secrets
Letter Extending Sales Representative Agreement	Agreement on Proprietary Rights	Acknowledgement of Temporary Employment
Change in Terms of Sales Representative Agreement	Employees Agreement on Confidentiality Data	Employer Indemnity Agreement
	Employee's Covenants	Employee Indemnity Agreement
Conflict of Interest Declaration	Employee Secrecy Agreement	Waiver of Liability
Consent for Drug/Alcohol Screen Testing		

Section 3

Processing New Employees

Rehire Form	New Personnel Checklist	Employee File
Hiring Authorization	Employee Agreement and Handbook Acknowledgement	New Employee Data
Relocation Expense Approval		Emergency Phone Numbers
Letter to New Employee 1	Job Description	Established Workday and Workweek Schedules and Policies
Letter to New Employee 2	Emergency Procedures	
Letter to New Employee 3	Summary of Employment Terms	Consent for Drug/Alcohol Screening
Letter to New Employee 4	Payroll Deduction Authorization	Receipt for Company Property
New Employee Announcement	Payroll Deduction Direct Deposit Authorization	Samples and Documents Receipt
Employee Background Verification		EEO Analysis of New Hires
New Employee Orientation Checklist	Direct Deposit Authorization	
New Employee Checklist	Withholding Tax Information	

(continued)

TABLE 3-B1 (*continued*)

Section 4

Personnel Management

Employment Record	Department Overtime Report	Employee Absence Report
Personnel Data Change	Department Payroll	Absence Report
Employee Information Update	Expense Report	Department Absence Report
Employee Salary Record	Mileage Reimbursement Report	Annual Attendance Record
Employment Changes	Payroll Change Notice	Employee Suggestion
Personnel Data Sheet	Pay Advice	Suggestion Plan 1
Personnel File Access Log	Payroll Summary	Suggestion Plan 2
Request to Inspect Personnel File	Vacation Request Memo	Suggestion Plan 3
Consent to Release Information	Vacation Request	Memo Regarding Drug Testing
Telephone Reference Record	Employee Health Record	Test Notice—Polygraph
Personnel Activity Report	Accident Report	Information Notice—Polygraph
Personnel Requirement Projections	Illness Report	Notice of Affirmative Action Policy
Temporary Employment Requisition	Injury Report	Affirmative Action Notice to Suppliers
Temporary Personnel Requisition	Disability Certificate	Affirmative Action Self-Identification
Employee Flextime Schedule	Physician's Report	Affirmative Action Supplier's Compliance Certificate
Weekly Work Schedule	Employee Sympathy Letter 1	
Daily Time Record	Employee Sympathy Letter 2	Affirmative Action Summary
Employee Daily Time Record	Employee Sympathy Letter 3	Equal Employment Opportunity Policy
Weekly Time Record	Employee Sympathy Letter 4	Current EEO Workforce Analysis
Hourly Employees' Weekly Time Sheet	Absence Request	EEO Analysis of Promotions
Department Overtime Request	Funeral Leave Request	Employee Transfer Request
Overtime Permit	Leave Request/Return from Leave	Off-Duty Employment Request
Overtime Authorization	Military Duty Absence	Grievance Form
Overtime Report	Late Report	

Section 5

Performance Evaluation

Employee Consultation	Disciplinary Notice	Standard Evaluation
Employee Counseling Activity Sheet	Disciplinary Warning	Temporary Employee Evaluation
Critical Incidents Report	Disciplinary Report	Employee Performance Review
Incident Report	Suspension Without Pay Notice	Performance Appraisal Interview Report
Notice of Ongoing Investigation—Polygraph	Employee Self-Evaluation	Employee Rating Response
Notice of 30-Day Evaluation	Performance Analysis Employee Worksheet	Performance Objectives
Notice of Probation	Employee Performance Checklist	Coaching Form
Notice of Extended Probation	New Employee Evaluation	Employee Performance Improvement Plan
Excessive Absenteeism Warning	Managerial Evaluation	Letter of Commendation
First Warning Notice	Performance Evaluation	Salary Change Request
Second Warning Notice	Production Personnel Evaluation	
	Sales Personnel Evaluation	

TABLE 3-B1 (*continued*)

Section 6

Benefits

Accrued Benefits Statements	Resolution—Paid-Up Annuity Plan	Resolution—Tuition Benefit
Employee Benefits Analysis	Resolution—Relocation Allowance	Resolution—Scholarship Aid Program
Benefits Planning Checklist	Resolution—Performance Bonus	Resolution—Financial Counseling Plan
Employee Benefits Survey	Resolution—Low-Interest Loan	Resolution—Sabbatical Leave
Employee Benefits List	Resolution—Company Car	Resolution—Child Care Plan
Combined Resolution—Incentive Stock Option Plan	Resolution—Club Membership	Resolution—Wage Continuation Plan
Resolution—Signing Bonus	Resolution—At-Home Entertainment Allowance	Resolution—Merchandise Discount Program

Section 7

Termination/Separation

Retirement Checklist	Termination Letter for Intoxication on the Job	Employee Separation Report
Resignation		Unemployment Compensation Record
Termination Checklist	Letter Terminating Sales Representative	EEO Analysis of Terminations
Notice of Dismissal	Employee Checkout Record	Reference Report
Notice of Termination Due to Absence	General Release	Employment Reference Response
Notice of Termination Due to Work Rules Violation	Mutual Release	Refusal to Grant References
	Employee Release	Notice of Confidentiality Agreement
Reduction in Workforce Notice	Employee Exit Interview	COBRA Letter to Terminating Employee
Termination Letter for Excessive Absenteeism	Seperation Notice	COBRA Employee Information Letter
Termination Letter for Lack of Work	Personnel Separation Report	COBRA Compliance

Source: Mario German, Personnel Director (Deerfield Beach, FL: EZ Legal Books, 1994), pp. vi, vii, and viii.

the Table of Contents of a compilation of HR agreements and forms.[7] A reasonable way to obtain the basic component forms of a manual HR system is to start with a compilation of forms book like that one. Another example is James Jenks, *The Hiring, Firing (and Everything in Between) Personnel Forms Book* (Ridgefield, CT: Roundlake Publishing, 1996). The forms you want can then be adapted from these sources for your particular situation. Office supply stores (such as Office Depot and Office Max) also sell packages of personnel forms. For example, Office Depot sells packages of individual personnel forms as well as a "Human Resource Kit" containing 10 copies of each of the following: Application, Employment Interview, Reference Check, Employee Record, Performance Evaluation, Warning Notice, Exit Interview and Vacation Request, plus a Lawsuit-Prevention Guide.[8] Also available (and highly recommended) is a package of Employee Record Folders. Use the folders to maintain a file on each individual employee; on the outside of the pocket is printed a form for recording information such as name, start date, company benefits, and so on.

Several direct-mail catalog companies similarly offer a variety of HR materials. For example, HRdirect (100 Enterprise Place, Dover, DE, 19901, phone: 1-800-346-1231) offers packages of personnel forms including ones to be used for: Short- and Long-Form Employee Applications, Applicant Interviews, Mail Reference Checking, Employee Performance Reviews, Job Descriptions, Exit Interviews, Absentee Calendars and Reports, and Sexual

Harassment Charge Investigation forms. Various legal-compliance forms including standardized No Weapons Policy, Harassment Policy, FMLA Notice forms, as well as posters (for instance, covering legally required postings for matters such as the Americans with Disabilities Act and Occupational Safety and Health Act) are similarly available.

G. Neil Company of Sunrise, Florida (phone: 1-800-999-9111), is another direct-mail catalog personnel materials source. In addition to a complete line of personnel forms, documents, and posters, it also offers manual paper-based systems for keeping track of matters such as attendance history, conducting job analyses, and for tracking vacation requests and safety records. A complete HR "start-up" kit is available containing 25 copies of each of the following basic components of a manual HR system: Long Form Application for Employment; Attendance History; Performance Appraisal; Payroll/Status Change Notice; Absence Report; Vacation Request & Approval; W-4 Form; I-9 Form; New Employee Data Records; Separation Notice; Interview Evaluation; Self-Appraisal; Weekly Time Sheets; Accident/Illness Report; Exit Interview; Pre-Employment Phone Reference Check; Employee Warning Notice; Performance Appraisal-Exempt Positions; and tabbed dividers, all organized in a file box.

Automating Individual HR Tasks

As your company grows, it becomes increasingly unwieldy and uncompetitive to rely exclusively on manual HR systems. For a company with 40 or 50 employees or more, the amount of management time devoted to conducting appraisals can multiply into weeks. It is therefore at about this stage that most small- to medium-sized firms begin computerizing individual HR tasks.

Here again there are a variety of resources available. For example, at the Web site for the International Association for Human Resource Information Management, (http://www.ihrim.org), you'll find, within the Products & Services tab, a categorical buyers' guide listing software vendors. These firms provide software solutions for virtually all personnel tasks, ranging from benefits management to compensation, compliance, employee relations, outsourcing, payroll, and time and attendance systems.

Off-the-shelf software is available elsewhere, too. For example, the G. Neil Company sells off-the-shelf software packages for controlling attendance, employee record keeping, writing job descriptions, writing employee policy handbooks, and conducting computerized employee appraisals. HRdirect offers software for writing employee policy manuals, writing performance reviews, creating job descriptions, tracking attendance and hours worked for each employee, employee scheduling, writing organizational charts, managing payroll, conducting employee surveys, scheduling and tracking employee training activities, and managing OSHA compliance. A program called People Manager maintains employee records on items such as marital status, number of dependents, emergency contact and phone numbers, hire date, and job history. It also enables employers to quickly produce 30 standard reports on matters such as attendance, benefits, and ethnic information.

Establishing Human Resource Information Systems (HRIS)

Why an HRIS?   Larger companies typically integrate their separate HR systems into integrated human resource information systems (HRIS). An HRIS may be defined as interrelated components working together to collect, process, store, and disseminate information to support decision making, coordination, control, analysis, and visualization of an organization's human resource management activities.[9]

There are at least three reasons for installing such a system. First is competitiveness; an HRIS can significantly improve the efficiency of the HR operation and therefore a company's bottom line. For example, W. H. Brady Company, a Milwaukee-based manufacturer of identification products such as labels, reportedly cut several hundred thousand dollars a year from its HR budget through the use of HRIS.[10] Software producer PeopleSoft reportedly has a ratio of one HR staffer to each 110 employees, a savings of millions of dollars a year when compared with the traditional ratio of one HR staffer per 50–100 employees, and it credits that to its HRIS. The company expects the HR to employee ratio to shrink to 1:500.[11]

The HRIS can also bump the firm up to a new plateau in terms of the number and variety of HR-related reports it can produce. Citibank, for instance (part of Citigroup), has a global database of information on all employees including their compensation, a skills inventory bank of more than 10,000 of its managers, and a compensation and benefits practices database for each of the 98 countries in which the company has employees.[12]

Finally, the HRIS can also help shift HR's attention from transactions-processing to strategic HR. As the HRIS takes over tasks such as updating employee information and electronically reviewing resumes, the types of HR staff needed and their jobs tend to change. There is less need for entry-level HR data processors, for instance, and more for analysts capable of reviewing HR activities in relation to the company's plans and engaging in activities such as management development. Let's look more closely at how these advantages come about.

HRIS in Action How exactly can an HRIS achieve these kinds of performance improvements? At some point the employer will outgrow the separate (manual or computerized) component approach to managing HR. Some estimate that firms with fewer than 150 employees can efficiently use computerized component systems, each separately handling tasks such as attendance, and benefits and payroll management. However, beyond that point larger firms should turn to either off-the-shelf or customizable HRIS packages.[13] The advantages of moving from component systems to integrated human resource information systems arise from the following.

Improved Transaction Processing It's been said that "the bread and butter of HRIS is still basic transaction processing."[14] One study—conducted at a pharmaceuticals a company just before it implemented an HRIS—found that 71% of HR employees' time was devoted to transactional and administrative tasks, for instance. In other words, an enormous amount of time was devoted to tasks like checking leave balances, maintaining address records, and monitoring employee benefits distributions.[15] HRIS packages are intended to be comprehensive. They therefore generally provide relatively powerful computerized processing of a wider range of the firm's HR transactions than would be possible if individual systems for each HR task had to be used.

Online Processing Many HR information systems make it possible (or easier) to make the company's employees themselves literally part of the HRIS. For example, Merck installed employee kiosks at which employees can verify and correct their home address and work location. Estimated savings reportedly approach $640,000 for the maintenance of those data alone, and many companies report similar savings. At Provident Bank, an HR compensation system called Benelogic allows the bank's employees to enroll in all their desired benefits programs over the Internet at a secure site. One shipping company estimates it will reduce transaction processing and related paperwork from $50 down to $30 or less per employee using direct-access kiosks and integrative voice response (IVR) phone scripts.[16] Increasingly, firms like Dell are creating intranet-based HR sites. These allow managers and employees to process HR related information with little or no support required from the HR group itself. But using kiosks, or (increasingly) the intranet-based systems should not only move the burden of the record keeping from HR to the employees themselves. It also should "support employees' quest for 'what if' information relating to, for example, the impact on their take-home pay of various benefits options, W-4 changes, insurance coverage, retirement planning and more."[17] Some experts refer to advanced Internet-based HR service programs like these as electronic HR or ("e-HR"). It is the "application of conventional, Web, and voice technologies to improve HR administration, transactions, and process performance."

Improved Reporting Capability   Because the HRIS is comprehensive with respect to the number of HR tasks it handles, the installation of such a system significantly improves HR's reporting capabilities.

For most of these systems, the number and variety of reports possible is limited only by the manager's imagination. For a start, reports might be available (companywide and by department) for: health care cost per employee, pay and benefits as a percent of operating expense, cost per hire, report on training, volunteer turnover rates, turnover costs, time to fill jobs, and return on human capital invested (in terms of training and education fees, for instance).[18] Similarly, you might want to calculate and review: human resource cost information by business unit; personal and performance information on candidates for global assignments; demographics of the candidate pool to meet diversity reporting requirements; benefit plan funding requirements and controls; union membership information; information required for HR if a merger, acquisition, or divestiture is expected; and data on your global executive-level population for development, promotion, and transfer purposes.[19]

HR System Integration   Because its software components (record keeping, payroll, appraisal, and so forth) are integrated, a true HRIS enables an employer to dramatically reengineer its entire HR function by having the information system itself take over and integrate many of the tasks formerly carried out by HR employees.

The system installed at PeopleSoft (now part of Oracle Corporation) provides a good example of this:

> Sophisticated workflow technology routes promotions, salary increases, transfers, and other forms through the organization to the proper managers for approval. As one person signs off, it's routed to the next. If anyone forgets to process a document, a smart agent issues reminders until the task is completed. Training materials—including video—are almost entirely online, and all payroll checks are distributed electronically.
>
> But the company's hiring process may be the most futuristic aspect of all. Applications sent via the World Wide Web or fax are automatically deposited into a database; those submitted on paper are scanned into the computer and plugged into the same database. Once a hiring manager has selected an applicant for an interview, the system phones that person and asks him or her to select an interview time by punching buttons on a touchtone phone. At the end of the call, the client/server database notifies the interviewers of the appointment, and even offers a reminder the day of the interview. It's all handled without human interaction. And an orientation program for new hires works much the same way.[20]

HRIS Applications   Because of such capabilities, even many midsize firms are installing HR information systems today. For example, Grand Casinos, Inc., installed an HRIS called the Human Resource Manager, a package from PDS, Inc., to help with the hiring of several thousand new casino employees. "This system consolidates the human resources operations of Grand Casinos' nine separate properties, and lets these operations share resumes and other applicant information."[21] State Capital Credit Union in Madison, Wisconsin, with 105 employees, installed a desktop version of an HRIS called Spectrum HR/1100. This system "tracks applicant history and status, salary and staffing changes across departments, benefits plan participation, pension plan contributions, employee training, and turnover. It maintains compliance statistics, . . . and wage and hour information."[22] State Capital's system also performs other HR tasks including internal job postings, benefits billing, payroll reconciliation, and personalized letters and labels for applicant and employee correspondence.[23] For larger installations, major IT firms including IBM provide the required HR Systems integration. For example, IBM provides software under its "On-Demand Workplace Program." Under this program IBM offers integratable HR software from several developers, including Workbrain (for instance, for labor scheduling, and time and attendance), and StorePerform (for work load optimization in retail stores). Similarly, when Chiron Corp., a large pharmaceutical and biotechnology company, found it needed to integrate its existing computer-based HR system component solutions, it turned to the large information systems firm SAP. For example, SAP was able to integrate its own proprietary human resource information system with an online recruiting tool from hire.com that Chiron had been using and wanted to continue to use.

HRIS Implementation Pitfalls As most everyone knows by now, implementing a sophisticated information system is often more of a challenge than the client expects, and several potential pitfalls account for this. Cost is one problem; for example, a representative from Allstate Insurance Company reported that the costs of moving to a new HRIS had increased 10% per year for five years and that additional investment would be required to make the transition.[24] Other systems run into management resistance. At one pharmaceuticals firm, for instance, the new HRIS requires line managers to input some information (such as on performance appraisals) into the HR system, and some object to doing tasks previously performed by HR.[25] Others trigger resistance by including inconvenient or unworkable user interfaces for the employees to use; still others are installed without enough thought being given to whether or not the new HRIS will be compatible with the firm's existing HR information systems. Inadequate documentation or training can undermine the system's utility, and increase resistance to the system by exactly those employees and managers who are supposed to aid in its use.[26]

Actually installing the HRIS therefore needs to be viewed as a whole but also as a process composed of separate projects, each of which must be planned and realistically scheduled.[27] Given these sorts of hurdles a careful needs assessment obviously should be done prior to adopting an HRIS. Particularly for firms with less than 150 employees, consideration should be given to depending more on individual software packages for managing separate tasks such as attendance, benefits and payroll, and OSHA compliance.[28]

HRIS Vendors Many firms today offer HRIS packages. At the Web site for the International Association for Human Resource Information Management (mentioned earlier), for instance, Automatic Data Processing, Inc., Business Information Technology, Inc., Human Resource Microsystems, Lawson Software, Oracle Corporation, PeopleSoft, Inc., Restrac Web Hire, SAP America, Inc., and about 25 other firms are listed as HRIS vendors. As another example, Business Computer Systems (www.bcs-tx.com), offers a line of ABRA software products for firms ranging in size from 20 to 10,000 employees. As one example, you can point and click to find a list of employees reporting to a particular supervisor, and print over a hundred reports such as salary lists, employee profiles, and EEO reports.[29]

HR and Intranets As noted above, employers are creating internal intranet-based HR information systems. For example, LG&E Energy Corporation uses its intranet for benefits communication.[30] Employees can access the benefits homepage and (among other things) review the company's 401(k) plan investment options, get answers to frequently asked questions about the company's medical and dental plans, and report changes in family status (such as marriage) that may impact the employee's benefits.

A list of other HR-related ways in which employers use the intranet include: create an electronic employee directory; automate job postings and applicant tracking; set up training registration; provide electronic pay stubs; publish an electronic employee handbook; offer more enticing employee communications and newsletters; let employees update their personal profiles and access their accounts, such as 401(k)s; conduct open benefits enrollments; provide leave status information; conduct performance and peer reviews; manage succession planning (in part by locating employees with the right skill set to fill openings); and create discussion groups or forums.[31]

APPENDICES A, B ENDNOTES

1. The idea for the HR Scorecard derives from a broader measurement tool managers call the balanced scorecard. This does for the company as a whole what the HR Scorecard does for HR, summarizing instead the impact of various functions including HRM, sales, production, and distribution. The "balanced" in balanced scorecard refers to a balance of goals—financial and non-financial.
2. Quoted in Bill Macalear and Jones Shannon, "Does HR Planning Improve Business Performance?" *Industrial Management*, January/February 2003, p. 20.
3. This section is adapted in part from Becker, Huselid, and Ulrich, *The HR Scorecard: Linking People, Strategy, and Performance.*
4. Arthur Thompson, Jr. and A. J. Strickland III, *Strategic Management: Concepts and Cases* (New York: McGraw-Hill, 2001), pp. 129–131.
5. *Human Resource Department Management Report* (December 2002), p. 8; "Watson Wyatt Worldwide Creates the HR Scorecard Alliance," *InfoTrac*, downloaded September 19, 2003.
6. "Creating the HR Scorecard, Preliminary Findings from the Business Intelligence Report," www.business-intelligence.co.uk/hrscorecard (2001).
7. Mario German, *Personnel Director* (Deerfield Beach, FL: E-Z Legal Books, 1994), pp. vi, vii, and viii.
8. Office Depot, Winter 2003 Catalog (Delray Beach, FL: Office Depot, 2003).
9. Adapted from Kenneth Laudon and Jane Laudon, *Management Information Systems: New Approaches to Organization and Technology* (Upper Saddle River, NJ: Prentice Hall, 1998), p. G7. See also, Michael Barrett and Randolph Kahn, "The Governance of Records Management," Directors and Boards 26, no. 3 (Spring 2002), pp. 45–48; and Anthony Hendrickson, "Human Resource Information Systems: Backbone Technology of Contemporary Human Resources," Journal of Labor Research, Summer 2003, vol. 24, issue 3, pp. 381–395.
10. Samuel Greengard, "Finding Time to Be Strategic," *Personnel Journal*, October 1996, pp. 84–89.
11. Samuel Greengard, "Client/Server: HR's Helping Hand?" *Personnel Journal*, May 1996, p. 92.
12. Linda Stroh, "Integrated HR Systems Help Develop Global Leaders," *HR Magazine* 43, no. 5 (April 1998), pp. 14–18.
13. Tony Berardine, "Human Resource Information Systems Improve Management Decision-Making," *Canadian Manager* 22, no. 5 (Winter 1997), pp. 17–18. See also, Nona Tobin, "Can Technology Ease the Pain of Salary Surveys?" *Public Personnel Management* 31, no. 1 (Spring 2002), pp. 65–78.
14. Gerald Groe, "Information Technology and HR," *Human Resource Planning* 19, no. 1 (March 1996), pp. 56–62. See also, France Lampron, "Is an ESS Right for Your Company?" *HR Magazine* 47, no. 12 (December 2002), pp. 77–80.
15. "HR Execs Trade Notes on Human Resource Information Systems," *BNA Bulletin to Management* December 3, 1998, p. 1. See also, Brian Walter, "But They Said Their Payroll Program Complied with the FLSA," *Public Personnel Management* 31, no. 1 (Spring 2002), pp. 79–94.
16. Marc Miller, "Great Expectations: Is Your HRIS Meeting Them?" *HR Focus* 75, no. 4 (April 1998), pp. 1–3. See also, Vicki Gerson, "Provident Bank Automates Benefits Administration: Web-Based Offering from Benelogic Cuts Employee Benefits Enrollment Costs," *Bank Systems + Technology*, September 2003, vol. 40, issue 9, p. 19.

17. Ibid., p. 2. See also, Ali Velshi, "Human Resources Information," *The Americas Intelligence Wire*, February 11, 2004.

18. Jac Fitz-enz, "Top Ten Calculations for Your HRIS," *HR Focus* 75, no. 4 (April 1998), p. 3.

19. Linda Stroh, "Integrated HR Systems," p. 16.

20. Samuel Greengard, "Client/Server: HR's Helping Hand?" *Personnel Journal*, May 1996, p. 92.

21. Stephanie Wilkinson, "Hire and Higher: Client/Server and Web-Based Systems Raise the Stakes for Solving HR Headaches," *PC Week*, July 8, 1996, pp. 45–47.

22. Mary Mink, "Software Eases HR Tasks," *Credit Union Executive* no. 6 (November–December 1996), p. 35. See also, Janet Wiscombe, "Using Technology to Cut Costs," *Workforce*, September 2001, pp. 46–51; and, "PILAT NAI Expands Its World-Class Talent Management Offerings with Web-Based Strategic Staffing Solutions," *Internet Wire*, January 26, 2004.

23. Ibid. See also, "Technology Trends 2002," *Workforce*, November 2001, pp. 55–58; Christina Blank and Michael G. A. R. R. Y., "Managing Smart: To Improve Hiring and Managing of In-Store Employees and to Reduce Paperwork, Retailers Are Turning to a Host of New Applications," Supermarket News, May 3, 2004, p. 149; and, "How Chiron Corp. Updated an Old Human Resource Information System," Human Resource Department Management Report, May 2003, p. 15.

24. "HR Execs Trade Notes on Human Resource Information Systems," p. 2.

25. Ibid, p. 1.

26. Victor Haines and Andre Petit, "Conditions for Successful Human Resource Information Systems," *Human Resource Management* 36, no. 2 (Summer 1997), pp. 261–276; see also "Five Critical "-tions" Help You Select New or Replacement HRIS," Human Department Management Report, August 2003, p. 1.

27. James Schultz, "Avoid the DDTs of HRIS Implementation," *HR Magazine* 42, no. 5 (May 1997), pp. 37–41. See also, Bill Roberts, "The New HRIS: Good Deal or $6 Million Paperweight?" *HR Magazine* 43, no. 3, (February 1998), p. 40.

28. Tony Berardine, "Human Resource Information Systems Improve Management Decision Making," *Canadian Manager* 22, no. 4 (Winter 1997), pp. 17–19. See also, MaryAnn Hammers, "HR in a Time of Caution: Recharging Your HRMS," *Workforce*, September 2002, p. 38.

29. Jim Meade, "Below Cost Alternative to the Traditional HRIS: Best Imperative HRMS Offers Great Value," *HR Magazine* 43, no. 9 (August 1998), pp. 37–40. Note that increasing numbers of HRIS depend on so-called client/server systems. For more information see, for instance, Eric Baker, "Do You Need a Client/Server System?" *HR Magazine*, February 1997, pp. 37–43.

30. Frank Kuzmits, "Communicating Benefits: A Double Click Away," *Compensation and Benefits Review*, September/October 1998, pp. 60–64.

31. Samuel Greengard, "Increase the Value of Your Intranet," *Workforce*, March 1997, pp. 88–94; Samuel Greengard, "Achieving Greater Intranet Efficiency," *Workforce*, September 1998, pp. 71–77.

PART I VIDEO CASES APPENDIX

Video 1: Introduction to Human Resource Management, and Strategic Human Resource Management

Video Title: Showtime

Showtime Networks operates cable networks and pay-per-view cable channels across the United States and in several countries abroad. As this video illustrates, its HR function supports corporate strategy by helping to determine what kind of employees are needed to keep the company in peek performance, and then by providing the company and its employees with the HR activities that these employees need to do their jobs. For example, you'll see that Showtime offers many development and training programs, as well as personal development type activities including mentoring programs and career oriented development activities. The firm's performance management process (which the employees helped develop) focuses specifically on the work activities and results that help achieve departmental and corporate goals. In this video, Matthew, the firm's CEO, emphasizes that it's essential to use human resources as a strategic partner, and the video then goes on to provide something of a summary of the basic human resource management functions.

Discussion Questions

1. What concrete evidence do you see in this video that HR at Showtime helps the company achieve its strategic goals?
2. What specific HR functions does the video mention, at least in passing?
3. Why do you think management at Showtime places such a heavy emphasis on personal development and quality of work issues such as open door policies, mentoring programs, and allowing employees to swap jobs?

Video 2: Managing Equal Opportunity and Diversity

Video Title: IQ Solutions

IQ solutions is in the business of providing health-care system services. It says one of its aims is lessening the inequality that they say exists in America's health-care system, and the company uses its very diverse employee base to better serve and attract a broad client base. Employees at IQ solutions work together in teams to achieve the company's goals. As we see in this video, the company itself is indeed very diverse: for example, employees speak about 18 languages. The company capitalizes on this diversity in many ways. For example, they let their employees share their ethnically unique holidays, and provide special training and other benefits that support diversity.

Discussion Questions

1. To what extent does diversity management at IQ solutions contribute to the company achieving its strategic goals?
2. Based upon what you read in this part of the book, which diversity management programs can you identify in use at IQ solutions?

4 Job Analysis

When Daimler-Chrysler opened its Mercedes Benz assembly plant in Arkansas, its managers faced a dilemma. They could not hire, train, or pay the plant employees unless the managers knew what each employee was expected to do—they needed, for each person, a list of job duties, a "job description." But in this plant, self-managing teams of employees would assemble the vehicles, and their jobs and duties might change every day. How does one list job duties, when the duties are a moving target? •

After studying this chapter, you should be able to:

1 Discuss the nature of job analysis, including what it is and how it's used.
2 Use at least three methods of collecting job analysis information, including interviews, questionnaires, and observation.
3 Write job descriptions, including summaries and job functions, using the Internet and traditional methods.
4 Write job specifications using the Internet as well as your judgment.
5 Explain job analysis in a "jobless" world, including what it means and how it's done in practice.

The main purpose of this chapter is to show you how to analyze a job and write job descriptions. We'll see that analyzing jobs involves determining in detail what the job entails and what kind of people the firm should hire for the job. We discuss several techniques for analyzing jobs, and how to use the Internet and more traditional methods to draft job descriptions and job specifications. Then, in the next chapter, "Personnel Planning and Recruiting," we'll turn to the methods managers use to actually find the employees they need.

THE BASICS OF JOB ANALYSIS

> ❶ Discuss the nature of job analysis, including what it is and how it's used.

job analysis
The procedure for determining the duties and skill requirements of a job and the kind of person who should be hired for it.

job description
A list of a job's duties, responsibilities, reporting relationships, working conditions, and supervisory responsibilities—one product of a job analysis.

job specifications
A list of a job's "human requirements," that is, the requisite education, skills, personality, and so on—another product of a job analysis.

Organizations consist of jobs that have to be staffed. **Job analysis** is the procedure through which you determine the duties of these positions and the characteristics of the people to hire for them.[1] Job analysis produces information used for writing **job descriptions** (a list of what the job entails) and **job specifications** (what kind of people to hire for the job).

The supervisor or human resources specialist normally collects one or more of the following types of information via the job analysis:

- *Work activities.* First, he or she collects information about the job's actual work activities, such as cleaning, selling, teaching, or painting. This list may also include how, why, and when the worker performs each activity.
- *Human behaviors.* The specialist may also collect information about human behaviors like sensing, communicating, deciding, and writing. Included here would be information regarding job demands such as lifting weights or walking long distances.
- *Machines, tools, equipment, and work aids.* This category includes information regarding tools used, materials processed, knowledge dealt with or applied (such as finance or law), and services rendered (such as counseling or repairing).
- *Performance standards.* The employer may also want information about the job's performance standards (in terms of quantity or quality levels for each job duty, for instance). Management will use these standards to appraise employees.
- *Job context.* Included here is information about such matters as physical working conditions, work schedule, and the organizational and social context—for instance, the number of people with whom the employee would normally interact. Information regarding incentives might also be included here.
- *Human requirements.* This includes information regarding the job's human requirements, such as job-related knowledge or skills (education, training, work experience) and required personal attributes (aptitudes, physical characteristics, personality, interests).

Uses of Job Analysis Information

As Figure 4-1 summarizes, employers use job analysis information to support several human resource management activities.

Recruitment and Selection   Job analysis provides information about what the job entails and what human characteristics are required to perform these activities. This information, in the form of job descriptions and specifications, helps managers decide what sort of people to recruit and hire.

Compensation   Job analysis information is indispensable for estimating the value of each job and its appropriate compensation. Compensation (such as salary and bonus) usually depends on the job's required skill and education level, safety hazards, degree of responsibility, and so on—all factors you can assess through job analysis. Furthermore, many employers group jobs into classes (say, secretary III and IV). Job analysis provides the information to determine the relative worth of each job—and thus its appropriate class.

FIGURE 4-1

Uses of Job Analysis Information

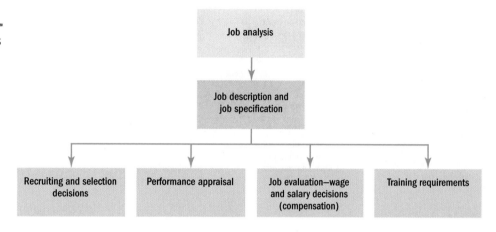

Training The job description lists the job's specific duties and requisite skills—and therefore the training—that the job requires.

Performance Appraisal A performance appraisal compares each employee's actual performance with his or her performance standards. Doing so requires knowledge of the job's duties and standards. Managers use job analysis to find out what these duties and performance standards are.

Discovering Unassigned Duties Job analysis can also help reveal unassigned duties. For example, your company's production manager says she's responsible for a dozen or so duties, such as production scheduling and raw material purchasing. Missing, however, is any reference to managing raw material inventories. On further study, you learn that none of the other manufacturing people are responsible for inventory management, either. You know from your review of other jobs like these that someone should be managing inventories. You've uncovered an essential unassigned duty, thanks to job analysis.

EEO Compliance Job analysis also plays a big role in EEO compliance. U.S. Federal Agencies' Uniform Guidelines on Employee Selection stipulate that job analysis is a crucial step in validating all major human resources activities.[2] For example, to comply with the Americans with Disabilities Act, employers should know each job's essential job functions—which in turn requires a job analysis.

Steps in Job Analysis

There are six steps in doing a job analysis. Let's look at each of them.

Step 1: Decide how you'll use the information, since this will determine the data you collect and how you collect them. Some data collection techniques—like interviewing the employee and asking what the job entails—are good for writing job descriptions and selecting employees for the job. Other techniques, like the position analysis questionnaire we describe later, do not provide qualitative information for job descriptions. Instead, they provide numerical ratings for each job; these can be used to compare jobs for compensation purposes.

Step 2: Review relevant background information such as organization charts, process charts, and job descriptions.[3] **Organization charts** show the organizationwide division of work, how the job in question relates to other jobs, and where the job fits in the overall organization. The chart should show the title of each position and, by means of interconnecting lines, who reports to whom and with whom the job incumbent communicates.

organization chart
A chart that shows the organizationwide distribution of work, with titles of each position and interconnecting lines that show who reports to and communicates to whom.

FIGURE 4-2

Process Chart for Analyzing a Job's Workflow

Source: Compensation Management: Rewarding Performance by Richard J. Henderson. Reprinted by permission of Pearson Education, Upper Saddle River, NJ.

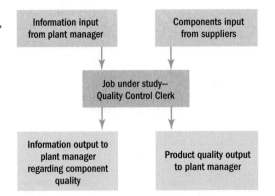

process chart

A work flow chart that shows the flow of inputs to and outputs from a particular job.

A **process chart** provides a more detailed picture of the work flow. In its simplest form a process chart (like that in Figure 4-2) shows the flow of inputs to and outputs from the job you're analyzing. (In Figure 4-2 the quality control clerk is expected to review components from suppliers, check components going to the plant managers, and give information regarding component's quality to these managers.) Finally, the existing job description, if there is one, usually provides a starting point for building the revised job description.

Step 3: Select representative positions. There may be too many similar jobs to analyze them all. For example, it is usually unnecessary to analyze the jobs of 200 assembly workers when a sample of 10 jobs will do.

Step 4: Actually analyze the job—by collecting data on job activities, required employee behaviors, working conditions, and human traits and abilities needed to perform the job. For this step, use one or more of the job analysis methods explained later in this chapter.

Step 5: Verify the job analysis information with the worker performing the job and with his or her immediate supervisor. This will help confirm that the information is factually correct and complete. This review can also help gain the employee's acceptance of the job analysis data and conclusions, by giving that person a chance to review and modify your description of the job activities.

Step 6: Develop a job description and job specification. These are two tangible products of the job analysis. The *job description* (to repeat) is a written statement that describes the activities and responsibilities of the job, as well as its important features, such as working conditions and safety hazards. The *job specification* summarizes the personal qualities, traits, skills, and background required for getting the job done. It may be in a separate document or in the same document as the job description.

In some firms, job analysis is still a time consuming process. It might take several days to interview 5 or 6 sample employees and their managers, and to try to explain to them the process and the reason for the analysis. Increasingly, however, the same process might take just three or four hours. The steps might include: (1) Greet participants, and conduct very brief introductions; (2) briefly explain the job analysis process and the participants' roles in this process; (3) spend about 15 minutes determining the scope of the job you're about to analyze, by getting agreement on the job's basic summary; (4) identify the job's broad functional or duty areas, such as "administrative" and "supervisory"; (5) identify tasks within each duty area, using a flip chart or collaboration software; and, finally (6) print the task list and get the group to sign off on it.[4]

> Use at least three methods of collecting job analysis information, including interviews, question-naires, and observation.

METHODS FOR COLLECTING JOB ANALYSIS INFORMATION

There are various ways (interviews, or questionnaires, for instance) to collect information on the duties, responsibilities, and activities of a job. We discuss the most important ones in this section. In practice, you could use any one of them, or combine several. The basic rule is to use those that best fit your purpose. Thus, an interview might be appropriate for creating a listing of job duties and job description, whereas the more quantitative Position Analysis Questionnaire may be best for quantifying each job's relative worth for compensation purposes.

Some Job Analysis Guidelines

In any event, there are several practical considerations to keep in mind.

First, conducting the job analysis usually involves a joint effort by a human resources specialist, the worker, and the worker's supervisor. The human resources specialist (perhaps a human resources manager, job analyst, or consultant) might observe and analyze the job and then develop a job description and specification. Often the supervisor and worker fill out questionnaires listing the subordinate's duties and activities. The supervisor and worker may then review and verify the job analyst's conclusions regarding the job's activities and duties.

Second, job analysis almost always requires collecting job analysis information from several people familiar with the job (called "subject matter experts") such as job incumbents and their supervisors, using questionnaires and interviews. For example the job incumbent or his or her supervisor alone will not suffice.

Third, if there are several employees doing the same job (as you might find for instance with the jobs of "programmer," "assembler," or "sales clerk"), it is typical to collect job analysis information from several of them from different departments, and then average up your results, to determine how much time a typical employee on that job spends on each job duty. The caveat is that employees who have the same job title but work in different departments may experience very different pressures. Therefore, simply adding up and averaging the amount of time that, say, recruiters in the engineering office and assembly plant each need to devote to "interviewing candidates" could end in misleading results. The point is that you must understand the job's departmental context: The way someone with a particular job title spends his or her time is not necessarily the same from department to department.

Fourth, make sure the questions and surveys are clear and understandable to the respondents.

Fifth, if possible, observe and question respondents early enough in the job analysis process to catch any problems while there's still time to correct the job analysis procedure (such as the questions) you're using.

Interviews, questionnaires, observations, and diary/logs are the most popular methods for gathering job analysis data. They all provide realistic information about what job incumbents actually do. Managers use them for developing job descriptions and job specifications.

It is helpful to spend several minutes prior to collecting job analysis information explaining the process that you will be following.

The Interview

Interviews are popular methods for obtaining job-related information. They may range from completely unstructured interviews ("Tell me about your job") to highly structured ones in which job analysts follow detailed questionnaires in asking their questions.

Managers may conduct individual interviews with each employee, group interviews with groups of employees who have the same job, and/or supervisor interviews with one or more supervisors who know the job. They use group interviews when a large number of employees are performing similar or identical work, since it can be a quick and inexpensive way to gather information. As a rule, the workers' immediate supervisor attends the group session; if not, you can interview the supervisor separately to get that person's perspective on the job's duties and responsibilities.

Whichever kind of interview you use, you need to be sure the interviewee fully understands the reason for the interview, because there's a tendency for such interviews to be viewed, rightly or wrongly, as "efficiency evaluations." If so, interviewees may hesitate to describe their jobs accurately.

Pros and Cons   The interview is probably the most widely used method for identifying a job's duties and responsibilities, and its wide use reflects its advantages. It's a simple and quick way to collect information, including information that might never appear on a written form. For instance, a skilled interviewer can unearth important activities that occur only occasionally, or informal contacts that wouldn't be obvious from the organization chart. The interview also provides an opportunity to explain the need for and functions of the job analysis. And the employee can vent frustrations that might otherwise go unnoticed by management.

Distortion of information is the main problem—whether due to outright falsification or honest misunderstanding.[5] Job analysis is often a prelude to changing a job's pay rate. Employees therefore may legitimately view the interview as some sort of "efficiency evaluation" that may affect their pay. They may then tend to exaggerate certain responsibilities while minimizing others. In one study researchers listed possible job duties either as simple task statements ("record phone messages and other routine information"), or as ability statements ("ability to record phone messages and other routine information"). Respondents were much more likely to include the ability based versions of the statements than they were to include the simple task statements. There may be a tendency for people to inflate their job's importance when abilities are involved, so as to impress the perceptions of others.[6] Obtaining valid information can thus be a slow process, and prudent analysts get multiple inputs.

Typical Questions   Despite their drawbacks, interviews are widely used. Some typical interview questions include:

What is the job being performed?

What are the major duties of your position? What exactly do you do?

What physical locations do you work in?

What are the education, experience, skill, and [where applicable] certification and licensing requirements?

In what activities do you participate?

What are the job's responsibilities and duties?

What are the basic accountabilities or performance standards that typify your work?

What are your responsibilities? What are the environmental and working conditions involved?

What are the job's physical demands? The emotional and mental demands?

What are the health and safety conditions?

Are you exposed to any hazards or unusual working conditions?

Structured interviews   Many interviewers follow structured or checklist formats. Figure 4-3 (pages 131–132) presents one example, in this case, a job analysis questionnaire.

FIGURE 4-3

Job Analysis Questionnaire for Developing Job Descriptions

Note: Use a questionnaire like this to interview job incumbents, or have them fill it out.

Source: www.hr.blr.com. Reprinted with permission of the publisher Business and Legal Reports, Inc., Old Saybrook, CT © 2004.

Job Analysis Information Sheet

Job Title_____   Date _____

Job Code_____ Dept. _____

Superior's Title _____

Hours Worked _____ AM to _____ PM

Job Analyst's Name _____

1. **What is the job's overall purpose?**

_____

2. **If the incumbent supervises others,** list them by job title; if there is more than one employee with the same title, put the number in parentheses following.

_____

3. **Check those activities** that are part of the incumbent's supervisory duties.

☐ Training
☐ Performance appraisal
☐ Inspecting work
☐ Budgeting
☐ Coaching and/or counseling
☐ Others (please specify) _____

4. **Describe the type and extent of supervision** received by the incumbent.

_____

5. **JOB DUTIES:** Describe briefly WHAT the incumbent does and, if possible, HOW he/she does it. Include duties in the following categories:

    a. daily duties (those performed on a regular basis every day or almost every day)

    _____

    b. periodic duties (those performed weekly, monthly, quarterly, or at other regular intervals)

    _____

    c. duties performed at irregular intervals

    _____

6. Is the incumbent performing duties he/she considers unnecessary? If so, describe.

_____

7. Is the incumbent performing duties not presently included in the job description? If so, describe.

_____

8. **EDUCATION:** Check the box that indicates the educational requirements for the job (not the educational background of the incumbent).

☐ No formal education required
☐ High school diploma (or equivalent)
☐ 4-year college degree (or equivalent)

☐ Eighth grade education
☐ 2-year college degree (or equivalent)
☐ Graduate work or advanced degree
    Specify: _____

☐ Professional license
    Specify: _____

FIGURE 4-3

(*continued*)

9. **EXPERIENCE:** Check the amount of experience needed to perform the job.

☐ None   ☐ Less than one month

☐ One to six months   ☐ Six months to one year

☐ One to three years   ☐ Three to five years

☐ Five to ten years   ☐ More than ten years

10. **LOCATION:** Check location of job and, if necessary or appropriate, describe briefly.

☐ Outdoor   ☐ Indoor

☐ Underground   ☐ Excavation

☐ Scaffold   ☐ Other (specify)

11. **ENVIRONMENTAL CONDITIONS:** Check any objectionable conditions found on the job and note afterward how frequently each is encountered (rarely, occasionally, constantly, etc.).

☐ Dirt   ☐ Dust

☐ Heat   ☐ Cold

☐ Noise   ☐ Fumes

☐ Odors   ☐ Wetness/humidity

☐ Vibration   ☐ Sudden temperature changes

☐ Darkness or poor lighting   ☐ Other (specify)

12. **HEALTH AND SAFETY:** Check any undesirable health and safety conditions under which the incumbent must perform and note how often they are encountered.

☐ Elevated workplace   ☐ Mechanical hazards

☐ Explosives   ☐ Electrical hazards

☐ Fire hazards   ☐ Radiation

☐ Other (specify)

13. **MACHINES, TOOLS, EQUIPMENT, AND WORK AIDS:** Describe briefly what machines, tools, equipment, or work aids the incumbent works with on a regular basis:

14. Have concrete work standards been established (errors allowed, time taken for a particular task, etc.)? If so, what are they?

15. Are there any personal attributes (special aptitudes, physical characteristics, personality traits, etc.) required by the job?

16. Are there any exceptional problems the incumbent might be expected to encounter in performing the job under normal conditions? If so, describe.

17. Describe the successful completion and/or end results of the job.

18. What is the seriousness of error on this job? Who or what is affected by errors the incumbent makes?

19. To what job would a successful incumbent expect to be promoted?

[**Note:** this form is obviously slanted toward a manufacturing environment, but it can be adapted quite easily to fit a number of different types of jobs.]

It includes a series of detailed questions regarding matters like the general purpose of the job; supervisory responsibilities; job duties; and education, experience, and skills required. Of course, structured lists are not just for interviewers: Job analysts who collect information by personally observing the work or by using questionnaires—two methods explained below—can also use lists like these.[7] Figure 4-4 (pages 134–136) is a questionnaire intended for completing online.

Interviewing Guidelines   Keep several things in mind when conducting a job analysis interview.

- *First*, the job analyst and supervisor should work together to identify the workers who know the job best—and preferably those who'll be most objective in describing their duties and responsibilities.
- *Second*, quickly establish rapport with the interviewee. Know the person's name, speak in easily understood language, briefly review the interview's purpose, and explain how the person was chosen for the interview.
- *Third*, follow a structured guide or checklist, one that lists questions and provides space for answers. This ensures you'll identify crucial questions ahead of time and that all interviewers (if there's more than one) cover all the required questions. (However, also make sure to give the worker some leeway in answering questions, and provide some open-ended questions like, "Was there anything we didn't cover with our questions?")
- *Fourth*, when duties are not performed in a regular manner—for instance, when the worker doesn't perform the same duties over and over again many times a day—ask the worker to list his or her duties in order of importance and frequency of occurrence. This will ensure that you don't overlook crucial but infrequently performed activities—like a nurse's occasional emergency room duties.
- *Fifth*, after completing the interview, review and verify the data. Specifically, review the information with the worker's immediate supervisor and with the interviewee.

Questionnaires

Having employees fill out questionnaires to describe their job-related duties and responsibilities is another popular way to obtain job analysis information.

Here, you have to decide how structured the questionnaire should be and what questions to include. Some questionnaires are very structured checklists. Each employee gets an inventory of perhaps hundreds of specific duties or tasks (such as "change and splice wire"). He or she is asked to indicate whether or not he or she performs each task and, if so, how much time is normally spent on each. At the other extreme, the questionnaire can be open-ended and simply ask the employee to "describe the major duties of your job."

In practice, the best questionnaire often falls between these two extremes. As illustrated in Figure 4-3, a typical job analysis questionnaire might have several open-ended questions (such as "state your jobs' overall purpose") as well as structured questions (concerning, for instance, previous education required). Figure 4-4 is another example.

Whether structured or unstructured, questionnaires have both pros and cons. A questionnaire is a quick and efficient way to obtain information from a large number of employees; it's less costly than interviewing hundreds of workers, for instance. However, developing the questionnaire and testing it (perhaps by making sure the workers understand the questions) can be expensive and time-consuming.

Observation

Direct observation is especially useful when jobs consist mainly of observable physical activities—assembly-line worker and accounting clerk are examples. On the other hand,

NEW COLLEGE OF FLORIDA
POSITION DESCRIPTION USPS & OPS

CURRENT DESCRIPTIVE DATA		FOR COMPLETION BY HR UPON FINAL ACTION				Position Number:		
		Approved Class Title:				Approved Class Code:		
1. Position Number:	2. Requested Classification Action: (__) Establish Position (__) Update (__) Change	Transaction:				Effective Date:		
3. Class Code:	4. Class Title:							
5. Department:	6. Department Head:	Org ID#:	Fund Code	FTE	Pay Plan	Pay Grade	EEO-6 Code	CBU Code
7. Grant Funded:	8. Contract:							
9. City: Sarasota	10. County: Sarasota	Signature of HR Director:				Date:		

ATTACH AN ADDITIONAL SHEET IF NEEDED TO PROPERLY DESCRIBE THE POSITION

In accordance with the Americans with Disabilities Act (ADA), identify essential functions of the job required to be performed with or without reasonable accommodations. Requests for reasonable accommodations to facilitate the performance of essential functions will be given careful consideration. **For purposes of the ADA, these functions are marginal only to individuals who are unable to perform the functions with or without reasonable accommodations because of a covered disability.

11. Describe functions in terms of outcomes/results rather than method used or how a job is normally accomplished.

11a. Essential Functions of the Job:* (List % of time for each function. Total % of time should add up to 100%.)

11b. Marginal Functions of the Job:

12. List the class titles and position numbers of positions under the direct supervision of this position.

13. List machines and equipment used regularly and percentage of time in the operations of each.

14. Describe the type and extent of instructions normally given to the incumbent of this position by the immediate supervisor.

14a. Working Hours (including any variations, split shifts, on call status, and/or rotations):

14b. Total hours per week:

FIGURE 4-4 Example of Position/Job Description Intended for Use Online

Source: www.ncf.edu/humanresources/documents/A&P%20Final.doc, accessed May 10, 2007.

15. **Education/Training/Experience** - In order of importance, state any specific education, training and experience and knowledge, skills and abilities required for this position. Note that these requirements must be related to the essential functions and at least equal to the minimum qualifications stated on the official class specification.

[ ]

Specialized Minimum Qualifications:

Preferred Qualifications:

Knowledge, Skills, & Abilities:

Language Skills:

Mathematical Skills:

Reasoning Ability:

Computer Skills:

16. **Required Licenses/Certifications and Other Specific Requirements of Law** - Review the statements below and check all that apply.

[ ]

17. **Other Characteristics of the Position** - Describe physical, mental and environmental factors critical to the satisfactory performance of the functions of the position or other characteristics which have not otherwise been described above.

[ ]

Physical Demands: The physical demands described here are representative of those that must be met by an employee to successfully perform the essential functions of this job. Reasonable accommodations may be made to enable individuals with disabilities to perform the essential functions.

[ ]

Work Environment:

[ ]

| _____ This position requires a post-offer employment physical | _____ This position requires a police background check | _____ This position requires fingerprinting | _____ This position required licensure, certification or other special requirements, as specified below |
| _____ This position requires a child care provider security check as required under Sections 402.305 and 402.3055, Florida Statutes | _____ This position is responsible for meeting the requirements of Section 215.422, Florida Statutes, as amended, regarding the approval and/or processing of vendors' invoices and/or distribution of warrants to vendors | _____ This position requires a classified driver's license appropriate to the type of vehicle operated in accordance with Section 332.60, Florida Statutes | _____ Other, as specified below |

FIGURE 4-4 (*continued*)

Signatures

18. I certify that I have reviewed and been provided a copy of the current position description for the position to which I am assigned.

_____   _____   _____
Name of Employee   Signature   Date

19. I certify that the statements above, to the best of my knowledge, accurately describe the position. I understand that intentional falsification of this documentation is in violation of State statutes and may result in disciplinary action or prosecution.

_____   _____   _____   _____
Name of Immediate Supervisor   Class Title   Signature   Date

20. **Reviewing Authority:**

_____   _____   _____
Name and Class Title   Signature   Date

21.   **REQUEST FOR CLASSIFICATION ACTION**
      Complete this section if requesting one or more of the types of actions listed; check all actions that apply.

___New Position   ___Class Change   ___Funding Change   ___FTE Change   ___Pay Grade Change   ___Organizational Unit Change

    Proposed Class Title _____   FTE _____   Acct. # _____   Pay Grade _____

FIGURE 4-4   *(continued)*

observation is usually not appropriate when the job entails a lot of mental activity (lawyer, design engineer). Nor is it useful if the employee only occasionally engages in important activities, such as a nurse who handles emergencies. And *reactivity*—the worker's changing what he or she normally does because you are watching—can also be a problem.

Managers often use direct observation and interviewing together. One approach is to observe the worker on the job during a complete work cycle. (The *cycle* is the time it takes to complete the job; it could be a minute for an assembly-line worker or an hour, a day, or longer for complex jobs.) Here you take notes of all the job activities. Then, after accumulating as much information as possible, you interview the worker. Ask the person to clarify points not understood and to explain what other activities he or she performs that you didn't observe. You can also observe and interview simultaneously, asking questions while the worker performs his or her job.

Participant Diary/Logs

diary/log
Daily listings made by workers of every activity in which they engage along with the time each activity takes.

Another approach is to ask workers to keep a **diary/log** of what they do during the day. For every activity he or she engages in, the employee records the activity (along with the time) in a log. This can produce a very complete picture of the job, especially when supplemented with subsequent interviews with the worker and the supervisor. The employee, of course, might try to exaggerate some activities and underplay others. However, the detailed, chronological nature of the log tends to mediate against this.

Diary/logs have gone high-tech. Some firms give employees pocket dictating machines and pagers. Then at random times during the day, they page the workers, who dictate what they are doing at that time. This approach can avoid one pitfall of the traditional diary/log method: relying on workers to remember what they did hours earlier when they complete their logs at the end of the day.

Quantitative Job Analysis Techniques

Qualitative approaches like interviews and questionnaires are not always suitable. For example, if your aim is to compare jobs for pay purposes, you may need to say that, in effect, "Job A is twice as challenging as Job B, and so is worth twice the pay." To do this, it can help to be able to assign quantitative values to each job. The position analysis questionnaire and the Department of Labor approach are popular quantitative methods.

position analysis questionnaire (PAQ)
A questionnaire used to collect quantifiable data concerning the duties and responsibilities of various jobs.

Position Analysis Questionnaire The **position analysis questionnaire (PAQ)** is a very structured job analysis questionnaire.[8] The PAQ contains 194 items, each of which (such as "written materials") represents a basic element that may or may not play an important role in the job. The job analyst decides if each item plays a role and, if so, to what extent. In Figure 4-5, for example, "written materials" received a rating of 4, indicating that written materials (like books, reports, and office notes) play a considerable role in this job. The analyst can do this online (see www.paq.com).

The advantage of the PAQ is that it provides a quantitative score or profile of any job in terms of how that job rates on five basic activities: (1) having decision-making/ communication/social responsibilities, (2) performing skilled activities, (3) being physically active, (4) operating vehicles/equipment, and (5) processing information. The PAQ's real strength is thus in classifying jobs. In other words, it lets you assign a quantitative score to each job based on its decision-making, skilled activity, physical activity, vehicle/equipment operation, and information-processing characteristics. You can therefore use the PAQ results to quantitatively compare jobs to one another,[9] and then assign pay levels for each job.[10]

U.S. Department of Labor (DOL) job analysis procedure
A standardized method by which different jobs can be quantitatively rated, classified, and compared based on data, people, and things scored.

Department of Labor (DOL) Procedure The **U.S. Department of Labor job analysis procedure** also provides a standardized method by which to quantitatively rate, classify, and compare different jobs. The heart of this analysis is a data, people, and things rating for each job.

It works as follows. As Table 4-1 shows, the DOL method uses a set of standard basic activities called *worker functions* to describe what a worker can do with respect to data, people, and things. With respect to data, for instance, the basic functions include synthesizing, coordinating, and copying. With respect to people, they include mentoring, negotiating, and supervising. With respect to things, the basic functions include manipulating, tending, and handling.

Note also that each worker function gets an importance level. Thus, "coordinating" is 1, whereas "copying" is 5. If you were analyzing the job of a receptionist/clerk, for example, you might label the job 5, 6, 7, which would represent copying data, speaking/signaling people, and handling things. On the other hand, you might code a psychiatric aide in a hospital 1, 7, 5 in relation to data, people, and things. In practice, you would analyze each task that the worker performed in terms of data, people, and things. Then the highest combination (say 4, 6, 5) would be used to identify the job, since this is the highest level that a job incumbent would be expected to attain.

As illustrated in Figure 4-6, the schedule produced from the DOL procedure contains several types of information. The job title, in this case dough mixer in a bakery, is listed first. Also listed are the industry in which this job is found and the industry's standard industrial classification code. There is a one- or two-sentence summary of the job, and the worker function ratings for data, people, and things—in this case 5, 6, 2. These numbers mean that in terms of difficulty, a dough mixer copies data, speaks/signals with people, and operates/controls with respect to things. Finally, the schedule specifies the human requirements of the job, for instance, in terms of training time required, aptitudes, temperaments. As you can see, each job ends up with a numerical score (such as 5, 6, 2). You can thus group together (and assign the same pay to) all jobs with similar scores, even for very different jobs like dough mixer and mechanic's helper.

FIGURE 4-5

Portion of a Completed Page from the Position Analysis Questionnaire

The 194 PAQ elements are grouped into six dimensions. This exhibits 11 of the "information input" questions or elements. Other PAQ pages contain questions regarding mental processes, work output, relationships with others, job context, and other job characteristics.

Information Input

1 Information Input

1.1 Sources of Job Information
Rate each of the following items in terms of the extent to which it is used by the worker as a source of information in performing his job.

	Extent of Use (U)
NA	Does not apply
1	Nominal/very infrequent
2	Occasional
3	Moderate
4	Considerable
5	Very substantial

1.1.1 Visual Sources of Job Information

1 **4** Written materials (books, reports, office notes, articles, job instructions, signs, etc.)

2 **2** Quantitative materials (materials which deal with quantities or amounts, such as graphs, accounts, specifications, tables of numbers, etc.)

3 **1** Pictorial materials (pictures or picturelike materials used as *sources* of information, for example, drawings, blueprints, diagrams, maps, tracing, photographic films, x-ray films, TV pictures, etc.)

4 **1** Patterns/related devices (templates, stencils, patterns, etc., used as *sources* of information when *observed* during use; do *not* include here materials described in item 3 above)

5 **2** Visual displays (dials, gauges, signal lights, radarscopes, speedometers, clocks, etc.)

6 **5** Measuring devices (rulers, calipers, tire pressure gauges, scales, thickness gauges, pipettes, thermometers, protractors, etc., used to obtain visual information about physical measurements; do *not* include here devices describe in item 5 above)

7 **4** Mechanical devices (tools, equipment, machinery, and other mechanical devices which are *sources* of information when observed during use of operation)

8 **3** Materials in process (parts, material, objects, etc., which are *sources* of information when being modified, worked on, or otherwise processed, such as bread dough being mixed, workpiece being turned in a lathe, fabric being cut, shoe being resoled, etc.)

9 **4** Materials *not* in process (parts, materials, objects, etc., not in the process of being changed or modified, which are *sources* of information when being inspected, handled, packaged, distributed, or selected, etc., such as items or materials in inventory, storage, or distribution channels, items being inspected, etc.)

10 **3** Features of nature (landscapes, fields, geological samples, vegetation, cloud formations, and other features of nature which are observed or inspected to provide information)

11 **2** Man-made features of environment (structures, buildings, dams, highways, bridges, docks, railroads, and other "man-made" or altered aspects of the indoor environment which are *observed* or *inspected* to provide job information; do not consider equipment, machines, etc., that an individual uses in his work, as covered by item 7)

functional job analysis
A method for classifying jobs similar to the DOL method, but additionally taking into account the extent to which instructions, reasoning, judgment, and mathematical and verbal ability are necessary for performing job tasks.

Another technique, **functional job analysis** is similar to the DOL method, but rates the job not just on data, people, and things, but also on the extent to which performing the task requires specific instructions, reasoning and judgment, mathematical ability, and verbal and language facilities.

TABLE 4-1 Basic Department of Labor Worker Functions

	Data	People	Things
Basic Activities	0 Synthesizing	0 Mentoring	0 Setting up
	1 Coordinating	1 Negotiating	1 Precision working
	2 Analyzing	2 Instructing	2 Operating/controlling
	3 Compiling	3 Supervising	3 Driving/operating
	4 Computing	4 Diverting	4 Manipulating
	5 Copying	5 Persuading	5 Tending
	6 Comparing	6 Speaking/signaling	6 Feeding/offbearing
		7 Serving	7 Handling
		8 Taking instructions/helping	

Note: Determine employee's job "score" on data, people, and things by observing his or her job and determining, for each of the three categories, which of the basic functions illustrates the person's job. "0" is high; "6," "8," and "7" are lows in each column.

FIGURE 4-6

Sample Report Based on Department of Labor Job Analysis Technique

Job Analysis Schedule

1. Established Job Title ___DOUGH MIXER___

2. Ind. Assign ___(bake prod.)___

3. SIC Code(s) and Title(s) ___2051 Bread and other bakery products___

4. JOB SUMMARY:

Operates mixing machine to mix ingredients for straight and sponge (yeast) doughs according to established formulas, directs other workers in fermentation of dough, and curls dough into pieces with hand cutter.

5. WORK PERFORMED RATINGS:

	D	P	(T)
Worker Functions	Data	People	Things
	5	6	2

Work Field ___Cooking, Food Preparing___

6. WORKER TRAITS RATING (to be filled in by analyst):

Training time required
Aptitudes
Temperaments
Interests
Physical demands
Environment conditions

You may find both the DOL and functional job analysis methods in use. However, job analysts increasingly rely on the use of other methods instead. These include the U.S. government's online O*NET initiatives, which we'll discuss below.

Internet-Based Job Analysis

Most of these job analysis methods suffer from one or more of several problems. Face-to-face interviews and observations can be slow and time-consuming. The information (usually collected orally or in writing) is difficult to update quickly. Collecting the information from internationally dispersed employees is challenging.[11]

Internet-based job analysis is an obvious solution: "The use of online methodologies for surveys, including job analysis surveys, has increased dramatically in recent years, and most companies choose to use the Internet or intranet to collect this type of data."[12] Thus the human resource department may distribute standardized job analysis questionnaires to geographically disbursed employees via their company intranets, with instructions to complete the forms and return them by a particular date.

Although widely used, this practice creates its own problems. Most importantly, without a job analyst/facilitator actually sitting there and interacting with the employee or supervisor, there's always a chance that important points won't be uncovered or that misunderstandings will cloud the results.

The U.S. Navy Project   A recent report describes how a new Web-based job analysis procedure for the U.S. Navy helps overcome this problem. "The challenge was to develop a system that would allow the collection of job-related information with minimal intervention and guidance, so that the system could be used in a distributed manner using the World Wide Web to access the system."[13] The basic aim was to reduce ambiguities by having respondents complete step-by-step, structured forms.

In this procedure, the system doesn't ask the subject matter experts (the job incumbents, supervisors, or others who know the jobs) about the jobs in question as a whole. Instead, the process is as follows:

- It presents them with a set of general work activities obtained from the Department of Labor online job analysis systems O*NET work activities list. (Figure 4-7 lists some of these activities, such as "Information Input Category" and "Interacting with Others Category" (the others are accessible at http://online.onetcenter.org/).
- It directs them to select those work activities that are relevant to their job.
- It asks them to list specific duties of their jobs that fit each of those selected standard work activities. (For instance, if an employee chose "getting information" as a work activity that was relevant to his or her job, he might here list one or more specific job duties from the job that are relevant to "getting information," perhaps such as "watch for new orders from our customers and bring them to the boss's attention."

The method proved to be a reliable and valid way to collect job-related related information online.[14]

A Final Point: Use Multiple Sources to Collect the Data

We've seen that there are many ways to obtain job analysis information, including from individual workers, groups, or supervisors; or from the observations of job analysts. You can use interviews, observations, or questionnaires.

Some firms use a single approach, like having the job analyst do interviews with current job incumbents. Yet one study suggests that using just one source is not wise.[15] The problem is that any single approach has potential drawbacks. For example, in a group interview, some group members may feel pressure to go along with the group's consensus; or an employee

FIGURE 4-7

Selected O*NET General Work Activities Categories

Information input category

Where and how are the information and data gained that are needed to perform the job?

- Getting information: observing, receiving, and otherwise obtaining information from all relevant sources
- Identifying objects, actions, and events: identifying information by categorizing, estimating, recognizing differences or similarities, and detecting changes in circumstances or events

Interacting with others category

What interactions with other persons or supervisory activities occur while performing this job?

- Assisting and caring for others: providing personal assistance, medical attention, emotional support, or other personal care to others such as coworkers, customers, or patients
- Coaching and developing others: identifying the developmental needs of others and coaching, mentoring, or otherwise helping others to improve their knowledge or skills

Mental processes category

What processing, planning, problem-solving, decision-making, and innovating activities are performed with job-relevant information?

- Analyzing data or information: identifying the underlying principles, reasons, or facts of information by breaking down information or data into separate parts
- Making decisions and solving problems: analyzing information and evaluating results to choose the best solution and solve problems

Work output category

What physical activities are performed, what equipment and vehicles are operated, and what complex/technical activities are accomplished as job outputs?

- Controlling machines and processes: using either control mechanisms or direct physical activity to operate machines or processes (not including computers or vehicles)
- Interacting with computers: using computers and computer systems (including hardware and software) to write software, set up functions, or enter data

may be careless about how he or she completes a questionnaire. Collecting job analysis data from just interviews, or just observations, may thus lead to inaccurate conclusions. It's better to use several sources.[16] For example, where possible, collect job analysis data from several types of respondents—groups, individuals, observers, supervisors, and analysts.

WRITING JOB DESCRIPTIONS

Write job descriptions, including summaries and job functions, using the Internet and traditional methods.

The employer almost always uses the job analysis to (at least) produce a job description. A job description is a written statement of what the worker actually does, how he or she does it, and what the job's working conditions are. You use this information to write a job specification; this lists the knowledge, abilities, and skills required to perform the job satisfactorily.

There is no standard format for writing a job description. However, most descriptions contain sections that cover:

1. Job identification
2. Job summary
3. Responsibilities and duties
4. Authority of incumbent
5. Standards of performance
6. Working conditions
7. Job specifications

Figures 4-8 and 4-9 present two sample forms of job descriptions.

JOB TITLE: Telesales Respresentative	JOB CODE:	100001
RECOMMENDED SALARY GRADE:	EXEMPT/NONEXEMPT STATUS:	Nonexempt
JOB FAMILY: Sales	EEOC:	Sales Workers
DIVISION: Higher Education	REPORTS TO:	District Sales Manager
DEPARTMENT: In-House Sales	LOCATION:	Boston
	DATE:	April 2007

SUMMARY (Write a brief summary of job.)

The person in this position is responsible for selling college textbooks, software, and multimedia products to professors, via incoming and outgoing telephone calls, and to carry out selling strategies to meet sales goals in assigned territories of smaller colleges and universities. In addition, the individual in this position will be responsible for generating a designated amount of editorial leads and communicating to the publishing groups product feedback and market trends observed in the assigned territory.

SCOPE AND IMPACT OF JOB

Dollar responsibilities (budget and/or revenue)

The person in this position is responsible for generating approximately $2 million in revenue, for meeting operating expense budget of approximately $4000, and a sampling budget of approximately 10,000 units.

Supervisory responsibilities (direct and indirect)

None

Other

REQUIRED KNOWLEDGE AND EXPERIENCE (Knowledge and experience necessary to do job)

Related work experience

Prior sales or publishing experience preferred. One year of company experience in a customer service or marketing function with broad knowledge of company products and services is desirable.

Formal education or equivalent

Bachelor's degree with strong acedemic performance or work equivalent experience.

Skills

Must have strong organizational and persuasive skills. Must have excellent verbal and written communications skills and must be PC proficient.

Other

Limited travel required (approx 5%)

FIGURE 4-8

Sample Job Description, Pearson Education

Source: Courtesy of HR Department, Pearson Education.

PRIMARY RESPONSIBILITIES (List in order of importance and list amount of time spent on task.)

Driving Sales (60%)
- Achieve quantitative sales goal for assigned territory of smaller colleges and universities.
- Determine sales priorities and strategies for territory and develop a plan for implementing those strategies.
- Conduct 15–20 professor interviews per day during the academic sales year that accomplishes those priorities.
- Conduct product presentations (including texts, software, and Web site); effectively articulate author's central vision of key titles; conduct sales interviews using the PSS model; conduct walk-through of books and technology.
- Employ telephone selling techniques and strategies.
- Sample products to appropriate faculty, making strategic use of assigned sampling budgets.
- Close class test adoptions for first edition products.
- Negotiate custom publishing and special packaging agreements within company guidelines.
- Initiate and conduct in-person faculty presentations and selling trips as appropriate to maximize sales with the strategic use of travel budget. Also use internal resources to support the territory sales goals.
- Plan and execute in-territory special selling events and book-fairs.
- Develop and implement in-territory promotional campaigns and targeted email campaigns.

Publishing (editorial/marketing) 25%
- Report, track, and sign editorial projects.
- Gather and communicate significant market feedback and information to publishing groups.

Territory Management 15%
- Track and report all pending and closed business in assigned database.
- Maintain records of customer sales interviews and adoption situations in assigned database.
- Manage operating budget strategically.
- Submit territory itineraries, sales plans, and sales forecasts as assigned.
- Provide superior customer service and maintain professional bookstore relations in assigned territory.

Decision-Making Responsibilities for This Position:
Determine the strategic use of assigned sampling budget to most effectively generate sales revenue to exceed sales goals.
Determine the priority of customer and account contacts to achieve maximum sales potential.
Determine where in-person presentations and special selling events would be most effective to generate most sales.

Submitted By: Jim Smith, District Sales Manager	Date: April 10, 2007
Approval:	Date:
Human Resources:	Date:
Corporate Compensation:	Date:

FIGURE 4-8

(continued)

FIGURE 4-9

Marketing Manager Description from Standard Occupational Classification

Source: www.bls.gov/soc/ soc_a2c1.htm, accessed May 10, 2007.

U.S. Department of Labor
Bureau of Labor Statistics
Standard Occupational Classification

www.bls.gov   Advanced Search | A-Z Index

BLS Home | Programs & Surveys | Get Detailed Statistics | Glossary | What's New | Find It! In DOL

11-2021 Marketing Managers

Determine the demand for products and services offered by a firm and its competitors and identify potential customers. Develop pricing strategies with the goal of maximizing the firm's profits or share of the market while ensuring the firm's customers are satisfied. Oversee product development or monitor trends that indicate the need for new products and services.

Job Identification

As in Figure 4-8, the job identification section (on top) contains several types of information.[17] The *job title* specifies the name of the job, such as supervisor of data processing operations, marketing manager, or inventory control clerk. The *FLSA status* section permits quick identification of the job as exempt or nonexempt. (Under the Fair Labor Standards Act, certain positions, primarily administrative and professional, are exempt from the act's overtime and minimum wage provisions.) *Date* is the date the job description was actually written.

There may also be a space to indicate who approved the description and perhaps a space that shows the location of the job in terms of its facility/division and department/ section. This section might also include the immediate supervisor's title and information regarding salary and/or pay scale. There might also be space for the grade/level of the job, if there is such a category. For example, a firm may classify programmers as programmer II, programmer III, and so on.

Job Summary

The job summary should of course summarize the essence of the job, and include only its major functions or activities. Thus (in Figure 4-8), the telesales rep ". . . is responsible for selling college textbooks. . . . " For the job of materials manager, the summary might state that the "materials manager purchases economically, regulates deliveries of, stores, and distributes all material necessary on the production line." For the job of mailroom supervisor, "the mailroom supervisor receives, sorts, and delivers all incoming mail properly, and he or she handles all outgoing mail including the accurate and timely posting of such mail."[18]

While it's common to do so, include general statements like "performs other assignments as required" with care. Such statements do give supervisors more flexibility in assigning duties. Some experts, however, state unequivocally that "one item frequently found that should never be included in a job description is a 'cop-out clause' like 'other duties, as assigned,' "[19] since this leaves open the nature of the job—and the people needed to staff it. However, to avoid any ambiguities in case the assignment does not work out, it's advisable to make it clear in the job summary that the employer expects the job incumbent to carry out his or her duties efficiently, attentively, and conscientiously.

Relationships

There may be a "relationships" statement (not in the example), which shows the jobholder's relationships with others inside and outside the organization. For a human resource manager, such a statement might look like this:[20]

> **Reports to:** Vice president of employee relations.
>
> **Supervises:** Human resource clerk, test administrator, labor relations director, and one secretary.
>
> **Works with:** All department managers and executive management.
>
> **Outside the company:** Employment agencies, executive recruiting firms, union representatives, state and federal employment offices, and various vendors.[21]

Responsibilities and Duties

This is the heart of the job description. It should present a list of the job's significant responsibilities and duties. As in Figure 4-8, list each of the job's major duties separately, and describe it in a few sentences. In the figure, for instance, the job's duties include "achieve quantitative sales goal . . . ," and "determine sales priorities. . . . " Typical duties for other jobs might include maintaining balanced and controlled inventories, making accurate postings to accounts payable, maintaining favorable purchase price variances, and repairing production-line tools and equipment.

This section may also define the limits of the jobholder's authority, including his or her decision-making authority, direct supervision of other personnel, and budgetary authority. For example, the jobholder might have authority to approve purchase requests up to $5,000, grant time off or leaves of absence, discipline department personnel, recommend salary increases, and interview and hire new employees.

The manager's basic question here is, "How do I know what the job's duties are?" The answer, first, is from the job analysis itself; this should reveal what the employees on each job are doing now. Second, the manager will turn to various sources of standardized job description information. For many years the U.S. Labor Department's *Dictionary of Occupational Titles* was the basic source that human resource managers both within and outside the government turned to for standard job descriptions. However, the government replaced the *Dictionary* with the new **Standard Occupational Classification (SOC)** (www.bls.gov/soc/socguide.htm). The SOC classifies all workers into one of 23 major groups of jobs (see Table 4-2). These in turn contain 96 minor groups of jobs, and these in turn include 821 detailed occupations, such as the marketing manager description in Figure 4-9. The employer can use descriptions like these to identify the job's specific duties and responsibilities, such as "Determine the demand for products." From a practical point of view, the employer may also use other popular sources of job descriptions and job duties, such as www.jobdescription.com; more on this below.

The list of job duties looms large in employers' efforts to comply with ADA regulations: See the "Know Your Employment Law" feature following.

Standard Occupational Classification (SOC)
Classifies all workers into one of 23 major groups of jobs which are subdivided into minor groups of jobs and detailed occupations.

Standards of Performance and Working Conditions

Some job descriptions contain a "standards of performance" section. This lists the standards the employee is expected to achieve under each of the job description's main duties and responsibilities.

Setting standards is never an easy matter. However, most managers soon learn that just telling subordinates to "do their best" doesn't provide enough guidance. One

Know Your Employment LAW
Writing Job Descriptions That Comply with the ADA

Congress enacted the Americans with Disabilities Act (ADA) to reduce or eliminate serious problems of discrimination against disabled individuals. Under the ADA, the individual must have the requisite skills, educational background, and experience to perform the job's essential functions. A job function is essential when it is the reason the position exists or when the function is so specialized that the firm hired the person doing the job for his or her expertise or ability to perform that particular function. If the disabled individual can't perform the job as currently structured, the employer is required to make a "reasonable accommodation," unless doing so would present an "undue hardship."

As we said earlier, the ADA does not require job descriptions, but it's probably advisable to have them. Virtually all ADA legal actions will revolve around the question, "What are the essential functions of the job?" Without a job description that lists such functions, it will be hard to convince a court that the functions are essential to the job. The corollary is that you should clearly identify the essential functions: Don't just list them among the job description's other duties.

Essential job functions are the job duties that employees must be able to perform, with or without reasonable accommodation.[22] Is a function essential? Questions to ask include:

1. What three or four main activities actually constitute the job? Is each really necessary? (For example a secretary types, files, answers the phone, takes dictation.)

2. What is the relationship between each task? Is there a special sequence which the tasks must follow?

3. Do the tasks necessitate sitting, standing, crawling, walking, climbing, running, stooping, kneeling, lifting, carrying, digging, writing, operating, pushing, pulling, fingering, talking, listening, interpreting, analyzing, seeing, coordinating, etc.?

4. How many other employees are available to perform the job function? Can the performance of that job function be distributed among any other employees?

5. How much time is spent on the job performing each particular function? Are the tasks performed less frequently as important to success as those done more frequently?

6. Would removing a function fundamentally alter the job?

7. What happens if a task is not completed on time?

8. Does the position exist to perform that function?

9. Are employees in the position actually required to perform the function?[23]

10. Is there a limited number of other employees available to perform the function?

11. What is the degree of expertise or skill required to perform the function?

12. What is the actual work experience of present or past employees in the job?

13. What is the amount of time an individual actually spends performing the function?

14. What are the consequences of not requiring the performance of the function?

straightforward way of setting standards is to finish the statement, "I will be completely satisfied with your work when. . . . " This sentence, if completed for each duty listed in the job description, should result in a usable set of performance standards.[24] Here are some examples:

Duty: Accurately Posting Accounts Payable

1. Post all invoices received within the same working day.
2. Route all invoices to proper department managers for approval no later than the day following receipt.
3. An average of no more than three posting errors per month.

TABLE 4-2 SOC Major Groups of Jobs

11-0000	Management Occupations
13-0000	Business and Financial Operations Occupations
15-0000	Computer and Mathematical Occupations
17-0000	Architecture and Engineering Occupations
19-0000	Life, Physical, and Social Science Occupations
21-0000	Community and Social Services Occupations
23-0000	Legal Occupations
25-0000	Education, Training, and Library Occupations
27-0000	Arts, Design, Entertainment, Sports, and Media Occupations
29-0000	Healthcare Practitioners and Technical Occupations
31-0000	Healthcare Support Occupations
33-0000	Protective Service Occupations
35-0000	Food Preparation and Serving-Related Occupations
37-0000	Building and Grounds Cleaning and Maintenance Occupations
39-0000	Personal Care and Service Occupations
41-0000	Sales and Related Occupations
43-0000	Office and Administrative Support Occupations
45-0000	Farming, Fishing, and Forestry Occupations
47-0000	Construction and Extraction Occupations
49-0000	Installation, Maintenance, and Repair Occupations
51-0000	Production Occupations
53-0000	Transportation and Material Moving Occupations
55-0000	Military Specific Occupations

Note: Within these major groups are 96 minor groups, 449 broad occupations, and 821 detailed occupations.

Duty: Meeting Daily Production Schedule

1. Produces no less than 426 units per working day.
2. Next work station rejects no more than an average of 2% of units.
3. Weekly overtime does not exceed an average of 5%.

The job description may also list the working conditions involved on the job. These might include things like noise level, hazardous conditions, or heat.

Using the Internet for Writing Job Descriptions

Most employers probably still write their own job descriptions, but more are turning to the Internet. One site, www.jobdescription.com, illustrates why. The process is simple. Search by alphabetical title, keyword, category, or industry to find the desired job title. This leads you to a generic job description for that title—say, "Computers & EDP systems sales representative." You can then use the wizard to customize the generic description for this position. For example, you can add specific information about your organization, such as job title, job codes, department, and preparation date. And you can indicate whether the job has supervisory abilities, and choose from a number of possible desirable competencies and experience levels.

O*NET The U.S. Department of Labor's occupational information network, called O*NET, is an increasingly popular Web tool (you'll find it at http://online.onetcenter.org). It allows users to see the most important characteristics of occupations, as well as the experience, education, and knowledge required to do each job well. Both the Standard Occupational Classification and O*NET include the specific tasks associated with many occupations. O*NET also provides skills, including basic skills such as reading and writing, process skills such as critical thinking, and transferable skills such as persuasion and negotiation. An O*NET listing also includes information on worker requirements (required knowledge, for instance), occupation requirements (based on work activities such as compiling, coding, and categorizing data), and experience requirements (including education and job training). You can also check the job's labor market characteristics (such as employment projections and earnings data).[25] The "When You're On Your Own" feature on pages 150–152 shows you how to use O*NET for this.

WRITING JOB SPECIFICATIONS

④ Write job specifications using the Internet as well as your judgment.

The job specification takes the job description and answers the question, "What human traits and experience are required to do this job well?" It shows what kind of person to recruit and for what qualities that person should be tested. The job specification may be a section of the job description, or a separate document entirely. Often—as in Figure 4-8 on pages 142–143—the employer presents it as part of the job description.[26]

Specifications for Trained Versus Untrained Personnel

Writing job specifications for trained employees is relatively straightforward. For example, suppose you want to fill a position for a bookkeeper (or counselor or programmer). In cases like these, your job specifications might focus mostly on traits like length of previous service, quality of relevant training, and previous job performance. Thus, it's usually not too difficult to determine the human requirements for placing already trained people on a job.

The problems are more complex when you're filling jobs with untrained people (with the intention of training them on the job). Here you must specify qualities such as physical traits, personality, interests, or sensory skills that imply some potential for performing or for being trained to do the job.

For example, suppose the job requires detailed manipulation in a circuit board assembly line. Here you might want to ensure that the person scores high on a test of finger dexterity. Your goal, in other words, is to identify those personal traits—those human requirements—that validly predict which candidates would do well on the job and which would not. Employers identify these human requirements through a subjective, judgmental approach or through statistical analysis (or both). Let's examine both approaches.

Specifications Based on Judgment

Most job specifications come from the educated guesses of people like supervisors and human resource managers. The basic procedure here is to ask, "What does it take in terms of education, intelligence, training, and the like to do this job well?"

Filling jobs with untrained employees requires identifying the personal traits that predict performance.

There are several ways to get educated guesses or judgments. You could simply review the job's duties, and deduce from those what human traits and skills the job requires. You can also choose them from the competencies listed in Web-based job descriptions like those at www.jobdescription.com. (For example, the typical job description there lists competencies like, "Generates creative solutions" and "Manages difficult or emotional customer situations.") O*NET online is another good option. Job listings there include complete listings of educational and other experience and skills required.

Use Common Sense In any case use common sense when compiling a list of the job's human requirements. Certainly, job-specific human traits like those unearthed through job analysis—manual dexterity, say, or educational level—are important. However, don't ignore the fact that some work behaviors may apply to almost any job (although they might not normally surface through a job analysis).

For example, one researcher collected supervisor ratings and other information from 18,000 employees in 42 different hourly entry-level jobs in predominantly retail settings.[27] Regardless of the job, here are the work behaviors (with examples) that he found to be "generic"—in other words, that seem to be important to all jobs:

Job-Related Behavior	Some Examples
Industriousness	Keeps working even when other employees are standing around talking; takes the initiative to find another task when finished with regular work.
Thoroughness	Cleans equipment thoroughly, creating a more attractive display; notices merchandise out of place and returns it to the proper area.
Schedule flexibility	Accepts schedule changes when necessary; offers to stay late when the store is extremely busy.
Attendance	Arrives at work on time; maintains good attendance.
Off-task behavior (reverse)	Uses store phones to make personal unauthorized calls; conducts personal business during work time; lets joking friends be a distraction and interruption to work.
Unruliness (reverse)	Threatens to bully another employee; refuses to take routine orders from supervisors; does not cooperate with other employees.
Theft (reverse)	(As a cashier) Underrings the price of merchandise for a friend; cheats on reporting time worked; allows nonemployees in unauthorized areas.
Drug misuse (reverse)	Drinks alcohol or takes drugs on company property; comes to work under the influence of alcohol or drugs.

Similarly, in doing the job analysis, don't miss the forest for the trees. Consider a study of 50 testing engineers at a Volvo plant in Sweden. When asked what determined job competence for a testing engineer, most of the engineers focused on traditional criteria such as "to make the engine perform according to specifications." But the most effective testing engineers defined the job's main task differently: "to make sure the engine provides a customer with a good driving experience." As a result, these engineers went about their jobs testing and tuning the engines "not as engineers trying to hit a number, but as ordinary drivers—imagining themselves as seniors, students, commuters, or vacationers." This subgroup of the testing engineers worked hard to develop their knowledge of customers' driving needs, even when it meant reaching out to people outside their own group, such as

When You're on Your OWN   Using O*NET
HR for Line Managers and Entrepreneurs

Without their own job analysts or (in many cases) human resource managers, many small business owners face two hurdles when doing job analyses and job descriptions. First, they often need a more streamlined approach than those provided by questionnaires like the one shown in Figure 4-3. Second, there is always the reasonable fear that in writing their job descriptions they will overlook duties that subordinates should be assigned, or assign duties not usually associated with such positions. What they need is an encyclopedia listing all the possible positions they might encounter, including a detailed listing of the duties normally assigned to these positions.

Help is at hand: The small business owner has at least three options. The *Standard Occupational Classification*, mentioned earlier, provides detailed descriptions of thousands of jobs and their human requirements. Web sites like www.jobdescription.com provide customizable descriptions by title and industry. And the Department of Labor's O*NET is a third alternative. We'll focus on using O*NET in this feature (http://online.onetcenter.org).

Step 1. Decide on a Plan
Start by developing at least the broad outline of a corporate plan. What do you expect your sales revenue to be next year, and in the next few years? What products do you intend to emphasize? What areas or departments in your company do you think will have to be expanded, reduced, or consolidated, given where you plan to go with your firm over the next few years? What kinds of new positions do you think you'll need in order to accomplish your strategic plans?

Step 2. Develop an Organization Chart
Next, develop an organization chart for the firm. Show who reports to the president and to each of his or her subordinates. Complete the chart by showing who reports to each of the other managers and supervisors in the firm. Start by drawing up the organization chart as it is now. Then, depending upon how far in advance you're planning, produce a chart showing how you'd like your chart to look in the immediate future (say, in two months) and perhaps

two or three other charts showing how you'd like your organization to evolve over the next two or three years.

You can use several tools here. For example, Microsoft's MS Word includes an organization charting function: On the Drawing Toolbar, click Diagram or Organization Chart. Then click the organization chart diagram and then click OK. Software packages such as OrgPublisher from TimeVision of Irving, Texas, are another option.[28]

Step 3. Use a Job Analysis/Description Questionnaire
Next, use a job analysis questionnaire to determine what the job(s) entails. You can use one of the more comprehensive questionnaires (see Figure 4-3); however, the job description questionnaire in Figure 4-10 is a simpler and often satisfactory alternative. Fill in the required information, then ask the supervisors and/or employees to list the job's duties (in the middle of the page), breaking them into daily duties, periodic duties, and duties performed at irregular intervals. You can distribute a sample of one of these duties (Figure 4-11) to supervisors and/or employees to facilitate the process.

Step 4. Obtain Lists of Job Duties from O*NET
The list of job duties you uncovered in the previous step may or may not be complete. We'll therefore use O*NET to compile a more comprehensive list. (Refer to the visual examples below as you read along.) Start by going to http://online.onetcenter.org (A). Here, click on *Find Occupations*. Assume you want to create job descriptions for a retail salesperson. Type in *Retail Sales* for the occupational titles, and *Sales and Related* from the "job families" drop-down box. Click *Find Occupations* to continue, which brings you to the *Find Occupations Search Result* (B). Clicking on *Retail Salespersons*-summary produces the job summary and specific occupational duties for retail salespersons (C). For a small store, you might want to combine the duties of the "retail

FIGURE 4-10

Preliminary Job Description Questionnaire

Source: Reprinted from www.hr.blr.com with the permission of the publisher. Business and Legal Reports, Inc., Old Saybrook, CT © 2004.

Instructions: Distribute copies of this questionnaire to supervisors, managers, personnel staff members, job analysts, and others who may be involved in writing job descriptions. Ask them to record their answers to these questions in writing.

1. What is the job title? _____

2. Summarize the job's more important, regularly performed/duties in a <u>Job Summary.</u>

3. In what department is the job located? _____

4. What is the title of the supervisor or manager to whom the job holder must report?

5. Does the job holder supervise other employees? If so, give their job titles and a brief description of their responsibilites.

Position Supervised	Responsibilites

6. What essential function duties does the job holder perform regularly? List them in order of importance.

Duty	Percentage of Time Devoted to This Duty
1.	
2.	
3.	
4.	
5.	
6.	

7. Does the job holder perform other duties periodically? Infrequently? If so, please list, indicating frequency.

8. What are the working conditions? List such items as noise, heat, outside work, and exposure to bad weather.

9. How much authority does the job holder have in such matters as training or guiding other people?

10. How much education, experience, and skill are required for satisfactory job performance?

11. At what stage is the job holder's work reviewed by the supervisor?

12. What machines or equipment is the job holder responsible for operating?

13. If the job holder makes a serious mistake or error in performing required duties, what would be the cost to management?

(continued)

FIGURE 4-11

Background Data for Examples

> **Example of Job Title:** Customer Service Clerk
>
> **Example of Job Summary:** Answers inquiries and gives directions to customers, authorizes cashing of customers' checks, records and returns lost charge cards, sorts and reviews new credit applications, works at customer service desk in department store.
>
> **Example of One Job Duty:** Authorizes cashing of checks: authorizes cashing of personal or payroll checks (up to a specified amount) by customers desiring to make payment by check. Requests identification—such as driver's license—from customers and examines check to verify date, amount, signature, and endorsement. Initials check and sends customer to cashier.

salesperson" with those of "first-line supervisors/managers of retail sales workers."

Step 5. Compile the Job's Human Requirements from O*NET

Next, return to the *Snapshot* (summary) *for Retail Salesperson* (C). Here, instead of choosing occupation-specific information, choose, for example, *Worker Experiences, Occupational Requirements*, and *Worker Characteristics*. Use this information to help develop a job specification for recruiting, selecting, and training the employees.

Step 6. Complete Your Job Description

Finally, perhaps using Figure 4-10 as a guide, write an appropriate job summary for the job. Then use the information obtained in Steps 4 and 5 to create a complete listing of the tasks, duties, and human requirements of each of the jobs you will need to fill.

Shown in the three screen captures, O*Net easily allows the user to develop job descriptions.

Source: O*Net™ is a trademark of the U.S. Department of Labor, Employment and Training Administration. Reprinted by permission of O*Net.

designers or marketers. So, the job specifications for effective engineers turned out to be quite different than the initial survey revealed.

The point, says the researcher, is that in developing the job description and job specification, make sure you really understand the reason for the job and therefore the skills a person actually needs to be competent at it.[29]

Job Specifications Based on Statistical Analysis

Basing job specifications on statistical analysis is the more defensible approach, but it's also more difficult. The aim here is to determine statistically the relationship between (1) some *predictor* or human trait, such as height, intelligence, or finger dexterity; and (2) some indicator or *criterion* of job effectiveness, such as performance as rated by the supervisor.

The procedure has five steps: (1) analyze the job and decide how to measure job performance; (2) select personal traits like finger dexterity that you believe should predict successful performance; (3) test candidates for these traits; (4) measure these candidates' subsequent job performance; and (5) statistically analyze the relationship between the human trait (finger dexterity) and job performance. Your objective is to determine whether the former predicts the latter.

This method is more defensible than the judgmental approach because equal rights legislation forbids using traits that you can't prove distinguish between high and low job performers. For example, hiring standards that discriminate based on sex, race, religion, national origin, or age may have to be shown to predict job performance. Ideally, this is done with a statistical validation study, as in the five-step approach above. In practice, most employers probably rely more on judgmental approaches.

Many employers and managers turn to the Web for a practical approach for creating job descriptions and specifications, as the "When You're on Your Own" feature illustrates.

JOB ANALYSIS IN A "JOBLESS" WORLD

> ⑤ Explain job analysis in a "jobless" world, including what it means and how it's done in practice.

Job is generally defined as "a set of closely related activities carried out for pay," but over the years the concept of a job has actually changed quite dramatically. In a nutshell, jobs tend to be much more varied and loosely defined than in the past. For example, when an employer like Daimler-Chrysler moves from traditional assembly-line production to using self-managing teams, the employees' jobs move from narrowly defined to broad and flexible (some call this "dejobbing"). This obviously has ramifications for what job descriptions look like. The "New Workforce" feature below illustrates this.

A (Very) Brief History: From Specialized to Enlarged Jobs

job enlargement
Assigning workers additional same-level activities, thus increasing the number of activities they perform.

job rotation
Systematically moving workers from one job to another to enhance work team performance and/or to broaden his or her experience and identify strong and weak points to prepare the person for an enhanced role with the company.

The term *job* as we know it today is largely an outgrowth of the industrial revolution's emphasis on efficiency. During this time, people like economist Adam Smith and consultant Frederick Taylor wrote enthusiastically of the positive correlation between specialized jobs (doing the same small thing over and over) and efficiency. Jobs and job descriptions, until quite recently, tended to follow their prescriptions and to be fairly detailed and specific.

By the mid-1900s other writers were reacting to what they viewed as the "dehumanizing" aspects of pigeonholing workers into highly repetitive and specialized jobs. Many proposed solutions like job enlargement, job rotation, and job enrichment. **Job enlargement** means assigning workers additional same-level activities, thus increasing the number of activities they perform. Thus, the worker who previously only bolted the seat to the legs might attach the back as well. **Job rotation** means systematically moving workers from one job to another.

The NEW Workforce Global Job Analysis Applications

When Daimler-Chrysler opened its new Mercedes-Benz factory in Alabama, it gave the company an opportunity to start with a "clean sheet" for designing a car-building system for the twenty-first century.

The system Daimler chose is similar to the "lean production systems" that Japanese manufacturers like Toyota have long used. It emphasizes *just-in-time* inventory methods, so that inventories stay negligible due to the arrival "just in time" of parts for the assembly line. It emphasizes *stable production flows*, since reducing surprises (such as cars reaching the end of the line with defects that the workers must then repair) boosts quality. The new system organizes employees into *work teams*, and emphasizes the fact that all employees must dedicate themselves to *continuous improvement*.

Job analysis plays a modified role in this factory. Rather than having dozens or hundreds of different job descriptions, there are just a relatively few different job descriptions or jobs. There is also a method to this apparent madness. Unconstrained by detailed descriptions listing dozens of specific duties showing what "my job" should be, it's easier for employees to move from job to job as they work on teams. It also encourages employees to look beyond their own jobs to find ways to improve the plant's operations. In just a few months' time, for instance, one team found a $.23 plastic prong that worked better than the previous $2.50 prong the plant was using to keep car doors open during painting. The same team also redesigned the racks that the assembly parts move on, saving assembly workers thousands of steps per year (and thereby improving productivity and quality).

Now that this new system has proved itself in Alabama, Daimler is extending it to plants around the world. For example, its other plants in the United States, as well as in South Africa, Brazil, and Germany, now use this new production system, including the simpler and broader job descriptions.

Source: Lindsey Chappell, "Mercedes Factories Embrace a New Order," *Automotive News*, May 28, 2001.

---

job enrichment
Redesigning jobs in a way that increases the opportunities for the worker to experience feelings of responsibility, achievement, growth, and recognition.

Psychologist Frederick Herzberg argued that the best way to motivate workers is to build opportunities for challenge and achievement into their jobs via job enrichment. **Job enrichment** means redesigning jobs in a way that increases the opportunities for the worker to experience feelings of responsibility, achievement, growth, and recognition—for instance, by letting the worker plan and control his or her own work instead of having it controlled by outsiders. Employees here, said Herzberg, would do their jobs well because they wanted to, and quality and productivity would rise. That philosophy, in one form or another, is the theoretical basis for the team-based self-managing jobs in factories like Daimler-Chryslers today.

Why Managers Are "Dejobbing" Their Companies

dejobbing
Broadening the responsibilities of the company's jobs, and encouraging employees not to limit themselves to what's on their job descriptions.

Daimler's Alabama Mercedes factory actually presents in microcosm a picture of why companies are moving to broader, simpler descriptions of jobs—to **dejobbing**, in other words. Companies are grappling with challenges like rapid product and technological change, global competition, deregulation, political instability, demographic changes, and a shift to a service economy. This has increased the need for firms to be responsive, flexible, and much more competitive. In turn, the organizational methods managers use to accomplish this have helped weaken the meaning of *job* as a well-defined and clearly delineated set of responsibilities. Requiring that employees limit themselves to narrow jobs runs counter to the need to have them willingly switch from task to task as jobs and team assignments change. Here is a sampling of organizational factors that have contributed to encouraging workers not to limit themselves to narrowly defined jobs.

Flatter Organizations Instead of traditional, pyramid-shaped organizations with seven or more management layers, flat organizations with just three or four levels are more prevalent. This assumedly puts top managers in closer touch with customers. But the implication is that the remaining managers each have more subordinates reporting to them (a "wider span of control"). The remaining managers thus can supervise the subordinates less, and the subordinates' jobs end up bigger in terms of responsibilities.

Self-Managing Work Teams Managers increasingly organize tasks around teams and processes rather than around specialized functions. For example, at Chesebrough-Ponds USA, a subsidiary of Unilever, managers replaced a traditional pyramidal factory organization with multiskilled, cross-functional, and self-directed teams; the latter now run the plant's four product areas. Hourly employees make employee assignments, schedule overtime, establish production times and changeovers, and even handle cost control, requisitions, and work orders. They also are solely responsible for quality control under the plant's continuous quality improvement program. In an organization like this, employees' jobs change daily, so management intentionally avoids having employees view their jobs as a specific, narrow set of responsibilities.

| reengineering | **Reengineering** In many companies, work processes are a little like relay races. For example, for a bank to approve a loan application, the application might be handed from department to department, such as from applications, to credit analysis, to loan approval, to the loan closing group. This can be very time consuming. **Reengineering** (technically, "business process reengineering"), usually means redesigning a business process so that small self-managing teams of employees working together (or virtually) get the task done together, all at once. The aim, say the method's early proponents, is ". . . to achieve dramatic improvements in critical contemporary measures of performance, such as cost, quality, service, and speed."[30] |

reengineering
The fundamental rethinking and radical redesign of business processes to achieve dramatic improvements in critical, contemporary measures of performance, such as cost, quality, service, and speed.

Reengineering has implications for writing job descriptions. Typically, in reengineered situations, workers become collectively responsible for overall results rather than just for their own tasks: "They share joint responsibility with their team members for performing the whole process, not just a small piece of it."[31] As a result, employee's jobs tend to change fairly continuously, and it's actually counterproductive to have employees thinking solely in terms of "just doing my job."

Competency-Based Job Analysis

Not coincidently, many employers and job analysis experts say traditional job analysis procedures can't go on playing a central role in HR management.[32] Their basic concern is this: that in high-performance work environments like Daimler's, in which employers need workers to seamlessly move from job to job and exercise self-control, job descriptions based on lists of job-specific duties may actually inhibit (or fail to encourage) the flexible behavior companies need. Employers are therefore shifting toward newer approaches for describing jobs. We focus on one, competency-based analysis, next.

What Are Competencies? Competency-based job analysis basically means writing job descriptions based on competencies rather than job duties. It emphasizes what the employee must be capable of doing, rather than on a list of the duties he or she must perform. We can simply define **competencies** as demonstrable characteristics of the person that enable performance. Job competencies are always observable and measurable behaviors comprising part of a job.

competencies
Demonstrable characteristics of a person that enable performance of a job.

At a Nissan factory in Tokyo, Japan, workers meet at a productivity session, surrounded by unfinished car frames hanging along the assembly line. Work teams like this are part of the trend toward a multiskilled, cross-functional, self-directed team organization that allows workers greater autonomy in meeting goals. In plants like these, broadly described jobs that emphasize employees' required competencies are replacing narrowly defined jobs.

competency-based job analysis
Describing a job in terms of the measurable, observable, behavioral competencies an employee must exhibit to do a job well.

performance management
Basing your employees' training, appraisals, and rewards on fostering and rewarding the skills and competencies he or she needs to achieve his or her goals.

Unfortunately, once we get beyond those simple definitions, there's some confusion over what exactly "competencies" means. Different organizations define "competencies" in somewhat different ways. Some define them more broadly, and use "competencies" synonymously with the knowledge, or skills, or abilities a person needs to do the job. Others define competencies more narrowly, in terms of measurable behaviors. Here, you would identify the job's required competencies by simply completing the phrase, "In order to perform this job competently, the employee should be able to: . . ."

We can say formally that **competency-based job analysis** means describing the job in terms of the measurable, observable, behavioral competencies (knowledge, skills, and/or behaviors) that an employee doing that job must exhibit to do the job well. This contrasts with the traditional way of describing the job in terms of job duties and responsibilities.[33] Traditional job analysis focuses on "what" is accomplished—on duties and responsibilities. Competency analysis focuses more on "how" the worker meets the job's objectives or actually accomplishes the work.[34] Traditional job analysis is thus job focused. Competency-based analysis is worker focused—specifically, what must he or she be competent to do?

Three Reasons to Use Competency Analysis   There are three reasons to describe jobs in terms of competencies rather than duties.

First, as mentioned earlier, traditional job descriptions (with their lists of specific duties) may actually backfire if a *high-performance work system* is your goal. The whole thrust of these systems is to encourage employees to work in a self-motivated way, by organizing the work around teams, by encouraging team members to rotate freely among jobs (each with its own skill set), by pushing more responsibility for things like day-to-day supervision down to the workers, and by organizing work around projects or processes in which jobs may blend or overlap. Employees here must be enthusiastic about learning and moving among jobs. Giving someone a job description with a list of specific duties may simply breed a "that's-not-my-job" attitude, by pigeonholing workers too narrowly.

Second, describing the job in terms of the skills, knowledge, and competencies the worker needs is *more strategic*. For example, Canon's strategic emphasis on miniaturization and precision manufacturing means it should encourage some employees to develop their expertise in these two strategically crucial areas.

Third, we'll see later in this book that measurable skills, knowledge, and competencies supports the employer's *performance management process*. As at Canon, achieving a firm's strategic goals means that employees must exhibit certain skills and competencies. **Performance management** means basing your employees' training, appraisals, and rewards on fostering and rewarding the skills and competencies he or she needs to achieve his or her goals. Understanding what those required competencies are is a prerequisite. Describing the job in terms of skills and competencies facilitates this.

Examples of Competencies   In practice, managers often write paragraph-length competencies for jobs, and organize these into two or three clusters. For example, the job's required competencies might include *general competencies* (such as reading, writing, and mathematical reasoning), *leadership competencies* (such as leadership, strategic thinking, and teaching others), and *technical competencies* (which focus on the specific technical competencies required for specific types of jobs and/or occupations).

So, some technical competencies for the job of systems engineer might include the following:

- Design complex software applications, establish protocols, and create prototypes.
- Establish the necessary platform requirements to efficiently and completely coordinate data transfer.
- Prepare comprehensive and complete documentation including specifications, flow diagrams, process patrols, and budgets.[35]

Similarly, for a corporate treasurer, technical competencies might include:

- Formulate trade recommendations, by studying several computer models for currency trends, and using various quantitative techniques to determine the financial impact of certain financial trades.
- Recommend specific trades and when to make them.
- Present recommendations and persuade others to follow the recommended course of action.[36] (Note that exhibiting this competency presumes the treasurer has certain knowledge and skills that one could measure.)

O*NET lists various skills within six skill groups (accessible at http://online.onetcenter. org/skills/) A sampling includes "Mathematics—using mathematics to solve problems," "Speaking—talking to others to convey information effectively," "Complex problem-solving—identifying complex problems and reviewing related information to develop and evaluate options and implement solutions," and "Negotiation—bringing others together and trying to reconcile differences."

Comparing Traditional Versus Competency-Based Job Analysis   In practice, if you pick up almost any job description today, you'll probably find that some of the job's listed duties and responsibilities are competency-based, while most are not. For example, consider the typical duties you might find in a marketing manager's job description. Which of the duties would complete the phrase, "In order to perform this job competently, the employee should be able to: . . . ?"

Some familiar duties and responsibilities would not easily fit these requirements. For example, "works with writers and artists and overseas copywriting, design, layout, and production of promotional materials" is not particularly measurable. How could you measure the extent to which the employee "works with writers and artists" or "overseas copywriting, design, and layout?" Put another way, if you had to devise a training program for this job's incumbent, how would you determine whether you'd adequately trained the person to work with writers and artists? In fact, what sort of training would that duty and responsibility even imply? It's not clear at all.

On the other hand, some of the job's typical duties and responsibilities are more easily expressed as competencies. For example, we could easily complete the phrase, "to perform this job competently, the employee should be able to" with "conduct marketing surveys on current and new-product concepts; prepare marketing activity reports; and develop and execute marketing plans and programs."

How to Write Job Competencies-Based Job Descriptions   Defining the job's competencies and writing them up involves a process that is similar in most respects to traditional job analysis. In other words, the manager will interview job incumbents and their supervisors, ask open-ended questions regarding job responsibilities and activities, and perhaps identify critical incidents that pinpoint success on the job. There are also off-the-shelf competencies databanks. One is that of the Department of Labor's Office of Personnel Management (see www.opm.gov).

An Example: BP's Matrices

In practice, developing competency-based job descriptions often comes down to listing the specific skills the job requires. This simple method then links in with the employer's pay plan. For instance: The employee's pay goes up every time he or she shows by testing that that skill is mastered.

In one firm—British Petroleum's exploration division—the need for more efficient, flexible, flatter organizations and empowered employees prompted management to replace job descriptions with matrices listing skills and skill levels. Senior managers wanted to shift employees' attention from a job description/"that's-not-my-job" mentality to one that would motivate them to obtain the new skills and competencies they needed to accomplish their broader responsibilities.[37]

The solution was a skills matrix like that in Figure 4-12. They created skills matrices for various jobs held by two groups of employees, those on a management track and those whose aims lay elsewhere (such as to stay in engineering). The human resource department prepared a matrix for each job or job family (such as drilling manager). As in Figure 4-12, the matrix listed (1) the basic skills needed for that job (such as technical expertise and business awareness) and (2) the minimum level of each skill required for that job or job family. As you can see, the emphasis is no longer on specific job duties. Instead, the focus is on specifying and developing the new skills (technical expertise, business awareness, and so on) needed for the employees' broader, empowered, and relatively undefined responsibilities.

The skills matrix triggered other HR changes, and supported a performance management effort. For example, the matrices gave employees a constant reminder of what skills they must improve. The firm instituted a new skill-based pay plan that awards raises based on skills improvement. Performance appraisals now focus more on skills acquisitions. And training emphasizes developing broad skills like leadership and planning—skills applicable across a wide range of responsibilities and jobs.

FIGURE 4-12

The Skills Matrix for One Job at BP

Note: The light blue boxes indicate the minimum level of skill required for the job.

Technical expertise	Business awareness	Communication and interpersonal	Decision-making and initiative	Leadership and guidance	Planning and organizational ability	Problem-solving
H	H	H	H	H	H	H
G	G	G	G	G	G	G
F	F	F	F	F	F	F
E	E	E	E	E	E	E
D	D	D	D	D	D	D
C	C	C	C	C	C	C
B	B	B	B	B	B	B
A	A	A	A	A	A	A

REVIEW

SUMMARY

1. Developing an organization structure results in jobs that have to be staffed. Job analysis is the procedure through which you find out (1) what the job entails and (2) what kinds of people you should hire for the job. It involves six steps: (1) determine the use of the job analysis information, (2) collect background information, (3) select the positions to be analyzed, (4) collect job analysis data, (5) review information with participants, and (6) develop a job description and job specification.

2. You can use four basic techniques to gather job analysis data: interviews, direct observation, questionnaires, and participant diary logs. These are good for developing job descriptions and specifications. The Department of Labor, functional job analysis, and PAQ approaches result in quantitative ratings of each job and are usually useful for classifying jobs for pay purposes.

3. The job description should portray the work of the position so well that the duties are clear without reference to other job descriptions. Always ask, "Will the new employee understand the job if he or she reads the job description?"

4. The job specification takes the job description and uses it to answer the question, "What human traits and experience are necessary to do this job well?" It tells what kind of person to recruit and for what qualities that person should be tested. Job specifications are usually based on the educated guesses of managers; a more accurate statistical approach to developing job specifications can also be used, however.

5. Use the Standard Occupational Classification to help you write job descriptions. Find and reproduce the descriptions that relate to the job you're describing. Then use those descriptions to "anchor" your own description and particularly to suggest duties to be included. You can also use Internet sources like jobdescription.com.

6. Firms increasingly use O*NET to create job descriptions. To use this tool, start at http://online.onetcenter.org.

7. Dejobbing is ultimately a product of the rapid changes taking place in business today. As firms try to speed decision making by taking steps such as reengineering, individual jobs are becoming broader and much less specialized. Increasingly, firms don't want employees to feel limited by a specific set of responsibilities like those listed in a job description. As a result, more employers are substituting brief job summaries, perhaps combined with summaries of the skills required for the position.

8. Competency-based analysis means describing a job in terms of measurable, observable, behavioral competencies that an employee doing the job must exhibit to do well. For example, these might include "create prototypes" and "design complex software programs."

DISCUSSION QUESTIONS

1. What items are typically included in the job description? What items are typically not shown?

2. What is job analysis? How can you make use of the information it provides?

3. We discussed several methods for collecting job analysis data—questionnaires, the position analysis questionnaire, and so on. Compare and contrast these methods, explaining what each is useful for and listing the pros and cons of each.

4. Describe the types of information typically found in a job specification.
5. Explain how you would conduct a job analysis.
6. Do you think companies can really do without detailed job descriptions? Why or why not?
7. In a company with only 25 employees, is there less need for job descriptions? Why or why not?

INDIVIDUAL AND GROUP ACTIVITIES

1. Working individually or in groups, obtain copies of job descriptions for clerical positions at the college or university where you study, or the firm where you work. What types of information do they contain? Do they give you enough information to explain what the job involves and how to do it? How would you improve on the description?

2. Working individually or in groups, use O*NET to develop a job description for your professor in this class. Based on that, use your judgment to develop a job specification. Compare your conclusions with those of other students or groups. Were there any significant differences? What do you think accounted for the differences?

3. The HRCI "Test Specifications" appendix at the end of this book (pages 726–735) lists the knowledge someone studying for the HRCI certification exam needs to have in each area of human resource management (such as in Strategic Management, Workforce Planning, and Human Resource Development). In groups of four to five students, do four things: (1) review that appendix now; (2) identify the material in this chapter that relates to the required knowledge in the appendix lists; (3) write four multiple choice exam questions on this material that you believe would be suitable for inclusion in the HRCI exam; and (4) if time permits, have someone from your team post your team's questions in front of the class, so the students in other teams can take each others' exam questions.

EXPERIENTIAL EXERCISE

The Instructor's Job Description

Purpose: The purpose of this exercise is to give you experience in developing a job description, by developing one for your instructor.

Required Understanding: You should understand the mechanics of job analysis and be thoroughly familiar with the job analysis questionnaires. (See Figures 4-3 and 4-4 and the job description questionnaire, Figure 4-10.)

How to Set Up the Exercise/Instructions: Set up groups of four to six students for this exercise. As in all exercises in this book, the groups should be separated and should not converse with each other. Half the groups in the class will develop the job description using the job analysis questionnaire (4-3), and the other half of the groups will develop it using the job description questionnaire (4-10). Each student should review his or her questionnaire (as appropriate) before joining his or her group.

1. Each group should do a job analysis of the instructor's job: Half the groups will use the Figure 4-3 job analysis questionnaire for this purpose, and half will use the Figure 4-10 job description questionnaire.

2. Based on this information, each group will develop its own job description and job specification for the instructor.

3. Next, each group should choose a partner group, one that developed the job description and job specification using the alternate method. (A group that used the

job analysis questionnaire should be paired with a group that used the job description questionnaire.)

4. Finally, within each of these new combined groups, compare and critique each of the two sets of job descriptions and job specifications. Did each job analysis method provide different types of information? Which seems superior? Does one seem more advantageous for some types of jobs than others?

APPLICATION CASE

Tropical Storm Wilma

In August 2005, tropical storm Wilma hit North Carolina and the Optima Air Filter Company. Many employees' homes were devastated, and the firm found that it had to hire almost three completely new crews, one for each of its shifts. The problem was that the "old-timers" had known their jobs so well that no one had ever bothered to draw up job descriptions for them. When about 30 new employees began taking their places, there was general confusion about what they should do and how they should do it.

The storm quickly became old news to the firm's out-of-state customers, who wanted filters, not excuses. Phil Mann, the firm's president, was at his wits' end. He had about 30 new employees, 10 old-timers, and his original factory supervisor, Maybelline. He decided to meet with Linda Lowe, a consultant from the local university's business school. She immediately had the old-timers fill out a job questionnaire that listed all their duties. Arguments ensued almost at once: Both Phil and Maybelline thought the old-timers were exaggerating to make themselves look more important, and the old-timers insisted that the lists faithfully reflected their duties. Meanwhile, the customers clamored for their filters.

Questions

1. Should Phil and Linda ignore the old-timers' protests and write up the job descriptions as they see fit? Why? Why not? How would you go about resolving the differences?
2. How would you have conducted the job analysis? What should Phil do now?

CONTINUING CASE

Carter Cleaning Company

The Job Description

Based on her review of the stores, Jennifer concluded that one of the first matters she had to attend to involved developing job descriptions for her store managers.

As Jennifer tells it, her lessons regarding job descriptions in her basic management and HR management courses were insufficient to fully convince her of the pivotal role job descriptions actually played in the smooth functioning of an enterprise. Many times during her first few weeks on the job, Jennifer found herself asking one of her store managers why he was violating what she knew to be recommended company policies and procedures. Repeatedly, the answers were either "Because I didn't know it was my job" or "Because I didn't know that was the way we were supposed to do it." Jennifer knew that a job description, along with a set of standards and procedures that specified what was to be done and how to do it, would go a long way toward alleviating this problem.

In general, the store manager is responsible for directing all store activities in such a way that quality work is produced, customer relations and sales are maximized, and profitability is maintained through effective control of labor, supply, and energy costs. In accomplishing that general aim, a specific store manager's duties and responsibilities include quality control, store appearance and cleanliness, customer relations, bookkeeping and cash management, cost control and productivity, damage control, pricing, inventory control, spotting and cleaning, machine maintenance, purchasing, employee safety, hazardous waste removal, human resource administration, and pest control.

The questions that Jennifer had to address follow.

Questions

1. What should be the format and final form of the store manager's job description?
2. Is it practical to specify standards and procedures in the body of the job description, or should these be kept separate?
3. How should Jennifer go about collecting the information required for the standards, procedures, and job description?
4. What, in your opinion, should the store manager's job description look like and contain?

TRANSLATING STRATEGY INTO HR POLICIES AND PRACTICES CASE:
THE HOTEL PARIS

Job Descriptions

The Hotel Paris's competitive strategy is "To use superior guest service to differentiate the Hotel Paris properties, and to thereby increase the length of stay and return rate of guests, and thus boost revenues and profitability." HR manager Lisa Cruz must now formulate functional policies and activities that support this competitive strategy, by eliciting the required employee behaviors and competencies.

As an experienced human resource director, the Hotel Paris's Lisa Cruz knew that recruitment and selection processes invariably influenced employee competencies and behavior and, through them, the company's bottom line. Everything about the workforce—its collective skills, morale, experience, and motivation—depended on attracting and then selecting the right employees.

In reviewing the Hotel Paris's employment systems, she was therefore concerned that virtually all the company's job descriptions were out of date, and that many jobs had no descriptions at all. She knew that without accurate job descriptions, all her improvement efforts would be in vain. After all, if you don't know a job's duties, responsibilities, and human requirements, how can you decide who to hire or how to train them? To create human resource policies and practices that would produce employee competencies and behaviors needed to achieve the hotel's strategic aims, Lisa's team first had to produce a set of usable job descriptions.

A brief analysis, conducted with her company's CFO, reinforced that observation. They chose departments across the hotel chain that did and did not have updated job descriptions. While they understood that many other factors might be influencing the results, they believed that the statistical relationships they observed did suggest that having job descriptions had a positive influence on various employee behaviors and competencies. Perhaps having the descriptions facilitated the employee selection process, or perhaps the departments with the descriptions just had better managers.

She knew the Hotel Paris's job descriptions would have to include traditional duties and responsibilities. However, most should also include several competencies unique to each job. For example, job descriptions for the front-desk clerks might include "able to check a guest in or out in five minutes or less." Most service employees' descriptions included the competency, "able to exhibit patience and guest supportiveness even when busy with other activities."

Questions:

In teams or individually:

1. Based on the hotel's stated strategy, list at least four important employee behaviors for the Hotel Paris' staff.
2. If time permits, spend some time prior to class observing the front desk clerk at a local hotel. In any case, create a job description for a Hotel Paris front desk clerk.

KEY TERMS

ENDNOTES

1. For a good discussion of job analysis, see James Clifford, "Job Analysis: Why Do It, and How Should It Be Done?" *Public Personnel Management* 23, no. 2 (Summer 1994), pp. 321–340.
2. James Clifford, "Manage Work Better to Better Manage Human Resources: A Comparative Study of Two Approaches to Job Analysis," *Public Personnel Management*, Spring 1996, pp. 89–102.
3. Richard Henderson, *Compensation Management: Rewarding Performance* (Upper Saddle River, NJ: Prentice Hall, 1994), pp. 139–150.
4. Darin, Hartley, "Job Analysis at the Speed of Reality," *Training and Development*, (September 2004): 20–22.
5. Wayne Cascio, *Applied Psychology in Human Resource Management* (Upper Saddle River, NJ: Prentice Hall, 1998), p. 142. See also, Michael Lundell et al., "Relationships Between Organizational Content and Job Analysis Task Ratings," *Journal of Applied Psychology* 83, no. 5 (1998), pp. 769–776.
6. Frederick Morgeson, et al., "Self Presentation Processes in Job Analysis: A Field Experiment Investigating Inflation in Abilities, Tasks, and Competencies," *Journal of Applied Psychology* 89, no. 4 (November 4, 2004): 674–686.
7. See Henderson, *Compensation Management*, pp. 148–152.
8. Note that the PAQ (and other quantitative techniques) can also be used for job evaluation, which is explained in Chapter 11.
9. Again, we will see that job evaluation is the process through which jobs are compared to one another and their values determined. Although usually viewed as a job analysis technique, the PAQ is, in practice, actually as much or more of a job evaluation technique and could therefore be discussed in either this chapter or in Chapter 11. For a discussion of how to use PAQ for classifying jobs for pay purposes, see Edwin Cornelius III, Theodore Carron, and Marianne Collins, "Job Analysis Models and Job Classifications," *Personnel Psychology* 32 (Winter 1979), pp. 693–708. See also, Edwin Cornelius III, Frank Schmidt, and Theodore Carron, "Job Classification Approaches and the Implementation of Validity Generalization Results," *Personnel Psychology* 37, no. 2 (Summer 1984), pp. 247–260.
10. Jack Smith and Milton Hakel, "Comparisons Among Data Sources, Response Bias, and Reliability and Validity of a Structured Job Analysis Questionnaire," *Personnel Psychology* 32 (Winter 1979), pp. 677–692. See also, Edwin Cornelius III, Angelo DeNisi, and Allyn Blencoe, "Expert and Naïve Raters Using the PAQ: Does It Matter?" *Personnel Psychology* 37, no. 3 (Autumn 1984), pp. 453–464; Robert J. Harvey et al., "Dimensionality of the Job Element Inventory: A Simplified Worker-Oriented Job Analysis Questionnaire," *Journal of Applied Psychology*, November 1988, pp. 639–646, Frederick Morgenson and Stephen Humphrey, "The Work Design Questionaire (WDQ): Developing and Validating a Comprehensive Measure for Assessing Job Design and the Nature of Work," *Journal of Applied Psychology* 91, no. 6 (2006), pp. 1321–1339.
11. Roni Reiter-Palmon, et al., "Development of an O*NET Web-Based Job Analysis and Its Implementation in the U.S. Navy: Lessons Learned," Human Resource Management Review 16, 2006, pp. 294–309.

12. Ibid., p. 294.

13. Ibid., p. 295.

14. Digitizing the information also enables the employer to quantify, tag, and electronically store and access it more readily. Lauren McIntire et al., "Innovations in Job Analysis: Development and Application of Metrics to Analyze Job Data," *Human Resource Management Review*, vol. 16, 2006, pp. 310–323.

15. Frederick P. Morgeson and Michael A. Campion, "Social and Cognitive Sources of Potential Inaccuracy in Job Analysis," *Journal of Applied Psychology* 82, no. 5 (1997), pp. 627–655.

16. Ibid., p. 648.

17. Regarding this discussion, see Henderson, *Compensation Management*, pp. 175–184. See also, Louisa Wah, "The Alphabet Soup of Job Titles," *Management Review* 87, no. 6, pp. 40–43.

18. James Evered, "How to Write a Good Job Description," *Supervisory Management*, April 1981, pp. 14–19; Roger J. Plachy, "Writing Job Descriptions That Get Results," Personnel, October 1987, pp. 56–58. See also, Matthew Mariani, "Replace with a Database," *Occupational Outlook Quarterly* 43, no. 1 (Spring 1999), pp. 2–9.

19. Ibid., p. 16.

20. Ibid., p. 16.

21. Ibid., p. 16.

22. Deborah Kearney, *Reasonable Accommodations: Job Descriptions in the Age of ADA, OSHA, and Workers Comp* (New York: Van Nostrand Reinhold, 1994), p. 9. See also, Paul Starkman, "The ADA's Essential Job Function Requirements: Just How Essential Does an Essential Job Function Have to Be?" *Employee Relations Law Journal* 26, no. 4 (Spring 2001), pp. 43–102.

23. Michael Esposito, "There's More to Writing Job Descriptions Than Complying with the ADA," *Employment Relations Today*, Autumn 1992, p. 279. See also, Richard Morfopoulos and William Roth, "Job Analysis and the Americans with Disabilities Act," *Business Horizons* 39, no. 6 (November 1996), pp. 68–72; and Kristin Mitchell, George Alliger, and Richard Morfopoulos, "Toward an ADA-Appropriate Job Analysis," *Human Resource Management Review* 7, no. 1 (Spring 1997), pp. 5–16.

24. James Evered, "How to Write a Good Job Description," p. 18.

25. Matthew Mariani, "Replace with a Database: O*NET Replaces the *Dictionary of Occupational Titles*," *Occupational Outlook Quarterly* 43 (Spring 1999), pp. 2–9.

26. Based on Ernest J. McCormick and Joseph Tiffin, *Industrial Psychology* (Upper Saddle River, NJ: Prentice Hall, 1974), pp. 56–61.

27. Steven Hunt, "Generic Work Behavior: An Investigation into the Dimensions of Entry-Level, Hourly Job Performance," *Personnel Psychology* 49 (1996), pp. 51–83.

28. David Shair, "Wizardry Makes Charts Relevant," *HR Magazine*, April 2000, p. 127.

29. Jorgen Sandberg, "Understanding Competence at Work," *Harvard Business Review*, March 2001, p. 28.

30. Michael Hammer and James Champy, *Reengineering the Corporation* (New York: Harper Business, 1993), p. 32. Note that some recent research suggests that job redesign that leads to semi-autonomous teams may only translate into improved performance when often activities such as the firms feedback and reward systems are relatively ineffective. See Frederick Morgeson et al., "understanding reactions to job redesign: a quasi-experimenta investigation of the moderating effects of organizational context on perceptions of performance behavior," *Personnel Psychology* 59, no. 2, Summer 2006, pp. 333–363.

31. Ibid., p. 68.

32. Jeffrey Shippmann et al., "The Practice of Competency Modeling," *Personnel Psychology* 53, no. 3 (2000), p. 703.

33. Ibid.

34. Ibid.

35. Adapted from Richard Mirabile, "Everything You Wanted to Know About Competency Modeling," *Training and Development* 51, no. 8 (August 1997), pp. 73–78.

36. Dennis Kravetz, "Building a Job Competency Database: What the Leaders Do," Kravetz Associates (Bartlett, Illinois, 1997).

37. Milan Moravec and Robert Tucker, "Job Descriptions for the 21st Century," *Personnel Journal*, June 1992, pp. 37–44.

5 | Personnel Planning and Recruiting

With 110 restaurants open, and adding 20 more per year, The Cheesecake Factory must attract and hire 24,000 people per year. That's a lot of recruits, and for Ed Eynon, the firm's senior vice president for human resources, that means casting a wide net when it comes to recruiting—"You don't find all the people you need from one source," he says. Perhaps even more so than in the typical firm, having the right recruiting sources is crucial to The Cheesecake Factory's success.[1] •

After studying this chapter, you should be able to:

1. Explain the main techniques used in employment planning and forecasting.
2. List and discuss the main outside sources of candidates.
3. Effectively recruit job candidates.
4. Name and describe the main internal sources of candidates.
5. Develop a help wanted ad.
6. Explain how to recruit a more diverse workforce.

In Chapter 4, we discussed job analysis and the methods managers use to create job descriptions and job specifications. The purpose of this chapter is to improve your effectiveness in recruiting candidates. The topics we discuss include personnel planning and forecasting, recruiting job candidates, and developing and using application forms.

THE RECRUITMENT AND SELECTION PROCESS

Job analysis defines the duties and human requirements of the company's jobs. The next step is to recruit and select employees. We can envision the *recruitment and selection process* as a series of hurdles (Figure 5-1):

1. Decide what positions to fill, through *personnel planning and forecasting*.
2. Build a pool of candidates for these jobs, by *recruiting* internal or external candidates.
3. Have candidates complete *application forms* and perhaps undergo initial screening interviews.
4. Use *selection tools* like tests, background investigations, and physical exams to identify viable candidates.
5. Decide who to make an offer to, by having the supervisor and perhaps others *interview* the candidates.

We discuss recruitment and selection in this and the next two chapters. This chapter focuses on personnel planning and forecasting, and on recruiting techniques. Chapter 6 addresses selection techniques, including tests, background checks, and physical exams. Chapter 7 focuses on interviewing—by far the most widely used selection technique.

PLANNING AND FORECASTING

employment or personnel planning
The process of deciding what positions the firm will have to fill, and how to fill them.

The recruitment and selection process starts with **employment or personnel planning**. This is the process of deciding what positions the firm will have to fill, and how to fill them. *Personnel planning* embraces all future positions, from maintenance clerk to CEO. However, most firms call the process of deciding how to fill executive jobs *succession planning*.

Employment planning should flow from the firm's strategic plans. Plans to enter new businesses, build new plants, or reduce costs all influence the types of positions the firm will need to fill (or eliminate). For example, JDS Uniphase (which designs and manufactures fiber optics products), decided to expand its Florida operations. Its managers knew

FIGURE 5-1

Steps in Recruitment and Selection Process

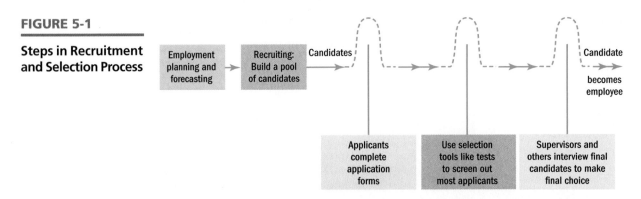

The recruitment and selection process is a series of hurdles aimed at selecting the best candidate for the job.

FIGURE 5-2

Linking Employer's Strategy to Plans

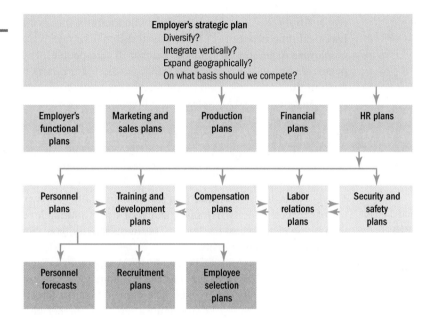

they'd have to expand its employment there from 140 people to almost 750. The human resources team thus knew they'd need plans for who to hire, how to screen applicants, and when to put the plans into place. Figure 5-2 summarizes the link between strategic and personnel planning.

One big question HR managers like those at JDS Uniphase need to answer is whether to fill their projected openings from within or from outside the firm. Each option produces its own set of personnel plans. Current employees may require training, development, and coaching. Going outside requires deciding what recruiting sources to use, among other things.

Like all good plans, management builds employment plans on basic forecasts, in this case of three things: personnel needs, the supply of inside candidates, and the supply of outside candidates. We'll start with personnel needs.

Forecasting Personnel Needs

❶ Explain the main techniques used in employment planning and forecasting.

Managers should consider several factors when forecasting personnel needs.[2] The usual process is to forecast revenues and then, from that, estimate the size of the staff required to achieve this sales volume. However, in practice, the manager will need to consider other factors as well, such as projected turnover (resignations or dismissals), decisions to upgrade (or downgrade) products or services, technological changes, and the department's financial resources. In any case, managers use several simple tools for projecting personnel needs, as follows.

trend analysis
Study of a firm's past employment needs over a period of years to predict future needs.

Trend Analysis   **Trend analysis** means studying variations in your firm's employment levels over the last few years. For example, you might compute the number of employees at the end of each of the last five years, or perhaps the number in each subgroup (like sales, production, secretarial, and administrative). The purpose is to identify trends that might continue into the future.

Trend analysis can provide an initial estimate of future staffing needs, but employment levels rarely depend just on the passage of time. Other factors (like changes in sales volume and productivity) also affect staffing needs.

ratio analysis
A forecasting technique for determining future staff needs by using ratios between, for example, sales volume and number of employees needed.

Ratio Analysis   Another approach, **ratio analysis**, means making forecasts based on the historical ratio between (1) some causal factor (like sales volume) and (2) the number of employees required (for instance, number of salespeople). For example, suppose a salesperson traditionally generates $500,000 in sales. If the sales revenue to salespeople ratio remains the same, you would require six new salespeople next year (each of whom produces an extra $500,000) to produce a hoped-for extra $3 million in sales.

Like trend analysis, ratio analysis assumes that productivity remains about the same—for instance, that each salesperson can't be motivated to produce much more than $500,000 in sales. If sales productivity were to rise or fall, the ratio of sales to salespeople would change. A forecast based solely on historical ratios would then no longer be accurate.

scatter plot
A graphical method used to help identify the relationship between two variables.

The Scatter Plot   A **scatter plot** shows graphically how two variables—such as a measure of business activity like sales, and your firm's staffing levels—are related. If they are, then if you can forecast the level of business activity, you should also be able to estimate your personnel requirements.

For example, assume a 500-bed hospital expects to expand to 1,200 beds over the next five years. The director of nursing and the human resource director want to forecast the requirement for registered nurses. The human resource director decides to determine the relationship between size of hospital (in terms of number of beds) and number of nurses required. She calls eight hospitals of various sizes and gets the following figures:

Size of Hospital (Number of Beds)	Number of Registered Nurses
200	240
300	260
400	470
500	500
600	620
700	660
800	820
900	860

Figure 5-3 shows hospital size on the horizontal axis. Number of nurses is shown on the vertical axis. If the two factors are related, then the points will tend to fall along a straight line, as they do here. If you carefully draw in a line to minimize the distances between the line and each one of the plotted points, you will be able to estimate the number of nurses needed for each hospital size. Thus, for a 1,200-bed hospital, the human resource director would assume she needs about 1,210 nurses.[3]

While simple, there are several drawbacks to techniques like trend or ratio analysis and scatter plots.[4]

1. They generally focus almost exclusively on projected sales volume and historical sales/personnel relationships, and generally assume that the firm's existing structure and activities will continue into the future.
2. They generally do not consider the impact the company's strategic initiatives may have on future staffing levels.
3. They tend to support outdated compensation plans that reward managers for managing ever-larger staffs, and don't reveal managers who expand their staffs irrespective of the company's strategic needs.

FIGURE 5-3

Determining the Relationship Between Hospital Size and Number of Nurses

Note: After fitting the line, you can project how many employees you'll need, given your projected volume.

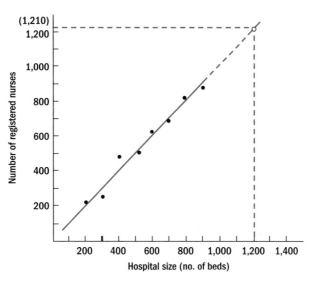

4. They tend to "bake in" the nonproductive idea that increases in staffs are inevitable.

5. They tend to validate and institutionalize existing planning processes and ways of doing things, even in the face of rapid change.

In summary, using these techniques requires a heavy dose of realism and common sense.

computerized forecast

Determination of future staff needs by projecting sales, volume of production, and personnel required to maintain this volume of output, using software packages.

Using Computers to Forecast Personnel Requirements   **Computerized forecasts** enable the manager to include more variables into his or her personnel projections.[5] These variables might include direct labor hours required to produce one unit of product (a measure of productivity), and three sales projections—minimum, maximum, and probable—for the product line in question. Based on such input, a typical program generates average staff levels required to meet product demands, as well as separate computerized forecasts for direct labor (such as assembly workers), indirect staff (such as secretaries), and exempt staff (such as executives).

With programs like these, employers can more accurately translate projected productivity and sales levels into forecasted personnel needs. And, they can estimate the effects of various productivity and sales level assumptions on personnel requirements.[6]

Many firms use automated computerized employee forecasting systems. In retailing, for instance, automated labor scheduling systems help retailers estimate required staffing needs based on sales forecasts and estimated store traffic.[7]

Whichever method you use, *managerial judgment* will play a big role. It's rare that any historical trend, ratio, or relationship will simply continue unchanged into the future. You will therefore have to modify the forecast based on factors—such as projected turnover or a desire to enter new markets—you believe will be important.

Forecasting the Supply of Inside Candidates

Knowing your staffing needs satisfies only half the staffing equation. Next, you have to estimate the likely supply of both inside and outside candidates. Most firms start with the inside candidates.

The main task here is determining which current employees might be qualified for the projected openings. For this you need to know current employees' skills sets—their current qualifications. Sometimes it's obvious how you have to proceed. For example, when Bill

Gates needed someone to lead Microsoft's new user interface project, his first question was, "Where's Kai-Fu?" His firm's voice recognition expert, Kai-Fu Lee, was in China at the time establishing a new research lab for the firm.[8] (Kai-Fu later went to work for Google China.)

Sometimes it's not so obvious, and managers turn to **qualifications inventories**. These contain data on employees' performance records, educational background, and promotability. Whether manual or computerized, these help managers determine which employees are available for promotion or transfer.

Manual Systems and Replacement Charts   Department managers or owners of smaller firms may still use several simple manual devices to track employee qualifications. A *personnel inventory and development record form* compiles qualifications information on each employee. The information includes education, company-sponsored courses taken, career and development interests, languages, desired assignments, and skills. **Personnel replacement charts** (Figure 5-4) are another option, particularly for the firm's top positions. They show the present performance and promotability for each position's potential replacement. As an alternative, you can develop a **position replacement card**. Here, create a card for each position, showing possible replacements as well as their present performance, promotion potential, and training.

Computerized Information Systems   Companies don't generally track the qualifications of hundreds or thousands of employees manually. Most firms computerize this information, using various packaged software systems. Increasingly, as we'll see, they also link these with their other human resources systems. So, for instance, the employee's skills inventory might automatically update based on his or her annual performance appraisal, or training.

Most computerized skills inventories work more or less the same. The employees, their supervisors, and/or human resources professionals enter information about the

qualifications inventories
Manual or computerized records listing employees' education, career and development interests, languages, special skills, and so on, to be used in selecting inside candidates for promotion.

personnel replacement charts
Company records showing present performance and promotability of inside candidates for the most important positions.

position replacement card
A card prepared for each position in a company to show possible replacement candidates and their qualifications.

FIGURE 5-4

Management Replacement Chart Showing Development Needs of Potential Future Divisional Vice Presidents

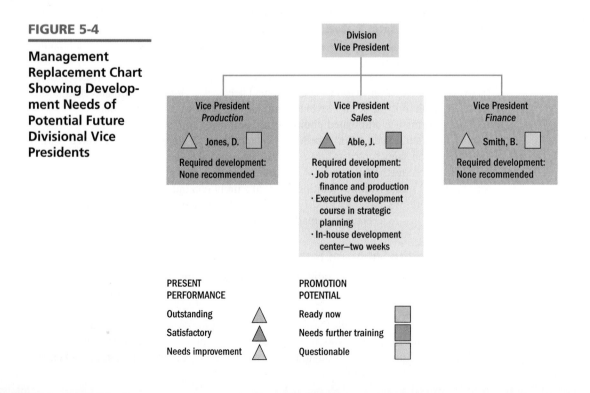

employee's background, experience, and skills, usually via the company intranet. Then, when a manager needs a person for a position, he or she describes the position's specifications (for instance, in terms of education and skills). After scanning its database, the system produces a list of qualified candidates. Computerized skills inventory data typically include *work experience codes; product knowledge*, the employee's *level of familiarity* with the employer's product lines or services; the person's *industry experiences*, since for some positions work in related industries is very useful; and *Formal education*.

The Matter of Privacy The employer should secure the data in the firm's personnel data banks. First, there is a lot of employee information in most data banks, often of a personal nature. Second, Internet/intranet access means it is relatively easy today for more people to access these data.[9] Third, legislation gives employees legal rights regarding who has access to information about them. The legislation includes the Federal Privacy Act of 1974 (which applies to federal workers), the New York Personal Privacy Act of 1985, HIPAA (which regulates use of medical records), and the Americans with Disabilities Act.

Balancing (1) the employer's right to make this information accessible to those in the firm who need it with (2) the employees' rights to privacy isn't easy. One solution is to incorporate an access matrix in the database management system. These matrices define the rights of users (specified by name, rank, or functional identification) to various kinds of access (such as "read only" or "write only") to each database element. So, the system might authorize employees in accounting to read information such as the employee's address and Social Security number. The human resource director, on the other hand, could both read and write all items. Figure 5-5 summarizes some guidelines for keeping employee data safe.

Forecasting the Supply of Outside Candidates

If there won't be enough inside candidates to fill the anticipated openings (or you want to go outside for another reason), the employer may want to forecast the availability of outside candidates. Unemployment rates of less than 4% in the U.S. in early 2007 signaled to HR managers that they may have to ramp up their recruitment to fill their open positions.

Information like this is easy to find, both online and in print format. For example, look for economic projections online, for instance from the U.S. Congressional Budget Office (CBO), http://www.cbo.gov/showdoc.cfm?index=1824&sequence=0; the Bureau of Labor Statistics (BLS), http://www.bls.gov/news.release/ecopro.toc.htm; and from private sources such as economists at the Bank of America, http://www.bankofamerica.com/newsroom/press/press.cfm?PressID=press.20040312.02.htm. For hard copy formats, *BusinessWeek* presents a weekly snapshot of the economy on its Outlook page, as well as a yearly forecast in December. *Fortune* magazine has a monthly forecast for the coming year.

FIGURE 5-5

Keeping Data Safe

Source: Dan Caternicchia, "Safeguarding HR Information," *HR Magazine*, Nov. 2005, p. 57. Reprinted by permission of Society for Human Resource Management via Copyright Clearance Center.

Since intruders can strike from outside an organization or from within, HR departments can help screen out potential identity thieves by following four basic rules:

- Perform background checks on anyone who is going to have access to personal information.
- If someone with access to personal information is out sick or on leave, don't hire a temporary employee to replace him or her. Instead, bring in a trusted worker from another department.
- Perform random background checks such as random drug tests. Just because someone passed five years ago doesn't mean their current situation is the same.
- Limit access to information such as SSNs, health information, and other sensitive data to HR managers who require it to do their jobs.

The planning may also require that you forecast the availability of potential job candidates in specific occupations such as nurse, computer programmer, or teacher. Recently, for instance, there has been an undersupply of nurses. O*NET (discussed in Chapter 4) includes online projections for most occupations. The Bureau of Labor Statistics of the U.S. Department of Labor publishes annual occupational projections both online and in the *Monthly Labor Review* and in *Occupational Outlook Quarterly*. The National Science Foundation regularly forecasts labor market conditions in the science and technology fields. Other federal agencies that provide occupational forecasts include the U.S. Public Health Service, the U.S. Employment Service, and the U.S. Office of Education.

EFFECTIVE RECRUITING

② List and discuss the main outside sources of candidates.

Assuming the company authorizes you to fill a position, the next step is to develop, through recruiting, an applicant pool. **Employee recruiting** means finding and/or attracting applicants for the employer's open positions.

employee recruiting
Finding and/or attracting applicants for the employer's open positions.

Why Recruiting Is Important

It's hard to overemphasize the importance of effective recruiting. If only two candidates apply for two openings, you may have little choice but to hire them. But if 10 or 20 applicants appear, you can use techniques like interviews and tests to screen out all but the best.

Effective recruiting is increasingly important. Barring some dramatic change, there will soon be an undersupply of workers. The Bureau of Labor Statistics estimates the United States will have created 22 million new jobs between 2003 and 2010, but only about 17 million new entrants will join the workforce. Several things could change this scenario. If the country continues to export white-collar jobs, then the number of new jobs added domestically will diminish. However, the supply-demand trend through 2010 seems to favor the worker.[10]

Even high unemployment, as in 2003–2004, doesn't necessarily mean that it is easy to find good candidates. For example, a survey during that period by the Department of Labor found that about half of respondents said they had "difficulty" finding qualified applicants. About 40% said it was "hard to find" good candidates.[11] Effective recruiting is thus not just important when the unemployment rate is low.

Recruiting's Complexities

Recruiting does not just involve placing ads or calling employment agencies. There are several things that make it more complex.

First, recruitment efforts should make sense in terms of the company's strategic plans. For example, decisions to expand abroad or to fill a large number of anticipated openings imply that you've carefully thought through when and how you will do your recruiting.

Second, we'll see that some recruiting methods are superior to others, depending on the type of job you are recruiting for.

Third, the success you have recruiting depends greatly on non-recruitment issues and policies. For example, paying 10% more than most firms in your locale should, other things equal, help you build a bigger applicant pool faster.[12]

Fourth, good recruiting preferably always requires simultaneously pre-screening employees—if only by listing the job's requirements in the ad, or by providing a realistic preview of the job during the initial call or contact. It's useless to waste time on applicants who have no real interest in the job.

Fifth, the firm's image affects its recruiting results. For example, ". . . a poor diversity reputation can make it particularly difficult for firms to recruit talent, especially among female and minority job seekers." Projecting the right message here might include using minority-targeted media outlets, highly diverse ads, emphasizing inclusiveness in policy statements, and using minority and female recruiters.[13]

Last but not least, (see the Know Your Employment Law feature) employment law prescribes what recruiter managers can and cannot do.

Know Your *Employment* LAW   Preemployment Activities

As we explained in Chapter 2, numerous federal, state, and local laws and court decisions restrict what employers can and cannot do when recruiting job applicants. For example, employers can't rely on word-of-mouth dissemination of information about job opportunities when its workforce is all, or substantially all, white or all members of some other class such as all female or all Hispanic.[14] Similarly, it is unlawful to give false or misleading information to members of any group, or to fail or to refuse to advise them of work opportunities and the procedures for obtaining them.

In practice, "the key question in all recruitment procedures is whether the method limits qualified applicants from applying."[15] So, for example, gender-specific ads that call for "busboy," or "firemen" would obviously raise red flags.[16] The bottom line is that it is generally best to avoid limiting recruitment efforts to just one recruitment method; use multiple sources to reach out as widely as possible.

In choosing what to ask on the application form, some suggest thinking of the selection process as consisting of two stages. Use the first stage to determine if the applicant is qualified. Limit application form questions to identification and work history, and to questions that will enable you to determine if the applicant has the skills to perform the functions of the job. This includes determining, perhaps through testing, if the person has the knowledge and skills to do the job.

If the answer is affirmative, then make a conditional job offer, but make it clear that failing to meet any of the following "second stage" conditions may result in rejection. Then, you may ask acceptable conditional job offer questions[17] such as "How long have you lived at the present address?" and "Do you have adequate means of transportation to get to work?" (see Figure 5-6).

There are two reasons to ensure that applicants complete the application form fully, and sign a statement on it indicating that the information the person provided is true. First, "The court will almost always support a discharge for falsifying information when applying for work."[18] Second, a less-than-complete job of filling in the form may reflect poor work habits. Some applicants will simply scribble "see résumé attached" on the application; this should not be acceptable.

FIGURE 5-6

Sample Acceptable Questions Once Conditional Offer Is Made

Source: Kenneth L. Sovereign, *Personnel Law*, 4th edition © 1999. Reprinted by permission of Pearson Education, Inc., Upper Saddle River, NJ.

1. Do you have any responsibilities that conflict with the job vacancy?
2. How long have you lived at your present address?
3. Do you have any relatives working for this company?
4. Do you have any physical defects that would prevent you from performing certain jobs where, to your knowledge, vacancies exist?
5. Do you have adequate means of transportation to get to work?
6. Have you had any major illness (treated or untreated) in the past 10 years?
7. Have you ever been convicted of a felony or do you have a history of being a violent person? (This is a very important question to avoid a negligent hiring or retention charge.)
8. What is your educational background? (The information required here would depend on the job-related requirements of the position.)

Organizing the Recruitment Function

Larger firms, in particular, must decide if they will conduct all their recruiting company-wide from a central recruitment office, or decentralize recruiting to the firm's various offices.

There are advantages to centralizing recruitment. First, doing so makes it easier to apply the company's *strategic priorities* companywide. For example, each of GM's geographical units, including its manufacturing plants, formerly did its own recruiting. GM decided to centralize recruitment because it wanted to strengthen its employment brand. Too many potential applicants erroneously viewed GM as somewhat old-fashioned. "We wanted to break away from the old views and be portrayed more realistically" says GM's manager of talent acquisition. About 45 professionals in GM's "talent acquisition department" now handle recruiting for all of GM's North American plants.[19]

Recruiting centrally has other advantages. It *reduces duplication* (having several recruitment offices instead of one), makes it easier to *spread the cost* of new technologies (such as Internet-based recruitment and prescreening solutions) over more departments, builds a *team of recruitment experts*, and makes it easier to identify why *recruitment efforts* are going well (or badly). It also produces *synergies*. For instance, instead of looking for one financial analyst, you can recruit for five related positions from the same applicant pool.[20] The accountants Deloitte & Touche Tohmatsu recently created a global recruitment site, thus eliminating the need to maintain 35 separate local recruiting Web sites.[21]

On the other hand, if the firm's divisions are autonomous, or their recruitment needs are varied, it may be more sensible to decentralize the recruitment function.

Line and Staff Cooperation   The human resources professional charged with recruiting for a vacant job is seldom responsible for supervising its performance. He or she must therefore know exactly what the job entails. This means speaking with the supervisor. For example (in addition to needing to know exactly what the job entails and its job specifications), the recruiter might want to know about the supervisor's leadership style and about the work group—is it a tough group to get along with, for instance? He or she might also want to visit the work site, to review the job description with the supervisor to ensure that the job hasn't changed, and to obtain any additional insight into the skills and talents the new worker will need. Line and staff coordination is therefore essential.

Measuring Recruiting Effectiveness

❸ Effectively recruit job candidates.

Even small employers may spend tens of thousands of dollars per year recruiting applicants, yet few firms assess their recruitment efforts' effectiveness. Is it more cost-effective to advertise for applicants on the Web, or in Sunday's paper? Should we use this employment agency or that one? One survey found that only about 44% of the 279 firms surveyed made formal attempts to evaluate the outcomes of their recruitment efforts.[22] Such inattention flies in the face of common sense.[23]

What to Measure   The question is what to measure and how to measure it. In terms of *what* to measure, one answer is, "how many applicants did we generate through each of our recruitment sources?" This makes sense. If more applicants are generated than there are positions to fill, the firm can be more selective.[24]

The problem is that more is not always better. The employer needs qualified, hirable applicants, not just applicants. An Internet ad may generate thousands of applicants, many from so far away that there's no chance they're viable. Even with computerized prescreening and tracking software (discussed below), there are still costs involved in managing applicant pools: more applicants to correspond with and screen, for instance.[25] Furthermore,

TABLE 5-1 Selection Devices That Could Be Used to Initially Evaluate Applicants

Selection Device	Validity for Predicting Job Performance*
Tests	
General mental ability tests	.51
Conscientiousness tests	.31
Integrity tests	.41
Method	
Work sample tests	.54
Job knowledge tests	.48
Structured interviews	.51
Biographical data	.35
Grade point average	.23
Ratings of training and experience	.11

Note: *Higher is better.

Source: Adapted from Kevin Carlson et al., "Recruitment Evaluation: The Case for Assessing the Quality of Applicants Attracted," *Personnel Psychology* 55 (2002), p. 470.

more applicants may not mean more selectivity. Realistically, the manager looking to hire five engineers probably won't be twice as selective with 20,000 applicants as with 10,000. So, it is not just quantity but quality.

How to Measure How then to measure each recruiting source's effectiveness? One way is to assess applicants from each source using simple prescreening selection devices.[26] For example, (see Table 5-1) having applicants perform several job tasks (a "work sample" test), or testing the applicant's job knowledge, are simple ways to assess the quality of the applicants from each source. Having assessed the quality of each recruitment source, the employer may then want to redirect recruiting dollars from sources that produce more applicants but lower-quality ones to sources that produce fewer but better candidates.

A High-Performance Example GE Medical uses another approach. The company hires about 500 technical workers a year to invent and make sophisticated medical devices such as CT scanners and magnetic resonance imagers. Since GE Medical must compete for talent with the likes of Microsoft, it's notable that it has cut its hiring costs by 17%, reduced time to fill the positions by 20% to 30%, and cut in half the percentage of new hires who don't work out.[27]

GE Medical accomplished this by applying best-practices management techniques.[28] For example, GE Medical draws up a "multigenerational staffing plan" to go with each of its products' multiyear product plan. That way, management can predict two or three years ahead its specific hiring needs.

GE Medical has also applied some of its purchasing techniques to its dealings with recruiters. For example, it called a meeting several years ago and told 20 recruiters that it would work with only the 10 best. To measure "best," the company created measurements inspired by manufacturing techniques, such as "percentage of résumés that result in interviews" and "percentage of interviews that lead to offers." Similarly, GE Medical discovered that current employees are very effective as references for new high-tech employees. For instance, GE Medical interviews just 1% of applicants whose résumés it receives,

FIGURE 5-7

Recruiting Yield Pyramid

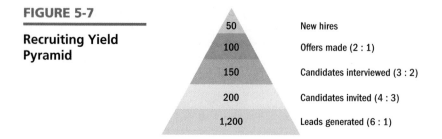

50	New hires
100	Offers made (2 : 1)
150	Candidates interviewed (3 : 2)
200	Candidates invited (4 : 3)
1,200	Leads generated (6 : 1)

while 10% of employee referrals result not only in interviews, but in actual hires. So GE Medical took steps to double the number of employee referrals. It simplified the referral forms, eliminated bureaucratic submission procedures, and added a small reward like a Sears gift certificate for referring a qualified candidate. GE also upped the incentive—$2,000 if someone referred is hired, and $3,000 if he or she is a software engineer.

The Recruiting Yield Pyramid

recruiting yield pyramid
The historical arithmetic relationships between recruitment leads and invitees, invitees and interviews, interviews and offers made, and offers made and offers accepted.

Some employers use a **recruiting yield pyramid** to calculate the number of applicants they must generate to hire the required number of new employees. In Figure 5-7, the company knows it needs 50 new entry-level accountants next year. From experience, the firm also knows the following:

- The ratio of offers made to actual new hires is 2 to 1.
- The ratio of candidates interviewed to offers made is 3 to 2.
- The ratio of candidates invited for interviews to candidates actually interviewed is about 4 to 3.
- Finally, the firm knows that of six leads that come in from all its recruiting sources, only one applicant typically gets invited for an interview—a 6-to-1 ratio.

Given these ratios, the firm knows it must generate 1,200 leads to be able to invite 200 viable candidates to its offices for interviews. The firm will then get to interview about 150 of those invited, and from these it will make 100 offers. Of those 100 offers, about 50 will accept. (The employer may also want to factor in the number of people it must hire, given the number that typically depart in the first year.)

④ Name and describe the main internal sources of candidates.

INTERNAL SOURCES OF CANDIDATES

Recruiting typically brings to mind Monster.com, employment agencies, and classified ads, but (as at GE Medical), internal sources—in other words, current employees or "promotions from within"—are often the best source of candidates.

Internal Sources: Pros and Cons

Filling open positions with inside candidates has several advantages. First, there is really no substitute for knowing a candidate's strengths and weaknesses, as you assumedly do after working with them for some time. Current employees may also be more committed to the company. Morale may rise if employees see promotions as rewards for loyalty and competence. And inside candidates should require less orientation and (perhaps) training than outsiders.

However, hiring from within can also backfire. Employees who apply for jobs and don't get them may become discontented; telling unsuccessful applicants why they were rejected and what remedial actions they might take to be more successful in the future is crucial. Many employers require managers to post job openings and interview all inside candidates. Yet the manager often knows ahead of time exactly whom he or she wants to hire. Requiring the person to interview a stream of unsuspecting inside candidates can be a waste of time for all concerned. Inbreeding is another potential drawback. When all managers come up through the ranks, they may have a tendency to maintain the status quo, when a new direction is required.

Finding Internal Candidates

job posting
Publicizing an open job to employees (often by literally posting it on bulletin boards) and listing its attributes, like qualifications, supervisor, working schedule, and pay rate.

To be effective, promotion from within requires using job posting, personnel records, and skills banks. **Job posting** means publicizing the open job to employees (usually by literally posting it on company intranets or bulletin boards). These list the job's attributes, like qualifications, supervisor, work schedule, and pay rate.

Qualifications inventory tools like those described earlier (such as computerized skills banks) also play a role. Thus, perusing the skill bank database may reveal persons who have potential for further training or who have the right background for the open job.

Rehiring

Should you rehire someone who left your employ? It depends. On the plus side, former employees are known quantities (more or less), and are already familiar with the company's culture, style, and ways of doing things. On the other hand, employees who were let go may return with less-than-positive attitudes. Hiring former employees who resigned back into better positions may signal current employees that the best way to get ahead is to leave the firm.

In any event, there are several ways to reduce the chance of adverse reactions.[29] After rehired employees have been back on the job for a certain period, credit them with the years of service they had accumulated before they left. In addition, inquire (before rehiring them) about what they did during the layoff and how they feel about returning to the firm: "You don't want someone coming back who feels they've been mistreated," said one manager.[30]

Succession Planning

succession planning
The ongoing process of systematically identifying, assessing, and developing organizational leadership to enhance performance.

Forecasting the availability of inside executive candidates is particularly important in **succession planning**—the ongoing process of systematically identifying, assessing, and developing organizational leadership to enhance performance. Where *succession planning* aims to identify and develop employees to fill specific slots, talent management is a broader activity. *Talent management* involves identifying, recruiting, hiring, and developing high potential employees.[31] About 36% of employers have formal succession planning programs in place.[32]

Succession planning entails three steps: identifying and analyzing key jobs, creating and assessing candidates, and selecting those who will fill the key positions.

First, based on the firm's strategic goals, top management and the HR director identify what the company's future key position needs will be, and formulate job descriptions and specifications for them. Thus, plans to expand abroad may suggest bulking up the management talent in the firm's international division. As one succession planning expert says, "A strategic business plan can only be realized when the right people are at the right place and at the right times to do the right things."[33]

After identifying future key position needs, management turns to the job of creating and assessing candidates for these jobs. "Creating" means identifying potential internal and external candidates for future key positions, and then providing them with the developmental experiences they require to be viable candidates when it's time to fill the positions. Organizations develop high-potential employees through a variety of means. Most use internal training and cross-functional experiences; they also use job rotation, external training, and global/regional assignments.[34]

Finally, succession planning requires assessing these candidates and selecting those who will actually fill the key positions.[35]

Improving Productivity Through HRIS: Succession Planning Systems

More large employers rely on software to facilitate the succession planning process. For example, when Larry Kern became president of Dole Food Co., Inc., it was highly decentralized. Each of its separate operating companies handled most of their own human resource activities, including succession planning. Kern's strategy involved improving financial performance by reducing redundancies and centralizing certain activities, including succession planning.[36]

Technology helped Dole do this. Instead of maintaining its own expensive human resource information (HRIS) system, Dole outsourced these activities. It contracted with application system providers (ASPs) to handle things like payroll management. For succession management, Dole chose special software from Pilat NAI, which runs the software and keeps all the data on its own servers for a monthly fee.

The Pilat succession planning system is easy for Dole's managers to use. They get access to the program via the Web using a password. They fill out online résumés for themselves, including career interests, and note special considerations such as geographic restrictions. The managers also assess themselves on four competencies. When the manager completes his or her succession planning input, the program automatically notifies that manager's boss. The latter then assesses his or her subordinate and indicates whether the person should be promoted. The person's manager also assesses his or her overall potential. This assessment and the online résumés then go automatically to the division head and the divisional HR director. Dole's senior vice president for human resources for North America then uses the information to create a career development plan for each manager, including seminars and other programs.[37]

OUTSIDE SOURCES OF CANDIDATES

Firms can't always get all the employees they need from their current staff, and sometimes they just don't want to. We'll look at the sources firms use to find outside candidates next.

Recruiting via the Internet

Most people today go online to look for jobs. One survey found that on a typical day, more than 4 million people turn to the Web looking for jobs.[38] Surveys show that for most employers and for most jobs, Internet-based ads and recruiting is far and away the recruiting source of choice.[39] The Cheesecake Factory gets about a third of its management applicants via the Web. Figure 5-8 lists some top online recruiting job sites.

Rather than place their own Internet ads on their own sites or sites like Monster.com, many managers do keyword searches on sites like HotJobs' résumé database. For example, when the HR manager for one hydraulic products company placed a Sunday ad in his local newspaper, it cost $3,000 and produced about 30 résumés, 10% of which were relevant.[40] By comparison, he found that keyword search of the HotJob database produced 52 résumés, many of which included the necessary industry experience. "I find more qualified candidates by searching for résumés than posting ads" he says.[41] New sites are capitalizing on the popularity of social networking to provide recruiting assistance. For example, users register by supplying their name, location, and the kind of work they do on sites like monster networking, and LinkIn.com. These sites facilitate developing personal relationships for networking, hiring, and employee referrals.[42]

Advantages   In general, the Web is a cost-effective way to publicize openings; it generates more responses quicker and for a longer time at less cost, than just about any other method. For example, Marsha Wheatley, human resource director for the Washington, DC–based American Crop Protection Association, no longer runs $400 ads in the

RANK '06	RANK '05	Company name and URL	Average number of job listings for most recent quarter (percentage change)	Number of client companies currently posting jobs on the board (percentage change)	Reach per million users*	Key clients
1.	**1.**	CAREERBUILDER.COM www.careerbuilder.com	1.5 million (50 percent)	250,000 (25 percent**)	3,090	Yum Brands, RadioShack, General Electric, Sprint, Deloitte, Morgan Stanley
2.	**2.**	MONSTER www.monster.com	1.1 million (38 percent)	275,000 (38 percent)	3,515	Home Depot, Nordstrom, McDonald's, Johnson & Johnson, Countrywide Financial, PepsiCo
3.	**3.**	COLLEGERECRUITER.COM www.collegerecruiter.com	250,000 (36 percent)	12,500 (20 percent)	39	Army National Guard, Red Lobster, RadioShack, Wells Fargo, CIA
4.	**5.**	CAREERJOURNAL.COM www.careerjournal.com	125,000 (67 percent)	4,468 (12 percent)	117.5	Accenture, Allstate, Deloitte, UBS, Edward Jones, Medtronic, Xerox
5.	**6.**	DICE INC. www.dice.com	89,286 (32 percent**)	8,300 (38 percent**)	574	IBM, Sun Microsystems, Microsoft, BearingPoint, Rockwell Collins, Sogeti, AOL
6.	**7.**	NATIONJOB www.nationjob.com	61,997 (8 percent)	6,000 (17 percent)	55.5	Wyeth, Dow Corning, Lockheed Martin, Mayo Clinic, Northrop Grumman
7.	**8.**	TRUECAREERS www.truecareers.com	35,000 (no change)	90 (-10 percent)	25.5	Deloitte, Procter & Gamble, Colgate-Palmolive, Merrill Lynch
8.	**N/A**	THELADDERS.COM www.theladders.com	30,000 (200 percent)	8,632 (-15 percent)	223	Wachovia, Microsoft, UnitedHealth Group, Aetna, Oracle, ADP, KPMG
9.	**9.**	EXECUNET www.execunet.com	25,000 (19 percent)	Would not disclose (N/A)	45	A.T. Kearney, Spencer Stuart, Merrill Lynch, DHR, Wachovia
10.	**11.**	VETJOBS www.vetjobs.com	21,000 (28 percent)	600 (100 percent)	1.05	BNSF Railway, CIA, Defense Intelligence Agency, Home Depot, Oracle Consulting
11.	**12.**	CAREERBANK www.careerbank.com	18,000 (50 percent)	1,230 (79 percent)	51	PricewaterhouseCoopers, Deloitte, KPMG, Wachovia, Lehman Brothers, Robert Half International
12.	**13.**	MEDZILLA www.medzilla.com	10,000 (no change)	3,500 (no change)	15.5	Aventis, Genentech, Allergan, Merck, Pfizer, Alcon, Amgen

*Data from Alexa.com. **Figures were revised from last year's list; companies acknowledged that they provided incorrect information in 2005.

Note: America's Job Bank and its subsidiary USAJobs.com as well as Vault.com and Yahoo HotJobs declined to participate. Job board aggregators do not meet the criteria for this list; only job boards with direct listings are included.

Sources: Companies, Alexa.com

FIGURE 5-8

Top Job Boards Ranked According to Average Number of Job Listings

Source: *Workforce Management*, May 22, 2006, p. 12. Copyright Crain Communications, Inc.

Washington Post when she's looking for professionals. Instead, ads on WashingtonPost.com cost only $200. "Instead of a tiny ad that says, 'ACPA needs an accountant,' I get a whole page to describe the job, give information about the association, and include a link to our Web site."[43] She estimates that she averages nine times as many applicants via the online ad. A newspaper ad might have a life span of perhaps 10 days, whereas the Internet ad may keep attracting applications for 30 days or more.

Disadvantages   Internet recruiting has two potential problems that employers must address.

First, fewer older people and certain minorities use the Internet, so automated online application gathering and screening may inadvertently exclude higher numbers of older applicants and certain minorities. To prove they've complied with EEOC laws, employers should keep track of each applicant's race, sex, and ethnic group. However, it's so easy to submit resumes online that many applications are unsolicited and not job specific. Therefore, many applicants may not be "applicants" for EEOC purposes. The interagency uniform guidelines on employee selection procedures define an Internet applicant as follows:

- The employer has acted to fill a particular position.
- The individual has followed the employer's standard procedures for submitting an application.
- The individual has indicated an interest in the particular position.

Note that under this definition, the employer probably need not keep track of "non-applicants' " race, sex, or ethnic group.[44]

The second challenge is that Internet recruiting is often too much of a good thing: employers end up deluged with resumes. There are several ways to handle this. The Cheesecake Factory, as noted earlier, posts detailed job duties listings, so those not interested need not apply. Another approach is to have job seekers complete a short online pre-screening questionnaire, and then use these responses to identify those that may proceed in the hiring process. (This carries legal risks, particularly if the device disproportionately screens out minority or women applicants.) Most employers also use applicant tracking systems, to which we now turn.[45]

Using Applicant Tracking ASP   Web-based ads tend to generate so many applicants that most firms are installing applicant tracking systems to support their on- and offline recruiting efforts. **Applicant tracking systems** (from firms such as recruitsoft.com, and Itrack-IT solutions) are online systems that help employers attract, gather, screen, compile, and manage applicants.[46] They also provide several services, including requisitions management (for monitoring the firm's open jobs), applicant data collection (for scanning applicants' data into the system), and reporting (to create various recruiting-related reports such as cost per hire and hire by source).[47]

applicant tracking systems
Online systems that help employers attract, gather, screen, compile, and manage applicants.

For example, with 10,000 job openings per year, Sutter Health Corporation turned to online recruiting. But this actually complicated things for Sutter.[48] Online postings did generate many more applications—over 300,000 a year. Sutter Health had so many résumés coming in by e-mail and through its Web site that the applications ended up in a pile, waiting for Sutter affiliates' HR departments to get to them.

Sutter Health's solution was to sign on with Recruitsoft, Inc., of San Francisco. Recruitsoft is a recruiting applications service provider (ASP). It now does all the work of hosting Sutter Health's job site. As an applications service provider, Recruitsoft doesn't just post Sutter Health job openings and collect its résumés; it also gives Sutter Health "an automated way to evaluate, rank and match IT and other job candidates with specific openings." For example, Recruitsoft's system automatically screens incoming résumés, compares them with Sutter's job requirements, and flags high-priority applicants. This helped Sutter cut its recruiting process from weeks to days, and thereby helped keep Sutter's expansion strategy on track.

Designing Effective Internet Ads and Systems   Designing effective Internet ads and systems is important. For one thing, some estimate that employers have only about four minutes "before online applicants will turn their attention elsewhere."[49] Employers are therefore making it easy to use their Web sites to hunt for jobs: 71% of the Standard & Poor's 500 place employment information just one click away from their home pages.[50] Job seekers can submit their résumés online at almost all *Fortune* 500 Web sites; fewer give job seekers the option of completing online applications, although it is the method many applicants prefer, according to one expert.[51]

The best Web ads don't just transpose your newspaper ads to the Web. As one specialist put it, "getting recruiters out of the 'shrunken want ad mentality' is a big problem." Figure 5-9 is an example of recycling a print ad to the Web. The ineffective Web ad is poorly written, has many needless abbreviations, and doesn't say much about why the job seeker should want that job or that employer.[52]

Now look at the effective Web ad in Figure 5-9. It uses compelling keywords such as "Excellent Commissions" and "Outstanding." It provides good reasons (such as "No Travel") why you would want to work for this company. And, it starts off with an attention-grabbing heading.

One survey of 256 alumni from graduate business schools showed why many firms' Web-based recruiting turned them off. The objections included:

- Job openings lacked relevant information (such as job descriptions).
- It was often difficult to format résumés and post them in the form required for the employer's recruitment site.
- Many respondents expressed concerns about the privacy of the information they provided.
- Poor graphics often made it difficult to use the Web site.
- And slow feedback from the employers (in terms of follow-up responses and receiving online applications) was also annoying.[53]

INEFFECTIVE WEB AD	EFFECTIVE WEB AD
Unix Solaris Admin./ Windows 2000 Administrator	**Work for the World's Best Boss...You!**
Exciting opportunity on ground floor project for telecom/Internet venture—local candidates only at this time. ***Might also consider subcontract if candidate has over 6 years of Solaris admin exp.*** Solaris Unix Solaris Systems Admin. MUST have Windows 2000 Admin experience. MUST have at least 3–4 years plus of System Admin experience. MUST have at least 3 solid years of Solaris exp. Looking for someone who has solid experience working with data storage and how it works in enterprise systems. (Looking for experience like RAID.) Also must have: Windows 2000 and looking for someone with specific Cisco switches and routers (5500 and 6500 Series).	Now you can be in business for yourself, have your own office, schedule your own time, and advance to management within a year. Add to that a six-figure income in the second year . . . and you have the dream career your talents deserve. We have over 140 offices nationally with over 60,000 clients. Currently, our office in Tampa seeks entrepreneurial, success-driven professionals who will welcome the independence and advantages of being a sales professional. You must have the interpersonal/communication skills and highly professional image to promote our indispensable services to the business and medical communities. We offer: · Excellent commissions · Proven repeat business · Outstanding training · No travel, nights or weekends

FIGURE 5-9

Ineffective and Effective Web Ads

Source: Workforce, December 2001, © Crain Communications, Inc. Reprinted with permission.

Finally, note that online recruiting always requires caution on the part of the applicants. Many job boards do little to assure the legitimacy of the "recruiters" who they let access their sites. Furthermore, many applicants fill out online forms with personal details such a Social Security numbers, not realizing that the sites they're using are actually run by ASP companies, rather than the one to which they're applying for employment.[54]

⑤ Develop a help wanted ad.

Advertising

While Web-based recruiting is rapidly replacing help wanted ads, a glance at almost any paper or business or professional magazine will confirm that print ads are still popular. To use help wanted ads successfully, employers have to address two issues: the advertising medium and the ad's construction.

The Media   The selection of the best medium—be it the local paper, the *Wall Street Journal*, TV, (or some other)—depends on the positions for which you're recruiting. For example, the local newspaper is often the best source for local blue-collar help, clerical employees, and lower-level administrative employees. On the other hand, if recruiting for workers with special skills—such as furniture finishers—you'd probably want to advertise in the Carolinas or Georgia, even if your plant is in Tennessee. The point is to target your ads where they'll reach your prospective employees.

For specialized employees, you can advertise in trade and professional journals like *American Psychologist, Sales Management, Chemical Engineering, Electronics News, Travel Trade*, and *Women's Wear Daily*. Help wanted ads in papers like the *Wall Street Journal* and *International Herald Tribune* can be good sources of middle- or senior-management personnel. Most of these print outlets now include online ads with the purchase of print help wanted ads.

Technology is enabling companies to be more creative about how they advertise for job applicants. For example, Electronic Arts, the world's largest video game publisher, knows that "our best [job] candidates hang out online and read gaming magazines."[55] The company therefore uses its products to help solicit job applicants. For example, Electronic Arts includes information about its internship program on the back of its video game manuals. Thanks to non-traditional techniques like these, the firm now has a database of over 200,000 potential job candidates. It also uses special tracking software to identify potential applicants with specific skills, and to facilitate ongoing communications (via e-mail) with everyone in its database.

Constructing the Ad   Experienced advertisers use a four-point guide labeled AIDA (attention, interest, desire, action) to construct ads. You must, of course, attract attention to the ad, or readers may just miss or ignore it. Figure 5-10 shows an ad from one paper's classified section. Why does this ad attract attention? The words "next key player" certainly help. Employers usually advertise key positions in separate display ads like this one.

Next, develop interest in the job. You can create interest by the nature of the job itself, with lines such as "are you looking to make an impact?" You can also use other aspects of the job, such as its location, to create interest.

Create desire by spotlighting the job's interest factors with words such as *travel* or *challenge*. As an example, having a graduate school nearby may appeal to engineers and professional people.

Finally, the ad should prompt action, with a statement like "call today," or "please forward your résumé." (And, of course, as explained earlier in this chapter, the ad should comply with equal employment laws, avoiding features like, "man wanted.")

FIGURE 5-10

Help Wanted Ad That Draws Attention

Source: Giombetti Associates, Hampden, MA. Reprinted with permission.

Are You Our Next Key Player?

PLANT CONTROLLER | Northern New Jersey

Are you looking to make an impact? Can you be a strategic business partner and team player, versus a classic, "bean counter"? Our client, a growing **Northern New Jersey** manufacturer with two locations, needs a high-energy, self-initiating, technically competent Plant Controller. Your organizational skills and strong understanding of general, cost, and manufacturing accounting are a must. We are not looking for a delegator, this is a hands-on position. If you have a positive can-do attitude and have what it takes to drive our accounting function, read oh!

Responsibilities and Qualifications:

- Monthly closings, management reporting, product costing, and annual budget.
- Accurate inventory valuations, year-end physical inventory, and internal controls.
- 4-year Accounting degree, with 5–8 years experience in a manufacturing environment.
- Must be proficient in Microsoft Excel and have general computer skills and aptitude.
- Must be analytical and technically competent, with the leadership ability to influence people, situations, and circumstances.

If you have what it takes to be our next key player, tell us in your cover letter, *"Beyond the beans, what is the role of a Plant Controller?"* **Only cover** letters addressing that question will be considered. Please indicate your general salary requirements in your cover letter and email or fax your resume and cover letter to:

Rich Frigon
Giombetti Associates
2 Allen Street, P.O. Box 720
Hampden, MA 01036
Email: rfrigon@giombettiassoc.com
Fax: (413) 566-2009

GIOMBETTI ASSOCIATES
INSTITUTE OF LEADERSHIP

Employment Ads and Image   Smart employers don't just use ads to attract recruits, they also use them to create the company image they want to project.[56] For example, in one study, researchers surveyed 133 students who were graduating with bachelor's or master's degrees in engineering. For these students, job-related ads were significantly related to their perceptions of the company. The results suggest that employers should try to create positive impressions of their companies through their job postings, Web sites, and other means. Building word-of-mouth reputation is also important: "From a practical standpoint, the results indicate that expanding and capitalizing on word-of-mouth endorsements will [prove] a highly effective and economical method for increasing applicant [inquiries]."

Employment Agencies

There are three main types of employment agencies: (1) public agencies operated by federal, state, or local governments; (2) agencies associated with nonprofit organizations; and (3) privately owned agencies.

Public and Nonprofit Agencies   Every state has a public, state-run employment service agency. The U.S. Department of Labor supports these agencies, in part through grants, and in part through other assistance such as a nationwide computerized job bank. The National Job Bank enables agency counselors in one state to advise applicants about available jobs not just in their local area, but in other areas as well.

These agencies are an important source of workers, but some employers have had mixed experiences with them. For one thing, applicants for unemployment insurance are required to register and to make themselves available for job interviews. Some of these people are not interested in getting back to work, so employers can end up with applicants who have little or no desire for immediate employment. And fairly or not, employers probably view some of these local agencies as rather lethargic in their efforts to fill area employers' jobs.

Yet these agencies are actually quite useful. Beyond just filling jobs, for instance, counselors will visit an employer's work site, review the employer's job requirements, and even assist the employer in writing job descriptions. Most states have turned their local state employment service agencies into "one-stop" shops—neighborhood training/employment/educational services centers.[57] One user says of the Queens New York Career Center in Jamaica: "I love it: I've made this place like a second home."[58] Services available to employers include recruitment services, tax credit information, training programs, and access to local and national labor market information.[59] More employers should probably be taking advantage of these centers (formerly the "unemployment offices" in many cities). Relatively few do.

Most (non-profit) professional and technical societies, such as the Institute for Electrical and Electronic Engineers (IEEE), have units that help members find jobs. Many public welfare agencies try to place people who are in special categories, such as those who are physically disabled or are war veterans.

Private Agencies   Private employment agencies are important sources of clerical, white-collar, and managerial personnel. They charge fees (set by state law and posted in their offices) for each applicant they place. Most are "fee-paid" jobs, in which the employer pays the fee. Fee-paid is generally the best way to attract currently employed applicants, who might not be so willing to pursue other jobs if they had to pay the fees.

Why use an agency? Reasons include:

1. Your firm doesn't have its own human resources department and is not geared to doing recruiting and screening.
2. Your firm has found it difficult in the past to generate a pool of qualified applicants.
3. You must fill a particular opening quickly.
4. There is a perceived need to attract a greater number of minority or female applicants.
5. You want to reach currently employed individuals, who might feel more comfortable dealing with agencies than with competing companies.
6. You want to cut down on the time you're devoting to recruiting.[60]

Yet using employment agencies requires avoiding potential pitfalls. For example, the employment agency's screening may let poor applicants bypass the preliminary stages of your own selection process. Unqualified applicants may go directly to the supervisors responsible for hiring, who may in turn naively hire them. Conversely, improper testing and screening at the employment agency could block potentially successful applicants from entering your applicant pool.

To help avoid problems:

1. Give the agency an accurate and complete job description.
2. Make sure tests, application blanks, and interviews are part of the agency's selection process.
3. Periodically review EEOC data on candidates accepted or rejected by your firm, and by the agency.
4. Screen the agency. Check with other managers or human resource people to find out which agencies have been the most effective at filling the sorts of positions you need filled. Review the Internet and classified ads to discover the agencies that handle the positions you want.

5. Make sure to supplement the agency's reference checking by conscientiously checking at least the final candidate's references yourself.

Temp Agencies and Alternative Staffing

Employers increasingly supplement their permanent workforces by hiring contingent or temporary workers, often through temporary help employment agencies. Also known as *part-time* or *just-in-time workers*, the *contingent workforce* is big and growing. It accounts for about 20% of all new jobs created in the United States.

The contingent workforce isn't limited to clerical or maintenance staff. It includes thousands of engineering, science, or management support occupations, for instance, including temporary chief financial officers, human resource managers, and CEOs.

Employers can hire temp workers either through direct hires or through temporary staff agencies. Direct hiring involves simply hiring workers and placing them on the job. The employer usually pays these people directly, as it does all its employees, but classifies them separately from regular employees, as casual, seasonal, or temporary employees, and often pays few if any benefits.[61] The other approach is to retain a temp agency to supply the employees. Here the agency handles all the recruiting, screening, and payroll administration for the temps. Thus Nike recently hired Kelly Services to manage Nike's temp needs.

Benefits and Costs   Contingent staffing is on the rise for several reasons. Historically, of course, employers have always used "temps" to fill in for permanent employees who were out sick or on vacation. But today's desire for ever-higher productivity also contributes to temp workers' growing popularity. Productivity is measured in terms of output per hour paid for, and temps are generally paid only when they're working—not for days off, in other words. Many firms also use temporary hiring to give prospective employees a trial run before hiring them as regular employees.[62]

The benefits of contingent staff don't come without a price. They may be more productive and less expensive to recruit and train, but generally cost employers 20% to 50% more than comparable permanent workers (per hour or per week), since the agency gets a fee. Furthermore, "people have a psychological reference point to their place of employment. Once you put them in the contingent category, you're saying they're expendable."[63] The Employment Law feature (page 186) addresses relevant law.

The numbers of temporary and freelance workers are increasing all over the world. Alemi Takada is a noted Japanese freelance animator who manages her workload and does projects for companies all over the world through an Internet agency that represents about 15,000 freelancers in media and publishing.

Know Your Employment LAW   Contingent Workers

Federal agents recently rounded up about 250 illegal "contract" workers in 60 Wal-Mart stores. The raid underscores that employers must understand the status of the contract employees who work on their premises under the auspices of outside firms, handling activities like security, foodservice, (or, as in Wal-Mart's case) after-hours store cleaning.[64]

Whether hired directly or through agencies, temp workers can pose legal risks to employers. One problem is that these "temps" are often temps in name only—they are really regular employees. Microsoft Corp.—certainly a sophisticated company—had to pay a $97 million settlement several years ago to employees it had mischaracterized as "temporary." Microsoft did not pay these employees certain benefits. A federal court held that despite their temp titles, these "temps" were actually regular Microsoft employees, eligible for the benefits.

Under the law, it is not the label (such as "temporary worker") that counts, but the facts of the case. The more control the employer and its managers and supervisors exercise over the agency's "temp" employees, the more likely it is that the court will view the temporary employees as regular employees (as at Microsoft).

Furthermore, as two lawyers put it, "for purposes of most employment laws, with certain limited exceptions, employees of temporary staffing firms working in an employer's workplace will be considered to be employees both of the agency and of the employer."[65] Managers and supervisors must therefore keep in mind that even for staffing company employees, the more control they exercise over the employee, the more likely it is that the law will view the employees as regular employees of the firm, and so eligible, for instance, for the employer's benefits. The prescription is to treat the temp employees as if the temp agency is in fact his or her employer. Figure 5-11 summarizes what this involves. For instance, do not train the temp employee, or negotiate pay with him or her. Let the agency do that.

Managers must also guard against treating temporary workers who come from temp agencies as if they have no employee rights. For example, some supervisors may assume that they can dismiss these employees arbitrarily, or ignore federal wage and hour laws. In fact, temporary workers, like all workers, have significant legal rights.

FIGURE 5-11

Guidelines for Using Temporary Employees

Source: Adapted from Bohner and Selasco, "Beware the Legal Risks of Hiring Temps," *Workforce*, October 2000, p. 53.

1. **Do not train your contingent workers.** Ask their staffing agency to handle training.
2. **Do not negotiate the pay rate of your contingent workers.** The agency should set pay.
3. **Do not coach or counsel a contingent worker on his/her job performance.** Instead, call the person's agency and request that it do so.
4. **Do not negotiate a contingent worker's vacations or personal time off.** Direct the worker to his or her agency.
5. **Do not routinely include contingent workers in your company's employee functions.**
6. **Do not allow contingent workers to utilize facilities intended for employees.**
7. **Do not let managers issue company business cards, nameplates, or employee badges to contingent workers without HR and legal approval.**
8. **Do not let managers discuss harassment or discrimination issues with contingent workers.**
9. **Do not discuss job opportunities and the contingent worker's suitability for them directly.** Instead, refer the worker to publicly available job postings.
10. **Do not terminate a contingent worker directly.** Contact the agency to do so.

Concerns   In order to make temp relationships as fruitful as possible, managers supervising temps should understand these employees' main concerns. In one survey, six key concerns emerged. They said they were:

1. Treated by employers in a dehumanizing, impersonal, and ultimately discouraging way.
2. Insecure about their employment and pessimistic about the future.

3. Worried about their lack of insurance and pension benefits.
4. Misled about their job assignments and in particular about whether temporary assignments were likely to become full-time positions.
5. "Underemployed" (particularly those trying to return to the full-time labor market).
6. In general angry toward the corporate world and its values; participants repeatedly expressed feelings of alienation and disenchantment.[66]

Guidelines   When working with temporary agencies, ensure that basic policies and procedures are in place, including:

- *Invoicing.* Get a sample copy of the agency's invoice. Make sure it fits your company's needs.
- *Time sheets.* With temps, the time sheet is not just a verification of hours worked. Once the worker's supervisor signs it, it's usually an agreement to pay the agency's fees.
- *Temp-to-perm policy.* What is the policy if the client wants to hire one of the agency's temps as a permanent employee?
- *Recruitment of and benefits for temp employees.* Find out how the agency plans to recruit employees and what sorts of benefits it pays.
- *Dress code.* Specify the appropriate attire at each of your offices or plants.
- *Equal employment opportunity statement.* Get a document from the agency stating that it is not discriminating when filling temp orders.
- *Job description information.* Have a procedure whereby you can ensure the agency understands the job to be filled and the sort of person, in terms of skills and so forth, you want to fill it.[67] The Know Your Employment Law feature on the previous page explains relevant legal issues.

alternative staffing
The use of nontraditional recruitment sources.

Alternative Staffing   Temporary employees are examples of **alternative staffing**—basically, the use of nontraditional recruitment sources. Other alternative staffing arrangements include "in-house temporary employees" (people employed directly by the company, but on an explicit short-term basis), and "contract technical employees" (highly skilled workers like engineers, who are supplied for long-term projects under contract from an outside technical services firm).

Offshoring/Outsourcing White-Collar and Other Jobs

Hiring workers abroad to do the jobs of those who would otherwise work in the United States may not be the first thing managers think of when "recruitment" comes to mind.[68] However, outsourcing is an increasingly important employment option. As explained in chapter one, current projections show that about three million white-collar jobs in occupations ranging from call-center employee to radiologist will be moving abroad in the next five or six years. To take just a few recent examples, GE's Transportation division announced that it was shifting 17 mid-level drafting jobs from Erie, Pennsylvania to India. Surveys conducted in California suggest that almost 7% of employers there are or would consider offshoring IT jobs (as well as many others).

As also discussed in Chapter 1, the issue of sending jobs abroad is contentious; there are staunch advocates of both the employers' and employees' points of view. However, regardless of the pros and cons, there seems little doubt that most managers will have to deal with outsourcing.

Main Issues   The question is, what specific issues should the human resources manager keep in mind when formulating plans to outsource jobs abroad? One is the potential for instability or military tension in countries such as India, the Philippines, and Russia. Other issues include: the likelihood of cultural misunderstandings (between your customers and the employees abroad, or between your employees here and employees there); security and privacy concerns (some U.S. customers may object to giving credit card information to strangers abroad, for instance); and the need to deal with foreign contract, liability, and legal systems issues.

Instituting outsourcing programs (for instance, a call-center in India) also requires careful attention to various other potential obstacles. For example, the employees need special training (for instance, in learning to speak with American idioms and to use pseudonyms like "Jim" without discomfort). Also understand that all the expected cost savings probably won't materialize. The employee abroad may earn only 10% of what someone in the United States would earn. However, the companies supplying and managing the foreign labor will retain a portion of the savings. And, the human resource manager's plans should include how to deal with the anxiety of its U.S.-based employees and unions.

Executive Recruiters

Executive recruiters (also called headhunters) are special employment agencies retained by employers to seek out top-management talent for their clients. The percentage of your firm's positions filled by these services might be small. However, these jobs include key executive and technical positions. For executive positions, headhunters may be your only source of candidates. The employer always pays the fees.

There are two types of executive recruiters—contingent and retained. Members of the Association of Executive Search Consultants usually focus on executive positions paying $150,000 or more, and on "retained executive search." This means they are paid regardless of whether or not the employer eventually hires the executive through the efforts of the research firm. *Contingency-based recruiters* tend to handle junior- to middle-level management job searches in the $50,000 to $150,000 range. Whether retained or contingent, fees are beginning to drop from the usual 30% or more of the executive's first-year pay. For example, in one survey about 96% of clients paying executive search fees paid the full 30% in 2000. This dropped to 77% in 2001, and to 70% in 2002.[69]

Two trends—technology and specialization—are changing the executive search business. Most recruiting firms have or use Internet-linked computerized databases, the aim of which, according to one senior recruiter, is "to create a long list [of potential candidates] by pushing a button."[70] Korn/Ferry has an Internet service called Futurestep, to draw more managerial applicants into its files.[71]

Executive recruiters are also becoming more specialized, and the large ones are creating new businesses aimed specifically at specialized functions or industries. For example, LAI Ward Howell launched a new business specializing in financial executives, with bases in London and New York.[72]

Pros and Cons   Recruiters are often irreplaceable. They have many contacts and are especially adept at contacting qualified, currently employed candidates who aren't actively looking to change jobs. They can also keep your firm's name confidential until late into the search process. The recruiter can save top management's time by advertising for the position and screening what could turn out to be hundreds of applicants. The recruiter's fee might actually turn out to be insignificant compared with the cost of the executive time saved.

But there are pitfalls. As an employer, it is essential to explain completely what sort of candidate is required—and why. Some recruiters also may be more interested in persuading you to hire a candidate than in finding one who will really do the job. Recruiters also claim that what their clients say they want is often not really what the clients want. Therefore, be prepared for some in-depth dissecting of your request. (See also the accompanying "When You're on Your Own" feature.)

When You're on Your OWN

HR for Line Managers and Entrepreneurs

Recruiting 101

There comes a time in the life of most small businesses when it dawns on the owner that his or her managers are incapable of taking the company to the next level. If the company is to expand, the owner must hire from outside. Should the owner recruit this person? Or is an outside expert required?

While most large firms don't think twice about hiring executive search firms, small-firm owners will understandably hesitate before committing to a fee that could reach $70,000 or so for a marketing manager. As an entrepreneur, however, you should keep in mind that such thinking can be shortsighted.

Engaging in a search like this by yourself is not at all like looking for secretaries, supervisors, or data entry clerks. When you are looking to hire a key executive to help run your firm, chances are you are not going to find him or her by placing ads or using most of the other traditional sources. For one thing, the person you seek is probably not reading the want ads.

So, what you'll end up with is a drawer of résumés of people who are, for one reason or another, out of work, unhappy with their work, or unsuited for your job. It will then fall on you to try to find several gems in this group by devoting the time to interview and assess these applicants.

This is harder than it sounds, even for someone familiar with the basics of HR. First, you may not even know where to place or how to write the ads; you won't know where to search, who to contact, or how to do the sort of job that needs to be done to screen out the laggards and misfits who may appear on the surface to be viable candidates. You also won't know enough to really do the kind of background checking that a position at this level requires. Second, this process is going to be time-consuming and will divert your attention from other duties. Many business owners find that when they

consider the opportunity costs (of not making sales calls, for instance), they are not saving any money at all.

If you do decide to do the job yourself (or even if you retain a recruiter), consider retaining an industrial psychologist to spend four or five hours assessing the problem-solving ability, personality, interests, and energy level of the two or three candidates in which you are most interested. The input can provide a valuable perspective on the candidates.

Exercise special care when recruiting applicants from competing companies. Always check to see if applicants are bound by noncompete or nondisclosure agreements, for instance. In general, even without a written contract, courts generally hold that employees have a duty of loyalty to their current employers during their employment. For example, they are generally expected to maintain the confidentiality of employer information such as customer lists. To the extent that the hiring manager participates in any breach of that loyalty—for instance, inquiring about customers' buying patterns or about new products under development—the hiring manager may share in the liability for the breach.[73]

If you're a department manager with an open position to fill in a *Fortune* 500 company, even you may find you have a dilemma. You may find that your local HR office will do little recruiting, other than, perhaps, placing an ad on Monster.com or other recruiting Web sites. On the other hand, your firm almost surely will not let you place your own help wanted ads. What to do? Use word of mouth to "advertise" your open position within and outside your company. Make sure everyone in your company who may conceivably know of a candidate knows that the position is open, and what it entails. And, contact your friends and colleagues in other firms to let them know you are recruiting, and to watch out for possible candidates.

Guidelines In choosing a recruiter, guidelines include:[74]

1. Make sure the firm is capable of conducting a thorough search. Under their ethics code, a recruiter can't approach the executive talent of a former client for a period of two years after completing a search for that client. Since former clients are off limits for two years, the recruiter must search from a constantly diminishing pool.

2. Meet the individual who will actually handle your assignment.

3. Make sure to ask how much the search firm charges. Get the agreement in writing.[75]

4. *Never* rely solely on the executive recruiter (or other search professional, such as employment agency) to do all the reference checking. Certainly, let them check the candidates' references, but get notes of these references in writing from the recruiter (if possible). And, in any event, make sure to check at least the final candidate's references yourself.

On Demand Recruiting Services

On demand recruiting services (ODRS) provide short-term specialized recruiting assistance to support specific projects without the expense of retaining traditional search firms. They are basically recruiters who get paid by the hour or project, instead of a percentage fee. For example, when the human resource manager for a biotech firm had to hire several dozen people with scientific degrees and experience in pharmaceuticals, she decided an ODRS firm was her best option. A traditional recruiting firm might charge 20 to 30% of each hire's salary, a prohibitive amount for a small company. The ODRS firm charged by time, rather than per hire. It handled recruiting, analysis, and prescreening, and left the client with a short list of qualified candidates to put through the employer's own internal screening process.[76]

College Recruiting

College recruiting—sending an employer's representatives to college campuses to prescreen applicants and create an applicant pool from the graduating class—is an important source of management trainees, promotable candidates, and professional and technical employees. One study several years ago concluded, for instance, that new college grads filled about 38% of all externally filled jobs requiring a college degree.[77]

The problem is that on-campus recruiting is expensive and time-consuming if done right. Schedules must be set well in advance, company brochures printed, records of interviews kept, and much time spent on campus. And recruiters themselves are sometimes ineffective, or worse. Some recruiters are unprepared, show little interest in the candidate, and act superior. Many don't screen candidates effectively. Such experiences underscore the need to train recruiters in how to interview candidates, how to explain what the company has to offer, and how to put candidates at ease.

On-Campus Recruiting Goals

The campus recruiter has two main goals. One is to determine if a candidate is worthy of further consideration. Exactly which traits to look for will depend on your company's specific needs. Usual traits to assess include communication skills, education, experience, and interpersonal skills.

The other aim is to attract good candidates. A sincere and informal attitude, respect for the applicant as an individual, and prompt follow-up letters can help sell the employer to the interviewee.

Employers have to choose recruiters and schools carefully. For recruiters, employers naturally seek employees who can do (and, preferably, who have done) the best job of identifying and attracting top applicants. Factors in selecting schools include the school's reputation and the performance of previous hires from that source.

Building close ties with a college's career center can help employers achieve these goals. Doing so provides recruiters with useful feedback regarding things like labor market conditions and the effectiveness of one's on- and off-line recruiting ads.[78] Shell reduced the list of schools its recruiters visit, using factors such as quality of academic program, number of students enrolled, and diversity of the student body.[79]

On-Site Visits   Employers generally invite good candidates to the office or plant for an on-site visit.

There are several ways to make this visit fruitful. The invitation letter should be warm and friendly but businesslike, and should give the person a choice of dates to visit the company. Someone should be assigned to meet the applicant, preferably at the airport or at his or her hotel, and to act as host. A package containing the applicant's schedule as well as other information regarding the company—such as annual reports and employee benefits—should be waiting for the applicant at the hotel.

Plan the interviews carefully and adhere to the schedule. Avoid interruptions; give the candidate the undivided attention of each person with whom he or she interviews. Luncheon should be hosted by one or more other recently hired graduates with whom the applicant may feel more at ease. Make an offer, if any, as soon as possible, preferably at the time of the visit. If this is not possible, tell the candidate when to expect a decision. If an offer is made, keep in mind that the applicant may have other offers, too. Frequent follow-ups to "find out how the decision process is going" or to "ask if there are any other questions" may help to tilt the applicant in your favor.

What sorts of things turn job candidates on or off? A study of 96 graduating students from a major Northeast university reveals some positive and negative factors. For example, 53% said that "on-site visit opportunities to meet with people in positions similar to those applied for, or with higher-ranking persons" had a positive effect. Fifty-one percent mentioned "impressive hotel/dinner arrangements and having well-organized site arrangements." On the other hand, 41% were turned off by "disorganized, unprepared interviewer behavior, or uninformed, useless answers." Similarly, 40% mentioned "unimpressive cheap hotels, disorganized arrangements, or inappropriate behavior of hosts" as having negative effects.[80]

Internships   Many college students get their jobs through college internships. Internships can be win–win situations for both students and employers. For students, it may mean being able to hone business skills, learn more about potential employers, and discover their career likes (and dislikes). And employers, of course, can use the interns to make useful contributions while evaluating them as possible full-time employees. One survey reports that employers offer jobs to over 70% of their interns.[81]

Referrals and Walk-Ins

"Employee referral" campaigns are an important recruiting option. The firm posts announcements of openings and requests for referrals on its intranet Web site, bulletin, and/or wallboards. Prizes or cash awards are offered for referrals that lead to hirings. AmeriCredit uses its "you've got friends, we want to meet them" employee referral program. Employees making a successful referral receive $1,000 awards, with the payments spread over a year. As the head of recruiting says, "Quality people know quality people. If you give employees the opportunity to make referrals, they automatically suggest high caliber people because they are stakeholders."[82] The Container Store uses a successful variant of the employee referrals campaign. They train their employees to recruit new employees from among the firm's customers.

Pros and Cons   The biggest advantage here—and the reason why so many employers favor this approach—is that referrals tend to generate high-quality candidates. Current employees will usually provide accurate information about the job applicants they are referring, especially since they're putting their own reputations on the line.[83] The new employees may also come with a more realistic picture of what working in the firm is like. Referrals can also facilitate diversifying your workforce. One survey found 70% of minority/ethnic candidates search for jobs on corporate Web sites; 67% use sites like Monster, 53%

classified ads, 52% referrals, and 35% headhunter/agencies. However, only 6% listed "corporate Web site" as one of the top five ways they actually found jobs; 25% listed referrals.[84]

A survey by the Society for Human Resource Management (SHRM) found that of 586 employer respondents, 69% said employee referral programs are more cost-effective than other recruiting practices and 80% specifically said they are more cost-effective than employment agencies. On average, referral programs cost between $400 and $900 per hire in incentives and rewards.[85]

However, the success of the campaign obviously depends on employee morale.[86] And the campaign can backfire if the firm rejects the employee's referral, and he or she becomes dissatisfied. As noted, relying on referrals may also be discriminatory if most current employees (and their referrals) are male or white.

Particularly for hourly workers, walk-ins—direct applications made at your office—are a big source of applicants. Employers encourage walk-ins by posting HIRING signs on the property. Treat walk-ins courteously and diplomatically, for the sake of both the employer's community reputation and the applicant's self-esteem. Many employers give every walk-in a brief interview with someone in the HR office, even if it is only to get information on the applicant "in case a position should be open in the future." Good business practice also requires answering all letters of inquiry from applicants promptly and courteously. And from a practical point of view, simply posting a "Help Wanted" sign outside the door is a cost-effective way to attract good local applicants.

Recruiting Source Use and Effectiveness

Figure 5-12 summarizes a survey of best recruiting sources. Internet job boards garnered the most votes, followed by professional/trade job boards, and employee referral programs.[87]

Research also reveals several guidelines employers can use to improve their recruiting efforts' effectiveness (see Table 5-2). For example, some recruitment sources produce

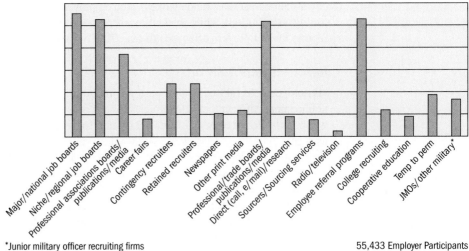

*Junior military officer recruiting firms   55,433 Employer Participants

FIGURE 5-12

Relative Recruiting Source Effectiveness Based on New Hires

Note: Internet job boards continue to be the most effective sources followed by employee referral programs and professional and trade media and associations.

Source: © Staffing.org, Inc., 2007. All Rights Reserved. The 2007 Recruiting Metrics and Performance Benchmark Report, 2nd Ed., is sponsored by NAS Recruitment Communications.

TABLE 5-2 Recruitment Research Findings and Applications

Research Finding[a]	Practical Applications
Recruitment sources affect the characteristics of applicants attracted.	Use sources such as referrals (e.g., from current employees) that yield applicants less likely to turnover and more likely to be better performers.
Recruitment materials have a more positive impact if they contain more specific information.	Provide applicants with information on aspects of the job that are important to them, such as salary, location, and diversity.
Organizational image influences applicants' initial reactions to employers.	Ensure all communications regarding an organization provide a positive message regarding the corporate image and the attractiveness of the organization as a place to work.
Applicants with a greater number of job opportunities are more attentive to and more influenced by early recruitment activities.	Ensure initial recruitment activities (e.g., Web site, brochure, on-campus recruiting) are as attractive to candidates as later activities.
Recruiter demographics have a relatively small effect on applicants' attraction to the organization.	Worry less about matching recruiter/applicant demographics and more about the content of recruiting messages and the organization's overall image in terms of diversity.
Realistic job previews (e.g., brochures, videos, group discussions that highlight both the advantages and the disadvantages of the job) reduce subsequent turnover.	Provide applicants with a realistic picture of the job and organization, not just the positives.
Applicants will infer job and organizational information based on the organizational image projected and their early interactions with the organization if the information is not clearly provided by the organization.	Provide clear, specific, and complete information in recruitment materials so that applicants do not make erroneous inferences about the nature of the job or the organization as an employer.
Recruiter warmth has a large and positive effect on applicants' decisions to accept a job.	Individuals who have contact with applicants should be chosen for their interpersonal skills.
Applicants' beliefs in a "good fit" between their values and the organization's influence their job-choice decisions.	Provide applicants with accurate information about what the organization is like so that they can make accurate fit assessments.

[a]Selected research principles from Taylor & Collins (2000).

Source: Ann Marie Ryan and Nancy Tippins, "Attracting and Selecting: What Psychological Research Tells Us" *Human Resource Management*, Winter 2004 43, no. 4, p. 311. Reprinted by permission of Society for Human Resource Management via Copyright Clearance Center.

higher quality candidates than do others. Thus referrals from current employees yield applicants who are less likely to turnover, and more likely to perform better.[88]

The Cheesecake Factory uses four recruiting sources, employee referrals, promotions of current employees, search firms, and online job postings. The firm's HR head, Ed Eynon, says the Web has become "our No. 1 source of recruitment, with between 30% and 35% of our new managers coming through it." The company does not just post short print-type help wanted ads on the Web. For most jobs it includes the entire job description.[89]

Image   Again, it's not just the ads, but the overall image the firm projects that is important in attracting top candidates. Borders and Barnes & Noble are both very successful bookseller chains, but they have very different approaches to staffing their stores. Borders wants employees who are specialists in and radiate excitement about particular types of books and music. It lets employees dress however they like, including piercings and tattoos. Barnes & Noble wants employees who are also passionate about books, but who will work the entire store and who generally have scholarly backgrounds. Employees here tend to wear collared shirts, and have a clean-cut look. The two chains translate these differing standards into the recruiting they do, with each projecting a different image in its ads.[90]

Improving Productivity Through HRIS: An Integrated Technology Approach to Recruiting

Employers may use several computerized systems to support their recruitment processes, preferably integrating them into a comprehensive employee recruitment system. Elements in such an integrated solution would include:

- A *requisition management system*, which facilitates requisition creation, routing, approval, and posting of job opening;
- A *recruiting solution*, including job advertisement, recruitment marketing, applicant tracking, and online recruitment vendor management, to increase and improve applicant pool quality;
- *Screening services*, such as background checks, and skills and behavioral assessment services.
- *Hiring management*, software to capture and manage candidate information while providing standard workflow practices.[91]

⑥ Explain how to recruit a more diverse workforce.

RECRUITING A MORE DIVERSE WORKFORCE

As we explained in Chapter 2, recruiting a diverse workforce isn't just socially responsible: It's a necessity, given globalization, the rapid increase in minority, older worker, and women candidates, and the 70% jobless rate among disabled people. Doing so means taking special steps to recruit people from these categories. (Many employers, such as Eastman Kodak Co., include disability under their diversity initiative umbrellas. This reflects their recognition that disabled people represent a large, untapped pool of potential employees.)[92]

Single Parents

About two-thirds of all single parents are in the workforce today; this group is an important source of candidates.

Attracting single parents begins with understanding the problems they face in balancing work and family life.[93] In one survey,

> Many described falling into bed exhausted at midnight without even minimal time for themselves . . . They often needed personal sick time or excused days off to care for sick children. As one mother noted, "I don't have enough sick days to get sick."[94]

Respondents viewed themselves as having "less support, less personal time, more stress, and greater difficulty balancing job and home life" than other working parents. Yet most were hesitant to dwell on their single-parent status at work; they feared that doing so would affect their jobs and careers adversely.

Given such concerns, the first step in attracting (and keeping) single mothers is to make the workplace as user friendly for them as

Not just single parents, but also their children may occasionally need some extra support.

is practical. Schedule flexibility can help. The problem is that "for some single mothers, this flexibility can help but it may not be sufficient to really make a difference in their ability to juggle work and family schedules."[95] In addition to flexibility, employers can and should train supervisors to be aware of and sensitive to the sorts of challenges single parents face. As two researchers conclude, "Very often, the single mother's relationships with her supervisor and co-workers is a significant factor influencing whether she perceives the work environment to be supportive."[96] Ongoing support groups at which single parents can share their concerns also help.

Older Workers

When it comes to hiring older workers, employers don't have much choice. Over the next few years, the fastest-growing labor force segment will be those from 45 to 64 years old. Those aged 25 to 34 will decline by almost three million, reflecting fewer births in the late 1960s and early 1970s. On the positive side, a survey by AARP (now one of the most powerful lobbies in Washington) and SHRM concluded that older workers tend to have lower absenteeism rates, more reliability, and better work habits than younger workers.[97] Furthermore, it's not just the workforce, the overall population is getting older as well. Firms like Home Depot capitalize on this by hiring older employees, who "serve as a powerful draw to baby boomer shoppers by mirroring their knowledge and perspective. . . ."[98]

It therefore makes sense for employers to encourage older workers to stay (or to come to work at the company). Here, employers should structure reward systems with older employees in mind. People's occupational needs and preferences change as they grow older. One survey found that getting a raise was the main motivator for 11% of those born in the 1960s and 1970s, but just 1% for those over 65.[99] Flexibility was the main concern for 71% of baby boomers, with those who continue working preferring to do so part-time.[100] At Wrigley Company, workers over 65 can progressively shorten their work schedules; another company uses "mini shifts" to accommodate those interested in working less than full time.[101] The following New Workforce feature illustrates another aspect of this. Retention aids for improving the chances of attracting and retaining older workers include:

- Management training to address age bias in the workplace.
- Phased retirement that allows workers to ease out of the workforce.
- Portable jobs for "snowbirds" who wish to live in warmer climates in the winter.
- Part-time projects for retirees.
- Full benefits for part-timers.[102]

As always in recruiting, projecting the right image is also essential here. For example, one study examined the impact of various organizational policies on the likelihood of attracting retirees interested in bridge employment (work after formal retirement). Using a mock newspaper ad, the researchers found that writing the ad so that it sent the message that the company was older worker–friendly was important. The most effective ads for attracting older workers emphasized schedule flexible and accentuated the firm's equal opportunity employment statement. This was much more effective than adding statements alluding to giving retirees opportunities to transfer their knowledge to the new work setting.[103]

Recruiting Minorities and Women

Basically the same prescriptions that apply to recruiting older workers apply to recruiting minorities and women. If there is a basic guideline, it is this: take the goal of recruiting more minorities and women seriously, and pursue that goal energetically. In practice, this

The NEW *Workforce*   Supervising Older Workers

Recruiting and hiring older employees is one thing; supervising them—especially when they're 20 or 30 years older than their supervisors—can be a challenge.

Gregg Levin's experiences provide an example. Levin, 31, is chief executive of Perfect Curve, a company in Sudbury, Massachusetts, that makes racks for baseball caps and related products. His father—one of his employees—doesn't use a computer, but instead "takes out his legal pad and spends an hour on something that takes me 4 1/2 minutes on a computer," says Gregg. Sometimes, he says, "I feel I'm just playing. A president is in his 50s or 60s, not 31." Maintaining authority is one of the challenges in a situation like this. Gregg Levin does this in part by dressing up: "I'm always in a suit and tie," he says. "If I'm going to represent my company, I've got to do it in a mature manner."

Mary Rodas was in a similar situation when, at 24, she helped start kardz.com (which then morphed into Your Free Presentation) and then became its vice president. Kardz.com delivered inexpensive gifts matched with greeting cards. Her five subordinates at that time were much older than she was. "When people meet me, their first reaction is: 'Who's this little kid?' Or else they say, 'Can I speak to your boss?' And I point to myself and say, 'That's her.'" She says she earns respect through hard work and getting to know her workers. "I know my business, and with time people realize that I'm talking to them as an individual and an equal. I've been in this industry for 11 years [she created a balloon ball at age 11 that brought in $70 million in sales for a toy company in New York], I know what I'm doing."[104]

requires a three-part effort: Understand the recruitment barriers; formulate the required recruitment plans; and institute the specific day-to-day programs.[105]

Understand   Understanding the barriers that prevent minorities and women from applying is the first step. For example, many minority applicants don't meet the educational or experience standards for the job, so many companies offer remedial training in basic arithmetic and writing. For many, lack of role models is a problem. For example, among life insurers and other financial services firms, a lack of women role models makes many hesitate to accept jobs as sales agents. In one retail store chain, it was similarly a lack of role models plus what the HR manager called the "rather macho culture" that stopped women from applying. Sometimes (as we saw) it's a lack of schedule flexibility, given the responsibility for caring and schooling of the children. Similarly, we saw that tolerant supervisors can be especially important when women size up potential employers.

Plan   After recognizing what the potential impediments are, the employer, preferably with the assistance of a diversity employment executive, should turn to formulating plans for attracting and retaining minorities and women. This may include reevaluating personnel policies, developing flexible work options, redesigning jobs, and offering flexible benefits plans.

Implement   Finally, translate these personnel plans into specific minority and women recruitment programs. For example, many jobseekers of Hispanic origin check with friends or relatives as a strategy for looking for jobs, so encouraging your Hispanic employees to assist in your recruitment efforts make sense. Other firms partner with professional organizations such as the black MBA Association, the national Society of

Hispanic MBAs, and the Organization of Chinese Americans. Specialized job search Web sites like those discussed elsewhere in this chapter are another option. In sum, to paraphrase one successful female financial services executive, the employer who is really interested in recruiting and retaining female employees has to fully commit to supporting them, coaching them, and offering them positive reinforcement.[106]

Welfare-to-Work

The Federal Personal Responsibility and Welfare Reconciliation Act of 1996 prompted many employers to implement "welfare-to-work" programs for attracting and assimilating former welfare recipients.

Some companies report difficulty in hiring and assimilating people previously on welfare. Applicants sometimes lack basic work skills such as reporting for work on time, working in teams, and "taking orders without losing their temper."[107] The key to a welfare-to-work program's success seems to be the employer's pretraining program, during which participants get counseling and basic skills training over several weeks.[108] For example, Marriott International hired 600 welfare recipients under its Pathways to Independence program. The heart of the program is six weeks of preemployment training focused on work and life skills and designed to rebuild self-esteem and instill positive attitudes about work.[109]

The Disabled

The EEOC estimates that nearly 70% of the disabled are jobless, but it certainly doesn't have to be that way.[110] In Germany, for instance, customers visiting Volkswagen's Wolfsburg plant are met by the receptionist, Mr. Janz. If they don't check the sign on his counter, they might assume he's ignoring them. In fact, Mr. Janz is blind, and the sign tells visitors to speak directly to him so he knows they are there.[111] Volkswagen recruited Mr. Janz because it has a policy of integrating people with disabilities into its workforce. Similarly, thousands of employers in the United States and elsewhere have found that disabled employees provide an excellent and largely untapped source of competent, efficient labor for jobs ranging from information technology to creative advertising to receptionist.

Employers can do several things to better tap this huge potential workforce. The U.S. Department of Labor's Office of Disability Employment Policy offers several programs, including one that helps link disabled college undergraduates who are looking for summer internships with potential employers.[112]

Employers also must use common sense if they want their recruiting efforts to reach the disabled. For example, employers who only post job openings online may miss potential employees who are visually impaired.[113] Beyond this, all states have local agencies (such as "Corporate Connections" in Tennessee) that provide placement services and other recruitment and training tools and information for employers seeking to hire the disabled.

DEVELOPING AND USING APPLICATION FORMS

Purpose of Application Forms

application form
The form that provides information on education, prior work record, and skills.

With a pool of applicants, the prescreening process can begin. The **application form** is usually the first step in this process (some firms first require a brief, prescreening interview or online test).

A filled-in form provides four types of information. First, you can make judgments on substantive matters, such as whether the applicant has the education and experience to do the job. Second, you can draw conclusions about the applicant's previous progress and growth, especially important for management candidates. Third, you can draw tentative conclusions about the applicant's stability based on previous work record (although years of downsizings and mergers signals the need for caution here). Fourth, you may be able to use the data in the application to predict which candidates will succeed on the job and which will not.

In practice, most organizations need several application forms. For technical and managerial personnel the form may require detailed answers to questions about education and training. The form for hourly factory workers might focus on tools and equipment.

Figure 5-13 presents one employer's approach to collecting application form information—the employment application for the FBI. In practice, most employers encourage online applications.

Employers should keep several practical application form guidelines in mind. In the "Employment History" section, request detailed information on each prior employer, including the name of the supervisor and his or her telephone number; this is all essential for following up on the reference. Also, in signing the application, the applicant should certify his or her understanding of several things: that falsified statements may be cause for dismissal; that investigation of credit and employment and driving record is authorized; that a medical examination may be required; that drug screening tests may be required; and that employment is for no definite period of time. Some applications also state an employer's "mandatory arbitration" policy for situations where problems arise. The feature on page 200 addresses this.

Application Forms and the Law

Employers should carefully review application forms to ensure that they comply with equal employment laws. Unfortunately, many application forms still do not. Questions to beware of include:

Education. A question on the dates of attendance and graduation from various schools—academic, vocational, or professional—is one potential violation. This question may be illegal insofar as it may reflect the applicant's age.

Arrest record. The courts have usually held that employers violate Title VII by disqualifying applicants from employment because of an arrest. This item has an adverse impact on minorities, and employers usually can't show it's required by business necessity.

Notify in case of emergency. It is generally legal to require the name, address, and phone number of a person to notify in case of emergency. However, asking the relationship of this person to the applicant could indicate the applicant's marital status or lineage.

Membership in organizations. Many forms ask the applicant to list memberships in clubs, organizations, or societies along with offices held. Employers should include instructions not to include organizations that would reveal race, religion, physical handicaps, marital status, or ancestry.

Physical handicaps. It is usually illegal to require the listing of an applicant's physical handicaps, defects, or past illnesses unless the application blank specifically asks only for those that "may interfere with your job performance." Similarly, it is generally illegal to ask whether the applicant has ever received workers' compensation.

Marital status. In general, the application should not ask whether an applicant is single, married, divorced, separated, or living with anyone, or the names, occupations, and ages of the applicants' spouse or children.

Housing. Asking whether an applicant *owns, rents,* or *leases* a house may also be discriminatory. It can adversely affect minority groups and is difficult to justify on grounds of business necessity.

	FIELD OFFICE USE ONLY

FEDERAL BUREAU OF INVESTIGATION

FIELD OFFICE USE ONLY
Right Thumb Print

Preliminary Application for
Special Agent Position
(Please Type or Print in Black Ink)

Div: Program:

Date: _____

I. PERSONAL HISTORY

Name in Full (Last, First, Middle)	List College Degree(s) Already Received or Pursuing, Major, School, and Month/Year:

Marital Status: ☐ Single ☐ Engaged ☐ Married ☐ Separated ☐ Legally Separated ☐ Widowed ☐ Divorced

Birth Date (Month, Day, Year) Birth Place:	Social Security Number: (Optional)	Do you understand FBI employment requires availability for assignment anywhere in the U.S.?

Current Address

Street   Apt. No.

Home Phone _____
                                                              Area Code   Number
Work Phone _____
City   State   Zip Code   Area Code   Number

Are you: CPA ☐ Yes ☐ No   Licensed Driver ☐ Yes ☐ No   U. S. Citizen ☐ Yes ☐ No

Have you served on active duty in the U. S. Military? ☐ Yes ☐ No If yes, indicate branch of service and dates (month/year) of active duty. Include military school attendance (month/year):

How did you learn or become interested in FBI employment as a Special Agent?	Have you previously applied for FBI employment? ☐ Yes ☐ No If yes, location and date:

Do you have a foreign language background? ☐ Yes ☐ No   List proficiency for each language on reverse side.

Have you ever been arrested for any crime (include major traffic violations such as Driving Under the Influence or While Intoxicated, etc.)?
☐ Yes ☐ No If so, list all such matters on a continuation sheet, even if not formally charged, or no court appearance or found not guilty, or matter settled by payment of fine or forfeiture of collateral. Include date, place, charge, disposition, details, and police agency on reverse side.

II. EMPLOYMENT HISTORY

Identify your most recent three years FULL-TIME work experience, after high school (excluding summer, part-time and temporary employment).

From Month/Year	To Month/Year	Title of Position and Description of Work	# of hrs. Per week	Name/Location of Employer

III. PERSONAL DECLARATIONS

Persons with a disability who require an accommodation to complete the application process are required to notify the FBI of their need for the accommodation.

Have you used marijuana during the last three years or more than 15 times? ☐ Yes ☐ No

Have you used any illegal drug(s) or combination of illegal drugs, other than marijuana, more than 5 times or during the last 10 years? ☐ Yes ☐ No

All Information provided by applicants concerning their drug history will be subject to verification by a preemployment polygraph examination.

Do you understand all prospective FBI employees will be required to submit to an urinalysis for drug abuse prior to employment? ☐ Yes ☐ No
Please do not write below this line.

I am aware that willfully withholding information or making false statements on this application constitutes a violation of Section 1001. Title 18, U.S. Code and if appointed, will be the basis for dismissal from the Federal Bureau of Investigation. I agree to these conditions and I hereby certify that all statements made by me on this application are true and complete, to the best of my knowledge.

_____
Signature of applicant as usually written (**Do Not Use Nickname**)

FIGURE 5-13

Employment Application

Know Your *Employment* LAW   Mandatory Arbitration

Different federal courts have taken different positions on the enforceability of mandatory alternative dispute resolution clauses. The basic situation now is that mandatory arbitration agreements are generally enforceable.

However, managers should keep two things in mind. First, courts can strike down individual agreements based on their merits.[114] Second, mandatory arbitration can inhibit recruiting. In one study, 389 professional and executive MBA students read simulated employment brochures. Mandatory employment arbitration had a significantly negative impact on the attractiveness to the subjects of the company as a place to work. Emphasizing the availability of due process and just cause protections lessened this to some extent.[115]

Therefore, employers must create such agreements with care. For example, the agreement should be a signed and dated separate agreement. Use simple wording. Provide for reconsideration and judicial appeal if there is an error of law.[116] The employer must absorb most of the cost of the arbitration process. The arbitration process should be reasonably swift. The employee, if he or she prevails, should be eligible to receive the full remedies that he or she would have had if he or she had had access to the courts. Finally, spell out proper due process and provide for written decisions.

Using Application Forms to Predict Job Performance

It is possible to use application form information to predict which candidates will be successful and which won't, in much the same way that one might use tests for screening. The basic process involves conducting statistical studies to analyze the relationship between (1) biodata responses on the application form (distance from work, for instance) and (2) measures of success on the job.

Here it is important to choose the biodata items (such as "does not own automobile" or "not living at home") with two things in mind. First, of course, equal employment law limits the items you'll want to use (don't use age, race, or gender, for instance). And, non-invasive questions are best. In one study, subjects perceived items such as "dollar sales achieved," "received cash bonus for good job," and "grade point average in math" as legitimate, and not invasive. Other items such as "birth order," and "frequent dates as senior in high school" were more invasive, and unacceptable. Basically, the items that subjects perceived as less invasive were more verifiable, more transparent in purpose, and more impersonal.[117]

REVIEW

SUMMARY

1. Developing personnel plans requires three forecasts: one for personnel requirements, one for the supply of outside candidates, and one for the supply of inside candidates. To predict the need for personnel, first project the demand for the product or service. Next, project the volume of production required to meet these estimates; finally, relate personnel needs to these production estimates.

2. With personnel needs projected, the next step is to build a pool of qualified applicants. There are several sources of candidates, both internal (promotion from within)

and external (advertising, employment agencies, executive recruiters, college recruiting, the Internet, and referrals and walk-ins).

3. Remember that it is unlawful to discriminate against any individual with respect to employment because of race, color, religion, sex, national origin, or age (unless religion, sex, or origin are bona fide occupational qualifications).

4. The initial selection screening in most organizations begins with an application form. Most managers use these just to obtain background data. However, you can use application form data to make predictions about the applicant's future performance.

DISCUSSION QUESTIONS

1. What are the pros and cons of five sources of job candidates?
2. What are the four main types of information that application forms provide?
3. How, specifically, do equal employment laws apply to personnel recruiting activities?
4. What are five things employers should keep in mind when using Internet sites to find job candidates?
5. What are the five main things you would do to recruit and retain a more diverse workforce?

INDIVIDUAL AND GROUP ACTIVITIES

1. Working individually or in groups, bring to class several classified and display ads from the Sunday help wanted ads. Analyze the effectiveness of these ads using the guidelines discussed in this chapter.

2. Working individually or in groups, develop a five-year forecast of occupational market conditions for five occupations such as accountant, nurse, and engineer.

3. Working individually or in groups, visit the local office of your state employment agency. Come back to class prepared to discuss the following questions: What types of jobs seem to be available through this agency, predominantly? To what extent do you think this particular agency would be a good source of professional, technical, and/or managerial applicants? What sorts of paperwork are applicants to the state agency required to complete before their applications are processed by the agency? What other services does the office provide? What other opinions do you form about the state agency?

4. Working individually or in groups, find at least five employment ads, either on the Internet or in a local newspaper, that suggest that the company is family-friendly and should appeal to women, minorities, older workers, and single parents. Discuss what they're doing to be family-friendly.

5. Working individually or in groups, interview a manager between the ages of 25 and 35 at a local business who manages employees age 40 or older. Ask the manager to describe three or four of his or her most challenging experiences managing older employees.

6. The HRCI "Test Specifications" appendix at the end of this book (pages 726–735) lists the knowledge someone studying for the HRCI certification exam needs to have in each area of human resource management (such as in Strategic Management, Workforce Planning, and Human Resource Development). In groups of four to five students, do four things: (1) review that appendix now; (2) identify the material in this chapter that relates to the required knowledge the appendix lists; (3) write four multiple choice exam questions on this material that you believe would be suitable

for inclusion in the HRCI exam; and (4) if time permits, have someone from your team post your team's questions in front of the class, so the students in other teams can take each others' exam questions.

EXPERIENTIAL EXERCISE

The Nursing Shortage

As of March 2004, the U.S. economy was improving in many respects, but unemployment was still disappointingly high, and employers were still obviously holding back on their hiring. However, while many people were unemployed, that was not the case with nurse professionals. Virtually every hospital was aggressively recruiting nurses. Many were turning to foreign-trained nurses, for example, by recruiting nurses in the Philippines. Experts expected nurses to be in very short supply for years to come.

Purpose: The purpose of this exercise is to give you experience creating a recruitment program.

Required Understanding: You should be thoroughly familiar with the contents of this chapter, and with the nurse recruitment program of a hospital such as Lenox Hill Hospital in New York (see http://www.lenoxhillhospital.org/nursing/index.jsp and http://www.lenoxhillhospital.org/careers/joblist.jsp).

How to Set Up the Exercise/Instructions: Set up groups of four to five students for this exercise. The groups should work separately and should not converse with each other. Each group should address the following tasks:

1. Based on information available on the hospital's Web site, create a hard-copy ad for the hospital to place in the Sunday edition of the *New York Times*. Which (geographic) editions of the *Times* would you use, and why?
2. Analyze and critique the hospital's current online nurses' ad. How would you improve on it?
3. Prepare in outline form a complete nurses' recruiting program for this hospital, including all recruiting sources your group would use.

APPLICATION CASE

Finding People Who Are Passionate About What They Do

Trilogy Enterprises Inc., of Austin, Texas, is a fast-growing software company, and provides software solutions to giant global firms for improving sales and performance. It prides itself on its unique and unorthodox culture. Many of its approaches to business practice are unusual, but in Trilogy's fast-changing and highly competitive environment they seem to work.

There is no dress code and employees make their own hours, often very long. They tend to socialize together (the average age is 26), both in the office's well-stocked kitchen and on company-sponsored events and trips to places like local dance clubs and retreats in Las Vegas and Hawaii. An in-house jargon has developed, and the shared history of the eight-year-old firm has taken on the status of legend. Responsibility is heavy and comes early, with a "just do it now" attitude that dispenses with long apprenticeships. New recruits are given a few weeks of intensive training, known as Trilogy University and described by participants as "more like boot camp than business school." Information is delivered as if with "a fire hose," and new employees are expected to commit their expertise and vitality to everything they do. Jeff Daniel, director of college recruiting, admits the intense and unconventional firm is not the employer for everybody. "But it's definitely an environment where people who are passionate about what they do can thrive."

The firm employs about 700 such passionate people. Trilogy's managers know the rapid growth they seek depends on having a staff of the best people they can find, quickly trained and given broad responsibility and freedom as soon as possible. Founder and CEO Joe Liemandt says, "At a software company, people are everything. You can't build the next great software company, which is what we're trying to do here, unless you're totally committed to that. Of course, the leaders at every company say, 'People are everything.' But they don't act on it."

Trilogy makes finding the right people (it calls them "great people") a companywide mission. Recruiters actively pursue the freshest, if least experienced, people in the job market, scouring college career fairs and computer science departments for talented overachievers with ambition and entrepreneurial instincts. Top managers conduct the first rounds of interviews, letting prospects know they will be pushed to achieve but will be well rewarded. Employees take top recruits and their significant others out on the town when they fly into Austin for the standard, three-day preliminary visit. A typical day might begin with grueling interviews but end with mountain biking, roller blading, or laser tag. Executives have been known to fly out to meet and woo hot prospects who couldn't make the trip.

One year, Trilogy reviewed 15,000 résumés, conducted 4,000 on-campus interviews, flew 850 prospects in for interviews, and hired 262 college graduates, who account for over a third of its current employees. The cost per hire was $13,000; Jeff Daniel believes it was worth every penny.

Questions

1. Identify some of the established recruiting techniques that underlie Trilogy's unconventional approach to attracting talent.
2. What particular elements of Trilogy's culture most likely appeal to the kind of employees it seeks? How does it convey those elements to job prospects?
3. Would Trilogy be an appealing employer for you? Why or why not? If not, what would it take for you to accept a job offer from Trilogy?
4. What suggestions would you make to Trilogy for improving its recruiting processes?

Source: Chuck Salter, "Insanity, Inc.," *Fast Company*, January 1999, pp. 101–108; and www. trilogy.com/ sections/careers/work, accessed August 24, 2007.

CONTINUING CASE

Carter Cleaning Company

Getting Better Applicants

If you were to ask Jennifer and her father what the main problem was in running their firm, their answer would be quick and short: hiring good people. Originally begun as a string of coin-operated laundromats requiring virtually no skilled help, the chain grew to six stores, each heavily dependent on skilled managers, cleaner–spotters, and pressers. Employees generally have no more than a high school education (often less), and the market for them is very competitive. Over a typical weekend literally dozens of want ads for experienced pressers or cleaner–spotters can be found in area newspapers. All these people are usually paid around $15.00 per hour, and they change jobs frequently. Jennifer and her father are thus faced with the continuing task of recruiting and hiring qualified workers out of a pool of individuals they feel are almost nomadic in their propensity to move from area to area and job to job. Turnover in their stores (as in the stores of many of their competitors) often approaches 400%. "Don't talk to me about human resources planning and trend analysis," says Jennifer. "We're fighting an economic war and I'm happy just to be able to round up enough live applicants to be able to keep my trenches fully manned."

In light of this problem, Jennifer's father asked her to answer the following questions:

Questions

1. First, how would you recommend we go about reducing the turnover in our stores?
2. Provide a detailed list of recommendations concerning how we should go about increasing our pool of acceptable job applicants so we are no longer faced with the need of hiring almost anyone who walks in the door. (Your recommendations regarding the latter should include completely worded online and hard-copy advertisements and recommendations regarding any other recruiting strategies you would suggest we use.)

TRANSLATING STRATEGY INTO HR POLICIES AND PRACTICES CASE: THE HOTEL PARIS

The New Recruitment Process

The Hotel Paris's competitive strategy is "To use superior guest service to differentiate the Hotel Paris properties, and to thereby increase the length of stay and return rate of guests, and thus boost revenues and profitability." HR manager Lisa Cruz must now formulate functional policies and activities that support this competitive strategy, by eliciting the required employee behaviors and competencies.

As a longtime HR professional, Lisa Cruz was well aware of the importance of effective employee recruitment. If the Hotel Paris didn't get enough applicants, it could not be selective about who to hire. And, if it could not be selective about who to hire, it wasn't likely that the hotels would enjoy the customer-oriented employee behaviors that the company's strategy relied on. She was therefore disappointed to discover that the Hotel Paris was paying virtually no attention to the job of recruiting prospective employees. Individual hotel managers slapped together help wanted ads when they had positions to fill, and no one in the chain had any measurable idea of how many recruits these ads were producing or which recruiting approaches worked the best (or worked at all). Lisa knew that it was time to step back and get control of the Hotel Paris's recruitment function.

As they reviewed the details of the Hotel Paris's current recruitment practices, Lisa Cruz and the firm's CFO became increasingly concerned. What they found, basically, was that the recruitment function was totally unmanaged. The previous HR director had simply allowed the responsibility for recruiting to remain with each separate hotel, and the hotel managers, not being human resources professionals, usually took the path of least resistance when a job became available, such as by placing help wanted ads in their local papers. There was no sense of direction from the Hotel Paris's headquarters regarding what sorts of applicants the company preferred, what media and alternative sources of recruits its managers should use, no online recruiting, and no measurement at all of recruitment process effectiveness. The company ignored recruitment-source metrics that other firms used effectively, such as number of qualified applicants per position, percentage of jobs filled from within, the offer-to-acceptance ratio, acceptance by recruiting source, turnover by recruiting source, and selection test results by recruiting source.

It was safe to say that achieving the Hotel Paris's strategic aims depended on the quality of the people that it attracted to and then selected for employment at the firm. "What we want are employees who will put our guests first, who will use initiative to see that our guests are satisfied, and who will work tirelessly to provide our guests with services that exceed their expectations" said the CFO. Lisa and the CFO both knew this process had to start with better recruiting. The CFO gave her the green light to design a new recruitment process.

Questions

1. Given the hotel's stated employee preferences, what recruiting sources would you suggest they use, and why?
2. What would a Hotel Paris help wanted ad look like?
3. How would you suggest they measure the effectiveness of their recruiting efforts?

KEY TERMS

employment or personnel planning, 166
trend analysis, 167
ratio analysis, 168
scatter plot, 168
computerized forecast, 169
qualifications inventories, 170
personnel replacement charts, 170
position replacement card, 170

employee recruiting, 172
recruiting yield pyramid, 176
job posting, 177
succession planning, 177
applicant tracking systems, 180
alternative staffing, 187
on demand recruiting services (ODRS), 190
application form, 197

ENDNOTES

1. "Help Wanted—and Found," *Fortune*, Oct 2, 2006, p. 40.
2. Bill Macaler and Jones Shannon, "Does HR Planning Improve Business Performance?" *Industrial Management*, January/February 2003, p. 20. See also, Michelle Harrison, et al., "Effective Succession Planning" *Training & Development*, October 2006, pp. 22–23.
3. Based on an idea in Elmer H. Burack and Robert D. Smith, *Personnel Management: A Human Resource Systems Approach* (St. Paul, MN: West, 1997), pp. 134–135. Reprinted by permission. Copyright 1997 by West Publishing Co. All rights reserved.
4. Macaler and Shannon, "Does HR Planning Improve Business Performance?" p. 16.
5. Glenn Bassett, "Elements of Manpower Forecasting and Scheduling," *Human Resource Management* 12, no. 3 (Fall 1973), pp. 35–43; Pat Sweet, "Model Future: Business Intelligence Software Is Giving Finance Directors the Time and Space to Think about the Future," *Accounting* 123 (March 1999), pp. 4–6.
6. For an example of a computerized, supply-chain-based personnel planning system, see Dan Kara, "Automating the Service Chain," *Software Magazine* 20 (June 2000), pp. 3, 42.
7. Shunyin Lam et al., "Retail Sales Force Scheduling Based on Store Traffic Forecasting," *Journal of Retailing* 74, no. 1 (Spring 1998), pp. 61–89.
8. John Markoff, "Bill Gates's Brain Cells, Dressed Down for Action," *New York Times*, March 25, 2001, pp. B1, B12.
9. This section is based on Ibid. See also, Bill Roberts, "Risky Business," *HR Magazine,* October 2006, pp. 69–72.
10. Jennifer Schramm, "A Worker Gap Ahead," *HR Magazine*, June 2003, p. 240.
11. "Employers Still in Recruiting Bind Should Seek Government Help, Chamber Suggests," *BNA Bulletin to Management*, May 29, 2003, pp. 169–170.
12. Tom Porter, "Effective Techniques to Attract, Hire, and Retain 'Top Notch' Employees for Your Company," *San Diego Business Journal* 21, no. 13 (March 27, 2000), p. b36.
13. Derek Avery and Patrick McKay, "Target Practice: An Organizational Impression Management Approach to Attracting Minority and Female Job Applicants," *Personnel Psychology,* 2006, vol. 59, pp. 157–189, p. 177.
14. Jonathan Segal, "Land Executives, Not Lawsuits," *HR Magazine*, October 2006, pp. 123–130.
15. Kenneth Sovereign, *Personnel Law* (Upper Saddle River, NJ: Prentice Hall, 1999), pp. 47–49.
16. Ibid., p. 48.
17. Ibid., p. 50.
18. Ibid., p. 51.
19. Michelle Martinez, "Recruiting Here and There," *HR Magazine*, September 2002, p. 95.
20. Ibid.
21. Jessica Marquez, "A Global Recruiting Site Helps Far-Flung Managers at the Professional Services Company Acquire the Talent they Need—and Saves One Half-Million Dollars a Year," *Workforce Management*, March 13, 2006, p. 22.
22. Kevin Carlson et al., "Recruitment Evaluation: The Case for Assessing the Quality of Applicants Attracted," *Personnel Psychology* 55 (2002), pp. 461–490.
23. Ibid., p. 461.

24. Ibid., p. 466.

25. Ibid., p. 466.

26. Ibid. See also, Diane Cadrain, "Mystery Shoppers Can Improve Recruitment," *HR Magazine*, November 2006, p. 26.

27. Thomas Stewart, "In Search of Elusive Tech Workers," *Fortune*, February 16, 1998, pp. 171–172.

28. Ibid., p. 171.

29. "Hiring Works the Second Time Around," *BNA Bulletin to Management*, January 30, 1997, p. 40.

30. Ibid.

31. Soonhee Kim, "Linking Employee Assessments to Succession Planning," *Public Personnel Management* 32, no. 4 (Winter 2003), pp. 533–547. See also, Michael Laff, "Talent Management: From Hire to Retire," *Training & Development*, November 2006, pp. 42–48.

32. Succession Management: Identifying and Developing Leaders," December 2003, vol. 21, no. 12, BNA Inc., 1231 25th St. NW Washington, DC 20037.

33. Quoted in Susan Wells, "Who's Next," *HR Magazine*, November 2003, p. 43.

34. See "Succession Management: Identifying and Developing Leaders," *BNA* 21, no. 12, (December 2003), p. 15.

35. Soonhee Kim, "Linking Employee Assessments to Succession Planning."

36. Bill Roberts, "Matching Talent with Tasks," *HR Magazine*, November 2002, pp. 91–96.

37. Ibid., p. 34.

38. Eric Krell, "Recruiting Outlook: Creative HR for 2003."

39. *Workforce Management,* December 2004, p. 98.

40. Sarah Gale, "Internet Recruiting: Better, Cheaper, Faster," *Workforce*, December 2001, p. 76.

41. Ibid.

42. Jennifer Berkshire, "Social Network Recruiting," *HR Magazine*, April 2005, pp. 95–98.

43. Ibid., p. 75.

44. Valerie Hoffman and Greg Davis, "OFCCP's Internet Applicant Definition Requires Overhaul of Recruitment and Hiring Policies," Legal Report, the Society for Human Resource Management, January/February 2006, p. 2.

45. Lisa Harpe, "Designing an Effective Employment Prescreening Program," *Employment Relations Today* 32, no. 3, Fall 2005, pp. 43–51.

46. William Dickmeyer, "Applicant Tracking Reports Make Data Meaningful," *Workforce*, February 2001, pp. 65–67.

47. Paul Gilster, "Channel the Resume Flood with Applicant Tracking Systems," *Workforce*, January 2001, pp. 32–34; Dickmeyer, "Applicant Tracking Reports," pp. 65–67.

48. Maria Seminerio, "E-Recruiting Takes Next Step," *The Week*, April 23, 2001, pp. 49–51.

49. Dawn Onley, "Improving Your Online Application Process," *HR Magazine*, 50, no. 10, October 2005, p. 109.

50. "Does Your Company's Website Click with Job Seekers?" *Workforce*, (August 2000), p. 260.

51. "Study Says Career Web Sites Could Snare More Job Seekers," *BNA Bulletin to Management*, February 1, 2001, p. 36.

52. Sarah Gale, "Internet Recruiting: Better, Cheaper, Faster," p. 75.

53. Daniel Feldman and Brian Klass, "Internet Job Hunting: A Field Study of Appliant Experiences with Online Recruiting," *Human Resource Management* 41, no. 2 (Summer 2002), pp. 175–192.

54. "Job Seekers Privacy Has Been Eroded with Online Job Searchers, Report Says," *BNA Bulletin to Management*, November 20, 2003, p. 369.

55. Erik Krell, "Recruiting Outlook: Creative HR for 2003," *Workforce*, December 2002, pp. 40–44.

56. Christopher Collins and Cynthia Stevens, "The Relationship Between Early Recruitment Related Activities and the Application Decisions of New Labor Market Entrants: A Brand Equity Approach to Recruitment," *Journal of Applied Psychology* 87, no. 6 (2002), pp. 1121–1133.

57. Find your nearest one stop center at www.servicelocator.org/.

58. Susan Saulney, "New Jobless Centers Offer More Than a Benefit Check," *New York Times*, September 5, 2001, p. A1.
59. Lynn Doherty and E. Norman Sims, "Quick, Easy Recruitment Help: From a State?" *Workforce*, May 1998, p. 36.
60. Ibid.
61. Robert Bohner Jr. and Elizabeth Salasko, "Beware the Legal Risks of Hiring Temps," *Workforce*, October 2002, pp. 50–57. See also, Fay Hansen, "A Permanent Strategy for Temporary Hires," *Workforce Management*, February 26, 2007, p. 27.
62. John Zappe, "Temp-to-Hire Is Becoming a Full-Time Practice at Firms," *Workforce Management*, June 2005, pp. 82–86.
63. Shari Caudron, "Contingent Workforce Spurs HR Planning," *Personnel Journal*, (July 1994), p. 60.
64. Carolyn Hirschman, "Are Your Contractors Legal?" *HR Magazine*, March 2004, pp. 59–63.
65. Ibid.
66. Daniel Feldman, Helen Doerpinghaus, and William Turnley, "Managing Temporary Workers: A Permanent HRM Challenge," *Organizational Dynamics* 23, no. 2 (Fall 1994), p. 49.
67. This is based on or quoted from Nancy Howe, "Match Temp Services to Your Needs," *Personnel Journal*, March 1989, pp. 45–51.
68. This section is based on Robyn Meredith, "Giant Sucking Sound," *Forbes*, September 29, 2003, vol. 172, issue 6, p. 158; Jim McKay, "Inevitable Outsourcing, Offshoring Stirred Passions at Pittsburgh Summit," *Knight Ridder/Tribune Business News*, March 11, 2004; Peter Panepento, "General Electric Transportation to Outsource Drafting Jobs to India," *Knight Ridder/Tribune Business News*, May 5, 2004; Julie Harbin, "Recent Survey Charts Execs' Willingness to Outsource Jobs," *San Diego Business Journal*, April 5, 2004, vol. 25, issue 14, pages 8–10; and Pamela Babcock, "America's Newest Export: White-Collar Jobs," *HR Magazine*, April 2004, vol. 49, no. 4, pp. 50–57.
69. Susan Wells, "Slow Times for Executive Recruiting," *HR Magazine*, April 2003, pp. 61–67.
70. "Search and Destroy," *Economist*, June 27, 1998, p. 63.
71. Ibid.
72. Ibid.
73. Jonathan Segal, "Strings Attached," *HR Magazine*, February 2005, pp. 119–123.
74. Michelle Martinez, "Working with an Outside Recruiter? Get It in Writing," *HR Magazine*, January 2001, pp. 98–105.
75. Bill Leonard, "Recruiting from the Competition," *HR Magazine*, February 2001, pp. 78–86.
76. Martha Frase-Blunt, "A Recruiting Spigot," *HR Magazine*, April 2003, pp. 71–79.
77. Sara Rynes, Marc Orlitzky, and Robert Bretz Jr., "Experienced Hiring Versus College Recruiting: Practices and Emerging Trends," *Personnel Psychology* 50 (1997), pp. 309–339. See also Lisa Munniksma, "Partnering with Collegiate Career Centers Offers Recruiters Access to Rich Source of Applicants," *HR Magazine*, 50, no. 2, February 2005, p. 93 FF.
78. Lisa Munniksma, "Career Matchmakers," *HR Magazine*, February 2005, pp. 93–96.
79. Joel Mullich, "Finding the Schools that Yield the Best Job Applicant ROI," *Workforce Management*, March 2004, pp. 67–68.
80. Wendy Boswell et al., "Individual Job Choice Decisions and the Impact of Job Attributes and Recruitment Practices: A Longitudinal Field Study," *Human Resource Management* 42, no. 1 (Spring 2003), pp. 23–37.
81. Roseanne Geisel, "Interns on the Payroll," *HR Magazine*, 49, no. 12, December 2004, p. 89 FF. And, "Internships Growing in Popularity Among Companies Seeking Fresh Talent and Ideas," *BNA Bulletin to Management*, March 20, 2007, pp. 89–90.
82. Michelle Martinez, "The Headhunter Within," *HR Magazine*, August 2001, pp. 48–56. See also, Jennifer Taylor Arnold, "Customers as Employees," *HR Magazine*, April 2007, pp. 77–82.
83. "Employee Referrals Improve Hiring," *BNA Bulletin to Management*, March 13, 1997, p. 88.
84. Ruth Thaler Carter, "Your Recruitment Advertising," *HR Magazine*, June 2001, pp. 93–100.
85. "Tell a Friend: Employee Referral Programs Earn High Marks for Low Recruiting Costs," *BNA Bulletin to Management*, June 28, 2001, p. 201.
86. Ibid., p. 13.

87. "The 2007 Recruiting Metrics and Performance Benchmark Report, 2nd ed.," Staffing.org, Inc., 2007.

88. Ann Marie Ryan and Nancy Tippins, "Attracting and Selecting: What Psychological Research Tells Us," *Human Resource Management*, Winter 2004, vol. 43, no. 4, p. 311.

89. "Help Wanted—and Found," *Fortune*, Oct 2, 2006, p. 40.

90. Sarah Gale, "The Bookstore Battle," *Workforce Management*, January 2004, pp. 51–56. See also David Allen et al., "Recruitment Communication Media: Impact on Prehire Outcomes," *Personnel Psychology*, 2004, vol. 57, pp. 143–171.

91. Quoted or paraphrased from Robert Neveu, "Making the Leap to Strategic Recruiting," special advertising supplement to *Workforce Management*, 2005, p. 3.

92. "Internship Programs Helps These Recruiters Toward Qualified Students with Disabilities," *BNA Bulletin to Management* (July 17, 2003), p. 225.

93. Unless otherwise noted, this section is based on Judith Casey and Marcie Pitt-Catsouphes, "Employed Single Mothers: Balancing Job and Home Life," *Employee Assistance Quarterly* 9, no. 324 (1994), pp. 37–53.

94. Ibid., p. 42.

95. Ibid., p. 48.

96. Ibid., p. 48.

97. Phaedra Brotherton, "Tapping into an Older Workforce," *Mosaics*, March/April 2000, Society for Human Resource Management.

98. Sue Shellenbarger, "Gray Is Good: Employers Make Efforts to Retain Older, Experienced Workers," the *Wall Street Journal*, December 1, 2005.

99. Allison Wellner, "Tapping a Silver Mine," *HR Magazine*, March 2002, p. 29.

100. Ibid.

101. For this and other examples here, see Robert Goddard, "How to Harness America's Gray Power," *Personnel Journal* (May 1987), p. 23.

102. Sue Shellenbarger, ibid.

103. Gary Adams and Barbara Rau, "Attracting Retirees to Apply: Desired Organizational Characteristics of Bridge Employment," *Journal of Organizational Behavior* 26, no. 6, September 2005, pp. 649–660.

104. Abby Ellin, "Supervising the Graybeards," *New York Times*, January 16, 2000, p. B16.

105. Susan Sweetser, "Women in Financial Services—An Ideal Match," *National Underwriter Life & Health—Financial Services Edition*, January 12, 2004, vol. 1, issue 2, pp. 14–16; Charles Lauer, "Keeping the Women on Board: Hospitals Must Work Overtime to Retain the Majority of their Employees," *Modern Health Care*, October 6, 2003, vol. 33, issue 40, p. 21.

106. "Recruitment: B&Q in Search of Female Managers," *Personnel Today*, September 2, 2003, p. 4; Dina Berta, "Brinker International's Gomez Keeps Recruitment of Women, Minorities on Company's Front Burner," *Nation's Restaurant News*, November 17, 2003, vol. 37, issue 46, p. 16.

107. "Welfare-to-Work: No Easy Chore," *BNA Bulletin to Management*, February 13, 1997, p. 56.

108. Herbert Greenberg, "A Hidden Source of Talent," *HR Magazine*, March 1997, pp. 88–91.

109. "Welfare to Work: No Easy Chore," p. 56.

110. Linda Moore, "Firms Need to Improve Recruitment, Hiring of Disabled Workers, EEO Chief Says," *Knight Ridder/Tribune Business News*, November 5, 2003, item 03309094.

111. Richard Donkin, "Making Space for a Wheelchair Workforce," *Financial Times*, November 13, 2003, p. 9.

112. "Students with Disabilities Available," *HR Briefing*, June 15, 2002, p. 5.

113. Moore, "Firms Need to Improve Recruitment."

114. "Supreme Court Denies Circuit Citiy's Bid for Review of Mandatory Arbitration," *BNA Bulletin to Management*, June 6, 2002, p. 177.

115. Douglas Mahoney, et al., "The Effects of Mandatory Employment Arbitration Systems on Applicants Attraction to Organizations," *Human Resource Management* 44, no. 4, Winter 2005, pp. 449–470.

116. "Supreme Court Gives the Employers Green Light to Hold Most Employees to Arbitration Pacts," *BNA Bulletin to Management*, March 29, 2001, pp. 97–98.

117. Fred Mael, Mary Connerley, and Ray Morath, "None of Your Business: Parameters of Biodata Invasiveness," *Personnel Psychology* 49 (1996), pp. 613–650.

6 Employee Testing and Selection

Google, Inc. recently changed its employee screening process. A few years ago, candidates went through a dozen or more grueling in person interviews. Then, the firm's selection team would routinely reject candidates with years of work experience if they had just average college grades. But, as Google's new head of human resources says, "Everything works if you're trying to hire 500 people a year, or 1000." Now, Google is hiring thousands of people per year, and can't be bogged down by such slow hiring process. They've lightened the interview load (down to about five on average) and, among other things, no longer put as much weight on college GPA as before. Other selection changes are in store.[1] •

After studying this chapter, you should be able to:

1. Explain what is meant by reliability and validity.
2. Explain how you would go about validating a test.
3. Cite and illustrate our testing guidelines.
4. Give examples of some of the ethical and legal considerations in testing.
5. List eight tests you could use for employee selection, and how you would use them.
6. Explain the key points to remember in conducting background investigations.

Chapter 5 focused on the methods managers use to build an applicant pool. The purpose of Chapter 6, Employee Testing and Selection, is to explain how to use various tools and techniques to select the best candidates for the job. The main topics we'll cover include the selection process, basic testing techniques, background and reference checks, ethical and legal questions in testing, types of tests, and work samples and simulations. In the following chapter, Interviewing Candidates, we turn to the techniques you can use to improve your skills with what is probably the most widely used screening tool, the selection interview.

WHY CAREFUL SELECTION IS IMPORTANT

Once you have a pool of applicants, the next step is to select the best candidates for the job. This usually means whittling down the applicant pool by using the screening tools explained in this chapter: tests, assessment centers, and background and reference checks. Then the prospective supervisor can interview likely candidates and decide who to hire.

Selecting the right employees is important for three main reasons: performance, costs, and legal obligations.

Performance   First, your own performance always depends in part on your subordinates. Employees with the right skills will do a better job for you and the company. Employees without these skills or who are abrasive or obstructionist won't perform effectively, and your own performance and the firm's will suffer. The time to screen out undesirables is before they are in the door, not after.

Cost   Second, it is important because it's costly to recruit and hire employees. Hiring and training even a clerk can cost $5,000 or more in fees and supervisory time. The total cost of hiring a manager could easily be 10 times as high once you add search fees, interviewing time, reference checking, and travel and moving expenses.

Legal Obligations   Third, it's important because of two legal implications of incompetent hiring. First, (as we saw in Chapter 2), equal employment laws require nondiscriminatory selection procedures for protected groups.

Second, courts will find the employer liable when employees with criminal records or other problems use access to customers' homes (or similar opportunities) to commit crimes. Lawyers call hiring workers with such backgrounds, without proper safeguards, **negligent hiring**.[2] In one case, *Ponticas v. K.M.S. Investments*, an apartment manager with a passkey entered a woman's apartment and assaulted her. The court found the apartment complex's owner negligent in not properly checking the manager's background. When lawyers recently sued Wal-Mart alleging that several employees with convictions for sexually related offenses had assaulted young girls, Wal-Mart instituted a new program of criminal background checks for qualified candidates.[3]

Negligent hiring highlights the need to think through what the job's human requirements really are.[4] For example, "nonrapist" isn't likely to appear as a required knowledge, skill, or ability in a job analysis of an apartment manager, but in situations like this screening for such tendencies is obviously required.[5]

Avoiding negligent hiring claims requires taking "reasonable" action to investigate the candidate's background. This includes:

- Making a systematic effort to gain relevant information about the applicant, and verifying all documentation;
- Scrutinizing all information supplied by the applicant, and following up on unexplained gaps in employment;

negligent hiring
Hiring workers with questionable backgrounds without proper safeguards.

- Keeping a detailed log of all attempts to obtain information, including names and dates for phone calls or other requests;
- Rejecting applicants who make false statements of material facts or who have conviction records for offenses directly related and important to the job in question;
- Balancing the applicant's privacy rights with others' "need to know," especially when you discover damaging information;
- Taking immediate disciplinary action if problems arise.[6]

BASIC TESTING CONCEPTS

1 Explain what is meant by reliability and validity.

Selection is thus important. We'll start with testing. A test is basically a sample of a person's behavior. Using a test (or other selection tool) assumes the device is both reliable and valid.

Reliability

reliability

The consistency of scores obtained by the same person when retested with the identical tests or with alternate forms of the same test.

Reliability is a test's first requirement and refers to its consistency: "A reliable test is one that yields consistent scores when a person takes two alternate forms of the test or when he or she takes the same test on two or more different occasions."[7]

Reliability is very important. If a person scores 90 on an intelligence test on a Monday and 130 when retested on Tuesday, you probably wouldn't have much faith in the test.

There are several ways to estimate consistency or reliability. You could administer the same test to the same people at two different points in time, comparing their test scores at time two with their scores at time one; this would be a *retest estimate*. Or you could administer a test and then administer what experts believe to be an equivalent test later; this would be an *equivalent form estimate*. The Scholastic Assessment Test (SAT) is an example of the latter.

A test's internal consistency is another reliability measure. For example, a psychologist includes 10 items on a test of vocational interests, believing that they all measure, in various ways, the test taker's interest in working outdoors. You administer the test and then statistically analyze the degree to which responses to these 10 items vary together. This would provide a measure of the internal reliability of the test. Psychologists refer to this as an *internal comparison estimate*. Internal consistency is one reason that you find apparently repetitive questions on some test questionnaires.

Many things could cause a test to be unreliable. For example, the questions may do a poor job of sampling the material; test one focuses more on Chapters 1, 3, 5, and 7, while test two focuses more on Chapters 2, 4, 5, and 8. Or there might be errors due to changes in the testing conditions; for instance, the room the test is in next month may be noisy.

Validity

Reliability, while indispensable, only tells you that the test is measuring something consistently. It does not prove that you are measuring what you intend to measure. A mismanufactured 33-inch yardstick will consistently tell you that 33-inch boards are 33 inches long. Unfortunately, if what you're looking for is a board that is one full yard long, then your 33-inch yardstick, though reliable, is misleading you by 3 inches.

What you need is a valid yardstick. Validity tells you whether the test (or yardstick) is measuring what you think it's supposed to be measuring.[8]

A test, as we said, is a sample of a person's behavior, but some tests are more clearly representative of the behavior being sampled than others. A typing test, for example, clearly corresponds to an on-the-job behavior. At the other extreme, there may be no apparent relationship between the items on the test and the behavior. This is the case with projective personality tests. Thus, in the Thematic Apperception Test illustrated in Figure 6-1, the psychologist asks the person to explain how he or she interprets an ambiguous picture. The

FIGURE 6-1

Sample Picture Card from Thematic Apperception Test

How do you interpret this picture?

Source: Reprinted by permission of the publishers from Henry A. Murray, THEMATIC APPERCEPTION TEST, Plate 12F, Cambridge, Mass: Harvard University Press, 1943.

psychologist uses that interpretation to draw conclusions about the person's personality and behavior. In such tests, it is more difficult to prove that the tests are measuring what they are said to measure, in this case some trait of the person's personality—that they're valid.

test validity

The accuracy with which a test, interview, and so on measures what it purports to measure or fulfills the function it was designed to fill.

Test Validity   Test validity answers the question, "Does this test measure what it's supposed to measure?" Put another way, *validity* refers to the correctness of the inferences that we can make based on the test. For example, if Jane gets a higher score on a mechanical comprehension tests than Jim,[9] can we be sure that Jane possesses more mechanical comprehension than Jim? With employee selection tests, *validity* often refers to evidence that the test is job related—in other words, that performance on the test is a valid predictor of subsequent performance on the job. A selection test must be valid since, without proof of validity, there is no logical or legally permissible reason to continue using it to screen job applicants. You would not be too comfortable taking the GRE, if you didn't think that your score on the GRE predicted, in some valid way, your likely performance in graduate school. Equal employment law calls for use of valid tests (see the feature on page 217). In employment testing, there are two main ways to demonstrate a test's validity: **criterion validity** and **content validity**.[10]

criterion validity

A type of validity based on showing that scores on the test (predictors) are related to job performance (criterion).

Criterion Validity   Demonstrating criterion validity means demonstrating that those who do well on the test also do well on the job, and that those who do poorly on the test do poorly on the job. Thus, the test has validity to the extent that the people with higher test scores perform better on the job. In psychological measurement, a *predictor* is the measurement (in this case, the test score) that you are trying to relate to a *criterion*, like performance on the job. The term *criterion validity* reflects that terminology.

content validity

A test that is content valid is one that contains a fair sample of the tasks and skills actually needed for the job in question.

Content Validity   Employers demonstrate the *content validity* of a test by showing that the test constitutes a fair sample of the content of the job. The basic procedure here is to identify job tasks that are critical to performance, and then randomly select a sample of those tasks to be tested. In selecting students for dental school, many schools give applicants chunks of chalk, and ask them to carve something that looks like a tooth. If the content you choose for the test is a representative sample of what the person needs to know for the job, then the test is probably content valid. Clumsy dental students need not apply.

Demonstrating content validity sounds easier than it is in practice. Demonstrating that (1) the tasks the person performs on the test are really a comprehensive and random sample of the tasks performed on the job, and (2) the conditions under which the person takes the test resemble the work situation is not always easy. For many jobs, employers opt to demonstrate other evidence of a test's validity—most often, criterion validity.

2 Explain how you would go about validating a test.

How to Validate a Test

In order for a selection test to be useful, you should be fairly sure test scores relate in a predictable way to performance on the job. Thus, other things being equal, students who score high on the graduate admissions tests also do better in graduate school. Applicants who score high on a mechanical comprehension test perform better as engineers. In other words, you should validate the test before using it by ensuring that scores on the test are a good predictor of some *criterion* like job performance. (In other words, demonstrate the test's *criterion validity*.)

This validation process is usually done by an industrial psychologist. The human resource department coordinates the effort. The supervisor's role is to describe the job and its requirements so that the human requirements of the job and its performance standards are clear to the psychologist. The validation process consists of five steps: analyze the job, choose your tests, administer the tests, relate the test scores and the criteria, and cross-validate and revalidate.

Step 1: Analyze the Job The first step is to analyze the job and write job descriptions and job specifications. Here, you need to specify the human traits and skills you believe are required for adequate job performance. For example, must an applicant be verbal, a good talker? Is programming required? Must the person assemble small, detailed components? These requirements become the predictors. These are the human traits and skills you believe predict success on the job.

In this first step, you also must define what you mean by "success on the job," since it's this success for which you want predictors. The standards of success are criteria. You could focus on production-related criteria (quantity, quality, and so on), personnel data (absenteeism, length of service, and so on), or judgments of worker performance (by persons like supervisors). For an assembler's job, your predictors might include manual dexterity and patience. Specific criteria then might include quantity produced per hour and number of rejects produced per hour.

Some employers make the mistake of carefully choosing predictors (such as manual dexterity) while virtually ignoring the question of how they're going to measure performance (the criteria). One study involved 212 gas utility company employees. The researchers found a significant relationship between the test battery that was used as a predictor and two performance criteria—supervisor ratings of performance and objective productivity indices. However, there was virtually no relationship between the same test battery and two other criteria, namely an objective quality index or employee self-ratings.[11]

Step 2: Choose the Tests Next, choose tests that you think measure the attributes (predictors, such as mechanical comprehension) important for job success. Employers usually base this choice on experience, previous research, and "best guesses." They usually don't start with just one test. Instead, they choose several tests and combine them into a test battery. The test battery aims to measure an array of possible predictors, such as aggressiveness, extroversion, and numerical ability.

FIGURE 6-2

Examples of Web Sites Offering Information on Tests or Testing Programs

- www.hr-guide.com/data/G371.htm
  Provides general information and sources for all types of employment tests.
- http://ericae.net/
  Provides technical information on all types of employment and nonemployment tests.
- www.ets.org/testcoll
  Provides information on over 20,000 tests.
- www.kaplan.com/
  Information from Kaplan test preparation on how various admissions tests work.
- www.assessments.biz
  One of many firms offering employment tests.

What tests are available and where do you get them? Given the EEO and ethical issues involved, the best advice is probably to use a professional, such as a licensed industrial psychologist. However, many firms publish tests. Psychological Assessment Resources, Inc., in Odessa, Florida, is typical. It publishes and distributes many tests; some are available to virtually any purchaser, but many are available only to qualified buyers (such as those with degrees in psychology or counseling). Figure 6-2 presents several Web sites that provide information about tests or testing programs.

Some companies publish employment tests that are generally available to anyone. For example, Wonderlic Personnel Test, Inc., publishes a well-known intellectual capacity test, and also other tests, including technical skills tests, aptitude test batteries, interest inventories, and reliability inventories. G. Neil Company of Sunrise, Florida, offers employment testing materials including, for example, a clerical skills test, telemarketing ability test, service ability test, management ability test, team skills test, and sales abilities test. Again, though, don't let the widespread availability of personnel tests blind you to this important fact: You should use the tests in a manner consistent with equal employment laws, and in a manner that is ethical and protects the test taker's privacy. We'll return to this point in a moment.

Step 3: Administer the Test   Next, administer the selected test(s) to employees. You have two choices here. One option is to administer the tests to employees presently on the job. You then compare their test scores with their current performance; this is *concurrent validation*. Its main advantage is that data on performance are readily available. The disadvantage is that current employees may not be representative of new applicants (who of course are really the ones for whom you are interested in developing a screening test). Current employees have already had on-the-job training and have been screened by your existing selection techniques.

Predictive validation is the second and more dependable way to validate a test. Here you administer the test to applicants before you hire them. Then hire these applicants using only existing selection techniques, not the results of the new tests. After they have been on the job for some time, measure their performance and compare it to their earlier test scores. You can then determine whether you could have used their performance on the new test to predict their subsequent job performance.

Step 4: Relate Your Test Scores and Criteria   The next step is to ascertain if there is a significant relationship between scores (the predictor) and performance (the criterion). The usual way to do this is to determine the statistical relationship between (1) scores on the test and (2) job performance using correlation analysis, which shows the degree of statistical relationship.

FIGURE 6-3

Expectancy Chart

Note: This expectancy chart shows the relation between scores made on the Minnesota Paper Form Board and rated success of junior draftspersons.

Example: Those who score between 37 and 44 have a 55% chance of being rated above average and those scoring between 57 and 64 have a 97% chance.

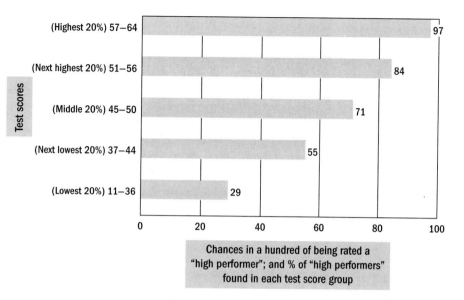

Chances in a hundred of being rated a "high performer"; and % of "high performers" found in each test score group

expectancy chart

A graph showing the relationship between test scores and job performance for a group of people.

If there is a correlation between test and job performance, you can develop an **expectancy chart**. This presents the relationship between test scores and job performance graphically. To do this, split the employees into, say, five groups according to test scores, with those scoring the highest fifth on the test, the second highest fifth, and so on. Then compute the percentage of high job performers in each of these five test score groups and present the data in an expectancy chart like that in Figure 6-3. In this case, someone scoring in the top fifth of the test has a 97% chance of being rated a high performer, while one scoring in the lowest fifth has only a 29% chance of being rated a high performer.[12]

Step 5: Cross-Validate and Revalidate   Before putting the test into use, you may want to check it by cross-validating, by again performing steps 3 and 4 on a new sample of employees. At a minimum, an expert should revalidate the test periodically. (Also see the Employment Law feature, page 217.)

Content Validation   The procedure you would use to demonstrate content validity differs from that used to demonstrate criterion validity (as described in steps 1 through 5). Content validity tends to emphasize judgment. Here, you first do a careful job analysis to identify the work behaviors required. Then combine several samples of those behaviors into a test. A typing and computer skills test for a clerk would be an example. The fact that the test is a comprehensive sample of actual, observable, on-the-job behaviors is what lends the test its content validity. Table 6-1 summarizes important testing guidelines such as "use tests as supplements."

❸ Cite and illustrate our testing guidelines.

Research Insight: Face Validity   What determines perceived test fairness?[13] Following good test practices—a quiet test-taking environment, privacy, and so on—is important.[14] Another factor is the obviousness of the link between the test and performing the job (in other words, the test's "face validity"). In one study, 259 college students from France and the United States rated the "favorability" of 10 selection procedures, and then specified what prompted them to rate some procedures as more favorable than others.[15] The "perceived face validity of the selection procedure was the strongest correlate of favorability reactions among both samples."[16] Students' reactions were highly favorable toward interviews and work sample tests, both of which had obvious links to the job

TABLE 6-1 Testing Program Guidelines

1. *Use tests as supplements.* Don't make tests your only selection tool; use them to supplement other tools like interviews and background checks.

2. *Validate the tests.* It's best to validate them in your own organization. However, the fact that the same tests have proven valid in similar organizations—called validity generalization—is usually adequate.

3. *Monitor your testing/selection program.* Ask questions such as, "What proportions of minority and nonminority applicants are rejected at each stage of the hiring process?" and "Why am I using this test—what does it mean in terms of actual behavior on the job?"

4. *Keep accurate records.* Record why you rejected each applicant. A general note such as "not sufficiently well qualified" is not enough. Your reasons for rejecting the person may be subject to validation at a later date.

5. *Use a certified psychologist.* Developing, validating, and using selection standards (including tests) generally require a qualified psychologist. Most states require persons who offer psychological services to the public to be certified or licensed. A Ph.D. degree (the bachelor's degree is never sufficient) is usually one qualification. Potential consultants should provide evidence of similar work and experience in test validation, and demonstrate familiarity with federal and state equal rights laws and regulations.

6. *Manage test conditions.* Administer tests in areas that are reasonably private, quiet, well lighted, and ventilated, and make sure all applicants take the tests under the same test conditions. Once completed, keep test results confidential. Give them only to individuals with a legitimate need for the information and the ability to understand and interpret the scores (including the applicant). Train your supervisors regarding test results confidentiality.

7. *Revalidate periodically.* Employers' needs and applicants' aptitudes change over time. You should have your testing program revalidated periodically.

itself. They were moderately favorable toward biographical information and written ability tests. Favorability reactions were neutral toward personality and honesty tests, and negative toward graphology. In general, reactions were more favorable when the students felt the employer had the right to obtain information with a particular technique, and when the procedure was widely used in industry. It may therefore sometimes make sense to substitute one valid test for another, if the new one comes across as more fair.[17] Amongst other things, fairness in selection is important because "applicants who hold positive perceptions about selection are more likely to view the organization favorably and report stronger intentions to accept job offers and recommend the employer to others."[18]

Test Takers' Individual Rights and Test Security

Give examples of some of the ethical and legal considerations in testing.

Test takers have rights to privacy and information under the American Psychological Association's (APA) standard for educational and psychological tests; these guide psychologists but are *not* legally enforceable. Test takers have the right to:

- The confidentiality of test results.
- The right to informed consent regarding use of these results.
- The right to expect that only people qualified to interpret the scores will have access to them, or that sufficient information will accompany the scores to ensure their appropriate interpretation.
- The right to expect the test is fair to all. For example, no one taking it should have prior access to the questions or answers.

Know Your Employment LAW — Equal Employment Opportunity Aspects of Testing

As explained in Chapter 2, various laws bar discrimination with respect to race, color, age, religion, sex, disability, and national origin. For example, a federal court recently ruled that Dial Corp discriminated against female job applicants at a meatpacking facility by requiring employees to take a preemployment strength test. The test had a disparate impact on women. Furthermore, there appeared to be no compelling need for strength on the job.[19] With respect to testing, the laws boil down to this: Once the plaintiff shows that one of your selection procedures has an *adverse impact* on his or her protected class, you must demonstrate the validity and selection fairness of the allegedly discriminatory test or item. Adverse impact means there is a significant discrepancy between rates of rejection of members of the protected groups and others. You must then be able to prove (1) that your tests are related to success or failure on the job (validity), and (2) that your tests don't unfairly discriminate against minority or nonminority subgroups.

Alternatives

Assume that you've used a test and that a rejected minority candidate has demonstrated adverse impact to the satisfaction of a court. (One way is to show that the selection rate for, say, the applicant's racial group, was less than four-fifths of that for the group with the highest selection rate.)

The employer would then have three alternatives with respect to its testing program. One is to institute a different, valid selection procedure that does not have an adverse impact. The second is to show that the test is valid—in other words, that it is a valid predictor of performance on the job. Ideally, you would do this by conducting your own validation study. In any event, the plaintiff would then have to prove that your explanation for using the test is inadequate.

A third alternative—in this case aimed at avoiding adverse impact rather than responding to it—is to monitor the selection test to see if it has disparate (adverse) impact. If not, it's generally permissible to use the device, even if it's not valid—but why would you want to?

Employers can't avoid EEO laws just by avoiding tests: EEO guidelines and laws apply to all selection devices, including interviews, applications, and references. You could have to prove the validity, fairness, and job relatedness of any screening or selection tool that has an adverse impact on a protected group.[20]

A complete discussion of the APA's "Ethical Principles of Psychologists and Code of Conduct" is beyond the scope of this book, but a summary of some of its headings helps to illustrate its concerns. Main subject headings include: competence; integrity; respect for people's dignity; concern for others' welfare; social responsibility; maintaining expertise; nondiscrimination; sexual harassment; personal problems and conflicts; avoiding harm; misuse of psychologists' influence; multiple relationships; exploitation of relationships; delegation to and supervision of subordinate; competence and appropriate use of assessments and interventions; obsolete tests; maintaining confidentiality; minimizing intrusions on privacy; confidential information and databases; familiarity with the ethics code; conflicts between ethics and organizational demands; and reporting ethical violations.[21]

Legal Privacy Issues   There are also privacy protections embedded in U.S. and common law. At the federal level, certain U.S. Supreme Court decisions do protect individuals from intrusive governmental action in a variety of contexts.[22] Furthermore, the Federal Privacy Act gives federal employees the right to inspect personnel files, and limits the disclosure of personnel information without the employee's consent, among other things.[23]

The common law of torts provides some protection against disclosing information about employees to people outside the company. The main application here involves defamation (either libel or slander). If your employer or former employer discloses information that is false and defamatory and that causes you serious injury, you may be able to sue for defamation of character.[24] Even if true, courts may view it as invasive and find for the plaintiff. Guidelines to follow here include:

1. Train your supervisors regarding the importance of employee confidentiality.[25]
2. Adopt a "need to know" policy. For example, if an employee has been rehabilitated after a period of drug use and that information is not relevant to his or her functioning in the workplace, then a new supervisor may not "need to know."
3. Disclose procedures. If you know your firm can't keep information—such as test results—confidential, you may limit your liability by disclosing that fact before testing. For example, if employees who test positive on drug tests will have to use the firm's employee assistance program, explain that before giving the tests.

Using Tests at Work

Many employers use selection tests. For example, about 41% of companies the American Management Association surveyed tested applicants for basic skills (defined as the ability to read instructions, write reports, and do arithmetic adequate to perform common workplace tasks).[26] About 67% of the respondents required employees to take job skills tests, and 29% required some form of psychological measurement.[27] To see what such tests are like, try the short test in Figure 6-4 to find out how prone you might be to on-the-job accidents.

CHECK YES OR NO   YES   NO

1. You like a lot of excitement in your life.

2. An employee who takes it easy at work is cheating on the employer.

3. You are a cautious person.

4. In the past three years you have found yourself in a shouting match at school or work.

5. You like to drive fast just for fun.

Analysis: According to John Kamp, an industrial psychologist, applicants who answered no, yes, yes, no, no to questions 1, 2, 3, 4, and 5 are statistically likely to be absent less often, to have fewer on-the-job injuries, and, if the job involves driving, to have fewer on-the-job driving accidents. Actual scores on the test are based on answers to 130 questions.

FIGURE 6-4

Sample Test

Source: Courtesy of NYT Permissions.

Tests are not just for lower-level workers. For example, Barclays Capital gives graduate and undergraduate job candidates aptitude tests instead of first-round interviews.[28] In general, as work demands increase (as represented by increasing skill requirements, training, and pay), employers tend to rely more on testing methods in the selection process.[29]

Employers don't use tests just to find good employees, but also to screen out bad ones. By some estimates, 75% of employees have stolen from their employers at least once; 33% to 75% have engaged in behaviors such as theft, vandalism, and voluntary absenteeism; almost 25% say they've had knowledge of illicit drug use among co-workers; and 7% of a sample of employees reported being victims of physical threats.[30] Occupational fraud and abuse reportedly cost U.S. employers about $400 billion annually, or about nine dollars per day per employee or 6% of annual revenues.[31] No wonder prudent employers test their applicants. The accompanying feature addresses gender related testing issues.

Outback Steakhouse   Testing isn't just for large employers. For example, Outback Steakhouse (which now has over 45,000 employees) began using preemployment tests in 1991, just two years after the company started. The testing is apparently quite successful. While annual turnover rates for hourly employees may reach 200% in the restaurant industry, Outback's turnover ranges from 40 to 60%. Outback is looking for employees who are highly social, meticulous, sympathetic, and adaptable, and uses a test to screen out applicants who don't fit the Outback culture. This personality assessment test is part of a three-step preemployment interview process. Applicants take the test, and managers then compare the candidates' results to the profile for Outback Steakhouse employees. Those who score low on certain traits (like compassion) don't move to the next step. Those who do, move on to be interviewed by two managers. The latter focus on behavioral questions such as "What would you do if a customer asked for a side dish we don't have on the menu?"[32]

Test Scoring   Tests come from test publishers, who provide various services to facilitate the testing process. Automated scoring and test interpretation is one such service. Some tests, such as the 16PF personality profile, must be professionally scored and interpreted. The 16PF is a 187-item personality profile psychologists use to measure management characteristics including creativity, independence, leadership, and self-control. Wonderlic, Inc., lets an employer administer the 16PF. The employer then faxes (or scans) the answer

The NEW *Workforce*   Gender Issues in Testing

Employers using selection tests should know that gender issues may distort the results. TV commercials for children's toys attest to the fact that gender-role socialization is a continuing reality. In particular, parents and others often socialize girls into traditionally female roles and boys into traditionally male roles. There is thus a "continuing overrepresentation of women in a small number of 'pink collar' jobs such as waitress and secretary and in the traditionally female professions, including nursing, teaching, and social work," and a continuing underrepresentation in traditional male areas such as engineering and the sciences. Such stereotypes are changing. One recent study found that both male and female managers "are rating women more as leaders than they did 15 and 30 years ago."[33]

Yet gender-role socialization does influence men's and women's test results. For example, it can influence the occupational interests for which candidates express a preference. Males tend to score higher on aptitude tests in what some view as male fields (such as mechanical reasoning). The test results may thus ironically perpetuate the narrowing of females' career options.

sheet to Wonderlic, which scores the candidate's profile and faxes (or scans) back the interpretive report in one day. Today, psychologists also easily score many psychological tests, including the MMPI personality test, online or using interpretive Windows-based software. Many tests, like the Wonderlic Personnel Test, the manager easily scores him or herself.

Computerized and Online Testing

Computerized testing is increasingly replacing conventional paper-and-pencil and manual tests. Many firms such as FedEx-Kinko's have applicants take online or offline computerized tests—sometimes by phone, using the touch-tone keypad, sometimes online—to quickly prescreen applicants prior to more in-depth interviews and background checks.[34] Service firms like Unicru process and score online preemployment tests from employers' applicants. The applicant tracking programs we discussed in chapter 5, often include an online prescreening test.[35]

Most of the tests we describe on the next pages are available in computerized form. These include numerical ability tests, reading comprehension tests, and clerical comparing and checking tests. Automated in-basket tests require job candidates to deal with a "virtual inbox" comprised of e-mails, phone calls, and documents and folders, to assess the candidates' decision-making and problem-solving skills. Candidates for architectural certification solve online architectural problems, for instance, designing building layouts to fit specified space constraints.[36]

City Garage Example   City Garage, a 200-employee chain of 25 auto service and repair shops in Dallas-Fort Worth, implemented a computerized testing program to improve its operations. The original hiring process consisted of a paper-and-pencil application and one interview, immediately followed by a hire/don't hire decision. The result was high turnover, and too few managers to staff new stores. This inhibited the firm's growth strategy.

City Garage's top managers' solution was to purchase the Personality Profile Analysis online test from Dallas-based Thomas International USA. Doing so added a third step to the application and interview process. After a quick application and background check, likely candidates take the 10-minute, 24-question PPA. City Garage staff then enter the answers into the PPA Software system, and test results are available in less than two minutes. These show whether the applicant is high or low in four personality characteristics; it also produces follow-up questions about areas that might cause problems. For example, applicants might be asked how they've handled possible weaknesses such as lack of patience in the past. If candidates answer those questions satisfactorily, they're asked back for extensive, all-day interviews, after which hiring decisions are made. The new process seems to have improved City's financial performance considerably.

Capital One Example   Several years ago, Capital One financial was using three paper-and-pencil tests for preemployment screening: a cognitive skills test, a math test, and a biodata job history test (which the firm used to predict job stability).[37] The process was time-consuming and inefficient: "In Tampa, we were having to process several thousand people a month just to hire 100," says a company officer. The company's new online system eliminates the paper-and-pencil process. Call center applicants working online

Person taking a Web-based employment test.

complete the application and the upgraded math and biodata tests (which might include number of years on last job, and distance from the nearest Capital One office, for instance). They also take an online role-playing call simulation. They put on a headset, and the program plays seven different customer situations. Applicants (playing the role of operators) answer multiple choice questions online as to how they would respond. The company is in the process of expanding its online preemployment testing program to the United Kingdom and France.

⑤ List eight tests you could use for employee selection, and how you would use them.

TYPES OF TESTS

We can conveniently classify tests according to whether they measure cognitive (mental) abilities, motor and physical abilities, personality and interests, or achievement.[38]

Tests of Cognitive Abilities

Cognitive tests include tests of general reasoning ability (intelligence) and tests of specific mental abilities like memory and inductive reasoning.

Intelligence Tests   Intelligence (IQ) tests are tests of general intellectual abilities. They measure not a single trait but rather a range of abilities, including memory, vocabulary, verbal fluency, and numerical ability.

Originally, IQ (intelligence quotient) was literally a quotient. The procedure was to divide a child's mental age (as measured by the intelligence test) by his or her chronological age, and then multiply the results by 100. If an 8-year-old child answered questions as a 10-year-old might, his or her IQ would be 10 divided by 8, times 100, or 125.

For adults, of course, the notion of mental age divided by chronological age wouldn't make sense. Therefore, an adult's IQ score is actually a derived score. It reflects the extent to which the person is above or below the "average" adult's intelligence score.

Intelligence is often measured with individually administered tests like the Stanford-Binet Test or the Wechsler Test. Employers can administer other IQ tests such as the Wonderlic to groups of people. Other intelligence tests include the Kaufman Adolescent and Adult Intelligence Test, the Slosson Intelligence Test, the Wide Range Intelligence Test, and the Comprehensive Test of Nonverbal Intelligence.

Specific Cognitive Abilities   There are also measures of specific mental abilities, such as inductive and deductive reasoning, verbal comprehension, memory, and numerical ability.

Psychologists often call such tests *aptitude tests*, since they purport to measure aptitude for the job in question. Consider the Test of Mechanical Comprehension in Figure 6-5, which tests the applicant's understanding of basic mechanical principles. It may reflect a person's aptitude for jobs—like that of machinist or engineer—that require

---

FIGURE 6-5

Type of Question Applicant Might Expect on a Test of Mechanical Comprehension

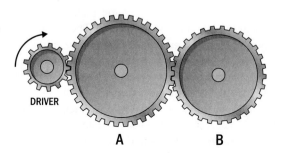

DRIVER

A   B

Which gear will turn the same way as the driver?

mechanical comprehension. Other tests of mechanical aptitude include the Mechanical Reasoning Test and the SRA Test of Mechanical Aptitude. The revised Minnesota Paper Form Board Test consists of 64 two-dimensional diagrams cut into separate pieces. It provides insights into an applicant's mechanical spatial ability; you'd use it for screening applicants for jobs such as designers, draftspeople, or engineers.

Tests of Motor and Physical Abilities

You might also want to measure motor abilities, such as finger dexterity, manual dexterity, and (if hiring pilots) reaction time. The Crawford Small Parts Dexterity Test is an example. It measures the speed and accuracy of simple judgment as well as the speed of finger, hand, and arm movements. Other tests here include the Stromberg Dexterity Test, the Minnesota Rate of Manipulation Test, and the Purdue Peg Board. The Roeder Manipulative Aptitude Test screens individuals for jobs where dexterity is a main requirement.

Tests of physical abilities may also be required. These include static strength (such as lifting weights), dynamic strength (like pull-ups), body coordination (as in jumping rope), and stamina.[39] Lifeguards, for example, must show they can swim a course before they're hired.

Measuring Personality and Interests

A person's cognitive and physical abilities alone seldom explain his or her job performance. Other factors, like motivation and interpersonal skills, are very important. As one consultant put it, most people are hired based on qualifications, but most are fired for nonperformance. And nonperformance (or performance) "is usually the result of personal characteristics, such as attitude, motivation, and especially, temperament."[40] Today, even some online dating services, like eHarmony.com, have prospective members take online personality tests, and reject those who its software judges are unmatchable.[41]

Employers use personality tests to measure and predict such intangibles. For example, as part of its selection process for CEO candidates, Hewlett-Packard put its eventual choice, Carleton Fiorina, and other finalists through a two-hour, 900-question personality test. Candidates had to indicate whether statements like "When I bump into a piece of furniture, I usually get angry" were true or false.[42] (A few years later, the board of directors asked Fiorina to resign.)

What Personality Tests Measure   Personality tests measure basic aspects of an applicant's personality, such as introversion, stability, and motivation.

Many of these tests are *projective*. The psychologist presents an ambiguous stimulus (like an ink blot or clouded picture) to the person. The person must then interpret or react to it. Since the pictures are ambiguous, the person supposedly projects into the picture his or her own emotional attitudes. A security-oriented person might describe the woman in Figure 6-1 (page 212) as "My mother worrying about what I'll do if I lose my job." Other projective techniques include Make a Picture Story (MAPS), House-Tree-Person (H-T-P), and the Forer Structured Sentence Completion Test.

Other personality tests are not projective. The Guilford-Zimmerman survey measures personality traits like emotional stability versus moodiness, and friendliness versus criticalness. The Minnesota Multiphasic Personality Inventory (MMPI) taps traits like hypochondria and paranoia. The Interpersonal Style Inventory is a self-report inventory composed of 300 true/false items covering scales such as sociable, sensitive, deliberate, stable, conscientious, trusting, and directive. Wonderlic's Personal Characteristics Inventory measures five personality dimensions, and links these dimensions to likely job performance. The manager administers this test, and scans or faxes it to Wonderlic. They

FIGURE 6-6

Sample Personality Test Items

Source: Elaine Pulakos, *Selection Assessment Methods*, SHRM Foundation, 2005, p. 9. Reprinted by permission of Society for Human Resource Management via Copyright Clearance Center.

It does not make sense to work hard on something if no one will notice.
- a. Definitely true
- b. Somewhat true
- c. Neither true nor false
- d. Somewhat false
- e. Definitely false

I tend to let others do most of the talking in conversations.
- a. Definitely ture
- b. Somewhat true
- c. Neither true nor false
- d. Somewhat false
- e. Definitely false

I have remained calm in situations where others have become upset.
- a. Definitely true
- b. Somewhat true
- c. Neither true nor false
- d. Somewhat false
- e. Definitely false

score it and return the report the same day. The Sales Achievement Predictor creates a report showing the person's percentile rank on scales such as "sales disposition" and "sales closing," and rates him or her as highly recommended, recommended, or not recommended for sales. You'll find sample personality tests online at www.psychtests.com. Figure 6-6 presents sample personality test items.

The "Big Five"   Industrial psychologists often emphasize the "big five" personality dimensions as they apply to personnel testing: extraversion, emotional stability/neuroticism, agreeableness, conscientiousness, and openness to experience.[43]

> Neuroticism represents a tendency to exhibit poor emotional adjustment and experience negative effects, such as anxiety, insecurity, and hostility. Extraversion represents a tendency to be sociable, assertive, active, and to experience positive effects, such as energy and zeal. Openness to experience is the disposition to be imaginative, nonconforming, unconventional, and autonomous. Agreeableness is the tendency to be trusting, compliant, caring, and gentle. Conscientiousness is comprised of two related facets: achievement and dependability.[44]

In one study, extraversion, conscientiousness, and openness to experience were strong predictors of leadership.[45] In another "big five" study, neuroticism was negatively related to motivation, while conscientiousness was positively related to it.[46] Components of the "big five"—in particular, extraversion and openness to experience—also correlate with career interests and occupational types.[47] And, "in personality research, conscientiousness has been the most consistent and universal predictor of job performance."[48]

Researchers in one study defined career success in terms of intrinsic success (job satisfaction) and extrinsic success (income and occupational status). Conscientiousness positively predicted both intrinsic and extrinsic career success. Neuroticism negatively predicted extrinsic success. (General mental ability also positively predicted extrinsic career success.)[49]

Caveats   Personality tests—particularly the projective type—are the most difficult tests to evaluate and use. An expert must analyze the test taker's interpretations and reactions and infer from them his or her personality. The usefulness of such tests for selection assumes that you can find a relationship between a measurable personality trait (like introversion) and success on the job. Measuring aberrant behavior is a particular challenge. For instance, personality tests may help predict if an employee's erratic behavior will pose a threat to workplace safety. However, they can also create legal problems—for instance, if rejected candidates claim the results are false or violate the Americans with Disabilities Act.[50] The Seventh U.S. Circuit Court of Appeals recently held that the MMPI is a medical test insofar as it can screen out applicants perceived to have a psychological impairment, so its use before an employment offer violates the ADA.[51]

Effectiveness   The difficulties notwithstanding, personality tests can help employers improve screening.[52] For example, three researchers concluded: "Personality constructs are indeed associated with work performance, with some traits such as conscientiousness predicting success across jobs. Other traits are correlated with specific [performance] criteria or specific occupations. For example, extraversion correlates with success in sales and management jobs, as well as with training performance."[53] The responsibility, socialization, and self-control scales of the California Psychological Inventory predicted dysfunctional job behaviors among law enforcement officers.[54] Emotional stability, extroversion, and agreeableness predicted whether expatriates would leave their overseas assignments early.[55] At another firm, employee testing predicted employee theft.[56]

A recent review of personality testing reached several conclusions. Employers are making increased use of personality testing. The weight of the evidence is that personality measures (and particularly the big five) contribute to predicting job performance. And, employers can reduce the possibility of personality test faking, by warning applicants that faking may reduce the chances of the person being hired.[57]

interest inventory
A personal development and selection device that compares the person's current interests with those of others now in various occupations so as to determine the preferred occupation for the individual.

Interest Inventories   **Interest inventories** compare your interests with those of people in various occupations. Thus, a person who takes the Strong-Campbell Interests Inventory would receive a report comparing his or her interests to those of people already in occupations like accounting, engineering, or management.

Such inventories have many uses. One example is career planning, since a person will likely do better in jobs that involve activities in which he or she is interested. They can also be useful as selection tools. Clearly, if you can select people whose interests are roughly the same as those of successful incumbents in the jobs for which you are recruiting, it is more likely that those applicants will be successful.

Achievement Tests

Achievement tests measure what a person has learned. Most of the tests you take in school are achievement tests. They measure your "job knowledge" in areas like economics, marketing, or human resources. Achievement tests are also popular at work. For example, the Purdue Test for Machinists and Machine Operators tests the job knowledge of experienced machinists with questions like, "What is meant by 'tolerance'?" Other tests are available for other occupations. In addition to job knowledge, achievement tests measure the applicant's abilities; a typing test is one example.

WORK SAMPLES AND SIMULATIONS

work samples
Actual job tasks used in testing applicants' performance.

With **work samples**, you present examinees with situations representative of the job for which they're applying, and evaluate their responses.[58] Experts consider these (and simulations like the assessment centers in this section) to be tests. However, they differ from most tests, because they measure job performance directly. For example, work samples for a cashier may include operating a cash register, and counting money; for a clerical position, work samples would include a typing test, and proofreading.[59]

Work Sampling for Employee Selection

work sampling technique

A testing method based on measuring performance on actual basic job tasks.

The **work sampling technique** tries to predict job performance by requiring job candidates to perform one or more samples of the job's basic tasks.

This approach has several advantages. It measures actual job tasks, so it's harder to fake answers. The work sample's content—the actual tasks the person must perform—is not as likely to be unfair to minorities as might a personnel test that possibly emphasized middle-class concepts and values.[60] Work sampling does not delve into the applicant's personality or psyche, so there's almost no chance of it being viewed as an invasion of privacy. Designed properly, work sampling tests also exhibit better validity than do other tests designed to predict performance.

Basic Procedure The basic procedure is to select a sample of several tasks crucial to performing the job, and to then test applicants on them.[61] An observer monitors performance on each task, and indicates on a checklist how well the applicant performs. Here is an example. In developing a work sampling test for maintenance mechanics, experts first listed all possible job tasks (like "install pulleys and belts" and "install and align a motor"). Four crucial tasks were installing pulleys and belts, disassembling and installing a gearbox, installing and aligning a motor, and pressing a bushing into a sprocket.

They then broke down these four tasks into the steps required to complete them. Mechanics could perform each step in a slightly different way, of course. Since some approaches were better than others, the experts gave a different weight to different approaches.

Figure 6-7 shows one of the steps required for installing pulleys and belts—"checks key before installing." As the figure shows, possible approaches here include checking the key against (1) the shaft, (2) the pulley, or (3) neither. The right of the figure lists the weights (scores) reflecting the worth of each method. The applicant performs the task, and the observer checks off the approach used.

Management Assessment Centers

management assessment center

A simulation in which management candidates are asked to perform realistic tasks in hypothetical situations and are scored on their performance. It usually also involves testing and the use of management games.

To select promotable managers, The Cheesecake Factory created its Professional Assessment and Development Center at its California headquarters. Candidates spend two days of exercises, simulations, and classroom learning to see if they have the skills for key management positions.[62] A **management assessment center** is a two- to three-day simulation in which 10 to 12 candidates perform realistic management tasks (like making presentations) under the observation of experts who appraise each candidate's leadership potential. The center itself may be a plain conference room, but it is often a special room with a one-way mirror to facilitate observation. Typical simulated exercises include:

- *The in-basket.* These exercises confront the candidate with an accumulation of reports, memos, notes of incoming phone calls, letters, and other materials collected in the actual or computerized in-basket of the simulated job he or she is about to start. The candidate must take appropriate action on each item. Trained evaluators then review the candidate's efforts.
- *Leaderless group discussion.* Trainers give a leaderless group a discussion question and tell members to arrive at a group decision. They then evaluate each group

FIGURE 6-7

Example of a Work Sampling Question

Checks key before installing against:	
—shaft	score 3
—pulley	score 3
—neither	score 1

Note: This is one step in installing pulleys and belts.

member's interpersonal skills, acceptance by the group, leadership ability, and individual influence.

- *Management games.* Participants solve realistic problems as members of simulated companies competing in a marketplace. They may have to decide, for instance, how to advertise and manufacture, and how much inventory to stock.
- *Individual presentations.* Trainers evaluate each participant's communication skills and persuasiveness by having each make an assigned oral presentation.
- *Objective tests.* A center typically includes tests of personality, mental ability, interests, and achievements.
- *The interview.* Most require an interview between at least one trainer and each participant, to assess the latter's interests, past performance, and motivation.

Supervisor recommendations usually play a big role in choosing center participants. Line managers usually act as assessors and typically arrive at their ratings through a consensus process.[63]

Effectiveness   Most experts view assessment centers as effective for selecting and promoting management candidates; the question is, are they worth their extra cost? They are expensive to develop, take much longer than conventional paper and pencil tests, require managers acting as assessors, and often require psychologists. One recent study of 40 police candidates found that such centers are worth the extra cost: "Assessment center performance shows a unique and substantial contribution to the prediction of future police work success, justifying the usage of such method." In this study, peers' evaluations of candidates during the center proved especially useful.[64]

Video-Based Situational Testing

situational test
A test that require examinees to respond to situations representative of the job.

video-based simulation
A situational test in which examinees respond to video simulations of realistic job situations.

Situational tests require examinees to respond to situations representative of the job. Work sampling (discussed above), and some assessment center tasks are examples, as are video-based tests (described next), and the situational interviews in Chapter 7.[65]

The typical **video-based simulation** presents the candidate with several online or PC-based videos scenarios, each followed by a multiple choice question. The scenario might depict an employee handling a situation on the job. At a critical moment, the scenario ends and the video asks the candidate to choose from several courses of action. For example:

(*A manager is upset about the condition of the department and takes it out on one of the department's employees.*)

Manager: Well, I'm glad you're here.

Associate: Oh? Why is that?

Manager: Look at this place, that's why! I take a day off and come back to find the department in a mess. You should know better.

Associate: But I didn't work late last night.

Manager: Maybe not. But there have been plenty of times before when you've left this department in a mess.

(*The scenario stops here.*)
If you were this associate, what would you do?
a. Let the other associates responsible for the mess know that you had to take the heat.
b. Straighten up the department, and try to reason with the manager later.
c. Suggest to the manager that he talk to the other associates who made the mess.
d. Take it up with the manager's boss.[66]

Results suggest that video-based situational tests can be useful for selecting employees.[67]

The Miniature Job Training and Evaluation Approach

miniature job training and evaluation
Training candidates to perform several of the job's tasks, and then evaluating the candidates' performance prior to hire.

Miniature job training and evaluation means training candidates to perform several of the job's tasks, and then evaluating the candidates' performance prior to hire. The approach assumes that a person who demonstrates that he or she can learn and perform the sample of tasks will be able to learn and perform the job itself.

Honda Example   When Honda decided to build a new plant in Alabama, it had to hire thousands of new employees in an area where few people worked in manufacturing. Honda began running help wanted ads. The ad sought applicants for a free training program Honda was offering as a precondition for applying for jobs at the new plant. Applicants had to have at least a high school diploma or GED, employment for the past two years with no unexplainable gaps, and Alabama residency. Soon 18,000 people had applied.

Honda and the Alabama state employment agency first screened the applications by eliminating those who lacked the education or experience, and then gave preference to applicants near the plant. About 340 applicants per six-week session received special training at a new facility about 15 miles from the plant, two evenings a week. It included classroom instruction, watching videos of current Honda employees in action, and actually practicing particular jobs. Some candidates who watched the videos dropped out when they saw the work's pace.

The training sessions enabled special assessors from the Alabama state agency to scrutinize the trainees' work and to rate them. They then invited those who graduated to apply for jobs at the plants. Honda teams, consisting of employees from HR and departmental representatives, do the final screening. They interview the candidates, review their training records, and decide which ones to hire. New employees get a one-time drug test, but there are no other paper-and-pencil tests or credentials required. New hires get a three-day orientation. Then, assistant managers in each department coordinate their actual day-to-day training.[68]

Employers such as Honda train and then have applicants perform several of the jobs tasks, and then evaluate the candidates before hiring them.

Pros and Cons The miniature job training approach tests applicants with actual samples of the job, so it's inherently content relevant and valid. The big problem is the expense involved in the individual instruction and training.

The "When You're on Your Own" feature shows how a manager who's on his or her own in a large company can apply these testing concepts and tools.

Realistic Job Previews

Sometimes, a dose of realism makes the best screening tool. For example, Wal-Mart found that associates who quit within the first 90 days did so because of conflict in their schedules

When You're on Your OWN
HR for Line Managers and Entrepreneurs
Employee Testing and Selection

The Manager

An irony of being a manager in even the largest company is that, when it comes to screening employees, you're often on your own. Some large firms' human resource departments may work with the hiring manager to design and administer screening tools. But in many of these firms, human resources does little more than some pre-screening (for instance, administering typing tests to clerical applicants), and background checks and drug and physical exams.

What should you do if you are, say, the marketing manager, and want to screen some of your job applicants more formally? It is possible to devise your own test battery, but caution is required. Purchasing and then using packaged intelligence tests or psychological tests or even tests of mechanical ability could be a problem. Doing so may violate company policy, raise questions of validity, and even expose your employer to EEO liability.

A preferred approach is to devise and use screening tools, the face validity of which is obvious. The work sampling test we discussed is one example. It's not unreasonable for the marketing manager to ask an advertising applicant to spend an hour designing an ad, or to ask a marketing research applicant to spend a half hour outlining a marketing research program for a hypothetical product.

However, even with relatively trouble-free tests like these, the hiring manager needs to keep the guidelines we discussed in mind. In particular, you should protect the test taker's privacy, take steps to ensure that the person's rights are protected, and endeavor to ensure that the tests you devise are indeed a valid sample of the job.

The Small Business Owner

For the small business, one or two hiring mistakes could wreak havoc. A formal testing program is thus advisable.

Some tests are so easy to use they are particularly good for smaller firms. One is the *Wonderlic Personnel Test*, which measures general mental ability. With questions somewhat similar to the SAT, it takes less than 15 minutes to administer the four-page booklet. The tester reads the instructions, and then keeps time as the candidate works through the 50 problems on the two inside sheets. The tester scores the test by totaling the number of correct answers. Comparing the person's score with the minimum scores recommended for various occupations shows whether the person achieved the minimally acceptable score for the type of job in question. The *Predictive Index* is another example. It measures work-related personality traits, drives, and behaviors—in particular dominance, extroversion, patience, and blame avoidance—on a two-sided sheet. A template makes scoring simple. The Predictive Index program includes 15 standard personality patterns. For example, there is the "social interest" pattern, for a person who is generally unselfish, congenial, persuasive, patient, and unassuming. This person would be good with people and a good personnel interviewer, for instance.

Computerized testing programs are especially useful for small employers. For example, many employers rely on informal typing tests when hiring office help. A better approach is to use a program like the Minnesota Clerical Assessment Battery published by Assessment Systems Corporation. It runs on a PC, and includes a typing test, proofreading test, filing test, business vocabulary test, business math test, and clerical knowledge test.

TABLE 6-2 Evaluation of Assessment Methods on Four Key Criteria

Assessment Method	Validity	Adverse Impact	Costs (Develop/ Administer)	Applicant Reactions
Cognitive ability tests	High	High (against minorities)	Low/low	Somewhat favorable
Job knowledge test	High	High (against minorities)	Low/low	More favorable
Personality tests	Low to moderate	Low	Low/low	Less favorable
Biographical data inventories	Moderate	Low to high for different types	High/low	Less favorable
Integrity tests	Moderate to high	Low	Low/low	Less favorable
Structured interviews	High	Low	High/high	More favorable
Physical fitness tests	Moderate to high	High (against females and older workers)	High/high	More favorable
Situational judgment tests	Moderate	Moderate (against minorities)	High/low	More favorable
Work samples	High	Low	High/high	More favorable
Assessment centers	Moderate to high	Low to moderate, depending on exercise	High/high	More favorable
Physical ability tests	Moderate to high	High (against females and older workers)	High/high	More favorable

Note: There was limited research evidence available on applicant reactions to situational judgment tests and physical ability tests. However, because these tests tend to appear very relevant to the job, it is likely that applicant reactions to them would be favorable.

Source: Elaine Pulakos, *Selection Assessment Methods*, SHRM Foundation, 2005, p. 17. Reprinted by permission of Society for Human Resource Management via Copyright Clearance Center.

or because they preferred to work in another geographic area. The firm then began explicitly explaining and asking about work schedules and work preferences.[69] One study even found that some applicants accepted jobs with the intention to quit, a fact that more realistic interviewing might have unearthed.[70]

Summary

Table 6-2 summarizes the validity and cost, and potential adverse impact of several popular selection of assessment methods.

BACKGROUND INVESTIGATIONS AND OTHER SELECTION METHODS

[6] Explain the key points to remember in conducting background investigations.

Testing is usually only part of an employer's selection process. Other tools may include background investigations and reference checks, preemployment information services, honesty testing, graphology, and substance abuse screening.

Background Investigations and Reference Checks

Most employers try to check and verify the job applicant's background information and references. In one survey of about 700 human resource managers, 87% said they conduct reference checks, 69% conduct background employment checks, 61% check employee criminal records, 56% check employees' driving records, and 35% sometimes or always check credit.[71] Commonly verified data include legal eligibility for employment (in compliance with immigration laws), dates of prior employment, military service (including discharge status), education, identification (including date of birth and address to confirm identity), county criminal records (current residence, last residence), motor vehicle record, credit, licensing verification, Social Security number; and reference checks.[72]

How deeply you search depends on the position you seek to fill. For example, a credit and education check would be more important for hiring an accountant than a groundskeeper. In any case, it is also advisable to periodically check, say, the credit ratings of employees (like cashiers) who have easy access to company assets, and the driving records of employees who routinely use company cars.

Aims   There are two main reasons to conduct preemployment background investigations and/or reference checks—to verify factual information provided by the applicant, and to uncover damaging information such as criminal records and suspended drivers' licenses.[73] Lying on one's application is not unusual. For example, BellSouth's security director estimates that 15% to 20% of applicants conceal a dark secret. As he says, "It's not uncommon to find someone who applies and looks good, and then you do a little digging and you start to see all sorts of criminal history."[74]

Even relatively sophisticated companies fall prey to criminal employees, in part because they haven't conducted proper background and reference checks. In Chicago, a major pharmaceutical firm discovered it had hired gang members in mail delivery and computer repair. The crooks were stealing close to a million dollars a year in computer parts, and then using the mail department to ship them to a nearby computer store they owned.[75] Thorough background checks might have prevented the losses.

Types of Background Checks   Most employers at least try to verify an applicant's current (or former) position and salary with his or her current (or former) employer by phone (assuming doing so was cleared with the candidate). Others call the applicant's current and previous supervisors to try to discover more about the person's motivation, technical competence, and ability to work with others (although many employers have policies against providing such information). Some employers get background reports from commercial credit rating companies. The latter can provide information about credit standing, indebtedness, reputation, character, and lifestyle. There are thousands of databases and sources for finding background information, including sex offender registries, workers' compensation histories, nurses' aid registries, and sources for criminal, employment, and educational histories.[76] Some employers ask for written references. Figure 6-8 shows a form used for phone references.

More employers are checking candidates' social networking sites' postings. One employer went to Facebook.com and found that a top candidate described his interests as smoking marijuana and shooting people. The student may have been kidding, but did not get the offer.[77]

Effectiveness   The background check is an inexpensive and straightforward way to verify factual information about the applicant, such as current and previous job titles, current salary range, dates of employment, and educational background. However, realistically, managers don't view reference letters as very useful. In one older study, only 12% replied that reference letters were "highly valuable," 43% called them "somewhat valuable," and 30% viewed them as having "little value," or (6%) "no value." Asked whether they preferred written or telephone references, 72% favored the telephone reference, because it allows a more candid assessment and provides a more personal exchange. In fact, reference letters ranked lowest—seventh out of seven—as selection tools. Ranked from top to

FIGURE 6-8

Reference Checking Form

Source: Society for Human Resource Management, © 2004. Reproduced with permission of Society for Human Resource Management in the Format Textbook via Copyright Clearance Center.

(Verify that the applicant has provided permission before conducting reference checks.)

Candidate
Name _____

Reference
Name _____

Company
Name _____

Dates of Employment
From: _____ To: _____

Position(s)
Held _____

Salary
History _____

Reason for
Leaving _____

Explain the reason for your call and verify the above information with the supervisor (including the reason for leaving)
_____
_____
_____

1. Please describe the type of work for which the candidate was responsible.
_____
_____

2. How would you describe the applicant's relationships with coworkers, subordinates (if applicable), and with superiors?
_____
_____

3. Did the candidate have a positive or negative work attitude? Please elaborate.
_____
_____

4. How would you describe the quantity and quality of output generated by the former employee?
_____
_____

5. What were his/her strengths on the job?
_____
_____

6. What were his/her weaknesses on the job?
_____
_____

7. What is your overall assessment of the candidate?
_____
_____

8. Would you recommend him/her for this position? Why or why not?
_____
_____

9. Would this individual be eligible for rehire? Why or why not?
_____
_____

Other comments?
_____
_____

bottom, the tools were interview, application form, academic record, oral referral, aptitude and achievement tests, psychological tests, and reference letters.[78]

One survey found that only 11% of respondents said the information they get about a candidate's violent or "bizarre" behavior is adequate. Fifty-four percent of the respondents said that they get inadequate information in this area. Of 11 types of information sought in background checks, only three were ranked by a majority of respondents as ones for which they received adequate information: dates of employment (96%), eligibility for rehire (65%), and job qualifications (56%). With regard to salary history, reasons for leaving a previous job, work habits, personality traits, human relations skills, special skills or knowledge, and employability, "fewer than half of HR managers responding to the survey said they were able to obtain adequate information."[79]

It's no secret why background checks often produce such useless information: legal issues loom large. Employers providing recommendations generally can't be successfully sued for defamation unless the employee can show "malice"—that is, ill will, culpable recklessness, or disregard of the employee's rights.[80] But the managers and companies providing the references understandably still don't want the grief. And, one U.S. Court of Appeals found that negative references may be adverse employment actions when they are retaliations for the employee having previously filed an EEOC claim.[81]

Legal Issues: Defamation   Federal laws that affect references include the Privacy Act of 1974 (which applies only to federal workers), the Fair Credit Reporting Act of 1970, the Family Education Rights and Privacy Act of 1974 (and Buckley Amendment of 1974), and the Freedom of Information Act of 1966. These laws give individuals and students (the Buckley Amendment) the right to know the nature and substance of information in their credit files and files with government agencies, and to review records pertaining to them from any private business that contracts with a federal agency. It is therefore quite possible that the person you're describing may be shown your comments.

Common law (and in particular the tort of defamation) applies to any information you supply. Communication is defamatory if it is false and tends to harm the reputation of another by lowering the person in the estimation of the community or by deterring other persons from associating or dealing with him or her. The rejected applicant has various legal remedies, including suing the source of the reference for defamation.[82] In one case, a court awarded a man $56,000 after he was turned down for a job because, among other things, the former employer called him a "character." In another, an employer fired four employees for "gross insubordination" after they disobeyed a supervisor's request to review their allegedly fabricated expense account reports. The jury found that the expense reports were honest. The employees then argued that although their employer didn't publicize the expense account matter to others, the employer should have known that the employees would have to admit the reason for their firing when explaining themselves to future employers. The court agreed and upheld jury awards to these employees totaling more than a million dollars. In another case, a manager who claimed he was wrongly accused of stealing from his former employer won $1.25 million in a slander suit.[83]

As if that's not enough, there are companies that, for a small fee, will call former employers on behalf of employees who believe they're getting bad references from the former employers. One supervisor left his job at a California telecommunications company, and thought his previous employer might bad-mouth him. He hired BadReferences.com to investigate. BadReferences.com (which uses trained court reporters for its investigations) found that a supervisor at the company suggested that the employee was "a little too obsessive, . . . and not comfortable with taking risks, or making big decisions." The former employee sued his previous employer, demanding an end to defamation and $45,000 in compensation.[84]

Legal Issues: Privacy   In any case, truth is not always a defense. Some states recognize common law as it applies to invasion of privacy. Employees can sue employers for disclosing to a large number of people true but embarrassing private facts about the employee. In invasion-of-privacy suits, truth is no defense.

One case involved a supervisor in a shouting match with an employee. The supervisor yelled out that the employee's wife had been having sexual relations with certain people. The employee and his wife sued the employer for invasion of privacy. The jury found the employer liable for invasion of the couple's privacy. It awarded damages to both of them, as well as damages for the couple's additional claim that the supervisor's conduct amounted to an intentional infliction of emotional distress.[85]

Supervisor Reluctance   Furthermore, realistically, many supervisors don't want to damage a former employee's chances for a job; others might prefer giving an incompetent employee good reviews if it will get rid of him or her. Even when checking references via phone, therefore, you have to be careful to ask the right questions. You must also try to judge whether the reference's answers are evasive and, if so, why.

Employer Guidelines   The net result is that most employers are very restrictive about who can give references, and what these people can say. As a rule, employers should ensure that only authorized managers provide information. Other suggested guidelines for defensible references include "Don't volunteer information," "Avoid vague statements," and "Do not answer trap questions such as, 'Would you rehire this person?'" In practice, many firms have a policy of not providing any information about former employees except for their dates of employment, last salary, and position titles.[86]

However, note that *not* disclosing relevant information can be dangerous, too. In one Florida case, an employee was fired for allegedly bringing a handgun to work. After his subsequent employer fired him (for absenteeism), he returned to the second company and shot a supervisor as well as the human resources director and three other people before taking his own life. The injured parties and the relatives of the murdered employees sued the original employer, who had provided the employee with a clean letter of recommendation. The letter stated his departure was not related to job performance, allegedly because that first employer didn't want to anger the employee over his firing.

Making Background Checks More Useful   So what is the prospective employer to do? Is there any way to obtain better information? Yes.

- First, include on the application form a statement for applicants to sign explicitly authorizing a background check, such as:

  I hereby certify that the facts set forth in the above employment application are true and complete to the best of my knowledge. I understand that falsified statements or misrepresentation of information on this application or omission of any information sought may be cause for dismissal, if employed, or may lead to refusal to make an offer and/or to withdrawal of an offer. I also authorize investigation of credit, employment record, driving record, and, once a job offer is made or during employment, workers' compensation background if required.

- Second, since telephone references apparently produce more candid assessments, it's probably best to rely on telephone references. Here use a form (as in Figure 6-8), and remember that you can probably get more accurate information regarding dates of employment, eligibility for rehire, and job qualifications than other background information (such as reasons for leaving a previous job).[87]
- Third, persistence and sensitivity to potential red flags improve results. For example, if the former employer hesitates or seems to qualify his or her answer when you ask,

"Would you rehire?" don't just go on to the next question. Instead, try to unearth what the applicant did to make the former employer pause.

- Fourth, use the references offered by the applicant as a source for other references. You might ask each of the applicant's references, "Could you please give me the name of another person who might be familiar with the applicant's performance?" In that way, you begin getting information from references who may be more objective, because they weren't referred directly by the applicant.
- Fifth, try to ask open-ended questions, such as, "How much structure does the applicant need in his/her work?" in order to get the references to talk more about the candidate.[88]

Using Preemployment Information Services

Numerous firms such as Hirecheck now provide employment screening services (see www.hirecheck.com). Firms like these use databases to accumulate information about matters such as workers' compensation and credit histories, and conviction and driving records. For example, a South Florida firm advertises that for under $50 it will do a criminal history report, motor vehicle/driver's record report, and (after the person is hired) a workers' compensation claims report history, plus confirm identity, name, and Social Security number.

There are two reasons to use caution when delving into an applicant's criminal, credit, and workers' compensation histories.[89] First (as discussed in Chapter 2), equal employment laws discourage or prohibit the use of such information in employee screening. For example, the ADA prohibits employers from making preemployment inquiries into the existence, nature, or severity of a disability. Therefore, asking about a candidate's previous workers' compensation claims before offering the person a job is usually unlawful. Similarly, asking about arrest records may be discriminatory.

Second, various federal and state laws govern how employers acquire and use applicants' and employees' background information. At the federal level, the Fair Credit Reporting Act is the main directive. In addition, at least 21 states impose their own requirements. Compliance with these laws essentially involves four steps, as follows:

Step 1: Disclosure and authorization Before requesting consumer or investigative reports from a consumer reporting agency, the employer must disclose to the applicant or employee that a report will be requested and that the employee/applicant may receive a copy.

Step 2: Certification The employer must certify to the reporting agency that the employer will comply with the federal and state legal requirements. (The reporting agency will generally provide the employer with a form for satisfying this requirement). The employer certifies, among other things, that the employer made the disclosures outlined above in step 1 and that it obtained written consent from the employee or applicant.

Step 3: Providing copies of reports Under federal law, the employer must provide copies of the report to the applicant or employee if adverse action (such as withdrawing an offer of employment) is contemplated. Under California law, applicants or employees must have the option of requesting a copy of the report regardless of action.

Step 4: Notice after adverse action After the employer provides the employee or applicant with copies of the consumer and investigative reports and a "reasonable period" has elapsed, the employer may take an adverse action (such as withdrawing an offer, or dismissing, or not promoting the applicant or employee). If the employer anticipates taking an adverse action, the employee or applicant must receive an adverse action notice. This notice contains information such as

TABLE 6-3 Collecting Background Information

Some suggestions for collecting background information include the following:

1. Check all applicable state laws.
2. Review the impact of federal equal employment laws.
3. Remember the Federal Fair Credit Reporting Act.
4. Do not obtain information that you're not going to use.
5. Remember that using arrest information will be highly suspect.
6. Avoid blanket policies (such as "we hire no one with a record of workers' compensation claims").
7. Use information that is specific and job related.
8. Keep information confidential and up to date.
9. Never authorize an unreasonable investigation.
10. Make sure you always get at least two forms of identification from the applicant.
11. Always require applicants to fill out a job application.
12. Compare the application to the résumé (people tend to be more imaginative on their résumés than on their application forms, where they must certify the information).
13. Particularly for executive candidates, include background checks of such things as involvement in lawsuits, and of articles about the candidate in local or national newspapers.
14. Separate the tasks of (1) hiring and (2) doing the background check (a recruiter or supervisor anxious to hire someone may cut corners when investigating the candidate's background).

Source: Adapted from Jeffrey M. Hahn, "Pre-Employment Services: Employers Beware?" *Employee Relations Law Journal* 17, no. 1 (Summer 1991), pp. 45–69; and Shari Caudron, "Who Are You Really Hiring?", *Workforce*, 81, no. 12 (November 2002), pp. 28–32.

the name, address, and telephone number of the consumer reporting agency; and a statement that the employee/applicant can dispute (with the consumer reporting agency) the report's accuracy or completeness.

The employee/applicant has various remedies under the applicable laws. For example, if the employer fails to provide the required notices and/or obtain the required consents, then the employee/applicant can sue the employer in federal or state court for damages.[90]

Table 6-3 summarizes suggestions for employers regarding the collection of background information. Top employee background checking providers include Kroll Background Screenings Group (www.Krollworldwide.com), Choicepoint (www.choicepoint.com), and First Advantage (www.FADV.com).[91]

The Polygraph and Honesty Testing

Some firms still use the polygraph (or lie detector) for honesty testing, although current law severely restricts its use. The polygraph is a device that measures physiological changes like increased perspiration. The assumption is that such changes reflect changes in emotional state that accompany lying.

Complaints about offensiveness plus grave doubts about the polygraph's accuracy culminated in the Employee Polygraph Protection Act of 1988. With a few exceptions, the law prohibits employers from conducting polygraph examinations of all job applicants and most employees. (Also prohibited under this law are other mechanical or electrical devices that attempt to measure honesty or dishonesty, including psychological stress evaluators and voice stress analyzers. Federal laws don't prohibit paper-and-pencil tests and chemical testing [as for drugs].)

Who Can Use the Polygraph Local, state, and federal government employers (including the FBI) can continue to use polygraph exams, but many local and state government

Employers can still use polygraph testing, but only under strictly limited circumstances.

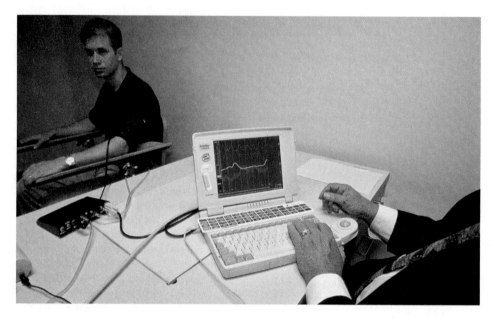

employers are further restricted under state laws. Other employers permitted to use polygraph tests include: industries with national defense or security contracts; certain businesses with nuclear-power-related contracts with the Department of Energy; businesses and consultants with access to highly classified information; those with counterintelligence-related contracts with the FBI or Department of Justice; and private businesses that are (1) hiring private security personnel, (2) hiring persons with access to drugs, or (3) doing ongoing investigations involving economic loss or injury to an employer's business, such as a theft.

Even in the case of ongoing investigations of theft, the law restricts employers' rights. To administer such a test during an ongoing investigation, an employer must meet four standards:

1. First, the employer must show that it suffered an economic loss or injury.
2. Second, it must show that the employee in question had access to the property.
3. Third, it must have a reasonable suspicion before asking the employee to take the polygraph.
4. Fourth, the employee must be told the details of the investigation before the test, as well as the questions to be asked on the polygraph test itself.

Paper-and-Pencil Honesty Tests   The virtual elimination of the polygraph as a screening device triggered a burgeoning market for paper-and-pencil honesty tests. These are psychological tests designed to predict job applicants' proneness to dishonesty and other forms of counterproductivity.[92] Most of these tests measure attitudes regarding things like tolerance of others who steal, acceptance of rationalizations for theft, and admission of theft-related activities. Tests include the Phase II profile. London House, Inc., and Stanton Corporation publish similar tests.[93] (see www.queendom.com/tests/career/honesty_access. html for an example.)

Psychologists initially raised concerns about the proliferation of paper-and-pencil honesty tests, but studies support these tests' validity. One study focused on 111 employees hired by a major retail convenience store chain to work at store or gas station counters.[94] The firm estimated that "shrinkage" equaled 3% of sales, and believed that internal theft accounted for much of this. Scores on an honesty test successfully predicted theft here, as measured by termination for theft. Subjects in another study included 329 federal prison inmates incarcerated for white-collar crime and 344 individuals from several midwestern firms employed in white-collar positions. Researchers administered the California Psychological Inventory (a personality inventory), the Employment Inventory (a second personality inventory), and a biodata scale. They concluded that "there are large and measurable psychological differences between white-collar offenders and nonoffenders . . ." and that it was possible to use a personality-based integrity test to differentiate between the two. One large-scale review of the use of such tests concluded that the "pattern of findings" regarding the usefulness of such tests "continues to be consistently positive."[95]

Some suggest that by possibly signaling mental illness, integrity tests may conflict with the Americans with Disabilities Act, but one review concludes these tests pose little such legal risk to employers.[96]

Honesty Testing Programs: What Employers Can Do   In practice, detecting dishonest candidates involves not just tests, but a comprehensive antitheft screening procedure:

- *Ask blunt questions.* [97] Ask direct questions in the face-to-face interview. For example, says one expert, there is nothing wrong with asking the applicant, "Have you ever stolen anything from an employer?" Other questions to ask include, "Have you recently held jobs other than those listed on your application?" "Have you ever been fired or asked to leave a job?" "What reasons would past supervisors give if they were asked why they let you go?" "Have past employers ever disciplined you or warned you about absences or lateness?" "Is any information on your application misrepresented or falsified?"
- *Listen, rather than talk.* Allow the applicant to do the talking so you can learn as much about the person as possible.
- *Do a credit check.* Include a clause in your application form that gives you the right to conduct background checks, including credit checks and motor vehicle reports.
- *Check all employment and personal references.*
- *Use paper-and-pencil honesty tests and psychological tests.*
- *Test for drugs.* Devise a drug-testing program and give each applicant a copy of the policy.
- *Establish a search-and-seizure policy and conduct searches.* Give each applicant a copy of the policy and require each to return a signed copy. The policy should state that all lockers, desks, and similar property remain the property of the company and may be inspected routinely.

The Adolf Coors Company uses a three-step honesty-screening program:

- First, it uses an outside lab to conduct a urinalysis test.
- Next, applicants take a Stanton Corporation paper-and-pencil survey on attitudes toward honesty and theft. Stanton provides a written report categorizing applicants by levels of risk.
- Finally, Equifax Services performs applicant references and background checks. These involve contacting previous employers and educational institutions.[98]

Honesty testing still requires some caution. Having just taken and "failed" what is fairly obviously an "honesty test," the candidate may leave the premises feeling his or her treatment was less than proper. Some "honesty" questions also pose invasion-of-privacy issues. And there are state laws to consider: For instance, Massachusetts and Rhode Island limit the use of paper-and-pencil honesty tests.

FIGURE 6-9

Handwriting Exhibit Used by Graphologist

Source: Kathryn Sackhein, *Handwriting Analysis and the Employee Selection Process* (New York: Quorum Books, 1990), p. 45. Reproduced with permission of Greenwood Publishing Group, Inc.

Graphology

Graphology refers to the use of handwriting analysis to determine the writer's basic personality traits. Graphology thus has some resemblance to projective personality tests, although graphology's validity is highly suspect.

In graphology, the handwriting analyst studies an applicant's handwriting and signature to discover the person's needs, desires, and psychological makeup. According to the graphologist, the writing in Figure 6-9 exemplifies "uneven pressure, poor rhythm, and uneven baselines." The variation of light and dark lines shows a "lack of control" and is "one strong indicator of the writer's inner disturbance."

Graphology's place in screening sometimes seems schizophrenic. Perhaps most importantly, studies suggest it is generally not valid, or that when graphologists do accurately size up candidates, it's because they are also privy to other background information. Yet some firms continue to use graphology—indeed, to swear by it. It tends to be bigger in Europe, where "countries like France or Germany have one central graphology institute, which serves as the certifying body."[99] Fike Corporation in Blue Springs, Missouri, a 325-employee maker of valves and other industrial products, uses profiles based on handwriting samples to design follow-up interviews. Sharon Stockham, senior human resources vice president for Exchange Bank in Santa Rosa, California, says her company "lives and dies" by handwriting analysis, using it as one element for screening officer candidates.[100]

Physical Exams

Once the employer extends the person a job offer, a medical exam is often the next step in the selection process (although it may also take place after the new employee starts work).

There are several reasons for preemployment medical exams. One is to verify that the applicant meets the physical requirements of the position; another is to discover any medical limitations you should take into account in placing the applicant. The exam will also establish a record and baseline of the applicant's health for future insurance or compensation claims. By identifying health problems, the examination can also reduce absenteeism and accidents and, of course, detect communicable diseases that may be unknown to the applicant.

In the largest firms, the employer's medical department performs the exam. Smaller employers retain the services of consulting physicians.

Under the Americans with Disabilities Act, a person with a disability can't be rejected for the job if he or she is otherwise qualified and can perform the essential job functions with reasonable accommodation. The ADA permits a medical exam during the period between the job offer and commencement of work if such exams are standard practice for all applicants for that job category.[101]

Substance Abuse Screening

Many employers conduct drug screenings. The most common practice is to test candidates just before they're formally hired. Many also test current employees when there is reason to believe the person has been using drugs—after a work accident, or in the presence of obvious behavioral symptoms such as chronic lateness or high absenteeism. Some firms routinely administer drug tests on a random or periodic basis, while others require drug tests when they transfer or promote employees to new positions.[102]

No drug test is foolproof. Some urine sample tests can't distinguish between legal and illegal substances; for example, Advil and Nuprin can produce positive results for marijuana. One medical review officer with health care provider Industrial Health Care, says "anyone" can go online and purchase drug-free samples to try to beat the tests.[103] In fact, "there is a swarm of products that promise to help employees (both male and female) beat drug tests."[104]

Other employers find such tests too personal, and use hair follicle testing. The method, radio-immunoassay of hair (RIAH), requires a small sample of hair, which the lab analyzes to detect prior ingestion of illicit drugs.[105] Hair follicle testing is less intrusive than urinalysis but can actually produce more personal information: A three-inch hair segment will record six months of drug use. And even here, classified ads advertise chemicals that can be added to specimens or rubbed on the scalp to fool the test.

Ethical Issues   Drug testing also raises ethical issues.[106] Unlike the roadside breathalizer tests given to inebriated drivers, urine and blood tests for drugs indicate only whether drug residues are present; they can't measure impairment or, for that matter, habituation or addiction.[107] Without strong evidence linking blood or urine drug levels to impairment, some argue that testing is not justifiable on the grounds of boosting workplace safety.[108] Many feel the testing procedures themselves are degrading and intrusive. Others argue that use of drugs during leisure hours might have little or no relevance to the job itself.[109] Many employers reasonably counter that they don't want drug-prone employees on their premises.

Legal Issues   Drug testing raises legal issues, too.[110] As one attorney writes, "It is not uncommon for employees to claim that drug tests violate their rights to privacy under common law or, in some states, a state statutory or constitutional provision."[111]

Several federal laws affect workplace drug testing. As one example, under the Americans with Disabilities Act, a court would probably consider a former drug user (who no longer uses illegal drugs and has successfully completed or is participating in a rehabilitation program) a qualified applicant with a disability.[112] Under the Drug Free Workplace Act of 1988, federal contractors must maintain a workplace free from illegal drugs. Under the U.S. Department of Transportation workplace regulations, firms with over 50 eligible employees in transportation industries must conduct alcohol testing on workers with sensitive or safety-related jobs. These include mass transit workers, air traffic controllers, train crews, and school bus drivers.[113] Other laws, including the Federal Rehabilitation Act of 1973 and various state laws, protect rehabilitating drug users or those who have a physical or mental addiction.

What to Do   What should an employer do when a job candidate tests positive? Most companies will not hire such candidates, and a few will immediately fire current employees who test positive. Current employees have more legal recourse. Employers must tell them the reason for dismissal if the reason is a positive drug test.[114]

However, particularly where sensitive jobs are concerned, courts tend to side with employers. In one case, the U.S. Court of Appeals for the First Circuit ruled that Exxon acted properly in firing a truck driver who failed a drug test. Exxon's drug-free workplace program included random testing of employees in safety-sensitive jobs. The employee drove a tractor-trailer carrying 12,000 gallons of flammable motor fuel and tested positive for cocaine. The union representing the employee challenged the firing, an arbitrator reduced the penalty to a two-month suspension. The appeals court reversed the arbitrator's decision. It ruled that the employer acted properly in firing the truck driver, given the circumstances.[115]

Complying with Immigration Law

Under the Immigration Reform and Control Act of 1986, employees hired in the United States must prove they are eligible to work in the United States. A person does not have to be a U.S. citizen to be employable. However, employers should ask a person they're about to hire whether he or she is a U.S. citizen or an alien lawfully authorized to work in the United States. To comply with this law, employers should follow procedures outlined in Figure 6-10.[116]

Proof Prospective employees can prove their eligibility for employment in two ways. One is to show a document such as a U.S. passport or alien registration card with photograph that proves both the person's identity and employment eligibility. Many prospective employees won't have either of these documents. So, the other way to verify employment eligibility is to see a document that proves the person's identity, along with a document showing the person's employment eligibility, such as a work permit.

Some documents may be fakes. For example, a few years ago INS agents seized over two million counterfeit documents ranging from green cards and Social Security cards to driver's licenses, from nine different states. The federal government is tightening restrictions on hiring undocumented workers. Realizing that many documents (such as Social Security cards) are faked, the government is putting the onus on the employers to make sure who they're hiring. The Department of Homeland Security recently began pressing criminal charges against suspected employer-violators.[117]

Employers protect themselves in several ways. Systematic background checks are the most obvious. Preemployment screening should include employment verification, criminal record checks, drug screens, and reference checks. You can verify Social Security cards by calling the Social Security Administration. Employers can avoid accusations of discrimination by verifying the documents of all applicants, not just those they may think suspicious.[118]

Discrimination Employers should not use the so-called I-9 Employment Eligibility Verification form (see Figure 6-10) to discriminate based on race or country of national origin. The requirement to verify eligibility does not provide any basis to reject an applicant just because he or she is a foreigner, or not a U.S. citizen, or an alien residing in the United States, as long as that person can prove his or her identity and employment eligibility. Since

---

FIGURE 6-10

Procedure in Complying with Immigration Law

1. Hire only citizens and aliens lawfully authorized to work in the United States.
2. Advise all new job applicants of your policy.
3. Require all new employees to complete and sign the verification form (the "I-9 form") designated by the Immigration and Naturalization Service (INS) to certify that they are eligible for employment.
4. Examine documentation presented by new employees, record information about the documents on the verification form, and sign the form.
5. Retain the form for three years or for one year past the employment of the individual, whichever is longer.
6. If requested, present the form for inspection by INS or Department of Labor officers. No reporting is required.

September 11, 2001, there has been a significant rise in allegations of religious and national origin discrimination, among both employees and applicants.

Today, almost all travelers who need visas have had to have interviews at their local American consulates. However, the Justice Department Appropriations Authorization bill, signed several years ago, authorizes the Justice Department to fight terrorism, but also actually makes it easier for foreign engineering specialists to get H-1B visas and jobs in the United States.[119]

Improving Productivity Through HRIS: Comprehensive Automated Applicant Tracking and Screening Systems

The applicant tracking systems we introduced in Chapter 5 (recruiting) do more than compile incoming Web-based résumés and track applicants during the hiring process. The new systems also do three things to help companies screen applicants.

First, most employers also use their applicant tracking systems (ATS) to "knock out" applicants who do not meet minimum, nonnegotiable job requirements, like submitting to drug tests or holding driver's licenses.

Second, employers use these advanced ATS to test and screen applicants online. This includes Web-based skills testing (in accounting, for instance), cognitive skills testing (such as for mechanical comprehension), and even psychological testing. Some design their ATS to screen for intangibles. For example, Recreation Equipment, Inc., needed a system that would match applicant skills with the company's culture, and in particular, identify applicants who were naturally inclined to work in teams. The company worked with its applicant tracking system vendor to customize its system to do that.[120]

Third, the newer systems don't just screen out candidates, but discover "hidden talents." Thanks to the Internet, applicants often send their résumés out across a wide range of job openings, hoping a shotgun approach will help them hit a match between their résumé-based qualifications and the listed job requirements. For most employers, this is simply a screening nuisance. But for those who design their ATS to do so, the ATS can identify talents in the candidate pool that lend themselves to job matches at the company that even the applicant didn't know existed when he or she applied. Figure 6-11 lists what the effective ATS should do.[121]

FIGURE 6-11

Checklist: What to Look for in an Applicant Tracking System (ATS)

The employer thinking of adopting an ATS should seek one that meets several minimum functionality requirements. Among other things, the ATS should be:

- Easy to use.
- Capable of being integrated into the company's existing HRIS platform, so that, for instance, data on a newly hired candidate can flow seamlessly into the HRIS payroll system.
- Able to capture, track, and report applicant EEO data.
- Able to provide employee selection performance metrics reports, including "time to fill," "cost to hire," and "applicant source statistics."
- Able to facilitate scheduling and tracking of candidate interviews, email communications, and completed forms, including job offers.
- Able to provide automated screening and ranking of candidates based upon job skill profiles.
- Able to provide an internal job posting service that supports applications from current employees and employee referral programs.
- Able to cross-post jobs to commercial job boards such as www.monster.com.
- Able to integrate the ATS job board with your company's own Web site, for instance, by linking it to your site's "careers" section.
- Able to provide for requisition creation and signoff approvals.

SUMMARY

1. In this chapter, we discussed techniques for screening and selecting job candidates; the first was testing.
2. As used by psychologists, the term *reliability* always means "consistency." One way to measure reliability is to administer the same (or equivalent) tests to the same people at two different points in time. Or you could focus on internal consistency, comparing the responses to roughly equivalent items on the same test.
3. Test validity answers the question, "What does this test measure?" We discussed criterion validity and content validity. Criterion validity means demonstrating that those who do well on the test do well on the job; content validity is demonstrated by showing that the test constitutes a fair sample of the content of the job.
4. There are many types of personnel tests in use, including intelligence tests, tests of physical skills, tests of achievement, aptitude tests, interest inventories, and personality tests.
5. For a selection test to be useful, scores should be predictably related to performance on the job; you must validate the test. This requires five steps: (1) analyze the job, (2) choose your tests, (3) administer the test, (4) relate test scores and criteria, and (5) cross-validate and validate the test.
6. Under equal rights legislation, an employer may have to prove that its tests are predictive of success or failure on the job. This usually requires a predictive validation study, although other means of validation are often acceptable.
7. Some basic testing guidelines include (a) use tests as supplements, (b) validate the tests for appropriate jobs, (c) analyze all current hiring and promotion standards, (d) beware of certain tests, (e) use a certified psychologist, and (f) maintain good test conditions.
8. The work sampling selection technique is based on the assumption that the best indicator of future performance is past performance. Here you use the applicant's actual performance on the same (or very similar) job to predict his or her future job performance. The steps are: (a) analyze the applicant's previous work experience, (b) have experts list component tasks for the open job, (c) select crucial tasks as work sample measures, (d) break down these tasks into steps, (e) test the applicant, and (f) relate the applicant's work sample score to his or her performance on the job.
9. Management assessment centers are another screening device and expose applicants to a series of real-life exercises. Performance is observed and assessed by experts, who then check their assessments by observing the participants when they are back at their jobs. Examples of "real-life" exercises include a simulated business game, an in-basket exercise, and group discussions.
10. Even though most people prefer not to give bad references, most companies still carry out some sort of reference check on their candidates. These can be useful in raising red flags, and questionnaires (page 231) can improve the usefulness of the responses you receive.
11. Other selection tools include the polygraph, honesty tests, and graphology. While graphology appears to have little predictive value, paper-and-pencil honesty tests have been used with success although they (and polygraphs) must be used with an eye toward the legal and ethical issues involved.

DISCUSSION QUESTIONS

1. What is the difference between reliability and validity? In what respects are they similar?
2. Explain how you would go about validating a test. How can this information be useful to a manager?

3. Explain why you think a certified psychologist who is specifically trained in test construction should (or should not) always be used by a small business that needs a test battery.
4. Give some examples of how to use interest inventories to improve employee selection. In doing so, suggest several examples of occupational interests that you believe might predict success in various occupations, including college professor, accountant, and computer programmer.
5. Why is it important to conduct preemployment background investigations? Outline how you would go about doing so.
6. Explain how you would get around the problem of former employers being unwilling to give bad references on their former employees.
7. How can employers protect themselves against negligent hiring claims?

INDIVIDUAL AND GROUP ACTIVITIES

1. Write a short essay discussing some of the ethical and legal considerations in testing.
2. Working individually or in groups, develop a list of specific selection techniques that you would suggest your dean use to hire the next HR professor at your school. Explain why you chose each selection technique.
3. Working individually or in groups, contact the publisher of a standardized test such as the Scholastic Assessment Test and obtain from it written information regarding the test's validity and reliability. Present a short report in class discussing what the test is supposed to measure and the degree to which you think the test does what it is supposed to do, based on the reported validity and reliability scores.
4. The HRCI "Test Specifications" appendix at the end of this book (pages 726–735) lists the knowledge someone studying for the HRCI certification exam needs to have in each area of human resource management (such as in Strategic Management, Workforce Planning, and Human Resource Development). In groups of four to five students, do four things: (1) review that appendix now; (2) identify the material in this chapter that relates to the required knowledge the appendix lists; (3) write four multiple choice exam questions on this material that you believe would be suitable for inclusion in the HRCI exam; and (4) if time permits, have someone from your team post your team's questions in front of the class, so the students in other teams can take each others' exam questions.

EXPERIENTIAL EXERCISE

A Test for a Reservation Clerk

Purpose: The purpose of this exercise is to give you practice in developing a test to measure *one specific ability* for the job of airline reservation clerk for a major airline. If time permits, you'll be able to combine your tests into a test battery.

Required Understanding: Your airline has decided to outsource its reservation jobs to Asia. You should be fully acquainted with the procedure for developing a personnel test and should read the following description of an airline reservation clerk's duties:

Customers contact our airline reservation clerks to obtain flight schedules, prices, and itineraries. The reservation clerks look up the requested information on our airline's online flight schedule systems, which are updated continuously. The reservation clerk must speak clearly, and deal courteously and expeditiously with the customer, and be able to quickly find alternative flight arrangements in order to provide the customer with the itinerary that fits his or her needs. Alternative flights and prices must be found quickly, so that the customer is not kept waiting, and so that our reservations operations group maintains its efficiency standards. It is often necessary to look under various routings, since there may be a dozen or more alternative routes between the customer's starting point and destination.

You may assume that we will hire about one-third of the applicants as airline reservation clerks. Therefore, your objective is to create a test that is useful in selecting a third of those available.

How to Set Up the Exercise/Instructions: Divide the class into teams of five or six students. The ideal candidate will obviously have to have a number of skills and abilities to perform this job well. Your job is to select a single ability and to develop a test to measure that ability. Use only the materials available in the room, please. The test should permit quantitative scoring and may be an individual or a group test.

Please go to your assigned groups and, as per our discussion of test development in this chapter, each group should make a list of the abilities relevant to success in the airline reservation clerk's job. Each group should then rate the importance of these abilities on a five-point scale. Then, develop a test to measure what you believe to be the top-ranked ability. If time permits, the groups should combine the various tests from each group into a test battery. If possible, leave time for a group of students to take the test battery.

APPLICATION CASE

Where's My Czar?

A few years ago, President Bush's White House team made what would seem to be a questionable hiring decision. It's not clear how much screening they did, or who did it, but almost as soon as the White House recommended Nebraska business executive Tony Raimondo to be the administration's assistant commerce secretary for manufacturing ("manufacturing czar"), Mr. Raimondo had to withdraw his name from consideration.

The candidate withdrew his name after blistering criticism from Democratic nominee John Kerry. Among other things, the president's manufacturing czar was supposed to develop strategies for beefing up U.S. manufacturing capacity and creating more manufacturing jobs in the United States (a crucial task, given the almost three million jobs the United States had lost in the previous three years). But, it turned out that Mr. Raimondo ran a Nebraska manufacturing business that had set up plants in China, and outsourced a portion of his company's jobs there. Senator Kerry said Mr. Raimondo therefore hardly seemed like the ideal person to champion keeping jobs in the United States.

The Bush administration said Raimondo's withdrawal was related to Nebraska political issues and not the fuss raised by Kerry. In an interview on CNBC, Commerce Secretary Don Evans said that the administration would continue to look for candidates. For a White House team known for working hard to be very corporate in the way it does things, the situation must have been somewhat embarrassing. Now, Mr. Bush has asked for your advice.

Questions

1. What should this position's job description look like?
2. What are the ideal job specifications for the person in this position?
3. How should we have gone about recruiting and screening for this position? What selection tools, specifically, would you use?
4. Where do you think we went wrong?

CONTINUING CASE

Honesty Testing at Carter Cleaning Company

Jennifer Carter, president of the Carter Cleaning Centers, and her father have what the latter describes as an easy but hard job when it comes to screening job applicants. It is easy because for two important jobs—the people who actually do the pressing and those who do the cleaning–spotting—the applicants are easily screened with about 20 minutes of on-the-job testing. As with typists, as Jennifer points out, "Applicants either know how to press clothes fast enough or how to use cleaning chemicals and machines, or they don't, and we find out very quickly by just trying them out on the job." On the other hand, applicant screening for the stores can also be frustratingly hard because of the nature of some of the other qualities that Jennifer would like to screen for. Two of the most critical problems facing her company are employee turnover and employee honesty. Jennifer and her father sorely need to implement practices that will reduce the rate of employee turnover. If there is a way to do this through employee testing and screening techniques, Jennifer would like to know about it because of the management time and money that are now being wasted by the never-ending need to recruit and hire new employees. Of even greater concern to Jennifer and her father is the need to institute new practices to screen out those employees who may be predisposed to steal from the company.

Employee theft is an enormous problem for the Carter Cleaning Centers, and one that is not just limited to employees who handle the cash. For example, the cleaner–spotter and/or the presser often open the store themselves, without a manager present, to get the day's work started, and it is not unusual to have one or more of these people steal supplies or "run a route." Running a route means that an employee canvasses his or her neighborhood to pick up people's clothes for cleaning and then secretly cleans and presses them in the Carter store, using the company's supplies, gas, and power. It would also not be unusual for an unsupervised person (or his or her supervisor, for that matter) to accept a one-hour rush order for cleaning or laundering, quickly clean and press the item, and return it to the customer for payment without making out a proper ticket for the item posting the sale. The money, of course, goes into the worker's pocket instead of into the cash register.

The more serious problem concerns the store manager and the counter workers who actually have to handle the cash. According to Jack Carter, "You would not believe the creativity employees use to get around the management controls we set up to cut down on employee theft." As one extreme example of this felonious creativity, Jack tells the following story: "To cut down on the amount of money my employees were stealing, I had a small sign painted and placed in front of all our cash registers. The sign said: YOUR ENTIRE ORDER FREE IF WE DON'T GIVE YOU A CASH REGISTER RE-CEIPT WHEN YOU PAY. CALL 552–0235. It was my intention with this sign to force all our cash-handling employees to place their receipts into the cash register where they would be recorded for my accountants. After all, if all the cash that comes in is recorded in the cash register, then we should have a much better handle on stealing in our stores, right? Well, one of our managers found a diabolical way around this. I came into the store one night and noticed that the cash register this particular manager was using just didn't look right, although the sign was dutifully placed in front of it. It turned out that every afternoon at about 5:00 P.M. when the other employees left, this character would pull his own cash register out of a box that he hid underneath our supplies. Customers coming in would notice the sign and of course the fact that he was meticulous in ringing up every sale. But unknown to them and us, for about five months the sales that came in for about an hour every day went into his cash register, not mine. It took us that long to figure out where our cash for that store was going."

Here is what Jennifer would like you to answer:

Questions

1. What would be the advantages and disadvantages to Jennifer's company of routinely administering honesty tests to all its employees?
2. Specifically, what other screening techniques could the company use to screen out theft-prone and turnover-prone employees, and how exactly could these be used?
3. How should her company terminate employees caught stealing, and what kind of procedure should be set up for handling reference calls about these employees when they go to other companies looking for jobs?

TRANSLATING STRATEGY INTO HR POLICIES AND PRACTICES CASE: THE HOTEL PARIS

Testing

The Hotel Paris's competitive strategy is "To use superior guest service to differentiate the Hotel Paris properties, and to thereby increase the length of stay and return rate of guests, and thus boost revenues and profitability." HR manager Lisa Cruz must now formulate functional policies and activities that support this competitive strategy, by eliciting the required employee behaviors and competencies. The HR Scorecard (inside back cover) outlines the relationships involved.

As she considered what she had to do next, Lisa Cruz, the Hotel Paris's HR director, knew that employee selection had to play a central role in her plans. The Hotel Paris currently had an informal screening process in which local hotel managers obtained application forms, interviewed applicants, and checked their references. However, a pilot project using an employment test for service people at the Chicago hotel had produced startling results. Lisa found consistent, significant relationships between test performance and a range of employee competencies and behaviors such as speed of check-in/out, employee turnover, and

percentage of calls answered with the required greeting. Clearly, she was on to something. She knew that employee capabilities and behaviors like these translated into just the sorts of improved guest services the Hotel Paris needed to execute its strategy. She therefore had to decide what selection procedures would be best.

Lisa's team, working with an industrial psychologist, wants to design a test battery that they believe will produce the sorts of high-morale, patient, people-oriented employees they are looking for. It should include, at a minimum, a work sample test for front-desk clerk candidates, and a personality test aimed at weeding out applicants who lack emotional stability.

Questions

1. Provide a detailed example of the front desk work sample test.
2. Provide a detailed example of two possible personality test questions.
3. What other tests would you suggest to Lisa, and why would you suggest them?

KEY TERMS

ENDNOTES

1. Kevin Delaney, "Google Adjusts Hiring Process as Needs Grow," *Wall Street Journal*, October 23, 2006, pp. B1,B8.
2. See, for example, Ann Marie Ryan and Marja Lasek, "Negligent Hiring and Defamation: Areas of Liability Related to Pre-employment Inquiries," *Personnel Psychology* 44, no. 2 (Summer 1991), pp. 293–319. See also, Jay Stuller, "Fatal Attraction," *Across the Board* 42, no. 6, November, December 2005, pp. 18–23.
3. Ryan Zimmerman, "Wal-Mart to Toughen Job Screening," *Wall Street Journal*, July 12, 2004, pp. B1–B8.
4. Ann Marie Ryan and Marja Lasek, op. cit.
5. Ibid.
6. Steven Mitchell Sack, "Fifteen Steps to Protecting Against the Risk of Negligent Hiring Claims," *Employment Relations Today*, August 1993, pp. 313–320; Fay Hansen, "*Taking 'Reasonable' Action to Avoid Negligent Hiring Claims*," *Workforce Management*, September 11, 2006, p. 31.
7. Kevin Murphy and Charles Davidshofer, *Psychological Testing: Principles and Applications* (Upper Saddle River, NJ: Prentice Hall, 2001), p. 73.
8. W. Bruce Walsh and Nancy Betz, *Tests and Assessment* (Upper Saddle River, NJ: Prentice Hall, 2001).
9. Murphy and Davidshofer, *Psychological Testing*, p. 74.
10. A third, less used, way to demonstrate a test's validity is *construct validity*. A construct is an abstract trait such as happiness or intelligence. Construct validity generally addresses the question of "validity of measurement," in other words, of whether the test is really measuring, say, intelligence. To prove construct validity, an employer has to prove that the test measures the construct. Federal agency guidelines make it difficult to prove construct validity, however, and as a result few employers use this approach as part of their process for satisfying the federal guidelines. See James Ledvinka, *Federal Regulation of Personnel and Human Resource Management* (Boston: Kent, 1982), p. 113; and Murphy and Davidshofer, *Psychological Testing*, pp. 154–165.
11. Murphy and Davidshofer, *Psychological Testing*, p. 73.
12. Experts sometimes have to develop separate expectancy charts and cutting points for minorities and nonminorities if the validation studies indicate that high performers from either group (minority or nonminority) score lower (or higher) on the test.
13. Mark Schmit and Ann Marie Ryan, "Applicant Withdrawal: The Role of Test-Taking Attitudes and Racial Differences," *Personnel Psychology* 50 (1997), pp. 855–876.
14. Robert Ployhart and Ann Marie Ryan, "Applicants' Reactions to the Fairness of Selection Procedures: The Effects of Positive Rule Violations and Time of Measurement," *Journal of Applied Psychology* 83, no. 1 (1998), pp. 3–16.
15. Walsh and Betz, *Tests and Assessment*, p. 425.
16. Ibid., p. 134.
17. Russell Cropanzano and Thomas Wright, "Procedural Justice and Organizational Staffing: A Tale of Two Paradigms," *Human Resource Management Review* 13, no. 1 (Spring 2003), pp. 7–39.
18. John Hausknecht, et al., "Applicant Reactions to Selection Procedures: An Updated Model and Meta-Analysis," *Personnel Psychology*, 2004, vol. 57, pp. 639–683; see also, Bradford Bell, Ann Marie Ryan, and Darin Wiechmann, "Consequences of Organizational Justice Expectations in a Selection System," *Journal of Applied Psychology*, 2006, vol. 91, no. 2, pp. 455–466.
19. "Hiring Based on Strength Test Discriminates Against Women," *BNA Bulletin to Management* February 22, 2005, p. 62.
20. Travis Gibbs and Matt Riggs, "Reducing Bias in Personnel Selection Decisions: Positive Effects of Attention to Irrelevant Information," *Psychological Reports* 74 (1994), pp. 19–26.
21. From "Ethical Principles of Psychologists and Code of Conduct," *American Psychologist* 47 (1992), pp. 1597–1611.
22. Susan Mendelsohn and Katheryn Morrison, "The Right to Privacy at the Work Place, Part I: Employee Searches," *Personnel*, July 1988, p. 20. See also Talya Bauer et al., "Applicant

Reactions to Selection: Development of the Selection Procedural Justice Scale," *Personnel Psychology* 54 (2001), pp. 387–419.

23. Mendelson and Morrison, "The Right to Privacy in the Work Place," p. 22.

24. Kenneth Sovereign, *Personnel Law*, (Upper Saddle River, NJ: Prentice Hall, 1999), pp. 204–206.

25. For a discussion of these see *Commerce Clearing House, Ideas and Trends*, October 16, 1987, pp. 165–166.

26. http://www.amanet.org/research/pdfs/bjp_2001.pdf. Downloaded August 22, 2004.

27. Ibid. See also, Alison Wolf and Andrew Jenkins, "Explaining Greater Test Use for Selection: The Role of HR Professionals in a World of Expanding Regulation," *Human Resource Management Journal*, 16, no. 2, 2006, pp. 193–213.

28. Rachel Emma Silverman, "Sharpen Your Pencil," *Wall Street Journal*, December 5, 2000.

29. Steffanie Wilk and Peter Capelli, "Understanding the Determinants of the Employer Use of Selection Methods," *Personnel Psychology* 56 (2003), p. 117.

30. See Rebecca Bennett and Sandra Robinson, "Development of a Measure of Workplace Deviance," *Journal of Applied Psychology* 85, no. 3 (2000), p. 349.

31. "Employees' Dirty Deeds Caused Companies 6% of Annual Revenue, Report Says," *BNA Bulletin to Management*, August 17, 2000, p. 257.

32. Sarah Gale, "Three Companies Cut Turnover with Tests," *Workforce*, Spring 2002, pp. 66–69.

33. Dirk Steiner and Stephen Gilliland, "Fairness Reactions to Personnel Selection Techniques in France and the United States," *Journal of Applied Psychology* 81, no. 2 (1996), pp. 134–141; Emily Duehr and Joyce Bono, "Men, Women, and Managers: Are Stereotypes Finally Changing?" *Personnel Psychology*, 2006, vol. 59, pp. 815–846.

34. Scott Hayes, "Kinko's Dials into Automated Applicants Screening," *Workforce*, November 1999, pp. 71–73; Gilbert Nicholson, "Automated Assessments for Better Hires," *Workforce*, December 2000, pp. 102–107.
Proctored Web-based and paper-and-pencil tests of applicants produce similar results, for instance on personality and judgment tests. However, a timed test may take longer for applicants on the Web, due to downloading problems and the fact that there are fewer items presented on the viewable page. Similarly, tests takers generally find it more difficult to go back and review their results on the web-based tests. Proctoring is another problem. There is "currently no way to completely prevent [online] test takers from cheating or copying items during testing" or to ensure there's not someone looking over the test taker's shoulder. See, Robert Plyhart et al., "Web-Based and Paper-and-Pencil Testing of Applicants in a Proctored Setting: Are Personality, Biodata and Situational Judgment Tests Comparable?," *Personnel Psychology* 56, (2003), pp. 733–752; Denise Potosky and Philip Bob Bobko, "Selection Testing Via the Internet: Practical Considerations and Exploratory Empirical Findings," *Personnel Psychology* 57, 2004, p. 1025.

35. Requiring job seekers to complete prescreening questionnaires and screening selected applicants out on this basis carries legal and business consequences. See for example Lisa Harpe, "Designing an Effective Employment Prescreening Program," *Employment Relations Today* 32, no. 3, Fall 2005, pp. 41–43.

36. Brian O'Leary et al., "Selecting the Best and Brightest," *Human Resource Management* 41, no. 3 (Fall 2002), pp. 25–34.

37. Gilbert Nicholson, "Automated Assessments for Better Hires," *Workforce*, December 2000, pp. 102–107.

38. Except as noted, this is based largely on Laurence Siegel and Irving Lane, *Personnel and Organizational Psychology* (Burr Ridge, IL: McGraw-Hill, 1982), pp. 170–185. See also Cabot Jaffe, "Measurement of Human Potential," *Employment Relations Today* 17, no. 2 (Summer 2000), pp. 15–27; Maureen Patterson, "Overcoming the Hiring Crunch; Tests Deliver Informed Choices," *Employment Relations Today* 27, no. 3 (Fall 2000), pp. 77–88; Kathryn Tyler, "Put Applicants' Skills to the Test," *HR Magazine*, January 2000, p. 74; Murphy and Davidshofer, *Psychological Testing*, pp. 215–403; Elizabeth Schoenfelt and Leslie Pedigo, "A Review of Court Decisions on Cognitive Ability Testing, 1992–2004," *Review of Public Personnel Administration* 25, no. 3, 2005, pp. 271–287.

39. As an example, results of meta-analyses in one study indicated that isometric strength tests were valid predictors of both supervisory ratings of physical performance, and performance on work

simulations. See Barry R. Blakley, Miguel Quinones, Marnie Swerdlin Crawford, and I. Ann Jago, "The Validity of Isometric Strength Tests," *Personnel Psychology* 47 (1994), pp. 247–274.

40. William Wagner, "All Skill, No Finesse," *Workforce*, June 2000, pp. 108–116.

41. James Spencer, "Sorry, You're Nobody's Type," *Wall Street Journal*, July 30, 2003, p. D1.

42. Cora Daniels, "Does This Man Need a Shrink?" *Fortune*, February 5, 2001, pp. 205–206.

43. See, for example, Douglas Cellar et al., "Comparison of Factor Structures and Criterion-Related Validity Coefficients for Two Measures of Personality Based on the Five Factor Model," *Journal of Applied Psychology* 81, no. 6 (1996), pp. 694–704; and Jesus Salgado, "The Five Factor Model of Personality and Job Performance in the European Community," *Journal of Applied Psychology* 82, no. 1 (1997), pp. 30–43.

44. Timothy Judge et al., "Personality and Leadership: A Qualitative and Quantitative Review," *Journal of Applied Psychology* 87, no. 4 (2002), p. 765.

45. Ibid.

46. Timothy Judge and Remus Ilies, "Relationship of Personality to Performance Motivation: A Meta Analytic Review," *Journal of Applied Psychology* 87, no. 4 (2002), pp. 797–807.

47. Murray Barrick et al., "Meta Analysis of the Relationship between the Five Factor Model of Personality and Holland's Occupational Types," *Personnel Psychology* 56, no. 1 (Spring 2003), pp. 45–74.

48. L. A. Witt et al., "The Interactive Effects of Conscientiousness and Agreeableness on Job Performance," *Journal of Applied Psychology* 87, no. 1 (2002), pp. 164–169.

49. Timothy Judge et al., "The Big Five Personality Traits, General Mental Ability, and Career Success Across the Lifespan," *Personnel Psychology* 52 (1999), pp. 621–652.

50. See "Can Testing Prevent Violence?" *BNA Bulletin to Management*, November 28, 1996, p. 384.

51. Diane Caudrain, "Reassess Personality Tests After Court Case," *HR Magazine* 50, no. 9, September 2005, p. 30 FF.

52. See, as one example of many, Michael Mount, et al., "Relationship of Personality Traits and Counterproductive Work Behaviors: the Mediating Effects of Job Satisfaction," *Personnel Psychology* 59, 2006, pp. 591–622.

53. Murray Barrick et al., "Personality and Job Performance: Test of the Immediate Effects of Motivation Among Sales Representatives," *Journal of Applied Psychology* 87, no. 1 (2002), p. 43.

54. Charles Sarchione et al., "Prediction of Dysfunctional Job Behaviors Among Law-Enforcement Officers," *Journal of Applied Psychology* 83, no. 6 (1998), pp. 904–912. See also Stephen Bates, "Personality Counts," *HR Magazine*, February 2002, pp. 28–34.

55. Paula Caligiuri, "The Big Five Personality Characteristics as Predictors of Expatriate's Desire to Terminate the Assignment and Supervisor Rated Performance," *Personnel Psychology* 53 (2000), pp. 67–68.

56. Brian Niehoff and Robert Paula, "Causes of Employee Theft and Strategies That HR Managers Can Use for Prevention," *Human Resource Management* 39, no. 1 (Spring 2000), pp. 51–64.

57. Mitchell Rothstein and Richard Goffin, "The New World of Work and Organizations: The Use of Personality Measures in Personnel Selection – What Does Current Research Support?" *Human Resource Management Review* 2006, vol. 16, pp. 155–180.

58. Jeff Weekley and Casey Jones, "Video-Based Situational Testing," *Personnel Psychology* 50 (1997), p. 25.

59. Elaine Pulakos, *Selection Assessment Methods*, SHRM Foundation, 2005, p. 14.

60. See, for example, George Burgnoli, James Campion, and Jeffrey Bisen, "Racial Bias in the Use of Work Samples for Personnel Selection," *Journal of Applied Psychology* 64, no. 2 (April 1979), pp. 119–123. See also Neal Schmitt and Amy Mills, "Traditional Tests and the Job Simulation: Minority and Majority Performance and Test Validity," *Journal of Applied Psychology* 86, no. 3 (2001), pp. 451–458; and Philip Roth, Philip Bobko, and Lynn McFarland, "A Meta-Analysis of Work Sample Test Validity: Updating and Integrating Some Classic Literature," *Personnel Psychology* 58, no. 4, Winter 2005, pp. 1009–1037.

61. Siegel and Lane, *Personnel and Organizational Psychology*, pp. 182–183.

62. "Help Wanted—and Found," *Fortune*, October 2, 2006, p. 40.

63. Annette Spychalski, Miguel Quinones, Barbara Gaugler, and Katja Pohley, "A Survey of Assessment Center Practices in Organizations in the United States," *Personnel Psychology* 50, no. 1 (Spring 1997), pp. 71–90. See also Winfred Arthur Jr. et al., "A Meta Analysis of the Criterion Related Validity of Assessment Center Data Dimensions," *Personnel Psychology* 56 (2003), pp. 124–154.

64. Kobi Dayan et al., "Entry-Level Police Candidate Assessment Center: An Efficient Tool or a Hammer to Kill a Fly?" *Personnel Psychology* 55 (2002), pp. 827–848.

65. Weekley and Jones, "Video-Based Situational Testing," p. 26.

66. Ibid., p. 30.

67. Ibid., p. 46.

68. Robert Grossman, "Made from Scratch," *HR Magazine*, April 2002, pp. 44–53.

69. Coleman Peterson, "Employee Retention, The Secrets Behind Wal-Mart's Successful Hiring Policies," *Human Resource Management* 44, no. 1, Spring 2005, pp. 85–88.

70. Murray Barrick and Ryan Zimmerman, "Reducing Voluntary, Avoidable Turnover Through Selection," *Journal of Applied Psychology* 90, no. 1, (2005): 159–166.

71. "Internet, E-mail Monitoring Common at Most Workplaces," *BNA Bulletin to Management*, February 1, 2001, p. 34. See also, "Are Your Background Checks Balanced? Experts Identify Concerns Over Verifications," *BNA Bulletin to Management*, May 13, 2004, p. 153.

72. Mary Mayer, "Background Checks in Focus," *HR Magazine*, January 2002, pp. 59–62; and Carroll Lachnit, "Protecting People and Profits with Background Checks," *Workforce*, February 2002, p. 52.

73. Seymour Adler, "Verifying a Job Candidate's Background: The State of Practice in a Vital Human Resources Activity," *Review of Business* 15, no. 2 (Winter 1993), p. 6.

74. Edward Robinson, "Beware—Job Seekers Have No Secrets," *Fortune*, December 29, 1997, p. 285.

75. This is based on Samuel Greengard, "Have Gangs Invaded Your Workplace?" *Personnel Journal*, February 1996, pp. 47–48.

76. Lachnit, "Protecting People and Profits with Background Checks," pp. 50.

77. Alan Finder, "When a Risqué Online Persona Undermines a Chance for a Job," *New York Times*, June 11, 2006, p. 1.

78. Thomas von der Embse and Rodney Wyse, "Those Reference Letters: How Useful Are They?" *Personnel* 62, no. 1 (January 1985), pp. 42–46.

79. "Reference Checks Hit Wall of Silence," *BNA Bulletin to Management*, July 6, 1995, p. 216.

80. Ibid., p. 55.

81. "Negative Reference Leads to Charge of Retaliation," *BNA Bulletin to Management*, October 21, 2004, p. 344.

82. For additional information, see Lawrence E. Dube Jr., "Employment References and the Law," *Personnel Journal* 65, no. 2 (February 1986), pp. 87–91. See also Mickey Veich, "Uncover the Resume Ruse," *Security Management*, October 1994, pp. 75–76.

83. "Jury Awards Manager Accused of Theft $1.25 Million," *BNA Bulletin to Management*, March 27, 1997, p. 97.

84. Eileen Zimmerman, "A Subtle Reference Trap for Unwary Employers," *Workforce*, April 2003, p. 22.

85. *Kehr v. Consolidated Freightways of Delaware*, Docket No. 86–2126, July 15, 1987, U.S. Seventh Circuit Court of Appeals. Discussed in *Commerce Clearing House, Ideas and Trends*, October 16, 1987, p. 165.

86. James Bell, James Castagnera, and Jane Patterson Yong, "Employment References: Do You Know the Law?" *Personnel Journal* 63, no. 2 (February 1984), pp. 32–36. In order to demonstrate defamation, several elements must be present: (a) the defamatory statement must have been communicated to another party; (b) the statement must be a false statement of fact; (c) injury to reputation must have occurred; and (d) the employer must not be protected under qualified or absolute privilege. For a discussion, see Ryan and Lasek, "Negligent Hiring and Defamation," p. 307. See also James Burns Jr., "Employment References: Is There a Better Way?" *Employee Relations Law Journal* 23, no. 2 (Fall 1997), pp. 157–168.

87. See Paul Taylor, et al., "Dimensionality and the Validity of a Structured Telephone Reference Check Procedure," *Personnel Psychology*, 2004, vol. 57, pp. 745–772, vol. 47 for a discussion of checking other work habits and traits.

88. "Getting Applicant Information Difficult but Still Necessary," *BNA Bulletin to Management*, February 5, 1999, p. 63. See also Robert Howie and Lawrence Shapiro, "Pre-Employment Criminal Background Checks: Why Employers Should Look Before They Leap," *Employee Relations Law Journal*, Summer 2002, pp. 63–77.

89. Jeffrey M. Hahn, "Pre-Employment Information Services: Employers Beware?" *Employee Relations Law Journal* 17, no. 1 (Summer 1991), pp. 45–69. See also "Pre-Employment Background Screenings Have Evolved, but so Have Liability Risks," *BNA Bulletin to Management*, November 1, 2005, p. 345.

90. Teresa Butler Stivarius, "Background Checks: Steps to Basic Compliance in a Multistate Environment," *Society for Human Resource Management Legal Report*, March–April 2003, pp. 1–8.

91. "Top Employee Background Checking and Screening Providers," *Workforce Management*, November 7, 2005, p. 289.

92. John Jones and William Terris, "Post-Polygraph Selection Techniques," *Recruitment Today*, May–June 1989, pp. 25–31.

93. Norma Fritz, "In Focus: Honest Answers—Post Polygraph," *Personnel*, April 1989, p. 8. See also Richard White Jr., "Ask Me No Questions, Tell Me No Lies: Examining the Uses and Misuses of the Polygraph," *Public Personnel Management* 30, no. 4 (Winter 2001), pp. 483–493.

94. John Bernardin and Donna Cooke, "Validity of an Honesty Test in Predicting Theft Among Convenience Store Employees," *Academy of Management Journal* 36, no. 5 (1993), pp. 1097–1108.

95. Judith Collins and Frank Schmidt, "Personality, Integrity, and White Collar Crime: A Construct Validity Study," *Personnel Psychology* 46 (1993), pp. 295–311; Paul Sackett and James Wanek, "New Developments in the Use of Measures of Honesty, Integrity, Conscientiousness, Dependability, Trustworthiness, and Reliability for Personnel Selection," *Personnel Psychology* 49 (1996), p. 821.

96. Christopher Berry et al., "A Review of recent Developments in Integrity Test Research," *Personnel Psychology*, 2007, pp. 271–301.

97. These are based on "Divining Integrity Through Interviews," *BNA Bulletin to Management*, June 4, 1987, p. 184; and *Commerce Clearing House, Ideas and Trends*, December 29, 1998, pp. 222–223.

98. This example is based on *BNA Bulletin to Management*, February 26, 1987, p. 65.

99. Bill Leonard, "Reading Employees," *HR Magazine*, April 1999, pp. 67–73.

100. Ibid.

101. Mick Haus, "Pre-Employment Physicals and the ADA," *Safety and Health*, February 1992, pp. 64–65.

102. Scott MacDonald, Samantha Wells, and Richard Fry, "The Limitations of Drug Screening in the Workplace," *International Labor Review* 132, no. 1 (1993), p. 98. Not all agree that drug testing is worthwhile. See, for example, Mark Karper, Clifford Donn, and Marie Lyndaker, "Drug Testing in the Transportation Industry: The Maritime Case," *Employee Responsibilities and Rights* 71, no. 3 (September 1994), pp. 219–233.

103. "Drug Testing: The Things People Will Do," *American Salesman* 46, no. 3 (March 2001), p. 20.

104. Diane Cadrain, "Are Your Employees' Drug Tests Accurate?" *HR Magazine*, January 2003, pp. 40–45.

105. Chris Berka and Courtney Poignand, "Hair Follicle Testing—An Alternative to Urinalysis for Drug Abuse Screening," *Employee Relations Today*, Winter 1991–1992, pp. 405–409.

106. MacDonald et al., "The Limitations of Drug Screening," pp. 102–104.

107. R. J. McCunney, "Drug Testing: Technical Complications of a Complex Social Issue," *American Journal of Industrial Medicine* 15, no. 5 (1989), pp. 589–600; discussed in MacDonald et al., "The Limitations of Drug Screening," p. 102.

108. MacDonald et al., "The Limitations of Drug Screening," p. 103.

109. For a discussion of this, see Ibid, pp. 105–106.

110. This is based on Ann M. O'Neill, "Legal Issues Presented by Hair Follicle Testing," *Employee Relations Today*, Winter 1991–1992, pp. 411–415.

111. Ibid., p. 411.

112. Ibid., p. 413.

113. Richard Lisko, "A Manager's Guide to Drug Testing," *Security Management* 38, no. 8 (August 1994), p. 92. See also Randall Kesselring and Jeffrey Pittman, "Drug Testing Laws and Employment Injuries," *Journal of Labor Research*, Spring 2002, pp. 293–301.

114. Michael A. McDaniel, "Does Pre-Employment Drug Use Predict On-the-Job Suitability?" *Personnel Psychology* 41, no. 4 (Winter 1988), pp. 717–729.

115. *Exxon Corp. v. Esso Workers Union, Inc.*, CA1#96–2241, 7/8/97; discussed in *BNA Bulletin to Management*, August 7, 1997, p. 249.

116. These are quoted from *Commerce Clearing House, Ideas and Trends*, May 1, 1987, pp. 70–71.

117. Susan Ladika, "Trouble on the Hiring Front," *HR Magazine*, October 2006, pp. 56–62.

118. Rusell Gerbman, "License to Work," *HR Magazine*, June 2000, pp. 151–160.

119. Gillian Flynn, "Hiring of Foreign Workers in a Post-911 World," *Workforce*, July 2002, p. 78. See also Mark Ivener, "Stopped at the Border," *HR Magazine*, June 2006, pp. 117–120.

120. Note that un-proctored Internet tests raise serious questions in employment settings. Nancy Tippins, et al., "Unproctored Internet Testing in Employment Settings," *Personnel Psychology*, 2006, vol. 59, pp. 189–225.

121. From Bob Neveu, "Applicant Tracking's Top 10: Do You Know What to Look for in Applicant Tracking Systems?" *Workforce*, October 2002, p. 10.

7 Interviewing Candidates

The Web site careerbuilder.com recently conducted a survey of more than 400 hiring managers, asking them to share "the most memorable blunders" that caused them to reject a particular candidate. Job interviews scored high on the list. For example, several job candidates displayed stunningly bored or arrogant attitudes during their interviews. Some samples: "He asked me to speed up the interview because he had a lunch date;" "He told me the only reason he was here was because his mother wanted him to get a job;" "The candidate used profanity when describing something negative about a previous boss;" and, "One candidate did not wear shoes to the interview."[1] •

After studying this chapter, you should be able to:

1. List the main types of selection interviews.
2. Explain and illustrate at least six factors that affect the usefulness of interviews.
3. Explain and illustrate each guideline for being a more effective interviewer.
4. Effectively interview a job candidate.

Chapter 6, Employee Testing and Selection, focused on important methods managers use to select employees. The purpose of the current chapter, Interviewing Candidates, is to improve your effectiveness at using what is perhaps the most important screening tool, the selection interview. The main topics we'll cover include types of interviews, the factors that can undermine an interview's usefulness, and designing and conducting an effective interview. In the following chapter, Training and Developing Employees, we'll turn to the techniques you can use to make sure the new employees you hire have the knowledge and skills they need to perform their jobs.

BASIC FEATURES OF INTERVIEWS

An *interview* is a procedure designed to obtain information from a person through oral responses to oral inquiries; a *selection interview*, which we'll focus on in this chapter, is "a selection procedure designed to predict future job performance on the basis of applicants' oral responses to oral inquiries."[2]

Since the interview is only one of several selection tools, you could reasonably ask, "Why devote a chapter to this one tool?" The answer, first, is that the interview is the most widely used personnel selection procedure. While not all employers use tests or even reference checks, it would be highly unusual for a manager not to interview someone before hiring them. Interviewing is thus an indispensable management tool. Second, most people tend to think they're better interviewers than they really are. In one study, less than 34% of interviewers had formal interview training, but "interviewers were confident that they could identify the best candidates regardless of the amount of interview structure employed."[3]

As we'll see below, experts have criticized the interview for its low validity.[4] However, recent reviews have been more favorable, and an interview—at least one done properly—can be "a much better predictor of performance than previously thought and is comparable with many other selection techniques."[5]

Types of Interviews

① List the main types of selection interviews.

Managers use several types of interviews in the work setting. For example, there are selection, appraisal, and exit interviews. An *appraisal interview* is a discussion, following a performance appraisal, in which supervisor and employee discuss the employee's rating and possible remedial actions. When an employee leaves a firm for any reason, one often conducts an *exit interview*. This interview aims at eliciting information that might give the employer some insight into what's right or wrong about the firm. Many techniques in this chapter apply equally to appraisal and exit interviews. However, we'll postpone a complete explanation of these types of interviews until Chapters 9 and 10, respectively, so we can focus here on *selection interviews*. We can classify selection interviews according to (1) how structured they are, (2) their "content"—the types of questions they contain—and (3) how the firm administers the interviews. Let's look at these.

Structured Versus Unstructured Interviews

unstructured or nondirective interview
An unstructured conversational-style interview in which the interviewer pursues points of interest as they come up in response to questions.

In **unstructured or nondirective interviews**, the manager generally follows no set format. The lack of structure allows the interviewer to ask follow-up questions and pursue points of interest as they develop. Interviewees for the same job may or may not get the same or similar questions. A few questions might be specified in advance, but they're usually not, and there is seldom a formal guide for scoring answers. This type of interview "could even be described as little more than a general conversation."[6]

structured or directive interview
An interview following a set sequence of questions.

At the other extreme, in **structured or directive interviews**, the employer specifies the questions ahead of time, and may also list and rate possible answers for appropriateness.[7] McMurray's patterned interview was one early example. The interviewer followed a printed form to ask a series of questions, such as "How was the person's present job obtained?" Comments printed beneath the questions (such as "Has he/she shown self-reliance in getting his/her jobs?") then guide the interviewer in evaluating the answers.

Some experts restrict the term "structured interview" to those interviews based on carefully selected job-oriented questions with predetermined answers that interviewers ask of all applicants. But in practice, the choice isn't "unstructured" versus "structured"; instead, structure is a matter of degree. Sometimes, for instance, the manager may just want to make sure he or she has a standard set of questions to ask, so he or she does not inadvertently skip any questions. Here the interviewer might just choose questions from a list like that in Figure 7-3 (page 271). The structured applicant interview guide in Figure 7-A2 (page 286–288) illustrates a more structured approach. As another example, the Department of Homeland Security uses the structured guide in Figure 7-1 (page 256–257) to help screen Coast Guard officer candidates. It contains a formal candidate rating procedure, and also enables geographically disbursed interviewers to complete the form over the Web. As we'll explain in more detail later in this chapter, there are different ways to structure an interview. Many of them have nothing to do with using structured guides like these.

Structured and nonstructured interviews each have pros and cons. In structured interviews, all interviewers generally ask all applicants the same questions. Partly because of this, these interviews tend to be more reliable and valid. Structured interviews can also help less talented interviewers conduct better interviews. Standardizing the interview also increases consistency across candidates, enhances job relatedness, reduces overall subjectivity (and thus the potential for bias), and may "enhance the ability to withstand legal challenge."[8] However, structured interviews don't always provide enough opportunity to pursue points of interest as they develop. The Know Your Employment Law feature presents some relevant issues.

Know Your Employment LAW Interviewing Candidates

Various equal employment laws, including Title VII of the Civil Rights Act of 1964 and the Civil Rights Act of 1991, require that employment interviewers exercise caution in which questions they ask, lest they expose their companies to accusations of discriminatory treatment. Questions regarding an applicant's race, color, religion, sex, age, national origin, or disability trigger red flags. Again, it is generally not illegal to ask a female job candidate about marital status, or an 80-year-old applicant "how old are you?" It certainly is not advisable to do so, but the manager can ask such questions as long as he or she can show either that the employer does not discriminate or that it can defend the selection practice (in this case the interview question) as a BFOQ or business necessity.

However, while inquiries like these may not be illegal, there are two reasons to avoid them. First, although federal law may not bar asking them, many state and local laws do. Second, the EEOC has said that it disapproves of such practices as asking women their marital status or applicants their age. Such questions may thus draw the attention of the EEOC and other regulatory agencies.

If a protected group member does bring a charge of discrimination against the employer, what will sway the court to find in favor of the employer? A study of federal district court cases involving alleged employment interview discrimination is relevant. The most important action seems to be to ensure that the interview process is structured and consistently applied. Three dimensions of interview structure, (1) having objective/job-related questions, (2) standardizing interview administration, and (3) having multiple interviewers, were related to verdicts in favor of employers.[9] In addition, ". . . endeavor to make it clear to applicants that the interview process is fair, that the interviewer treats the interviewee with courtesy and respect, and that the interviewer is willing to explain the interview process and the nature and rationale for the questions."[10]

Department of Homeland Security CG-5527 (04-03)	**Officer Programs Applicant Interview Form**	Date:

Name of Applicant (Last, First, MI)

DIRECTIONS: This interview form is designed to help the selection panel reach a consensus on the merits of the applicant under consideration. The form is heavily based on the Officer Evaluation Report. While it should be remembered that applicants are not yet Coast Guard Officers, they should have had opportunities to exhibit qualities that show they possess the character and potential necessary to be successful Officers. The scale for each category below is based on performance standards presented on the Officer Evaluation Report. Provide written comments in support of numeric markings for each category. Base these comments on what you observe during the interview or see in the supporting documentation in the applicant's package. Marks in the overall impression block should summarize the panel's recommendation on the applicant's suitability for service as a Coast Guard Officer.

Planning and Preparedness: Ability to determine goals, set priorities and deadlines and develop strategies.
1☐   2☐   3☐   4☐   5☐   6☐   7☐
Comments:

Using Resources: Ability to manage time, materials, information, money and people.
1☐   2☐   3☐   4☐   5☐   6☐   7☐
Comments:

Adaptability: Ability to modify work methods and priorities in response to new information, changing conditions or unexpected obstacles.
1☐   2☐   3☐   4☐   5☐   6☐   7☐
Comments:

Speaking and Listening: Ability to speak effectively and listen to understand.
1☐   2 ☐   3☐   4☐   5☐   6☐   7☐
Comments:

Looking out for Others: Ability to consider and respond to others *personal* needs and capabilities.
1☐   2 ☐   3☐   4☐   5☐   6☐   7☐
Comments:

FIGURE 7-1

Officer Programs Applicant Interview Form

Source: Adapted from http://www.uscg.mil/jobs/dc/DCPrograms/OProgramForms/PDFS/DCA/Interview%20CG-5527.pdf, accessed May 9, 2007.

Page 2 - CG-5527 (04-03)

Directing Others: Ability to influence or direct others in accomplishing tasks or goals.

1☐　　　2☐　　　3☐　　　4☐　　　5☐　　　6☐　　　7☐

Comments:

Teamwork: Ability to manage, lead and participate in teams, encourage cooperation and develop espirit de corps.

1☐　　　2☐　　　3☐　　　4☐　　　5☐　　　6☐　　　7☐

Comments:

Initiative: Ability to originate and act on new ideas and seek responsibility without guidance and supervision.

1☐　　　2☐　　　3☐　　　4☐　　　5☐　　　6☐　　　7☐

Comments:

Responsibility: Ability to act ethically, courageously, and dependably and inspire the same in others.

1☐　　　2☐　　　3☐　　　4☐　　　5☐　　　6☐　　　7☐

Comments:

Professional Presence: Ability to bring credit to the Coast Guard through one's actions, demeanor and appearance.

1☐　　　2☐　　　3☐　　　4☐　　　5☐　　　6☐　　　7☐

Comments:

Overall Impression: Compare this applicant to others you have interviewed, **blocks two through seven constitute a recommendation for selection.**

Unsatisfactory　　Qualified　　One of many competent applicants for this program　　Exceptional　　Distinguished

1☐　　　2☐　　　3☐　　　4☐　　　5☐　　　6☐　　　7☐

Names of Panel Members	Rank	Command/Unit	Signature	Interviews Conducted

FIGURE 7-1 *(continued)*

Interview Content (Types of Questions)

situational interview
A series of job-related questions that focus on how the candidate would behave in a given situation.

We can also classify interviews based on the "content" or the types of questions they contain. In a **situational interview**, you ask the candidate what his or her behavior would be in a given situation.[11] For example, you might ask a supervisory candidate how he or she would act in response to a subordinate coming to work late three days in a row. We'll see that often, the best interviews are both structured and situational; here you use predetermined situational questions and answers. In such a *structured situational interview*, you might evaluate the applicant on, say, his or her choice between letting the persistently late subordinate off with a warning versus suspending the subordinate for a week.

behavioral interviews
A series of job-related questions that focus on how the candidate reacted to actual situations in the past.

Whereas situational interviews ask interviewees to describe how they would react to a hypothetical situation today or tomorrow, **behavioral interviews** ask interviewees to describe how they reacted to actual situations in the past.[12] For example, when Citizen's Banking Corporation in Flint, Michigan, found that 31 of the 50 people in its call center quit in one year, Cynthia Wilson, the center's head, switched to behavioral interviews. Many of those who left did so because they didn't enjoy fielding questions from occasionally irate clients. So Wilson no longer tries to predict how candidates will act based on asking them if they want to work with angry clients. Instead, she asks behavioral questions like, "Tell me about a time you were speaking with an irate person, and how you turned the situation around." Wilson says this makes it much harder to fool the interviewer, and, indeed, only four people left her center in the following year.[13]

Situational questions start with phrases such as, "Suppose you were faced with the following situation . . . What would you do?" Behavioral questions might start with a phrase like, "Can you think of a time when . . . What did you do?"[14]

Behavioral or situational interviews can produce a lot of tension. "It's pretty intense," said one applicant for a consultant's job with Accenture, the consulting firm, "You can pretty much fake one or two answers, but the third time they come back to it you pretty much can't. You're pulling from real life, and you're nervous. [The interviewer] asked how I would prepare for something important. He came back to that again and again to make sure what I said was true. The whole time they are writing constantly."[15]

job-related interview
A series of job-related questions that focus on relevant past job-related behaviors.

In a **job-related interview**, the interviewer tries to deduce what the applicant's on-the-job performance will be based on his or her answers to questions about relevant past experiences. The questions here don't revolve around hypothetical or actual situations or scenarios. Instead, the interviewer asks job-related questions (such as, "Which courses did you like best in business school?"). The aim is to draw conclusions about, say, the candidate's ability to handle the financial aspects of the job to be filled.

stress interview
An interview in which the applicant is made uncomfortable by a series of often rude questions. This technique helps identify hypersensitive applicants and those with low or high stress tolerance.

In a **stress interview**, the interviewer seeks to make the applicant uncomfortable with occasionally rude questions. The aim is supposedly to spot sensitive applicants and those with low (or high) stress tolerance. The interviewer might first probe for weaknesses in the applicant's background, such as a job that the applicant left under questionable circumstances. The interviewer then zeroes in on these weaknesses, hoping to get the candidate to lose his or her composure. Thus, a candidate for customer relations manager who obligingly mentions having had four jobs in the past two years might be told that frequent job changes reflect irresponsible and immature behavior. If the applicant then responds with a reasonable explanation of why the job changes were necessary, the interviewer might pursue another topic. On the other hand, if the formerly tranquil applicant reacts explosively with anger and disbelief, the interviewer might deduce that the person has a low tolerance for stress.

Stress interviews may help unearth hypersensitive applicants who might overreact to mild criticism with anger and abuse. However, the stress interview's invasive and ethically questionable nature demands that the interviewer be both skilled in its use and sure the job really calls for a thick skin and an ability to handle stress. This is definitely not an approach for amateur interrogators or for those without the skills to keep the interview under control.

Puzzle questions are popular today. Recruiters occasionally likes to use them to see how candidates think under pressure. For example, an interviewer at Microsoft asked a tech service applicant this: "Mike and Todd have $21 between them. Mike has $20 more than Todd. How much money has Mike, and how much money has Todd?"[16] (You'll find the answer two paragraphs below.)

Administering the Interview

Interviews can also be administered in various ways: *one-on-one or by a panel of interviewers; sequentially or all at once;* and *computerized or personally.*

Most interviews are **one-on-one** and **sequential**. In a one-on-one interview, two people meet alone, and one interviews the other by seeking oral responses to oral inquiries. At the same time, the employer schedules the candidate's interviews to be sequential. In a *sequential (or serial) interview*, several persons interview the applicant, in sequence, one-on-one, before a decision is made. In such a serial interview, candidates may cover the same ground over and over again with each interviewer. In an **unstructured sequential interview**, each interviewer may ask different questions. In a **structured sequential interview**, each interviewer rates the candidates on a standard evaluation form, using standardized questions. The hiring manager then reviews and compares the evaluations before deciding who to hire.[17] (Answer: Mike had $20.50, Todd $.50).

Panel Interviews   A **panel interview**, also known as a board interview, is defined as "an interview conducted by a team of interviewers (usually two to three), who together interview each candidate, and then combine their ratings into a final panel score." This contrasts with the *one-on-one interview* (in which one interviewer meets one candidate), and a *serial interview* (where several interviewers assess a single candidate one-on-one, sequentially).[18] The panel format enables interviewers to ask follow-up questions, much as

unstructured sequential interview
An interview in which each interviewer forms an independent opinion after asking different questions.

structured sequential interview
An interview in which the applicant is interviewed sequentially by several persons; each rates the applicant on a standard form.

panel interview
An interview in which a group of interviewers questions the applicant.

In a **panel interview**, a team of interviewers together interview each candidate, and then combine their ratings into a final panel score.

reporters do in press conferences. This may elicit more meaningful responses than are normally produced by a series of one-on-one interviews.

On the other hand, some candidates find panel interviews more stressful, so they may actually inhibit responses. An even more stressful variant is the **mass interview**. Here a panel interviews several candidates simultaneously. The panel poses a problem and then sits back and watches to see which candidate takes the lead in formulating an answer.

It's not clear whether, as a rule, panel interviews are more or less reliable and valid than other types of interviews, because how the employer actually conducts the panel interview has a big effect on reliability and validity. For example, structured panel interviews are more reliable and valid than unstructured ones. In particular, panel interviews in which members use scoring sheets with descriptive scoring anchors for sample answers are more reliable and valid than those that don't. And, training the panel interviewers may boost the interview's reliability, but probably not its validity.[19]

mass interview
A panel interviews several candidates simultaneously.

Phone and Video Interviews   Some interviews are done entirely by *telephone*. These can actually be more accurate than face-to-face interviews for judging an applicant's conscientiousness, intelligence, and interpersonal skills. Here, neither party need worry about things like appearance or handshakes, so each can focus on substantive answers. Or perhaps candidates—somewhat surprised by an unexpected call from the recruiter—just give more spontaneous answers.[20] In a typical study, interviewers tended to evaluate applicants more favorably in telephone versus face-to-face interviews, particularly where the interviewees were less physically attractive. However, the interviewers came to about the same conclusions regarding the interviewees whether the interview was face-to-face or by *videoconference*. The applicants themselves preferred the face-to-face interviews.[21]

Computerized Interviews

A *computerized selection interview* is one in which a job candidate's oral and/or computerized replies are obtained in response to computerized oral, visual, or written questions and/or situations. Most computerized interviews present the applicant with a series of questions regarding his or her background, experience, education, skills, knowledge, and work attitudes that relate to the job for which the person has applied.[22] Some (video-based) computerized interviews also confront candidates with realistic scenarios (such as irate customers) to which they must respond.

Typical computerized interviews present questions in a multiple choice format, one at a time; the applicant is expected to respond to the questions on the screen by pressing a key. For example, a sample interview question for a person applying for a job as a retail store clerk might be:

How would your supervisor rate your customer service skills?

a. Outstanding
b. Above average
c. Average
d. Below average
e. Poor[23]

Questions on a computerized interview come in rapid sequence and require the applicant to concentrate.[24] The typical computerized interview program measures the response time to each question. A delay in answering certain questions—such as "Can you be trusted?"—can flag a potential problem.

Great Western Bank Example   Here's how the system works at Great Western Bank. When Bonnie Dunn, 20 years old, tried out for a teller's job at Great Western Bank, she faced a lineup of tough customers.[25] One young woman sputtered contradictory instructions about depositing a check and then blew her top when the transaction wasn't handled fast enough. Another customer had an even shorter fuse: "You people are unbelievably slow," he said.

Both tough customers appeared on a computer screen, as part of a 20-minute computerized job interview. Ms. Dunn was seated in front of a personal computer, responding via a touch screen and a microphone. She was tested on making change and on sales skills, as well as keeping cool in tense situations.

When applicants sit down facing the computer at Great Western's bank branches, they hear it say, "Welcome to the interactive assessment aid." The computer doesn't understand what applicants say at that point, although it records their comments for evaluation later. To begin the interview, applicants touch a label on the screen, eliciting an ominous foreword: "We'll be keeping track of how long it takes you and how many mistakes you make. Accuracy is more important than speed."

First, the computer tests the applicant on money skills, asking him or her to cash a check for $192.18, including at least three $5 bills and two dollars in quarters. Then, when an angry customer appears on the screen, the system expects candidates to grab the microphone and mollify him. Later, a bank official who listens to the recorded interviews gives applicants five points for maintaining a friendly tone of voice, plus up to 15 points for apologizing, promising to solve the customer's problem, and, taking a cue from the screen, suggesting that in the future he use the bank's deposit-only line.

The touchy young woman on the screen is tougher. Speaking fast, she says she wants to cash a $150 check, get $40 in cash, and put $65 in savings and the rest in checking. As an applicant struggles to sort that out, she quickly adds, "No, it has to be $50 in checking because I just wrote a check this morning." If the applicant then touches a label on the screen that says "?" the woman fumes, "How many times do I have to tell you?"

Great Western reports success with its system. It dramatically reduced useless personal interviewing of unacceptable candidates. And, partly because the candidates see what the job's really like, those hired are reportedly 26% less likely to quit or be fired within 90 days of hiring.

Pic 'n Pay Stores Example Employers often use computer-aided interviews to prescreen out unacceptable candidates. Pic 'n Pay stores, a chain of 915 self-service shoe stores headquartered in North Carolina, gives job applicants an 800 number to dial for a computerized interview. The interview contains 100 questions and lasts about 10 minutes. Applicants press 1 for *yes* and 0 for *no*. Every applicant then gets a follow-up live telephone interview, from one of the firm's six dedicated interviewers.

Web-Assisted Interviews Many firms use the Web to assist in the employee interview process. For instance, Cisco Systems, Inc. (which in 2006 expanded its core business to include video-conferencing equipment) equips Cisco recruiters with PC video cameras, so they can conduct preliminary interviews via online Webcasts. The recruiter instructs the applicant to use his or her own camera-supported PC (or go to a local FedEx Kinko's or similar business). Then, at the appointed time, he or she links to Cisco via Web video for the interview. Cisco doesn't plan to eliminate face-to-face interviews. However, the Web-video interviews do reduce travel and recruiting expenses, and make things easier for candidates. Jobs.com conducts frequent live, interactive online career fairs. Job seekers go to the jobs.com interactive career Web site and select a city and job category. They can then participate in a live, interactive career fair event. The U.S. Army also now does online recruiting at its recruiter chat site.

Pros and Cons Computer-aided interviews can be advantageous. Systems like those at Great Western and Pic 'n Pay reduce the time managers devote to interviewing unacceptable candidates.[26] Applicants are reportedly more honest with computers than they would be with people, presumably because computers aren't judgmental.[27] The computer can also be sneaky; if an applicant takes longer than average to answer certain questions, he or she may be summarily screened out, or at least questioned more deeply in that area by a human interviewer. Several of the interpersonal interview problems we'll discuss later in this chapter (such as making snap judgments about interviewees based on physical appearance) are also obviously avoided with this approach.[28] On the other hand, the mechanical nature of computer-aided interviews can leave applicants feeling that both the process and the employer were rather impersonal.

Are Interviews Useful?

While used by virtually all managers, interviews received low marks for reliability and validity in early studies. However, today (as noted previously), studies confirm that the "validity of the interview is greater than previously believed,"[29] and that the interview is "generally a much better predictor of performance than previously thought and is comparable with many other selection techniques[30].

But there are three caveats. First, you should *structure the interview*.[31] Structured interviews (particularly structured situational interviews) are more valid than unstructured interviews for predicting job performance. They are more valid partly because they are more reliable—for example, the same interviewer administers the interview more consistently from candidate to candidate.[32] Situational interviews yield a higher mean validity than do job-related (or behavioral) interviews, which in turn yield a higher mean validity than do psychological interviews, (which focus more on motives and interests).[33]

The second caveat is this: Be careful *what sorts of traits* you try to assess. A typical study illustrates why. Interviewers were able to size up the interviewee's extraversion and agreeableness. What they could *not* assess accurately were the traits that often matter most on jobs—like conscientiousness and emotional stability.[34] The implication seems to be to not focus (as many do) on hard-to-assess traits like conscientiousness. Limit yourself mostly to situational and job knowledge questions that help you assess how the candidate will actually respond to typical situations on that job. We'll explain how to do this later in the chapter. Third, it is clear that the manager must keep in mind the *various factors that can undermine* any interview's usefulness. We turn to these next.

❷ Explain and illustrate at least six factors that affect the usefulness of interviews.

WHAT CAN UNDERMINE AN INTERVIEW'S USEFULNESS?

Hiring the right people is an essential management job, and you can't do that job if you don't know how to interview. Several things can undermine an interview's usefulness.

First Impressions (Snap Judgments)

Perhaps the most consistent finding is that interviewers tend to jump to conclusions—make snap judgments—about candidates during the first few minutes of the interview (or even before the interview starts, based on test scores or résumé data). One researcher estimates that in 85% of the cases, interviewers had made up their minds before the interview even began, based on first impressions the interviewers gleaned from candidates' applications and personal appearance.[35] In one study giving interviewers the candidates' test scores biased the ultimate assessment of the candidates.[36]

First impressions are especially damaging when the prior information about the candidate is negative. In one study, interviewers who previously received unfavorable reference letters about applicants gave those applicants less credit for past successes and held them more personally responsible for past failures after the interview. And their final decisions (to accept or reject applicants) were always tied to what they expected of the applicants based on the references, quite aside from the applicants' actual interview performance.[37]

Add to this the fact that interviewers seem to have a consistently negative bias. They are more influenced by unfavorable than favorable information about the candidate. Furthermore, their impressions are much more likely to change from favorable to unfavorable than from unfavorable to favorable. Indeed, a common interviewing mistake is to turn the interview into a search for negative information.

In a sense, therefore, most interviews are probably loaded against the applicant. An applicant who starts well could easily end up with a low rating, because unfavorable information tends to carry more weight in the interview. An interviewee who starts out poorly will find it hard to overcome that first bad impression.[38]

One London-based psychologist who interviewed the chief executives of 80 top companies came to these conclusions about snap judgments in selection interviews:

> "Really, to make a good impression, you don't even get time to open your mouth . . . An interviewer's response to you will generally be preverbal—how you walk through the door, what your posture is like, whether you smile, whether you have a captivating aura, whether you have a firm, confident handshake. You've got about half a minute to make an impact and after that all you are doing is building on a good or bad first impression . . . It's a very emotional response."[39]

Misunderstanding the Job

Interviewers who don't have an accurate picture of what the job entails and what sort of candidate is best suited for it usually make their decisions based on incorrect impressions or stereotypes of what a good applicant is. They then erroneously match interviewees with their incorrect stereotypes.

One classic study involved 30 professional interviewers.[40] Half got just a brief description of the jobs for which they were recruiting: They were told the "eight applicants here represented by their application blanks are applying for the position of secretary." The other 15 interviewers got much more explicit job information, in terms of typing speed and bilingual ability, for instance.

More job knowledge translated into better interviews. The 15 interviewers who had more job information generally agreed among themselves about each candidate's potential, while those without complete job information did not. The latter also didn't discriminate as well among applicants—they tended to give them all high ratings.

Candidate-Order (Contrast) Error and Pressure to Hire

candidate-order error
An error of judgment on the part of the interviewer due to interviewing one or more very good or very bad candidates just before the interview in question.

Candidate-order (or contrast) error means that the order in which you see applicants affects how you rate them. In one study, managers had to evaluate a candidate who was "just average" after first evaluating several "unfavorable" candidates. They scored the average candidate more favorably than they might otherwise have done because, in contrast to the unfavorable candidates, the average one looked better than he actually was. This contrast effect can be huge: In some early studies, evaluators based only a small part of the applicant's rating on his or her actual potential.[41]

Pressure to hire accentuates problems like this. Researchers told one group of managers to assume they were behind in their recruiting quota. They told a second group they were ahead of their quota. Those "behind" evaluated the same recruits much more highly than did those "ahead."[42]

Nonverbal Behavior and Impression Management

The applicant's nonverbal behavior can also have a surprisingly large impact on his or her rating. In one study, 52 human resource specialists watched videotaped job interviews in which the applicants' verbal content was identical, but their nonverbal behavior differed markedly. Researchers told applicants in one group to exhibit minimal eye contact, a low energy level, and low voice modulation. Those in a second group demonstrated the opposite behavior. Of the 26 personnel specialists who saw the high-eye-contact, high-energy-level candidate, 23 would have invited him or her for a second interview. None who saw the low-eye-contact, low-energy-level candidate would have recommended a second interview.[43] It certainly seems to pay for interviewees to "look alive."

In another study, interviewers listened to audio interviews and watched video interviews. Vocal cues (such as the interviewee's pitch, speech rates, and pauses) and visual cues (such as physical attractiveness, smile, and body orientation) correlated with the evaluator's judgments of whether or not the interviewees could be liked and trusted, and were credible.[44]

Nonverbal behaviors are probably so important because interviewers infer the interviewee's personality from the way he or she acts in the interview. In one study, 99 graduating college seniors completed questionnaires both before and after their job interviews; the questionnaires included measures of personality, among other things.[45] The seniors then reported their success in generating follow-up job interviews and job offers. The interviewee's personality, particularly his or her level of extraversion, had a pronounced influence on whether or not he or she received follow-up interviews and job offers. In part, this seems to be because "interviewers draw inferences about the applicant's personality based on the applicant's behavior during the interview."[46] Extraverted applicants seem particularly prone to self-promotion, and self-promotion is strongly related to the interviewer's perceptions of candidate–job fit.[47]

Impression Management In fact, clever interviewees do say and do things to manage the impression they present. One study found that some used ingratiation to persuade interviewers to like them, for instance by praising them or appearing to agree with their opinions. Others used self-promotion tactics, for instance by making complimentary comments about their own accomplishments.[48] Ingratiation involves, for example, agreeing with the recruiter's opinions and thus signaling that they share similar beliefs. Knowing that a perceived similarity in attitudes or values may influence how the interviewer rates the applicant's competence, some interviewees may try to emphasize (or fabricate) such similarities.[49] Self-promotion means promoting one's own skills and abilities to create the impression of competence.[50]

Some researchers in this area question results like these. The problem is that much of the interviewing research uses students as raters and hypothetical jobs, so it's not clear that we can apply the findings to the real world. For example, "In operational settings, where actual jobs are at stake, faking or socially desirable responding may be more likely to distort personality measurement and obscure relationships."[51] But, realistically, anyone who has been through an interview probably recognizes that such impression management goes on (and probably works, at least up to a point).

Effect of Personal Characteristics: Attractiveness, Gender, Race

Interviewers also must guard against letting an applicant's *attractiveness* and *gender* distort their assessments.[52] For example, people usually ascribe more favorable traits and more successful life outcomes to attractive people.[53] In one study, subjects had to evaluate candidates for promotion based on photographs. They perceived men as being more suitable for hire and more likely to advance to a next executive level than they did equally qualified women; they preferred more attractive candidates, especially men, over less attractive ones.[54] "Even when female managers exhibited the same career-advancing behaviors as male managers, they still earned less money and were offered fewer career-progressing transfer opportunities."[55]

Race can also play a role, depending on how you conduct the interview. In one study, the interviewees appeared before three panels whose racial composition was either primarily black (75% black, 25% white), balanced (50% black, 50% white), or primarily white (75% white, 25% black).[56] On the primarily black panels, black and white raters judged black and white candidates similarly. In the primarily white and in the racially balanced panels, white interviewers rated white candidates higher, while black interviewers rated black candidates higher. In all cases, structured interviews produced less of a difference between minority and white interviewees on average than did unstructured interviews.[57]

Such findings don't necessarily apply to other EEOC-protected classes. In another study, candidates evidencing a wide range of attributes and disabilities (such as child-care demands, HIV-positive status, and being wheelchair-bound) had less chance of obtaining a positive decision, even when the person performed very well in the structured interview.[58] Because the applicant's "race, gender, hair style, teeth and even facial tics" can influence the interview process in a discriminatory way, the European Community is considering a new directive. It would require that employers conduct recruitment interviews with screens between the applicant and the interviewers, or over a room-to-room speakerphone.[59] "The New Workforce" expands on this topic.

The NEW Workforce — Applicant Disability and the Employment Interview

A study by the Research and Evaluation Center at the National Center for Disability Services provides some insight into what disabled people who use "assistive technology" at work expect and prefer from interviewers.[60] Researchers surveyed 40 disabled people from various occupations to arrive at their conclusions. The basic finding was that the disabled people felt that interviewers tend to avoid directly addressing the disability, and therefore make their decisions without getting all the facts.

What the disabled people prefer is an open discussion, one that would allow the employer to clarify his or her concerns and reach a knowledgeable conclusion. Among the questions disabled persons said they would like interviewers to ask were these:

- Is there any kind of setting or special equipment that will facilitate the interview process for you?
- Is there any specific technology that you currently use or have used in previous jobs that assists the way you work?
- Other than technology, what other kind of support did you have in previous jobs? If none, is there anything that would benefit you?

- Provide an example of how you would use technology to carry out your job duties.
- Is there any technology that you don't currently have that would be helpful in performing the duties of this position?
- In the past, did you experience any problems between your technology and the company's information systems?
- Do you foresee your technology needs changing in the near future? Why and how?
- Discuss a barrier or obstacle, if any, that you have encountered in any of your previous jobs. How was that addressed?
- Do you anticipate any transportation or scheduling issues with the work schedule expected of this position?

Remember that, under the Americans with Disabilities Act, the interviewer must limit his or her questions to whether the applicant has any physical or mental impairment that may interfere with his or her ability to perform the job's essential tasks.[61]

Employment discrimination is always abhorrent, but the use of employment discrimination "testers" makes nondiscriminatory interviewing even more important. As defined by the EEOC, testers are "individuals who apply for employment which they do not intend to accept, for the sole purpose of uncovering unlawful discriminatory hiring practices."[62] Although they're not really seeking employment, testers have legal standing, with the courts and with the EEOC.[63]

A case illustrates the usual approach. A private, nonprofit civil rights group sent four university students—two white, two black—to an employment agency, supposedly in pursuit of a job. The four testers were given backgrounds and training to make them appear almost indistinguishable from each other in terms of qualifications. However, the white applicants and black applicants were allegedly treated differently. For example, the white tester/applicants got interviews and job offers, while the black tester/applicants got neither interviews nor offers.[64]

Interviewer Behavior

Anyone who's been interviewed also knows that the *interviewer's* behavior also affects the interviewee's performance and rating.

Consider some examples. Some interviewers inadvertently telegraph the expected answers,[65] as in: "This job calls for handling a lot of stress. You can do that, can't you?" Even subtle cues (like a smile or nod) can telegraph the desired answer.[66] Some interviewers talk so much that applicants have no time to answer questions. At the other extreme, some interviewers let the applicant dominate the interview, and so don't ask all their questions.[67] When interviewers have favorable pre-interview impressions of the applicant, they tend to act more positively toward that person (smiling more, for instance), possibly because they want to increase the chance that the applicant will accept the job.[68] Other interviewers play district attorney. It's smart to be alert for inconsistencies, but uncivil to play "gotcha" by gleefully pouncing on them. Some interviewers play amateur psychologist, unprofessionally probing for hidden meanings in everything the applicants say.[69] And, of course, some interviewers are simply inept, unable to formulate decent questions, while others are gifted at drawing out the best in interviewees.

DESIGNING AND CONDUCTING AN EFFECTIVE INTERVIEW

There are two basic ways to avoid these interview problems. One is obvious: Keep them in mind and avoid them (don't make snap judgements, for instance). The second is not quite so obvious: Be careful how you design and structure the interview. Structured interviews can minimize many of the problems we discussed. Let's therefore look next at structuring the interview, and at some guidelines for effective interviews.

The Structured Situational Interview

There is little doubt that the structured situational interview—a series of job-oriented questions with predetermined answers that interviewers ask of all applicants for the job—produces superior results.[70] The basic idea is to write situational (what would you do) or behavioral (what did you do), or job knowledge questions, and have job experts (like those supervising the job) also write answers rated from good to poor. The raters typically use descriptively anchored rating scale answer sheets to rate the interviewees' answers; these use short descriptions to illustrate good, average, or poor performance).[71]

Structured employment interviews using either situational questions or behavioral questions tend to yield high validities. However, structured interviews with situational question formats yield the higher ratings. This may be because interviewers get more consistent (reliable) responses with situational questions (which force all applicants to apply the same scenario) than they do with behavioral questions (which require each applicant to find applicable experiences.)[72] In creating structured situational interviews, people familiar with the job develop questions based on the job's actual duties. They then reach consensus on what are and are not acceptable answers. The procedure is as follows.[73]

Step 1: Job Analysis   Write a job description with a list of job duties, required knowledge, skills, abilities, and other worker qualifications.

Step 2: Rate the Job's Main Duties   Identify the job's main duties. To do so, rate each job duty based on its importance to job success and on the time required to perform it compared to other tasks.

Step 3: Create Interview Questions   Create interview questions based on actual job duties, with more questions for the important duties.

Structured situational interviews may actually contain several types of questions. *Situational questions* pose a hypothetical job situation, such as "What would you do if the machine suddenly began heating up?" *Job knowledge questions* assess knowledge essential to job performance. These often deal with technical aspects of a job (such as "What is HTML?"). *Willingness questions* gauge the applicant's willingness and motivation to meet the job's requirements—to do repetitive physical work or to travel, for instance. *Behavioral questions* of course ask candidates how they've handled similar situations.

The people who create the questions usually write them in terms of critical incidents. For example, for a supervisory candidate, the interviewer might ask this situational question:

> Your spouse and two teenage children are sick in bed with colds. There are no relatives or friends available to look in on them. Your shift starts in three hours. What would you do in this situation?

Step 4: Create Benchmark Answers   Next, *for each question*, develop several descriptive answers and a five-point rating scale for each, with ideal answers for good (a 5 rating), marginal (a 3 rating), and poor (a 1 rating). For example, consider the preceding situational question, where the spouse and children are sick. Each member of the committee writes good, marginal, and poor answers based on things they have actually heard in an interview from people who then turned out to be good, marginal, or poor (as the case may be) on the job. After a group discussion, they reach consensus on the answers to use as benchmarks for each scenario. Three benchmark answers (from low to high) for the example question might be, "I'd stay home—my spouse and family come first" (1); "I'd phone my supervisor and explain my situation" (3); and "Since they only have colds, I'd come to work" (5).

Step 5: Appoint the Interview Panel and Conduct Interviews   Employers generally conduct structured situational interviews using a panel, rather than one-on-one or sequentially. The panel usually consists of three to six members, preferably the same ones who wrote the questions and answers. It may also include the job's supervisor and/or incumbent, and an HR representative. The same panel interviews all candidates for the job.[74]

The panel members generally review the job description, questions, and benchmark answers before the interview. One panel member usually introduces the applicant, and asks all questions of all applicants in this and succeeding interviews (to ensure consistency). However, all panel members record and rate the applicant's answers on the rating scale sheet. They do this by indicating where the candidate's answer to each question falls relative to the ideal poor, marginal, or good answers. At the end of the interview, someone explains the follow-up procedure and answers any questions the applicant has.[75]

Web-based programs help interviewers design and organize behavior based selection interviews. For example, SelectPro (www.selectpro.com) enables interviewers to create behavior-based selection interviews, custom interview guides, and automated online interviews.

⊗ Explain and illustrate each guideline for being a more effective interviewer.

How to Conduct a More Effective Interview

Yet in practice, some employers are quite successful without structured interviews. For example, the Container Store (which often tops the lists of best employers to work for) requires each applicant to have two to three screening interviews, each of which lasts two to three hours.[76] As one Container Store human resource manager puts it, "They are often more like noninterview discussions, so that our interviews do not put people off guard. They put people at ease."

You may not have the time or inclination to create actual structured situational interviews. However, there is still a lot you can do to make your interviews more effective. Suggestions include:

Structure Your Interview   There are several things you can do to help the interviewer ask more consistent and job-relevant questions, without actually creating a structured situational interview.[77] They include:[78]

1. Base questions on *actual job duties*. This will minimize irrelevant questions. It may also reduce the likelihood of bias, because there's less opportunity to "read" things into the answer.
2. Use *job knowledge, situational, or behavioral questions*, and objective criteria to evaluate the interviewee's responses. Questions that simply ask for opinions and attitudes, goals and aspirations, and self-descriptions and self-evaluations allow candidates to present themselves in an overly favorable manner or avoid revealing weaknesses. Structured interview questions can reduce subjectivity and therefore the chance for inaccurate conclusions, and bias.[79] Figure 7-2 illustrates some structured interview questions.

FIGURE 7-2

Examples of Questions That Provide Structure

Note: These questions provide structure, insofar as they are job-related and the employer can be consistent in asking them of all candidates.

Source: Michael Campion, David Palmer, and James Campion, "A Review of Structure in the Selection Interview," *Personnel Psychology* (1997), p. 668. Reprinted by permission of Wiley–Blackwell.

Situational Questions
1. Suppose a co-worker was not following standard work procedures. The co-worker was more experienced than you and claimed the new procedure was better. Would you use the new procedure?
2. Suppose you were giving a sales presentation and a difficult technical question arose that you could not answer. What would you do?

Past Behavior Questions
3. Based on your past work experience, what is the most significant action you have ever taken to help out a co-worker?
4. Can you provide an example of a specific instance where you developed a sales presentation that was highly effective?

Background Questions
5. What work experiences, training, or other qualifications do you have for working in a team-work environment?
6. What experience have you had with direct point-of-purchase sales?

Job Knowledge Questions
7. What steps would you follow to conduct a brainstorming session with a group of employees on safety?
8. What factors should you consider when developing a television advertising campaign?

3. *Train interviewers*. For example, review EEO laws with prospective interviewers and train them to avoid irrelevant or potentially discriminatory questions, and to avoid stereotyping minority candidates. Explain (with examples) the problems, like snap judgments, that undermine interviews. Emphasize the need to base questions on job-related information.

4. *Use the same questions* with all candidates. When it comes to asking questions, the prescription seems to be "the more standardized, the better." Using the same questions with all candidates improves reliability and can also reduce bias "because of the obvious fairness of giving all the candidates the exact same opportunity."

5. Use *descriptive rating scales* (excellent, fair, poor) to rate answers. For each question, if possible, provide several possible ideal answers and a score for each. Then you can rate each candidate's answers against this scale. This ensures that all interviewers are using the same standards.

6. Use *multiple interviewers* or panel interviews. Doing so can reduce bias by diminishing the importance of one interviewer's idiosyncratic opinions, and by bringing in more points of view.

7. If possible, use a *standardized interview form*. Interviews based on structured guides like the one in Figure 7-A2 (pages 286–288) usually result in better interviews.[80] At the very least, list your questions before the interview.

8. *Control the interview*. Techniques here include, limit the interviewers' follow-up questions (to ensure all interviewees get the same questions), use a larger number of questions, and prohibit questions from candidates until after the interview.[81]

9. Take *brief, unobtrusive notes* during the interview. Doing so may help overcome "the recency effect" (putting too much weight on the last few minutes of the interview). It may also help avoid making a snap decision based on inadequate information early in the interview, and may also help jog your memory once the interview is complete. (A study did confirm that note taking helped interviewers recall the interviewee's behavior. However, at least in this study, those who did take notes were no more accurate in sizing up interviewees than those who did not. The bottom line seems to be to take notes, but not copious ones, instead noting just the key points of what the interviewee says).[82]

Does it make sense for employers to ask applicants about their extracurricular activities? In one study, researchers had 618 college students complete online surveys assessing their extracurricular activities. The researchers then had the students participate in an assessment center. Here they evaluated the students in terms of four dimensions—communication, initiative, decision making, and teamwork. "The results revealed that extracurricular activities are significantly associated with each of the four interpersonal skill dimensions."[83]

Prepare for the Interview   The interview should take place in a private room where telephone calls are not accepted and you can minimize interruptions. Prior to the interview, review the candidate's application and résumé, and note any areas that are vague or that may indicate strengths or weaknesses. In one study, about 39% of the 191 respondents said interviewers were unprepared or unfocused.[84]

Most interviews probably fail to unearth the best candidate because the interviewer is unprepared, or overconfident, or just plain lazy. General questions like, "What are your main strengths?" or "Why did you leave your last job?" may not be totally useless. But what you really want to do is go into the interview with a set of specific questions that focus on the skills and experiences the ideal candidate for that job needs.

Here, remember, it's essential that you know the duties of the job, and the specific skills and abilities you should be looking for. At a minimum, review the job specifications. Go into

Go into the interview with an accurate picture of the traits of an ideal candidate, know what you're going to ask, and be prepared to keep an open mind about the candidate.

the interview with an accurate picture of the traits of an ideal candidate, and know what you're going to ask. Be prepared to keep an open mind about the candidate, and to keep a record of the answers, and review them after the interview. Make your decision then.

Establish Rapport   The main point of the interview is to find out about the applicant. To do this, you need to put the person at ease. Doing so improves interview performance. For example, researchers used a scale called the Measure of Anxiety in Selection Interviews (MASI) to study how interview stress affected the interview performance of two groups, a student sample (212 people) and job applicants in a field setting (276 people). The MASI scores correlated negatively with measures of interview performance. The results "attest to the potential value of reducing interview anxiety among job applicants."[85] Similarly, people who feel more self-confident about their interviewing skills perform better on interviews.[86]

Greet all applicants—even drop-ins—courteously and start the interview with a noncontroversial question—perhaps about the weather. Keep the applicant's status in mind. For example, if the person is unemployed, or is coming back to the workforce after many years, he or she may be exceptionally nervous, and you may want to take additional steps to put the person at ease.[87]

Ask Questions   Ideally here, it is best to ask situational or similarly structured questions, as we just explained. In any case:

- Follow your list of questions. (Figure 7-3 presents additional sample questions.)
- Some do's and don'ts for actually asking questions include:
  - don't ask questions that can be answered yes or no;
  - don't put words in the applicant's mouth or telegraph the desired answer;
  - don't interrogate the applicant as if the person is a criminal, and don't be patronizing, sarcastic, or inattentive;
  - don't monopolize the interview or let the applicant dominate the interview;

FIGURE 7-3

Suggested Supplementary Questions for Interviewing Applicants

Source: Reprinted from www.HR.BLR.com with permission of the publisher Business and Legal Reports, Inc. 141 Mill Rock Road East, Old Saybrook, CT © 2004.

1. How did you choose this line of work?
2. What did you enjoy most about your last job?
3. What did you like least about your last job?
4. What has been your greatest frustration or disappointment on your present job? Why?
5. What are some of the pluses and minuses of your last job?
6. What were the circumstances surrounding your leaving your last job?
7. Did you give notice?
8. Why should we be hiring you?
9. What do you expect from this employer?
10. What are three things you will not do in your next job?
11. What would your last supervisor say your three weaknesses are?
12. What are your major strengths?
13. How can your supervisor best help you obtain your goals?
14. How did your supervisor rate your job performance?
15. In what ways would you change your last supervisor?
16. What are your career goals during the next 1–3 years? 5–10 years?
17. How will working for this company help you reach those goals?
18. What did you do the last time you received instructions with which you disagreed?
19. What are some of the things about which you and your supervisor disagreed? What did you do?
20. Which do you prefer, working alone or working with groups?
21. What motivated you to do better at your last job?
22. Do you consider your progress on that job representative of your ability? Why?
23. Do you have any questions about the duties of the job for which you have applied?
24. Can you perform the essential functions of the job for which you have applied?

- do ask open-ended questions;
- do listen to the candidate to encourage him or her to express thoughts fully;
- and do draw out the applicant's opinions and feelings by repeating the person's last comment as a question (such as "You didn't like your last job?").

- To get more candid answers, mention that you're going to conduct reference checks. Ask, "If I were to arrange for an interview with your boss, and if the boss were very candid with me, what's your best guess as to what he or she would say as your strengths, weaker points, and overall performance?"[88]
- Finally, if you ask for general statements of a candidate's accomplishments, ask for examples.[89] If the candidate lists specific strengths or weaknesses, follow up with "What are specific examples that demonstrate each of your strengths?"

Close the Interview Leave time to answer any questions the candidate may have and, if appropriate, to advocate your firm to the candidate.

Try to end the interview on a positive note. Tell the applicant whether there is any interest and, if so, what the next step will be. Make rejections diplomatically: for instance, "Although your background is impressive, there are other candidates whose experience is closer to our requirements." If the applicant is still being considered but you can't reach a decision now, say so. If your policy is to inform candidates of their status in writing, do so within a few days of the interview.

In rejecting a candidate, one perennial question is, should you provide an explanation or not? In one study, rejected candidates who received an explanation detailing why the employer rejected them felt that the rejection process was fairer. These people were also more likely to give the employer a better recommendation, and to apply again for jobs with the firm. Unfortunately, providing detailed explanations may not be practical. As the researchers put it,

> "We were unsuccessful in a number of attempts to secure a site for our applied study. Of three organizations that expressed interest in our research, all eventually declined to participate in the study because they were afraid that any additional information in the rejection letters might increase legal problems. They were reluctant to give rejected applicants information that can be used to dispute the decision."[90]

④ Effectively interview a job candidate.

Review the Interview   Once the candidate leaves, and while the interview is fresh in your mind, review your notes and fill in the structured interview guide (if you

When You're on Your OWN
HR for Line Managers and Entrepreneurs

Employment Interviewing[91]

A practical, streamlined employment interview process is as follows:

Preparing for the Interview

Even a busy entrepreneur or manager can quickly specify the kind of person who would be best for the job. One way to do so is to focus on four basic required factors—knowledge and experience, motivation, intellectual capacity, and personality—and to ask the following questions:

- *Knowledge and experience:* What must the candidate know to perform the job? What experience is absolutely necessary to perform the job?
- *Motivation:* What should the person like doing to enjoy this job? Is there anything the person should not dislike? Are there any essential goals or aspirations the person should have? Are there any unusual energy demands on the job?
- *Intellectual capacity:* Are there any specific intellectual aptitudes required (mathematical, mechanical, and so on)? How complex are the problems the person must solve? What must a person be able to demonstrate he or she can do intellectually? How should the person solve problems (cautiously, deductively, and so on)?
- *Personality factor:* What are the critical personality qualities needed for success on the job (ability to

withstand boredom, decisiveness, stability, and so on)? How must the job incumbent handle stress, pressure, and criticism? What kind of interpersonal behavior is required in the job up the line, at peer level, down the line, and outside the firm with customers?

Specific Factors to Probe in the Interview

Next, ask a combination of situational questions, plus open-ended questions like those in Figure 7-3, to probe the candidate's suitability for the job. For example:

- *Intellectual factor.* Here, assess such things as complexity of tasks the person has performed, grades in school, test results (including scholastic aptitude tests, and so on), and how the person organizes his or her thoughts and communicates.
- *Motivation factor.* Probe such areas as: the person's likes and dislikes (for each thing done, what he or she liked or disliked about it); aspirations (including the validity of each goal in terms of the person's reasoning about why he or she chose it); and energy level, perhaps by asking what he or she does on, say, a "typical Tuesday."
- *Personality factor.* Here, probe by looking for self-defeating behaviors (aggressiveness, compulsive fidgeting, and so on) and by exploring the person's

used one and if you did not fill it in during the interview). Reviewing the interview shortly after the candidate leaves can also help minimize snap judgments and negative emphasis.

Another Practical Approach Prescriptions like "know the job," "know the skills you're looking for," and "structure the job interview" can be easier said than done, even if you're working at a *Fortune 500* company. All the corporate resources won't do you much good if, as often happens, the company hasn't made provisions to provide employment interview training and support for its managers. There you sit with a candidate about to arrive for her job interview.

What should you do? Following this chapter's guidelines is the preferred approach, but perhaps you don't have the time to create, say, a structured situational interview. What follows, in the accompanying "When You're On Your Own" feature is a streamlined procedure.

past interpersonal relationships. Ask questions about the person's past interactions (working in a group at school, working with fraternity brothers or sorority sisters, leading the work team on the last job, and so on). Also, try to judge the person's behavior in the interview itself—is the candidate personable? Shy? Outgoing?

• *Knowledge and experience factor.* Here, probe with situational questions such as "How would you organize such a sales effort?" "How would you design that kind of Web site?"

Conducting the Interview

• **Have a Plan** Devise and use a plan to guide the interview. According to interviewing expert John Drake, significant areas to cover include the candidate's:

- College experiences
- Work experiences—summer, part-time
- Work experience—full-time (one by one)
- Goals and ambitions
- Reactions to the job you are interviewing for
- Self-assessments (by the candidate of his or her strengths and weaknesses)
- Military experiences
- Present outside activities[92]

• **Follow Your Plan** Perhaps start with an open-ended question for each topic, such as, "Could you tell me about what you did when you were in high school?" Keep in mind that you are trying to elicit information about four main traits—intelligence, motivation, personality, and knowledge and experience. You can then accumulate the information in each of these four areas as the person answers. Follow up on particular areas that you want to pursue by asking questions like, "Could you elaborate on that, please?"

Match the Candidate to the Job

After following the interview plan and probing for the four factors, you should be able to draw conclusions about the person's intellectual capacity, knowledge and experience, motivation, and personality, and to summarize the candidate's general strengths and limitations. You should then compare your conclusions to both the job description and the list of behavioral requirements you developed when preparing for the interview. This should provide a rational basis for matching the candidate to the job—one based on an analysis of the traits and aptitudes the job actually requires.

You might use an interview evaluation form to compile your impressions (for instance, see Figure 7-4).

FIGURE 7-4

Interview Evaluation Form

Source: Reprinted from www.HR.BLR.com with permission of the publisher Business and Legal Reports Inc. 141 Mill Rock Road East, Old Saybrook, CT © 2004.

Name of candidate:

Date interviewed:

Position:

Completed by:

Date:

Instructions: Circle one number for each criterion, then add them together for a total.

KNOWLEDGE OF SPECIFIC JOB AND JOB-RELATED TOPICS

0. No knowledge evident.
1. Less than we would prefer.
2. Meets requirements for hiring.
3. Exceeds our expectations of average candidates.
4. Thoroughly versed in job and very strong in associated areas.

EXPERIENCE

0. None for this job; no related experience either.
1. Would prefer more for this job. Adequate for job applied for.
2. More than sufficient for job.
3. Totally experienced in job.
4. Strong experience in all related areas.

COMMUNICATION

0. Could not communicate. Will be severely impaired in most jobs.
1. Some difficulties. Will detract from job performance.
2. Sufficient for adequate job performance.
3. More than sufficient for job.
4. Outstanding ability to communicate.

INTEREST IN POSITION AND ORGANIZATION

0. Showed no interest.
1. Some lack of interest.
2. Appeared genuinely interested.
3. Very interested. Seems to prefer type of work applied for.
4. Totally absorbed with job content. Conveys feeling only this job will do.

OVERALL MOTIVATION TO SUCCEED

0. None exhibited.
1. Showed little interest in advancement.
2. Average interest in advancement.
3. Highly motivated. Strong desire to advance.
4. Extremely motivated. Very strong desire to succeed and advance.

POISE AND CONFIDENCE

0. Extremely distracted and confused. Displayed uneven temper.
1. Sufficient display of confusion or loss of temper to interfere with job performance.
2. Sufficient poise and confidence to perform job.
3. No loss of poise during interview. Confidence in ability to handle pressure.
4. Displayed impressive poise under stress. Appears unusually confident and secure.

COMPREHENSION

0. Did not understand many points and concepts.
1. Missed some ideas or concepts.
2. Understood most new ideas and skills discussed.
3. Grasped all new points and concepts quickly.
4. Extremely sharp. Understood subtle points and underlying motives.

_____ **TOTAL POINTS**

ADDITIONAL REMARKS:

REVIEW

SUMMARY

1. There are several basic types of interviews—situational, nondirective, structured, sequential, panel, stress, and appraisal interviews, for instance. We can classify interviews according to content, structure, and method of administration.
2. Several factors and problems can undermine the usefulness of an interview. These are making premature decisions, letting unfavorable information predominate, not knowing the requirements of the job, being under pressure to hire, the candidate-order effect, and sending visual cues to telegraph enthusiasm.
3. The five steps in the interview are: Plan, establish rapport, question the candidate, close the interview, and review the data.
4. Guidelines for interviewers include: Use a structured guide, know the requirements of the job, focus on traits you can more accurately evaluate, let the interviewee do most of the talking, delay your decision until after the interview, and remember the EEOC requirements.
5. Increasingly, employers use computers and the Web to assist in the employee interview process. As explained in this chapter, firms now conduct at least the preliminary interviews online, often using video-assisted scenarios. Several of the newer systems combine initial interviews with applicant tracking, to facilitate the employee selection process.
6. The steps in a structured or situational interview are: Analyze the job, evaluate the job duty information, develop interview questions with critical incidents, develop benchmark answers, appoint an interview committee, and implement.
7. A quick procedure for conducting an interview is to develop behavioral specifications; determine the basic intellectual, motivational, personality, and experience factors to probe for; use an interview plan; and then match the individual to the job.
8. As an interviewee, keep in mind that interviewers tend to make premature decisions and let unfavorable information predominate; your appearance and enthusiasm are important; you should get the interviewer to talk; it is important to prepare before walking in—get to know the job and the problems the interviewer wants solved; and you should stress your enthusiasm and motivation to work, and how your accomplishments match your interviewer's needs. (See the Appendix to this chapter, Guidelines for Interviewees.)

DISCUSSION QUESTIONS

1. Explain and illustrate the basic ways in which you can classify selection interviews.
2. Briefly describe each of the following possible types of interviews; unstructured panel interviews; structured sequential interviews; job-related structured interviews.
3. For what sorts of jobs do you think computerized interviews are most appropriate? Why?
4. Why do you think "situational interviews yield a higher mean validity than do job-related or behavioral interviews, which in turn yield a higher mean validity than do psychological interviews"?
5. Similarly, how would you explain the fact that structured interviews, regardless of content, are more valid than unstructured interviews for predicting job performance?
6. Briefly discuss and give examples of at least five common interviewing mistakes. What recommendations would you give for avoiding these interviewing mistakes?
7. Briefly discuss what an interviewer can do to improve his or her performance.

INDIVIDUAL AND GROUP ACTIVITIES

1. Prepare and give a short presentation titled, "How to Be Effective As an Employment Interviewer."

2. Use the Internet to find employers who now do preliminary selection interviews via the Web. Print out and bring examples to class. Do you think these interviews are useful? Why or why not? How would you improve them?

3. In groups, discuss and compile examples of "the worst interview I ever had." What was it about these interviews that made them so bad? If time permits, discuss as a class.

4. In groups, prepare an interview (including a sequence of at least 20 questions) you'll use to interview candidates for the job of teaching a course in Human Resources Management. Each group should present their interview questions in class.

5. Some firms swear by unorthodox interview methods. For example, Tech Planet, of Menlo Park, California, uses weekly lunches and "wacky follow-up sessions" as substitutes for first-round job interviews. During the informal meals, candidates are expected to mingle, and they're then reviewed by the Tech Planet employees they meet at the luncheons. One Tech Planet employee asks candidates to ride a unicycle in her office to see if "they'll bond with the corporate culture or not." Toward the end of the screening process, the surviving group of interviewees has to solve brainteasers, and then openly evaluate their fellow candidates' strengths and weaknesses. What do you think of a screening process like this? Specifically, what do you think are its pros and cons? Would you recommend a procedure like this? If so, what changes, if any, would you recommend?[93]

6. Several years ago, Lockheed Martin Corp. sued the Boeing Corp. in Orlando, Florida, accusing it of using Lockheed's trade secrets to help win a multibillion-dollar government contract. Among other things, Lockheed Martin claimed that Boeing had obtained those trade secrets from a former Lockheed Martin employee who switched to Boeing.[94] But in describing methods companies use to commit corporate espionage, one writer says that hiring away the competitor's employees or hiring people to through go its dumpster are just the most obvious methods companies use to commit corporate espionage. As he says, "one of the more unusual scams—sometimes referred to as 'help wanted'—uses a person posing as a corporate headhunter who approaches an employee of the target company with a potentially lucrative job offer. During the interview, the employee is quizzed about his responsibilities, accomplishments and current projects. The goal is to extract important details without the employee realizing there is no job."[95]

    Assume that you are the owner of a small high-tech company that is worried about the possibility that one or more of your employees may be approached by one of these sinister "headhunters." What would you do (in terms of employee training, or a letter from you, for instance) to try to minimize the chance that one of your employees will fall into that kind of a trap? Also, compile a list of ten questions that you think such a corporate spy might ask one of your employees.

7. The HRCI "Test Specifications" appendix at the end of this book (pages 726–735) lists the knowledge someone studying for the HRCI certification exam needs to have in each area of human resource management (such as in Strategic Management, Workforce Planning, and Human Resource Development). In groups of four to five students, do four things: (1) review that appendix now; (2) identify the material in this chapter that relates to the required knowledge the appendix lists; (3) write four multiple choice exam questions on this material that you believe would be suitable for inclusion in the HRCI exam; and (4) if time permits, have someone from your team post your team's questions in front of the class, so the students in other teams can take each others' exam questions.

EXPERIENTIAL EXERCISE

The Most Important Person You'll Ever Hire

Purpose: The purpose of this exercise is to give you practice using some of the interview techniques you learned from this chapter.

Required Understanding: You should be familiar with the information presented in this chapter, and read this: For parents, children are precious. It's therefore interesting that parents who hire "nannies" to take care of their children usually do little more than ask several interview questions and conduct what is often, at best, a perfunctory reference check. Given the often questionable validity of interviews, and the (often) relative inexperience of the father or mother doing the interviewing, it's not surprising that many of these arrangements end in disappointment. You know from this chapter that it is difficult to conduct a valid interview unless you know exactly what you're looking for and, preferably, also structure the interview. Most parents simply aren't trained to do this.

How to Set Up the Exercise/Instructions:

1. Set up groups of five or six students. Two students will be the interviewees, while the other students in the group will serve as panel interviewers. The interviewees will develop an interviewer assessment form, and the panel interviewers will develop a structured situational interview for a "nannie."

2. Instructions for the interviewees: The interviewees should leave the room for about 20 minutes. While out of the room, the interviewees should develop an "interviewer assessment form" based on the information presented in this chapter regarding factors that can undermine the usefulness of an interview. During the panel interview, the interviewees should assess the interviewers using the interviewer assessment form. After the panel interviewers have conducted the interview, the interviewees should leave the room to discuss their notes. Did the interviewers exhibit any of the factors that can undermine the usefulness of an interview? If so, which ones? What suggestions would you (the interviewees) make to the interviewers on how to improve the usefulness of the interview?

3. Instructions for the interviewers: While the interviewees are out of the room, the panel interviewers will have 20 minutes to develop a short structured situational interview form for a "nannie." The panel interview team will interview two candidates for the position. During the panel interview, each interview should be taking notes on a copy of the structured situational interview form. After the panel interview, the panel interviewers should discuss their notes. What were your first impressions of each interviewee? Were your impressions similar? Which candidate would you all select for the position and why?

APPLICATION CASE

The Out-of-Control Interview

Maria Fernandez is a bright, popular, and well-informed mechanical engineer who graduated with an engineering degree from State University in June 2003. During the spring preceding her graduation, she went out on many job interviews, most of which she thought were conducted courteously and were reasonably useful in giving both her and the prospective employer a good impression of where each of them stood on matters of importance to both of them. It was, therefore, with great anticipation that she looked forward to an interview with the one firm in which she most wanted to work: Apex Environmental. She had always had a strong interest in cleaning up the environment and firmly believed that the best use of her training and skills lay in working for a firm like Apex, where she thought she could have a successful career while making the world a better place.

The interview, however, was a disaster. Maria walked into a room in which five men—the president of the company, two vice presidents, the marketing director, and another engineer—began throwing questions at her that she felt were aimed primarily at tripping her up rather than finding out what she could offer through her engineering skills. The questions ranged from unnecessarily discourteous ("Why would you take a job as a waitress in college if you're such an intelligent person?") to irrelevant and sexist ("Are you planning on settling down and starting a family anytime soon?"). Then, after the interview, she met with two of the gentlemen individually (including the president), and the discussions focused almost exclusively on her technical expertise. She thought that these later discussions went fairly well. However, given the apparent aimlessness and even mean-spiritedness of the panel interview, she was astonished when several days later she got a job offer from the firm.

The offer forced her to consider several matters. From her point of view, the job itself was perfect—she liked what she would be doing, the industry, and the firm's location. And in fact, the president had been quite courteous in subsequent discussions, as had been the other members of the management team. She was left wondering whether the panel interview had been intentionally tense to see how she'd stand up under pressure, and, if so, why they would do such a thing.

Questions

1. How would you explain the nature of the panel interview Maria had to endure? Specifically, do you think it reflected a well-thought-out interviewing strategy on the part of the firm or carelessness on the part of the firm's management? If it was carelessness, what would you do to improve the interview process at Apex Environmental?
2. Would you take the job offer if you were Maria? If you're not sure, is there any additional information that would help you make your decision, and if so, what is it?
3. The job of applications engineer for which Maria was applying requires: (a) excellent technical skills with respect to mechanical engineering; (b) a commitment to working in the area of pollution control; (c) the ability to deal well and confidently with customers who have engineering problems; (d) a willingness to travel worldwide; and (e) a very intelligent and well-balanced personality. List 10 questions you would ask when interviewing applicants for the job.

CONTINUING CASE

Carter Cleaning Company

The Better Interview

Like virtually all the other HR-related activities at Carter Cleaning Centers, the company currently has no organized approach to interviewing job candidates. Store managers, who do almost all the hiring, have a few of their own favorite questions that they ask. But in the absence of any guidance from top management, they all admit their interview performance leaves something to be desired. Similarly, Jack Carter himself is admittedly most comfortable dealing with what he calls the "nuts and bolts" machinery aspect of his business and has never felt particularly comfortable having to interview management or other job applicants. Jennifer is sure that this lack of formal interviewing practices, procedures, and training account for some of the employee turnover and theft problems. Therefore, she wants to do something to improve her company's batting average in this important area. Here are her questions:

Questions

1. In general, what can Jennifer do to improve her employee interviewing practices? Should she develop interview forms that list questions for management and nonmanagement jobs, and if so how should these look and what questions should be included? Should she initiate a computer-based interview approach, and if so why and (specifically) how?

2. Should she implement a training program for her managers, and if so, specifically what should be the content of such an interview training program? In other words, if she did decide to start training her management people to be better interviewers, what should she tell them and how should she tell it to them?

TRANSLATING STRATEGY INTO HR POLICIES AND PRACTICE CASE: THE HOTEL PARIS

The New Interviewing Program

The Hotel Paris's competitive strategy is "To use superior guest service to differentiate the Hotel Paris properties, and to thereby increase the length of stay and return rate of guests, and thus boost revenues and profitability." HR manager Lisa Cruz must now formulate functional policies and activities that support this competitive strategy, by eliciting the required employee behaviors and competencies.

One thing that concerned Lisa Cruz was the fact that the Hotel Paris's hotel managers varied widely in their interviewing and hiring skills. Some were quite effective, most were not. Furthermore, the company did not have a formal employment interview-training program, nor, for that matter, did it have standardized interview packages that hotel managers around the world could use.

As an experienced HR professional, Lisa knew that the company's new testing program would go only so far. She knew that at best, employment tests accounted for perhaps 30% of employee performance. It was essential that she and her team design a package of interviews that her hotel managers could use to assess—on an interactive and personal basis—candidates for various positions. It was only in that way that the hotel could hire the sorts of employees whose competencies and behaviors would translate into the kinds of outcomes—such as improved guest services—that the hotel required to achieve its strategic goals.

Lisa receives budgetary approval to design a new employee interview system. She and her team start by reviewing the job descriptions and job specifications for the positions of front-desk clerk, assistant manager, security guard, car hop/door person, and housekeeper. Focusing on developing structured interviews for each position, the team sets about devising interview questions. For example, for the front-desk clerk and assistant manager, they formulate several *behavioral questions*, including, "Tell me about a time when you had to deal with an irate person, and what you did." And, "Tell me about a time when you had to deal with several conflicting demands at once, such as having to study for several final exams at the same time, while working. How did you handle the situation?" They also developed a number of *situational questions*, including "Suppose you have a very pushy incoming guest who insists on being checked in at once, while at the same time you're trying to process the checkout for another guest who must be at the airport in 10 minutes. How would you handle the situation?"

Questions

1. For the jobs of security guard or car hop, develop five situational, five behavioral, and five job knowledge questions, with descriptive good/average/poor answers.

2. Combine your questions into a complete interview process that you would give to someone who must interview candidates for these jobs.

KEY TERMS

unstructured or nondirective interview, 254
structured or directive interview, 254
situational interview, 258
behavioral interviews, 258
job-related interview, 258
stress interview, 258

unstructured sequential interview, 259
structured sequential interview, 259
panel interview, 259
mass interview, 260
candidate-order error, 263

ENDNOTES

1. "Hiring Managers Reveal Top Five Biggest Mistakes Candidates Make During Job Interviews in Careerbuilder.com Survey," *Internet Wire*, January 21, 2004, page N/A.
2. Michael McDaniel et al., "The Validity of Employment Interviews: A Comprehensive Review and Meta-analysis," *Journal of Applied Psychology* 79, no. 4 (1994), p. 599. See also Laura Graves and Ronald Karren, "The Employee Selection Interview: A Fresh Look at an Old Problem," *Human Resource Management* 35, no. 2 (Summer 1996), pp. 163–180.
3. Derek Chapman and David Zweig, "Developing a Nomological Network for Interview Structure: Antecedents and Consequences of the Structured Selection Interview," *Personnel Psychology* 2005, vol. 58, pp. 673–702.
4. Laura Gollub Williamson et al., "Employment Interview on Trial: Linking Interview Structure with Litigation Outcomes," *Journal of Applied Psychology* 82, no. 6 (1996), p. 900.
5. Alan Huffcutt et al., "A Meta-Analytic Investigation of Cognitive Ability in Employment Interview Evaluations: Moderating Characteristics and Implications for Incremental Validity," *Journal of Applied Psychology* 81, no. 5 (1996), p. 459. See also Richard Posthuma, Frederick Morgeson, and Michael Campion, "Beyond Employment Interview Validity: A Comprehensive Narrative Review of Recent Trends over Time," *Personnel Psychology* 55 (2002), p. 18.
6. Duane Schultz and Sydney Schultz, *Psychology and Work Today* (Upper Saddle River, NJ: Prentice Hall, 1998), p. 830. A recent study found that interview structure "was best described by four dimensions: questioning consistency, evaluation standardization, question sophistication, and rapport building." Derek Chapman and David Zweig, "Developing a Nomological Network for Interview Structure: Antecedents and Consequences of the Structured Selection Interview," *Personnel Psychology*, 2005, vol. 58, pp. 673–702.
7. McDaniel et al., "The Validity of Employment Interviews," p. 602.
8. Williamson et al., "Employment Interview on Trial," p. 908.
9. Posthuma, Morgeson, and Campion, "Beyond Employment Interview Validity," p. 47.
10. Ibid.
11. Ibid., p. 601.
12. McDaniel et al., "The Validity of Employment Interviews," p. 602.
13. Bill Stoneman, "Matching Personalities with Jobs Made Easier with Behavioral Interviews," *American Banker*, November 30, 2000, p. 8a.
14. Paul Taylor and Bruce Small, "Asking Applicants What They Would Do Versus What They Did: A Meta-Analytic Comparison of Situational and Past Behavior in Employment Interview Questions," *Journal of Occupational and Organizational Psychology* 75, no. 3 (September 2002), pp. 277–295.
15. "Job Hunt as Head Trip? More Companies Use Behavioral Interviews to Screen Candidates," *Los Angeles Times*, May 20, 2001, p. W.1.
16. Martha Frase-Blunt, "Games Interviewers Play," *HR Magazine*, January 2001, pp. 104–114.
17. Kevin Murphy and Charles David Shofer, *Psychological Testing*. (Upper Saddle River, NJ: Prentice Hall, 2001) pp. 430–431.
18. Marlene Dixon et al., "The Panel Interview: A Review of Empirical Research and Guidelines for Practice," *Public Personnel Management* 31, no. 3 (Fall 2002), pp. 397–429.
19. Ibid.
20. "Phone Interviews Might Be the Most Telling, Study Finds," *BNA Bulletin to Management*, September 1998, p. 273.

21. Susan Strauss et al., "The Effects of Videoconference, Telephone, and Face-to-Face Media on Interviewer and Applicant Judgments in Employment Interviews," *Journal of Management* 27, no. 3 (2001), pp. 363–381. If the employer records a video **interview** with the intention of sharing it with hiring managers who don't participate in the interview, it's advisable to first obtain the candidates written permission. Matt Bolch, "Lights, Camera… Interview!," *HR Magazine*, March 2007, pp. 99–102.

22. Douglas Rodgers, "Computer-Aided Interviewing Overcomes First Impressions," *Personnel Journal*, April 1987, pp. 148–152; see also Linda Thornburg, "Computer-Assisted Interviewing Shortens Hiring Cycle," *HR Magazine*, February 1998, p. 73ff.

23. Ibid.

24. Gary Robins, "Dial-an-Interview," *Stores*, June 1994, pp. 34–35.

25. This is quoted from or paraphrased from Bulkeley, "Replaced by Technology," pp. B1, B7.

26. William Bulkeley, "Replaced by Technology: Job Interviews," *Wall Street Journal*, August 22, 1994, pp. B1, B7.

27. Ibid.

28. For additional information on computer-aided interviewing's benefits, see, for example, Christopher Martin and Denise Nagao, "Some Effects of Computerized Interviewing on Job Applicant Responses," *Journal of Applied Psychology* 74, no. 1 (February 1989), pp. 72–80.

29. Timothy Judge et al., "The Employment Interview: A Review of Recent Research and Recommendations for Future Research," *Human Resource Management* 10, no. 4 (2000), p. 392.

30. For example, structured employment interviews using either situational questions or behavioral questions tend to yield high criterion-related validities (.63 versus .47). This is particularly so where the raters can use descriptively anchored rating scale answer sheets; these use short descriptors to illustrate good, average, or poor performance. Taylor and Small, "Asking Applicants What They Would Do Versus What They Did," pp. 277–295.

31. Williamson, "Employment Interview on Trial," p. 900.

32. Frank Schmidt and Ryan Zimmerman, "A Counterintuitive Hypothesis About Employment Interview Validity and Some Supporting Evidence," *Journal of Applied Psychology* 89, no. 3, (2004): 553–561.

33. This validity discussion and these findings are based on McDaniel et al., "The Validity of Employment Interviews," pp. 607–610; the validities for situational, job-related, and psychological interviews were (.50), (.39), and (.29), respectively.

34. Murray Barrick et al., "Accuracy of Interviewer Judgments of Job Applicant Personality Traits," *Personnel Psychology* 53 (2000), pp. 925–951.

35. McDaniel et al., "The Validity of Employment Interviews," p. 608.

36. Anthony Dalessio and Todd Silverhart, "Combining Biodata Test and Interview Information: Predicting Decisions and Performance Criteria," *Personnel Psychology* 47 (1994), p. 313.

37. S. W. Constantin, "An Investigation of Information Favorability in the Employment Interview," *Journal of Applied Psychology* 61 (1976), pp. 743–749. It should be noted that a number of the studies discussed in this chapter involve having interviewers evaluate interviews based on written transcripts (rather than face to face) and that a study suggests that this procedure may not be equivalent to having interviewers interview applicants directly. See Charles Gorman, William Grover, and Michael Doherty, "Can We Learn Anything About Interviewing Real People from 'Interviews' of Paper People? A Study of the External Validity Paradigm," *Organizational Behavior and Human Performance* 22, no. 2 (October 1978), pp. 165–192. See also John Binning et al., "Effects of Pre-interview Impressions on Questioning Strategies in Same and Opposite Sex Employment Interviews," *Journal of Applied Psychology* 73, no. 1 (February 1988), pp. 30–37; and Sebastiana Fisicaro, "A Reexamination of the Relation Between Halo Error and Accuracy," *Journal of Applied Psychology* 73, no. 2 (May 1988), pp. 239–246.

38. David Tucker and Patricia Rowe, "Relationship Between Expectancy, Causal Attribution, and Final Hiring Decisions in the Employment Interview," *Journal of Applied Psychology* 64, no. 1 (February 1979), pp. 27–34. See also Robert Dipboye, Gail Fontenelle, and Kathleen Garner, "Effect of Previewing the Application on Interview Process and Outcomes," *Journal of Applied Psychology* 69, no. 1 (February 1984), pp. 118–128.

39. Anita Chaudhuri, "Beat the Clock: Applying for Job? A New Study Shows That Interviewers Will Make Up Their Minds about You within a Minute," *The Guardian*, June 14, 2000, pp. 2–6.

40. Don Langdale and Joseph Weitz, "Estimating the Influence of Job Information on Interviewer Agreement," *Journal of Applied Psychology* 57 (1973), pp. 23–27; for a review of how to determine the human requirements of a job, see Anthony W. Simmons, "Selection Interviewing," *Employment Relations Today*, Winter 1991, pp. 305–309.

41. R. E. Carlson, "Effects of Applicant Sample on Ratings of Valid Information in an Employment Setting," *Journal of Applied Psychology* 20 (1967), pp. 259–280.

42. R. E. Carlson, "Selection Interview Decisions: The Effects of Interviewer Experience, Relative Quota Situation, and Applicant Sample on Interview Decisions," *Personnel Psychology* 20 (1967), pp. 259–280.

43. T. V. McGovern and H. E. Tinsley, "Interviewer Evaluations of Interviewees' Nonverbal Behavior," *Journal of Vocational Behavior* 13 (1978), pp. 163–171. See also Keith Rasmussen Jr., "Nonverbal Behavior, Verbal Behavior, Résumé Credentials, and Selection Interview Outcomes," *Journal of Applied Psychology* 60, no. 4 (1984), pp. 551–556; Robert Gifford, Cheuk Fan Ng, and Margaret Wilkinson, "Nonverbal Cues in the Employment Interview: Links Between Applicant Qualities and Interviewer Judgments," *Journal of Applied Psychology* 70, no. 4 (1984), pp. 729–736; Scott T. Fleishmann, "The Messages of Body Language in Job Interviews," *Employee Relations* 18, no. 2 (Summer 1991), pp. 161–166.

44. Tim DeGroot and Stephen Motowidlo, "Why Visual and Vocal Interview Cues Can Affect Interviewers' Judgments and Predicted Job Performance," *Journal of Applied Psychology*, December 1999, pp. 968–984.

45. David Caldwell and Jerry Burger, "Personality Characteristics of Job Applicants and Success in Screening Interviews," *Personnel Psychology* 51 (1998), pp. 119–136.

46. Ibid., p. 130.

47. Amy Kristof-Brown et al., "Applicant Impression Management: Dispositional Influences and Consequences for Recruiter Perceptions of Fit and Similarity," *Journal of Management* 28, no. 1 (2002), pp. 27–46. See also Linda McFarland et al., "Impression Management Use and Effectiveness Across Assessment Methods," *Journal of Management* 29, no. 5, (2003): 641–661.

48. C. K. Stevens and A. L. Kristof, "Making the Right Impression: A Field Study of Applicant Impression Management During Interviews," *Journal of Applied Psychology* 80, pp. 587–606; Schultz and Schultz, *Psychology and Work Today*, p. 82. See also Jay Stuller, "Fatal Attraction; *Across the Board*," 42, no. 6, November/December 2005, pp. 18–23.

49. Posthuma, Morgeson, and Campion, "Beyond Employment Interview Validity," 1–87.

50. Chad Higgins and Timothy Judge, "The Effect of Applicant Influences Tactics on Recruiter Perceptions of Fit and Hiring Recommendations: A Field Study," *Journal of Applied Psychology* 89, no. 4, (2004): 622–632.

51. Richard Posthuma, Frederick Morgeson, and Michael Campion, "Beyond Employment Interview Validity: A Comprehensive Narrative Review of Recent Trends Over Time," *Personnel Psychology* 55 (2002), p. 30.

52. See, for example, Madelaine Heilmann and Lewis Saruwatari, "When Beauty Is Beastly: The Effects of Appearance and Sex on Evaluation of Job Applicants for Managerial and Nonmanagerial Jobs," *Organizational Behavior and Human Performance* 23 (June 1979), pp. 360–372; and Cynthia Marlowe, Sondra Schneider, and Carnot Nelson, "Gender and Attractiveness Biases in Hiring Decisions: Are More Experienced Managers Less Biased?" *Journal of Applied Psychology* 81, no. 1 (1996), pp. 11–21.

53. Marlowe et al., "Gender and Attractiveness Biases," p. 11.

54. Ibid., p. 18.

55. Ibid., p. 11.

56. Amelia J. Prewett-Livingston et al., "Effects of Race on Interview Ratings in a Situational Panel Interview," *Journal of Applied Psychology* 81, no. 2 (1996), pp. 178–186.

57. Alan Huffcutt and Philip Roth, "Racial Group Differences in Employment Interview Evaluations," *Journal of Applied Psychology* 83, no. 2 (1998), pp. 179–189.

58. Michael Miceli et al., "Potential Discrimination in Structured Employment Interviews," *Employee Responsibilities and Rights* 13, no. 1 (March 2001), pp. 15–38.

59. "Screens Can be a Key to Unbiased Interview Process," *Personnel Today*, April 1, 2003, p. 3.

60. Andrea Rodriguez and Fran Prezant, "Better Interviews for People with Disabilities," *Workforce*, downloaded from workforce.com, November 14, 2003.

61. Pat Tammaro, "Laws to Prevent Discrimination Affect Job Interview Process and Will," *The Elected Business Journal*, June 16, 2000, p. 48.

62. This is based on John F. Wymer III and Deborah A. Sudbury, "Employment Discrimination: 'Testers'—Will Your Hiring Practices 'Pass'?" *Employee Relations Law Journal* 17, no. 4 (Spring 1992), pp. 623–633.

63. Bureau of National Affairs, Daily Labor Report, December 5, 1990, p. D1.

64. Wymer and Sudbury, "Employment Discrimination," p. 629.

65. Arthur Pell, "Nine Interviewing Pitfalls," *Managers Magazine*, January 1994, p. 20.

66. Thomas Dougherty, Daniel Turban, and John Callender, "Confirming First Impressions in the Employment Interview: A Field Study of Interviewer Behavior," *Journal of Applied Psychology* 79, no. 5 (1994), p. 663.

67. See Pell, "Nine Interviewing Pitfalls," p. 29; Parth Sarathi, "Making Selection Interviews Effective," *Management and Labor Studies* 18, no. 1 (1993), pp. 5–7.

68. Posthuma, Morgeson, and Campion, "Beyond Employment Interview Validity," pp. 1–87.

69. Pell, "Nine Interviewing Pitfalls," p. 30.

70. This section is based on Elliot Pursell et al., "Structured Interviewing," *Personnel Journal* 59, (November 1980), pp. 907–912; and G. Latham et al., "The Situational Interview," *Journal of Applied Psychology* 65 (1980), pp. 422–427. See also Campion, Pursell, and Brown, "Structured Interviewing," pp. 25–42; and Weekley and Gier, "Reliability and Validity of the Situational Interview," pp. 484–487.

71. .63 versus .47, op cit.; Taylor and Small, "Asking Applicants What They Would Do Versus What They Did," pp. 277–295.

72. There is some evidence that, for higher-level positions, situational question–based interviews are inferior to behavioral question–based ones, possibly because the situations are "just too simple to allow any real differentiation among candidates for higher level positions." Alan Huffcutt et al., "Comparison of Situational and Behavioral Description Interview Questions for Higher Level Positions," *Personnel Psychology* 54, no. 3 (2001), p. 619.

73. See also Phillip Lowry, "The Structured Interview: An Alternative to the Assessment Center?" *Public Personnel Management* 23, no. 2 (Summer 1994), pp. 201–215. See also Steven Maurer, "The Potential of the Situational Interview: Existing Research and Unresolved Issues," *Human Resource Management Review* 7, no. 2 (Summer 1997), pp. 185–201, and Todd Maurer and Jerry Solamon, "The Science and Practice of a Structured Employment Interview Coaching Program," *Personnel Psychology* 59, no. 2, Summer 2006, pp. 433–456.

74. Pursell et al., "Structured Interviewing," p. 910.

75. From a speech by industrial psychologist Paul Green and contained in *BNA Bulletin to Management*, June 20, 1985, pp. 2–3.

76. "Container Store Thinks Outside the Box: Award-Winning Employer Hires for Quality," *BNA Bulletin to Management*, March 1, 2001, p. 65.

77. Williamson et al., "Employment Interview on Trial," p. 901; Michael Campion, David Palmer, and James Campion, "A Review of Structure in the Selection Interview," *Personnel Psychology* 50 (1997), pp. 655–702. See also, Todd Maurer and Jerry Solamon "The Science and Practice of a Structured Employment Interview Coaching Program," *Personnel Psychology*, 2006, vol. 59, pp. 433–456.

78. Unless otherwise specified, the following are based on Williamson et al., "Employment Interview on Trial," pp. 901–902.

79. Campion, Palmer, and Campion, "A Review of Structure," p. 668.

80. Carlson, "Selection Interview Decisions," pp. 259–280.

81. Campion, Palmer, and Campion, "A Review of Structure," pp. 655–702.

82. Catherine Middendorf and Therese Macan, "Note Taking in the Employment Interview: Effects on Recall and Judgment," *Journal of Applied Psychology* 87, no. 2 (2002), pp. 293–303.

83. Robert Rubin et al., "Using Extracurricular Activity as an Indicator of Interpersonal Skill: Prudent Evaluation or Recruiting Malpractice?" *Human Resource Management* 41, no. 4 (Winter 2002), pp. 441–454.

84. "The Tables Have Turned," *American Management Association International*, September 1998, p. 6.

85. Julie McCarthy and Richard Goffin, "Measuring Job Interview Anxiety: Beyond Weak Knees and the Sweaty Palms," *Personnel Psychology*, 2004, vol. 57, pp. 607–637.

86. Cheryl Tay, Soon Ang, and Linn Van Dyne, "Personality, Biographical Characteristics, and Job Interview Success: A Longitudinal Study of the Mediating Effects of Interviewing Self-Efficacy and the Moderating Effects of Internal Locus of Causality," *Journal of Applied Psychology*, 2006, vol. 91, no 2, pp. 446–454.

87. Edwin Walley, "Successful Interviewing Techniques," *CPA Journal*, September 1993, p. 70.

88. Walley, "Successful Interviewing Techniques," p. 70.

89. Pamela Kaul, "Interviewing Is Your Business," *Association Management*, November 1992, p. 29.

90. Stephen Gilliland et al., "Improving Applicants' Reactions to Rejection Letters: An Application of Fairness Theory," *Personnel Psychology* 54 (2001), pp. 669–703.

91. This is based on John Drake, Interviewing for Managers: A Complete Guide to Employment Interviewing (New York, AMACOM, 1982).

92. Ibid.

93. Chris Maynard, "New High-Tech Recruiting Tools: Unicycles, Yahtzee and Silly Putty," *Wall Street Journal*, June 6, 2000, p. B14; see also Paul McNamara, "Extreme Interview," *Network World*, June 25, 2001, p. 65.

94. Tim Barker, "Corporate Espionage Takes Center Stage with the Boeing Revelation," *Knight Ridder/Tribune Business News*, June 15, 2003, item 03166010.

95. Ibid.

APPENDIX FOR CHAPTER 7

Guidelines for Interviewees

Before you get into a position where you have to do interviewing, you will probably have to navigate some interviews yourself. Here are some hints for excelling in your interview.

The first thing to understand is that interviews are often used to help employers determine what you are like as a person. In other words, information regarding how you get along with other people and your desire to work is often very important in the interview; your skills and technical expertise are often assessed through tests and a study of your educational and work history. Interviewers will look first for crisp, articulate answers. Specifically, whether you respond concisely, cooperate fully in answering questions, state personal opinions when relevant, and keep to the subject at hand are very important elements in influencing the interviewer's decision.

There are seven things to do to get that extra edge in the interview.

1. *Preparation is essential.* Before the interview, learn all you can about the employer, the job, and the people doing the recruiting. On the Web or at the library, look through business periodicals to find out what is happening in the employer's field. Who is the competition? How are they doing? Try to unearth the employer's problems. Be ready to explain why you think you would be able to solve such problems, citing some of your *specific accomplishments* to make your case.

2. *Uncover the interviewer's real needs.* Spend as little time as possible answering your interviewer's first questions and as much time as possible getting him or her to describe his or her needs. Determine what the person is expecting to accomplish, and the type of person he or she feels is needed. Use open-ended questions here such as, "Could you tell me more about that?"

3. *Relate yourself to the interviewer's needs.* Once you know the type of person your interviewer is looking for and the sorts of problems he or she wants solved, you are in a good position to describe your own accomplishments *in terms of the interviewer's needs*. Start by saying something like, "One of the problem areas you've said is important to you is similar to a problem I once faced." Then state the problem, describe your solution, and reveal the results.

4. *Think before answering.* Answering a question should be a three-step process: Pause—Think—Speak. *Pause* to make sure you understand what the interviewer is

driving at, *think* about how to structure your answer, and then *speak*. In your answer, try to emphasize how hiring you will help the interviewer solve his or her problem.

5. ***Remember that appearance and enthusiasm are important.*** Appropriate clothing, good grooming, a firm handshake, and the appearance of controlled energy are important. Remember that your *nonverbal behavior* may broadcast more about you than the verbal content of what you say. Here maintaining eye contact is very important. In addition, speak with enthusiasm, nod agreement, and remember to take a moment to frame your answer (pause, think, speak) so that you sound articulate and fluent.

6. ***Make a good first impression.*** Remember, studies show that in most cases interviewers make up their minds about the applicant during the early minutes of the interview. A good first impression may turn to bad during the interview, but it is unlikely. Bad first impressions are almost impossible to overcome. One expert suggests paying attention to the following key interviewing considerations.

   1. Appropriate clothing
   2. Good grooming
   3. A firm handshake
   4. The appearance of controlled energy
   5. Pertinent humor and readiness to smile
   6. A genuine interest in the employer's operation and alert attention when the interviewer speaks
   7. Pride in past performance
   8. An understanding of the employer's needs and a desire to serve them
   9. The display of sound ideas
   10. Ability to take control when employers fall down on the interviewing job

7. ***Ask questions.*** Sample questions you can ask are presented in Figure 7-A1.

FIGURE 7-A1

Interview Questions to Ask

Source: H. Lee Rust, *Job Search: The Complete Manual for Job Seekers*, 1991 H. Lee Rust. Published by AMACOM, division of American Management Assn. Intl., New York, NY. Used by permission of the publisher. All rights reserved.

1. What is the first problem that needs the attention of the person you hire?
2. What other problems need attention now?
3. What has been done about any of these to date?
4. How has this job been performed in the past?
5. Why is it now vacant?
6. Do you have a written job description for this position?
7. What are its major responsibilities?
8. What authority would I have? How would you define its scope?
9. What are the company's five-year sales and profit projections?
10. What needs to be done to reach these projections?
11. What are the company's major strengths and weaknesses?
12. What are its strengths and weaknesses in production?
13. What are its strengths and weaknesses in its products or its competitive position?
14. Whom do you identify as your major competitors?
15. What are their strengths and weaknesses?
16. How do you view the future for your industry?
17. Do you have any plans for new products or acquisitions?
18. Might this company be sold or acquired?
19. What is the company's current financial strength?
20. What can you tell me about the individual to whom I would report?
21. What can you tell me about other persons in key positions?
22. What can you tell me about the subordinates I would have?
23. How would you define your management philosophy?
24. Are employees afforded an opportunity for continuing education?
25. What are you looking for in the person who will fill this job?

Interview Guide

FIGURE 7-A2

Structured Interview Guide

Source: Copyright 1992. The Dartnell Corporation, Chicago, IL. Adapted with permission.

APPLICANT INTERVIEW GUIDE

To the interviewer: This Applicant Interview Guide is intended to assist in employee selection and placement. If it is used for all applicants for a position, it will help you to compare them, and it will provide more objective information than you will obtain from unstructured interviews.

Because this is a general guide, all of the items may not apply in every instance. Skip those that are not applicable and add questions appropriate to the specific position. Space for additional questions will be found at the end of the form.

Federal law prohibits discrimination in employment on the basis of sex, race, color, national origin, religion, disability, and in most instances, age. The laws of most states also ban some or all of the above types of discrimination in employment as well as discrimination based on marital status or ancestry. Interviewers should take care to avoid any questions that suggest that an employment decision will be made on the basis of any such factors.

Job Interest

Name _____ Position applied for _____

What do you think the job (position) involves? _____

Why do you want the job (position)? _____

Why are you qualified for it? _____

What would your salary requirements be? _____

What do you know about our company? _____

Why do you want to work for us? _____

Current Work Status

Are you now employed? _____ Yes _____ No. If not, how long have you been unemployed? _____

Why are you unemployed? _____

If you are working, why are you applying for this position? _____

When would you be available to start work with us? _____

Work Experience

(Start with the applicant's current or last position and work back. All periods of time should be accounted for. Go back at least 12 years, depending upon the applicant's age. Military service should be treated as a job.)

Current or last
employer _____ Address _____

Dates of employment: from _____ to _____

Current or last job title _____

What are (were) your duties? _____

Have you held the same job throughout your employment with that company? _____ Yes _____ No. If not,

describe the various jobs you have had with that employer, how long you held each of them, and the main

duties of each. _____

What was your starting salary? _____ What are you earning now? _____ Comments _____

_____

Name of your last or current supervisor _____

What did you like most about that job? _____

What did you like least about it? _____

Why are you thinking of leaving? _____

Why are you leaving right now? _____

Interviewer's comments or observations _____

_____

(continued)

FIGURE 7-A2

(continued)

What did you do before you took your last job? _____

Where were you employed? _____

Location _____ Job title _____

Duties _____

Did you hold the same job throughout your employment with that company? _____ Yes _____ No. If not, describe the jobs you held, when you held them, and the duties of each. _____

_____

What was your starting salary? _____ What was your final salary? _____

Name of your last supervisor _____

May we contact that company? _____ Yes _____ No

What did you like most about that job? _____

What did you like least about that job? _____

Why did you leave that job? _____

Would you consider working there again? _____

Interviewer: If there is any gap between the various periods of employment, the applicant should be asked about them. _____

Interviewer's comments or observations _____

_____

What did you do prior to the job with that company? _____

What other jobs or experience have you had? Describe them briefly and explain the general duties of each.

_____

Have you been unemployed at any time in the last five years? _____ Yes _____ No. What efforts did you make to find work? _____

What other experience or training do you have that would help qualify you for the job applied for? Explain how and where you obtained this experience or training. _____

_____

Educational Background

What education or training do you have that would help you in the job for which you have applied? _____

_____

Describe any formal education you have had. (Interviewer may substitute technical training, if relevant.) _____

_____

Off-Job Activities

What do you do in your off-hours? ___ Part-time job ___ Athletics ___ Spectator sports ___ Clubs ___ Other

Please explain. _____

Interviewer's Specific Questions

Interviewer: Add any questions to the particular job for which you are interviewing, leaving space for brief answers.

(Be careful to avoid questions that may be viewed as discriminatory.)

_____

_____

_____

Personal

Would you be willing to relocate? _____ Yes _____ No

Are you willing to travel? _____ Yes _____ No

(continued)

FIGURE 7-A2

(continued)

What is the maximum amount of time you would consider traveling? _____

_____

Are you able to work overtime? _____

What about working on weekends? _____

Self-Assessment

What do you feel are your strong points? _____

_____

What do you feel are your weak points? _____

_____

Interviewer: Compare the applicant's responses with the information furnished on the application for employment.

Clear up any discrepancies. _____

_____

Before the applicant leaves, the interviewer should provide basic information about the organization and the job opening, if this has not already been done. The applicant should be given information on the work location, work hours, the wage or salary, type of remuneration (salary or salary plus bonus, etc.), and other factors that may affect the applicant's interest in the job.

Interviewer's Impressions

Rate each characteristic from 1 to 4, with 1 being the highest rating and 4 being the lowest.

Personal Characteristics	1	2	3	4	Comments
Personal appearance					
Poise, manner					
Speech					
Cooperation with interviewer					
Job-related Characteristics					
Experience for this job					
Knowledge of job					
Interpersonal relationships					
Effectiveness					

Overall rating for job

1	2	3	4	5
___ Superior	___ Above Average	___ Average	___ Marginal	___ Unsatisfactory
	(well qualified)	(qualified)	(barely qualified)	

Comments or remarks _____

_____

_____

Interviewer _____   Date _____

PART II VIDEO CASES APPENDIX

Video 3: The HR Manager's Job, Job Analysis, Personnel Planning, and Recruitment

Video Title: Recruitment and Placement

In this video, Paul, the vice president of human resources at BMG faces the possibility that the wrong person was hired for a job. The senior director of music placement accuses Paul of sending her candidates that do not meet the criteria set by her department. A discussion takes place between the two, detailing information about the role of HR in the hiring process, and the recruitment process in general. And, the video delves into some of the technological aspects of recruiting.

As Paul explains, when we get a "recruitment request, we ask for job specifications, we interview several candidates, and we provide the hiring department with a short list of candidates." So, as Paul says, if the candidate turns out to be inadequate, it's not HR's problem, it's "your fault, since your supervisors picked him." She makes the point that "you only recruited in Rolling Stone magazine." Paul agrees, but points out that they did get 60 candidates. Furthermore, recruiting more extensively would involve considerably more cost. Again, though, one of the main issues revolves around whether the job specifications ("criteria") are correct, and whether there was an agreement on those job specs between HR and the hiring managers.

Discussion Questions

1. Do you agree or disagree with BMG's HR vice president when he tells the hiring manager that "your department picked him, so if the candidate did not work out it's your fault, not ours." What, if anything, does an approach like that say about the extent to which HR in this company views itself is a strategic partner?
2. If you had been in HR's shoes in this company, what if anything would you have done differently to make sure you understood the job specifications? And, whose responsibility was it to come up with those job specifications—HR, the hiring department, or both in partnership?
3. Do you think one good solution would be raising the salary of the position in order to get better candidates; if so, do you think it's really practical to do so?
4. Based on what you read in this textbook, how much legitimacy is there to the accusation that BMG did not throw out a wide enough net in recruiting (given the fact that they did get 60 candidates)?

Video 4: Testing and Selecting Employees

Video Title: Praendex

Using a proven, proprietary management tool called the Predictive Index (PI), Massachusetts-based Praendex Inc. enables employers of all types to hire and retain the right people. Mentioned in our textbook, the PI is a personality survey consisting of a two-sided sheet with 86 adjectives on each side. One side asks people to check off any words they feel describe how others perceive them, and the other side asks them to check off any words they believe pertain to themselves ("how you see yourself"). As the company's president says, our main purpose is "to help clients make the best use of their employees talents."

Discussion Questions

1. How would you classify the PI, in terms of the type of test that is?
2. What sort of information would you want from Praendex before deciding to use a survey like the PI in your company?
3. Why do you think the company's head described the PI, not simply as a selection tool, but as something that helps clients "make the best use of their employees' talents"?

8 Training and Developing Employees

In a Stanford University hospital training room, residents and medical students wearing virtual reality headsets control computer screen avatars. The avatars are computerized simulations dressed in medical scrubs. Each avatar plays a different role, such as nurse or emergency room technician. The residents and medical students use their key pads to control their avatar's every move in the virtual reality trauma center. One avatar props up the patient; another rushes to clear his airway. On the screen, the patient's vital signs react appropriately to the medical students' and residents' decisions. Later, instructors replay the scenario, showing trainees what they did right and wrong.[1] •

After studying this chapter, you should be able to:

1 Describe the basic training process.
2 Describe and illustrate how you would go about identifying training requirements.
3 Explain how to distinguish between problems you can fix with training and those you can't.
4 Explain how to use five training techniques.

Chapters 6 and 7 focused on the methods managers use to interview and select employees. Once employees are on board, the employer must train them. The purpose of this chapter is to increase your effectiveness as a trainer. The main topics we'll cover include orienting employees, the training process, training methods, training for special purposes, managerial development and training techniques, and evaluating the training effort.

ORIENTING EMPLOYEES

Carefully selecting employees doesn't guarantee they'll perform effectively. Potential is one thing, performance is another. Even high-potential employees can't do their jobs if they don't know what to do or how to do it. Therefore your next step is to ensure that your employees do know what to do and how to do it. This is the purpose of orienting and training employees. We will start with orientation.

Purpose of Orientation

employee orientation
A procedure for providing new employees with basic background information about the firm.

Employee orientation provides new employees with the basic background information they need to work in your company, such as information about company rules.

At a minimum, orientation should accomplish four things: The new employee should feel welcome and at ease; he or she should understand the organization in a broad sense (its past, present, culture, and vision of the future), as well as key facts such as policies and procedures; the employee should be clear about what is expected in terms of work and behavior; and the person should have begun the process of becoming socialized into the firm's ways of acting and doing things.[2]

However, orientation programs are moving away from mere discussions of rules, to explaining the company's mission and the employee's role in accomplishing it.[3] The assumption is that this will foster self-directed behavior that is more consistent with the company's needs. The Mayo Clinic recently revised its orientation program. Its new "heritage and culture" program now covers matters such as core principles, history, work atmosphere, teamwork, personal responsibility, innovation, integrity, diversity, customer service, and mutual respect.[4]

Don't underestimate orientation's importance. Without basic information on things like rules and policies, new employees may make time-consuming or even dangerous errors. Furthermore, orientation is not just about rules. It is also about making the new person feel welcome and at home and part of the team.

The Orientation Process

Orientation programs range from 10-minute discussions to week-long programs (at firms like Toyota). The human resource specialist (or, in smaller firms, the office manager) usually performs the first part of the orientation, by explaining basic matters like working hours, benefits, and vacations. That person then introduces the new employee to his or her new supervisor. The supervisor continues the orientation by explaining (see Figure 8-1) the organization of the department, and by introducing the person to his or her new colleagues, familiarizing the new employee with the workplace, and helping to reduce first-day jitters.

As in Figure 8-1, the orientation typically includes information on employee benefits, personnel policies, the daily routine, company organization and operations, and safety measures and regulations, as well as a facilities tour.[5] At a minimum, new employees should receive print or Internet-based *employee handbooks* covering matters like these.

More employers use technology to provide orientation. Some firms provide incoming managers with preloaded personal digital assistants. These contain information the new

UCSD Healthcare

NEW EMPLOYEE DEPARTMENTAL ORIENTATION CHECKLIST
(Return to Human Resources within 10 days of Hire)

NAME:	HIRE DATE:	SSN:	JOB TITLE:
DEPARTMENT:	NEO DATE:	DEPARTMENTAL ORIENTATION COMPLETED BY:	

TOPIC	DATE REVIEWED	N/A
1. HUMAN RESOURCES INFORMATION		
a. Departmental Attendance Procedures and UCSD Healthcare Work Time & Attendance Policy	a. _____	☐
b. Job Description Review	b. _____	☐
c. Annual Performance Evaluation and Peer Feedback Process	c. _____	☐
d. Probationary Period Information	d. _____	☐
e. Appearance/Dress Code Requirements	e. _____	☐
f. Annual TB Screening	f. _____	☐
g. License and/or certification Renewals	g. _____	☐
2. DEPARTMENT INFORMATION		
a. Organizational Structure-Department Core Values Orientation	a. _____	☐
b. Department/Unit Area Specific Policies & Procedures	b. _____	☐
c. Customer Service Practices	c. _____	☐
d. CQI Effort and Projects	d. _____	☐
e. Tour and Floor Plan	e. _____	☐
f. Equipment/Supplies	f. _____	☐
• Keys issued	_____	☐
• Radio Pager issued	_____	☐
• Other _____	_____	☐
g. Mail and Recharge Codes	g. _____	☐
3. SAFETY INFORMATION		
a. Departmental Safety Plan	a. _____	☐
b. Employee Safety/Injury Reporting Procedures	b. _____	☐
c. Hazard Communication	c. _____	☐
d. Infection Control/Sharps Disposal	d. _____	☐
e. Attendance at annual Safety Fair (mandatory)	e. _____	☐
4. FACILITES INFORMATION		
a. Emergency Power	a. _____	☐
b. Mechanical Systems	b. _____	☐
c. Water	c. _____	☐
d. Medical Gases	d. _____	☐
e. Patient Room	e. _____	☐
• Bed	_____	☐
• Headwall	_____	☐
• Bathroom	_____	☐
• Nurse Call System	_____	☐
5. SECURITY INFORMATION		
a. Code Triage Assignment	a. _____	☐
b. Code Blue Assignment	b. _____	☐
c. Code Red – Evacuation Procedure	c. _____	☐
d. Code 10 – Bomb Threat Procedure	d. _____	☐
e. Departmental Security Measures	e. _____	☐
f. UCSD Emergency Number 6111 or 911	f. _____	☐

This generic checklist may not constitute a complete departmental orientation or assessment. Please attach any additional unit specific orientation material for placement in the employee's HR file

I have been oriented on the items listed above_____

FIGURE 8-1

New Employee Departmental Orientation Checklist

Source: UCSDHealthcare. Used with permission.

managers need to better adjust to their new jobs, such as key contact information, main tasks to undertake, and even digital images of employees the new manager needs to know.[6] Other employers put all or some of their orientation media on the Web. At the University of Cincinnati for instance, new employees spend about 45 minutes online learning about their new employer's mission, organization, and policies and procedures.

The Employee Handbook   Note that under certain conditions, courts may find that the employee handbook's contents represent legally binding employment commitments. Therefore, employers often include disclaimers. These make it clear that statements of company policies, benefits, and regulations do not constitute the terms and conditions of an employment contract either expressed or implied. Also, companies generally do not insert statements such as "no employee will be fired without just cause" or statements that imply or state that employees have tenure. Indeed, it's best to emphasize that the employment relationship is strictly "at-will."

Not all new hires react to orientation in the same way.[7] Supervisors should therefore be vigilant, and follow up and encourage new employees to engage in those activities that will enable each to "learn the ropes" and quickly become productive.

THE TRAINING PROCESS

training
The process of teaching new employees the basic skills they need to perform their jobs.

Immediately after the orientation, training should begin. **Training** means giving new or present employees the skills they need to perform their jobs. This might mean showing a new Web designer the intricacies of your site, a new salesperson how to sell your firm's product, or a new supervisor how to fill out the firm's weekly payroll sheets. It might involve simply having the current job-holder explain the job to the new hire, or, at the other extreme, a multi-week process including classroom or Internet classes.

In any case, training is a hallmark of good management, and a task that managers ignore at their peril. Having high-potential employees doesn't guarantee they'll succeed. Instead, they must know what you want them to do and how you want them to do it. If they don't, they will improvise or do nothing productive at all.

Training's Strategic Context

Training used to focus mostly on teaching technical skills, such as training assemblers to solder wires. Today, as one trainer puts it: "We don't just concentrate on the traditional training objectives anymore . . . We sit down with management and help them identify strategic goals and objectives and the skills and knowledge needed to achieve them. Then we work together to identify whether our staff has the skills and knowledge, and when they don't, that's when we discuss training needs."[8] In other words, the firm's training programs must make sense in terms of the company's strategic goals.

Thus, when Wisconsin-based Signicast Corp. decided to build a new, high-tech plant, Terry Lutz, the firm's president, knew Signicast would need a new type of employee to run that plant, and new screening and training programs to hire and train them.

performance management
Taking an integrated, goal-oriented approach to assigning, training, assessing, and rewarding employees' performance.

Performance Management   Training also plays a key role today in the *performance management* process. **Performance management** means taking an integrated, goal-oriented approach to assigning, training, assessing, and rewarding employees' performance. Taking a performance management approach to training means that the training effort must make sense in terms of what the company wants each employee to contribute to achieving the company's goals.

These emphases on strategic, performance management-oriented training help explain why training is booming. Companies spent about $826 per employee for training in one recent year, and offered each about 28 hours of training.[9] Training has a fairly impressive record of influencing organizational effectiveness, scoring higher than appraisal and feedback, and just below goal setting in its effect on productivity.[10] One survey found that "establishing a linkage between learning and organizational perform-ance" was the number one pressing issue facing training professionals.[11] Training experts today increasingly use the phrase "workplace learning and performance" in lieu of training to underscore training's dual aims of employee learning and organizational per-formance.[12]

 Describe the basic training process.

The Five-Step Training and Development Process

Training programs consist of five steps.

1. The first, or *needs analysis* step, identifies the specific job performance skills needed, assesses the prospective trainees' skills, and develops specific, measurable knowl-edge and performance objectives based on any deficiencies.
2. In the second step, *instructional design*, you decide on, compile, and produce the training program content, including workbooks, exercises, and activities. Here, you'll probably use techniques like those discussed in this chapter, such as on-the-job training and computer-assisted learning.
3. There may be a third, *validation* step, in which the bugs are worked out of the train-ing program by presenting it to a small representative audience.
4. The fourth step is to *implement* the program, by actually training the targeted em-ployee group.
5. Fifth is an *evaluation* step, in which management assesses the program's successes or failures.

Most employers probably do not (and need not) create their own training materials (Step 2 above), since many materials are available online and offline. For example, the professional development site saba.com offers Web-based courses for employees. The Association for Training and Development (astd.org) lists training vendors. Many firms,

Most employers can build training programs like this one based on existing online and offline content offered by training content providers.

including American Media, Inc., of West Des Moines, Iowa, provide turnkey training packages. These include a training leader's guide, self-study book, and video for improving skills in areas such as customer service, and appraising performance.

Training, Learning, and Motivation

Training is futile if the trainee lacks the ability or motivation to benefit from it. In terms of *ability*, the trainee needs (among other things) the required reading, writing, and mathematics skills, and the required educational level, intelligence, and knowledge base. Effective employee selection is obviously important here. (As we first explained in Chapter 5, some employers use "miniature job training" to screen out low-potential trainees. It basically involves using sample tasks from the firm's training program to help decide who will and will not move on to training.)[13]

The employer can take several steps to increase the trainee's *motivation* to learn. Municipalities running driver education programs know there's often no more effective way to get a learner's attention than by graphically presenting a filmed auto accident. In other words, start the training by making the material meaningful. For example, show why it's important, provide an overview of the material, and use familiar examples to illustrate key points.[14] Providing opportunities for practice, and letting the trainee make errors also improve motivation and learning.[15] Feedback—including periodic performance assessments and more frequent verbal critiques—is also important.[16] We can summarize motivational points as follows.

Make the Learning Meaningful   It is easier for trainees to understand and remember material that is *meaningful*. Therefore:

1. At the start of training, provide a bird's-eye view of the material to be presented. Knowing the overall picture facilitates learning.
2. Use a variety of familiar examples.
3. Organize the information so you can present it logically, and in meaningful units.
4. Use terms and concepts that are already familiar to trainees.
5. Use as many visual aids as possible.

Make Skills Transfer Easy   Make it easy to *transfer* new skills and behaviors from the training site to the job site:

1. Maximize the similarity between the training situation and the work situation.
2. Provide adequate practice.
3. Label or identify each feature of the machine and/or step in the process.
4. Direct the trainees' attention to important aspects of the job. For example, if you're training customer service representatives to handle incoming calls, first explain the different types of calls they will encounter and how to recognize them.[17]
5. Provide "heads-up," preparatory information. For example, trainees learning to become first-line supervisors often face stressful conditions, high workload, and difficult subordinates back on the job. Studies suggest you can reduce the negative impact of such events by letting trainees know they might happen.[18]

Motivation Principles for Trainers

1. People learn best by doing. Try to provide as much realistic practice as possible.
2. Trainees learn best when the trainers immediately reinforce correct responses, perhaps with a quick "well done."

3. Trainees learn best at their own pace. If possible, let them pace themselves.

4. Create a perceived training need in trainees' minds.[19] In one study, pilots who experienced pretraining, accident-related events subsequently learned more from an accident-reduction training program than did those experiencing fewer such events.[20] Similarly, "Before the training, managers need to sit down and talk with the trainee about why they are enrolled in the class, what they are expected to learn and how they can use it on the job."[21] (The Employment Law feature below discusses some reasons training is crucial for *employers*.)

5. The schedule is important. The learning curve goes down late in the day, so that "full day training is not as effective as half the day or three-fourths of the day."[22]

② Describe and illustrate how you would go about identifying training requirements.

negligent training
A situation where an employer fails to train adequately, and the employee subsequently harms a third party.

Analyzing Training Needs

How you analyze training needs depends on whether you're training new or current employees. The main task in analyzing *new* employees' training needs is to determine what the job entails and to break it down into subtasks, each of which you then teach to the new employee.

Analyzing *current* employees' training needs is more complex, since you have the added task of deciding whether training is the solution. For example, performance may be

Know Your *Employment* LAW   Training and the Law

Managers should understand the legal implications of their training-related decisions, particularly with respect to discrimination, harassment, negligent training, and overtime pay.

With respect to *discrimination*, Title VII of the Civil Rights Act of 1964 and related legislation requires that the employer avoid discriminatory actions in all aspects of its human resource management process, and that applies to selecting which employees to train. Employers face much the same consequences for discriminating against protected individuals when selecting candidates for training programs as they would in selecting candidates for jobs, or for promotion or other related decisions.

As explained in Chapter 2, the U.S. Supreme Court ruled that courts could hold employers liable for the sexually harassing acts of their supervisors, but that employers could avoid liability by taking steps (including training) to prevent and rectify *harassment*. In practical terms, this means that many lower courts, in interpreting the Supreme Court's decision, rely on the adequacy of the employer's sexual harassment training to determine whether the employer did exercise reasonable care to prevent harassment.[23]

Inadequate training can also expose the employer to liability for **negligent training**. As one expert puts it, "it's clear from the case law that where an employer fails to train adequately and an employee subsequently does harm to third parties, the court will find the employer liable." Among other things, this means that the employer must confirm the applicant/employee's claims of skill and experience, provide adequate training (particularly where employees work with dangerous equipment), and evaluate the training to ensure that it is actually reducing risks.[24]

Given its frequent off-the-job nature, the question also often arises as to whether the employer must *pay the employee* for the time the latter spends being trained. Generally, if the training program is strictly voluntary, conducted outside working hours, not directly related to the trainee's job, and the trainee doesn't perform any productive work, then the trainee should not expect to be compensated. On the other hand, if the training is on the current employee's time and the employer tells him or her that the training is mandatory, then the employer may have to compensate the employee for the time spent in the program.[25]

down because the standards aren't clear or because the person is not motivated. Some trainers use special analytical software, such as from Saba Software, Inc., to diagnose performance gaps and their causes.

Task Analysis: Assessing New Employees' Training Needs

Particularly with lower-level workers, it's common to hire inexperienced personnel and train them. Your aim here is to give these new employees the skills and knowledge they need to do the job. You use task analysis to determine the new employees' training needs.

task analysis
A detailed study of a job to identify the specific skills required.

    Task analysis is a detailed study of the job to determine what specific skills—like Java (in the case of a Web developer) or interviewing (in the case of a supervisor)—the job requires. Job descriptions and job specifications are helpful here. These list the job's specific duties and skills and thus provide the basic reference point in determining the training required. You can also uncover training needs by reviewing performance standards, performing the job, and questioning current job holders and their supervisors.[26]

    Some employers supplement the job description and specification with a *task analysis record form*. This consolidates information regarding required tasks and skills in a form that's especially helpful for determining training requirements. As Table 8-1 illustrates, a task analysis record form contains six types of information, such as "Skills Required."

Performance Analysis: Assessing Current Employees' Training Needs

❸ Explain how to distinguish between problems you can fix with training and those you can't.

performance analysis
Verifying that there is a performance deficiency and determining whether that deficiency should be corrected through training or through some other means (such as transferring the employee).

For current employees, **performance analysis** is the process of verifying that there is a performance deficiency and determining if the employer should correct such deficiency through training or some other means (like transferring the employee).

    There are several methods you can use to identify a current employee's training needs. These include reviewing:

- performance appraisals;
- job-related performance data (including productivity, absenteeism and tardiness, grievances, waste, late deliveries, product quality, downtime, repairs, equipment utilization, and customer complaints);
- observations by supervisors or other specialists;
- interviews with the employee or his or her supervisor;
- tests of things like job knowledge, skills, and attendance;
- attitude surveys;
- individual employee daily diaries;
- and assessment center results.

    The first step is usually to compare the person's actual performance to what it should be. Examples of specific performance deficiencies include:

> I expect each salesperson to make ten new contracts per week, but John averages only six. Other plants our size average no more than two serious accidents per month; we're averaging five.

Can't Do/Won't Do   It is futile to spend time training an employee whose work is deficient because of insufficient motivation. Distinguishing between can't-do and won't-do problems is thus the heart of performance analysis.

    First, determine whether it is a *can't-do* problem and, if so, its specific causes. For example: The employees don't know what to do or what your standards are; there are obstacles in the system such as lack of tools or supplies; there are no job aids (such as

TABLE 8-1 Task Analysis Record Form

Task List	When and How Often Performed	Quantity and Quality of Performance	Conditions Under Which Performed	Skills or Knowledge Required	Where Best Learned
1. Operate paper cutter	4 times per day		Noisy pressroom: distractions		
1.1 Start motor					
1.2 Set cutting distance		± tolerance of 0.007 in.		Read gauge	On the job
1.3 Place paper on cutting table		Must be completely even to prevent uneven cut		Lift paper correctly	On the job
1.4 Push paper up to cutter				Must be even	On the job
1.5 Grasp safety release with left hand		100% of time, for safety		Essential for safety	On the job but practice first with no distractions
1.6 Grasp cutter release with right hand				Must keep both hands on releases	On the job but practice first with no distractions
1.7 Simultaneously pull safety release with left hand and cutter release with right hand					
1.8 Wait for cutter to retract		100% of time, for safety		Must keep both hands on releases	On the job but practice first with no distractions
1.9 Retract paper				Wait until cutter retracts	On the job but practice first with no distractions
1.10 Shut off		100% of time, for safety			On the job but practice first with no distractions
2. Operate printing press					
2.1 Start motor					

Note: Task analysis record form showing some of the tasks and subtasks performed by a printing press operator.

color-coded wires that show assemblers which wire goes where); you've hired people who haven't the skills to do the job; or inadequate training.

On the other hand, it might be a *won't-do* problem. Here employees could do a good job if they wanted to. One expert says, "perhaps the biggest trap that trainers fall into is [developing] training for problems that training just won't fix."[27] Perhaps you need to change the reward system.

If training is the solution, you need to set objectives. These specify what the trainee should be able to accomplish upon completing the training program—repair a copier in 30 minutes, program a simple Web site in half a day, or sell five advertising banners per day, for instance.[28]

Competency Models   Many companies, including Sharp Electronics, develop generic competency models for jobs or closely related groups of jobs. In this context, *competency* means knowledge, skills, and behaviors that enable employees to effectively perform their jobs. Sharp's process for identifying a job's competencies begins with interviews with senior executives, to crystallize the firm's strategy and objectives. Human resource specialists then conduct behavioral interviews with the job's top performers as well as focus groups, to identify the set of competencies (such as "demonstrates creativity," "communicates effectively," and "focuses on the customer") that together will comprise the job's competency model. Subsequent training and development then aim, in part, to develop these competencies.[29]

4 Explain how to use five training techniques.

TRAINING METHODS

Once you've decided to train employees and have identified their training needs and goals, you have to design the training program. This basically means deciding on the actual content (the courses and step-by-step instructions, for instance) as well as on how to deliver the training—on-the-job, or via the Web, for instance.

Some employers create their own training content, but there is also a vast selection of online and off-line content and packages from which to choose. You'll find turnkey, off-the-shelf programs on virtually any topic—from occupational safety to sexual harassment to Web design—from tens of thousands of online and off-line providers. (See, for example, www.astd.org; www.trainerswarehouse.com, and www.gneil.com, among thousands of such suppliers.)

In any case, there are various methods employers use to actually deliver the training. We'll start with what is probably the most popular: on-the-job training.

On-the-Job Training

on-the-job training
Training a person to learn a job while working on it.

On-the-job training (OJT) means having a person learn a job by actually doing it. Every employee, from mailroom clerk to CEO, gets on-the-job training when he or she joins a firm. In many firms, OJT is the only training available.[30] All too often the employer says, "Here's your desk . . . get started."

Types of On-the-Job Training   The most familiar type of on-the-job training is the *coaching or understudy method*. Here, an experienced worker or the trainee's supervisor trains the employee. This may involve simply acquiring skills by observing the supervisor, or (preferably) having the supervisor or job expert show the new employee the ropes, step-by-step. The Men's Wearhouse, with 455 stores nationwide, makes extensive use of on-the-job training. It has few full-time trainers. Instead, the Men's Wearhouse has a formal process of "cascading" responsibility for training: Every manager is formally accountable for the development of his or her direct subordinates.[31]

Job rotation, in which an employee (usually a management trainee) moves from job to job at planned intervals, is another OJT technique. Jeffrey Immelt progressed through such a process in becoming GE's new CEO. *Special assignments* similarly give lower-level executives firsthand experience in working on actual problems.

Advantages and Guidelines   OJT has several advantages. It is relatively inexpensive; trainees learn while producing; and there is no need for expensive off-site facilities like classrooms or programmed learning devices. The method also facilitates learning, since trainees learn by doing and get quick feedback on their performance.

But there are several guidelines to follow. Most important, don't take the success of an on-the-job training program for granted. Carefully train the trainers themselves (often the employees' supervisors), and provide the necessary training materials. Trainers should know, for instance, the principles of motivating learners. Low expectations on the trainer's part may translate into poorer trainee performance (a phenomenon researchers have called "the golem effect"). So, trainers should emphasize the high expectations they have for their trainees' success.

OJT Steps Here are some steps to help ensure OJT success.

Step 1: Prepare the Learner

1. Put the learner at ease.
2. Explain why he or she is being taught.
3. Create interest, find out what the learner already knows about the job.
4. Explain the whole job and relate it to some job the worker already knows.
5. Place the learner as close to the normal working position as possible.
6. Familiarize the worker with equipment, materials, tools, and trade terms.

Step 2: Present the Operation

1. Explain quantity and quality requirements.
2. Go through the job at the normal work pace.
3. Go through the job at a slow pace several times, explaining each step. Between operations, explain the difficult parts, or those in which errors are likely to be made.
4. Again go through the job at a slow pace several times; explain the key points.
5. Have the learner explain the steps as you go through the job at a slow pace.

Step 3: Do a Tryout

1. Have the learner go through the job several times, slowly, explaining each step to you. Correct mistakes and, if necessary, do some of the complicated steps the first few times.
2. Run the job at the normal pace.
3. Have the learner do the job, gradually building up skill and speed.
4. As soon as the learner demonstrates ability to do the job, let the work begin, but don't abandon him or her.

Step 4: Follow Up

1. Designate to whom the learner should go for help.
2. Gradually decrease supervision, checking work from time.
3. Correct faulty work patterns before they become a habit. Show why the learned method is superior.
4. Compliment good work.[32]

Apprenticeship Training

apprenticeship training
A structured process by which people become skilled workers through a combination of classroom instruction and on-the-job training.

Apprenticeship programs began in the Middle Ages. **Apprenticeship training** is a process by which people become skilled workers, usually through a combination of formal learning and long-term on-the-job training. It traditionally involves having the learner/apprentice study under the tutelage of a master craftsperson. When steelmaker Dofasco discovered that many of their employees would be retiring during the next five to 10 years, the company decided to revive its apprenticeship training program. Applicants are pre-screened. New recruits then spend about 32 months in an internal training program that emphasizes apprenticeship training, learning various jobs under the tutelage of experienced employees.[33]

The U.S. Department of Labor's Employment and Training Administration offers apprenticeship training, along with a number of other types of training programs. Figure 8-2 lists 25 popular recent apprenticeships.

FIGURE 8-2

The 25 Most Popular Apprenticeships*

* Listed alphabetically

Source: Olivia Crosby, "Apprenticeships," *Occupational Outlook Quarterly,* 46, no. 2 (Summer 2002), p. 5.

According to the U.S. Department of Labor apprenticeship database, the occupations listed below had the highest numbers of apprentices in 2001. These findings are approximate because the database includes only about 70% of registered apprenticeship programs—and none of the unregistered ones.

- Boilermaker
- Bricklayer (construction)
- Carpenter
- Construction craft laborer
- Cook (any industry)
- Cook (hotel and restaurant)
- Correction officer
- Electrician
- Electrician (aircraft)
- Electrician (maintenance)
- Electronics mechanic
- Firefighter
- Machinist
- Maintenance mechanic (any industry)
- Millwright
- Operating engineer
- Painter (construction)
- Pipefitter (construction)
- Plumber
- Power plant operator
- Roofer
- Sheet-metal worker
- Structural-steel worker
- Telecommunications technician
- Tool and die maker

Informal Learning

Surveys from the American Society for Training and Development estimate that as much as 80% of what employees learn on the job they learn not through formal training programs but through informal means, including performing their jobs on a daily basis in collaboration with their colleagues.[34]

Although managers don't arrange informal learning, there's still much they can do to ensure that it occurs. Most of the steps are simple. For example, Siemens Power Transmission and Distribution in Raleigh, North Carolina, places tools in cafeteria areas to take advantage of the work-related discussions taking place. Even installing white boards and keeping them stocked with markers can facilitate informal learning.

job instruction training (JIT)
Listing each job's basic tasks, along with key points, in order to provide step-by-step training for employees.

Job Instruction Training

Many jobs consist of a logical sequence of steps and are best taught step-by-step. This step-by-step process is called **job instruction training (JIT)**. To begin, list all necessary steps in the job, (see below) each in its proper sequence. Alongside each step also lists a

Steps	Key Points
1. Start motor	None
2. Set cutting distance	Carefully read scale—to prevent wrong-sized cut
3. Place paper on cutting table	Make sure paper is even—to prevent uneven cut
4. Push paper up to cutter	Make sure paper is tight—to prevent uneven cut
5. Grasp safety release with left hand	Do not release left hand—to prevent hand from being caught in cutter
6. Grasp cutter release with right hand	Do not release right hand—to prevent hand from being caught in cutter
7. Simultaneously pull cutter and safety releases	Keep both hands on corresponding releases—avoid hands being on cutting table
8. Wait for cutter to retract	Keep both hands on releases—to avoid having hands on cutting table
9. Retract paper	Make sure cutter is retracted; keep both hands away from releases
10. Shut off motor	None

corresponding "key point" (if any). The steps (as in the example) show what is to be done, and the key points show how it's to be done—and why.

Lectures

Lecturing has several advantages. It is a quick and simple way to present knowledge to large groups of trainees, as when the salesforce needs to learn a new product's features. While some correctly view lectures as boring and ineffective, studies and practical experience suggest that they can in fact be effective.[35] Here are some guidelines for presenting a lecture:[36]

- Don't start out on the wrong foot. For instance, don't open with an irrelevant joke or by saying something like, "I really don't know why I was asked to speak here today."
- Give your listeners signals. For instance, if you have a list of items, start by saying something like, "There are four reasons why the sales reports are necessary. . . . The first . . ."
- Be alert to your audience. Watch body language for negative signals like fidgeting and crossed arms.
- Maintain eye contact with the audience during your presentation.
- Make sure everyone in the room can hear. Repeat questions that you get from trainees before you answer.
- Control your hands. Get in the habit of leaving them hanging naturally at your sides.
- Talk from notes rather than from a script. Write out clear, legible notes on large index cards or on PowerPoint slides. Use these as an outline.
- Break a long talk into a series of five-minute talks. Speakers often give a short overview introduction, and then spend the rest of a one-hour presentation going point by point through their material. Unfortunately, most people quickly lose interest in your list. Experts suggest breaking the long talk into a series of five-minute talks, each with its own introduction. Write more, briefer, PowerPoint slides, and spend about a minute on each. Each introduction highlights what you'll discuss, why it's important to the audience, and your credibility—why they should listen to you.[37]
- Practice. If possible, rehearse under conditions similar to those under which you will actually give your presentation.

Programmed Learning

programmed learning
A systematic method for teaching job skills involving presenting questions or facts, allowing the person to respond, and giving the learner immediate feedback on the accuracy of his or her answers.

Whether the medium is a textbook, PC, or the Internet, **programmed learning** (or programmed instruction) is a step-by-step, self-learning method that consists of three parts:

1. Presenting questions, facts, or problems to the learner
2. Allowing the person to respond
3. Providing feedback on the accuracy of answers

Generally, programmed learning presents facts and follow-up questions frame by frame. The learner can then respond, and subsequent frames provide feedback on the accuracy of his or her answers. What the next question is often depends on the accuracy of the learner's answer to the previous question.

Intelligent tutoring systems are basically computerized supercharged programmed instruction programs. In addition to providing the trainee with guidance and directing the trainee toward the next instructional step, intelligent tutoring systems learn what questions and approaches worked and did not work and therefore adjust the suggested instructional sequence to the trainee's unique needs.

Programmed learning's main advantage is that it reduces training time.[38] It also facilitates learning because it lets trainees learn at their own pace, provides immediate feedback, and reduces the learner's risk of error. On the other hand, trainees do not learn much more from programmed learning than they would from a traditional textbook course. You must therefore weigh the cost of developing the programmed instruction against the faster but not improved learning.

Audiovisual-Based Training

Audiovisual-based training techniques like DVDs, films, PowerPoints, videoconferencing, audiotapes, and videotapes can be very effective and are widely used.[39] The Ford Motor Company uses videos in its dealer training sessions to simulate problems and sample reactions to various customer complaints, for example.

Audiovisuals are more expensive than conventional lectures but offer some advantages. Of course, they usually tend to be more interesting. In addition, consider using them in the following situations:

1. When there is a need to illustrate how to follow a certain sequence over time, such as when teaching fax machine repair. The stop-action, instant replay, and fast- or slow-motion capabilities of audiovisuals can be useful here.
2. When there is a need to expose trainees to events not easily demonstrable in live lectures, such as a visual tour of a factory or open-heart surgery.
3. When you need organizationwide training and it is too costly to move the trainers from place to place.

Simulated Training

simulated training
Training employees on special off-the-job equipment, as in airplane pilot training, so training costs and hazards can be reduced.

The Stanford University medical students in the virtual reality training room use simulated training. **Simulated training** (occasionally called vestibule training) is a method in which trainees learn on the actual or simulated equipment they will use on the job, but are actually trained off the job (perhaps in a separate room or *vestibule*).

Simulated training is necessary when it's too costly or dangerous to train employees on the job. Putting new assembly-line workers right to work could slow production, for instance, and when safety is a concern—as with pilots—simulated training may be the only practical alternative.

Simulated training may take place in a separate room with the same equipment the trainees will use on the job. However, it often involves the use of simulators. In pilot training, for instance, airlines use flight simulators for safety, learning efficiency, and cost savings. Simulated training is increasingly computer-based. In fact, computerized and Internet-based tools have revolutionized the training process.

Computer-Based Training

With computer-based training, the trainee uses interactive computer-based and/or DVD systems to increase his or her knowledge or skills. McDonald's developed about 11 different courses for its franchisees' employees, and put the programs on DVDs. The programs consist of graphics-supported lessons, and require trainees to make choices to show their understanding.[40]

Computer-based training (CBT) is increasingly interactive and realistic. For example, *interactive multimedia training* "integrates the use of text, video, graphics, photos, animation, and sound to produce a complex training environment with which the trainee interacts."[41] In training a physician, for instance, an interactive multimedia training system lets a medical student take a hypothetical patient's medical history, conduct an examination, analyze lab tests, and then (by clicking the "examine chest" button) choose a type of chest examination and even hear the sounds of the person's heart. The medical student can then interpret the sounds and draw conclusions upon which to base a diagnosis. As noted, *virtual reality training* takes this realism a step further. Virtual reality "puts the trainee in an artificial three-dimensional environment that simulates events and situations that might be experienced on the job."[42] Sensory devices transmit how the trainee is responding to the computer, and the trainee sees and feels and hears what is going on, assisted by special goggles and auditory and sensory devices.[43]

The U.S. Armed Forces are increasingly utilizing simulation-based training programs for soldiers and officers. For example, the army developed video-game-type training programs called Full-Spectrum Command and Full-Spectrum Warrior for training troops in urban warfare. According to one description, the two games offer extremely realistic features, within a context that emphasizes real-time leadership and decision-making skills.[44] Table 8-2 summarizes the main terminology of computer-based training.

TABLE 8-2 Names and Descriptions of Various Computer-Based Training Techniques

PI	Computer-based programmed instruction (PI) programs consist of text, graphics, and perhaps multimedia enhancements that are stored in memory and connected to one another electronically. Material to be learned is grouped into chunks of closely related information. Typically, the computer-based PI program presents the trainees with the information in the chunk, and then tests them on their retention of the information. If they have not retained the material, they are cycled back to the original information, or to remedial information. If they have retained the information they move on to the next information to be learned.
CBT	Training provided in part or in whole through the use of a computer. *Computer-based training* is the term most often used in private industry or the government for training employees using computer-assisted instruction.
CMI	Computer-managed instruction (CMI) uses a computer to manage the administrative functions of training, such as registration, record keeping, scoring, and grading.
ICAI	When the computer-based training system is able to provide some of the primary characteristics of a human tutor, it is often referred to as an intelligent computer-assisted instruction (ICAI) system. It is a more advanced form of PI. Expert systems are used to run the tutoring aspect of the training, monitor trainee knowledge within a programmed knowledge model, and provide adaptive tutoring based on trainee responses.
ITS	Intelligent tutoring systems (ITS) make use of artificial intelligence to provide tutoring that is more advanced than ICAI type tutoring. ITS "learns" through trainee responses the best methods of facilitating the trainee's learning.
Simulations	Computer simulations provide a representation of a situation and the tasks to be performed in the situation. The representation can range from identical (e.g., word processing training) to fairly abstract (e.g., conflict resolution). Trainees perform the tasks presented to them by the computer program and the computer program monitors their performance.
Virtual Reality	Virtual reality is an advanced form of computer simulation, placing the trainee in a simulated environment that is "virtually" the same as the physical environment. This simulation is accomplished by the trainee wearing special equipment such as head gear, gloves, and so on, which control what the trainee is able to see, feel, and otherwise sense. The trainee learns by interacting with objects in the electronic environment to achieve some goal.

Source: P. Nick Blanchard and James Thacker, *Effective Training: Systems, Strategies, and Practices* (Upper Saddle River, NJ: Pearson, 2003), p. 144.

Effectiveness   Interactive technologies (wherein trainees receive quick feedback) reduce learning time by an average of 50%.[45] They can also be cost-effective once designed and produced. Other advantages include instructional consistency (computers, unlike human trainers, don't have good days and bad days), mastery of learning (if the trainee doesn't learn it, he or she generally can't move on to the next step), increased retention, and increased trainee motivation (resulting from responsive feedback).

Specialist multimedia software houses like Graphic Media of Portland, Oregon, produce much of the content for CBT programs. They produce both custom titles and generic programs like a $999 package for teaching workplace safety.

Electronic Performance Support Systems (EPSS)

People don't remember everything they learn. Dell, for example, introduces about 80 new products per year, so it's unrealistic to expect Dell's technical support people to know everything about every product. Dell's training therefore focuses on providing its employees with the general knowledge they need every day, such as Dell's rules, culture and values, and systems and work processes. Performance support systems then deliver the rest of what they need to know, when they need it.[46]

electronic performance support systems (EPSS)
Sets of computerized tools and displays that automate training, documentation, and phone support, integrate this automation into applications, and provide support that's faster, cheaper, and more effective than traditional methods.

job aid
Is a set of instructions, diagrams, or similar methods available at the job site to guide the worker.

Electronic performance support systems (EPSS) are computerized tools and displays that automate training, documentation, and phone support.[47] When you call a Dell service rep about a problem with your new computer, he or she is probably asking questions that are prompted by an EPSS; it takes you both, step-by-step, through an analytical sequence. Without the EPSS, Dell would have to train its service reps to memorize an unrealistically large number of solutions. Aetna Insurance cut its 13-week instructor-led training course for new call-center employees by about two weeks, by providing the employees with performance support tools.[48]

Performance support systems are modern job aids. A **job aid** is a set of instructions, diagrams, or similar methods available at the job site to guide the worker.[49] Job aids work particularly well on complex jobs that require multiple steps, or where it's dangerous to forget a step. Airline pilots use job aids (such as a checklist of things to do prior to takeoff). The General Motors Electromotive Division gives workers job aids in the form of diagrams. These show, for example, where the locomotive wiring runs and which color wires go where.

Distance and Internet-Based Training

Firms today use various forms of distance learning methods for training. These range from paper-and-pencil correspondence courses, to teletraining, videoconferencing, and modern Internet-based courses.[50]

Teletraining   With teletraining, a trainer in a central location teaches groups of employees at remote locations via television hookups. Honda America began by using satellite television technology to train engineers, and now uses it for many other types of employee training. For example, its Ohio-based subsidiary purchases seminars from the National Technological University, a provider of satellite education that uses courses from various universities and specialized teaching organizations.

Videoconferencing   Videoconferencing allows people in one location to communicate live via a combination of audio and visual equipment with people in another city or country, or with groups in several cities. This may simply involve using PC-based video cameras and several remote trainees, or a dozen or more learners taking a class in a video-conference lecture room. Here, keypads allow audience interactivity. For instance, in a program at Texas Instruments, the keypad system lets instructors call on remote trainees and lets the latter respond.

There are several things to keep in mind before lecturing in front of the camera. For example, because the training is remote, it's particularly important to prepare a manual the learners can use to follow the points the trainer is making, and a script for the trainer to follow. A sampling of other hints would include: Avoid bright, flashy jewelry or heavily patterned clothing; arrive at least 20 minutes early; and test all equipment you will be using.

Internet-Based Training

Employers make extensive use of Web-based learning.[51] Many firms simply let their employees take online courses offered by online course providers such as saba.com. Others use their proprietary internal *intranets* to facilitate computer-based training.

Various products, like Blackboard and WebCT, support online learning endeavors. For example, WebCT provides a process for delivering course content via PowerPoint slides, enables learners and instructors to interact live and asynchronously via online chat rooms and discussion forums, and also delivers, grades, and compiles online exams and grades.

Having used Internet-based learning, many students are familiar with its advantages. When the Park Avenue Bank of Valdosta, Georgia, installed its e-training program, trainees could use it 24/7 from any computer. The bank's training program included a *learning management system* that helps trainers track employees' progress in completing courses.[52] Internet training can be *cost-effective*. For example, Delta Airlines customer service personnel receive about 70% of their annual required FAA training via the Internet. Delta likes it because "prior to online training, employees had to travel to one of five training centers, keeping them away from their jobs for at least the day."[53]

Effectiveness Researchers reviewed 96 studies reporting data from 19,331 trainees who participated in 168 training courses, both Web-based and classroom. In general: Web-based

Employers increasingly rely on video- and Internet-based training programs to create "virtual classrooms."

instruction was a bit more effective than classroom instruction for teaching declarative knowledge (memory of facts and principles); Web-based instruction and classroom instruction were equally effective for teaching procedural knowledge (information about how to perform a task or action); trainees were equally satisfied with Web-based instruction and classroom instruction; and Web-based instruction was much more effective than classroom instruction when the trainees could use the Web program to control the pace and selection of the content.[54] Another study, by Michigan State University researchers, found that on-site employee education programs produced better results than online training, in terms of subsequent test results.[55]

In any case, e-learning is booming. By one estimate, employer's annual use of e-learning exceeds $14.5 billion.[56]

The Virtual Classroom   Conventional Web-based learning tends to be limited to the sorts of online learning with which many college students are already familiar—reading PowerPoint presentations, participating in instant message–type chat rooms, and taking online exams, for instance.

virtual classroom

A learning environment that uses special collaboration software to enable multiple remote learners, using their PCs or laptops, to participate in live audio and visual discussions, communicate via written text, and learn via content such as PowerPoint slides.

The virtual classroom takes online learning to a new level. A **virtual classroom** uses special collaboration software to enable multiple remote learners, using their PCs or laptops, to participate in live audio and visual discussions, communicate via written text, and learn via content such as PowerPoint slides.

The virtual classroom combines the best of Web-based learning offered by systems like Blackboard and WebCT, with live video and audio. For example, Elluminate Inc. makes one popular virtual classroom system, Elluminate live! It enables learners to communicate with clear, two-way audio, build communities with user profiles and live video, collaborate with chat and shared whiteboards, and learn with shared applications such as PowerPoint slides.

Using E-Learning

There are several ways to improve e-based learning. The manager needs to consider that trainees tend to be slower taking online exams than they are paper-and-pencil ones. This is because Web test pages tend to have fewer questions, in larger font, than do paper quizzes, and because going back and reviewing answers tends to take longer online. It's also important to make sure that the trainee can actually use the extra control that Web-based learning should provide. For example, a Web-based course may give learners the opportunity to choose the content they'll focus on, and its sequence and pacing. Therefore, make sure trainees know the control they have, and how they can use it, such as how to change the learning sequence.[57]

In practice, it's usually not a choice of conventional versus online training. The trend is toward blended learning solutions. For example, Intuit (which makes accounting software such as TurboTax and QuickBooks) uses instructor led classroom training for bringing in new distributors and getting them up to speed. Then, they use their virtual classroom systems to provide additional training, for monthly meetings with distributors, and for short classes on special software features.[58]

MP3/Instant Messaging   Some employers, including J. P. Morgan, encourage employees to use instant messaging as a quick learning device. Figure 8-3 illustrates a sample IM learning incident. CapitalOne recently purchased 3000 iPods for trainees. The training department then had an Internet audio book provider create an audio learning site within CapitalOne's firewall. Employees used it to download training materials to their iPods.

FIGURE 8-3

IM Learning Incident

Source: Joshua Bronstein and Amy Newman, "IM 4 Learning," *Training and Development*, February 2006, p. 48. Copyright © 2007 from T&D. Reprinted with permission of American Society for Training & Development.

> Employee 1: do you know how to undo split screens?
> Employee 1: on excel?
> Employee 2: yup
> Employee 1: how?
> Employee 2: go into.. one sec
> Employee 2: ok highlight the column or row where the split is
> Employee 2: go into Window
> Employee 2: click freeze panes
> Employee 2: that should do it
> Employee 1: thanks!
> Employee 2: no prob

Improving Productivity Through HRIS: Learning Portals

Many firms employ business portals. Through its business portal, a firm's employees—secretaries, engineers, salespeople, and so on—can "get the tools you need to analyze data inside and outside your company, and see the customized content you need, like industry news and competitive data."[59]

Employers increasingly convey their employee training through learning portals. Learning portal suppliers such as skillsoft.com contract with employers to deliver online training courses to the firms' employees. (See learnitivity.com for a list of commercial learning portals.) They usually maintain the employers' learning portals on their own servers, which employees reach by clicking on their own firms' business portal training links. Skillsoft calls its portals Knowledge Centers. Some target specific industries with relevant offerings. Other firms create special courses for a firm's employees and customers.[60] The U.S. Post Office instituted one such system. It contracted a supplier to use the latter's learning management system (LMS) to expand the Postal Service's learning activities. The LMS gives employees access to state-of-the-art training, and lets the Postal Service's managers monitor their organization's training progress.[61]

The movement today is toward integrating the e-learning system with the company's overall, enterprisewide information systems. In that way, for instance, employers can more easily synchronize employees' training with their performance appraisal, skills inventory, and succession plans.[62]

Literacy Training Techniques

Functional illiteracy—the inability to handle basic reading, writing, and arithmetic tasks—is a serious problem at work. By one estimate, about 39 million people in the U.S. have a learning disability that makes it challenging for them to read, write, or do arithmetic.[63] Managers and trainers should therefore be ready to accommodate these people, for instance with additional, preparatory training, or by using different training media.

Employers are responding in two main ways. First, they are *testing* job candidates' basic skills. Second, they are *instituting* basic skills and literacy programs. The Life Skills program at the Bellwood plant of Borg-Warner Automotive is an example. Based on test scores, managers chose participants and placed them in classes of 15 students each. There were two trainers from a local training company. Employees could leave when they reached a predetermined literacy skill level, so that some were in the program for only 40 hours and others stayed the entire (200 hours) course. Classes were five days per week, two hours per day, with classes scheduled so that one hour was during the employee's personal time and the second was on company time. Employees were paired so that they could help each other

The NEW Workforce   Diversity Training

With an increasingly diverse workforce, we saw that more firms are implementing diversity training programs. Diversity training aims to create better cross-cultural sensitivity, with the goal of fostering more harmonious working relationships among a firm's employees. Such training typically includes improving interpersonal skills, understanding and valuing cultural differences, improving technical skills, socializing employees into the corporate culture, indoctrinating new workers into the U.S. work ethic, improving English proficiency and basic math skills, and improving bilingual skills for English-speaking employees.[64] Adams Mark Hotel & Resorts conducted a diversity training seminar for about 11,000 employees. It combined lectures, video, and employee role playing to emphasize sensitivity to race and religion.[65]

Most employers can probably opt for an off-the-shelf diversity training program such as *F.A.I.R.: a practical approach to diversity and the workplace*, from VisionPoint productions. The package includes a facilitator and discussion guide, participant materials and workbook, a DVD with print materials, PowerPoint slides, and two videos (the purchase price for the entire program is about $1,000). The first video provides an overview of diversity, explains what it means to be "culturally competent," and addresses the various categories of diversity such as race, religion, ethnicity, gender, and age. The second presents four vignettes illustrating such things as the importance of communicating, the potential pitfalls of stereotyping people, and bias in action (such as a worker whose colleagues treat his religion's holidays with less seriousness then their own).[66]

through a series of timed exercises in math and reading.[67] (Note that with minorities, the fastest-growing part of the U.S. workforce, language training no longer means just teaching English. In many industries or locales customers speak a variety of languages, and for a company to thrive, its workforce may have to be bilingual or multilingual.)[68]

Employees with weak reading, writing, or arithmetic skills may be reluctant to admit the problem. Supervisors therefore should watch for employees who avoid doing a particular job or using a particular tool; do not follow written directions or instructions; do not take written phone messages; take home forms to complete; or make the same mistakes repeatedly.[69] Literacy training is sometimes one aspect of diversity training programs, as "The New Workforce" feature illustrates.

MANAGEMENT DEVELOPMENT

It's not always easy to tell where "training" leaves off and "management development" begins. The latter, however, tends to emphasize longer term development and to focus on developing the capabilities of current or future managers. **Management development** is any attempt to improve managerial performance by imparting knowledge, changing attitudes, or increasing skills. The management development process consists of (1) assessing the company's strategic needs (for instance, to fill future executive openings, or to boost competitiveness), (2) appraising managers' current performance, and then (3) developing the managers (and future managers).[70]

management development
Any attempt to improve current or future management performance by imparting knowledge, changing attitudes, or increasing skills.

Research Insight Employers often talk about the need to "shatter the glass ceiling," the transparent but often impermeable barrier women face in trying to move to top management. While it makes sense to shatter the glass ceiling for equity's sake, there may be another reason. With the trend toward high-involvement work teams, consensus decision making, and empowerment, the sorts of leadership styles that women already exhibit may be much more appropriate than men's.

This conclusion is based on the assumption that female managers' leadership styles are different than males', and, based on research, that appears to be the case. Specifically, women scored higher than men on such traditional measures of transformational leadership as encouraging followers to question their old ways of doing things or to break with the past, providing simplified emotional appeals to increase awareness and understanding of mutually desired goals, and providing learning opportunities. Male managers were more likely to commend followers if they complied or to discipline them if they failed.[71]

Succession Planning Some management development programs are companywide and involve all or most new (or potential) managers. Thus, new MBAs may join Ford's management development program and rotate through various assignments and educational experiences. The dual aims are identifying their management potential and giving them breadth of experience (in, say, production and finance). The firm may then slot superior candidates onto a "fast track," a development program that prepares them more quickly for senior-level commands.

Other development programs aim to fill specific top positions, such as CEO. **Succession planning** refers to the process through which a company plans for and fills senior-level openings. For example, GE spent several years developing, testing, and watching potential replacements for CEO before finally choosing Jeffrey Immelt.

The typical succession planning process involves several steps: First, *anticipate management needs* based on strategic factors like planned expansion. Next, *review your firm's management skills* inventory (data on things like education and work experience, career preferences, and performance appraisals) to assess current talent. Then, *create replacement charts* that summarize potential candidates and each person's development needs. As in an earlier example (Figure 5-4, page 170), the development needs for a future division vice president might include job rotation, executive development programs—to provide training in strategic planning—and assignment for two weeks to the employer's in-house management development center. *Management development* can then begin, using methods like managerial on-the-job training, discussed below.

Assessment is usually part of such manager development programs. At frozen foods manufacturer Schawn, a committee of senior executives first whittles 40 or more candidates down to 10 or less. Then the program begins with a one-day assessment by outside consultants of each manager's leadership strengths and weaknesses. The assessment involves managers addressing a range of problems such as irate customers and employee conflict. The consultants assess 15 leadership competencies. This assessment becomes the basis for each manager's individual development plan. Action-learning (practical) projects then supplement individual and group training activities.[72]

An employer's succession plans and the manager's performance and potential all influence who is tapped for development. However, bear in mind that some deficiencies are easier to rectify. Knowledge is relatively easy to change, for instance through classroom courses, books, and e-learning. Skills and abilities are more difficult but still possible to change, for instance through coaching, mentoring, and (for a job abroad) a language immersion program. Changing personality tendencies is something else altogether. It's rare that a simple development course will suffice here, unless it's a major, life-altering assignment such as a posting abroad in a radically new culture.[73]

Managerial On-the-Job Training

Managerial on-the-job training methods include job rotation, the coaching/understudy approach, and action learning.

succession planning
A process through which senior-level openings are planned for and eventually filled.

job rotation
A management training technique that involves moving a trainee from department to department to broaden his or her experience and identify strong and weak points.

Job Rotation   **Job rotation** means moving management trainees from department to department to broaden their understanding of all parts of the business and to test their abilities. The trainee, often a recent college graduate, may spend several months in each department, fully involved in its operations. The trainee thus learns the department's business by actually doing it, while discovering what jobs he or she prefers.

Coaching/Understudy Approach   Here the trainee works directly with a senior manager or with the person he or she is to replace; the latter is responsible for the trainee's coaching. Normally, the understudy relieves the executive of certain responsibilities, giving the trainee a chance to learn the job.

action learning
A training technique by which management trainees are allowed to work full-time analyzing and solving problems in other departments.

Action Learning   **Action learning** programs give managers and others released time to work full-time analyzing and solving problems in departments other than their own. The basics include: carefully selected teams of five to 25 members; assigning the teams real world business problems that extend beyond their usual areas of expertise; and structured learning through coaching and feedback. The employer's senior managers usually choose the projects and decide whether to accept the teams' recommendations.[74] Many major firms around the world, from GE to Samsung and Deutsche Bank use action learning.[75]

For example, Pacific Gas & Electric Company's (PG&E) Action-Forum Process has three phases: (1) a "framework" phase of six to eight weeks—this is basically an intense planning period during which the team defines and collects data on an issue to work on; (2) the Action-Forum—two to three days at PG&E's learning center discussing the issue and developing action-plan recommendations; and (3) accountability sessions, when the teams meet with the leadership group at 30, 60, and 90 days to review the status of their action plans.

Off-the-Job Management Training and Development Techniques

There are also many off-the-job techniques for training and developing managers.

case study method
A development method in which the manager is presented with a written description of an organizational problem to diagnose and solve.

The Case Study Method   As most everyone knows, the **case study method** presents a trainee with a written description of an organizational problem. The person then analyzes the case, diagnoses the problem, and presents his or her findings and solutions in a discussion with other trainees.

Integrated case scenarios expand the case analysis concept by creating long-term, comprehensive case situations. For example, the FBI Academy created an integrated case scenario. It starts with "a concerned citizen's telephone call and ends 14 weeks later with a simulated trial. In between is the stuff of a genuine investigation, including a healthy sampling of what can go wrong in an actual criminal inquiry." To create such scenarios, scriptwriters (often employees in the firm's training group) write the scripts. The scripts include themes, background stories, detailed personnel histories, and role-playing instructions. In the case of the FBI, the scenarios are aimed at developing specific training skills, such as interviewing witnesses and analyzing crime scenes.[76]

management game
A development technique in which teams of managers compete by making computerized decisions regarding realistic but simulated situations.

Management Games   With computerized **management games**, trainees divide into five- or six-person groups, each of which competes with the others in a simulated marketplace. Each group typically must decide, for example, (1) how much to spend on advertising, (2) how much to produce, (3) how much inventory to maintain, and (4) how many of which product to produce. Usually, the game itself compresses a two- or three-year period into days, weeks, or months. As in the real world, each company team usually can't see what decisions (such as to boost advertising) the other firms have made, although these decisions do affect their own sales.

Management games can be effective. People learn best by being involved, and the games can gain such involvement. They help trainees develop their problem-solving skills, as well as to focus attention on planning rather than just putting out fires. The groups also usually elect their own officers and organize themselves. This can develop leadership skills and foster cooperation and teamwork.

Outside Seminars   Many companies and universities offer Web-based and traditional classroom management development seminars and conferences. For example, the American Management Association provides thousands of courses in areas ranging from accounting and controls to assertiveness training, basic financial skills, information systems, and total quality management.[77] Specialized associations, such as SHRM provide more specialized seminars for their own profession's members. The When You're on Your Own feature on pages 314–315 provides some practical training guidance.

University-Related Programs   Many universities provide executive education and continuing education programs in leadership, supervision, and the like. These can range from one- to four-day programs to executive development programs lasting one to four months. An increasing number of these are online.

The Advanced Management Program of the Graduate School of Business Administration at Harvard University is a well-known example. Students in this program consist of experienced managers from around the world. It uses cases and lectures to provide top-level management talent with the latest management skills, and with practice analyzing complex organizational problems. When Hasbro wanted to improve its executives' creativity skills, it turned to Dartmouth University's Amos Tuck Business School. Tuck provided a "custom approach to designing a program that would be built from the ground up to suit Hasbro's specific needs."[78]

Video-linked classrooms are another option. For example, a video link between the School of Business and Public Administration at California State University, Sacramento, and a Hewlett-Packard facility in Roseville, California, allows HP employees to take courses at their facility.

role playing
A training technique in which trainees act out parts in a realistic management situation.

Role Playing   The aim of **role playing** is to create a realistic situation and then have the trainees assume the parts (or roles) of specific persons in that situation.

Figure 8-4 presents a role from a classic role-playing exercise called the New Truck Dilemma. When combined with the general instructions and other roles for the exercise, role playing can trigger spirited discussions among the role player/trainees. The aim is to

FIGURE 8-4

Typical Role in a Role-Playing Exercise

Source: Normal R. F. Maier and Gertrude Casselman Verser, *Psychology in Industrial Organizations*, 5th ed., p. 190. © 1982 by Houghton Mifflin Company. Used by permission of the publishers.

Walt Marshall—Supervisor of Repair Crew

You are the head of a crew of telephone maintenance workers, each of whom drives a small service truck to and from the various jobs. Every so often you get a new truck to exchange for an old one, and you have the problem of deciding which of your crew members you should give the new truck. Often there are hard feelings, since each seems to feel entitled to the new truck, so you have a tough time being fair. As a matter of fact, it usually turns out that whatever you decide is considered wrong by most of the crew. You now have to face the issue again because a new truck, a Chevrolet, has just been allocated to you for assignment.

In order to handle this problem you have decided to put the decision up to the crew. You will tell them about the new truck and will put the problem in terms of what would be the fairest way to assign the truck. Do not take a position yourself, because you want to do what they think is most fair.

Creating Your Own Training Program

While it would certainly be ideal if supervisors in even the largest firms could tap into their companies' packaged training programs to train the new people that they hire, the fact is that many times they cannot. You often hire and are responsible for the performance of a new employee, only to find that your company provides little or no specialized training, beyond the new person's introductory orientation. If so, you have several options.

First, for either the individual manager or small business owner there are hundreds of suppliers of prepackaged training solutions. These range from self-study programs from the American Management Association (www.amanet.org/) and SHRM (www.shrm.org), to specialized programs (for example trade journals like *Occupational Hazards*, (www.occupationalhazards.com) contain information on specialized prepackaged training program suppliers (in this case, for occupational safety and health). Firms like elearningdepot.com offer various online courses.

Second, small-and medium-sized companies may also want to take advantage of the new trend toward

outsourced learning. Because major consulting firms such as Accenture, and IBM Global Services can obtain increased returns to scale by providing training solutions to multiple clients, a number of employers are now productively outsourcing their companies' entire learning functions to them.

Third, you can create your own training program, using the following process.

Step 1. Set Training Objectives

First, write down your training objectives. For example, your objective might be to reduce scrap, or to get new employees up to speed within two weeks.

Step 2. Write a Detailed Job Description

A detailed job description is the heart of any training program. It should list the daily and periodic tasks of each job, along with a summary of the steps in each task.

Step 3. Develop an Abbreviated Task Analysis Record Form

The individual manager or small business owner can use an abbreviated version of the Task Analysis

---

outsourced learning
The outsourcing of companies' learning functions to major consulting firms.

develop trainees' skills in areas like leadership and delegating. For example, a supervisor could experiment with both a considerate and an autocratic leadership style, whereas in the real world the person might not have the luxury of experimenting. It may also train someone to be more aware of and sensitive to others' feelings.[79]

behavior modeling
A training technique in which trainees are first shown good management techniques in a film, are asked to play roles in a simulated situation, and are then given feedback and praise by their supervisor.

Behavior Modeling **Behavior modeling** involves (1) showing trainees the right (or "model") way of doing something, (2) letting trainees practice that way, and then (3) giving feedback on the trainees' performance. Behavior modeling training is "one of the most widely used, well researched, and highly regarded psychologically based training interventions."[80] The basic procedure is as follows:

1. *Modeling.* First, trainees watch live or video examples that show models behaving effectively in a problem situation. The video might show a supervisor effectively disciplining a subordinate, if teaching how to discipline is the aim of the training program.
2. *Role playing.* Next, the trainees are given roles to play in a simulated situation; here they practice and rehearse the effective behaviors demonstrated by the models.
3. *Social reinforcement.* The trainer provides reinforcement in the form of praise and constructive feedback based on how the trainee performs in the role-playing situation.

Record Form (Table 8-1) containing just four columns. In the first, list *tasks* (including what is to be performed in terms of each of the main tasks, and the steps involved in each task). In column B, list *performance standards* (in terms of quantity, quality, accuracy, and so on). In column C, list *trainable skills* required, things the employee must know or do to perform the task. This column provides you with specific knowledge and skills (such as "Keep both hands on the wheel") that you want to stress. In the fourth column, list *aptitudes required*. These are the human aptitudes (such as mechanical comprehension, and so on) that the employee should have to be trainable for the task and for which the employee can be screened ahead of time.

Step 4. Develop a Job Instruction Sheet

Next develop a job instruction sheet for the job. As explained on page 302, a job instruction training sheet shows the steps in each task as well as key points for each.

Step 5. Prepare Training Program for the Job

At a minimum, your training package should include the job description, abbreviated Task Analysis Record Form, and job instruction sheet, all collected in a training manual. The latter should also contain a summary of the training program's objectives, and a listing of the trainable skills required for the trainee. The manual might also contain an introduction to the job, and an explanation of how the job fits with other jobs in the plant or office.

You also have to make a decision regarding which media to use in your training program. A simple but effective on-the-job training program using current employees or supervisors as trainers requires only the materials we just listed. However, it could turn out that the nature of the job or the number of trainees requires producing or purchasing special media, a PowerPoint slide presentation, or more extensive printed materials.

4. *Transfer of training.* Finally, trainees are encouraged to apply their new skills when they are back on their jobs.

Firms don't use behavior modeling just for teaching supervisory-type skills. For example, by one estimate, firms spend more of their training dollars on behavioral computer skills training than they do on sales training, supervisory training, or communication training.[81] Studies suggest that behavioral modeling results in significant improvements in knowledge and skill learning, but its effect on actual job behavior is less clear.[82]

in-house development center

A company-based method for exposing prospective managers to realistic exercises to develop improved management skills.

Corporate Universities   Many firms, particularly larger ones, establish **in-house development centers** (often called corporate universities). GE, McDonalds, and IBM are just a few examples. In-house development centers typically offer a catalogue of courses and special programs aimed at supporting the employers' management development needs. They typically do not produce all (or most) of their own training and development programs, although some do. In fact, employers are increasingly collaborating with academic institutions, training and development program providers, and Web-based educational portals to create packages of programs and materials appropriate to their employees' needs.[83]

For many firms, learning portals are becoming their virtual corporate universities. While firms such as GE have long had their own bricks-and-mortar corporate universities, learning portals let even smaller firms have corporate universities. Bain & Company, a management consulting firm, has such a Web-based virtual university for its employees. It provides a means not only for conveniently coordinating all the company's training efforts, but also for delivering Web-based modules that cover topics from strategic management to mentoring.[84]

executive coach

An outside consultant who questions the executive's associates in order to identify the executive's strengths and weaknesses, and then counsels the executive so he or she can capitalize on those strengths and overcome the weaknesses.

Executive Coaches   Many firms use executive coaches to develop their top managers' effectiveness. An **executive coach** is an outside consultant who questions the executive's boss, peers, subordinates, and (sometimes) family in order to identify the executive's strengths and weaknesses, and to counsel the executive so he or she can capitalize on those strengths and overcome the weaknesses.[85] Executive coaching can cost as much as $50,000 per executive. Experts therefore recommend using formal assessments prior to coaching, to uncover strengths and weaknesses and to provide more focused coaching.[86]

Executive coaching can be quite effective. Participants in one study included about 1,400 senior managers who had received "360 degree" performance feedback from bosses, peers, and subordinates. About 400 worked with an executive coach to review the feedback. Then, about a year later, these 400 managers and about 400 who didn't receive coaching again received multisource feedback. The managers who received executive coaching were more likely to set more effective, specific, goals for their subordinates, and to have received improved ratings from subordinates and supervisors.[87] Some firms, including Becton Dickinson & Co., encourage professional and management employees to coach each other.[88]

Because (as with most consulting) the coaching field is basically unregulated, employers or managers seeking coaches should do their due diligence. The International Coach Federation is one trade group.

The SHRM Learning System   SHRM, the Society for Human Resource Management, encourages HR professionals to qualify for certification by taking examinations. The Society offers several preparatory training programs. The self-study option includes text and DVD. The college/university option provides classroom interaction with instructors and other students.

MANAGING ORGANIZATIONAL CHANGE AND DEVELOPMENT

Helping firms manage change is a major issue for human resource managers. Professor Edward Lawler conducted an extensive survey of human resources practices. He concluded that as more employers face the need to adapt to rapid competitive change, "focusing on strategy, organizational development, and organizational change is a high payoff activity for the HR organization."[89]

What to Change

When she became CEO of a troubled Avon Products Company several years ago, Andrea Jung knew she had to renew her vast organization. Sales reps were leaving, customers were demanding new, more effective products, and the firm's whole "back end" operation—its purchasing, order-taking, distribution system—lacked automation.

Faced with situations like these, managers like Andrea Jung can change one or more of five aspects of their companies—their *strategy*, *culture*, *structure*, *technologies*, or the *attitudes and skills* of the employees.

Organizational renewal often starts with a change in the firm's strategy, mission, and vision—with *strategic change*. For example, faced with intense competition from firms like Estée Lauder, Avon under Ms. Jung more than doubled its expenditures on new-product development, with the aim of introducing a new product line that created younger

CEO Andrea Jung initiated a renewal program at Avon Products that demanded strategic change (doubling expenditures on new-product development) and cultural change (selling through retail outlets, not just door to door), as well as structural and technological changes to fulfill the new goals.

looking skin. Avon also expanded its strategy to selling through select department stores, rather than just door-to-door sales reps.

Strategic changes like these invariably trigger repercussions throughout the organization. For one thing (in Avon's case), going from strictly door-to-door to adding department stores meant *cultural change*, in other words, adopting new corporate values—new notions of what employees view as what they should or shouldn't do. Moving fast, embracing technology, and keeping lines of communication open were a few of the new values Avon management needed employees to adopt.

Avon's new expansion to department stores and product lines demanded *structural change*; in other words, reorganizing the company's departmental structure, coordination, span of control, reporting relationships, tasks, and decision-making procedures; as well as *technological change*, as Ms. Jung guided Avon to automate its purchasing/distribution chain.

Of course, strategic, cultural, structural, and technological changes like these, no matter how logical, will fail without the active support of a motivated and competent workforce. Organizational renewal therefore invariably involves bringing about *changes in the employees* themselves, and in their attitudes, skills, and behaviors.[90]

The Human Resource Manager's Role HR managers play a central role in organizational renewals like Avon's. For example, structural change may require performance reviews to decide who stays and who goes, as well as job analysis, personnel planning, and revised employee selection standards. Changing the employees' attitudes, skills, and behavior typically triggers a wide range of new human resource efforts—recruiting and selecting new employees, instituting new training programs, and changing how the firm appraises and rewards its personnel, for instance. The net effect is that human resource managers must be familiar with the techniques companies can use to bring about organizational change. At a minimum, this includes understanding three things—how to overcome resistance to change, how to organize and lead an organizational change, and how to use a technique known as organizational development. We turn to these three next.

Overcoming Resistance to Change: Lewin's Change Process

Often, the trickiest part of implementing an organizational change is overcoming employees' resistance to it. The change may require the cooperation of dozens or even hundreds of managers and supervisors, many of whom might well view the change as detrimental to their peace of mind. Resistance may therefore be considerable.

Psychologist Kurt Lewin formulated the classic explanation of how to implement change in the face of resistance. To Lewin, behavior was a product of two kinds of forces—those striving to maintain the status quo and those pushing for change. Implementing change thus meant either weakening the status quo forces or building up the forces for change. Lewin's change process consisted of these three steps:

1. *Unfreezing.* Unfreezing means reducing the forces that are striving to maintain the status quo, usually by presenting a provocative problem or event to get people to recognize the need for change and to search for new solutions.

2. ***Moving.*** Moving means developing new behaviors, values, and attitudes, sometimes through structural changes and sometimes through the sorts of HR-based organizational change and development techniques explained later in this chapter. The aim is to alter people's behavior.

3. ***Refreezing.*** Lewin assumed that organizations tend to revert to their former ways of doing things unless you reinforce the changes. How do you do this? By "refreezing" the organization into its new equilibrium. Specifically, Lewin advocated instituting new systems and procedures (such as new compensation plans and appraisal processes) to support and maintain the changes.[91]

How to Lead the Change

In practice, of course, the challenge is in the details of leading the organizational change. We can summarize these as follows.[92]

Unfreezing Phase

- Establish a sense of urgency. Most CEOs such as Avon's Andrea Jung start by creating a sense of urgency. This often takes creativity. For example, the CEO might present executives with an analyst's report describing the firm's lack of competitiveness.
- Mobilize commitment through joint diagnosis of problems. Having established a sense of urgency, the leader may then create one or more task forces to diagnose the problems facing the company. Such teams can produce a shared understanding of what they can and must improve, and thereby mobilize commitment.

Moving Phase

- Create a guiding coalition. No one can really implement changes like that at Avon alone. Most CEOs create a guiding coalition of influential people. They work together as a team to act as missionaries and implementers.
- Develop and communicate a shared vision. Organizational renewal requires a new leadership vision, "a general statement of the organization's intended direction that evokes emotional feelings in organization members." For example, when Barry Gibbons became CEO of Spec's Music some years ago, his vision of a leaner Spec's offering a diversified blend of concerts and retail music helped provide this direction. The key elements in communicating the vision are:

  - ***Keep it simple.*** Eliminate all jargon and wasted words. For example: "We are going to become faster than anyone else in our industry at satisfying customer needs."
  - ***Use multiple forums.*** Try to use every channel possible—big meetings and small, memos and newspapers, formal and informal interaction—to spread the word.
  - ***Use repetition.*** Ideas sink in deeply only after employees have heard them many times.
  - ***Lead by example.*** "Walk your talk"—make sure your behaviors and decisions are consistent with the vision you espouse.[93]

- Help employees make the change. Perhaps a lack of skills stands in the way; or policies, procedures, and the organization chart make it difficult to act; or some intransigent managers actually discourage employees from acting. When he was CEO at the former Allied Signal, Lawrence Bossidy put every one of his 80,000 people through quality improvement training.[94]
- Consolidate gains and produce more change. Aim for attainable short-term accomplishments, and use the credibility from these to change all the systems, structures, and policies that don't fit well with the company's new vision. Leaders continue to

produce more change by hiring and promoting new people; by identifying selected employees to champion the continuing change; and by providing additional opportunities for short-term wins by employees.[95]

Refreezing Phase

- Reinforce the new ways of doing things with changes to the company's systems and procedures. Use new appraisal systems and incentives to reinforce the desired behaviors. Change the culture by ensuring that the firm's managers take steps to role-model and communicate the company's new values.
- Finally, the leader must monitor and assess progress. In brief, this involves comparing where the company is today with where it should be, based on measurable milestones. At Avon, for instance, how many new products has the company introduced? How many new door-to-door sales reps has the firm added?

Using Organizational Development

organizational development

A special approach to organizational change in which employees themselves formulate and implement the change that's required.

There are many ways to find out what organizational change the firm requires, and to implement the change itself. One popular method is organizational development (OD). **Organizational development** is an approach to organizational change in which the employees themselves formulate the change that's required and implement it, often with the assistance of a trained consultant. Particularly in large companies, the OD process (including hiring of facilitators) is almost always handled through HR. As an approach to changing organizations, OD has several distinguishing characteristics:

1. It usually involves *action research*, which means collecting data about a group, department, or organization, and feeding the information back to the employees so they can analyze it and develop hypotheses about what the problems in the unit might be.
2. It applies behavioral science knowledge to improve the organization's effectiveness.
3. It changes the organization in a particular direction—toward improved problem solving, responsiveness, quality of work, and effectiveness.

There are four basic categories of OD applications: human process, technostructural, human resource management, and strategic applications (see Table 8-3). Action research—getting the employees themselves to collect the required data and to design and implement the solutions—is the basis of all four.

Human Process Applications   Human process OD techniques generally aim first at improving human relations skills. The goal is to give employees the insight and skills required to analyze their own and others' behavior more effectively, so they can then solve interpersonal and intergroup problems. These problems might include, for instance, conflict among employees, or a lack of interdepartmental communications. *Sensitivity training* is perhaps the most widely used technique in this category. Team building and survey research are others.

Sensitivity, laboratory, or t-group training's (the *t* is for "training") basic aim is to increase the participant's insight into his or her own behavior by encouraging an open expression of feelings in the trainer-guided t-group. Typically, 10 to 15 people meet, usually away from the job, with no specific agenda. Instead, the focus is on the feelings and emotions of the members in the group at the meeting. The facilitator encourages participants to portray themselves as they are in the group rather than in terms of past behaviors. The t-group's success depends on the feedback each person gets from the others, and on the participants' willingness to be candid. The process requires a climate of "psychological safety," so participants feel safe enough to expose their feelings.[96]

TABLE 8-3 Examples of OD Interventions

Interventions

Human Process

T-groups
Process consultation
Third-party intervention
Team building
Organizational confrontation meeting
Survey research

Technostructural

Formal structural change
Differentiation and integration
Cooperative union–management projects
Quality circles
Total quality management
Work design

Human Resource Management

Goal setting
Performance appraisal
Reward systems
Career planning and development
Managing workforce diversity
Employee wellness

Strategic

Integrated strategic management
Culture change
Strategic change
Self-designing organizations

T-group training is controversial. Its personal nature suggests that participation should be voluntary. Some view it as unethical because you can't consider participation "suggested" by one's superior as really voluntary.[97] Others argue that it can actually be a dangerous exercise if led by an inadequately prepared trainer.

OD's distinctive emphasis on action research is quite evident in *team building*. According to experts French and Bell, the typical team-building meeting begins with the consultant interviewing each of the group members and the leader before the meeting.[98] They are asked what their problems are, how they think the group functions, and what obstacles are keeping the group from performing better. The consultant then categorizes the interview data into themes (such as "inadequate communications") and presents the themes to the group at the start of the meeting. The group ranks the themes in terms of importance, and the most important ones become the agenda for the meeting. The group then explores and discusses the issues, examines the underlying causes of the problems, and begins devising solutions.

Survey research, another human process OD technique, requires that employees throughout the organization complete attitude surveys. The facilitator then uses those data as a basis for problem analysis and action planning. In general, such surveys are a convenient way to unfreeze a company's management and employees. They provide a comparative, graphic illustration of the fact that the organization does have problems to solve.[99]

Technostructural Interventions   OD practitioners are involved in changing firms' structures, methods, and job designs, using an assortment of technostructural interventions. For example, in a *formal structural change* program, the employees collect data on the company's existing organizational structure; they then jointly redesign and implement a new one.

Human Resource Management Applications   OD practitioners use action research to enable employees to analyze and change their firm's human resources practices. Targets of change here might include the performance appraisal and reward systems, as well as installing diversity programs.

Strategic OD Applications   Strategic interventions are organizationwide OD programs aimed at achieving a fit among a firm's strategy, structure, culture, and external environment. *Integrated strategic management* is one example. It consists of four steps: (1) managers and employees analyze current strategy and organizational design, (2) choose a desired strategy and organizational design, and (3) design a strategic change plan—"an action plan for moving the organization from its current strategy and organizational design to the desired future strategy and design."[100] Finally, (4) the team oversees implementing the strategic change plan, and reviewing the results to ensure that they are proceeding as planned.[101]

EVALUATING THE TRAINING EFFORT

With today's emphasis on measuring human resource management's impact, it is crucial that the manager evaluate the training program. There are basically three things you can measure: participants' *reactions* to the program; what (if anything) the trainees *learned* from the program; and to what extent their on-the-job *behavior* changed as a result of the program. In one survey of about 500 U.S. organizations, 77% evaluated their training programs by eliciting reactions, 36% evaluated learning, and about 10% to 15% assessed the program's behavior and/or results.[102]

There are actually two basic issues to address when evaluating training programs. The first is the design of the evaluation study and, in particular, whether to use controlled experimentation. The second issue is: What should we measure?

Designing the Study

In evaluating the training program, the first question should be how to design the evaluation study. The *time series design* is one option. Here, as in Figure 8-5, you take a series of measures before and after the training program. This can provide at least an initial reading on the program's effectiveness.[103]

controlled experimentation
Formal methods for testing the effectiveness of a training program, preferably with before-and-after tests and a control group.

Controlled experimentation is a second option, and is the evaluation process of choice. A controlled experiment uses both a training group and a control group that receives no training. Data (for instance, on quantity of sales or quality of service) are obtained both before and after the group is exposed to training and before and after a corresponding work period in the control group. This makes it possible to determine the extent to which any change in performance in the training group resulted from the training rather than from some organizationwide change like a raise in pay that would have affected employees in both groups equally.[104]

This approach is feasible, but, in terms of current practice, few firms use it. Most simply measure trainees' reactions to the program; some also measure the trainees' job performance before and after training.[105] The human resource manager should at least use an evaluation form like the one shown in Figure 8-6 to evaluate the training program.

FIGURE 8-5

Using a Time Series Graph to Assess a Training Program's Effects

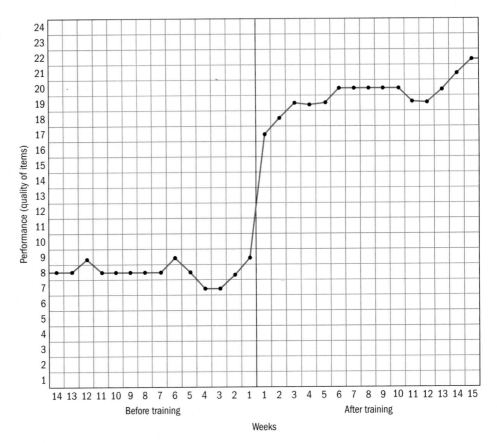

FIGURE 8-5

Using a Time Series Graph to Assess a Training Program's Effects

Training Effects to Measure

You can measure four basic categories of training outcomes:

1. *Reaction.* Evaluate trainees' reactions to the program. Did they like the program? Did they think it worthwhile?
2. *Learning.* Test the trainees to determine whether they learned the principles, skills, and facts they were supposed to learn.
3. *Behavior.* Ask whether the trainees' on-the-job behavior changed because of the training program. For example, are employees in the store's complaint department more courteous toward disgruntled customers?
4. *Results.* Probably most important, ask: What final results were achieved in terms of the training objectives previously set? For example, did the number of customer complaints about employees drop? Did the percentage of calls answered with the required greeting rise? Reactions, learning, and behavior are important. But if the training program doesn't produce measurable results, then it probably hasn't achieved its goals. But remember that the results may be poor because the problem could not be solved by training in the first place.

Evaluating any of these four is fairly straightforward. For example, Figure 8-6 presents one page from a sample evaluation questionnaire for assessing trainees' reactions. Similarly, you might assess trainees' learning by testing their new knowledge. The employer can assess the trainees' behavioral change directly or indirectly. Indirectly, you might assess the effectiveness of, say, a supervisory performance appraisal training program by asking that person's subordinates questions like, "Did your supervisor take the time to provide you with examples of good and bad performance when he or she appraised your

INSTRUCTOR HANDOUTS

United States Office of Personnel Management

TRAINING EVALUATION FORM

TITLE OF COURSE: "Work and Family Issues — A Module for Supervisors and Managers"

NAME OF INSTRUCTOR:

DATE OF TRAINING
Started:_____
Ended:_____

NAME: (Optional)	POSITION TITLE/GRADE:

AGENCY:	OFFICE PHONE: (Optional)	OFFICE ADDRESS: (Optional)

Rate Your Knowledge and Skill Level (Circle your rating)	Overall, how would you rate this course?
Before this course Low -----------------------------------High 1 2 3 4 5	__ Excellent __Very Good __ Good
After this course Low -----------------------------------High 1 2 3 4 5	__ Fair __ Poor

EVALUATION OF COURSE
(Check appropriate box)

ITEMS OF EVALUATION How did the course sharpen your knowledge or skills in:	Excellent	Very Good	Good	Fair	Poor	Not Applicable
1. What work and family programs are	°	°	°	°	°	°
2. Who uses work and family programs	°	°	°	°	°	°
3. How to recognize/solve work/family issues	°	°	°	°	°	°
4. Helping you take practical steps on the job	°	°	°	°	°	°

RATING OF INSTRUCTOR

	Excellent	Very Good	Good	Fair	Poor	Not Applicable
1. Presentation, organization, delivery	°	°	°	°	°	°
2. Knowledge and command of the subject	°	°	°	°	°	°
3. Use of audio-visuals or other training aids	°	°	°	°	°	°
4. Stimulation of an open exchange of ideas, participation, & group interaction	°	°	°	°	°	°

STRONG POINTS OF THE COURSE
- °
- °

WEAK POINTS OF THE COURSE
- °
- °
- °

ADDITIONAL DATA YOU WOULD LIKE TO HAVE COVERED IN COURSE
- °
- °

ADDITIONAL COMMENTS/OR RECOMMENDATIONS

FIGURE 8-6

A Sample Training Evaluation Form

Source: www.opm.gov/Employment_and_Benefits/WorkLife.

performance most recently? Or, you can directly assess a training program's results, for instance, by measuring, say, the percentage of phone calls answered correctly.

Suggestions   "Reaction" measures aren't good substitutes for measuring learning or results. Unfortunately, only about 10% to 35% of trainees are transferring what they learned to their jobs a year after training. Managers can improve this. *Prior to training*, get trainee and supervisor input in designing the program, institute a training attendance policy, and encourage employees to participate. *During training*, provide trainees with training experiences and conditions (surroundings, equipment) that resemble the actual work environment. *After training* reinforce what trainees learned, for instance, by appraising and rewarding employees for using new skills, and by ensuring they have the tools and materials they need to use their new skills.[106]

Computerization facilitates evaluation. For example, Bovis Lend Lease uses learning management software to monitor which employees are taking which courses, and the extent to which they're improving their skills.[107]

REVIEW

SUMMARY

1. The training process consists of five steps: needs analysis, instructional design, validation, implementation, and evaluation.
2. Principles of learning that are useful for training include: Make the material meaningful (by providing a bird's-eye view and familiar examples, organizing the material, splitting it into meaningful chunks, and using familiar terms and visual aids); make provision for transfer of training; and try to motivate trainees.
3. Basic training methods include on-the-job training, apprenticeship training, informal learning, job instruction training, lectures, programmed learning, audiovisual tools, simulated training, computer-based training, electronic performance support systems, and distance and Internet-based training.
4. On-the-job training is a common training technique. It might take the form of the understudy method, job rotation, or special assignments and committees. In any case, it should have four steps: preparing the learner, presenting the operation (or nature of the job), doing performance tryouts, and following up.
5. Management development prepares employees for future jobs by imparting knowledge, changing attitudes, or increasing skills.
6. Managerial on-the-job training methods include job rotation, coaching, and action learning. Basic off-the-job techniques include case studies, management games, outside seminars, university-related programs, role playing, behavior modeling, and in-house development centers.
7. In gauging the effectiveness of a training program, there are four categories of outcomes companies can measure: reactions, learning, behavior, and results. In some cases where training seems to have failed, it may be because training was not the appropriate solution to the problem.

DISCUSSION QUESTIONS

1. "A well-thought-out orientation program is essential for all new employees, whether they have experience or not." Explain why you agree or disagree with this statement.
2. Explain how you would apply our principles of learning in developing a lecture, say, on orientation and training.

3. "John Santos" is an undergraduate business student majoring in accounting. He has just failed the first accounting course, Accounting 101, and is understandably upset. Explain how you would use performance analysis to identify what, if any, are John's training needs.

4. What are some typical on-the-job training techniques? What do you think are some of the main drawbacks of relying on informal on-the-job training for breaking new employees into their jobs?

5. One reason for implementing global training programs is the need to avoid business losses "due to cultural insensitivity." What sort of cultural insensitivity do you think is referred to, and how might that translate into lost business? What sort of training program would you recommend to avoid such cultural insensitivity?

6. Describe the pros and cons of five management development methods.

7. Do you think job rotation is a good method to use for developing management trainees? Why or why not?

INDIVIDUAL AND GROUP ACTIVITIES

1. You're the supervisor of a group of employees whose task is to assemble disk drives that go into computers. You find that quality is not what it should be and that many of your group's devices have to be brought back and reworked; your boss says that "You'd better start doing a better job of training your workers."

   a. What are some of the "staffing" factors that could be contributing to this problem?
   b. Explain how you would go about assessing whether it is in fact a training problem.

2. Pick out some task with which you are familiar—mowing the lawn, making a salad, or studying for a test—and develop a job instruction training sheet for it.

3. Working individually or in groups, develop a short, programmed learning program on the subject "Guidelines for Giving a More Effective Lecture."

4. Working individually or in groups, use the phone or the Web to contact a provider of management development seminars. Obtain copies of its recent listings of seminar offerings. At what levels of managers are the seminar offerings aimed? What seem to be the most popular types of development programs? Why do you think that's the case?

5. Working individually or in groups, develop several specific examples to illustrate how a professor teaching human resource management could use at least four of the techniques described in this chapter in teaching his or her HR course.

6. Working individually or in groups, develop an orientation program for high school graduates entering your university as freshmen.

7. The HRCI "Test Specifications" appendix at the end of this book (pages 726–735) lists the knowledge someone studying for the HRCI certification exam needs to have in each area of human resource management (such as in Strategic Management, Workforce Planning, and Human Resource Development). In groups of four to five students, do four things: (1) review that appendix now; (2) identify the material in this chapter that relates to the required knowledge the appendix lists; (3) write four multiple choice exam questions on this material that you believe would be suitable for inclusion in the HRCI exam; and (4) if time permits, have someone from your team post your team's questions in front of the class, so the students in other teams can take each others' exam questions.

8. The U.S.-led coalition in Iraq was sending hundreds of trainers to that country to train new cadres of Iraqi workers, from teachers to police officers. Perhaps no training task was more pressing than that involved in creating the country's new police force. These were the people who were to help the coalition bring security to Iraq.

However, many new officers had no experience in police work. There were language barriers between trainers and trainees. And some trainees found themselves quickly under fire from insurgents when they went as trainees out into the field. Based on what you learned about training from this chapter, list the five most important things you would tell the officer in charge of training (a former U.S. big-city police chief) to keep in mind as he designs the training program.

EXPERIENTIAL EXERCISE

Flying the Friendlier Skies

Purpose: The purpose of this exercise is to give you practice in developing a training program for the job of airline reservation clerk for a major airline.

Required Understanding: You should be fully acquainted with the material in this chapter and should read the following description of an airline reservation clerk's duties:

Customers contact our airline reservation clerks to obtain flight schedules, prices, and itineraries. The reservation clerks look up the requested information on our airline's online flight schedule systems, which are updated continuously. The reservation clerk must deal courteously and expeditiously with the customer, and be able to quickly find alternative flight arrangements in order to provide the customer with the itinerary that fits his or her needs. Alternative flights and prices must be found quickly, so that the customer is not kept waiting, and so that our reservations operations group maintains its efficiency standards. It is often necessary to look under various routings, since there may be a dozen or more alternative routes between the customer's starting point and destination.

You may assume that we just hired 30 new clerks, and that you must create a three-day training program.

How to Set Up the Exercise/Instructions: Divide the class into teams of five or six students.

Airline reservation clerks obviously need numerous skills to perform their jobs. JetBlue Airlines has asked you to quickly develop the outline of a training program for its new reservation clerks. You may want to start by listing the job's main duties, and by reviewing any work you may have done for the exercise at the end of Chapter 6. In any case, please produce the requested outline, making sure to be very specific about what you want to teach the new clerks, and what methods and aids you suggest using to train them.

APPLICATION CASE

Reinventing the Wheel at Apex Door Company

Jim Delaney, president of Apex Door, has a problem. No matter how often he tells his employees how to do their jobs, they invariably "decide to do it their way," as he puts it, and arguments ensue between Jim, the employee, and the employee's supervisor. One example is the door-design department, where the designers are expected to work with the architects to design doors that meet the specifications. While it's not "rocket science," as Jim puts it, the designers invariably make mistakes—such as designing in too much steel, a problem that can cost Apex tens of thousands of wasted dollars, once you consider the number of doors in, say, a 30-story office tower.

The order processing department is another example. Jim has a very specific and detailed way he wants the order written up, but most of the order clerks don't understand how to actually use the multipage order form. They simply improvise when it comes to a detailed question such as whether to classify the customer as "industrial" or "commercial."

The current training process is as follows. None of the jobs has a training manual per se, although several have somewhat out-of-date job descriptions. The training for new people is all on the job. Usually, the person leaving the company trains the new person during the one- or two-week overlap period, but if there's no overlap, the new person is trained as well as possible by other employees who have filled in occasionally on the job in the past. The training is basically the same throughout the company—for machinists, secretaries, assemblers, engineers, and accounting clerks, for example.

Questions

1. What do you think of Apex's training process? Could it help to explain why employees "do things their way" and if so, how?
2. What role should job descriptions play in training at Apex?
3. Explain in detail what you would do to improve the training process at Apex. Make sure to provide specific suggestions, please.

CONTINUING CASE

Carter Cleaning Company

The New Training Program

At the present time the Carter Cleaning Centers have no formal orientation or training policies or procedures, and Jennifer believes this is one reason why the standards to which she and her father would like employees to adhere are generally not followed.

The Carters would prefer that certain practices and procedures be used in dealing with the customers at the front counters. For example, all customers should be greeted with what Jack refers to as a "big hello." Garments they drop off should immediately be inspected for any damage or unusual stains so these can be brought to the customer's attention, lest the customer later return to pick up the garment and erroneously blame the store. The garments are then supposed to be immediately placed together in a nylon sack to separate them from other customers' garments. The ticket also has to be carefully written up, with the customer's name and telephone number and the date precisely and clearly noted on all copies. The counterperson is also supposed to take the opportunity to try to sell the customer additional services such as waterproofing, or simply notify the customer that "Now that people are doing their spring cleaning, we're having a special on drapery cleaning all this month." Finally, as the customer leaves, the counterperson is supposed to make a courteous comment like "Have a nice day" or "Drive safely." Each of the other jobs in the stores—pressing, cleaning and spotting, periodically maintaining the coin laundry equipment, and so forth—similarly contain certain steps, procedures, and most important, standards the Carters would prefer to see upheld.

The company has had problems, Jennifer feels, because of a lack of adequate employee training and orientation. For example, two new employees became very upset last month when they discovered that they were not paid at the end of the week, on Friday, but instead were paid (as are all Carter employees) on the following Tuesday. The Carters use the extra two days in part to give them time to obtain everyone's hours and compute their pay. The other reason they do it, according to Jack, is that "frankly, when we stay a few days behind in paying employees it helps to ensure that they at least give us a few days' notice before quitting on us. While we are certainly obligated to pay them anything they earn, we find that psychologically they seem to be less likely to just walk out on us Friday evening and not show up Monday morning if they still haven't gotten their pay from the previous week. This way they at least give us a few days' notice so we can find a replacement."

Other matters that could be covered during orientation and training, says Jennifer, include company policy regarding paid holidays, lateness and absences, health and hospitalization benefits (there are none, other than workers' compensation), and general matters like the maintenance of a clean and safe work area, personal appearance and cleanliness, time sheets, personal telephone calls and mail, company policies regarding matters like substance abuse, and eating or smoking on the job (both forbidden).

Jennifer believes that implementing orientation and training programs would help to ensure that employees know how to do their jobs the right way. And she and her father further believe that it is only when employees understand the right way to do their jobs that there is any hope their jobs will in fact be accomplished the way the Carters want them to be accomplished.

Questions

1. Specifically what should the Carters cover in their new employee orientation program and how should they convey this information?
2. In the HR management course Jennifer took, the book suggested using a job instruction sheet to identify tasks performed by an employee. "Should we use a form like this for the counterperson's job, and if so, what would the filled-in form look like?"
3. Which specific training techniques should Jennifer use to train her pressers, her cleaner–spotters, her managers, and her counterpeople, and why?

TRANSLATING STRATEGY INTO HR POLICIES AND PRACTICES CASE: THE HOTEL PARIS

The New Training Program

The Hotel Paris's competitive strategy is "To use superior guest service to differentiate the Hotel Paris properties, and to thereby increase the length of stay and return rate of guests, and thus boost revenues and profitability." HR manager Lisa Cruz must now formulate functional policies and activities that support this competitive strategy, by eliciting the required employee behaviors and competencies.

As she reviewed her company's training processes, Lisa had reasons to be concerned. For one thing, the Hotel Paris relied almost exclusively on informal on-the-job training. New security guards attended a one-week program offered by a law enforcement agency, but all other new hires, from assistant manager to housekeeping crew, learned the rudiments of their jobs from their colleagues and their supervisors, on the job. Lisa noted that the drawbacks of this informality were evident when she compared the Hotel Paris's performance on various training metrics with those of other hotels and service firms. For example, in terms of number of hours training per employee per year, number of hours training for new employees, cost per trainee hour, and percent of payroll spent on training, the Hotel Paris was far from the norm when benchmarked against similar firms.

Indeed, as Lisa and the CFO reviewed the measures of the Hotel Paris's current training efforts, it was clear that (when compared to similar companies) some changes were in order. Most other service companies provided at least 40 hours of training per employee per year, while the Hotel Paris offered, on average, no more than five or six. Similar firms offered at least 40 hours of training per new employee, while the Hotel Paris offered, at most, 10. Even the apparently "good" metrics comparisons simply masked poor results. For example, whereas most service firms spend about 8% of their payrolls on training, the Hotel Paris spent less than 1%. The problem, of course, was that the Hotel Paris's training wasn't just inefficient, it was nonexistent. Given this and the commonsense links between (1) employee training and (2) employee performance, the CFO gave his go-ahead for Lisa and her team to design a comprehensive package of training programs for all Hotel Paris employees.

Questions

1. Based on what you read in this chapter, what do you suggest Lisa and her team do first with respect to training? Why?
2. Have Lisa and the CFO sufficiently investigated whether training is really called for? Why? What would you suggest?
3. Based on what you read in this chapter, and what you may access via the Web, develop a detailed training program for one of these hotel positions: security guard, housekeeper, or doorperson.

KEY TERMS

ENDNOTES

1. David Raths, "Virtual Reality in the OR," *Training and Development*, August 2006.
2. Sabrina Hicks, "Successful Orientation Programs," *Training and Development*, April 2000, p. 59. See also, Howard Klein and Natasha Weaver, "The Effectiveness of an Organizational Level Orientation Program in the Socialization of New Hires," *Personnel Psychology* 53 (2000), pp. 47–66, and Laurie Friedman, "Are You Losing Potential New Hires at Hello?", *Training & Development*, November 2006, pp. 25–27.
3. Charlotte Garvey, "The Whirlwind of a New Job," *HR Magazine*, June 2001, p. 111. See also, Talya Bauer, et al., "Newcomer Adjustment During Organizational Socialization: a Meta-analytic Review of Antecedents, Outcomes, and Methods," *Journal of Applied Psychology* 92, no. 3, 2007, pp. 707–721.
4. Sheila Hicks, et al., "Orientation Redesign," *Training and Development*, July 2006, pp. 43–46.
5. See for example, John Kammeyer-Mueller and Connie Wanberg, "Unwrapping the Organizational Entry Process: Disentangling Multiple Antecedents and Their Pathways to Adjustments," *Journal of Applied Psychology* 88, no. 5, (2003), pp. 779–794.
6. See Darin Hartley, "Technology Kicks Up Leadership Development," *Training and Development*, (March 2004), pp. 22–24.
7. Susan Ashford and Jay Stewart Black, "Proactivity During Organizational Entry: The Role of Desire for Control," *Journal of Applied Psychology* 81, no. 2 (1996), pp. 199–214.
8. Christine Ellis and Sarah Gale, "A Seat at the Table," *Training*, March 2001, pp. 90–96.
9. "Companies Invested More in Training Despite Economic Setbacks, Survey Says," *BNA Bulletin to Management*, March 7, 2002, p. 73. "Employee Training Expenditures on the Rise," *American Salesman*, Jan 2004, v49 i1, pp. 26–28.
10. "Companies Invested More in Training Despite Economic Setbacks, Survey Says," *BNA Bulletin to Management*, March 7, 2002, p. 73. "Employee Training Expenditures on the Rise," *American Salesman* Jan 2004 v49 i1, pp. 26–28.
11. Nancy DeViney and Brenda Sugrue, "Learning Outsourcing: A Reality Check," *Training and Development*, (December 2004): 41.
12. Brenda Sugrue, et al., "What in the World is WLP?," *Training and Development*, (January, 2005): pp. 51–54.
13. Kenneth Wexley and Gary Latham, *Developing and Training Human Resources in Organizations* (Upper Saddle River, NJ: Prentice Hall, 2002) p. 107.
14. Ibid., p. 90.
15. Ibid., p. 82.
16. Ibid., p. 87.

17. Janice A. Cannon-Bowers et al., "Framework for Understanding Pre-Practice Conditions and Their Impact on Learning," *Personnel Psychology* 51 (1998), pp. 291–320.
18. Ibid., p. 305.
19. Ibid., p. 305.
20. Ibid.
21. Kathryn Tyler, "Focus on Training," *HR Magazine*, May 2000, pp. 94–102.
22. Ibid.
23. Mindy Chapman, "The Return on Investment for Training," *Compensation & Benefits Review*, January/February 2003, pp. 32–33.
24. Ibid., p. 33.
25. Ibid., pp. 216–217.
26. P. Nick Blanchard and James Thacker, *Effective Training: Systems, Strategies and Practices* (Upper Saddle River, NJ: Prentice Hall, 1999), pp. 138–139. See also, Matthew Casey and Dennis Doverspike, "Training Needs Analysis and Evaluation for New Technologies Through the Use of Problem Based Inquiry," *Performance Improvement Quarterly* 18, no. 1, 2005, pp. 110–124.
27. Tom Barron, "When Things Go Haywire," *Training and Development*, February 1999, pp. 25–27.
28. For an additional perspective, see Danny Langdon, "Objectives: Get Over Them," *Training and Development*, February 1999, pp. 54–58. See also Joan Brett and Don VandeWalle, "Goal Orientation and Goal Content As Predictors of Performance in a Training Program," *Journal of Applied Psychology* 84, no. 6 (1999), pp. 863–873.
29. Richard Montier, et al., "Competency Models Develop Top Performance," *Training and Development*, July 2006, pp. 47–50.
30. Kenneth Wexley and Gary Latham, *Developing and Training Human Resources in Organizations* (Upper Saddle River, NJ: Prentice Hall, 2002), pp. 78–79.
31. Donna Goldwasser, "Me a Trainer?" *Training*, April 2001, pp. 60–66.
32. Four steps in on-the-job training based on William Berliner and William McLarney, *Management Practice and Training* (Burr Ridge, IL: McGraw-Hill, 1974), pp. 442–443. See also Robert Sullivan and Donald Miklas, "On-the-Job Training That Works," *Training and Development Journal* 39, no. 5 (May 1985), pp. 118–120; Stephen B. Wehrenberg, "Supervisors as Trainees: The Long-Term Gains of OJT," *Personnel Journal* 66, no. 4 (April 1987), pp. 48–51.
33. Cindy Waxer, "Steelmaker Revives Apprentice Program to Address Graying Workforce, Forge Next Leaders," *Workforce Management*, January 30, 2006, p. 40.
34. Robert Weintraub and Jennifer Martineau, "The Just in Time Imperative," *Training and Development* (June 2002), p. 52.
35. Arthur Winfred Jr. et al., "Effectiveness of Training in Organizations: A Meta Analysis of Design and Evaluation Features," *Journal of Applied Psychology* 88, no. 2 (2003), pp. 234–245.
36. Donald Michalak and Edwin G. Yager, *Making the Training Process Work* (New York: Harper & Row, 1979), pp. 108–111. See also Richard Wiegand, "Can All Your Trainees Hear You?" *Training and Development Journal* 41, no. 8 (August 1987), pp. 38–43.
37. Jacqueline Schmidt and Joseph Miller, "The Five-Minute Rule for Presentations," *Training and Development*, March 2000, pp. 16–17.
38. G. N. Nash, J. P. Muczyk, and F. L. Vettori, "The Role and Practical Effectiveness of Programmed Instruction," *Personnel Psychology* 24 (1971), pp. 397–418; Duane Schultz and Sydney Ellen Shultz, *Psychology and Work Today* (Upper Saddle River, NJ: Prentice Hall, 1998), pp. 181–183.
39. Wexley and Latham, *Developing and Training*, pp. 131–133. See also Teri O. Grady and Mike Matthews, "Video . . . Through the Eyes of the Trainee," *Training* 24, no. 7 (July 1987), pp. 57–62. Erica Schroeder, "Training Takes Off, Using Multimedia," *PC Week*, August 29, 1994, pp. 33–34.
40. Dina Berta, "Computer-Based Training Clicks with both Franchisees and Their Employees," *Nation's Restaurant News*, July 9, 2001, pp. 1, 18; see also Daniel Cable and Charles Parsons, "Socialization Tactics and Person–Organization Fit," *Personnel Psychology*, 54 (2001), pp. 1–23.

41. P. Nick Blanchard and James Thacker, *Effective Training: Systems, Strategies, and Practices* (Upper Saddle River, NJ: Pearson, 2003), p. 247. See also, Michael Laff, "Simulations: Slowly Proving Their Worth," *Training & Development*, June 2007, pp. 30–34.

42. Ibid., p. 248.

43. Ibid., p. 249. See also, Kim Kleps, "Virtual Sales Training Scores a Hit," *Training & Development*, December 2006, pp. 63–64.

44. Paul Harris, "Simulation: The Game Is On," *Training and Development*, October 2003, p. 49. See also, Jenni Jarventaus, "Virtual Threat, Real Sweat," *Training & Development*, May 2007, pp. 72–78.

45. These are summarized in Rockley Miller, "New Training Looms," *Hotel and Motel Management*, April 4, 1994, pp. 26, 30.

46. Tyler, "Focus on Training," p. 96. See also Allison Rosset and Erica Mohr, "Performance Support Tools: Where Learning, Work, and Results Converge," *Training and Development*, February 2004, pp. 35–37.

47. Craig Marion, "What Is the EPSS Movement and What Does It Mean to Information Designers?" http://www.chesco.com/~cmarion/pcd/epssimplications.html.

48. Josh Bersin and Karen O'Leonard, "Performance Support Systems," *Training and Development*, April 2005, p. 68.

49. Blanchard and Thacker, *Effective Training*, p. 163.

50. Michael Blotzer, "Distance Learning," *Occupational Hazards*, March 2000, pp. 53–54.

51. See for example, Michael Tucker, "E-Learning Evolves," *HR Magazine* 50, no. 10, October 2005, pp. 74–78.

52. Larry Stevens, "The Internet: Your Newest Training Tool?" *Personnel Journal*, July 1996, pp. 27–31; see also Kenneth Brown, "Using Computers to Deliver Training: Which Employees Learn and Why?" *Personnel Psychology* 54, no. 2 (Summer 2001), pp. 271–296; Jason Lewis and Dan Michaluk, "Four Steps to Building E-Learning Success," *Workforce*, May 2002, p. 42.

53. Ellen Zimmerman, "Better Training Is Just a Click Away," *Workforce*, January 2001, pp. 36–42.

54. Traci Sitzmann, et al., "The Comparative Effectiveness of Web-Based and Classroom Instruction: A Meta-Analysis," *Personnel Psychology*, 2006, vol. 59, pp. 623–664.

55. Helen Beckett, "Blended Skills for a Better Class of E-Learning," *Computer Weekly*, January 20, 2004, p. 20.

56. "Lessons of Mass Instruction: E-Learning Adds Cost-Cutting Muscle to HR Strategy," *BNA Bulletin to Management*, (August 21, 2003): 265. See also, "Less Classroom, More Technology," *Training and Development*, May 2005, p. 24.

57. Renee DeRouin, et al., "Optimizing E-Learning: Research-Based Guidelines for Learner Controlled Training," *Human Resource Management* 43, no. 2, (Summer/Fall 2004), pp. 147–162.

58. Ruth Clark, "Harnessing the Virtual Classroom," *Training and Development*, November 2005, pp. 40–46. See also, Elizabeth Agnvall, "Just-In-Time Training," *HR Magazine*, May 2006, pp. 67–78.

59. Tom Barron, "A Portrait of Learning Portals," www.learningcircuits.com/may2000/barron.html.

60. "The U.S. Postal Service Turns to Thinq's LMS to Streamline Operations," *Training and Development*, December 2003, pp. 72–73.

61. Eileen Granger, "Goodbye Training, Hello Learning," *Workforce*, July 2002, pp. 35–42.

62. "The Next Generation of Corporate Learning," *Training and Development*, June 2003, p. 47.

63. Paula Ketter, "The Hidden Disability," *Training and Development*, June 2006, pp. 34–40.

64. Willie Hopkins, Karen Sterkel-Powell, and Shirley Hopkins, "Training Priorities for a Diverse Workforce," *Public Personnel Management* 23, no. 3 (Fall 1994), p. 433.

65. "Adams Mark Hotel & Resorts Launches Diversity Training Program," *Hotel and Motel Management* 216, no. 6 (April 2001), p. 15.

66. Matthew Reis, "Do-It-Yourself Diversity," *Training and Development*, March 2004, pp. 80–81.

67. Valerie Frazee, "Workers Learn to Walk So They Can Run," *Personnel Journal* (May 1996): 115–20. See Also, Kathryn Tyler, "I Say Potato, You Say Patata: As Workforce and Customer Diversity Grow, Employers Offer Foreign Language Training to Staff," *HR Magazine* 49, no. 1, (January 2004), pp. 85–87.

68. Jennifer Salopek, "Trends: Lost in Translation," *Training and Development*, December 2003, p. 15.

69. Kathryn Tyler, "Brushing Up on the Three Rs," *HR Magazine*, October 1999, p. 88. See also, Michael Eisenstein, "Test, Then Train," *Training and Development*, May 2005, p. 26.

70. For a discussion of leadership development tools, see John Beeson, "Building Bench Strength: A Tool Kit for Executive Development," *Business Horizons* 47, no. 6, November 2004, pp. 3–9. See also, Rita Smith and Beth Bledsoe, "Grooming Leaders for Growth," *Training and Development*, August 2006, pp. 47–50.

71. Bernard Bass and Bruce Avolio, "Shatter the Glass Ceiling: Women May Make Better Managers," *Human Resource Management* 33, no. 4 (Winter 1994), pp. 549–560.

72. Ann Pomeroy, "Head of the Class," *HR Magazine*, (January 2005): 57.

73. Paula Caligiuri, "Developing Global Leaders," *Human Resource Management Review* 16, 2006, pp. 219–228.

74. "Thrown into Deep End, Workers Surface as Leaders," *BNA Bulletin to Management*, July 11, 2002, p. 223. See also, Ann Locke and Arlene Tarantino, "Strategic Leadership Development," *Training & Development*, December 2006, pp. 53–55.

75. Michael Marquardt, "Harnessing the Power of Action Learning," *Training and Development*, June 2004, pp. 26–32.

76. Chris Whitcomb, "Scenario-Based Training at the FBI," *Training and Development*, June 1999, pp. 42–46. See also, Michael Laff, "Serious Gaming: the Trainer's New Best Friend," *Training & Development*, January 2007, pp. 52–57.

77. American Management Association, Catalog of Seminars: April–December, 2003.

78. Ann Pomeroy, "Head of the Class," *HR Magazine*, (January 2005), p. 57. See also, Michael Laff, "Centralized Training Leads to Nontraditional Universities," *Training & Development*, January 2007, pp. 27–29, and see also, Chris Musselwhite, "University Executive Education Gets Real," *Training & Development*, May 2006, p. 57.

79. Norman Maier, Allen Solem, and Ayesha Maier, *The Role Play Technique* (San Diego, CA: University Associates, 1975), pp. 2–3. See also, Alan Test, "Why I Do Not Like to Role Play," *American Salesman*, August 1994, pp. 7–20.

80. Paul Taylor, et al., "A Meta-Analytic Review of Behavior Modeling Training," *Journal of Applied Psychology* 90, 2005, no. 4, pp. 692–719.

81. See Tom Barron, "The Link Between Leadership Development and Retention," *Training and Development*, (April 2004), pp. 58–65.

82. Paul Taylor et al., op. cit.

83. Martha Peak, "Go Corporate U!" *Management Review* 86, no. 2 (February 1997), pp. 33–37. See also, Jeanne Meister, "Universities Put to the Test," *Workforce Management*, December 11, 2006, pp. 27–30.

84. Russell Gerbman, "Corporate Universities 101," *HR Magazine*, February 2000, pp. 101–106.

85. "Executive Coaching: Corporate Therapy," *The Economist*, November 15, 2003, p. 61.

86. "As Corporate Coaching Goes Mainstream, Key Prerequisite Overlooked: Assessment," *BNA Bulletin to Management*, May 16, 2006, p. 153.

87. James Smither et al., "Can Working with an Executive Coach Improve Multisource Feedback Ratings Over Time?" *Personnel Psychology* 56, no. 1 (Spring 2003), pp. 23–44.

88. Joseph Toto, "Untapped World of Peer Coaching," *Training and Development*, April 2006, pp. 69–72.

89. Paul Harris, "A New Market Emerges," *Training and Development*, September 2003, pp. 30–38.

90. Edward Lawler III and Susan Mohrman, "Beyond the Vision: What Makes HR Effective?" *Human Resource Planning* 23, no. 4 (December 2000), p. 10.

91. One organizational change expert says, "Successful change agents I've observed employ three distinct but linked campaigns in their initiatives. A *political campaign* creates a coalition strong enough to support and guide the initiative. A *marketing campaign* taps into employees' thoughts and feelings and also effectively communicates messages about the prospective program's theme and benefits. And finally, a *military campaign* deploys executives' attention and time to actually carry out the change. Let us look more closely at how to actually lead the organizational

change process. Larry Hirschhorn, "Campaigning for Change," *Harvard Business Review*, July 2002, p. 98.

92. The 10 steps are based on Michael Beer, Russell Eisenstat, and Burt Spector, "Why Change Programs Don't Produce Change," *Harvard Business Review*, November–December 1990, pp. 158–166; Thomas Cummings and Christopher Worley, *Organization Development and Change* (Minneapolis, MN: West Publishing Company, 1993); John P. Kotter, "Leading Change: Why Transformation Efforts Fail," *Harvard Business Review*, March–April 1995, pp. 59–66; and John P. Kotter, *Leading Change* (Boston: Harvard Business School Press, 1996). Change doesn't necessarily have to be painful. See, for example, Eric Abrahamson, "Change Without Pain," *Harvard Business Review*, July–August 2000, pp. 75–79, and Michael Beer and Nitin Nohria, "Cracking the Code of Change," *Harvard Business Review*, June 2000, pp. 133–141. And, some people are just more open to change than are others. As just one example, self-esteem and optimism were related to higher levels of change acceptance in one recent study: Connie Wanberg, "Predictors and Outcomes of Openness to Changes in a Reorganizing Workplace," *Journal of Applied Psychology* 85, no. 1 (2000), pp. 132–142.

93. Kotter, "Leading Change," p. 85.

94. Noel Tichy and Ram Charan, "The CEO as Coach: An Interview with Allied Signal's Lawrence A. Bossidy," *Harvard Business Review*, March–April 1995, p. 77. See also Nicholas DiFonzo and Prashant Borgia, "A Tale of Two Corporations: Managing Uncertainty During Organizational Change," *Human Resource Management* 37, nos. 3 & 4 (Winter 1998), pp. 95–304.

95. Beer, Eisenstat, and Spector, "Why Change Programs Don't Produce Change," p. 164.

96. Beer, Eisenstat, and Spector, "Why Change Programs Don't Produce Change," p. 164.

97. Robert J. House, *Management Development* (Ann Arbor, MI: Bureau of Industrial Relations, University of Michigan, 1967), p. 71; Louis White and Kevin Wooten, "Ethical Dilemmas in Various Stages of Organizational Development," *Academy of Management Review* 8, no. 4 (1983), pp. 690–697.

98. Wendell French and Cecil Bell Jr., *Organization Development* (Upper Saddle River, NJ: Prentice Hall, 1995), pp. 171–193.

99. Benjamin Schneider, Steven Ashworth, A. Catherine Higgs, and Linda Carr, "Design Validity, and Use of Strategically Focused Employee Attitude Surveys," *Personnel Psychology* 49 (1996), pp. 695–705.

100. Cummings and Worley, *Organization Development and Change*, p. 501.

101. For a description of how to make OD a part of organizational strategy, see Aubrey Mendelow and S. Jay Liebowitz, "Difficulties in Making OD a Part of Organizational Strategy," *Human Resource Planning* 12, no. 4 (1995), pp. 317–329.

102. Wexley and Latham, *Developing and Training Human Resources in Organizations*, p. 128.

103. Ibid., p. 153.

104. See, for example, Charlie Morrow, M. Quintin Jarrett, and Melvin Rupinski, "An Investigation of the Effect and Economic Utility of Corporate-Wide Training," *Personnel Psychology* 50 (1997), pp. 91–119.

105. See, for example, Antonio Aragon-Sanchez, et al., "Effects of Training on Business Results," *International Journal of Human Resource Management* 14, no. 6, (September 2003), pp. 956–980.

106. Alan Saks and Monica Belcourt, "An Investigation of Training Activities and Transfer of Training in Organizations," *Human Resource Management*, Winter 2006, vol. 45, no. 4, pp. 629–648.

107. Todd Raphel, "What Learning Management Reports Do for You," *Workforce*, June 2001, pp. 56–58.

9 | Performance Management and Appraisal

With over 100,000 employees in 36 countries, administering employee performance appraisals is a complicated process at TRW Inc. Several years ago, the firm was deeply in debt. TRW's top management knew it had to make the firm more competitive and performance driven. One way to do that was to systematize how the company set standards for and appraised its employees. At the time, most of TRW's far-flung departments used their own paper-based appraisal systems. Top management decided that a companywide appraisal system was a top priority. •

After studying this chapter, you should be able to:

1   Evaluate and improve the appraisal form in Figure 9-1.
2   Describe the appraisal process.
3   Develop, evaluate, and administer at least four performance appraisal tools.
4   Explain and illustrate the problems to avoid in appraising performance.
5   List and discuss the pros and cons of six appraisal methods.
6   Perform an effective appraisal interview.
7   Discuss the pros and cons of using different raters to appraise a person's performance.

Chapters 6–8 addressed selecting, training, and developing employees. After they've been on the job for some time, you should appraise their performance. The purpose of this chapter is to show you how to appraise employees' performance. The main topics we cover include the performance management process, appraisal methods, appraisal performance problems and solutions, and the appraisal interview. Career planning is a logical consequence of appraisal: We'll turn to career planning in Chapter 10.

BASIC CONCEPTS IN PERFORMANCE MANAGEMENT AND APPRAISAL

Virtually all companies have some formal or informal means of appraising their employees' performance. We may define **performance appraisal** as any procedure that involves (1) setting work standards, (2) assessing the employee's actual performance relative to those standards, and (3) providing feedback to the employee with the aim of motivating him or her to eliminate performance deficiencies or to continue to perform above par.

For most people, "performance appraisal" brings to mind appraisal tools like the teaching appraisal form in Figure 9-1. However, forms are only part of the appraisal process. Performance appraisal also assumes that the employee knew what the performance standards were, and received the feedback required to remove any performance deficiencies. The aim should always be to improve the employee's, and, thereby, the company's performance.

Comparing Performance Appraisal and Performance Management

While the idea that appraisals should improve employee and company performance is nothing new, many managers take the integrated nature of that process—of setting goals, training employees, and then appraising and rewarding them—more seriously today than they have in the past. They call the total, integrated process *performance management*. We may define **performance management** as a process that unites goal setting, performance appraisal, and development into a single, common system whose aim is to ensure that the employee's performance is supporting the company's strategic aims. The distinguishing feature of performance management is that *it explicitly measures the employee's training, standards-setting, appraisal, and feedback relative to how his or her performance should be and is contributing to achieving the company's goals.*[1]

Performance management therefore never just means meeting with a subordinate once or twice a year to "review your performance." It means setting goals that make sense in terms of the company's strategic aims. It means daily or weekly interactions to ensure continuous improvement in the employee's capacity and performance.[2] And it means ensuring that the employee has the training he or she needs to perform the job. "The distinction is the contrast between a year-end event—the completion of the appraisal form—and a process that starts the year with performance planning and is integral to the way people are managed throughout the year"; Figure 9-2 summarizes performance management's building blocks.[3]

Why Performance Management?

If one were to spend several days in Toyota's Lexington, Kentucky, Camry plant, the absence of "appraisal" as most of us know it would soon be apparent. Supervisors don't sit down with individual employees to fill out forms and appraise them. Instead, teams of employees monitor their own results, continuously adjusting how they do things to align those results with the work team's standards and with the plant's overall quality and productivity needs. The fact that managers are emphasizing such a performance management approach reflects several things.

performance appraisal
Evaluating an employee's current and/or past performance relative to his or her performance standards.

performance management
A process that consolidates goal setting, performance appraisal, and development into a single, common system, the aim of which is to ensure that the employee's performance is supporting the company's strategic aims.

FIGURE 9-1

Classroom Teaching Appraisal by Students

Source: Richard I. Miller, *Evaluating Faculty for Promotion and Tenure* (San Francisco: Jossey-Bass Publishers, 1987), pp. 164–165. © 1987, Jossey-Bass Inc., Publishers. All rights reserved. Reprinted with permission of John Wiley & Sons, Inc.

❶ Evaluate and improve the appraisal form in Figure 9-1.

Evaluating Faculty for Promotion and Tenure
Classroom Teaching Appraisal by Students

Teacher _____ Course _____

Term _____ Academic Year _____

Thoughtful student appraisal can help improve teaching effectiveness. This questionnaire is designed for that purpose, and your assistance is appreciated. Please do not sign your name.

Use the back of this form for any further comments you might want to express.

Directions: Rate your teacher on each item, giving the highest scores for exceptional performances and the lowest scores for very poor performances. Place in the blank space before each statement the rating that most closely expresses your view.

Exceptional		Moderately Good			Very Poor		Don't Know
7	6	5	4	3	2	1	X

_____ 1. How do you rate the agreement between course objectives and lesson assignments?

_____ 2. How do you rate the planning, organization, and use of class periods?

_____ 3. Are the teaching methods and techniques employed by the teacher appropriate and effective?

_____ 4. How do you rate the competence of the instructor in the subject?

_____ 5. How do you rate the interest of the teacher in the subject?

_____ 6. Does the teacher stimulate and challenge you to think and to question?

_____ 7. Does he or she welcome differing points of view?

_____ 8. Does the teacher have a personal interest in helping you in and out of class?

_____ 9. How would you rate the fairness and effectiveness of the grading policies and procedures of the teacher?

_____ 10. Considering all the above items, what is your overall rating of this teacher?

_____ 11. How would you rate this teacher in comparison with all others you have had in the college or university?

Total Quality It reflects, first, the total quality management (TQM) concepts advocated by management experts like W. Edwards Deming. Basically, Deming argued that an employee's performance is more a function of things like training, communication, tools, and supervision than of his or her own motivation. Performance management's emphasis on the integrated nature of goal setting, appraisal, and development reflects this assumption.

Appraisal Issues Second, it reflects the fact that traditional performance appraisals are often not just useless but tense and counterproductive.[4]

Strategic Focus Third, performance management recognizes that in today's globally competitive environment, every employee's competencies and efforts must focus on helping the company achieve its strategic goals. The basic idea is that management and each worker and work team should continuously monitor performance relative to goals, and continuously improve results. *Continuous improvement* is a management philosophy. It

FIGURE 9-2

The Building Blocks of an Effective Performance Management Process

Direction sharing means communicating the organization's higher-level goals (including its vision, mission, values, and strategy) throughout the organization and then translating these into doable departmental goals.

Role clarification means clarifying each employee's role in terms of his or her day-to-day work.

Goal setting and planning means translating organizational and departmental goals into specific goals for each employee.

Goal alignment means having a process in place that allows any manager to see the link between an employee's goals and those of the department and organization.

Developmental goal setting involves ensuring that each employee "thinks through, at the start of any performance period, 'what do I have to do to achieve my goals?'"

Ongoing performance monitoring includes using computer-based systems that measure and then email progress and exception reports based on the person's progress toward meeting his or her performance goals.

Ongoing feedback includes both face-to-face and computer-based feedback regarding progress toward goals.

Coaching and support should be an integral part of the feedback process.

Performance assessment (appraisal) is just one element in the performance management process. The focus in performance management should be on planning and influencing how the employee's performance produces improved company results.

Rewards, recognition, and compensation all play a role in providing the consequences needed to keep the employee's goal-directed performance on track.

Workflow, process control, and return on investment management means making sure that the employee's performance is linked in a meaningful way via goal setting to the company's overall measurable performance.

means continuously setting and meeting ever-higher quality, cost, delivery, and availability goals. Central to this philosophy is the idea that each employee and team must continuously improve performance, from one period to the next.[5]

Defining the Employee's Goals and Work Standards

As you can see, the idea that the employee's effort should be goal directed is central to performance management and appraisal.[6] Managers should appraise employees based on the specific standards by which the employees expected to be measured. And, the employees' goals and performance standards should make sense in terms of the company's strategic goals.

In practice, clarifying what you expect from employees is trickier than it may appear. Job descriptions are rarely the answer. Employers usually write job descriptions not for specific jobs, but for groups of jobs, and the descriptions rarely include specific goals. Your sales manager's job description may list duties like "supervise salesforce." But, for strategic purposes, you may expect your sales manager to personally sell at least $600,000 worth of products per year by handling the division's two largest accounts; and to keep the salesforce happy.

The most straightforward way to do this (for the sales manager job above, for instance) is to set measurable standards for each objective. You might measure the "personal selling" activity in terms of how many dollars of sales your manager is to generate personally; perhaps measure "keeping the salesforce happy" in terms of turnover (on the assumption that less than 10% of the salesforce will quit in any given year if morale is high).[7] Guidelines for effective goal setting include the following.

Assign Specific Goals   Employees with specific goals usually perform better.

Assign Measurable Goals   Express goals in quantitative terms and include target dates or deadlines.[8] Goals set in absolute terms (such as "an average daily output of

300 units") are less confusing than goals set in relative terms (such as "improve production by 20%"). If measurable results will not be available, then "satisfactory completion"—such as "satisfactorily attended workshop" or "satisfactorily completed his or her degree"—is the next best thing. In any case, always include target dates or deadlines.

Assign Challenging but Doable Goals   Goals should be challenging, but not so difficult that they appear impossible or unrealistic.[9] When is a goal "too difficult" or "too hard"? One expert says:

> A goal is probably too easy if it calls for little or no improvement in performance when conditions are becoming more favorable, or if the targeted level of performance is well below that of most other employees in comparable positions. A goal is probably too difficult if it calls for a large improvement in performance when conditions are worsening, or if the targeted level of performance is well above that of people in comparable positions.[10]

Encourage Participation   A perennial management question is, "Should I just tell my employees what their goals are? Or, Should I let them participate with me in setting their goals?"

Research provides an answer. The evidence suggests that participatively set goals *do not* consistently result in higher performance than assigned goals, nor do assigned goals consistently result in higher performance than participatively set ones. *It is only when the participatively set goals are more difficult than the assigned ones that the participatively set goals produce higher performance.* In practice, participatively set goals do tend to be set higher. It's the fact that the goal is more difficult, not that it was participatively set, that explains the higher performance.[11]

As a shorthand way of remembering how to set goals, many managers use the acronym, SMART. Goals should be *specific*, and clearly state the desired results. They are *measurable*, and answer the question "how much." They are *attainable*, and not too tough or too easy. They are *relevant*, and clearly derive from what the manager and company want to achieve. And, they are *timely*, and reflect deadlines and milestones.

AN INTRODUCTION TO APPRAISING PERFORMANCE

Although many progressive employers, such as Toyota, have essentially eliminated formal appraisals, doing so may not be practical for most employers. At firms like Toyota, eliminating appraisals is a by-product of a broader effort. New employees endure a week or more of screening, and then several weeks of training. Enormous efforts go into fostering employee commitment and teamwork. Incentives support company-oriented thinking. Not all employers can or necessarily would benefit from such systems. Conventional appraisals are therefore still the norm. They are also, as most people know, more often than not occasions for tension and grief.

Why Appraise Performance?

There are four reasons to appraise subordinates' performance.

- First, from a practical point of view, most employers still base pay and promotional decisions on the employee's appraisal.[12]
- Second, appraisals play an integral role in the employer's performance management process. It does little good to translate the employer's strategic goals into specific employees' goals, if you don't periodically review performance.

- Third, the appraisal lets the boss and subordinate develop a plan for correcting any deficiencies, and to reinforce the things the subordinate does right.
- Fourth, appraisals should serve a useful career planning purpose. They provide an opportunity to review the employee's career plans in light of his or her exhibited strengths and weaknesses.

Realistic Appraisals

In reviewing the appraisal tools we discuss below, don't miss the forest for the trees. It doesn't matter which tool you use if you're less than candid when your subordinate is underperforming. Not all managers are devotees of such candor, but some firms, like GE, are famous for hard-hearted appraisals. GE's former CEO Jack Welch once said, for instance, that there's nothing crueler than telling someone who's doing a mediocre job that he or she is doing well.[13] Someone who might have had the chance to correct bad behavior or find a more appropriate vocation may instead spend years in a dead-end situation, only to have to leave when a more demanding boss comes along.

There are many practical motivations for giving soft appraisals: the fear of having to hire and train someone new; the appraisee's unpleasant reactions; or a company appraisal process that's not conducive to candor, for instance. Ultimately, it is the person doing the appraising who must decide if the potential negatives of less-than-candid appraisals outweigh the assumed benefits. They rarely do.

The Supervisor's Role

Appraising performance is both a difficult and an essential supervisory skill. The supervisor—not HR—usually does the actual appraising, and a supervisor who rates his or her employees too high or too low (or all average) is doing a disservice to them and to the company. Supervisors must therefore be familiar with appraisal techniques, understand and avoid problems that can cripple appraisals, and know how to conduct appraisals fairly.

The human resources department serves a policy-making and advisory role. Generally, human resources provides advice and assistance regarding the appraisal tool to use, but leaves final decisions on procedures to operating division heads. (In some firms, human resources prepares detailed forms and procedures for all departments). The human resource team should also be responsible for training supervisors to improve their appraisal skills, for monitoring the appraisal system's effectiveness, and for ensuring that it complies with EEO laws.

Supervisors must be familiar with appraisal techniques, understand and avoid problems that can cripple appraisals, and know how to conduct appraisals fairly.

Steps in Appraising Performance

🔵 Describe the appraisal process.

The performance appraisal process itself contains three steps: define the job, appraise performance, and provide feedback. *Defining the job* means making sure that you and your subordinate agree on his or her duties and job standards. *Appraising performance* means comparing your subordinate's actual performance to the standards that have been set; this usually involves some type of rating form. Third, performance appraisal usually requires one or more *feedback sessions*. Here the two of you discuss the subordinate's performance and progress, and make plans for any development required.

The NEW *Workforce*   Performance Appraisals and Joint Venture Collaboration

For an international joint venture in which employees from, say, the United States and Japan, or England and Spain, must work collaboratively for the venture to succeed, fostering collaboration is often the key to whether the venture succeeds. Designing the appraisal system can help in that regard.

A study looked at what managers can do to foster that sort of collaboration. The study involved a survey of U.S. participants in U.S.-based joint ventures between U.S. and Japanese auto supply companies. The study focused on the variables that influenced the U.S. employees' collaborative attitudes.

The researchers found that, among other things, the joint venture's appraisal system influenced collaboration. Specifically, to encourage collaboration, employee performance appraisal systems "should include measures of initiative and success in developing productive working relationships with counterparts." For example, appraise such employees in part based on information-sharing with counterparts, and on participation in sponsored events and informal get-togethers. Managers often say, "you get what you measure." That certainly appears to apply to encouraging global joint ventures' employees to be collaborative.[14]

The Appraisal Method   The manager generally conducts the appraisal itself with the aid of a predetermined and formal tool like one or more of those described next. The two basic considerations in designing the actual appraisal tool are *what to measure* and *how to measure* it. For example, in terms of *what to measure*, we may measure the employee's performance in terms of generic dimensions such as quality, quantity, and timeliness of work. Or, we may measure performance with respect to developing one's competencies (as in the ability to use Java), or achieving one's goals. "The New Workforce" illustrates why carefully choosing what to measure is important.

In terms of *how to measure* it, there are various methodologies, including graphic rating scales, the alternation ranking method, and "MBO."

Graphic Rating Scale Method

⊗ Develop, evaluate, and administer at least four performance appraisal tools.

graphic rating scale
A scale that lists a number of traits and a range of performance for each. The employee is then rated by identifying the score that best describes his or her level of performance for each trait.

The **graphic rating scale** is the simplest and most popular method for appraising performance. Figure 9-3 shows a typical rating scale. A graphic rating scale lists traits (such as quality and reliability) and a range of performance values (from unsatisfactory to outstanding) for each trait. The supervisor rates each subordinate by circling or checking the score that best describes his or her performance for each trait. The assigned values for the traits are then totaled.

What to Measure?   As noted earlier, the employer must decide exactly what aspects of the job's performance to measure. There are three basic options.

- As in Figure 9-3, the manager may opt for *generic dimensions* such as communications, teamwork, know-how, and quantity.
- Another option is to appraise performance based on the *job's actual duties*. For example, Figure 9-4 shows part of an appraisal form for an administrative secretary. The form assesses the job's five main sets of duties, one of which is "maintaining records." Here you would assess how well the employee did in exercising each of these five sets of duties.

Sample Performance Rating Form

Employee's Name _____   Level: Entry-level employee

Manager's Name _____

Key Work Responsibilities   Results/Goals to be Achieved
1. _____   1. _____
2. _____   2. _____
3. _____   3. _____
4. _____   4. _____

Communication

1	2	3	4	5

Below Expectations	Meets Expectations	Role Model
Even with guidance, fails to prepare straightforward communications, including forms, paperwork, and records, in a timely and accurate manner; products require minimal corrections.	With guidance, prepares straightforward communications, including forms, paperwork, and records, in a timely and accurate manner; products require minimal corrections.	Independently prepares communications, such as forms, paperwork, and records, in a timely, clear, and accurate manner; products require few, if any, corrections.
Even with guidance, fails to adapt style and materials to communicate straightforward information.	With guidance, adapts style and materials to communicate straightforward information.	Independently adapts style and materials to communicate information.

Organizational Know-How

1	2	3	4	5

Below Expectations	Meets Expectations	Role Model
<performance standards appear here>	<performance standards appear here>	<performance standards appear here>

Personal Effectiveness

1	2	3	4	5

Below Expectations	Meets Expectations	Role Model
<performance standards appear here>	<performance standards appear here>	<performance standards appear here>

Teamwork

1	2	3	4	5

Below Expectations	Meets Expectations	Role Model
<performance standards appear here>	<performance standards appear here>	<performance standards appear here>

Achieving Business Results

1	2	3	4	5

Below Expectations	Meets Expectations	Role Model
<performance standards appear here>	<performance standards appear here>	<performance standards appear here>

Source: Adapted from Elaine Pulakos, *Performance Management* (SHRM Foundation, 2004) pp. 16–17. Reprinted by permission of Society for Human Resource Management via Copyright Clearance Center.

FIGURE 9-3

Sample Graphic Rating Performance Rating Form

Results Assessment

Accomplishment 1: _____

	1		2		3		4		5	

Low Impact	Moderate Impact	High Impact
The efficiency or effectiveness of operations remained the same or improved only minimally. The quality of products remained the same or improved only minimally.	The efficiency or effectiveness of operations improved quite a lot. The quality of products improved quite a lot.	The efficiency or effectiveness of operations improved tremendously. The quality of products improved tremendously.

Accomplishment 2: _____

	1		2		3		4		5	

Low Impact	Moderate Impact	High Impact
The efficiency or effectiveness of operations remained the same or improved only minimally. The quality of products remained the same or improved only minimally.	The efficiency or effectiveness of operations improved quite a lot. The quality of products improved quite a lot.	The efficiency or effectiveness of operations improved tremendously. The quality of products improved tremendously.

Narrative

_____

_____

_____

_____

_____

Areas to be Developed	Actions	Completion Date

Manager's Signature _____ Date _____

Employee's Signature _____ Date _____

The above employee signature indicates receipt of, but not necessarily concurrence with, the evaluation herein.

FIGURE 9-3 (*continued*)

Name: ______ Rating period: from ______ to ______ Rater name: ______ Rater title: ______ Department: ______	Rating Scale Key [1] Fails to meet job requirements [2] Meets most job requirements [3] Fully meets all job requirements [4] Exceeds all job requirements

Part II: Rating Scales for Task Areas

Position: Administrative Secretary Duties and Responsibilities		
Duty: Maintaining Departmental Personnel Records	PCT. (30%)	RATING: 1 ☐ 2 ☐ 3 ☐ 4 ☐
Using spreadsheets and other computerized forms: Ensure all recorded personnel information is up to date and accurate, including name, address, and contact information; maintain accurate records of all personal leave taken annually, as well as vacation schedules; maintain accurate records of all employees' benefits.		Comments

FIGURE 9-4

Portion of an Administrative Secretary's Performance Appraisal Form Showing Task(s) to Appraise

Source: Janes Boford Jr., Bebby Borkhalter, and Grover Jacobs, "Link Job Description to Performance Appraisals," *Personnel Journal*, June 1988, pp. 135–136. Reprinted with permission, Workforce, June 1988. Copyright Crain Communications, Inc.

- *Competency-based appraisals* are another option. Here, the idea is to focus on the extent to which the employee exhibits the behaviorally recognizable competencies essential for the job. *Performance management* systems focus more on competencies. This is because behavioral competencies such as "builds a culture that is open and receptive to improved clinical care" connect in a more clear and meaningful way to achieving a company's strategic aims then would a traditional listing of duties like "supervise one dozen nurses."[15]

Some forms measure several things. Thus, Figure 9-5 (parts I, II, III) explicitly measures both competencies and objectives. With respect to competencies, the employee is expected to develop and exhibit competencies (Section II) such as "identifies and analyzes problems" (Problem Solving), and "maintains harmonious and effective work relationships with co-workers and constituents" (Teamwork). The employee and supervisor would fill in the "objectives" section (Section I) at the start of the year, and then set new ones as part of the appraisal.

alternation ranking method
Ranking employees from best to worst on a particular trait, choosing highest, then lowest, until all are ranked.

paired comparison method
Ranking employees by making a chart of all possible pairs of the employees for each trait and indicating which is the better employee of the pair.

Alternation Ranking Method

Ranking employees from best to worst on a trait or traits is another option. Since it is usually easier to distinguish between the worst and best employees, an **alternation ranking method** is most popular. First, list all subordinates to be rated, and then cross out the names of any not known well enough to rank. Then, on a form like that in Figure 9-6 (page 349) indicate the employee who is the highest on the characteristic being measured and also the one who is the lowest. Then choose the next highest and the next lowest, alternating between highest and lowest until all employees have been ranked.

Paired Comparison Method

The **paired comparison method** helps make the ranking method more precise. For every trait (quantity of work, quality of work, and so on), you pair and compare every subordinate with every other subordinate.

**Case Western Reserve University
Performance Management Outline
for the Development and Evaluation of Professional Staff**

Case Western Reserve University is a leading independent center for education, research and community citizenship. The University achieves its goals through the performance and excellence of each individual. The University expects all its staff employees to exemplify its values through committed leadership and concern for human relationships. As an organization, we value:

A working environment that encourages:

• Mutual respect and open communication
• Innovation and continuous learning
• A cooperative spirit and teamwork
• Respect for diversity and inclusiveness
• Personal growth and celebration of accomplishments
• Safety orientation

Personal responsibility based on:

• Integrity and ethics
• Accountability for results
• Clear goals and empowerment
• Dependability
• Protecting resources against waste, loss, or misuse

A customer-focused service orientation which exhibits:

• Concern for the customer's goals and needs
• Economy, efficiency, and flexibility
• Courtesy
• Responsiveness with good judgment
• Continuous and measurable improvements

Employee Name _____

Job Title _____

Department _____

Evaluator _____

Objectives & Development Planning Period:

#HR40100101   From _____ Through _____

Human **R**esources
C · W · R · U

FIGURE 9-5

Appraisal Form for Assessing Both Competencies and Specific Objectives

Source: http://www.case.edu/finadmin/humres/policies/perfExempt.pdf, Accessed May 17, 2007. Used by permission of Case Western Reserve University.

Suppose you have five employees to rate. In the paired comparison method, you make a chart, as in Figure 9-7 (page 349), of all possible pairs of employees for each trait. Then, for each trait, indicate (with a + or −) who is the better employee of the pair. Next, add up the number of +s for each employee. In Figure 9-7, Maria ranked highest (has the most + marks) for quality of work, whereas Art was ranked highest for creativity.

Forced Distribution Method

forced distribution method

Similar to grading on a curve; predetermined percentages of ratees are placed in various performance categories.

The **forced distribution method** is similar to grading on a curve. With this method, you place predetermined percentages of ratees into several performance categories. The proportions in each category need not be symmetrical; GE used top 20%, middle 70%, and bottom 10% for managers. One practical, if low-tech, way to do this is to write each employee's name on a separate index card. Then, for each trait (quality of work, creativity, and so on), place the employee's card in the appropriate performance category.

SECTION I	**Responsibilities/Objectives and Performance Standards in Support of Departmental Goals** *"Maximizing one's professional qualifications to make a difference"*		

Primary Performance Expectations: Responsibilities/Objectives and Standards	Mid-Year Progress Notes	End of Period Rating of Success and Effectiveness Comment and Place X on Scale to Rate Not Strong ———— Very Strong
Objective 1:		⊢—┼—┼—┼—⊣
Objective 2:		⊢—┼—┼—┼—⊣
Objective 3:		⊢—┼—┼—┼—⊣
Objective 4:		⊢—┼—┼—┼—⊣
Objective 5:		⊢—┼—┼—┼—⊣

Objectives for new rating period reviewed and agreed to:		Mid-Year Review:			
Evaluator	Date	Employee	Date	Evaluator	Date	Employee	Date

FIGURE 9-5 (*continued*)

Sun Microsystems force-ranks all its 43,000 employees. Managers appraise employees in groups of about 30, and those in the bottom 10% of each group get 90 days to improve. If they're still in the bottom 10% in 90 days, they can resign and take severance pay. Some decide to stay, but "If it doesn't work out," the firm fires them without severance.[16] This dismissal policy seems somewhat standard. It reflects the fact that top employees often outperform average or poor ones by as much as 100%.[17] Sometimes attempting to implement forced ranking fails; Jacques Nasser, a former Ford CEO, famously left in part due to resistance to his advocacy of such a plan. About a fourth of Fortune 500 companies including Microsoft, Conoco, and Intel use versions of forced distribution.[18] GE, which first popularized forced ranking, has recently been injecting more flexibility into its system. For instance it now tells managers to use more common sense in assigning rankings, and no longer strictly adheres to its famous 20/70/10 split.[19]

As most students know, forced distribution grading systems are more unforgiving than most other appraisal methods. With a forced distribution system, you're either in the top 5% or 10% (and thus get that "A"), or you're not. And, if you're in the bottom 5% or 10%, you get an "F," no questions asked. Your professor hasn't the wiggle room to give everyone As, Bs, and Cs. Some students have to fail.

SECTION II	Performance Competencies "Making a Difference by Working and Learning Together."	
	Mid-Year Progress Notes	End of Period Rating of Success and Effectiveness Comment and Place X on Scale to Rate Not Strong ———————— Very Strong
Job Knowledge/Competency: Demonstrates the knowledge and skills necessary to perform the job effectively. Understands the expectations of the job and remains current regarding new developments in areas of responsibility. Performs responsibilities in accordance with job procedures and policies. Acts as a resource person upon whom others rely for assistance.		⊢—+—+—+—⊣
Quality/Quantity of Work: Completes assignments in a thorough, accurate, and timely manner that achieves expected outcomes. Exhibits concern for the goals and needs of the department and others that depend on services or work products. Handles multiple responsibilities in an effective manner. Uses work time productively.		⊢—+—+—+—⊣
Planning/Organization: Establishes clear objectives and organizes duties for self based on the goals of the department, division, or management center. Identifies resources required to meet goals and objectives. Seeks guidance when goals or priorities are unclear.		⊢—+—+—+—⊣
Initiative/Commitment: Demonstrates personal responsibility when performing duties. Offers assistance to support the goals and objectives of the department and division. Performs with minimal supervision. Meets work schedule/attendance expectations for the position.		⊢—+—+—+—⊣
Problem Solving/Creativity: Identifies and analyzes problems. Formulates alternative solutions. Takes or recommends appropriate actions. Follows up to ensure problems are resolved.		⊢—+—+—+—⊣
Teamwork and Cooperation: Maintains harmonious and effective work relationships with co-workers and constituents. Adapts to changing priorities and demands. Shares information and resources with others to promote positive and collaborative work relationships.		⊢—+—+—+—⊣
Interpersonal Skills: Deals positively and effectively with coworkers and constituents. Demonstrates respect for all individuals.		⊢—+—+—+—⊣
Communication (Oral and Written): Effectively conveys information and ideas both orally and in writing. Listens carefully and seeks clarification to ensure understanding.		⊢—+—+—+—⊣

Competencies Reviewed and Discussed:	Mid-Year Review	
Evaluator	Date	Employee Date

FIGURE 9-5 *(continued)*

One survey found that 77% of responding employers using this approach were at least "somewhat satisfied" with forced ranking, while the remaining 23% were dissatisfied. The biggest complaints: 44% said it damages morale. Forty-seven percent said it creates interdepartmental inequities: "High performing teams must cut 10% of their workers while low performing teams are still allowed to retain 90% of theirs."[20] Some writers refer unkindly to forced ranking as "Rank and Yank."[21]

Given this, employers need to be doubly careful to protect such appraisals from managerial abuse. Office politics and managerial bias can taint ratings. Furthermore, choosing performance extremes is usually not even the problem: "It is not difficult to identify the good performer and the bad performer . . . The challenge is for processes to differentiate meaningfully between the other 80%."[22]

SECTION III   **End of Period Summary Performance Rating**

Based on a review of Section I, Success and Effectiveness in Position Responsibilities/Accomplishing Objectives and Standards, and Section II, Performance Competencies, provide a summary performance rating:

Comments: _____

_____

_____

_____

_____

_____

- ◼ Performance consistently and significantly above standards in virtually all areas; far exceeds normal expectations.

- ◼ Performance well above standards in many important aspects; usually exceeds normal expectations.

- ◼ Performance meets standards in all important aspects; good contributor.

- ◼ Performance slightly below standards in some important aspects, but meets standards in others; performance generally acceptable but improvement needed to fully achieve functional performance level.

- ◼ Performance below standards in a number of critical aspects; substantial improvement needed.

_____   _____
Evaluator Signature   Date

I have read this appraisal and it had been discussed with me. I understand that signing this appraisal does not necessarily mean I agree with all of the information in it or that I forfeit my right for review.

_____   _____
Employee Signature   Date

FIGURE 9-5 (continued)

To protect against unfairness, and bias claims, employers should take several steps.[23] Appoint a review committee to review any employee's low ranking. Train raters to be objective, and consider using multiple raters in conjunction with the forced distribution approach.

Critical Incident Method

critical incident method
Keeping a record of uncommonly good or undesirable examples of an employee's work-related behavior and reviewing it with the employee at predetermined times.

With the **critical incident method**, the supervisor keeps a log of positive and negative examples (critical incidents) of a subordinate's work-related behavior. Every six months or so, supervisor and subordinate meet to discuss the latter's performance, using the incidents as examples.

This method has several advantages. It provides examples of good and poor performance the supervisor can use to explain the person's rating. It makes the supervisor think about the subordinate's appraisal all during the year (so the rating does not just reflect the

FIGURE 9-6

Scale for Alternate Ranking of Appraiseer

ALTERNATION RANKING SCALE

Trait: _____

For the trait you are measuring, list all the employees you want to rank. Put the highest-ranking employee's name on line 1. Put the lowest-ranking employee's name on line 20. Then list the next highest ranking on line 2, the next lowest ranking on line 19, and so on. Continue until all names are on the scale.

Highest-ranking employee

1. _____   11. _____
2. _____   12. _____
3. _____   13. _____
4. _____   14. _____
5. _____   15. _____
6. _____   16. _____
7. _____   17. _____
8. _____   18. _____
9. _____   19. _____
10. _____   20. _____

Lowest-ranking employee

FIGURE 9-7

Ranking Employees by the Paired Comparison Method

Note: + means "better than." − means "worse than." For each chart, add up the number of +'s in each column to get the highest-ranked employee.

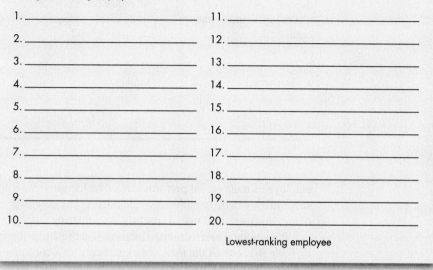

FOR THE TRAIT "QUALITY OF WORK"

As Compared to:	A Art	B Maria	C Chuck	D Diane	E José
A Art		+	+	−	−
B Maria	−		−	−	−
C Chuck	−	+		+	−
D Diane	+	+	−		+
E José	+	+	+	−	

Maria ranks highest here

FOR THE TRAIT "CREATIVITY"

As Compared to:	A Art	B Maria	C Chuck	D Diane	E José
A Art		−	−	−	−
B Maria	+		−	+	+
C Chuck	+	+		−	+
D Diane	+	−	+		−
E José	+	−	−	+	

Art ranks highest here

TABLE 9-1 Examples of Critical Incidents for Assistant Plant Manager

Continuing Duties	Targets	Critical Incidents
Schedule production for plant	90% utilization of personnel and machinery in plant; orders delivered on time	Instituted new production scheduling system; decreased late orders by 10% last month; increased machine utilization in plant by 20% last month
Supervise procurement of raw materials and inventory control	Minimize inventory costs while keeping adequate supplies on hand	Let inventory storage costs rise 15% last month; overordered parts "A" and "B" by 20%; underordered part "C" by 30%
Supervise machinery maintenance	No shutdowns due to faulty machinery	Instituted new preventative maintenance system for plant; prevented a machine breakdown by discovering faulty part

employee's most recent performance). The list provides examples of what specifically the subordinate can do to eliminate deficiencies. The downside is that without some numerical rating, this method is not too useful for comparing employees or for salary decisions.

It's common to accumulate incidents that relate to the employee's performance goals. In Table 9-1, one of the assistant plant manager's continuing duties was to supervise procurement and to minimize inventory costs. The critical incident log shows that the assistant plant manager let inventory storage costs rise 15%; this provides an example of what performance she must improve in the future.

Narrative Forms

All or part of the written appraisal may be in narrative form. Figure 9-8 presents one example. Here, the person's supervisor is responsible for providing an assessment of the employee's past performance and required areas of improvement. This narrative assessment aids the employee in understanding where his or her performance was good or bad, and how to improve that performance.

Behaviorally Anchored Rating Scales

behaviorally anchored rating scale (BARS)

An appraisal method that aims at combining the benefits of narrative critical incidents and quantified ratings by anchoring a quantified scale with specific narrative examples of good and poor performance.

A **behaviorally anchored rating scale (BARS)** is an appraisal tool that anchors a numerical rating scale with specific behavioral examples of good or poor performance. It thus combines the benefits of narratives, critical incidents, and quantified (graphic rating type) scales. Its proponents say it provides better, more equitable appraisals than do the other tools we discussed.[24]

Developing a BARS typically requires five steps:

1. *Generate critical incidents.* Ask persons who know the job (jobholders and/or supervisors) to describe specific illustrations (critical incidents) of effective and ineffective performance.
2. *Develop performance dimensions.* Have these people cluster the incidents into a smaller set of (5 or 10) performance dimensions, and define each dimension, such as "salesmanship skills."
3. *Reallocate incidents.* To verify, have another group of people who also know the job reallocate the original critical incidents. They get the cluster definitions (from step 2)

FIGURE 9-8

Appraisal-Coaching Worksheet

Source: Reprinted from www.HR.BLR.com with permission of the publisher *Business and Legal Reports, Inc.* 141 Mill Rock Road East, Old Saybrook, CT © 2004.

Appraisal-Coaching Worksheet

Instructions: This form is to be filled out by supervisor and employee prior to each performance review period.

Employee: _____ Position: _____

Supervisor: _____ Department: _____

Date: _____ Period of Work under Consideration: from _____ to _____

1. What areas of the employee's work performance are meeting job performance standards?

2. In what areas is improvement needed during the next six to twelve months?

3. What factors or events that are beyond the employee's control may affect (positively or negatively) his or her ability to accomplish planned results during the next six to twelve months?

4. What specific strengths has the employee demonstrated on this job that should be more fully used during the next six to twelve months?

5. List two or three areas (if applicable) in which the employee needs to improve his or her performance during the next six to twelve months (gaps in knowledge or experience, skill development needs, behavior modifications that affect job performance, etc.).

6. Based on your consideration of items 1–5 above, summarize your mutual objectives:

A. What supervisor will do:

B. What employee will do:

C. Date for next progress check or to re-evaluate objectives:

D. Data/evidence that will be used to observe and/or measure progress.

_____

Employee Signature   Supervisor Signature

_____

Date

and the critical incidents, and must reassign each incident to the cluster they think it fits best. Retain a critical incident if some percentage (usually 50% to 80%) of this second group assigns it to the same cluster as did the first group.

4. *Scale the incidents.* This second group then rates the behavior described by the incident as to how effectively or ineffectively it represents performance on the dimension (7- to 9-point scales are typical).

5. *Develop a final instrument.* Choose about six or seven of the incidents as the dimension's behavioral anchors.[25]

Research Insight   Three researchers developed a BARS for grocery checkout clerks.[26] They collected critical incidents, and then clustered these into eight performance dimensions:

Knowledge and Judgment

Conscientiousness

Skill in Human Relations

Skill in Operation of Register

Skill in Bagging

Organizational Ability of Check-stand Work

Skill in Monetary Transactions

Observational Ability

They then developed behaviorally anchored rating scales (similar to the one in Figure 9-9) for each of these dimensions. Each contained a scale (ranging from 1 to 9) for rating performance from "extremely poor" to "extremely good." Then a specific critical

FIGURE 9-9

Example of a Behaviorally Anchored Rating Scale for the Dimension *Salesmanship Skills*

Source: Walter C. Borman, "Behavior Based Rating Scales," in Ronald A. Berk (ed.), *Performance Assessment: Methods and Applications* (Baltimore, MD: Johns Hopkins University Press, 1986), p. 103. Reprinted with the permission of the John Hopkins University Press.

SALESMANSHIP SKILLS

Skillfully persuading prospects to join the Navy; using Navy benefits and opportunities effectively to sell the Navy; closing skills; adapting selling techniques appropriately to different prospects; effectively overcoming objectives to joining the Navy.

9 — A prospect stated he wanted the nuclear power program or he would not sign up. When he did not qualify, the recruiter did not give up; instead, he talked this young man into electronics by emphasizing the technical training he would receive.

8 — The recruiter treats objections to joining the Navy seriously; he works hard to counter the objections with relevant, positive arguments for a Navy career.

7 — When talking to a high school senior, the recruiter mentions names of other seniors from that school who have already enlisted.

6 — When an applicant qualifies for only one program, the recruiter tries to convey to the applicant that it is a desirable program.

5 — When a prospect is deciding on which service to enlist in, the recruiter tries to sell the Navy by describing Navy life at sea and adventures in port.

4 — During an interview, the recruiter said to the applicant. "I'll try to get you the school you want, but frankly it probably won't be open for another three months, so why don't you take your second choice and leave now."

3 — The recruiter insisted on showing more brochures and films even though the applicant told him he wanted to sign up right now.

2 — When a prospect states an objection to being in the Navy, the recruiter ends the conversation because he thinks the prospect must not be interested.

1 —

incident (such as "by knowing the price of items, this checker would be expected to look for mismarked and unmarked items") helped anchor or specify what was meant by "extremely good" (9) performance. Similarly, they used several other critical incident anchors along the performance scale from (8) down to (1).

Advantages   While more time-consuming than other appraisal tools, BARS seems to have some advantages.

1. *A more accurate gauge.* People who know and do the job and its requirements better than anyone develop the BARS. This should produce a good gauge of job performance.
2. *Clearer standards.* The critical incidents along the scale make clear what to look for in terms of superior performance, average performance, and so forth.
3. *Feedback.* The critical incidents make it easier to explain the ratings to appraisees.
4. *Independent dimensions.* Systematically clustering the critical incidents into five or six performance dimensions (such as "salesmanship skills") should help to make the performance dimensions more independent of one another. For example, a rater should be less likely to rate an employee high on all dimensions simply because he or she was rated high in "salesmanship skills."
5. *Consistency.*[27] BARS-based evaluations seem to be relatively reliable, in that different raters' appraisals of the same person tend to be similar.

Management by Objectives

management by objectives (MBO)

Involves setting specific measurable goals with each employee and then periodically reviewing the progress made.

Stripped to its basics, **management by objectives (MBO)** requires the manager to set specific measurable goals with each employee and then periodically discuss the latter's progress toward these goals. You could engage in a modest and informal MBO program with subordinates by jointly setting goals and periodically providing feedback. However, the term *MBO* generally refers to a comprehensive and formal organizationwide goal-setting and appraisal program consisting of six steps:

1. *Set the organization's goals.* Establish, based on the firm's strategic plan, an organizationwide plan for next year, and, from this, set specific company goals.
2. *Set departmental goals.* Next, department heads take these company goals (like "boost 2008 profits by 20%") and, with their superiors, jointly set goals for their departments.
3. *Discuss departmental goals.* Department heads discuss the department's goals with all subordinates, often at a departmentwide meeting. They ask employees to set their own preliminary individual goals. In other words, how can each employee contribute to the department's goals?
4. *Define expected results* (set individual goals). Department heads and their subordinates set short-term individual performance targets.
5. *Performance reviews.* Department heads compare each employee's actual and targeted performance.
6. *Provide feedback.* Department heads and employees discuss and evaluate the latters' progress.

There are three problems in using MBO. Setting unclear objectives is one. An objective such as "will do a better job of training" is useless. On the other hand, "will have four subordinates promoted during the year" is a measurable objective.

Second, MBO is time-consuming. Setting objectives, measuring progress, and giving feedback can take several hours per employee per year, over and above the time you already spend doing each person's appraisal.

Third, setting objectives with the subordinate sometimes turns into a tug-of-war, with you pushing for higher quotas and the subordinate pushing for lower ones. To motivate performance, the objectives must be fair and attainable. The more you know about the job and the person's ability, the more confident you can be about the standards you set.

Computerized and Web-Based Performance Appraisal

Several inexpensive performance appraisal software programs are available. These generally enable managers to keep computerized notes on subordinates during the year, and then to combine these with ratings of employees on several performance traits. The software programs then generate written text to support each part of the appraisal.

Example   Employee Appraiser (developed by the Austin-Hayne Corporation, San Mateo, California) presents a menu of more than a dozen evaluation dimensions, including dependability, initiative, communication, decision making, leadership, judgment, and planning and productivity. Within each dimension are various performance factors, again in menu form. For example, under "communication" are separate factors for writing, verbal communication, and listening skills. When the supervisor clicks on a performance factor, the person sees a sophisticated version of a graphic rating scale. Instead of a scale with numbers, however, Employee Appraiser uses behaviorally anchored examples. For example, for verbal communication, there are six choices, ranging from "presents ideas clearly" to "lacks structure." After the manager picks the phrase that most accurately describes the worker, Employee Appraiser generates sample text for the employee's appraisal. Evaluators rated two other appraisal packages outstanding: PeopleSoft HR management, and SAP r/3 hr.[28]

About a third of employers use online performance management tools to facilitate the appraisal process, at least for some employees.[29] Doing so of course enables supervisors and subordinates to complete and transfer the appraisal forms remotely, and helps the employer to ensure a relatively standardized appraisal process.

Online Appraisals   For example, PerformanceReview.com, from KnowledgePoint of Petaluma, California, lets managers evaluate employees online based on their competencies, goals, and development plans. Managers can choose from standard competencies such as "communications," or create their own.[30] The Web site decwise.com/360Demo/ directs employees to a 360 online appraisal they can use for their supervisor.[31]

Electronic performance monitoring is, in some respects, the ultimate in computerized appraising. **Electronic performance monitoring (EPM)** means having supervisors electronically observe the employee's output or whereabouts. This typically involves using computer networks and wireless audio or video links to monitor and record employees' work activities. It includes, for instance, monitoring a data clerk's hourly keystrokes, tracking via GPS the whereabouts of delivery drivers, and monitoring the calls of customer service clerks.

How do employees react to EPM? Studies suggest two things. First, "[Employees] with the ability to delay or prevent electronic performance monitoring indicated higher feelings of personal control and demonstrated superior task performance." In other words, let employees have some control over how and when they're monitored.[32] If you can't, then the findings suggest this: Don't let them know when you're monitoring them. Participants who knew exactly when the monitoring was taking place expressed lower feelings of personal control than did those who did not know when the monitoring was on.

electronic performance monitoring (EPM)
Having supervisors electronically monitor the amount of computerized data an employee is processing per day, and thereby his or her performance.

Many employers today make use of online appraisals for evaluating employee performance.

Merging the Methods

Creating an appraisal form is not an either-or process. The best forms merge several approaches. For example, Figure 9-3 (pages 342–343) merges a graphic rating scale with behavioral incidents. This form illustrates an important fact regarding appraisals. Even if the company does not choose to use a full behaviorally anchored rating scale approach, anchoring the scale, as here, with behavioral descriptions can improve the reliability and validity of the appraisal scale. Figure 9-3 is basically a graphic rating scale supported with specific behavioral competency expectations. These expectations pinpoint what raters should look for.

APPRAISING PERFORMANCE: PROBLEMS AND SOLUTIONS

Few things managers do are fraught with more peril than appraising subordinates' performance. Employees in general are overly optimistic about what their ratings will be. You and they know their raises, career progress, and peace of mind may well hinge on how you rate them. This alone makes it difficult to rate performance. However, of perhaps greater concern are the technical problems that can cast doubt on how fair the whole process is. Let's turn to some of these more technical appraisal problems and how to solve them, and to several other pertinent appraisal issues.

Potential Rating Scale Appraisal Problems

Most employers use graphic-type rating scales to appraise performance, but these scales are especially susceptible to several problems: unclear standards, halo effect, central tendency, leniency or strictness, and bias.

unclear standards
An appraisal that is too open to interpretation.

Unclear Standards   Table 9-2 illustrates the **unclear standards** problem. This graphic rating scale seems objective. However, it would probably result in unfair appraisals, because the traits and degrees of merit are ambiguous. For example, different supervisors would

TABLE 9-2 A Graphic Rating Scale with Unclear Standards

	Excellent	Good	Fair	Poor
Quality of work				
Quantity of work				
Creativity				
Integrity				

Note: For example, what exactly is meant by "good," "quantity of work," and so forth?

probably define "good" performance, "fair" performance, and so on differently. The same is true of traits such as "quality of work" or "creativity."

The best way to fix this problem is to develop and include descriptive phrases that define each trait, as in Figure 9-3. That form spells out what measures like "Role Model," or "Below Expectations" mean. This specificity results in more consistent and more easily explained appraisals.

halo effect

In performance appraisal, the problem that occurs when a supervisor's rating of a subordinate on one trait biases the rating of that person on other traits.

Halo Effect   Experts define **halo effect** as "the influence of a rater's general impression on ratings of specific ratee qualities."[33] For example, supervisors often rate unfriendly employees lower on all traits, rather than just for the trait "gets along well with others." Being aware of this problem is a big step toward avoiding it. Supervisory training can also alleviate the problem, as can using a BARS (on which, recall, the performance dimensions are usually quite independent of each other).

central tendency

A tendency to rate all employees the same way, such as rating them all average.

Central Tendency   Some supervisors stick to the middle when filling in rating scales. For example, if the rating scale ranges from 1 to 7, they tend to avoid the highs (6 and 7) and lows (1 and 2) and rate most of their people between 3 and 5. **Central tendency** basically means rating all employees average. Doing so distorts the evaluations, making them less useful for promotion, salary, or counseling purposes. Ranking employees instead of using graphic rating scales can reduce this problem, since ranking means you can't rate them all average.

strictness/leniency

The problem that occurs when a supervisor has a tendency to rate all subordinates either high or low.

Leniency or Strictness   Other supervisors tend to rate all their subordinates consistently high (or low), just as some instructors are notoriously high or low graders. This **strictness/leniency** problem is especially severe with graphic rating scales. On the other hand, ranking forces supervisors to distinguish between high and low performers.

There are several solutions. One is for the employer to recommend that supervisors avoid giving all their employees high (or low) ratings. A second is to basically enforce a distribution—that, say, about 10% of the people should be rated "excellent," 20% "good," and so forth.

bias

The tendency to allow individual differences such as age, race, and sex to affect the appraisal ratings employees receive.

Bias   The number of things that can lead to biased appraisals is pretty much limitless. One study focused on how personality influenced the evaluations students gave their peers. Raters who scored higher on "conscientiousness" tended to give their peers lower ratings—they were stricter, in other words; those scoring higher on "agreeableness" gave higher ratings—they were more lenient.[34] Another study found that raters may actually penalize successful women for their success.[35] Even the appraisal's purpose biases the results. Two researchers concluded that "performance appraisal ratings obtained for administrative purposes [such as pay raises or promotions] were nearly one-third [higher] than those obtained for research or employee development purposes."[36]

Then there is the intensely interpersonal nature of the appraisal process. As one writer puts it, "performance ratings amplify the quality of the personal relationship between boss and employee." Good relationships tend to create good experiences, bad relationships bad ones."[37]

Appraisees' personal characteristics (such as age, race, and sex) can affect their ratings. Appraisals frequently say more about the appraiser than about the appraised.[38] A 36-year-old supervisor ranked a 62-year-old subordinate at the bottom of the department's rankings, and then terminated him. The U.S. Court of Appeals for the 10th circuit held that the decision to terminate might have been influenced by the discriminatory motives of the younger boss.[39] In one study, promoted women had to receive higher performance ratings than promoted men to get promoted, "suggesting that women were held to stricter standards for promotion."[40] In sum, studies suggest that "rater idiosyncratic biases account for the largest percentage of the observed variances in performance ratings."[41]

Research Insight   A study illustrates how bias can influence the way one person appraises another. In this study, researchers sought to determine the extent to which pregnancy biases performance appraisals.[42] The subjects were 220 undergraduate students between the ages of 17 and 43 attending a midwestern university.

Two videotapes of a female "employee" were shown. Each video showed three five-minute scenarios in which this "employee" interacted with another woman. For example, she acted as a customer representative to deal with an irate customer, tried to sell a computer system to a potential customer, and dealt with a problem subordinate. In each case, the employee's performance level was designed to be average or slightly above average. The employee was the same in both videotapes, and the videotapes were identical—except for one difference. Researchers shot the first videotape in the employee's ninth month of pregnancy, the second about five months later.

Several groups of student raters watched either the "pregnant" or "not pregnant" tape. They rated the "employee" on a 5-point graphic rating scale for individual characteristics such as "ability to do the job," "dependability," and "physical mannerisms." Despite seeing otherwise identical behavior by the same woman, the student raters "with a remarkably high degree of consistency" assigned lower performance ratings to a pregnant woman as opposed to a nonpregnant one.[43]

One company posts potential rating errors on its Web site's performance management section as part of its rater training. See Figure 9-10.[44]

How to Avoid Appraisal Problems

4 Explain and illustrate the problems to avoid in appraising performance.

It's probably safe to say that problems like these can make having an appraisal worse than having no appraisal at all. Would an employee not be better off with no appraisal than with a seemingly objective but actually biased one? However, problems like these aren't inevitable, and you can minimize them.

Know Problems   *First*, learn and understand the potential problems and their solutions. Understanding the problem can help you avoid it.

Use Right Tool   *Second*, use the right appraisal tool. Each has its own pros and cons. For example, the ranking method avoids central tendency but can cause bad feelings when employees' performances are in fact all "high." Table 9-3 summarizes each tool's pros and cons.

5 List and discuss the pros and cons of six appraisal methods.

Train Supervisors   *Third*, train supervisors to reduce rating errors such as halo, leniency, and central tendency. In one training program, raters watched a video of people at work, and then rated the workers. The trainers then placed the supervisors' ratings of these workers on

FIGURE 9-10

Potential Rating Errors

- *Focusing on one or two critical incidents:* Basing assessments on one or two big incidents and disregarding the person's total performance.
- *Lower rating for less challenge:* Rating some employees lower than others because they are in jobs that you believe are less challenging.
- *Nobody can be that good:* Strictness error; in other words, being overly stringent, believing that no one can be that effective.
- *Similarity:* Giving high ratings to employees who strike you as very similar to you in background, work habits, or experiences.
- *Being influenced by prior performance:* Believing, based on the person's prior performance ratings, that you must be wrong about how you appraise his or her current performance, and that you must have overlooked something.
- *Rating for retention:* Giving your employees higher ratings because you're afraid you'll lose them.
- *Style differences:* Lowering an employee's rating because he or she approaches the task differently than you might.
- *Emotional rating:* Allowing strong feelings about individuals to influence the rating (positively or negatively).
- *Recent performance only:* Also called the recency effect, letting what the employee has done recently to blind you to what his or her performance has been over the year.
- *Friendships:* Letting personal relationships outside the office influence employee's rating.

TABLE 9-3 Important Advantages and Disadvantages of Appraisal Tools

Tool	Advantages	Disadvantages
Graphic rating scale	Simple to use; provides a quantitative rating for each employee.	Standards may be unclear; halo effect, central tendency, leniency, bias can also be problems.
BARS	Provides behavioral "anchors." BARS is very accurate.	Difficult to develop.
Alternation ranking	Simple to use (but not as simple as graphic rating scales). Avoids central tendency and other problems of rating scales.	Can cause disagreements among employees and may be unfair if all employees are, in fact, excellent.
Forced distribution method	End up with a predetermined number or % of people in each group.	Employees' appraisal results depend on your choice of cutoff points.
Critical incident method	Helps specify what is "right" and "wrong" about the employee's performance; forces supervisor to evaluate subordinates on an ongoing basis.	Difficult to rate or rank employees relative to one another.
MBO	Tied to jointly agreed-upon performance objectives.	Time-consuming.

a flip chart, and explained and illustrated the various errors, such as leniency and halo. But beware: One problem with training raters to avoid rating errors is that, sometimes, what appears to be an error—such as leniency—isn't an error at all, as when all subordinates really are superior performers.[45] (Packaged training programs are available. For example, Harvard Business School Publishing offers *Assessing Performance*, for about $150. It lists the steps and things to consider in preparing for and conducting the appraisal interview).[46]

Control Outside Influences   *Fourth*, training isn't always enough to overcome the supervisor's outside distractions. In practice, several factors—including the extent to which employees' pay is tied to performance ratings, union pressure, employee turnover, time constraints, and the need to justify ratings—may be more important than training. This means that improving appraisal accuracy also requires reducing the effects of outside factors such as union pressure and time constraints.

Keep a Diary   *Fifth*, keep a diary of employees' performance over the year.[47] One study involved 112 first-line supervisors from a large electronics firm. Some attended a special training program on diary keeping. The program explained the role of critical incidents, and how the supervisors could compile these incidents into a diary or incident file to use later as a reference for a subordinate's appraisal. There was then a practice session, followed by a feedback and group discussion session aimed at reinforcing the importance of recording positive and negative incidents.

The conclusion of this and similar studies is that you can reduce the adverse effects of appraisal problems by having raters compile positive and negative critical incidents as they occur during the appraisal period. Maintaining such records instead of relying on memories is definitely the preferred approach.[48]

Diary keeping is preferred but not foolproof.[49] In one study, raters actually seemed to seek out and record incidents that were consistent with how they felt about the ratees. In any case, it's apparent that as a rater you must always keep the cognitive nature of the appraisal process in mind. Raters bring to the task a bundle of biases, inclinations, and decision-making shortcuts (such as stereotyping people based on age), so that, potentially at least, the appraisal is bound to be a victim of the rater's biases and inclinations.

Knowing the employment law that applies to appraisals is also important, as in the "Know Your Employment Law" feature below.

Who Should Do the Appraising?

Traditionally, the person's direct supervisor appraises his or her performance. However, other options are available and are increasingly used. We'll look at the main ones.

The Immediate Supervisor   Supervisors' ratings are the heart of most appraisals. This makes sense: The supervisor usually is in the best position to observe and evaluate the subordinate's performance, and is responsible for that person's performance.

Peer Appraisals   With more firms using self-managing teams, peer or team appraisals—the appraisal of an employee by his or her peers—are becoming more popular. Typically, an employee chooses an appraisal chairperson each year. That person then selects one supervisor and three or four other peers to evaluate the employee's work.

Peer appraisals can predict future management success. In one study of military officers, peer ratings were quite accurate in predicting which officers would be promoted.[50] Peer ratings have other benefits. One study involved placing undergraduates into self-managing work groups. The researchers found that peer appraisals had "an immediate positive impact on [improving] perception of open communication, task motivation, social loafing, group viability, cohesion, and satisfaction."[51] However, *logrolling*—when several peers collude to rate each other highly—can be a problem.

Rating Committees   Many employers use rating committees. These committees usually contain the employee's immediate supervisor and three or four other supervisors.

Using multiple raters makes sense. While there may be a discrepancy among ratings by individual supervisors, the composite ratings tend to be more reliable, fair, and valid.[52]

Know Your Employment LAW   Appraising Performance

Courts have often found that the inadequacies of an employer's appraisal system lay at the root of illegal discriminatory actions, particularly in cases concerning layoffs, promotions, discharges, merit pay, or combinations of these.[53]

An illustrative case involved layoff decisions. The court held that the firm had violated Title VII when it laid off several Hispanic-surnamed employees on the basis of poor performance ratings. The court concluded that the practice was illegal because:

1. The firm based the appraisals on subjective supervisory observations.
2. It didn't administer and score the appraisals in a standardized fashion.
3. Two of the three supervisory evaluators did not have daily contact with the employees.

Personal bias, unreasonably rating everyone high (or low), and relying just on recent events are some other reasons courts gave for deciding that firms' appraisal processes and subsequent personnel actions were unfair.[54] Here are some guidelines for developing a legally defensible appraisal process.[55]

1. Clarify what you mean by "successful performance." Conduct a job analysis to establish the criteria and standards.
2. Incorporate these criteria and standards into a rating instrument.
3. Communicate performance standards to employees and to those rating them, in writing.
4. When using graphic rating scales, avoid abstract trait names (such as "loyalty" or "honesty"), unless you can define them in terms of observable behaviors.

5. Use subjective supervisory ratings (essays) as only one component of the appraisal.
6. Train supervisors to use the rating instrument properly. At least provide raters with written instructions for using the rating scale.
7. Allow appraisers substantial daily contact with the employees they're evaluating.
8. Base your appraisals on separate ratings for each of the job's performance dimensions. Using a single overall rating of performance is usually not acceptable to the courts, which often characterize such systems as vague.[56]
9. Whenever possible, have more than one appraiser, and conduct all such appraisals independently.
10. One appraiser should never have absolute authority to determine a personnel action.
11. Give employees the opportunity to review and make comments, and have a formal appeals process.
12. Document all information: "Without exception, courts condemn informal performance evaluation practices that eschew documentation."[57]
13. Where appropriate, provide corrective guidance to assist poor performers in improving their performance.

If your case gets to court, which of these guidelines will most influence the judge's decision? A review of almost 300 U.S. court decisions is informative. Actions reflecting fairness and due process were most important. Performing a *job analysis*, providing raters with *written instructions*, permitting employee *review* of results, and obtaining *agreement* among raters were the four practices that seemed to have the most consistent impact. The courts placed little emphasis on whether or not the employers formally validated their performance appraisal processes.[58]

Using several raters can also help cancel out problems like bias and halo effects. Furthermore, when there are differences in ratings, they usually stem from the fact that raters at different levels observe different facets of an employee's performance, and the appraisal ought to reflect these differences. Even when a committee is not used, it is customary to have the manager immediately above the one who makes the appraisal review it.

Self-Ratings   Should employees appraise themselves? The basic problem, of course, is that employees usually rate themselves higher than they are rated by supervisors or peers.

The basic problem with self-ratings is that employees usually rate themselves higher than they are rated by supervisors or peers.

One study found that when asked to rate their own job performances, 40% of employees in jobs of all types placed themselves in the top 10% ("one of the best"), while virtually all remaining employees rated themselves either in the top 25% ("well above average"), or at least in the top 50% ("above average").[59] Usually no more than 1 or 2% will place themselves in a below-average category. One study concludes that individuals do not necessarily always have such positive illusions about their own performances, although even here group members did give their own groups unrealistically high ratings.[60]

Supervisors requesting self-appraisals to accompany their own should therefore know that doing so may accentuate differences and rigidify positions, rather than aid the process. Furthermore, even if you don't ask for a self-appraisal, your employees will almost certainly attend their performance reviews with their own self-appraisals in mind, and this will usually be higher than your rating. Therefore, come prepared for a dialogue, with specific critical incidents to make your point.

Appraisal by Subordinates   Many employers let subordinates anonymously rate their supervisor's performance, a process some call *upward feedback*. The process helps top managers diagnose management styles, identify potential "people" problems, and take corrective action with individual managers as required. At firms such as FedEx, subordinate ratings are especially valuable when used for developmental rather than evaluative purposes. Managers who receive feedback from subordinates who identify themselves view the upward appraisal process more positively than do managers who receive anonymous feedback. However, subordinates (not surprisingly) are more comfortable giving anonymous responses, and those who have to identify themselves tend to provide inflated ratings. Sample upward feedback items include: I can tell my manager what I think; and, my manager tells me what is expected.

Research Insight   One study involved 92 managers who were rated by one or more subordinates in each of four administrations of an upward feedback survey over two years.[61] The subordinates rated themselves and their managers on 33 behavioral statements. The feedback managers received included a review of results from previous administrations of the survey, so they could track their performance over time.

The results were impressive. According to the researchers, "managers whose initial level of performance (defined as the average rating from subordinates) was 'low' improved between administrations one and two, and sustained this improvement two years later."[62] The results also suggest that it's not necessarily the specific feedback that caused the performance improvement (since low-performing managers seemed to improve over time even if they didn't receive any feedback). Instead, learning what the critical supervisory behaviors were (as a result of themselves filling out the appraisal surveys), plus knowing their subordinates would be appraising them, may have been enough to prompt the improved behavior.

360-Degree Feedback   Many firms have expanded the idea of upward and peer feedback into "360-degree feedback." Here ratings are collected "all around" an employee, from supervisors, subordinates, peers, and internal or external customers.[63] Employers generally use the feedback for development rather than for pay increases.

Most 360-degree feedback systems contain several common features. Appropriate parties—peers, supervisors, subordinates, and customers, for instance—complete surveys on an individual. The surveys often include items such as "returns phone calls promptly," "listens well," or "[my manager] keeps me informed." Computerized and Web-based systems then compile this feedback into individualized reports, just for the ratees. They then meet with their own supervisors and sometimes with their subordinates and share the information they feel is pertinent for self-improvement.

Some doubt the practicality of 360-degree feedback. Employees usually do these reviews anonymously, so those with an ax to grind can misuse them. A "Dilbert" cartoon, announcing that evaluations by co-workers will help decide raises, has one character asking, "If my co-workers got small raises, won't there be more available in the budget for me?"[64]

Thus, 360-degree appraisal is the subject of considerable debate. One study found significant correlations between (1) 360-degree ratings (by peers and managers) and (2) conventional performance ratings.[65] Another study concluded that multi-source feedback leads to "generally small" performance improvements on subsequent ratings.[66] However, anchoring 360-degree appraisals with behavioral competencies improves the ratings' reliability; in one study, the competency-based 360-degree assessments were strongly predictive of how the managers performed in a subsequent assessment center.[67] The consulting firm Watson Wyatt, found that companies using 360-degree-type feedback have lower market value (in terms of stock price), perhaps due to the methods' complications.[68]

All in all, the findings suggest that firms should carefully assess the potential costs of the program, focus any feedback very clearly on concrete goals, carefully train the people that are giving and receiving the feedback, and not rely solely on 360-degree feedback. And, the company should make sure that the feedback is productive, unbiased, and development-oriented.[69]

The use of 360-degree appraisals seems to be diminishing. Some firms, like GE, backed off from using it. Some found the paperwork overwhelming; others found that some employees colluded with peers to give each other high ratings. But others still argue that progressive executives welcome 360-degree feedback, since "by laying themselves open to praise and criticism from all directions and inviting others to do the same, they guide their organizations to new capacities for continuous improvement."[70]

appraisal interview
An interview in which the supervisor and subordinate review the appraisal and make plans to remedy deficiencies and reinforce strengths.

THE APPRAISAL INTERVIEW

An appraisal typically culminates in an **appraisal interview**. Here, supervisor and subordinate review the appraisal and make plans to remedy deficiencies and reinforce strengths. Interviews like these are often uncomfortable. Few people like to receive—or give—negative feedback. Adequate preparation and effective implementation are therefore essential.

Types of Appraisal Interviews

There are four basic types of appraisal interviews, each with its own objectives:

Satisfactory—Promotable is the easiest interview: The person's performance is satisfactory and there is a promotion ahead. Your objective is to discuss the person's career plans and to develop a specific action plan for the educational and professional development the person needs to move up.

Satisfactory—Not promotable is for employees whose performance is satisfactory but for whom promotion is not possible. Perhaps there is no more room in the company. Perhaps he or she is happy as is and doesn't want a promotion. The objective here is to maintain satisfactory performance. The best option is usually to find incentives that are important to the person and enough to maintain satisfactory performance. These might include extra time off, a small bonus, additional authority to handle a slightly enlarged job, and reinforcement, perhaps in the form of an occasional "well done!"

When the person's performance is *unsatisfactory but correctable*, the interview objective is to lay out an action plan (see Figure 9-11) for correcting the unsatisfactory performance.

If the employee is *unsatisfactory* and the situation is *uncorrectable*, you can usually skip the interview. You either tolerate the person's poor performance for now, or dismiss the person.

FIGURE 9-11

Performance Contract

Source: David Antonion, "Improving the Performance Management Process Before Discontinuing Performance Appraisals," *Compensation and Benefits Review* May–June 1994, pp. 33, 34. Reprinted by permission of Sage Publications, Inc.

PERFORMANCE CONTRACT

Within the next year, I understand that our organization's objectives are _____

_____

and that the goals of our department are _____ . I also

understand that our work unit goals are _____ .

My key internal customers are _____ and their

work needs and expectations are _____ .

To make my contribution toward attaining the goals stated above, I understand that I am expected to do the following:

My individual performance goals are _____ .

My goals for improving work methods (process) are _____ .

My goals for improving specific interpersonal work behaviors when I interact with the following

_____ are _____ .

I believe these goals are acceptable and attainable. I also understand that I will be evaluated by multiple appraisal sources (supervisor, peers, internal, and, if appropriate, external customers).

Compensation for my work performance will be based on whether my performance was (1) outstanding, (2) fully competent, or (3) unsatisfactory. I understand that the following forms of compensation will be considered: (1) merit award for my individual performance goal attainment, (2) enhancement and utilization of my skills, (3) my work unit's or team's performance (gainsharing), and (4) our organization's performance (profit sharing).

_____   _____
Your Signature   Supervisor's Signature

⑥ Perform an effective appraisal interview.

How to Conduct the Appraisal Interview

Preparation is essential. Review the person's job description, compare performance to the standards, and review the employee's previous appraisals. Give the employee at least a week's notice to review his or her work, analyze problems, and gather questions and comments.

Find a mutually agreeable time for the interview and allow enough time for the entire interview. Interviews with lower-level personnel like clerical workers and maintenance staff should take no more than an hour. Interviews with management employees often take two or three hours. Be sure the interview is done in a private place where you won't be interrupted.

Guidelines   There are four things to keep mind when actually conducting the interview:

1. *Talk in terms of objective work data.* Use examples such as absences, tardiness, quality records, orders processed, productivity records, order processing time, accident reports, and so on.
2. *Don't get personal.* Don't say, "You're too slow in producing those reports." Instead, try to compare the person's performance to a standard. ("These reports should normally be done within 10 days.") Similarly, don't compare the person's performance to that of other people. ("He's quicker than you are.")
3. *Encourage the person to talk.* Stop and listen to what the person is saying; ask open-ended questions such as, "What do you think we can do to improve the situation?" Use a command such as "Go on." Restate the person's last point as a question, such as, "You don't think you can get the job done?"
4. *Don't tiptoe around.* Don't get personal, but do make sure the person leaves knowing specifically what he or she is doing right and doing wrong. Make sure before he or she leaves there is agreement on how things will be improved, and by when. Write up an action plan with targets and dates.

How to Ensure the Interview Leads to Improved Performance   Many managers bring to the appraisal an erroneous (and unstated) assumption: that simply revealing the gap between where the employee should be and is will trigger improved performance. But in most human endeavors, that's not enough. For example, if getting someone to lose weight merely required a scale, there'd be little need for all the diet programs on the market. Similarly, identifying the gap is just the first step in improving an employee's performance. Doing so often requires providing the tools and support the person needs to move ahead.[71] Here, clearing up job-related problems with the employee and setting measurable performance targets and a schedule for achieving them—an action plan—are essential.

How to Handle a Defensive Subordinate   Defenses are an important and familiar aspect of our lives. When a supervisor tells someone his or her performance is poor, the first reaction is often denial. By denying the fault, the person avoids having to question his or her own competence. Others react to criticism with anger and aggression. This helps them let off steam and postpones confronting the immediate problem until they are able to cope with it. Still others react to criticism by retreating into a shell.

In any event, understanding and dealing with defensiveness is an important appraisal skill. In his book *Effective Psychology for Managers*, psychologist Mortimer Feinberg suggests the following:

1. Recognize that defensive behavior is normal.
2. Never attack a person's defenses. Don't try to "explain someone to themselves" by saying things like, "You know the real reason you're using that excuse is that you can't bear to be blamed." Instead, concentrate on the act ("sales are down").
3. Postpone action. Sometimes it is best to do nothing. People frequently react to sudden threats by instinctively hiding behind their "masks." But given sufficient time, a more rational reaction takes over.

4. Recognize your own limitations. The supervisor should not try to be a psychologist. Offering understanding is one thing; trying to deal with psychological problems is another matter entirely.

How to Criticize a Subordinate   When you must criticize, do it in a manner that lets the person maintain his or her dignity. Criticize in private, and do it constructively. Provide examples of critical incidents and specific suggestions of what could be done and why. Avoid once-a-year "critical broadsides" by giving feedback on a daily basis, so that the formal review contains no surprises. Never say the person is "always" wrong (since no one is ever "always" wrong or right). Criticism should be objective and free of any personal biases on your part.

Whether subordinates express satisfaction with their appraisal interview depends on factors such as (1) not feeling threatened during the interview; (2) having an opportunity to present their ideas and feelings and to influence the course of the interview; and (3) having a helpful and constructive supervisor conduct the interview.

How to Handle a Formal Written Warning   An employee's performance may be so poor that it requires a formal written warning. Such written warnings serve two purposes: (1) They may serve to shake your employee out of his or her bad habits, and (2) they can help you defend your rating, both to your own boss and (if needed) to the courts.

Written warnings should identify the standards by which the employee is judged, make it clear that the employee was aware of the standard, specify any deficiencies relative to the standard, and show the employee had an opportunity to correct his or her performance. Figure 9-12 provides an appraisal interview checklist.

FIGURE 9-12

Checklist During the Appraisal Interview

Source: Reprinted from www.HR.BLR.com with permission of the publisher *Business and Legal Reports, Inc.* 141 Mill Rock Road East, Old Saybrook, CT © 2004.

CHECKLIST DURING THE APPRAISAL INTERVIEW

	Yes	No
• Did you discuss each goal or objective established for this employee?	☐	☐
• Are you and the employee clear on the areas of agreement? disagreement?	☐	☐
• Did you and the employee cover all positive skills, traits, accomplishments, areas of growth, etc.? Did you reinforce the employee's accomplishments?	☐	☐
• Did you give the employee a sense of what you thought of his or her potential or ability?	☐	☐
• Are you both clear on areas where improvement is required? expected? demanded? desired?	☐	☐
• What training or development recommendations did you agree on?	☐	☐
• Did you indicate consequences for noncompliance, if appropriate?	☐	☐
• Did you set good objectives for the next appraisal period?	☐	☐
• Objective?	☐	☐
• Specific?	☐	☐
• Measurable?	☐	☐
• Did you set a standard to be used for evaluation?	☐	☐
• Time frame?	☐	☐
• Did you set a time for the next evaluation?	☐	☐
• Did you confirm what your part would be? Did the employee confirm his or her part?	☐	☐
• Did you thank the employee for his or her efforts?	☐	☐

⑦ Discuss the pros and cons of using different raters to appraise a person's performance.

Appraisals in Practice

Surveys shed light on how and why companies appraise employees.[72] In one survey, about 89% (of 250) SHRM members reported they required performance appraisals for all their employees. About 32% said they used MBO, 24% used the graphic rating scale, 10% used "other," and, about 34% used a narrative essay format; here raters take an open-ended approach to describing their employees' behaviors. None of those responding used behaviorally anchored rating scales. Eighty percent conduct annual evaluations; most of the rest do semiannual appraisals, and 92% require a review and feedback session as part of the appraisal process. A second survey found that of 100 large organizations, 52% use appraisals for promotions, 60% do *not* link appraisals to pay raises, and 68% say they don't even link the appraisals to determining other rewards, such as bonuses. About half used appraisals for succession planning.

CREATING THE TOTAL PERFORMANCE MANAGEMENT PROCESS

We have seen that for many employers, performance appraisal is just part of the firm's overall performance management process. In a sense, performance management starts at the end and works back. Top management says, "What is our strategy and what are our goals?" Each manager in the chain of command then asks, "What does this mean for the goals we set for our employees, for the competencies that they must exhibit, and for how we train, appraise, promote, and reward them?"

Perhaps the best way to illustrate how to create a total performance management process is to look at how one company, TRW, did so.

Improving Productivity Through HRIS: TRW's New Performance Management System

With over 100,000 employees in 36 countries on five continents, administering employee appraisals and managing performance is a complicated process in a company like TRW.[73] Several years ago, the firm was deeply in debt. TRW's top management knew it had to take steps to make the firm more competitive and performance driven. At the time, most of the firm's far-flung departments used their own paper-based appraisal systems. Top management decided that a companywide performance management system was a top priority.

Top management identified a special team and charged it with creating a "one company, one system" performance management system. The team consisted of several information technology experts, and key HR representatives from the business units. Because team members were scattered around the world, the team and its team meetings were entirely Web-based and virtual. Their aim was to quickly develop a performance management system that was *consistent* in that employees in all of TRW's far-flung organization could use the same system. It also had to be *comprehensive* in that it consolidated the various components of performance management into a single common system. For TRW, these components included goal setting, performance appraisal, professional development, and succession planning.

The team created an online system, one in which most TRW employees and supervisors worldwide could input and review their data electronically. (The team subsequently created an equivalent paper-based system, for use by certain employees abroad, who did not have easy access to the Web.) The Web-based performance management system included the information in Figure 9-13.

FIGURE 9-13

Information Required for TRW's Web-Based Performance Management System

Source: D. Bradford Neary, "Creating a Company-Wide, Online, Performance Management System: A Case Study at TRW, Inc.," *Human Resource Management* 41, no. 4 (Winter 2002), p. 495. Reprinted by permission of Society for Human Resource Management via Copyright Clearance Center.

Page 1 biographical data

Identification information

Education

Experience summary

Pages 2–3 performance summary

Accomplishments against previous year goals
  TRW behaviors
  TRW initiatives
Legal and ethical conduct/diversity and
  cultural sensitivity
Previous year's professional development
  activities
Employee comments

Overall performance—manager's overall rating and comments

Page 4 development summary

Demonstrated strengths
Improvement opportunities
Performance goals for the upcoming year
Professional development activities for the
  upcoming year
Future potential/positions (employee
  perspective)
Future potential/positions (manager perspective)
Electronic sign-off from both employee and
  manager

To facilitate filling in the online form's pages, the team created a wizard that leads the user from step to step. The system also includes embedded prompts, and pull-down menus. For example, in the "demonstrated strengths" area, the pull-down menus allow the user to select specific competencies such as "financial acumen."

In practice, either the employee or the manager can trigger the performance management process by completing the appraisal and sending it to the other, (although it's usually the employee that begins the process). Once the employee finishes the online form, a system-generated e-mail notifies the manager that the form is ready for review. Then the two fine-tune the appraisal by meeting in person, and by interacting online.

The new performance management system has produced many benefits. It focuses everyone's attention on goal-oriented performance, specifically on what that employee needs to do to contribute to achieving TRW's strategic goals. It identifies development needs that are both relevant to TRW's needs, and to the employee. It gives managers instant access to employee performance data. (For example, by clicking a "managing employees" function on the online system, a manager can see an onscreen overview of the assessment status of each of his or her subordinates.) It gives all managers access to an employee database (so, for instance, a search for an engineer with Chinese language skills takes just a few minutes) And, the system lets the manager quickly review the development needs of all his or her employees. The result is an integrated, goal-oriented employee development and appraisal Performance Management Process.

REVIEW

SUMMARY

1. Most companies have some formal or informal means of appraising their employees' performance. *Performance appraisal* means evaluating an employee's current and/or past performance relative to his or her performance standards.

2. We defined *performance management* as a process that consolidates goal setting, performance appraisal, and development into a single, common system, the aim of which is to ensure that the employee's performance is supporting the company's strategic aims.

3. Performance management includes practices through which the manager defines the employee's goals and work, develops the employee's capabilities, and evaluates and rewards the person's effort.

4. The employer must decide exactly what sort of performance to measure. The employer may opt for *generic dimensions* such as quality and quantity, or appraise performance on the *job's actual duties*. With *competency-based appraisals* the idea is to focus on the extent to which the employee exhibits the competencies that the employer values for this job. The employer may also want to appraise the employee based on the extent to which he or she is achieving his or her *objectives*.

5. Performance appraisal tools include the graphic rating scale, alternation ranking method, forced distribution method, BARS, MBO, critical incident method, and computer and Web-based methods.

6. Appraisal problems to beware of include unclear standards, halo effect, central tendency, leniency or strictness problems, and bias.

7. Most subordinates probably want a specific explanation or examples regarding why they were appraised high or low, and for this, compiling a record of positive and negative critical incidents can be useful.

8. There are three types of appraisal interviews: unsatisfactory but correctable performance; satisfactory but not promotable; and satisfactory—promotable.

9. To bring about constructive change in a subordinate's behavior, get the person to talk in the interview. Use open-ended questions, state questions in terms of a problem, use a command question, use questions to try to understand the feelings underlying what the person is saying, and restate the person's last point as a question. On the other hand, don't do all the talking, don't use restrictive questions, don't be judgmental, don't give free advice, and don't get involved with name calling, ridicule, or sarcasm.

DISCUSSION QUESTIONS

1. What is the purpose of a performance appraisal?
2. Discuss the pros and cons of four performance appraisal tools.
3. Explain how you would use the alternation ranking method, the paired comparison method, and the forced distribution method.
4. Explain in your own words how you would go about developing a behaviorally anchored rating scale.
5. Explain the problems to be avoided in appraising performance.
6. Discuss the pros and cons of using different potential raters to appraise a person's performance.
7. Compare and contrast performance management and performance appraisal.
8. Answer the question, "How would you get the interviewee to talk during an appraisal interview?"

INDIVIDUAL AND GROUP ACTIVITIES

1. Working individually or in groups, develop a graphic rating scale for the following jobs: secretary, professor, directory assistance operator.
2. Working individually or in groups, describe the advantages and disadvantages of using the forced distribution appraisal method for college professors.
3. Working individually or in groups, develop, over the period of a week, a set of critical incidents covering the classroom performance of one of your instructors.

4. The HRCI "Test Specifications" appendix at the end of this book (pages 726–735) lists the knowledge someone studying for the HRCI certification exam needs to have in each area of human resource management (such as in Strategic Management, Workforce Planning, and Human Resource Development). In groups of four to five students, do four things: (1) review that appendix now; (2) identify the material in this chapter that relates to the required knowledge the appendix lists; (3) write four multiple choice exam questions on this material that you believe would be suitable for inclusion in the HRCI exam; and (4) if time permits, have someone from your team post your team's questions in front of the class, so the students in other teams can take each others' exam questions.

5. Every week, like clockwork, during the 2004 TV season, Donald Trump told another "apprentice," "You're fired." Review recent (or archived) episodes of Donald Trump's *Apprentice* show and answer this: What performance appraisal system did Mr. Trump use, and do you think it resulted in valid appraisals? What techniques discussed in this chapter did he seem to apply? How would you suggest he change his appraisal system to make it more effective?

EXPERIENTIAL EXERCISE

Grading the Professor

Purpose: The purpose of this exercise is to give you practice in developing and using a performance appraisal form.

Required Understanding: You are going to develop a performance appraisal form for an instructor and should therefore be thoroughly familiar with the discussion of performance appraisals in this chapter.

How to Set Up the Exercise/Instructions: Divide the class into groups of four or five students.

Instructions

1. First, based on what you now know about performance appraisal, do you think Figure 9-1 is an effective scale for appraising instructors? Why? Why not?

2. Next, your group should develop its own tool for appraising the performance of an instructor. Decide which of the appraisal tools (graphic rating scales, alternation ranking, and so on) you are going to use, and then design the instrument itself.

3. Next, have a spokesperson from each group put his or her group's appraisal tool on the board. How similar are the tools? Do they all measure about the same factors? Which factor appears most often? Which do you think is the most effective tool on the board?

4. The class should select the top 10 factors from all of the appraisal tools presented to create what the class perceives to be the most effective tool for appraising the performance of the instructor.

APPLICATION CASE

Appraising the Secretaries at Sweetwater U

Rob Winchester, newly appointed vice president for administrative affairs at Sweetwater State University, faced a tough problem shortly after his university career began. Three weeks after he came on board in September, Sweetwater's president, Rob's boss, told Rob that one of his first tasks was to improve the appraisal system used to evaluate secretarial and clerical performance at Sweetwater U. Apparently, the main difficulty was that the performance appraisal was traditionally tied directly to salary increases given at the end of the year. So most administrators were less than accurate when they used the graphic rating forms that were the basis of the clerical staff evaluation. In fact, what usually happened was that each administrator simply rated his or her clerk or secretary as "excellent." This cleared the way for all support staff to receive a maximum pay increase every year.

But the current university budget simply did not include enough money to fund another "maximum" annual increase for every staffer. Furthermore, Sweetwater's president felt that the custom of providing invalid feedback to each secretary on his or her year's performance was not productive, so he had asked the new vice president to revise the system. In October, Rob sent a memo to all administrators telling them that in the future no more than half the secretaries reporting to any particular administrator could be appraised as "excellent." This move, in effect, forced each supervisor to begin ranking his or her secretaries for quality of performance. The vice president's memo met widespread resistance immediately—from administrators, who were afraid that many of their secretaries would begin leaving for more lucrative jobs in private industry; and from secretaries, who felt that the new system was unfair and reduced each secretary's chance of receiving a maximum salary increase. A handful of secretaries had begun quietly picketing outside the president's home on the university campus. The picketing, caustic remarks by disgruntled administrators, and rumors of an impending slowdown by the secretaries (there were about 250 on campus) made Rob Winchester wonder whether he had made the right decision by setting up forced ranking. He knew, however, that there were a few performance appraisal experts in the School of Business, so he decided to set up an appointment with them to discuss the matter.

He met with them the next morning. He explained the situation as he had found it: The present appraisal system had been set up when the university first opened 10 years earlier, and the appraisal form had been developed primarily by a committee of secretaries. Under that system, Sweetwater's administrators filled out forms similar to the one shown in Table 9-2. This once-a-year appraisal (in March) had run into problems almost immediately, since it was apparent from the start that administrators varied widely in their interpretations of job standards, as well as in how conscientiously they filled out the forms and supervised their secretaries. Moreover, at the end of the first year it became obvious to everyone that each secretary's salary increase was tied directly to the March appraisal. For example, those rated "excellent" received the maximum increases, those rated "good" received smaller increases, and those given neither rating received only the standard across-the-board cost-of-living increase. Since universities in general—and Sweetwater in particular—have paid secretaries somewhat lower salaries than those prevailing in private industry, some secretaries left in a huff that first year. From that time on, most administrators simply rated all secretaries excellent in order to reduce staff turnover, thus ensuring each a maximum increase. In the process, they also avoided the hard feelings aroused by the significant performance differences otherwise highlighted by administrators.

Two Sweetwater experts agreed to consider the problem, and in two weeks they came back to the vice president with the following recommendations. First, the form used to rate the secretaries was grossly insufficient. It was unclear what "excellent" or "quality of work" meant, for example. They recommended instead a form like that in Figure 9-3. In addition, they recommended that the vice president rescind his earlier memo and no longer attempt to force university administrators to arbitrarily rate at least half their secretaries as something less than excellent. The two consultants pointed out that this was, in fact, an unfair procedure since it was quite possible that any particular administrator might have staffers who were all or virtually all excellent—or conceivably, although less likely, all below standard. The experts said that the way to get all the administrators to take the appraisal process more seriously was to stop tying it to salary increases. In other words, they recommended that every administrator fill out a form like that in Figure 9-3 for each secretary at least once a year and then use this form as the basis of a counseling session. Salary increases would have to be made on some basis other than the performance appraisal, so that administrators would no longer hesitate to fill out the rating forms honestly.

Rob thanked the two experts and went back to his office to ponder their recommendations. Some of the recommendations (such as substituting the new rating form for the old) seemed to make sense. Nevertheless, he still had serious doubts as to the efficacy of any graphic rating form, particularly if he were to decide in favor of his original forced ranking approach. The experts' second recommendation—to stop tying the appraisals to automatic salary increases—made sense but raised at least one very practical problem: If salary increases were not to be based on performance appraisals, on what were they to be based? He began wondering whether the experts' recommendations weren't simply based on ivory tower theorizing.

Questions

1. Do you think that the experts' recommendations will be sufficient to get most of the administrators to fill out the rating forms properly? Why? Why not? What additional actions (if any) do you think will be necessary?
2. Do you think that Vice President Winchester would be better off dropping graphic rating forms, substituting instead one of the other techniques we discussed in this chapter, such as a ranking method? Why?
3. What performance appraisal system would you develop for the secretaries if you were Rob Winchester? Defend your answer.

CONTINUING CASE

Carter Cleaning Company

The Performance Appraisal

After spending several weeks on the job, Jennifer was surprised to discover that her father had not formally evaluated any employee's performance for all the years that he had owned the business. Jack's position was that he had "a hundred higher-priority things to attend to," such as boosting sales and lowering costs, and, in any case, many employees didn't stick around long enough to be appraisable anyway. Furthermore, contended Jack, manual workers such as those doing the pressing and the cleaning did periodically get positive feedback in terms of praise from Jack for a job well done, or criticism, also from Jack, if things did not look right during one of his swings through the stores. Similarly, Jack was never shy about telling his managers about store problems so that they, too, got some feedback on where they stood.

This informal feedback notwithstanding, Jennifer believes that a more formal appraisal approach is required. She believes that there are criteria such as quality, quantity, attendance, and punctuality that should be evaluated periodically even if a worker is paid on piece rate. Furthermore, she feels quite strongly that the managers need to have a list of quality standards for matters such as store cleanliness, efficiency, safety, and adherence to budget on which they know they are to be formally evaluated.

Questions

1. Is Jennifer right about the need to evaluate the workers formally? The managers? Why or why not?
2. Develop a performance appraisal method for the workers and managers in each store.

TRANSLATING STRATEGY INTO HR POLICIES AND PRACTICE CASE:
THE HOTEL PARIS

The New Performance Management System

The Hotel Paris's competitive strategy is "To use superior guest service to differentiate the Hotel Paris properties, and to thereby increase the length of stay and return rate of guests, and thus boost revenues and profitability." HR manager Lisa Cruz must now formulate functional policies and activities that support this competitive strategy, by eliciting the required employee behaviors and competencies.

Lisa knew that the Hotel Paris's performance appraisal system was archaic. When the founders opened their first hotel, they went to an office-supply store, and purchased a pad of performance appraisal forms. The hotel chain uses these to this day. Each form is a two-sided page. Supervisors indicate whether the employee's performance in terms of various standard traits including quantity of work, quality of work, and dependability was excellent, good, fair, or poor. Lisa knew that, among other flaws, this appraisal tool did not force either the employee or the supervisor to focus the appraisal on the extent to which the employee was helping the Hotel Paris to achieve its strategic goals. She wanted a system that focused the employee's attention on taking those actions that would contribute to helping the company achieve its goals, for instance, in terms of improved customer service.

Lisa and her team also wanted a performance management system that focused on both competencies and objectives. In designing the new system, their starting point was the job descriptions they had created for the hotel's employees. These descriptions each included required competencies. Consequently, using a form similar to Figure 9-5 (page 345–348), the front-desk clerks' appraisals now focus on competencies such as "able to check a guest in or out in five minutes or less." Most service employees' appraisals include the competency, "able to exhibit patience and guest support of this even when busy with other activities." There were other required competencies. For example, the Hotel Paris wanted all service employees to show initiative in helping guests, to be customer oriented, and to be team players (in terms of sharing information and best practices). Each of these competencies derives from the Hotel's aim of becoming more service-oriented.

Questions

1. Pick out one job, such as front-desk clerk. Based on any information you have (including job descriptions you may have created in other chapters) write a list of duties, competencies, and performance standards for that chosen job.
2. Based on that, create a performance appraisal form for appraising that job.

KEY TERMS

ENDNOTES

1. Peter Glendinning, "Performance Management: Pariah or Messiah," *Public Personnel Management* 31, no. 2 (Summer 2002), pp. 161–178.
2. Clinton Wingrove, "Developing an Effective Blend of Process and Technology in the New Era of Performance Management," *Compensation and Benefits Review*, January/February 2003, p. 27.

3. Howard Risher, "Getting Serious about Performance Management," *Compensation and Benefits Review*, November/December 2005, p. 19.

4. Mushin Lee and Byoungho Son, "The Effects of Appraisal Review Content on Employees' Reactions and Performance," *International Journal of Human Resource Management* 1 (February 1998), p. 283; David Antonioni, "Improve the Management Process Before Discontinuing Performance Appraisals," *Compensation and Benefits Review*, May–June 1994, p. 29. See also Jonathan Siegel, "86 Your Appraisal Process?" *HR Magazine*, October 2000, pp. 199–206; Steve Bates, "Performance Appraisals: Some Improvement Needed," *HR Magazine* April 2003, p. 12.

5. Clinton Wingrove, "Developing an Effective Blend of Process and Technology" p. 27; See also, "IBM Was Named a Recipient of Intel Corporation's Prestigious 2003 Supplier Continuous Improvement Award," *Purchasing*, May 6, 2004, v133, i8, p. 26.

6. Vesa Vuutari and Marja Tahbanainen, "The Antecedents of Performance Management Among Finnish Expatriates," *Journal of Human Resource Management* 13, no. 1 (February 2002), pp. 53–75.

7. See, for example, Doug Cederblom and Dan Pemerl, "From Performance Appraisal to Performance Management: One Agency's Experience," *Personnel Management* 31, no. 2 (Summer 2002), pp. 131–140.

8. Gary Yukl, *Skills for Managers and Leaders* (Upper Saddle River, NJ: Prentice Hall, 1991), pp. 132–33; see also Gary Latham, "Cognitive and Motivational Effects of Participation: A Mediator Study," *Journal of Organizational Behavior*, January 1994, pp. 49–64.

9. Yukl, *Skills for Managers and Leaders*, p. 133. See also Miriam Erez, Daniel Gopher, and Nira Arzi, "Effects of Goal Difficulty, Self-Set Goals, and Monetary Rewards on Dual Task Performance," *Organizational Behavior and Human Decision Processes*, December 1990, pp. 247–269; and Thomas Lee, "Explaining the Assigned Goal-Incentive Interaction: The Role of Self-Efficacy and Personal Goals," *Journal of Management*, July–August 1997, pp. 541–550.

10. Yukl, *Skills for Manager and Leaders*, p. 133.

11. See, for example, Robert Renn, "Further Examination of the Measurement of Properties of Leifer & McGannon's 1998 Goal Acceptance and Goal Commitment Scales," *Journal of Occupational and Organizational Psychology*, March 1999, pp. 107–114.

12. Experts debate the pros and cons of tying appraisals to pay decisions. One side argues that doing so distorts the appraisals. A recent study concludes the opposite. Based on an analysis of surveys from over 24,000 employees in more than 6000 workplaces in Canada, the researchers concluded: (1) linking the employees' pay to their performance appraisals contributed to improved pay satisfaction; (2) even when appraisals are *not* directly linked to pay, they apparently contributed to pay satisfaction, "probably through mechanisms related to perceived organizational justice;" and (3) whether or not the employees received performance pay, "individuals who do not receive performance appraisals are significantly less satisfied with their pay." Mary Jo Ducharme, et al., "Exploring the Links between Performance Appraisals and Pay Satisfaction," *Compensation and Benefits Review*, September/October 2005, pp. 46–52. See also Robert Morgan, "Making the Most of Performance Management Systems," *Compensation and Benefits Review*, September/October 2006, pp. 22–27.

13. John (Jack) Welch, broadcast interview at Fairfield University, C-Span (May 5, 2001).

14. Kurt H. Loess and Ugur Yavas, "Human Resource Collaboration Issues in International Joint Ventures: A Study of U.S.-Japanese Auto Supply IJVs," *Management International Review* 43, no. 13 (July 2003), p. 311.

15. Howard Risher, "Getting Serious about Performance Management," *Compensation and Benefits Review*, November/December 2005, pp. 18–26.

16. Del Jones, "More Firms Cut Workers Ranked at Bottom to Make Way for Talent," *USA Today*, May 30, 2001, p. B01.

17. Steve Bates, "Forced Ranking," *HR Magazine*, June 2003, pp. 63–68.

18. Steven Cullen, et al., "Forced Distribution Rating Systems and the Improvement of Workforce Potential: A Baseline Simulation," *Personnel Psychology* 58, (2005): 1.

19. Jena McGregor, "The Struggle to Measure Performance," *BusinessWeek*, January 9, 2006, p. 26.

20. "Survey Says Problems with Forced Ranking Include Lower Morale and Costly Turnover," *BNA Bulletin to Management*, (September 16, 2004), p. 297.

21. Steve Bates, "Forced Ranking: Why Grading Employees on a Scale Relative to Each Other Forces a Hard Look at Finding Keepers, Losers May Become Weepers," *HR Magazine* 48, no. 6, (June 2003), p. 62.

22. Clinton Wingrove, "Developing an Effective Blend of Process and Technology," p. 26.

23. "Straight Talk About Grading Employees on a Curve," *BNA Bulletin to Management*, November 1, 2001, p. 351.

24. See, for example, Timothy Keaveny and Anthony McGann, "A Comparison of Behavioral Expectation Scales and Graphic Rating Scales," *Journal of Applied Psychology*, 60 (1975), pp. 695–703. See also John Ivancevich, "A Longitudinal Study of Behavioral Expectation Scales: Attitudes and Performance," *Journal of Applied Psychology* 30, no. 3 (Autumn 1986), pp. 619–628.

25. Based on Donald Schwab, Herbert Heneman III, and Thomas DeCotiis, "Behaviorally Anchored Scales: A Review of the Literature," *Personnel Psychology*, 28 (1975), pp. 549–562. For a discussion, see also Uco Wiersma and Gary Latham, "The Practicality of Behavioral Observation Scales, Behavioral Expectation Scales, and Trait Scales," *Personnel Psychology* 30, no. 3 (Autumn 1986), pp. 619–689.

26. Lawrence Fogli, Charles Hullin, and Milton Blood, "Development of First Level Behavioral Job Criteria," *Journal of Applied Psychology* 55 (1971), pp. 3–8. See also Terry Dickenson and Peter Fellinger, "A Comparison of the Behaviorally Anchored Rating and Fixed Standard Scale Formats," *Journal of Applied Psychology*, April 1980, pp. 147–154; and Joseph Maiorca, "How to Construct Behaviorally Anchored Rating Scales (BARS) for Employee Evaluations," *Supervision*, August 1997, pp. 15–19.

27. Kevin R. Murphy and Joseph Constans, "Behavioral Anchors as a Source of Bias in Rating," *Journal of Applied Psychology* 72, no. 4 (November 1987), pp. 573–577; Aharon Tziner, "A Comparison of Three Methods of Performance Appraisal with Regard to Goal Properties, Goal Perception, and Ratee Satisfaction," *Group and Organization Management* 25, no. 2 (June 2000), pp. 175–191.

28. "Appraisal Puts 15 Leading HRIS's to the Test," *BNA Bulletin to Management*, October 26, 2000, p. 340.

29. "Software Simplifies Performance Reviews, But Is It Affecting Employee Development," *BNA Bulletin to Management*, March 27, 2003, p. 97.

30. Gary Meyer, "Performance Reviews Made Easy, Paperless," *HR Magazine*, October 2000, pp. 181–184.

31. Ann Harrington, "Workers of the World, Rate Your Boss?" *Fortune*, 2000, pp. 340–342.

32. Jeffrey Stanton and Janet Barnes-Farrell, "Effects of Electronic Performance Monitoring on Personal Control, Task Satisfaction, and Task Performance," *Journal of Applied Psychology* 81, no. 6 (1996), p. 738. See also Stoney Alder and Maureen Ambrose, "Towards Understanding Fairness Judgments Associated with Computer Performance Monitoring: An Integration of the Feedback, Justice, and Monitoring Research," *Human Resource Management Review* 15, no. 1, March 2005, pp. 43–67.

33. Andrew Solomonson and Charles Lance, "Examination of the Relationship Between True Halo and Halo Effect in Performance Ratings," *Journal of Applied Psychology* 82, no. 5 (1997), pp. 665–674. Andrew Solomonson and Charles Lance, "Examination of the Relationship Between True Halo and Halo Effect in Performance Ratings," *Journal of Applied Psychology* 82, no. 5 (1997), pp. 665–674.

34. Ted Turnasella, "Dagwood Bumstead, Will You Ever Get That Raise?" *Compensation and Benefits Review*, September–October 1995, pp. 25–27. See also Solomonson and Lance, "Examination of the Relationship Between True Halo and Halo Effect," pp. 665–674.

35. Madeleine Heilman, et al., "Penalties for Success: Reactions to Women Who Succeed at Male Gender Type Tasks," *Journal of Applied Psychology* 89, no. 3 (2004): 416–427. Managers may not rate successful female managers negatively (for instance, in terms of likeability and boss desirability) when they see the woman as supportive, caring, and sensitive to their needs. Madeleine Heilmann and Tyler Okimoto, "Why Are Women Penalized for Success at Male Tasks?: The Implied Communality Deficit," *Journal of Applied Psychology* 92, no. 1, 2007, pp. 81–92.

36. I. M. Jawahar and Charles Williams, "Where All the Children Are Above Average: The Performance Appraisal Purpose Effect," *Personnel Psychology* 50 (1997), p. 921.

37. Annette Simmons, "When Performance Reviews Fail," *Training and Development* 57, no. 9 (September 2003), pp. 47–53.

38. Clinton Wingrove, "Developing an Effective Blend of Process and Technology," pp. 25–30.

39. "Flawed Ranking System Revives Workers' Bias Claim," *BNA Bulletin to Management*, June 28, 2005, p. 206.

40. Karen Lyness and Madeline Heilman, "When Fit Is Fundamental: Performance Evaluations and Promotions Of Upper-Level Female and Male Managers," *Journal of Applied Psychology*, 2006, vol. 91, no. 4, pp. 777–75.

41. Gary Gregures et al., "A Field Study of the Effects of Rating Purpose on the Quality of Multisource Ratings," *Personnel Psychology* 56 (2003), pp. 1–21.

42. Jane Halpert, Midge Wilson, and Julia Hickman, "Pregnancy as a Source of Bias in Performance Appraisals," *Journal of Organizational Behavior* 14 (1993), pp. 649–663.

43. Ibid., p. 655.

44. Manuel London, Edward Mone, and John C. Scott, "Performance Management and Assessment: Methods for Improved Rater Accuracy and Employee Goal Setting," *Human Resource Management*, Winter 2004, vol. 43, no. 4, pp. 319–336.

45. Manuel London, Edward Mone, and John C. Scott, "Performance Management and Assessment: Methods for Improved Rater Accuracy and Employee Goal Setting," *Human Resource Management*, Winter 2004, vol. 43, no. 4, pp. 319–336.

46. "Assessing Performance," *Training and Development* 55, no. 5 (May 2001), p. 133.

47. Angelo DeNisi and Lawrence Peters, "Organization of Information in Memory and the Performance Appraisal Process: Evidence from the Field," *Journal of Applied Psychology* 81, no. 6 (1996), pp. 717–737.

48. Juan Sanchez and Philip DeLaTorre, "A Second Look at the Relationship Between Rating and Behavioral Accuracy in Performance Appraisal," *Journal of Applied Psychology* 81, no. 1 (1996), p. 7.

49. Arup Varna et al., "Interpersonal Affect and Performance Appraisal: A Field Study," *Personnel Psychology* 49 (1996), pp. 341–360.

50. R. G. Downey, F. F. Medland, and L. G. Yates, "Evaluation of a Peer Rating System for Predicting Subsequent Promotion of Senior Military Officers," *Journal of Applied Psychology* 61 (April 1976); see also Julie Barclay and Lynn Harland, "Peer Performance Appraisals: The Impact of Rater Competence, Rater Location, and Rating Correctability on Fairness Perceptions," *Group and Organization Management* 20, no. 1 (March 1995), pp. 39–60.

51. Vanessa Druskat and Steven Wolf, "Effects and Timing of Developmental Peer Appraisals in Self-Managing Workgroups," *Journal of Applied Psychology* 84, no. 1 (1999), pp. 58–74.

52. Chockalingam Viswesvaran, Denize Ones, and Frank Schmidt, "Comparative Analysis of the Reliability of Job Performance Ratings," *Journal of Applied Psychology* 81, no. 5 (1996), pp. 557–574. See also Kevin Murphy, et al., "Raters Who Pursue Different Goals Give Different Ratings," *Journal of Applied Psychology*, 2004, vol. 89, no. 1, pp. 158–164.

53. David Martin et al., "The Legal Ramifications of Performance Appraisal: The Growing Significance," *Public Personnel Management* 29, no. 3 (Fall 2000), pp. 381–383.

54. This is based on Kenneth L. Sovereign, *Personnel Law* (Upper Saddle River, NJ: Prentice Hall, 1994), pp. 113–114. See also "Avoiding HR Lawsuits," *Credit Union Executive*, November–December 1999, p. 6.

55. Wayne Cascio and H. John Bernardin, "Implications of Performance Appraisal Litigation for Personnel Decisions," *Personnel Psychology*, Summer 1981, pp. 211–212; Gerald Barrett and Mary Kernan, "Performance Appraisal and Terminations: A Review of Court Decisions since *Brito v. Zia* with Implications for Personnel Practices," *Personnel Psychology* 40, no. 3 (Autumn 1987), pp. 489–504; Elaine Pulakos, *Performance Management*, SHRM Foundation, 2004.

56. James Austin, Peter Villanova, and Hugh Hindman, "Legal Requirements and Technical Guidelines Involved in Implementing Performance Appraisal Systems," in Gerald Ferris and

M. Ronald Buckley (eds.), *Human Resources Management*, 3rd ed. (Upper Saddle River, NJ: Prentice Hall, 1996), pp. 271–288.

57. Ibid., p. 282.

58. Jon Werner and Mark Bolino, "Explaining U.S. Courts of Appeals' Decisions Involving Performance Appraisal: Accuracy, Fairness, and Validation," *Personnel Psychology* 50 (1997), pp. 1–24.

59. George Thornton III, "Psychometric Properties of Self-Appraisal of Job Performance," *Personnel Psychology* 33 (Summer 1980), p. 265. See also Cathy Anderson, Jack Warner, and Cassie Spencer, "Inflation Bias in Self-Assessment Evaluations: Implications for Valid Employee Selection," *Journal of Applied Psychology* 69, no. 4 (November 1984), pp. 574–580; and Shaul Fox and Vossi Dinur, "Validity of Self-Assessment: A Field Evaluation," *Personnel Psychology* 41, no. 3 (Autumn 1988), pp. 581–592. Yet, such findings may be culturally related. One study compared self and supervisor ratings in "other-oriented" cultures (as in Asia, where values tend to emphasize teams). It found here that self and supervisor ratings were related. M. Audrey Korsgaard, et al., "The Effect of Other Orientation on Self–Supervisor Rating Agreement," *Journal of Organizational Behavior* 25, no. 7, November 2004, pp. 873–891.

60. Forest Jourden and Chip Heath, "The Evaluation Gap in Performance Perceptions: Illusory Perceptions of Groups and Individuals," *Journal of Applied Psychology* 81, no. 4 (August 1996), pp. 369–379. See also Sheri Ostroff, "Understanding Self-Other Agreement: A Look at Rater and Ratee Characteristics, Context, and Outcomes," *Personnel Psychology* 57, no. 2, (Summer 2004), pp. 333–375.

61. Richard Reilly, James Smither, and Nicholas Vasilopoulos, "A Longitudinal Study of Upward Feedback," *Personnel Psychology* 49 (1996), pp. 599–612.

62. Ibid., p. 599.

63. "360-Degree Feedback on the Rise, Survey Finds," *BNA Bulletin to Management*, January 23, 1997, p. 31. See also Christopher Mabey, "Closing the Circle: Participant Views of a 360-Degree Feedback Program," *Human Resource Management Journal* 11, no. 1 (2001), pp. 41–53.

64. Carol Hymowitz, "Do 360-Degree Job Reviews by Colleagues Promote Honesty or Insults?" p. B-1.

65. Terry Beehr et al., "Evaluation of 360-Degree Feedback Ratings: Relationships with Each Other and with Performance and Selection Predictors," *Journal of Organizational Behavior* 22, no. 7 (November 2001), pp. 775–778.

66. James Smither et al., "Does Performance Improve Following Multi-Score Feedback? A Theoretical Model, Meta Analysis, and Review of Empirical Findings," *Personnel Psychology* 58, (2005): 33–36.

67. Christine Hagan, et al., "Predicting Assessment Center Performance With 360-Degree, Top-Down, and Customer-Based Competency Assessments," *Human Resource Management,* Fall 2006, vol. 45, no. 3, pp. 357–390.

68. Bruce Pfau and Ira Kay, "Does a 360-Degree Feedback Negatively Affect the Company Performance?" *HR Magazine*, June 2002, pp. 55–59.

69. Scott Wimer, "The Dark Side of 360-Degree Feedback," *Training and Development*, September 2002, pp. 37–42.

70. Maury Pieperl, "Getting 360-Degree Job Feedback Right," *Harvard Business Review*, January 2001, p. 147. See also, Leanne Atwater, et al., "Multisource Feedback: Lessons Learned and Implications for Practice," *Human Resource Management*, Summer 2007, vol. 46, no. 2, p. 285.

71. Annette Simmons, "When Performance Reviews Fail," *Training and Development* 57, no. 9 (September 2003), pp. 47–53.

72. Brian Smith et al., "Current Trends in Performance Appraisal: An Examination of Managerial Practice," *SAM Advanced Management Journal* 61, no. 3 (Summer 1996), p. 16; "Companies Appraise to Improve Development," *Personnel Today*, Feb. 25, 2003, p. 51.

73. D. Bradford Neary, "Creating a Company-Wide, Online, Performance Management System: A Case at TRW, Inc.," *Human Resource Management* 41, no. 4, (Winter 2002), pp. 491–498.

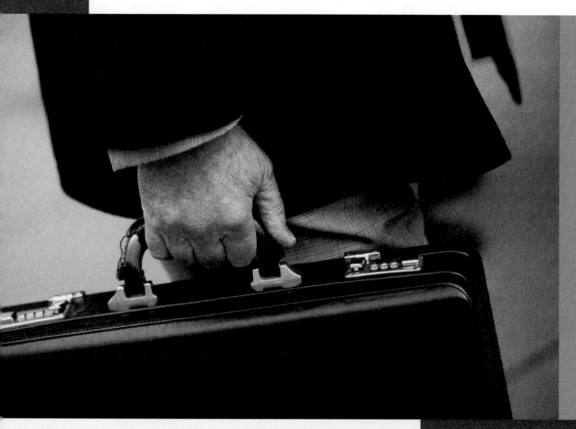

10 Managing Careers

Reviewing demographic trends, pharmacy chain CVS knew it had a problem. As a retail chain, CVS relied on an army of young people to staff its stores—to restock shelves, be cashiers, and serve as clerks in each store's various departments. The problem was that the number of young people entering the workforce was beginning to shrink, while the number of older workers was rising. CVS executives knew they needed some way to tap into this growing pool of older workers. •

After studying this chapter, you should be able to:

1 Compare employers' traditional and career planning-oriented HR focuses.
2 Explain the employee's, manager's, and employer's career development roles.
3 Describe the issues to consider when making promotion decisions.
4 Describe the methods for enhancing diversity through career management.
5 Answer the question: How can career development foster employee commitment?

Chapter 9 focused on appraising employees' performance. After appraising performance, it is advisable to address the employees' career-related issues. The main purpose of this chapter is to help you be more effective at managing your employees' careers. We discuss the employee's, manager's, and employer's roles in career development, and the procedures for managing promotions and transfers. We also discuss enhancing diversity through career management, and, finally, the career management steps an employer can take to foster employee commitment. The appendix to this chapter provides specific career-related tools and techniques. This chapter completes Part 3, which addressed training, appraisal, and development. Once you've trained and appraised employees, you need to turn to the question of how to pay them, the topic we cover in the next three chapters.

THE BASICS OF CAREER MANAGEMENT

career
The occupational positions a person has had over many years.

We may define **career** as the "occupational positions a person has had over many years." Many people look back on their careers, knowing that what they might have achieved they did achieve, and that their career goals were satisfied. Others are less fortunate and feel that, at least in their careers, their lives and their potential went unfulfilled.

career management
The process for enabling employees to better understand and develop their career skills and interests, and to use these skills and interests more effectively.

Employers have a big effect on employees' careers. Some institute formal *career management* processes, while others do little. We can define **career management** as a process for enabling employees to better understand and develop their career skills and interests, and to use these skills and interests most effectively both within the company and after they leave the firm. Specific career management activities might include providing realistic career-oriented appraisals, posting open jobs, and offering formal career development activities. **Career development** is the lifelong series of activities (such as workshops) that contribute to a person's career exploration, establishment, success, and fulfillment. **Career planning** is the deliberate process through which someone becomes aware of his or her personal skills, interests, knowledge, motivations, and other characteristics; acquires information about opportunities and choices; identifies career-related goals; and establishes action plans to attain specific goals.

career development
The lifelong series of activities that contribute to a person's career exploration, establishment, success, and fulfillment.

career planning
The deliberate process through which someone becomes aware of personal skills, interests, knowledge, motivations, and other characteristics; and establishes action plans to attain specific goals.

Careers Today

Careers today are not what they were several years ago. People traditionally viewed careers as a sort of upward staircase from job to job, more often than not with just one or, at most, a few firms. Today, mergers, outsourcings, consolidations, and more or less endless downsizings have changed the ground rules, at least for most people. Many people do still move up from job to job. But more often they find themselves having to re-invent themselves—thus, the sales rep, laid off by a publishing firm that's just merged, may reinvent her career for the next few years as an account executive at a media-oriented accounting firm.[1]

Careers today differ in other ways from a few years ago. With increasing numbers of women pursuing professional and managerial careers, families must balance the challenges associated with dual career pressures. At the same time, what people want from their careers seems to be changing. Whereas baby boomers—those retiring in the next 10 or so years—by and large were job and employer-focused, those entering the job market now often value work arrangements that provide more opportunities for having more balanced lives.

These changes have implications for the human resource function. A few years ago, the assumption—the "psychological contract" between employer and employee—was, often, "You be loyal to us, and we'll take care of you." Today, employees know they must take care of themselves. The psychological contract is more like, "I'll do my best for you, but I expect you to provide me with the development and learning that will prepare me for

TABLE 10-1 Traditional Versus Career Development Focus

HR Activity	Traditional Focus	Career Development Focus
Human resource planning	Analyzes jobs, skills, tasks—present and future. Projects needs. Uses statistical data.	Adds information about individual interests, preferences, and the like to replacement plans.
Recruiting and placement	Matching organization's needs with qualified individuals.	Matches individual and jobs based on variables including employees' career interests and aptitudes.
Training and development	Provides opportunities for learning skills, information, and attitudes related to job.	Provides career path information. Adds individual development plans.
Performance appraisal	Rating and/or rewards.	Adds development plans and individual goal setting.
Compensation and benefits	Rewards for time, productivity, talent, and so on.	Adds tuition reimbursement plans, compensation for non-job-related activities such as United Way.

Source: Adapted from Fred L. Otte and Peggy G. Hutcheson, *Helping Employees Manage Careers* (Upper Saddle River, NJ: Prentice Hall, 1992), p. 10, and www.ge.com.cn/careers/career_management.html, accessed May 18, 2007.

the day I must move on, and for having the work-life balance that I desire."[2] John Madigan, vice president of HR for the Hartford Insurance Company's 3,500-member IT group, discovered how important development activities can be. He conducted a survey. Of the employees who left the organization, "Ninety percent of people who left voluntarily talked about [the lack of] career and professional development and the level of support their managers gave them in this area," he says.[3]

① Compare employers' traditional and career planning-oriented HR focuses.

Career Development Today

This shift in philosophy means that many employers have strengthened the career focus of their human resources activities. The focus is no longer just, "how can you best serve our company?" Today, the reality for most people is that they'll have to change employers (and perhaps careers) several times during their work lives. Employees therefore expect activities like selection, training, and appraisal to serve their own longer-term career needs, too. The emphasis now is thus on using HR activities and milestones (like annual appraisals) to facilitate career self-analysis, development, and management.[4] Table 10-1 summarizes how employers can use activities such as training and appraisal to support such a **career planning and development** focus.

career planning and development
The deliberate process through which a person becomes aware of personal career-related attributes and the lifelong series of steps that contribute to his or her career fulfillment.

Career development programs needn't be complicated. Employees report that receiving performance feedback, having individual development plans, and having access to non-technical skills training would probably reduce the likelihood they'd leave their firms. Yet, only about a fourth of the respondents in one survey had individual development plans.[5] Figure 10-1 illustrates a simple career plan that can derive from such an approach.[6]

John Madigan's experience at the Hartford Insurance Company illustrates why it's not just the employees who benefit from this newer career development approach. Certainly, it helps employees. They get the skills they need to understand their career options, and, often, the support required to pursue them. However employers also gain. As two experts put it, "employers provide the tools, environment, and skill development opportunities for employees, and then employees are better equipped to serve the company and build it to its potential."[7] Furthermore, it can foster commitment and assist in the firm's employee recruitment and retention efforts: "The most attractive proposition an employer can make

FIGURE 10-1

Employee Career Development Plan

Source: Reprinted from www.HR.BLR.com with permission of the publisher *Business and Legal Reports Inc.*, 141 Mill Rock Road East, Old Saybrook, CT © 2004.

Employee Career Development Plan

Employee: _____   Position: _____

Manager: _____   Department: _____

Date of Appraisal: _____

1. What is the next logical step up for this employee, and when do you think he or she will be ready for it?

Probable Next Job:	When Ready:			
	Now	6 Months	1 Year	2 Years
1.	☐	☐	☐	☐
2.	☐	☐	☐	☐
3.	☐	☐	☐	☐

2. What is the highest probable promotion within five years?

3. What does this employee need to prepare for promotion?

• Knowledge: _____
  _____

  Action Plan: _____
  _____

• Still Training: _____
  _____

  Action Plan: _____
  _____

• Management Training: _____
  _____

  Action Plan: _____
  _____

today is that in five years the employee will have more knowledge and be more employable than now. That should be the acid test for any career development program."[8]

ROLES IN CAREER PLANNING AND DEVELOPMENT

❷ Explain the employee's, manager's, and employer's career development roles.

Ideally, the employer, employee, and manager all play roles in planning, guiding, and developing the employee's career (see Table 10-2). We'll look at each.

The Employee's Role

While the employer and manager play roles in guiding employees' careers, this is one task that no employee should ever abandon to his or her manager or employer. For the individual

TABLE 10-2 Roles in Career Development

Individual

- Accept responsibility for your own career.
- Assess your interests, skills, and values.
- Seek out career information and resources.
- Establish goals and career plans.
- Utilize development opportunities.
- Talk with your manager about your career.
- Follow through on realistic career plans.

Manager

- Provide timely and accurate performance feedback.
- Provide developmental assignments and support.
- Participate in career development discussions with subordinates.
- Support employee development plans.

Employer

- Communicate mission, policies, and procedures.
- Provide training and development opportunities including workshops.
- Provide career information and career programs.
- Offer a variety of career paths.
- Provide career-oriented performance feedback.
- Provide mentoring opportunities to support growth and self-direction.
- Provide employees with individual development plans.
- Provide academic learning assistance programs.

Source: Adapted from Fred L. Otte and Peggy G. Hutcheson, *Helping Employees Manage Careers* (Upper Saddle River, NJ: Prentice Hall, 1992), p. 56; www.ge.com.cn/careers/career_management.html; and www_03.ibm.com/employment/us.cd_career_dev.shtml, accessed May 18, 2007.

employee, *career planning* means matching individual strengths and weaknesses with occupational opportunities and threats. In other words, the person wants to pursue occupations, jobs, and a career that capitalize on his or her interests, aptitudes, values, and skills. He or she wants to choose occupations, jobs, and a career that make sense in terms of projected future demand for various types of occupations. The consequences of a bad choice (or of no choice) are too severe to leave such decisions to others.

Of course, career planning is no guarantee. Several years ago, a career as a systems analyst or computer engineer seemed like a ticket to success, at least until many firms began outsourcing jobs like these to Asia. Yet, uncertainties like these only underscore the need for monitoring the job market, so as to be better positioned to move when a career change is required. Luck, as someone once said, tends to come to those who are best prepared. The appendix to this chapter, "Managing Your Career" (see page 402) explains the career planning process from the employee's point of view.

Many people make the mistake of changing jobs or occupations when a smaller change would suffice. Dissatisfied at work, they assume it must be the job or the occupation. But, why decide to switch from being a lawyer to a teacher, when it's not the profession but that law firm's 80-hour weeks that's the problem?

The employee needs to use a process of elimination. For example, some people may like their occupations and the employers for whom they work, but not how their specific jobs are structured. Others may find their employers' ways of doing things are the problem. Or, it may in fact be the occupation.

In any case, the solution needs to fit the cause. For example, if, after thinking it through, you are satisfied with your occupation and where you work, but not with your job as it's organized now, try reconfiguring it. For example, consider alternative work arrangements such as flexible hours or telecommuting; delegate or eliminate the job functions you least prefer; and seek out a "stretch assignment" that will let you work on something you find more challenging.[9]

Mentors   Studies also suggest that having a mentor—a senior person who can be a sounding board for your career questions and concerns, and provide career-related guidance and assistance—can significantly enhance career satisfaction and success.[10] Here, the employer can play an important role, for instance by encouraging senior managers to serve as mentors. But it is still usually the employee's responsibility to find a mentor and to maintain a productive relationship. Suggestions for doing so include:

- Choose an appropriate potential mentor. The mentor should be objective enough to offer good career advice, so someone who's not your direct boss may be best. Many people seek out someone who is one or two levels above their current boss.
- Don't be surprised if you're turned down. Not everyone is willing to undertake this time-consuming commitment.
- Make it easier for a potential mentor to agree to your request by making it clear ahead of time what you expect in terms of time and advice.
- Have an agenda. Bring an agenda to your first mentoring meeting that lays out key issues and topics for discussion.
- Respect the mentor's time. Be selective about the work-related issues that you bring to the table. Furthermore, the mentoring relationship generally should not involve personal problems or issues.[11]

Mentoring may be formal or informal. Informally, mid- and senior-level managers may voluntarily help less-experienced employees—for instance, by giving them career advice and helping them navigate office politics. Other informal means include increasing the opportunities for networking and interactions among diverse employees. We'll see below that many firms also have formal mentoring programs. For instance, the employer may pair protégés with potential mentors, and provide training to help mentor and protégé better understand their respective responsibilities.

In this chapter, we'll focus primarily on the manager's and the employer's role in the employee's career development process (again, see the appendix for what the employee can do). The "When You're on Your Own" feature illustrates the manager's role in the process. Let's turn now to the employer's role.

The Employer's Role

All or most of the employer's human resources activities can support career development efforts. Table 10-3 presents a list of such organizational career planning and management practices.

A survey illustrates the popularity of various employer career management practices. The researchers studied 524 organizations in the United Kingdom to determine how they used 17 career management practices. "Posting job openings" was the most popular practice. The other top career practices, in descending order, were: formal education;

When You're on Your OWN

Employee Career Development

Whether or not the employer has a career development program, the individual manager can do several things to support his or her subordinates' career development needs. For example, when the subordinate first begins his or her job, discuss the importance of developing a career plan, as well as ways in which you can help the employee achieve career goals. The manager can schedule regular performance appraisals and, at these reviews,

focus on the extent to which the employee's current skills and performance are consistent with the person's career goals. The manager can provide the employee with an informal career development plan like that in Figure 10-1. And, the manager can provide mentoring assistance, and keep subordinates informed about how they can utilize the firm's current career-related benefits.[12]

TABLE 10-3 Possible Employer Career Planning and Development Practices

Job postings

Formal education/tuition reimbursement

Performance appraisal for career planning

Counseling by manager

Lateral moves/job rotations

Counseling by HR

Pre-retirement programs

Succession planning

Formal mentoring

Common career paths

Dual ladder career paths

Career booklets/pamphlets

Written individual career plans

Career workshops

Assessment center

Upward appraisal

Appraisal committees

Training programs for managers

Orientation/induction programs

Special needs (highfliers)

Special needs (dual-career couples)

Diversity management

Expatriation/repatriation

Source: Yehuda Baruch, "Career Development in Organizations and Beyond: Balancing Traditional and Contemporary Viewpoints," *Human Resource Management Review*, vol. 16, 2006, p. 131.

career-oriented performance appraisals; counseling by managers; lateral, developmental moves; counseling by HR; retirement preparation; and succession planning.[13] Many firms, like Sun Microsystems, have relatively formal programs. Sun maintains a career development center staffed by certified counselors. It helps employees fill development gaps and choose Sun career opportunities. The firm believes its program helps explain why its average employee tenure of four years is more than twice that estimated at other Silicon Valley firms.[14]

reality shock
Results of a period that may occur at the initial career entry when the new employee's high job expectations confront the reality of a boring, unchallenging job.

Life-Cycle Career Management   The employer's career development responsibilities depend somewhat on how long the employee has been with the firm. Before hiring, *realistic job previews* can help candidates gauge whether the job is indeed for them, and particularly whether a job's demands are a good fit with a candidate's skills and interests. Especially for recent college graduates, the first job can be crucial for building confidence and a more realistic picture of what he or she can and cannot do: Providing *challenging first jobs* (rather than relegating new employees to "jobs where they can't do any harm"), and having an experienced *mentor* who can help the person learn the ropes, are thus important. Some refer to this as preventing **reality shock**, a phenomenon that occurs when a new employee's high expectations and enthusiasm confront the reality of a boring, unchallenging job.

job rotation
Moving an employee through a preplanned series of positions in order to prepare the person for an enhanced role with the company.

After the person has been on the job for a while, an employer can take steps to help further the employee's career. *Career-oriented appraisals*—in which the manager is trained not just to appraise the employee but also to match the person's strengths and weaknesses with a feasible career path and required development work—is one important step. Similarly, providing periodic, planned **job rotation** can help the person develop a more realistic picture of what he or she is (and is not) good at, and thus the sort of future career moves that might be best. Formal *job postings, promotion-from-within policies*, and *training* help ensure employees can continue to use their skills to the best advantage. Dow Chemical instituted a "People Success System" to facilitate employees' career planning and development. The system includes a list of competencies for every job at Dow. Employees can review the competencies required for their own jobs (or for others they might be interested in), and identify their own developmental needs. *Pre-retirement counseling* and *transition policies* (such as phased retirement with part-time work) then play a role toward the end of the employee's career.

Mentoring can be formal or informal, but usually consists of mid- or senior-level managers helping less-experienced colleagues with career advice and tips on how to avoid political problems and move up the ladder.

Mentoring Programs   Many companies, including Marriott International, Charles Schwab, and Bank of America have formal mentoring programs. Here more senior professionals and managers team with less experienced protégés with the aim of assisting the protégés to improve their performance and career progress.[15] The accounting firm KPMG made an online mentoring program part of its "employer of choice" initiative, which also includes job-sharing time off, flexible work schedules, and community volunteer opportunities with pay and benefits.[16] Dow Chemical Co. has a Web-based mentor technology similar to a Google search. It enables Dow employees who seek a mentor to create a list of names of potential Dow mentors.[17]

mentoring

Formal or informal programs in which mid- and senior-level managers help less-experienced employees—for instance, by giving them career advice and helping them navigate political pitfalls.

Studies suggest several ways to improve a **mentoring** program's effectiveness. For example, one study found no evidence that it mattered whether participation was mandatory or voluntary. However, having input into choosing the mentor was important. Thus both the mentor and protégé should have some input into the matching. Providing the participants with training aimed at enabling them to get the most out of the mentoring relationship was also important.[18]

Innovative Corporate Career Development Initiatives

Employers' corporate career development initiatives may also include innovative programs like those listed below.

1. *Provide each employee with an individual budget.* He or she can use this budget for learning about career options and personal development.[19]
2. *Offer on-site or online career centers.* These include a Web-based or off-line library of career development materials, career workshops, workshops on related topics (such as time management), and individual career coaches for career guidance. The employer may organize an online career center using tools like those in the chapter appendix. First USA Bank has what it calls the Opportunity Knocks program. Its purpose is to help employees crystallize their career goals and achieve them within the company. In addition to career development training and follow-up support, First USA Bank outfitted special career development facilities at its work sites that employees can use on company time. These contain materials such as career assessment and planning tools.[20]
3. *Encourage role reversal.* Have employees temporarily work in different positions in order to develop a better appreciation of their occupational strengths and weaknesses.
4. *Establish a "corporate campus."* Make career and development courses and programs available, perhaps through partnerships with local colleges or consultants.
5. *Help organize "career success teams."* These are small groups of employees from the same or different departments who meet periodically to network and support one another in achieving their career goals.
6. *Provide career coaches.* For example, Allmerica Financial Corp., hired 20 career development coaches to assist its 850-person information technology staff. This coaching program was part of a broader organizational change program, to centralize information technology and create small information technology teams. The coaches help individual employees identify their development needs, and obtain the training, professional development, and networking opportunities that they need to satisfy those needs.[21]

   Career coaches usually work one-on-one with individual employees to help them use career assessment tools and identify their training and development options.[22] However, a new breed of coach is emerging. Used mostly for companies' highest-level managers, these "executive coaches" provide assessment and advice that often digs quite deeply into the executive's personality, and into how the person's personal life may be influencing his or her career.

   Career coaches should help employees create clear one- to five-year plans showing where their careers with the firm may lead. Then, base developmental plans on the skills employees will need to move up.[23]
7. *Provide career planning workshops.* A career planning workshop is "a planned learning event in which participants are expected to be actively involved, completing career planning exercises and inventories and participating in career skills practice sessions."[24] A typical workshop includes a self-assessment, an environmental assessment, and goal-setting and action-planning segment. See Figure 10-2 for a typical agenda.

Before the program—Two weeks prior to the workshop participants receive a letter confirming their participation in the program and package of work to be completed before coming to the workshop. The exercises in this package include skills inventory, values identification, life accomplishments inventory, and a reading describing career direction options.

Day 1

8:30–10:00 Introduction and Overview of Career Planning

Welcome and Introduction to Program

> Welcome by general manager
> Overview of agenda and outcomes
> Participant introductions (statements of expectations for the program)

Overview of Career Development

> Company's philosophy
> Why career planning is needed
> What career planning is and is not
> Career planning model

10:00–Noon Self-Assessment: Part 1

Individual Self-Assessment: Values

> Values card sort exercise
> Reconciling with values pre-work
> Introduce career planning summary work sheet

Individual Self-Assessment: Skills

> Motivated skills exercise
> Examining life accomplishments (synthesize with pre-work)
> Identifying accomplishment themes
> Preferred work skills (from pre-work inventory)
> Fill in career planning summary work sheet

1:00–3:00 Self-Assessment: Part 2

Individual Self-Assessment: Career Anchors

> Career anchoring pattern exercise
> Small group discussions
> Fill in career planning summary work sheet

Individual Self-Assessment: Preferences

> What success means to me
> Skills, knowledge, personal qualities
> Fill in career planning summary work sheet

Individual Self-Assessment: Career Path Pattern

> Synthesize with direction options from pre-work
> Fill in career planning summary work sheet

3:30–4:30 Environmental Assessment

Information About the Company

> Goals, growth areas, expectations, turnover, competition for jobs, skills for the future
> Fill in career planning summary work sheet
> Personal career profile
> Reality test, how you see self at this point by sharing

Day 2

8:30–10:00 Goal Setting

> Warm-Up Exercise
> Review of where we've been and where we're going
> Setting goals—where do I want to be?
> Creating an ideal future
> Future skills and accomplishments
> Desired lifestyle
> Life and career goals

10:15–1:30 Environmental Assessment: Part 2

> Career resources in the company
> Introduce support services and hand out information
> Marketing yourself—what it takes to achieve your goals here
> Describe resource people who will be with the group for lunch and brainstorm questions/issues to be discussed
> Lunch with resource people
> Review lunch discussions

1:30–4:30 Developing Career Action Plans

> Making career decisions
> Identifying long-range alternatives
> Identifying short-range alternatives
> Improving career decisions
> Decision styles and ways to enhance them
> Creating your career plan
> Reconciling your goals with options
> Next career steps
> Development action plan
> Contingency planning
> Making it happen—Making commitments to next steps
> Summary and adjourn

FIGURE 10-2

Sample Agenda—Two-Day Career Planning Workshop

Source: Fred L. Otte and Peggy Hutcheson, *Helping Employees Manage Careers* (Upper Saddle River, NJ: Prentice Hall), 1992, pp. 22–23.

8. *Make computerized on- and off-line programs available for improving the organizational career planning process.* For example, WorkforceVision from Criterion, Inc., supplies online systems that help the company analyze an employee's training needs. Clicking on the employee's name launches his or her work history, competencies, career path, and other information. For each competency (such as leadership and customer focus), a bar chart graphically shows "gap analysis" highlighting the person's strengths and weaknesses. The firm can then organize developmental activities around the person's needs.[25] For both the employer and employee, it often makes more sense to merge the firm's career development and training and appraisal systems together as an integrated online package, as follows.

Improving Productivity Through HRIS: Career Planning and Development

Realistically, it doesn't make much sense to isolate activities like career planning, succession planning, performance appraisal, and training from each other. For example, the employee's career planning and development needs should ideally reflect the strengths and weaknesses that the performance appraisal brings to light. Similarly, eliminating the weaknesses should involve helping the employee tap into the firm's training and development offerings. At the same time, top management and HR should have an integrated information system that gives them a bird's-eye view of their employees' career interests, progress, and appraisal results, so as to expedite the firm's succession planning process.

Therefore, more employers are integrating their career planning and development systems with their firms' performance appraisal, succession planning, and training and development information systems. For example, Alyeska, the company that manages the trans-Alaska pipeline, has a user-friendly portal that lets employees "see their full training history, development plans and upcoming deadlines, register for courses, or do career planning—usually without having to ask for help."[26] At the same time, "managers can get a quick picture of the training needs for a particular group, or see all the employees who have a specific qualification."[27]

One information system that lets employers integrate appraisal, career development, training, and succession planning systems is Kenexa CareerTracker. CareerTracker "helps organizations optimize workforce productivity by providing an easily accessible platform for ongoing employee performance management, succession planning, and career development."[28]

promotions
Advancements to positions of increased responsibility.

transfers
Reassignments to similar positions in other parts of the firm.

⑧ Describe the issues to consider when making promotion decisions.

MANAGING PROMOTIONS AND TRANSFERS

Promotions and transfers are important parts of most people's careers. **Promotions** traditionally refer to advancements to positions of increased responsibility; **transfers** are reassignments to similar positions in other parts of the firm.

Making Promotion Decisions

Most people look forward to promotions, which usually mean more pay, responsibility, and (often) job satisfaction. For employers, promotions can provide opportunities to reward exceptional performance, and to fill open positions with tested and loyal employees. Yet the promotion process isn't always a positive experience for either employee or employer. Unfairness, arbitrariness, or secrecy can diminish the effectiveness of the process. Several decisions, therefore, loom large in any firm's promotion process.

Decision 1: Is Seniority or Competence the Rule?   Probably the most important decision is whether to base promotion on seniority or competence, or some combination of the two.

Today's focus on competitiveness favors competence, as does the fact that promotion based on competence is the superior motivator. However, a company's ability to use competence as the criterion depends on several things, most notably whether or not union agreements or civil service requirements govern promotions. Union agreements sometimes contain clauses that emphasize seniority, such as: "In the advancement of employees, employees with the highest seniority will be given preference, where skills and performance are approximately equal." And civil service regulations that stress seniority rather than competence often govern promotions in many public-sector organizations.

Decision 2: How Should We Measure Competence?   If the firm opts for competence, how should it define and measure competence? Defining and measuring past performance is relatively straightforward: Define the job, set standards, and use one or more appraisal tools to record performance. But promotions require something more: You also need a valid procedure for predicting a candidate's future performance.

Most employers use prior performance as a guide, and assume that (based on his or her prior performance) the person will do well on the new job. This is the simplest procedure. Others use tests or assessment centers to evaluate promotable employees and to identify those with executive potential.

An increasing number of employers take a more comprehensive approach. For example (particularly given the public safety issues involved), police departments have traditionally taken a relatively systematic approach when evaluating candidates for promotion to command positions. Traditional promotional reviews here include a written knowledge test, an assessment center, credit for seniority, and a score based on recent performance appraisal ratings. Other departments are adding a personnel records review. This includes evaluation of job-related dimensions such as supervisory-related education and experience, ratings from multiple sources, and systematic evaluation of behavioral evidence.[29]

Decision 3: Is the Process Formal or Informal?   Many firms have informal promotion processes. They may or may not post open positions, and key managers may use their own "unpublished" criteria to make decisions. Here employees may (reasonably) conclude that factors like "who you know" are more important than performance, and that working hard to get ahead—at least in this firm—is futile.

Many employers establish formal, published promotion policies and procedures. These have several components. Employees get a *formal promotion policy* describing the criteria by which the firm awards promotions. A *job-posting policy* states the firm will post open positions and their requirements, and circulate these to all employees. As explained in Chapter 5, many employers also maintain *employee qualification databanks*, and use replacement charts and computerized employee information systems.

Decision 4: Vertical, Horizontal, or Other?   Promotions aren't necessarily as simple as they may appear. For example, how do you motivate employees with the prospect of promotion when your firm is downsizing? And how do you provide promotional opportunities for those, like engineers, who may have little or no interest in managerial roles?

Several options are available. Some firms, such as the exploration division of British Petroleum, create two parallel career paths, one for managers, and another for "individual contributors" such as high-performing engineers. At BP, individual contributors can move up to nonsupervisory but senior positions, such as "senior engineer." These jobs have most

Employers are transferring employees less often, partly because of family resistance.

of the financial rewards attached to management-track positions at that level.

Another option is to move the person horizontally. For instance, move a production employee to human resources so as to develop his or her skills and to test and challenge his or her aptitudes. And in a sense, "promotions" are possible even when leaving the person in the same job. For example, you can usually enrich the job, and provide training to enhance the opportunity for assuming more responsibility. The "Know Your Employment Law" feature below explains some legal aspects of promotions.

Handling Transfers

A *transfer* is a move from one job to another, usually with no change in salary or grade. Employees seek transfers for many reasons, including personal enrichment, more interesting jobs, greater convenience—better hours, location of work, and so on—or to jobs offering greater advancement possibilities. Employers may transfer a worker to vacate a position where he or she is no longer needed, to fill one where he or she is needed, or more generally to find a better fit for the employee within the firm. Many firms today boost productivity by consolidating positions. Transfers are a way to give employees who might have nowhere else to go a chance for another assignment and, perhaps, some personal growth.

Many firms have had policies of routinely transferring employees from locale to locale, either to expose them to a wider range of jobs or to fill open positions with trained employees. Such easy-transfer policies have now fallen into disfavor. This is partly because of the cost of relocating employees (paying moving expenses, and buying back the employee's current home, for instance) and partly because firms assumed that frequent transfers had a damaging effect on transferees' family life.

④ Describe the methods for enhancing diversity through career management.

ENHANCING DIVERSITY THROUGH CAREER MANAGEMENT

Sources of Bias and Discrimination in Promotion Decisions

Women and people of color still experience relatively less career progress in organizations, and bias and more subtle barriers are often the cause. Yet this is not necessarily the result of decision makers' racist sentiments. Instead, secondary factors—such as having few people of color employed in the hiring department—may be the cause. In any case, the bottom line seems to be that whether it's bias or some other reason, questionable barriers like these do exist, and need to be found and eliminated.

Similarly, women still don't make it to the top of the career ladder in numbers proportionate to their numbers in U.S. industry. Women constitute 40% of the workforce, but hold less than 2% of top-management positions. Blatant or subtle discrimination accounts for most of this. Some hiring managers erroneously believe that "women belong at home and are not committed to careers." The "old-boy network" of informal friendships forged over lunch, at social events, or at club meetings is usually not open to women, although it's often here that promotional decisions are made. A lack of women mentors makes it harder for women to find the role models and supporters they need to help guide their careers. Unlike many men, women must also make the "career versus family" decision, since the

Know Your Employment LAW | Establish Clear Guidelines for Managing Promotions

In general, the employer's promotion processes must comply with all the same anti-discrimination laws as do procedures for recruiting and selecting employees or any other such actions. For example, Title VII of the 1964 Civil Rights Act states, "it shall be an unlawful employment practice for an employer to fail or refuse to hire or to discharge an individual or otherwise to discriminate against any individual with respect to his/her compensation, terms, conditions, or privileges of employment, because of such individual's race, color, religion, sex, or national origin." Similarly, the Age Discrimination in Employment Act of 1967 made it unlawful to discriminate against older employees or applicants for employment in any manner, including promotion.

Beyond such general caveats, there are several specific things to keep in mind regarding the employment law aspects of promotional decisions. One concerns potential problems caused by claims of *retaliation*. Most federal and state employment laws contain anti-retaliation provisions. As long as the employee (or former employee) was acting in good faith when he or she filed the EEOC (or other protected) claim against the employer, the employee may claim retaliation if he or she subsequently suffers an adverse employment action.[30] In such charges, the employee basically claims that (1) the employee tried to blow the whistle on the company for doing something illegal, or filed an EEOC charges or workers' compensation claim, or safety complaint, or lawsuit against the company; (2) the employer then fired, demoted, failed to promote, or cut the pay of that employee; and (3) the HR action was caused by the employee's legally protected activity.

For example, the Fifth U.S. Circuit Court of Appeals allowed her claim of retaliation to proceed when a female employee provided evidence that she was turned down for promotion because a supervisor she had previously accused of sexual harassment made comments that persuaded her current supervisor not to promote her.[31] The evidence confirmed that in a meeting at which supervisors reviewed the person's performance, the former supervisor (and object of the sexual harassment accusation) made comments regarding the employee's "ability to work effectively with others."

One way for the employer to defend against such claims is to ensure that its promotion procedures are objective. For example, the Eighth U.S. Circuit Court of Appeals recently held that a company's failure to set objective guidelines and procedures for promoting current employees may suggest employment discrimination.[32] (In this case, the court found that a community college did not consistently use the same procedures for hiring and promotions at different times, did not clarify when and under what conditions vacant positions were announced, or whether or not there were application deadlines.) In another case, the employer turned down the 61-year-old applicant for a promotion because of his interview performance; the person who interviewed him said he did not "get a real feeling of confidence" from the candidate.[33] In this case, "the court made it clear that while subjective reasons can justify adverse employment decisions, an employer must articulate any clear and reasonably specific factual bases upon which it based its decision." In other words, you should be able to provide objective evidence supporting your subjective assessment for promotion.

responsibilities of raising the children and managing the household still fall disproportionately on women:

> Balancing work and family life can be a challenge. For example, Brenda Barnes gave up her job as head of PepsiCo's North American beverage business in order to spend more time with her family. Linda Noonan, an auditor with Deloitte & Touche, left to join a smaller accounting firm after trying to balance a 70-hour workweek

with her responsibilities as a new mother. Her situation also illustrates what employers can do to resolve such work–family conflicts. When Deloitte instituted a new flexible work schedule, Noonan went back to work there. She signed an agreement to work 80% of the hours normally expected of her position. She also arranged to work more hours from January to March (when the workload is heaviest), and to take more time off the rest of the year to spend with her two daughters.[34]

Different Career Challenges   Women and men also face different challenges as they advance through their careers. Women report greater barriers (such as being excluded from informal networks) than do men, and greater difficulty getting developmental assignments and geographic mobility opportunities. Women had to be more proactive to get such assignments. Because developmental experiences like these are so important, "organizations that are interested in helping female managers advance should focus on breaking down the barriers that interfere with women's access to developmental experiences."[35]

In these matters, minority women seem particularly at risk. Over the past few years, the number of African American, Asian American, and Hispanic women in the U.S. workforce grew by 35%, 78%, and 25%, respectively. Yet women of color hold only a small percentage of professional and managerial private-sector positions. One survey asked minority women what they saw as the barriers to a successful career. The minority women in this survey reported that the main barriers to advancement included not having an influential mentor (47%), lack of informal networking with influential colleagues (40%), lack of company role models for members of the same racial or ethnic group (29%), and a lack of high-visibility assignments (28%).[36]

Adding to the problem is the fact that some corporate career development programs are inconsistent with the needs of minority and nonminority women. For example, many such programs underestimate the role played by family responsibilities in many women's (and men's) lives. Similarly, some programs assume that career paths are orderly, sequential, and continuous; yet the need to stop working for a time to attend to family needs may well punctuate the career paths of many people of color and women (and perhaps men).[37] And, in any case, a study of male and female corporate expatriates concluded that several types of career development programs—fast-track programs, individual career counseling, and career planning workshops—were less available to women than to men.[38] Many refer to this totality of subtle and not-so-subtle barriers to womens' career progress as the *glass ceiling*.

Taking Steps to Enhance Diversity: Women's and Minorities' Prospects

Employers can take steps to enhance women's and minorities' promotional and career prospects. Perhaps the most important thing is to focus on *taking the career interests of women and minority employees seriously*. In other words, accept that there are problems, and work on eliminating the barriers. Other advisable steps include the following.

Eliminate Institutional Barriers   Many practices (such as required late-night meetings) may seem gender neutral but in fact disproportionately affect women and minorities. Employers need to identify such practices and make their practices more accommodating.

Improve Networking and Mentoring   To improve female employees' networking opportunities, Marriott International instituted a series of leadership conferences for women. Speakers offered practical tips for career advancement, and shared their experiences. More important, the conferences provided numerous informal opportunities—over lunch, for instance—for the Marriott women to meet and forge business relationships. Accountants Deloitte & Touche instituted a formal mentoring program.

Retail businesses, with a higher proportion of women managers, often have more flexible schedules and career tracks.

Eliminate the Glass Ceiling Eliminating glass ceiling barriers requires more than an order from the CEO, because the problem is usually systemic. As one expert puts it, "the roots of gender discrimination are built into a platform of work practices, cultural norms and images that appear unbiased . . . People don't even notice them, let alone question them. But they create a subtle pattern of disadvantage that blocks all women." Complicating things is the fact that when they come up against these obstacles, women may attribute them not to structural ("glass ceiling") barriers, but to their own personal inadequacies. For example, numerous after-hours meetings may be the norm in a fast-driving company. For women with family responsibilities, not being able to attend could cripple their advancement prospects. Rescheduling late meetings will therefore (as noted above) make a difference for women with child-care responsibilities.

Institute Flexible Schedules and Career Tracks Inflexible promotional ladders (such as "you must work eight years of 70-hour weeks to apply for partner) can put women—who often have more responsibility for child-raising chores—at a disadvantage. In many large accounting firms, for instance, "more men successfully logged the dozen or so years normally needed to apply for a position as partner. But fewer women stuck around, so fewer applied for or earned these prized positions."[39] One solution, as at Deloitte & Touche, is to institute career tracks (including reduced hours, and more flexible year-round work schedules) that enable women to periodically reduce their time at work, but still remain on a partnership track.

CAREER MANAGEMENT AND EMPLOYEE COMMITMENT

⑤ Answer the question: How can career development foster employee commitment?

The globalization of the world economy has been a boon in many ways. For products and services ranging from cars to computers to air travel, it has powered lower prices, better quality, and higher productivity and living standards.

But these advances haven't come without a price. At least in the short run, the same cost-efficiencies, belt-tightening, and productivity improvements that globalization produced have also triggered numerous and ongoing workforce dislocations. The desire for efficiencies drove firms to downsize, and to "do more with less." It prompted thousands of mergers, large and small, many of which—as when NCNB bought BankAmerica—aimed specifically to "eliminate redundancies;" in other words, to close duplicate branches and back office operations. And with every buyout, merger, and downsizing, more employees found themselves out of work.

The New Psychological Contract

Changes like these understandably prompt many employees to ask why they should be loyal to their employers. "Why," they might ask, "should I be loyal to you if you're just going to dump me when you decide to cut costs again?" To paraphrase the author of the book *Pack Your Own Parachute*, the smart employee today thus tends to think of him or herself as a free agent, there to do a good job but also to prepare for the next career move, to another firm. As we noted earlier in this chapter, yesterday's employee–employer "psychological contract" may have been something like, "do your best and be loyal to us, and we'll take care of your career." Today, it is "do your best for us and be loyal to us for as long as you're here, and we'll provide you with the developmental opportunities you'll need to move on and have a successful career." In such situations, employers must think through what they're going to do to maintain employee commitment, if they are to minimize voluntary departures, and maximize employee effort.

Commitment-Oriented Career Development Efforts

The employer's career planning and development activities can and should play a central role here. Managed effectively, the employer's career development process should send the signal that the employee cares about the employee's career success, and thus deserves the employee's commitment. Career development programs and career-oriented appraisals can facilitate this.

Career Development Programs   For example, we've seen that most large (and many smaller) employers provide career planning and development services. Consider the program at Saturn Corporation's Spring Hill, Tennessee, plant. A career workshop uses vocational guidance tools (including a computerized skills assessment program and other career gap analysis tools) to help employees identify career-related skills and the development needs they possess. This workshop helps employees to assess themselves, and to identify their weaknesses and strengths. Tuition reimbursement and other development aids are also available to help employees develop the skills they need to get ahead.

Programs like these can help foster employee commitment. Here is how one Saturn employee put it:

> I'm an assembler now, and was a team leader for two-and-a-half years. My goal is to move into our people-systems [HR] unit. I know things are tight now, but I know that the philosophy here is that the firm will look out for me—they want people to be all they can be. I know here I'll go as far as I can go; that's one reason I'm so committed to Saturn.[40]

Career-Oriented Appraisals   Similarly, the annual or semi-annual appraisal provides an excellent opportunity to review career-related issues. Performance appraisals should not only be about telling someone how he or she has done. They also provide the ideal occasion to link the employee's performance, career interests, and developmental needs into a coherent career plan. A form like the one in Figure 10-3 can facilitate this process, by helping the manager and employee to translate the latter's performance-based experiences for the year into tangible development plans and goals.

RETIREMENT

retirement
The point at which one gives up one's work, usually between the ages of 60 and 65.

preretirement counseling
Counseling provided to employees who are about to retire, which covers matters such as benefits advice, second careers, and so on.

Retirement for many employees is a mixed blessing. The employee may be free of the daily demands of his or her job, but at the same time be slightly adrift due to not having a job to go to. In a recent survey, 78% of employees said they expect to continue working in some capacity after normal retirement age (64% said they want to do so part-time). Only about a third said they plan to continue work for financial reasons; about 43% said they just wanted to remain active.[41] About 30% of the employers in one survey therefore reported having formal **preretirement counseling** aimed at easing the passage of their employees into retirement. The most common preretirement practices were:

Explanation of Social Security benefits (reported by 97% of those with preretirement education programs)

Leisure time counseling (86%)

Financial and investment counseling (84%)

HR Management Checklists

A. Employee's Major Strengths
    1. _____
    2. _____
    3. _____

B. Areas for Improvement/Development
    1. _____
    2. _____
    3. _____

C. Development Plans: Areas for Development
    1. _____
    2. _____
    3. _____
    4. _____

Development Strategy:
    _____
    _____
    _____

D. Employee's Comments on This Review: _____
    _____
    _____
    _____

E. Reviewer's Comments: _____
    _____
    _____
    _____

    Growth potential in present position and future growth potential for increased
    responsibilities: _____
    _____
    _____

Employer's Signature:_____ Date:_____
Reviewer's Signature:_____ Date:_____
Reviewer's Manager's Signature:_____ Date:_____

FIGURE 10-3

Sample Performance Review Development Plan

Source: Reprinted from www.HR.BLR.com with permission of the publisher *Business and Legal Reports, Inc.*, 141 Mill Rock Road East, Old Saybrook, CT © 2004.

Health counseling (82%)

Psychological counseling (35%)

Counseling for second careers outside the company (31%)

Counseling for second careers inside the company (4%)

Retirement planning does not just benefit soon-to-be retirees; it's also increasingly important for employers. In the United States, the 25- to 34-year-old segment is growing relatively slowly, and the 35–44 group is declining. Employers like CVS pharmacy therefore face a labor shortage. Many have wisely chosen to fill their staffing needs in part with current or soon-to-be retirees. As one study concluded, "in the past few years, companies have been so focused on downsizing to contain costs that they largely neglected a looming threat to their competitiveness . . . A severe shortage of talented workers."[42] Therefore, "retirement planning" is no longer just for helping current employees quietly slip into retirement.[43] It should also enable the employer to retain, in some capacity, the skills and brain power of those who would normally retire and leave the firm.

Doing so requires a change in emphasis on the part of most employers. In general, human resource policies tend to discourage older workers' employment. Suggestions include:

Create a Culture that Honors Experience   At many employers, the work environment and human resource practices "are often explicitly or implicitly biased against older workers." Changing this culture, and making the workplace more attractive to those of retirement age, requires concrete actions. For example, CVS executives took several steps to make their company more "retiree-friendly." Thus, knowing that traditional recruiting channels such as want ads and help-wanted signs might not attract older workers, the pharmacy chain now works through The National Council on Aging, city agencies, and community organizations to find new employees. They've also made it clear to retirees with their policies that they welcome older workers: "I'm too young to retire. [CVS] is willing to hire older people. They don't look at your age but your experience" said one dedicated older worker.[44] Other employers modify testing procedures. For example, one British bank stopped using psychometric tests, replacing them with role-playing exercises to gauge how candidates deal with customers.

Offer Flexible Work   Companies, ". . . need to design jobs such that staying on is more attractive than leaving." One of the simplest ways to do this is through flexible work, specifically, making where one works (as with telecommuting) and when the work is performed flexible.

Offer Part-Time Work   Another trend is granting part-time employment to employees as an alternative to outright retirement. Several surveys of blue- and white-collar employees showed that about half of all employees over age 55 would like to continue working part-time after they retire.

One need not wait until someone is ready to retire to provide retirement planning assistance. For example, American Express introduced an online asset allocation tool for use by its employer-clients' retirement plan participants. The Web-based tool, called Retirement Guidance Planner, lets an employer's retirement plan participants calculate and keep track of progress toward retirement income goals and more easily allocate assets among different investments online.[45] Many firms, including Vanguard, and Fidelity, offer similar online programs.

Retirement procedures must comply with the law. For example, current and former agents of New York Life Insurance Company filed a suit alleging that the company defrauded about 10,000 agents of their retirement and health insurance benefits. Among other things, the suit claims that agents were systematically forced out as they got close to the 20 years of service that would qualify them for full retirement benefits. New York Life says most of the terminations were for other reasons, such as compliance problems or the agents' own decisions to move on.[46]

REVIEW

SUMMARY

1. We may define *career* as the occupational positions a person has had over many years. *Career planning* is the deliberate process through which someone becomes aware of personal skills, interests, knowledge, motivations, and other characteristics; acquires information about opportunities and choices; identifies career-related goals; and establishes action plans to attain specific goals.

2. Corporate career development programs used to focus on the employee's future with that particular firm. Today, the emphasis is more on self-analysis, development, and career management to enable the individual to develop the career plans and skills he or she will need to move on to the next step in his or her career, quite probably with another employer.

3. Employers play an important role in the career management process. Among other things, the employer may provide on-site or online career centers, implement formal mentoring programs, and provide career coaches and/or mentors.

4. Studies suggest that having a mentor can be an important element in furthering an employee's career. Guidelines here include: Choose an appropriate potential mentor, don't be surprised if you're turned down, have an agenda, and respect the mentor's time.

5. In making promotion decisions, the employer must decide between seniority and competence, a formal or informal system, and ways to measure competence.

6. Enhancing diversity through career management requires some special preparations on the part of the employer. Guarding against intentional or unintentional bias and discrimination in promotion decisions is one issue. For example, blatant or subtle discrimination often explains the relatively low success rate in women moving to the top rungs of organizational career ladders.

7. Career management-related steps to enhance diversity include: Eliminate institutional barriers, improve networking and mentoring, eliminate the glass ceiling barriers, and institute flexible schedules.

8. The employer's career planning and development process can and should play a central role in helping employees crystallize their career goals and thereby increase their commitment to the employer. Career development programs and career-oriented appraisals are two important components in this process.

DISCUSSION QUESTIONS

1. What is the employee's role in the career development process? The manager's role? The employer's role?

2. Describe the specific corporate career development initiatives that an employer can take.

3. What are four specific steps employees can take to support diverse employees' career progress?

4. Give several examples of career development activities that employers can use to foster employee commitment.

INDIVIDUAL AND GROUP ACTIVITIES

1. Write a one-page essay stating, "Where I would like to be career-wise 10 years from today."
2. Explain the career-related factors to keep in mind when making the employee's first assignments.
3. In groups of four or five students, meet with several administrators and faculty members in your college or university, and, based on this, write a two-page paper on the topic, "The faculty promotion process at our college." What do you think of the process? Could you make any suggestions for improving it?
4. In groups of four or five students, at your place of work or at your college, interview the HR manager with the aim of writing a two-page paper addressing the topic, "Steps we are taking in this organization to enhance diversity through career management."
5. Develop a résumé for yourself, using the guidelines presented in this chapter's appendix.
6. Working individually or in groups, choose three occupations (such as management consultant, HR manager, or salesperson) and use some of the sources described in the appendix to this chapter to make an assessment of the future demand for this occupation in the next 10 years or so. Does this seem like a good occupation to pursue? Why or why not?
7. The HRCI "Test Specifications" appendix at the end of this book (pages 726–735) lists the knowledge someone studying for the HRCI certification exam needs to have in each area of human resource management (such as in Strategic Management, Workforce Planning, and Human Resource Development). In groups of four to five students, do four things: (1) review that appendix now; (2) identify the material in this chapter that relates to the required knowledge the appendix lists; (3) write four multiple choice exam questions on this material that you believe would be suitable for inclusion in the HRCI exam; and (4) if time permits, have someone from your team post your team's questions in front of the class, so the students in other teams can take each others' exam questions.
8. A survey of recent college graduates in the United Kingdom found that although many hadn't found their first jobs, most were already planning "career breaks" and to keep up their hobbies and interests outside work. As one report of the findings put it, "the next generation of workers is determined not to wind up on the hamster wheel of long hours with no play."[47] Part of the problem seems to be that many already see their friends "putting in more than 48 hours a week" at work. Career experts reviewing the results concluded that many of these recent college grads "are not looking for high pay, high-profile jobs anymore."[48] Instead, they seem to be looking to "compartmentalize" their lives; to keep the number of hours they spend at work down, so they can maintain their hobbies and outside interests. So, do you think these findings are as popular in the United States as they appear to be in the United Kingdom? If so, if you were mentoring one of these people at work, what three specific bits of career advice would you give him or her?

EXPERIENTIAL EXERCISE

Where Am I Going . . . and Why?

Purpose: The purpose of this exercise is to provide you with experience in analyzing your career preferences.

Required Understanding: Students should be thoroughly familiar with the "Managing Your Career" appendix to this chapter.

How to Set Up the Exercise/Instructions: Using at least three of the methods described in this chapter's appendix (identify your occupational orientation, identify your career directions, and so forth), analyze your career-related inclinations (you can take the self-directed search for about eight dollars at www.self-directed-search.com). Based on this analysis, answer the following questions (you may, if you wish, do this analysis in teams of three or four students).

1. What does your research suggest to you about what would be your preferable occupational options?
2. Based on research sources like those we listed in the appendix to this chapter, what are the prospects for these occupations?
3. Given these prospects and your own occupational inclinations, outline a brief, one-page career plan for yourself including current occupational inclinations, career goals, and an action plan listing four or five development steps you will need to take in order to get from where you are now career-wise to where you want to be, based on your career goals.

APPLICATION CASE

The Mentor Relationship Turns Upside Down

"I wish I could talk this problem over with Walter," Carol Lee thought. Walter Lemaire had been her mentor for several years at Larchmont Consulting, yet now he was her problem.

Carol thought back to the beginning of her association with Larchmont and with Walter. She had joined the firm as a writer and editor; her job during those early years had been to revise and polish the consultants' business reports. The work brought her into frequent contact with Walter, who was a senior vice president at the time. Carol enjoyed discussing the consultants' work with him, and when she decided to try to join the consulting team, she asked for his help. Walter became her mentor as well as her boss and guided her through her successful transition to consultant and eventually partner.

At each promotion to various supervisory jobs along the way to partner, Carol cemented her relationship with her new subordinates by acknowledging the inevitable initial awkwardness and by meeting with each person individually to forge a new working relationship. Her career prospered, and when Walter moved on to run a start-up software publishing venture for Larchmont, Carol was promoted to take his place. However, his new venture faltered, and the partners decided someone else would have to step in. Despite the fact that Carol was much younger than Walter and once had worked for him, she was given the assignment of rescuing the start-up operation.

Carol's discomfort over the assignment only grew as she began to review the history of the new venture. Her rescue mission was going to entail undoing much of what Walter had done, reversing his decisions about everything from product design to marketing and pricing. Carol was so reluctant to second-guess her old mentor and boss that she found herself all but unable to discuss any of her proposed solutions with him directly. She doubted that any of her past experience had prepared her to assume the role of Walter's boss, and in these difficult circumstances her need to turn the operation around would be, she felt, like "pouring salt on his wounds."

Questions

1. What is Carol's role in Walter's career development now? Should Larchmont have any such role? Why or why not?
2. What advice would you offer Carol for approaching Walter?
3. If Carol has to dismiss Walter, how specifically would you suggest she proceed?

4. Assume Carol has heard a rumor that Walter has considered resigning. What should she do about it?

Note: The incident in this case is based on an event at an unidentified firm described in Jennifer Frey, "Pride and Your Promotion," *Working Woman*, October 1996.

CONTINUING CASE

Carter Cleaning Company

The Career Planning Program

Career planning has always been a pretty low-priority item for Carter Cleaning, since "just getting workers to come to work and then keeping them honest is enough of a problem," as Jack likes to say. Yet Jennifer thought it might not be a bad idea to give some thought to what a career planning program might involve for Carter. A lot of their employees had been with them for years in dead-end jobs, and she frankly felt a little badly for them: "Perhaps we could help them gain a better perspective on what they want to do," she thought. And she definitely believed that the store management group needed better career direction if Carter Cleaning was to develop and grow.

Questions

1. What would be the advantages to Carter Cleaning of setting up such a career planning program?
2. Who should participate in the program? All employees? Selected employees?
3. Outline and describe the career development program you would propose for the cleaners, pressers, counterpeople, and managers at the Carter Cleaning Centers.

TRANSLATING STRATEGY INTO HR POLICIES AND PRACTICES CASE: THE HOTEL PARIS

The New Career Management System

The Hotel Paris's competitive strategy is "To use superior guest service to differentiate the Hotel Paris properties, and to thereby increase the length of stay and return rate of guests, and thus boost revenues and profitability." HR manager Lisa Cruz must now formulate functional policies and activities that support this competitive strategy, by eliciting the required employee behaviors and competencies.

Lisa Cruz knew that as a hospitality business, the Hotel Paris was uniquely dependent upon having committed, high-morale employees. In a factory or small retail shop, the employer might be able to rely on direct supervision to make sure that the employees were doing their jobs. But in a hotel, just about every employee is "on the front line." There is usually no one there to supervise the limousine driver when he or she picks up a guest at the airport, or when the valet takes the guest's car, or the front-desk clerk signs the guest in, or the housekeeping

clerk needs to handle a guest's special request. If the hotel wanted satisfied guests, they had to have committed employees who did their jobs as if they owned the company, even when the supervisor was nowhere in sight. But for the employees to be committed, Lisa knew the Hotel Paris had to make it clear that the company was also committed to its employees.

From her experience, she knew that one way to do this was to help her employees have successful and satisfying careers, and she was therefore concerned to find that the Hotel Paris had no career management process at all. Supervisors weren't trained to discuss employees' developmental needs or promotional options during the performance appraisal interviews. Promotional processes were informal. And the firm made no attempt to provide any career development services that might help its employees to develop a better understanding of what their career options were, or should be. Lisa was sure that

(Continued)

committed employees were key to improving the experiences of its guests, and that she couldn't boost employee commitment without doing a better job of attending to her employees' career needs.

For Lisa and the CFO, their preliminary research left little doubt about the advisability of instituting a new career management system at the Hotel Paris. The CFO therefore gave the go-ahead to design and institute a new Hotel Paris career management program. Lisa and her team knew that they already had some of the building blocks in place, thanks to the new performance management system they had instituted just a few weeks earlier (as noted in the previous chapter). For example, the new performance management system required that the supervisor appraise the employee based on goals and competencies that were driven by the company's strategic needs; and the appraisal itself produced new goals for the coming year and specific development plans for the employee.

Questions

1. "Many hotel jobs are inherently, "dead end,"—maids, laundry workers, and valets, for instance, either have no great aspirations to move up, or are just using these jobs temporarily, for instance to help out with household expenses." First, do you agree with this statement—why, or why not? Second, list three specific career activities you would recommend Lisa implement for these employees.

2. Build on the company's current performance management system by recommending two other specific career development activities the hotel should implement.

3. What specific career development activities would you recommend in light of the fact that the Paris's hotels and employees are disbursed around the world?

KEY TERMS

career, 378
career management, 378
career development, 378
career planning, 378
career planning and development, 379
reality shock, 384
job rotation, 384
mentoring, 385
promotions, 387
transfers, 387
retirement, 393

preretirement counseling, 393
career cycle, 402
growth stage, 402
exploration stage, 402
establishment stage, 403
trial substage, 403
stabilization substage, 403
midcareer crisis substage, 403
maintenance stage, 403
decline stage, 403
career anchors, 406

ENDNOTES

1. For example, see *The Career Mystique*, Phyllis Moen and Patricia Roehling, Rowman and Littlefield Publishers, Boulder Colorado, 2005.

2. See for example, Andreas Liefooghe, et al., "Managing the Career Deal: The Psychological Contract as a Framework for Understanding Career Management, Organizational Commitment and Work Behavior," *Journal of Organizational Behavior* 26, no. 7, November 2005, pp. 821–838.

3. Carla Joinson, "Career Management and Commitment," *HR Magazine*, May 2001, pp. 60–64.

4. Jan Selmer, "Usage of Corporate Career Development Activities by Expatriate Managers and the Extent of Their International Adjustment," *International Journal of Commerce and Management* 10, no. 1 (Spring 2000), p. 1.

5. Carla Joinson, "Employee, Sculpt Thyself with a Little Help," *HR Magazine*, May 2001, pp. 61–64.

6. Jim Bright, "Career Development: Empowering Your Staff to Excellence," *Journal of Banking and Financial Services* 17, no. 3 (July 2003), p. 12.

7. Barbara Greene and Liana Knudsen, "Competitive Employers Make Career Development Programs a Priority," *San Antonio Business Journal* 15, no. 26 (July 20, 2001), p. 27.
8. Bright, "Career Development: Empowering Your Staff to Excellence," p. 12.
9. Deb Koen, "Revitalize Your Career," *Training and Development*, January 2003, pp. 59–60.
10. Michael Doody, "A Mentor Is a Key to Career Success," *Health-Care Financial Management* 57, no. 2 (February 2003), pp. 92–94.
11. "Preparing Future Leaders in Health-Care," Leaders, c/o Witt/Kieffer, 2015 Spring Road, Suite 510, Oak Brook, IL 60523.
12. Bill Hayes, "Helping Workers with Career Goals Boosts Retention Efforts," *Boston Business Journal* 21, no. 11 (April 20, 2001), p. 38.
13. Yehuda Baruch and Maury Pieperl, "Career Management Practices: An Empirical Survey and Implications," *Human Resource Management* 39, no. 4 (Winter 2000), pp. 347–366.
14. "Career Guidance Steers Workers Away from Early Exits," *BNA Bulletin to Management*, September 7, 2000, p. 287.
15. Tammy Allen, et al., "The Relationship between Formal Mentoring Program Characteristics and Perceived Program Effectiveness," *Personnel Psychology*, vol. 59, 2006, pp. 125–153.
16. Donna Owens, "Virtual Mentoring," *HR Magazine*, March 2006, pp. 15–17.
17. Eve Tahmincioglu, "Looking for a Mentor? Technology Can Help Make the Right Match," *Workforce Management*, December 2004, pp. 863–865.
18. Tammy Allen, et al., "The Relationship between Formal Mentoring Program Characteristics and Perceived Program Effectiveness," *Personnel Psychology*, vol. 59, 2006, pp. 125–153.
19. Greene and Knudsen, "Competitive Employers Make Career Development Programs a Priority," p. 27.
20. Patrick Kiger, "First USA Bank, Promotions and Job Satisfaction," *Workforce*, March 2001, pp. 54–56.
21. Julekha Dash, "Coaching to Aid IT Careers, Retention," *Computerworld*, March 20, 2000, p. 52.
22. P. Sandlin, "Coaching Takes to the Couch: CEO's Increasing Use of Coaches," *Chief Executive*, December 2002, pp. 42–46.
23. David Foote, "Wanna Keep Your Staff Happy? Think Career," *Computerworld*, October 9, 2000, p. 38.
24. Fred Otte and Peggy Hutcheson, *Helping Employees Manage Careers* (Upper Saddle River, NJ: Prentice Hall, 1992), p. 143.
25. Jim Meade, "Boost Careers and Succession Planning," *HR Magazine*, October 2000, pp. 175–178.
26. Tim Harvey, "Enterprise Training System Is Trans Alaska Pipeline's Latest Safety Innovation," *Pipeline and Gas Journal* 229, no. 12 (December 2002), pp. 28–32.
27. Ibid.
28. "Kenexa Announces a Latest Version of Kenexa Career Tracker," *Internet Wire*, March 22, 2004, p. NA.
29. George Thornton III and David Morris, "The Application of Assessment Center Technology to the Evaluation of Personnel Records," *Public Personnel Management* 30, no. 1 (Spring 2001), p. 55.
30. Robin Shay, "Don't Get Caught in the Legal Wringer When Dealing with Difficult to Manage Employees," www.shrm.org.
31. *Gee v. Pincipi*, 5th Cir., number 01-50159, April 18, 2002, "Alleged Harasser's Comments Tainted Promotion Decision," www.shrm.org, downloaded March 2, 2004.
32. Maria Danaher, "Unclean Promotion Procedures Smack of Discrimination," www.shrm.org, downloaded March 2, 2004.
33. Elaine Herskowitz, "The Perils of Subjective Hiring and Promotion Criteria," www.shrm.org.
34. In Susan Wells, "Smoothing the Way," *HR Magazine*, June 2001, pp. 52–58.
35. Karen Lyness and Donna Thompson, "Climbing the Corporate Ladder: Do Female and Male Executives Follow the Same Route?" *Journal of Applied Psychology* 85, no. 1 (2000), pp. 86–101.
36. "Minority Women Surveyed on Career Growth Factors," *Community Banker* 9, no. 3 (March 2000), p. 44.

37. In Ellen Cook et al., "Career Development of Women of Color and White Women: Assumptions, Conceptualization, and Interventions from an Ecological Perspective," *Career Development Quarterly* 50, no. 4 (June 2002), pp. 291–306.

38. Jan Selmer and Alicia Leung, "Are Corporate Career Development Activities Less Available to Female than to Male Expatriates?" *Journal of Business Ethics*, March 2003, pp. 125–137.

39. Kathleen Melymuka, "Glass Ceilings & Clear Solutions," *Computerworld*, May 29, 2000, p. 56.

40. Personal interview, March 1992.

41. "Employees Plan to Work Past Retirement, but Not Necessarily for Financial Reasons," *BNA Bulletin to Management*, February 19, 2004, pp. 57–58. Employers should conduct the necessary numerical analyses for dealing with the prospect of retirements. This assessment should include a demographic analysis (including a census of the company's employees); a determination of the average retirement age for the company's employees; and a review of how retirement is going to impact the employer's health care and pension benefits. The employer can then determine the extent of the "retirement problem," and take fact-based steps to address it. Luis Fleites, and Lou Valentino, "The Case for Phased Retirement," *Compensation & Benefits Review*, March and/April 2007, pp. 42–46.

42. Ken Dychtwald et al., "It's Time to Retire Retirement," *Harvard Business Review*, March 2004, p. 49.

43. See for example, Matt Bolch, "Bidding Adieu," *HR Magazine*, June 2006, pp. 123–127.

44. Dychtwald et al., op. cit., p. 52.

45. "American Express Adds Tools to Retirement Section," *Financial Net News* 6, no. 17 (April 30, 2001), p. 3. See also Katherine Dalton, "The Art of the Graceful Exit," *Business Horizons* 48, no. 2, March 2005, pp. 91–93.

46. "Agents Sue New York Life Over Retirement Benefits," *National Underwriter Life and Health Financial Services Edition* 105, no. 10 (March 5, 2001), pp. 49–50.

47. "New Trend in Career Hunt," *Europe Intelligence Wire*, February 10, 2004, p. NA.

48. Ibid.

APPENDIX FOR CHAPTER 10

Managing Your Career

Managing your career has never been as important as it is today.[1] The individual must be responsible for creating and managing his or her own career. And, in today's job marketplace, employee ability replaces job security.

The first step in planning a career for yourself or someone else is to learn as much as possible about your interests, aptitudes, and skills.

Making Career Choices

Identify Your Career Stage   Each person's career goes through stages, and the stage you are in will influence your knowledge of and preference for various occupations. The main stages of this **career cycle** follows.[2]

Growth Stage   The **growth stage** lasts roughly from birth to age 14 and is a period during which the person develops a self-concept by identifying with and interacting with other people such as family, friends, and teachers. Toward the beginning of this period, role playing is important, and children experiment with different ways of acting; this helps them to form impressions of how other people react to different behaviors and contributes to their developing a unique self-concept or identity. Toward the end of this stage, the adolescent (who by this time has developed preliminary ideas about what his or her interests and abilities are) begins to think realistically about alternative occupations.

Exploration Stage   The **exploration stage** is the period (roughly from ages 15 to 24) during which a person seriously explores various occupational alternatives. The person attempts to match these alternatives with what he or she has learned about them and about his or her own interests and abilities from school, leisure activities, and work. Tentative broad occupational choices are usually made during the beginning of this period. Then toward the end of this period, a seemingly appropriate choice is made and the person tries out for a beginning job.

Probably the most important task the person has in this and the preceding stage is that of developing a realistic understanding of his or her abilities and talents. Similarly, the person must make sound educational decisions based on reliable sources of information about occupational alternatives.

Establishment Stage   The **establishment stage** spans roughly ages 24 to 44 and is the heart of most people's work lives. During this period, it is hoped a suitable occupation is found and the person engages in those activities that help him or her earn a permanent place in it. Often, and particularly in the professions, the person locks onto a chosen occupation early. But in most cases, this is a period during which the person is continually testing his or her capabilities and ambitions against those of the initial occupational choice.

The establishment stage is itself comprised of three substages. The **trial substage** lasts from about ages 25 to 30. During this period, the person determines whether or not the chosen field is suitable; if it is not, several changes might be attempted. (Jane Smith might have her heart set on a career in retailing, for example, but after several months of constant travel as a newly hired assistant buyer for a department store, she might decide that a less travel-oriented career such as one in market research is more in tune with her needs.) Roughly between the ages of 30 and 40, the person goes through a **stabilization substage**. Here firm occupational goals are set and the person does more explicit career planning to determine the sequence of promotions, job changes, and/or any educational activities that seem necessary for accomplishing these goals.

Finally, somewhere between the mid-thirties and mid-forties, the person may enter the **midcareer crisis substage**. During this period, people often make a major reassessment of their progress relative to original ambitions and goals. They may find that they are not going to realize their dreams (such as being company president) or that having been accomplished, their dreams are not all they were purported to be. Also during this period, people have to decide how important work and career are to be in their lives. It is often during this midcareer substage that some people face, for the first time, the difficult choices between what they really want, what really can be accomplished, and how much must be sacrificed to achieve it.

Maintenance Stage   Between the ages of 45 and 65, many people simply slide from the stabilization substage into the **maintenance stage**. During this latter period, the person has typically created a place in the world of work and most efforts are now directed at maintaining that place.

Decline Stage   As retirement age approaches, there is often a deceleration period in the **decline stage**. Here many people face the prospect of having to accept reduced levels of power and responsibility and learn to accept and develop new roles as mentor and confidante for those who are younger. There is then the more or less inevitable retirement, after which the person hopefully finds alternative uses for the time and effort formerly expended on his or her occupation.

Identify Your Occupational Orientation   Career-counseling expert John Holland says that personality (including values, motives, and needs) is one career choice determinant. For example, a person with a strong social orientation might be attracted to careers that entail interpersonal rather than intellectual or physical activities and to occupations such as social work. Based on research with his Vocational Preference Test (VPT), Holland found six basic personality types or orientations (see www.self-directed-search.com).[3]

1. *Realistic orientation.* These people are attracted to occupations that involve physical activities requiring skill, strength, and coordination. Examples include forestry, farming, and agriculture.
2. *Investigative orientation.* Investigative people are attracted to careers that involve cognitive activities (thinking, organizing, understanding) rather than affective activities (feeling, acting, or interpersonal and emotional tasks). Examples include biologist, chemist, and college professor.
3. *Social orientation.* These people are attracted to careers that involve interpersonal rather than intellectual or physical activities. Examples include clinical psychology, foreign service, and social work.
4. *Conventional orientation.* A conventional orientation favors careers that involve structured, rule-regulated activities, as well as careers in which it is expected that the employee subordinate his or her personal needs to those of the organization. Examples include accountants and bankers.
5. *Enterprising orientation.* Verbal activities aimed at influencing others characterize enterprising personalities. Examples include managers, lawyers, and public relations executives.
6. *Artistic orientation.* People here are attracted to careers that involve self-expression, artistic creation, expression of emotions, and individualistic activities. Examples include artists, advertising executives, and musicians.

Most people have more than one occupational orientation (they might be social, realistic, and investigative, for example), and Holland believes that the more similar or compatible these orientations are, the less internal conflict or indecision a person will face in making a career choice. To help illustrate this, Holland suggests placing each orientation in one corner of a hexagon, as in Figure 10-A1. As you can see, the model has six corners, each of which represents one personal orientation (for example, enterprising). According to Holland's research, the closer two orientations are in this figure, the more compatible they are. If your number-one and number-two orientations fall side by side, you will have an easier time choosing a career. However, if your orientations turn out to be opposite (such as realistic and social), you may experience more indecision in making a career choice because your interests are driving you toward very different types of careers. In Table 10-A1, we have summarized some of the occupations found to be the best match for each of these six orientations. You can, for about $8.00 take Holland's SDS online (see www.self-directed-search.com).

FIGURE 10-A1

Choosing an Occupational Orientation

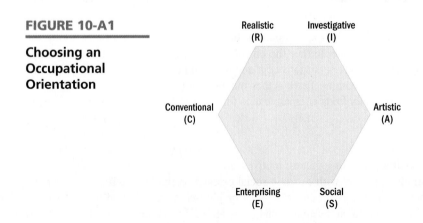

TABLE 10-A1 Example of Some Occupations That May Typify Each Occupational Theme

Realistic	Investigative	Artistic	Social	Enterprising	Conventional
				A Wide Range of Managerial Occupations, including:	
Engineers	Physicians	Advertising Executives	Auto Sales Dealers	Military Officers	Accountants
Carpenters	Psychologists	Public Relations Executives	School Administrators	Chamber of Commerce Executives	Bankers
	Research and Development Managers			Investment Managers	Credit Managers
				Lawyers	

The SDS has an excellent reputation, but the career seeker needs to be somewhat wary of some of the other online career assessment sites. One study of 24 no-cost online career assessment Web sites concluded that they were easy to use, but suffered from a lack of validation, limited confidentiality controls, and limited information on test interpretation. However, a number of online career assessment instruments such as the career key (www.careerkey.org/english) do reportedly provide validated and useful information.[4]

Identify Your Career Directions MBA students at the Harvard Business School sometimes take a quiz to help them identify career directions and make career choices in which they'll be happy.[5] To take a short-form version of this quiz, you'll need three types of information. First (see Figure 10-A2), this approach assumes that all executive work is based on one or more of eight core activities such as "quantitative analysis" and "managing people." Begin by reading each of those activities.

Next (see Figure 10-A3), quickly go through each of the second figure's pairs of statements and indicate which one is more interesting to you. Then add the letters for your total score on each core function and record that score in the second figure.

Then, use Figure 10-A4 to see what kind of successful businesspeople share your career direction's interests. For example, if you scored high in Figure 10-A3 on "Enterprise Control" and "Managing People," then CEOs, Presidents, Division Managers, and General Managers are the sorts of people whose career interests are most similar to yours.

Identify Your Skills Successful performance also depends on ability. You may have a conventional orientation, but whether you have *the skills* to be an accountant, banker, or credit manager will largely determine which occupation you ultimately choose. Therefore, you have to identify your skills.

An Exercise One useful exercise for identifying occupational skills is to take a blank piece of paper and head it "The School or Occupational Tasks I Was Best At." Then write a short essay that describes the tasks. Make sure to go into as much detail as you can about your duties and responsibilities and what it was about each task that you found enjoyable. (In writing your essay, by the way, notice that it's not necessarily the most enjoyable *job* you've had, but the most enjoyable *task* you've had to perform; you may have had jobs

Business Career Interest Inventory (BC II)

Part 1: *All executive work is based on one or more of the following eight core activities. Read them.*

Application of Technology: Taking an engineering-like approach to business problems and using technology to solve them (operations process analysis, process redesign, production planning).

Quantitative Anaysis: Problem-solving that relies on mathmatical and financial analysis (determining the most advantageous debt/equity structure, analyzing market research).

Theory Development and Conceptual Thinking: Taking a broadly conceptual, quasi-academic approach to business problems (developing a new general economic theory or model of market behavior).

Creative Production: Highly creative activities (the generation of new business ideas such as line extensions or additional markets, the development of new marketing concepts).

Counseling and Mentoring: Developing a variety of personal relationships in the workplace and helping others in their careers (human-resources coaching, training, and mentoring).

Managing People: Accomplishing business goals through working directly with people (particularly as a front-line manager, team leader, director, or direct supervisor).

Enterprise Control: Having ultimate stategy and decision-making authority as well as resource control for an operation (as a division manager, president, CEO, partner in a professional firm, or entrepreneur).

Influence Through Language and Ideas: Exercising influence through the skillful use of persuasion (negotiating, deal-making, sales functions, and relationship development).

FIGURE 10-A2

Finding the Job You *Should* Want (Part 1)

Source: James Waldroop and Timothy Butler, "Finding the Job You *Should* Want," *Fortune*, March 2, 1998, p. 211. Copyright © 1998 Time Inc. Reprinted by permission. All rights reserved.

that you really didn't like except for one of the specific duties or tasks in the job, which you really enjoyed.) Next, on other sheets of paper, do the same thing for two other tasks you have had. Now go through your three essays and underline the skills that you mentioned the most often. For example, did you enjoy putting together and coordinating the school play when you worked in the principal's office one year? Did you especially enjoy the hours you spent in the library doing research for your boss when you worked one summer as an office clerk?[6]

Aptitudes and Special Talents   For career planning purposes, a person's aptitudes are usually measured with a test battery such as the general aptitude test battery (GATB), which most state one stop career centers make available. This instrument measures various aptitudes including intelligence and mathematical ability. You can also use specialized tests, such as for mechanical comprehension. However, even Holland's Self Directed Search will provide some insights into your aptitudes.[7]

Identify Your Career Anchors   Edgar Schein says that career planning is a continuing process of discovery—one in which a person slowly develops a clearer occupational self-concept in terms of what his or her talents, abilities, motives, needs, attitudes, and values are. Schein also says that as you learn more about yourself, it becomes apparent that you have a dominant **career anchor**, *a concern or value that you will not give up if a [career] choice has to be made.*

Part 2: *Reread the brief description of the eight sets of activities on the previous page, then quickly go through each of the following pairs and indicate which one is more interesting to you by placing the bold letter for that choice in the box to the left. Don't leave any out and don't record any ties. Mark your first intuitive response.*

☐ 1. Creative **P**roduction or **I**nfluence Through Language and Ideas

☐ 2. **M**anaging People or Creative **P**roductions

☐ 3. **E**nterprise Control or **A**pplication of Technology

☐ 4. **T**heory Development or Creative **P**roduction

☐ 5. **M**anaging People or **C**ounseling and Mentoring

☐ 6. **Q**uantitative Analysis or **T**heory Development

☐ 7. **I**nfluence Through Language and Ideas or **E**nterprise Control

☐ 8. **Q**uantitative Analysis or **E**nterprise Control

☐ 9. **A**pplication of Technology or **I**nfluence Through Language and Ideas

☐ 10. **I**nfluence Through Language and Ideas or **Q**uantitative Analysis

☐ 11. **T**heory Development or **C**ounseling and Mentoring

☐ 12. **A**pplication of Technology or Creative **P**roduction

☐ 13. **A**pplication of Technology or **M**anaging People

☐ 14. **T**heory Development or **I**nfluence Through Language and Ideas

☐ 15. Creative **P**roduction or **C**ounseling and Mentoring

☐ 16. **C**ounseling and Mentoring or **Q**uantitative Analysis

☐ 17. **T**heory Development or **E**nterprise Control

☐ 18. **E**nterprise Control or Creative **P**roduction

☐ 19. **M**anaging People or **T**heory Development

☐ 20. **A**pplication of Technology or **T**heory Development

☐ 21. **E**nterprise Control or **C**ounseling and Mentoring

☐ 22. Creative **P**roduction or **Q**uantitative Analysis

☐ 23. **C**ounseling and Mentoring or **I**nfluence Through Language and Ideas

☐ 24. **Q**uantitative Analysis or **M**anaging People

☐ 25. **E**nterprise Control or **M**anaging People

☐ 26. **A**pplication of Technology or **C**ounseling and Mentoring

☐ 27. **M**anaging People or **I**nfluence Through Language and Ideas

☐ 28. **A**pplication of Technology or **Q**uantitative Analysis

Add the bold letters for your total score on each core function and record that score below:

☐ **Application of Technology**

☐ **Counseling and Mentoring**

☐ **Quantitative Analysis**

☐ **Managing People**

☐ **Theory Development and Conceptual Thinking**

☐ **Enterprise Control**

☐ **Creative Production**

☐ **Influence Through Language and Ideas**

Based on the scores above, identify your most significant interests. Most people will find one to three clear leaders. What does it all mean? Turn the page to find out.

FIGURE 10-A3

Finding the Job You *Should* Want (Part 2)

Source: James Waldroop and Timothy Butler, "Finding the Job You *Should* Want," *Fortune*, March 2, 1998, p. 212. Copyright © 1998 Time Inc. Reprinted by permission. All rights reserved.

Part 3: *Now that you know which combinations you prefer, see what kind of success-ful business people share your interests.*

ENTERPRISE CONTROL and MANAGING PEOPLE: CEOs, presidents, division managers, and general managers who enjoy both strategy and the operations aspects of the position—the CEO who enjoys playing the COO role as well.

ENTERPRISE CONTROL and QUANTITATIVE ANALYSIS: Investment bankers, other financial professionals who enjoy deal making, partners in Big Six firms, top-level executives in commercial and investment banks, investment managers.

APPLICATION OF TECHNOLOGY and QUANTITATIVE ANALYSIS: Individual contributors who have a strong interest in engineering analysis (systems analysis, tech consultants, process consultants); production and operations managers.

CREATIVE PRODUCTION and INFLUENCE THROUGH LANGUAGE AND IDEAS: Advertising executives, brand managers, corporate trainers, salespeople, public relations specialists; people in the fashion, entertainment, and media industries.

COUNSELING AND MENTORING and MANAGING PEOPLE: Human resources managers, managers who enjoy coaching and developing the people reporting to them, managers in nonprofit organizations with an altruistic mission.

ENTERPRISE CONTROL and INFLUENCE THROUGH LANGUAGE AND IDEAS: Executives (CEOs, presidents, general managers) whose leadership style relies on persuasion and consensus building, marketing managers, salespeople.

APPLICATION OF TECHNOLOGY and ENTERPRISE CONTROL: Managers and senior executives in high technology, telecommunications, biotech, information systems (internally or consulting), and other engineering-related fields.

THEORY DEVELOPMENT and QUANTITATIVE ANALYSIS: Economic-model builders quantitative analysis, "knowledge base" consultants, market forecasters, business professors.

CREATIVE PRODUCTION and ENTERPRISE CONTROL: Solo entrepreneurs, senior executives in industries where the product or service is of a creative nature (fashion, entertainment, advertising, media).

CREATIVE PRODUCTION: Entrepreneurs who partner with a professional manager, short-term project managers, new-product developers, advertising "creatives," individual contributors in fashion, entertainment, and media.

FIGURE 10-A4

Finding the Job You *Should* Want (Part 3)

Source: James Waldroop and Timothy Butler, "Finding the Job You *Should* Want," *Fortune*, March 2, 1998, p. 214. Copyright © 1998 Time Inc. Reprinted by permission. All rights reserved.

Career anchors, as their name implies, are the pivots around which a person's career swings; a person becomes conscious of them as a result of learning, through experience, about his or her talents and abilities, motives and needs, and attitudes and values. Based on his research at the Massachusetts Institute of Technology, Schein believes that career anchors are difficult to predict because they are evolutionary and a product of a process of discovery. Some people may never find out what their career anchors are until they have to make a major choice—such as whether to take the promotion to the headquarters staff or strike out on their own by starting a business. It is at this point that all the person's past work experiences, interests, aptitudes, and orientations converge into a meaningful pattern that helps show what (career anchor) is the most important factor in driving the person's career choices.

Based on his study of MIT graduates, Schein identified five career anchors.[8]

Technical/Functional Competence   People who had a strong technical/functional career anchor tended to avoid decisions that would drive them toward general management. Instead, they made decisions that would enable them to remain and grow in their chosen technical or functional fields.

Managerial Competence   Other people show a strong motivation to become managers and their career experience enabled them to believe they had the skills and values required. A management position of high responsibility is their ultimate goal. When pressed to explain why they believed they had the skills necessary to gain such positions, many in Schein's research sample answered that they were qualified for these jobs because of what they saw as their competencies in a combination of three areas: (1) analytical competence (ability to identify, analyze, and solve problems under conditions of incomplete information and uncertainty); (2) interpersonal competence (ability to influence, supervise, lead, manipulate, and control people at all levels); and (3) emotional competence (the capacity to be stimulated by emotional and interpersonal crises rather than exhausted or debilitated by them, and the capacity to bear high levels of responsibility without becoming paralyzed).

Creativity   Some of the graduates had gone on to become successful entrepreneurs. To Schein these people seemed to have a need "to build or create something that was entirely their own product—a product or process that bears their name, a company of their own, or a personal fortune that reflects their accomplishments." For example, one graduate had become a successful purchaser, restorer, and renter of townhouses in a large city; another had built a successful consulting firm.

Autonomy and Independence   Some seemed driven by the need to be on their own, free of the dependence that can arise when a person elects to work in a large organization where promotions, transfers, and salary decisions make them subordinate to others. Many of these graduates also had a strong technical/functional orientation. Instead of pursuing this orientation in an organization, they had decided to become consultants, working either alone or as part of a relatively small firm. Others had become professors of business, freelance writers, and proprietors of a small retail business.

Security   A few of the graduates were mostly concerned with long-run career stability and job security. They seemed willing to do what was required to maintain job security, a decent income, and a stable future in the form of a good retirement program and benefits. For those interested in *geographic security*, maintaining a stable, secure career in familiar surroundings was generally more important than pursuing superior career choices, if choosing the latter meant injecting instability or insecurity into their lives by forcing them to pull up roots and move to another city. For others, security meant *organizational security*. They might today opt for government jobs, where tenure still tends to be a way of life. They were much more willing to let their employers decide what their careers should be.

Assessing Career Anchors   To help you identify career anchors, take a few sheets of blank paper and write out your answers to the following questions:[9]
1. What was your major area of concentration (if any) in high school? Why did you choose that area? How did you feel about it?
2. What is (or was) your major area of concentration in college? Why did you choose that area? How did you feel about it?
3. What was your first job after school? (Include military if relevant.) What were you looking for in your first job?

4. What were your ambitions or long-range goals when you started your career? Have they changed? When? Why?

5. What was your first major change of job or company? What were you looking for in your next job?

6. What was your next major change of job, company, or career? Why did you initiate or accept it? What were you looking for? (Do this for each of your major changes of job, company, or career.)

7. As you look back over your career, identify some times you have especially enjoyed. What was it about those times that you enjoyed?

8. As you look back, identify some times you have not especially enjoyed. What was it about those times you did not enjoy?

9. Have you ever refused a job move or promotion? Why?

10. Now review all your answers carefully, as well as the descriptions for the five career anchors (managerial competence, technical/functional, security, creativity, autonomy). Based on your answers to the questions, rate, for yourself, each of the anchors from 1 to 5; 1 equals low importance, 5 equals high importance.

Managerial competence _____

Technical/functional competence _____

Security _____

Creativity _____

Autonomy _____

What Do You Want to Do?   We have explained occupational orientations, skills, and career anchors and the role these play in choosing a career. But there is at least one more exercise that can prove enlightening. On a sheet of paper, answer the question: "If you could have any kind of job, what would it be?" Invent your own job if need be, and don't worry about what you can do—just what you want to do.[10]

Identify High-Potential Occupations   Learning about yourself is only half the job of choosing an occupation. You also have to identify those occupations that are right (given your occupational orientations, skills, career anchors, and occupational preferences) as well as those that will be in high demand in the years to come.

Not surprisingly, the most efficient way to learn about and compare and contrast occupations is through the Internet. The U.S. Department of Labor's online *Occupational Outlook Handbook* (www.bls.gov/oco/), updated each year, provides detailed descriptions and information on hundreds of occupations (see Figure 10-A5). The New York State Department of Labor (http://nycareerzone.org) similarly provides excellent information on careers categorized in clusters, such as Arts and Humanities, Business and Information Systems, and Engineering and Technology. Both these sites include information regarding demand for and employment prospects for the occupations they cover. Figure 10-A6 lists some other sites to turn to both for occupational information and for information on where to turn to when searching for a job—the subject to which we ourselves now turn.

The U.S. government's One-Stop Career Centers are another excellent source. In them, job seekers can now apply for unemployment benefits, register with the state job service, talk to career counselors, use computers to write résumés and access the Internet, take tests, and use career libraries, which offer books and videos on various employment topics. In some centers job hunters can even make use of free telephones, fax machines, and photocopiers to facilitate job searches.

FIGURE 10-A5

Occupational Outlook Handbook Online

Source: http://www.bls.gov//oco/, accessed May 18, 2007.

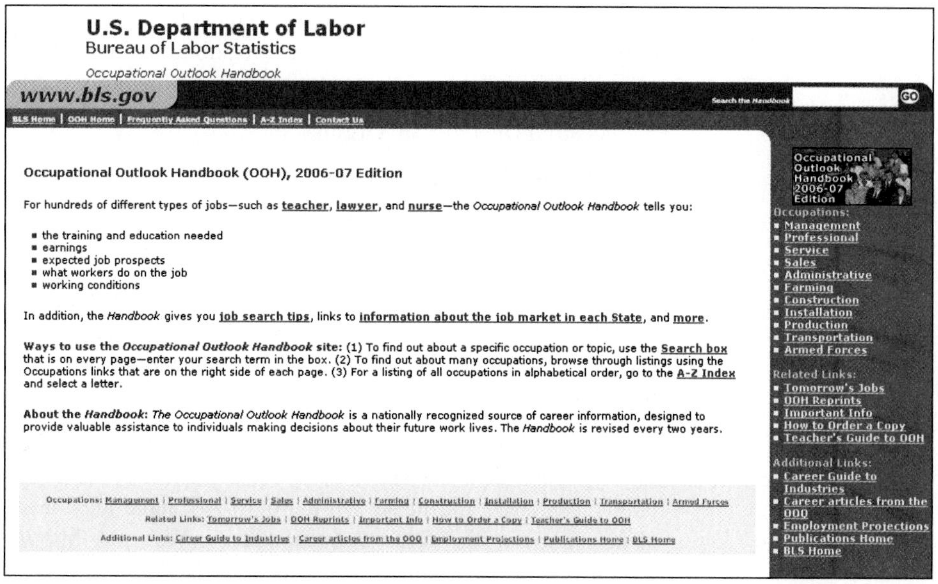

FIGURE 10-A6

Some Online Sources of Occupational Information

Source: Printed with permission from Mapping Your Future, a public service Web site providing career, college, financial aid, and financial literacy information and services to students, families, and schools (http://mapping-your-future.org/features/resources.cfm#CareerGuidance/JobSearch). Accessed August 25, 2007.

Career Guidance / Job Search

- All Star Jobs
- America's Career InfoNet
- America's Job Bank
- Campus Career Center
- Career Magazine
- Career Resource Library - New York State Department of Labor
- CareerExplorer
- College Central Network
- College Grad Job Hunter--WWW Home Page
- Cool Works
- ERI's Career Salary and Cost of Living Calculators
- hotjobs.com
- Jammin Jobs!
- Job Options
- Job Web
- JobGusher
- JobProfiles.com
- JobSniper
- mJob
- Monster.com
- NationJob
- Occupational Outlook Handbook
- Quintessential Careers
- Snag a Job
- Streaming Futures (career advice from industry leaders through online streaming video)
- True Careers

Finding the Right Job

You have identified your occupational orientation, skills, and career anchors and have picked out the occupation you want and made plans for a career. If necessary, you have embarked on the required education and training. Your next step is to find a job that you want in the company and locale in which you want to work.

Job Search Techniques

Do Your Own Local Research   Perhaps the most direct way of unearthing the job you want, where you want it, is to pick out the geographic area in which you want to work, and find out all you can about the companies in that area that appeal to you, and the people you have to contact in those companies to get the job you want. Sometimes this research is decidedly low-tech. For example, the reference librarian in one Fairfax County, Virginia, library suggested the following sources for patrons seeking information about local businesses:

Industrial Directory of Virginia

Industrial Directory of Fairfax County

Principal Employers of the Washington Metro Area

The Business Review of Washington

Other general reference materials you can use includes *Who's Who in Commerce and Industry, Who's Who in America, Who's Who in the East*, and *Poor's Register*. Using these guides, you can find the person in each organization who is ultimately responsible for hiring people in the position you seek.

Online Job Boards   But the Internet is generally a better bet, especially if you're in one city and your ideal job would be in another. Most of the large online job search sites such as monster.com (and those in Figure 10-A6) have local-area search capabilities, for instance. Use the *Wall Street Journal*'s career Web site (http://www.careerjournal.com/) to search for jobs by occupation and location (see Figure 10-A7). And, most big-city newspapers have their own (or links to) online local job listings.

In addition to the giant general-purpose career Web sites (like Monster), most large companies, industries, and crafts have their own specialized sites.[11] For example, the Air Conditioning Contractors in America (www.acca.org/careers/) and Financial Executives International (www.fei.org) make it easy for industry employers and prospective employees to match their needs.

When job hunting, you can post your résumé on the Web. But while many people do so, Web-based résumés can cause problems. "Once I put my résumé on the Internet, I couldn't

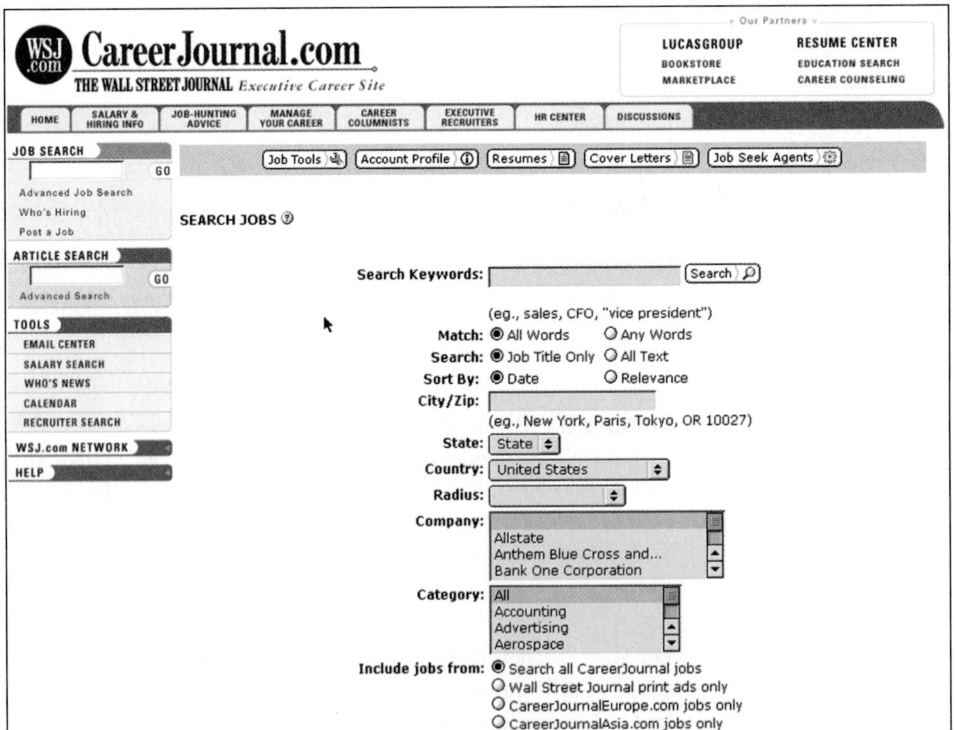

FIGURE 10-A7

CareerJournal.com

Source: Wall Street Journal by CareerJournal.com Reproduced with permission of Dow Jones & Co. Inc. via Copyright Clearance Center © 2004. The job search url is http://jobs.careerjournal. com/careers/jobsearch? clientid=cj. Accessed August 25, 2007.

do anything to control it," said one technical consultant after his boss had stumbled across the fact that several months before he had been job hunting. If you do post your résumé on the Web, experts suggest taking precautions. At a minimum, date your résumé (in case it lands on your boss's desk two years from now); insert a disclaimer forbidding unauthorized transmission by headhunters; check ahead of time to see who has access to the database on which you're posting your résumé; and try to cloak your identity by listing your capabilities but not your name or employer—just an anonymous e-mail account to receive inquiries.[12]

Personal Contacts   Generally, the most popular way to seek job interviews is to rely on personal contacts such as friends and relatives.[13] So, let as many responsible people as possible know that you are in the market for a job and specifically what kind of job you want. (Beware, though, if you are currently employed and don't want your job search getting back to your current boss. If that is the case, better just pick out two or three very close friends and tell them it is absolutely essential that they be discreet in seeking a job for you.)

No matter how close your friends or relatives are to you, by the way, you don't want to impose too much on them. It is usually best to ask them for the name of someone they think you should talk to in the kind of firm in which you'd like to work, and then do the digging yourself.

Answering Advertisements   Most experts agree that answering ads is a low-probability way to get a job, and it becomes increasingly less likely that you will get a job this way as the level of jobs increases. Answering ads, in other words, is fine for jobs that pay under $30,000 per year, but it's highly unlikely that as you move up in management you are going to get your job by simply answering classified ads. Nevertheless, good sources of classified ads for professionals and managers include the *New York Times*, the *Wall Street Journal*, and specialized journals in your field that list job openings. All these sources also post the positions online, of course.

In responding to ads, be sure to create the right impression with the materials you submit; check the typing, style, grammar, neatness, and so forth, and check your résumé to make sure it is geared to the job for which you are applying. In your cover letter, be sure to have a paragraph or so in which you specifically address why your background and accomplishments are appropriate to the job being advertised; you must respond clearly to the company's identified needs.[14]

Be very careful in replying to blind ads, however (those with just a post office box). Some executive search firms and companies will run ads even when no position exists just to gauge the market, and there is always the chance that you can be trapped into responding to your own firm.

Employment Agencies   Agencies are especially good at placing people in jobs paying up to about $40,000, but they can be useful for higher-paying jobs as well. Their fees for professional and management jobs are usually paid by the employer. Assuming you know the job you want, review a few back issues of your paper's Sunday classified ads to identify the agencies that consistently handle the positions you want. Approach three or four initially, preferably in response to specific ads, and avoid signing any contract that gives an agency the exclusive right to place you.

Executive Recruiters   Executive recruiters are retained by employers to seek out top talent for their clients, and their fees are always paid by the employer. They do not do career counseling, but if you know the job you want, it pays to contact a few. Send your résumé and a cover letter summarizing your objective in precise terms, including job title and the size of company you want, work-related accomplishments, current salary, and salary requirements. Firms are usually listed in the Yellow Pages under "Executive Search Consultants." However, beware, because some firms today call themselves executive search or career consultants but do no searches: They just charge a (often hefty) fee to help you manage your search. Remember that with a search firm you never pay a fee.

What sorts of things will the headhunter look for? Ten important items include:[15] You have demonstrated the ability to get results; you come well recommended by your peers and competitors; you understand who the search consultant works for and what he is trying to do; you are likeable and presentable, and your ego is in check; you can think strategically and understand how to institute change in an organized direction; you have achieved the results you have because of the way you treat others, not in spite of it; you can sell yourself concisely; you have at least some of the key specific experiences that the job entails; you are honest, fair, and a good source and even take the time when somebody calls you as a source to give them other sources that you believe are high potential; and you know who you are and what you want.[16]

Career Counselors   Career counselors will not help you find a job per se; rather, they specialize in aptitude testing and career counseling. They are listed under "Career Counseling" or "Vocational Guidance." Their services usually cost $300 or so and include psychological testing and interviews with an experienced career counselor. Check the firm's services, prices, and history as well as the credentials of the person you will be dealing with.

Executive Marketing Consultants   Executive marketing consultants manage your job-hunting campaign. They generally are not recruiters and do not have jobs to fill. Depending on the services you choose, your cost will range from $400 to $5,000 or more. The process may involve months of weekly meetings. Services include résumé and letter writing, interview skill building, and developing a full job-hunting campaign. Before approaching a consultant, though, you should definitely do in-depth self-appraisal (as explained in this chapter) and read books like Richard Bolles's *The Quick Job Hunting Map* and *What Color Is Your Parachute?*

Then check out three or four of these firms (they are listed in the Yellow Pages under "Executive Search Consultants") by visiting each and asking: What exactly is your program? How much does each service cost? Are there any extra costs, such as charges for printing and mailing résumés? What does the contract say? After what point will you get no rebate if you're unhappy with the services? Then review your notes, check the Better Business Bureau, and decide which of these firms (if any) is for you.

Employers' Web Sites   With more and more companies listing job openings on their Web sites any serious job hunter should be using this valuable source. Doing so requires some special résumé preparations, as we'll see next.

Writing Your Résumé   Your résumé is probably your most important selling document, one that can determine whether you get offered a job interview. Here are some résumé pointers, as offered by employment counselor Richard Payne and other experts.[17] Figure 10-A8 presents one example of an effective résumé.

Introductory Information   Start your résumé with your name, home and e-mail address, and telephone number. Using your office phone number can indicate either that (1) your employer knows you are leaving or (2) you don't care whether he or she finds out. You're usually better off using your home or cell phone number.

Job Objective   State your job objective next. This should summarize in one sentence the specific position you want, where you want to do it (type and size of company), and a special reason an employer might have for wanting you to fill the job. For example, "Production manager in a medium-size manufacturing company in a situation in which strong production scheduling and control experience would be valuable." Always try to put down

CONRAD D. STAPLETON
77 Pleasantapple Way
Coltsville, NY 10176
747-1012 conrad@Pearson.com

CONFIDENTIAL

JOB OBJECTIVE *Senior Production Manager* in a situation requiring extensive advertising and promotion experience.

PRESENT POSITION VALUE-PLUS DIVISION, INTERCONTINENTAL CORPORATION

2000–Present *Product Manager,* NEW PRODUCTS, LAUDRYON SOAP and CARBOLENE CLEANER, reporting to Group Product Manager.

Recommended and obtained test market authorization, then managed all phases of development of THREE test brands, scheduled for introduction during Fall/Winter 2003. Combined first year national volume projects to $20 million, with advertising budget of $6 million. Concurrently developing several new products for 2004 test marketing.

Also responsible for two established brands: LAUNDRYON SOAP, a $7 million brand, and CARBOLENE CLEANER, a $4 million regional brand. Currently work with three advertising agencies on test and established brands.

1997–2000 *Product Manager,* WEEKENDER PAINTS, a $6 million brand.

Developed and implemented a repositioning of this brand (including new copy and new package graphics) to counter a 10-year sales downtrend averaging 10% a year. Repositioning increased test market volume 16%, and national volume 8% the following year.

Later initiated development of new, more competitive copy than advertising used during repositioning. Test area sales increased 35%. National airing is scheduled for Fall 1999.

Developed plastic packaging that increased test market volume 10%.

Also developed and implemented profit improvement projects which increased net profit 33%.

1996 *Product Manager,* SHINEZY CAR WASH, a $4 million brand.

Initiated and test marketed an improved aerosol formula and a liquid refill. Both were subsequently expanded nationally and increased brand volume 26%.

RICHARDS-DONALDS COMPANY

1995–1996 *Assistant Product Manager,* reporting to Product Manager.

Concurrent responsibility on PAR and SHIPSHAPE detergents. Developed locally tailored annual promotion plans. These resulted in 30% sales increase on PAR and stabilization of SHIPSHAPE volume.

1994–1995 *Product Merchandising Assistant*

Developed and implemented SUNSHINE SUDS annual promotion plan.

1993–1994 Academic Leave of Absence to obtain MBA.

1991–1993 *Account Manager,* Field Sales.

Account Manager for Shopper's Pal, the most difficult chain in metropolitan Westchester. Achieved sales increase of 10% and distribution of all Lever products, introduced while I was on territory. Based on this performance was awarded Food'N Things Cooperatives, the second most difficult account, and achieved similar results.

1990–1991 READING SCHOOL, University of Maryland

MBA in Marketing Management. Average grade 3.5 out of 4.0. Thesis: "The Distribution of Pet Supplies through Supermarkets," graded 4.0 out of 4.0. Courses included quantitative methods, finance, accounting, and international business.

1986–1990 ELTON COLLEGE, Kansas City, Missouri

BA in Liberal Arts. Was one of 33, out of freshman class of 110, who completed four years of this academically rigorous program. Judge in Student Court during senior year.

FIGURE 10-A8

Example of a Good Résumé

Source: Adapted from Richard Payne, *How to Get a Better Job Quicker* (New York: Signet) 1988, pp. 80–81.

the most senior title you know you can expect to secure, keeping in mind the specific job for which you are applying.

Job Scope   Indicate the scope of your responsibility in each of your previous jobs, starting with your most recent position. For each of your previous jobs, write a paragraph that shows job title, whom you reported to directly and indirectly, who reported to you, how many people reported to you, the operational and human resource budgets you controlled, and what your job entailed (in one sentence).

Your Accomplishments   Next (and this is very important), indicate your "worth" in each of the positions you held. This is the heart of your résumé. It shows for each of your previous jobs: (1) the concrete action you took and why you took it and (2) the specific result of your action—the "payoff." For example, "As production supervisor, I introduced a new process to replace costly hand soldering of component parts. The new process reduced assembly time per unit from 30 to 10 minutes and reduced labor costs by over 60%." Use several of these worth statements for each job.

Length   Keep your résumé to two pages or less, and list education, military service (if any), and personal background (hobbies, interests, associations) on the last page.

Personal Data   Do not put personal data regarding age, marital status, or dependents on top of page one. If you must include it, do so at the end of the résumé, where it will be read after the employer has already formed an opinion of you.

Finally, two last points. First, do not produce a slipshod résumé: Avoid overcrowded pages, difficult-to-read copies, typographical errors, and other problems of this sort. Second, do not use a make-do résumé—one from 10 years ago. Produce a new résumé for each job you are applying for, gearing your job objective and worth statements to the job you want.

Make Your Résumé Scannable   For many job applications it's important to write a scannable résumé, in other words, one that is electronically readable by a computer system. Many medium- and larger-sized firms that do extensive recruiting and hiring—especially online and with the aid of applicant tracking systems—now use software to quickly and automatically review large numbers of résumés, screening out those that don't seem to match (often based on the absence of certain key words that the employer is looking for).

There are several guidelines to keep in mind for writing scannable résumés.[18] These can be summarized as follows:

Use type no smaller than 10 points and no larger than 14 points.

Do not use italicized type, and do not underline words.

Use type styles that work well for résumés and can be scanned as well as read, such as Helvetica, Futura, Optima, Times Roman, New Century Schoolbook, Courier, Univers, and Bookman.

When submitting hard copies, submit only high-resolution documents. Documents produced on a laser printer work best. Many photocopies and faxes are not clean enough for scanning.

Make sure to present your qualifications using powerful key words appropriate to the job or jobs for which you are applying. For example, trainers might use key words and phrases such as: computer-based training, interactive video, and group facilitator.

Online Bios Today, employers often encourage or require their professionals and managers to post brief biographies on corporate intranets or Web sites. These bios let other employees know about their colleagues' expertise. Tips for writing such bios include:[19]

Fill it with details. "The more information you enter, the more likely a person seeking someone with your background will find you . . . ."

Avoid touchy subjects. For example, avoid discussing religion and politics.

Look the part. Your profile may require posting photos. If so, dress in professional attire.

Make it search friendly. Make sure your profile contains the key words you think someone searching for someone with your background and expertise would be looking for, such as "manager," "supervisor," or "engineer."

Use abbreviations. Abbreviations are important. For example, someone searching the site might more readily punch in "MBA" then "Masters in Business Administration."

Say it with numbers. Describe specifically how your work has contributed to your current employer's and past employer's bottom lines.

Proofread. Carefully proofread your online profile, as you would your résumé.

Handling the Interview   You have done all your homework and now the big day is almost here; you have an interview next week with the person who is responsible for hiring for the job you want. What must you do to excel in the interview? Here are some suggestions.

Prepare, Prepare, Prepare First, remember that preparation is essential. Before the interview, learn all you can about the employer, the job, and the people doing the recruiting. Search the Internet (or your library) to find out what is happening in the employer's field. Who is the competition? How are they doing?

Uncover the Interviewer's Needs Spend as little time as possible answering your interviewer's first questions and as much time as possible getting the person to describe his or her needs—what the person is looking to get accomplished and the type of person needed. Use open-ended questions, such as "Could you tell me more about that?"

Relate Yourself to the Person's Needs Once you understand the type of person your interviewer is looking for and the sorts of problems he or she wants solved, you are in a good position to describe your own accomplishments in terms of the interviewer's needs. Start by saying something like, "One of the problem areas you've indicated is important to you is similar to a problem I once faced." Then state the problem, describe your solution, and reveal the results.

Think Before Answering Answering a question should be a three-step process: pause, think, speak. Pause to make sure you understand what the interviewer is driving at, think about how to structure your answer, and then speak. In your answer, try to emphasize how hiring you will help the interviewer solve his or her problem.

Make a Good Appearance and Show Enthusiasm Appropriate clothing, good grooming, a firm handshake, and the appearance of controlled energy are important. Remember that studies of interviews show that in almost 80% of the cases, interviewers make up their minds about the applicant during the first few moments of the interview. A good first impression may turn bad during the interview, but it is unlikely. Bad first impressions are almost impossible to overcome.

APPENDIX GLOSSARY

career cycle The various stages a person's career goes through.

growth stage The period from birth to age 14 during which a person develops a self-concept by identifying with and interacting with other people.

exploration stage The period (roughly from ages 15 to 24) during which a person seriously explores various occupational alternatives.

establishment stage Spans roughly ages 24 to 44 and is the heart of most people's work lives.

trial substage Period that lasts from about ages 25 to 30 during which the person determines whether or not the chosen field is suitable; if not, changes may be attempted.

stabilization substage Firm occupational goals are set and the person does more explicit career planning.

midcareer crisis substage Period during which people often make major reassessments of their progress relative to original ambitions and goals.

maintenance stage Period between ages 45 and 65 when many people slide from the stabilization substage into an established position and focus on maintaining that place.

decline stage Period where many people face having to accept reduced levels of power and responsibility, and must learn to develop new roles as mentors or confidantes for younger people.

career anchors Pivots around which a person's career swings; require self-awareness of talents and abilities, motives and needs, and attitudes and values.

APPENDIX ENDNOTES

1. Rebecca Sohn, "Career Management in a Jobless Economy," *Westchester County Business Journal,* April 5, 2004, v 43, i14, p. 4.
2. The classic discussion of career stages is in Donald Super et al., *Vocational Development: A Framework for Research* (New York: Teachers College Press, 1975), and Edgar Schein, *Career Dynamics: Matching Individual and Organizational Needs* (Reading, MA: Addison-Wesley, 1978).
3. John Holland, *Making Vocational Choices: A Theory of Careers* (Upper Saddle River, NJ: Prentice Hall, 1973).
4. Edward Levinson et al., "A Critical Evaluation of the Web-Based Version of the Career Key," *Career Development Quarterly* 50, no. 1 (September 1, 2002), pp. 26–36.
5. This is based on James Waldroop and Timothy Butler, "Finding the Job You *Should* Want," *Fortune*, March 2, 1998, pp. 211–214.
6. Richard Bolles, *What Color Is Your Parachute?* (Berkeley, CA: Ten Speed Press, 2003), pp. 5–6.
7. Ibid., p. 5. Researchers and career specialists are working with the U.S. government's O*NET to devise a methodology that will enable individuals to make better use of O*NET in identifying and choosing career paths. See, for example, Patrick Converse et al., "Matching Individuals to Occupations Using Abilities and the O*NET: Issues and an Application in Career Guidance," *Personnel Psychology*, 2004, vol. 57, pp. 451–47.
8. Edgar Schein, *Career Dynamics*, (Reading, MA; Addison Wesley, 1978) pp. 128–129; and Edgar Schein, "Career Anchors Revisited: Implications for Career Development in the 21st Century," *Academy of Management Executive* 10, no. 4 (1996), pp. 80–88.
9. Ibid., pp. 257–262. For a recent test of Schein's career anchor is concept, see Yvon Martineau et al., "Multiple Career Anchors of Québec Engineers: Impact on Career Path and Success," *Relations Industrielles/Industrial Relations* 60, no. 3, Summer 2005, p. 45; pp. 455–482.

10. This example is based on Richard Bolles, *The Three Boxes of Life* (Berkely, CA: Ten Speed Press, 1976). See also Richard Bolles, *What Color Is Your Parachute?*

11. "Resume Banks Launched," *Financial Executives* 17, no. 6 (September 2001), p. 72; James Siegel, "The ACCA Launches Online Career Center," *A/C, Heating & Refrigeration News*, June 16, 2003, p. 5.

12. "Read This Before You Put a Resume Online," *Fortune*, May 24, 1999, pp. 290–291.

13. See, John Wareham, "How to Make a Headhunter Call You," *Across-the-Board* 32, no. 1 (January 1995), pp. 49–50, and Deborah Wright Brown and Alison Konrad, "Job Seeking in a Turbulent Environment: Social Networks and the Importance of Cross-Industry Ties to An Industry Change," *Human Relations*, August 2001, v 54, i8, p. 1018.

14. See, for example, "Job Search Tips The America's Intelligence Wire," May 17, 2004, and "What to Do When Your Job Search Stalls," *BusinessWeek* online, March 16, 2004.

15. John Rau, "And the Winner Is . . . ," *Across-the-Board* 54, no. 10 (November/December 1997), pp. 38–42.

16. Based on Ibid., pp. 32–42.

17. Richard Payne, "How to Get a Better Job Quicker," (New York, Mentor, 1987) pp. 54–87. See also Larry Salters, "Resume Writing for the 1990s," *Business and Economics Review* 40, no. 3 (April 1994), pp. 11–18.

18. Erica Gordon Sorohan, "Electrifying a Job Search," *Training and Development*, October 1994, pp. 7–9; "Electronic Resumes Help Searchers Get in Job Hunt," Knight Ridder/Tribune Business News, April 6, 2004, ITEM 04097013.

19. Sara Needleman, "Posting a Job Profile Online? Keep it Polished," August 29, 2006, the *Wall Street Journal*, p. B7.

PART III VIDEO CASES APPENDIX

Video 5: The HR Manager's Job, Job Analysis, Training and Developing Employees

Video Title: Training and Development

In this video, the director of training and development turns a somewhat confrontational meeting with the firm's marketing director into something more positive. The marketing director is making the case that there are several performance problems among employees of the company, and that she believes that inadequate training and development is the reason why. For her part, the training and development manager, Jenny Herman, says that she understands that the company, Loews Hotels, is getting complaints from customers, but that the firm's training program has been following the employee performance standards now in place. The problem is "there are standards, but employees are still falling down." After discussing the matter between the two of them, they agree that the training and development program was not revised for the company's new needs, and that among other things Jenny would "like to revise the new hire certification process." She emphasizes that "we need to hear more from the field what the training and development needs are, and then try these out, and then roll out the final program."

Discussion Questions

1. Could the inadequate performance be a result, not of inadequate training, but of something else—such as inadequate motivation, or inadequate employee selection?

2. How would you go about finding out, based upon what you read in this part of the book?

3. The concluding discussion of the video about how human resource managers actually choose training techniques raises some useful questions. For example, do you agree that classroom training is particularly appropriate for hotel employees "because they like classroom training?"

Video 6: Performance Management and Appraisal, Career Management

Video Title: Ernst & Young

Ernst & Young, a large U.S. accounting firm, increased its employee retention rate by 5% as a result of a human resource initiative "to put people first." By creating a performance feedback—rich culture, building great résumés for its 160,000 people in New York City and around the world, and giving them time and freedom to pursue personal goals, Ernst & Young operationalized the idea of "people first" and thereby created a more motivated work force. In this video, you'll see the company uses mandatory goal setting, provides employees with learning opportunities in their areas of interest, and measures HR processes using an employee survey to evaluate the workplace environment. While the first segment of this video is necessarily relevant for our needs, the segment on Ernst & Young, in which Kevin, the senior auditor describes his experience at Ernst & Young, illustrates both what performance management means in practice, and the effect that it can have on employees.

Discussion Questions

1. In what ways to the HR practices that Ernst & Young (such as goal setting, and providing people with learning opportunities in their areas of interest) illustrate what performance management means in practice?
2. How important do you think it is that Ernst & Young measure HR practices using an employee survey? Why? How would you do so?
3. What role should such a survey place in the firm's performance management program, and in its strategic human resource efforts?

11 Establishing Strategic Pay Plans

The retail grocery business traditionally has low profit margins and is highly competitive. So when Wal-Mart moves into a grocery's area, the knee-jerk reaction is usually to cut costs, particularly wage rates and benefits. For example, several years ago, Safeway Stores cut employee health-care benefits, precipitating a strike by its California employees. As Wegman's Food Markets Inc. adds more stores and increasingly confronts competition from Wal-Mart, its management similarly needs to decide what to do about pay. Should they cut pay-related expenses to better compete based on cost, or pursue a different compensation policy?[1] •

After studying this chapter, you should be able to:

1 List the basic factors in determining pay rates.
2 Explain in detail how to establish pay rates.
3 Explain how to price managerial and professional jobs.
4 Discuss competency-based pay and other current trends in compensation.

employee compensation
All forms of pay or rewards going to employees and arising from their employment.

Once employees have done their jobs and been appraised, they expect to be paid. Each employee's pay should make sense in terms of the company's overall pay plan. The main purpose of this chapter is to show you how to establish a pay plan. We explain *job evaluation*—techniques for finding the relative worth of a job—and how to conduct online and offline salary surveys. We also explain how to price the jobs in your firm by developing pay grades and ranges and an overall pay plan. The next chapter focuses specifically on pay-for-performance and incentive plans.

❶ List the basic factors in determining pay rates.

BASIC FACTORS IN DETERMINING PAY RATES

direct financial payments
Pay in the form of wages, salaries, incentives, commissions, and bonuses.

Employee compensation refers to all forms of pay going to employees and arising from their employment. It has two main components, **direct financial payments** (wages, salaries, incentives, commissions, and bonuses), and **indirect financial payments** (financial benefits like employer-paid insurance and vacations).

indirect financial payments
Pay in the form of financial benefits such as insurance.

In turn, there are basically two ways to make direct financial payments to employees: base them on increments of time, or on performance. Time-based pay is still the foundation of most employers' pay plans. Blue-collar and clerical workers get hourly or daily wages, for instance, and others, like managers or Web designers, tend to be salaried and paid by the week, month, or year. The second direct payment option is to pay for performance. Piecework is an example. It ties compensation to the amount of production (or number of "pieces") the worker turns out. For instance, you divide a worker's target hourly wage by the standard number of units he or she is to produce in one hour. Then for each unit he or she produces, the person earns the calculated rate per piece. Sales commissions are another example of performance-based (in this case, sales-based) compensation. Of course, employers also devise pay plans in which employees receive some combination of time-based pay plus incentives.

Davis-Bacon Act (1931)
A law that sets wage rates for laborers employed by contractors working for the federal government.

In this chapter, we explain how to formulate plans for paying employees a time-based wage or salary; subsequent chapters cover performance-based financial incentives and bonuses (Chapter 12), and employee benefits (Chapter 13).

Walsh-Healey Public Contract Act (1936)
A law that requires minimum wage and working conditions for employees working on any government contract amounting to more than $10,000.

Several factors determine the design of any pay plan: legal, union, company policy, and equity. We'll start with legal factors.

Legal Considerations in Compensation

Title VII of the 1964 Civil Rights Act
This act makes it unlawful for employers to discriminate against any individual with respect to hiring, compensation, terms, conditions, or privileges of employment because of race, color, religion, sex, or national origin.

Various laws specify things like minimum wages, overtime rates, and benefits.[2] For example, the 1931 **Davis-Bacon Act** allows the secretary of labor to set wage rates for laborers and mechanics employed by contractors working for the federal government. Amendments provide for paid employee benefits. The 1936 **Walsh-Healey Public Contract Act** sets basic labor standards for employees working on any government contract that amounts to more than $10,000. It contains minimum wage, maximum hour, and safety and health provisions, and requires time-and-a-half pay for work over 40 hours a week. **Title VII of the 1964 Civil Rights Act** makes it unlawful for employers to discriminate against any individual with respect to hiring, compensation, terms, conditions, or privileges of employment because of race, color, religion, sex, or national origin. We'll look next at other important compensation-related laws.

Fair Labor Standards Act (1938)
This act provides for minimum wages, maximum hours, overtime pay, and child labor protection. The law has been amended many times and covers most employees.

The 1938 Fair Labor Standards Act The **Fair Labor Standards Act**, originally passed in 1938 and since amended many times, contains minimum wage, maximum hours, overtime pay, equal pay, record-keeping, and child labor provisions that are familiar to most working people. It covers the majority of U.S. workers—virtually all those engaged in the production and/or sale of goods for interstate and foreign commerce. In addition, agricultural workers and those employed by certain larger retail and service companies are included. State fair labor standards laws cover most employers not covered by the FLSA.[3]

One familiar provision governs *overtime pay*. It says employers must pay overtime at a rate of at least one-and-a-half times normal pay for any hours worked over 40 in a workweek. Thus, if a worker covered by the act works 44 hours in one week, he or she must be paid for four of those hours at a rate equal to one-and-a-half times the hourly or weekly base rate the person would have earned for 40 hours. For example, if the person earns $8 an hour (or $320 for a 40-hour week), he or she would be paid at the rate of $12 per hour (8 times 1.5) for each of the four overtime hours worked, or a total of $48 extra. If the employee instead receives time off for the overtime hours, the employer must also compute the number of hours granted off at the one-and-a-half-times rate. So the person would get six hours off for the four hours of overtime, in lieu of overtime pay.

Violating these provisions can be costly. For example, several years ago a federal judge ordered the owners of a Colorado beef processing plant to pay nearly $2 million in back wages to 5,071 employees. The firm violated the Fair Labor Standards Act by not paying those employees one-and-a-half times their regular pay rate for hours worked in excess of 40 per week, and for not keeping required records.[4]

The act also sets a *minimum wage*, which sets a floor for employees covered by the act (and usually bumps up wages for practically all workers when Congress raises the minimum). The minimum wage will rise in steps from $5.85 per hour in 2007 for the majority of those covered by the act to $7.25 in 2009. Many states have their own minimum wage laws. For example, the minimum wage in California as of June 2007, was $6.75. About 80 localities, including Boston and Chicago, require businesses that have contracts with the city to pay employees wages ranging from $6 to $12 an hour.[5] *Child labor provisions* prohibit employing minors between 16 and 18 years old in hazardous occupations, and carefully restrict employment of those under 16.

Exempt/Non-Exempt   Specific categories of employees are *exempt* from the act or certain provisions of the act, and particularly from the act's overtime provisions—they are "exempt employees." A person's exemption depends on his or her responsibilities, duties, and salary. Bona fide executive, administrative (like office managers), and professional employees (like architects) are generally exempt from the minimum wage and overtime requirements of the act.[6] A white-collar worker earning more than $100,000 and performing any one exempt administrative, executive, or management duty is automatically ineligible for overtime pay. Other employees can generally earn up to $23,660 per year and still automatically get overtime pay, so most employees earning less than $455 per week are non-exempt and earn overtime.[7] Up until a few years ago, only workers earning up to $8,060 per year automatically received overtime pay.[8] Figure 11-1 provides examples of those who are and are not exempt.

If an employee is exempt from the FLSA's minimum wage provisions, then he or she is also exempt from its overtime pay provisions. However, certain employees are always exempt from overtime pay provisions. They include, among others: agricultural employees; live-in household employees; taxicab drivers; and motion picture theater employees.[9] Figure 11-2 summarizes important guidelines governing white-collar exemptions.

Equal Pay Act (1963)
An amendment to the Fair Labor Standards Act designed to require equal pay for women doing the same work as men.

1963 Equal Pay Act   The **Equal Pay Act**, an amendment to the Fair Labor Standards Act, states that employees of one sex may not be paid wages at a rate lower than that paid to employees of the opposite sex for doing roughly equivalent work. Specifically, if the work requires equal skills, effort, and responsibility and involves similar working conditions, employees of

FIGURE 11-1

Who Is Exempt?
Who Is Not Exempt?

Source: Jeffrey Friedman, "The Fair Labor Standards Act Today: A Primer," *Compensation*, January/February 2002, p. 53. Reprinted with permission of Sage Publications, Inc. *Note:* These lists are general in nature, and exceptions exist. Any questionable allocation of exemption status should be reviewed by labor legal counsel.

Exempt, Nonexempt Examples

Exempt Professionals

Attorneys
Physicians
Dentists
Pharmacists
Optometrists
Architects
Engineers
Teachers
Certified public accountants
Scientists
Computer systems analysts

Nonexempt

Paralegals
Nonlicensed accountants
Accounting clerks
Newspaper writers

Exempt Executives

Corporate officers
Supervisors
Superintendents
General managers
Individual who is in sole charge
  of an "independent establishment"
  or branch

Nonexempt

Working foreman/forewoman
Working supervisor
Lead worker
Management trainees

Exempt Administrators

Executive assistant to the
  president
Personnel directors
Accountants
Purchasing agents

Nonexempt

Secretaries
Clerical employees
Inspectors
Statisticians

FIGURE 11-2

Main Duties Determining Which White Collar Employees Are Exempt Employees

Source: André Honoreé, "The New Fair Labor Standards Act Regulations and the Sales Force: Who Is Entitled to Pay?" *Compensation & Benefits Review*, January/February 2006, p. 31. Reprinted by permission of Sage Publications, Inc.

Executive (Three Duties Are Required)

1. Management of the enterprise in which the employee is employed or of a permanent department or subdivision; **AND**

2. Who customarily and regularly directs the work of two or more other employees; **AND**

3. Who has the authority to hire or fire other employees or whose suggestions and recommendations are given particular weight.

Administrative (Both Duties Are Required)

1. Performance of office or nonmanual work directly related to the management or general business operations of the employer or the employer's customers; **AND**

2. The exercise of discretion and independent judgment with respect to matters of significance.

Professional (Either Duty Is Sufficient)

1. Performance of work requiring knowledge of an advanced type in a field of science or learning customarily acquired by a prolonged course of specialized intellectual instructions; **OR**

2. Performance of work requiring invention, imagination, originality, or talent in a recognized field of artistic or creative endeavor.

Employee Retirement Income Security Act (ERISA)

The law that provides government protection of pensions for all employees with company pension plans. It also regulates vesting rights (employees who leave before retirement may claim compensation from the pension plan).

both sexes must receive equal pay, unless the differences in pay stem from a seniority system, a merit system, the quantity or quality of production, or "any factor other than sex."

1974 Employee Retirement Income Security Act (ERISA)   The **Employee Retirement Income Security Act** This act provided for the creation of government-run, employer-financed corporations to protect employees against the failure of their employers'

Two executives discuss a print layout; one happens to be in a wheelchair. Federal law mandates that the wheelchair-bound employee not suffer discrimination in compensation.

pension plans. In addition, it sets regulations regarding vesting rights (*vesting* refers to the equity or ownership the employees build up in their pension plans should their employment be terminated before retirement). ERISA also regulates *portability rights* (the transfer of an employee's vested rights from one organization to another) and contains fiduciary standards to prevent dishonesty in pension plan funding.

Other Legislation Affecting Compensation   Various other laws influence compensation decisions. For example, the *Age Discrimination in Employment Act* prohibits age discrimination against employees who are 40 years of age and older in all aspects of employment, including compensation.[10] The *Americans with Disabilities Act* prohibits discrimination against qualified persons with disabilities in all aspects of employment, including compensation. The *Family and Medical Leave Act* aims to entitle eligible employees, both men and women, to take up to 12 weeks of unpaid, job-protected leave for the birth of a child or for the care of a child, spouse, or parent. And various executive orders require employers that are federal government contractors or subcontractors to not discriminate, and to take affirmative action in certain employment areas, including compensation.

Each state has its own *workers' compensation laws*. Among other things, these aim to provide prompt, sure, and reasonable income to victims of work-related accidents. The *Social Security Act of 1935* (as amended) provides for unemployment compensation for workers unemployed through no fault of their own for up to 26 weeks, and for retirement benefits. (We'll discuss Social Security benefits in Chapter 13.) The federal wage garnishment law limits the amount of an employee's earnings that employers can withhold (garnish) per week, and protects the worker from discharge due to garnishment. The "Know Your Employment Law" feature explains some special applications of compensation law.

Union Influences on Compensation Decisions

Unions and labor relations laws also influence pay plan design. The National Labor Relations Act of 1935 (Wagner Act) and related legislation and court decisions legitimized the labor movement. It gave unions legal protection and granted employees the right to unionize, to bargain collectively, and to engage in concerted activities for the purpose of collective bargaining or other mutual aid or protection. Historically, the wage rate has been the main issue in collective bargaining. However, unions also negotiate other pay-related issues, including time off with pay, income security (for those in industries with periodic layoffs), cost-of-living adjustments, and health care benefits.

The 1935 Act created the National Labor Relations Board (NLRB) to oversee employer practices and ensure that employees receive their rights. Its rulings underscore the need to involve union officials in developing the compensation package. For example, employers must give the union a written explanation of the employer's "wage curves"—the graph that relates job to pay rate. The union is also entitled to know its members' salaries.[11]

Competitive Strategy, Corporate Policies, and Compensation

The compensation plan should further the firm's strategic aims—management should produce an *aligned reward strategy*. The employer's basic task here is to create a bundle

Know Your *Employment* **LAW** | **Some Special Common Pay Applications**

Making the Offer

The manager needs to exercise care in how he or she words the letter of offer. Some employers quote an annual salary, (often because a modest hourly pay rate may look more impressive when annualized— $20,000 per year sounds better than $10 per hour, for instance). The problem with making offers in terms of annual salaries is that in some jurisdictions doing so can create an implied (one-year) contract between employer and new employee. Not many courts have taken that position, but as one labor lawyer points out, "The problem in the use of annual salary is that it creates exposure to a lawsuit win or lose."[12] It's therefore usually safer to describe prospective pay in terms of hourly pay rate or monthly salary.

The Workday

Employers should be vigilant about employees who arrive early or leave late, lest the extra time spent on the employer's property obligate the employer to compensate the employee for that time. For example, a diligent employee may get dropped off at work early and spend, say, 20 minutes before his or her day actually starts doing work-related chores such as compiling a list of clients to call that day. While there is no hard and fast rule, some courts follow the rule that employees who arrive 15 or more minutes early are presumed to be working unless the employer can prove otherwise.[13] If using time clocks, employers should always instruct employees not to clock in more than 5–10 minutes early (or out 5–10 minutes late).

FIGURE 11-3

Independent Contractor

Source: Reprinted from www.HR.BLR.com with permission of the publisher *Business and Legal Reports Inc.*, 141 Mill Rock Road East, Old Saybrook, CT © 2004.

Independent Contractor

Managers are to use the following checklist to classify individuals as independent contractors. If more than three questions are answered "yes," the manager will confer with human resources regarding the classification. (EE = Employees, IC = Independent Contractors)

<u>Factors which show control:</u>

	Yes/EE	No/IC	N/A
1. Worker must comply with instructions.	☐	☐	☐
2. Worker is trained by person hired.	☐	☐	☐
3. Worker's services are integrated in business.	☐	☐	☐
4. Worker must personally render services.	☐	☐	☐
5. Worker cannot hire or fire assistants.	☐	☐	☐
6. Work relationship is continuous or indefinite.	☐	☐	☐
7. Work hours are present.	☐	☐	☐
8. Worker must devote full time to this business.	☐	☐	☐
9. Work is done on the employer's premises.	☐	☐	☐
10. Worker cannot control order or sequence.	☐	☐	☐
11. Worker submits oral or written reports.	☐	☐	☐
12. Worker is paid at specific intervals.	☐	☐	☐
13. Worker's business expenses are reimbursed.	☐	☐	☐
14. Worker is provided with tools or materials.	☐	☐	☐
15. Worker has no significant investment.	☐	☐	☐
16. Worker has no opportunity for profit/loss.	☐	☐	☐
17. Worker is not engaged by many different firms.	☐	☐	☐
18. Worker does not offer services to public.	☐	☐	☐
19. Worker may be discharged by employer.	☐	☐	☐
20. Worker can terminate without liability.	☐	☐	☐

The Independent Contractor

Whether the person is an employee or an *independent contractor* is a continuing issue for employers.

The problem is that many so-called independent contractor relationships are not really independent contractor relationships. The U.S. Department of Labor says there is no single rule or test for determining whether an individual is an independent contractor or a bona fide employee. Instead, it is the total activity or situation at which the courts will look. The major consideration is this: The more the employer controls what the worker does, the more likely it is that the courts will find the worker is actually an employee. Figure 11-3 lists some factors the courts will consider here.

For employers, there are advantages to claiming that someone doing work for them is an independent contractor (basically, a person like a consultant who is his or her own boss). For one thing, the FLSA's requirements do not apply. For another, the employer does not have to pay unemployment compensation payroll taxes, Social Security taxes, or city, state, and federal income taxes or compulsory workers' compensation for that worker. If the person is truly an independent contractor, the relationship can also be advantageous to him or her. For example, it gives the worker more flexibility regarding things like when and where he or she works, and often gives the person more options, for instance, in terms of deducting business expenses.

Penalties for the employer who misclassifies an employee as an independent contractor can be severe. For example, the employer can be retroactively liable for the IRS taxes that it did not withhold (plus penalties), as well as for overtime pay, unemployment compensation taxes, and back Social Security taxes plus interest. Even major firms allegedly misclassify some employees. Microsoft paid almost $97 million to settle one such suit, for instance.[14]

of rewards—a total reward package—aimed at eliciting the employee behaviors the firm needs to support and achieve its competitive strategy. Table 11-1 summarizes this cause-and-effect process.

The employer's compensation strategy will manifest itself in *pay policies*. For example, a top hospital like Johns Hopkins might have a policy of starting nurses at a wage of 20% above the prevailing market wage. (Note that paying higher salaries is no guarantee

TABLE 11-1 Developing an Aligned Reward Strategy

Questions to Ask:

1. What must our company do, to be successful in fulfilling its mission or achieving its desired competitive position?

2. What are the employee behaviors or actions necessary to successfully implement this competitive strategy?

3. What compensation programs should we use to reinforce those behaviors? What should be the purpose of each program in reinforcing each desired behavior?

4. What measurable requirements should each compensation program meet to be deemed successful in fulfilling its purpose?

5. How well do our current compensation programs match these requirements?

Source: Adapted from Jack Dolmat-Connell, "Developing a Reward Strategy that Delivers Shareholder and Employee Value," *Compensation and Benefits Review*, March–April 1999, p. 51.

the employer will hire more qualified employees; many factors influence the quality of hires, for example, union pressure and company reputation.)[15]

The employer will formulate pay policies covering various pay related issues. One is whether to emphasize seniority or performance. For example, it takes 18 years for a U.S. federal employee to progress from step one to step nine of the government's pay scale. Seniority-based pay may be advantageous to the extent that seniority as an objective standard. One disadvantage is that top performers may get the same raises as poor ones. Seniority-based pay might seem to be a relic reserved for some government agencies and unionized firms, but one recent survey found that 60% of employees responding thought it was the people who'd been with their companies the longest that received the most pay; about 35% said their companies paid high performers more.[16]

Distinguishing between high and low performers is a related policy issue. For example, for many years Payless ShoeSource was fairly paternal in how it distributed raises. However, after seeing its market share drop over several years, management decided on a turnaround plan. The plan included revising its compensation policies to differentiate more aggressively between top performers and others.[17] Other policies usually cover the pay cycle, how to award salary increases and promotions, overtime pay, probationary pay, and leaves for military service, jury duty, and holidays.

salary compression
A salary inequity problem, generally caused by inflation, resulting in longer-term employees in a position earning less than workers entering the firm today.

Salary Compression How to handle salary compression is another policy issue. **Salary compression**, which means longer-term employees' salaries are lower than those of workers entering the firm today, is a creature of inflation. Prices (and starting salaries) go up faster than the company's salaries, and firms need a policy to handle it. On the one hand, you don't want to treat current employees unfairly or to have them leave with their knowledge and expertise. However, mediocre performance or lack of assertiveness, not salary compression, may explain some low salaries. One policy is to install a more aggressive merit pay program. Others authorize supervisors to recommend "equity" adjustments for selected employees who are both highly valued and victims of pay compression.

Geography Geography also plays a policy role. For example, the average base pay for an executive secretary ranges from $37,300 in Albuquerque, New Mexico, to $41,900 (Tampa, Florida), $59,800 (New York, New York), and $60,100 (San Francisco, California).[18]

Employers handle cost-of-living differentials in several ways. One is to give the transferred person a nonrecurring payment, usually in a lump sum or perhaps spread over one to three years. Others pay a differential for ongoing costs in addition to a one-time allocation. For example, one employer pays a differential of $6,000 per year to people earning $35,000 to $45,000 whom it transfers from Atlanta to Minneapolis. Others simply raise the employee's base salary. Compensating expatriate employees is still another policy problem, as "The New Workforce" feature illustrates.

IBM Example IBM is a classic example of organizational renewal. It dominated its industry into the 1980s. But by the 1990s, it was failing to exploit new technologies and losing touch with its customers.[19] Its board hired Louis Gerstner as CEO. His first strategic aim was to transform IBM from a sluggish giant to a lean winner. His actions illustrate how employers use compensation policies to support strategic aims.

Transforming IBM into a "lean winner" meant doing more than downsizing; Gerstner had to transform IBM's culture—the shared values, attitudes, and behavior patterns that guided employees' behavior. He sought to emphasize winning, execution, speed, and decisiveness. He wisely decided to use the compensation plan to support IBM's strategic aims.[20]

IBM's existing compensation pay plan did the opposite. Everyone was in a job whose relative worth for pay purposes was based on a decades-old "point-factor" system which

The **NEW** *Workforce*

Globalization and Diversity: Compensating Expatriate Employees

How should employers compensate expatriate employees—those it sends overseas? Two basic international compensation policies are popular: home-based and host-based plans.[21]

With a *home-based salary plan*, an international transferee's base salary reflects his or her home country's salary. The employer then adds allowances for cost-of-living differences—housing and schooling costs, for instance. This is a reasonable approach for short-term assignments, and avoids the problem of having to change the employee's base salary every time he or she moves.

In the *host-based plan*, the firm ties the international transferee's base salary to the host country's salary structure. In other words, the manager from New York who is sent to France would have his or her base salary changed to the prevailing base salary for that position in France,

rather than keep the New York base salary. The firm usually tacks on cost-of-living, housing, schooling, and other allowances here as well.

Most multinational enterprises set expatriates' salaries according to their home-country base pay. (Thus, a French manager assigned to Kiev by a U.S. multinational will generally have a base salary that reflects the salary structure in the manager's home country, in this case France.) In addition, the person typically gets allowances including cost-of-living, relocation, housing, education, and hardship allowances (the latter for countries with a relatively hard quality of life, such as China).[22] The employer also usually pays any extra tax burdens resulting from taxes the manager is liable for over and above those he or she would have to pay in the home country.

meticulously assigned points to each job's duties. Maintaining the point system for over 100,000 employees required "a massive and cumbersome" attention to point-factor-manual-based evaluations. This approach also cultivated a preoccupation with internal equity rather than with market-driven, competitive rates of pay. Gerstner knew he had to change the pay plan to drive the new culture he sought to create.

To change this situation, Gerstner's team made four main changes in what became the firm's new strategic compensation plan:

1. ***The marketplace rules.*** The company switched from its previous single salary structure (for nonsales employees) to different salary structures and merit budgets for different job families. This enabled IBM to concentrate on paying employees in different job families (accountants, engineers, and so on) in a more market-oriented way. The new approach sent the strong cultural signal that "a market-driven company must watch the market closely and act accordingly."[23]

2. ***Fewer jobs, evaluated differently, in broadbands.*** Second, IBM scrapped its point-factor job evaluation system and its 24 traditional salary grades. The new system has no points at all. The old system contained 10 different "compensable factors" for assessing a job's worth; the new one slots jobs into 10 bands based on just three factors (skills, leadership requirements, and scope/impact).

   In the United States, the number of separate job titles dropped from over 5,000 to fewer than 1,200[24] and 24 salary grades dropped to 10 broadbands. This communicated a new organizational model: IBM was to be a flatter organization that could "deliver goods and services to market faster."[25]

3. ***Managers manage.*** The previous compensation plan based raises on a complex formula that linked performance appraisal scores to salary increases measured in

tenths of a percent. The new system is streamlined. Managers get a budget and some coaching, the essence of which is: "Either differentiate the pay you give to stars versus acceptable performers or the stars won't be around too long."[26] The new approach lets managers rank employees on a variety of factors (such as critical skills and results). The managers decide which factors are used and what weights they're given.

4. *Big stakes for stakeholders.* As IBM was floundering in the early 1990s, every nonexecutive employee's cash compensation (outside the sales division) consisted of base salary (plus overtime, shift premiums, and some other adjustments). Pay for performance was a foreign concept. Within a year or two after Gerstner arrived, most IBM employees around the world "had 10% or more of their total cash compensation tied to performance."[27] In the new system, there are only three performance appraisal ratings. "A top-rated employee receives two-and-one-half times the award of an employee with the lowest ranking."[28]

The changes at IBM illustrate the nuts and bolts of *strategic compensation*, which means using the compensation plan to support the company's strategic aims. IBM's new pay plan refocused its employees' attention on the values of winning, execution, and speed.

Wegman's Example   It may seem counterintuitive, but cutting pay rates does not always translate into higher profits, since one must also take productivity and quality into account. Wegman's Food Market's compensation policies illustrate this. Facing competition from Wal-Mart and other chains, Wegman's chose to pay above average wages and provide all its employees with free health coverage. Management's assumption, said their human resources head, is that "if we take care of our employees, they will take care of our customers."[29]

Wegman's pay strategy seems to be working. Their larger stores each average about $950,000 a week in sales, compared to the national average of about $361,564 for grocery stores. Similarly, Wegman's employee retention figures are well above national averages for retail stores. Wegman's management decided that its competitive strategy was to compete with other grocery chains (including Wal-Mart's) based on productivity and quality of service. Its compensation strategy effectively supports that competitive strategy.

Equity and Its Impact on Pay Rates

In studies at Emory University, researchers investigated how Capuchin monkeys reacted to inequitable pay. They trained monkeys to trade pebbles for food. Some monkeys got grapes in return for pebbles, others got cucumber slices. Those receiving the sweeter grapes willingly traded in their pebbles. But if a monkey receiving a cucumber slice saw one of its neighbors get grapes, it slammed down the pebble or refused to eat the cucumber.[30] The moral seems to be that even lower primates are genetically programmed to demand fair treatment when it comes to pay.

Equity Theory of Motivation   Higher up the primate line, *the equity theory of motivation* postulates that people are strongly motivated to maintain a balance between what they perceive as their inputs or contributions, and their rewards. Equity theory states that if a person perceives an inequity, a tension or drive will develop in the person's mind, and the person will be motivated to reduce or eliminate the tension and perceived inequity. Research tends to support equity theory, particularly as it applies to people who are underpaid.[31] One recent study found that turnover of retail buyers is significantly lower when the buyers perceive fair treatment in the amount or rewards and in the methods by which employers allocate rewards.[32]

With respect to compensation, managers should address four forms of equity: *external, internal, individual,* and *procedural.*[33]

- *External equity* refers to how a job's pay rate in one company compares to the job's pay rate in other companies.
- *Internal equity* refers to how fair the job's pay rate is, when compared to other jobs within the same company (for instance, is the sales manager's pay fair, when compared to what the production manager is earning?).
- *Individual equity* refers to the fairness of an individual's pay as compared with what his or her co-workers are earning for the same or very similar jobs within the company, based on each individual's performance.
- *Procedural equity* refers to the "perceived fairness of the processes and procedures used to make decisions regarding the allocation of pay."[34]

Addressing Equity Issues   Managers use various methods to address each of these equity issues. For example, they use salary surveys (surveys of what other employers are paying) to monitor and maintain external equity. They use job analysis and job evaluation (discussed below) to maintain internal equity. They use performance appraisal and incentive pay to maintain individual equity. And they use communications, grievance mechanisms, and employees' participation in developing the company's pay plan to help ensure that employees view the pay process as transparent and procedurally fair. Some firms administer surveys to monitor employees' attitudes regarding the pay plan. Questions typically include, "How satisfied are you with your pay?" and "What factors do you believe are used when your pay is determined?"

Even large, sophisticated companies aren't immune to pay inequities. With morale down due to widespread concerns about racial discrimination suits, layoffs, and possibly inequitable salaries, Coca-Cola Co. undertook a salary review of companies ranging from PepsiCo to Procter & Gamble and Yahoo. Management then announced raises ranging from about $1,000 to as much as $15,000 for most of its employees.

When inequities do arise, conflict can ensue. To head off discussions that might prompt feelings of internal inequity, some firms maintain strict secrecy over pay rates, with mixed results. For external equity, online pay forum sites like Salary.com make it easy for employees to discover that they could earn more elsewhere.

ESTABLISHING PAY RATES

> 2 Explain in detail how to establish pay rates.

The process of establishing pay rates while ensuring external, internal, and (to some extent) procedural equity consists of five steps:

1. Conduct a salary survey of what other employers are paying for comparable jobs (to help ensure external equity).
2. Determine the worth of each job in your organization through job evaluation (to ensure internal equity).
3. Group similar jobs into pay grades.
4. Price each pay grade by using wave curves.
5. Fine-tune pay rates.

We start with the salary survey.

Step 1. The Salary Survey

salary survey
A survey aimed at determining prevailing wage rates. A good salary survey provides specific wage rates for specific jobs. Formal written questionnaire surveys are the most comprehensive, but telephone surveys and newspaper ads are also sources of information.

It's difficult to set pay rates if you don't know what others are paying, so **salary surveys**—surveys of what others are paying—play a big role in pricing jobs. Virtually every employer conducts at least an informal telephone, newspaper, or Internet salary survey.[35]

Employers use these surveys in three ways. First, they use survey data to price **benchmark jobs**. Benchmark jobs are the anchor jobs around which they slot their other jobs, based on each job's relative worth to the firm. (*Job evaluation*, explained next, helps determine the relative worth of each job.) Second, employers typically price 20% or more of their positions directly in the marketplace (rather than relative to the firm's benchmark jobs), based on a formal or informal survey of what comparable firms are paying for comparable jobs. (Google might do this for jobs like Web programmer, whose salaries fluctuate widely and often.) Third, surveys also collect data on benefits like insurance, sick leave, and vacations to provide a basis for decisions regarding employee benefits.

Salary surveys can be formal or informal. Informal phone or Internet surveys are good for checking specific issues, such as when a bank wants to confirm the salary at which to advertise a newly open teller's job, or if some banks are really paying tellers an incentive. Some large employers can afford to send out their own formal surveys to collect compensation information from other employers. Most of these ask about things like number of employees, overtime policies, starting salaries, and paid vacations.

Commercial, Professional, and Government Salary Surveys   Many employers use surveys published by consulting firms, professional associations, or government agencies. For example, the U.S. Department of Labor's Bureau of Labor Statistics (BLS) conducts three annual surveys: (1) area wage surveys; (2) industry wage surveys; and (3) professional, administrative, technical, and clerical (PATC) surveys.

The 200 or so annual *area wage surveys* provide salary data for clerical and manual occupations ranging from secretary to messenger. Area wage surveys also provide data on weekly work schedules, paid holidays and vacation practices, health insurance and pension plans, as well as on shift operations and differentials. *Industry wage surveys* provide similar data, but by industry. They also provide national pay data for workers in selected jobs for industries like building, trucking, and printing. *PATC surveys* collect pay data on 80 professional and technical occupations, including those in accounting, legal services, human resource management, and engineering. They provide information about earnings as well as production bonuses, commissions, and cost-of-living increases. The BLS organizes its various pay surveys into a national compensation survey, and publishes this information on the Web (http://stats.bls.gov).

Private consulting and/or executive recruiting companies like Hay Associates, Heidrick and Struggles, and Hewitt Associates publish data covering compensation for top and middle management and members of boards of directors. Professional organizations like the Society for Human Resource Management and the Financial Executives Institute publish surveys of compensation practices among members of their associations.

Watson Wyatt Data Services of Rochelle Park, New Jersey, publishes several compensation surveys.[36] Its top management compensation surveys cover dozens of top positions, including chief executive officer, top real estate executive, top financial executive, top sales executive, and top claims executive, all categorized by function and industry. Watson Wyatt also offers middle management compensation surveys, supervisory management compensation surveys, sales and marketing personnel surveys, professional and scientific personnel surveys, and surveys of technician trades, skilled trades, and office personnel, among others. The surveys generally cost about $700 each, but can help employers avoid the dual hazards of (1) paying too much or (2) suffering turnover due to uncompetitive pay.

benchmark job
A job that is used to anchor the employer's pay scale and around which other jobs are arranged in order of relative worth.

TABLE 11-2 Some Pay Data Web Sites

Sponsor	Internet Address	What It Provides	Downside
Salary.com	Salary.com	Salary by job and zip code, plus job and description, for hundreds of jobs	Adapts national averages by applying local cost-of-living differences
Wageweb	www.wageweb.com	Average salaries for more than 150 clerical, professional, and managerial jobs	Charges $169 for breakdowns by industry, location, etc.
U.S. Office of Personnel Management	www.opm.gov/oca/07tables/	Salaries and wages for U.S. government jobs, by location	Limited to U.S. government jobs
Job Smart	http://jobstar.org/tools/salary/sal-prof.php	Profession-specific salary surveys	Necessary to review numerous salary surveys for each profession
Monster.com	http://salary.monster.com/	Median salaries for thousands of jobs, by city	Doesn't consider factors like company size or benefits
cnnmoney.com	cnnmoney.com	Input your current salary and city, and this gives you comparable salary in destination city	Based on national averages adapted to cost of living differences

Source: Adapted from Joarm S. Cublin, "Web Transforms Art of Negotiating Raises," *Wall Street Journal*, Sept. 22, 1998, p. B1. See also Susan Marks, "Can the Internet Help You Hit the Salary Mark?" *Workforce* 80, no. 1 (Jan. 2001), pp. 86–93. Accessed August 25, 2007.

Using the Internet to Do Compensation Surveys   A rapidly expanding array of Internet-based options makes it easy for anyone to access published compensation survey information. Table 11-2 shows some popular salary survey Web sites.

Many of these sites, such as Salary.com, provide national salary levels for jobs that are then arithmetically adjusted to each locale based on cost-of-living formulas. To get a real-time picture of what employers in your area are actually paying for, say, accounting clerks, it's useful to access the online Internet sites of one or two of your local newspapers. For example, the *South Florida Sun-Sentinel* uses a site called careerbuilder. It lists career opportunities—in other words, just about all the jobs listed in the newspaper by category and, in many instances, their wage rates (http://www.sun-sentinel.com/classified/jobs). From this listing, you'll find jobs listed for "Accounts receivable clerks—$10.00 per hour," "Accounting clerk—$25k," "Accounting clerk—credit clerk, to $22k," and "Accounts payable clerk, $22–26k," among many others. Switching to the *Miami Herald*'s Web site (www.miami.com/mld/miamiherald/classifieds/employment) classifieds, you similarly find a list of several dozen related job listings. For example, there is a "Payroll clerk, Doral area, $25k," an "Accounting clerk—City of Hialeah starting at $594 biweekly," and "Accounting assistant—Miami Lakes area, to $29k."

The Internet also provides numerous fee-based sources of international salary data. For example, William M. Mercer, Inc. (http://www.mercer.com) publishes an annual global compensation planning report summarizing compensation trends for more than 40 countries plus representative pay data for four common benchmark jobs.[37]

Employers usually use salary survey data to price benchmark jobs, around which other jobs are then slotted based on the job's relative worth. Determining the relative worth of a job is the purpose of job evaluation, which we'll address next.

job evaluation
A systematic comparison done in order to determine the worth of one job relative to another.

Step 2. Job Evaluation

Job evaluation is aimed at determining a job's relative worth. It is *a formal and systematic comparison of jobs to determine the worth of one job relative to another*, and eventually results in a wage or salary structure or hierarchy (the latter shows what various jobs or groups of jobs will earn). The basic principle of job evaluation is this: Jobs that require greater qualifications, more responsibilities, and more complex job duties should be paid more highly than jobs with lesser requirements.[38] The basic procedure is to compare the jobs in relation to one another—for example, in terms of required effort, responsibility, and skills. Suppose you know (based on your salary survey) how to price key benchmark jobs, and then use job evaluation to determine the relative worth of all the other jobs in your firm relative to these key jobs. You are then well on your way to being able to price all the jobs in your organization equitably.

Compensable Factors You can use two basic approaches to compare several jobs. First, you can take an intuitive approach. You might decide that one job is more important than another and not dig any deeper into why. As an alternative, you could compare the jobs by focusing on certain basic factors the jobs have in common. Compensation management specialists call these **compensable factors**. They are the factors that establish how the jobs compare to one another, and that determine the pay for each job.

compensable factor
A fundamental, compensable element of a job, such as skills, effort, responsibility, and working conditions.

Some employers develop their own compensable factors. However, most use factors popularized by packaged job evaluation systems or by federal legislation. For example, the Equal Pay Act focuses on four compensable factors—skills, effort, responsibility, and working conditions. The method popularized by the Hay consulting firm focuses on three factors: know-how, problem solving, and accountability. Wal-Mart bases its wage structure on knowledge, problem solving skills, and accountability requirements.

Identifying compensable factors plays a central role in job evaluation. You usually compare each job with all comparable jobs using the same compensable factors. However, the compensable factors you use depend on the job and the job evaluation method. For example, you might choose to include "decision making" for a manager's job, though it might be inappropriate for a cleaner's job.[39]

Preparing for the Job Evaluation Job evaluation is a judgmental process and demands close cooperation among supervisors, HR specialists, and employees and union representatives. The main steps include identifying the need for the program, getting cooperation, and then choosing an evaluation committee. The committee then performs the actual evaluation.

Identifying the need for job evaluation should not be difficult. For example, dissatisfaction reflected in high turnover, work stoppages, or arguments may result from paying employees different rates for similar jobs. Managers may express uneasiness with an informal way of assigning pay rates, accurately sensing that a more systematic assignment would be more equitable.

Next (since employees may fear that a systematic evaluation of their jobs may actually reduce their pay rates), *getting employees to cooperate* in the evaluation is important. You can tell employees that as a result of the impending job evaluation program, pay rate decisions will no longer be made just by management whim; that job evaluation will provide a mechanism for considering the complaints they have been expressing; and that no present employee's rate will be adversely affected as a result of the job evaluation.

Next, *choose a job evaluation committee.* There are two reasons for doing so. First, the committee should include several people who are familiar with the jobs in question, each of whom may have a different perspective regarding the nature of the jobs. Second, if the committee is composed at least partly of employees, the committee approach can help ensure greater employee acceptance of the job evaluation results.

So the composition of the committee is important. The group usually consists of about five members, most of whom are employees. Management has the right to serve on such committees, but employees may view this with suspicion. However, a human resource

The job evaluation committee typically includes at least several employees, and has the important task of evaluating the worth of each job using compensable factors.

specialist can usually be justified on the grounds that he or she has a more impartial outlook than line managers and can provide expert assistance. Perhaps have this person serve in a nonvoting capacity. Union representation is possible. In most cases, though, the union's position is that it is accepting the results of the job evaluation only as an initial decision and is reserving the right to appeal actual job pricing decisions through grievance or bargaining channels.[40] Once appointed, each committee member should receive a manual explaining the job evaluation process, and instructions that explain how to conduct the job evaluation.

The evaluation committee performs three main functions. First, it usually identifies 10 or 15 key benchmark jobs. These will be the first jobs to be evaluated and will serve as the anchors or benchmarks against which the relative importance or value of all other jobs can be compared. Next, the committee may select compensable factors (although the human resources department will usually choose these as part of the process of determining the specific job evaluation technique the firm will use). Finally, the committee performs its most important function—actually evaluating the worth of each job. For this, the committee will probably use one of the following methods: ranking, job classification, point method, or factor comparison.

Job Evaluation Methods: Ranking   The simplest job evaluation method ranks each job relative to all other jobs, usually based on some overall factor like "job difficulty." There are several steps in the job **ranking method**.

ranking method
The simplest method of job evaluation that involves ranking each job relative to all other jobs, usually based on overall difficulty.

1. ***Obtain job information.*** Job analysis is the first step: Job descriptions for each job are prepared, and the information they contain about the job's duties is usually the basis for ranking jobs. (Sometimes job specifications are also prepared. However, the ranking method usually ranks jobs according to the whole job, rather than a number of compensable factors. Therefore, job specifications—which list the job's demands in terms of problem solving, decision making, and skills, for instance—are not as necessary with this method as they are for other job evaluation methods.)
2. ***Select and group jobs.*** It is often not practical to make a single ranking for all jobs in an organization. The usual procedure is to rank jobs by department or in clusters (such as factory workers or clerical workers). This eliminates the need for direct comparison of, say, factory jobs and clerical jobs.

TABLE 11-3 Job Ranking by Olympia Health Care

Ranking Order	Annual Pay Scale
1. Office manager	$43,000
2. Chief nurse	42,500
3. Bookkeeper	34,000
4. Nurse	32,500
5. Cook	31,000
6. Nurse's aide	28,500
7. Orderly	25,500

3. *Select compensable factors.* In the ranking method, it is common to use just one factor (such as job difficulty) and to rank jobs based on the whole job. Regardless of the number of factors you choose, it's advisable to explain the definition of the factor(s) to the evaluators carefully so that they evaluate the jobs consistently.

4. *Rank jobs.* For example, give each rater a set of index cards, each of which contains a brief description of a job. Then they rank these cards from lowest to highest. Some managers use an "alternation ranking method" for making the procedure more accurate. Here you take the cards, first choosing the highest and the lowest, then the next highest and next lowest, and so forth until you've ranked all the cards.

   Table 11-3 illustrates a job ranking. Jobs in this small health facility are ranked from orderly up to office manager. The corresponding pay scales are on the right. After ranking, it is possible to slot additional jobs between those already ranked and to assign an appropriate wage rate.

5. *Combine ratings.* Usually, several raters rank the jobs independently. Then the rating committee (or the employer) can simply average the raters' rankings.

This is the simplest job evaluation method, as well as the easiest to explain. And it usually takes less time than other methods.

Some of its drawbacks derive more from how it's used than from the method itself. For example, there's a tendency to rely too heavily on "guesstimates" (of things like overall difficulty, since ranking usually does not use compensable factors). Similarly, ranking provides no yardstick for quantifying the value of one job relative to another. For example, job number 4 may in fact be five times "more valuable" than job number 5, but with the ranking system all you know is that one job ranks higher than the other. Ranking is usually more appropriate for small organizations that can't afford the time or expense of developing a more elaborate system.

Job Evaluation Methods: Job Classification   **Job classification** (or **job grading**) is a simple, widely used method in which raters categorize jobs into groups; all the jobs in each group are of roughly the same value for pay purposes. The groups are called **classes** if they contain similar jobs, or **grades** if they contain jobs that are similar in difficulty but otherwise different. Thus, in the federal government's pay grade system, a "press secretary" and a "fire chief" might both be graded "GS-10" (GS stands for "General Schedule"). On the other hand, in its job class system, the state of Florida might classify all "secretary IIs" in one class, all "maintenance engineers" in another, and so forth.

There are several ways to actually categorize jobs. One is to write class or grade descriptions (similar to job descriptions) and place jobs into classes or grades based on how well they fit these descriptions. A second is to write a set of compensable factor-based rules

job classification (or grading) method
A method for categorizing jobs into groups.

classes
Grouping jobs based on a set of rules for each group or class, such as amount of independent judgment, skill, physical effort, and so forth, required. Classes usually contain similar jobs.

grades
A job classification system like the class system, although grades often contain dissimilar jobs, such as secretaries, mechanics, and firefighters. Grade descriptions are written based on compensable factors listed in classification systems.

Grade	Nature of Assignment	Level of Responsibility
GS-7	Performs specialized duties in a defined functional or program area involving a wide variety of problems or situations; develops information, identifies interrelationships, and takes actions consistent with objectives of the function or program served.	Work is assigned in terms of objectives, priorities, and deadlines; the employee works independently in resolving most conflicts; completed work is evaluated for conformance to policy; guidelines, such as regulations, precedent cases, and policy statements require considerable interpretation and adaptation.

FIGURE 11-4

Example of a Grade Level Definition

This is a summary chart of the key grade level criteria for the GS-7 level of clerical and assistance work. Do not use this chart alone for classification purposes; additional grade level criteria are in the Web-based chart.

Source: www.opm.gov/fedclass/gscler.pdf. Accessed May 18, 2007.

grade definition
Written descriptions of the level of, say, responsibility and knowledge required by jobs in each grade. Similar jobs can then be combined into grades or classes.

for each class (for instance, how much independent judgment, skill, physical effort, and so on, does the class of jobs require?). Then categorize the jobs according to these rules.

The most popular procedure is to choose compensable factors and then develop class or grade descriptions for each class or grade in terms of the amount or level of the compensable factor(s) in those jobs. For example, the U.S. government's federal classification system uses the following compensable factors: (1) difficulty and variety of work, (2) supervision received and exercised, (3) judgment exercised, (4) originality required, (5) nature and purpose of interpersonal work relationships, (6) responsibility, (7) experience, and (8) knowledge required. Based on these compensable factors, raters write a **grade definition** like that in Figure 11-4. This one shows one grade description (GS-7) for the federal government's pay grade system. Then the evaluation committee reviews all job descriptions and slots each job into its appropriate grade, by comparing each job description to the rules in each grade description. For instance, the federal government system classifies the positions automotive mechanic, welder, electrician, and machinist in grade GS-10.

The classification method has several advantages. The main one is that most employers usually end up grouping jobs into classes anyway, regardless of the evaluation method they use. They do this to avoid having to work with and price separately dozens or hundreds of jobs. Of course the job classification automatically groups the employer's jobs into classes. The disadvantages are that it is difficult to write the class or grade descriptions, and considerable judgment is required to apply them. Yet many employers use this method with success.

point method
The job evaluation method in which a number of compensable factors are identified and then the degree to which each of these factors is present on the job is determined.

Job Evaluation Methods: Point Method   The **point method** is a more quantitative technique. It involves identifying (1) several compensable factors, each having several degrees, as well as (2) the degree to which each of these factors is present in the job. Assume there are five degrees of "responsibility" a job could contain. Further assume you assign a different number of points to each degree of each factor. Once the evaluation committee determines the degree to which each compensable factor (like "responsibility" and "effort") is present in the job, it can calculate a total point value for the job by adding up the corresponding points for each factor. The result is a quantitative point rating for each job. The point method is probably the most widely used job evaluation method; the appendix to this chapter explains it in detail.

factor comparison method
A widely used method of ranking jobs according to a variety of skill and difficulty factors, then adding up these rankings to arrive at an overall numerical rating for each given job.

Job Evaluation Methods: Factor Comparison   The **factor comparison method** is actually a refinement of the ranking method. With the ranking method, you generally look at each job as an entity and rank the jobs on some overall factor like job difficulty. With the factor comparison method, you rank each job several times—once for each of several compensable factors. For example, you might first rank jobs in terms of the compensable factor "skill." Then rank them according to their "mental requirements," and so forth. Then combine the rankings for each job into an overall numerical rating for the job. This too is a widely used method, also found in more detail in the appendix to this chapter.

Computerized Job Evaluations   Using quantitative job evaluation methods such as the point or factor comparison plans can be time-consuming. Accumulating the information about "how much" of each compensable factor the job contains involves a tedious process in which evaluation committees debate the level of each compensable factor in a job. They then write down their consensus judgments and manually compute each job's point values.

Computer-aided job evaluation can streamline this process. Most of these computerized systems have two main components. There is, first, a structured questionnaire. This contains items such as "enter total number of employees who report to this position." Second, all such systems use statistical models. These allow the computer program to price jobs more or less automatically, by assigning points or factor comparison rankings to things like number of employees reporting to the positions, prices of benchmark jobs, and current pay.

Step 3. Group Similar Jobs into Pay Grades

pay grade
A pay grade is comprised of jobs of approximately equal difficulty.

Once the committee has used job evaluation to determine the relative worth of each job, it can turn to the task of assigning pay rates to each job; however, it will usually want to first group jobs into **pay grades**.[41] It could, of course, just assign pay rates to each individual job. But for a large employer, such a plan would be difficult to administer, since there might be different pay rates for hundreds or even thousands of jobs. And even in smaller organizations, there's a tendency to try to simplify wage and salary structures as much as possible. Therefore, the committee will probably group similar jobs (in terms of their ranking or number of points, for instance) into grades for pay purposes. So, instead of having to deal with hundreds of pay rates, it might only have to focus on, say, 10 or 12.

A pay grade is comprised of jobs of approximately equal difficulty or importance as established by job evaluation. If the committee used the point method, then the pay grade consists of jobs falling within a range of points. With the ranking method, the grade consists of all jobs that fall within two or three ranks. The classification method automatically categorizes jobs into classes or grades. (With the factor comparison method, the grade consists of a specified range of pay rates, as the appendix to this chapter explains.) Ten to 16 grades per "job cluster" (a *cluster* is a logical grouping, such as factory jobs, clerical jobs, and so on) are now common. However, as we'll explain shortly, there's a trend toward including more jobs—and a broader range of jobs—within each cluster.

Step 4. Price Each Pay Grade—Wage Curves

wage curve
Shows the relationship between the value of the job and the average wage paid for this job.

The next step is to assign pay rates to your pay grades. (Of course, if you chose not to slot jobs into pay grades, you would have to assign individual pay rates to each individual job.) You'll typically use a *wage curve* to help assign pay rates to each pay grade (or to each job).

The **wage curve** *shows the pay rates currently paid for jobs in each pay grade, relative to the points or rankings assigned to each job or grade by the job evaluation.* Figure 11-5 presents an example. Note that it shows pay rates on the vertical axis, and pay grades (in terms of points) along the horizontal axis. The purpose of the wage curve is to show the relationships between (1) the value of the job as determined by one of the job evaluation methods and (2) the current average pay rates for your grades.

The pay rates on the wage curve are traditionally those now paid by the employer. However, if there is reason to believe the current pay rates are out of step with the market rates for

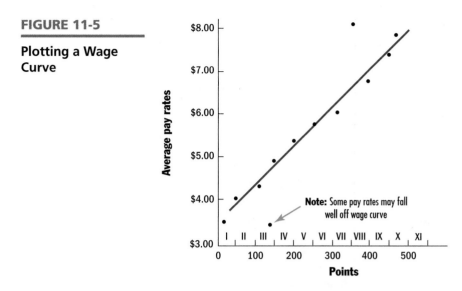

FIGURE 11-5

Plotting a Wage Curve

these jobs, choose benchmark jobs within each pay grade, and price them via a compensation survey. These new market-based pay rates then replace the current rates on the wage curve. Then slot in your other jobs (and their pay rates) around the benchmark jobs.[42]

Here is how to price jobs with a wage curve. First, find the average pay for each pay grade, since each of the pay grades consists of several jobs. Next, plot the average pay rates for each pay grade as was done in Figure 11-5. Then fit a line, called a *wage line*, through the points just plotted. You can do this freehand or by using a statistical method. Finally, price the jobs. For this, wages along the wage line are the target wages or salary rates for the jobs in each pay grade. If the current rates being paid for any of your jobs or grades fall well above or below the wage line, raises or a pay freeze for that job may be in order. Your next step, then, is to fine-tune your pay rates.

Step 5. Fine-Tune Pay Rates

Fine-tuning involves (1) developing pay ranges and (2) correcting out-of-line rates.

pay ranges
A series of steps or levels within a pay grade, usually based upon years of service.

Developing Pay Ranges Most employers do not pay just one rate for all jobs in a particular pay grade. For example, GE Medical won't want to pay all its accounting clerks, from beginners to long tenure, at the same rate. Instead, employers develop vertical pay (or "rate") ranges for each of the horizontal pay grades (or pay classes). These **pay ranges** often appear as vertical boxes within each grade, showing minimum, maximum, and midpoint pay rates for that grade, as in Figure 11-6. (Specialists call this graph a *wage structure*. It graphically depicts the range of pay rates—in this case, per hour—paid for each pay grade.) Or, you may depict the pay range found on the vertical axis as steps or levels, with specific corresponding pay rates for each step within each grade in tabular form. Table 11-4 shows the pay rates and steps for some federal government grades. As of the time of this pay schedule, for instance, employees in positions classified in grade GS-10 could be paid annual salaries between $50,169 and $65,218, depending on the level or step at which they were hired into the grade, the amount of time they were in the grade, and their merit increases (if any).

The wage line or curve usually anchors the pay rate for each pay range. The firm might then arbitrarily decide on a maximum and minimum rate for each grade, such as 15% above and below the wage line. As an alternative, some employers allow the pay range for each grade to become wider (covering more pay rates) for the higher pay ranges,

FIGURE 11-6

Wage Structure

Note: This shows overlapping wage classes and maximum/minimum wage ranges.

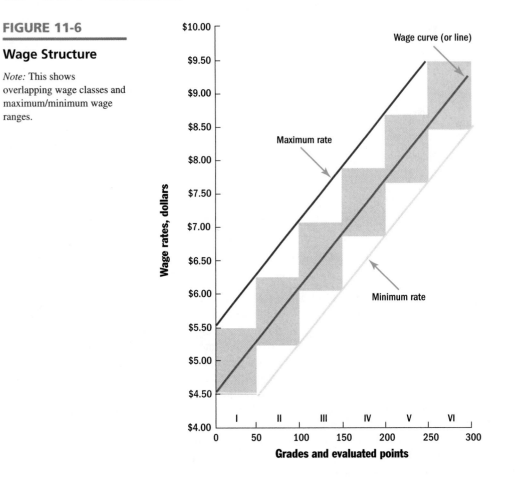

TABLE 11-4 Federal Government Pay Schedule: Grades GS-8, GS-9, GS-10, GS-11 for Dallas-Fort Worth, Texas

	EFFECTIVE JANUARY 2007 *Annual Rates by Grade and Step*								
GS-8	41,246	42,621	43,997	45,372	46,747	48,122	49,498	50,873	52,248	53,623
GS-9	45,556	47,074	48,593	50,111	51,630	53,148	54,666	56,185	57,703	59,221
GS-10	50,169	51,841	53,513	55,185	56,857	58,529	60,201	61,873	63,545	65,218
GS-11	55,119	56,957	58,794	60,632	62,469	64,307	66,145	67,982	69,820	71,657

Source: http://opm.gov/oca/07tables/pdf/DFW.pdf, accessed May 18, 2007.

reflecting the greater demands and performance variability inherent in more complex jobs. As in Figure 11-6, most employers structure their pay ranges to overlap a bit, so an employee in one grade who has more experience or seniority may earn more than an entry-level position in the next higher pay grade.

There are several reasons to use pay ranges for each pay grade. First, it lets the employer take a more flexible stance in the labor market. For example, it makes it easier to attract experienced, higher-paid employees into a pay grade at the top of the range, since the starting salary for the pay grade's lowest step may be too low to attract them. Pay ranges also let companies provide for performance differences between employees within the same grade or between those with different seniorities.

Correcting Out-of-Line Rates   The wage rate for a particular job may now fall well off the wage line or well outside the rate range for its grade, as shown in Figure 11-5. This means that the average pay for that job is currently too high or too low, relative to other jobs in the firm. For underpaid jobs, the solution is clear: raise the wages of underpaid employees to the minimum of the rate range for their pay grade.

Current pay rates falling above the rate range are a different story. These are "red circle," "flagged," or "overrates," and there are several ways to cope with this problem. One is to freeze the rate paid to these employees until general salary increases bring the other jobs into line. A second option is to transfer or promote the employees involved to jobs for which you can legitimately pay them their current pay rates. The third option is to freeze the rate for six months, during which time you try to transfer or promote the overpaid employees. If you cannot, then cut the rate you pay these employees to the maximum in the pay range for their pay grade.

The "When You're on Your Own" feature below outlines a practical method for creating a wage structure in a small firm.

③ Explain how to price managerial and professional jobs.

PRICING MANAGERIAL AND PROFESSIONAL JOBS

Developing compensation plans for managers or professionals is similar in many respects to developing plans for any employee. The basic aim is the same: to attract and keep good employees. And job evaluation—classifying jobs, ranking them, or assigning points to them, for instance—is about as applicable to managerial and professional jobs as to production and clerical ones.

There are some big differences, though. Managerial jobs tend to stress harder-to-quantify factors like judgment and problem solving more than do production and clerical jobs. There is also more emphasis on paying managers and professionals based on results—based on their performance or on what they can do—rather than on the basis of static job demands like working conditions. And there is also the considerable challenge of having to compete in the marketplace for executives who by some standards are paid like rock stars. So, job evaluation, while still important, usually plays a secondary role to non-salary issues like bonuses, incentives, market rates, and benefits.

Compensating Executives and Managers

Compensation for a company's top executives usually consists of four main elements: base pay, short-term incentives, long-term incentives, and executive benefits and perks.[43] *Base pay* includes the person's fixed salary as well as, often, guaranteed bonuses such as "10% of pay at the end of the fourth fiscal quarter, regardless of whether or not the company makes a profit." *Short-term incentives* are usually cash or stock bonuses for achieving short-term goals, such as year-to-year increases in sales revenue. *Long-term incentives* aim to encourage the executive to take actions that drive up the value of the company's stock, and include things like stock options; these generally give the executive the right to purchase stock at a specific price for a specific period. Finally, *executive benefits and perks* might include supplemental executive retirement pension plans, supplemental life insurance, and health insurance without a deductible or coinsurance. With so many complicated elements, employers must also be alert to the tax and securities law implications of their executive compensation decisions.[44]

When You're on Your OWN   Developing a Workable Pay Plan
HR for Line Managers and Entrepreneurs

Developing a pay plan is as important in a small firm as a large one. Paying wage rates that are too high may be unnecessarily expensive, and paying less may guarantee inferior help and high turnover. Furthermore, internally inequitable wage rates will reduce morale and cause endless badgering by employees demanding raises "the same as Joe down the hall." The owner who wants to concentrate on major issues like sales would thus do well to install a rational pay plan.

First, conduct a wage survey. Four sources can be especially useful. The Sunday classified newspaper ads should yield useful information on wages offered for jobs similar to those you are trying to price. Second, local Job Service "One Stop" offices can provide a wealth of information, as they compile extensive information on pay ranges and averages for many of the jobs listed on in BLS online wage surveys. Third, local employment agencies, always anxious to establish ties that could grow into business relationships, should be able to provide good data. Fourth, the Internet and Web sites like Salary.com can yield a wealth of information on area pay rates.

Smaller firms are using the Internet in other ways. For example, StockHouse Media Corp., has 210 employees from the United States to Canada, Japan, and Singapore. Shawnee Love, the firm's global HR director, makes extensive use of the Web for determining salaries for all the firm's personnel. For example, she uses e-mail to request salary data from professional groups like the Society for Human Resource Management, and surfs the Internet to monitor rates and trends by periodically checking job boards, company Web sites, and industry associations. "We source information that is both industry related as well as functionally related and of varying geographies, such as state, provincial, countrywide versus marketing, sales, HR, tech, etc.," she says.[45]

If you employ more than 20 employees or so, conduct at least a rudimentary job evaluation. You will need job descriptions, since these will be the source of data regarding the nature and worth of each job. Checking a Web site like JobDescription.com can be useful here.

You may find it easier to split employees into three clusters—managerial/professional, office/clerical, and plant personnel. For each of the three groups, choose compensable factors and then rank or assign points to each job based on the job evaluation. For each job or class of jobs (such as assemblers), you will want to create a pay range. In general, you should choose as the midpoint of that range the target salary required by your job evaluation, and then produce a range of about 30% around this average, broken into a total of five steps. (Thus, the assemblers in one pay grade might earn from $6.00 to $9.60 per hour, in five steps.)

As noted earlier in this chapter, compensation policies are important. For example, you need a policy on when and how to compute raises. Many small business owners make the mistake of appraising employees on their anniversary date, a year after they are hired. The problem here is that the raise for one employee then becomes the standard for the next, as employees have time to compare notes. This produces a never-ending cycle of appraisals and posturing for ever-higher raises.

The better alternative is to have a policy of once-a-year raises following a standard one-week appraisal period, preferably about four weeks before you produce the budget for next year. In this way, the administrative headache of conducting these appraisals and awarding raises is dealt with during a one-week (or two-week) period, and the raises are known before the budget is compiled. Other required compensation policies include amount of holiday and vacation pay (as explained in Chapter 13), overtime pay policy, method of pay (weekly, biweekly, monthly), garnishments, and time card or sign-in sheet procedures. (For sources of sample policies, see the human resources systems discussion in the Chapter 3 Appendix B.) The business owner can use the checklist in Figure 11-7 to judge the new plan's completeness.

FIGURE 11-7

Compensation Administration Checklist

A good compensation administration program is comprehensive and flexible and ensures optimum performance from employees at all levels. The following checklist may be used to evaluate a company's program. The more questions answered "yes," the more thorough has been the planning for compensation administration.

Source: Reprinted from www.HR.BLR.com with permission of the publisher Business and Legal Reports Inc., 141 Mill Rock Road East, Old Saybrook, CT © 2004.

	Yes	No
• Is your plan for salary administration in writing?	☐	☐
• Do you have stated goals for your plan, such as:		
–Compliance with applicable law?	☐	☐
–Consistently rewarding performance?	☐	☐
–Attracting quality employees?	☐	☐
–Reducing turnover?	☐	☐
• Does your plan include the following topics?	☐	☐
–Annual wage and hour surveys?	☐	☐
–Explanations for salary schedules?	☐	☐
–Evaluations of job classifications?	☐	☐
–Premium, bonus, vacation pay?	☐	☐
–Paid medical leave, long-term disability?	☐	☐
–Temporary positions, part-time positions?	☐	☐
• Is there a written analysis for each job in your company?	☐	☐
• Does each analysis include a listing of the following job requirements?	☐	☐
–Knowledge/skills/experience/personal characteristics?	☐	☐
• Do you periodically review and update each job description?	☐	☐
• Have you set salary ranges for each job category?	☐	☐
• Do you provide regular, written performance evaluations for employees?	☐	☐
• Are the evaluations used to decide promotions and pay increases?	☐	☐
• Do you communicate your job evaluation plan to your employees through:	☐	☐
–Orientation/supervisors?	☐	☐
–Bulletin boards/handbooks?	☐	☐
• Have you developed a written system of merit increases?	☐	☐
• Do you have stated goals for the system, such as:	☐	☐
–Increase productivity/quality?	☐	☐
–Reduce errors/cost?	☐	☐
• Do you respond to suggestions from employees about your compensation plan?	☐	☐

What Determines Executive Pay? The traditional wisdom is that company size and performance significantly affects top managers' salaries. Yet studies show that company size and company performance explain only about 30% of the variation in CEO pay. Instead, each firm seems to take a unique approach: "In reality, CEO pay is set by the board taking into account a variety of factors such as the business strategy, corporate trends, and most importantly where they want to be in a short and long term."[46] Another study concluded that CEOs' pay depends on the complexity and unpredictability of the decisions they make.[47] In this study, complexity was a function of such things as the number of businesses controlled by the CEO's firm, the number of corporate officers in each firm, and the level of R&D and capital investment activity.[48] In practice, CEOs may have considerable influence over the boards of directors who theoretically set their pay. So, while some CEOs may be paid like top athletes, their pay is sometimes not based on the arms-length market-based negotiations that the athletes' (or rock stars') are.[49]

However, we'll see that shareholder activism has tightened the restrictions on what companies pay top executives. For example, shareholders in pharmaceuticals firm GlaxoSmithKline voted to reject the board's recommendation to pay its chief executive $35 million if he lost his job and to enhance the pension plans of both him and his wife.[50]

Elements of Executive Pay Salary is traditionally the cornerstone of executive compensation; it's the element on which employers layer benefits, incentives, and perquisites—all normally conferred in proportion to base pay. Executive compensation emphasizes performance incentives more than do other employees' pay plans, since organizational results are likely to reflect executives' contributions more directly than lower-echelon employees'.[51] Indeed, boards are boosting the emphasis on performance-based pay (in part due to shareholder activism). The big issue here is identifying the appropriate performance standards and then determining how to link these to pay. Typical short-term measures of shareholder value include revenue growth and operating profit margin. Long-term shareholder value measures include rate of return above some predetermined base, and what is known as economic value added. We'll discuss short- and long-term incentives in Chapter 12.

Performance-based pay can focus a manager's attention. When heavy truck production tumbled, CEO Joseph Magliochetti saw sales of auto parts maker Dana Corp. drop by 6%, and profits by 44%. At the end of the year, he still got his $850,000 salary. But his board eliminated his bonus and stock grant, which the year before had earned him $1.8 million. The board said he had failed to beat the profit goals it had set for him.[52]

Managerial Job Evaluation Despite questions about the rationality behind executive pay, job evaluation is still important in pricing executive and managerial jobs in most large firms. The basic approach is to classify all executive and management positions into a series of grades, to which a series of salary ranges is attached.

As with nonmanagerial jobs, one alternative is to rank the executive and management positions in relation to each other, grouping those of equal value. However, firms also use the job classification and point evaluation methods, with compensable factors like position scope, complexity, difficulty, and creative demands. Job analysis, salary surveys, and the fine-tuning of salary levels around wage curves also play central roles.

Compensating Professional Employees

Compensating professional employees like engineers and scientists presents unique problems.[53] Analytical jobs like these emphasize creativity and problem solving, compensable factors not easily compared or measured. Furthermore, how do you measure performance? For example, the success of an engineer's invention depends on many factors, like how well the firm markets it.

Employers can use job evaluation for professional jobs. Compensable factors here tend to focus on problem solving, creativity, job scope, and technical knowledge and expertise. Firms use the point method and factor comparison methods, although job classification seems most popular. (Here, recall that you slot jobs into grades based on grade descriptions.) Yet in practice, firms rarely use traditional job evaluation methods for pricing professional jobs, since it is so difficult to quantify the factors, such as creativity, that make a difference in professional work.

Most employers use a market-pricing approach. They price professional jobs in the marketplace as best they can, to establish the values for benchmark jobs. Then they slot these benchmark jobs and their other professional jobs into a salary structure. Each professional discipline (like engineering or R&D) usually ends up having four to six grade levels, each with a broad salary range. This helps employers remain competitive when bidding for professionals whose skills and attainments vary widely, and who literally have global employment possibilities.[54]

④ Discuss competency-based pay and other current trends in compensation.

COMPETENCY-BASED PAY

Introduction

We've seen that employers traditionally base a job's pay rate on the relative worth of the job. The compensation team compares jobs using compensable factors such as effort and responsibility. This allows them (1) to compare jobs to one another (as in, "based on its duties, this job seems to require about twice the effort of that one"), and (2) to assign internally equitable pay rates for each job. Thus, the pay rate for the job principally depends on the job itself, not on who is doing it.

For reasons which we'll explain shortly, an increasing number of compensation experts and employers are moving away from assigning pay rates to jobs based on the jobs' numerically rated, intrinsic duties. Instead, they advocate basing the job's pay rate on the level of "competencies" the job demands of those who fill it.[55] "Title and tenure have been replaced with performance and competencies," is how one expert puts it.[56] Compensation specialists call this second approach *competency-based pay*.

What Is Competency-Based Pay?

competency-based pay

Where the company pays for the employee's range, depth, and types of skills and knowledge, rather than for the job title he or she holds.

In a nutshell, **competency-based pay** means the company pays for the employee's range, depth, and types of skills and knowledge, rather than for the job title he or she holds.[57] Experts variously call this competence-, knowledge-, or skill-based pay. With competency-based pay, an employee in a class I job who could (but may not have to at the moment) do class II work gets paid as a class II worker, not a class I.

Different organizations define "competencies" in somewhat different ways. Most, like the U.S. Office of Personnel Management, use "competencies" synonymously with the knowledge, or skills, or abilities required to do the job. Another approach is to express competencies somewhat more narrowly, in terms of measurable behaviors, such as "design a Web site."[58] Here, you would identify the job's required competencies by completing the phrase, "In order to perform this job competently, the employee should be able to . . ."[59] We can simply define **competencies** as demonstrable knowledge, skills, and behaviors that enable performance.[60]

competencies

Demonstrable characteristics of a person, including knowledge, skills, and behaviors, that enable performance.

In practice, competency-based pay usually comes down to using one or both of two basic types of pay programs: *pay for knowledge* or *skill-based pay*.[61] Pay-for-knowledge pay plans reward employees for learning organizationally relevant knowledge—for instance Microsoft pays new programmers more as they learn the intricacies of Windows Vista. Skill-based pay tends to be used more for workers with manual jobs—thus carpenters earn more as they become more proficient at finishing cabinets.

Several things distinguish the competency-based pay approach.

- First, employees build job competencies (knowledge and/or skills) through *experience* on the same or similar jobs.
- Second, competence-based pay ties the person's pay to his or her competencies—pay is more *person oriented*. Employees here get paid based on what they know or can do—even if, at the moment, they don't have to do it.
- Traditional job evaluation-based pay plans tie the worker's pay to the worth of the job based on the job description—pay here is more *job oriented*.

Why Use Competency-Based Pay?

Why pay employees based on the skill, knowledge, or competency level they achieve, rather than based on the duties of the jobs they're assigned to? For example, why pay an Accounting Clerk III who has achieved a certain mastery of accounting techniques the same (or more than) someone who is an Accounting Clerk IV? There are three good (and interrelated) reasons for doing so.

Support High-Performance Work Systems   First, traditional pay plans may actually backfire if a *high-performance work system* is your goal. The whole thrust of these systems is to encourage employees to work in a self-motivated way, by organizing the work around teams, by encouraging team members to rotate freely among jobs (each with its own skill set), by pushing more responsibility for things like day-to-day supervision down to the workers, and by organizing work around projects or processes where jobs may blend or overlap. In such systems, you obviously want employees to be enthusiastic about learning and moving among other jobs. Pigeonholing workers by classifying them too narrowly into jobs based on the job's points may actually discourage such enthusiasm and flexibility.

Studies suggest that analytical types of job evaluation (such as the point or factor comparison methods) may conflict with the high-performance work approach.[62] In one study, the researchers found that "workplaces in which the high-performance approach has been most fully implemented are less likely to have the more formal, analytical type of job evaluation. Furthermore, those [workplaces] with both analytical job evaluation and the high-performance work system are less likely to have high above average financial performance than those with either of these on a single basis."[63] The less quantitative job evaluation methods such as classifying, grading, or ranking jobs didn't seem to be a problem.

Support Strategic Aims   Second, paying for skills, knowledge, and competencies is *more strategic*. For example, Canon Corp. needs competencies in miniaturization and precision manufacturing to design and produce its cameras and copiers. It thus makes sense for Canon to reward some employees based on the skills and knowledge they develop in these two strategically crucial areas, not just based on the jobs to which they're assigned.

Support Performance Management   *Performance management* means aligning employees' goals, training, appraisals, and rewards so that they support the company's strategic goals. The manager can influence an employee's competencies (skills or knowledge). There is not much a manager can do to "manage" the employee's job duties. So, (third) paying for competencies rather than duties thus gives the employer more control over managing the employee's performance. At Canon, this might mean training, appraising, and paying some employees based on their miniaturization and precision manufacturing competencies.

Competency-Based Pay in Practice

In practice, skill/competency/knowledge-based pay programs generally contain four main elements:

1. a system for defining specific skills, and a process for tying the person's pay to his or her skill level;
2. a training system that lets employees seek and acquire skills;
3. a formal competency testing system; and
4. a work design that lets employees move among jobs to permit work assignment flexibility.[64]

General Mills Example   For example, a General Mills manufacturing plant pays workers based on attained skill levels.[65] Management created four clusters of jobs, corresponding to the plant's four production areas: mixing, filling, packaging, and materials. Within each cluster, workers could attain three levels of skill. Level 1 indicates limited ability, such as knowledge of basic facts and ability to perform simple tasks without direction.[66] Level 2 means the employee attained partial proficiency and could, for instance, apply technical principles on the job. Attaining Level 3 means the employee is fully competent in the area and could, for example, analyze and solve production problems. Each of the four production clusters had a different average wage rate. There were, therefore, 12 pay levels in the plant (four clusters with three pay levels each).

General Mills set the wages for the 12 skill levels in part by making the pay for the lowest of the three pay levels in each cluster equal to the average entry-level pay rate for similar jobs in the community. A new employee could start in any cluster, but always at Level 1. If after several weeks he or she was certified at the next higher skill level, General Mills raised his or her salary. Employees freely rotated from cluster to cluster, as long as they could achieve Level 2 performance within their current cluster.

Competency-Based Pay: Pros, Cons, and Results

Competency-based pay has its detractors. Many companies reported competency-based pay implementation problems.[67] Some experts note that competency-based pay "ignores

Many employers, such as General Mills, pay certain workers based on attained skill levels.

the cost implications of paying [employees] for knowledge, skills and behaviors even if they are not used."[68] There may also be simpler ways to encourage the necessary learning. For example, one aerospace firm has a quasi-skill-based pay program. It has all exempt employees negotiate "learning contracts" with their supervisors. The employees then get raises for meeting learning (skills-improvement) objectives.[69]

Whether skill-based pay improves productivity is an open question. When used in conjunction with team-building and worker involvement and empowerment programs, it does appear to lead to higher quality as well as lower absenteeism rates and fewer accidents.[70] However, the findings in another firm, which are not conclusive, suggest that productivity was higher at its non-skill-based-pay facility.[71]

OTHER COMPENSATION TRENDS

How employers pay employees has been evolving. Today's shift towards competency-based pay is just one example. Overall, there is less emphasis on basing pay on seniority, and more on the employee's contribution, performance, and value to the business; less emphasis on the job's duties, and more on the person's skills and competencies and on how his or her contribution fits with the firm's overall strategic needs; finally, there's less emphasis on narrowly defined pay ranges and jobs, and more on broader jobs and pay ranges. This section looks at four important trends: broadbanding, comparable worth, board oversight of executive pay, and automating compensation administration.[72]

Broadbanding

Most firms end up with pay plans that slot jobs into classes or grades, each with its own vertical pay rate range. For example, the U.S. government's pay plan consists of 18 main grades (GS-1 to GS-18), each with its own pay range. For an employee whose job falls in one of these grades, the pay range for that grade dictates his or her minimum and maximum salary.

The question is, "How wide should the salary grades be, in terms of the number of job evaluation points they include?" (For example, might the U.S. government want to collapse its 18 salary grades into six or seven broader bands?) There is a downside to having (say, 18) narrow grades. For instance, if you want someone whose job is in grade 2 to fill in for a time in a job that happens to be in grade 1, it's difficult to reassign that person without lowering his or her salary. Similarly, if you want the person to learn about a job that happens to be in grade 3, the employee might object to the reassignment without a corresponding raise to grade 3 pay. Traditional grade pay plans thus breed inflexibility.

broadbanding

Consolidating salary grades and ranges into just a few wide levels or "bands," each of which contains a relatively wide range of jobs and salary levels.

That is why some firms are broadbanding their pay plans. **Broadbanding** means collapsing salary grades into just a few wide levels or bands, each of which contains a relatively wide range of jobs and salary levels. Figure 11-8 illustrates this. In this case the company's previous six pay grades are consolidated into two broadbands.

A company may create broadbands for all its jobs, or for specific groups such as managers or professionals. The pay rate range of each broadband is relatively large, since it ranges from the minimum pay of the lowest grade the firm merged into the broadband up to the maximum pay of the highest merged grade. Thus, for example, instead of having 10 salary grades, each of which contains a salary range of $15,000, the firm might collapse the 10 grades into three broadbands, each with a set of jobs such that the difference between the lowest- and highest-paid jobs might be $40,000 or more. For the jobs that fall in this broadband, there is therefore a much wider range of pay rates. You can move employees from job to job within the broadband more easily, without worrying about the employees moving outside the relatively narrow rate range associated with a traditional narrow pay grade. Broadbanding therefore breeds flexibility.

FIGURE 11-8

Broadbanded Structure and How It Relates to Traditional Pay Grades and Ranges

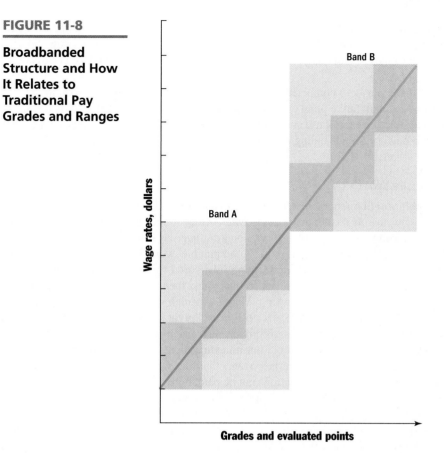

Pros and Cons Companies broadband for several reasons. Broadbanding's basic advantage is that it injects greater flexibility into employee assignments.[73] It is especially sensible where firms flatten their hierarchies and organize into self-managing teams. The new, broad salary bands can include both supervisors and subordinates and also facilitate moving employees slightly up or down along the pay scale, without bumping the person into a new salary range. For example, "the employee who needs to spend time in a lower-level job to develop a certain skill set can receive higher-than-usual pay for the work, a circumstance considered impossible under traditional pay systems."[74] One expert argues that traditional quantitative evaluation plans actually reward unadaptability.[75] He argues that jobs narrowly defined by compensable factors such as "know-how" are unlikely to encourage job incumbents to be flexible. Instead, the tendency may be for workers to take a "that's not my job" attitude and to concentrate on their specific tasks.

However, broadbanding can be unsettling, particularly for new employees. For example, Home Depot has used broadbanding for over 10 years, and "when employees want to learn something new, they play to the level [on that project] that they're capable of," says the firm's head of information systems. That is motivating once you get used to it. However, it can make a new employee feel adrift: "There's a sense of permanence in the set of job responsibilities often attached to job titles," he says. That sense of permanence isn't nearly as clear when employees can (and are expected to) move frequently from project to project and job to job.[76]

Use A survey of 783 employers found that about 15% were using broadbanding.[77] One British company does so to support its strategy of cutting costs and flattening and downsizing the organization. The flattening meant fewer job titles, each of which had broader responsibilities, and broadbanding made it easier to get employees to assume their new, broader roles.[78] Dow Jones & Company implemented broadbanding for its 1,000 IT professionals several years ago.

Note that even with competence/skill-based pay and broadbanding, 60% to 70% of U.S. firms use quantitative point and factor comparison plans to create pay structures. Job evaluation's relative ease of use and familiarity are probably the main reasons. And neither skill-based pay nor broadbanding eliminates the need for evaluating the worth of one job relative to others.[79]

Comparable Worth

comparable worth
The concept by which women who are usually paid less than men can claim that men in comparable rather than in strictly equal jobs are paid more.

Comparable worth refers to the requirement to pay men and women equal wages for jobs that are of *comparable* (rather than strictly *equal*) value to the employer. Thus, comparable worth may mean comparing quite dissimilar jobs, such as nurses to truck mechanics or secretaries to technicians. The question "comparable worth" seeks to address is this: Should you pay women who are performing jobs *equal* to men's or just *comparable* to men's the same as men? If it's only for equal jobs, then the tendency may be to limit women's pay to that of the other lower paid jobs in which women tend to predominate.

County of Washington v. Gunther (1981) was a pivotal case for comparable worth. It involved Washington County, Oregon, prison matrons who claimed sex discrimination. The county had evaluated comparable but nonequal men's jobs as having 5% more "job content" (based on a point evaluation system) than the women's jobs, but paid the men 35% more.[80] Should the women matrons not be paid more then they were, even though the comparable (in terms of points) men's jobs were "unequal" to (not the same as) theirs? After seesawing through the courts to the U.S. Supreme Court, Washington County finally agreed to pay 35,000 employees in female-dominated jobs almost $500 million in pay raises over seven years to settle the suit.

Comparable worth has implications for job evaluation. Virtually every comparable worth case that reached a court involved the use of the point method of job evaluation. By assigning points to jobs, point plans facilitate comparability ratings among different jobs. Should employers still use point-type plans? Perhaps the wisest approach is for employers to price their jobs as they see fit (with or without point plans), but to ensure that women have equal access to all jobs. In other words, eliminate wage discrimination issue by eliminating sex-segregated jobs.

The Pay Gap All this notwithstanding, the fact is that women in the United States still earn only about 77% as much as men, although the gap is narrowing a bit.[81]

What accounts for the difference? One pay specialist cites four factors: women's starting salaries are traditionally lower because employers traditionally view them as having less leverage; salary increases for women in professional jobs do not reflect their above-average performance, (men with equal performance receive bigger raises); in white-collar jobs, men tend to change jobs more frequently, which enables them to be promoted to higher-level jobs over women with more seniority; and in blue-collar jobs, women tend to be placed in departments with lower-paying jobs.[82] Education may reduce the wage gap. Studies suggest that schooling's impact on earnings is greater for females than for males, other things equal. This may be because education increases both women's and men's productivity but also reduces the male–female earnings gap attributable to female discrimination.[83]

Board Oversight of Executive Pay

For 15 years, the Board of Directors of UnitedHealth Group Inc. supported its CEO, with almost $2 billion in compensation. Recently, the board ousted him, allegedly because, as the Wall Street Journal put it, "his explanation for a pattern of unusually well-timed stock option grants didn't add up."[84]

There are various reasons why boards like United Healthcare's are clamping down on executive pay. As of 2005, the Financial Accounting Standards Board requires that most public companies recognize as an expense the fair value of the stock options they grant.[85] The Securities and Exchange Commission (SEC) now requires filing more compensation related information. The Sarbannes Oxley Act makes executives personally liable, under certain conditions, for corporate financial oversight lapses. Writing in the Harvard Business Review, the chief justice of Delaware's Supreme Court recently said that governance issues, shareholder activism, and other changes have "created a new set of expectations for directors."[86] The net result is that lawyers specializing in executive pay suggest that boards of directors ask themselves these questions:

- Has our compensation committee thoroughly identified its duties and processes?
- Is our compensation committee being appropriately advised? (Government regulators and commentators strongly encourage this).
- Are there particular executive compensation issues that our committee should address?
- Do our procedures demonstrate diligence and independence? (This demands careful deliberations and records).
- Is our committee appropriately communicating its decisions? How will shareholders react?[87]

Improving Productivity Through HRIS: Automating Compensation Administration

Usually, the employer identifies set times during the year (called "focal reviews") when all the firm's managers review employees' performance, and match these with budgetary constraints and formulate pay raise recommendations for the coming year.[88] As employers moved toward linking their compensation plans more closely to strategic considerations, the job of developing salary raise recommendations has become more complex. It's no longer just a case of allocating raises across the board, or based on performance appraisals. Instead, numerous issues (including strategic concerns, geographic considerations, paying employees based on competencies, and the need to factor in various elements including bonus payments and stock option grants) make allocating raises while staying within budget a challenge.

Making raise decisions has always been cumbersome. Traditionally, employers used spreadsheets to administer these compensation decisions. The human resource department would create individual spreadsheets for each manager. The manager would then use these spreadsheets to record their salary increase recommendations for their subordinates. Human resources would then compile the spreadsheets by unit, department, division, and, finally, companywide to add up who was spending what. This was a labor-intensive and costly process.

Today, companies more often use server-based intranet compensation planning programs to keep track of who can spend what, and who is spending what. This Web-based method has many advantages. The employer can quickly update its compensation programs (such as how much is available, and how much can each manager allocate for various criteria), without having to modify the software on individual managers' computers. And automating the system reduces costs, by eliminating manual processes. For example, one company estimated that it cost them about $35 to complete a single manual compensation transaction (such as combining the raise budgets for two departments), but about $16 if it automated this process. Using a centralized application saves money in other ways. For example, employers often assign pay raise budgets to all their managers, only to find that (once the various department budgets all come together) the accumulated excess raises amount to millions of dollars. This generally doesn't happen with an automated system. And, a compensation administration system that is compatible with the employer's HRIS can also automatically administer other pay actions, such as updating employee's pay checks.

REVIEW

SUMMARY

1. There are two bases on which to pay employee compensation—increments of time and volume of production. The former includes hourly or daily wages and salaries. Basing pay on volume of production ties compensation directly to the amount of product (or number of "pieces") the worker generates.
2. Establishing pay rates involves five steps: Conduct salary surveys, evaluate jobs, develop pay grades, use wage curves, and fine-tune pay rates.
3. Job evaluation determines the relative worth of a job. It compares jobs to one another based on their content, which is usually defined in terms of compensable factors like skills, effort, responsibility, and working conditions.
4. The five-step ranking method of job evaluation is simple to use, but there is a tendency to rely too heavily on estimates. The classification (or grading) method is a second qualitative approach that categorizes jobs based on a class description or classification rules for each class.
5. Quantitative methods include the point method, which requires identifying a number of compensable factors and then determining the degree to which each of these factors is present in the job. The factor comparison method entails deciding which jobs have more of certain compensable factors than others.
6. Most managers group similar jobs into wage or pay grades for pay purposes. These are comprised of jobs of approximately equal difficulty or importance as determined by job evaluation.
7. Developing a compensation plan for executive, managerial, and professional personnel is complicated by the fact that factors like performance and creativity must take precedence over static factors like working conditions. Market rates, performance, and incentives and benefits thus play a much greater role than does job evaluation for these employees.
8. Competence-, knowledge-, or skill-based pay means paying for the employee's range, depth, and types of skills and knowledge, rather than for the job title he or she holds. We defined *competencies* as "demonstrable characteristics of the person, including knowledge, skills, and behaviors, that enable performance."
9. We listed three reasons for considering a competency-based pay plan. First, traditional pay plans may actually backfire if a *high-performance work system* is your goal. Second, paying for skills, knowledge, and competencies is *more strategic*. Third, measurable skills, knowledge, and competencies are the heart of any company's *performance management process*.
10. Other trends in compensation include broadbanding, strategic compensation, and adjustments for comparable worth.

DISCUSSION QUESTIONS

1. What is the difference between exempt and nonexempt jobs?
2. Should the job evaluation depend on an appraisal of the jobholder's performance? Why? Why not?

3. What is the relationship between compensable factors and job specifications?
4. Compare and contrast the following methods of job evaluation: ranking, classification, factor comparison, and point method.
5. What are the pros and cons of broadbanding, and would you recommend your current employer (or some other firm you're familiar with) use it? Why or why not?
6. It was recently reported in the news that the average pay for most university presidents ranged around $250,000 per year, but that a few earned much more. For example, the new president of Vanderbilt received $852,000 in one year. Discuss why you would (or would not) pay university presidents as much or more than many corporate CEO's.
7. Do small companies need to develop a pay plan? Why or why not?

INDIVIDUAL AND GROUP ACTIVITIES

1. Working individually or in groups, conduct salary surveys for the following positions: entry-level accountant and entry-level chemical engineer. What sources did you use, and what conclusions did you reach? If you were the HR manager for a local engineering firm, what would you recommend that you pay for each job?
2. Working individually or in groups, develop compensation policies for the teller position at a local bank. Assume that there are four tellers: two were hired in May and the other two were hired in December. The compensation policies should address the following: appraisals, raises, holidays, vacation pay, overtime pay, method of pay, garnishments, and time cards.
3. Working individually or in groups, access relevant Web sites to determine what equitable pay ranges are for these jobs: chemical engineer, marketing manager, and HR manager, all with a bachelor's degree and five years of experience in the following cities: New York, New York; San Francisco, California; Houston, Texas; Denver, Colorado; Miami, Florida; Atlanta, Georgia; Chicago, Illinois; Birmingham, Alabama; Detroit, Michigan; and Washington, D.C. For each position in each city, what are the pay ranges and the average pay? Does geographical location impact the salaries of the different positions? If so, how?
4. The HRCI "Test Specifications" appendix at the end of this book (pages 726–735) lists the knowledge someone studying for the HRCI certification exam needs to have in each area of human resource management (such as in Strategic Management, Workforce Planning, and Human Resource Development). In groups of four to five students, do four things: (1) review that appendix now; (2) identify the material in this chapter that relates to the required knowledge the appendix lists; (3) write four multiple choice exam questions on this material that you believe would be suitable for inclusion in the HRCI exam; and (4) if time permits, have someone from your team post your team's questions in front of the class, so the students in other teams can take each others' exam questions.
5. Some of America's CEOs came under fire recently because their pay seemed to some to be excessive, given their firms' performances. To choose just two of very many: former Citigroup CEO Sandy Weill got a $29 million cash bonus, and Sprint's CEO Gary Forsee got $14 million. However, big institutional investors are no longer sitting back and not complaining. For example, TV's *Nightly Business Line* says that pension manager TIAA-CREF is talking to 50 companies about executive pay. What do you think it was about the period 2000–2005 that got so many big investors to rebel against "excessive" executive pay? Do you think they were right to make a fuss? Why?

EXPERIENTIAL EXERCISE

Ranking the College's Administrators

Purpose: The purpose of this exercise is to give you experience in performing a job evaluation using the ranking method.

Required Understanding: You should be thoroughly familiar with the ranking method of job evaluation and obtain job descriptions for your college's dean, department chairperson, director of admissions, library director, registrar, and your professor.

How to Set Up the Exercise/Instructions: Divide the class into groups of four or five students. The groups will perform a job evaluation of the positions of dean, department chairperson, and professor using the ranking method.

1. Perform a job evaluation by ranking the jobs. You may use one or more compensable factors.
2. If time permits, a spokesperson from each group can put his or her group's rankings on the board. Did the groups end up with about the same results? How did they differ? Why do you think they differed?

APPLICATION CASE

Salary Inequities at Acme Manufacturing

Joe Black was trying to figure out what to do about a problem salary situation he had in his plant. Black recently took over as president of Acme Manufacturing. The founder and former president, Bill George, had been president for 35 years. The company was family owned and located in a small eastern Arkansas town. It had approximately 250 employees and was the largest employer in the community. Black was a member of the family that owned Acme, but he had never worked for the company prior to becoming president. He had an MBA and a law degree, plus five years of management experience with a large manufacturing organization, where he was senior vice president for human resources before making his move to Acme.

A short time after joining Acme, Black started to notice that there was considerable inequity in the pay structure for salaried employees. A discussion with the human resources director led him to believe that salaried employees' pay was very much a matter of individual bargaining with the past president. Hourly paid factory employees were not part of the problem because they were unionized and their wages were set by collective bargaining. An examination of the salaried payroll showed that there were 25 employees, ranging in pay from that of the president to that of the receptionist. A closer examination showed that 14 of the salaried employees were female. Three of these were front-line factory supervisors and one was the human resources director. The other 10 were nonmanagement.

This examination also showed that the human resources director appeared to be underpaid, and that the three female supervisors were paid somewhat less than any of the male supervisors. However, there were no similar supervisory jobs in which there were both male and female job incumbents. When asked, the HR director said she thought the female supervisors may have been paid at a lower rate mainly because they were women, and perhaps George, the former president, did not think that women needed as much money because they had working husbands. However, she added she personally thought that they were paid less because they supervised less-skilled employees than did the male supervisors. Black was not sure that this was true.

The company from which Black had moved had a good job evaluation system. Although he was thoroughly familiar with and capable in this compensation tool, Black did not have time to make a job evaluation study at Acme. Therefore, he decided to hire a compensation consultant from a nearby university to help him. Together, they decided that all 25 salaried jobs should be in the same job evaluation cluster; that a modified ranking method of job evaluation should be used; and that the job descriptions recently completed by the HR director were current, accurate, and usable in the study.

The job evaluation showed that the HR director and the three female supervisors were being underpaid relative to comparable male salaried employees.

Black was not sure what to do. He knew that if the underpaid female supervisors took the case to the local EEOC office, the company could be found guilty of sex discrimination and then have to pay considerable back wages. He was afraid that if he gave these women an immediate salary increase large enough to bring them up to where they should be, the male supervisors would be upset and the female supervisors might comprehend the total situation and want back pay. The HR director told Black that the female supervisors had never complained about pay differences.

The HR director agreed to take a sizable salary increase with no back pay, so this part of the problem was solved. Black believed he had four choices relative to the female supervisors:

1. To do nothing.
2. To gradually increase the female supervisors' salaries.
3. To increase their salaries immediately.
4. To call the three supervisors into his office, discuss the situation with them, and jointly decide what to do.

Questions

1. What would you do if you were Black?
2. How do you think the company got into a situation like this in the first place?
3. Why would you suggest Black pursue the alternative you suggested?

Source: This case was prepared by Professor James C. Hodgetts of the Fogelman College of Business and Economics of the University of Memphis. All names are disguised. Used by permission.

CONTINUING CASE

Carter Cleaning Company

The New Pay Plan

Carter Cleaning Centers does not have a formal wage structure nor does it have rate ranges or use compensable factors. Wage rates are based mostly on those prevailing in the surrounding community and are tempered with an attempt on the part of Jack Carter to maintain some semblance of equity between what workers with different responsibilities in the stores are paid.

Needless to say, Carter does not make any formal surveys when determining what his company should pay. He peruses the want ads almost every day and conducts informal surveys among his friends in the local chapter of the laundry and cleaners trade association. While Jack has taken a "seat-of-the-pants" approach to paying employees, his salary schedule has been guided by several basic pay policies. While many of his colleagues adhere to a policy of paying absolutely minimum rates, Jack has always followed a policy of paying his employees about 10% above what he feels are the prevailing rates, a policy that he believes reduces turnover while fostering employee loyalty. Of somewhat more concern to Jennifer is her father's informal policy of paying men about 20% more than women for the same job. Her father's explanation is, "They're stronger and can work harder for longer hours, and besides they all have families to support."

Questions

1. Is the company at the point where it should be setting up a formal salary structure based on a complete job evaluation? Why?
2. Is Jack Carter's policy of paying 10% more than the prevailing rates a sound one, and how could that be determined?
3. Similarly, is Carter's male–female differential wise and if not, why not?
4. Specifically, what would you suggest Jennifer do now with respect to her company's pay plan?

TRANSLATING STRATEGY INTO HR POLICIES AND PRACTICES CASE:
THE HOTEL PARIS

The New Compensation Plan

The Hotel Paris's competitive strategy is "To use superior guest service to differentiate the Hotel Paris properties, and to thereby increase the length of stay and return rate of guests, and thus boost revenues and profitability." HR manager Lisa Cruz must now formulate functional policies and activities that support this competitive strategy, by eliciting the required employee behaviors and competencies.

Like several other HR systems at the Hotel Paris, the compensation program was unplanned and unsophisticated. The company has a narrow target range for what it will pay employees in each job category (front-desk clerk, security guard, and so forth). Each hotel manager decides where to start a new employee within that narrow pay range. The company has given little thought to tying general pay levels or individual employees' pay to the company's strategic goals. For example, the firm's policy is simply to pay its employees a "competitive salary," by which it means about average for what other hotels in the city are paying for similar jobs. Lisa knows that pay policies like these may actually run counter to what the company wants to achieve strategically, in terms of creating an extraordinarily service-oriented workforce. How can you hire and retain a top workforce, and channel their behaviors toward high-quality guest services, if you don't somehow link performance and pay? She and her team therefore turn to the task of assessing and redesigning the company's compensation plan.

So, even a casual review by Lisa Cruz and the CFO made it clear that the company's compensation plan wasn't designed to support the firm's new strategic goals. For one thing, they knew that they should pay somewhat more, on average, than did their competitors if they expected employees to consistently exceed expectations when it came to serving guests. Yet their review of a variety of metrics (including the Hotel Paris's salary/competitive salary ratios, the total compensation expense per employee, and the target percentile for total compensation) suggested that in virtually all job categories the Hotel Paris paid no more than average, and, occasionally, paid somewhat less.

The current compensation policies had also bred what one hotel manager called an "I don't care" attitude on the part of most employees. What she meant was that most Hotel Paris employees quickly learned that regardless of what their performance was, they always ended up getting paid about the same as employees who performed better and worse than they did. So, the firm's compensation plan actually created a disconnect between pay and performance: It was not channeling employees' behaviors toward those required to achieve the company's goals. In some ways, it was doing the opposite.

Lisa and the CFO knew they had to institute a new, strategic compensation plan. They wanted a plan that improved employee morale, contributed to employee commitment, reduced employee turnover, and rewarded (and thus encouraged) the sorts of service-oriented behaviors that boosted guest satisfaction. After meeting with the company's CEO and the Board, the CFO gave Lisa the go-ahead to redesign the company's compensation plan, with the overall aim of creating a new plan that would support the company's strategic aims.

Questions

1. Draw a diagram showing with arrows how compensation at Hotel Paris should influence employee performance, which should in turn influence Hotel Paris performance. Include at each level specific examples of compensation policies, employee behavior, and Hotel Paris outcomes.
2. Would you suggest Hotel Paris implement a competency-based pay plan for its non-managerial staff—why or why not?
3. Devise a ranking job evaluation system for the Hotel Paris' non-managerial employees (housekeepers, valets, front desk clerks, phone operators, waitstaff, groundskeepers, and security guards), and use it to show the worth of these jobs relative to one another.

KEY TERMS

ENDNOTES

1. Elayne Robertson Demby, "Two Stores Refused to Join the Race to the Bottom for Benefits and Wages," *Workforce Management*, February 2004, pp. 57–59.
2. Richard Henderson, *Compensation Management* (Reston, VA: Reston, 1980); See also Barry Gerhart and Sara Rynes, Compensation: Theory, Evidence, and Strategic Implications, Sage Publications, Thousand Oaks California, 2003, and Joseph Martocchio, *Strategic Compensation*, (Upper Saddle River, NJ: Prentice Hall, 2004), pp. 44–60.
3. Also note that 18 states have their own rules governing overtime. The states are: Alaska, Arkansas, California, Colorado, Connecticut, Hawaii, Illinois, Kentucky, Maryland, Minnesota, Montana, New Jersey, North Dakota, Oregon, Pennsylvania, Washington, West Virginia, and Wisconsin. "DOL's Final Rule Is Not the Final Word on Overtime for Employers in 18 States," *BNA Bulletin to Management*, June 3, 2004, p. 55; p. 177.
4. www.dol.gov/_sec/media/speeches/541_Side_By_Side.htm, and "FLSA Exemptions Flow Chart," www.SHRM.org.
5. "The Evolution of Compensation," *Workplace Visions*, The Society for Human Resource Management, 2002, p. 2, www.dol.gov/esa/minwage/america.htm, accessed June 3, 2004.
6. For a description of exemption requirements see Jeffrey Friedman, "The Fair Labor Standards Act Today: A Primer," *Compensation*, (January/February 2002) pp. 51–54.
7. "Employer Ordered to Pay $2 Million in Overtime," *BNA Bulletin to Management*, September 26, 1996, pp. 308–309. See also "Restaurant Managers Awarded $2.9 Million in Overtime Wages for Nonmanagement Work," *BNA Bulletin to Management*, August 30, 2001, p. 275.
8. Stephanie Rosseau, "Department of Labor Changes White-Collar Overtime Exemptions," *Compensation and Benefits Review*, (July/August 2004) pp. 36–40; See also Scott Carroll and Steven Miller, "Federal Regulations Update for Summer 2004," *Employment Relations Today* 31, no. 2, Summer 2004, pp. 89–98; "Overtime Rules, Offshoring, Employers' Handling of Reservists Top Events in 2004," *BNA Bulletin to Management*, (January 4, 2005), p. 1.
9. Because the overtime and minimum wage rules only changed in 2004, exactly how to apply these rules is still in a state of flux. If there's doubt about exemption eligibility, it's probably best to check with the local Department of Labor Wage and Hour office. See for example "Attorneys Say FLSA Draws a Fine Line between Exempt/Nonexempt Employees," *BNA Bulletin to Management*, July 5, 2005, p. 219; "DOL Releases Letters on Administrative Exemption, Overtime," *BNA Bulletin to Management*, October 18, 2005, p. 335.
10. Robert Nobile, "How Discrimination Laws Affect Compensation," *Compensation and Benefits Review*, July/August 1996, pp. 38–42.

11. Henderson, *Compensation Management*, pp. 101–127; see also Barry Hirsch and Edward Schumacher, "Unions, Wages, and Skills," *Journal of Human Resources* 33, no. 1 (Winter 1998), p. 115.

12. Kenneth Sovereign, *Personnel Law* (Upper Saddle River, NJ: Prentice Hall, 1999), p. 165.

13. Ibid., p. 215.

14. "Microsoft Agrees to Pay $96.9 Million to Settle Contingent Workers' Lawsuits," *BNA Bulletin to Management*, December 14, 2000, p. 395.

15. David Figlio, "Better Qualified Teachers?" *Industrial and Labor Relations Review* 55, no. 4 (July 2002), pp. 686–700.

16. Peg Buchenroth, "Driving Performance: Making Pay Work for the Organization," *Compensation & Benefits Review*, May/June 2006, pp. 30–35.

17. Jessica Marquez, "Raising the Performance Bar," *Workforce Management*, April 24, 2006, pp. 31–32.

18. "Salaries for Similar Jobs Very Significantly across the United States," *Compensation & Benefits Review*, January/February 2006, p. 9.

19. Andrew Richter, "Paying the People in Black at Big Blue," *Compensation and Benefits Review*, May/June 1998, p. 51. See also McNabb and Whitfield, "Job Evaluation and High-Performance Work Practices," pp. 293–313.

20. Ibid., pp. 53–54.

21. This is based on ibid.

22. Bobby Watson, Jr. and Gangaram Singh, "Global Pay Systems: Compensation in Support of Multinational Strategy," *Compensation and Benefits Review*, (January/February 2005), pp. 33–36.

23. Ibid., p. 54.

24. Ibid.

25. Ibid.

26. See ibid., p. 55.

27. Ibid., p. 56.

28. Ibid., p. 56.

29. Elayne Robertson Demby, "Two Stores Refuse to Join the Race to the Bottom for Benefits and Wages," *Workforce Management*, February 2004, p. 57.

30. Nicholas Wade, "Play Fair: Your Life May Depend on It," *New York Times*, September 12, 2003, p. 12.

31. Robert Bretz and Stephen Thomas, "Perceived Inequity, Motivation, and Final Offer Arbitration in Major League Baseball," *Journal of Applied Psychology*, June 1992, pp. 280–289.

32. James DeConick and Dane Bachmann, "An Analysis of Turnover among Retail Buyers," *Journal of Business Research* 58, no. 7, July 2005, pp. 874–882.

33. David Terpstra and Andre Honoree, "The Relative Importance of External, Internal, Individual, and Procedural Equity to Pay Satisfaction," *Compensation and Benefits Review*, November/December 2003, pp. 67–74.

34. Ibid., p. 68.

35. Henderson, *Compensation Management*, pp. 260–269. See also "Web Access Transforms Compensation Surveys," *Workforce Management*, April 24, 2006, p. 34.

36. For more information on these surveys, see the company's brochure, "Domestic Survey References," Watson Wyatt Data Services, 218 Route 17 North, Rochelle Park, NJ 07662.

37. "International Sources of Salary Data," *Compensation and Benefits Review*, May/June 1998, p. 23.

38. Martocchio, *Strategic Compensation*, p. 138. See also Nona Tobin, "Can Technology Ease the Pain of Salary Surveys?" *Public Personnel Management* 31, no. 1 (Spring 2002), pp. 65–78.

39. You may have noticed that job analysis as discussed in Chapter 4 can be a useful source of information on compensable factors, as well as on job descriptions and job specifications. For example, a quantitative job analysis technique like the position analysis questionnaire generates quantitative information on the degree to which the following five basic factors are present in each job: having decision-making/communication/social responsibilities, performing skilled activities, being physically active, operating vehicles or equipment, and processing information. As a result, a job analysis technique like the PAQ is actually as (or some say, more) appropriate as a job evaluation technique (than for job analysis) in that jobs can be quantitatively compared to one another on those five dimensions and their relative worth thus ascertained.

Another point worth noting is that you may find that a single set of compensable factors is not adequate for describing all your jobs. This is another reason why many managers therefore divide their jobs into job clusters. For example, you might have a separate job cluster for factory workers, for clerical workers, and for managerial personnel. You would then probably have a somewhat different set of compensable factors for each job cluster.

40. Michael Carrell and Christina Heavrin, Labor Relations and Collective Bargaining (Upper Saddle River, NJ: Prentice Hall, 2004) pp. 300–303.

41. If you used the job classification method, then of course the jobs are already classified.

42. In other words, on the graph, plot the benchmark jobs' points (as determined by job evaluation) and their corresponding market pay rates (as determined by the salary survey). Then slot in the other jobs based on their evaluations, to determine what their target pay rates should be.

43. Mark Meltzer and Howard Goldsmith, "Executive Compensation for Growth Companies," *Compensation and Benefits Review*, November/December 1997, pp. 41–50.

44. Douglas Tormey, "Executive Compensation: Creating 'Legal' Checklist," *Compensation and Benefits Review*, July/August 1996, pp. 12–36. See also Bruce Ellig, "Executive Pay: A Primer," *Compensation and Benefits Review*, January/February 2003, pp. 44–50.

45. Susan Marks, "Can the Internet Help You Hit the Salary Mark?" *Workforce*, January 2001, pp. 86–93.

46. James Reda, "Executive Pay Today and Tomorrow," *Corporate Board* 22, no. 126 (January 2001), p. 18.

47. Andrew Henderson and James Frederickson, "Information-Processing Demands as a Determinant of CEO Compensation," *Academy of Management Journal* 39, no. 2 (1996), pp. 576–606.

48. Ibid., pp. 585–586.

49. For example, one recent book argues that executives of large companies use their power to have themselves compensated in ways that are not sufficiently related to performance. Lucian Bebchuck and Jessie Fried, Pay Without Performance: The Unfulfilled Promise of Executive Compensation, Harvard University Press, Boston, 2004.

50. "Revolting Shareholders," *The Economist*, May 24, 2003, p. 13.

51. See for example, Fay Hansen, "Current Trends in Compensation and Benefits," *Compensation and Benefits Review* 36, no. 2 (March/April 2004), pp. 7–8.

52. Louis Lavelle, "While the CEO Gravy Train May Be Slowing Down, It Hasn't Jumped the Rails," *BusinessWeek*, April 16, 2001, pp. 76–80. See also David Backin and Michele Swift, "Top Management Team Compensation in High-Growth Technology Ventures," *Human Resource Management Review* 16, no. 1, March 2006, pp. 1–11.

53. See for example Martocchio, *Strategic Compensation*, and Patricia Zingheim and Jay Schuster, "Designing Pay and Rewards in Professional Services Companies," *Compensation and Benefits Review*, January/February 2007, pp. 55–62.

54. Dimitris Manolopoulos, "What Motivates Research and Development Professionals? Evidence from Decentralized Laboratories in Greece," *International Journal of Human Resource Management* 17, no. 4, April 2006, pp. 616–647.

55. See, for example, Robert Henneman and Peter LeBlanc, "Development of and Approach for Valuing Knowledge Work," *Compensation and Benefits Review*, July/August 2002, p. 47.

56. Kevin Foote, "Competencies in the Real World: Performance Management for the Rationally Healthy Organization," *Compensation and Benefits Review*, July/August 2001, p. 25.

57. Gerald Ledford Jr., "Paying for the Skills, Knowledge, and Competencies of Knowledge Workers," *Compensation and Benefits Review*, July/August 1995, p. 56; see also Richard Sperling and Larry Hicks, "Trends in Compensation and Benefits Strategies," *Employment Relations Today* 25, no. 2 (Summer 1998), pp. 85–99.

58. Foote, "Competencies in the Real World," p. 29.

59. Duncan Brown, "Using Competencies and Rewards to Enhance Business Performance and Customer Service at The Standard Life Assurance Company," *Compensation and Benefits Review*, July/August 2001, pp. 17, 19.

60. Ledford, "Three Case Studies on Skill-Based Pay," *Compensation and Benefits Review*, (March/April 1991), p. 12. See also Kathryn Cofsky, "Critical Keys to Competency-Based Pay," *Compensation and Benefits Review*, November/December 1993, pp. 46–52; Brian Murray and Barry Gerhart, "Skill-Based Pay and Skills Seeking," *Human Resource Management Review* 10, no. 3 (2000), pp. 271–287.

61. Joseph Martocchio, *Strategic Compensation*, p. 168.

62. Robert McNabb and Keith Whitfield, "Job Evaluation and High-Performance Work Practices: Compatible or Conflictual?" *Journal of Management Studies* 38, no. 2 (March 2001), pp. 294–311.

63. Ibid., p. 293.

64. Gerald Ledford, "Three Case Studies on Skill-Based Pay," p. 12. See also Cofsky, "Critical Keys to Competency-Based Pay," pp. 46–52; Murray and Gerhart, "Skill-Based Pay and Skills Seeking," pp. 271–287.

65. Gerald Ledford Jr., and Gary Bergal, "Skill-Based Pay Case Number 1: General Mills," *Compensation and Benefits Review*, March/April 1991, pp. 24–38; see also Gerald Barrett, "Comparison of Skill-Based Pay with Traditional Job Evaluation Techniques," *Human Resource Management Review* 1, no. 2 (Summer 1991), pp. 97–105; Barbara Dewey, "Changing to Skill-Based Pay: Disarming the Transition Land Mines," *Compensation and Benefits Review*, January/February 1994, pp. 38–43.

66. This is based on Ledford and Bergal, "Skill-Based Pay Case Number 1," pp. 28–29.

67. Brown, "Using Competencies and Rewards," p. 14.

68. Robert Henneman and Peter LeBlanc, "Work Evaluation Addresses the Shortcomings of Both Job Evaluation and Market Pricing," *Compensation and Benefits Review*, January/February 2003, p. 8.

69. Ledford, "Paying for the Skills, Knowledge, and Competencies of Knowledge Workers," p. 55.

70. Kevin Parent and Carline Weber, "Case Study: Does Paying for Knoweldge Pay Off?" *Compensation and Benefits Review*, September/October 1994, pp. 44–50; and Edward Lawler III, Gerald Ledford Jr., and Lei Chang, "Who Uses Skill-Based Pay, and Why?" *Compensation and Benefits Review*, November/December 1996, pp. 20–26.

71. Parent and Weber, "Case Study." For a good discussion of the conditions under which competency based pay is more effective, see Edward Lawler III, "Competencies: A Poor Foundation for the New Pay," *Compensation and Benefits Review*, November/December 1996, pp. 20–26.

72. Patricia Zingheim and Jay Schuster, "The Next Decade for Pay and Rewards," *Compensation and Benefits Review*, (January/February 2005), p. 29, and Patricia Zingheim and Jay Schuster, "What are Key Pay Issues Right Now," *Compensation & Benefits Review*, May/June 2007, pp. 51–55.

73. David Hofrichter, "Broadbanding: A 'Second Generation' Approach," *Compensation and Benefits Review*, September/October 1993, pp. 53–58. See also "The Future of Salary Management," *Compensation and Benefits Review*, July/August 2001, pp. 7–12.

74. Ibid., p. 55.

75. For example, see Sondra Emerson, "Job Evaluation: A Barrier to Excellence?" *Compensation and Benefits Review*, January/February 1991, pp. 39–52; Nan Weiner, "Job Evaluation Systems: A Critique," *Human Resource Management Review* 1, no. 2 (Summer 1991), pp. 119–132; and Brian Klass, "Compensation in the Jobless Organization," *Human Resource Management Review* 12, no. 1 (Spring 2002), pp. 43–62.

76. Dawne Shand, "Broadbanding the IT Worker," *Computerworld* 34, no. 41 (October 9, 2000).

77. "Broadbanding Pay Structures Does Not Receive Flat-Out Support from Employers, Survey Finds," *BNA Bulletin to Management*, January 13, 2000, p. 11.

78. Duncan Brown, "Broadbanding: A Case Study of Company Practices in the United Kingdom," *Compensation and Benefits Review*, November/December 1996, p. 43.

79. Emerson, "Job Evaluation," p. 39.

80. *County of Washington v. Gunther*, U.S. Supreme Court, no. 80–426, June 8, 1981.

81. "Generation X Women Earn More Than Predecessors," *BNA Bulletin to Management*, June 6, 2002, p. 181.

82. "Women Still Earned Less Than Men, BLS Data Show," *BNA Bulletin to Management*, June 8, 2000, p. 72. However, there is some indication that there is less gender-based pay gap among full-time workers ages 21 to 35 living alone. Kent Hoover, "Study Finds No Pay Gap for Young, Single Workers," *Tampa Bay Business Journal* 20, no. 19 (May 12, 2000), p. 10.

83. Christopher Dougherty, "Why are the Returns to Schooling Higher for Women than for Men?" *Journal of Human Resources* 40, no. 4, Fall 2005, pp. 969–988.

84. Jamison Bandler and Charles Forelle, "How a Giant Insurer Decided to Oust Hugely Successful CEO," *Wall Street Journal*, December 7, 2006, p. A1.

85. Mark Poerio and Eric Keller, "Executive Compensation 2005: Many Forces, One Direction," *Compensation and Benefits Review*, May/June 2005, pp. 34–40.

86. Ibid., p. 38.

87. Ibid. See also, Brent Cougnecker and James Krueger, "The Next Wave of Compensation Disclosure; *Compensation & Benefits Review*, January/February 2007, pp. 50–54.

88. Al Wright, "Tools for Automating Complex Compensation Programs," *Compensation and Benefits Review*, November/December 2003, pp. 53–61.

APPENDIX FOR CHAPTER 11

Quantitative Job Evaluation Methods

Using the Factor Comparison Job Evaluation Method   The factor comparison technique is a *quantitative* job evaluation method. It has many variations and appears to be the most accurate, the most complex, and one of the most widely used job evaluation methods.

It is actually a refinement of the ranking method and entails deciding which jobs have more of certain compensable factors. With the ranking method you generally look at each job as an entity and rank the jobs. With the factor comparison method you rank each job *several times—once for each compensable factor you choose*. For example, jobs might be ranked first in terms of the factor "skill." Then they are ranked according to their "mental requirements." Next they are ranked according to their "responsibility," and so forth. Then these rankings are combined for each job into an overall numerical rating for the job. Here are the required steps.

Step 1. Obtain Job Information   This method requires a careful, complete job analysis. First, job descriptions are written. Then job specifications are developed, preferably in terms of the compensable factors the job evaluation committee has decided to use. For the factor comparison method, these compensable factors are usually (1) mental requirements, (2) physical requirements, (3) skill requirements, (4) responsibility, and (5) working conditions. Typical definitions of each of these five factors are presented in Figure 11-A1.

Step 2. Select Key Benchmark Jobs   Next, 15 to 25 key jobs are selected by the job evaluation committee. These jobs will have to be representative benchmark jobs, acceptable reference points that represent the full range of jobs to be evaluated.

Step 3. Rank Key Jobs By Factor   Here evaluators are asked to rank the key jobs on each of the five factors (mental requirements, physical requirements, skill requirements, responsibility, and working conditions). This ranking procedure is based on job descriptions and job specifications. Each committee member usually makes this ranking individually, and then a meeting is held to develop a consensus on each job. The result of this process is a table, as in Table 11-A1. This shows how each key job ranks on each of the five compensable factors.

Step 4. Distribute Wage Rates by Factors   This is where the factor comparison method gets a bit more complicated. In this step the committee members have to divide up the present wage now being paid for each key job, distributing it among the five compensable factors. They do this in accordance with their judgments about the importance to the job of each factor. For example, if the present wage for the job of laborer in Mexico is $4.26, our evaluators might distribute this wage as follows:

Mental requirements	$0.36
Physical requirements	$2.20
Skill requirements	$0.42
Responsibility	$0.28
Working conditions	$1.00
Total	$4.26

FIGURE 11-A1

Sample Definitions of Five Factors Typically Used in Factor Comparison Method

Source: Jay L. Otis and Richard H. Leukart, *Job Evaluation: A Basis for Sound Wage Administration*, p. 181. © 1954, revised 1983. Reprinted by permission of Prentice Hall, Upper Saddle River, NJ.

1. **Mental Requirements**

Either the possession of and/or the active application of the following:

   A. (inherent) Mental traits, such as intelligence, memory, reasoning, facility in verbal expression, ability to get along with people, and imagination.
   B. (acquired) General education, such as grammar and arithmetic; or general information as to sports, world events, etc.
   C. (acquired) Specialized knowledge such as chemistry, engineering, accounting, advertising, etc.

2. **Skill**

   A. (acquired) Facility in muscular coordination, as in operating machines, repetitive movements, careful coordinations, dexterity, assembling, sorting, etc.
   B. (acquired) Specific job knowledge necessary to the muscular coordination only; acquired by performance of the work and not to be confused with general education or specialized knowledge. It is very largely training in the interpretation of sensory impressions.

   Examples

   1. In operating an adding machine, the knowledge of *which* key to depress for a subtotal would be skill.
   2. In automobile repair, the ability to determine the significance of a certain knock in the motor would be skill.
   3. In hand-firing a boiler, the ability to determine from the appearance of the firebed how coal should be shoveled over the surface would be skill.

3. **Physical Requirements**

   A. Physical effort, such as sitting, standing, walking, climbing, pulling, lifting, etc.; both the amount exercised and the degree of the continuity should be taken into account.
   B. Physical status, such as age, height, weight, sex, strength, and eyesight.

4. **Responsibilities**

   A. For raw materials, processed materials, tools, equipment, and property.
   B. For money or negotiable securities.
   C. For profits or loss, savings or methods' improvement.
   D. For public contact.
   E. For records.
   F. For supervision.

   1. Primarily the complexity of supervision *given* to subordinates; the number of subordinates is a secondary feature. Planning, direction, coordination, instruction, control, and approval characterize this kind of supervision.
   2. Also, the degree of supervision *received*. If Jobs A and B gave no supervision to subordinates, but A received much closer immediate supervision than B, then B would be entitled to a higher rating than A in the supervision factor.

      To summarize the four degrees of supervision:
      Highest degree—gives much—gets little
      High degree—gives much—gets much
      Low degree—gives none—gets little
      Lowest degree—gives none—gets much

5. **Working Conditions**

   A. Environmental influences such as atmosphere, ventilation, illumination, noise, congestion, fellow workers, etc.
   B. Hazards—from the work or its surroundings.
   C. Hours.

TABLE 11-A1 Ranking Key Jobs by Factors[1]

	Mental Requirements	Physical Requirements	Skill Requirements	Responsibility	Working Conditions
Welder	1	4	1	1	2
Crane operator	3	1	3	4	4
Punch press operator	2	3	2	2	3
Security guard	4	2	4	3	1

[1]1 is high, 4 is low.

TABLE 11-A2 Ranking Key Jobs by Wage Rates[1]

	Hourly Wage	Mental Requirements	Physical Requirements	Skill Requirements	Responsibility	Working Conditions
Welder	$9.80	4.00(1)	0.40(4)	3.00(1)	2.00(1)	0.40(2)
Crane operator	5.60	1.40(3)	2.00(1)	1.80(3)	0.20(4)	0.20(4)
Punch press operator	6.00	1.60(2)	1.30(3)	2.00(2)	0.80(2)	0.30(3)
Security guard	4.00	1.20(4)	1.40(2)	0.40(4)	0.40(3)	0.60(1)

[1]1 is high, 4 is low.

You make such a distribution for all key jobs.

Step 5. Rank Key Jobs According to Wages Assigned to Each Factor   Here you again rank each job, factor by factor, but the ranking is based on the wages assigned to each factor. As shown in Table 11-A2, for example, for the "mental requirements" factor, the welder job ranks first, whereas the security guard job ranks last.

Each member of the committee first makes this distribution working independently. Then the committee meets and arrives at a consensus concerning the money to be assigned to each factor for each key job.

Step 6. Compare the Two Sets of Rankings to Screen Out Unusable Key Jobs   You now have two sets of rankings for each key job. One was your original ranking (from step 3). This shows how each job ranks on each of the five compensable factors. The second ranking reflects for each job the wages assigned to each factor. You can now draw up a table like the one in Table 11-A3.

For each factor, this shows both rankings for each key job. On the left is the ranking from step 3. On the right is the ranking based on wages paid. For each factor, the ranking based on the amount of the factor (from step 3) should be about the same as the ranking based on the wages assigned to the job (step 5). (In this case they are.) If there's much of a discrepancy, it suggests that the key job might be unusable, and from this point on, it is no longer used as a key job. (Many managers don't bother to screen out unusable key jobs. To simplify things, they skip over our steps 5 and 6, going instead from step 4 to step 7; this is an acceptable alternative.)

TABLE 11-A3 Comparison of Factor and Wage Rankings

	Mental Requirements		Physical Requirements		Skill Requirements		Responsibility		Working Conditions	
	A[1]	$[2]	A[1]	$[2]	A[1]	$[2]	A[1]	$[2]	A[1]	$[2]
Welder	1	1	4	4	1	1	1	1	2	2
Crane operator	3	3	1	1	3	3	4	4	4	4
Punch press operator	2	2	3	3	2	2	2	2	3	3
Security guard	4	4	2	2	4	4	3	3	1	1

[1]Amount of each factor based on step 3.
[2]Ratings based on distribution of wages to each factor from step 5.

Step 7. Construct the Job-Comparison Scale   Once you've identified the usable, true key jobs, the next step is to set up the job-comparison scale (Table 11-A4). (Note that there's a separate column for each of the five comparable factors.) To develop it, you'll need the assigned wage tables from steps 4 and 5.

For each of the factors for all key jobs, you write the job next to the appropriate wage rate. Thus, in the assigned wage rate table (Table 11-A2), the welder job has $4.00 assigned to the factor "mental requirements." Therefore, on the job-comparison scale (Table 11-A4) write "welder" in the "mental requirements" factor column, next to the "$4.00" row. Do the same for all factors for all key jobs.

Step 8. Use the Job-Comparison Scale   Now all the other jobs to be evaluated can be slotted, factor by factor, into the job-comparison scale. For example, suppose you have a job of plater that you want to slot in. You decide where the "mental requirements" of the plater job would fit as compared with the "mental requirements" of all the other jobs listed. It might, for example, fit between punch press operator and inspector. Similarly, you would ask where the "physical requirements" of the plater's job fit as compared with the other jobs listed. Here you might find that it fits just below crane operator. You would do the same for each of the remaining three factors.

An Example   Let us work through an example to clarify the factor-comparison method. We'll just use four key jobs to simplify the presentation—you'd usually start with 15 to 25 key jobs.

Step 1: First, we do a job analysis.
Step 2: Here we select our four key jobs: welder, crane operator, punch press operator, and security guard.
Step 3: Based on the job descriptions and specifications, here we rank key jobs by factor, as in Table 11-A1.
Step 4: Here we distribute wage rates by factor, as in Table 11-A2.
Step 5: Then we rank our key jobs according to wage rates assigned to each key factor. These rankings are shown in parentheses in Table 11-A2.
Step 6: Next compare your two sets of rankings (see Table 11-A3). In each left-hand column (marked A) is the job's ranking from step 3 based on the amount of the compensable factor. In each right-hand column (marked $) is the job's ranking from step 5 based on the wage assigned to that factor. In this case, there are no differences between any of the pairs of A (amount) and $ (wage) rankings, so

TABLE 11-A4 **Job (Factor)-Comparison Scale**

	Mental Requirements	Physical Requirements	Skill Requirements	Responsibility	Working Conditions
.20				Crane Operator	Crane Operator
.30					Punch Press Operator
.40		Welder	Sec. Guard	Sec. Guard	Welder
.50					
.60					Sec. Guard
.70					
.80				Punch Press Operator	
.90					
1.00				(Plater)	
1.10					
1.20	Sec. Guard				
1.30		Punch Press Operator			
1.40	Crane Operator	Sec. Guard	(Inspector)	(Plater)	
1.50		(Inspector)			(Inspector)
1.60	Punch Press Operator				
1.70	(Plater)				
1.80			Crane Operator	(Inspector)	
1.90					
2.00		Crane Operator	Punch Press Operator	Welder	
2.20		(Plater)			
2.40	(Inspector)				(Plater)
2.60					
2.80					
3.00			Welder		
3.20					
3.40					
3.60					
3.80					
4.00	Welder				
4.20					
4.40					
4.60					
4.80					

all our key jobs are usable. If there had been any differences (for example, between the A and $ rankings for the welder job's "mental requirements" factor), we would have dropped that job as a key job.

Step 7: Now we construct our job-comparison scale as in Table 11-A4. For this, we use the wage distributions from step 4. For example, let us say that in steps 4 and 5 we assigned $4.00 to the "mental requirements" factor of the welder's job. Therefore, we now write "welder" on the $4.00 row under the "mental requirements" column as in Table 11-A4.

Step 8: Now all our other jobs can be slotted, factor by factor, into our job-comparison scale. We do not distribute wages to each of the factors for our other jobs to do this. We just decide where, factor by factor, each of our other jobs should be slotted. We've done this for two other jobs in the factor comparison scale: They're shown in parentheses. Now we also know what the wages for these two jobs should be, and we can also do the same for all our jobs.

A Variation There are several variations to this basic factor-comparison method. One converts the dollar values on the factor comparison chart (Table 11-A4) to points. (You can do this by multiplying each of the dollar values by 100, for example.) The main advantage in making this change is that your system would no longer be "locked in" to your present wage rates. Instead, each of your jobs would be compared with one another, factor by factor, in terms of a more constant point system.

Pros and Cons We've presented the factor-comparison method at some length because it is (in one form or another) a very widely used job evaluation method. Its wide use derives from several advantages: First, it is an accurate, systematic, quantifiable method for which detailed, step-by-step instructions are available. Second, jobs are compared to other jobs to determine a relative value. Thus, in the job-comparison scale you not only see that a welder requires more mental ability than a plater; you also can determine about *how much* more mental ability is required—apparently about twice as much ($4.00 versus $1.70). (This type of calibration is not possible with the ranking or classification methods.) Third, this is also a fairly easy job evaluation system to explain to employees.

Complexity is probably the most serious disadvantage of the factor-comparison method. Although it is fairly easy to explain the factor-comparison scale and its rationale to employees, it is difficult to show them how to build one. In addition, the use of the five factors is an outgrowth of the technique developed by its originators. However, using the same five factors for all organizations and for all jobs in an organization may not always be appropriate.

The Point Method of Job Evaluation The point method is widely used. It requires identifying several compensable factors (like skills and responsibility), each with several degrees, and also the degree to which each of these factors is present in the job. A different number of points is usually assigned for each degree of each factor. So once you determine the degree to which each factor is present in the job, you need only add up the corresponding number of points for each factor and arrive at an overall point value for the job.[1] Here are the steps:

Step 1. Determine Clusters of Jobs to Be Evaluated Because jobs vary widely by department, you usually will not use one point-rating plan for all jobs in the organization. Therefore, the first step is usually to cluster jobs, for example, into shop jobs, clerical jobs, sales jobs, and so forth. Then the committee will generally develop a point plan for one group or cluster at a time.

Step 2. Collect Job Information This means performing a job analysis and writing job descriptions and job specifications.

Step 3. Select Compensable Factors Here select compensable factors, like problem solving, physical requirements, or skills. Each cluster of jobs may require its own compensable factors.

Step 4. Define Compensable Factors Next, carefully define each compensable factor. This is done to ensure that the evaluation committee members will each apply the factors with consistency. Figure 11-A2 (top) shows one such definition. The definitions are often drawn up or obtained by the human resource specialist.

Step 5. Define Factor Degrees Next define each of several degrees for each factor so that raters may judge the amount or degree of a factor existing in a job. Thus, for the factor "complexity" you might choose to have six degrees, ranging from "seldom confronts new problems" through "uses independent judgement." (Definitions for each degree are shown in Figure 11-A2.) The number of degrees usually does not exceed five or six, and the actual number depends mostly on judgment. Thus, if all employees either work in a quiet, air-conditioned office or in a noisy, hot factory, then two degrees would probably suffice for the factor "working conditions." You need not have the same number of degrees for each factor, and you should limit degrees to the number necessary to distinguish among jobs.

Step 6. Determine Relative Values of Factors The next step is to decide how much weight (or how many total points) to assign to each factor. This is important because for

FIGURE 11-A2

Example of One Factor (Complexity/ Problem Solving) in a Point Factor System

Source: Richard W. Beatty and James R. Beatty, "Job Evaluation," in Ronald A. Berk (ed.), *Performance Assessment: Methods and Applications* (Baltimore, MD: Johns Hopkins University Press, 1986), p. 322. Reprinted by permission.

The mental capacity required to perform the given job as expressed in resourcefulness in dealing with unfamiliar problems, interpretation of data, initiation of new ideas, complex data analysis, creative or developmental work.

Level	Point Value	Description of Characteristics and Measures
0	0	Seldom confronts problems not covered by job routine or organizational policy; analysis of data is negligible. *Benchmark*: Telephone operator/receptionist.
1	40	Follows clearly prescribed standard practice and demonstrates straightforward application of readily understood rules and procedures. Analyzes noncomplicated data by established routine. *Benchmark*: Statistical clerk, billing clerk.
2	80	Frequently confronts problems not covered by job routine. Independent judgment exercised in making minor decisions where alternatives are limited and standard policies established. Analysis of standardized data for information of or use by others. *Benchmark*: Social worker, executive secretary.
3	120	Exercises independent judgment in making decisions involving nonroutine problems with general guidance only from higher supervision. Analyzes and evaluates data pertaining to nonroutine problems for solution in conjunction with others. *Benchmark*: Nurse, accountant, team leader.
4	160	Uses independent judgment in making decisions that are subject to review in the final stages only. Analyzes and solves nonroutine problems involving evaluation of a wide variety of data as a regular part of job duties. Makes decisions involving procedures. *Benchmark*: Associate director, business manager, park services director.
5	200	Uses independent judgment in making decisions that are not subject to review. Regularly exercises developmental or creative abilities in policy development. *Benchmark*: Executive director.

each cluster of jobs some factors are bound to be more important than others. Thus, for executives the "mental requirements" factor would carry far more weight than would "physical requirements." The opposite might be true of factory jobs.

The process of determining the relative values or weights that should be assigned to each of the factors is generally done by the evaluation committee. The committee members carefully study factor and degree definitions and then determine the relative value of the factors for the cluster of jobs under consideration. Here is one method for doing this:

First, assign a value of 100% to the highest-ranking factor. Then assign a value to the next highest factor as a percentage of its importance to the first factor, and so forth. For example,

Decision making	100%
Problem solving	85%
Knowledge	60%

Next, sum up the total percentage (in this case 100% + 85% + 60% = 245%). Then convert this 245% to a 100% system as follows:

Decision making:	$100 \div 245 = 40.82 = 40.8\%$
Problem solving:	$85 \div 245 = 34.69 = 34.7\%$
Knowledge:	$60 \div 245 = 24.49 = 24.5\%$
Totals	100.0%

Step 7. Assign Point Values to Factors and Degrees   In step 6, total weights were developed for each factor in percentage terms. Now assign points to each factor as in Table 11-A5. For example, suppose it is decided to use a total number of 500 points in the point plan. Because the factor "decision making" had a weight of 40.8%, it would be assigned a total of $40.8\% \times 500 = 204$ points.

Thus, it was decided to assign 204 points to the decision-making factor. This automatically means that the highest degree for the decision-making factor would also carry 204 points. Then assign points to the other degrees for this factor, usually in equal amounts from the lowest to the highest degree. For example, divide 204 by the number of degrees (say, 5); this equals 40.8. Then the lowest degree here would carry about 41 points. The second degree would carry 41 plus 41, or 82 points. The third degree would carry 123 points. The fourth degree would carry 164 points. Finally, the fifth and highest degree would carry 204 points. Do this for each factor (as in Table 11-A5).

Step 8. Write the Job Evaluation Manual   Developing a point plan like this usually culminates in a *point manual* or *job evaluation manual*. This simply consolidates the factor and degree definitions and point values into one convenient manual.

TABLE 11-A5   **Evaluation Points Assigned to Factors and Degrees**

	First-Degree Points	Second-Degree Points	Third-Degree Points	Fourth-Degree Points	Fifth-Degree Points
Decision making	41	82	123	164	204
Problem solving	35	70	105	140	174
Knowledge	24	48	72	96	123

Step 9. Rate the Jobs   Once the manual is complete, the actual evaluations can begin. Raters (usually the committee) use the manual to evaluate jobs. Each job based on its job description and job specification is evaluated factor by factor to determine the number of points that should be assigned to it. First, committee members determine the degree (first degree, second degree, and so on) to which each factor is present in the job. Then they note the corresponding points (see Table 11-A5) that were previously assigned to each of these degrees (in step 7). Finally, they add up the points for all factors, arriving at a total point value for the job. Raters generally start with rating key jobs and obtain consensus on these. Then they rate the rest of the jobs in the cluster.

"Packaged" Point Plans   Developing a point plan of one's own can obviously be a time-consuming process. For this reason a number of groups (such as the National Electrical Manufacturer's Association and the National Trade Association) have developed standardized point plans. These have been used or adapted by thousands of organizations. They contain ready-made factor and degree definitions and point assessments for a wide range of jobs and can often be used with little or no modification.

Pros and Cons   Point systems have their advantages, as their wide use suggests. This is a quantitative technique that is easily explained to and used by employees. On the other hand, it can be difficult to develop a point plan, and this is one reason many organizations have opted for ready-made plans. In fact, the availability of a number of ready-made plans probably accounts in part for the wide use of point plans in job evaluation.

APPENDIX ENDNOTE

1. For a discussion, see, for example, Roger Plachy, "The Point Factor Job Evaluation System: A Step-by-Step Guide, Part I," *Compensation and Benefits Review*, July/August 1987, pp. 12–27; Roger Plachy, "The Case for Effective Point-Factor Job Evaluation, Viewpoint I," *Compensation and Benefits Review*, March/April 1987, pp. 45–48; Roger Plachy, "The Point-Factor Job Evaluation System: A Step-by-Step Guide, Part II," *Compensation and Benefits Review*, September/October 1987, pp. 9–24; and Alfred Candrilli and Ronald Armagast, "The Case for Effective Point-Factor Job Evaluation, Viewpoint II," *Compensation and Benefits Review*, March/April 1987, pp. 49–54. See also Robert J. Sahl, "How to Install a Point-Factor Job Evaluation System," *Personnel* 66, no. 3 (March 1989), pp. 38–42.

12 Pay for Performance and Financial Incentives

Like many successful companies, Home Depot Inc. knew it needed a way to get its store employees more involved in helping the company cut costs and compete with companies like Lowe's. Also like many companies, Home Depot already had a bonus program in place for its managers and executives. The question facing Home Depot's top management was whether to institute such a bonus program for workers in all its stores, and if so how to do so. •

After studying this chapter, you should be able to:

1 Discuss the main incentives for individual employees.
2 Discuss the pros and cons of incentives for salespeople.
3 Name and define the most popular organizationwide variable pay plans.
4 Describe the main incentives for managers and executives.
5 Outline the steps in developing effective incentive plans.

Chapter 11 focused on developing pay plans and on salaries and wages. The main purpose of this chapter is to explain how to use performance-based incentives to motivate employees. We'll discuss incentives for individual employees, and for managers and executives, salespeople, and professionals, as well as organizationwide incentive plans. We'll explain why incentive plans fail, and creating an effective plan. In the next chapter, Benefits and Services, we'll turn to the financial and non-financial benefits and services, which are the final part of the employee's compensation package.

MONEY AND MOTIVATION: AN INTRODUCTION

financial incentives
Financial rewards paid to workers whose production exceeds some predetermined standard.

Frederick Taylor popularized using **financial incentives**—financial rewards paid to workers whose production exceeds some predetermined standard—in the late 1800s. As a supervisory employee of the Midvale Steel Company, Taylor was concerned with what he called "systematic soldiering"—the tendency of employees to work at the slowest pace possible and to produce at the minimum acceptable level. What especially intrigued him was the fact that some of these workers had the energy to run home and work on their houses, even after a 12-hour day. Taylor knew that if he could harness this energy during the workday, Midvale Steel could achieve huge productivity gains.

fair day's work
Output standards devised based on careful, scientific analysis.

At the time, primitive piecework incentive plans were already in use, but were generally ineffective (due to employers' propensities for arbitrarily assigning and changing incentive rates). Taylor made three contributions. He saw the need for formulating what he called a **fair day's work**, namely standards of output which employers should devise for each job based on careful, scientific analysis. He spearheaded the **scientific management movement**, a management approach that emphasized improving work methods through observation and analysis. And, he popularized the use of incentive pay.

scientific management
Management approach based on improving work methods through observation and analysis.

Performance and Pay

Today, as we explained in Chapter 11, tying workers' pay to their performance is widely popular. Indeed, with the emphasis on competitiveness, productivity, and delivering measurable bottom line results, the trend for virtually all employers is to tie at least some portion of their workers' pay to the workers' and/or the company's performance.[1]

The problem is that doing so is easier said than done. Many such programs are ineffective or worse (one plan, at Levi's, is widely assumed to have been the last nail in the coffin of Levi's U.S.-based production). Mercer Human Resource Consulting found that just 28% of the 2,600 U.S. workers it surveyed said they were personally motivated by their companies' incentive plans. Only 29% said their firms rewarded their performance when they did a good job. "Employees don't see a strong connection between pay and performance, and their performance is not particularly influenced by the company's incentive plan," said one Mercer expert.[2] About 95% of companies tie employee pay to their individual work performance to some extent, according to consultants Hewitt Associates. About 83% of companies with such programs say their programs are only somewhat successful or not successful at all.[3]

There are, as we'll see, many reasons for such dismal results. Many employers, perhaps ignorant of Taylor and history, institute and change their plans' standards arbitrarily. Others ignore the fact that incentive pay is, at its heart, psychologically based. Therefore, not everyone reacts to a reward in the same way, and not all rewards are suited to all situations. Compensation experts therefore argue that managers should be aware of the motivational bases of incentive plans.[4] We'll review some of this basic motivation information next.

FIGURE 12-1

Employee Preferences for Noncash Incentives

Source: Darryl Hutson, "Shopping for Incentives," *Compensation and Benefits Review*, March/April 2002, p. 76. Reprinted with permission of Sage Publications, Inc.

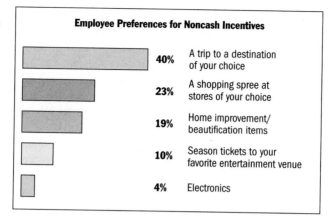

Employee Preferences for Noncash Incentives

40%	A trip to a destination of your choice
23%	A shopping spree at stores of your choice
19%	Home improvement/ beautification items
10%	Season tickets to your favorite entertainment venue
4%	Electronics

Motivation and Incentives

While it may seem obvious, the manager devising an incentive plan should first remember that different people react to different incentives in different ways. To choose just one example, one study focused on high and low "positive affective" (PA) individuals. High PAs are energetic, active, and alert. Low PAs are more lethargic, listless, and apathetic.[5] In this study, the low PAs actually responded much more favorably to merit raises than did the high PAs, (perhaps because the raise gave the relatively unhappy low PAs relatively more to be happy about).[6] A survey of how employees react to noncash incentive recognition rewards (such as gift certificates) further illustrates how differences affect incentive choice. Figure 12-1 summarizes employee preferences for noncash incentives based on the survey.

Several motivation theories have particular relevance to designing incentive plans. These include theories associated with the psychologists Frederick Herzberg, Edward Deci, Victor Vroom, and B.F. Skinner.

Frederick Herzberg   Frederick Herzberg said the best way to motivate someone is to organize the job so that doing it provides the feedback and challenge that helps satisfy the person's "higher-level" needs for things like accomplishment and recognition. These needs are relatively insatiable, says Herzberg, so recognition and challenging work provide a sort of built-in motivation generator. Satisfying "lower level" needs for things like better pay and working conditions just keep the person from becoming dissatisfied.

Herzberg says the factors ("hygienes") that satisfy lower-level needs are different from those ("motivators") that satisfy or partially satisfy higher-level needs. If *hygiene* factors (factors outside the job itself, such as working conditions, salary, and incentive pay) are inadequate, employees become dissatisfied. However, adding more of these hygienes (like incentives) to the job (supplying what Herzberg calls extrinsic motivation) is an inferior way to try to motivate someone, because lower-level needs are quickly satisfied. Soon the person simply says, in effect, "What have you done for me lately? I want another raise."

Instead of relying on hygienes, says Herzberg, the employer interested in creating a self-motivated workforce should emphasize "job content" or *motivator* factors. Managers do this by enriching workers' jobs so that the jobs are more challenging, and by providing feedback and recognition—make the job itself intrinsically motivating, in other words. Here, the motivation, in a sense, come from within the person, and just doing the job provides the motivation. Among other things, Herzberg's theory makes the point that relying exclusively on financial incentives is risky. The employer should also provide the recognition and challenging work that most people desire.

Edward Deci   Psychologist Edward Deci's work highlights another potential downside to relying too heavily on extrinsic rewards: they may backfire. Deci found that extrinsic rewards could at times actually detract from the person's intrinsic motivation.[7] For example, a Samaritan who risks danger by rushing to an accident victim's aid might be insulted if the victim said, "Thanks, here's some money for your trouble." The point may be stated thusly: Be cautious in devising incentive pay for highly motivated employees, lest you inadvertently demean and detract from the desire they have to do the job out of a sense of responsibility.

Victor Vroom   Another important motivational fact is that, in general, people won't pursue rewards they find unattractive, or where the odds of success are very low. Psychologist Victor Vroom's motivation theory echoes these commonsense observations. He says a person's motivation to exert some level of effort depends on three things: the person's **expectancy** (in terms of probability) that his or her effort will lead to performance;[8] **instrumentality**, or the perceived connection (if any) between successful performance and actually obtaining the rewards; and **valence**, which represents the perceived value the person attaches to the reward.[9] In Vroom's theory, motivation is thus a product of three things: Motivation = (E × I × V), where, of course, E represents expectancy, I instrumentality, and V valence. If E or I or V is zero or inconsequential, there will be no motivation.

Vroom's theory has three implications for how managers design incentive plans.

- First, if employees don't *expect* that effort will produce performance, no motivation will occur. So, managers must ensure that their employees have the skills to do the job, and believe they can do the job. Thus training, job descriptions, and confidence building and support are important.
- Second, Vroom's theory suggests that employees must see the *instrumentality* of their efforts—they must believe that successful performance will in fact lead to getting the reward. Managers can accomplish this, for instance, by creating easy to understand incentive plans.
- Third, the reward itself must be of *value* to the employee. So ideally, the manager should take individual employee preferences into account. Endeavor to use extrinsic and intrinsic rewards that make sense in terms of the specific behaviors you want to encourage.

Behavior Modification/Reinforcement Theory   Using incentives also reflects the idea that to understand behavior one must understand the consequences of that behavior.[10] Psychologist BF Skinner's findings provide the foundation for much of what we know about this. Managers apply Skinner's principles by using *behavior modification*. **Behavior modification** means changing behavior through rewards or punishments that are contingent on performance. Behavior modification has two basic principles: (1) That behavior that appears to lead to a positive consequence (reward) tends to be repeated, while behavior that appears to lead to a negative consequence (punishment) tends not to be repeated; and (2) that, therefore, managers can get someone to change his or her behavior by providing the properly scheduled rewards (or punishment).

Incentive Pay Terminology

Managers often use two terms synonymously with incentive plans.[11] Traditionally, all incentive plans are *pay-for-performance* plans. They pay all employees based on the employees' performance. **Variable pay** is generally a group incentive plan that ties pay to some measure of the firm's (or the facility's) overall profitability;[12] *profit-sharing plans* (discussed below) are one example.[13] However, confusing as it may be, some experts do use the term variable pay to include incentive plans for individual employees.[14]

---

expectancy
A person's expectation that his or her effort will lead to performance.

instrumentality
The perceived relationships between successful performance and obtaining the reward.

valence
The perceived value a person attaches to the reward.

behavior modification
Using contingent rewards or punishment to change behavior.

variable pay
Any plan that ties pay to productivity or profitability, usually as one-time lump payments.

Know Your Employment LAW   Incentives

Several federal laws apply to employer incentive plans. For one thing, the employer must comply with the overtime provisions of the Fair Labor Standards Act when designing and administering its incentive plans. If the incentive is in the form of a prize or cash award, the employee generally must include the value of that award when calculating the worker's overtime pay for that pay period.[15] Overtime rates are paid to nonexempt employees based on their previous week's earnings. Unless you structure the incentive bonuses properly, the bonus itself becomes part of the week's wages. It must then be included in base pay when computing any overtime that week.

Certain bonuses are excludable from overtime pay calculations. For example, Christmas and gift bonuses that are not based on hours worked, or are so substantial that employees don't consider them a part of their wages, do not have to be included in overtime pay calculations. Similarly, purely discretionary bonuses in which the employer retains discretion over how much if anything to pay are excludable.

Other types of incentive pay must be included. Under the FLSA, bonuses to be included in overtime pay computations include those promised to newly hired employees, those provided in union contracts or other agreements, and those announced to induce employees to work more productively, steadily, rapidly, or efficiently or to induce them to remain with the company. Such bonuses would include individual and group production bonuses, bonuses for quality and accuracy of work, efficiency bonuses, attendance bonuses, and sales commissions.

The Sarbanes-Oxley act of 2002, affects how employers formulate their executive incentive programs. Congress passed Sarbanes-Oxley to inject a higher level of responsibility into executives' and board members' decisions. It makes them personally liable for violating their fiduciary responsibilities to their shareholders. The act also requires that CEOs and CFOs of public companies repay any bonuses, incentives, or equity-based compensation received from the company during the 12-month period following the issuance of a financial statement that the company must restate due to material noncompliance with a financial reporting requirement as a result of misconduct.[16]

To structure our discussion, we will organize the remainder of this chapter around individual employee incentive and recognition programs, sales compensation programs, team/group-based variable pay programs, organizationwide incentive programs, and executive incentive compensation programs. The "Know Your Employment Law" feature briefly looks at some legal aspects of incentive pay.

❶ Discuss the main incentives for individual employees.

INDIVIDUAL EMPLOYEE INCENTIVE AND RECOGNITION PROGRAMS

Several incentive plans are particularly suited for use with individual employees.

Piecework Plans

piecework
A system of pay based on the number of items processed by each individual worker in a unit of time, such as items per hour or items per day.

Piecework is the oldest individual incentive plan and is still the most widely used. Here you pay the worker a sum (called a *piece rate*) for each unit he or she produces. Thus, if Tom the Web surfer gets $0.40 for each e-mail sales lead he finds for the firm, he would make $40 for bringing in 100 a day and $80 for 200.

In a perfect world, developing a workable piece rate plan requires industrial engineering (that's how Frederick Taylor got his start). The crucial issue is the production standard, and industrial engineers usually set this—for instance, in terms of a standard number of e-mail leads per hour or a standard number of minutes per e-mail lead. In Tom's case, a job evaluation indicated that his Web surfing job was worth $8 an hour. The industrial engineer determined that 20 good leads per hour was the standard production rate. Therefore, the piece rate (for each lead) was $8 divided by 20, or $0.40 per sales lead. (Of course, we need to ensure that Tom makes at least the minimum wage, so we'd probably pay him $5.85 per hour—the minimum wage in July 2007—whether or not he brought in 15 leads, and then pay him $0.40 per lead for each over 15.) In practice, most employers set the piece rates more informally.

straight piecework

An incentive plan in which a person is paid a sum for each item he or she makes or sells, with a strict proportionality between results and rewards.

Straight Piecework   Piecework generally implies **straight piecework**, which entails a strict proportionality between results and rewards regardless of output. However, some piecework plans allow for sharing productivity gains between employer and worker, such that the worker receives extra income for some above-normal production.[17] So if Tom starts bringing in 30 leads per hour instead of the "standard" 20, his piece rate for leads above 25 might bump to $.45 each.

standard hour plan

A plan by which a worker is paid a basic hourly rate but is paid an extra percentage of his or her rate for production exceeding the standard per hour or per day. Similar to piecework payment but based on a percent premium.

Standard Hour Plans   The **standard hour plan** is like the piece rate plan, with one difference. Instead of getting a rate per piece, the worker gets a premium equal to the percent by which his or her performance exceeds the standard. So if Tom's standard is 160 leads per day (and thus $64 per day), and he brings in 200 leads, he'd get an extra 25% (40/160), or $80 total for the day. Some firms find that expressing the incentive in percentages reduces the workers' tendency to link their production standard to pay (thus making the standard easier to change). It also eliminates the need to recompute piece rates whenever hourly wage rates are changed.

Pros and Cons   Piecework plans have pros and cons. They are understandable, appear equitable in principle, and can be powerful incentives, since rewards are proportionate to performance. However, workers on piecework may resist attempts to revise production standards, even if the change is justified. Indeed, these plans may promote rigidity: Employees concentrate on output and are less willing to concern themselves with meeting quality standards or switching from job to job (since doing so could reduce their productivity).[18] Attempts to introduce new technology or processes may trigger resistance, for much the same reason. Options in such an event include team-based incentives and gainsharing programs, both discussed below.

In some industries, the term *piecework* has a poor reputation, (and not just because managers have a history of changing the production standards). For example, some garment manufacturers had operators assemble items (like shirts) in their homes, and paid them for each piece they completed. Unfortunately, the hourly pay for this work didn't always fulfill the Wage and Hour Act's minimum wage requirements. More recently, an electronics firm had a woman who assembled cables for the firm during the day take home parts to assemble at night. Working with her sister, the two assembled cables in their downtown San Jose, California, apartment, allegedly averaging only $2 to $2.50 an hour for the piecework.[19]

While still widely used, even industries that traditionally stressed piecework incentive plans, such as textiles, are moving to other plans. "People did work harder under these programs, but they posed problems. For one thing, they created quality problems," says one expert.[20] More firms are therefore moving to the team incentive plans, gainsharing plans, and organizationwide incentive pay programs we'll discuss later in this chapter.

Merit Pay as an Incentive

merit pay (merit raise)

Any salary increase awarded to an employee based on his or her individual performance.

Merit pay or a **merit raise** is any salary increase the firm awards to an individual employee based on his or her individual performance. It is different from a bonus in that it usually becomes part of the employee's base salary, whereas a bonus is a one-time payment. Although the term *merit pay* can apply to the incentive raises given to any employee—exempt or nonexempt, office or factory, management or nonmanagement—the term is more often used for white-collar employees and particularly professional, office, and clerical employees.

Merit pay is the subject of much debate. Advocates argue that only performance-based rewards (like merit pay) can motivate improved performance. They contend that awarding pay raises across the board (without regard to individual merit) may actually detract from performance, by showing employees they'll be rewarded regardless of how they perform.

Detractors present good reasons why merit pay can backfire. One problem is that almost every employee thinks he or she is an above-average performer, so getting a below-average merit increase can be demoralizing. Another is the dubious nature of many firms' appraisal processes. Since many appraisals are unfair, so too will be the merit pay you base them on.[21] Similarly, supervisors often give most employees about the same raise, either because of a reluctance to alienate some employees or because of a desire to give everyone a raise that will at least help them stay even with the cost of living.

Research results tend to be mixed. One study focused on the relationship between performance ratings and merit pay raises for 218 workers in a nuclear waste facility. The researchers found a "very modest relationship between merit pay increase and performance rating."[22] Researchers have recently focused their efforts on the effects of tying merit pay increases to teachers' or faculty members' research and/or teaching performance. Results here, too, tend to be mixed. They suggest that merit pay is more clearly linked with research productivity than with teaching effectiveness.[23]

The solution is not to throw out merit raises, but to design them so they are effective. Among other things, this means establishing effective appraisal procedures, and ensuring that managers in fact tie merit pay awards to performance.

Merit Pay Options

Two more recent adaptations of merit pay plans are popular. One awards merit raises in a lump sum once a year and does *not* make the raises part of the employee's salary (making them, in effect, short-term bonuses for lower-level workers). Traditional merit increases are cumulative, but most *lump-sum merit raises* are not. This produces two potential benefits. First, the rise in payroll expenses can be significantly slowed. (Traditionally, someone with a salary of $30,000 per year might get a 5% merit increase. This moves the employee to a new base salary of $31,500. If the employee gets another 5% increase next year, then the new merit increase of 5% is tacked on not just to the $30,000 base salary, but to the extra $1,500 the employee received last year.) Lump-sum merit increases can also be more dramatic motivators than traditional merit pay raises. For example, a 5% lump-sum merit payment to our $30,000 employee is $1,500 cash, as opposed to a traditional weekly merit payout of $29 for 52 weeks.

The other adaptation ties merit awards to both individual and organizational performance. Table 12-1 presents a sample matrix for doing so. In this example, you might measure the company's performance by, say, rate on return, or sales divided by payroll costs. Company performance and the employee's performance (using his or her performance appraisal) receive equal weight in computing the merit pay. Here an outstanding performer would receive 70% of his or her maximum lump-sum award even if the organization's performance were marginal. However, employees with marginal or unacceptable performance would get no lump-sum awards even in years in which the firm's performance was outstanding. The bonus plan at Discovery Communications is an example. Executive assistants can receive bonuses of up to 10% of their salaries. The boss's evaluation of

TABLE 12-1 Lump-Sum Award Determination Matrix (an Example)

The Employee's Performance Rating (Weight = 0.50)	The Company's Performance (Weight = 0.50)				
	Outstanding	Excellent	Good	Marginal	Unacceptable
Outstanding	1.00	0.90	0.80	0.70	0.00
Excellent	0.90	0.80	0.70	0.60	0.00
Good	0.80	0.70	0.60	0.50	0.00
Marginal	—	—	—	—	—
Unacceptable	—	—	—	—	—

To determine the dollar value of each employee's incentive award: (1) multiply the employee's annual, straight-time wage or salary as of June 30 times his or her maximum incentive award and (2) multiply the resultant product by the appropriate percentage figure from this table. For example, if an employee had an annual salary of $20,000 on June 30 and a maximum incentive award of 7% and if her performance and the organization's performance were both "excellent," the employee's award would be $1,120: ($20,000 × 0.07 × 0.80 = $1,120).

the assistant's individual performance accounts for 80% of the potential bonus; 10% is based on how the division does, and 10% on how the company as a whole does.[24]

Incentives for Professional Employees

Professional employees are those whose work involves the application of learned knowledge to the solution of the employer's problems. They include lawyers, doctors, economists, and engineers.

Making incentive pay decisions for professional employees can be challenging. For one thing, firms usually pay professionals well anyway. For another, they're already driven—by the desire to produce high-caliber work and receive recognition from colleagues. In some cases, (as experts like Deci would argue) offering financial rewards to people like these may actually diminish their intrinsic motivation—not add to it.

However, it would be unrealistic to assume that people like the systems analysts and programmers at Microsoft and Google work only for professional gratification. A survey of 300 IT departments found that 77% were paying bonuses and incentives, including stock options and profit sharing, to IT professionals.[25] Texas Instruments began offering stock option grants to about a third of its engineers when it discovered it was losing about 15% of them to the competition.[26] Several firms, including IBM and Motorola, award bonuses to employees whose work wins patents for the firms.[27]

Recognition-Based Awards

Recognition is one of several types of non-financial incentives. The term *recognition program* usually refers to formal programs, such as employee-of-the-month programs. *Social recognition program* refers to more informal manager-employee exchanges such as praise, approval, or expressions of appreciation for a job well-done. *Performance feedback* is similar to social recognition, but means "providing quantitative or qualitative information on task performance for the purpose of changing or maintaining performance and specific ways."[28]

Recognition (ranging from "good job" to more material awards) has a positive impact on performance, either alone or in conjunction with financial rewards. For example, in one study, combining financial rewards with non-financial ones (like recognition), produced a 30% performance improvement in service firms, almost twice the effect of using each

Many firms, like Spartech Corporation, hold annual awards and recognitions meetings to recognize and thank selected employees for their contributions to the firm.

reward alone.[29] The Minnesota Department of Natural Resources conducted one study of recognition. Respondents said they "highly valued" day-to-day recognition from supervisors, peers, and team members. More than two-thirds said it was important to believe that others appreciated their work.[30]

Employers are therefore increasingly using performance-based recognition programs today.[31] Texas Instruments, for instance, offers bonuses as well as non-financial recognition, including personalized plaques, parties, movie tickets, golf lessons, and team shirts and jackets. In one year over 80,000 Texas Instrument employees were so rewarded.[32] Managers at American Skandia, which provides insurance and financial planning products and services, regularly evaluate their customer service reps based on specific standards. Those who exceed those standards receive a plaque, a $500 check, their photo and story on the firm's internal Web site, and a dinner for them and their teams.[33]

Combining Financial and Non-Financial Incentives   Most employers use both financial and non-financial incentives. In a survey of 235 managers by Northwestern University researchers, the most used rewards to motivate employees were (from most used to least used) were:[34]

- Employee recognition
- Gift certificates
- Special events
- Cash rewards
- Merchandise incentives
- E-mail/print communications
- Training programs
- Work/life benefits
- Variable pay
- Group travel
- Individual travel
- Sweepstakes

Supporting Incentives and Recognition Programs with Technology

If there's a downside to incentives and recognition programs, it's that they can both be expensive to administer. For example, with over 1,000 sales representatives, First Tennessee Bank was having problems managing its sales incentive programs.[35] Bank employees had to laboriously enter by hand sales information for each of the 1,000 sales reps onto Excel spreadsheets. The process, said one officer, "was more labor-intensive than it needed to be" and "had begun to spiral out of control."

Incentives are also becoming more complicated. More employees now receive incentives. Furthermore, the range of behaviors for which employees can earn incentives extends from better cost to cutting cost to answering more calls per hour.[36] Tracking performance of dozens or hundreds of measures like these and then computing individual employees' incentives is obviously very time-consuming.

The solution is that firms such as Incentives Systems Inc., provide sophisticated automated support for calculating, monitoring, and awarding and maintaining such pay plans. Compensation experts refer to this software as enterprise incentive management (EIM). As one says, "EIM software automates the planning, calculation, modeling and management of incentive compensation plans, enabling companies to align their employees with corporate strategy and goals."[37]

Administering recognition programs is similarly challenging. If a company has an employee anniversary recognition program, for instance, someone (probably in human resources) needs to compile a prizes catalog, distribute it, and keep track of who gets what. Many employers therefore outsource the logistics of their recognition programs to online incentive firms. Management consultant Hewitt Associates uses www.bravanta.com to help its managers recognize exceptional employee service with special awards. The system not only does the heavy lifting associated with administering the awards; it also makes recognizing employees and letting them choose the awards easier: "the gifts are good and easy to order from the desktop . . . and we value the ability to update gift choices easily, so the program doesn't become stagnant," says the Hewitt program administrator.[38] Texas Instruments has an online "TI Mall" that helps its 102 divisional managers provide merchandise and individual travel awards to employees who do a good job.[39] Internet recognition sites include bravanta.com, premierchoiceaward.com, incentivecity.com, netcentives.com, salesdriver.com, and kudoz.com.

INCENTIVES FOR SALESPEOPLE

> ❷ Discuss the pros and cons of incentives for salespeople.

Sales compensation plans typically rely heavily on incentives in the form of sales commissions. However, some salespeople get straight salaries, and most receive a combination of salary and commissions.

Salary Plan

Some firms pay salespeople fixed salaries (perhaps with occasional incentives in the form of bonuses, sales contest prizes, and the like).[40] Straight salaries particularly make sense when the main task involves prospecting (finding new clients), or when it mostly involves account servicing, (such as executing product training programs for a customer's salesforce or participating in trade shows). This is why technology-based industries like aerospace and transportation equipment tend to emphasize sales salary plans.

The straight salary approach has pros and cons. Straight salary makes it easier to switch territories or to reassign salespeople, and it can foster sales staff loyalty. Commissions tend to shift the salesperson's emphasis to making the sale rather than to prospecting and cultivating long-term customers. The main disadvantage, of course, is that pay isn't proportionate to results.[41] This can demotivate potentially high-performing salespeople.

Commission Plan

Straight commission plans pay salespeople for results, and only for results. Under these plans salespeople have the greatest incentive. Commission plans tend to attract high-performing salespeople who see that effort clearly produces rewards. Sales costs are proportionate to sales rather than fixed, and the company's fixed sales costs are thus lower. It's a plan that's easy to understand and compute.

However, problems abound. Salespeople tend to focus on making the sale and on high-volume items, and may neglect nonselling duties like servicing small accounts, cultivating dedicated customers, and pushing hard-to-sell items. Wide variations in pay may occur; this can make some feel the plan is inequitable. Misjudging sales potential can lead to excessively high commissions, and to a cycle in which sales commission rates need to be cut. In addition, salespersons' pay may be excessive in boom times and low in recessions. Furthermore, sales performance—like any performance—reflects not just motivation, but ability too. If the person hasn't the sales skills, commissions won't produce sales.

Another potential drawback of commission-only plans is that working without a financial safety net can be unsettling. As one sales representative in a study put it,

> If I go on vacation, I lose money. If I'm sick, I lose money. If I'm not willing to drop everything on a moment's notice to close with a customer, I lose money. I can't see how anyone could stay in this job for long. It's like a trapeze act and I'm working without a net.[42]

In this study, paying salespersons 100% based on commissions was the situation with by far the highest turnover. Turnover was much lower when salespersons received a combination of a base pay plus commissions. However, the results did depend a lot on the salesperson's skills and personality. The findings suggested that 100% commissions can drive higher sales by focusing strong-willed salespeople on maximizing sales. However, it also undermines the desire of less-strong-willed salespeople to stay. (Sometimes, of course, such outcomes are exactly what the employer wants).

In another study, data were collected from 214 business-to-business salespeople. It concluded that certain salespeople respond positively to fixed salary plans while others respond positively to incentives.[43]

Combination Plan

Most companies pay salespeople a combination of salary and commissions, usually with a sizable salary component. An incentive mix of about 70% base salary/30% incentive seems typical; this cushions the salesperson's downside risk (of earning nothing), while limiting the risk that the commissions could get out of hand from the firm's point of view.[44]

Combination plans have pros and cons. They give salespeople a floor to their earnings, let the company specify what services the salary component is for (such as servicing current accounts), and still provide an incentive for superior performance. However, the salary component isn't tied to performance, so the employer is obviously trading away some incentive value. Combination plans also tend to become complicated, and misunderstandings can result.

The latter might not be a problem with a simple salary-plus-commission plan, but most plans are not so simple. For example, in a "commission-plus-drawing-account" plan, a salesperson is paid on commissions but can draw on future earnings to get through low sales periods. Similarly, in the "commission-plus-bonus" plan, the firm pays its salespeople mostly based on commissions. However, they also get a small bonus for directed activities like selling slow-moving items.

An example can help illustrate the complexities of the typical combination plan. In one company, the following three-step formula is applied:

Step 1: For sales volume up to $18,000 a month. Base salary plus 7% of gross profits plus 0.5% of gross sales.

Step 2: For sales volume from $18,000 to $25,000 a month. Base salary plus 9% of gross profits plus 0.5% of gross sales.

Step 3: Over $25,000 a month. Base salary plus 10% of gross profits plus 0.5% of gross sales.

In all cases, base salary is paid every two weeks, while the earned percentage of gross profits and gross sales is paid monthly.[45]

Sales Awards   The salesforce also may get various special awards. Metiom, Inc., a New York–based e-commerce infrastructure firm, calls its sales award program "inner circle." After meeting specific sales quotas, the firm's 30 top salespeople and their significant others got a trip to Paradise Island in the Bahamas. The program not only motivated the company's salesforce, but had the added benefit of encouraging family support for the salesperson's success.[46]

As noted earlier, employers increasingly use the Web to support their incentive programs. For example, SalesDriver, (Maynard, Massachusetts), runs Web-based sales-performance-based incentive programs. Firms like these specialize in setting up online sales incentive programs. SalesDriver can help a company launch a campaign template in a day or less. Using the template, the sales manager can select from a catalog of 1,500 reward items, and award these to sales and marketing reps for meeting quotas for things like lead generation and total sales.[47]

Setting Sales Quotas

There are several things to consider when choosing sales quotas.

Commission Rate/Sales Quota   In setting sales quotas and commission rates, the employer wants to motivate sales activity but avoid having commissions become excessive. Unfortunately, there is a tendency to set commission rates informally, without considering how much each sale must contribute to covering expenses. Each salesperson's effort should contribute to covering his or her share of fixed costs and variable costs, and to the company's profit. Fixed costs include the person's salary and benefits, as well as his or her share of office space, utilities, and salaries for support staff and management. Variable costs include telephone charges and travel expenses. In computing the sales commission rates, ensure that what's left over from the sale (after commissions) contributes to profits, too.[48]

Lock In or Not?   Experts traditionally suggested "locking in" sales quotas and incentive plans, on the assumption that frequent changes undermine motivation and morale. But in today's fast-changing business scene, such inflexibility is usually not advisable. One expert says, "Now that product life cycles are often in the six-month to even six-week range, the traditional approaches to most sales plans cannot accommodate the pace. The sales organization and its emphasis must become more flexible than it has been." Firms therefore tend to review their sales compensation plans and quotas more often.[49]

A Checklist To better judge the commission plan's effectiveness, questions to ask include:

- Have we communicated quotas to the salesforce within one month of the start of the period?
- Does the salesforce know exactly how its quotas are set?
- Do you combine bottom-up information (like account forecasts) with top-down requirements (like the company business plan)?
- Do 60 to 70% of the salesforce generally hit their quota?
- Do high performers hit their targets consistently?
- Do low performers show improvement over time?
- Are quotas stable through the performance period? Are returns and debookings reasonably low?
- Has your firm generally avoided compensation-related lawsuits?[50]
- Is 10% of the salesforce achieving higher performance than previously?
- And, is 5 to 10% of the salesforce achieving below quota performance and receiving coaching?[51]

Auto Dealer Example Commission rates vary by industry, but a look at how auto dealers set their salespersons' commission rates provides some insights into how to set rates to achieve specific aims. Compensation for car salespeople ranges from a high of 100% commission to a small base salary with commission accounting for most of total compensation. Traditionally, commission is based on the net profit on the car when it's delivered to the buyer. This promotes precisely the sorts of behaviors the car dealer wants to encourage. For example, it encourages the salesperson to hold firm on the retail price, and to push "after-sale products" like floor mats, side moldings, undercoating, and car alarms. Car dealers also use short-term incentives. For helping sell slow-moving vehicles, the salesperson may be offered a "spiff"—a car dealer term for an extra incentive bonus over commission.

However, while commission plans still predominate in auto dealerships, they are not as popular as they were, with many dealerships substituting salary plus bonus plans for commissions. The transition to salary plus bonus reflects the growing emphasis on "one price no hassle" pricing, and the desire on the part of more dealers to make the purchase process less tense. For example, one sales manager gives his sales staff a choice of salary and bonus or commission (most start with the former, but then move to commission). In another dealership, each salesperson's compensation is based on the number sold, regardless of price (to avoid efforts to "sell customers up"). For example, salespeople receive $250 per vehicle for the first 10 sold each month (new or used), and average $63,000 annually. Others are substituting salary plus bonus plans. One dealership reviews salaries monthly and pays a bonus starting with the eighth sale. Another bases salary on a rolling six-month average of vehicles sold. This dealership adjusts salaries every three months, and with bonuses, salespeople make $30,000 to $85,000 a year.[52]

Strategic Sales Incentives

Employers increasingly link sales commissions to non-sales related strategic measures. Procter & Gamble rewards its salespeople (its "customer consultants") commissions based on their success in helping customers lower their inventories. At Siebel systems, about 40% of each salesperson's incentive is based on factors like customers' reported satisfaction with service. The firm's vice president of technical services says, "I think our people are better sales reps because of it. There's a lot of value to using this metric as opposed to using only traditional quotas."[53]

A recent survey of sales effectiveness by consultants Watson Wyatt reveals several current trends in sales compensation. It found that, among other things, salespeople at high-performing companies:

- Receive 40% more of their total compensation in the form of sales-related variable pay (38% of total cash compensation, compared with 27% for salespeople at low-performing companies), and,
- Are twice as likely to receive stock, stock options, or other equity pay than their counterparts at low-performing companies (36% versus 18%).

The survey results also provide a reminder that salesforce success reflects more than just pay practices. For example, salespeople at high-performing companies:

- Spend 264 more hours per year on high-value sales activities (e.g., prospecting, making sales presentations, and closing) than salespeople at low-performing companies,
- Spend 40% more time each year with their best potential customers—qualified leads and prospects they know—than salespeople at low-performing companies,
- Compared with salespeople at low-performing companies, spend nearly 25% less time on administration, allowing them to allocate more time to core sales activities, such as prospecting leads and closing sales, and,
- Had a much clearer understanding of their companies' strategies and goals.[54]

TEAM/GROUP INCENTIVE PLANS

How to Design Team Incentives

team or group incentive plan
A plan in which a production standard is set for a specific work group, and its members are paid incentives if the group exceeds the production standard.

Firms increasingly rely on teams to manage their work. They therefore need incentive plans that encourage teamwork and focus team members' attention on performance. Many world-class facilities, such as those run by some major automakers, rely almost exclusively on team and facility-wide incentives. **Team (or group) incentive plans** pay incentives to the team based on the team's performance.

The main question here is how to reward the team's performance. One approach is to tie rewards to some overall standard of group performance, such as "total labor hours per car." Doing so avoids the need for a precisely engineered piecework standard (in terms of wheels installed per hour, for instance).[55] One company established such an overall standard for its teams. If the firm reached 100% of its goal, the employees would share in about 5% of the improvement (in labor costs saved). The firm divided the 5% pool by the number of employees to compute the value of a "share." If the firm achieved less than 100% of its goal, the bonus pool was lower. The results of this plan—in terms of changing employee attitudes and focusing teams on strategic goals—were reportedly "extraordinary." (Employers also use such team incentives to improve top management team performance.)[56]

Engineered Standards   Some set an engineered production standard based on the output of the group (again, such as in terms of wheels installed per hour, for instance). This approach can use the piece rate or standard hour plan, but the latter is more prevalent. All members then typically receive the same share of the team's incentive pay. Occasionally, the employer may want to pay all team members according to some other formula. For instance, instead of paying everyone on the team based on how well the team as a whole does, pay everyone based on how well the *best* team member does. This counterintuitive sounding option may make sense when an employer has reason to believe the new team incentive plan might demotivate high-performing team members (who may not covet being paid based on the team average). Thus a team incentive plan at Levi's reportedly failed when high-performing workers suddenly found their rewards reduced to a lower team average.

Team incentives can foster a sense of cooperation and unanimity

Pros and Cons of Team Incentives

Team incentives often make sense. Project teams publish books, assembly teams assemble cars, and new-product teams launch new products. Performance here reflects not just individual but team effort. Team-based incentive plans reinforce team planning and problem solving, and help ensure collaboration. In Asia in general and Japan in particular the tendency is to reward the group—to reduce jealousy, to make group members indebted to one another, and to encourage a sense of cooperation. Team incentives also facilitate training, since each member has an interest in getting new members trained as fast as possible.

The main disadvantage is that a worker's pay may not be proportionate to his or her personal efforts. As at Levi's this may demotivate top workers. Workers who share in the team's pay but don't put their hearts into the effort (what economists call "free riders") are a related problem. Solutions include having team members commit in writing to putting the goals of the team before their own, and basing part of each worker's pay on individual (not just team) performance.[57]

The "When You're on Your Own" feature below illustrates some incentives the supervisor can easily use.

ORGANIZATIONWIDE INCENTIVE PLANS

❸ Name and define the most popular organizationwide variable pay plans.

organizationwide incentive plans
Incentive plans in which all or most employees can participate.

Organizationwide incentive plans are plans in which all or most employees can participate, and which generally tie the reward to some measure of companywide performance. Also called variable pay plans, they include profit sharing, employee stock ownership (ESOP), and Scanlon/gainsharing plans.

Profit-Sharing Plans

profit-sharing plan
A plan whereby employees share in the company's profits.

Profit-sharing plans are plans in which all or most employees receive a share of the firm's annual profits. Research on such plans' effectiveness is sketchy. One study concludes that there is ample evidence that profit-sharing plans boost productivity and morale, but that their effect on profits is insignificant, once you factor in the costs of the plans' payouts.[58]

When You're on Your OWN

HR for Line Managers and Entrepreneurs

Incentives Supervisors Can Use

The individual line manager probably should not rely just on the employer's incentive plans for motivating subordinates. Those plans may not be very complete, and there are simply too many opportunities to motivate employees every day to let those opportunities pass. There are three guides to follow.

First, the best option for motivating employees is also the simplest—make sure the employee has a doable *goal* and that he or she agrees with that. It makes little sense to try to motivate employees in other ways (such as with financial incentives) if they don't know their goals or don't agree with them. Psychologist Edwin Locke and his colleagues have consistently found that specific, challenging goals lead to higher task performance than specific, unchallenging goals, or vague goals or no goals. You should set SMART goals—make them Specific, Measurable, Attainable, Relevant, and Timely.

Second, *recognizing an employee's contribution* is a simple and powerful motivation tool. Studies show that recognition has a positive impact on performance, either alone or in combination with financial rewards. For example, in one study (noted earlier), combining financial rewards with recognition produced a 30% performance improvement in service firms, almost twice the effect of using each reward alone. When the Minnesota Department of Natural Resources conducted a study of recognition, more than two-thirds of respondents said it was important to believe that others appreciated their work.

Third, remember, as noted earlier, that there are numerous *positive reinforcement rewards* you can use on a day-to-day basis, independent of your company's incentive plans. A short list would include:[59]

- Challenging work assignments
- Freedom to choose own work activity
- Having fun built into work
- More of preferred task
- Role as boss's stand-in when he or she is away
- Role in presentations to top management
- Job rotation
- Encouragement of learning and continuous improvement
- Being provided with ample encouragement
- Being allowed to set own goals
- Compliments
- Expression of appreciation in front of others
- Note of thanks
- Employee-of-the-month award
- Special commendation
- Bigger desk
- Bigger office or cubicle

There are several types of profit-sharing plans. In *cash plans* the firm simply distributes a percentage of profits (usually 15 to 20%) as profit shares to employees at regular intervals. The *Lincoln incentive system*, first instituted at the Lincoln Electric Company of Ohio, is more complex. In one version, employees work on a guaranteed piecework basis, and the firm distributes total annual profits (less taxes, 6% dividends to stockholders, and a reserve) each year among employees based on their merit rating. The Lincoln plan also includes a suggestion system that pays individual workers rewards for savings resulting from their suggestions. The plan has been quite successful.

There are also *deferred profit-sharing plans*: The firm places a predetermined portion of profits in each employee's account under a trustee's supervision. There is a tax advantage here, since employees' income taxes on the distributions are deferred, often until the employee retires, when the money is assumedly taxed at a lower rate.

Home Depot instituted a bonus program for all its store workers. Starting in 2003, it started paying store associates a bonus if their stores meet certain financial goals. In one recent year, Home Depot distributed a total of $90 million under that companywide incentive plan.[60]

Employee Stock Ownership Plan (ESOP)

employee stock ownership plan (ESOP)

A corporation contributes shares of its own stock to a trust in which additional contributions are made annually. The trust distributes the stock to employees on retirement or separation from service.

Employee stock ownership plans are companywide plans in which a corporation contributes shares of its own stock—or cash to be used to purchase such stock—to a trust established to purchase shares of the firm's stock for employees. The firm generally makes these contributions annually in proportion to total employee compensation, with a limit of 15% of compensation. The trust holds the stock in individual employee accounts, and distributes it to employees upon retirement (or other separation from service), assuming the person has worked long enough to earn ownership of the stock. (*Stock options*, as discussed later in this chapter, go directly to the employees individually to use as they see fit, rather than into a retirement trust.)

ESOPs have several advantages. The company gets a tax deduction equal to the fair market value of the shares that are transferred to the trustee, and can also claim an income tax deduction for dividends paid on ESOP-owned stock. Employees, as noted, aren't taxed until they receive a distribution from the trust, usually at retirement when their tax rate is lower. The Employee Retirement Income Security Act (ERISA) allows a firm to borrow against employee stock held in trust and then repay the loan in pretax rather than after-tax dollars, another tax incentive for using such plans.[61]

ESOPs can also help the shareholders of closely held corporations (in which, for instance, a family owns virtually all the shares) to diversify their assets, by placing some of their own shares of the company's stock into the ESOP trust and purchasing other marketable securities for themselves in their place.[62]

Research suggests that ESOPs do encourage employees to develop a sense of ownership in and commitment to the firm. They do so in part because the ESOPs provide increased financial incentives, create a sense of ownership, and help build teamwork. Those responsible for the funds—usually, the firm's top executives—must be fastidious in executing their fiduciary responsibilities for the fund.[63]

Thermacore Example The annual employee bonus at Thermacore, Inc., is one example. All employees of Thermacore and its parent corporation, DTX, are eligible. The unique aspect of the program is that all employees receive the same amount of bonus regardless of total compensation, seniority, or position in the company.

The bonus pool is based on pretax income minus a minimum, threshold guarantee to the stockholders. The guarantee to stockholders is typically 15% of the firm's equity at the beginning of the year. The amount of income to place in the bonus pool is determined by multiplying (1) company income (less the 15%-of-equity guarantee) by (2) an employee bonus pool percentage rate established by the board of directors and senior management. Regular employees then receive a full share, and part-time employees receive a share based on the percentage of time worked. In one year, the bonus pool rate was 12%, and the full bonus share was more than $1,300 per employee.

Thermacore also has an employee stock ownership plan. Each year, the stockholders and the board of directors approve a dollar value of stock to offer to employees. For example, the board may decide to make available $100,000 of company stock. No one employee may subscribe for more than $10,000 worth of stock. Thermacore is a private company, so the stock trades only within the company. The firm sells shares to the employees at a discount. The company has the right of first refusal should the employee wish to leave the company or sell stock. Employees can pay for the stock in cash or by payroll deduction.[64]

Scanlon and Other Gainsharing Plans

Few would argue with the fact that the most powerful way of ensuring employee commitment is to synchronize the company's goals with those of its employees—to ensure that the two sets of goals overlap, and that by pursuing his or her goals, the worker pursues the employer's

Scanlon plan

An incentive plan developed in 1937 by Joseph Scanlon and designed to encourage cooperation, involvement, and sharing of benefits.

goals as well. Experts have proposed many techniques for attaining this idyllic state. However few are used as widely or successfully as the **Scanlon plan**, an incentive plan developed in 1937 by Joseph Scanlon, a United Steel Workers Union official.[65] It is still popular today.

The Scanlon plan is remarkably progressive, considering that it is now about 70 years old. Scanlon plans have five basic features.[66] The first is Scanlon's *philosophy of cooperation*. This philosophy assumes that managers and workers must rid themselves of the "us" and "them" attitudes that normally inhibit employees from developing a sense of ownership in the company.

A second feature is what its practitioners call *identity*. This means that to focus employee involvement, the company must clearly articulate its mission or purpose, and employees must understand how the business operates in terms of customers, prices, and costs. *Competence* is a third basic feature. The program, say three experts, "explicitly recognizes that a Scanlon plan demands a high level of competence from employees at all levels."[67] This suggests careful selection and training.

The fourth feature of the plan is the *involvement system*. Employees present improvement suggestions to the appropriate departmental-level committees, which transmit the valuable ones to the executive-level committee. The latter then decides whether to implement the suggestion.

The fifth element of the plan is the *sharing of benefits formula*. If a suggestion is implemented and successful, all employees usually share in 75% of the savings. For example, assume that the normal monthly ratio of payroll costs to sales is 50%. (Thus, if sales are $600,000, payroll costs should be $300,000.) Assume the firm implements suggestions that result in payroll costs of $250,000 in a month when sales were $550,000 and payroll costs should have been $275,000 (50% of sales). The savings attributable to these suggestions is $25,000 ($275,000 minus $250,000). Workers would typically share in 75% of this ($18,750), while $6,250 would go to the firm. In practice, the firm sets aside a portion, usually one-quarter of the $18,750, for the months in which payroll costs exceed the standard.

Gainsharing Plans

gainsharing plan

An incentive plan that engages employees in a common effort to achieve productivity objectives and share the gains.

The Scanlon plan is one early version of what we call today a **gainsharing plan**. Gainsharing is an incentive plan that engages many or all employees in a common effort to achieve a company's productivity objectives, with any resulting cost-savings gains shared among employees and the company.[68] In addition to the Scanlon plan, other popular gainsharing plans include the Rucker and Improshare plans.

The basic difference among these plans is the formula employers use to determine employee bonuses. The Scanlon formula divides payroll expenses by total sales (or, sometimes, by total sales plus increases in inventory). The Rucker plan uses a value-added formula. Here the employer divides the value added for the period (basically, net sales minus the cost of materials, supplies, and services such as utilities) by total payroll expenses. With the Improshare plan, the bonus basically depends on the difference between how many labor hours the company should have used for the period, compared with how many it actually used. Most firms use custom-designed versions of these plans.

Implementing a Gainsharing Plan   There are eight basic steps in implementing a gainsharing plan:[69]

1. Establish general plan objectives, such as boosting productivity or lowering labor costs.
2. Choose specific performance measures. For example, use productivity measures such as labor hours per unit produced, or financial measures like return on assets.
3. Decide on a funding formula. What portion of gains will employees receive? In the Scanlon example above, employees receive about 75% of the gains.

4. Decide on a method for dividing and distributing the employees' share of the gains. Standard methods include equal percentage of pay or equal shares; however, some plans modify awards based on individual performance.
5. Choose the form of payment. This is usually cash, but occasionally is common stock.
6. Decide how often to pay bonuses. Firms tend to compute financial performance measures for this purpose annually, and labor productivity measures quarterly or monthly.
7. Develop the involvement system. The most commonly used elements include steering committees, update meetings, suggestion systems, coordinators, problem-solving teams, department committees, training programs, newsletters, inside auditors, and outside auditors. (Note that the Scanlon and Rucker include employee involvement elements; Improshare does not.)
8. Implement the plan.

As an example, assume a supplier wants to boost quality. Doing so would translate into fewer customer returns, less scrap and rework, and therefore higher profits. Historically, $10 million in output results in $200,000 (2%) scrap, returns, and rework. The company tells its employees that if next month's production results in only 1% scrap, returns, and rework, the 1% saved would be a gain, to be split 50/50 with the workforce, less a small amount for reserve for months in which scrap exceeds 2%. The firm announces awards monthly but allocates them quarterly (to even out up and down months). Recent results—from various efforts in hospitals, as well as manufacturing plants—suggest quite clearly that gainsharing plans can improve productivity and patient care, and reduce grievances, but also entail often considerable implementation costs.[70]

At-Risk Variable Pay Plans

at-risk variable pay plans

Plans that put some portion of the employee's weekly pay at risk, subject to the firm's meeting its financial goals.

At-risk variable pay plans (sometimes called risk-sharing plans) are plans that put some portion of the employee's weekly, monthly, or yearly pay at risk. Then, if employees meet or exceed their goals, they earn back not only the portion of their pay that was at risk, but also an incentive. If they fail to meet their goals, they forego some of the pay they would normally have earned. One DuPont division set employee's at-risk pay at 6%. Employees could then match or exceed their usual full pay if their department reached certain predetermined financial goals.

INCENTIVES FOR MANAGERS AND EXECUTIVES

> ❹ Describe the main incentives for managers and executives.

Managers play a crucial role in divisional and companywide profitability, and most firms therefore put considerable thought into how to reward them. Most managers get short-term and long-term incentives in addition to salary.[71] For firms offering short-term incentive plans, virtually all—96%—provide those incentives in cash. For those offering long-term incentives, about 48% offer them as stock options. The latter are intended to motivate and reward management for long-term corporate growth, prosperity, and shareholder value. For mature companies, executives' base salary, short-term incentives, long-term incentives, and benefits might be 60%, 15%, 15%, and 10%, respectively. For growth companies, the corresponding figures might be 40%, 45%, 25%, and 10%.[72] About 69% of companies in one survey had short-term incentives, although nearly a third of those said they didn't consider them effective in boosting employee performance.[73] We'll look at short- and long-term incentives.

Short-Term Incentives: The Annual Bonus

annual bonus

Plans that are designed to motivate short-term performance of managers and are tied to company profitability.

As noted, most firms have **annual bonus** plans aimed at motivating managers' and executives' short-term performance. Short-term bonuses can easily result in plus or minus

Even in retail stores, it would not be unusual to compensate the store managers partly based on the stores short term sales and profit performance

adjustments of 25% or more to total pay. There are three basic issues to consider when awarding short-term incentives: eligibility, fund size, and individual awards.

Eligibility   Most firms include both top- and lower-level managers, and mainly decide who's eligible in several ways. Most base eligibility on a combination of factors, including job level/title, base salary, and discretionary considerations (such as key jobs having a measurable impact on profits). Some simply base eligibility on job level or job title. A few base eligibility on salary level alone.[74]

The percentage size of the bonus is usually greater for top-level executives. Thus, an executive earning $150,000 in salary may be able to earn another 80% of his or her salary as a bonus, while a manager in the same firm earning $80,000 can earn only another 30%. Similarly, a supervisor might be able to earn up to 15% of his or her base salary in bonuses. A typical breakdown might be executives 45% of base salary, managers 25%, and supervisory personnel 12%.

Fund Size   The employer must also decide the total amount of bonus money to make available—fund size. Some use a *nondeductible formula*. They use a straight percentage (usually of the company's net income) to create the short-term incentive fund. Others use a *deductible formula*, on the assumption that the fund should start to accumulate only after the firm has met a specified level of earnings. Some firms don't use a formula at all, but make that decision on a totally discretionary basis.[75]

There are no hard-and-fast rules about the proportion of profits to pay out. One alternative is to reserve a minimal amount of the profits, say, 10%, for safeguarding stockholders' investments, and then to establish a fund for bonuses equal to, say, 20% of the corporate operating profit before taxes in excess of this safeguard amount. So here, if the operating profits were $200,000, (after putting away 10% to safeguard stockholders) then the management bonus fund might be 20% of $200,000 or $40,000. Other illustrative formulas might include:

1. Twelve percent of net earnings after deducting 6% of net capital.
2. Ten percent of the amount by which net income exceeds 5% of stockholders' equity.

Individual Awards   The third task is deciding the actual individual awards. Typically, a target bonus (as well as maximum bonus, perhaps double the target bonus) is set for each eligible position. The actual award then reflects the person's performance. The firm computes performance ratings for each manager, computes preliminary total bonus estimates, and compares the total amount of money required with the bonus fund available. If necessary, it then adjusts the individual bonus estimates. The basic rule should be: Outstanding managers should receive at least their target bonuses, and marginal ones should receive at best below-average awards. Give the money you save from the poor performers to the outstanding ones.

One question is whether managers will receive bonuses based on individual performance, corporate performance, or both. Firms usually tie top-level executive bonuses mostly to overall corporate results (or divisional results if the executive heads a major division). This makes sense because, to a large extent, the company's results are their own. But as one moves farther down the chain of command, corporate profits become a less accurate gauge of a manager's contribution. For, say, supervisors or the heads of functional departments, it often makes more sense to tie the bonus more closely to individual performance.

Many firms therefore end up tying short-term bonuses to both organizational and individual performance. Perhaps the simplest method is the split-award plan. This basically makes the manager eligible for two bonuses, one based on his or her individual effort and one based on the organization's overall performance. Thus, a manager might be eligible for an individual performance bonus of up to $10,000, but receive only $2,000 at the end of the year, based on his or her individual performance evaluation. But the person might also receive a second bonus of $3,000, based on the firm's profits for the year.

One drawback to this approach is that it may give marginal performers too much—for instance, someone could get a company-based bonus, even if his or her own performance is mediocre. One way to avoid this is to use the multiplier method. In other words, make the bonus a product of both individual and corporate performance. As Table 12-2 illustrates, multiply the target bonus by 1.00 or .80 or zero (if the firm's performance is excellent, and the person's performance is excellent, good, fair, or poor). Here a manager whose own performance is poor does not even receive the company-based bonus.

Long-Term Incentives

Employers use long-term incentives to inject a long-term perspective into their executives' decisions. With only short-term criteria to shoot for, a manager could conceivably boost profitability by reducing plant maintenance, for instance; this tactic might catch up with the company two or three years later. Long-term incentives are also "golden handcuffs"—they motivate executives to stay with the company, by letting them accumulate capital

TABLE 12-2   Multiplier Approach to Determining Annual Bonus

Individual Performance (based on appraisal. weight = 0.50)	Company Performance (Based on Sales Targets, Weight = 0.50)			
	Excellent	Good	Fair	Poor
Excellent	1.00	0.90	0.80	0.70
Good	0.80	0.70	0.60	0.50
Fair	0.00	0.00	0.00	0.00
Poor	0.00	0.00	0.00	0.00

Note: To determine the dollar amount of a manager's award, multiply the maximum possible (target) bonus by the appropriate factor in the matrix.

(usually options to buy company stock) that they can only cash in after a certain number of years. Popular long-term incentives include cash, stock, stock options, stock appreciation rights, and phantom stock. We'll look at each.

stock option

The right to purchase a stated number of shares of a company stock at today's price at some time in the future.

Stock Options   A **stock option** is the right to purchase a specific number of shares of company stock at a specific price during a specific period of time. The executive thus hopes to profit by exercising his or her option to buy the shares in the future but at today's price. The assumption is that the price of the stock will go up. Unfortunately, this depends partly on considerations outside the manager's control, such as general economic and market conditions. When the market for Internet stocks plummeted several years ago, many managers saw their options go "underwater." Many of these firms then had to scramble to sweeten their managers' incentive plans. One study compared performance of 229 "new economy" firms offering broad-based stock options to that of their non-stock-option counterparts. Those offering the stock options had higher shareholder returns than did those not offering the options.[76]

The chronic problem with stock options is that firms have traditionally used them to reward managers for even lackluster performance. There is therefore a trend toward using options tied more explicitly to specific goals. For example, with *indexed options*, the option's exercise price fluctuates with the performance of, say, a market index. Then, if the company's stock does no better than the index, the manager's options are worthless. With *premium priced options*, the exercise price is higher than the stock's closing price on the date of the grant, so the executive can't profit from the options until the stock has made significant gains.[77]

Stock Option Problems   Firms have begun deemphasizing stock option plans, for several reasons. Many blame enormous stock options in part for incentivizing questionable managerial decisions and for helping to trigger the numerous corporate scandals in the past few years. Recently, many companies have had to explain why they often "backdated" their stock option grants, thus enabling some executives to make exquisitely well-timed stock option acquisitions. Furthermore, until recently, most companies did not treat the stock options they awarded as an expense. (So, while the stock options were very much a part of each manager's compensation, the cost of those stock options didn't show up as an expense on the companies' financial statements.) Today, regulatory reform means more companies are expensing stock options. This reduces, to some degree, the attractiveness to the companies of awarding the options. As one compensation consultant puts it, "The fact that this is now 'costing' them something will mean that they will have to do more of the cost/benefit analysis to see which [compensation plan] design will give them the best return for their dollar."[78]

Finally, too many stock options can be too much of a good thing. "Executives with increasingly large stock option holdings have an added incentive to undertake riskier business strategies." Their options provide an incentive to go for spectacular results, but since they have not actually bought the stock yet, they don't risk their own money. The solution is to draft the option plan so it forces recipients to convert their options to stock more quickly.[79]

Broad-Based Stock Options   Plans for key employees (such as top executives) typically provide for a very significant upside in the value of stock the employee can receive. On the other hand, more companies today are implementing broad-based stock option plans in which the potential appreciation is relatively modest, but in which all or most employees can participate. The basic thinking here is that most employers rely on empowered, self-motivated employees, and that sharing ownership in the company with employees therefore makes motivational and practical sense.

The NEW Workforce — Long-Term Incentives for Overseas Executives

Developing long-term incentives for a firm's overseas employees presents some tricky problems, particularly with regard to taxation. For example, it's not unusual for an executive to be taxed $40,000 on $140,000 of stock option income if he or she is based in the United States. However, if that person receives the same stock option income while stationed overseas, he or she may be subject to both the $40,000 U.S. tax and a foreign income tax (depending on the country) of $90,000 or more. The employer therefore either has to forego the stock options' incentive value, or pay the extra taxes itself. In any case, firms cannot assume that they can simply export their executives' incentive programs. Instead, they must consider various factors, including tax treatment, the regulatory environment, and foreign exchange controls.

Recently, several companies including Time Warner, Microsoft, Aetna, and Charles Schwab announced they were discontinuing distributing stock options to most employees. Some of them, including Microsoft, are instead awarding stock. With companies now having to show the options as an expense when awarded, firms like Microsoft apparently feel awarding stock instead of stock options is a more direct and immediate way to link pay to performance.[80]

Other Plans   There are several other stock-related long-term incentive plans. *Stock appreciation rights* permit the recipient to exercise the stock option (by buying the stock) or to take any appreciation in the stock price in cash, stock, or some combination of these. A *performance achievement plan* awards shares of stock for the achievement of predetermined financial targets, such as profit or growth in earnings per share. With *restricted stock plans*, the firm usually awards shares without cost to the executive: The employee can sell the stock (for which he or she paid nothing), but is restricted from doing so for, say, five years. Under *phantom stock plans*, executives receive not shares but "units" that are similar to shares of company stock. Then at some future time, they receive value (usually in cash) equal to the appreciation of the "phantom" stock they own. "The New Workforce" illustrates some global aspects of the executive pay issue.

Other Executive Incentives

golden parachutes
Payments companies make in connection with a change in ownership or control of a company.

Companies also provide various incentives to persuade executives to remain with the firm. This is especially important when there is reason to believe the firm is being stalked by another company that wants to buy it. The target company might then install *golden parachute* incentives. **Golden parachutes** (as opposed to golden handcuffs) are extraordinary payments companies make to executives in connection with a change in ownership or control of a company. For example, a company's golden parachute clause might state that, should there be a change in ownership of the firm, the executive would receive a one-time payment of $2 million. Under IRS regulations, companies cannot deduct all golden parachute payments made to executives, and the executive must pay a 20% excise tax on the golden parachute payments.[81]

Other firms, perhaps more dubiously, guarantee large loans as incentives to directors and officers, for instance, to buy company stock. Thus, directors and officers of Conseco Inc., owed the company more than $500 million for such loans when shares of the company stock dropped precipitously.[82]

Strategy and Executive Compensation

Few human resource practices can have as profound or obvious an impact on strategic success as the company's long-term incentives. Whether expanding through joint ventures abroad, consolidating operations, or pursuing some other strategy, few firms can fully implement strategies in just one or two years. Therefore, the long-term signals you send managers and executives regarding what you will (or won't) reward can have a big effect on whether the firm's strategy succeeds.

Employers designing long-term incentives thus ignore their firm's strategy at their peril. Compensation experts suggest first defining the strategic context for the executive compensation plan, and then creating the compensation package itself in what is basically a strategy-mapping-type process. In brief, decide what long term behaviors the executives must exhibit to achieve the firm's strategic goals, and put in place long-term incentives to reward those behaviors:

1. Define the strategic context for the executive compensation program, including the internal and external issues that face the company, and the firm's business objectives. For example, ask: What are our organization's long-term goals, and how can the compensation structure support them? What competitive challenges do we face?[83] Preferably, translate goals and aims into measurable terms.

2. Based on your strategic aims, shape each component of the executive compensation package (base salary, short-term incentives, long-term incentives, and benefits and perquisites), and then group the components into a balanced plan that makes sense in terms of motivating executive behavior to achieve these aims. Each component should help to focus the manager's attention on the behaviors required to achieve the company's strategic goals.

3. Check the executive compensation plan for compliance with all legal and regulatory requirements and for tax effectiveness.

4. Install a process for reviewing and evaluating the executive compensation plan whenever a major business change occurs.

This process may be more complicated than it may at first appear. The challenge is to zero in on the financial factors that really drive the company's results. One expert says, "In many companies, a careful analysis of historical financials shows that well over 90% of economic value change is driven by a few simple items that can be separated out."[84] For example, you may find that about 10 or 15 financial items—pricing, discounts, raw material costs, and net sales, for instance—are the controllable factors that drive the improvements in the value of the company and the value of the shareholders' investment.[85] These are the sorts of items the employer will want to tie its incentives to.

⑤ Outline the steps in developing effective incentive plans.

DESIGNING EFFECTIVE INCENTIVE PROGRAMS

As we saw at the start of this chapter, roughly 70% of employees feel that their firms' incentive plans are ineffective. We turn here to why such plans fail, and to how to improve their effectiveness.[86]

Why Incentive Plans Fail

Experts have proposed many explanations for why incentive plans fail. We can summarize their reasoning with the following points:

- ***Performance pay can't replace good management.*** Performance pay is supposed to motivate workers, but lack of motivation is not always the culprit. Ambiguous instructions, lack of clear goals, inadequate employee selection and training, unavailability of tools, and a hostile workforce (or management) are some other factors that impede performance.

- *You get what you pay for.* An incentive plan that rewards a group based on how many pieces they produce may lead to rushed production and lower quality. A plantwide incentive for reducing accidents may simply reduce the number of reported accidents.

- *"Pay is not a motivator."* Recall that psychologist Frederick Herzberg says employers should provide adequate financial rewards, and then build other, more effective motivators (like opportunities for achievement) into jobs. More challenging jobs and employee regulations often make more sense than do financial incentive plans.

- *Rewards punish.* Many view punishment and reward as two sides of the same coin. Herzberg says, "Do this and you'll get that" is not very different from "Do this or you won't get that."

- *Rewards rupture relationships.* Incentive plans have the potential for encouraging individuals (or individual groups) to pursue self-interest at the expanse of teamwork.

- *Rewards can have unintended consequences.* People tend to put their efforts where they think they're being measured. So, for instance, reward only productivity and you may end up with poor quality.

- *Rewards may undermine responsiveness.* When employees' main focus is on achieving some specific goal like cutting costs, any changes or distractions make achieving that goal harder for the employees. Requests from management for assistance in implementing a needed change (for instance in factory design) may therefore trigger resistance.

- *Rewards undermine intrinsic motivation.* Edward Deci said that contingent financial rewards (incentives) may actually undermine the intrinsic motivation that often results in optimal performance.[87] The argument is that financial incentives undermine the feeling that the person is doing a good job voluntarily.

How to Implement Effective Incentive Plans

What then can the manager do to make an incentive plan more effective? Some guidelines follow:

1. *Ask: Are performance levels inadequate due to motivation?* It makes sense to use an incentive plan when motivation (and not ability) is the problem, and where: there is a clear relationship between employee effort and quantity or quality of output; the job is standardized; the work flow is regular; delays are few or consistent; and quality is less important than quantity—or, if quality is important, employees can easily measure and control it.[88]

2. *Link the incentive with your strategy.* Decide how the incentive plan will contribute to implementing the firm's strategy and objectives. The key thing is that, "in the best of all possible worlds, each item on your awards menu earns its keep by delivering on its promise, whether to inspire higher performance, reduce costs or any of a range of results that fit your business and its strategic plan."[89] For example, one incentive program at Sun Microsystems supports the firm's customer satisfaction strategy. Employees receive incentives based on achieving improvements in activities like on-time delivery and customer returns.[90] About 43% of employers surveyed by consultants Watson Wyatt Worldwide recently said they were linking their rewards to business strategy, up from 35% in 1996.[91]

3. *Make sure the program is motivational.* Ideally, the incentive plan should reward employees in direct proportion to increased productivity or quality. Employees must also perceive that they can actually do the tasks required. The standard has to be attainable, and employees should have the necessary tools, equipment, and training.[92] Victor Vroom would say there should be a clear link between effort and performance, and between performance and reward, and that the reward must be attractive to the employee.

4. *Make the plan easy for employees to understand.* Employees should be able to calculate their rewards for various levels of effort.

5. *Set effective standards.* Make standards high but reasonable—there should be about a 60 to 70% chance of success. And the goal should be specific—this is much more effective than telling someone to "do your best."

6. *View the standard as a contract with employees.* Once the plan is working, use caution before decreasing the size of the incentive. Rate cuts have long been the nemesis of incentive plans.

7. *Get employees' support for the plan.* Restrictions by members of the work group can undermine the plan.

8. *Use good measurement systems.* In the case of merit pay, for instance, the process used to appraise performance must be clear and fair if the plan is to be of any use.

9. *Use a complete set of standards.* For example, just paying assembly workers for quantity may be shortsighted. Quality issues, as well as longer-term improvements like those deriving from work-improvement suggestions are often equally important.

10. *Make the incentive plan part of a comprehensive, commitment-oriented approach.* From the employees' point of view, incentive plans don't exist in isolation. For example, trying to motivate employees with a new incentive plan when they don't have the skills to do the job, or are demoralized by unfair supervisors or a lack of respect might well fail. Therefore, the most successful plans, like Scanlon's, are part of comprehensive programs that promote employee competence and commitment.

    Human resources activities that contribute to building commitment include: clarifying and communicating the company's goals; guaranteeing organizational justice—for instance, by having a comprehensive grievance procedure; creating a sense of community by encouraging employees to interact; supporting employee development and career-enhancing activities; and generally committing to being supportive of employees.[93]

Finally, it's hard to imagine many things more wasteful than distributing incentives that don't have the desired effects. Therefore, the manager should clarify ahead of time what measures or metrics he or she intends to improve by instituting the incentive plan. And, the manager should use statistical analysis to measure the effects of the incentive on these measures over time.[94]

Research Insight: The Impact of Financial and Non-financial Incentives

Two researchers studied the impact of financial and non-financial incentives on business performance in 21 stores of a fast food franchise in the Midwest.[95] In this study, the researchers carefully compared performance over time in stores that did and did not use financial and non-financial employee incentives. Each store had about 25 subordinates and two managers. The managers were trained to identify critical, observable, measurable employee behaviors that were currently deficient but that could impact store performance. Example behaviors included "keeping both hands moving at the drive-through window," "working during idle time," and "repeating the customer's order back to him or her."[96] The researchers measured store performance in terms of three things, gross profitability (revenue minus expenses), drive-through time, and employee turnover.

Financial Incentives   Some employees in some of the stores received financial incentives for exhibiting the desired behaviors. The financial incentives consisted of lump-sum bonuses in the workers' paychecks. For example, if the manager observed a work-team exhibiting up to 50 behaviors during the observation period, he or she added $25 to the paychecks of all store employees that period; 50 to 100 behaviors added $50 per paycheck, and over 100 behaviors added $75 per paycheck. Payouts rose over time as the employees learned more about the behaviors they were to exhibit. Specifically, payouts rose from about $33 average per employee per month during the three months just after training, to about $54 per employee per month during the next three months, to about $70 per employee per month during the final three months of the study.

Non-Financial Incentives   The researchers also trained the managers to deliver non-financial incentives in the form of performance feedback and social recognition. For example, for *performance feedback* managers maintained charts showing the drive-through times at the end of each day. They placed the charts by the time clocks, so all the store employees could keep track of their store's performance on things like drive-through times. The researchers also trained managers to administer *recognition* to employees, such as, "I noticed that today the drive-through times were really good. That is great since that is what we're really focusing on these days."[97]

Results   The results of this study indicated that both financial and non-financial incentives improved employee and store performance, and that these improvements were sustained over time.[98] For example, store profits rose 30% for those units where managers used financial rewards. Store profits rose 36% for those units where managers used non-financial rewards. During the same nine-month period, drive-through times decreased 19% for the financial incentives group, and 25% for the non-financial incentives groups. Turnover improved 13% for the financial incentives group, and 10% for the non-financial incentives group. Initially, financial incentives had a greater impact than non-financial incentives on profits and customer service, but their effects became equally effective over time. (Financial incentives had a more significant impact on employee turnover than did non-financial incentives over time, however.)

Incentive Plans in Practice: Nucor

Nucor Corp. is the largest steel producer in the United States, and also has the highest productivity, highest wages, and lowest labor cost per ton in the American steel industry.[99] Employees earn bonuses of 100% or more of base salary, and all Nucor employees participate in one of four performance-based incentive plans. With the *production incentive plan*, operating and maintenance employees and supervisors get weekly bonuses based on their work groups' productivity. The *department manager incentive plan* pays department managers annual incentive bonuses based mostly on the ratio of net income to dollars of assets employed for their division. With the *professional and clerical bonus plan*, employees who are not in one of the two previous plans get bonuses based on their divisions' net income return on assets.[100] Finally, under the *senior officer incentive plan*, Nucor senior managers (whose base salaries are lower than those of executives in comparable firms) get bonuses based on Nucor's annual overall percentage of net income to stockholders equity.[101]

REVIEW

SUMMARY

1. The scientific use of financial incentives can be traced back to Frederick Taylor. Although such incentives subsequently became somewhat less popular, most writers today agree that they can be quite effective.

2. Different people react to different incentives in different ways. Psychologists explain this with what they call the law of individual differences, the fact that people differ in personality, abilities, values, and needs.

3. Psychologists distinguish between intrinsic and extrinsic motivation. Abraham Maslow argued that people have a hierarchy of five increasingly higher-level needs which he called physiological, security, social, self-esteem, and self-actualization. Similarly, Frederick Herzberg's hygiene-motivator motivation theory divides Maslow's hierarchy into lower-level and higher-level needs. Victor Vroom says a person's motivation to exert some level of effort is a function of three things: the person's expectancy that his or her effort will lead to performance, instrumentality, and valence.

4. Piecework, where a worker is paid a piece rate for each unit he or she produces, is the oldest type of incentive plan. With a straight piecework plan, workers are paid on the basis of the number of units produced. With a guaranteed piecework plan, each worker receives his or her base rate (such as the minimum wage) regardless of how many units he or she produces.

5. Other useful incentive plans include the standard hour plan and group incentive plans. The former rewards workers by a percent premium that equals the percent by which their performance is above standard. Group incentive plans are useful where the workers' jobs are highly interrelated.

6. Most sales personnel are paid on some type of salary plus commission (incentive) basis. Management employees are often paid according to a bonus formula that ties the bonus to, for example, increased sales. Stock options are one of the most popular executive incentive plans.

7. Profit sharing and the Scanlon plan are examples of organizationwide incentive plans. Gainsharing and merit plans are two other popular plans. The problem with such plans is that the link between a person's efforts and rewards is sometimes unclear. On the other hand, such plans may contribute to developing a sense of commitment among employees.

8. Incentive plans work best when units of output are easily measured, when employees can control output, when the effort—reward relationship is clear, when work delays are under employees' control, when quality is not paramount, and when the organization must know precise labor costs anyway (to stay competitive).

DISCUSSION QUESTIONS

1. Compare and contrast six types of incentive plans.
2. Explain five reasons why incentive plans fail.
3. Describe the nature of some important management incentives.

4. When and why would you pay a salesperson a combined salary and commission?

5. What is merit pay? Do you think it's a good idea to award employees merit raises? Why or why not?

6. In this chapter, we listed a number of reasons experts give for not instituting a pay-for-performance plan (such as "rewards punish"). Do you think these points (or any of them) are valid? Why or why not?

7. What is a Scanlon plan? Based on what you've read in this chapter, what features of an effective incentive program does the Scanlon plan include?

8. Give four examples of when you would suggest using team or group incentive programs rather than individual incentive programs.

INDIVIDUAL AND GROUP ACTIVITIES

1. Working individually or in groups, develop an incentive plan for the following positions: chemical engineer, plant manager, used-car salesperson. What factors did you have to consider in reaching your conclusions?

2. A state university system in the Southeast instituted a "Teacher Incentive Program" (TIP) for its faculty. Basically, faculty committees within each university's colleges were told to award $5,000 raises (not bonuses) to about 40% of their faculty members based on how good a job they did teaching undergraduates, and how many they taught per year. What are the potential advantages and pitfalls of such an incentive program? How well do you think it was accepted by the faculty? Do you think it had the desired effect?

3. The HRCI "Test Specifications" appendix at the end of this book (pages 726–735) lists the knowledge someone studying for the HRCI certification exam needs to have in each area of human resource management (such as in Strategic Management, Workforce Planning, and Human Resource Development). In groups of four to five students, do four things: (1) review that appendix now; (2) identify the material in this chapter that relates to the required knowledge the appendix lists; (3) write four multiple choice exam questions on this material that you believe would be suitable for inclusion in the HRCI exam; and (4) if time permits, have someone from your team post your team's questions in front of the class, so the students in other teams can take each others' exam questions.

4. In March 2004, the pension plan of the Utility Workers Union of America proposed changing the corporate bylaws of Dominion Resources, Inc., so that in the future, management had to get shareholder approval of executive pay exceeding $1 million, as well as detailed information about the firm's executive incentive plans. Many unions—most of which have pension funds with huge investments in U.S. companies—are taking similar steps. They point out that, usually, under Internal Revenue Service regulations, corporations can't deduct more than $1 million in pay for any of a company's top five paid executives. Under the new rules the unions are pushing, boards of directors will no longer be able to approve executive pay above $1 million; instead, shareholders would have to vote on it. In terms of effectively running a company, what do you think are the pros and cons of the unions' recommendations? Would you vote for or against the unions' recommendation? Why or why not?

EXPERIENTIAL EXERCISE

Motivating the Salesforce at Express Auto

Purpose: The purpose of this exercise is to give you practice developing an incentive plan.

Required Understanding: Be thoroughly familiar with this chapter, and read the following:

Express Auto, an automobile megadealership with over 600 employees that represents 22 brands, has just received a very discouraging set of survey results. Customer satisfaction scores have fallen for the ninth straight quarter. Customer complaints include:

- It was hard to get prompt feedback from mechanics by phone.
- Salespeople often did not return phone calls.
- The finance people seemed "pushy."
- New cars were often not properly cleaned or had minor items that needed immediate repair or adjustment.
- Cars often had to be returned to have repair work redone.

Table 12-3 describes Express Auto's current compensation system.

How to Set Up the Exercise/Instructions: Divide the class into groups of four to five students. Assign one or more groups to analyzing each of the five teams in column one. Each student group should analyze the compensation package for its Express Auto team. Each group should address these questions:

1. In what ways might your team's compensation plan contribute to the customer service problems?
2. What recommendations would you make to improve the compensation system in a way that would likely improve customer satisfaction?

TABLE 12-3 Express Auto Compensation System

Express Auto Team	Responsibility of Team	Current Compensation Method
1. Sales force	Persuade buyer to purchase a car.	Very small salary (minimum wage) with commissions. Commission rate increases with every 20 cars sold per month.
2. Finance office	Help close the sale; persuade customer to use company finance plan.	Salary, plus bonus for each $10,000 financed with the company.
3. Detailing	Inspect cars delivered from factory, clean, and make minor adjustments	Piecework paid on the number of cars detailed per day.
4. Mechanics	Provide factory warranty service, maintenance, and repair.	Small hourly wage, plus bonus based on (1) number of cars completed per day and (2) finishing each car faster than the standard estimated time to repair.
5. Receptionists/phone service personnel	Primary liaison between customer and salesforce, finance, and mechanics.	Minimum wage.

APPLICATION CASE

Inserting the Team Concept into Compensation—or Not

One of the first things Sandy Caldwell wanted to do in his new position at Hathaway Manufacturing was improve productivity through teamwork at every level of the firm. As the new human resource manager for the suburban plant, Sandy set out to change the culture to accommodate the team-based approach he had become so enthusiastic about in his most recent position.

Sandy started by installing the concept of team management at the highest level, to oversee the operations of the entire plant. The new management team consisted of manufacturing, distribution, planning, technical, and human resource plant managers. Together they developed a new vision for the 500-employee facility, which they expressed in the simple phrase "Excellence Together." They drafted a new mission statement for the firm that focused on becoming customer driven and team based, and that called upon employees to raise their level of commitment and begin acting as "owners" of the firm.

The next step was to convey the team message to employees throughout the company. The communication process went surprisingly well, and Sandy was happy to see his idea of a "workforce of owners" begin to take shape. Teams trained together, developed production plans together, and embraced the technique of 360-degree feedback, in which an employee's performance evaluation is obtained from supervisors, subordinates, peers, and internal or external customers. Performance and morale improved, and productivity began to tick upward. The company even sponsored occasional celebrations to reward team achievements, and the team structure seemed firmly in place.

Sandy decided to change one more thing. Hathaway's long-standing policy had been to give all employees the same annual pay increase. But Sandy felt that in the new team environment, outstanding performance should be the criterion for pay raises. After consulting with CEO Regina Cioffi, Sandy sent a memo to all employees announcing the change to team-based pay for performance.

The reaction was immediate and 100% negative. None of the employees was happy with the change, and among their complaints, two stood out. First, because the 360-degree feedback system made everyone responsible in part for someone else's performance evaluation, no one was comfortable with the idea that pay raises might also somehow be linked to peer input. Second, there was a widespread perception that the way the change was decided upon, and the way it was announced, put the firm's commitment to team effort in doubt. Simply put, employees felt left out of the decision process.

Sandy and Regina arranged a meeting for early the next morning. Sitting in her office over their coffee, they began a painful debate. Should the new policy be rescinded as quickly as it was adopted, or should it be allowed to stand?

Questions

1. Does the pay-for-performance plan seem like a good idea? Why or why not?
2. What advice would you give Regina and Sandy as they consider their decision?
3. What mistakes did they make in adopting and communicating the new salary plan? How might Sandy have approached this major compensation change a little differently?
4. Assuming the new pay plan were eventually accepted, how would you address the fact that in the new performance evaluation system, employees' input affects their peers' pay levels?

Note: The incident in this case is based on an actual event at Frito-Lay's Kirkwood, New York, plant, as reported in C. James Novak, "Proceed with Caution When Paying Teams," *HR Magazine,* April 1997, p. 73.

CONTINUING CASE

Carter Cleaning Company

The Incentive Plan

The question of whether to pay Carter Cleaning Center employees an hourly wage or an incentive of some kind has always intrigued Jack Carter.

His basic policy has been to pay employees an hourly wage, except that his managers do receive an end-of-year bonus depending, as Jack puts it, "on whether their stores do well or not that year."

He is, however, considering using an incentive plan in one store. Jack knows that a presser should press about 25 "tops" (jackets, dresses, blouses) per hour. Most of his pressers do not attain this ideal standard, though. In one instance, a presser named Walt was paid $8 per hour, and Jack noticed that regardless of the amount of work he had to do, Walt always ended up going home at about 3:00 P.M., so he earned about $300 at the end of the week. If it was a holiday week, for instance, and there were a lot of clothes to press, he might average 22 to 23 tops per hour (someone else did pants) and so he'd earn perhaps $300 and still finish up each day in time to leave by 3:00 P.M. so he could pick up his children at school. But when things were very slow in the store, his productivity would drop to perhaps 12 to 15 pieces an hour, so that at the end of the week he'd end up earning perhaps $280, and in fact not go home much earlier than he did when it was busy.

Jack spoke with Walt several times, and while Walt always promised to try to do better, it gradually became apparent to Jack that Walt was simply going to earn his $300 per week no matter what. While Walt never told him so directly, it dawned on Jack that Walt had a family to support and was not about to earn less than his "target" wage regardless of how busy or slow the store was. The problem was that the longer Walt kept pressing each day, the longer the steam boilers and compressors had to be kept on to power his machines, and the fuel charges alone ran close to $6 per hour. Jack clearly needed some way short of firing Walt to solve the problem, since the fuel bills were eating up his profits.

His solution was to tell Walt that instead of an hourly $8 wage he would henceforth pay him $0.33 per item pressed. That way, said Jack to himself, if Walt presses 25 items per hour at $0.33 he will in effect get a small raise. He'll get more items pressed per hour and will therefore be able to shut the machines down earlier.

On the whole, the experiment worked well. Walt generally presses 25 to 35 pieces per hour now. He gets to leave earlier, and with the small increase in pay he generally earns his target wage. Two problems have arisen, though. The quality of Walt's work has dipped a bit, plus, his manager has to spend a minute or two each hour counting the number of pieces Walt pressed that hour. Otherwise Jack is fairly pleased with the results of his incentive plan and he's wondering whether to extend it to other employees and other stores.

Questions

1. Should this plan in its present form be extended to pressers in the other stores?
2. Should other employees (cleaner–spotters, counter people) be put on a similar plan? Why? Why not? If so, how, exactly?
3. Is there another incentive plan you think would work better for the pressers?
4. A store manager's job is to keep total wages to no more than 30% of sales and to maintain the fuel bill and the supply bill at about 9% of sales each. Managers can also directly affect sales by ensuring courteous customer service and by ensuring that the work is done properly. What suggestions would you make to Jennifer and her father for an incentive plan for store managers?

TRANSLATING STRATEGY INTO HR POLICIES AND PRACTICES CASE: THE HOTEL PARIS

The New Incentive Plan

The Hotel Paris's competitive strategy is "To use superior guest service to differentiate the Hotel Paris properties, and to thereby increase the length of stay and return rate of guests, and thus boost revenues and profitability." HR manager Lisa Cruz must now formulate functional policies and activities that support this competitive strategy, by eliciting the required employee behaviors and competencies.

One of Lisa Cruz's biggest pay-related concerns is that the Hotel Paris compensation plan does not link pay to performance in any effective way. Because salaries were historically barely competitive, supervisors tended to award merit raises across the board. So, employees who performed well got only about the same raises as did those who performed poorly. Similarly, there was no bonus or incentive plan of any kind aimed at linking employee performance to strategically relevant employee capabilities and behaviors such as greeting guests in a friendly manner or providing expeditious check-ins and checkouts.

Based on their analysis, Lisa Cruz and the CFO concluded that by any metric, their company's incentive plan was totally inadequate. The percentage of the workforce whose merit increase or incentive pay is tied to performance is effectively zero, because managers awarded merit pay across the board. No more than 5% of the workforce (just the managers) was eligible for incentive pay. And, the percentage of difference in incentive pay between a low-performing and a high-performing employee was less than 2%. Lisa knew from industry studies that in top firms, over 80% of the workforce had merit pay or incentive pay tied to performance. She also knew that in high-performing

firms, there was at least a 5 or 6% difference in incentive pay between a low-performing and a high-performing employee. The CFO authorized Lisa to design a new strategy-oriented incentive plan for the Hotel Paris's employees. Their overall aim was to incentivize the pay plans of just about all the company's employees.

Lisa and the company's CFO laid out three measurable criteria that the new incentive plan had to meet. First, at least 90% (and preferably all) of the Hotel Paris's employees must be eligible for a merit increase or incentive pay that is tied to performance. Second, there must be at least a 10% difference in incentive pay between a low-performing and high-performing employee. Third, the new incentive plan had to include specific bonuses and evaluative mechanisms that linked employee behaviors in each job category with strategically relevant employee capabilities and behaviors. For example, front-desk clerks were to be rewarded in part based on the friendliness and speed of their checkins and checkouts, and the housecleaning crew was to be evaluated and rewarded in part based on the percentage of room cleaning infractions.

Questions

1. Discuss what you think of the measurable criteria Lisa and the CFO set for their new incentive plan.
2. Given what you know about the Hotel Paris' strategic goals, list 3–4 specific behaviors you would incentivize for each of the following groups of employees: front desk clerks; hotel managers; valets; housekeepers.
3. Lay out a complete incentive plans (including all long and short-term incentives) for the Hotel Paris' hotel managers.

KEY TERMS

ENDNOTES

1. Even the traditional holiday bonus is being replaced by performance-based pay. A recent survey by consultants Hewitt Associates found that only about 5% of employers surveyed planned to distribute holiday cash bonuses. About 78% said they were offering performance based awards, up from 51% about 15 years ago. "Cash Bonuses Are Ghosts of Holidays Past, Survey Says," *BNA Bulletin to Management*, December 13, 2005, p. 396. See also, "Aligning Rewards with the Changing Employment Deal: 2006/2007 Strategic Rewards® Report," http://www.watsonwyatt.com/research/resrender.asp?id=2006-US-0038&page=1, accessed May 20, 2007.

2. "Few Employees See the Pay for Performance Connection," *Compensation and Benefits Review*, June 2003, vol. 17, issue 2, "Most Workers Not Motivated by Cash," *Incentive Today*, July–August 2004, p. 19, and "Pay-for-Performance Plans' Impact Uncertain: Study," *Modern Healthcare*, May 24, 2004, p. 34.

3. Kathy Chu, "Employers See Lackluster Results Linking Salary to Performance," *Wall Street Journal*, June 15, 2004, page d2.

4. James Shaw et al., "Reactions to Merit Pay Increases: A Longitudinal Test of a Signal Sensitivity Perspective," *Journal of Applied Psychology* 88, no. 3 (2003), pp. 538–544.

5. Ibid.

6. Ted Turnasella, "Pay and Personality," *Compensation and Benefits Review*, March/April 2002, pp. 45–59.

7. See, for example, Edward Deci, *Intrinsic Motivation* (New York: Plenum, 1975).

8. Kanfer, "Motivation Theory," p. 113.

9. For a discussion, see John P. Campbell and Robert Prichard, "Motivation Theory in Industrial and Organizational Psychology," in Marvin Dunnette (ed.), *Industrial and Organizational Psychology* (Chicago: Rand McNally, 1976), pp. 74–75; and Kanfer, "Motivation Theory," pp. 115–116.

10. See for example Aubrey Daniels, et al., "The Leader's Role in Pay Systems and Organizational Performance," *Compensation and Benefits Review*, May/June 2006, pp. 58–60, and Suzanne Peterson and Fred Luthans, "The Impact of Financial and Non-Financial Incentives on Business Unit Outcomes Over Time," *Journal of Applied Psychology* 91, no. 1, 2006, pp. 156–165.

11. See for example Mary Ducharne and Mark Podolsky, "Variable Pay: Its Impact on Motivation and Organisation Performance," *International Journal of Human Resources Development and Management*, May 9, 2006, vol. 6, p. 68.

12. Ibid.

13. "Employers Use Pay to Lever Performance," *BNA Bulletin to Management*, August 21, 1997, p. 272.

14. See, for example, Kenan Abosch, "Variable Pay: Do We Have the Basics in Place?" *Compensation and Benefits Review*, July/August 1998, pp. 2–22.

15. See, for example, Diane Cadrain, "Cash Versus Non-Cash Rewards," *HR Magazine*, April 2003, pp. 81–87.

16. "Impact of Sarbanes-Oxley on Executive Compensation," downloaded December 11, 2003, from www.thelenreid.com, Thelen, Reid, and Priest L. L. P.

17. Richard Henderson, *Compensation Management* (Upper Saddle River, NJ: Prentice Hall, 2000), p. 463.

18. For a discussion of these, see Thomas Wilson, "Is it Time to Eliminate the Piece Rate Incentive System?" *Compensation and Benefits Review*, March/April 1992, pp. 43–49.

19. Oanh Ha, "California Workers Named in Articles Not Asked to Help in Piecework Probe," *Knight Ridder/Tribune News*, March 23, 2000, item 0008408e.

20. William Atkinson, "Incentive Pay Programs that Work in Textile," *Textile World* 151, no. 2 (February 2001), pp. 55–57.

21. Donald Campbell et al., "Merit Pay, Performance Appraisal, and Individual Motivation: An Analysis and Alternative," *Human Resource Management* 37, no. 2 (Summer 1998), pp. 131–146.

22. The average uncorrected cross-sectional correlation was 17. Michael Harris et al., "A Longitudinal Examination of a Merit Pay System: Relationships Among Performance Ratings, Merit

Increases, and Total Pay Increases," *Journal of Applied Psychology* 83, no. 5 (1998), pp. 825–831.

23. Eric R. Schulz and Denise Marie Tanguay, "Merit Pay in a Public Higher Education Institution: Questions of Impact and Attitudes," *Public Personnel Management*, Spring 2006, v35 i1 p. 71(18). Thomas S. Dee and Benjamin J. Keys, "Does Merit Pay Reward Good Teachers? Evidence from a Randomized Experiment," *Journal of Policy Analysis & Management*, Summer 2004, v23 i3 pp. 471–488. See also, David N. Figlio and Lawrence W. Kenny, "Individual Teacher Incentives and Student Performance," *The Journal of Public Economics*, June 2007, v91 i5-6 p. 901(14).

24. Jonathan Glater, "Varying the Recipe Helps TV Operations Solve Morale Problem," *New York Times*, March 7, 2001, p. C1.

25. Esther Shein, "Team Spirit: IT is Getting Creative with Compensation to Foster Collaboration," *PC Week*, May 11, 1998, pp. 69–72. See also, Fay Hansen, "Short-Term Incentive Programs Are Most Effective in Driving IT Performance," *Compensation and Benefits Review*, November/ December 2003, pp. 11–12.

26. Ann Harrington, "Saying 'We Love You' with Stock Options," *Fortune*, October 11, 1999, p. 316.

27. Betty Sosin, "A Patent on the Back," *HR Magazine*, March 2000, pp. 107–112.

28. Suzanne Peterson and Fred Luthans, "The Impact of Financial and Non-Financial Incentives on Business Unit Outcomes Over Time," *Journal of Applied Psychology* 91, no. 1, 2006, p. 158.

29. Scott Hays, "Pros and Cons of Pay for Performance," *Workforce*, February 1999, pp. 69–74, and "Incentives: Is Employee Recognition Key to Corporate Goals?" *Occupational Hazards*, November 2003, vol. 65, issue iii, p. 23.

30. Bob Nelson, *1001 Ways to Reward Employees* (New York: Workmen Publishing, 1994), p. 5. For a recent short survey of noncash incentives, see "Cash Rewards Blend into Paychecks While Noncash Awards Stand Out," *Report on Salary Surveys*, Feb. 2004, i04-02, p. 8.

31. "Round-the-Clock Recognition: Any Time Is a Good Time to Give Workers Their Due," *BNA Bulletin to Management*, February 13, 2003, p. 49.

32. Libby Estell, "I See London, I See France . . . ," *Incentives*, August 2001, pp. 58–62. See also, Scott Jeffrey and Victoria Schaffer, "The Motivational Properties of Tangible Incentives," *Compensation & Benefits Review*, May/June 2007, pp. 44–50.

33. Ibid. See also, Chris Taylor, "On-the-Spot Incentives," *HR Magazine*, May 2004, pp. 80–85.

34. Charlotte Huff, "Recognition That Resonates," *Workforce Management*, Sept. 11, 2006, pp. 25–29.

35. Jeremy Wuittner, "Plenty of Incentives to Use E.I.M. Software Systems," *American Banker* 168, no. 129 (July 8, 2003), p. 680.

36. William Bulkeley, "Incentives Systems Fine-Tune Pay/Bonus Plans," *Wall Street Journal*, August 16, 2001, p. B4.

37. Nina McIntyre, "EIM Technology to Successfully Motivate Employees," *Compensation and Benefits Review*, July/August 2001, pp. 57–60.

38. Paul Glister, "Online Incentives Sizzle—and You Shine," *Workforce*, January 2001, p. 46. See also Andrea Poe, "On-line Recognition," *HR Magazine*, June 2002, pp. 95–103.

39. "Striking a Chord: Texas Instruments Uses All the Right Tools to Recognize Top Performers," *Incentives* 177, no. 3 (March 2003), p. 34.

40. Straight salary by itself is not, of course, an incentive compensation plan as we use the term in this chapter.

41. Sonjun Luo, "Does Your Sales Incentive Plan Pay for Performance?" *Compensation and Benefits Review*, January/ February 2003, pp. 18–24.

42. David Harrison, Meghan Virick, and Sonja William, "Working Without a Net: Time, Performance, and Turnover Under Maximally Contingent Rewards," *Journal of Applied Psychology* 81, no. 4 (1996), p. 332.

43. Ibid., pp. 331–345. See also, James M. Pappas and Karen E. Flaherty, "The Moderating Role of Individual-Difference Variables in Compensation Research," *Journal of Managerial Psychology*, Jan. 2006, v21 i1 pp. 19–35, and Tara Burnthorne Lopez, Christopher D. Hopkins and Mary Anne Raymond, "Reward Preferences of Salespeople: How Do Commissions Rate?," *Journal of Personal Selling & Sales Management*, Fall 2006, v26 i4 p381(10).

44. Bill O'Connell, "Dead Solid Perfect: Achieving Sales Compensation Alignment," *Compensation and Benefits Review*, March/April 1996, pp. 46–47.

45. In the salary bonus plan, salespeople are paid a basic salary and are then paid a bonus for carrying out specific activities.

46. Jeanie Casisom, "Jumpstart Motivation," *Incentives* 175, no. 5 (May 2001), p. 77.

47. Kathleen Cholewka, "Tech Tools," *Sales and Marketing Management* 152, no. 7 (July 2001), p. 24.

48. David Cocks and Dennis Gould, "'Sales Compensation' A New Technology—The Enabled Strategy," *Compensation and Benefits Review*, January/February 2001, pp. 27–31.

49. Bill Weeks, "Setting Sales Force Compensation in the Internet Age," *Compensation and Benefits Review*, March/April 2000, pp. 25–34, and David Fiedler, "Should You Adjust Your Sales Compensation?" *HR Magazine*, February 2003, pp. 78–80.

50. S. Scott Sands, "Ineffective Quotas: The Hidden Threat to Sales Compensation Plans," *Compensation and Benefits Review*, March/April 2000, pp. 35–42.

51. Peter Gundy, "Sales Compensation Programs: Built to Last," *Compensation and Benefits Review*, September/October 2002, pp. 21–28.

52. Peter Glendinning, "Kicking the Tires of Automotive Sales Compensation," *Compensation and Benefits Review*, September/October 2000, pp. 47–53, and Michele Marchetti, "Why Sales Contests Don't Work," *Sales and Marketing Management*, January 2004, vol. 156, p. 19. See also, "Salary and Bonus Gain Favor in Sales Pay (for Motor Vehicle Salespeople)," *Automotive News*, Feb. 5, 2001, v75 i5915 p. 50.

53. Eileen Zimmerman, "Quota Busters," *Sales and Marketing Management* 153, no. 1 (January 2001), pp. 58–63.

54. "Driving Profitable Sales Growth: 2006/2007 Report on Sales Effectiveness," source http://www.watsonwyatt.com/research/resrender.asp?id=2006-US-0060&page=1, accessed May 20, 2007.

55. Other suggestions are as follows: equal payments to all members on the team; differential payments to team members based on their contributions to the team's performance; and differential payments determined by a ratio of each group member's base pay to the total base pay of the group. See Kathryn Bartol and Laura Hagmann, "Team Based Pay Plans: A Key to Effective Team Work," *Compensation and Benefits Review*, November–December 1992, pp. 24–29. See also, Charlotte Garvey, "Steer Teams with the Right Pay," *HR Magazine*, May 2002, pp. 70–71.

56. Richard Seaman, "The Case Study: Rejuvenating an Organization with Team Pay," *Compensation and Benefits Review*, September/October 1997, pp. 25–30. See also, Mark Kroll, Jeffrey A. Krug, Michael Pettus and Peter Wright, "Influences of Top Management Team Incentives on Firm Risk Taking," *Strategic Management Journal*, Jan. 2007, v28 i1, pp. 81–89.

57. Robert Heneman and Courtney Von Hippel, "Balancing Group and Individual Rewards: Rewarding Individual Contributions to the Team," *Compensation and Benefits Review*, July/August 1995, pp. 63–68.

58. Seongsu Kim, "Does Profit Sharing Increase Firms' Profits?" *Journal of Labor Research* (Spring 1998), pp. 351–371. See also Jacqueline Coyle-Shapiro et al., "Using Profit-Sharing to Enhance Employee Attitudes: A Longitudinal Examination of the Effects on Trust and Commitment," *Human Resource Management* 41, no. 4 (Winter 2002), pp. 423–449.

59. Nelson, *1001 Ways to Reward Employees*, p. 19. See also, Sunny C. L. Fong and Margaret A. Shaffer, "The Dimensionality and Determinants of Pay Satisfaction: A Cross-cultural Investigation of a Group Incentive Plan," *International Journal of Human Resource Management*, June 2003, v14 i4 p. 559(22).

60. Kaja Whitehouse, "More Companies Offer Packages Linking Pay Plans to Performance," the *Wall Street Journal*, December 13, 2005, p. b4.

61. For a discussion of the effects of employee stock ownership on employee attitudes, see John Gamble, "ESOPs: Financial Performance and Federal Tax Incentives," *Journal of Labor Research* 19, no. 3 (Summer 1998), pp. 529–542.

62. Steven Etkind, "ESOPs Create Liquidity for Share Holders and Help Diversify Their Assets," *Estate Planning* 24, no. 4 (May 1998), pp. 158–165.

63. William Smith, Harold Lazarus, and Harold Murray Kalkstein, "Employee Stock Ownership Plans: Motivation and Moral Issues," *Compensation and Benefits Review*, September/October

1990, pp. 37–46. See also, "ESOP Trustees Breached Their Fiduciary Duties under ERISA by Failing to Make Prudent Investigation into Value of Stock Purchased by ESOP," *Tax Management Compensation Planning Journal*, Oct. 4, 2002, v30 i10 p. 301(1), and Jeffery D. Mamorsky, "Court Approves ERISA Action Against ENRON Executives, Trustee, and Plan Auditor for Retirement Plan Losses," *Journal of Compensation and Benefits*, Jan.–Feb. 2004, v20 i1 p. 46(7).

64. Best Manufacturing Practices Center of Excellence, copyright 1998.
65. Brian Moore and Timothy Ross, *The Scanlon Way to Improved Productivity: A Practical Guide* (New York: Wiley, 1978), p. 2.
66. These are based in part on Steven Markham, K. Dow Scott, and Walter Cox Jr., "The Evolutionary Development of a Scanlon Plan," *Compensation and Benefits Review*, March/April 1992, pp. 50–56. See also, Woodruff Imberman, "Are You Ready to Boost Productivity with a Gainsharing Plan? To Survive and Prosper in Our Hyper-competitive Environment, Board Converters Must Motivate Employees at All Levels," *Official Board Markets*, Nov. 25, 2006, v82 i47 p. 5(2), and James Reynolds and Daniel Roble, "Combining Pay for Performance with Gainsharing," *Healthcare Financial Management*, Nov. 2006, v60 i11 p. 50(6).
67. Markham et al., "The Evolutionary Development of a Scanlon Plan," p. 51.
68. Barry W. Thomas and Madeline Hess Olson, "Gainsharing: The Design Guarantees Success," *Personnel Journal*, May 1998, pp. 73–79.
69. Paul Rossler and C. Patrick Koelling, "The Effect of Gainsharing on Business Performance at a Paper Mill," *National Productivity Review* (Summer 1993), pp. 365–382.
70. Paraphrased from Woodruff Imbermann, "Boosting Plant Performance with Gainsharing," *Business Horizons*, November–December 1992, pp. 77. See also, Max Reynolds and Joane Goodroe, "The Return of Gainsharing: Gainsharing Appears to Be Enjoying a Renaissance," *Healthcare Financial Management*, Nov. 2005, v59 i11 p. 114(6) and Dong-One Kim, "The Benefits and Costs of Employee Suggestions Under Gainsharing," *Industrial and Labor Relations Review*, July 2005, v58 i4 p. (631)(22).
71. Mark Meltzer and Howard Goldsmith, "Executive Compensation for Growth Companies," *Compensation and Benefits Review*, November/December 1997, pp. 41–50, and Barbara Kiviat, "Everyone into the Bonus Pool," *Time*, December 15, 2003, vol. 162, issue 24, p. A5.
72. Ibid. See also, Eric Krell, "Getting a Grip on Executive Pay," *Workforce*, February 2003, pp. 30–32.
73. "Short-Term Incentives Considered Ineffective, Survey Reveals," *Society for Human Resource Management*, January 2000, p. 5. See also, Steven Balsam and Setiyono Miharjo, "The Effect of Equity Compensation on Voluntary Executive Turnover," *The Journal of Accounting and Economics*, March 2007, v43 i1 p. 95(25).
74. Meltzer and Goldsmith, "Executive Compensation for Growth Companies," pp. 44–45. See also Robert E. Wood et al., "Bonuses, Goals, and Instrumentality Effects," *Journal of Applied Psychology* 84, no. 5 (1999), pp. 703–720.
75. Ibid., pp. 188. Meltzer and Goldsmith, "Executive Compensation for Growth Companies," p. 44. Fay Hansen, "Salary and Wage Trends," *Compensation and Benefits Review*, March/April 2004, pp. 9–10.
76. James Sesil et al., "Broad-Based Employee Stock Options in U.S. New Economy Firms," *British Journal of Industrial Relations* 40, no. 2 (June 2002), pp. 273–294.
77. Louis Lavelle, "How to Hold the Options Express," *BusinessWeek*, September 9, 2002.
78. Elaine Denby, "Weighing Your Options," *HR Magazine*, November 2002, pp. 44–49. See also, Brent Longnecker and James Krueger, "The Next Wave of Compensation Disclosure," *Compensation & Benefits Review*, January/February 2007, pp. 50–54.
79. "Study Finds That Directly Owning Stock Shares Leads to Better Results," *Compensation and Benefits Review*, March/April 2001, p. 7. See also, Ira Kay, "Whither the Stock Option? While Stock Options Lose More Luster as Executive Motivatiors, Compensation Committees Face Challenges, Including Selecting Other Forms of Stock Incentives," *Financial Executive*, March–April 2004, v20 i2 p. 46(3), and Lucian A. Bebchuk and Jesse M. Fried, "Pay Without Performance: Overview of the Issues," *The Academy of Management Perspectives*, Feb. 2006, v20 i1 p. 5(20).
80. "Time Warner Stops Granting Stock Options to Most of Staff," the *New York Times*, February 19, 2005, p. na, no. 128921996.

81. "Final Regs Issued for Golden Parachute Payments," *Executive Tax and Management Report* 66, no. 17 (September 2003), p. 1.

82. "Conseco Not Alone on Executive Perks," *Knight-Ridder/Tribune Business News*, August 28, 2003, item 03240015. See also, "Realities of Executive Compensation—2006/2007 Report on Executive Pay and Stock Options," http://www.watsonwyatt.com/research/resrender. asp?id=2006-US-0085&page=1), accessed May 20, 2007.

83. This section is based on Meltzer and Goldsmith, "Executive Compensation for Growth Companies," pp. 41–50. See also, Patricia Zingheim and Jay Schuster, "Designing Pay and Rewards in Professional Companies," *Compensation & Benefits Review*, January/February 2007, pp. 55–62.

84. Richard Semler, "Developing Management Incentives That Drive Results," *Compensation and Benefits Review*, July/August 1998, pp. 41–48.

85. Ibid., p. 47.

86. Peter Kurlander, "Building Incentive Compensation Management Systems: What Can Go Wrong?" *Compensation and Benefits Review*, July/August 2001, pp. 52–56. Employers may be moving to emphasize merit increases and deemphasize performance pay. The average percentage of payroll employers spent on broad-based performance pay plans pay rose till 2005, and then fell for the past few years. "Companies pull back from performance pay," *Workforce Management*, October 23, 2006, p. 26.

87. Ibid.; See also, Bruce Tulgan, "Real Pay for Performance," *Journal of Business Strategy* 22, no. 3 (May/June 2001), pp. 19–22.

88. Reed Taussig, "Managing Cash Based Incentives," *Compensation and Benefits Review*, March/April 2002, pp. 65–68. See also Nigel Nicholson, "How to Motivate Your Problem People," *Harvard Business Review*, January 2003, pp. 57–65, and "Incentives, Motivation and Workplace Performance," Incentive Research Foundation, www.incentivescentral.org/employees/whitepapers, accessed May 19, 2007.

89. "Frameworks for a More ROI Minded Rewards Plan," *Pay for Performance Report*, (February 2003), p. 1, and Alan Robinson and Dean Schroeder, "Rewards That Really Work," *Security Management*, July 2004, pp. 30–34. See also, Patricia Zingheim and Jay Schuster, "What Are Key Pay Issues Right Now?", *Compensation & Benefits Review*, May/June 2007, pp. 51–55.

90. Jennifer Schott, "Compensation Ties Incentives to Change," *ebusiness*, March 12, 2001, p. 4.

91. Kaja Whitehouse, "More Companies Offer Packages Linking Pay Plans to Performance," *Wall Street Journal*, December 13, 2005, p. b4.

92. See, for example, James Gutherie and Edward Cunningham, "Pay for Performance: The Quaker Oats Alternative," *Compensation and Benefits Review*, March/April 1992, pp. 18–23.

93. Gary Dessler, "How to Earn Your Employees' Commitment," *Academy of Management Executive* 13, no. 2 (1999), pp. 58–67; Steven Gross and Jeffrey Bacher, "The New Variable Pay Programs: How Some Succeed, Why Some Don't," *Compensation and Benefits Review*, January/ February 1993, pp. 55–56. See also Nina Gupta and Jason Shaw, "Financial Incentives Are Effective!" *Compensation and Benefits Review*, March/April 1998, pp. 28–32.

94. Theodore Weinberger, "Evaluating the Effectiveness of an Incentive Plan Design within Company Constraints," *Compensation and Benefits Review*, November/December 2005, pp. 27–33.

95. Suzanne Peterson and Fred Luthans, "The Impact of Financial and Non-Financial Incentives on Business Unit Outcomes Over Time," *Journal of Applied Psychology* 91, no. 1, 2006, pp. 156–165.

96. Op. cit., p. 159.

97. Op. cit., p. 159.

98. Op. cit., p. 162.

99. Janet Wiscombe, "Can Pay for Performance Really Work?" *Workforce*, August 2001, p. 30.

100. Susan Marks, "Incentives That Really Reward and Motivate," *Workforce*, June 2001, pp. 108–114.

101. While not an issue at Nucor, the employer needs to beware of instituting so many incentive plans (cash bonuses, stock options, recognition programs, and so on) tied to so many different behaviors that employees don't have a clear priority of the employer's priorities. See for example, Stephen Rubenfeld and Jannifer David, "Multiple Employee Incentive Plans: Too Much of a Good Thing?" *Compensation and Benefits Review*, March/April 2006, pp. 35–43.

13 | Benefits and Services

Verizon Communications, facing intense competition and the need to reduce its workforce after several mergers, needed a way to persuade thousands of its employees to take early retirement. In doing so, Verizon required a plan that was economically sensible, as well as one that complied with the various laws that apply to retirement and other benefits. •

After studying this chapter, you should be able to:

1 Name and define each of the main pay for time not worked benefits.
2 Describe each of the main insurance benefits.
3 Discuss the main retirement benefits.
4 Outline the main employees' services benefits.
5 Explain the main flexible benefit programs.

Chapters 11 and 12 addressed compensation and incentive plans. The main purpose of Chapter 13 is to explain employee benefit plans. We discuss four main types of plans: supplemental pay benefits (such as sick leave and vacation pay); insurance benefits (such as workers' compensation); retirement benefits (such as pensions); and employee services (such as child-care facilities). Because legal considerations loom large in any benefits decision, we cover applicable federal laws and their implications for managers.

This chapter completes our discussion of employee compensation and benefits. The next chapter, Ethics, Justice, and Fair Treatment, starts a new part of this book, and focuses on another important human resources task, employee relations.

THE BENEFITS PICTURE TODAY

benefits

Indirect financial and non-financial payments employees receive for continuing their employment with the company.

"What are your benefits?" is the first thing many applicants ask. **Benefits**—indirect financial and non-financial payments employees receive for continuing their employment with the company—are an important part of just about everyone's compensation.[1] They include things like health and life insurance, pensions, time off with pay, and child-care assistance.

Most full-time employees in the United States receive benefits. Virtually all employers—99%—offer some health insurance coverage.[2] About 62% of Americans receive job-based health insurance.[3] Benefits account for about one-third of wages and salaries (or about 30% of total payrolls), with legally required benefits (Social Security, for instance) the most expensive single benefit cost; health insurance usually ranks second.[4] As Figure 13-1 summarizes, annual health care costs rose steadily till 2002, but the rate of increase had moderated lately. By one estimate, the cost of medical coverage recently was about $314 per month for employee-only coverage, $627 per month for employee plus one dependent coverage, and $888 per month for family coverage.[5] Figure 13-2 summarizes the breakdown of benefits as a percentage of wages and salaries.[6]

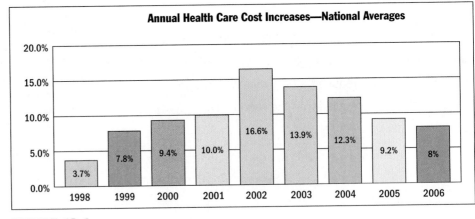

FIGURE 13-1

Annual Health Care Cost Increases—National Averages

Sources: Eric Parmenter, "Controlling Health Care Costs," *Compensation and Benefits Review*, September/October 2002, p. 44; Leah Carlson, "Health Care Cost Increases Easing," *Employee Benefit News*, Oct. 1, 2004, Item 04274002; Trevor Thomas, "Studies Hint at Slowing Health Care Cost Increases," *National Underwriter Life & Health*, Oct. 24, 2005, vol. 109, p. 8; "Health Care Cost Increases Expected to Slow in 2006," *Managing Benefits Plans*, April 2006, p. 9.

FIGURE 13-2

Private-Sector Employer Compensation Costs, December 2006

Source: "Employer Costs for Employer Compensation— December 2006," *Bureau of Labor Statistics*, Washington D.C. 20212, www.bls.gov/ news.release/pdf/ecec.pdf, accessed May 21, 2007.

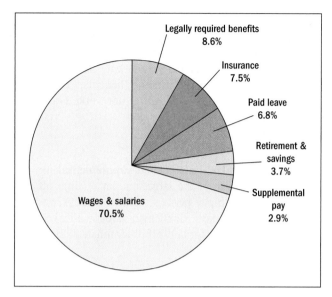

Employees understand the value of health benefits. One study concluded that employees whose firms provided such benefits accepted wages about 20% lower than what they would have received working at firms without them.[7] But another survey found that only 43% of surveyed employees were satisfied with their health plans' overall performance. Less than half trust their employers to design health plans that provide the coverage they need.[8]

Policy Issues   Employers therefore need to design benefits packages with care. A short list of policy issues would include: what benefits to offer; who receives coverage; whether to include retirees in the plan; whether to deny benefits to employees during initial "probationary" periods; how to finance benefits; the degree of employee choice in determining benefits; cost-containment procedures; and how to communicate benefits options to employees.[9]

Some benefits are required by federal or state law, while others are discretionary (see Table 13-1). However, we'll see that even the "discretionary" benefits are often regulated

TABLE 13-1 Some Required and Discretionary Benefits

Benefits Required by Federal or Most State Law	Benefits Discretionary on Part of Employer*
Social Security	Disability, Health, and Life Insurance
Unemployment Insurance	Pensions
Workers' Compensation	Paid Time Off for Vacations, Holidays, Sick Leave, Personal Leave, Jury Duty, etc.
Leaves under Family Medical Leave Act	Employee Assistance and Counseling Programs
	"Family Friendly" benefits for Child Care, Elder Care, Flexible Work Schedules, etc.
	Executive Perquisites

*While not required under federal law, all these benefits are regulated in some way by federal law, as explained in this chapter.

by federal law. Of course, employers also must adhere to the laws of the states in which they do business. For example, California requires most state contractors to provide domestic partner benefits for employees who are in same-sex relationships.[10]

There are many benefits and various ways to classify them. We will classify them as (1) pay for time not worked, (2) insurance benefits, (3) retirement benefits, and (4) services. We start our discussion with pay for time not worked.

PAY FOR TIME NOT WORKED

1 Name and define each of the main pay for time not worked benefits.

supplemental pay benefits
Benefits for time not worked such as unemployment insurance, vacation and holiday pay, and sick pay.

unemployment insurance
Provides benefits if a person is unable to work through some fault other than his or her own.

Pay for time not worked—also called **supplemental pay benefits**—is one of the most costly benefits, because of the large amount of time off that many employees receive. Common time-off-with-pay periods include holidays, vacations, jury duty, funeral leave, military duty, personal days, sick leave, sabbatical leave, maternity leave, and unemployment insurance payments for laid-off or terminated employees.

Unemployment Insurance

All states have **unemployment insurance** or **compensation** laws. These provide benefits if a person is unable to work through no fault of his or her own. The benefits derive from a tax on employers that can range from 0.1 to 5% of taxable payroll in most states. An employer's unemployment tax rate reflects its rate of employee terminations. States have their own unemployment laws, but they all follow federal guidelines.

Firms aren't required to just let everyone they dismiss receive unemployment benefits—only those released through no fault of their own. Thus, strictly speaking, a worker fired for chronic lateness can't legitimately claim benefits. But many managers take a lackadaisical attitude toward protecting their employers against unwarranted claims. Employers therefore spend thousands of dollars per year on unemployment taxes that would not be necessary if they protected themselves.

Following the checklist in Table 13-2 can help protect the employer. Determine whether you could answer "yes" to questions such as, "Do you have a rule that three days' absence without calling is reason for automatic discharge?" Doing so should enable you to

Unemployment insurance/compensation laws provide short term benefits to people who lose their jobs through no fault of their own.

TABLE 13-2 An Unemployment Insurance Cost-Control To-Do Checklist

Do You:

1. Keep documented history of lateness, absence, and warning notices
2. Warn chronically late employees before discharging them
3. Have policy that three days' absence without calling in is reason for automatic discharge
4. Request doctor's note on return to work after absence
5. Make written approval for personal leave mandatory
6. Stipulate date for return to work from leave
7. Obtain a signed resignation statement
8. Mail job abandonment letter if employee fails to return on time
9. Require new employees to stipulate in writing their availability to work overtime, night shifts, etc.
10. Set probationary periods to evaluate new employees
11. Conduct follow-up interviews one to two months after hire
12. Document all instances of poor performance, recording when and how employees did not meet job requirements
13. Require supervisors to document the steps taken to remedy the situation
14. Require supervisors to document employee's refusal of advice and direction
15. Make sure all policies and rules of conduct are understood by all employees
16. Require all employees to sign a statement acknowledging acceptance of firm's policies and rules
17. File the protest against a former employee's unemployment claim on time (usually within 10 days)
18. Use proper terminology on claim form and attach documented evidence regarding separation
19. Attend hearings and appeal unwarranted claims
20. Check every claim against the individual's personnel file
21. Routinely conduct exit interviews to produce information for protesting unemployment claims
22. Hold periodic workshops with supervisors to review procedures and support effort to reduce turnover costs
23. Identify turnover problems as they occur by
    a. location
    b. department
    c. classification of employee

better demonstrate that a dismissal was a result of the person's inadequate performance rather than lack of work or some other cause beyond his or her control.

Vacations and Holidays

The number of paid employee vacation days varies considerably from employer to employer. In the United States, the average is about 10 days per year. However, even for the same employer, long-term employees traditionally get more vacation days. Thus, based on the U.S. Bureau of Labor Statistics March 2006 survey, a typical U.S. company's policy might call for:

1. Eight to 9 days after 1 year of service;
2. Eleven days after 3 years of service;

3. Thirteen days after 5 years of service;

4. Sixteen to 19 days thereafter.

The number of paid holidays also varies considerably from employer to employer, from about 5 days to 13 or more; as of 2006, the average was 8. The most common paid holidays include New Year's Day, Memorial Day, Independence Day, Labor Day, Thanksgiving Day, and Christmas Day. Other common holidays include Martin Luther King, Jr. Day, Good Friday, Presidents' Day, Veterans' Day, the Friday after Thanksgiving, the day before Christmas Day, and the day before New Year's Day.[11]

Firms have to address several holiday- and vacation-related policy issues. They must decide, of course, how many days off employees will get, and which (if any) will be the paid holidays. Other vacation policy decisions include:

- Will employees get their regular base pay while on vacation, or vacation pay based on average earnings (which may include overtime)?
- Will employees get paid for accrued vacation time if they leave before taking their vacations?
- Will we pay employees for a holiday if they don't come to work the day before and the day after the holiday?
- And, should we pay some premium—such as time and a half—when employees must work on holidays?

Wage surveys and Web sites like hrtools.com provide sample vacation policies for inclusion in the firm's employee manual. The "Know Your Employment Law" feature describes some legal aspects to consider.

Know Your Employment LAW   Vacations and Holidays

While federal law does not require vacation benefits, the employer must still formulate vacation policy with care. As an example, the employer generally must pay the employee for his or her earned but unused vacation when the employee terminates. However, the employer defines "earned." For example, if the employer's vacation policy requires that a new employee pass his or her first employment anniversary before becoming entitled to a vacation, the employee gets no vacation pay if he or she leaves for any reason during that first year. Similarly, if the vacation policy simply says that an employee receives, say, a two-week vacation after two years with the company, he or she may not be eligible for any pro rata vacation if he or she leaves before the end of two years. Many employers write a vacation policy that says vacation pay accrues, say, on a biweekly basis. By doing so they obligate themselves to pay employees pro rata vacation pay when they leave the firm.

One question that may arise is whether the employer has the right to cancel an employee's scheduled vacation, for instance, due to a rush of orders. Here it's important that the employer formulate its vacation policy so it is clear that the employer reserves the right to require vacation cancellation and rescheduling if production so demands. If the employee works during what would otherwise be his or her vacation period, the employee should then be paid both his or her regular pay and vacation pay for the period ("pay in lieu of vacation"), assuming the employer does not simply reschedule the vacation.

Sick Leave

sick leave

Provides pay to an employee when he or she is out of work because of illness.

Sick leave provides pay to employees when they're out of work due to illness. Most sick leave policies grant full pay for a specified number of sick days—usually up to about 12 per year. The sick days usually accumulate at the rate of, say, one day per month of service.

Sick leave pay causes trouble for many employers. The problem is that while many employees use their sick days only when they are legitimately sick, others use it for personal leave and as extensions to vacations, whether sick or not. In one survey, personal illnesses accounted for only about 45% of unscheduled sick leave absences. Family issues (27%), personal needs (13%), a mentality of "entitlement" (9%), and stress (6%) were other reasons cited.[12] One survey found that the average cost of absenteeism per employee per year was $789, with personal illness accounting for about a third of the absences.[13]

Cost-Reduction Tactics   Employers have tried several tactics to reduce excessive sick-leave absence. Some repurchase unused sick leave at the end of the year by paying their employees a sum for each sick leave day not used. The drawback is that the policy can encourage legitimately sick employees to come to work despite their illness. Others have experimented with holding monthly lotteries in which only employees with perfect monthly attendance are eligible for a cash prize. Marriott has a program called BeneTrade through which employees can trade the value of some sick days for other benefits. Others aggressively investigate all absences, for instance, by calling the absent employees at their homes when they are out sick.[14]

Many employers—about 66%—use pooled paid leave plans.[15] These plans lump together sick leave, vacation, and holidays into a single leave pool. For example, one hospital previously granted new employees 25 days off per year (10 vacation days, three personal days, and 12 sick days). Employees used, on average, five of those 12 sick days (as well as all vacations and personal days).[16] The pooled paid leave plan allowed new employees to accrue 18 days to use as they saw fit. ("Catastrophic leaves"—defined as short-term illnesses causing absences for more than five consecutive workdays, as well as special absences like jury duty and bereavement leave—were handled with separate accounts.) The pooled plan reportedly resulted in a saving of almost $400,000 over three years in lower overtime, and $350,000 in reduced temporary help.

Many of the manager's day-to-day leaves-related questions involve legal issues. The "Know Your Empoyment Law" feature below addresses some pertinent issues.

Parental Leave and the Family and Medical Leave Act

Parental leave is an important benefit. About half of workers are women, and about 80% will become pregnant during their work lives. Furthermore, many women and men are heads of single-parent households. Under the Pregnancy Discrimination Act, employers must treat women applying for pregnancy leave as they would any employee requesting a leave under the employer's policies. Beyond this, congress passed, as we noted, the Family and Medical Leave Act of 1993 (FMLA). Among other things (see Figure 13-3), the law stipulates that:

1. Private employers of 50 or more employees must provide eligible employees (women or men) up to 12 weeks of unpaid leave for their own serious illness, the birth or adoption of a child, or the care of a seriously ill child, spouse, or parent.
2. Employers may require employees to take any unused paid sick leave or annual leave as part of the 12-week leave provided in the law.

Dealing with requests for leaves is a common supervisory issue, and so managers must be familiar with the basics of leaves-related laws such as the *Family and Medical Leave Act (FMLA)*.

Under the *Family and Medical Leave Act*, the *Americans with Disabilities Act (ADA)*, or state *workers' compensation laws*, some leaves are statutorily required. For example, under the FMLA the employer must grant

Your Rights
under the
Family and Medical Leave Act of 1993

FMLA requires covered employers to provide up to 12 weeks of unpaid, job-protected leave to "eligible" employees for certain family and medical reasons. Employees are eligible if they have worked for their employer for at least one year, and for 1,250 hours over the previous 12 months, and if there are at least 50 employees within 75 miles. The FMLA permits employees to take leave on an intermittent basis or to work a reduced schedule under certain circumstances.

Reasons for Taking Leave:

Unpaid leave must be granted for *any* of the following reasons:

• to care for the employee's child after birth, or placement for adoption or foster care;

• to care for the employee's spouse, son or daughter, or parent who has a serious health condition; or

• for a serious health condition that makes the employee unable to perform the employee's job.

At the employee's or employer's option, certain kinds of *paid* leave may be substituted for unpaid leave.

Advance Notice and Medical Certification:

The employee may be required to provide advance leave notice and medical certification. Taking of leave may be denied if requirements are not met.

• The employee ordinarily must provide 30 days advance notice when the leave is "foreseeable."

• An employer may require medical certification to support a request for leave because of a serious health condition, and may require second or third opinions (at the employer's expense) and a fitness for duty report to return to work.

Job Benefits and Protection:

• For the duration of FMLA leave, the employer must maintain the employee's health coverage under any "group health plan."

• Upon return from FMLA leave, most employees must be restored to their original or equivalent positions with equivalent pay, benefits, and other employment terms.

• The use of FMLA leave cannot result in the loss of any employment benefit that accrued prior to the start of an employee's leave.

Unlawful Acts by Employers:

FMLA makes it unlawful for any employer to:

• interfere with, restrain, or deny the exercise of any right provided under FMLA.

• discharge or discriminate against any person for opposing any practice made unlawful by FMLA or for involvement in any proceeding under or relating to FMLA.

Enforcement:

• The U.S. Department of Labor is authorized to investigate and resolve complaints of violations.

• An eligible employee may bring a civil action against an employer for violations.

FMLA does not affect any Federal or State law prohibiting discrimination, or supersede any State or local law or collective bargaining agreement which provides greater family or medical leave rights.

For Additional Information:

If you have access to the Internet visit our FMLA website: **http://www.dol.gov.** To locate your nearest Wage-Hour Office, telephone our Wage-Hour toll-free information and help line at 1-866-4USWAGE (1-866-487-9243); a customer service representative is available to assist you with referral information from 8am to 5pm **in your time zone;** or log onto our Home Page at **http://www.wagehour.dol.gov.**

U.S. Department of Labor
Employment Standards Administration
Wage and Hour Division
Washington, D.C. 20210

WH Publication 1420
Revised August 2001

FIGURE 13-3

Your Rights under the Family and Medical Leave Act of 1993

an employee 12 weeks of leave in a 12-month period for the birth or care of a newborn child; placement of a child for adoption or foster care; to care for a spouse, child, or parent with a serious health condition; or to care for the employee's own serious health condition. Figure 13-3 ("Your Rights under the Federal Family and Medical Leave Act of 1993") presents the Department of Labor's employment poster outlining the FMLA's basic requirements. Under the *Americans with Disabilities Act*, a qualified employee with a disability may be eligible for a leave if such a leave is necessary to reasonably accommodate the employee. Under various state *workers' compensation laws*, employees may be eligible for medical expense reimbursement and disability income and leave in connection with work-related injuries.

Leave decisions get particularly tricky when two or more federal laws apply. For example, an employee's workers compensation leave can count against that person's FMLA leave entitlement "provided the reason for the absence is due to a qualifying serious illness or injury and the employer properly notifies the employee in writing that the leave will be counted as FMLA leave."[17] Similarly, an employer can count leave taken due to pregnancy complications against the 12 weeks of FMLA leave for the birth and care of a child. See www.dol.gov/elaws for further guidelines.

Most employers also grant personal leave for things like non-health-related personal crises.[18] The main legal obligation here is to ensure that the company awards and extends personal leaves in a nondiscriminatory manner. If the employee fails to return once the unpaid personal leave expires, then the manager should invoke the company's job abandonment or attendance discipline policies.[19]

3. Employees taking leave are entitled to receive health benefits while they are on unpaid leave, under the same terms and conditions as when they were on the job.
4. Employers must guarantee most employees the right to return to their previous or equivalent position with no loss of benefits at the end of the leave.

FMLA Employer Concerns FMLA leaves are usually unpaid (see Figure 13-4), but they're not costless. The costs associated with hiring temporary replacements, training them, and compensating for their lower productivity can be considerable.

Employers have expressed some dissatisfaction with the FMLA. A survey of 416 human resource professionals found that about half said they approved leaves they believed were not legitimate, but felt they had to grant because of vague interpretations of the law.[20] For example, a "serious health condition that makes the employee unable to form the job" is one reason for FMLA leave; unfortunately, it's not clear what this means. The Act seems to exclude short-term conditions. However, the Department of Labor's FMLA regulations seem to set a lower bar; that serious health conditions include those where an employee sees a health care provider once, gets a prescription, and is told by the health care provider to call back if the symptoms don't improve.[21]

FMLA Guidelines Therefore, the employer who wants to avoid granting nonrequired FMLA leaves needs to understand some FMLA details (as the poster in Figure 13-3 summarizes). For example, to be eligible for leave under the FMLA, the employee must have worked for the employer for at least a total of 12 months and have worked (not just been paid, as someone might be if on leave) for 1,250 or more hours in the past 12 consecutive months.[22] If these do not apply, no leave is required.

Policy issues therefore loom large. For example, if the employer uses a calendar or fiscal year for its 12-month FMLA period, then an employee could conceivably take two

Please send this request and the U.S. Department of Labor Certification of Health Care Provider form to Human Resources, University Service

Employee Name _____ University ID# _____

Telephone _____ (work) _____ (home) _____ (cell)

Department _____

Supervisor Name _____ Telephone _____

Leave Coordinator Name _____ Telephone _____

Leave to Begin ___/ /_____ Return to Work ___/ /_____

While on Family Illness Leave I plan to use: (check all that apply)

☐ **Leave Without Pay (LWOP)**   ☐ **Sick Leave**   ☐ **Comp Time**
☐ **Annual Leave**   ☐ **Bonus Leave**

I understand that if I am taking this leave as leave without pay, I will pay for my health benefits should I want them to continue while I am on Family Illness Leave. I also understand that I must provide written notice of my intention to return to work prior to the end of my leave and return to duty within or at the end of the time granted. Failure to report at the expiration of a leave, unless an extension has been requested and approved, may be considered as a resignation.

Employee Signature _____ **Date** _____

Supervisor Signature _____ **Date** _____

Human Resources Signature _____ **Date** _____

FIGURE 13-4

University Family Illness Leave Request

12-week leaves back-to-back. To avoid this, write the policy so the clock starts again on the date the employee returns from his or her last leave. Similarly, keep in mind that under the FMLA the employee must give the employer 30 days' advance notice if the need is foreseeable.

Employers obviously need clear procedures for leaves of absence (including those awarded under the Family and Medical Leave Act). These include:

- In general, no employee should be given a leave until it's clear what the leave is for.
- If the leave is for medical or family reasons, the employer should obtain medical certification from the attending physician or medical practitioner.

- A standard form should also place on record the employee's expected return date, and the fact that without an authorized extension, the firm may terminate his or her employment.
- One employment lawyer says employers should "kind of bend over backward" when deciding if an employee is eligible for leave based on an FMLA situation.[23] However, employers can require independent medical assessments before approving paid FMLA disability leaves.[24]

Some employers are enriching their parental leave plans to make it more attractive for mothers to return from maternity leave. Tactics include: increasing maternity leave pay; communicating benefits and supports proactively; keeping in touch throughout the maternity leave; offering meaningful jobs with reduced travel and hours; giving mothers fair access to bonuses and incentives; and facilitating longer leaves.[25]

Severance Pay

severance pay
A one-time payment some employers provide when terminating an employee.

Many employers provide **severance pay**—a one-time separation payment when terminating an employee. Severance pay makes sense. It is a humanitarian gesture, and good public relations. In addition, most managers expect employees to give them one or two weeks' notice if they plan to quit, so it seems appropriate to provide a few weeks' severance pay when dismissing an employee. Avoiding litigation from disgruntled former employees is another reason. Severance pay plans also help reassure employees who stay on after the employer downsizes its workforce that they'll receive some financial help if they're let go, too.

For whatever reason, severance pay is common. In one survey of 3,000 human resource managers, 82% of responding organizations (ranging from 66% for very small firms to over 90% for larger firms) reported having a severance policy.[26] Just about all full time employees of "old economy" U.S. companies (such as steel and autos) and about half their part time workers are eligible for severance pay.

The reason for the dismissal affects whether the employee gets severance pay. For example, about 95% of employees dismissed due to downsizings got severance pay, while only about a third of employers offered severance in cases of termination for poor performance. Those who quit or are dismissed for cause rarely get severance. About half the employees receiving severance pay get lump-sum amounts; the others receive salary continuation for a time. The average maximum severance is 39 weeks for executives and about 30 weeks for other downsized employees.[27] Severance pay at the rate of one and one half of severance pay for each year of service seems about average.

Severance Pay and ERISA   While federal law generally doesn't require severance pay, an employer could well find its voluntary severance plan covered by ERISA rules.[28] Whether the plan becomes subject to ERISA depends on two things. If the employer has a *legal obligation* (for instance, under a union contract) to make severance payments, then the plan comes under ERISA. Second, a voluntary plan could come under ERISA if the employer identifies it (for instance in employee handbooks or even by verbal assurances) as a plan or program established or maintained by the employer.

Guidelines   In any event, there are several things to keep in mind when crafting the severance plan. These include,

- Cover the situations for which the firm will pay severance, such as layoffs resulting from internal reorganizations. Indicate that action regarding other situations will be determined by management is necessary.
- Require signing of a waiver/general release prior to remittance of any severance pay, absolving the employer from employment related liability. Note that to be an

effective release, the signing of the release must be knowing and voluntary, and there are additional legal requirements.

- Reserve the right to terminate or alter the policy.
- Make it clear that any severance payments continue until only the deadline, or until the employee gets a new job, whichever occurs first.
- Remember that as with all personnel actions, the employer must make severance payments, if any, equitably.[29]

supplemental unemployment benefits
Provide for a "guaranteed annual income" in certain industries where employers must shut down to change machinery or due to reduced work. These benefits are paid by the company and supplement unemployment benefits.

Supplemental Unemployment Benefits

In some industries such as automaking, shutdowns to reduce inventories or change machinery are common, and laid-off or furloughed employees must depend on unemployment insurance. Some companies pay **supplemental unemployment benefits**. As the name implies, these cash payments supplement the employee's unemployment compensation, to help the person maintain his or her standard of living while out of work. They generally cover three contingencies: layoffs, reduced workweeks, and facility relocations.

❷ Describe each of the main insurance benefits.

INSURANCE BENEFITS

Most employers also provide a number of required or voluntary insurance benefits, such as workers' compensation and health insurance.

Workers' Compensation

workers' compensation
Provides income and medical benefits to work-related accident victims or their dependents regardless of fault.

Workers' compensation laws aim to provide sure, prompt income and medical benefits to work-related accident victims or their dependents, regardless of fault. Every state has its own workers' compensation law and commission, and some run their own insurance programs. However, most require employers to carry workers' compensation insurance with private, state-approved insurance companies. Neither the state nor the federal government contributes any funds for workers' compensation.

How Benefits Are Determined   Workers' compensation benefits can be monetary or medical. In the event of a worker's death or disablement, the person's dependents receive a cash benefit based on prior earnings—usually one-half to two-thirds the worker's average weekly wage, per week of employment. In most states, there is a set time limit—such as 500 weeks—for which benefits can be paid. If the injury causes a specific loss (such as an arm), the employee may receive additional benefits based on a statutory list of losses, even though he or she may return to work. In addition to these cash benefits, employers must furnish medical, surgical, and hospital services as required for the employee.

For workers' compensation to cover an injury or work-related illness, one must only prove that it arose while the worker was on the job. It does not matter that he or she may have been at fault; if the person was on the job when the injury occurred, he or she is entitled to workers' compensation. For example, suppose you instruct all employees to wear safety goggles when at their machines. One worker does not and experiences an injury while on the job. The company must still provide workers' compensation benefits.

The ADA   The employment provisions of the Americans with Disabilities Act (ADA) influence employers' workers' compensation procedures. For one thing, ADA provisions generally prohibit employers from inquiring about an applicant's workers' compensation history, a practice that was widespread before the Act's passage. Furthermore, the ADA makes it more important that injured employees get back to work quickly or be accommodated if their injury leads to a disability. Failing to let an employee who is on injury-related workers' compensation return to work, or not accommodate him or her, could lead to law-suits under ADA.

Controlling Workers' Compensation Costs   It is important to control workers' compensation claims (and therefore costs). While it's usually the employer's insurance company that pays the claim, the costs of the employer's premiums reflect the amount of claims. These costs recently grew by 3.5% overall while wages grew by just 2.4%.[30] Workers' comp claims also tend to correlate with injuries, and so fewer claims is usually a sign of fewer accidents.

In practice, there are several ways to reduce workers' compensation claims. Screen out accident-prone workers. Reduce accident-causing conditions in your facilities. And reduce the accidents and health problems that trigger these claims—for instance, by instituting effective safety and health programs and complying with government safety standards. Furthermore, while many workers' compensation claims are legitimate, some are not. Supervisors should therefore watch for typical fraudulent claim red flags, including: vague accident details; minor accidents resulting in major injuries; lack of witnesses; injuries occurring late Friday or very early Monday; and late reporting.[31]

It's also important to get injured employees back on the job as fast as possible, since workers' compensation costs accumulate as long as the person is out of work. Many firms have rehabilitation programs. These include physical therapy; career counseling to guide injured employees into new, less strenuous jobs; and nursing assistance to help reintegrate recipients back into your workforce.[32]

case management

Treating injured workers on a case-by-case basis using an assigned case manager, who coordinates the employee's treatments.

Case management is a popular cost-control option. It is "the treatment of injured workers on a case-by-case basis by an assigned manager, usually a registered nurse, who coordinates with the physician and health plan to determine which care settings are the most effective for quality care and cost."[33] Respondents in one survey found that safety/injury protection and case management were the most common workers' compensation cost-containment measures. Other workers' comp cost control techniques include monitoring health care providers for compliance with their fee schedules, and auditing medical bills.[34] Employers can also select insurers based on their level of service and flexibility in negotiating rates.[35]

Hospitalization, Health, and Disability Insurance

Health insurance looms large in many people's choice of employer, because such insurance is so expensive. Most employers therefore offer some type of hospitalization, medical, and disability insurance. Figure 13-5 illustrates the prevalance of health-related benefits.

Hospitalization, health, and disability insurance helps protect employees against hospitalization costs and the loss of income arising from off-the-job accidents or illness. Many employers purchase the insurance from life insurance companies, casualty insurance companies, or Blue Cross (for hospital expenses) and Blue Shield (for physician expenses) organizations. Others contract with health maintenance organizations or preferred provider organizations.

Coverage   Most health insurance plans provide at least basic hospitalization and surgical and medical insurance for all eligible employees at group rates. Insurance is generally available to all employees—including new nonprobationary ones—regardless of health or physical condition. Most basic plans pay for hospital room and board, surgery charges, and medical expenses (such as doctors' visits to the hospital). Some also provide major medical coverage to meet the high medical expenses resulting from long-term or serious illnesses.

FIGURE 13-5

Access to and Participation by Workers for Selected Benefits, Private Industry, March 2006

Source: "National Compensation Survey: Employee Benefits in Private Industry in the United States, March 2006," U.S. Department of Labor, U.S. Bureau of Labor Statistics, August 2006.

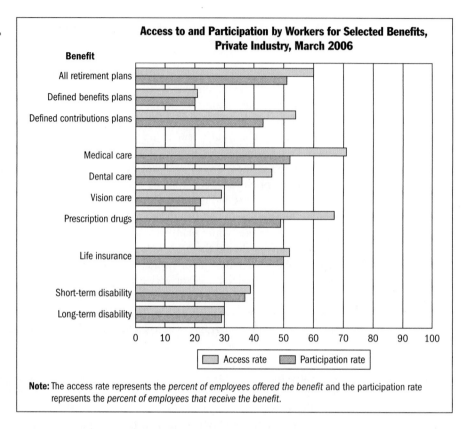

Access to and Participation by Workers for Selected Benefits, Private Industry, March 2006

Note: The access rate represents the *percent of employees offered the benefit* and the participation rate represents the *percent of employees that receive the benefit.*

Most employers' insurance plans cover health-related expenses like doctors' visits, eye care, and dental services. Other plans pay for general and diagnostic visits to the doctor's office, vision care, hearing aids, and prescription drugs. In most employer-sponsored dental plans, employees pay a specific amount of deductible dental expenses before the plan kicks in with benefits. *Disability insurance* provides income protection for salary loss due to illness or accident. Payments usually start when normal sick leave payments end, and may continue until age 65 or beyond. The benefits usually range from 50 to 75% of the employee's base pay if he or she is disabled.

HMOs Many employers offer membership in a **health maintenance organization (HMO)** as a hospital/medical option. The HMO is a medical organization consisting of specialists (surgeons, psychiatrists, and so on), often operating out of a health care center. It provides routine medical services to employees who pay a nominal fee. Employees often have general practitioner "gatekeeper" doctors who need to approve appointments with specialist doctors. The HMO receives a fixed annual fee per employee from the employer (or employer and employee), regardless of whether it provides that person service.

PPOs **Preferred provider organizations (PPOs)** are a cross between HMOs and the traditional doctor–patient arrangement: They are "groups of health care providers that contract with employers, insurance companies, or third-party payers to provide medical care services at a reduced fee."[36] Unlike HMOs (whose relatively limited lists of health care providers are often located in one health care center), PPOs let employees select providers (like doctors) from a relatively wide list, and see them in their offices, often without gatekeeper doctor approval. The providers agree to provide discounts and submit to certain utilization controls, such as on the number of diagnostic tests they can order.[37]

health maintenance organization (HMO)
A prepaid health care system that generally provides routine round-the-clock medical services as well as preventive medicine in a clinic-type arrangement for employees, who pay a nominal fee in addition to the fixed annual fee the employer pays.

preferred provider organizations (PPOs)
Groups of health care providers that contract with employers, insurance companies, or third-party payers to provide medical care services at a reduced fee.

Mental Health Benefits Mental illnesses account for a large portion of the disabilities in the United States, Canada, and Western Europe. The World Health Organization estimates that more than 34 million people in the United States between the ages of 18 and 64 suffer from mental illness.[38] Mental illnesses represent about 24% of all reported disabilities, considerably more than disabling injuries, respiratory diseases, cardiovascular diseases, and cancer combined.

Mental health treatment costs are rising because of widespread drug and alcohol problems, an increase in the number of states that require employers to offer a minimum package of mental health benefits, and the fact that other health care claims are higher for employees with high mental health claims. Some employers are slowing the rise in mental health benefits by monitoring the benefit's costs, and by instituting utilization reviews to certify treatment and offering increased outpatient benefits. The Mental Health Parity Act of 1996 sets minimum mental health care benefits at the national level.

Various other laws impact health care benefits; we discuss this in the "Know Your Employment Law" feature below.

Trends in Health Care Cost Control

Employers are taking steps to try to rein in spiraling health care costs. Many do this in conjunction with *cost-containment specialists*—companies that specialize in helping employers reduce their health care costs. We'll address several important cost-control trends.

Communication, Involvement, and Empowerment Getting employees more *involved and empowered* in the health care program is important. One cost control expert said, "the biggest criticism of managed care . . . is that the health care consumer has little financial stake in treatment decisions. Today's typical patients consume as much health care as they wish, and someone else pays for it."[39] In one recent survey, 75% of human resource managers said consumer education would be the most critical tactic driving cost control in the years immediately ahead.[40]

How to do this? One solution is to *make sure employees know the costs* of the medical decisions they're making, and to involve them more in plan administration. For example, employers use their intranets to provide employees with access to basic health care coverage and benefits information, promote in-network services to employees, and encourage employees to reevaluate their health care market options frequently. *Online selection software* allows employees to choose the best of the employer's health care offerings based on input from employees concerning matters like doctor visits, prescriptions, and use of specialists.

Premiums and Co-Pays More employers are requiring employees to pay higher premiums or a greater share of out-of-pocket costs in the form of higher deductibles and copayments.[41]

Prevention Programs Many illnesses are preventable. Almost all large employers (and perhaps 80% of small ones) therefore offer some form of preventive services as benefits. *Clinical prevention* programs include things like mammograms, immunizations, and routine checkups. *Health promotion and disease prevention* programs include things like seminars and incentives aimed at improving health by changing unhealthy behaviors or modifying lifestyles. In one study "employers who undertook prevention programs aimed at cardiovascular disease, the most costly preventable illness, reported an average 28% reduction in sick leave, a 26% reduction in direct health-care costs, and a 30% reduction in workers compensation and disability cause."[42]

Know Your Employment LAW Health Care Benefits

Various federal laws influence employers' health care insurance decisions. For example, the Employee Retirement Income Security act of 1974 (ERISA) sets minimum standards for most voluntarily established pension and health plans in private industry. Among other things, it requires plans to provide participants with plan information (including plan features and funding), and outlines fiduciary responsibilities for those who manage the plans.[43] (We'll discuss ERISA again below, under pensions).

The Newborn Mother's Protection Act of 1996 prohibits an employer's health plan from using incentives to encourage employees to leave the hospital after childbirth after less than the legislatively determined minimum stay. *The Mental Health Parity Act of 1996* limits health plans' ability to set annual or lifetime maximums on mental and nervous disorders benefits.

Employers who provide health care services (such as in-house counseling or medical facilities) must follow the privacy rules of the *Health Insurance Portability and Accountability Act of 1996 (HIPAA)*. These rules set minimum requirements for protecting individuals' health care data accessibility and confidentiality.[44] While most closely identified with protecting Americans' medical records privacy, HIPAA also limits exclusions for certain pre-existing conditions, and prohibits discrimination against employees and dependants based on their health status.

Employers must provide the same health care benefits to employees over the age of 65 that they do to younger workers, even though the older workers

Detailed record keeping is crucial for COBRA compliance. The following checklist is designed to ensure that the proper records are maintained for problem-free COBRA compliance.

	Yes	No
• Do you maintain records so that is easily determined who is covered by your group health care plan?	☐	☐
• Do you record terminations of covered employees as soon as terminations occur?	☐	☐
• Do you track reduction of hours of employees covered by group health care plans?	☐	☐
• Do you track deaths of employees covered by group health care plans?	☐	☐
• Do you track leaves of absence of employees covered by group health care plans?	☐	☐
• Do you track Medicare eligibility of employees covered by group health care plans?	☐	☐
• Do you track the disability status of employees covered by group health care plans?	☐	☐
• Do you track retirees covered by group health care plans?	☐	☐
• Do you maintain current addresses of employees?	☐	☐
• Do you maintain current addresses of individuals receiving COBRA benefits?	☐	☐
• Do you require employees to provide a written acknowledgement that they have received notice of their COBRA rights?	☐	☐
• Do you have a system to determine who has paid COBRA premiums on time?	☐	☐
• Do you have a system to determine who has obtained other group health coverage so that they are no longer eligible for COBRA under your plan?	☐	☐
• Do you maintain a telephone log of calls received about COBRA?	☐	☐
• Do you maintain a record of changes in your plan?	☐	☐
• Do you maintain a record of how premiums are calculated?	☐	☐
• Do you maintain a log of those employees who are denied COBRA coverage?	☐	☐
• Do you maintain a log of why employees are denied COBRA coverage?	☐	☐

FIGURE 13-6

COBRA Record-Keeping Compliance Checklist

Source: Reprinted from www.HR.BLR.com with permission of the publisher *Business and Legal Reports, Inc.*, 141 Mill Rock Road East, Old Saybrook, CT © 2004.

are eligible for federally funded Medicare health insurance. Employers' health and hospitalization plans must also comply with the *Americans with Disabilities Act*. For example, the plan generally shouldn't make distinctions based on disability.

As explained earlier, the *Pregnancy Discrimination Act* requires employers to treat women affected by pregnancy, childbirth, or related medical conditions the same as any employees not able to work, with respect to all benefits, including disability benefits and health and medical insurance.

COBRA Requirements

The ominously titled COBRA—Consolidated Omnibus Budget Reconciliation Act—requires most private employers to continue to make health benefits available to terminated or retired employees and their families for a period of time, generally 18 months.[45] The former employee must pay for the coverage, as well as a small fee for administrative costs.

Employers who ignore COBRA's regulations do so at their peril. For example, you don't want terminated or retired employees to be injured and then claim you never told them they could have continued their insurance coverage. Therefore, when a new employee first becomes eligible for your company's insurance plan, that person must receive (and acknowledge receiving) an explanation of his or her COBRA rights. Similarly, all employees separated from the company for any reason should sign a form acknowledging that they received and understand the information about their COBRA rights. Figure 13-6 provides a COBRA checklist. COBRA and HIPAA are both amendments to ERISA.

Health Savings Accounts   The Medicare Modernization Act of 2003 contains a provision allowing employers to establish tax-free health savings accounts (HSA). After depositing pre-tax pay in their HSAs, employees or their families can use these to pay for "low dollar" (not catastrophic) medical expenses. Employers typically combine HSA plans with health care plans that have large out-of-pocket deductibles. The assumption is that this will motivate employees to take steps to utilize less expensive health care options, and thus avoid having to pay big deductibles. The basic idea is to encourage employees to make more educated health care decisions.[46]

Claim Audits   It makes little sense to initiate things like prevention plans or HSAs when employers are paying out thousands or millions of dollars in erroneous claims. Unfortunately, with health care plans becoming ever-more customized and therefore complicated, it's increasingly easy for medical claims errors to occur. Human Resource consultants Towers Perrin recently conducted a survey of claims payments. Industry standards for percentage of claims with financial errors is 3%, but in two recent years Towers Perrin found the *actual* percentage of claims with financial errors were 6.3% and 6.6%. The industry standard for percentage of claims dollars actually paid in error was 1%; in two recent years the *actual* percentage of claims dollars paid in error were 3.5% and 3.3%. Setting standards for errors, and then aggressively auditing the claims being paid may be the most direct way to reduce employer health care expenses.[47]

Other Cost-Control Options   Employers are taking other steps. Savings come from *automating health care plan administration*, for instance, by making online enrollment mandatory.[48] Other employers are using *defined contribution health care plans*. Under these plans, each employee has a specific dollar amount medical allotment that he or she can use for copayments or discretionary medical costs, rather than a specified health care benefits package with open-ended costs.[49] *Outsourcing* health care plan administration to outside companies for a fee is another option. For example,[50] 84% of firms in one survey said they were outsourcing employee assistance and counseling and 53% were outsourcing health care benefits administration. Many firms are reducing or *eliminating retiree health care coverage*. One study found that about 13% of surveyed employers had reduced subsidized health benefits for their future retirees in the previous two years.[51] (About 17,000 unionized blue-collar employees at GE staged a two-day strike protesting increased premiums for the firm's 25,000 early retirees.)[52] Small firms are joining *benefits purchasing alliances*. By banding together to purchase health care benefits, these employers hope to obtain better choice and purchasing power. Other employers are encouraging employees to have non-urgent medical procedures abroad, where costs are lower.[53]

Long-Term Care

Today, the oldest baby boomers are in their 60s, and long-term care insurance—care to support things like nursing assistance to former employees in their old age—is a key employee benefit. The Health Insurance Portability and Accountability Act, enacted in 1996, lets employers and employees deduct the cost of long-term care insurance premiums from their annual income taxes, making this particular benefit even more attractive.[54] Employers can provide insurance benefits for several types of long-term care, such as adult day care, assisted living, and custodial care.

Life Insurance

group life insurance
Provides lower rates for the employer or employee and includes all employees, including new employees, regardless of health or physical condition.

In addition to hospitalization and medical benefits, most employers provide **group life insurance** plans. Employees can usually obtain lower rates in a group plan. And group plans usually accept all employees—including new nonprobationary ones—regardless of health or physical condition.

In many cases, the employer pays 100% of the base premium, which usually provides life insurance equal to about two years' salary. The employee then pays for any additional coverage. In some cases, the cost of the base premium is split 50/50 or 80/20 between employer and employee. In general, there are three key personnel policies to address: the benefits-paid schedule (the amount of life insurance benefits is usually tied to the employee's annual earnings), supplemental benefits (continued life insurance coverage after retirement, for instance); and financing (the amount and percent that the employee contributes).

Accidental death and dismemberment coverage provides a lump-sum benefit in addition to life insurance benefits when death is accidental. It also provides benefits in case of accidental loss of limbs or sight.

Benefits for Part-Time and Contingent Workers

The Bureau of Labor Statistics, which defines part-time work as less than 35 hours a week, says about 19 million people work part-time. More phased (gradual) retirement programs, a desire to better balance work and family life issues, and more women in the workforce help explain this phenomenon. In any case, about 80% of firms surveyed provide holiday, sick leave, and vacation benefits to part-timers, and over 70% offer some form of health care benefits to part-time workers.[55]

A related issue concerns misclassifying as "independent contractors" or "consultants" contingent workers whose ongoing relationships with the employer actually make them employees. As three attorneys put it, "Short-term, just-in-time workers provided by staffing agencies are not an issue. However the employer's policy for workers who are still on the job after 1,000 to 1,500 hours should require that they be provided with benefits, either through the staffing agency or by outsourcing their administration to an administrative employer who can provide benefits."[56]

RETIREMENT BENEFITS

❸ Discuss the main retirement benefits.

The first contingent of baby boomers turns 65 in the year 2011, and many reportedly won't wait till 65 to retire. This presents two challenges for employers. First, many employees, facing the inevitable aging process, are seeking (or demanding) enhanced retirement benefits. Second, we'll see that employers, facing a looming employee shortage, are taking steps to entice older workers to keep working in some capacity.[57] The major retirement benefits are the federal Social Security program and employer pension/retirement plans, like the 401(k).

Social Security

Social Security

Federal program that provides three types of benefits: retirement income at the age of 62 and thereafter; survivor's or death benefits payable to the employee's dependents regardless of age at time of death; and disability benefits payable to disabled employees and their dependents. These benefits are payable only if the employee is insured under the Social Security Act.

Most people assume that **Social Security** provides income only when they are over 62, but it actually provides three types of benefits. The familiar *retirement benefits* provide an income if you retire at age 62 or thereafter and are insured under the Social Security Act. Second are *survivor's* or *death benefits*. These provide monthly payments to your dependents regardless of your age at death, again assuming you are insured under the Social Security Act. Finally, there are *disability payments*. These provide monthly payments to employees who become totally disabled (and to their dependents) if they work and meet certain requirements. The Social Security system also administers the Medicare program, which provides a wide range of health services to people 65 or over. "Full retirement age" traditionally was 65—the usual age for retirement. However, full retirement age to collect Social Security rose gradually till 1960. It is now 67 for those born in 1960 or later.

A tax on the employee's wages, shared equally by employees and employers, funds Social Security (technically, it is called "Federal Old Age and Survivor's Insurance"). As of 2007, the maximum amount of earnings subject to Social Security tax was $97,500.[58] Employer and employee each paid 7.65%.

Pension Plans

pension plans

Plans that provide a fixed sum when employees reach a predetermined retirement age or when they can no longer work due to disability.

Pensions plans are financial programs that provide income to individuals in their retirement. About half of full-time workers participate in some type of pension plan at work. However, the actual rate of participation depends on several things. For example, older workers tend to have a higher participation rate, and employees of larger firms have participation rates as much as three times as high as those in small firms.

We can classify pension plans in three basic ways: *contributory versus noncontributory* plans; *qualified versus nonqualified* plans; and *defined contribution versus defined benefit* plans.[59] The employee contributes to the contributory pension plan, while the employer makes all contributions to the noncontributory pension plan. Employers derive tax benefits from contributing to qualified pension plans, such as tax deductions for pension plan contributions (they are "qualified" for improved tax treatment); nonqualified pension plans get less favorable tax treatment for employees and employers.

defined benefit pension plan

A plan that contains a formula for determining retirement benefits.

Defined Benefits Plans With **defined benefit plans**, employees know ahead of time the pension benefits they will receive (the benefit is "defined" or specified by amount or formula). The defined pension benefit itself is usually set by a formula that ties the person's retirement pension to an amount equal to a percentage of the person's preretirement pay (for instance, to a fraction of an average of his or her last five years of employment), multiplied by the number of years he or she worked for the company.

defined contribution pension plan
A plan in which the employer's contribution to employees' retirement savings funds is specified.

portability
Instituting policies that enable employees to easily take their accumulated pension funds when they leave employer.

Defined Contribution Plans   In contrast, **defined contribution plans** specify what contribution the employee and/or employer will make to the employee's retirement or savings fund. Here, in other words, the contribution is defined, not the pension. With a defined benefit plan, the employee knows what his or her retirement benefits will be upon retirement. With a defined contribution plan, the person's pension will depend on the amounts contributed to the fund and on the retirement fund's investment earnings. Defined contribution plans prevail among employers today, because of their relative ease of administration, favorable tax treatment, and other factors. **Portability**—making it easier for employees who leave the firm prior to retirement to take their accumulated pension funds with them—is enhanced by switching from defined benefit to defined contribution plans. The former are therefore more appropriate for employees who plan to stay with the firm until retirement.

A MANAGED PORTFOLIO REALLY MAKES A LOT OF SENSE. DEPENDING, OF COURSE, ON WHO'S MANAGING IT.

Firms such as Vanguard, Fidelity, and others can establish online, fully Web-based 401(k) plans even for small firms with 10 to 50 employees.

401(k) plan
A defined contribution plan based on section 401(k) of the Internal Revenue Code.

401(k) Plans   The most popular defined contribution plans are based on section 401(k) of the Internal Revenue Code, and called 401(k) plans. The employee authorizes the employer to deduct a sum of money from his or her paycheck before taxes, and to invest it in the bundle of investments in his or her 401(k). The deduction is pre-tax, so the employee pays no tax on those set-aside dollars until after he or she retires (or removes the money from the 401(k) plan). The person can decide to deduct any amount up to the legal maximum (the IRS sets an annual dollar limit—now about $15,000). The employer arranges, usually with an investment company such as Fidelity Investments, to actually manage the 401(k) plan and to make various investment options available to the company's 401(k) plan. The options typically include mutual stock funds and bond funds.

Employers should choose their 401(k) providers with care, because of the employer's responsibility to its employees, and because changing 401(k) providers can be a "grueling venture."[60] In addition to trustworthiness, employers want a 401(k) plan provider that makes it easy for employer and employee to participate in the plan. Firms such as Vanguard, Fidelity, and others can establish online, fully Web-based 401(k) plans even for small firms with 10 to 50 employees. Employees get various online tools—such as an "asset allocation planner."

Other Defined Contribution Plans   The 401(k) plan is one example of a **savings and thrift plan**.[61] In any savings and thrift plan, employees contribute a portion of their earnings to a fund, and the employer usually matches this contribution in whole or in part. The employer's contributions can be considerable, particularly where competition for employees is intense. Harleysville Group, Inc., matches up to 100% of an employee's contribution up to 6% of his or her salary, in an effort to attract and retain information technology workers. Radio Shack matches 401(k) contributions at 159%.[62]

savings and thrift plan
Plan in which employees contribute a portion of their earnings to a fund; the employer usually matches this contribution in whole or in part.

In a **deferred profit-sharing plan**, employers contribute a portion of their profits in cash to the pension fund, regardless of the level of employee contribution (income taxes on those contributions are deferred until the employee retires or leaves the employer). An **employee stock ownership plan (ESOP)** is a qualified, tax-deductible defined contribution plan in which employers contribute stock to a trust for eventual use by employees who retire.

deferred profit-sharing plan
A plan in which a certain amount of profits is credited to each employee's account, payable at retirement, termination, or death.

employee stock ownership plan (ESOP)
A qualified, tax-deductible stock bonus plan in which employers contribute stock to a trust for eventual use by employees.

cash balance plans
Defined benefit plans under which the employer contributes a percentage of employees' current pay to employees' pension plans every year, and employees earn interest on this amount.

Overall, about 91% of employers offer 401(k) type plans; 67% also offer defined benefit pension plans alongside their 401(k)s, and 18% offer other deferred profit-sharing savings plans.[63]

Cash Balance Pension Plans   These are defined benefit plans for federal tax purposes, but they have the portability advantages of defined contribution plans. In a defined benefit plan, the employer typically multiplies the employee's average pay over the last few years of his or her pre-retirement employment by a predetermined multiple, based on years with the firm, and the result represents the person's annual retirement income. To get the maximum benefit, the person generally must "put in" his or her full 30 or so years with the firm. This approach tends to favor older employees (whose income is often higher and who have been with the firm for a number of years).

Younger employees and/or those who want the option of moving on with their vested pension benefits) after say 7 or 8 years might prefer defined contribution plans. Here the employee gets the full vested value to that point of his or her pension.

Cash balance plans are a hybrid. Under these plans, the employer contributes a percentage of employees' current pay to the employees' pension plans every year, and employees earn interest on this amount. Cash balance plans provide the portability of defined contribution plans with the more predictable benefits of defined benefit plans.[64]

Switching to cash balance plans can be problematic for employers, since doing so typically puts older employees at a disadvantage. Partly in response to numerous lawsuits over this, in August, 2006 President Bush signed into law the Pension Protection act. This makes it clear that employers who offer cash balance pension plans or other plans generally do *not* violate the Age Discrimination in Employment Act.[65]

Pension Planning and the Law

Many federal laws impact pension planning, and in most cases it is basically impossible to formulate a plan without expert help. Most notably, the **Employee Retirement Income Security Act of 1975 (ERISA)** requires that employers have written pension plan documents and adhere to certain guidelines, for instance regarding who is eligible for the employer's plan, and at what point the employer's contribution becomes the employee's (more on this below).[66] ERISA protects the employer's pension or health plans' assets by requiring that those who control the plans act responsibly. The Department of Labor says "the primary responsibility of *fiduciaries* is to run the plan solely in the interest of participants and beneficiaries."

Employee Retirement Income Security Act (ERISA)
Signed into law by President Ford in 1974 to require that pension rights be vested and protected by a government agency, the PBGC.

Employers (and employees) also usually want their pension contributions to be "qualified," or tax deductible, so they must adhere to the pertinent *income tax codes*. Under *labor relations laws*, the employer must let their unions participate in pension plan administration. The *Job Creation and Worker Assistance Act* provides guidelines regarding what rates of return employers should use in computing their pension plan values.

Pension Benefits Guarantee Corporation (PBGC)
Established under ERISA to ensure that pensions meet vesting obligations; also insures pensions should a plan terminate without sufficient funds to meet its vested obligations.

PBGC   ERISA established the **Pension Benefits Guarantee Corporation (PBGC)** to oversee and insure pensions should a plan terminate without sufficient funds. (The PBGC guarantees only defined benefit plans, not defined contribution plans. Furthermore, it will only pay an individual a pension of up to maximum of about $49,000 per year for someone 65 years of age with a plan terminating in 2007. So, high income workers such as airline pilots may still see most of their expected pensions evaporate if their employers go bankrupt).

In developing pension plans to meet their needs, employers must address several key policy issues:

Membership Requirements   For example, what is the minimum age or minimum service at which employees become eligible for a pension? Under the Tax Reform Act of 1986, an employer can require that an employee complete a period of no more than two years' service to the company before becoming eligible to participate in the plan. However, if it requires more than one year of service before eligibility, the plan must grant employees full and immediate vesting rights at the end of that period.

vested funds

Money placed in a pension fund that cannot be forfeited for any reason.

Vesting Vested funds   are the money employer and employee have placed in the latter's pension fund that cannot be forfeited for any reason. The employees' contributions are always theirs, of course. However, until the passage of ERISA, the *employer's* contribution in many pension plans didn't vest until the employee retired. So, you could have worked for a company for 30 years and been left with no pension if the company went bust one year before you were to retire. That generally can't happen today, although as we saw, that's no guarantee that some employees won't get lower pensions than they expected if their plans fail.

Today (the rules changed in 2002) employers can choose one of two minimum vesting schedules (employers can allow funds to vest faster if they wish). With so called *cliff vesting*, the time period for acquiring a nonforfeitable right in employer matching contributions (if any) is three years. So, the employee must have nonforfeitable rights to these funds by the end of three years. With the second option (*graded vesting*) participants in pension plans must receive nonforfeitable rights to the matching contributions as follows: 20% after 2 years, and then 20% for each succeeding year, with a 100% nonforfeitable right by the end of 6 years.

Benefit Formula   This usually ties the (defined) pension to the employee's final earnings, or an average of his or her last three or four years' earnings.

Plan Funding   How will you fund the plan? Will it be contributory or noncontributory?

Early Retirement

To trim their workforces or for other reasons, many employers including GM and Verizon have been encouraging employees to retire early. Many plans take the form of **early retirement window** arrangements in which specific employees (often age 50-plus) are eligible to participate. The "window" means that for a limited time, the company opens up the opportunity for employees to retire earlier than usual. The financial incentive is generally a combination of improved or liberalized pension benefits plus a cash payment.

early retirement window

A type of offering by which employees are encouraged to retire early, the incentive being liberal pension benefits plus perhaps a cash payment.

Employers should use such programs cautiously. Unless structured properly, early retirement programs can be challenged as de facto methods for forcing the discharge of older employees against their will. While it is generally legal to use incentives to encourage individuals to choose early retirement, the employee's decision must be voluntary. In one case (*Paolillo v. Dresser Industries, Inc.*), the employer told employees on October 12 that they were eligible to retire under a "totally voluntary" early retirement program, and must inform the company of their decision by October 18. However, employees didn't get the details of the program until October 15. The employees subsequently sued, claiming coercion. The U.S. Court of Appeals for the Second Circuit (New York) agreed with them, arguing that an employee's decision to retire must be voluntary and made without undue strain.[67]

Waivers Employers must therefore exercise caution in encouraging employees to take early retirement. The Older Workers' Benefit Protection Act (OWBPA) imposes limitations on waivers that purport to release a terminating employee's potential claims against his or her employer based on age discrimination. The waiver of future claims must:

- Be knowing and voluntary,
- Not provide for the release of prospective rights or claims,
- Not be an exchange for benefits to which the employee was already entitled.
- Give the employee ample opportunity to think over the agreement and to seek legal advice.

Early retirement plans can backfire in other ways. When Verizon Communications offered enhanced pension benefits to encourage what it hoped would be 12,000 employees to retire, more than 21,000 took the plan. Verizon had to replace 16,000 managers.[68]

Phased Retirement and the Aging Workforce

In a recent SHRM survey, human resource professionals said the number one demographic trend impacting employers was the aging workforce. The demographic fact of an aging workforce has two implications for employers. First, with the population aging and with the overall workforce growing more slowly, employers will need to attract and retain more older workers. Second, employers will need policies to deal with employees who are older than traditional workers, and who may therefore have somewhat different needs and work preferences.

Employers are dealing with these issues in various ways. A SHRM survey found that 41% of surveyed employers are bringing retirees back into the workforce; 34% are conducting studies to determine projected retirement rates in the organization; and 31% are offering employment options designed to attract and retain semiretired workers.[69]

Given that three out of four employees approaching retirement age say they would rather cut back gradually than retire abruptly, one way to attract and retain these people is to offer *phased retirement programs*. Here, for instance, retirement-eligible employees may get the option to work half-time for several years beyond normal retirement age, before retiring. Only about 16% of employers now offer such phased retirement plans. However, SHRM reports that "the movement toward phased retirement could gain steam if employers have difficulty recruiting skilled workers and need a strategy that retains talent and organizational knowledge."[70]

Improving Productivity Through HRIS: Benefits Management Systems

With health care and drug costs rising fast, human resource managers are struggling to find ways to make their benefits dollars go further. As we noted earlier, they are therefore implementing various health care cost-control strategies. One is to utilize more Web-based technology. One survey found that about 57% of the 192 HR and benefits managers who responded said they will focus on getting more out of existing benefits technology and automation, while 30% of benefits managers said they would be investing in new benefits technology soon.[71]

The motivation for this is that benefits administration can be enormously labor-intensive and time-consuming. Left unautomated, it can require the employer to devote hundreds or thousands of human resource professionals' hours to transactions such as answering employees' questions about comparative benefits, and updating employees' benefits information. Typical questions include, "In which option of the medical plan am I enrolled?" and, "If I retire in two years, what will be my monthly retirement income?" Tasks like these clearly demand intranet-based self-service benefits management applications.

BeneLogic   For example, when the organization that assists Pennsylvania school districts with their insurance needs decided to assist the school boards with automating their benefits administration, they interviewed four solution providers. They chose a company called BeneLogic.[72] The solution, called the Employee Benefit Electronic Service Tool, "lets users manage all aspects of benefits administration, including enrollment, plan descriptions, eligibility, and premium reconciliation, via Microsoft Internet Explorer and Netscape Navigator."[73]

BeneLogic's benefits management system provides the school boards with numerous advantages. BeneLogic hosts and maintains the Web support application on its own servers, and creates customized, Web-based applications for each school district. The system facilitates Web-based employee benefit enrollment, provides centralized call center support for benefit-related questions, and even handles benefits-related payroll, HRIS, and similar functions by partnering with companies like ADP (which manages many of the school boards' payroll functions), and Oracle PeopleSoft (which provides and services many of the school boards' human resource information systems). Each school board employee accesses the BeneLogic site via a link on his or her own board's Web site.

Small Businesses   Systems like these are not just for large employers. For example, consider the paperwork involved when an employee asks, "Can I take my vacation next week?" Answering may require digging through time cards, spreadsheets, and HR folders, and then considering whether the request falls under the Family and Medical Leave Act or COBRA. Even smaller firms therefore often use software like HROffice, from Ascentis Software Corporation. HROffice includes over 100 built-in reports on matters ranging from attendance and benefits to performance reviews and bonuses.[74]

PERSONAL SERVICES AND FAMILY-FRIENDLY BENEFITS

Outline the main employees' services benefits.

While time off, insurance, and retirement benefits account for the lion's share of benefits costs, most employers also provide various services benefits. These include personal services (such as legal and personal counseling), job-related "family-friendly" services (such as child-care facilities), educational subsidies, and executive perquisites (such as company cars for its executives).

Personal Services

Many companies provide the sorts of personal services that most employees need at one time or another. These include credit unions, legal services, counseling, and social and recreational opportunities. (Some employers use the term *voluntary benefits* to cover personal services benefits that range from things like pet insurance to automobile insurance.)[75]

Credit Unions   Credit unions are usually separate businesses established with the employer's assistance to help employees with borrowing and saving needs. Employees usually become members by purchasing a share of the credit union's stock for a small fee—perhaps $5 or $10. Members can then deposit savings that accrue interest at a rate determined by the credit union's board of directors. Loan eligibility and the loan's rate of interest are usually more favorable than those of banks and finance companies.

employee assistance program
A formal employer program for providing employees with counseling and/or treatment programs for problems such as alcoholism, gambling, or stress.

Employee Assistance Programs   **Employee assistance programs (EAPs)** provide counseling and advisory services, such as personal legal and financial services, child and elder care referrals, adoption assistance, mental health counseling, and life event planning.[76] EAPs are increasingly popular, with more than 60% of larger firms offering such programs.

One study found that personal mental health was the most common problem addressed by employee assistance programs, followed by family problems.[77]

For the employer, EAPs produce advantages, not just costs. For example, sick family members and problems like depression account for many of the sick days employees take. Employee assistance programs can reduce such absences by providing expert advice on issues like elder care referrals and disease management.[78]

Key steps for launching a successful EAP program include:

- *Develop a policy statement.* Define the program's purpose, employee eligibility, the roles and responsibilities of various personnel in the organization, and procedures for using the plan.
- *Ensure professional staffing.* Consider the professional and state licensing requirements.
- *Maintain confidential record-keeping systems.* Everyone involved with the EAP, including supervisors, secretaries, and support staff, must understand the importance of confidentiality. Also ensure files are locked, access is limited and monitored, and identifying information is minimized.
- *Be aware of legal issues.* For example, in most states counselors must disclose suspicions of child abuse to appropriate state agencies. Get legal advice on establishing the EAP, carefully screen the credentials of the EAP staff, and obtain professional liability insurance for the EAP.[79]

Family-Friendly Benefits

Several trends are changing the landscape of benefits administration: There are more households where both adults work; more one-parent households; more women in the workforce; more workers over 55; and there's the "time bind"—people working harder and longer, without the time to do all they'd like to do. The issues involve working men, as well as women. One expert on work and family issues says that "for men, particularly the younger ones, it has become more socially acceptable to take time off or flexible schedules to take care of the kids, and employers are responding to this change by granting to fathers the time required."[80]

The pressures of balancing work and family life have led many employers to bolster what they call their **family-friendly benefits**. These generally include benefits like child care, elder care, fitness facilities, and flexible work schedules, benefits that help employees balance their family and work lives.[81]

family-friendly benefits
Benefits such as child care and fitness facilities that make it easier for employees to balance their work and family responsibilities.

Use A survey by the Society for Human Resource Management (SHRM) found that about 29% of employers provided at least some type of child-care assistance.[82] The SHRM survey also found that, of the firms responding, 55% offer flextime, 31% offer compressed workweeks, and 34% permit some telecommuting.[83] (We'll discuss flextime as one of several possible flexible benefits, below). Family-friendly firms routinely turn up on "best companies to work for" lists.[84] We'll look more closely at four family-friendly benefits, subsidized child care, sick-child care, time off, and elder care.

Subsidized Child Care Fulfilling one's work responsibilities while raising a family is a challenge, particularly for single parents. Most working people make private provisions to take care of their children. For example, relatives accounted for 48% of all child-care providers in one study.[85] Organized day care centers accounted for another 30% of child-care arrangements, and nonrelatives accounted for most of the remaining arrangements.

Employers who want to reduce the distractions associated with finding reliable child care can help in various ways. Some employers (about 18% recently) simply investigate

Software giant SAS Institute, Inc., offers generous employee benefits. The North Carolina firm keeps turnover at 4% in an industry where 20% is typical, in large part by offering family-friendly benefits like paid maternity leave, day care on site, lunchtime piano concerts, massages, and yoga classes like this one.

the day care facilities in their communities and recommend certain ones to interested employees. But more employers are setting up company-sponsored and subsidized day care facilities, both to attract employees and to reduce absenteeism. For example, Abbott Laboratories built a $10 million childcare center at its headquarters north of Chicago, daytime home to about 400 children on Abbott employee.[86]

By establishing subsidized day care centers, employers can benefit via improved recruiting results, lower absenteeism, improved morale, favorable publicity, and lower turnover. But, good planning is required. This often starts with a questionnaire to employees to answer questions like, "What would you be willing to pay for care for one child in a child-care center near work?" and "Have you missed work during the past six months because you needed to find new care arrangements?"

Sick Child Benefits What to do when your child is sick and you need to get to work? One study found that unexpected absences climbed to about 2.4% of payroll hours recently, with a cost per absence to employers of about $600 per episode (for temp employees and reduced productivity, for instance). More employers are thus offering emergency child-care benefits, for instance for when a young child's regular babysitter is a no-show. Texas Instruments built a Web database its employees use to find last-minute child care providers. Others, like Canadian financial services company CIBC are expanding their on-site child care centers to handle last-minute emergencies.[87]

Elder Care Elder care benefits are important for much the same reasons as are childcare benefits: The responsibility for caring for an aging relative can affect the employee's performance at work.[88] One study found that, to care for an older relative, 64% of employees took sick days or vacation time, 33% decreased work hours, 22% took leaves of absence, 20% changed their job status from full- to part-time, 16% quit their jobs, and 13% retired early. The problem will grow more acute as the segment of the population over age 65 rises. One survey found that about 120 million Americans are now or have in the past cared for an adult relative or friend.[89]

So, often citing the "human toll on caregivers," more employers are providing elder care services. For example, the United Auto Workers and Ford Motor Company provide elder care referral service for Ford's salaried employees. They provide a detailed assessment of the elderly relative's needs, and recommendations on the care that would be best.[90] The National Council on Aging has a useful Web site to help elders and caregivers find benefit programs: www.benefitscheckup.org.

Time Off   One survey found that about half the 2,586 workers surveyed felt they were working too much, and putting too little time into "other things in life that really matter." In response, employers such as Hartford Financial Services Group, and Nationwide Mutual Insurance are changing their time off policies. For example, they are handing out time off as a performance reward; tracking employees time off to avert burnout; giving new hires more vacation; and offering employees more long weekends on holidays.[91]

Effect on Performance   Do family-friendly programs improve productivity? Many firms that implement these plans do so as part of broader commitment-building programs (also emphasizing developmental activities, and fair treatment programs, for instance). Studies suggest such work/life benefits may in fact contribute to employees' willingness to "go the extra mile" for their employers. And, employee who experience work-family conflict may experience anger that affects performance, a situation family-type benefits may improve.[92]

On the other hand, benefits like these don't come cheap. For example, Aetna found it saved $400,000 by making employees at its Blue Bell, Pennsylvania, office buy their own coffee and tea.[93]

Other Job-Related Benefits

Employers provide various other job-related benefits. Some provide subsidized *employee transportation*. Google's website lists benefits such as adoption assistance, the Google Child Care Center, free shuttle service from San Francisco, onsite dry cleaning, backup childcare assistance, and on-site physician and dental care at their Mountain View and Seattle facilities. *Food services* are provided in some form by many employers; they let employees purchase meals, snacks, or coffee, usually at relatively low prices.

Educational Subsidies   *Educational subsidies* such as tuition refunds are popular benefits for employees seeking to continue their educations. Payments range from all tuition and expenses to some percentage of expenses to a flat fee of several hundred dollars per year. One survey found that about 72% of the 579 companies surveyed pay for college courses related to an employee's present job. Many employers also reimburse non-job-related courses (such as a Web designer taking an accounting class) that pertain to the company business. Some employers pay for self-improvement classes, such as foreign language study, even though they are unrelated to company business or the employee's job, (although there seems to be a trend toward reducing such benefits).[94] Many employers provide college programs, taught on the employer's premises. Other in-house educational programs include remedial work in basic literacy and training for improved supervisory skills.

College tuition subsidies may help employers attract recruits, retain some employees, and provide promotable employees with the educations they need to move up. However, that same enhanced mobility makes it easier for employees to leave. Two researchers studied how employer-sponsored part-time college education reimbursements impacted job mobility. They focused on the U.S. Navy's tuition assistance program. Tuition assistance usage significantly decreased the probability of staying in the Navy.[95]

"The New Workforce" feature describes another personal/family benefit.

The NEW *Workforce*   Domestic Partner Benefits

A survey by the Society for Human Resource Management found that of 578 companies responding, about 23% offer same-sex domestic partner benefits, 31% offer opposite-sex partner benefits, and about 2% plan to do one or both.[96] For example, Northrop Grumman Corp., extends domestic partner benefits to the 9,500 salaried workers at its Newport News shipyard.[97]

When employers provide *domestic partner benefits* to employees, it generally means that employees' same-sex or opposite-sex domestic partners are eligible to receive the same benefits (health care, life insurance, and so forth) as do the husband, wife, or legal dependent of one of the firm's employees. Under Internal Revenue Service guidelines, "dependents" include the taxpayer's son or daughter or a descendant of either, stepson or stepdaughter, brother, sister, stepbrother or stepsister, father, mother or ancestor of either, stepfather or stepmother, niece or nephew, aunt or uncle, or in-law for whom the taxpayer pays more than half the support.[98] With the passage of the Defense of Marriage Act, Congress provided that employers may not treat same-sex domestic partners the same as employees' spouses for purposes of federal law, so there is some doubt as to whether the benefits extended to domestic partners will be federal tax free, as they generally are for the relatives enumerated above.

Executive Perquisites

When you reach the pinnacle of the organizational pyramid—or at least get close to the top—you will find, waiting for you, the Executive Perk. Perquisites (perks, for short) usually only go to top executives. Perks can range from substantial (company planes) to relatively insignificant (private bathrooms).

Many popular perks fall between these extremes. These include *management loans* (which typically enable senior officers to exercise their stock options); *salary guarantees* (also known as golden parachutes), to protect executives if their firms become targets of acquisitions or mergers; *financial counseling* (to handle top executives' investment programs); and *relocation benefits*, often including subsidized mortgages, purchase of the executive's current house, and payment for the actual move.[99] A selection of other executive perks includes time off with pay (including sabbaticals and severance pay), outplacement assistance, company cars, chauffeured limousines, security systems, company planes and yachts, executive dining rooms, physical fitness programs, legal services, tax assistance, liberal expense accounts, club memberships, season tickets, company credit cards, and children's educational subsidies. As you can see, employers have many ways of making their hardworking executives' lives as pleasant as possible!

FLEXIBLE BENEFITS PROGRAMS

When given the opportunity, employees prefer choice in their benefits plans. In one survey of working couples, 83% took advantage of flexible hours, 69% took advantage of the sorts of flexible-style benefits options packages we'll discuss next; and 75% said that flexible-style benefits plans are the sorts of plans they would like to see their companies offer. About 70% of employers in one survey chose flexible health care options.[100] The online job listing service jobtrak.com asked college students and recent graduates, "Which benefit do you desire most?" Thirty-five percent sought flexible hours; 19% stock options; 13% more vacation time; 12% a better health plan; and 9% wanted a signing bonus. Most of the preferred benefits had to do with lifestyle issues rather than

Indicate the level of importance of the following benefits to you and your family:

	Low Importance	High Importance
Single health coverage	_____	_____
Family health coverage	_____	_____
Preventive health care	_____	_____
Flexibility in choice of physician	_____	_____
Prescription coverage	_____	_____
Vision coverage	_____	_____
Dependent care assistance	_____	_____
Educational assistance	_____	_____
Paid maternity leave	_____	_____
Disability insurance	_____	_____

Indicate any two benefits listed below that you feel can be enhanced by the company, and include a comment suggesting how:

Health care coverage	_____
Prescription coverage	_____
Vision coverage	_____
Dependent care assistance	_____
Educational assistance	_____
Maternity leave	_____
Disability insurance	_____

If the company could spend additional money on benefits, rank in order of importance (1 = *most important*; 7 = *least important*) which of the following benefits you suggest should be funded:

_____	Health care coverage
_____	Prescription coverage
_____	Vision coverage
_____	Dependent care assistance
_____	Educational assistance
_____	Maternity leave

FIGURE 13-7

Sample Survey of Employee Needs

Source: Michelle Buckley, "Checkup for Health Benefit Offerings," *Compensation and Benefits Review*, September/October 2000, p. 43. Reprinted by permission of Sage Publications, Inc.

financial ones. At the same time, employers tend to misjudge employees' preferences for various benefits.[101]

Given findings like these, it is prudent to survey employees' benefits preferences, perhaps using a form like that in Figure 13-7. In any case, it's apparent that employers must provide opportunities for choice when designing benefits plans.

The Cafeteria Approach

flexible benefits plan/cafeteria benefits plan
Individualized plans allowed by employers to accommodate employee preferences for benefits.

Because employees do have different preferences for benefits, employers often let employees individualize their benefits plans. The "cafeteria" approach is one way to do this. (The terms **flexible benefits plan** and **cafeteria benefits plan** are generally used synonymously.) A *cafeteria plan* is one in which the employer gives each employee a benefits fund budget, and lets the person spend it on the benefits he or she prefers, subject to two constraints. First, the employer must of course limit the total cost for each employee's benefits package. Second, each employee's benefits plan must include certain required items—for example, Social Security, workers' compensation, and unemployment insurance. Employees can often make midyear changes to their plans if, for instance, their dependent care costs rise and they want to divert more contributions to this expense.[102]

Types of Plans   Cafeteria plans come in several varieties. To give employees more flexibility in what benefits they use, about 70% of employers offer *flexible spending accounts* for medical and other expenses. This option lets employees pay for certain benefits expenses with pretax dollars (so the IRS, in effect, subsidizes some of the employee's expense). During the open enrollment period, the employee may choose how much of his or her pay the employer will deposit in this account. To encourage employees to use this option without laying out cash, some firms are offering *debit cards* that employees can use at their medical provider or pharmacy.[103] *Core plus option plans* establish a core set of benefits (such as medical insurance), which are usually mandatory for all employees. Beyond the core, employees can then choose from various benefits options.[104]

The "Life Plan" at Pitney Bowes provides an example.[105] Pitney Bowes attaches a "price" to every benefit offered and allows employees to "shop" for the benefits they need each year. Each employee gets a certain number of "flex dollars" to spend each year on the benefits he or she prefers. Employees can buy whatever benefits they want up to the limit of their available flex dollars; they can even supplement that amount with their personal funds if they so choose.

Many businesses—particularly smaller ones—don't have the resources or employee base to support the cost of many of the benefits we discussed in this chapter. The "When You're on Your Own" feature below describes one solution.

Flexible Work Arrangements

⑤ Explain the main flexible benefit programs.

Flextime   **Flextime** is a plan whereby employees' workdays are built around a core of mid-day hours, such as 11:00 A.M. to 2:00 P.M. Workers determine their own starting and stopping hours. For example, they may opt to work from 7:00 A.M. to 3:00 P.M. or from 11:00 A.M. to 7:00 P.M. The number of employees in formal flextime programs—from 4% of operators to 17% of executive employees—doesn't tell the whole story. Many more employees, about 46%, actually take advantage of informal flexible work schedules.[106]

Flextime
A work schedule in which employees' workdays are built around a care of mid day hours, and employees determine, within limits, what other hours they will work.

In practice, most employers hold fairly close to the traditional 9:00 A.M. to 5:00 P.M. workday. In about half the firms, employees can't start work later than 9:00 A.M., and employees in about 40% of the firms must be in by 10:00 A.M. Therefore, the effect of flextime for most employees is to give them about one hour of leeway before 9:00 A.M. or after 5:00 P.M.

compressed workweek
Schedule in which employee works fewer but longer days each week.

Compressed Workweeks   Many employees, like airline pilots, do not work conventional five-day, 40-hour workweeks. Similarly, hospitals may want doctors and nurses to provide continuing care to a patient, or manufacturers may want to reduce the productivity lost whenever workers change shifts. Firefighters usually work for several days straight. Workers like these typically have **compressed workweek** schedules, which mean they work fewer days each week, but each day they work longer hours.

When You're on Your OWN
HR for Line Managers and Entrepreneurs

Benefits and Employee Leasing

The 40 employees at First Weigh Manufacturing in Sanford, Florida, may not work for a giant company, but they get employee benefits and human resource services as if they do. That's because Tom Strasse, First Weigh's owner, signed up with ADP Total Source, a professional employee organization that now handles all First Weigh's HR processes. "I didn't have the time or the personnel to deal with the human resources, safety and OSHA regulations," Strasse says. "We were always looking for new insurance."[107]

Strasse's experience is typical of small businesses that turn to *employee leasing*. Employee leasing firms (generally called professional employer organizations or staff leasing firms) basically assume all the employer's human resources chores; they also become the employer of record for the employer's employees, by transferring them all to the employee leasing firm's payroll. The leasing firm thus becomes the employees' legal employer, and usually handles all employee-related activities such as recruiting, hiring (with client firms' supervisors' approvals), and paying taxes (Social Security payments, unemployment insurance, and so on).

Advantages
Insurance and benefits are usually the big attraction. Getting health and other insurance is a problem for smaller firms. Even group rates for life or health insurance can be quite high when only 20 or 30 employees are involved. First Weigh Manufacturing's health insurance carrier dropped the firm after its first two years, and Strasse had to go scrambling to find a new carrier—which he did, with premiums that were 30% higher.

That's where the leasing firm comes in. Remember that the leasing firm is the legal employer of your employees. The employees therefore are absorbed into a much larger insurable group, along with other employers' former employees. As a result, a small business owner may be able to get insurance for its people that it couldn't otherwise afford.

An added benefit: The association that represents employee leasing firms estimates that the average cost of regulations, paperwork, and tax compliance for smaller firms is about $5,000 per employee per year.[108] Many small business owners therefore figure what they save on not managing their own human resource activities pays for the employee leasing firm's fees. For instance, when Strasse has a question about employee legal issues or safety concerns, he just calls his representative at the employee leasing firm.

Caveats
Employee leasing may sound too good to be true, and it often is. Many employers aren't comfortable letting a third party become the legal employer of their employees (who literally have to be terminated by the employer and rehired by the leasing firm). However, there are other, more concrete risks to consider. Several years ago, for instance, the employee leasing industry tarnished itself when one or two firms manipulated the pension benefits offered to higher-paid employees.[109] Employee leasing can also raise liability concerns. For example, in the typical employee leasing arrangement, the leasing firm and the client employer agree to share certain employee-related responsibilities, a concept known as co-employment. So, for instance, in states where courts have not universally upheld workers' compensation as the sole remedy for injuries at work (there are some such states), one must specify whether the client company or the leasing firm is insuring the workers' compensation exposure.[110]

Nonconventional workweeks come in many flavors. Some firms have four-day workweeks, with four 10-hour days. Some workers—in hospitals, for instance—work three 12-hour shifts, and then are off for the next four days. About half of 500 employers in one survey said they use 12-hour shifts for many of their employees.[111]

Effectiveness of Flextime and Compressed Workweek Programs Flexible work schedules do have positive effects on employee productivity, job satisfaction, satisfaction with work schedule, and employee absenteeism; the positive effect on absenteeism was much greater than on productivity. Compressed workweeks positively affected job satisfaction and satisfaction with work schedule; absenteeism did not increase, and productivity was not positively affected. Highly flexible programs were actually less effective than less flexible ones.[112]

Some experts argue that longer, 12-hour shifts may increase fatigue and accidents. However, one report suggests 12-hour shifts can actually be safer, in some respects. For example, 12-hour shifts reduce the "general workplace confusion" that often occurs during shift changes, since there are fewer shift changes per day. To further reduce potential side effects, employers take steps such as installing treadmills and exercise bikes, and special "light boxes" that mimic daylight.

job sharing

Allows two or more people to share a single full-time job.

work sharing

Refers to a temporary reduction in work hours by a group of employees during economic downturns as a way to prevent layoffs.

telecommuting

Where employees work at home, usually with computers, and use phones and the Internet to transmit letters, data, and completed work to the home office.

Other Flexible Work Arrangements   Employers are taking other steps to accommodate employees' scheduling needs. **Job sharing** allows two or more people to share a single full-time job. For example, two people may share a 40-hour-per-week job, with one working mornings and the other working afternoons. About 22% of the firms questioned in one survey indicated that they allow job sharing.[113] These include Gannett newspapers and PepsiCo, which has offered it for more than 20 years.[114] (Job sharing can be particularly useful for retirement-aged employees, in that it allows them to reduce their hours while enabling the company to retain their expertise.)[115] **Work sharing** refers to a temporary reduction in work hours by a group of employees during economic downturns as a way to prevent layoffs. Thus, 400 employees may all agree to work (and get paid for) only 35 hours per week, to avoid a lay-off of 30 workers.

With **telecommuting**, employees work at home, usually with computers, and use phones and the Internet to transmit letters, data, and completed work to the home office.[116]

REVIEW

SUMMARY

1. Financial incentives are usually paid to specific employees whose work is above standard. Employee benefits, on the other hand, are available to all employees based on their membership in the organization.
2. There are four basic types of benefits plans: pay supplements, insurance, retirement benefits, and services.
3. Supplemental pay benefits provide pay for time not worked. They include unemployment insurance, vacation and holiday pay, severance pay, and supplemental unemployment benefits.
4. Insurance benefits include workers' compensation, group hospitalization, accident and disability insurance, and group life insurance.
5. Employee benefits are highly regulated by federal and state laws. Benefits required by federal or most state law include Social Security, unemployment insurance, workers' compensation, and leaves under the Family Medical Leave Act. Discretionary (non-legally required) benefits include disability, health and life insurance, pensions, and paid time off for vacations and holidays.
6. Employers are trying to rein in spiraling health care costs, and taking several specific steps to do this. These include using cost-containment specialists, getting employees more involved and empowered in the health care program, moving toward defined contribution health care plans, and outsourcing benefits such as employee assistance and counseling.

7. Retirement benefits include Social Security and pension plans. Social Security does not cover just retirement benefits but survivor's and disability benefits as well. Pension plans include defined benefit plans, defined contribution plans, deferred profit sharing, and savings plans. One of the critical issues in pension planning is vesting. ERISA basically ensures that pension rights become vested and protected after a reasonable amount of time.
8. Most employers also provide benefits in the form of employee services. These include food services, recreational opportunities, legal advice, credit unions, and counseling.
9. The employee's age, marital status, and sex clearly influence choice of benefits. This suggests the need for individualizing the organization's benefits plans.
10. Flexible benefits plans, also called the cafeteria approach, allow the employee to put together his or her own benefits plan, subject to total cost limits and the inclusion of certain nonoptional items. Many firms have installed cafeteria plans; they require considerable planning and computer assistance.

DISCUSSION QUESTIONS

1. You are applying for a job as a manager and are at the point of negotiating salary and benefits. What questions would you ask your prospective employer concerning benefits? Describe the benefits package you would try to negotiate for yourself.
2. What is unemployment insurance? Is an organization required to pay unemployment benefits to all dismissed employees? Explain how you would go about minimizing your organization's unemployment insurance tax.
3. Explain how ERISA protects employees' pension rights.
4. What is "portability"? Why do you think it is (or isn't) important to a recent college graduate?
5. What are the provisions of the FMLA?

INDIVIDUAL AND GROUP ACTIVITIES

1. Working individually or in groups, research the unemployment insurance rate and laws of your state. Write a summary detailing your state's unemployment laws. Assuming Company X has a 30% rate of annual personnel terminations, calculate Company X's unemployment tax rate in your state.
2. Assume you run a small business. Working individually or in groups, visit the Web site www.dol.gov/elaws. (See the Small Business Retirement Savings Advisor.) Write a two-page summary explaining: (1) the various retirement savings programs available to small business employers, and (2) which retirement savings program you would choose for your small business and why.
3. You are the HR consultant to a small business with about 40 employees. At the present time the firm offers only five days of vacation, five paid holidays, and legally mandated benefits such as unemployment insurance payments. Develop a list of other benefits you believe it should offer, along with your reasons for suggesting them.
4. The HRCI "Test Specifications" appendix at the end of this book (pages 726–735) lists the knowledge someone studying for the HRCI certification exam needs to have in each area of human resource management (such as in Strategic Management, Workforce Planning, and Human Resource Development). In groups of four to five students, do four things: (1) review that appendix now; (2) identify the material in

this chapter that relates to the required knowledge the appendix lists; (3) write four multiple choice exam questions on this material that you believe would be suitable for inclusion in the HRCI exam; and (4) if time permits, have someone from your team post your team's questions in front of the class, so the students in other teams can take each others' exam questions.

EXPERIENTIAL EXERCISE

Revising the Benefits Package

Purpose: The purpose of this exercise is to provide practice in developing a benefits package for a small business.

Required Understanding: Be very familiar with the material presented in this chapter. In addition, review Chapter 11 to reacquaint yourself with sources of compensation survey information, and come to class prepared to share with your group the benefits package for the small business in which you work or in which someone with whom you're familiar works.

How to Set Up the Exercise/Instructions: Divide the class into groups of four or five students. Your assignment is as follows: Maria Cortes runs a small personnel recruiting office in Miami and has decided to start offering an expanded benefits package to her 25 employees. At the current time, the only benefits are seven paid holidays per year and five sick days per year. In her company, there are two other managers, as well as 17 full-time recruiters and five secretarial staff members. In the time allotted, your group should create a benefits package in keeping with the size and requirements of this firm.

APPLICATION CASE

Striking for Benefits

By February 2004, the strike by Southern California grocery workers against the state's major supermarket chains was almost five months old. Because so many workers were striking (70,000), and because of the issues involved, unions and employers across the country were closely following the negotiations. Indeed, grocery union contracts were set to expire in several cities later in 2004, and many believed the California settlement—assuming one was reached—would set a pattern.

The main issue was employee benefits, and specifically how much (if any) of the employees' health care costs the employees should pay themselves. Based on their existing contract, Southern California grocery workers had unusually good health benefits. For example, they paid nothing toward their health insurance premiums, and paid only $10 co-payments for doctor visits. However, supporting these excellent health benefits cost the big Southern California grocery chains over $4.00 per hour per worker.

The big grocery chains were not proposing cutting health care insurance benefits for their existing employees. Instead, they proposed putting any new employees hired after the new contract went into effect into a separate insurance pool, and contributing $1.35 per hour for their health insurance coverage. That meant new employees' health insurance would cost each new employee perhaps $10 per week. And, if that $10 per week wasn't enough to cover the cost of health care, then the employees would have to pay more, or do without some of their benefits.

It was a difficult situation for all the parties involved. For the grocery chain employers, skyrocketing health care costs were undermining their competitiveness; and the current employees feared any step down the slippery slope that might eventually mean cutting their own health benefits. The unions didn't welcome a situation in which they'd end up representing two classes of employees, one (the existing employees) who had excellent health insurance benefits, and another (newly hired employees) whose benefits were relatively meager, and who might therefore be unhappy from the moment they took their jobs and joined the union.

Questions

1. Assume you are mediating this dispute. Discuss five creative solutions you would suggest for how the grocers could reduce the health insurance benefits and the cost of their total benefits package without making any employees pay more.
2. From the grocery chains' point of view, what is the downside of having two classes of employees, one of which has superior health insurance benefits? How would you suggest they handle the problem?
3. Similarly, from the point of view of the union, what are the downsides of having to represent two classes of employees, and how would you suggest handling the situation?

Source: Based on "Settlement Nears for Southern California Grocery Strike," *Knight-Ridder/Tribune Business News,* February 26, 2004, item 04057052.

CONTINUING CASE

Carter Cleaning Company

The New Benefit Plan

Carter Cleaning Centers has traditionally provided only legislatively required benefits for its employees. These include participation in the state's unemployment compensation program, Social Security, and workers' compensation (which is provided through the same insurance carrier that insures the stores for such hazards as theft and fire). The principals of the firm—Jack, Jennifer, and their families—have individual, family-supplied health and life insurance.

At the present time, Jennifer can see several potential problems with the company's policies regarding benefits and services. One is turnover. She wants to do a study to determine whether similar companies' experiences with providing health and life insurance benefits suggest they enable these firms to reduce employee turnover and perhaps pay lower wages. Jennifer is also concerned with the fact that her company has no formal policy regarding vacations or paid days off or sick leave. Informally, at least, it is understood that employees get one week's vacation after one year's work, but in the past the policy regarding paid vacations for days such as New Year's Day and Thanksgiving Day has been very inconsistent. Sometimes employees who had been on the job only two or three weeks were paid fully for one of these holidays, while at other times employees who had been with the firm for six months or more had been paid for only half a day. Jennifer knows that this policy must be made more consistent.

She also wonders whether it would be advisable to establish some type of day care center for the employees' children. She knows that many of the employees' children either have no place to go during the day (they are preschoolers) or have no place to go after school, and she wonders whether a benefit such as day care would be in the best interests of the company.

Questions

1. Draw up a policy statement regarding vacations, sick leave, and paid days off for Carter Cleaning Centers.
2. What would you tell Jennifer are the advantages and disadvantages to Carter Cleaning Centers of providing its employees with health, hospitalization, and life insurance programs?
3. Would you advise establishing some type of day care center for the Carter cleaning employees? Why or why not?

TRANSLATING STRATEGY INTO HR POLICIES AND PRACTICES CASE: THE HOTEL PARIS

The New Benefits Plan

The Hotel Paris's competitive strategy is "To use superior guest service to differentiate the Hotel Paris properties, and to thereby increase the length of stay and return rate of guests, and thus boost revenues and profitability." HR manager Lisa Cruz must now formulate functional policies and activities that support this competitive strategy, by eliciting the required employee behaviors and competencies.

While the Hotel Paris's benefits (in terms of things like holidays and health care) were comparable to other hotels', Lisa Cruz knew they weren't good enough to support the high-quality service behaviors her company sought. Indeed, the fact that they were roughly comparable to those of similar firms didn't seem to impress the Hotel Paris's employees, at least 60% of whom consistently said they were deeply dissatisfied with the benefits they were getting. Lisa's concern (with which the CFO concurred) was that dissatisfaction with benefits contributed to morale and commitment being below what they should be, and thus to inhibiting the Hotel Paris from achieving its strategic aims. Lisa therefore turned to the task of assessing and redesigning the company's benefits plans.

As they reviewed the numbers relating to their benefits plan, Lisa Cruz and the CFO became increasingly concerned. They computed several benefits-related metrics for their firm, including *benefits costs as a percentage of payroll*, *sick days per full-time equivalent employee per year*, *benefits cost/competitor's benefits cost ratio*, and *workers' compensation experience ratings*. The results, as the CFO put it, offered a "good news–bad news" situation. On the good side, the ratios were generally similar to those of most competing hotels. The bad news was that the measures were strikingly below what they were when compared with the results for high-performing

service-oriented businesses. The CFO authorized Lisa to design and propose a new benefits plan.

Lisa knew there were several things she wanted to accomplish with this plan. She wanted a plan that contributed to improved employee morale and commitment. And, she wanted the plan to include elements that made it easier for her employees to do their jobs—so that, as she put it, "they could come to work and give their full attention to giving our guests great service, without worrying about child care and other major family-oriented distractions."

One of the metrics Lisa and her team specifically wanted to address was the relatively high absence rate at the Hotel Paris. Because so many of these jobs are front-line jobs—car hops, limousine drivers, and front-desk clerks, for instance—it's impossible to do without someone in the position if there is absence. As a result, poor attendance had a particularly serious effect on metrics like overtime pay and temporary help costs. Here, at the urging of her compensation consultant, Lisa decided to look into a system similar to Marriott's "BENETRADE." With this benefit program, employees can trade the value of some sick days for other benefits. As Lisa put it, "I'd rather see our employees using their sick day pay for things like additional health care benefits, if it means they'll think twice before taking a sick day to run a personal errand."

Questions

1. Because employers typically make benefits available to all employees, they may not have the motivational effects of incentive plans. Given this, list five employee behaviors you believe Hotel Paris could try to improve through an enhanced benefits plan, and explain why you chose them.
2. Given your answer to question 1, explain specifically what benefits you would recommend the Hotel Paris implement to achieve these behavioral improvements.

KEY TERMS

benefits, 510
supplemental pay benefits, 512
unemployment insurance, 512
sick leave, 515
severance pay, 519
supplemental unemployment benefits, 520
workers' compensation, 520
case management, 521
health maintenance organization
   (HMO), 522
preferred provider organizations (PPOs), 522
group life insurance, 526
Social Security, 527
pension plans, 527
defined benefit pension plan, 527
defined contribution pension plan, 528
portability, 528
401(k) plan, 528
savings and thrift plan, 528

deferred profit-sharing plan, 528–529
employee stock ownership plan
   (ESOP), 528–529
cash balance plans, 529
Employee Retirement Income Security
   Act (ERISA), 529
Pension Benefits Guarantee Corporation
   (PBGC), 529
vested funds, 530
early retirement window, 530
employee assistance program, 532
family-friendly benefits, 533
flexible benefits plan/cafeteria
   benefits plan, 538
flextime, 538
compressed workweek, 538
job sharing, 540
work sharing, 540
telecommuting, 540

ENDNOTES

1. Based on Frederick Hills, Thomas Bergmann, and Vida Scarpello, *Compensation Decision Making* (Fort Worth, TX: The Dryden Press, 1994), p. 424. See also L. Kate Beatty, "Pay and Benefits Break Away from Tradition," *HR Magazine*, November 1994, pp. 63–68, and Fay Hansen, "The Cutting Edge of Benefit Cost Control," *Workforce*, March 2003, pp. 36–42.

2. "Survey Finds 99 Percent of Employers Providing Health-Care Benefits," *Compensation and Benefits Review*, September/October 2002, p. 11. About 69% of workers in private in the private industry have access to employer-sponsored medical care plans, and 53% participate in such plans. See, "New Bureau of Labor Statistics Benefit Data Have Been Released," *Compensation and Benefits Review*, January/February 2005, p. 15.

3. "Decline in Job Based Health Coverage Links to Growth of U.S. Uninsured," *BNA Human Resources Report*, December 8, 2003, p. 30.

4. Eric Parmenter, "Controlling Health-Care Costs," *Compensation and Benefits Review*, September/October 2002, p. 44. See also "Benefits Vary Widely by Industry," *Compensation and Benefits Review*, March/April 2005, pp. 11–12.

5. "Employers Face Fifth Successive Year of Major Health Cost Increases, Survey Finds," *BNA Human Resources Report*, October 6, 2003, p. 1050.

6. It's not clear why, but between 1992/1993 and 2003, the percentage of private-sector workers participating in employer provided medical care plans declined, as did those participating in retirement plans. "These declines may be the result of shifts in the composition of the labor force, changes in employer decisions to offer coverage, or employee decisions to choose coverage or some combination of these and other factors. William Wiatrowski, "Medical and Retirement Plan Coverage: Exploring the Decline in Recent Years," *Monthly Labor Review* 127, no. 8, August 2004, pp. 29–36.

7. Craig Olson, "Will Workers Accept Lower Wages in Exchange for Health Benefits?" *Journal of Labor Economics* 20, no. 2 (April 2002), pp. S91–S114.

8. "Survey Finds 57 Percent of Employees Satisfied with Health Plans," *Compensation and Benefits Review*, March/April 2002, p. 11.

9. Joseph Martocchio, *Strategic Compensation* (Upper Saddle River, NJ: Prentice Hall, 2001), p. 262.

10. "California Domestic Partner Benefits Mandate Carries Likely Impact Beyond State's Borders," *BNA Bulletin to Management*, November 6, 2003, p. 353.

11. "National Compensation Survey: Employee Benefits in Private Industry in the United States, March 2006," U.S. Department of Labor, U.S. Bureau of Labor Statistics, August 2006.

12. Ibid., p. 116. See also, "Spurious Sick-Notes Spiral Upwards," *The Safety and Health Practitioner*, June 2004, vol. 22, issue 6, p. 3.

13. "Unscheduled Employee Absences Cost Companies More Than Ever," *Compensation and Benefits Review*, March/April 2003, p. 19.

14. "Making Up for Lost Time: How Employers Can Curb Excessive Unscheduled Absences," *BNA Human Resources Report*, October 20, 2003, p. 1097.

15. "SHRM Benefits Survey Finds Growth in Employer Use of Paid Leave Pools," *BNA Bulletin to Management*, March 21, 2002, p. 89.

16. This is based on M. Michael Markowich and Steve Eckberg, "Get Control of the Absentee-Minded," *Personnel Journal*, March 1996, pp. 115–120. See also, "Exploring the Pluses, Minuses, and Myths of Switching to Paid Time Off Banks," *BNA Bulletin to Management*, June 17, 2004, vol. 55, no. 25, pp. 193–194.

17. www.dol.gov/elaws

18. Based on Dennis Grant, "Managing Employee Leaves: A Legal Primer," *Compensation and Benefits Review*, July/August 2003, pp. 36–46.

19. Ibid., pp. 36–37.

20. "Ten Years After It Was Signed into Law, FMLA Needs Makeover, Advocates Contend," *BNA Bulletin to Management*, February 20, 2003, p. 58.

21. "As Employers Grapple with FMLA Malaise, DOL Remains Unsure of Timing of Revisions," *BNA Bulletin to Management*, December 2, 2004, vol. 55, no. 49, p. 385.

22. Based on Dennis Grant, "Managing Employee Leaves: A Legal Primer," p. 41.

23. Gillian Flynn, "Employers Need an FMLA Brush-Up," *Workforce*, April 1997, pp. 101–104. See also "Worker Who Was Employee for Less than One Year Can Pursue FMLA Claim, Federal Court Determines," *BNA Fair Employment Practices*, April 26, 2001, p. 51.

24. "Workers Who Come and Go Under FMLA Complicate Attendance Policies, Lawyer Says," *BNA Bulletin to Management*, March 16, 2000, p. 81.

25. Sue Shellenbarger, "The Mommy Drain: Employers Beef Up Perks to Lure New Mothers Back to Work," *Wall Street Journal*, September 28, 2006, p. D1.

26. "Severance Practices," *BNA Bulletin to Management*, January 11, 1996, pp. 12, 13, and Neil Grossman, "Shrinking the Workforce in an Economic Slowdown," *Compensation and Benefits Review*, Spring 2002, pp. 12–23.

27. Ibid., and, "Severance/Retention Practices: 2002; Pension Benefits, October 2002, p. 11; "Severance Pay," July 2007, Culpepper Compensation & Benefits Surveys.

28. Terry Baglieri, "Severance Pay," www.SHRM.org, downloaded December 23, 2006.

29. Ibid.

30. "Workers' Compensation Costs are Rising Faster Than Wages," *BNA Bulletin to Management*, July 31, 2003, p. 244.

31. "Workers' Comp Claims Rise with Layoffs, But Employers Can Identify, Prevent Fraud," *BNA Bulletin to Management*, October 4, 2001, p. 313.

32. See, for example, Betty Bialk, "Cutting Workers' Compensation Costs," *Personnel Journal*, July 1987, pp. 95–97.

33. "Using Case Management in Workers' Compensation," *BNA Bulletin to Management*, June 6, 1996, p. 181.

34. "Firms Cite Own Efforts as Key to Controlling Costs," *BNA Bulletin to Management*, March 21, 1996, p. 89. See also "Workers' Compensation Outlook: Cost Control Persists," *BNA Bulletin to Management*, January 30, 1997, pp. 33–44, and Annmarie Lipold, "The Soaring Costs of Workers' Comp," *Workforce*, February 2003, p. 42ff.

35. Steve Lattanzio, "What Can Employer Do to Influence the Cost of Its Workers' Compensation Program?" *Compensation and Benefits Review*, 1997, pp. 20–30.

36. Hills, Bergmann, and Scarpello, *Compensation Decision Making*, p. 137.

37. George Milkovich and Jerry Newman, *Compensation* (Burr Ridge, IL: McGraw-Hill, 1993), p. 445.

38. "Mental Health Trends," *Workplace Editions,* no. 2, Society for Human Resource Management, Alexandria, VA.

39. Ibid., p. 40. See also, "Employers Explore Range of Tactics to Rein in Rising Health Costs for 2005 Plan Year," *BNA Bulletin to Management*, July 1, 2004, vol. 55, no. 27, p. 219.

40. Allen Cohen, "Decision-Support in the Benefits Consumer Age," *Compensation and Benefits Review*, March/April 2006, pp. 46–51.

41. "Study: Employers Shifting to Deflect Health Expenses," *BNA Bulletin to Management*, June 10, 2004, p. 188.

42. Ron Finch, "Preventive Services: Improving the Bottom Line for Employers and Employees," *Compensation and Benefits Review*, March/April 2005, p. 18. Note that prevention/wellness programs can run afoul of the Americans with Disabilities Act. So, for instance, employers should not make participation in such plans mandatory, nor use information obtained in such programs in such a way that violates ADA confidentiality requirements or discriminates against employees who are not physically fit. Here, see "Despite Good Intentions, Wellness Plans Can Run Afoul of ADA, Attorney Cautions," *BNA Bulletin to Management*, December 20, 2005, vol. 56, no. 51, p. 41.

43. www.DOL.gov, downloaded December 23, 2006.

44. Larri Short and Eileen Kahanar, "Unlocking the Secrets of the New Privacy Rules," *Occupational Hazards*, September 2002, pp. 51–54.

45. See for example, Karli Dunkelberger, "Avoiding COBRA's Bite: Three Keys to Compliance," *Compensation and Benefits Review*, March/April 2005, pp. 44–48.

46. Michael Bond, et al., "Using Health Savings Accounts to Provide Low-Cost Health-Care," *Compensation and Benefits Review*, March/April 2005, pp. 29–32.

47. Vanessa Fuhrmanns, "Oops! As Health Plans Become More Complicated, They're also Subject to a Lot More Costly Mistakes," *Wall Street Journal*, January 24, 2005, p. r4.

48. "As Workers Feel the Effect of Cost Hikes, Employers Turn to Health Remedies," *BNA Bulletin to Management*, April 18, 2002, p. 121.

49. "High Deductible Plans Might Catch On," *BNA Human Resources Report*, September 15, 2003, p. 967.

50. "HR Outsourcing: Managing Costs and Maximizing Provider Relations," *BNA, Inc.* 21, no. 11 (Washington, DC: November 2003), p. 10.

51. "One in Five Big Firms May Drop Coverage for Future Retirees, Health Survey Finds," *BNA Bulletin to Management*, December 12, 2002, p. 393. See also James McElligott Jr. "Retiree Medical Benefit Developments in the Courts, Congress, and EEOC," *Compensation and Benefits Review*, March/April 2005, pp. 23–28.

52. Dale Busse, "Health Care," *HR Magazine*, April 2003, pp. 49–51.

53. Robert Christadore, "Benefits Purchasing Alliances: Creating Stability in an Unstable World," *Compensation and Benefits Review*, September/October 2001, pp. 49–53. Betty Liddick, "Going the Distance for Health Savings," *HR Magazine*, March 2007, pp. 51–55.

54. Carolyn Hirschman, "Will Employers Take the Lead in Long-Term Care?" *HR Magazine*, March 1997, pp. 59–66.

55. Bill Leonard, "Recipes for Part-Time Benefits," *HR Magazine*, April 2000, pp. 56–62.

56. Bob Lanza et al., "Legal Status of Contingent Workers," *Compensation and Benefits Review*, July/August 2003, pp. 47–60.

57. Brenda Pol Sunoo, "Millions May Retire," *Workforce*, December 1997, p. 48. See also "Many Older Workers Choose to 'Un-Retire' or Not Retire at All," *Knight Ridder/Tribune Business News*, September 28, 2003, item 03271012, "Older Workers: Recent Trends in Employment and Retirement, Patrick Purcell, *Journal of Deferred Compensation*, Spring 2003, vol. 8, issue 3, pp. 30–54, and "For Many Seniors, a Job Beats Retirement," *Knight Ridder/Tribune Business News*, February 9, 2003, item 3040001.

58. "Update 2007: SSA Publication no. 05-10003, January 2007," www.SSA.Gov/pubs/10003.html#offset, accessed May 21, 2007.

59. Martocchio, *Strategic Compensation*, pp. 245–248; Lin Grensing-Pophal, "A Pension Formula that Pays Off," *HR Magazine*, February 2003, pp. 58–62; Jim Morris, "The Changing Pension Landscape," *Compensation and Benefits Review*, September/October 2005, pp. 30–34.

60. Lindsay Wyatt, "401(k) Conversion: It's as Easy as Riding a Bike," *Workforce*, April 1997, p. 66. See also Carolyn Hirschman, "Growing Pains. Employers and Employees Alike Have Lots to Learn About 401(k) Plans," *HR Magazine*, June 2002, pp. 30–38.

61. Wyatt, "401(k) Conversion," p. 20.

62. Matt Hamblin, "Benefits and Then Some: When It Comes to Basic Job Perks, IT Pros Want Them All—Plus a Fat Paycheck," *Computerworld*, July 19, 2000.

63. Victor Infante, "Retirement Plan Trends," *Workforce*, November 2000, pp. 69–76.

64. Harold Burlingame and Michael Culotta, "Cash Balance Pension Plan Facilitate Restructuring the Workforce at AT&T," *Compensation and Benefits Review*, November/December 1998, pp. 25–31; Eric Lekus, "When Are Cash Balance Pension Plans the Right Choice?" *BNA Bulletin to Management*, January 28, 1999, p. 7.

65. "New Pension Law Plus a Recent Court Ruling Doom Age-Related Suits, Practitioners Say," *BNA Bulletin to Management*, September 5, 2006, vol. 57, no. 36, pp. 281–282.

66. This is based on Eric Parmenter, "Employee Benefit Compliance Checklist," *Compensation and Benefits Review*, May/June 2002, pp. 29–38.

67. *Paolillo v. Dresser Industries*, 821F.2d81 (2d cir., 1987).

68. Patrick Kiger., "Early-Retirement Plans Backfire, Driving Up Costs Instead of Cutting Them," *Workforce Management*, January 2004, pp. 66–68.

69. Jennifer Schramm, "Exploring the Future of Work: Workplace Visions," *Society for Human Resource Management*, no. 2, 2005, p. 6.

70. Ibid.

71. "Benefits Cost Control Solutions to Consider Now," *HR Focus* 80, no. 11 (November 2003), p. 1.

72. Johanna Rodgers, "Web Based Apps Simplify Employee Benefits," *Insurance and Technology* 28, no. 11 (November 2003), p. 21.

73. Ibid.

74. Jim Meade, "Affordable HRIS Strong on Benefits," *HR Magazine*, April 2000, pp. 132–135.

75. Carolyn Hirschman, "Employees' Choice," *HR Magazine*, February 2006, pp. 95–99.

76. Joseph O'Connell, "Using Employee Assistance Programs to Avoid Crises," *Long Island Business News*, April 19, 2002, p. 10.

77. See Scott MacDonald et al., "Absenteeism and Other Workplace Indicators of Employee Assistance Program and Matched Controls," *Employee Assistance Quarterly* 15, no. 3 (2000), pp. 51–58. See also, Paul Courtis, "Performance Measures in the Employee Assistance Program," *Employer Assistance Quarterly* 19, no. 3, 2004, pp. 45–58.

78. See for example Donna Owens, "EAPs for a Diverse World," *HR Magazine*, October 2006, pp. 91–96.

79. See Harry Turk, "Questions and Answers: Avoiding Liability for EAP Services," *Employment Relations Today*, Spring 1992, pp. 111–114.

80. "Fathers Fighting to Keep Work–Life Balance Are Finding Employers Firmly in their Corner," *BNA Bulletin to Management*, June 14, 2005, vol. 56, no. 24, p. 185.

81. Maureen Hannay and Melissa Northam, "Low-Cost Strategies for Employee Retention," *Compensation and Benefits Review*, July/August 2000, pp. 65–72. See also Roseanne Geisel, "Responding to Changing Ideas of Family," *HR Magazine*, August 2004, pp. 89–98.

82. Mary Burke, Euren Esen, and Jessica Cullison, *2003 Benefits Survey*, SHRM/SHRM Foundation, 1800 Duke Street, Alexandria, VA, 2003, pp. 8–9.

83. Ibid.

84. Jerry Useem, "Welcome to the New Company Town," *Fortune*, January 10, 2000, pp. 62–70.

85. "Child Care Options," *BNA Bulletin to Management*, July 4, 1996, p. 212. See also, "Child Care Report Boasts of Its Benefit to California Economy," *Knight Ridder/Tribune Business News*, January 9, 2003, item 03009011.

86. Patrick Kiger, "A Case for Childcare," *Workforce Management*, April 2004, pp. 34–40.

87. www.SHRM.org/rewards/library, downloaded December 23, 2006. See also, Kathy Gurchiek, "Give us Your Sick," *HR Magazine*, January 2007, pp. 91–93.

88. Kelli Earhart, R. Dennis Middlemist, and Willi Hopkins, "Elder Care: An Emerging Assistance Issue," *Employee Assistance Quarterly* 8, no. 3 (1993), pp. 1–10. See also, "Finding a Balance Between Conflicting Responsibilities: Work and Caring for Aging Parents," *Monday Business Briefing*, July 7, 2004, and "Employers Feel Impact of Eldercare: Some Expanded Benefits for Workers," *Knight Ridder/Tribune Business News*, June 13, 2004, item 04165011.

89. "Employers Gain from Elder Care Programs by Boosting Workers' Morale, Productivity," *BNA Bulletin to Management*, March 7, 2006, vol. 57, no. 10, pp. 73–74.

90. Rudy Yandrick, "Elder Care Grows Up," *HR Magazine*, November 2001, pp. 72–77.

91. Sue Shellenbarger, "Companies Retool Time Off Policies to Prevent Burnout, Reward Performance," *Wall Street Journal*, January 5, 2006, p. D1.

92. Susan Lambert, "Added Benefits: The Link Between Work Life Benefits and Organizational Citizenship Behavior," *Academy of Management Journal* 43, no. 5 (2000), pp. 801–815. Timothy Junge, et al., "Work Family Conflict and Emotions: Effects at Work and Home," *Personnel Psychology*, vol. 59, 2006, pp. 779–814.

93. Mathew Boyle, "How to Cut Perks Without Killing Morale," *Fortune*, February 19, 2001, pp. 241–244.

94. SHRM, 2003 Benefits Survey, op cit, p. 30. See also Michael Laff, "U.S. Employers Tighten Reins on Tuition Reimbursement," *Training and Development*, July 2006, p. 18.

95. Richard Buddin and Kanika Kapur, "The Effect of Employer-Sponsored Education on Job Mobility: Evidence from the U.S. Navy," *Industrial Relations* 44, no. 2, April 2005, pp. 341–363.

96. SHRM/SHRM Foundation, 2003 Benefits Survey, p. 2.

97. Carolyn Shapiro, "More Companies Cover Benefits for Employee's Domestic Partners," *Knight-Ridder/Tribune Business News*, July 20, 2003.

98. "What You Need to Know to Provide Domestic Partner Benefits," *HR Focus* 80, no. 3 (August 2003), p. 3.

99. Martocchio, *Strategic Compensation*, pp. 308–309.

100. "Couples Want Flexible Leave, Benefits," *BNA Bulletin to Management*, February 19, 1998, p. 53, SHRM, 2003 Benefits Survey, op. cit., p. 14. See also, Paul Harris, "Flexible Work Policies Mean Business," *Training & Development*, April 2007, pp. 32–36.

101. "Money Isn't Everything," *Journal of Business Strategy* 21, no. 2 (March 2000), p. 4; see also, Kaven Kroll, "Let's Get Flexible," *HR Magazine*, April 2007, vol. 52, pp. 97–100, and "CEOs in the Dark on Employees' Benefits Preferences," *Employee Benefits News*, Sept. 1, 2006, ITEM 06244007, accessed May 21, 2007.

102. Carolyn Hirshman, "Kinder, Simpler Cafeteria Rules," *HR Magazine*, January 2001, pp. 74–79.

103. "Debit Cards for Health-Care Expenses Received Increased Employer Attention," *BNA Bulletin to Management*, September 25, 2003, p. 305.

104. Martocchio, *Strategic Compensation*, p. 263.

105. David Hom, "How Pitney Bowes Broadens Benefit Choices with Value-Added Services," *Compensation and Benefits Review*, March/April 1996, pp. 60–66.

106. "Slightly More Workers Are Skirting 9–5 Tradition," *BNA Bulletin to Management*, June 20, 2002, p. 197.

107. Jane Applegate, "Employee Leasing Can Be a Savior For Small Firms," *Business Courier Serving Cincinnati–Northern Kentucky*, January 28, 2000, p. 23.

108. Harriet Tramer, "Employee Leasing Agreement Can Ease Personnel Concerns," *Cranes Cleveland Business*, July 24, 2000, p. 24.

109. Applegate, "Employee Leasing Can Be Savior for Small Firms," p. 23.

110. Diana Reitz, "Employee Leasing Breeds Liability Questions," *National Underwriter Property and Casualty Risk and Benefits Management* 104, no. 18 (May 2000), p. 12.

111. "Improving Well-Being and Morale 24 Hours a Day," *BNA Bulletin to Management*, August 19, 1999.

112. Boris Baltes et al., "Flexible and Compressed Workweek Schedules: A Meta-Analysis of Their Effects on Work-Related Criteria," *Journal of Applied Psychology* 84, no. 4 (1999), pp. 496–513. See also Charlotte Hoff, "With Flextime, Less Can Be More," *Workforce Management*, May 2005, pp. 65–66.

113. "2003 Benefits Survey," SHRM, op. cit., p. 2.

114. Judith Letterman, "Two People, One Job," *New York Times*, January 14, 2001, p. 8.

115. "With Job Sharing Arrangements, Companies Can Get Two Employees for the Price of One," *BNA Bulletin to Management*, November 22, 2005, vol. 56, no. 47, pp. 369–370.

116. William Van Winkle, "Your Away-from-Home Office," *Home Office Computing* 19, no. 1 (January 2001), p. 54.

PART IV VIDEO CASES APPENDIX

Video 7: Compensating Employees

Video Title: Compensation

In this video, two HR staff members, Cheryl and Gina, must determine if an employee, Angelo, is worthy of a pay raise. The company, Focus Pointe, provides market research services. One of these services involves recruiting consumer, medical, and other respondents for the market research industry. It's important to get good, qualified respondents. To distinguish itself from its competitors, Focus Pointe uses a special "triple screening" process to ensure that the respondents it recruits meets its clients' specifications. In this case, Angelo seems to be recruiting inadequate respondents. The two HR staff members are trying to determine if giving Angelo a raise would solve the problem.

As Angelo says in the video, he'd like to be better compensated. Cheryl and Gina point out to him that his pay is falling because his recruits often don't qualify. They ask him what he would like, an increase in salary, or an increase in the amount per recruit that he is paid. He responds that he'd like both. They tell them they will go along with his request but that they must see higher levels of recruit qualifications within three months. As the panel's human resource managers (including Paul, from BMG) point out in assessing this video, they don't necessarily agree with giving someone who is underperforming a raise. As Paul says, "they should have just told him to improve first."

Discussion Questions

1. Do you think Angelo is underperforming as a result of motivation, or something else, such as the need for improved training? How would you find out?
2. Is it a good idea to give someone who is underperforming a raise? Does it send the wrong signal, insofar as it seems to suggest that poor performance leads to rewards?
3. Do you think the idea of paying recruiters like Angelo per recruit might actually backfire, and if so how?

Video 8: Compensating Employees

Video Title: Nova Soft Information Technology

Nova Soft has grown from a New Jersey-based business with one employee to an international company employing more than 400 people around the world. Neal, the firm's founder and head, believes in doing whatever it takes to keep a promise to a client, even if it means working all weekend or staying up all night. While that's fine for the owner, it raises the question of how you keep your employees committed to that sort of continuously high level of effort. At Nova Soft, part of the answer is to provide an enticing incentives and benefits packages. High performers can earn things like overseas vacations for two, a Mercedes-Benz, or Rolex watch when they meet their objectives.

Discussion Questions

1. What role do you think employee benefits plays in maintaining the kind of employee commitment Nova Soft must maintain, and why?
2. From the video, what benefits could you identify at Nova Soft now?
3. Would you consider items like a Mercedes-Benz, holidays, and laptops benefits or incentives (or a little of both), and why?

14 Ethics, Justice, and Fair Treatment in HR Management

Wal-Mart recently instituted a new employee scheduling system, to improve the way the firm utilizes its personnel. Formerly, employees had predictable work shifts, for instance Tuesday–Friday, noon–5. With the new system, employees must list, on "availability forms," what hours during the day and night they were ready and willing to work. Then, as the store's customer traffic rises and falls, supervisors will call into work or send home employees to meet demand. This is good for the stores' staffing needs. However, many Wal-Mart critics felt that by forcing employees to work relatively unpredictable hours, the new system would rip apart many employees' family lives, and so was unethical and unfair. •

After studying this chapter, you should be able to:

1 Explain what is meant by ethical behavior at work.
2 Discuss important factors that shape ethical behavior at work.
3 Describe at least four specific ways in which HR management can influence ethical behavior at work.
4 Employ fair disciplinary practices.
5 List at least four important factors in managing dismissals effectively.

This chapter starts a new part of the book. Part 4 focused on salaries, incentives, and benefits. Now, in Part 5 we turn to issues relating to employee justice, safety, and union relations. This chapter focuses on ethics, justice, and fair treatment in human resource management, matters at the heart of excellent employee relations. Topics we'll cover include ethics and fair treatment at work, the factors that shape ethical behavior at work, HR's role in fostering improved workplace ethics, employee discipline and privacy, and managing dismissals.

ETHICS AND FAIR TREATMENT AT WORK

① Explain what is meant by ethical behavior at work.

People face ethical choices every day. Is it wrong to use company e-mail for personal messages? Is a $50 gift to a client unacceptable? Compare your answers to those of Americans by answering the quiz in Figure 14-1.

Managers' human resource decisions often trigger ethical issues. For example, the executive director of the Ethics Officer Association notes that supervisory activities such as disciplinary actions and performance appraisals often raise ethical questions.[1] One survey of 747 human resource professionals found that 54% had observed misconduct ranging from

Office Technology

1. Is it wrong to use company e-mail for personal reasons?
   ❏ Yes ❏ No

2. Is it wrong to use office equipment to help your children or spouse do schoolwork?
   ❏ Yes ❏ No

3. Is it wrong to play computer games on office equipment during the workday?
   ❏ Yes ❏ No

4. Is it wrong to use office equipment to do Internet shopping?
   ❏ Yes ❏ No

5. Is it unethical to blame an error you made on a technological glitch?
   ❏ Yes ❏ No

6. Is it unethical to visit pornographic Web sites using office equipment?
   ❏ Yes ❏ No

Gifts and Entertainment

7. What's the value at which a gift from a supplier or client becomes troubling?
   ❏ $25 ❏ $50 ❏ $100

8. Is a $50 gift to a boss unacceptable?
   ❏ Yes ❏ No

9. Is a $50 gift *from* the boss unacceptable?
   ❏ Yes ❏ No

10. Of gifts from suppliers: Is it OK to take a $200 pair of football tickets?
    ❏ Yes ❏ No

11. Is it OK to take a $120 pair of theater tickets?
    ❏ Yes ❏ No

12. Is it OK to take a $100 holiday food basket?
    ❏ Yes ❏ No

13. Is it OK to take a $25 gift certificate?
    ❏ Yes ❏ No

14. Can you accept a $75 prize won at a raffle at a supplier's conference?
    ❏ Yes ❏ No

Truth and Lies

15. Due to on-the-job pressure, have you ever abused or lied about sick days?
    ❏ Yes ❏ No

16. Due to on-the-job pressure, have you ever taken credit for someone else's work or idea?
    ❏ Yes ❏ No

FIGURE 14-1

The *Wall Street Journal* Workplace-Ethics Quiz

Note: The spread of technology into the workplace has raised a variety of new ethical questions, and many old ones still linger. Compare your answers with those of other Americans surveyed, on page 588.

Source: Wall Street Journal, October 21, 1999, pp. B1–B4. Reproduced with permission via Copyright Clearance Center.

TABLE 14-1 Specific Observed Unethical Behaviors

Abusive or intimidating behavior toward employees	21%
Lying to employees, customers, vendors, or to the public	19%
A situation that places employee interests over organizational interests	18%
Violations of safety regulations	16%
Misreporting of actual time worked	16%
E-mail and Internet abuse	13%
Discrimination on the basis of race, color, gender, age, or similar categories	12%
Stealing or theft	11%
Sexual harassment	9%
Provision of goods or services that fail to meet specifications	8%
Misuse of confidential information	7%
Alteration of documents	6%
Falsification or misrepresentation of financial records or reports	5%
Improper use of competitors' inside information	4%
Price fixing	3%
Giving or accepting bribes, kickbacks, or inappropriate gifts	3%

Source: From *2005 National Business Ethics Survey: How Employees Perceive Ethics at Work*, 2005, p. 25. Copyright © 2006, Ethics Resource Center (ERC). Used with permission of the ERC, 1747 Pennsylvania Ave., N.W., Suite 400, Washington, DC 2006, www.ethics.org. Reprinted in O. C. Ferrell, John Fraedrich, and Linog Ferrell, *Business Ethics* (Boston: Houghton Mifflin, 2008) p. 61.

violations of Title VII, to violations of the Occupational Safety and Health Act, to employees falsifying work records.[2] Another survey found that 6 of the 10 most serious ethical issues—workplace safety, security of employee records, employee theft, affirmative action, comparable work, and employee privacy rights—were HR related.[3] A U.S. Supreme Court decision (*Reeves v. Sanderson Plumbing Products*) suggests that poor employee relations—for instance, untruthful or incomplete communications with or about employees—may overwhelm otherwise good defenses to discrimination claims when the claims reach the courts.[4] Table 14-1 lists the percentage of employees observing various unethical behaviors.

All managers thus need to understand the basics of ethics, and of the ethical dimensions of their human resource decisions. Let's look first at what *ethics* means.

The Meaning of *Ethics*

ethics
The principles of conduct governing an individual or a group; specifically, the standards you use to decide what your conduct should be.

Ethics refers to "the principles of conduct governing an individual or a group."[5]

Ethical decisions always involve two things. First, they involve *normative judgments*.[6] A normative judgment implies that something is good or bad, right or wrong, better or worse. "You are wearing a skirt and blouse" is a nonnormative statement; "That's a great outfit!" is a normative one.

Ethical decisions also involve morality. *Morality* is society's accepted standards of behavior. Moral standards address behaviors of serious consequence to society's well-being, such as murder, lying, and slander. They cannot be established or changed by decisions of authoritative bodies like legislatures. They should override self-interest. Many people believe that moral judgments are never situational. They say something that is morally right (or wrong) in one situation is right (or wrong) in another. Moral judgments also tend to trigger strong emotions. Violating moral standards may therefore make individuals feel ashamed or remorseful.[7]

It would simplify things if it was always clear which decisions were ethical and which were not. Unfortunately, it is not. If the decision makes the person feel ashamed or remorseful, or involves doing something with serious consequence such as murder, then chances are it's unethical. The problem for managers is that many decisions seem to fall "on the line."

Ethics and the Law

Furthermore, asking, "Is it legal?" is not a perfect guide about what is ethical. You can make a decision that involves ethics (such as firing an employee) using what's legal as a guide. However, that doesn't mean the decision will be ethical. Firing a 39-year-old employee with 20 years' tenure without notice or cause may be legal, but many would view doing so as unethical. Patrick Gnazzo, vice president for business practices at United Technologies Corp. (and a former trial lawyer), put it this way: "Don't lie, don't cheat, don't steal. We were all raised with essentially the same values. Ethics means making decisions that represent what you stand for, not just what the laws are."[8] Sometimes behavior is both illegal and unethical. For example, one huge meat processor had to respond to a federal indictment charging it with smuggling illegal immigrants from Mexico to cut factory costs.[9]

Ethics, Fair Treatment, and Justice

Managing human resources often requires making decisions in which fairness plays a role. You hire one candidate and reject another, promote one and demote another, pay one more and one less, and settle one's grievances while rejecting another's. How employees react to these decisions depends, to some extent, on whether they think the decisions and the processes that led up to them were fair.

Fairness is inseparable from what most people think of as "justice." A company that is *just* is, among other things, equitable, fair, impartial, and unbiased in how it does things. With respect to employee relations, experts generally define *organizational justice* in terms of its three components—distributive justice, procedural justice, and interpersonal or interactive justice.

distributive justice
The fairness and justice of a decision's result.

procedural justice
The fairness of the process.

interactional (interpersonal) justice
The manner in which managers conduct their interpersonal dealings with employees.

- **Distributive justice** refers to the fairness and justice of the decision's *result* (for instance, Did I get an equitable pay raise?).
- **Procedural justice** refers to the fairness of the *process* (for instance, Is the process my company uses to allocate merit raises fair?).
- **Interactional** or **interpersonal justice** refers to "the *manner* in which managers conduct their interpersonal dealings with employees," and, in particular, to the degree to which they treat employees with dignity as opposed to abuse or disrespect.[10]

Employees tend to correlate fairness, justice, and ethics with each other when it comes to employers. One study focused on how employees reacted to fair treatment. It concluded that "to the extent that survey respondents believed that employees were treated fairly . . . [they] reported less unethical behavior in their organizations. They also reported that employees and their organizations were more aware of ethical issues [and] more likely to ask for ethical advice.[11] Similarly, "[H]iring, performance evaluation, discipline, and terminations can be ethical issues because they all involve honesty, fairness, and the dignity of the individual.[12] Most employees associate fairness with ethical behavior.[13] In practice, fair treatment reflects concrete actions such as "employees are trusted," "employees are treated with respect," and "employees are treated fairly" (see Figure 14-2).[14] The bottom line is that ethics, fairness, and justice tend to be intertwined.

FIGURE 14-2

Perceptions of Fair Interpersonal Treatment Scale

Sources: Michelle A. Donovan et al., "The Perceptions of Their Interpersonal Treatment Scale: Development and Validation of a Measure of Interpersonal Treatment in the Workplace," *Journal of Applied Psychology*, 83, no. 5 (1998), p. 692.

What is your organization like most of the time? Circle Yes if the item describes your organization, No if it does not describe your organization, and ? if you cannot decide.

IN THIS ORGANIZATION:

1. Employees are praised for good work	Yes	?	No
2. Supervisors yell at employees (R)	Yes	?	No
3. Supervisors play favorites (R)	Yes	?	No
4. Employees are trusted	Yes	?	No
5. Employees' complaints are dealt with effectively	Yes	?	No
6. Employees are treated like children (R)	Yes	?	No
7. Employees are treated with respect	Yes	?	No
8. Employees' questions and problems are responded to quickly	Yes	?	No
9. Employees are lied to (R)	Yes	?	No
10. Employees' suggestions are ignored (R)	Yes	?	No
11. Supervisors swear at employees (R)	Yes	?	No
12. Employees' hard work is appreciated	Yes	?	No
13. Supervisors threaten to fire or lay off employees (R)	Yes	?	No
14. Employees are treated fairly	Yes	?	No
15. Coworkers help each other out	Yes	?	No
16. Coworkers argue with each other (R)	Yes	?	No
17. Coworkers put each other down (R)	Yes	?	No
18. Coworkers treat each other with respect	Yes	?	No

Note: R = the item is reverse scored.

❷ Discuss important factors that shape ethical behavior at work.

WHAT SHAPES ETHICAL BEHAVIOR AT WORK?

Whether a person acts ethically at work is usually not a consequence of any one thing. For example, it's not just the employee's *ethical tendencies*, since even "ethical" employees can have their actions influenced by *organizational* factors. So, the manager's first task is to understand what shapes ethical behavior, and then to take concrete steps to ensure that employees make ethical choices. Let's look first at the factors that shape ethical behavior. Then, in the following section, we turn to the steps the human resource manager can take to encourage ethical behavior.

Individual Factors

Because people bring to their jobs their own ideas of what is morally right and wrong, the individual must shoulder much of the credit (or blame) for the ethical choices he or she makes. For example, one survey of CEOs explored their intention to engage (or to not engage) in two questionable business practices: soliciting a competitor's technological secrets and making payments to foreign government officials to secure business. The researchers concluded that personal predispositions more strongly affected decisions than did environmental pressures or organizational characteristics.[15] Employers' experience with honesty testing (discussed in Chapter 6) shows that some people are more inclined toward making the wrong ethical choice. How would you rate your own ethics? Figure 14-3 presents a short self-assessment survey to help you answer that question.

Self-Deception   Personal tendencies are also important because self-deception has a bigger influence in ethical choice than most people realize. For example, "corrupt individuals tend not to view themselves as corrupt."[16] They rationalize their unethical acts as being somehow okay. As the president of the Association of Certified Fraud Examiners puts it,

Instrument

Indicate your level of agreement with these 15 statements using the following scale:

1 = Strongly disagree
2 = Disagree
3 = Neither agree nor disagree
4 = Agree
5 = Strongly agree

1. The only moral of business is making money.	1	2	3	4	5
2. A person who is doing well in business does not have to worry about moral problems.	1	2	3	4	5
3. Act according to the law, and you can't go wrong morally.	1	2	3	4	5
4. Ethics in business is basically an adjustment between expectations and the ways people behave.	1	2	3	4	5
5. Business decisions involve a realistic economic attitude and not a moral philosophy.	1	2	3	4	5
6. "Business ethics" is a concept for public relations only.	1	2	3	4	5
7. Competitiveness and profitability are important values.	1	2	3	4	5
8. Conditions of a free economy will best serve the needs of society. Limiting competition can only hurt society and actually violates basic natural laws.	1	2	3	4	5
9. As a consumer, when making an auto insurance claim, I try to get as much as possible regardless of the extent of the damage.	1	2	3	4	5
10. While shopping at the supermarket, it is appropriate to switch price tags on packages.	1	2	3	4	5
11. As an employee, I can take home office supplies; it doesn't hurt anyone.	1	2	3	4	5
12. I view sick days as vacation days that I deserve.	1	2	3	4	5
13. Employees' wages should be determined according to the laws of supply and demand.	1	2	3	4	5
14. The business world has its own rules.	1	2	3	4	5
15. A good businessperson is a successful businessperson.	1	2	3	4	5

ANALYSIS AND INTERPRETATION

Rather than specify "right" answers, this instrument works best when you compare your answer to those of others. With that in mind, here are mean responses from a group of 243 management students. How did your responses compare?

1. 3.09	6. 2.88	11. 1.58
2. 1.88	7. 3.62	12. 2.31
3. 2.54	8. 3.79	13. 3.36
4. 3.41	9. 3.44	14. 3.79
5. 3.88	10. 1.33	15. 3.38

FIGURE 14-3

How Do My Ethics Rate?

Source: Adapted from A. Reichel and Y. Neumann, *Journal of Instructional Psychology*, March 1988, pp. 25–53.

people who have engaged in corrupt acts " . . . excuse their actions to themselves, by viewing their crimes as non-criminal, justified, or part of a situation which they do not control."[17]

Organizational Factors

That happens all the time. Several years ago, WorldCom's former chief financial officer (CFO) pleaded guilty to helping the firm's former chairman mask WorldCom's deteriorating financial situation. Among other things, the government accused the CFO of instructing underlings to fraudulently book accounting entries, and of filing false statements with the SEC. Why would the CFO do such a thing? "I took these actions, knowing they were wrong, in a misguided attempt to preserve the company to allow it to withstand what I believed were temporary financial difficulties."[18]

As in WorldCom's case, the scary thing about unethical behavior at work is that it's usually not driven just by personal interests. Table 14-2 summarizes the results of one survey of the principal causes of ethical lapses, as reported by six levels of employees and managers. As you can see, being under the gun to meet scheduling pressures was the number-one reported factor in causing ethical lapses. For most of these employees, "meeting overly aggressive financial or business objectives," and "helping the company survive" were the two other top causes. "Advancing my own career or financial interests" ranked toward the bottom of the list. Thus (at least in this case) most ethical lapses seemed to occur because employees said they felt pressured to help their companies. Guarding against such pressures is one way to head off ethical lapses.

Whistleblower policies can help reduce the occurrence of employer unethical behaviors. Whistleblowers are individuals, frequently employees, who use procedural or legal channels

TABLE 14-2 Principal Causes of Ethical Compromises

	Senior Mgmt.	Middle Mgmt.	Front-Line Supv.	Prof. Non-Mgmt.	Admin. Salaried	Hourly
Meeting schedule pressure	1	1	1	1	1	1
Meeting overly aggressive financial or business objectives	3	2	2	2	2	2
Helping the company survive	2	3	4	4	3	4
Advancing the career interests of my boss	5	4	3	3	4	5
Feeling peer pressure	7	7	5	6	5	3
Resisting competitive threats	4	5	6	5	6	7
Saving jobs	9	6	7	7	7	6
Advancing my own career or financial interests	8	9	9	8	9	8
Other	6	8	8	9	8	9

Note: 1 is high, 9 is low.

Sources: O. C. Ferrell and John Fraedrich, *Business Ethics*, 3rd ed. (New York: Houghton Mifflin, 1997), p. 28; adapted from Rebecca Goodell, *Ethics in American Business: Policies, Programs, and Perceptions* (1994), p. 54. Permission provided courtesy of the Ethics Resource Center, 1120 6th Street NW, Washington, DC: 2005.

to report incidents of unethical behavior to company ethics officers or to legal authorities. While many employers fear whistleblowers, others encourage them to come forward, for instance by instituting ethics hotlines.[19]

The Boss's Influence

The boss often has a determining effect on whether his or her employees do the ethical thing. According to one report, for instance, "the level of misconduct at work dropped dramatically when employees said their supervisors exhibited ethical behavior." Only 25% of employees who agreed that their supervisors "set a good example of ethical business behavior" said they had observed misconduct in the last year, compared with 72% of those who did not feel that their supervisors set good ethical examples.[20] A study by the American Society of Chartered Life Underwriters found that 56% of all workers felt some pressure to act unethically or illegally.[21]

Here are examples of how supervisors knowingly (or unknowingly) lead subordinates astray:

- Tell staffers to do whatever is necessary to achieve results.
- Overload top performers to ensure that work gets done.
- Look the other way when wrongdoing occurs.
- Take credit for others' work or shift blame.[22]

Ethics Policies and Codes

ethics code

A document that memorializes the standards the employer expects its employees to adhere to.

An **ethics code** memorializes the standards to which the employer expects its employees to adhere, for instance with respect to bribery, and accurate reporting.

Basically, all publicly traded companies doing business in the United States need ethics codes. The Sarbanes-Oxley Act (passed after a series of top corporate management ethical lapses) requires companies to declare if they have a code of conduct. Federal sentencing guidelines reduce penalties for companies convicted of ethics violations if they have codes of conduct.

Having a code does not guarantee ethical behavior. About three-fourths of U.S. firms have formal ethics codes, and most (about 95%) offer ethics training. Yet about four of every 10 employees in the United States say they have witnessed serious legal or ethical problems where they work. The energy company Enron collapsed due to falsified accounting. Enron's Web site stated, among other things, that "as a partner in the communities in which we operate, Enron believes it has a responsibility to conduct itself according to certain basic principles." Those include, "respect, integrity, communication, and excellence."[23]

However, in general, ethics codes do have a positive impact on employees' ethical behavior. Researchers interviewed 766 subjects over a two-year period.[24] Respondents who worked for companies having a code of ethics judged subordinates, co-workers, themselves, and supervisors and top managers to be more ethical than respondents employed in organizations not having a formal code of ethics. Employees in companies with an ethics code also gave higher ratings of the company's support for ethical behavior, and felt somewhat less pressure to behave unethically than respondents from companies without an ethics code.

Some firms urge employees to apply a quick "ethics test" to evaluate whether what they're about to do fits the company's code of conduct. For example, the Raytheon Company asks employees who are faced with ethical dilemmas to ask:

- Is the action legal?
- Is it right?
- Who will be affected?
- Does it fit Raytheon's values?

- How will it "feel" afterwards?
- How will it look in the newspaper?
- Will it reflect poorly on the company?[25]

The Organization's Culture

organizational culture
The characteristic values, traditions, and behaviors a company's employees share.

One reason why ethics codes (and even what the boss says) does not always determine how ethically employees act is that it is not what the boss or employer says but what they do that's important. Organizational psychologists refer to this phenomenon as *organizational culture*. **Organizational culture** is the characteristic values, traditions, and behaviors a company's employees share. A *value* is a basic belief about what is right or wrong, or about what you should or shouldn't do. ("Honesty is the best policy" would be a value.) Values are important because they guide and channel behavior. Managing people and shaping their behavior therefore depends on shaping the values they use as behavioral guides. The firm's culture should therefore send clean signals about what is and isn't acceptable behavior.

To an outside observer, a company's culture reveals itself in several ways. You can see it in employees' *patterns of behavior*, such as ceremonial events and written and spoken commands. For example, managers and employees may engage in behaviors such as hiding information, politicking, or expressing concern when a colleague is bending ethical rules. You can also see it in the *physical manifestations* of a company's behavior, such as written rules, office layout, organizational structure, and ethics codes. In turn, these cultural symbols and behaviors tend to reflect the firm's shared *values*, such as "the customer is always right" or "be honest." If management and employees really believe "honesty is the best policy," the written rules they follow and the things they do should reflect this value. JetBlue Airlines' Founder, David Neeleman, wants all employees get the message that, "we're all in this together." You'll therefore sometimes still find him helping out at the gate, or handing luggage up into the plane.

The Manager's Role   Managers have to think through ways to send the right signals to their employees. Techniques include:

- *Clarify Expectations.* First, they make clear their expectations with respect to the values they want subordinates to follow. One way to do this is to publish a corporate

David Neeleman, JetBlue's Founder and former CEO, helps set his company's culture by getting up and helping to serve passengers himself.

ethics code. For example, the Johnson & Johnson code says, "We believe our first responsibility is to the doctors, nurses and patients, to mothers and fathers and all others who use our products and services."

- *Use Signs and Symbols.* Symbolism—what the manager actually does and thus the signals he or she sends—ultimately does the most to create and sustain the company's culture. Managers need to "walk the talk." They cannot expect to say "don't fudge the financials," and then do so themselves.
- *Provide Physical Support.* The physical manifestations of the manager's values—the firm's incentive plan, appraisal system, and disciplinary procedures, for instance— send strong signals regarding what employees should and should not do. Does the firm reward ethical behavior or penalize it?
- *Use Stories.* Stories can illustrate important company values. IBM has such stories, like the one about how IBM salespeople drove through storms to get parts to customers.
- *Organize Rites and Ceremonies.* At JCPenney, new management employees are inducted into the "Penney Partnership." Each inductee receives an HCSC lapel pin. The letters stand for JCPenney's core values of honor, confidence, service, and cooperation.

Ethics programs are not just important for large companies. The "When You're on Your Own" feature illustrates this.

When You're on Your OWN   Small Business Ethics
HR for Line Managers and Entrepreneurs

When people think of unethical corporate behavior, big headline-grabbing companies like Enron come to mind. Yet small firms have problems too. One study of 20 small to midsize firms found that bribery, corrupt dealings, payoffs to local gangsters, and a general tone of dishonesty were all often "business as usual."[26] Sometimes, these firms were clever about their corrupt dealings. When doing business abroad, one U.S. business tried to keep its hands clean by forming a "strategic alliance" with a local firm. The latter then did the dirty work, handling the local bribes.

Smaller firms have to be particularly alert to the possibility of unethical behavior. For one thing, their employees may tend to be careless, on the assumption that "we're one big family" and so are all operating from the same ethical rulebook. Smaller firms also don't have the resources for things like ethics hotlines, extensive ethics code–building, and ethics training that big firms have.[27]

There are several steps a small business owner can take to establish a workable, simple ethics *program:*

First, *size up your company's current ethics-related activities*. Doing an audit based on guidelines like those in this chapter (the availability of an ethics code, ethics training, internal controls to monitor ethical behavior, and so on) can be worthwhile.

Second, *create a code of conduct*, and make it clear to all employees that you take it seriously.

Third, *train your people*. For example, have your managers develop scenarios illustrating which behaviors are ethical and which are not, and discuss these.

Fourth, make it easier to *solicit feedback* from your employees, so that they can more easily report suspicions of unethical behavior.

Fifth, *walk the talk*. Particularly in a small business, the owner or CEO is so visible that employees will take their ethical signals from him or her.

❸ Describe at least four specific ways in which HR management can influence ethical behavior at work.

HUMAN RESOURCE MANAGEMENT'S ROLE IN PROMOTING ETHICS AND FAIR TREATMENT

We've seen that employers can take various steps to ensure ethical behavior by their employees. Many steps are within the realm of human resource management policies and practices. We'll consider some specific examples.

Human Resource Management–Related Ethics Activities

Selection   One writer says, "The simplest way to tune up an organization, ethically speaking, is to hire more ethical people."[28] This can start before the applicant even applies, by creating recruitment materials with explicit references to the firm's emphasis on ethics. (The U.S. Datatrust site in Figure 14-4 is an example.) Employers can then use tools such as honesty tests and meticulous background checks (discussed in Chapter 6) to screen out undesirables.[29] Also, ask behavioral questions such as, "Have you ever observed someone stretching the rules at work? What did you do about it? And, "Have you ever had to go against company guidelines or procedures in order to get something done?"[30]

The apparent fairness of the selection process is important. For example, "If prospective employees perceive that the hiring process does not treat people fairly, they may assume that ethical behavior is not important in the company, and that 'official' pronouncements

FIGURE 14-4

U.S. Data Trust WebSite

Source: Reprinted with permission of U.S. Data Trust Corporation. www.US DataTrust.com/company.

U.S.DataTrust

| | Contact Us | Support | Company |

Call Sales: (888) DATA-SAFE

Search

LiveVault Service
Features & Benefits
How It Works
Information Kit
Customer Testimonials
Plans & Pricing
30-Day Risk-Free Trial
Request Information

Solutions
Exchange® Servers
SQL® Servers
Disaster Recovery

Resource Center
White Papers
Data Risk Survey
Web Seminars

Questions?

Call Our Sales Team:
888-DATA-SAFE

Or Contact Us Online

About The Company

Overview | Media | Employment | Contact Us

Dedication. Integrity.

U.S. Data Trust is committed to attracting, developing and retaining talented, intelligent, highly motivated individuals. We expect our employees to be professional, well trained, and dedicated to the highest standards of performance, quality and integrity.

In turn, we provide an atmosphere where employees can excel, and we reward superior achievement. Our employees also participate in U.S. Data Trust's success through their ownership of company stock.

Our greatest asset is our people, and our objective is to build long-term relationships with them. They are essential to the accomplishment of our mission.

Employment opportunities are regularly available at U.S. Data Trust for recent college graduates, support staff and individuals seeking professional and managerial positions. Please see our **open position listing** below.

Equal Opportunity Employer

U.S. Data Trust is firmly committed to a policy affording equal employment opportunity to every employee and job applicant in a manner wholly consistent with federal, state and city laws, and without regard to race, color, religion, religious affiliation, sex, sexual preference, national origin, marital status, disability or age.

This policy applies to recruitment, hiring terms and conditions of employment, the administration of compensation rates, opportunities for education and training, participation in social and recreational programs, benefit programs and opportunities for advancement at U.S. Data Trust.

Open Position Listing

There are currently no positions available at this time. However, please check back again in the future.

Thank you for your interest.

U.S.DataTrust

about the importance of ethics can be discounted."[31] The manager can do several things to ensure that others view the firm's assessment methods as fair:

- The employee will tend to view the *formal procedure* (such as the selection interview) as fair to the extent that it tests job-related criteria, provides an opportunity to demonstrate competence, provides a way of redressing an error, and is used consistently with all applicants (or employees).
- The person's *interpersonal treatment* reflects such things as the propriety of the questions, the politeness and respect of the person doing the assessing, and the degree to which there was an opportunity for two-way communication.
- Candidates appreciate employers' *providing explanations*. Individuals see a system as fair to the extent that the employer provides useful knowledge both about the employee's or candidate's own performance and about the employer's assessment procedures.[32]
- Applicants or employees tend to view some *selection tools* as fairer than others. For example, to the extent that work sample tests (discussed in Chapter 6) are clearly job-related, give applicants an opportunity to perform, and provide specific feedback, applicants tend to view them as fair. Subjects in several studies preferred honesty tests or urinalysis to personality assessment tests, probably because of the lack of obvious job relevance of personality assessment.
- Effective interviews that provide for *two-way communication*, let the applicant display skills, offer feedback, and have high face validity (in terms of measuring what they're purported to measure), are also viewed as fair.

Ethics Training   For all practical purposes, ethics training is mandatory. Federal sentencing guidelines reduced penalties for employers accused of misconduct who implemented codes of conduct and ethics training. An amendment to those guidelines now outlines stricter ethics training requirements.[33] Ethics training usually includes showing employees how to recognize ethical dilemmas, how to use ethical frameworks (such as codes of conduct) to resolve problems, and how to use human resource activities (such as interviews and disciplinary practices) in ethical ways.

Training like this needn't be complicated. Lockheed Martin provides its employees with short, "what-if" ethical scenarios that highlight how to identify and deal with conflict of interest situations. The training should also emphasize the moral underpinnings of the ethical choice and the company's deep commitment to integrity and ethics. Top managers' participation underscores that commitment.[34]

Ethics training is often Internet-based. For example, Lockheed Martin's 160,000 employees also take ethics and legal compliance training via the firm's intranet. Lockheed's online ethics program software also keeps track of how well the company and its employees are doing in terms of maintaining high ethical standards. The program helped top management see that in one year, 4.8% of the company's ethics allegations involved conflicts of interest, and that it takes about 30 days to complete an ethics violation internal investigation.[35] Online ethics training tools include Business Ethics, from skillsoft.com, and two online courses, Ethical Decision-Making, and Managerial Business Ethics, both from netG.com.[36]

Figure 14-5 summarizes the tools and techniques employers use as part of their ethics training programs. As you can see, new-hire orientation, annual refresher training, and distributing the companies' policies and handbooks are all quite important.

Performance Appraisal   Performance appraisals are uniquely personal and important matters to most employees, and employees therefore enter the appraisal interview with a heightened sensitivity regarding fair treatment. To most employees, unfairness here

FIGURE 14-5

The Role of Training in Ethics

Source: Susan Wells, "Turn Employees into Saints," *HR Magazine*, December 1999, p. 52. Reproduced with permission via Copyright Clearance Center.

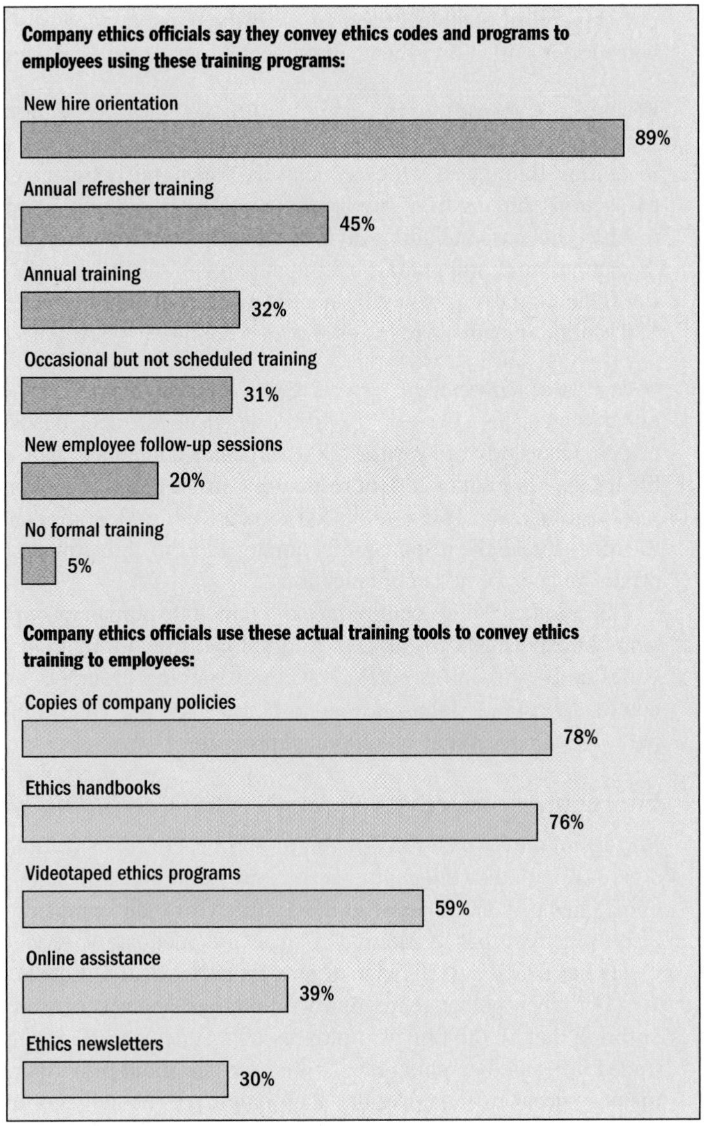

Company ethics officials say they convey ethics codes and programs to employees using these training programs:

New hire orientation
89%

Annual refresher training
45%

Annual training
32%

Occasional but not scheduled training
31%

New employee follow-up sessions
20%

No formal training
5%

Company ethics officials use these actual training tools to convey ethics training to employees:

Copies of company policies
78%

Ethics handbooks
76%

Videotaped ethics programs
59%

Online assistance
39%

Ethics newsletters
30%

reflects not just the supervisor's actions, but also the employer's inaction, in having not taken the necessary steps to prevent the unjust treatment.

How the supervisors do the appraisals is important. Studies (and practical experience) confirm that, in practice, some managers ignore accuracy and honesty in performance appraisals and instead use the process for political purposes (such as encouraging employees with whom they don't get along to leave the firm).[37] Few things can send a more damaging signal about how fair and ethical the company is. To send the signal that fairness is paramount, standards should be clear, employees should understand the basis upon which they're going to be appraised, and the appraisals themselves should be performed objectively and fairly.

Reward and Disciplinary Systems   To the extent that behavior is a function of its consequences, the employer needs to reward ethical behavior and penalize unethical behavior. Research suggests that "employees expect the organization to dole out relatively harsh punishment for unethical conduct."[38] If the company does not deal swiftly with unethical behavior, it's often the ethical employees, not the unethical ones, who feel punished.

Workplace Aggression and Violence Workplace aggression and violence are increasingly serious problems, as well as problems that often stem from real or perceived inequities. Employees who see themselves as unfairly treated or underpaid may take negative actions ranging from employee theft to destruction of company property. Many human resource actions, including layoffs, being passed over for promotion, terminations, and discipline can prompt unfair treatment perceptions that translate into dysfunctional behavior. (One employee, believing his dismissal was inhumane, retaliated by causing almost $20 million in damage to his employer's computer systems.)

HR's Ethics Compliance Activities In today's post-Sarbanes-Oxley Act era, usually either human resources or the firm's legal department heads up its ethical compliance efforts. One study of *Fortune* 500 companies concluded than an HR officer was responsible for the program in 28% of responding firms. Another 28% gave the firm's legal officers responsibility, and 16% established separate ethics or compliance departments. The rest of the firms spread the responsibility among auditing departments, or positions such as public affairs and corporate communications.[39]

Employers' ethics committees often include human resource professionals. Every two years Lockheed Martin surveys its employees regarding their adherence to the Lockheed ethics code. It then institutes new ethics training programs based on the feedback it receives. Johnson & Johnson uses its famous "credo" (its set of core ethical principles) as part of its management development programs.[40]

Improving Productivity Through HRIS: *Complying with Sarbanes-Oxley*

Passage of the Sarbanes-Oxley Act of 2002 made ethics compliance obligatory and expensive. Among other things, the act requires that the CEO and the CFO of publicly traded companies personally attest to the accuracy of their companies' financial statements, and also to the fact that its internal controls are adequate.[41] As one lawyer put it, "Sarbanes-Oxley has added a wide range of new issues to the traditional compliance function."[42]

With their personal credibility on the line, the act focused top managers' attention on ensuring that all the firm's employees take ethics very seriously. This means big, publicly traded firms are becoming much more serious about providing ethics-related training, and making sure they can prove that their employees actually got trained.

The problem is, training and following up programs like this can be very expensive. Larger firms need a cost-effective way of making such training available. For this they often go online. When DTE Energy's 14,000 employees needed ethics training, DTE turned to a Web-based program from Integrity Interactive Corp. Now, all the company's employees have easy access to a standardized ethics training program through their PCs, and DTE can easily track who has taken the training and who has not. The employees can take the training when they want to, and the company can monitor their progress.[43]

Why Treat Employees Fairly?

We've seen that a main way employers foster ethical behavior is by ensuring that they treat employees fairly. For most people the answer to, "Why treat employees fairly?" is obvious, since most learn, at an early age, some version of the golden rule.

But there are also concrete, reasons to treat employees fairly. *Arbitrators and the courts* will consider the fairness of the employer's disciplinary procedures when reviewing disciplinary and discharge decisions. Fairness also relates to a wide range of *positive employee outcomes*. These include enhanced employee commitment, enhanced satisfaction with the organization, job, and leader, and to "organizational citizenship behaviors" (the steps employees take to support their employers' interests).[44] *Job applicants* who felt they were treated unfairly expressed more desire to appeal the outcome. Those who view the firm's testing programs as fair react more favorably to the selection procedure, and view the company and the job as more attractive. Employees who view the firm's drug testing program as unfair are less satisfied and committed.[45]

Research Insight   A study provides an illustration. College instructors completed surveys regarding the extent to which they saw their colleges as treating them with procedural and distributive justice. Procedural justice questions included, for example, "In general, the department/college's procedures allow for requests for clarification for additional information about a decision." Distributive justice questions included, "I am fairly rewarded considering the responsibilities I have." The instructors also completed attitude surveys. These included questions such as, "I am proud to tell others that I am part of this department/ college." Their students also completed surveys. These contained items such as "The instructor put a lot of effort into planning the content of this course," "The instructor was sympathetic to my needs," and "The instructor treated me fairly."

The results were impressive. Instructors who perceived high distributive and procedural justice reported being more committed to the college and to their jobs. Their students reported higher levels of instructor effort, pro-social behaviors, and fairness. "Overall, . . . the results imply that fair treatment of employees has important organizational consequences."[46]

Behaving Unfairly

Workplace unfairness is often subtle, but can be blatant. Some supervisors are workplace bullies, yelling at or even threatening subordinates. The employer should, of course, always prohibit such behavior. Many firms do have anti-harassment policies. (For example, at the Oregon Department of Transportation, "It is the policy of the department that all employees, customers, contractors, and visitors to the work site are entitled to a positive, respectful, and productive work environment, free from behavior, actions, [and] language constituting workplace harassment.")[47] Not surprisingly, employees of abusive supervisors are more likely to quit their jobs, and to report lower job and life satisfaction and higher stress if they remain in those jobs.[48] Mistreatment makes it more likely the employee will also show higher levels of "work withdrawal," in other words show up for work, but not do his or her best.[49]

What Causes Unfair Behavior?

Some of the things that motivate managers to be fair may (or may not) be surprising. For one thing, the saying, "the squeaky wheel gets the grease" seems to be true. One study investigated the extent to which assertiveness on the subordinate's part influenced the fairness with which the person's supervisor treated him or her.[50] Supervisors treated pushier employees more fairly: "Individuals who communicated assertively were more likely to be treated fairly by the decision maker." Supervisors exposed to procedural injustice in turn exhibit abusive behavior against subordinates who they see as vulnerable or provocative.[51] Studies also suggest that large organizations have to work particularly hard to set up procedures that make the workplace seem fair to employees.[52] Hopefully, however, fair treatment stems more from the quality of the supervisors the company hires and from their training, and from the human resource policies and practices the company puts in place; we'll discuss this below.

Supervisory Fairness Guidelines

What seems "fair" to one person may seem unfair to another. People tend to rate their own performance more highly than do outsiders, and to be sensitive to issues of equity and fairness. As a result, even supervisors who work hard to be fair can expect to have subordinates occasionally say, "You treated me unfairly." Here, the best approach is probably not to deny the unfairness or debate the issue. Instead, suggestions include:[53]

- Ask questions and listen carefully. For example, say, "Can you tell me exactly what you see as unfair about my decision?"
- Set aside your defensive reactions. Instead, perhaps say something like, "I can see why you might feel that way."
- Tactfully deflect distracting statements. For instance, don't get into debates comparing the person's salary raise to someone else's. Instead say, "In fairness to that other person, let's just discuss your situation—you wouldn't want me discussing your salary with him or her."
- Ask, "What would you like me to do?" It could turn out the employee just wants to be heard.
- Deal with specifics. If the employee does want you to change the decision, ask him or he to outline specific reasons for the request.

Building Two-Way Communication

Opportunities for two-way communication effect our perceptions of how fairly we're being treated. One study concluded that three actions contributed to perceived fairness in business settings: *engagement* (involving individuals in the decisions that affect them by asking for their input and allowing them to refute the merits of others' ideas and assumptions); *explanation* (ensuring that everyone involved and affected understands why final decisions are made and the thinking that underlies the decisions); and *expectation clarity* (making sure everyone knows up front by what standards they will be judged and the penalties for failure).[54] For this reason, many employers take explicit steps to facilitate communications.

Facilitating Two-Way Communication   For example, Lexington, Kentucky-based Toyota Motor Manufacturing's *hotline* gives employees an anonymous method of bringing questions or problems to management's attention. The plant hotline is available 24 hours a day. Employees can pick up any phone, dial the hotline extension (the number is posted on the plant bulletin boards), and deliver their message to the recorder. The human resource manager reviews and answers all messages. The FedEx Survey Feedback Action (SFA) program includes an anonymous survey that lets employees express their feelings about the company and their managers. Sample questions include:

- I can tell my manager what I think.
- My manager tells me what is expected.
- My manager listens to my concerns.
- My manager keeps me informed.

Each manager then has an opportunity to discuss the department results with subordinates, and create an action plan for improving work group commitment.

EMPLOYEE DISCIPLINE AND PRIVACY

❹ Employ fair disciplinary practices.

The purpose of *discipline* is to encourage employees to behave sensibly at work (where *sensible* means adhering to rules and regulations). Discipline is called for when an employee violates one of the rules.[55]

Basics of a Fair and Just Disciplinary Process

The employer wants its discipline process to be both effective (in terms of discouraging unwanted behavior) and fair. Such a process is based on three pillars: clear rules and regulations, a system of progressive penalties, and an appeals process.

Rules and Regulations First, rules and regulations address issues such as theft, destruction of company property, drinking on the job, and insubordination. Examples include:

- *Poor performance is not acceptable.* Each employee is expected to perform his or her work properly and efficiently and to meet established standards of quality.
- *Alcohol and drugs do not mix with work.* The use of either during working hours and reporting for work under the influence of either are both prohibited.
- *The vending of anything in the plant without authorization is not allowed; nor is gambling in any form permitted.*

Rules inform employees ahead of time what is and is not acceptable behavior. Upon hiring, tell employees, preferably in writing, what is not permitted. The employee handbook usually contains the rules and regulations.

Progressive Penalties A system of progressive penalties is a second pillar of effective discipline. Penalties typically range from oral warnings to written warnings to suspension from the job to discharge.

The severity of the penalty is usually a function of the type of offense and the number of times the offense has occurred. For example, most companies issue warnings for the first unexcused lateness (see form in Figure 14-6). For a fourth offense, discharge is the usual disciplinary action.

The "When You're on Your Own" feature provides specific guidance for the front-line supervisor.

When You're *on Your* OWN Disciplining an Employee
HR for Line Managers and Entrepreneurs

Even if you're a manager in a *Fortune* 500 company, you may find yourself without company guidelines when disciplining an employee for violating company rules. Supervisors traditionally apply the four points of what they call the "hot stove rule" when applying discipline. When touching a hot stove that says "don't touch," one has *warning*, and the pain is *consistent, impersonal,* and *immediate.* Specific fair discipline guidelines would include:[56]

- Make sure the evidence supports the charge of employee wrongdoing.
- Ensure that the employee's due process rights are protected.
- Warn the employee of the disciplinary consequences.
- The rule that was allegedly violated should be "reasonably related" to the efficient and safe operation of the particular work environment.

- Fairly and adequately investigate the matter before administering discipline.
- The investigation should produce substantial evidence of misconduct.
- Rules, orders, or penalties should be applied even-handedly.
- The penalty should be reasonably related to the misconduct and to the employee's past work history.
- Maintain the employee's right to counsel.
- Don't rob a subordinate of his or her dignity.
- Remember that the burden of proof is on you.
- Get the facts. Don't base a decision on hearsay or on your general impression.
- Don't act while angry.
- In general, do not attempt to deal with an employee's "bad attitude." Instead, focus on improving the specific behaviors creating the workplace problem.[57]

FIGURE 14-6

Disciplinary Action Form

Source: Reprinted from www.HR.BLR.com with permission of the publisher *Business and Legal Reports, Inc.*, 141 Mill Rock Road East, Old Saybrook CT © 2004.

Disciplinary Action Form

Date: _____

Name: _____

Dept.: _____

Disciplinary Action:

❏ Verbal*   ❏ Written   ❏ Written & Suspension   ❏ Discharge

To the employee:

Your performance has been found unsatisfactory for the reasons set forth below. Your failure to improve or avoid a recurrence will be cause for further disciplinary action.

Details: _____

_____

_____

_____

_____

_____

A copy of this warning was personally delivered to the above employee by:

Supervisor: _____

Date: _____

I have received and read this warning notice. I have been informed that a copy of this notice will be placed in my personnel file.

Employee: _____

Date: _____

*If action is *verbal,* completion of this form shall serve as documentation only and should not be filed in the employee's personnel file.

When disciplinary decisions reach arbitration, clarity and fairness loom large. One study surveyed 45 published arbitration awards in which tardiness had triggered discipline and/or discharge. When arbitrators overturned employers' decisions, it was usually because the employer had failed to clarify what it meant by "tardy," or because there was a lack of clarity regarding how often an employee may be late over a given period, or because of an inappropriately severe penalty.

The NEW Workforce — Comparing Males and Females in a Discipline Situation

Watching a movie like *King Arthur* may lead you to the conclusion that chivalry in general and a protective attitude toward women in particular is a well-established value in many societies, but that may not be the case. Not only is chivalry not necessarily a prevailing value, but there is even a competing hypothesis in the research literature. What several researchers call the "Evil Woman Thesis" certainly doesn't argue that women are evil. Instead it "argues that women who commit offenses violate stereotypic assumptions about the proper behavior of women. These women will be penalized for their inappropriate sex role behavior in addition to their other offenses."

In other words, the unfortunately titled "Evil Woman Thesis" argues that when a woman doesn't act the way other men and women think she should act, they tend to overreact and treat her more harshly than they might if the alleged misdeed was done by a man.

While such a thesis might seem ridiculous on its face, the results of at least one careful study seem to indicate that it may in fact have considerable validity. In this study, 360 graduate and undergraduate university business school students in a southern city reviewed a labor arbitration case. The case involved two employees, one male and one female, with similar work records and tenure with their employers. Both were discharged for violation of company rules related to alcohol and drugs. The case portrays one worker's behavior as a more serious breach of company rules: The more culpable worker (a male in half the study and a female in the other half) had brought the intoxicant to work. The male and female decision-maker students were asked to express their agreement with two alternative approaches to arbitrating the dispute that arose after the discharge.

In their study, the researchers found bias against the culpable woman employee by both the male and female students. The culpable female workers in the case received recommendations for harsher treatment from both the men and women student decision makers. As the researchers conclude, ". . . women, as decision makers, appear to be as willing as men to impose harsher discipline on women than upon men."

In this study, it was student decision makers who were asked to come to some conclusions regarding discipline based on what they read in the case. There is no way to conclude based solely on this study that the findings would necessarily apply in real-world settings or under different conditions. However, the results of this study suggest that women just might be treated more harshly than men in a discipline situation.

Overly severe disciplinary procedures can backfire in other ways. For example, an unfair disciplinary procedure (such as one with harsh supervisory behaviors) can trigger retaliatory employee mischief, and thus actually encourage misbehavior.[58] Particularly in light of the top executives' ethics problems in the headlines recently, it's also important for the company to send the right signals by also disciplining executives who misbehave.

"The New Workforce" feature addresses gender disciplinary issues.[59]

Formal Disciplinary Appeals Processes

In addition to rules and progressive penalties, the disciplinary process requires an appeals procedure (see Figure 14-7).

Virtually all union agreements contain disciplinary appeal procedures, but such procedures are not limited to unionized firms. For example, FedEx calls its appeals procedure *guaranteed fair treatment:*

- In *step 1, management review,* the complainant submits a written complaint to a member of management (manager, senior manager, or managing director) within seven calendar days of the occurrence of the eligible issue.

FIGURE 14-7

Grievance Form as Part of Appeal Process

Source: http://www.wfu.edu/ hr/forms/staff-grievance.pdf, accessed May 24, 2007. Used with permission.

STAFF GRIEVANCE FORM

HUMAN RESOURCES DEPARTMENT

This form is to be used by staff employees of Wake Forest University to initiate a **formal** grievance (Step II) that seeks resolution of a work-related problem or condition of employment that an employee believes to be unfair, inequitable, or a hindrance to his/her effective job performance. An employee who wishes to pursue a formal grievance must first have attempted to resolve the grievance informally through a discussion with his/her immediate supervisor (Step I) as outlined in *Staff Employee Grievance and Appeal Process.* Upon completion, this form is to be submitted to the Human Resources Department (Employee Relations), 116 Reynolda Hall.

Grievant: _____ Telephone #: _____

Job Title: _____

Employing Department/Office: _____

Name of Immediate Supervisor: _____

Date Grievance was informally discussed with immediate supervisor (Step I): _____

EMPLOYEE STATEMENT OF GRIEVANCE: (Provide a concise statement of facts, including dates, to identify the work-related problem or condition of employment you believe to be unfair, inequitable, or a hindrance to your effective job performance – attach a continuation page, if necessary)

REMEDY OR REDRESS SOUGHT BY THE GRIEVANT: (Be specific as to what resolution you are seeking)

_____   _____
Grievant's Signature   Date

Date the grievance was received by Human Resources: _____ Initials: _____

WFU-HR-0013
Issued: 5-17-00
Revised: 5-16-01

- If not satisfied with that decision, then in *step 2, officer complaint*, the complainant submits a written appeal to the vice president or senior vice president of the division within seven calendar days of the step 1 decision.
- Finally, in *step 3, executive appeals review*, the complainant may submit a written complaint within seven calendar days of the step 2 decision to the employee relations department. This department then investigates and prepares a case file for the executive review appeals board. The appeals board—the CEO, the COO, the chief personnel officer, and three senior vice presidents—then reviews all relevant information and makes a decision to uphold, overturn, or initiate a board of review, or to take other appropriate action.

Some companies establish independent ombudsman, neutral counselors outside the normal chain of command to whom employees who believe they were treated unfairly can turn for confidential advice.[60]

Discipline without Punishment   Traditional discipline has two potential drawbacks. First, no one likes being punished. Second, punishment tends to gain short-term compliance, but not the sort of long-term cooperation employers often prefer.

Discipline without punishment (or **nonpunitive discipline**) aims to avoid these drawbacks. It does this by gaining employees' acceptance of the rules and by reducing the punitive nature of the discipline itself. Here is how it works:[61]

nonpunitive discipline
Discipline without punishment, usually involving a system of oral warnings and paid "decision-making leaves" in lieu of more traditional punishment.

1. *Issue an oral reminder.* The goal is to get the employee to agree to avoid future infractions.
2. *Should another incident arise within six weeks, issue a formal written reminder, a copy of which is placed in the employee's personnel file.* In addition, hold a second private discussion with the employee, again without any threats.
3. *Give a paid, one-day "decision-making leave."* If another incident occurs in the next six weeks or so, tell the employee to take a one-day leave with pay, and to stay home and consider whether the job is right for him or her and whether he or she wants to abide by the company's rules. When the employee returns to work, he or she meets with you and gives you a decision regarding whether or not he or she will follow the rules.
4. *If no further incidents occur in the next year or so, purge the one-day paid suspension from the person's file.* If the behavior is repeated, the next step is dismissal (see later discussion).

The process would not apply to exceptional circumstances. Criminal behavior or in-plant fighting might be grounds for immediate dismissal, for instance. And if several incidents occurred at very close intervals, the supervisor might skip step 2—the written warning.

Employee Privacy

For most people, invasions of their privacy are neither ethical nor fair.[62] The four main types of employee privacy violations upheld by courts are intrusion (locker room and bathroom surveillance), publication of private matters, disclosure of medical records, and appropriation of an employee's name or likeness for commercial purposes.[63] Background checks, monitoring off-duty conduct and lifestyle, drug testing, workplace searches, and monitoring of workplace activities trigger most privacy violations.[64] We'll look more closely at monitoring.

Employee Monitoring   Monitoring today has gone far beyond methods like listening in on phone lines or video-monitoring employees. Biometrics—using physical traits such as fingerprints or iris scans for identification—is one example. With fingerprint technology, the user typically passes his or her fingertip over an optical reader, or presses it onto a computer chip. Bronx Lebanon Hospital in New York uses biometric scanners, for instance to ensure that the employee that clocks in in the morning is really who he or she says he is.[65] Iris scanning tends to be the most accurate authorization device. Some organizations like the Federal Aviation Authority use it to control employees' access to its network information systems.[66]

Location monitoring is becoming pervasive. As its name implies, this involves checking the location and movement of employees.[67] Employers ranging from United Parcel Service to the City of Oakland, California use GPS units to monitor their truckers' and street sweepers' whereabouts. Federal law required all new cell phones to have GPS capabilities by December 31, 2005, so this may expand their use by employers.[68] Similarly, cheaper GPS-type technologies will contribute to wider use of location monitoring.

Employee monitoring is widespread. One survey found that about two-thirds of companies monitor e-mail activity, three-quarters monitor employee Internet use, and about 40% monitor phone calls.[69] Employers say they do so mostly to improve productivity and protect themselves from computer viruses, leaks of confidential information, and harassment suits.[70] Furthermore, employees who use company computers to do things like swap and download music can ensnare employers in illegal activities—another reason to clarify what employees can and can't use company computers for.[71] In one case, an employer in New Jersey was found liable when one of its employees used his company computer at work to distribute child pornography. (Someone had previously alerted the employer to the suspicious activity and the employer had not taken action.)[72]

When Turner Broadcasting System Inc., noticed that employees at its CNN London business bureau were piling up overtime, they installed software to monitor every Web page workers used. As the firm's network security specialist puts it, "If we see people were surfing the Web all day, then they don't have to be paid for that overtime."[73]

Electronic Communications Privacy Act (ECPA)
Intended in part to restrict interception and monitoring of oral and wire communications, but with two exceptions: employers who can show a legitimate business reason for doing so, and employers who have employees' consent to do so.

Restrictions   There are two main restrictions on workplace monitoring: the **Electronic Communications Privacy Act (ECPA)**, and *common-law protections* against invasion of privacy. The ECPA is a federal law intended to help restrict interception and monitoring of oral and wire communications. It contains two exceptions. The "business purpose exception" permits employers to monitor communications if they can show a legitimate business reason for doing so. The second, "consent exception" lets employers monitor communications if they have their employees' consent to do so.[74]

More employers are using iris scanning to verify employee identity.

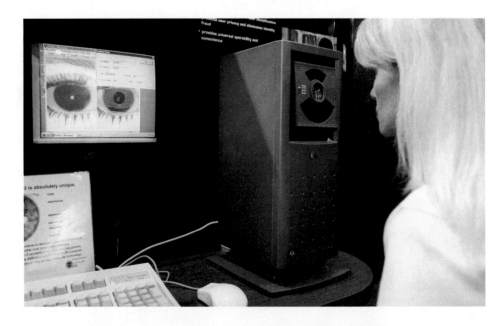

FIGURE 14-8

Sample Telephone Monitoring Acknowledgement Statement

Source: Reprinted with permission from *Bulletin to Management* (BNA Policy and Practice Series) 48, no. 14, Part II, (April 3, 1997), p. 7. © 1997 by The Bureau of National Affairs, Inc.

I understand that my telephone and e-mail communications will be monitored periodically by my supervisor and other [company] management staff. I understand that the purpose of this monitoring is to improve:

- The quality of customer service provided to policyholders and prospective customers
- My product knowledge and presentation skills

Signature   Date

Print Name   Department

Legality   Electronic eavesdropping is legal—at least to a point. For example, federal law and most state laws allow employers to monitor employees' phone calls in the ordinary course of business, but they must stop listening once it becomes clear that a conversation is personal rather than business related. You can also intercept e-mail service to protect the property rights of the e-mail provider. However, to be safe, employers often issue e-mail and online service usage policies. These warn employees that those systems are meant to be used for business purposes only. Employers also have employees sign e-mail and telephone monitoring acknowledgment statements like that in Figure 14-8.

One reason for explicit, signed policy statements is that employers can be liable for illegal acts their employees commit by via e-mail. For example, messages sent by supervisors that contain sexual innuendo or defame an employee can ensnare employers that haven't taken steps to prohibit e-mail system misuse.

Videotaped workplace monitoring calls for more legal caution than, for instance, e-mail monitoring. In one case, the U.S. Court of Appeals for the First Circuit ruled that an employer's continuous video surveillance of employees in an office setting did not constitute an unconstitutional invasion of privacy.[75] But a Boston employer had to pay over $200,000 to five workers it secretly videotaped in an employee locker room, after they sued.[76]

⑤ List at least four important factors in managing dismissals effectively.

dismissal

Involuntary termination of an employee's employment with the firm.

MANAGING DISMISSALS

Dismissal is the most drastic disciplinary step the employer can take. Because of this, it requires special care. There should be sufficient cause for dismissal, and dismissal should preferably occur only after all reasonable steps to rehabilitate or salvage the employee failed. However, there will undoubtedly be times when dismissal is required, perhaps at once.

The best way to "handle" a dismissal is to avoid it in the first place. Many dismissals start with bad hiring decisions. Using effective selection practices including assessment tests, reference and background checks, drug testing, and clearly defined job descriptions can reduce the need for many dismissals.

termination at will

means that without a contract, either the employer or the employee can terminate at will the employment relationship.

Termination at Will and Wrongful Discharge

For more than 100 years, *termination at will* was the prevailing dismissal-related rule in the United States. **Termination at will** means that without a contract, either the employer or the employee could *terminate at will* the employment relationship. The employee can resign for any reason, at will, and the employer can dismiss an employee for any reason, at will.[77]

Today, however, dismissed employees are increasingly taking their cases to court, and many employers are discovering they no longer have a blanket right to fire. Instead, EEO and other laws and court rulings increasingly limit management's right to dismiss employees. For example, firing a whistleblower might trigger "public policy" exceptions to firing at will. Or, a statement in an employee handbook may imply a contractual agreement to keep an employee on.

wrongful discharge

An employee dismissal that does not comply with the law or does not comply with the contractual arrangement stated or implied by the firm via its employment application forms, employee manuals, or other promises.

Wrongful Discharge   **Wrongful discharge** refers to a dismissal that violates the law or that fails to comply with contractual arrangements stated or implied by the employer, for instance in application forms or employee manuals.

Three main protections against wrongful discharge have eroded the termination-at-will doctrine—statutory exceptions, common law exceptions, and public policy exceptions.

First, in terms of *statutory exceptions*, federal and state equal employment and workplace laws prohibit specific types of dismissals. For example, Title VII of the Civil Rights Act of 1964 prohibits discharging employees based on race, color, religion, sex, or national origin. The Age Discrimination in Employment Act prohibits discrimination against persons 40 years or older. The Family and Medical Leave Act provides employees with up to 12 weeks of protected unpaid leave for things like serious health conditions. Occupational safety laws prohibit firing employees for reporting dangerous workplace conditions.[78]

Second, numerous *common law exceptions* exist. For example, some state courts recognize the concept of *implied contracts* in employment. Thus a court may decide that an employee handbook promising termination only "for just cause" may create an exception to the at-will rule. Similarly, an employer may create "an impression of secure employment by incorporating in its handbook progressive discipline policies or a series of procedures they will follow before taking adverse employment actions."[79] Torts are special protections created by the courts. One is against intentional infliction of emotional distress. Here a state court may deem an employer's actions toward the employee so extreme and outrageous that it overturns a dismissal.[80]

Finally, under the *public policy exception*, courts have held a discharge to be wrongful when it was against an explicit, well-established public policy (for instance, the employer fired the employee for refusing to break the law).

Grounds for Dismissal

There are four bases for dismissal: unsatisfactory performance, misconduct, lack of qualifications for the job, and changed requirements of (or elimination of) the job. We'll discuss each.

Unsatisfactory performance means persistent failure to perform assigned duties or to meet prescribed job standards.[81] Specific grounds include excessive absenteeism, tardiness, a persistent failure to meet normal job requirements, or an adverse attitude toward the company, supervisor, or fellow employees. **Misconduct** is deliberate and willful violation of the employer's rules and may include stealing, rowdy behavior, and insubordination. The "Know Your Employment Law" feature discusses an extreme example, gross misconduct.

Lack of qualifications for the job is an employee's inability to do the assigned work although he or she is diligent. Because the employee may be trying to do the job, it is reasonable for the employer to do what's possible to salvage him or her—perhaps by assigning the person to another job, or retraining the person. *Changed requirements of the job* refers to an employee's inability to do the job after the employer changed the nature of the job. Again, the employee may be industrious, so it is reasonable to retrain or transfer this person, if possible.

unsatisfactory performance

Persistent failure to perform assigned duties or to meet prescribed standards on the job.

misconduct

Deliberate and willful violation of the employer's rules.

insubordination

Willful disregard or disobedience of the boss's authority or legitimate orders; criticizing the boss in public.

Insubordination   **Insubordination** is a form of misconduct, and basically refers to disobedience and/or rebelliousness. While things like stealing, chronic tardiness, and poor-quality

Know Your *Employment* **LAW** | Gross Misconduct Checklist

There are instances in which the employee's conduct is so outrageous that it qualifies as "gross misconduct." Employers who fire employees for gross misconduct frequently do so without going through the usual warning steps, and tend to be much less flexible about letting employees like this return to work. Furthermore, the employer is not obligated under the COBRA law to provide the usual ongoing COBRA benefits for these employees.

Congress did not make it clear what it meant by "gross misconduct" when it wrote it into COBRA. Given this ambiguity, courts will tend to decide in favor of the employee. However, the following Gross Misconduct Checklist provides an idea of what gross misconduct involves.[82] (The more Yes's, the more likely it was gross misconduct.)

- Was anyone physically harmed? How badly?
- Has the employee violated the same rule several times before?
- Did the employee realize the seriousness of his or her actions?
- Will the employee be denied unemployment benefits based on the conduct?
- Did the conduct seriously harm the business of the employer?
- Was work severely disrupted?
- Were other employees significantly affected?
- Was the employer exposed to bad publicity that would greatly harm its business?

- Was the employer's reputation severely damaged?
- Will the employer lose significant business or otherwise suffer economic harm because of the misconduct?
- Will the employer be heavily fined because of the misconduct?
- Could the employer lose its business license because of the employee's misconduct?
- Has the harm to the employer already occurred?
- Will the employee lose any license needed to work for the employer (e.g., driver's license)?
- Was there criminal activity involved?
- Was it a felony?
- Does it involve harm to a person?
- Was fraud involved?
- Was any safety statute violated?
- Was any civil statute violated?
- Was the conduct purposeful?
- Was the conduct on duty?
- Is the policy violated well-known to employees?
- Does the conduct justify immediate termination?
- Has the employer immediately fired other employees who did something similar?
- Did the employee have an opportunity to explain the conduct prior to the determination that it was gross misconduct?

work are easily understood grounds for dismissal, insubordination is sometimes harder to translate into words. However, some acts are usually clearly insubordinate. These include, for instance:

1. Direct disregard of the boss's authority.
2. Direct disobedience of, or refusal to obey, the boss's orders, particularly in front of others.
3. Deliberate defiance of clearly stated company policies, rules, regulations, and procedures.
4. Public criticism of the boss.
5. Blatant disregard of reasonable instructions.
6. Contemptuous display of disrespect; making insolent comments, for example, and portraying these feelings while on the job.

7. Disregard for the chain of command, shown by frequently going around the immediate supervisor with complaints, suggestions, or political maneuvers.

8. Participation in (or leadership of) an effort to undermine and remove the boss from power.[83]

Fairness in Dismissals   Dismissals are never pleasant, but there are several things you can do to ensure that the person views the dismissal as fair.[84] First, one study found that "individuals who reported that they were given *full explanations* of why and how termination decisions were made were more likely to perceive their layoff as fair, endorse the terminating organization, and indicate that they did not wish to take the past employer to court." Second, instituting a formal *multistep procedure* (including warning) and a neutral appeal process also fosters fairness.

Third, *who actually does the dismissing* is important. Employees in one study whose managers informed them of an impending layoff viewed the dismissal procedure as much fairer than did those told by, say, a human resource manager. (The quality of the pre-layoff relationship between the employee and the manager did affect whether or not the employee preferred to get the news from the manager.) Based on this, one has to question the common practice of having the human resource department handle such notifications.

Amazon.com took what some feel was an even less diplomatic approach to dismissing some employees in the Seattle area. The firm had an in-person meeting to announce the downsizing, but telecommuter employees who were unable to attend got the news by e-mail, once the meeting was underway.

Security Measures   Facility security measures are important whenever dismissals occur. Common sense requires using a checklist to ensure that dismissed employees return all keys and company property, and (often) accompanying them out of their offices and out of the building. The employer should disable Internet-related passwords and accounts of former employees, plug holes that could allow an ex-employee to exploit someone else's user account to gain illegal access, and have formal rules for return of company laptops and handhelds. "Measures range from simply disabling access and changing passwords to reconfiguring the network and changing IP addresses, remote access procedures, and telephone numbers," says one chief technology officer. When Verizon terminates an employee, it's that person's immediate supervisor who must ensure that all access privileges are cut off and all accounts deleted; the company's security group then checks to make sure the manager followed procedures.[85]

Avoiding Wrongful Discharge Suits

As noted earlier, wrongful discharge occurs when an employee's dismissal does not comply with the law or with the contractual arrangement stated or implied by the employer. (In a *constructive discharge* claim, the plaintiff argues that he or she quit, but had no choice because the employer made the situation so intolerable at work.)[86]

Avoiding wrongful discharge suits requires a two-pronged approach.[87] *First*, create employment policies and, specifically, grievance/dispute resolution procedures (like those in this chapter) that make employees feel they are treated fairly. People who are fired and who walk away feeling embarrassed or treated unfairly are more likely to seek retribution in court. In that regard, employers can use severance pay to blunt a dismissal's sting. Figure 14-9 summarizes typical severance policies in manufacturing and service industries. There is no way to make termination pleasant, but the first line of defense is to handle it with fairness and justice.

Second, review and refine all employment related policies, procedures, and documents. Pay particular attention to the employee handbook. It should include an acknowledgment form as in Figure 14-10. This makes clear that the material in the handbook does not constitute a contract.

FIGURE 14-9

Typical Severance Pay

Source: www.shrm.org, downloaded March 6, 2004. Reprinted by permission of Society for Human Resource Management via Copyright Clearance Center.

- *Nonexempt employee*—one week of pay for each year with a minimum of four weeks and maximum of two months.
- *Exempt employee to $90,000*—two weeks for each year with a minimum of two months and a maximum of six months.
- *Exempt employee over $90,000 to director or VP level*—two to three weeks for each year with a minimum of three months and maximum of nine months.
- *Director or VP to company officer*—three weeks for each year with a minimum of four months and maximum of a year.
- *Officer*—usually covered by an employment contract or Change of Control provisions and can be all the way from one year of pay to three or four years, with other perks that may be continued.

FIGURE 14-10

TJP Inc. Employee Handbook Acknowledgment Form

TJP INC. EMPLOYEE HANDBOOK ACKNOWLEDGMENT FORM

This employee handbook has been given to _____

on (date) _____

by _____ (title) _____

Employee's effective starting date _____

Employee's pay period _____

Employee's hours and workweek are _____

Welcome to TJP Inc. Below are a list of your benefits with their effective date:

Benefit	**Effective Date**
Hospitalization _____	_____
Life insurance _____	_____
Retirement _____	_____
Vacation _____	_____
Sick leave _____	_____
Holidays _____	_____
Personal days _____	_____
Bereavement _____	_____
Worker's compensation _____	_____
Social Security _____	_____
Your first performance appraisal will be on _____	_____

I understand that my employee handbook is for informational purposes only and that I am to read and refer to the employee handbook for information on employment work rules and company policies. TJP Inc. may modify, revoke, suspend, or terminate any and all policies, rules, procedures, and benefits at any time without prior notice to company employees. This handbook and its statements do not create a contract between TJP Inc. and its employees. This handbook and its statements do not affect in any way the employment-at-will relationship between TJP Inc. and its employees.

Employee's signature _____

Date _____

Avoiding Wrongful Discharge Suits

To reduce exposure to a wrongful discharge suit, a manager may ask the following:

1. Is the employee's employment covered by any type of written agreement, including a collective bargaining agreement?
2. Have written or oral representations been made to form a contract?
3. Is a defamation claim likely?
4. Is there a possible discrimination allegation?
5. Is there any workers' compensation involvement?
6. Have reasonable rules and regulations been communicated and enforced?
7. Has employee been given an opportunity to explain any rule violations or to correct poor performance?
8. Have all monies been paid within 24 hours after separation?
9. Has employee been advised of his or her rights under COBRA?
10. Has employee been advised of what the employer will tell a prospective employer in response to a reference inquiry?[88]

Other steps for employers to take include the following:

- Have applicants sign the employment application. Make sure it contains a clear statement that employment is for no fixed term, and that the employer can terminate at any time. It should also inform applicants that "nothing on this application can be changed."
- Review your employee manual to find and delete statements that could prejudice your defense in a wrongful discharge case. For example, delete any reference to things like, "employees can be terminated only for just cause" (unless you really mean that).
- Have clear written rules listing infractions that may require discipline and discharge, and then follow the rules.
- If a rule is broken, get the worker's side of the story in front of witnesses, and preferably get it signed.
- Appraise employees in writing at least annually. If an employee shows evidence of incompetence, give that person a warning and provide an opportunity to improve.
- Keep careful confidential records of all actions such as employee appraisals, warnings or notices, memos outlining how improvement should be accomplished, and so on.

The "When You're on Your Own" feature presents some specific suggestions for supervisors to follow.

Personal Supervisory Liability

Courts sometimes hold managers personally liable for their supervisory actions, particularly with respect to actions covered by the Fair Labor Standards Act and the Family and Medical Leave Act.[89] The former defines *employer* to include "any person acting directly or indirectly in the interest of an employer in relation to any employee . . . " This can mean the individual supervisor.

There are several ways to avoid personal liability. Managers should be fully familiar with applicable federal, state, and local *statutes* and know how to uphold their requirements. *Follow company policies and procedures* (since an employee may initiate a claim against an individual supervisor whom he or she alleges did not follow company policies and procedures). The essence of many charges is that the plaintiff was treated differently than others, so *consistent application* of the rule or regulation is important. Administer the discipline in a manner that does not add to the *emotional hardship* on the employee (as would dismissing them in the middle of the day, when they must publicly collect their belongings and leave the office). Most employees will try to present *their side* of the story, and allowing them to do so can provide the employee some measure of satisfaction. *Do not act in anger*, since doing so undermines any appearance of objectivity. Finally, *utilize the human resources department* for advice on how to handle difficult disciplinary matters.

While some managers try to avoid arguments or hurting the terminated employee's feelings, not being honest can backfire. A U.S. Supreme Court decision suggests that in certain cases an employee who simply shows that the employer's stated reason for discharging him or her is a lie could have the right to take the case to a jury.[90]

The Termination Interview

termination interview
The interview in which an employee is informed of the fact that he or she has been dismissed.

Dismissing an employee is one of the most difficult tasks a manager faces at work. During one five-year period, physicians interviewed 791 working people who had just undergone heart attacks to find out what might have triggered them. The researchers concluded that the stress associated with firing someone doubled the usual risk of a heart attack for the person doing the firing, during the week following the dismissal.[91] Furthermore, the dismissed employee, even if forewarned warned many times, may still react with disbelief or even violence.[92] Guidelines for the **termination interview** itself are as follows:

1. *Plan the interview carefully.* According to experts at Hay Associates, this includes:
   - Make sure the employee keeps the appointment time.
   - Allow 10 minutes as sufficient time for the interview.
   - Use a neutral site, not your own office.
   - Have employee agreements and release announcements prepared in advance.
   - Have phone numbers ready for medical or security emergencies.
2. *Get to the point.* Avoid small talk. *As soon as the employee enters*, give the person a moment to get comfortable and then inform him or her of your decision.
3. *Describe the situation.* Briefly explain why the person is being let go. For instance, "Production in your area is down 6%. We have talked about these problems several times in the past three months, and the solutions are not being followed through. We have to make a change." Stress the situation, rather than the employee and his or her shortcomings. Emphasize that the decision is final and irrevocable.
4. *Listen.* To the extent practical, continue the interview for several minutes until the person seems to be talking freely and reasonably calmly about the reasons for his or her termination and the support package (including severance pay).
5. *Review all elements of the severance package.* Describe severance payments, benefits, access to office support people, and how references will be handled. However, under no conditions should any promises or benefits beyond those already in the support package be implied.
6. *Identify the next step.* The terminated employee may be disoriented and unsure what to do next. Explain where the employee should go upon leaving the interview. It's often best to have someone escort him or her until the person is out the door.

outplacement counseling
A systematic process by which a terminated person is trained and counseled in the techniques of self-appraisal and securing a new position.

Outplacement Counseling **Outplacement counseling** is a systematic process by which someone you've terminated is trained and counseled in the techniques of conducting a self-appraisal and securing a new job appropriate to his or her needs and talents. As the term is generally used, outplacement does not imply that the employer takes responsibility for placing the person in a new job. Instead, it is a counseling service whose purpose is to provide the person with advice, instructions, and a sounding board to help formulate career goals and successfully execute a job search him or herself. Outplacement counseling is part of the terminated employee's support or severance package and is often done by specialized outside firms.

Outplacement firms do more than counsel displaced employees; they also help the employer devise its dismissal plan. For example, prior to announcing a downsizing, it might be sensible to work with an outplacement firm to decide things like how to break the news and deal with dismissed employees' emotional reactions, what benefits to offer (including severance pay and outplacement), and equal opportunity employment considerations.

exit interviews

Interviews with employees who are leaving the firm, conducted for the purpose of obtaining information about the job or related matters, to give the employer insight about the company.

Exit Interview   Many employers conduct **exit interviews** with employees who are leaving the firm for any reason. These are interviews, usually conducted by a human resource professional just prior to the employee leaving, that elicit information about the job or related matters with the aim of giving employers insights into what is right—or wrong—about their companies.

Exit interview questions include: How were you recruited? Why did you join the company? Was the job presented correctly and honestly? Were your expectations met? What was the workplace environment like? What was your supervisor's management style like? What did you like most/least about the company? Were there any special problem areas? Why did you decide to leave, and how was the departure handled?[93] Figure 14-11 presents a form for this purpose.

The assumption of course is that because the employee is leaving, he or she will be candid. However, one study suggests that the information one gets from exit interviews is questionable.[94] The researchers found that at the time of separation, 38% of those leaving blamed salary and benefits, and only 4% blamed supervision. Followed up 18 months later, however, 24% blamed supervision and only 12% blamed salary and benefits. Getting to the real problem during the exit interview may thus require some heavy digging. Yet these interviews can be useful. When Blue Cross of Northeastern Pennsylvania laid off employees, many said, in exit interviews, "This is not a stable place to work." The firm took steps to correct that misperception for those who stayed with Blue Cross.

Layoffs, Downsizing, and the Plant Closing Law

Nondisciplinary separations are a fact of corporate life. For the employer, reduced sales or profits may required *layoffs* or *downsizing*. *Layoff* generally refers to having selected employees take time off, with the expectation that they will come back to work. *Downsizing* refers to permanently dismissing a relatively large proportion of employees in an attempt to improve productivity and competitiveness. Similarly, employees may *resign* to *retire* or to look for better jobs.

The Plant Closing Law   Until 1989, there were no federal laws requiring notification of employees when an employer decided to close a facility. However, in that year the Worker Adjustment and Retraining Notification Act (popularly known as the *plant closing law*) became law. It requires employers of 100 or more employees to give 60 days' notice before closing a facility or starting a layoff of 50 people or more. The law does not prevent the employer from closing down, nor does it require saving jobs. It simply gives employees time to seek other work or retraining by giving them advance notice of the shutdown.

The law says employers must give advance notice to employees who will (or who might reasonably be expected to) experience a covered "employment loss." *Covered employment losses* include *terminations* (other than discharges for cause; voluntary departures, or retirement); *layoffs* exceeding six months, and *reductions* of more than 50% in employee's work hours during each month of any six-month period. Generally, the firm need *not* notify workers it reassigns or transfers to another company location within a reasonable commuting distance. While there are exceptions, the penalty for failing to give notice is one day's pay and benefits to each employee for each day's notice that should have been given, up to 60 days.

FIGURE 14-11

Employee Exit Interview Questionnaire

Source: http://www.fin.ucar. edu/forms/HR/exit_form/ exit.pdf, accessed May 24, 2007. Used with permission.

University Corporation for Atmospheric Research

EXIT INTERVIEW

Employee Name _____   Supervisor _____

Division _____   Job Title _____

Hire Date _____   Termination Date _____

1. **Why are you leaving UCAR?**

   _____

   _____

   _____

2. **What circumstances would have prevented your departure?**

   _____

   _____

3. **What did you like most about your job?**

   _____

   _____

4. **What did you like least about your job?**

   _____

   _____

5. **What did you think of your supervisor on the following points:**

	Almost Always	Usually	Sometimes	Never
Was consistently fair	( )	( )	( )	( )
Provided recognition	( )	( )	( )	( )
Resolved complaints	( )	( )	( )	( )
Was sensitive to employees' needs	( )	( )	( )	( )
Provided feedback on performance	( )	( )	( )	( )
Was receptive to open communication	( )	( )	( )	( )
Followed UCAR's policies	( )	( )	( )	( )

FIGURE 14-11

(*continued*)

6. **How would you rate the following:**

	Excellent	Good	Fair	Poor
Cooperation within your division/program	( )	( )	( )	( )
Cooperation with other divisions	( )	( )	( )	( )
Personal job training	( )	( )	( )	( )
Equipment provided (materials, resources, facilities)	( )	( )	( )	( )
Company's performance review system	( )	( )	( )	( )
Company's new employee orientation program	( )	( )	( )	( )
Rate of pay for your job	( )	( )	( )	( )
Career development/Advancement opportunities	( )	( )	( )	( )
Physical working conditions	( )	( )	( )	( )

Comments: _____

_____

7. **Was the work you were doing approximately what you expected it would be?**

Yes _____ No _____

Comments: _____

8. **Was your workload usually:** Too heavy ( )   About right ( )   Too light ( )

9. **How did you feel about the employee benefits provided by the company?**

	Excellent	Good	Fair	Poor	No Opinion
Paid holidays	( )	( )	( )	( )	( )
Paid vacation	( )	( )	( )	( )	( )
Medical plan	( )	( )	( )	( )	( )
Dental plan	( )	( )	( )	( )	( )
Vision plan	( )	( )	( )	( )	( )
Flexible spending plans	( )	( )	( )	( )	( )
Sick leave	( )	( )	( )	( )	( )
Retirement plan	( )	( )	( )	( )	( )
Educational assistance	( )	( )	( )	( )	( )

10. **Would you recommend the company to a friend as a good organization to work for?**

Most definitely ( )   With reservations ( )   No ( )

11. **What suggestions do you have to make UCAR a better place to work?:** _____

_____

_____

_____

_____   _____

Human Resources Representative   Employee

Date: _____   Date: _____

The law is not entirely clear about how to notify employees. However, a paragraph that might suit the purpose would be as follows:

Please consider this letter to be your official notice, as required by the federal plant closing law, that your current position with the company will end 60 days from today because of a [layoff or closing] that is now projected to take place on [date]. After that day your employment with the company will be terminated, and you will no longer be carried on our payroll records or be covered by any company benefit programs. Any questions concerning the plant closing law or this notice will be answered in the HR office.[95]

The Layoff Process   A study helps illustrate one firm's layoff process. In this company, senior management first met to make strategic decisions about the size and timing of the layoffs. These managers also debated the relative importance of the skill sets they thought the firm needed going forward. Front-line supervisors assessed their subordinates, rating their nonunion employees either A, B, or C (union employees were covered by a union agreement making layoffs dependant on seniority). The front-line supervisors than informed each of their subordinates about his or her A, B, or C rating, and told each that those employees with C grades were designated "surplus" and most likely to be laid off.[96]

Dismissal's Effects   Dismissal's " . . . tend to result in deleterious psychological and physical health outcomes for employees who lose their jobs" as well as for the survivors who, witnessing the layoffs of their coworkers and friends, face uncertainty and discomfort.[97]

Furthermore, it is not just the "victims" and "survivors" who suffer negative effects. Researchers collected data from 410 managers who either had or had not been in the position of having to inform subordinates about expected mass layoffs. None of the managers were layoff targets. The researchers " . . . found that the more managers were personally responsible for handing out warning notices to employees, regardless of their age, gender, and marital status, the more likely they were to report physical health problems, to seek treatment for these problems, and to complain of disturbed sleep . . . "[98]

Bumping/Layoff Procedures   As noted above, *layoff* generally refers to having selected employees take time off, with the expectation that they will come back to work. With layoffs, three conditions are usually present: (1) there is no work available for these employees, (2) management expects the no-work situation to be temporary and probably short term, and (3) management intends to recall the employees when work is again available. A layoff is therefore not a termination, which is a permanent severing of the employment relationship. Some employers, however, use the term *layoff* as a euphemism for discharge or termination.

Employers who encounter frequent business slowdowns may have bumping/layoff procedures that let employees use their seniority to remain on the job. Most such **bumping/layoff procedures** have these features in common:

bumping/layoff procedures
Detailed procedures that determine who will be laid off if no work is available; generally allow employees to use their seniority to remain on the job.

1. Seniority is usually the ultimate determinant of who will work.
2. Seniority can give way to merit or ability, but usually only when no senior employee is qualified for a particular job.
3. Seniority is usually based on the date the employee joined the organization, not the date he or she took a particular job.
4. Because seniority is usually companywide, an employee in one job can usually bump or displace an employee in another job, provided the more senior person can do the job without further training. When the New York Stock Exchange eliminated all "reporter" jobs on the exchange, many of these people applied for and "bumped" lower seniority employees, for instance, from "messenger" jobs.

Layoff and Downsizing Alternatives   Layoffs and (especially) downsizings are usually painful for all involved, and have the added disadvantage of stripping the company of well-trained personnel. Employers therefore often try to find alternatives to wholesale dismissals, where possible. Suggestions include finding volunteers who are interested in reducing hours or part-time work; using attrition; and networking with local employers concerning temporary or permanent redeployments.

There are also other alternatives. With the *voluntary reduction in pay plan*, all employees agree to reductions in pay to keep everyone working. Other employers arrange for all or most employees to *concentrate their vacations* during slow periods. They don't have to hire temporary help for vacationing employees during peak periods, and staffing auto-matically declines when business declines. For example, Sun (as well as many Silicon Valley employers) had all employees stay home for a week when the economy slowed. Other employees agree to take *voluntary time off*, which again has the effect of reducing the employer's payroll and avoiding layoffs.

Many employers hire temporary employees, often as independent contractors, with the understanding their work is temporary. When layoffs are required, they are the first to leave. Some seek volunteers as an alternative to dismissing large numbers of employees. For example, GM and Ford recently offered *early retirement* buyout packages to many of their employees.

Adjusting to Downsizings and Mergers

downsizing

The process of reducing, usually dramatically, the number of people employed by a firm.

Firm's usually **downsize** to improve their financial positions. Yet many firms discover profits don't rise after major personnel cuts. Low morale among those remaining is often part of the problem.

It therefore makes sense to think through how the firm is going to reduce the surviving employees' uncertainty and boost their morale.[99] When Duracell, Inc. (now part of Dow), downsized, their program included post-downsizing announcement activities, including a full staff meeting at the facility; an immediate follow-up in which remaining employees were split into groups with senior managers to express their concerns and have their questions answered; and long-term support, for instance, by encouraging supervisors to meet with employees frequently and informally to encourage an open-door atmosphere. The Diners Club subsidiary of Citigroup used attitude surveys to help management monitor how postdownsizing efforts are progressing.

Downsizing/Layoff Guidelines   Guidelines for implementing a reduction in force include:[100]

- *Identify objectives and constraints.* For example, decide how many positions to eliminate at which locations, and what criteria to use to identify the employees to whom you'll offer any voluntary exit incentives.
- *Form a downsizing team.* This management team should prepare a communication strategy for explaining the downsizing; establish hiring and promotion levels; produce a downsizing schedule; and supervise the displaced employees' benefit programs.
- *Address legal issues.* Ensure that others won't view the downsizing as a subterfuge to lay off protected classes of employees. Review factors such as age, race, and gender before finalizing and communicating any dismissals.
- *Plan post-implementation actions.* Activities such as surveys and explanatory meetings can help maintain morale. Similarly, some suggest a hiring freeze of at least six months after the layoffs have taken effect.
- *Address security concerns.* With any large layoffs, it may be wise to have security personnel in place in case there's a problem from one or two employees.

One lawyer says that when employees seek out lawyers after mass layoffs it's often because they're unhappy with how the employer handled the layoff. Yet mass layoffs and downsizings need not trigger the horror stories one occasionally finds in the press. *Information sharing* (providing advanced notice regarding the layoff), and *interpersonal sensitivity* (in terms of the manager's demeanor during layoffs) can both help mitigate the otherwise negative effects.[101] The people who announce the downsizing and deal with the employee questions should factually and truthfully explain what is happening and what the employees' rights are.

Merger Guidelines In terms of dismissal, *mergers and acquisitions* are usually one-sided. One company essentially acquires the other, and it is often the employees of the latter who find themselves looking for new jobs. In such situations, the acquired firm's surviving employees may be hypersensitive to mistreatment of their soon-to-be former colleagues. Seeing your former colleagues fired is bad enough for morale. Seeing them fired under conditions that smack of unfairness poisons the relationship. It thus behooves the manager to treat those whom you let go fairly. As a rule, therefore:

- Avoid the appearance of power and domination.
- Avoid win–lose behavior.
- Remain businesslike and professional in all dealings.
- Maintain as positive a feeling about the acquired company as possible.
- Remember that the degree to which your organization treats the acquired group with care and dignity will affect the confidence, productivity, and commitment of those who remain.[102]

For example, Jack Brown, chairman of Slater Brothers, knew it was crucial to maintain good relations with the employees of the 33 Albertson's and 10 Lucky Stores his company acquired. Slater first created a transition team headed by a top executive. Among other things, they offered jobs to all employees of the 43 stores. He and his firm also devoted a great deal of time and effort to communicating with the new employees.[103]

R E V I E W

SUMMARY

1. Ethics refers to the principles of conduct governing an individual or a group, and specifically to the standards you use to decide what your conduct should be.
2. Ethical decisions are always characterized by two things. First, they always involve normative judgments. Second, ethical decisions also always involve morality, which is society's accepted standards of behavior.
3. Numerous factors shape ethical behavior at work. These include individual factors, organizational factors, the boss's influence, ethics policies and codes, and the organization's culture.
4. HR management can influence ethics and fair treatment at work in numerous ways. Some examples: A fair and open selection process can emphasize the company's stress on integrity and ethics, the company can have special ethics training programs, employees' adherence to high ethical standards can be measured during performance appraisals, and ethical (or unethical) work-related behavior can be rewarded or punished.
5. A fair and just discipline process is based on three prerequisites: rules and regulations, a system of progressive penalties, and an appeals process. Following discipline guidelines is important.
6. The basic aim of discipline without punishment is to gain an employee's acceptance of the rules by reducing the punitive nature of the discipline itself.
7. Managing dismissals is an important part of any supervisor's job. Among the reasons for dismissal are unsatisfactory performance, misconduct, lack of qualifications, changed job requirements, and insubordination. In dismissing one or more employees, however, remember that termination at will as a policy has been weakened by exceptions in many states. Furthermore, great care should be taken to avoid wrongful discharge suits.
8. Dismissing an employee is always difficult, and the termination interview should be handled properly. Plan the interview carefully (for instance, early in the week), get to

the point, describe the situation and then listen until the person has expressed his or her feelings. Then discuss the severance package and identify the next step.

9. Nondisciplinary separations such as layoffs and retirement occur all the time. The plant closing law (the Worker Adjustment and Retraining Notification Act) outlines requirements to be followed with regard to official notice before operations with 50 or more people are to be closed down.

DISCUSSION QUESTIONS

1. Explain how you would ensure fairness in disciplining, discussing particularly the prerequisites to disciplining, disciplining guidelines, and the discipline without punishment approach.
2. Why is it important in our highly litigious society to manage dismissals properly?
3. What techniques would you use as alternatives to traditional discipline? What do such alternatives have to do with "organizational justice?" Why do you think alternatives like these are important, given industry's need today for highly committed employees?
4. Provide three examples of behaviors that would probably be unethical but legal, and three that would probably be illegal but ethical.
5. List ten things your college or university does to encourage ethical behavior by students and/or faculty.
6. You need to select a nanny for your or a relative's child, and want someone ethical. Based on what you read in this chapter, what would you do to help ensure you ended up hiring someone ethical?
7. You believe your employee is being insubordinate. How would you verify this and what would you do about it if true?
8. Wal-Mart instituted a new scheduling system that makes it more difficult for its employees to know for sure what hours they would be working, (please see chapter vignette). Based on what you read in this chapter, is the new system ethical? Why or why not? Is it fair? What would you do if you were a Wal-Mart employee?

INDIVIDUAL AND GROUP ACTIVITIES

1. Working individually or in groups, interview managers or administrators at your employer or college in order to determine the extent to which the employer or college endeavors to build two-way communication, and the specific types of programs used. Do the managers think they are effective? What do the employees (or faculty members) think of the programs in use at the employer or college?
2. Working individually or in groups, obtain copies of the student handbook for your college and determine to what extent there is a formal process through which students can air grievances. Based on your contacts with other students, has it been an effective grievance process? Why or why not?
3. Working individually or in groups, determine the nature of the academic discipline process in your college. Do you think it is effective? Based on what you read in this chapter, would you recommend any modifications?
4. The HRCI "Test Specifications" appendix at the end of this book (pages 726–735) lists the knowledge someone studying for the HRCI certification exam needs to have in each area of human resource management (such as in Strategic Management, Workforce Planning, and Human Resource Development). In groups of four to five students, do four things: (1) review that appendix now; (2) identify the material in

this chapter that relates to the required knowledge the appendix lists; (3) write four multiple choice exam questions on this material that you believe would be suitable for inclusion in the HRCI exam; and (4) if time permits, have someone from your team post your team's questions in front of the class, so the students in other teams can take each others' exam questions.

5. In a recent research study at Ohio State University, a professor found that even honest people, left to their own devices, will steal from their employers.[104] In this study, the researchers gave financial services workers the opportunity to steal a small amount of money after participating in an after-work project for which the pay was inadequate. Would the employees steal to make up for the underpayment? In most cases, yes. Employees who scored low on an honesty test stole whether or not their office had an ethics program that said stealing from the company was illegal. Employees who scored high on the honesty test also stole, but only if their office did not have such an employee ethics program—the "honest" people didn't steal if there was an ethics policy.

In groups of four or five students, answer these questions: Do you think findings like these are generalizable? In other words, would they apply across the board to employees in other types of companies and situations? If your answer is yes, what do you think this implies about the need for and wisdom of having an ethics program?

EXPERIENTIAL EXERCISE

Discipline or Not?

Purpose: The purpose of this exercise is to provide you with some experience in analyzing and handling an actual disciplinary action.

Required Understanding: Students should be thoroughly familiar with the following case, titled "Botched Batch." **Do not read the "award" or "discussion" sections until after the groups have completed their deliberations.**

How to Set Up the Exercise/Instructions: Divide the class into groups of four or five students. Each group should take the arbitrator's point of view and assume that they are to analyze the case and make the arbitrator's decision. Review the case again at this point, but please do not read the award and discussion.

Each group should answer the following questions:
1. Based on what you read in this chapter, including all relevant guidelines, what would your decision be if you were the arbitrator? Why?
2. Do you think that after their experience in this arbitration the parties will be more or less inclined to settle grievances by themselves without resorting to arbitration?

Botched Batch

Facts: A computer department employee made an entry error that botched an entire run of computer reports. Efforts to rectify the situation produced a second set of improperly run reports. As a result of the series of errors, the employer incurred extra costs of $2,400, plus a weekend of overtime work by other computer department staffers. Management suspended the employee for three days for negligence, and also revoked a promotion for which the employee had previously been approved.

Protesting the discipline, the employee stressed that she had attempted to correct her error in the early stages of the run by notifying the manager of computer operations of her mistake. Maintaining that the resulting string of errors could have been avoided if the manager had followed up on her report and stopped the initial run, the employee argued that she had been treated unfairly because the manager had not been disciplined even though he compounded the problem, whereas she was severely punished. Moreover, citing her "impeccable" work record and management's acknowledgment that she had always been a "model employee," the employee insisted that the denial of her previously approved promotion was "unconscionable."

*(Please do **not** read beyond this point until after you have answered the two questions.)*

Award: The arbitrator upholds the three-day suspension, but decides that the promotion should be restored.

Discussion: "There is no question," the arbitrator notes, that the employee's negligent act "set in motion the train of events that resulted in running two complete sets of reports reflecting improper information." Stressing that the employer incurred substantial cost because of the error, the arbitrator cites "unchallenged" testimony that management had commonly issued three-day suspensions for similar infractions in the past. Thus, the arbitrator decides, the employer acted with just cause in meting out an "evenhanded" punishment for the negligence.

Turning to the denial of the already approved promotion, the arbitrator says that this action should be viewed "in the same light as a demotion for disciplinary reasons." In such cases, the arbitrator notes, management's decision normally is based on a pattern of unsatisfactory behavior, an employee's inability to perform, or similar grounds. Observing that management had never before reversed a promotion as part of a disciplinary action, the arbitrator says that by tacking on the denial of the promotion in this case, the employer substantially varied its disciplinary policy from its past practice. Because this action on management's part was not "evenhanded," the arbitrator rules, the promotion should be restored.[105]

Ethics Quiz Answers

Quiz is on page 552—Figure 14-1.

1. 34% said personal e-mail on company computers is wrong.
2. 37% said using office equipment for schoolwork is wrong.
3. 49% said playing computer games at work is wrong.
4. 54% said Internet shopping at work is wrong.
5. 61% said it's unethical to blame your error on technology.
6. 87% said it's unethical to visit pornographic sites at work.
7. 33% said $25 is the amount at which a gift from a supplier or client becomes troubling, while 33% said $50, and 33% said $100.
8. 35% said a $50 gift to the boss is unacceptable.
9. 12% said a $50 gift *from* the boss is unacceptable.
10. 70% said it's unacceptable to take the $200 football tickets.
11. 70% said it's unacceptable to take the $120 theater tickets.
12. 35% said it's unacceptable to take the $100 food basket.
13. 45% said it's unacceptable to take the $25 gift certificate.
14. 40% said it's unacceptable to take the $75 raffle prize.
15. 11% reported they lie about sick days.
16. 4% reported they take credit for the work or ideas of others.

APPLICATION CASE

Fire My Best Salesperson?

Greg Johns, sales director for International Widget Industries (IWI) had a problem. He was just told that his top salesperson, Bob Pollock, was stealing from the company. Pollock had been inflating expense reports and exaggerating his sales (by double-booking sales orders).

He therefore got higher expense reimbursements and commissions than he deserved. The accounting department had proof that Pollock was stealing. IWI's CEO has told Johns to either rectify the situation or lose his own job. Johns is in a quandary about what to do. He doesn't want to lose his best salesperson, and he thinks perhaps there might be extenuating circumstances—such as family pressures—that explain Pollock's behavior. The question is, what should Johns do now?[106]

Questions

Assume you are Johns. Specifically,

1. What should you do now?
2. Why should you do it?
3. How would you do it?

Please answer that three-part question before moving on to see what actually happened, by reading the following:

In this case, there's no question of what to do. The company must terminate this salesperson. According to the people who are actually involved in this situation, no company can tolerate stealing on the part of its employees. If you cannot trust the salesperson, his presence with your company will have a corrosive effect on all that he deals with, including customers and coworkers.

The consensus is to confront him. First, confirm that the information is accurate. Show him the evidence, get his response, and assuming the accusations are true, have the person surrender all his company account information and leads in return for a quiet termination.

Now, knowing what IWI actually did, what do you think of their response? What, if anything, would you have done differently?

CONTINUING CASE

Carter Cleaning Company

Guaranteeing Fair Treatment

Being in the laundry and cleaning business, the Carters have always felt strongly about not allowing employees to smoke, eat, or drink in their stores. Jennifer was therefore surprised to walk into a store and find two employees eating lunch at the front counter. There was a large pizza in its box, and the two of them were sipping colas and eating slices of pizza and submarine sandwiches off paper plates. Not only did it look messy, but there were also grease and soda spills on the counter and the store smelled from onions and pepperoni, even with the four-foot-wide exhaust fan pulling air out through the roof. In addition to being a turnoff to customers, the mess on the counter increased the possibility that a customer's order might actually become soiled in the store.

While this was a serious matter, neither Jennifer nor her father felt that what the counter people were doing was grounds for immediate dismissal, partly because the store manager had apparently condoned their actions. The problem was, they didn't know what to do. It seemed to them that the matter called for more than just a warning but less than dismissal.

Questions

1. What would you do if you were Jennifer, and why?
2. Should a disciplinary system be established at Carter's Cleaning Centers?
3. If so, what should it cover, and how would you suggest it deal with a situation such as the one with the errant counter people?
4. How would you deal with the store manager?

TRANSLATING STRATEGY INTO HR POLICIES AND PRACTICES CASE:
THE HOTEL PARIS

The Hotel Paris's New Ethics, Justice, and Fair Treatment Process

The Hotel Paris's competitive strategy is "To use superior guest service to differentiate the Hotel Paris properties, and to thereby increase the length of stay and return rate of guests, and thus boost revenues and profitability." HR manager Lisa Cruz must now formulate functional policies and activities that support this competitive strategy, by eliciting the required employee behaviors and competencies.

As the head of HR for the Hotel Paris, Lisa Cruz was especially concerned about her company maintaining the highest ethical standards. Her concerns were twofold. First, from a practical point of view, there are, in a hotel chain, literally thousands of opportunities on any given day for guests to have bad ethical experiences. For example, in any single hotel each day there are at least a dozen people (including housekeepers, front-desk clerks, security guards, and so on) with easy access to guests' rooms, and to their personal belongings. Guests—many younger, and many unwary—are continually walking the halls unprotected. So, in a service company like this, there is simply no margin for ethical errors.

But she was concerned about ethics for a second reason. She'd been around long enough to know that employees do not like being treated unfairly, and that unfairness in any form could manifest itself in low morale, commitment, and performance. Indeed, perhaps her employees' low morale and commitment—as measured by her firm's attitude surveys—stemmed, in part, from what they perceived as unjust treatment by the hotel's managers. Lisa therefore turned to the task of assessing and redesigning the Hotel Paris's ethics, justice, and fair treatment practices.

To do this, Lisa and her team wanted to proceed methodically through the company's entire HR process, starting with recruitment and selection. For example, working with the company's general counsel, they produced and presented to the CEO a new Hotel Paris code of ethics, as well as a more complete set of ethical guidelines. These now appear on the Hotel Paris's careers Web site link, and are part of each new employee's orientation packet. They contracted with a vendor to provide a customized, Web-based ethics training program, and made it clear that the first employees to participate in it were the company's top executives. However, she knew this was just the start.

Questions

1. List three specific steps Hotel Paris should take with respect to each individual human research function (selection, training, and so on) to improve the level of ethics in the company.
2. Based on what you read in this chapter, create in outline form a strategy map showing how the Hotel's HR functions can foster better employee service.
3. Based on what you learned in this chapter, write a short (less than one page) explanation Lisa can use to sell to top management the need to improve the hotel chain's fairness and justice processes.

KEY TERMS

ethics, 553
distributive justice, 554
procedural justice, 554
interactional (interpersonal) justice, 554
ethics code, 558
organizational culture, 559
nonpunitive discipline, 571
Electronic Communications Privacy Act (ECPA), 572
dismissal, 573

termination at will, 573
wrongful discharge, 574
unsatisfactory performance, 574
misconduct, 574
insubordination, 574
termination interview, 579
outplacement counseling, 579
exit interviews, 580
bumping/layoff procedures, 583
downsizing, 584

ENDNOTES

1. "What Role Should HR Play in Corporate Ethics?" *HR Focus* 81, no. 1 (January 2004), p. 3. See also Dennis Moberg, "Ethics Blind Spots in Organizations: How Systematic Errors in Person's Perception Undermine Moral Agency," *Organization Studies* 27, no. 3, 2006, pp. 413–428.

2. Paul Schumann, "A Moral Principles Framework for Human Resource Management Ethics," *Human Resource Management Review* 11 (2004), p. 94.

3. Kevin Wooten, "Ethical Dilemmas in Human Resource Management: An Application of a Multidimensional Framework, A Unifying Taxonomy, and Applicable Codes," *Human Resource Management Review* 11 (2001), p. 161. See also Sean Valentine et al., "Employee Job Response As a Function of Ethical Context and Perceived Organization Support," *Journal of Business Research* 59, no. 5, 2006, pp. 582–588.

4. William Kandel, "After Reeves: Proving Pretext, Imprecision, or Imperfection?" *Employee Relations Law Journal* 26, no. 3 (Winter 2000), pp. 5–29.

5. Manuel Velasquez, *Business Ethics: Concepts and Cases* (Upper Saddle River, NJ: Prentice Hall, 1992), p. 9. See also Kate Walter, "Ethics Hot Lines Tap into More Than Wrongdoing," *HR Magazine*, September 1995, pp. 79–85; Skip Kaltenheuser, "Bribery Is Being Outlawed Virtually Worldwide," *Business Ethics*, May 1998, p. 11; and Wendy Fischman et al., *Making Good: How Young People Cope with Moral Dilemmas at Work*, (Boston, MA: Harvard University Press, 2004).

6. The following discussion, except as noted, is based on Manuel Velasquez, *Business Ethics*, pp. 9–12.

7. For further discussion of ethics and morality, see Tom Beauchamp and Norman Bowie, *Ethical Theory and Business* (Upper Saddle River, NJ: Prentice Hall, 2001), pp. 1–19.

8. Richard Osborne, "A Matter of Ethics," *Industry Week*, September 4, 2000, pp. 41–42.

9. Carroll Lachnit, "Recruiting Trouble for Tyson," *Workforce, HR Trends and Tools for Business Results* 81, no. 2 (February 2002), p. 22.

10. Daniel Skarlicki and Robert Folger, "Fairness and Human Resources Management," *Human Resource Management Review* 13, no. 1 (2003), p. 1.

11. Gary Weaver and Linda Trevino, "The Role of Human Resources in Ethics/Compliance Management: A Fairness Perspective," *Human Resource Management Review* 11 (2001), p. 115.

12. Linda Trevino and Katherine Nelson, *Managing Business Ethics* (New York: John Wiley & Sons, 1999), p. 134.

13. Weaver and Trevino, "The Role of Human Resources," pp. 113–134.

14. Michelle Donovan et al., "The Perceptions of Their Interpersonal Treatment Scale: Development and Validation of a Measure of Interpersonal Treatment in the Workplace," *Journal of Applied Psychology* 83, no. 5 (1998), pp. 683–692.

15. Sara Morris et al., "A Test of Environmental, Situational, and Personal Influences on the Ethical Intentions of CEOs," *Business and Society*, August 1995, pp. 119–247.

16. Vikas Anand et al., "Business as Usual: The Acceptance and Perpetuation of Corruption in Organizations," *Academy of Management Executive*, 2004, vol. 18, no. 2, pp. 40–41.

17. Ibid.

18. "Former CEO Joins WorldCom's Indicted," *Miami Herald*, March 3, 2004, p. 4C.

19. See for example, Roberta Johnson, *Whistleblowing: When it Works—and Why*, (L. Reimer, 2003).

20. "Ethics Policies are Big with Employers, but Workers See Small Impact on the Workplace," *BNA Bulletin to Management*, June 29, 2000, p. 201.

21. Discussed in Samuel Greengard, "Cheating and Stealing," *Workforce*, October 1997, pp. 45–53.

22. From Guy Brumback, "Managing Above the Bottom Line of Ethics," *Supervisory Management*, December 1993, p. 12.

23. James Kunen, "Enron Division (and Values) Thing," *New York Times*, January 19, 2002, p. A19. For another example, see Heather Tesoriero and Avery Johnson, "Suit Details How J&J Pushed Sales of Procrit," *The Wall Street Journal*, April 10, 2007.

24. Janet Adams et al., "Code of Ethics as Signals for Ethical Behavior," *Journal of Business Ethics*, February 2001, vol. 29, no. 3, pp. 199–211.

25. Dayton Fandray, "The Ethical Company," *Workforce*, December 2000, pp. 74–77.

26. "Ethics: It Isn't Just the Big Guys," *The American Intelligence Wire*, July 28, 2003, p. 10.

27. Ibid.

28. J. Krohe Jr., "The Big Business of Business Ethics," *Across the Board* 34 (May 1997), pp. 23–29; Deborah Wells and Marshall Schminke, "Ethical Development and Human Resources Training: An Integrator Framework," *Human Resource Management Review* 11 (2001), pp. 135–158.

29. Editorial: "Ethical Issues in the Management of Human Resources," *Human Resource Management Review* 11 (2001), p. 6; See also Joel Lefkowitz, "The Constancy of Ethics amidst the Changing World of Work," *Human Resource Management Review*, vol. 16, 2006, pp. 245–268.

30. William Byham, "Can You Interview for Integrity?" *Across-The-Board* 41, no. 2, (March/April 2004): 34–38. For a description of how the United States Military Academy uses its student admission and socialization processes to promote character development, see Evan Offstein and Ronald Dufresne, "Building Strong Ethics and Promoting Positive Character Development: The Influence of HRM at the United States Military Academy at West Point," *Human Resource Management*, Spring 2007, vol. 46, no. 1, pp. 95–114.

31. Weaver and Trevino, "The Role of Human Resources," p. 123. See also Linda Andrews, "The Nexus of Ethics," *HR Magazine*, August 2005, pp. 53–58.

32. Cropanzano and Wright, "Procedural Justice and Organizational Staffing," pp. 7–40.

33. Kathryn Tyler, "Do the Right Thing, Ethics Training Programs Help Employees Deal with Ethical Dilemmas," *HR Magazine*, (February 2005): 99–102.

34. Weaver and Trevino, "The Role of Human Resources," p. 123.

35. M. Ronald Buckley et al., "Ethical Issues in Human Resources Systems," *Human Resource Management Review* 11, nos. 1, 2 (2001), pp. 11, 29. See also Ann Pomeroy, "The Ethics Squeeze," *HR Magazine*, March 2006, pp. 48–55.

36. Tom Asacker, "Ethics in the Workplace," *Training and Development*, (August 2004): 44.

37. Weaver and Trevino, "The Role of Human Resources," pp. 113–134.

38. Weaver and Trevino, "The Role of Human Resources," p. 114.

39. "Corporations' Drive to Embrace Ethics Gives HR Leaders Chance to Take Reins," *BNA Bulletin to Management*, November 7, 2002, p. 353.

40. Max Rexroad and Joyce Ostrosky, "Sarbanes-Oxley: What It Means to the Marketplace," *Journal of Accountancy* 197, no. 2 (February 2004), pp. 43–48.

41. Michael Burr, "Corporate Governance: Embracing Sarbanes-Oxley," *Public Utilities Fortnightly*, October 15, 2003, pp. 20–22.

42. Ibid.

43. W. Chan Kim and Rene Mauborgne, "Fair Process: Managing in the Knowledge Economy," *Harvard Business Review*, July/August 1997, pp. 65–75.

44. Weaver and Trevino, "The Role of Human Resources," p. 117.

45. Russell Cropanzano and Thomas Wright, "Procedural Justice and Organizational Staffing: A Tale of Two Paradigms," *Human Resource Management Review* 13, no. 1 (2003), pp. 7–40.

46. Suzanne Masterson, "A Trickle-Down Model of Organizational Justice: Relating Employees' and Customers' Perceptions of and Reactions to Fairness," *Journal of Applied Psychology* 86, no. 4 (2001), pp. 594–601.

47. Rudy Yandrick, "Lurking in the Shadows," *HR Magazine*, October 1999, pp. 61–68. See also, Helge Hoel and David Beale, "Workplace Bullying, Psychological Perspectives and Industrial Relations: Towards a Contextualized and Interdisciplinary Approach," *British Journal of Industrial Relations* 44, no. 2, June 2006, pp. 239–262.

48. Bennett Tepper, "Consequences of Abusive Supervision," *Academy of Management Journal* 43, no. 2 (2000), pp. 178–190. See also Samuel Aryee, et al, "Antecedents and Outcomes of Abusive Supervision: A Test of a Trickle-Down Model," *Journal of Applied Psychology*, vol. 1992, no. 1, 2007, pp. 191–201.

49. Wendy Boswell and Julie Olson-Buchanan, "Experiencing Mistreatment at Work: The Role of Grievance Filing, Nature of Mistreatment, and Employee Withdrawal," *Academy of Management Journal*, vol. 47, 2004, no. 1, pp. 129–139.

50. M. Audrey Korsgaard, Loriann Roberson, and R. Douglas Rymph, "What Motivates Fairness? The Role of Subordinate Assertive Behavior on Managers' Interactional Fairness," *Journal of Applied Psychology* 83, no. 5 (1998), pp. 731–744.

51. Bennett Tepper, et al., "Procedural Injustice, Victim Precipitation, and Abusive Supervision," *Personnel Psychology*, vol. 59, 2006, pp. 11–23.

52. Marshall Schminke et al., "The Effect of Organizational Structure on Perceptions of Procedural Fairness," *Journal of Applied Psychology* 85, no. 2 (2000), pp. 294–304.

53. Kelly Mollica, "Perceptions of Fairness," *HR Magazine*, June 2004, pp. 169–171.

54. W. Chan Kim and Rene Mauborgne, "Fair Process: Managing in the Knowledge Economy," *Harvard Business Review*, July/August 1997, pp. 65–75.

55. Lester Bittel, *What Every Supervisor Should Know* (New York: McGraw-Hill, 1974), p. 308; Paul Falcone, Fundamentals of Progressive Discipline," *HR Magazine*, February 1997, pp. 90–92.

56. Ibid.

57. Dick Grote, "Attitude Adjustments: To Deal with an Employee's Bad Attitude, Focus on His or Her Specific Behaviors," *HR Magazine* 50, no. 7, July 2005, pp. 105–107.

58. David Campbell et al., "Discipline Without Punishment—At Last," *Harvard Business Review*, July/August 1995, pp. 162–178.

59. Robert Grossman, "Executive Discipline," *HR Magazine* 50, no. 8, August 2005, pp. 46–51. "The Evil Women Theses" based on Sandva Hartman, et al., "Males and Females in a Discipline Situation Exploratory Research on Competing Hypotheses," *Journal of Managerial Issues*, 6, no. 1, Spring 1994, pp. 57, 64–68; "A Woman's Place," *The Economist* 356, no. 8184, August 19, 2000, p. 56.

60. "Employers Turn to Corporate Ombuds to Defuse Internal Ticking Time Bombs," *BNA Bulletin to Management*, August 9, 2005, p. 249.

61. Dick Grote, "Discipline without Punishment," *Across the Board* 38, no. 5 (September 2001), pp. 52–57.

62. Milton Zall, "Employee Privacy," *Journal of Property Management* 66, no. 3 (May 2001), p. 16.

63. Morris Attaway, "Privacy in the Workplace on the Web," *Internal Auditor* 58, no. 1 (February 2001), p. 30.

64. Declam Leonard and Angela France, "Workplace Monitoring: Balancing Business Interests with Employee Privacy Rights," *Society for Human Resource Management Legal Report*, May–June 2003, pp. 3–6.

65. "Time Clocks Go High Touch, High Tech to Keep Workers From Gaming the System," *BNA Bulletin to Management*, (March 25, 2004): 97.

66. Andrea Poe, "Make Foresight 20/20," *HR Magazine*, February 2000, pp. 74–80.

67. Gundars Kaupin et al., "Recommended Employee Location Monitoring Policies," www.SHRM.org, downloaded January 2, 2007.

68. "Do You Know Where Your Workers Are? GPS Units Aid Efficiency, Raise Privacy Issues," *BNA Bulletin to Management*, (July 22, 2004): 233. See also, www.WORKRIGHTS.ORG/issue_electronic/NWI_GPS_report.pdf, downloaded January 2, 2007.

69. Eileen Zimmerman, "HR Must Know When Employee Surveillance Crosses the Line," *Workforce*, February 2002, pp. 38–44. See also, Rita Zeidner, "Keeping E-Mail in Check," *HR Magazine*, June 2007, pp. 70–74.

70. "Workers Sharing Music, Movies at Work Violates Copyrights, Employer Finds," *BNA Bulletin to Management*, June 19, 2003, p. 193.

71. Cynthia Kemper, "Big Brother," *Communication World* 18, no. 1 (December 2000/January 2001), pp. 8–12.

72. "After Employer Found Liable for Worker's Child Porn, Policies May Need to be Revisited," *BNA Bulletin to Management*, March 21, 2006, p. 89.

73. Leonard and France, "Workplace Monitoring," p. 4.

74. *Vega-Rodriguez v. Puerto Rico Telephone Company*, CA1, #962061, 4/8/97, discussed in "Video Surveillance Withstands Privacy Challenge," *BNA Bulletin to Management*, April 17, 1997, p. 121.

75. "Secret Videotaping Leads to $200,000 Settlement," *BNA Bulletin to Management*, January 22, 1998, p. 17.

76. Bill Roberts, "Are You Ready for Biometrics?" *HR Magazine*, March 2003, pp. 95–96.

77. Charles Muhl, "The Employment at Will Doctrine: Three Major Exceptions," *Monthly Labor Review* 124, no. 1 (January 2001), pp. 3–11.

78. Robert Lanza and Morton Warren, "United States: Employment at Will Prevails Despite Exceptions to the Rule," *Society for Human Resource Management Legal Report*, October–November 2005, pp. 1–8.

79. Ibid.

80. Ibid.

81. Joseph Famularo, *Handbook of Modern Personnel Administration*, (New York, McGraw Hill, 1982), pp. 65.3–65.5.

82. Kenneth Sovereign, *Personnel Law* (Upper Saddle River, NJ: Prentice Hall, 1999); Connie Wanderg et al., "Perceived Fairness of Layoffs Among Individuals Who Have Been Laid Off: A Longitudinal Study," *Personnel Psychology* 2 (1999), pp. 59–84.

83. Famularo, op. cit., pp. 65.4–64.5.

84. Connie Wanderg, et al., "Perceived Unfairness of Layoffs Among Individuals Who Have Been Laid Off: A Longitudinal Study," *Personnel Psychology*, vol. 2, 1999, pp. 59–84; Brian Klass and Gregory Dell'omo, "Managerial Use of Dismissal: Organizational Level Determinants," *Personnel Psychology*, vol. 50, 1997, pp. 927–953; Nancy Hatch Woodward, "Smoother Separations," *HR Magazine*, June 2007, pp. 94–97.

85. Jaikumar Vijayan, "Downsizings Leave Firms Vulnerable to Digital Attacks," *Computerworld* 25 (2001), pp. 6–7.

86. Paul Falcon, "Give Employees the (Gentle) Hook," *HR Magazine*, April 2001, pp. 121–128.

87. Based on James Coil III and Charles Rice, "Three Steps to Creating Effective Employee Releases," *Employment Relations Today*, Spring 1994, pp. 91–94, and "Fairness to Employees Can Stare Off Litigation," *BNA Bulletin to Management*, Nov. 27, 1999, p. 377. See also Jeffrey Conner, "Disarming Terminated Employees," *HR Magazine*, January 2000, pp. 113–116; Richard Bayer, "Termination with Dignity," *Business Horizons* 43, no. 5 (September 2000), pp. 4–10; and Betty Sosnin, "Orderly Departures," *HR Magazine* 50, no. 11, November 2005, pp. 74–78.

88. Sovereign, op. cit., p. 185; Gillian Flynn, "Grounds for Dismissal," *Workforce*, August 2000, pp. 86–90.

89. Based on Coil and Rice, "Three Steps to Creating Effective Employee Releases," pp. 91–94.

90. Gillian Flynn, "Grounds for Dismassal," *Workforce* 79, August 2000, no. 8, pp. 86–90. See also, Edward Isler et al., "Personal Liability and Employee Discipline," *Society for Human Resource Management Legal Report*, September–October 2000, pp. 1–4.

91. "One More Heart Risk: Firing Employees," *Miami Herald*, March 20, 1998, pp. C1, C7.

92. Kemba Dunham, "The Kinder Gentler Way to Lay Off Employees—More Human Approach Helps," *Wall Street Journal*, March 13, 2001, p. B-1.

93. Paul Brada, "Before You Go . . . ," *HR Magazine*, December 1998, pp. 89–102; Marlene Piturro, "Alternatives to Downsizing," *Management Review*, October 1999, pp. 37–42; "How Safe Is Your Job?" *Money*, December 1, 2001, p. 130.

94. Joseph Zarandona and Michael Camuso, "A Study of Exit Interviews: Does the Last Word Count," *Personnel* 62, no. 3 (March 1981), pp. 47–48. For another point of view, see "Firms Can Profit from Data Obtained from Exit Interviews," *Knight-Ridder/Tribune Business News*, February 13, 2001, Item 0104 4446.

95. See Nancy Ryan, "Complying with the Worker Adjustment and Retraining Notification Act (WARNACT)," *Employee Relations Law Journal*, 18, no. 1, Summer 1993, pp. 169–76; and Emily Nelson, "The Job Cut Buyouts Favored by P&G Pose Problems," *Wall Street Journal*, June 12, 2001, p. B01.

96. Leon Grunberg, Sarah Moore, and Edward Greenberg, "Managers' Reactions to Implementing Layoffs: Relationship to Health Problems and Withdrawal Behaviors," *Human Resource Management*, Summer 2006, vol. 45, no. 2, pp. 159–178.

97. Ibid.

98. In one recent year, U.S. employers implemented about 1,200 mass layoffs, involving a total of almost 144,000 workers. "Workers Hit by Mass Layoffs Rose to 143,977 in February," *BNA Bulletin to Management*, April 3, 2007, p. 109.

99. See, for example, "Cushioning the Blow as Layoffs," *BNA Bulletin to Management*, July 3, 1997, p. 216.

100. These are suggested by attorney Ethan Lipsig and discussed in "The Lowdown on Downsizing," *BNA Bulletin to Management*, January 9, 1997, p. 16. See also, Stephen Gilliland and Donald Schepers, "Why We Do the Things We Do: A Discussion and Analysis of Determinants of Just Treatment in Layoff Implementation Decisions," *Human Resource Management Review* 13, no. 1 (2003), pp. 59–84.

101. "Communication Can Reduce Problems, Litigation After Layoffs, Attorneys Say," *BNA Bulletin to Management*, April 24, 2003, p. 129.

102. Steve Weinstein, "The People Side of Mergers," *Progressive Grocer* 80, no. 1 (January 2001), pp. 29–31.

104. Based on "Theft Is Unethical," *HE Solutions* 34 (October 2002), p. 66.

105. Bureau of National Affairs, *Bulletin to Management*, Sept. 13, 1985, p. 3.

106. Based on "What Would You Do?" *Sales & Marketing Management* 155 (January 2003), pp. 52–54.

15 Labor Relations and Collective Bargaining

The U.S. Department of Labor's National Labor Relations Board (NLRB) recently accused Starbucks of breaking the law in trying to prevent workers in some of its New York shops from unionizing. Among other things, the NLRB accused managers in those stores of retaliating against workers who wanted to unionize, by firing two of them and illegally interrogating others about their union inclinations. A Starbucks spokesperson said the company believes the allegations are baseless and that the firm will vigorously defend itself.[1] •

After studying this chapter, you should be able to:

1 Give a brief history of the American labor movement.
2 Discuss the main features of at least three major pieces of labor legislation.
3 Present examples of what to expect during the union drive and election.
4 Describe five ways to lose an NLRB election.
5 Illustrate with examples bargaining that is not in good faith.
6 Develop a grievance procedure.

The previous chapter focused on employee ethics and justice—important topics in determining employees' tendencies to join unions. The main purpose of this chapter is to provide you with information you'll need to deal effectively with unions and grievances. After briefly discussing the history of the American labor movement, we describe some basic labor legislation, including the subject of unfair labor practices. We explain labor negotiations, including the union actions you can expect during the union campaign and election. And we explain what you can expect during the actual bargaining sessions, and how to handle grievances, an activity often called "contract administration." In the next chapter, Employee Safety and Health, we'll turn to the techniques managers use to provide employees with a safe and healthy workplace.

THE LABOR MOVEMENT

The union movement is important. Just over 15 million U.S. workers belong to unions—around 12% of the total number of men and women working in this country.[2] Many are still traditional blue-collar workers, but more and more are white-collar workers. For instance, workers including doctors, psychologists, graduate teaching assistants, government office workers, and even fashion models are forming or joining unions.[3] Federal, state, and local governments employ about seven million union members, who account for almost 40% of total government employees. And in some industries—including transportation and public utilities, where over 26% of employees are union members—it's still hard to get a job without joining a union.[4] Union membership in other countries is declining, but is still very high relative to the United States: over 35% of employed workers in Canada, Mexico, Brazil, and Italy, for instance.

Furthermore, it can be a mistake to always assume, as a knee-jerk reaction, that unions only negatively impact employers. For example, perhaps by professionalizing the staff and/or systematizing company practices, unionization may also improve performance. Thus in one study, researchers concluded that heart attack mortality among patients in hospitals with unionized registered nurses were 5 to 9% lower than in nonunion hospitals.[5] Another study found a significant, negative relationship between union membership and employees' intent to leave their jobs.[6]

Why are unions important? How did they get that way? Why do workers join them? How do employers and unions hammer out agreements? These are questions we'll address in this chapter.

1 Give a brief history of the American labor movement.

A Brief History of the American Union Movement

To understand what unions are and what they want, it is useful to understand "where they've been." The history of the union movement in the United States has been one of alternate expansion and contraction. As early as 1790, skilled craftsmen (shoemakers, tailors, printers, and so on) organized themselves into trade unions. They posted their minimum wage demands and had "tramping committees" go from shop to shop to ensure that no member accepted a lesser wage. Union membership grew until a major depression around 1837 resulted in a membership decline. Membership then began increasing as the United States entered its industrial revolution. In 1869, a group of tailors met and formed the Knights of Labor. The Knights were interested in political reform. By 1885, they had 100,000 members, which (as a result of winning a major strike against a railroad) exploded to 700,000 the following year. Partly because of their focus on social reform, and partly due to a series of unsuccessful strikes, the Knights' membership dwindled rapidly thereafter, and the group dissolved in 1893.

Making fenders at an early Ford factory in Ypsilanti, Michigan. In addition to heavy physical labor, workers faced health hazards—poor lighting, dust, and dangerous machinery.

In 1886, Samuel Gompers formed the American Federation of Labor. It consisted mostly of skilled workers and, unlike the Knights, focused on practical, bread-and-butter gains for its members. The Knights of Labor had engaged in a class struggle to alter the form of society, and thereby get a bigger chunk of benefits for its members. Gompers aimed to reach the same goal by raising day-to-day wages and improving working conditions. The AFL grew rapidly until after World War I, at which point its membership exceeded 5.5 million people.

The 1920s was a period of stagnation and decline for the U.S. union movement. This was a result of several events, including a postwar depression, manufacturers' renewed resistance to unions, Samuel Gompers's death, and the apparent prosperity of the 1920s. By late 1929, due to the Great Depression, millions of workers (including many union members) had lost their jobs, and by 1933 union membership was down to under three million workers.

Membership began to rise again in the mid-1930s. As part of his New Deal programs, President Franklin Delano Roosevelt passed the National Industrial Recovery Act, which made it easier for labor to organize. Other federal laws as well as prosperity and World War II also contributed to the rapid increase in members, which topped out at about 21 million workers in the 1970s. Union membership has consistently fallen since then, due to factors such as the shift from manufacturing to service jobs, and new legislation (such as occupational safety laws) that provide the sorts of protections that workers could once only obtain from their unions. Indeed, hundreds of local, state, and federal laws and regulations now address the sorts of concerns that helped drive the early union movement.[7]

Why Do Workers Organize?

Experts have spent much time and money trying to discover why workers unionize, and they've proposed many theories. Yet there is no simple answer to the question, partly because each worker probably joins for his or her own reasons.

However, workers don't unionize just to get more pay or better working conditions, though these are important factors. For example, recent median weekly wages for union workers was $781, while that for nonunion workers was $612.[8] Union workers also generally receive significantly more holidays, sick leave, unpaid leave, insurance plan benefits, long-term disability benefits, and various other benefits than do nonunion workers. Unions also seem to have been able to somewhat reduce the impact of (but obviously not eliminate) downsizings and wage cuts in most industries.[9]

Studies suggest that two factors—employer unfairness, and the union's clout—explain why employees unionize. In one Australia-based firm, researchers found that "Individuals who believe that the company rules or policies were administered unfairly or to their detriment were more likely to turn to unions . . .".[10] But, to vote pro-union, the employees also had to believe the union could improve their wages, benefits, and treatment.

The Bottom Line   The bottom line is that the urge to unionize often seems to boil down to the belief on the part of workers that it is only through unity that they can protect themselves from unilateral management whims. Sometimes, even when the employer is trustworthy and benevolent, employees feel they need unity to protect themselves. When Kaiser Permanente's San Francisco Medical Center cut back on vacation and sick leave for its pharmacists and other workers, the pharmacists' union, the Guild for Professional Pharmacists, won back the lost vacation days. As one staff pharmacist said, "Kaiser is a pretty benevolent employer, but there's always the pressure to squeeze a little."[11] One labor relations lawyer puts it this way, "the one major thing unions offer is making you a "for cause" instead of an "at will" employee, which guarantees a hearing and arbitration if you're fired."[12] So, in practice, low morale, fear of job loss, and arbitrary management actions help foster unionization. Employers ignore that at their peril.

In some respects, these factors have not changed in years. Here is how one writer describes the motivation behind the early unionization of automobile workers:

> In the years to come, economic issues would make the headlines when union and management met in negotiations. But in the early years the rate of pay was not the major complaint of the autoworkers. . . . Specifically, the principal grievances of the autoworkers were the speed-up of production and the lack of any kind of job security. As production tapered off, the order in which workers were laid off was determined largely by the whim of foremen and other supervisors. . . . The worker had no way of knowing when he would be laid off, and had no assurance when, or whether, he would be recalled. . . . Generally, what the workers revolted against was the lack of human dignity and individuality, and a working relationship that was massively impersonal, cold, and nonhuman. They wanted to be treated like human beings—not like faceless clockcard numbers.[13]

What Do Unions Want?

We can generalize by saying that unions have two sets of aims, one for *union security* and one for *improved wages, hours, working conditions*, and *benefits* for their members.

Union Security   First and probably foremost, unions seek security for themselves. They fight hard for the right to represent a firm's workers, and to be the exclusive bargaining agent for all employees in the unit. (As such, they negotiate contracts for all employees, including those not members of the union.) Five types of union security are possible:

1. *Closed shop.* The company can hire only union members. Congress outlawed this in 1947, but it still exists in some industries (such as printing).
2. *Union shop.* The company can hire nonunion people, but they must join the union after a prescribed period of time and pay dues. (If not, they can be fired.)
3. *Agency shop.* Employees who do not belong to the union still must pay union dues on the assumption that the union's efforts benefit all the workers.

---

closed shop
A form of union security in which the company can hire only union members. This was outlawed in 1947 but still exists in some industries (such as printing).

union shop
A form of union security in which the company can hire nonunion people, but they must join the union after a prescribed period of time and pay dues. (If they do not, they can be fired.)

agency shop
A form of union security in which employees who do not belong to the union must still pay union dues on the assumption that union efforts benefit all workers.

open shop
Perhaps the least attractive type of union security from the union's point of view, the workers decide whether or not to join the union; and those who join must pay dues.

right to work
A term used to describe state statutory or constitutional provisions banning the requirement of union membership as a condition of employment.

4. ***Open shop.*** It is up to the workers whether or not they join the union—those who do not, do not pay dues.
5. Maintenance of membership arrangement. Employees do not have to belong to the union. However, union members employed by the firm must maintain membership in the union for the contract period.

Not all states give unions the right to require union membership as a condition of employment. **Right to work** "is a term used to describe state statutory or constitutional provisions banning the requirement of union membership as a condition of employment."[14] Section 14(b) of the Taft-Hartley Act (discussed below) permits states to forbid the negotiation of compulsory union membership provisions, not just for firms engaged in interstate commerce, but those in intrastate commerce, too. Right to work laws don't outlaw unions. They do outlaw (within those states) any of the forms of union security. This understandably inhibits union formation in those states. Twenty-two "right to work states," from Florida to Mississippi to Wyoming, ban all forms of union security. Several years ago, Oklahoma became the 22nd state to pass Right to Work legislation. Some believe that this—combined with a loss of manufacturing jobs—explains why Oklahoma's union membership dropped dramatically in the next three years.[15]

Improved Wages, Hours, and Benefits Once the union ensures its security at the company, it fights to improve its members' wages, hours, and working conditions. The typical labor agreement also gives the union a role in other human resource activities, including recruiting, selecting, compensating, promoting, training, and discharging employees.

The AFL-CIO

The American Federation of Labor and Congress of Industrial Organizations (AFL-CIO) is a voluntary federation of about 100 national and international labor unions in the United States. The separate AFL and CIO merged in 1955, with the AFL's George Meany as its first president. For many people in the United States, the AFL-CIO is synonymous with the word *union*.

There are three layers in the structure of the AFL-CIO (and other U.S. unions). First, there is the local union. This is the union the worker joins, and to which he or she pays dues. The local union also usually signs the collective bargaining agreement determining the wages and working conditions. The local is in turn a single chapter in the national union. For example, if you were a teacher in Detroit, you would belong to the local union there, which is one of hundreds of local chapters of the American Federation of Teachers, their national union. The third layer in the structure is the national federation, in this case, the AFL-CIO.

Many people tend to think of the AFL-CIO as the most important part of the labor movement, but it is not. The AFL-CIO itself really has little power, except what its constituent unions let it exercise. Thus, the president of the teachers' union wields more power in that capacity than in her capacity as a vice president of the AFL-CIO. Yet as a practical matter, the AFL-CIO does act as a spokesperson for labor, and its president, John Sweeney, has political clout far in excess of a figurehead president.

However, dramatic changes are taking place. Four big unions—the Service Employees' International Union (SEIU), the International Brotherhood of Teamsters, the United Food and Commercial Workers, and UNITE recently announced they were leaving the AFL-CIO and establishing their own Federation, called the Change to Win Coalition. Together, the departing unions represented about one quarter of the AFL-CIO's membership and budget. Other unions are reportedly contemplating leaving the AFL-CIO and joining Change to Win. Among other things, Change to Win plans to be much more aggressive about organizing workers than they say the AFL-CIO was.[16]

UNIONS AND THE LAW

Until about 1930, there were no special labor laws. Employers were not required to engage in collective bargaining with employees and were virtually unrestrained in their behavior toward unions; the use of spies, blacklists, and firing of union agitators were widespread. "Yellow dog" contracts, whereby management could require nonunion membership as a condition for employment, were widely enforced. Most union weapons—even strikes—were illegal.

This one-sided situation lasted until the Great Depression (around 1930). Since then, in response to changing public attitudes, values, and economic conditions, labor law has gone through three clear periods: from "strong encouragement" of unions, to "modified encouragement coupled with regulation," and finally to "detailed regulation of internal union affairs."[17]

② Discuss the main features of at least three major pieces of labor legislation.

Norris-LaGuardia Act (1932)
This law marked the beginning of the era of strong encouragement of unions and guaranteed to each employee the right to bargain collectively "free from interference, restraint, or coercion."

National Labor Relations (or Wagner) Act
This law banned certain types of unfair practices and provided for secret-ballot elections and majority rule for determining whether or not a firm's employees want to unionize.

National Labor Relations Board (NLRB)
The agency created by the Wagner Act to investigate unfair labor practice charges and to provide for secret-ballot elections and majority rule in determining whether or not a firm's employees want a union.

Period of Strong Encouragement: The Norris-LaGuardia (1932) and National Labor Relations or Wagner Acts (1935)

The **Norris-LaGuardia Act of 1932** set the stage for a new era in which union activity was encouraged. It guaranteed to each employee the right to bargain collectively "free from interference, restraint, or coercion." It declared yellow dog contracts unenforceable. And it limited the courts' abilities to issue injunctions (stop orders) for activities such as peaceful picketing and payment of strike benefits.

Yet this act did little to restrain employers from fighting labor organizations by whatever means they could find. So in 1935, Congress passed the **National Labor Relations (or Wagner) Act** to add teeth to Norris-LaGuardia. It did this by (1) banning certain unfair labor practices; (2) providing for secret-ballot elections and majority rule for determining whether a firm's employees would unionize; and (3) creating the **National Labor Relations Board (NLRB)** to enforce these two provisions.

As part of its duties, the NLRB periodically issues interpretive rulings. For example, the NLRB ruled that temporary employees could join the unions of permanent employees in the companies where their temporary employment agencies assign them to work.[18]

Unfair Employer Labor Practices   The Wagner Act deemed "statutory wrongs" (but not crimes) five unfair labor practices used by employers:

1. It is unfair for employers to "interface with, restrain, or coerce employees" in exercising their legally sanctioned right of self-organization.
2. It is unfair for company representatives to dominate or interfere with either the formation or the administration of labor unions. Among other specific management actions found to be unfair under these first two practices (1 and 2) are bribing employees, using company spy systems, moving a business to avoid unionization, and black-listing union sympathizers.
3. Employers are prohibited from discriminating in any way against employees for their legal union activities.
4. Employers are forbidden to discharge or discriminate against employees simply because the latter file unfair practice charges against the company.
5. Finally, it is an unfair labor practice for employers to refuse to bargain collectively with their employees' duly chosen representatives.

Unions file an unfair labor practice charge (see Figure 15-1) with the National Labor Relations Board. The board then investigates the charge and decides if it should take action. Possible actions include dismissal of the complaint, request for an injunction against the employer, or an order that the employer cease and desist.

FIGURE 15-1

**NLRB Form 501:
Filing an Unfair
Labor Practice**

FORM NLRB 501
(2 81)

FORM EXEMPT UNDER
44 U.S.C. 3512

UNITED STATES OF AMERICA
NATIONAL LABOR RELATIONS BOARD
CHARGE AGAINST EMPLOYER

INSTRUCTIONS: File an original and 4 copies of this charge with NLRB Regional Director for the region in which the alleged unfair labor practice occurred or is occurring.	DO NOT WRITE IN THIS SPACE	
	CASE NO.	DATE FILE

1. EMPLOYER AGAINST WHOM CHARGE IS BROUGHT

a. NAME OF EMPLOYER	b. NUMBER OF WORKERS EMPLOYED	
c. ADDRESS OF ESTABLISHMENT (*street and number, city, State, and ZIP code*)	d. EMPLOYER REPRESEN-TATIVE TO CONTACT	e. PHONE NO.
f. TYPE OF ESTABLISHMENT (*factory, mine, wholesaler, etc.*)	g. IDENTIFY PRINCIPAL PRODUCT OR SERVICE	

h. THE ABOVE-NAMED EMPLOYER HAS ENGAGED IN AND IS ENGAGING IN UNFAIR LABOR PRACTICES WITHIN THE MEANING OF SECTION 8(a), SUBSECTIONS (1) AND _____ OF THE NATIONAL
(*list subsections*)
LABOR RELATIONS ACT, AND THESE UNFAIR LABOR PRACTICES ARE UNFAIR LABOR PRACTICES AFFECTING COMMERCE WITHIN THE MEANING OF THE ACT.

2. BASIS OF THE CHARGE (*be specific as to facts, names, addresses, plants involved, dates, places, etc.*)

BY THE ABOVE AND OTHER ACTS, THE ABOVE-NAMED EMPLOYER HAS INTERFERED WITH, RESTRAINED, AND COERCED EMPLOYEES IN THE EXERCISE OF THE RIGHTS GUARANTEED IN SECTION 7 OF THE ACT.

3. FULL NAME OF PARTY FILING CHARGE (*if labor organization, give full name, including local name and number*)

4a. ADDRESS (*street and number, city, State, and ZIP code*)	4b. TELEPHONE NO.

5. FULL NAME OF NATIONAL OR INTERNATIONAL LABOR ORGANIZATION OF WHICH IT IS AN AFFILIATE OR CONSTITUENT UNIT (*to be filled in when charge is filed by a labor organization*)

6. DECLARATION

I declare that I have read the above charge and that the statements therein are true to the best of my knowledge and belief.

By _____
(signature of respresentative or person filing charge)   (title, if any)

Address _____
(telephone number)   (date)

WILLFULLY FALSE STATEMENTS ON THIS CHARGE CAN BE PUNISHED BY FINE AND IMPRISONMENT
(*U.S. CODE, TITLE 18, SECTION 1001*)

Such complaints are not unusual. When the former Knight Ridder company consolidated the separate online operations of several of its papers into the new KnightRidder.com, it triggered a labor dispute. Citing possible unfair labor practices, the unions asked the NLRB to investigate whether KnightRidder.com violated labor law by not negotiating the transfer of workers with the union.[19]

From 1935 to 1947   Union membership increased quickly after passage of the Wagner Act in 1935. Other factors such as an improving economy and aggressive union leadership contributed to this rise. But by the mid-1940s, after the end of World War II, the tide had begun to turn. Largely because of a series of massive postwar strikes, public policy began to shift against what many viewed as union excesses. The stage was set for passage of the Taft-Hartley Act.

Period of Modified Encouragement Coupled with Regulation: The Taft-Hartley Act (1947)

Taft-Hartley Act (1947)
Also known as the Labor Management Relations Act, this law prohibited unfair union labor practices and enumerated the rights of employees as union members. It also enumerated the rights of employers.

The **Taft-Hartley (or Labor Management Relations) Act of 1947** reflected the public's less enthusiastic attitude toward unions. It amended the National Labor Relations (Wagner) Act by limiting unions in four ways: (1) prohibiting unfair union labor practices, (2) enumerating the rights of employees as union members, (3) enumerating the rights of employers, and (4) allowing the president of the United States to temporarily bar national emergency strikes.

Unfair Union Labor Practices   The Taft-Hartley Act enumerated several labor practices that unions were prohibited from engaging in:

1. First, it banned unions from restraining or coercing employees from exercising their guaranteed bargaining rights. Some specific union actions the courts have held illegal under this provision include stating to an anti-union employee that he or she will lose his or her job once the union gains recognition, and issuing patently false statements during union organizing campaigns.
2. It is also an unfair labor practice for a union to cause an employer to discriminate in any way against an employee in order to encourage or discourage his or her membership in a union. In other words, the union cannot try to force an employer to fire a worker because he or she doesn't attend union meetings, opposes union policies, or refuses to join a union. There is one exception: Where a closed or union shop prevails (and union membership is therefore a prerequisite to employment), the union may demand discharge for a worker who fails to pay his or her initiation fees and dues.
3. It is an unfair labor practice for a union to refuse to bargain in good faith with the employer about wages, hours, and other employment conditions. Certain strikes and boycotts are also unfair practices.
4. It is an unfair labor practice for a union to engage in "featherbedding" (requiring an employer to pay an employee for services not performed).

Rights of Employees   The Taft-Hartley Act also protected the rights of employees against their unions. For example, many people felt that compulsory unionism violated the basic right of freedom of association. Legitimized by Taft-Hartley, new right-to-work laws quickly sprang up in 19 (now 22) states (mainly in the South and Southwest). These outlawed labor contracts that made union membership a condition for keeping one's job. In New York, for example, many printing firms have union shops. You can't work as a press operator unless you belong to a printers' union. In Florida, such union shops—except those covered by the Railway Labor Act—are illegal, and printing shops typically employ both union and nonunion press operators. Even today, union membership varies widely by state, from a high of 26.8% in New York to a low of 3.7% in South Carolina (other representative membership densities are California, 16.5%; Florida, 7.4%; Texas, 6.5%; Michigan, 23.9%; and Ohio, 19.4%).[20] This employee rights provision also allowed an employee to present grievances directly to the employer (without going through the union). And it required the employee's authorization before the union could have dues subtracted from his or her paycheck.

In general, the National Labor Relations Act does not restrain unions from unfair labor practices to the extent that it does employers. Unions may not restrain or coerce employees. However "violent or otherwise threatening behavior or clearly coercive or intimidating union activities are necessary before the NLRB will find an unfair labor practice."[21] Examples here would include physical assaults or threats of violence, economic reprisals, and mass picketing that restrains the lawful entry or leaving of a work site. In one typical case, *Pattern Makers v. National Labor Relations Board*, the U.S. Supreme Court found the union guilty of an unfair labor practice when it tried to fine some members for resigning from the union and returning to work during a strike.[22]

Rights of Employers   The Taft-Hartley Act also explicitly gave employers certain rights. First, it gave them full freedom to express their views concerning union organization. For example, you as a manager can tell your employees that in your opinion unions are worthless, dangerous to the economy, and immoral. You can even, generally speaking, hint that unionization and subsequent high-wage demands might result in the permanent closing of the plant (but not its relocation). Employers can set forth the union's record concerning violence and corruption, if appropriate. In fact, the only major restraint is that employers must avoid threats, promises, coercion, and direct interference with workers who are trying to reach a decision. There can be no threat of reprisal or force or promise of benefit.[23]

Furthermore, the employer (1) cannot meet with employees on company time within 24 hours of an election or (2) suggest to employees that they vote against the union while they are at home or in the employer's office, although he or she can do so while in their work area or where they normally gather.

National Emergency Strikes   The Taft-Hartley Act also allows the U.S. president to intervene in **national emergency strikes**. These are strikes (for example, on the part of railroad workers) that might "imperil the national health and safety." The president may appoint a board of inquiry and, based on its report, apply for an injunction restraining the strike for 60 days. If the parties don't reach a settlement during that time, the president can have the injunction extended for another 20 days. During this last period, employees take a secret ballot to ascertain their willingness to accept the employer's last offer.

national emergency strikes
Strikes that might "imperil the national health and safety."

Period of Detailed Regulation of Internal Union Affairs: The Landrum-Griffin Act (1959)   In the 1950s, Senate investigations revealed unsavory practices on the part of some unions, and the result was the **Landrum-Griffin Act** (officially, the **Labor Management Reporting and Disclosure Act) of 1959**. An overriding aim of this act was to protect union members from possible wrongdoing on the part of their unions. Like Taft-Hartley, it also amended the National Labor Relations (Wagner) Act.

First, the law contains a bill of rights for union members. Among other things, it provides for certain rights in the nomination of candidates for union office. It also affirms a member's right to sue his or her union and ensures that no member can be fined or suspended without due process, which includes a list of specific charges, time to prepare a defense, and a fair hearing.

This act also laid out rules regarding union elections. For example, national and international unions must elect officers at least once every five years, using some type of

Landrum-Griffin Act (1959)
The law aimed at protecting union members from possible wrongdoing on the part of their unions.

New Economy Entrepreneurs and Unions

High-tech "new economy" entrepreneurs are getting an unexpected lesson in labor relations. Many assumed that jobs like Web designer were immune from union efforts. But with several e-commerce firms (including Amazon. com) facing union organizing efforts, it's obvious they are not.

There are many reasons why these firms are not as immune to unions as their entrepreneur founders thought they'd be. For one thing, many employees at "new economy" online companies like Amazon are doing "old economy" jobs like loading and unloading trucks. And even jobs like Web designers and programmers aren't immune from unionization if conditions in their companies warrant it.

Furthermore, when it comes to attracting unions, many entrepreneurs are their own worst enemies. Focusing on sales and on meeting customer demand, many pay little attention to writing personnel policies, developing effective performance appraisal systems, or staying in touch with employees' concerns. As one labor attorney puts it, "they have been lax about overtime, pay scales, and just having an employee handbook with policies and procedures clearly defined. . . . The high-tech industry has always been so confident that none of their own would ever want the union that they've been amazingly ignorant of basic labor law."[24] Even the entrepreneurs' intranets may work against them. For example, many store all personal information regarding employees in computer files that are easily accessed by employees who want to start union organizing campaigns.

For the owner/entrepreneur, the solution is to improve human resource and employee relations practices. For example, revise personnel policies and practices, to ensure, for instance, fair and equitable treatment and to show potential union organizers that the company is well run. Improve the security of employee files. And (since unionization attempts in even high-tech firms tend to focus on support services such as call centers, distribution, and help desks)—one labor lawyer says—"Don't lose touch with the people taking the calls. And don't think it is just about compensation. It is also the work environment. An hourly call center employee who punches a clock day after day while watching the engineers come and go as they please may get ideas."

secret-ballot mechanism. And it regulates the kind of person who can serve as a union officer. For example, persons convicted of felonies (bribery, murder, and so on) are barred from holding union officer positions for a period of five years after conviction.

Senate investigators also discovered flagrant examples of employer wrongdoing. Employers and their "labor relations consultants" had bribed union agents and officers, for example. That had been a federal crime starting with the passage of the Taft-Hartley Act. But Landrum-Griffin greatly expanded the list of unlawful employer actions. For example, companies can no longer pay their own employees to entice them not to join the union. The act also requires reports from unions and employers covering such practices as the use of labor relations consultants.

Union laws like these aren't just issues for big companies like FedEx and GE. They're increasingly an issue for high-tech entrepreneurs too, as the "When You're on Your Own" above illustrates.

THE UNION DRIVE AND ELECTION

③ Present examples of what to expect during the union drive and election.

It is through the union drive and election that a union tries to be recognized to represent employees. This process has five basic steps.

Step 1. Initial Contact

During the initial contact stage, the union determines the employees' interest in organizing, and establishes an organizing committee.

The initiative for the first contact between the employees and the union may come from the employees, from a union already representing other employees of the firm, or from a union representing workers elsewhere. In any case, there is an initial contact between a union representative and a few employees.

Once an employer becomes a target, a union official usually assigns a representative to assess employee interest. The representative visits the firm to determine whether enough employees are interested to make a union campaign worthwhile. He or she also identifies employees who would make good leaders in the organizing campaign and calls them together to create an organizing committee. The objective here is to educate the committee about the benefits of forming a union and the law and procedures involved in forming a local union.

The union must follow certain rules when it starts contacting employees. The law allows organizers to solicit employees for membership as long as the effort doesn't endanger the performance or safety of the employees. Therefore, much of the contact takes place off the job, for example, at home or at eating places near work. Organizers can also safely contact employees on company grounds during off hours (such as lunch or break time). Yet, in practice, there will be much informal organizing going on at the workplace as employees debate the merits of organizing. In any case, this initial contact stage may be deceptively quiet. Sometimes the first inkling management has of the campaign is the distribution or posting of handbills soliciting union membership.

Technology, for instance in the form of e-mail, is important in the organizing process. However, preventing union employees from sending pro-union e-mail messages on company e-mail is easier said than done. Prohibiting only union e-mail may violate NLRB decisions, for instance. And instituting a rule barring workers from using e-mail for all non-work-related topics may also be futile if the company actually does little to stop e-mail other than pro-union messages.

Labor Relations Consultants   Both management and unions typically use "labor relations consultants," and these are increasingly influencing the unionization process. Coca-Cola and ConAgra foods are among firms using labor consultants in the past few years. The consultants may be law firms, researchers, psychologists, labor relations specialists, or public relations firms. Some are former union organizers who now represent the employers.[25]

In any case, their role is to provide advice and related services not just when a vote is expected (although this is when most of them are used), but at other times, too. For the employer, the consultant's services may range from ensuring that the firm properly fills out routine forms to managing the whole union campaign. Unions may use public relations firms to improve their image, or specialists to manage corporate campaigns aimed at pressuring shareholders and creditors to get management to agree to the union's demands.

The widespread use of such consultants—only some of whom are actually lawyers—raises the question of whether some have advised their clients to engage in activities that are illegal or questionable under labor laws. One tactic, for instance, is to delay the union vote with lengthy hearings at the NLRB. The longer the delay in the vote, they argue, the more time the employer has to drill anti-union propaganda into the employees.

union salting
A union organizing tactic by which workers who are in fact employed full-time by a union as undercover organizers are hired by unwitting employers.

Union Salting   Unions are not without creative ways to win elections. The National Labor Relations Board defines **union salting** as "placing of union members on nonunion job sites for the purpose of organizing." However critics claim that "salts" also often interfere with business operations and harass employees.[26] A U.S. Supreme Court decision held the tactic to be legal.[27] The U.S. Supreme Court has also ruled that union salts are "employees" under the National Labor Relations Act, and the NLRB will require that employers pay salts if they fire them for trying to organize the workplace.[28] For employers, the solution is to make sure you know who you're hiring.[29]

However, employers must proceed with care. For instance, the National Labor Relations Board concluded that an employer did commit an unfair labor practice by refusing to consider hiring nine members of Plumbers and Pipe Fitters, Local 520. Not hiring the people simply because as members of the local union they might be pro-union or union salts would be discriminatory.[30]

Step 2. Obtaining Authorization Cards

authorization cards

In order to petition for a union election, the union must show that at least 30% of employees may be interested in being unionized. Employees indicate this interest by signing authorization cards.

For the union to petition the NLRB for the right to hold an election, it must show that a sizable number of employees may be interested in organizing. The next step is thus for union organizers to try to get the employees to sign **authorization cards**. Among other things, these usually authorize the union to seek a representation election and state that the employee has applied to join the union. Thirty percent of the eligible employees in an appropriate bargaining unit must sign before the union can petition the NLRB for an election.

During this stage, both union and management use various forms of propaganda. The union claims it can improve working conditions, raise wages, increase benefits, and generally get the workers better deals. Management can attack the union on ethical and moral grounds and cite the cost of union membership. Management can also explain its track record, express facts and opinions, and explain the law applicable to organizing campaigns. However, neither side can threaten, bribe, or coerce employees. And an employer may not make promises of benefits to employees or make unilateral changes in terms and conditions of employment that were not planned to be implemented prior to the onset of union organizing activity.

Steps to Take   Management can take several steps with respect to the authorization cards themselves. For example, the NLRB ruled an employer may lawfully inform employees of their right to revoke their authorization cards, even when employees have not solicited such information. The employer can also distribute pamphlets that explain just how employees can revoke their cards. However, management can go no further than explaining to employees the procedure for card revocation and furnishing resignation language. The law prohibits any material assistance such as postage or stationery. The employer also cannot check to determine which employees have actually signed or revoked their authorization cards.

What else can you do to educate employees who have not yet decided whether to sign their cards? It is an unfair labor practice to tell employees they can't sign a card. What you can do is prepare supervisors so they can explain what the card actually authorizes the union to do. For example, the typical authorization card actually does three things. It lets the union seek a representation election (it can be used as evidence that 30% of your employees have an interest in organizing). It designates the union as a bargaining representative in all employment matters. And it states that the employee has applied for membership in the union and will be subject to union rules and bylaws. The latter is especially important. The union, for instance, may force the employee to picket and fine any member who does not comply with union instructions. Explaining the serious legal and practical implications of signing the card can thus be an effective management weapon.

One thing management should *not* do is look through signed authorization cards if confronted with them by union representatives. The NLRB could construe that as an unfair labor practice, as spying on those who signed. It could also later form the basis of a charge alleging discrimination due to union activity, if the firm subsequently disciplines someone who signed a card.

During this stage, unions can picket the company, subject to three constraints: (1) The union must file a petition for an election within 30 days after the start of picketing; (2) the firm cannot already be lawfully recognizing another union; and (3) there cannot have been a valid NLRB election during the past 12 months. Unions today use the Internet to distribute and collect authorization cards.

Step 3. Hold a Hearing

Once the union collects the authorization cards, one of three things can occur. If the employer chooses not to contest *union recognition* at all, then the parties need no hearing, and a special "consent election" is held. If the employer chooses not to contest the union's *right to an election*, and/or the scope of the bargaining unit, and/or which employees are eligible to vote in the election, no hearing is needed and the parties can stipulate an election. If an employer *does* wish to contest the union's right, it can insist on a hearing to determine those issues. An employer's decision about whether to insist on a hearing is a strategic one based on the facts of each case and whether it feels it needs additional time to try to persuade a majority of its employees not to elect a union to represent them.

Most companies do contest the union's right to represent their employees, claiming that a significant number of them don't really want the union. It is at this point that the National Labor Relations Board gets involved. The union usually contacts the NLRB, which requests a hearing. The regional director of the NLRB then sends a hearing officer to investigate. The examiner sends both management and union a notice of representation hearing (NLRB Form 852; see Figure 15-2) that states the time and place of the hearing.

bargaining unit
The group of employees the union will be authorized to represent.

The hearing addresses several issues. First, does the record indicate there is enough evidence to hold an election? (For example, did 30% or more of the employees in an appropriate bargaining unit sign the authorization cards?) Second, the examiner must decide what the bargaining unit will be. The latter is a crucial matter for the union, for employees, and for the employer. The **bargaining unit** is the group of employees that the union will be authorized to represent and bargain for collectively. If the entire organization is the bargaining unit, the union will represent all nonsupervisory, nonmanagerial, and nonconfidential employees, even though the union may be oriented mostly toward blue-collar workers. (Professional and nonprofessional employees can be included in the same bargaining unit only if the professionals agree to it.) If your firm disagrees with the examiner's decision regarding the bargaining unit, it can challenge the decision. This will require a separate step and NLRB ruling.

The NLRB hearing addresses other questions. These include: "Does the employer qualify for coverage by the NLRB?" "Is the union a labor organization within the meaning of the National Labor Relations Act?" and, "Do any existing collective bargaining agreements or prior elections bar the union from holding a representation election?"

If the results of the hearing are favorable for the union, the NLRB will order holding an election. It will issue a Notice of Election (NLRB Form 707) to that effect, for the employer to post.

Step 4. The Campaign

During the campaign that precedes the election, union and employer appeal to employees for their votes. The union emphasizes that it will prevent unfairness, set up grievance and seniority systems, and improve wages. Union strength, they'll say, will give employees a voice in determining wages and working conditions. Management will stress that improvements like the union promises don't require unionizing, and that wages are equal to or better than they would be with a union. Management will also emphasize the financial cost of

FIGURE 15-2

NLRB Form 852:
Notice of
Representation
Hearing

FORM NLRB-852
(6-61)

**UNITED STATES OF AMERICA
BEFORE THE NATIONAL LABOR RELATIONS BOARD**

Case No.

NOTICE OF REPRESENTATION HEARING

The Petitioner, above named, having heretofore filed a Petition pursuant to Section 9 (c) of the National Labor Relations Act, as amended, 29 U.S.C. Sec 151 et seq., copy of which Petition is hereto attached, and it appearing that a question affecting commerce has arisen concerning the representation of employees described by such Petition.

YOU ARE HEREBY NOTIFIED that, pursuant to Section 3(b) and 9(c) of the Act, on the day of   , 20   , at

a hearing will be conducted before a hearing officer of the National Labor Relations Board upon the question of representation affecting commerce which has arisen, at which time and place the parties will have the right to appear in person or otherwise, and give testimony.

Signed at   on the   day of   , 20

_____
Regional Director, Region
National Labor Relations Board

union dues; the fact that the union is an "outsider"; and that if the union wins, a strike may follow. It can even attack the union on ethical and moral grounds, while insisting that employees will not be as well off and may lose freedom. But neither side can threaten, bribe, or coerce employees.

Step 5. The Election

The election is held within 30 to 60 days after the NLRB issues its Decision and Direction of Election. The election is by secret ballot; the NLRB provides the ballots (see Figure 15-3), voting booth, and ballot box, and counts the votes and certifies the results.

The union becomes the employees' representative if it wins the election, and winning means getting a majority of the votes *cast*, not a majority of the total workers in the

FIGURE 15-3

Sample NLRB Ballot

UNITED STATES OF AMERICA

National Labor Relations Board

OFFICIAL SECRET BALLOT

FOR CERTAIN EMPLOYEES OF

_____

Do you wish to be represented for purposes of collective bargaining by —

_____

MARK AN "S" IN THE SQUARE OF YOUR CHOICE

YES   NO

DO NOT SIGN THIS BALLOT. Fold and drop in ballot box.
If you spoil this ballot return it to the Board Agent for a new one.

bargaining unit. (Also keep in mind that if an employer commits an unfair labor practice, the NLRB may reverse a "no union" election. As representatives of their employer, supervisors must therefore be careful not to commit unfair practices.) Several things influence whether the union wins the certification election. Unions have a higher probability of success in geographic areas with a higher percentage of union workers, in part because union employees enjoy higher wages and benefits. High unemployment seems to lead to poorer results for the union, perhaps because employees fear that unionization efforts might result in reduced job security or employer retaliation. Unions usually carefully pick the size of their bargaining unit (all clerical employees in the company, only those at one facility, and so on), because it's clear that the larger the bargaining unit, the smaller the probability of union victory. The more workers vote, the less likely a union victory, probably because more workers who are not strong supporters vote. The union is important, too: The Teamsters union is less likely to win a representation election than other unions, for instance.[31]

4 Describe five ways to lose an NLRB election.

How to Lose an NLRB Election

Over the past few years, unions typically won about 55% of elections held each year.[32] According to expert Mathew Goodfellow, there is no sure way employers can win elections. However, there are five sure ways to lose one.[33]

Reason 1. Asleep at the Switch In one study, in 68% of the companies that lost to the union, executives were caught unaware. In these companies, turnover and absenteeism had increased, productivity was erratic, and safety was poor. Grievance procedures were rare. When the first reports of authorization cards began trickling back to top managers, they usually responded with a barrage of letters describing how the company was "one big family" and calling for a "team effort." As Goodfellow observes,

> Yet the best strategy is to not be caught asleep in the first place: Overall, prudence dictates that management spend time and effort even when the atmosphere is calm testing the temperature of employee sentiments and finding ways to remove irritants. Doing that cuts down on the possibility that an election will ever take place.[34]

Reason 2. Appointing a Committee   Of the losing companies, 36% formed a committee to manage the campaign. According to the expert, there are three problems in doing so: (1) Promptness is essential in an election situation, and committees are notorious for moving slowly. (2) Most committee members are NLRB neophytes. Their views therefore are mostly reflections of wishful thinking rather than experience. (3) A committee's decision is usually a compromise decision. The result is often close to the most conservative opinion—but not necessarily the most knowledgeable or most effective one. This expert suggests giving full responsibility to a single, decisive executive. A human resource director and a consultant or adviser with broad experience in labor relations should in turn assist this person.

Reason 3. Concentrating on Money and Benefits   In 54% of the elections studied, the company lost because top management concentrated on the wrong issues: money and benefits. As this expert puts it:

> Employees may want more money, but quite often if they feel the company treats them fairly, decently, and honestly, they are satisfied with reasonable, competitive rates and benefits. It is only when they feel ignored, uncared for, and disregarded that money becomes a major issue to express their dissatisfaction.[35]

Reason 4. Industry Blind Spots   The researcher found that in some industries, employees felt more ignored and disregarded than in others. In highly automated industries (such as paper manufacturing and automobiles), there was some tendency for executives to ignore hourly employees, although this is changing today as firms implement more quality improvement programs. Here (as in reason 3), the solution is to pay more attention to employees' needs and attitudes.

Reason 5. Delegating Too Much to Divisions   For companies with plants scattered around the country, organizing several of the plants gives the union a wedge to tempt other plants' workers. Unionizing one or more plants tends to lead to unionizing others. Part of the solution is to keep the first four reasons above in mind, and thus diminish the union's ability to organize those first few plants. Also, don't abdicate all personnel and industrial relations decisions to plant managers.[36] Dealing effectively with unions—monitoring employees' attitudes, reacting properly when the union appears, and so on—generally requires centralized guidance from the main office and its HR staff.

The Supervisor's Role

Supervisors are an employer's first line of defense when it comes to the unionizing effort. They are often in the best position to sense evolving employee attitude problems, for instance, and to discover the first signs of union activity. Unfortunately, there's another side to that coin: They can also inadvertently take actions that hurt their employer's union-related efforts.

Supervisors therefore need special training. Specifically, they must be knowledgeable about what they can and can't do to legally hamper organizing activities. Unfair labor practices could (1) cause the NLRB to hold a new election after your company has won a previous election, or (2) cause your company to forfeit the second election and go directly to contract negotiation.

In one case, a plant superintendent reacted to a union's initial organizing attempt by prohibiting distribution of union literature in the plant's lunchroom. Since solicitation of off-duty workers in nonwork areas is generally legal, the company subsequently allowed the union to post union literature on the company's bulletin board and to distribute union literature in nonworking areas inside the plant. However, the NLRB still ruled that the initial act of prohibiting distribution of the literature was an unfair labor practice, one not "made right" by the company's subsequent efforts. The NLRB used the superintendent's action as one reason for invalidating an election that the company had won.

The "When You're on Your Own" feature provides guidelines for the front-line manager.

Rules Regarding Literature and Solicitation

The employer can take steps to legally restrict union organizing activity.[37]

1. Employers can always bar nonemployees from soliciting employees during their work time—that is, when the employee is on duty and not on a break. Thus, if the company cafeteria is open to whomever is on the premises, union organizers can solicit off-duty employees who are in the cafeteria, but not the cafeteria workers (such as cooks) who are not on a break.
2. Employers can usually stop employees from soliciting other employees for any purpose if one or both employees are on paid-duty time and not on a break.
3. Most employers (generally not including retail stores, shopping centers, and certain other employers) can bar nonemployees from the building's interiors and work areas as a right of private property owners. They can also sometimes bar nonemployees from exterior private areas—such as parking lots—if there is a business reason (such as safety) and the reason is not just to interfere with union organizers.[38]
4. Employers can deny on- or off-duty employees access to interior or exterior areas only if they can show the rule is required for reasons of production, safety, or discipline.

Such restrictions are valid only if the employer doesn't discriminate against the union. For example, if the employer lets employees collect money for wedding, shower, and baby gifts, to sell Avon products or Tupperware, or to engage in other solicitation during their working time, it may not be able to lawfully prohibit them from union soliciting during work time. To do so would discriminate based on union activity, which is an unfair labor practice. Here are two examples of specific rules aimed at limiting union organizing (or other) activity:

> Solicitation of employees on company property during working time interferes with the efficient operation of our business. Nonemployees are not permitted to solicit employees on company property for any purpose. Except in break areas where both employees are on break or off the clock, no employee may solicit another employee during working time for any purpose.
>
> Distribution of literature on company property not only creates a litter problem but also distracts us from our work. Nonemployees are not allowed to distribute literature on company property. Except in the performance of his or her job, an employee may not distribute literature unless both the distributor and the recipient are off the clock or on authorized break in a break area or off company premises. Special exceptions to these rules may be made by the company for especially worthwhile causes such as United Way, but written permission must first be obtained and the solicitation will be permitted only during break periods.[39]

Decertification Elections: Ousting the Union

Winning an election and signing an agreement do not necessarily mean that the union is in the company to stay. The same law that grants employees the right to unionize also gives

The Supervisor's Role in the Unionizing Effort

One company helps its supervisors remember what they may and may not do with respect to unionization with the acronyms TIPS and FORE.[40] Use TIPS to remember what *not* to do:

T—Threaten. Do not threaten or imply the company will take adverse action of any kind for supporting the unions.[41] Do not threaten to terminate employees because of their union activities, and don't threaten to close the facility if the union wins the election.

I—Interrogate. Don't interrogate or ask employees their position concerning unions, or how they are going to vote in an election.

P—Promise. Don't promise employees a pay increase, special favors, better benefits, or promotions.

S—Spy. Don't spy at any union activities or attend a union meeting, even if invited.

Use FORE to remember what the supervisor *may do* to discourage unionization.

F—Facts. Do tell employees that by signing the authorization card the union may become their legal representative in matters regarding wages and hours, and do tell them that by signing a union authorization card it does not mean they must vote for the union.

O—Opinion. You may tell employees that management doesn't believe in third-party representation, and that management believes in having an open-door policy to air grievances.

R—Rules. Provide factually correct advice such as telling employees that the law permits the company to permanently replace them if there's a strike, and that the union can't make the company agree to anything it does not want to during negotiations.

E—Experience. The supervisor may share personal experiences he or she may have had with a union.[42]

Figure 15-4 summarizes some other things to avoid.

FIGURE 15-4

Union Avoidance: What Not to Do

Source: From the BLR Newsletter "Best Practices in HR." Business & Legal Reports, Inc., 141 Mill Rock Road East, Old Saybrook, CT © 2004. Reprinted with permission of the publisher.

Human resources professionals must be very careful to do the following during union activities at their companies:

- Watch what you say. Angry feelings of the moment may get you in trouble.
- Never threaten workers with what you will do or what will happen if a union comes in. Do not say, for example, that the business will close or move, that wages will go down or overtime will be eliminated, that there will be layoffs, etc.
- Don't tell union sympathizers that they will suffer in any way for their support. Don't terminate or discipline workers for engaging in union activities.
- Don't interrogate workers about union sympathizers or organizers.
- Don't ask workers to remove union screensavers or campaign buttons if you allow these things for other organizations.
- Don't treat pro-union or anti-union workers any differently.
- Don't transfer workers on the basis of union affiliation or sympathies.
- Don't ask workers how they are going to vote or how others may vote.
- Don't ask employees about union meetings or any matters related to unions. You can listen, but don't ask for any details.
- Don't promise workers benefits, promotions, or anything else if they vote against the union.
- Avoid becoming involved—in any way—in the details of the union's election or campaign, and don't participate in any petition movement against the union.
- Don't give financial aid or any support to any unions.

Any one of these practices may result in a finding of "unfair labor practices," which may in turn result in recognition of a union without an election, as well as fines for your company.

The NEW *Workforce*   Unions Go Global

Wal-Mart, a company that traditionally works hard to prevent its stores from going union recently had to agree to let the workers in its stores in China join unions. Any company that thinks it can avoid unionization by sending manufacturing and jobs abroad is mistaken.

For example, U.S. unions are helping Mexican unions to organize, especially in U.S.-owned factories. Thus, the United Electrical Workers is subsidizing organizers at Mexican plants of the General Electric Company. And when the Campbell Soup Company threatened to move some operations to Mexico, the Farm Labor Organizing Committee, a midwestern union, discouraged the move

by helping its Mexican counterpart win a stronger contract, one that would have cost Campbell Soup higher wages if it made the move.

Reebok's experience provides another example of how unions reach across national boundaries. It has been working with the AFL-CIO to make the unions representing its overseas factories' employees more effective in protecting its workers' human rights. And the head of the Service Employees International union recently met with China's All China Federation of Trade Unions to help the latter organize China's Wal-Mart stores.[43].

decertification

Legal process for employees to terminate a union's right to represent them.

them a way to legally terminate their union's right to represent them. The process is **decertification**. There are around 450 to 500 decertification elections each year, of which unions usually win only around 30%.[44] That's actually a more favorable win rate for management than the rate for the original, representation elections.

Decertification campaigns don't differ much from certification campaigns.[45] The union organizes membership meetings and house-to-house visits, mails literature into the homes, and uses phone calls, NLRB appeals, and (sometimes) threats and harassment to win the election.[46] For its part, management uses meetings—including one-on-one meetings, small-group meetings, and meetings with entire units—as well as legal or expert assistance, letters, improved working conditions, and subtle or not-so-subtle threats to try to influence the votes.

"The New Workforce" illustrates some global aspects of union–management relations.

THE COLLECTIVE BARGAINING PROCESS

What Is Collective Bargaining?

When and if the union becomes your employees' representative, a day is set for management and labor to meet and negotiate a labor agreement. This agreement will contain specific provisions covering wages, hours, and working conditions.

collective bargaining

The process through which representatives of management and the union meet to negotiate a labor agreement.

What exactly is **collective bargaining**? According to the National Labor Relations Act:

> For the purpose of [this act,] to bargain collectively is the performance of the mutual obligation of the employer and the representative of the employees to meet at reasonable times and confer in good faith with respect to wages, hours, and terms and conditions of employment, or the negotiation of an agreement, or any question arising thereunder, and the execution of a written contract incorporating any agreement reached if requested by either party, but such obligation does not compel either party to agree to a proposal or require the making of a concession.

In plain language, this means that both management and labor are required by law to negotiate wage, hours, and terms and conditions of employment "in good faith." In a moment, we will see that the specific terms that are negotiable (since "wages, hours, and conditions of employment" are too broad to be useful in practice) have been clarified by a series of court decisions.

What Is Good Faith?

⑤ Illustrate with examples bargaining that is not in good faith.

good faith bargaining
Both parties are making every reasonable effort to arrive at agreement; proposals are being matched with counterproposals.

Good faith bargaining is the cornerstone of effective labor–management relations. It means that both parties communicate and negotiate, that they match proposals with counterproposals, and that both make every reasonable effort to arrive at an agreement. It does not mean that one party compels another to agree to a proposal. Nor does it require that either party make any specific concessions (although as a practical matter, some may be necessary).

When is bargaining not in good faith? As interpreted by the NLRB and the courts, a violation of the requirement for good faith bargaining may include the following:

1. *Surface bargaining.* Going through the motions of bargaining without any real intention of completing a formal agreement.
2. *Inadequate concessions.* Unwillingness to compromise, even though no one is required to make a concession.
3. *Inadequate proposals and demands.* The NLRB considers the advancement of proposals to be a positive factor in determining overall good faith.
4. *Dilatory tactics.* The law requires that the parties meet and "confer at reasonable times and intervals." Obviously, refusal to meet with the union does not satisfy the positive duty imposed on the employer.
5. *Imposing conditions.* Attempts to impose conditions that are so onerous or unreasonable as to indicate bad faith.
6. *Making unilateral changes in conditions.* This is a strong indication that the employer is not bargaining with the required intent of reaching an agreement.
7. *Bypassing the representative.* The duty of management to bargain in good faith involves, at a minimum, recognition that the union representative is the one with whom the employer must deal in conducting negotiations.
8. *Committing unfair labor practices during negotiations.* Such practices may reflect poorly upon the good faith of the guilty party.
9. *Withholding information.* An employer must supply the union with information, upon request, to enable it to understand and intelligently discuss the issues raised in bargaining.
10. *Ignoring bargaining items.* Refusal to bargain on a mandatory item (one must bargain over these) or insistence on a permissive item (one may bargain over these).[47]

Of course, requiring good faith bargaining doesn't mean that negotiations can't grind to a halt. For example, Northwest Airlines wouldn't let its negotiators meet with mechanics' union representatives because, Northwest said, the union didn't respond to company proposals the last three times they met.[48] Claiming that Bryant College negotiators were not sufficiently responsive with respect to wages and benefits, the Service Employees International Union, Local 134, filed an unfair labor practice claiming Bryant failed to negotiate in good faith.[49]

The Negotiating Team

Both union and management send a negotiating team to the bargaining table, and both teams usually go into the bargaining sessions having "done their homework." Union representatives will have sounded out union members on their desires and conferred with representatives of related unions.

Management uses several techniques to prepare for bargaining. First, it prepares the data on which to build its bargaining position.[50] It compiles data on pay and benefits that include comparisons with local pay rates and to rates paid for similar jobs within the industry. Data on the distribution of the workforce (in terms of age, sex, and seniority, for instance) are also important, because these factors determine what the company will actually pay out in benefits. Internal economic data regarding cost of benefits, overall earnings levels, and the amount and cost of overtime are important as well.

Management will also "cost" the current labor contract and determine the increased cost—total, per employee, and per hour—of the union's demands. It will use information from grievances and feedback from supervisors to determine what the union's demands might be, and prepare counteroffers and arguments.[51] Other popular tactics are attitude surveys to test employee reactions to various sections of the contract that management may feel require change, and informal conferences with local union leaders to discuss the operational effectiveness of the contract and to send up trial balloons on management ideas for change.

Collective bargaining experts emphasize the need to carefully cost the union's demands. One says,

> "The mistake I see most often is [HR professionals who] enter the negotiations without understanding the financial impact of things they put on the table. The thing you give up can make or break your employer. . . . For example, the union wants three extra vacation days. That doesn't sound like a lot, except that in some states, if an employee leaves, you have to pay them for unused vacation time. [So] now your employer has to carry that liability on their books at all times."[52]

Bargaining Items

Labor law sets out categories of items that are subject to bargaining: These are mandatory, voluntary, and illegal items.

Voluntary (or permissible) bargaining items are neither mandatory nor illegal; they become a part of negotiations only through the joint agreement of both management and union. Neither party can compel the other to negotiate over voluntary items. You cannot hold up signing a contract because the other party refuses to bargain on a voluntary item. Benefits for retirees might be an example.

Illegal bargaining items are forbidden by law. A clause agreeing to hire union members exclusively would be illegal in a right-to-work state, for example.

Table 15-1 presents some of the 70 or so **mandatory bargaining items**, over which bargaining is mandatory under the law. They include wages, hours, rest periods, layoffs, transfers, benefits, and severance pay. Others, such as drug testing, are added as the law evolves.

Bargaining Stages

The actual bargaining typically goes through several stages.[53] First, each side presents its demands. At this stage, both parties are usually quite far apart on some issues. Second, there is a reduction of demands. At this stage, each side trades off some of its demands to gain others. Third come the subcommittee studies; the parties form joint subcommittees to try to work out reasonable alternatives. Fourth, the parties reach an informal settlement, and each group goes back to its sponsor. Union representatives check informally with their superiors and the union members; management representatives check with top management. Finally, once everything is in order, the parties fine-tune and sign a formal agreement.

Bargaining Hints

Expert Reed Richardson has the following advice for bargainers:

1. Be sure to set clear objectives for every bargaining item, and be sure you understand the reason for each.
2. Do not hurry.

---

voluntary bargaining items
Items in collective bargaining over which bargaining is neither illegal nor mandatory—neither party can be compelled against its wishes to negotiate over those items.

illegal bargaining items
Items in collective bargaining that are forbidden by law; for example, a clause agreeing to hire "union members exclusively" would be illegal in a right-to-work state.

mandatory bargaining items
Items in collective bargaining that a party must bargain over if they are introduced by the other party—for example, pay.

TABLE 15-1 Bargaining Items

Mandatory	Permissible	Illegal
Rates of pay	Indemnity bonds	Closed shop
Wages	Management rights as to union affairs	Separation of employees based on race
Hours of employment		
Overtime pay	Pension benefits of retired employees	Discriminatory treatment
Shift differentials		
Holidays	Scope of the bargaining unit	
Vacations	Including supervisors in the contract	
Severance pay		
Pensions	Additional parties to the contract such as the international union	
Insurance benefits		
Profit-sharing plans		
Christmas bonuses	Use of union label	
Company housing, meals, and discounts	Settlement of unfair labor changes	
Employee security	Prices in cafeteria	
Job performance	Continuance of past contract	
Union security	Membership of bargaining team	
Management–union relationship		
Drug testing of employees	Employment of strike breaker	

Source: Michael R. Carrell and Christina Heavrin, *Labor Relations and Collective Bargaining: Cases, Practices, and Law* (Upper Saddle River, NJ: Prentice Hall, 2001), p. 177.

3. When in doubt, caucus with your associates.
4. Be well prepared with firm data supporting your position.
5. Always strive to keep some flexibility in your position.
6. Don't concern yourself just with what the other party says and does; find out why.
7. Respect the importance of face saving for the other party.
8. Be alert to the real intentions of the other party—not only for goals, but also for priorities.
9. Be a good listener.
10. Build a reputation for being fair but firm.
11. Learn to control your emotions and use them as a tool.
12. As you make each bargaining move, be sure you know its relationship to all other moves.
13. Measure each move against your objectives.
14. Pay close attention to the wording of every clause negotiated; they are often a source of grievances.
15. Remember that collective bargaining is a compromise process. There is no such thing as having all the pie.
16. Try to understand people and their personalities.
17. Consider the impact of present negotiations on those in future years.[54]

Impasses, Mediation, and Strikes

impasse

Collective bargaining situation that occurs when the parties are not able to move further toward settlement, usually because one party is demanding more than the other will offer.

In collective bargaining, an **impasse** occurs when the parties are not able to move further toward settlement. An impasse usually occurs because one party is demanding more than the other will offer. Sometimes an impasse can be resolved through a third party—a disinterested person such as a mediator or arbitrator. If the impasse is not resolved in this way, the union may call a work stoppage, or strike, to put pressure on management.

mediation

Intervention in which a neutral third party tries to assist the principals in reaching agreement.

Third-Party Involvement   Negotiators use three types of third-party interventions to overcome an impasse: mediation, fact finding, and arbitration. With **mediation**, a neutral third party tries to assist the principals in reaching agreement. The mediator usually holds meetings with each party to determine where each stands regarding its position, and then uses this information to find common ground for further bargaining. The mediator is always a go-between, and does not have the authority to dictate terms or make concessions. He or she communicates assessments of the likelihood of a strike, the possible settlement packages available, and the like.

fact finder

A neutral party who studies the issues in a dispute and makes a public recommendation for a reasonable settlement.

In certain situations, as in a national emergency dispute, a fact finder may be appointed. A **fact finder** is a neutral party who studies the issues in a dispute and makes a public recommendation for a reasonable settlement.[55] Presidential emergency fact-finding boards have successfully resolved impasses in certain critical transportation disputes.

arbitration

The most definitive type of third-party intervention, in which the arbitrator usually has the power to determine and dictate the settlement terms.

Arbitration is the most definitive type of third-party intervention, because the arbitrator often has the power to determine and dictate the settlement terms. Unlike mediation and fact finding, arbitration can guarantee a solution to an impasse. With *binding arbitration*, both parties are committed to accepting the arbitrator's award. With *nonbinding arbitration*, they are not. Arbitration may also be voluntary or compulsory (in other words, imposed by a government agency). In the United States, voluntary binding arbitration is the most prevalent.

There are two main topics of arbitration. *Interest arbitration* always centers on working out a labor agreement; the parties use it when such agreements do not yet exist or when one or both parties are seeking to change the agreement. *Rights arbitration* really means "contract interpretation arbitration." It usually involves interpreting existing contract terms, for instance, when an employee questions the employer's right to have taken some disciplinary action.[56]

Sources of Third-Party Assistance   Various public and professional agencies make arbitrators and mediators available. For example, the American Arbitration Association (AAA) represents and provides the services of thousands of arbitrators and mediators to employers and unions requesting their services. The U.S. government's Federal Mediation and Conciliation Service provides both arbitrators and mediators. For example, its Office of Arbitration Services maintains a roster of arbitrators qualified to hear and decide disputes over the interpretation or application of collective-bargaining agreements, and provides the parties involved with lists and panels of arbitrators. In fiscal year 2006, its arbitration panels decided about 2,400 cases. In addition, most states provide arbitrator and mediation services. For example, New York State's Employment Relations Board provides mediation services to assist in settling grievance disputes and in the collective-bargaining process.

Figure 15-5 (see page 618) shows the form employers or unions use to request arbitrator or mediator services from the U.S. government's Federal Mediation and Conciliation Service (FMCS).

FMCS Form F-53
Revised 5-92

Form Approved
OMB No. 3076-0

FEDERAL SECTOR LABOR RELATIONS
NOTICE TO FEDERAL MEDIATION AND CONCILIATION SERVICE

Mail
To:

Notice Processing Unit
FEDERAL MEDIATION AND CONCILIATION SERVICE
2100 K Street, N.W.
Washington, D.C. 20427

THIS NOTICE IS IN REGARD TO: (MARK "X")

(1) ☐ AN INITIAL CONTRACT   (INCLUDED FLRA CERTIFICATION NUMBER) # _____
    ☐ A CONTRACT REOPENER   REOPENER DATE _____
    ☐ THE EXPIRATION OF AN EXISTING AGREEMENT   EXPIRATION DATE: _____

    ☐ *OTHER REQUESTS FOR THE ASSISTANCE OF FMCS IN BARGAINING*   *(MARK "X")*
(2)
    SPECIFY TYPE OF ISSUE(S)

    ☐ *REQUEST FOR GRIEVANCE MEDIATION (SEE ITEM #10)*   *(MARK "X")*
(3)
    ISSUE(S)

(4) NAME OF FEDERAL AGENCY   NAME OF SUBDIVISION OR COMPONENT, IF ANY

    STREET ADDRESS OF AGENCY   CITY   STATE   ZIP

    AGENCY OFFICIAL TO BE CONTACTED   AREA CODE & PHONE NUMBER

(5) NAME OF NATIONAL UNION OR PARENT BODY   NAME AND/OR LOCAL NUMBER

    STREET ADDRESS   CITY   STATE   ZIP

    UNION OFFICIAL TO BE CONTACTED   AREA CODE & PHONE NUMBER

    LOCATION OF NEGOTIATIONS OR WHERE MEDIATION WILL BE HELD
    STREET ADDRESS   CITY   STATE   ZIP
(6)

(7) APPROX. # OF EMPLOYEES IN BARGAINING UNIT(S) >>   IN ESTABLISHMENT >>

(8) THIS NOTICE OR REQUEST IS FILED ON BEHALF OF *(MARK "X")*   ☐ UNION   ☐ AGENCY

(9) NAME AND TITLE OF OFFICIAL(S) SUBMITTING THIS NOTICE OR REQUEST   AREA CODE AND PHONE NUMBER

    STREET ADDRESS   CITY   STATE   ZIP

    FOR GRIEVANCE MEDIATION, THE SIGNATURES OF BOTH PARTIES ARE REQUIRED: *

(10) SIGNATURE (AGENCY)   DATE   SIGNATURE (UNION)   DATE

*Receipt of this form does not commit FMCS to offer its services. Receipt of this form will not be acknowledged in writing by FMCS. While use of this form is voluntary, its use will facilitate FMCS service to respondents. Public reporting burden for this collection of information is estimated to average 10 minutes per response, including time for reviewing the collection of information. Send comments regarding this burden estimate or any other aspect of this collection of information, including suggestions for reducing this burden, to FMCS Division of Administrative Services, Washington, D.C. 20427, and to the Office of Management and Budget, Paperwork Reduction Project, Washington, D.C. 20603, accessed September 4, 2006.

FIGURE 15-5

Form to Request Mediation Services

strike
A withdrawal of labor.

economic strike
A strike that results from a failure to agree on the terms of a contract that involve wages, benefits, and other conditions of employment.

unfair labor practice strike
A strike aimed at protesting illegal conduct by the employer.

wildcat strike
An unauthorized strike occurring during the term of a contract.

sympathy strike
A strike that takes place when one union strikes in support of the strike of another.

picketing
Having employees carry signs announcing their concerns near the employer's place of business.

Strikes   A **strike** is a withdrawal of labor, and there are four main types of strikes. An **economic strike** results from a failure to agree on the terms of a contract. Unions call **unfair labor practice strikes** to protest illegal conduct by the employer. A **wildcat strike** is an unauthorized strike occurring during the term of a contract. A **sympathy strike** occurs when one union strikes in support of the strike of another union.[57] For example, in sympathy with employees of the *Detroit News, Detroit Free Press*, and *USA Today*, the United Auto Workers enforced a nearly six-year boycott that prevented the papers from being sold at Detroit-area auto plants, cutting sales by about 20,000 to 30,000 copies a day.[58]

The number of major work stoppages (those involving 1,000 workers or more) peaked at about 400 per year between 1965 and 1975, and today average around 20.

Picketing, or having employees carry signs announcing their concerns near the employer's place of business, is one of the first activities to occur during a strike. Its purpose is to inform the public about the existence of the labor dispute and often to encourage others to refrain from doing business with the struck employer.

Employers can make several responses when they become the object of a strike. One is to shut down the affected area and halt operations until the strike is over. A second is to contract out work in order to blunt the effects of the strike. A third response is to continue operations, perhaps using supervisors and other nonstriking workers to fill in for the striking workers. A fourth alternative is hiring replacements for the strikers.

Diminished union leverage plus competitive pressures now prompt more employers to *replace* (or at least consider replacing) *strikers* with permanent replacement workers. One study of human resource managers found that of those responding, 18% "would not consider striker replacements" in the event of a strike, while 31% called it "not very likely," 23% "somewhat likely" and 21% "very likely."[59] When Northwest Airlines began giving permanent jobs to 1,500 substitute workers it hired to replace striking mechanics, the strike, by the Aircraft Mechanics Fraternal Association basically fell apart.[60]

Employers generally can replace strikers. In one very important labor relations case known as *Mackay*, the U.S. Supreme Court ruled that while the National Labor Relations Act does prohibit employers from interfering with employees' right to strike, employers still have the right to continue their operations and, therefore, to replace strikers.

Picketing is one of the first activities to occur during a strike. The purpose is to inform the public about the labor dispute

Subsequent decisions by the National Labor Relations Board put some limitations on *Mackay*. For example, employers cannot permanently replace strikers who are protesting unfair labor practices, cannot grant replacement workers pay raises not offered to strikers, and must rehire strikers who apply for reinstatement unconditionally.

When a strike is imminent, the employer should make plans to deal with it. For example, as negotiations between the Hibbing Taconite Steel Plant in Minnesota and the United Steelworkers of America headed toward a deadline, the firm began preparations that included bringing in security workers and trailers to house them.

Two experts say that, with a strike imminent, following these guidelines can minimize confusion:

- Pay all striking employees what you owe them on the first day of the strike.
- Secure the facility. Management should control access to the property. The company should consider hiring guards to protect replacements coming to and from work and to watch and control the picketers, if necessary.
- Notify all customers, and prepare a standard official response to all queries.
- Contact all suppliers and other persons who will have to cross the picket line. Establish alternative methods of obtaining supplies.
- Make arrangements for overnight stays in the facility and for delivered meals in case the occasion warrants such action.
- Notify the local unemployment office of your need for replacement workers.
- Photograph the facility before, during, and after picketing. If necessary, install video-tape equipment and devices to monitor picket line misconduct.
- Record all facts concerning strikers' demeanor and activities and such incidents as violence, threats, mass pickets, property damage, or problems. Record the police response to requests for assistance.
- Gather the following evidence: number of pickets and their names; time, date, and location of picketing; wording on every sign carried by pickets; and descriptions of picket cars and license numbers.[61]

Other Alternatives   Management and labor each have other weapons they can use to try to break an impasse and achieve their aims. The union, for example, may resort to a corporate campaign. A **corporate campaign** is an organized effort by the union that exerts pressure on the employer by pressuring the company's other unions, shareholders, corporate directors, customers, creditors, and government agencies, often directly. Thus, the union might surprise individual members of the board of directors by picketing their homes, and organizing a **boycott** of the company's banks.[62]

The Web is another potent union tool. For example, when the Hotel Employees and Restaurant Employees Union, Local 2, wanted to turn up the heat on the San Francisco Marriott, it launched a new Web site. The site explained the union's eight-month boycott and provided a helpful list of union-backed hotels where prospective guests can stay. It also listed organizations that decided to stay elsewhere in response to the boycott.[63]

Inside games are another union tactic, one often used in conjunction with corporate campaigns. **Inside games** are union efforts to convince employees to impede or to disrupt production—for example, by slowing the work pace, refusing to work overtime, filing mass charges with government agencies, refusing to do work without receiving detailed instructions from supervisors, and engaging in other disruptive activities such as sick-outs.[64] Inside games are basically strikes—albeit "strikes" in which the employees are being supported by the company, which continues to pay them. In one inside game at Caterpillar's Aurora, Illinois, plant, United Auto Workers' grievances in the final stage before arbitration rose from 22 to 336. The effect was to clog the grievance procedure and tie up workers and management in unproductive endeavors on company time.[65]

corporate campaign
An organized effort by the union that exerts pressure on the corporation by pressuring the company's other unions, shareholders, directors, customers, creditors, and government agencies, often directly.

boycott
The combined refusal by employees and other interested parties to buy or use the employer's products.

inside games
Union efforts to convince employees to impede or to disrupt production—for example, by slowing the work pace.

lockout
A refusal by the employer to provide opportunities to work.

For their part, employers can try to break an impasse with lockouts. A **lockout** is a refusal by the employer to provide opportunities to work. It (sometimes literally) locks out employees and prohibits them from doing their jobs (and getting paid). The NLRB generally doesn't view lockouts as an unfair labor practice. For example, if your product is a perishable one (such as vegetables), then a lockout may be a legitimate tactic to neutralize or decrease union power. The NLRB views lockouts as an unfair labor practice only when the employer acts for a prohibited purpose. It is not a prohibited purpose to try to bring about a settlement on terms favorable to the employer. Lockouts are not widely used today; employers are usually reluctant to cease operations when employees are willing to continue working (even though there may be an impasse at the bargaining table).

Both employers and unions can seek an injunction from the courts if they believe the other side is taking actions that could cause irreparable harm to the other party. An **injunction** is a court order compelling a party or parties either to resume or to desist from a certain action.[66]

injunction
A court order compelling a party or parties either to resume or to desist from a certain action.

The Contract Agreement

The actual contract agreement may be a 20- or 30-page document; or it may be even longer. It may contain just general declarations of policy, or detailed rules and procedures. The tendency today is toward the longer, more detailed contract. This is largely a result of the increased number of items the agreements have been covering.

The main sections of a typical contract cover subjects such as these:

(1) management rights, (2) union security and automatic payroll dues deduction, (3) grievance procedures, (4) arbitration of grievances, (5) disciplinary procedures, (6) compensation rates, (7) hours of work and overtime, (8) benefits: vacations, holidays, insurance, pensions, (9) health and safety provisions, (10) employee security seniority provisions, and (11) contract expiration date.

Develop a grievance procedure.

GRIEVANCES

Hammering out a labor agreement is not the last step in collective bargaining. No labor contract can cover all contingencies and answer all questions. For example, suppose the contract says you can only discharge an employee for "just cause." You subsequently discharge someone for speaking back to you in harsh terms. Was it within your rights to discharge this person? Was speaking back to you harshly "just cause"?

grievance procedure
Any factor involving wages, hours, or conditions of employment that is used as a complaint against the employer.

The labor contract's grievance procedure usually handles problems like these. The **grievance procedure** provides an orderly system whereby both employer and union determine whether some action violated the contract.[67] It is the vehicle for administering the contract on a day-to-day basis. The grievance process allows both parties to interpret and give meaning to various clauses, and transforms the contract into a "living organism." Remember, though, that this involves interpretation only; it usually doesn't involve negotiating new terms or altering existing ones.

Sources of Grievances

From a practical point of view, it is probably easier to list those items that *don't* precipitate grievances than to list the ones that do. Employees may use just about any factor involving wages, hours, or conditions of employment as the basis of a grievance.

However, certain grievances are more serious, since they're usually more difficult to settle. Discipline cases and seniority problems including promotions, transfers, and layoffs would top this list. Others would include grievances growing out of job evaluations and work assignments, overtime, vacations, incentive plans, and holidays.[68] Here are four examples of grievances:

- *Absenteeism.* An employer fired an employee for excessive absences. The employee filed a grievance stating that there had been no previous warnings or discipline related to excessive absences.
- *Insubordination.* An employee on two occasions refused to obey a supervisor's order to meet with him, unless a union representative was present at the meeting. As a result, the employee was discharged and subsequently filed a grievance protesting the discharge.
- *Overtime.* The employer discontinued Sunday overtime work after a department was split. Employees affected filed a grievance protesting loss of the overtime work.
- *Plant rules.* The plant had a posted rule barring employees from eating or drinking during unscheduled breaks. The employees filed a grievance claiming the rule was arbitrary.[69]

A grievance is often a symptom of an underlying problem. Sometimes, bad relationships between supervisors and subordinates are to blame: This is often the cause of grievances over "fair treatment," for instance. Organizational factors such as automated jobs or ambiguous job descriptions that frustrate or aggravate employees also cause grievances. Union activism is another cause; the union may solicit grievances from workers to underscore ineffective supervision. Problem employees are yet another underlying cause of grievances. These are individuals, who, by their nature, are negative, dissatisfied, and prone to complaints. Discipline and dismissal, explained in Chapter 14, are also both major sources of grievances.

The Grievance Procedure

Most collective bargaining contracts contain a specific grievance procedure. It lists the various steps in the procedure, time limits associated with each step, and specific rules such as "all charges of contract violation must be reduced to writing." Virtually every labor agreement signed today contains a grievance procedure clause. (Nonunionized employers need such procedures, too, as explained in Chapter 14.)

Union grievance procedures differ from firm to firm. Some contain simple, two-step procedures. Here the grievant, union representative, and company representative meet to discuss the grievance. If they don't find a satisfactory solution, the grievance is brought before an independent, third-party arbitrator, who hears the case, writes it up, and makes a decision. Figure 15-6 shows a Grievance Record Form.

At the other extreme, the grievance procedure may contain six or more steps. The first step might be for the grievant and shop steward to meet informally with the grievant's supervisor to try to find a solution. If they don't find one, the employee files a formal grievance, and there's a meeting with the employee, shop steward, and the supervisor's boss. The next steps involve the grievant and union representatives meeting with higher-level managers. Finally, if top management and the union can't reach agreement, the grievance may go to arbitration.

Sometimes the grievance process gets out of hand. For example, several years ago, members of American Postal Workers Union, Local 482, filed 1,800 grievances at the Postal Service's Roanoke mail processing facility (the usual rate is about 800 grievances per year). The employees apparently were responding to job changes, including transfers triggered by the Postal Service's efforts to further automate its processes.[70]

Guidelines for Handling Grievances

The best way to handle a grievance is to develop a work environment in which grievances don't occur in the first place. Hone your ability to recognize, diagnose, and correct the

FIGURE 15-6

A Standard Grievance Record Form

Source: Michael Carrell and Christina Heavrin, *Labor Relations and Collective Bargaining* (Upper Saddle River, NJ: Prentice Hall, 2001), p. 415.

GRIEVANCE NUMBER *97-007*   DATE FILED *4/23/07*   UNION *Local 1233*

NAME OF GRIEVANT(S) *Davis, Henry*   CLOCK # *0379*

DATE CAUSE OF GRIEVANCE OCCURRED *4/20/07*

CONTRACTUAL PROVISIONS CITED *Articles III, VII, and others*

STATEMENT OF THE GRIEVANCE

On April 20, Foreman George Moore asked Henry Davis to go temporarily to the Rolling Mill for the rest of the turn. Davis said he preferred not to, and that he was more senior to others who were available. The foreman never ordered Davis to take the temporary assignment. He only requested that Davis do so.

Davis was improperly charged with insubordination and suspended for three days. The foreman did not have just cause for the discipline.

RELIEF SOUGHT:

Reinstatement with full back pay and seniority.

GRIEVANT'S SIGNATURE _____*Henry Davis*_____ DATE *4/22/07*

STEWARD'S SIGNATURE _____*Jim Bob Smith*_____ DATE *4/23/07*

STEP 1

DISPOSITION:

Foreman Moore gave Davis clear instructions to report temporarily to the Rolling Mill for the remainder of the shift. Davis refused to do so and was warned that it could result in discipline. When he again refused the foreman's directive, he was disciplined.

The discipline was for just cause. The grievance is rejected.

SIGNATURE OF
EMPLOYER REPRESENTATIVE _____*Paul Roberts*_____ DATE *4/26/07*

_____ Grievance Withdrawn or __✓__ Referred to Step 2

SIGNATURE OF
UNION REPRESENTATIVE _____*Jim Bob Smith*_____ DATE *4/28/07*

causes of potential employee dissatisfaction (such as unfair appraisals, inequitable wages, or poor communications) before they become grievances.

The manager is on the firing line and must steer a course between treating employees fairly and maintaining management's rights and prerogatives. One expert has developed a list of do's and don'ts as useful guides in handling grievances.[71] Some critical ones include:

Do:

1. Investigate and handle each case as though it may eventually result in arbitration.
2. Talk with the employee about his or her grievance; give the person a full hearing.
3. Require the union to identify specific contractual provisions allegedly violated.
4. Comply with the contractual time limits for handling the grievance.
5. Visit the work area of the grievance.
6. Determine whether there were any witnesses.
7. Examine the grievant's personnel record.
8. Fully examine prior grievance records.
9. Treat the union representative as your equal.
10. Hold your grievance discussions privately.
11. Fully inform your own supervisor of grievance matters.

Don't:

12. Discuss the case with the union steward alone—the grievant should be there.
13. Make arrangements with individual employees that are inconsistent with the labor agreement.
14. Hold back the remedy if the company is wrong.
15. Admit to the binding effect of a past practice.
16. Relinquish to the union your rights as a manager.
17. Settle grievances based on what is "fair." Instead, stick to the labor agreement.
18. Bargain over items not covered by the contract.
19. Treat as subject to arbitration claims demanding the discipline or discharge of managers.
20. Give long written grievance answers.
21. Trade a grievance settlement for a grievance withdrawal.
22. Deny grievances because "your hands have been tied by management."
23. Agree to informal amendments in the contract.

THE UNION MOVEMENT TODAY AND TOMORROW

About 35% of the nonfarm U.S. workforce belonged to unions in the 1960s. Recently, that figure dropped to about 12%. Why has this occurred and what is the future for the union movement?

Why Union Membership Is Down

As we said earlier, several things contributed to union membership decline. *Laws* like OSHA and Title VII of the Civil Rights Act reduced the need for the traditional protective role unions play. Increased global *competition* and *new technologies* like the Internet and just-in-time production systems forced employers to reduce inefficiencies and cut costs—often by reducing payrolls by automating or by sending jobs abroad. This squeezes unions. For example, with GM's performance stumbling, the United Auto Workers recently agreed to "give back" rights to benefits they previously won.[72] New *foreign-owned* auto plants from Toyota, Nissan, BMW, and DaimlerChrysler largely stayed union free. Only about 15% of U.S. workers are now employed in *manufacturing and construction*, so unions' traditional membership sources shrank. Some union leaders also believe that new labor–management cooperation tactics (like employee participation teams) undermine unions' traditional prerogatives.

An Upswing for Unions?

However, the news is not all bleak.[73] For one thing, the 12% unionization figure conceals the real impact unions have on the U.S. economy. Union membership varies widely by state, so unions are still quite influential in some states (such as Michigan and New York). And, fully 35% of the nation's blue-collar workers—in particular those in manufacturing and construction jobs—belong to unions. Furthermore, a slight majority of all union members (about 51%), are now white-collar, which suggests unions are having success tapping this growing portion of the workforce. For example, an optical physicist at the National Aeronautics and Space Administration is also the president of his local union.[74] White collar union members include about 40% of all college faculty members, 45,000 physicians, 50,000 engineers, and almost 100,000 nurses who belong to unions (as do most major league baseball, football, basketball, and hockey players). About 40% of all federal, state, and local government employees belong to unions. Recently, the union win rate in elections increased a bit, to 57.8% of elections held.[75] Union membership declines seem to have leveled off.[76] And, as we'll see, unions themselves are becoming much more aggressive.

Public Employees and Unions

One bright spot for the union movement is their success in organizing federal, state, and municipal workers. With at least 7 million public-sector union members, the public sector represents at least 44% of total U.S. union membership. Three public unions—the National Education Association, the American Federation of State, County and Municipal Employees, and the American Federation of Teachers—are among the largest nine U.S. unions.

The unions' success in organizing public employees reflects, in part, years of changes in public sector collective bargaining and labor relations legislation. The National Labor Relations Act does not cover public employees. However, other laws do extend to public employees much the same rights. For example, in 1962, President John F. Kennedy signed executive order 10988. This recognized federal employees' rights to join or refrain from joining labor organizations and granted recognition to those organizations. In 1978, Congress passed the Civil Service Reform Act of 1978. Title VII of this act (known as the Federal Labor Relations Act) is similar to the National Labor Relations Act. It gave the new Federal Labor Relations Authority new authority to oversee federal public-sector labor relations. Among other things, this Title VII prohibits the government from restraining or coercing employees in the exercise of their organizational rights, or from encouraging or discouraging union membership. Similarly, labor organizations may not interfere with the employees' rights to unionize or to refrain from organizing.[77]

Organizing Professionals and White-Collar Employees

As noted, unions are also making inroads into traditionally hard-to-organize worker segments like professionals and white-collar workers, as even these employees see their job security and perquisites under attack. Recent reports of IBM sending systems analysts' jobs abroad, of Merrill Lynch having more security analysis done abroad by foreign nationals, and of hospitals having digitized X-rays read and interpreted by doctors abroad illustrate the concerns many professionals have. As noted above, thousands of teachers, doctors, nurses, and professionals have already joined unions, and employers' continuing attempts to squeeze ever more productivity out of these workers may well prompt more to

Unions are making inroads into traditionally hard-to-organize worker segments like professionals and white-collar workers.

consider doing so. Several years ago Boeing began focusing more on cost cutting and financial results and (from its engineers' point of view) less on engineering excellence. Engineers' morale reportedly dropped, and Boeing was caught by surprise when its engineers joined the Seattle Professional Engineering Employees Association.[78]

New Union Tactics

Unions are also becoming much more aggressive. Unions are pushing Congress to pass the Employee Free Choice Act. This would, among other things, make it more difficult for employers to inhibit workers from trying to form a union. Unions are also pushing for a new means of obtaining union recognition. Instead of secret ballots elections, they want a "card check" system. Here the union would win recognition when a majority of workers signed authorization card saying they want to union. Several large companies, including Cingular Wireless agreed to the card check process.[79] Unions are also using class action lawsuits to support employees in nonunionized companies, so as to pressure employers. For example, unions recently used class action lawsuits to support workers claims under the fair labor standards act, and the equal pay act.[80]

The steps that UNITE took against Cintas Corp. illustrate some of unions' new aggressive tactics. In their organizing effort against Cintas, UNITE did not petition for an NLRB election. Instead, UNITE proposed using the "card-check" process. They also filed a $100 million class-action suit against the company in support of its sales representatives. Then Cintas workers in California filed a lawsuit claiming that the company was violating a nearby municipality's "living wage" law. UNITE then joined forces with the Teamsters union, which in turn began targeting Cintas' delivery people.[81]

Change to Win   The priorities of the Change to Win Coalition (whose members broke off from the AFL-CIO), help illustrate what may be the new union strategies. They,

> Make it our first priority to help millions more workers form unions so we can build a strong movement for rewarding work in America; unite the strength of everyone who works in the same industry so we can negotiate with today's huge global corporations for everyone's benefit; reflect the diversity and commitment to change of today's workforce; build a growing, independent voice for working people in politics based on economic issues, and party; modernize the strategies, structure and priorities of the AFL-CIO to make these changes possible.[82]

In practice, this means several things. Change to Win will be very aggressive about in organizing workers, will focus on organizing women and minority workers, will focus more on organizing temporary or contingent workers, and will target specific multinational companies for international campaigns.[83]

Other unions are taking a different tack. For years the head of Ford's United Auto Workers union fought hard for increased benefits for his members. But recently, he's been urging his colleagues to accept productivity enhancing plans, such as outsourcing Ford's factory jobs to lower paid workers. "Ford is in a desperate situation" he says, and "if this company goes down, I want to be able to look in the mirror and say I did everything I could."[84]

Improving Productivity Through HRIS

Furthermore, employers are not the only ones benefiting from technology. As one expert recently asked, "If faster and more powerful ways of communicating enable companies to compete in a quickly changing and challenging environment, shouldn't they also make unions stronger and more efficient as organizations and workplace representatives?"[85]

In fact, the Internet is revolutionizing union activity, much as it revolutionized how firms do business. E-mail and the Internet mean unions can mass e-mail announcements to collective bargaining unit members, and use mass e-mail to reach supporters and government officials for their corporate campaigns.

Union-based Web sites are now integral parts of many such unionization campaigns; Alliance@IBM provides one example. Managed by the Communications Workers of America, Alliance@IBM seeks to encourage IBM employees to join the Communications Workers of America. It does so by providing information on a range of issues, such as why IBM employees need a union, questions and concerns about unions, and how employees can join the union and get involved. For example, one page contains background information and instructions for Alliance organizers at IBM. It contains downloadable, online flyers for distribution; articles on topics like "Renewing a Union in the New Economy" and "Working Hard, Earning Less: The Story of Job Growth in America." The site even includes a downloadable authorization card.

The Web site for the United Farmworkers (www.ufw.org) provides another example. For example, it provides an efficient way for the union to organize its Gallo campaign, and to sign up new contributors for its other efforts.

Employee Participation Programs and Unions

As noted above, unions are grappling with how to deal with employee participation programs. Many unions believe that the effects, if not the motives, of such programs is to usurp unions' traditional duties. In one such program, at UPS, hourly employees in self-directed teams establish priorities on how to do their jobs.

To understand the problem, it's useful to know that one goal of the National Labor Relations (or Wagner) Act was to outlaw "sham unions." Two years before passage of the NLRA, the National Recovery Act (1933) tried to give employees the right to organize and to bargain collectively. This triggered an increase in unions that were actually company-supported organizations aimed at keeping legitimate unions out. This helped lead to passage of the National Labor Relations Act. The problem is that, because of how the courts often interpret the NLRA, courts might view some participative programs like UPS's as sham unions. If the committees focus just on issues such as quality and productivity improvement, courts are more likely to view them as outside the scope of the National Labor Relations Act. Being involved in union-type matters such as wages, working conditions, and hours of work may be more questionable.

Employers can take these steps to avoid having their employee participation programs viewed as sham unions:[86]

- Involve employees in the formation of these programs to the greatest extent practical.
- Continually emphasize to employees that the committees exist for the exclusive purpose of addressing issues such as quality and productivity. They are not intended as vehicles for dealing with management on mandatory bargaining-type items such as pay and working conditions.
- Don't try to establish such committees at the same time union organizing activities are beginning in your facility.
- Fill the committees with volunteers rather than elected employee representatives, and rotate membership to ensure broad employee participation.
- Minimize your participation in the committees' day-to-day activities, to avoid unlawful interference or, worse, the perception of domination.

SUMMARY

1. Union membership has been alternately growing and shrinking since as early as 1790. A major milestone was the creation in 1886 of the American Federation of Labor (AFL) by Samuel Gompers. Today, the AFL-CIO is a national federation of about 100 national and international unions. Most recently the trend in unionization has been toward organizing white-collar workers, particularly since the proportion of blue-collar workers has been declining.

2. In addition to improved wages and working conditions, unions seek security when organizing. We discussed five possible arrangements, including the closed shop, the union shop, the agency shop, the open shop, and maintenance of membership.

3. The Norris-LaGuardia Act and the Wagner Act marked a shift in labor law from repression to strong encouragement of union activity. They did this by banning certain types of unfair labor practices, by providing for secret-ballot elections, and by creating the National Labor Relations Board.

4. The Taft-Hartley Act reflected the period of modified encouragement coupled with regulation. It enumerated the rights of employees with respect to their unions, enumerated the rights of employers, and allowed the U.S. president to temporarily bar national emergency strikes. Among other things, it also enumerated certain unfair union labor practices. And employers were explicitly given the right to express their views concerning union organization.

5. The Landrum-Griffin Act reflected the period of detailed regulation of internal union affairs. It grew out of discoveries of wrongdoing on the part of both management and union leadership and contained a bill of rights for union members.

6. There are five steps in a union drive and election: the initial contact, obtaining authorization cards, holding a hearing with the NLRB, the campaign, and the election itself. The union need only win a majority of the votes cast, not a majority of the workers in the bargaining unit eligible to vote.

7. There are five surefire ways to lose an NLRB election: Be caught sleeping at the switch, form a committee, emphasize money and benefits, have an industry blind spot, and delegate too much to divisions.

8. Bargaining collectively in good faith is the next step if and when the union wins the election. Good faith means that both parties communicate and negotiate, and that proposals are matched with counterproposals. Bargaining items are categorized as mandatory, voluntary, or illegal.

9. An impasse occurs when the parties aren't able to move further toward settlement. Third-party involvement—namely, arbitration, fact finding, or mediation—is one alternative. Sometimes, though, a strike occurs. Boycotts and lockouts are two other anti-impasse weapons sometimes used by labor and management.

10. Grievance handling has been called day-to-day collective bargaining. It involves the continuing interpretation of the collective bargaining agreement but usually not its renegotiation.

11. Most agreements contain a carefully worded grievance procedure ranging from two to six or more steps. The steps usually involve union-management meetings at each step up the chain of command until (if agreement isn't reached) the grievance goes to arbitration. Grievance handling is as important in nonunion organizations as in those that are unionized.

12. Several things contributed to the union movement's declining membership. These include laws, like OSHA and Title VII, global competition and new technologies,

declining numbers of U.S. manufacturing jobs, and possibly, the new attempts at labor–management cooperation such as employee participation teams.

13. There are some bright spots for labor unions. For example, many professional employees belong to unions, as do about 40% of all federal, state, and local government employees. The unions' success in organizing public employees reflects, in part, years of changes in public-sector collective bargaining and labor relations legislation. In 1962, President John F. Kennedy signed executive order 10988. This recognized federal employees' rights to join or refrain from joining labor organizations and granted recognition to those organizations. And, in 1978, Congress passed the Civil Service Reform Act.

DISCUSSION QUESTIONS

1. Why do employees join unions? What are the advantages and disadvantages of being a union member?
2. Discuss five sure ways to lose an NLRB election.
3. Describe important tactics you would expect the union to use during the union drive and election.
4. Briefly illustrate how labor law has gone through a cycle of repression and encouragement.
5. Explain in detail each step in a union drive and election.
6. What is meant by good faith bargaining? Using examples, explain when bargaining is not in good faith.
7. Define impasse, mediation, and strike, and explain the techniques that are used to overcome an impasse.

INDIVIDUAL AND GROUP ACTIVITIES

1. You are the manager of a small manufacturing plant. The union contract covering most of your employees is about to expire. Working individually or in groups, discuss how to prepare for union contract negotiations.
2. Working individually or in groups, use Internet resources to find situations where company management and the union reached an impasse at some point during their negotiation process, but eventually resolved the impasse. Describe the issues on both sides that led to the impasse. How did they move past the impasse? What were the final outcomes?
3. The HRCI "Test Specifications" appendix at the end of this book (pages 726–735) lists the knowledge someone studying for the HRCI certification exam needs to have in each area of human resource management (such as in Strategic Management, Workforce Planning, and Human Resource Development). In groups of four to five students, do four things: (1) review that appendix now; (2) identify the material in this chapter that relates to the required knowledge the appendix lists; (3) write four multiple choice exam questions on this material that you believe would be suitable for inclusion in the HRCI exam; and (4) if time permits, have someone from your team post your team's questions in front of the class, so the students in other teams can take each others' exam questions.
4. In October 2003, 8,000 Amtrak workers agreed not to disrupt service by walking out, at least not until a court hearing was held. Amtrak had asked the courts for a temporary restraining order, and the Transport Workers Union of America was actually

pleased to postpone its walkout. The workers were apparently not upset at Amtrak, but at Congress, for failing to provide enough funding for Amtrak. What if anything can an employer do when employees threaten to go on strike, not because of what the employer did, but what a third party—in this case, Congress—has done or not done? What laws would prevent the union from going on strike in this case?

EXPERIENTIAL EXERCISE

The Union-Organizing Campaign at Pierce U.

Purpose: The purpose of this exercise is to give you practice in dealing with some of the elements of a union organizing campaign.

Required Understanding: You should be familiar with the material covered in this chapter, as well as the following incident, "An Organizing Question on Campus."

INCIDENT: An Organizing Question on Campus: Art Tipton is human resource director of Pierce University, a private university located in a large urban city. Ruth Zimmer, a supervisor in the maintenance and housekeeping services division of the university, has just come into Art's office to discuss her situation. Zimmer's division is responsible for maintaining and cleaning physical facilities of the university. Zimmer is one of the department supervisors who supervises employees who maintain and clean on-campus dormitories.

In the next several minutes, Zimmer proceeds to express her concerns about a union organizing campaign that has begun among her employees. According to Zimmer, a representative of the Service Workers Union has met with several of her employees, urging them to sign union authorization cards. She has observed several of her employees "cornering" other employees to talk to them about joining the union and to urge them to sign union authorization (or representation) cards. Zimmer even observed this during working hours as employees were going about their normal duties in the dormitories. Zimmer reports that a number of her employees have come to her asking for her opinions about the union. They told her that several other supervisors in the department had told their employees not to sign any union authorization cards and not to talk about the union at any time while they were on campus. Zimmer also reports that one of her fellow supervisors told his employees that anyone who was caught talking about the union or signing a union authorization card would be disciplined and perhaps dismissed.

Zimmer says that her employees are very dissatisfied with their wages and with the conditions that they have endured from students, supervisors, and other staff people. She says that several employees told her that they had signed union cards because they believed that the only way university administration would pay attention to their concerns was if the employees had a union to represent them. Zimmer says that she made a list of employees whom she felt had joined or were interested in the union, and she could share these with Tipton if he wanted to deal with them personally. Zimmer closed her presentation with the comment that she and other department supervisors need to know what they should do in order to stomp out the threat of unionization in their department.

How to Set Up the Exercise/Instructions: Divide the class into groups of four or five students. Assume that you are labor relations consultants retained by the university to identify the problems and issues involved and to advise Art Tipton on the university's rights and what to do next. Each group will spend about 45 minutes discussing the issues. Then, outline those issues, as well as an action plan for Tipton. What should he do next?

If time permits, a spokesperson from each group should list on the board the issues involved and the group's recommendations. What should Art do?

APPLICATION CASE

Disciplinary Action

The employee, a union shop steward, was on her regularly scheduled day off at home. She was called by her supervisor and told to talk to three union members and instruct them to attend a work function called a "Quest for Quality Interaction Committee" meeting. The Quest for Quality program was a high priority with the employer for improving patient care at the hospital facility and was part of a corporate program. The union had objected to the implementation of the Quest for Quality program and had taken the position that employees could attend the program if their jobs were threatened, but they should do so under protest and then file a grievance afterward.

On the day in question, the union shop steward, in a conference call with the three employees, said she would not order them to attend the Quest for Quality meeting, although her supervisor had asked her to. The supervisor who had called the union shop steward had herself refused to order the employees to attend the meeting, but relied on the union shop steward to issue the order to the employees. When the shop steward failed to order the employees to attend the meeting, the employer suspended her for two weeks. She grieved the two-week suspension.

The union position was that the company had no authority to discipline the union shop steward on her day off for failure to give what it termed a "management direction to perform the specific job function of attending a mandatory corporate meeting." The union pointed out that it was unfair that the employer refused to order the employees directly to attend the meeting but then expected the union shop steward to do so. The union argued that while it is not unusual to call a union shop steward for assistance in problem solving, the company had no right to demand that he or she replace supervisors or management in giving orders and then discipline the union official for refusing to do so.

The company position was that the opposition of the union to the Quest for Quality meetings put the employees in a position of being unable to attend the meetings without direction from the union shop steward; that the union shop steward was given a job assignment of directing the employees to attend the meeting; and that failure to follow that job assignment was insubordination and just cause for her suspension.

Nonetheless, the union contended that the arbitrator must examine the nature of the order when deciding whether the insubordination was grounds for discipline. As to the nature of the order in this case, the employer had to demonstrate that the order was directly related to the job classification and work assignment of the employee disciplined. The refusal to obey such an order must be shown to pose a real challenge to supervisory authority. The employee did not dispute the fact that she failed to follow the orders given to her by her supervisor, but pointed out that she was not on duty at the time and that the task being given to her was not because of her job with the company but because of her status as a union shop steward.

Questions

1. As the arbitrator, do you think the employer had just cause to discipline the employee? Why or why not?
2. If the union's opposition to the Quest for Quality program encouraged the employees not to participate, why shouldn't the union be held responsible for directing the employees to attend?

Source: Adapted from Cheltenham Nursing Rehabilitation Center 89 LA 361 (1987); discussion in Michael Carrell and Christina Heavrin, *Labor Relations and Collective Bargaining* (Upper Saddle River, NJ: Prentice Hall, 1995), pp. 100–101.

CONTINUING CASE

Carter Cleaning Company

The Grievance

On visiting one of Carter Cleaning Company's stores, Jennifer was surprised to be taken aside by a long-term Carter employee, who met her as she was parking her car. "Murray (the store manager) told me I was suspended for two days without pay because I came in late last Thursday," said George. "I'm really upset, but around here the store manager's word seems to be law, and it sometimes seems like the only way anyone can file a grievance is by meeting you or your father like this in the parking lot." Jennifer was very disturbed by this revelation and promised the employee she would look into it and discuss the situation with her father. In the car heading back to headquarters she began mulling over what Carter Cleaning Company's alternatives might be.

Questions

1. Do you think it is important for Carter Cleaning Company to have a formal grievance process? Why or why not?
2. Based on what you know about the Carter Cleaning Company, outline the steps in what you think would be the ideal grievance process for this company.
3. In addition to the grievance process, can you think of anything else that Carter Cleaning Company might do to make sure that grievances and gripes like this one get expressed and also get heard by top management?

TRANSLATING STRATEGY INTO HR POLICIES AND PRACTICES CASE: THE HOTEL PARIS

The Hotel Paris's New Labor Relations Practices

The Hotel Paris's competitive strategy is "To use superior guest service to differentiate the Hotel Paris properties, and to thereby increase the length of stay and return rate of guests, and thus boost revenues and profitability." HR manager Lisa Cruz must now formulate functional policies and activities that support this competitive strategy, by eliciting the required employee behaviors and competencies.

Lisa Cruz's parents were both union members, and she had no strong philosophical objections to unions. However, as the head of human resources for the Hotel Paris, she did feel very strongly that her employer should do everything legally possible to remain union-free. She knew that this is what the hotel chain's owners and top executives wanted. Furthermore, the evidence seemed to support their position. At least one study that she'd seen concluded that firms with 30% or more of their eligible workers in unions were in the bottom 10% in terms of performance, while those with 8% to 9% of eligible workers in unions scored in the top 10%.[87] The problem was that the Hotel Paris really had no specific policies and procedures in place to help its managers and supervisors deal with union activities. With all the laws regarding what employers and their managers could and could not do to respond to a union's efforts, Lisa knew her company was "a problem waiting to happen." She turned her attention to deciding what steps she and her team should take with regard to labor relations and collective bargaining.

Lisa and the CFO knew that unionization was a reality for the Hotel Paris. About 5% of the hotel chain's U.S. employees were already unionized, and unions in this area were quite active. For example, as they were surfing the Internet to better gauge the situation, Lisa and the CFO came across an interesting Web site from the Boston Hotel Employees and Restaurant Employees Union, Local 26, (www.bostonhotelunion.org). It describes their success in negotiating a contract and their accomplishments at several local hotels including ones managed by the Westin and Sheraton chains. The CFO and Lisa agreed that it was important that she and her team develop and institute a new set of policies and practices that would enable the Hotel Paris to reduce the likelihood of further unionization and deal more effectively with their current unions. They set about that task with the aid of a labor-management attorney.

Questions

1. How specifically should the reality of the Hotel Paris's strategy influence the new union-related practices (perhaps such as grievance procedures) it establishes?

2. List and briefly describe what you believe are the three most important steps Hotel Paris management can take to reduce the likelihood unions will organize more of its employees.

3. Write a detailed two-page outline for a, "What You Need to Know When the Union Calls" manual. Lisa will distribute this manual to her company's supervisors and managers, telling them what they need to know about looking out for possible unionizing activity, and how to handle actual organizing process–related supervisory tasks.

KEY TERMS

closed shop, 598
union shop, 598
agency shop, 598
open shop, 599
right to work, 599
Norris-LaGuardia Act (1932), 600
National Labor Relations (or Wagner) Act, 600
National Labor Relations Board (NLRB), 600
Taft-Hartley Act (1947), 602
national emergency strikes, 603
Landrum-Griffin Act (1959), 603
union salting, 605
authorization cards, 606
bargaining unit, 607
decertification, 613
collective bargaining, 613
good faith bargaining, 614
voluntary bargaining items, 615

illegal bargaining items, 615
mandatory bargaining items, 615
impasse, 617
mediation, 617
fact finder, 617
arbitration, 617
strike, 619
economic strike, 619
unfair labor practice strike, 619
wildcat strike, 619
sympathy strike, 619
picketing, 619
corporate campaign, 620
boycott, 620
inside games, 620
lockout, 621
injunction, 621
grievance procedure, 621

ENDNOTES

1. Steven Greenhouse, "Board Accuses Starbucks of Trying to Block Union," *The New York Times*, April 3, 2007, p. B2.
2. "Union Members Summary," www.bls.gov/news.release/unions.toc.htm, accessed May 25, 2007.
3. Ibid.
4. Ibid.
5. Michael Ash and Jean Seago, "The Effect of Registered Nurses' Unions on Heart Attack Mortality," *Industrial and Labor Relations Review* 57, no. 3, (April 2004): 422–442.

6. Steven Abraham et al., "The Impact of Union Membership on Intent to Leave: Additional Evidence on the Voice Face of Unions," *Employee Responsibilities and Rights* 17, no. 4, 2005, pp. 21–23.

7. James Bennett and Jason Taylor, "Labor Unions: Victims of Their Political Success?" *Journal of Labor Research* 22, no. 2 (Spring 2001), pp. 261–273.

8. Paul Monies, "Unions Hit Hard by Job Losses, Right to Work," *The Daily Oklahoman*, (via *Knight Ridder/Tribune Business News*), (February 1, 2005), downloaded May 25, 2005.

9. Dale Belman and Paul Voos, "Changes in Union Wage Effects by Industry: A Fresh Look at the Evidence," *Industrial Relations* 43, no. 3, (July 2004): 491–519.

10. Donna Buttigieg, et al., "An Event History Analysis of Union Joining and Leaving," *Journal of Applied Psychology* 92, no. 3, 2007, pp. 829–839.

11. Kris Maher, "The New Union Worker," *Wall Street Journal*, September 27, 2005, pp. B1, B11.

12. Robert Grossman, "Unions Follow Suit," *HR Magazine*, May 2005, p. 49.

13. Warner Pflug, *The UAW in Pictures* (Detroit: Wayne State University Press, 1971), pp. 11–12.

14. Benjamin Taylor and Fred Witney, *Labor Relations Law* (Upper Saddle River, NJ: Prentice Hall, 1992), pp. 170–171.

15. "Unions Hit Hard by Job Losses, Right to Work," *The Daily Oklahoman*, (via *Knight Ridder/Tribune Business News*), (February 1, 2005), downloaded May 25, 2005.

16. Steven Greenhouse, "4th Union Quits AFL-CIO in a Dispute over Organizing," *New York Times*, Sept. 15, 2005, p. A14.

17. The following material is based on Arthur Sloane and Fred Witney, *Labor Relations* (Upper Saddle River, NJ: Prentice Hall, 2001), pp. 46–124.

18. Karen Robinson, "Temp Workers Gain Union Access," *HR News, Society for Human Resource Management* 19, no. 10 (October 2000), p. 1.

19. Elizabeth Bennett, "Online Staffers in Dispute with Papers," *Philadelphia Business Journal*, January 12, 2001, p. 6.

20. "Union Membership by State and Industry," *BNA Bulletin to Management*, May 29, 1997, pp. 172–173; "Regional Trends: Union Membership by State and Multiple Jobholding by State," *Monthly Labor Review* 123, no. 9 (September 2000), pp. 40–41.

21. Michael Carrell and Christina Heavrin, *Labor Relations and Collective Bargaining* (Upper Saddle River, NJ: Pearson, 2004), p. 180.

22. Ibid., p. 179.

23. Sloane and Witney, *Labor Relations*, p. 121.

24. Ben Foster, "Tech Firms a New Target for Union Organizers," *Baltimore Business Journal*, February 16, 2001, p. 14; Mark Leon, "A Union of Their Own," *InfoWorld*, March 12, 2001, pp. 41–42; Loretta Prencipe, "E-mail and the Internet Are Changing the Labor/Management Powerplay," *InfoWorld*, March 12, 2001, p. 46; Scott Tillett, "Dot-com Workers Take New Path to Unions," *Internet Week*, January 15, 2001, p. 9.

25. Kris Maher, "Unions' New Foe: Consultants," *Wall Street Journal*, August 15, 2005, p. B1.

26. "Some Say Salting Leaves to Bitter Taste for Employers," *BNA Bulletin to Management*, March 4, 2004, p. 79.

27. For a discussion, see Cory Fine, "Beware the Trojan Horse," *Workforce*, May 1998, pp. 45–51.

28. "Spurned Union Salts Entitled to Back Pay, D.C. Court Says, Affirming Labor Board," *BNA Bulletin to Management*, June 21, 2001, p. 193.

29. Cory Fine, "Beware the Trojan Horse," p. 46.

30. Diane Hatch and James Hall, "Salting Cases Clarified by NLRB," *Workforce*, August 2000, p. 92. For a management lawyer's perspective, see www.fklaborlaw.com/union_salt-objectives.html, accessed May 25, 2007.

31. Edwin Arnold et al., "Determinants of Certification Election Outcomes in the Service Sector," *Labor Studies Journal* 25, no. 3 (Fall 2000), p. 51.

32. "Number of Elections, Union Wins Increased in 2002," *BNA Bulletin to Management*, June 19, 2003, p. 197.

33. This section is based on Matthew Goodfellow, "How to Lose an NLRB Election," *Personnel Administrator* 23 (September 1976), pp. 40–44. See also Gillian Flynn, "When the Unions Come Calling," *Workforce*, November 2000, pp. 82–87.

34. Ibid.

35. Ibid.

36. Harry Katz, "The Decentralization of Collective Bargaining: A Literature Review and Comparative Analysis," *Industrial and Labor Relations Review* 47, no. 1 (October 1993), p. 11.

37. Jonathon Segal, "Unshackle Your Supervisors to Stay Union Free," *HR Magazine*, June 1998, pp. 62–65.

38. Whether employers must give union representatives permission to organize on employer-owned property at shopping malls is a matter of legal debate. The U.S. Supreme Court ruled in *Lechmere, Inc. v. National Labor Relations Board* that employers may bar nonemployees from their property if the nonemployees have reasonable alternative means of communicating their message to the intended audience. However, if the employer lets other organizations like the Salvation Army set up at their workplaces, the NLRB may view discriminating against the union organizers as an unfair labor practice. See for example, "Union Access to Employer's Customers Restricted," *BNA Bulletin to Management*, February 15, 1996, p. 49; "Workplace Access for Unions Hinges on Legal Issues," *BNA Bulletin to Management*, April 11, 1996, p. 113.

39. Ibid., pp. 4–65. The appropriateness of these sample rules may be affected by factors unique to an employer's operation, and they should therefore be reviewed by the employer's attorney before implementation.

40. Carrell and Heavrin, *Labor Relations and Collective Bargaining*.

41. Ibid., p. 166.

42. Ibid., pp. 167–168.

43. Doug Cahn, "Reebok Takes the Sweat Out of Sweatshops," *Business Ethics* 14, no. 1 (January 2000), p. 9, and Mei Fong and Kris Maher, "U.S. Labor Chief Moves into China," *The Wall Street Journal Asia*, June 22–24, 2007, p. 1.

44. "Union Decertifications Up in First Half of 1998," *BNA Bulletin to Management*, December 24, 1998, p. 406. See also, Clyde Scott and Edwin Arnold, "Deauthorization and Decertification Elections: An Analysis and Comparison of Results," *Working USA*, Winter 2003, vol. 7, issue 3, pp. 6–20, and http://www.nlrb.gov/workplace_rights/i_am_new_to_this_website/how_do_i_file_a_petition_to_start_or_remove_a_union.aspx, accessed May 25, 2007.

45. Carrell and Heavrin, *Labor Relations and Collective Bargaining*, pp. 120–121.

46. See for example David Meyer and Trevor Bain, "Union Decertification Election Outcomes: Bargaining Unit Characteristics and Union Resources," *Journal of Labor Research* 15, no. 2 (Spring 1994), pp. 117–136.

47. Carrell and Heavrin, *Labor Relations and Collective Bargaining*, pp. 176–177.

48. "No Talks Until Mechanics Union Softens Demand, Northwest Airlines Says," *Knight-Ridder/Tribune Business News*, March 28, 2001, Item 01087165.

49. "Bryant Union Says College Is Bargaining in Good Faith," *Providence Business News*, March 12, 2001, p. 19.

50. John Fossum, *Labor Relations* Dallas: BPI, 1982, pp. 246–250.

51. Boulwareism is the name given to a strategy, now generally held in disfavor, by which the company, based on an exhaustive study of what it thought its employees wanted, made but one offer at the bargaining table and then refused to bargain any further unless convinced by the union on the basis of new facts that its original position was wrong. The NLRB subsequently found that the practice of offering the same settlement to all units, insisting that certain parts of the package could not differ among agreements, and communicating to the employees about how negotiations were going amounted to an illegal pattern. Fossum, *Labor Relations*, p. 267. See also William Cooke, Aneil Mishra, Gretchen Spreitzer, and Mary Tschirhart, "The Determinants of NLRB Decision-Making Revisited," *Industrial and Labor Relations Review* 48, no. 2 (January 1995), pp. 237–257.

52. Kathryn Tyler, "Good-Faith Bargaining," *HR Magazine*, (January 2005): 52.

53. See for example, Arthur Sloane and Fred Witney, *Labor Relations* (Upper Saddle River, NJ, Prentice Hall, 2004) pp. 177–218.

54. Reed Richardson, *Collective Bargaining by Objectives* (Upper Saddle River, NJ: Prentice Hall, 1977) p. 150.

55. Fossum, *Labor Relations*, p. 312. See also Thomas Watkins, "Assessing Arbitrator Competence," *Arbitration Journal* 47, no. 2 (June 1992), pp. 43–48.
56. Carrell and Heavrin, *Labor Relations and Collective Bargaining*, p. 501.
57. Fossum, *Labor Relations*, p. 317.
58. Mark Fitzgerald, "UAW Lifts Boycott," *Editor and Publisher*, February 26, 2001, p. 9.
59. "Striker Replacements," *BNA Bulletin to Management*, February 6, 2003, p. S7.
60. Micheline Maynard and Jeremey Peters, "Northwest Airlines Threatens to Replace Strikers Permanently," *New York Times*, August 26, 2005, p. C3.
61. Stephen Cabot and Gerald Cuerton, "Labor Disputes and Strikes: Be Prepared," *Personnel Journal* 60 (February 1981), pp. 121–126. See also Brenda Sunoo, "Managing Strikes, Minimizing Loss," *Personnel Journal* 74, no. 1 (January 1995), pp. 50ff.
62. For a discussion, see Herbert Northrup, "Union Corporate Campaigns and Inside Games as a Strike Form," *Employee Relations Law Journal* 19, no. 4 (Spring 1994), pp. 507–549.
63. Jessica Materna, "Union Launches Web Site to Air Grievances Against San Francisco Marriott," *San Francisco Business Times*, May 4, 2001, p. 15.
64. Northrup, "Union Corporate Campaigns and Inside Games," p. 513.
65. Ibid., p. 518.
66. Clifford Koen Jr., Sondra Hartmen, and Dinah Payne, "The NLRB Wields a Rejuvenated Weapon," *Personnel Journal*, December 1996, pp. 85–87.
67. Sloane and Witney, *Labor Relations*, 10th ed., pp. 221–227.
68. Carrell and Heavrin, *Labor Relations and Collective Bargaining*, pp. 417–418.
69. Richardson, *Collective Bargaining*.
70. Duncan Adams, "Worker Grievances Consume Roanoke, VA Mail Distribution Center," *Knight-Ridder/Tribune Business News*, March 27, 2001, Item 01086009.
71. See Newport, Supervisory Management, p. 273, for an excellent checklist. See also Mark Lurie, "The Eight Essential Steps in Grievance Processing," *Dispute Resolution Journal* 54, no. 4 (November 1999), pp. 61–65.
72. See for example, Kris Maher, "Demand for Labor Give Backs to Grow More Aggressive," *Wall Street Journal*, October 27, 2005, p. 81
73. See for example Jo Blandon, et al., "Have Unions Turned the Corner? New Evidence on Recent Trends in Union Recognition in UK Firms," *British Journal of Industrial Relations*, and vol. 44, no. 2, June 2006, pp. 169–190.
74. Kris Maher, "The New Union Worker," *Wall Street Journal*, September 27, 2005, pp. B1, B11.
75. "Number of Union Elections Decreased in 2003," *BNA Bulletin to Management*, August 1, 2004, p. 215.
76. Andy Meisler, "Who Will Fold First?" op. cit., p. 30.
77. Carrell and Heavrin, *Labor Relations and Collective Bargaining*, pp. 34–36.
78. Woodrow Timberman, "Why Engineers Strike: The Boeing Story," *Business Horizons* 44, no. 6 (November 2001), pp. 35–39.
79. "The Limits of Solidarity," *The Economist*, September 23, 2006, p. 34.
80. "Unions Using Class Actions to Pressure Nonunion Companies," *BNA Bulletin to Management*, August 22, 2006, p. 271.
81. Andy Meisler "Who Will Fold First?" *Workforce Management*, January 2004, pp. 28–38.
82. Jennifer Schramm, "The Future of Unions," *Society of Human Resource Management*, Workplace Visions, no. 4, 2005, pp. 1–8.
83. Ibid.
84. Jeffrey McCracken, "Desperate to Cut Costs, Ford Gets Union's Help," *The Wall Street Journal*, March 2, 2007, pp. A1, A9.
85. Gary Chaison, "Information Technology: The Threat to Unions," *Journal of Labor Research* 23, no. 2 (Spring 2002), pp. 249–260.
86. "Employer's System of Worker Empowerment Does Not Fall Prey to Labor Act, NLRB Rules," *BNA Bulletin to Management*, August 2, 2001, p. 241.
87. Brian Becker et al., *The HR Scorecard* (Boston: Harvard Business School Press, 2001), p. 16.

16 Employee Safety and Health

After an accident in which four workers lost their lives, management at the Golden Eagle refinery east of San Francisco Bay knew they had to ensure that no such tragedy occurred again. They shut down the facility for four months, retrained all employees in safety methods, and created six new safety management positions. Then they turned their attention to other steps they could take.[1] •

After studying this chapter, you should be able to:

1 Explain the basic facts about OSHA.
2 Explain the supervisor's role in safety.
3 Minimize unsafe acts by employees.
4 Explain how to deal with important occupational health problems.

Chapter 15 focused on union–management relations, and the issues unions and employers typically concentrate on when negotiating agreements. Employee safety is usually one of these issues. Now, the main purpose of this chapter is to provide you with the basic knowledge you'll need to deal more effectively with workplace safety and health problems. Every manager needs a working knowledge of OSHA—the Occupational Safety and Health Act—and we discuss its purpose, standards, and inspection procedures, as well as employees' and employers' rights and responsibilities under OSHA. We'll see that there are three basic causes of accidents: chance occurrences, unsafe conditions, and unsafe acts—and several techniques for preventing accidents. And we discuss important employee health problems, such as substance abuse and workplace violence.

Why Safety Is Important

Safety and accident prevention concerns managers for several reasons, one of which is the staggering number of work-related accidents. In one recent year, 5,559 U.S. workers died in workplace incidents. There were also over 4.4 million occupational injuries and illnesses resulting from accidents at work—roughly five cases per hundred full-time workers in the United States per year.[2] One recent study estimates that such Bureau of Labor Statistics (which calculates workplace injuries and illnesses by sampling employers' injury and illness logs) may actually underestimate the real number of injuries and illnesses by two or three times.[3]

Injuries are not just a problem in traditionally dangerous industries like mining and construction. For example, every year over 15,000 reportable injuries or illnesses occur among semiconductor workers, and another 15,000 occur at manufacturers of computers and computer peripherals. Commercial kitchens have hazards like knives and slippery floors.[4] New computers contribute to "sick building syndrome"—symptoms like headaches and sniffles, which some experts blame on poor ventilation and dust and fumes from on-site irritants.[5] (Two engineers found that new computers emit chemical fumes which, however, diminish after the computer runs constantly for a week.)[6] And office work is susceptible to other health and safety problems, including "repetitive trauma injuries related to computer use, respiratory illnesses stemming from indoor air quality, and high levels of stress, which are associated with a variety of factors, including task design."[7]

The Hidden Story   But even facts like these don't tell the whole story. They don't reflect the human suffering incurred by the injured workers and their families or the real economic costs incurred by employers. For example, the direct injury costs of a forklift accident might be $4,500, but the indirect costs for things like forklift damage, lost production time, maintenance time, and emergency supplies could raise the bill to $18,000 or more.[8] Nor do they reflect the legal implications. When a boiler explosion at Ford's Rouge Power Plant killed six workers and injured 14, Ford was slapped with a $1.5 million fine, and also agreed to spend almost $6 million instituting various safety measures.[9] One senator was planning to introduce legislation making it a federal crime punishable by up to 10 years' imprisonment to cause a worker's death through willfully violating OSHA regulations.[10]

Yet, even with all of this attention, there still are employers who seem to take safety less seriously then they should. For example, the *New York Times* described, in a story entitled "A Family's Profits, Wrung from Blood and Sweat," a cast-iron business that "has been cited for more than 400 safety violations since 1995, four times more than its six major competitors combined," and an environment in which managers allegedly marked for dismissal employees who protested unsafe conditions.[11]

❶ Explain the basic facts about OSHA.

Occupational Safety and Health Act
The law passed by Congress in 1970 "to assure so far as possible every working man and woman in the nation safe and healthful working conditions and to preserve our human resources."

Occupational Safety and Health Administration (OSHA)
The agency created within the Department of Labor to set safety and health standards for almost all workers in the United States.

OCCUPATIONAL SAFETY LAW

Congress passed the **Occupational Safety and Health Act** in 1970 "to assure so far as possible every working man and woman in the nation safe and healthful working conditions and to preserve our human resources."[12] The only employers it doesn't cover are self-employed persons, farms in which only immediate members of the employer's family work, and some workplaces already protected by other federal agencies or under other statutes. The act covers federal agencies, but its provisions usually don't apply to state and local governments in their role as employers.

The act created the **Occupational Safety and Health Administration (OSHA)** within the Department of Labor. OSHA's basic purpose is to administer the act and to set and enforce the safety and health standards that apply to almost all workers in the United States. The Department of Labor enforces the standards, and OSHA has inspectors working out of branch offices around the country to ensure compliance.

OSHA Standards and Record Keeping

OSHA operates under the "general" standard clause that each employer:

> . . . shall furnish to each of his [or her] employees employment and a place of employment which are free from recognized hazards that are causing or are likely to cause death or serious physical harm to his [or her] employees.

To carry out this basic mission, OSHA is responsible for promulgating legally enforceable standards. These are contained in five volumes covering general industry standards, maritime standards, construction standards, other regulations and procedures, and a field operations manual.

The standards are very complete and seem to cover just about every conceivable hazard in great detail. (Figure 16-1 presents a small part of the standard governing handrails for scaffolds.) And OSHA regulations don't just list specific chemical or structural-type standards for employers to adhere to. For example, OSHA's respiratory protection standard also includes standards for program administration; work-site-specific procedures; requirements regarding the selection, use, cleaning, maintenance, and repair of respirators; employee training; respirator fit tests; and medical evaluations of the employees who use the respirators.[13]

Under OSHA, employers with 11 or more employees must maintain records of and report certain occupational injuries and occupational illnesses. An **occupational illness** is any abnormal condition or disorder caused by exposure to environmental factors associated with employment. This includes acute and chronic illnesses caused by inhalation, absorption, ingestion, or direct contact with toxic substances or harmful agents.

occupational illness
Any abnormal condition or disorder caused by exposure to environmental factors associated with employment.

Guardrails not less than 2″ × 4″ or the equivalent and not less than 36″ or more than 42″ high, with a midrail, when required, of a 1″ × 4″ lumber or equivalent, and toeboards, shall be installed at all open sides on all scaffolds more than 10 feet above the ground or floor. Toeboards shall be a minimum of 4″ in height. Wire mesh shall be installed in accordance with paragraph [a] (17) of this section.

FIGURE 16-1

OSHA Standards Example

Source: http://www.osha.gov/pls/oshaweb/owadisp.show_document?p_id=9720&p_table=STANDARDS, accessed May 25, 2007.

FIGURE 16-2

What Accidents Must Be Reported under the Occupational Safety and Health Act (OSHA)?

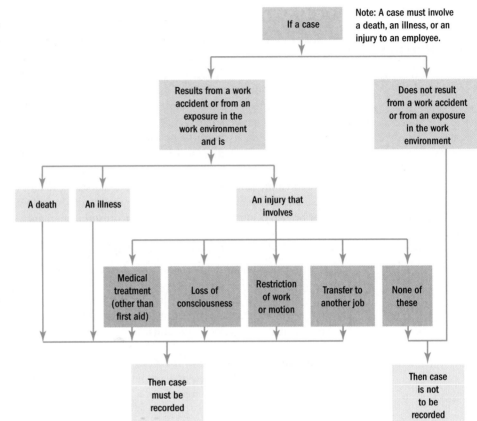

What the Employer Must Report As summarized in Figure 16-2, employers must report all occupational illnesses.[14] They must also report most occupational injuries, specifically those that result in medical treatment (other than first aid), loss of consciousness, restriction of work (one or more lost workdays), restriction of motion, or transfer to another job.[15] If an on-the-job accident results in the death of an employee or in the hospitalization of five or more employees, all employers, regardless of size, must report the accident in detail to the nearest OSHA office.

OSHA's latest record-keeping rules streamline the job of reporting occupational injuries or illnesses.[16] The rules continue to presume that an injury or illness that resulted from an event in or exposure to the work environment is "work related." However, it allows the employer to conclude that the event was *not* work related (and needn't be reported) if the facts so warrant—such as if a worker breaks an ankle after catching his foot on his car's seat belt when parked on the company lot.

However, OSHA's record-keeping requirements are still broader than you might expect, because OSHA's definition of occupational injuries and illnesses is so broad.[17] Examples of recordable conditions include: food poisoning suffered by an employee after eating in the employer's cafeteria, colds compounded by drafty work areas, and ankle sprains that occur during voluntary participation in a company softball game at a picnic the employee was required to attend.

OSHA pursues record-keeping violations during investigations, so it behooves employers to carefully record injuries or illnesses. Figure 16-3 shows the OSHA form for reporting occupational injuries or illness.

OSHA's FORM 301

Injury and Illness Incident Report

U.S. Department of Labor
Occupational Safety and Health Administration

Form approved OMB no. 1218-0176

Attention: This form contains information relating to employee health and must be used in a manner that protects the confidentiality of employees to the extent possible while the information is being used for occupational safety and health purposes.

This *Injury and Illness Incident Report* is one of the first forms you must fill out when a recordable work-related injury or illness has occurred. Together with the *Log of Work-Related Injuries and Illnesses* and the accompanying *Summary*, these forms help the employer and OSHA develop a picture of the extent and severity of work-related incidents.

Within 7 calendar days after you receive information that a recordable work-related injury or illness has occurred, you must fill out this form or an equivalent. Some state workers' compensation, insurance, or other reports may be acceptable substitutes. To be considered an equivalent form, any substitute must contain all the information asked for on this form.

According to Public Law 91-596 and 29 CFR 1904, OSHA's recordkeeping rule, you must keep this form on file for 5 years following the year to which it pertains.

If you need additional copies of this form, you may photocopy and use as many as you need.

Completed by _____

Title _____

Phone (_____) _____ – _____   Date ___/___/___

Information about the employee

1) Full name _____

2) Street _____
   City _____ State ___ ZIP ___

3) Date of birth ___/___/___

4) Date hired ___/___/___

5) ☐ Male
   ☐ Female

Information about the physician or other health care professional

6) Name of physician or other health care professional _____

7) If treatment was given away from the worksite, where was it given?
   Facility _____
   Street _____
   City _____ State ___ ZIP ___

8) Was employee treated in an emergency room?
   ☐ Yes
   ☐ No

9) Was employee hospitalized overnight as an in-patient?
   ☐ Yes
   ☐ No

Information about the case

10) Case number from the *Log* _____ *(Transfer the case number from the Log after you record the case.)*

11) Date of injury or illness ___/___/___

12) Time employee began work _____ AM/PM

13) Time of event _____ AM/PM
    ☐ Check if time cannot be determined

14) **What was the employee doing just before the incident occurred?** Describe the activity, as well as the tools, equipment, or material the employee was using. Be specific. *Examples:* "climbing a ladder while carrying roofing materials"; "spraying chlorine from hand sprayer"; "daily computer key-entry."

15) **What happened?** Tell us how the injury occurred. *Examples:* "When ladder slipped on wet floor, worker fell 20 feet"; "Worker was sprayed with chlorine when gasket broke during replacement"; "Worker developed soreness in wrist over time."

16) **What was the injury or illness?** Tell us the part of the body that was affected and how it was affected; be more specific than "hurt," "pain," or sore." *Examples:* "strained back"; "chemical burn, hand"; "carpal tunnel syndrome."

17) **What object or substance directly harmed the employee?** *Examples:* "concrete floor"; "chlorine"; "radial arm saw." *If this question does not apply to the incident, leave it blank.*

18) **If the employee died, when did death occur?** Date of death ___/___/___

Public reporting burden for this collection of information is estimated to average 22 minutes per response, including time for reviewing instructions, searching existing data sources, gathering and maintaining the data needed, and completing and reviewing the collection of information. Persons are not required to respond to the collection of information unless it displays a current valid OMB control number. If you have any comments about this estimate or any other aspects of this data collection, including suggestions for reducing this burden, contact: US Department of Labor, OSHA Office of Statistical Analysis, Room N-3644, 200 Constitution Avenue, NW, Washington, DC 20210. Do not send the completed forms to this office.

FIGURE 16-3

Form Used to Record Occupational Injuries and Illnesses

Source: U.S. Department of Labor.

Inspections and Citations

OSHA enforces its standards through inspections and (if necessary) citations. The inspection is almost always unannounced. OSHA may not conduct warrantless inspections without an employer's consent. However, it may inspect after acquiring an authorized search warrant or its equivalent.[18] Like many government agencies, OSHA has wide-ranging compliance responsibilities but relatively limited funds. As a result, OSHA is trying to encourage cooperative safety programs rather than relying just on inspections and citations.

Inspection Priorities   Such efforts notwithstanding, OSHA does of course still make extensive use of inspections. OSHA takes a "worst-first" approach in setting inspection priorities. Priorities include, from highest to lowest, reports of imminent dangers-accidents about to happen; fatalities or accidents serious enough to send three or more workers to the hospital; employee complaints; referrals from other government agencies; targeted inspections-such as on employers that report high injury and illness rates; and finally, follow-up inspections.[19] In one recent year, OSHA conducted just over 39,000 inspections. Of these, about 9,200 were prompted by complaints or accidents, about 21,500 were high hazard targeted, and about 8,400 were prompted by follow-ups and referrals.[20] Random inspections and reinspections generally have last priority.

Under its priority system, OSHA conducts an inspection within 24 hours when a complaint indicates an immediate danger, and within three working days when a serious hazard exists. For a "nonserious" complaint filed in writing by a worker or a union, OSHA will respond within 20 working days. OSHA handles other nonserious complaints by writing to the employer and requesting corrective action.

The Inspection   The inspection itself begins when the OSHA officer arrives at the workplace.[21] He or she displays official credentials and asks to meet an employer representative. (Always insist on seeing the officer's credentials, which include photograph and serial number.) The officer explains the visit's purpose, the scope of the inspection, and the standards that apply. An authorized employee representative accompanies the officer during the inspection. The inspector can also stop and question workers (in private, if necessary) about safety and health conditions. The act protects each employee from discrimination for exercising his or her disclosure rights. OSHA rules require employee involvement in OSHA's on-site consultations, and that employees be informed of the inspections' results.[22]

OSHA inspectors look for all types of violations, but some potential problem areas—such as scaffolding and fall protection—seem to grab more of their attention. The five most frequent OSHA inspection violation areas are scaffolding, fall protection, hazard communication, lockout/tagout (electrical repairs), and respiratory problems.

Finally, after checking the premises and employer's records, the inspector holds a closing conference with the employer's representative. Here the inspector discusses apparent violations for which OSHA may issue or recommend a **citation** and penalty. At this point, the employer can produce records to show compliance efforts. Figure 16-4 lists the hazards that accounted for the greatest number of citations in one recent year. As noted, inadequate or unsafe scaffolding was the most frequently cited hazard.

citation
Summons informing employers and employees of the regulations and standards that have been violated in the workplace.

Penalties   OSHA can impose penalties. These generally range from $5,000 up to $70,000 for willful or repeat serious violations, although in practice the penalties can be far higher—$1.5 million at the Ford Rouge plant, for instance. The parties settle many OSHA cases before litigation, in "pre-citation settlements." Here, OSHA issues the citation and agreed-on penalties simultaneously, after negotiations with the employer.[23] There

FIGURE 16-4

Ten Safety Standards OSHA Cited for Penalties Most Frequently, 2005–2006.

Source: http://www.osha.gov/ pls/imis/citedstandard.sic?p_ esize=&p_state=FEFederal& p_sic=all, accessed May 26, 2007.

U.S. Department of Labor
Occupational Safety & Health Administration

www.osha.gov   MyOSHA   Search [   ] GO Advanced Search | A-Z Index

Standards Cited for SIC ALL; All sizes; Federal

ALL *SIC Codes*

Listed below are the standards which were cited by **Federal OSHA** for the specified SIC during the period October 2005 through September 2006. Penalties shown reflect current rather than initial amounts. For more information, see definitions.

Standard	#Cited	#Insp	$Penalty	Description
Total	111529	28183	89370521	
19260451	9774	3756	10369193	Scaffolds—General requirements.
19101200	7124	3627	1546760	Hazard Communication.
19260501	6886	6134	8346946	Duty to have fall protection.
19100134	4654	1922	1393672	Respiratory Protection.
19100147	3976	2115	3763302	The control of hazardous energy (lockout/tagout).
19100178	3183	2130	2050999	Powered industrial trucks.
19100305	3028	1863	1433020	Wiring methods, components, and equipment for general use.
19100212	2866	2310	4031408	General requirements for all machines.
19261053	2541	1910	1329484	Ladders.
19100303	2267	1692	1181507	Electrical equipment installation—General requirements.

is also a maximum of $7,000 a day in penalties for failure to correct a violation. Other-than-serious violations often carry no penalties.

In general, OSHA calculates penalties based on the gravity of the violation, and usually takes into consideration factors like the size of the business, the firm's compliance history, and the employer's good faith.[24] In practice, OSHA must have a final order from the independent Occupational Safety and Health Review Commission (OSHRC) to enforce a penalty.[25] An employer who files a notice of contest can drag out an appeal for years. Many employers do appeal their citations, at least to the OSHA district office.

To the chagrin of some employers, OSHA is publicizing its inspection results online. For example, OSHA's Web site (www.osha.gov) gives you easy access to your company's (or your competitors') OSHA enforcement history. The "When You're on Your Own" feature shows how OSHA can help smaller businesses comply with safety rules and laws.

Inspection Guidelines What should managers do when OSHA inspectors unexpectedly show up? Suggestions include:

Initial Contact

- Refer the inspector to your OSHA coordinator.
- Check the inspector's credentials.
- Ask the inspector why he or she is inspecting your workplace: Complaint? Regular scheduled visit? Fatality or accident follow-up? Imminent danger?
- If the inspection stems from a complaint, you are entitled to know whether the person is a current employee, though not the person's name.
- Notify your counsel, who should review all requests for documents and information, as well as documents and information you provide.

Free On-Site Safety and Health Services for Small Businesses

Small businesses have unique challenges when it comes to managing safety. Without HR or safety departments, they often don't know where to turn for advice on promoting employee safety. Many even have the (inaccurate) notion that the Occupational Safety and Health Act doesn't cover small firms.[26]

OSHA provides free on-site safety and health services for small businesses. This service uses safety experts from state governments, and provides consultations, usually at the employer's workplace. Employers can contact their nearest OSHA Area Office to speak to the compliance assistance specialist, and check out training available at the OSHA Training Institute in the Chicago area or at one of 20 education centers located at U.S. colleges and universities. According to OSHA, its safety and health consultation program is completely separate from the OSHA inspection effort, and no citations are issued or penalties proposed.

The employer triggers the process by requesting a voluntary consultation. There is then an opening conference with a safety expert, a walk-through, and a closing conference at which the employer and safety expert discuss the latter's observations. The consultant then sends you a detailed report explaining the findings. The employer's only obligation is to commit to correcting serious job safety and health hazards in a timely manner.

For example, when Jan Anderson, president of her own steel installation company in Colorado, realized her workers' compensation costs were higher than her payroll, she knew she had to do something. OSHA helped draft new safety systems, created educational materials, and provided inspections that were more cooperative than adversarial. As a result, says Anderson, "Our workers' compensation costs have decreased significantly, we have had no accidents, and there is an awareness that we take safety seriously."[27]

Opening Conference

- Establish the focus and scope of the planned inspection.
- Discuss the procedures for protecting trade secret areas.
- Show the inspector you have safety programs in place. He or she may not go to the work floor if paperwork is complete and up to date.

Walk-Around Inspection

- Accompany the inspector and take detailed notes.
- If the inspector takes a photo or video, you should, too.
- Ask for duplicates of all physical samples and copies of all test results.
- Be helpful and cooperative, but don't volunteer information.
- To the extent possible, immediately correct any violation the inspector identifies.[28]

Responsibilities and Rights of Employers and Employees

Both employers and employees have responsibilities and rights under the Occupational Safety Health Act. *Employers* are responsible for providing "a workplace free from recognized hazards," for being familiar with mandatory OSHA standards, and for examining workplace conditions to make sure they conform to OSHA standards. Employers have the right to seek advice and off-site consultation from OSHA, request and receive proper identification of the OSHA compliance officer before inspection, and to be advised by the compliance officer of the reason for an inspection.

Employees have rights and responsibilities under OSHA standards, such as to wear their hardhats, but OSHA can't cite them if they violate their responsibilities.

Employees also have rights and responsibilities, but OSHA can't cite them for violations of their responsibilities. Employees are responsible, for example, for complying with all applicable OSHA standards, for following all employer safety and health rules and regulations, and for reporting hazardous conditions to the supervisor. Employees have a right to demand safety and health on the job without fear of punishment. The act prohibits employers from punishing or discriminating against workers who complain to OSHA about job safety and health hazards. (See the accompanying OSHA safety poster, in Figure 16-5.)

Dealing with Employee Resistance   While employees have a responsibility to comply with OSHA standards, they often resist; the employer usually remains liable for any penalties. The refusal of some workers to wear hard hats as mandated by the OSHA requirements typifies this problem.

Employers have attempted to defend themselves against penalties for such noncompliance by citing worker intransigence and their own fear of wildcat strikes and walkouts. In most cases, courts have still held employers liable for workplace safety violations, regardless of the fact that employee resistance caused the violations.

Yet employers can reduce their liability, since "courts have recognized that it is impossible to totally eliminate all hazardous conduct by employees."[29] In the event of a problem, the courts may take into consideration facts such as whether the employer's safety procedures were adequate; whether the training really gave employees the understanding, knowledge, and skills required to perform their duties safely; and whether the employer really required employees to follow the procedures.

There are several other ways to reduce liability.[30] The employer can bargain with its union for the right to discharge or discipline any employee who disobeys an OSHA standard. A formal employer–employee arbitration process could provide a relatively quick method for resolving an OSHA-related dispute. Other employers turn to positive reinforcement and training for gaining employee compliance; more on this shortly. The independent three-member Occupational Safety and Health Review Commission that reviews OSHA decisions says employers must make "a diligent effort to discourage, by discipline if necessary, violations of

FIGURE 16-5

OSHA Safety Poster

safety rules by employees."[31] However, the only surefire way to eliminate liability is to ensure that no safety violations occur.

Staying Out of Trouble with OSHA

The magazine *Occupational Hazards* conducted a survey of 12 health and safety experts, and asked them to identify the "10 best ways" to get into trouble with OSHA. Here's what they said (starting with the top way to incur OSHA's wrath):[32]

1. Ignore or retaliate against employees who raise safety issues.
2. Antagonize or lie to OSHA during an inspection.
3. Keep inaccurate OSHA logs and have disorganized safety files.
4. Do not correct hazards OSHA has cited you for and ignore commonly cited hazards.

5. Fail to control the flow of information during and after an inspection. (The employer should not hand over to the OSHA inspector any information he or she does not ask for, and should also keep tabs on everything the employer has given to the inspector.)
6. Do not conduct a safety audit, or identify a serious hazard and do nothing about it.
7. Do not use appropriate engineering controls.
8. Do not take a systemic approach toward safety. (As one expert put it, "an OSHA officer can see right away if [your company] does not place a priority on safety.")
9. Do not enforce safety rules.
10. Ignore industrial hygiene issues. (Day-to-day physical safety problems tend to be more apparent than hygiene issues such as often invisible airborne contaminants.)

TOP MANAGEMENT'S ROLE IN SAFETY

On the next few pages, we'll see that reducing accidents often boils down to reducing accident-causing conditions and accident-causing acts. However, safety experts would agree that employers should not miss the forest for the trees. Telling supervisors to "watch for spills" and employees to "work safely" is futile if everyone thinks management's not serious about safety. The point is that workplace safety always starts with and depends on top management's genuine commitment to safety.

Historically, for instance, DuPont's accident rate has been much lower than that of the chemical industry as a whole. This good safety record is partly due to an organizational commitment to safety, which is evident in the following description:

> One of the best examples I know of in setting the highest possible priority for safety takes place at a DuPont Plant in Germany. Each morning at the DuPont Polyester and Nylon Plant the director and his assistants meet at 8:45 to review the past 24 hours. The first matter they discuss is not production, but safety. Only after they have examined reports of accidents and near misses and satisfied themselves that corrective action has been taken do they move on to look at output, quality, and cost matters.[33]

What Top Management Can Do

In brief, evidencing top management's commitment requires several things. Top management should be personally involved in safety activities; give safety matters high priority in meetings and production scheduling; give the company safety officer high rank and status; and include safety training in new workers' training. Ideally, "safety is an integral part of the system, woven into each management competency and a part of everyone's day-to-day responsibilities."[34] In addition top management (usually working through human resource management) should:

- Institutionalize management's commitment with a safety policy, and publicize it.
- Analyze the number of accidents and safety incidents and then set specific achievable safety goals. Georgia-Pacific reduced its workers' compensation costs with a policy that forces managers to halve accidents or forfeit 30% of their bonuses.

Committing to safety is not just a case of legal compliance or humanitarianism.[35] Safety programs also pay for themselves. One safety program at a Missouri ABB plant resulted in total OSHA cases reduced 80% in one year; OSHA lost-time rate reduced 86% in one year; and $560,000 contributed to profit. One study of two organizations concluded that their safety activities paid for themselves by a ratio of 10 to 1, just in direct savings of workers' compensation expenses over four years.[36]

WHAT CAUSES ACCIDENTS?

There are three basic causes of workplace accidents: chance occurrences, unsafe conditions, and employees' unsafe acts. Chance occurrences (such as walking past a window just as someone hits a ball through it) are more or less beyond management's control. We will therefore focus on unsafe conditions and unsafe acts.

Unsafe Conditions and Other Work-Related Factors

unsafe conditions
The mechanical and physical conditions that cause accidents.

Unsafe conditions are a main cause of accidents. They include things like:

- Improperly guarded equipment
- Defective equipment
- Hazardous procedures in, on, or around machines or equipment
- Unsafe storage—congestion, overloading
- Improper illumination—glare, insufficient light
- Improper ventilation—insufficient air change, impure air source[37]

The solution here is to identify and eliminate the unsafe conditions. The main aim of the OSHA standards is to address these mechanical and physical accident-causing conditions. The employer's safety department (if any), and its human resource managers and top managers should take responsibility for identifying unsafe conditions. However, front-line supervisors play a big role too, as the "When You're on Your Own" feature explains.

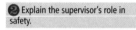 Explain the supervisor's role in safety.

Danger Zones While accidents can happen anywhere, there are some high-danger zones. About one-third of industrial accidents occur around forklift trucks, wheelbarrows, and other handling and lifting areas. The most serious accidents usually occur by metal and

When You're on Your OWN
HR for Line Managers and Entrepreneurs

The Supervisor's Role in Accident Prevention

After inspecting a work site in which workers were installing sewer pipes in a four-foot trench, an OSHA inspector cited an employer for violating the OSHA rule requiring employers to have a "stairway, ladder, ramp, or other safe means of egress" in trench excavations that are four or more feet in depth.[38] In the event the trench caved in, workers needed a quick way out.

As in most such cases, the employer and its top management had the primary responsibility for the safety breakdown, but the local supervisor was responsible for the day-to-day inspections. The OSHA rule for which the company was cited requires that a competent person make daily inspections of trenches like this to make sure that its walls aren't shifting and its ladders are functioning properly. Here, the supervisor did not properly do his daily inspection. The trench collapsed, and several employees were severely injured.

The moral is that whether one is manager of an IT department or managing an excavation or dry cleaning store, safety inspections should always be part of the supervisor's daily routine. For example, "a daily walk-through of your workplace—whether you are working in outdoor construction, indoor manufacturing, or any place that poses safety challenges—is an essential part of your work."[39]

Exactly what to look for depends on the workplace. For example, construction sites and dry cleaning stores have hazards all their own. However, in general you can use a checklist of unsafe conditions such as the one in Figure 16-6 to spot problems. We present another, more extensive checklist in Figure 16-11 at the end of this chapter. And you may use a checklist such as Figure 16-7 for inspecting office work areas.

I. GENERAL HOUSEKEEPING

Adequate and wide aisles—no materials protruding into aisles

Parts and tools stored safely after use—not left in hazardous positions that could cause them to fall

Even and solid flooring—no defective floors or ramps that could cause falling or tripping accidents

Waste cans and sand pails—safely located and properly used

Material piled in safe manner—not too high or too close to sprinkler heads

Floors—clean and dry

Firefighting equipment—unobstructed

Work benches orderly

Stockcarts and skids safely located, not left in aisles or passageways

Aisles kept clear and properly marked; no air lines or electric cords across aisles

II. MATERIAL HANDLING EQUIPMENT AND CONVEYANCES

On all conveyances, electric or hand, check to see that the following items are all in sound working conditions:

Brakes—properly adjusted

Not too much play in steering wheel

Warning device—in place and working

Wheels—securely in place; properly inflated

Fuel and oil—enough and right kind

No loose parts

Cables, hooks, or chains—not worn or otherwise defective

Suspended chains or hooks conspicuous

Safely loaded

Properly stored

III. LADDERS, SCAFFOLD, BENCHES, STAIRWAYS, ETC.

The following items of major interest to be checked:

Safety feet on straight ladders

Guardrails or handrails

Treads, not slippery

No cracked, or rickety

Properly stored

Extension ladder ropes in good condition

Toeboards

IV. POWER TOOLS (STATIONARY)

Point of operation guarded

Guards in proper adjustment

Gears, belts, shafting, counterweights guarded

Foot pedals guarded

Brushes provided for cleaning machines

Adequate lighting

Properly grounded

Tool or material rests properly adjusted

Adequate work space around machines

Control switch easily accessible

Safety glasses worn

Gloves worn by persons handling rough or sharp materials

No gloves or loose clothing worn by persons operating machines

V. HAND TOOLS AND MISCELLANEOUS

In good condition—not cracked, worn, or otherwise defective

Properly stored

Correct for job

Goggles, respirators, and other personal protective equipment worn where necessary

VI. WELDING

Arc shielded

Fire hazards controlled

Operator using suitable protective equipment

Adequate ventilation

Cylinder secured

Valves closed when not in use

VII. SPRAY PAINTING

Explosion-proof electrical equipment

Proper storage of paints and thinners in approved metal cabinets

Fire extinguishers adequate and suitable; readily accessible

Minimum storage in work area

VIII. FIRE EXTINGUISHERS

Properly serviced and tagged

Readily accessible

Adequate and suitable for operations involved

FIGURE 16-6

Checklist of Mechanical or Physical Accident-Causing Conditions

Source: Courtesy of the American Insurance Association. From "A Safety Committee Man's Guide," pp. 1–64.

FORM **CD-574**
(2/03)

U.S. Department of Commerce
Office Safety Inspection Checklist for
Supervisors and Program Managers

Name:	Division:
Location:	Date:
Signature:	

This checklist is intended as a guide to assist supervisors and program managers in conducting safety and health inspections of their work areas. It includes questions relating to general office safety, ergonomics, fire prevention, and electrical safety. Questions which receive a "NO" answer require corrective action. If you have questions or need assistance with resolving any problems, please contact your safety office. More information on office safety is available through the Department of Commerce Safety Office website at **http://ohrm.doc.gov/safetyprogram/safety.htm**.

Work Environment

Yes	No	N/A	
O	O	O	Are all work areas clean, sanitary, and orderly?
O	O	O	Is there adequate lighting?
O	O	O	Is the noise level within an acceptable range?
O	O	O	Is ventilation adequate?

Walking / Working Surfaces

Yes	No	N/A	
O	O	O	Are aisles and passages free of stored material that may present trip hazards?
O	O	O	Are tile floors in places like kitchens and bathrooms free of water and slippery substances?
O	O	O	Are carpet and throw rugs free of tears or trip hazards?
O	O	O	Are hand rails provided on all fixed stairways?
O	O	O	Are treads provided with anti-slip surfaces?
O	O	O	Are step ladders provided for reaching overhead storage areas and are materials stored safely?
O	O	O	Are file drawers kept closed when not in use?
O	O	O	Are passenger and freight elevators inspected annually and are the inspection certificates available for review on-site?
O	O	O	Are pits and floor openings covered or otherwise guarded?
O	O	O	Are standard guardrails provided wherever aisle or walkway surfaces are elevated more than 48 inches above any adjacent floor or the ground?
O	O	O	Is furniture free of any unsafe defects?
O	O	O	Are heating and air conditioning vents clear of obstructions?

Ergonomics

Yes	No	N/A	
O	O	O	Are employees advised of proper lifting techniques?
O	O	O	Are workstations configured to prevent common ergonomic problems? (Chair height allows employees' feet to rest flat on the ground with thighs parallel to the floor, top of computer screen is at or slightly below eye level, keyboard is at elbow height. Additional information on proper configuration of workstations is available through the Commerce Safety website at http://ohrm.doc.gov/safetyprogram/safety.htm)
O	O	O	Are mechanical aids and equipment, such as; lifting devices, carts, or dollies provided where needed?
O	O	O	Are employees surveyed annually on their ergonomic concerns?

Emergency Information (Postings)

Yes	No	N/A	
O	O	O	Are established emergency phone numbers posted where they can be readily found in case of an emergency?
O	O	O	Are employees trained on emergency procedures?
O	O	O	Are fire evacuation procedures/diagrams posted?
O	O	O	Is emergency information posted in every area where you store hazardous waste?
O	O	O	Is established facility emergency information posted near a telephone?
O	O	O	Are the OSHA poster, and other required posters displayed conspicuously?
O	O	O	Are adequate first aid supplies available and properly maintained?
O	O	O	Are an adequate number of first aid trained personnel available to respond to injuries and illnesses until medical assistance arrives?
O	O	O	Is a copy of the facility fire prevention and emergency action plan available on site?
O	O	O	Are safety hazard warning signs/caution signs provided to warn employees of pertinent hazards?

FIGURE 16-7 Supervisor's Safety Checklist

Source: http://www.sefsc.noaa.gov/PDFdocs/CD-574OfficeInspectionChecklistSupervisors.pdf, accessed May 26, 2007.

FORM **CD-574**
(2/03)

Fire Prevention

Yes	No	N/A	
O	O	O	Are flammable liquids, such as gasoline, kept in approved safety cans and stored in flammable cabinets?
O	O	O	Are portable fire extinguishers distributed properly (less than 75 feet travel distance for combustibles and 50 feet for flammables)?
O	O	O	Are employees trained on the use of portable fire extinguishers?
O	O	O	Are portable fire extinguishers visually inspected monthly and serviced annually?
O	O	O	Are areas around portable fire extinguishers free of obstructions and properly labeled ?
O	O	O	Is heat-producing equipment used in a well ventilated area?
O	O	O	Are fire alarm pull stations clearly marked and unobstructed?
O	O	O	Are proper clearances maintained below sprinkler heads (i.e., 18" clear)?

Emergency Exits

Yes	No	N/A	
O	O	O	Are doors, passageways or stairways that are neither exits nor access to exits and which could be mistaken for exits, appropriately marked "NOT AN EXIT," "TO BASEMENT," "STOREROOM," etc.?
O	O	O	Are a sufficient number of exits provided?
O	O	O	Are exits kept free of obstructions or locking devices which could impede immediate escape?
O	O	O	Are exits properly marked and illuminated?
O	O	O	Are the directions to exits, when not immediately apparent, marked with visible signs?
O	O	O	Can emergency exit doors be opened from the direction of exit travel without the use of a key or other significant effort when the building is occupied?
O	O	O	Are exits arranged such that it is not possible to travel toward a fire hazard when exiting the facility?

Electrical Systems

(Please have your facility maintenance person or electrician accompany you during this part of the inspection)

Yes	No	N/A	
O	O	O	Are all cord and cable connections intact and secure?
O	O	O	Are electrical outlets free of overloads?
O	O	O	Is fixed wiring used instead of flexible/extension cords?
O	O	O	Is the area around electrical panels and breakers free of obstructions?
O	O	O	Are high-voltage electrical service rooms kept locked?
O	O	O	Are electrical cords routed such that they are free of sharp objects and clearly visible?
O	O	O	Are all electrical cords grounded?
O	O	O	Are electrical cords in good condition (free of splices, frays, etc.)?
O	O	O	Are electrical appliances approved (Underwriters Laboratory, Inc. (UL), etc)?
O	O	O	Are electric fans provided with guards of not over one-half inch, preventing finger exposures?
O	O	O	Are space heaters UL listed and equipped with shutoffs that activate if the heater tips over?
O	O	O	Are space heaters located away from combustibles and properly ventilated?
O	O	O	In your electrical rooms are all electrical raceways and enclosures securely fastened in place?
O	O	O	Are clamps or other securing means provided on flexible cords or cables at plugs, receptacles, tools, equipment, etc., and is the cord jacket securely held in place?
O	O	O	Is sufficient access and working space provided and maintained about all electrical equipment to permit ready and safe operations and maintenance? (This space is 3 feet for less than 600 volts, 4 feet for more than 600 volts)

Material Storage

Yes	No	N/A	
O	O	O	Are storage racks and shelves capable of supporting the intended load and materials stored safely?
O	O	O	Are storage racks secured from falling?
O	O	O	Are office equipment stored in a stable manner, not capable of falling?

FIGURE 16-7

(*continued***)**

woodworking machines and saws, or around transmission machinery like gears, pulleys, and flywheels. Falls on stairs, ladders, walkways, and scaffolds are the third most common cause of industrial accidents. Hand tools (like chisels and screwdrivers) and electrical equipment (extension cords, electric droplights, and so on) are other major causes of accidents.[40]

Certain jobs are inherently more dangerous. For example, the job of crane operator results in about three times more accident-related hospital visits than does the job of supervisor. "High-quality jobs"—those that involved extensive training, variety, and autonomy—trigger fewer accidents.[41]

Work schedules and fatigue also affect accident rates. Accident rates usually don't increase too noticeably during the first five or six hours of the workday. But after that, the accident rate increases faster than the increase in the number of hours worked. This is due partly to fatigue and partly to the fact that accidents occur more often during night shifts.

Unfortunately, some of the most important working-condition-related causes of accidents are not as obvious, because they involve workplace "climate" or psychology. One researcher reviewed the official hearings regarding fatal accidents offshore oil workers suffered in the British sector of the North Sea.[42] A strong pressure within the organization to complete the work as quickly as possible, employees who are under a great deal of stress, and a poor safety climate—for instance, supervisors who never mention safety— were a few of the psychological conditions leading to accidents. Similarly, accidents occur more frequently in plants with a high seasonal layoff rate and where there is hostility among employees, many garnished wages, and blighted living conditions.

What Causes Unsafe Acts? (A Second Basic Cause of Accidents)

Unsafe acts can undo even the best attempts to reduce unsafe conditions. The problem is that there are no easy answers to the question of what causes people to act recklessly.

It may seem intuitively obvious that some people are simply accident prone, but the research isn't all that clear.[43] On closer inspection it turns out that some "accident repeaters" were just unlucky, or may have been more meticulous about reporting their accidents.[44] However, there is growing evidence that people with specific traits may indeed by accident prone. For example, people who are impulsive, sensation seeking, extremely extroverted, and less conscientious (in terms of being less fastidious and dependable) are more likely to have accidents.[45]

Furthermore, the person who is accident prone on one job may not be so on a different job. Driving is one familiar example. Personality traits that correlate with filing vehicular insurance claims include *entitlement* "bad drivers think there's no reason they should not speed or run lights," *impatience* "drivers with high claim frequency were 'always in a hurry,'" *aggressiveness* "always the first to want to move when the red light turns green," and *distractability* "easily and frequently distracted by cell phones, eating, drinking, and so on." A study in Thailand similarly found that drivers who are naturally competitive and prone to anger are particularly risky drivers.[46]

We'll turn to how employers reduce unsafe acts and conditions next.

HOW TO PREVENT ACCIDENTS

In practice, accident prevention boils down to two basic activities: (1) reducing unsafe conditions and (2) reducing unsafe acts. In large facilities, the chief safety officer (often called the "Environmental Health and Safety Officer") is responsible for this.[47] In smaller firms, various other managers including those from human resources, plant management, and first line managers share these responsibilities.

Reducing Unsafe Conditions

Reducing unsafe conditions is always an employer's first line of defense in accident prevention. Safety engineers should design jobs so as to remove or reduce physical hazards. In addition, supervisors and managers play a role in reducing unsafe conditions. Checklists like the ones in Figures 16-6 and 16-7 or the self-inspection checklist in Figure 16-11 can help identify and remove potential hazards.

Employers increasingly use computerized tools to design safer equipment. For example, Designsafe (from Designsafe Engineering, Ann Arbor, Michigan) helps automate the

FIGURE 16-8

Cut-Resistant Gloves Web Ad

Source: Courtesy of Occupational Hazards, Penton Media, Inc.

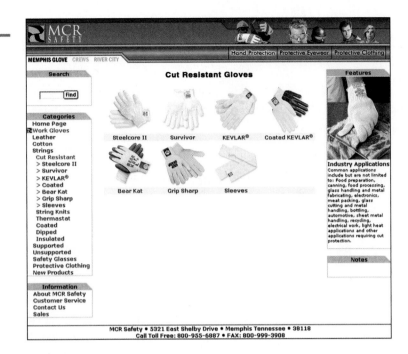

tasks of hazard analysis, risk assessment, and identifying safety options. First, Designsafe helps the safety designer identify the job's main processes and subprocesses, and the worker behaviors associated with each of them. It then helps the designer choose the most appropriate safety control device for keeping the worker safe, from a list of devices such as adjustable enclosures, presence-sensing devices, and personal protective equipment.[48]

Sometimes the solution for eliminating an unsafe condition is obvious, and sometimes it's more subtle. For example, slips and falls are often the result of debris or a slippery floor.[49] Relatively obvious remedies for problems like these include slip-reducing floor coatings, floor mats, better lighting, and a system to quickly block off spills. But perhaps less obviously, personal safety gear can also reduce the problems associated with otherwise unsafe conditions. For example, slip-resistant footwear with grooved soles can reduce slips and falls. Cut-resistant gloves reduce the hazards of working with sharp objects. Figure 16-8 illustrates what's available.

Personal Protective Equipment Getting employees to wear personal protective equipment can be a famously difficult chore. Wearability is important. In addition to providing reliable protection and durability, protective gear should fit properly; be easy to care for, maintain, and repair; be flexible and lightweight; provide comfort and reduce heat stress; have rugged construction; be relatively easy to put on and take off; and be easy to clean, dispose of, and recycle.[50] Including the employees in planning the safety program, reinforcing appropriate behaviors, and addressing comfort issues contribute to employees' willingness to use the protective gear.[51]

Again, however, reducing unsafe conditions (such as by enclosing noisy equipment) and having managers watch for hazards is always the employer's first line of defense. Then come administrative controls, such as job rotation to reduce long-term exposure to the hazard. Only then should you turn to personal protective equipment.[52] The accompanying "The New Workforce" feature below addresses a related issue.

The NEW Workforce   Protecting Vulnerable Workers

In designing safe and healthy environments, employers need to pay special attention to vulnerable workers, those who are "unprepared to deal with hazards in the workplace," either due to lack of education, ill-fitting personal protective equipment, physical limitations, or cultural reasons. Among others, these may include young workers, immigrant workers, aging workers, and women workers.[53] (Even young people need special protection. The Fair Labor Standards Act strictly limits young people's exposure to dangerous jobs, but about 64 workers under age 18 died from work-related injuries in one recent year.)[54]

For example, although about half of all workers today are women, most machinery and personal protective equipment (like gloves) are designed for men. Women may thus have to use makeshift platforms or stools to reach machinery controls, or safety goggles that don't really fit. The solution is to make sure the equipment and machines women use are appropriate for their size.[55]

Similarly, with more workers postponing retirement, older workers are doing a rising percentage of manufacturing jobs. They can do these jobs effectively. However, there are numerous physical changes associated with aging, including loss of strength, loss of muscular flexibility, reduced grip strength, reduced blood flow, and reduced reaction time.[56] This means that employers may have to make some special provisions, for instance providing mechanical assists, and providing older workers with additional insulation if they work for long periods in the cold.[57] The fatality rate for older workers in one recent year was about three times that of younger workers.[58]

Reducing unsafe acts—by emphasizing safety and through screening, training, or incentive programs, for example—is the second basic way to reduce accidents. Let's look at how to do this.

3 Minimize unsafe acts by employees.

Reducing Unsafe Acts by Emphasizing Safety

As mentioned above, it is the supervisor's responsibility to set the tone so subordinates want to work safely. This involves more than talking up safety, ensuring that workers wipe up spills, or enforcing safety rules, although such things are important. It's also necessary to show by both word and deed that safety is crucial. For example, supervisors should:

- Praise employees when they choose safe behaviors;
- Listen when employees offer safety suggestions, concerns, or complaints;
- Be a good example, for instance, by following every safety rule and procedure;
- Visit plant areas regularly;
- Maintain open safety communications—for instance, by telling employees as much as possible about safety activities such as testing alarms;
- Link managers' bonuses to safety improvements.[59]

Creating the right safety climate isn't just academic. One study assessed safety climate in terms of items such as "my supervisor says a good word whenever he sees the job done according to the safety rules." The study found that (1) employees did develop consistent perceptions concerning supervisory safety practices, and (2) these safety climate perceptions predicted safety records in the months following the survey.[60]

Reducing Unsafe Acts Through Selection and Placement

Proper employee screening and placement can reduce unsafe acts. Here, the employer's aim is to identify the trait (such as visual skill) that might predict accidents on the job in question, and then screen candidates for this trait. For example, a test like the Employee Reliability Inventory (ERI) can help employers reduce unsafe acts at work. The ERI (see http://www.ramsaycorp.com/products/eriphone.asp) purportedly measures reliability dimensions such as emotional maturity, conscientiousness, safe job performance, and courteous job performance.[61] While the findings of one study were not definitive, using the ERI in the selection process did seem to be associated with reductions in work-related accidents. Similarly, using job simulation tests (which attempt to measure the applicant by simulating physically demanding work activities) and physical capabilities tests (which measure muscle strength and motion) also seem to predict who will have more accidents. Using simulation and capabilities tests reflect the common-sense view that people do best on jobs that they're capable of doing well.[62]

Also, ask several safety-related questions during the selection interview—for instance, "What would you do if you saw another employee working in an unsafe way?" and "What would you do if your supervisor gave you a task, but didn't provide any training on how to perform it safely?"[63]

Asking about a candidate's workers compensation history might at first glance seem a sensible thing to do. However, under the Americans with Disability Act it is unlawful to inquire (prior to hiring) about an applicant's workers' compensation injuries and claims. You also cannot ask applicants whether they have a disability, or require them to take tests that tend to screen out those with disabilities. However, you can usually ask whether an applicant has the ability to perform a job. You can even ask, "Do you know of any reason why you would not be able to perform the various functions of the job you are seeking?"[64]

Reducing Unsafe Acts Through Training

Safety training is another way to reduce unsafe acts, especially for new employees. You should instruct them in safe practices and procedures, warn them of potential hazards, and work on developing a safety-conscious attitude. OSHA has published two useful booklets, "Training Requirements Under OSHA" and "Teaching Safety and Health in the Workplace." "The New Workforce" feature below provides an additional perspective.

Note that the employer cannot just provide training and assume it will be effective; they must show that employees learned what to do. For example, OSHA's respiratory protection standard requires that each employee be able to demonstrate how to inspect, put on, remove, use, and check respirator seals.[65]

Reducing Unsafe Acts Through Motivation: Posters, Incentives, and Positive Reinforcement

Employers also use various tools to motivate workers to work safely. *Safety posters* are one. Safety posters can apparently increase safe behavior, but they are no substitute for a comprehensive safety program. Employers should combine them with other techniques (like screening and training) to reduce unsafe conditions and acts, and also change the posters often.

Incentive programs are also successful at reducing workplace injuries.[66] Management at the Golden Eagle refinery in California instituted one such safety incentive plan. Employees earn "WINGS" points for engaging in one or more of 28 safety activities, such as conducting safety meetings, and taking emergency response training. Employees can earn up to $20 per month per person by accumulating points.[67]

Some contend that safety incentive programs are misguided. OSHA has argued, for instance, that they don't cut down on actual injuries or illnesses, but only on injury and illness *reporting*. One expert argues that by encouraging habitual behavior they can lull employees

The NEW Workforce   Safety Training for Hispanic Workers

With increasing numbers of largely Spanish speaking workers in the United States, experts express concern about their safety. For example, while total fatalities in the relatively dangerous construction industry only rose about 1% from 1997 to 2002, the number of Hispanic fatalities in construction rose by almost 50%, because so many more Hispanics are now working in construction jobs.[69]

Faced with statistics like these, many construction companies are offering specialized training programs for Hispanic workers. One example is a 40-hour training course provided for construction workers at the Dallas-Fort Worth airport expansion project. The construction firms here credit part of the airport site's safety record improvements to the new training program.

Based on this program's apparent success, there are several useful conclusions one can draw about what a program like this should look like.

- First, the program should *speak the workers' language*. OSHA requirements already demand this.
- Second, teaching the program in Spanish (or another appropriate language) is only part of "speaking the workers' language." The employer should also recruit instructors who are from the ethnic groups they are training, and try to use instructors who worked in (in this case) construction.
- Third, provide for some *multilingual cross-training* for specific phrases. For example, the course teaches non-Hispanic trainees to say "peligro" [danger] or "cuidado" (be careful) if you see someone with his or her back to dangerous equipment.[70]
- Fourth, address *cultural differences*. For example, in the Dallas airport program, they found that some workers, such as those from Panama, usually want to be greeted first, instead of just told, "you are doing something wrong."
- Fifth, *Don't skimp on training*. Because of the added cultural and multilingual aspects, experts contend that a 24-hour course is the absolute minimum. The 40-hour course at Dallas-Fort Worth airport cost about $500 tuition per student (not counting the worker's wages).

into letting their guard down.[68] One option is to emphasize "nontraditional" incentives. For instance, give employees recognition awards for identifying hazards, or for demonstrating their safety and health proficiency.[71] In any case, for ". . . an incentives program to be successful, all other pieces/parts of a comprehensive safety program need to be in place," says one expert.[72]

Research Insight: Positive Reinforcement   Many employers successfully use *positive reinforcement programs* to improve safety. Such programs provide workers with continuing positive feedback, usually in the form of graphical performance reports and supervisory support, to shape the workers' safety-related behavior.

Researchers introduced one program in a wholesale bakery.[73] An analysis of the safety-related conditions in the plant before the study suggested areas that needed improvement. For example, new hires received no formal safety training, and managers rarely mentioned safety.

The new safety program included training and positive reinforcement. The researchers set and communicated a reasonable safety goal (in terms of observed incidents performed safely). Next, employees participated in a 30-minute training session, by viewing pairs of slides depicting scenes that the researchers staged in the plant. One slide, for example, showed the supervisor climbing over a conveyor; the parallel slide showed the supervisor walking around the conveyor. After viewing an unsafe act, employees had to describe what

One way to motivate and encourage safety in a factory is to tell employees how much management values it: This safety poster on an exterior factory wall tells employees how well they are doing.

was wrong ("what's unsafe here?"). Then, the researchers demonstrated the same incident again but performed in a safe manner, and explicitly stated the safe-conduct rule ("go around, not over or under, conveyors").

At the conclusion of the training phase, supervisors showed employees a graph with their pretraining safety record (in terms of observed incidents performed safely) plotted. Supervisors then encouraged workers to consider increasing their performance to the new safety goal for their own protection, to decrease costs, and to help the plant get out of its last place in safety ranking. Then the researchers posted the graph and a list of safety rules.

Whenever observers walked through the plant collecting safety data, they posted on the graph the percentage of incidents they had seen performed safely by the group as a whole, thus providing the workers with positive feedback. Workers could compare their current safety performance with both their previous performance and their assigned goal. In addition, supervisors praised workers when they performed selected incidents safely. Safety in the plant subsequently improved markedly.

Use Behavior-Based Safety

behavior-based safety
Identifying the worker behaviors that contribute to accidents and then training workers to avoid these behaviors.

Behavior-based safety means identifying the worker behaviors that contribute to accidents and then training workers to avoid these behaviors. For example, Tenneco Corporation (which manufactures automobile exhaust systems and Monroe brand suspensions) implemented a behavior-based safety program at its 70 manufacturing sites in 20 countries. The firm selected internal consultants from among its quality managers, training managers, engineers, and production workers. After training, the internal consultants identified five critical behaviors for Tenneco's first safety program, such as: *Eyes on task: Does the employee watch his or her hands while performing a task?* The consultants made observations, collected data regarding the behaviors, and then successfully instituted on-site training programs to get employees to perform these five behaviors properly.[74]

Use Employee Participation

There are two good reasons to get the employees involved in designing the safety program. First, employees are often management's best source of ideas about what the potential

FIGURE 16-9

Employee Safety Responsibilities Checklist

Source: Reprinted from www.HR.BLR.com with permission of the publisher Business and Legal Reports, Inc., 141 Mill Rock Road East, Old Saybrook, CT © 2004.

Employee Safety Responsibilities Checklist

❑ Know what constitutes a safety hazard.
❑ Be constantly on the lookout for safety hazards.
❑ Correct or report safety hazards immediately.
❑ Know and use safe work procedures.
❑ Avoid unsafe acts.
❑ Keep the work area clean and uncluttered.
❑ Report accidents, injuries, illnesses, exposures to hazardous substances, and near misses immediately.
❑ Report acts and conditions that don't seem right even if you aren't sure if they're hazards.
❑ Cooperate with internal inspections and job hazard analyses.
❑ Follow company safety rules.
❑ Look for ways to make the job safer.
❑ Participate actively in safety training.
❑ Treat safety as one of your most important job responsibilities.

problems are and how to solve them. Second, employee involvement tends to encourage employees to accept the safety program.

For example, when the International Truck and Engine Corp. began designing its new robot-based plant in Springfield, Ohio, management chose to involve employees in designing the new facility.[75]

Employee participation took several forms. Management appointed joint labor–management safety teams for each department. Several years before the equipment was to arrive, project engineers began speaking with safety teams to start designing safeguards for the robot equipment. The company sent one safety team, including the union safety chairman, to Japan to watch the robot machines in action, and to develop a checklist of items that the safety teams needed to address. Then, back in Ohio, members of this team worked with employees to identify possible hazards and to develop new devices such as color-coded locks to better protect the employees.[76]

Once they are committed to the idea of safety, a checklist as in Figure 16-9 can provide employees with a useful reminder of what to watch out for.

Conduct Safety and Health Audits and Inspections

Again, however, reducing unsafe acts is no substitute for eliminating hazards. Managers should therefore routinely inspect for possible problems, using checklists as aids. Investigate all accidents and "near misses." Enable employees to notify managers about hazards.[77] Use employee safety committees to inspect. Committees should evaluate safety adequacy, monitor safety audit findings, and suggest strategies for improving health and safety performance.[78]

Managers expedite the safety audits by using personal digital assistants. For example, one Microsoft Windows application for designing and completing safety audit questionnaires is called Process and Performance Measurement (PPM). To use this application, the manager gives the safety audit a name, enters the audit questions, and lists possible answers. Typical questions for a fire extinguisher audit might include, "Are fire extinguishers clearly identified and accessible?" and "Are only approved fire extinguishers used in the workplace?"[79] The supervisor or employee then uses the PDA to record the audit and to automatically transmit it to the firm's safety office.

Research Insight: High-Performance Systems and Safety

Finally, as noted earlier it is important not to miss the forest for the trees. Individual practices like training and incentives may be no more effective than the overall management system of which they are part.

A recent study illustrates this. At several points in this book we've seen that *high-performance work systems* are associated with superior organizational performance, including profitability and customer service. While there's no hard and fast rule about what comprises high-performance work systems, most organizational psychologists would agree they include practices like employment security, selective hiring, extensive training, self-managed teams and decentralized decision making, reduced status distinctions between managers and workers, information sharing, contingent rewards, transformational leadership (for instance, in terms of inspirational motivation), measurement of management practices, and an emphasis on high-quality work.[80]

This study found that high-performance work systems also produce fewer occupational injuries. As the researchers conclude, ". . . We can no longer assume that occupational safety is the primary prerogative of individual workers, ergonomic design, and government regulations of collective agreements. Rather, our data demonstrates that a high-performance work system is significantly associated with occupational safety."[81]

Table 16-1 summarizes actions for reducing unsafe conditions and acts.[82]

Controlling Workers' Compensation Costs

In the event an accident does occur, the employee may turn to the employer's workers' compensation insurance to cover his or her expenses and losses. In turn, the employer's workers' compensation premiums reflect the number and size of its claims. There is, therefore, both a

---

TABLE 16-1   Reducing Unsafe Conditions and Acts: A Summary

Reduce Unsafe Conditions

Identify and eliminate unsafe conditions.

Use administrative means, such as job rotation.

Use personal protective equipment.

Reduce Unsafe Acts

Emphasize top management commitment.

Emphasize safety.

Establish a safety policy.

Reduce unsafe acts through selection.

Provide safety training.

Use posters and other propaganda.

Use positive reinforcement.

Use behavior-based safety programs.

Encourage worker participation.

Conduct safety and health inspections regularly.

---

humanitarian and financial impetus for reducing claims. Workers compensation claims tend to spike on Mondays, possibly because some workers represent weekend injuries as work-related ones.[83]

Before the Accident The time to start "controlling" workers' compensation claims is before the accident happens. This involves taking all the safety steps described above.[84] The approach doesn't have to be complicated. For example, LKL Associates, Inc., of Orem, Utah, cut its workers' compensation premiums in half by communicating written safety and substance abuse policies to workers and then strictly enforcing those policies.[85]

After the Accident The injury can be traumatic for the employee, and how the employer handles it is important. The employee will have questions, such as where to go for medical help and whether he or she gets paid for time off. It's also usually at this point that the employee decides whether to retain a workers' compensation attorney to plead his or her case.

Here it is important for the employer to be supportive and proactive. Provide first aid, and make sure the worker gets quick medical attention; make it clear that you are interested in the injured worker and his or her fears and questions; document the accident; file required accident reports; and encourage a speedy return to work.[86]

It doesn't help that half the employees who return after workers' comp face indifference, criticism, or dismissal.[87] Perhaps the most important thing an employer can do is develop an aggressive return-to-work program, including making light-duty work available. The best solution, for both employer and employee, is for the worker to become a productive member of the company again instead of a victim living on benefits.[88]

Analyzing Claims Claims-tracking software is crucial for helping employers understand what's causing their workers' compensation claims. For example, a health services agency in Bangor, Maine, purchased CompWatch, a workers' compensation claims management and tracking program, from Benefit Software, Inc. CompWatch enables an employer to track and analyze each of its workers' compensation claims. The agency entered all its previous claims, including near-miss incidents, and used CompWatch to analyze trends. For example, CompWatch could divide automobile accidents into those in which its driver was at fault, and those in which another person caused the accident (or the responsibility could not be determined). The agency discovered some of the auto accidents were apparently due to its drivers' need for training, so the agency introduced a driver safety program. Doing so reduced accidents. In one department, this apparently led to a 42% reduction in auto accidents from one year to the next.[89]

Explain how to deal with important occupational health problems.

WORKPLACE HEALTH HAZARDS: PROBLEMS AND REMEDIES

Most workplace health hazards aren't obvious ones like unguarded equipment or slippery floors. Many are unseen hazards (like mold) that the company inadvertently produces as part of its production processes. Other problems, like drug abuse, the employees may create for themselves. In either case, these health hazards are often as much or more dangerous to workers' health and safety than are obvious hazards like slippery floors. The manager must therefore address them. Typical workplace exposure hazards may include:

1. Chemicals and other hazardous materials.
2. Excessive noise and vibrations.
3. Temperature extremes.

TABLE 16-2 OSHA Substance-Specific Health Standards

Substance	Permissable Exposure Limits
Asbestos	.1001
Vinyl chloride	.1017
Inorganic arsenic	.1018
Lead	.1025
Cadmium	.1027
Benzene	.1028
Coke oven emissions	.1029
Cotton dust	.1043
1,2-Dibromo-3-chloropropane	.1044
Acrylonitrile	.1045
Ethylene oxide	.1047
Formaldehyde	.1048
4,4′-Methylene-dianaline	.1050
Methylene chloride	.1051

Source: John F. Rekus, "If You Thought Air Sampling Was Too Difficult to Handle, This Guide Can Help You Tackle Routine Sampling with Confidence, Part I," *Occupational Hazards*, May 2003, p. 43.

4. Biohazards including those that are normally occurring (such as mold) and man-made (such as anthrax).
5. Ergonomic hazards (such as poorly designed equipment that forces workers to do their jobs while contorted in unnatural positions).
6. And, familiar safety-related hazards such as slippery floors and blocked passageways.[90]

OSHA standards list permissible exposure limits for about 600 chemicals. Table 16-2 lists some OSHA substance-specific health standards. Hazardous substances like these require air sampling and other preventive and precautionary measures. They are also more widespread than most managers realize. For example, cadmium pigments provide color to many paints and coatings, and ethyl alcohol is often used as a solvent in industrial processes.

The Basic Industrial Hygiene Program

Managing exposure hazards like these comes under the category of *industrial hygiene*, and involves recognition, evaluation, and control. First, the facility's health and safety officers (possibly working with teams of supervisors and employees) must *recognize* possible exposure hazards. This typically involves conducting plant/facility walk-around surveys, employee interviews, records reviews, and reviews of government and nongovernmental standards regarding various occupational exposure hazards.

Having identified a possible hazard, the *evaluation* phase involves determining how severe the hazard is. This requires measuring the exposure, comparing the measured exposure to some benchmark (as in Table 16-2), and determining whether the risk is within tolerances.[91]

Finally, the hazard *control* phase involves eliminating or reducing the hazard. Note that personal protective gear such as face masks are generally the *last* option for dealing with such problems. Before relying on these, the employer must install engineering

Exposure to asbestos is a major potential source of occupational respiratory disease. This worker wears protective clothing and a respirator to remove asbestos from ceiling panels in a classroom.

material safety data sheets (MSDS)
Sheets that describe the precautions required by OSHA that employees are to take when dealing with hazardous chemicals, and what to do if problems arise.

controls (such as process enclosures or ventilation), and administrative controls (including training and improved housekeeping); this is mandatory under OSHA.

Asbestos Exposure at Work

There are four major sources of occupational respiratory diseases: asbestos, silica, lead, and carbon dioxide. Of these, asbestos has become a major concern, in part because of publicity surrounding asbestos in buildings such as schools constructed before the mid-1970s. Major efforts are still under way to rid these buildings of the substance.

OSHA standards require several actions with respect to asbestos. Companies must monitor the air whenever an employer expects the level of asbestos to rise to one-half the allowable limit. (You would therefore have to monitor if you expected asbestos levels of 0.1 fibers per cubic centimeter.) Engineering controls—walls, special filters, and so forth—are required to maintain an asbestos level that complies with OSHA standards. Only then can employers use respirators if additional efforts are required to achieve compliance.

Improving Productivity Through HRIS: *Internet-Based Safety Improvement Solutions*

In today's business environment, companies need to obtain efficiencies wherever they can, and Internet-based systems can help them manage their safety programs much more efficiently. For example, any employees handling hazardous chemicals must be familiar with those chemicals' **material safety data sheets (MSDS)**. These sheets, from OSHA, describe the precautions employees are to take when dealing with the chemicals, and what to do if problems arise. In a dry cleaning store, for instance, the cleaner–spotter is supposed to be knowledgeable about the MSDS for chemicals like hydrafluorous acid (used for stain removal) and perchloroethylene (used for cleaning).

Particularly for large firms, managing the MSDS can cost millions of dollars annually. The employer needs to distribute the appropriate MSDS to each employee, ensure that the employees study and learn their contents, and continually update the data sheets based on new OSHA information. Many firms are therefore putting their MSDS programs online. The Web-based systems provide a platform upon which the employer can mount all its relevant MSDS, make these available to the employees who need them, monitor and test employees on the sheets' use, and update the MSDS as required. Systems like these provide an inexpensive way to boost the productivity and effectiveness of one essential aspect of an employer's safety and health program.[92]

Employers also turn to the Web to support their safety training programs. For example, PureSafety (www.puresafety.com) enables firms to create their own training Web sites, complete with a "message from the safety director." Once an employer installs the PureSafety Web site, it can populate the site with courses from companies that supply health and safety courses via PureSafety.com. The courses themselves are available in various formats, including digital versions of videotape training, and PowerPoint presentations. PureSafety.com also develops or modifies existing courses for employers.

Sites like PureSafety.com make it easy for an employer to quickly organize and launch a health and safety program for its employees, and to efficiently deliver individual courses to employees, when and where they want them.[93]

Infectious Diseases

With many employees traveling to and from international destinations, monitoring and controlling infectious diseases like Ebola and SARS has become an important safety issue.[94]

Employers can take steps to prevent the entry or spread of infectious diseases like these into their workplaces. These include:

1. Closely monitor Centers for Disease Control (CDC) travel alerts. The CDC issues travel advisories (which may recommend deferring nonessential travel) and travel alerts (which simply inform travelers of health concerns and provides precautions). Access this information at www.cdc.gov.
2. Provide daily medical screenings for employees returning from SARS or other infected areas.
3. Deny access to your facility for 10 days to employees or visitors returning from affected areas, particularly those who have had contact with suspected infected individuals.
4. Tell employees to stay home if they have a fever or respiratory system symptoms.
5. Clean work areas and surfaces regularly.
6. Stagger breaks. Offer several lunch periods to reduce overcrowding.
7. Emphasize to employees the importance of frequent handwashing, and make sanitizers containing alcohol easily available throughout the workplace.

Alcoholism and Substance Abuse

Alcoholism and substance abuse are serious and widespread problems at work. A recent study concluded that about 15% of the U.S. workforce (just over 19 million workers) "has either been hungover at work, been drinking shortly before showing up for work, or been drinking or impaired while on the job at least once during the previous year."[95] While the percentage of full-time U.S. workers engaging in illegal drug use has reportedly dropped in the last 15 years or so, about 15% of workers still report having used illicit drugs in one recent year. Drug-using employees are over three and a half times more likely to be involved in workplace accidents.[96] Some experts estimate that as many as 50% of all "problem employees" are actually alcoholics. One estimate places the cost of a substance abuser's damage to a company at $7,000 per abuser per year.[97]

Effects of Alcohol Abuse   The effects of alcoholism on the worker and work are severe.[98] Both the quality and quantity of the work decline, in the face of a sort of on-the-job absenteeism. The alcoholic's on-the-job accidents usually don't increase significantly, apparently because he or she becomes much more cautious. However, the off-the-job accident rate is higher than for nonalcoholics. Morale of other workers drops as they have to shoulder the alcoholic's burdens.

Recognizing the alcoholic on the job is a problem. Early symptoms such as tardiness are similar to those of other problems and thus hard to classify. The supervisor is not a psychiatrist, and without specialized training, identifying—and dealing with—the alcoholic is difficult.

Table 16-3 presents a chart showing observable behavior patterns that indicate alcohol-related problems. As you can see, alcohol-related problems range from tardiness in the earliest stages of alcohol abuse to prolonged, unpredictable absences in its later stages.

Dealing with Substance Abuse   As explained earlier in this book, most firms test applicants and (often) current employees for drugs.

TABLE 16-3 Observable Behavior Patterns Indicating Possible Alcohol-Related Problems

Stage	Absenteeism	General Behavior	Job Performance
I Early	Tardiness Quits early Absence from work situations ("I drink to relieve tension")	Complaints from fellow employees for not doing his or her share Overreaction Complaints of not "feeling well" Makes untrue statements	Misses deadlines Commits errors (frequently) Lower job efficiency Criticism from the boss
II Middle	Frequent days off for vague or implausible reasons ("I feel guilty about sneaking drinks"; "I have tremors") Does not return from lunch ("I don't feel like eating"; "I don't want to talk about it"; "I like to drink alone")	Marked changes Undependable statements Avoids fellow employees Borrows money from fellow employees Exaggerates work accomplishments Frequent hospitalization Minor injuries on the job (repeatedly) Financial difficulties (garnishments, and so on) More frequent hospitalization Resignation: Does not want to discuss problems Problems with the laws in the community	General deterioration Cannot concentrate Occasional lapses of memory Warning from boss
III Late	Frequent days off; several days at a time	Aggressive and belligerent behavior Domestic problems interfere with work	Far below expectation Punitive disciplinary action
IV Approaching Terminal Stage	Prolonged unpredictable absences ("My job interferes with my drinking")	Drinking on the job (probably) Completely undependable Repeated hospitalization Serious financial problems Serious family problems: divorce	Uneven Generally incompetent Faces termination or hospitalization

Note: Based on content analysis of files of recovering alcoholics in five organizations. From *Managing and Employing the Handicapped: The Untapped Potential*, by Gopal C. Patl and John I. Adkins Jr., with Clenn Morrison (Lake Forest, IL: Brace-Park, Human Resource Press, 1981).

Source: Gopal C. Patl and John I. Adkins Jr., "The Employer's Role in Alcoholism Assistance," *Personnel Journal* 62, no. 7 (July 1983), p. 570. Recent evidence supports these earlier studies. See for example, http://pubs.niaaa.nih.gov/publications/aa44.htm, http://www.nmsu.edu/~personel/dahandbook/albob.html, and http://www.usda.gov/da/pdsd/Security%20Guide/Eap/Alcohol.htm#Warning%20Signs, all accessed May 26, 2007.

Such testing is generally effective. Preemployment drug testing discourages those on drugs from applying for work or coming to work for employers who do testing. One study found that over 30% of regular drug users employed full-time said they were less likely to work for a company that conducted preemployment screening.[99] Some applicants or employees may try to evade the test, for instance, by purchasing "clean" specimens to use. Several states, including New Jersey, North Carolina, Virginia, Oregon, South Carolina, Pennsylvania, Louisiana, Texas, and Nebraska have laws making drug-test fraud a crime.[100]

The big question is what to do when a *current* employee tests positive. Disciplining, discharge, in-house counseling, and referral to an outside agency are the four traditional prescriptions. Most professionals seem to counsel treatment rather than outright dismissal, at least initially, and also emphasize that whether it's the supervisor or just a friend that notices the employee's problem, the worst thing to do is ignore it.

In practice, each employer tends to develop its own approach to dealing with substance abuse. One human resource manager says: "We present the employee with the option of a mandatory professional assessment (which may result in rehab and/or counseling depending on the results of the assessment). If the employee refuses the professional assessment, employment is terminated."[101] Another describes her company's policy this way:

> Some employers have zero tolerance and terminate immediately. Some employers don't have a choice (pharmaceutical labs, for example). Others are lenient. Our policy is a three-strikes-and-you're-out process. The first step is a warning notification and permission given to us to test the employee at any time we want—for a period of five years. The second step is a mandatory substance abuse rehabilitation program at the employee's own expense . . . the third step is immediate termination for cause.[102]

Substance Abuse Policies   Employers should establish and communicate a substance abuse policy. This policy should state management's position on alcohol and drug abuse and on the use and possession of illegal drugs on company premises. It should also list the methods (such as urinalysis) used to determine the causes of poor performance; state the company's views on rehabilitation, including workplace counseling; and specify penalties for policy violations. Additional steps employers take include conducting workplace inspections (searching employees for illegal substances) and using undercover agents.

Supervisor Training   Training supervisors to identify alcoholics or drug abusers and the problems they create is advisable. However, supervisors are in a tricky position: They should be the company's first line of defense in combating workplace drug abuse, but should avoid becoming detectives or medical diagnosticians. Guidelines supervisors should follow include these:

- If an employee appears to be under the influence of drugs or alcohol, ask how the employee feels and look for signs of impairment such as slurred speech. Send an employee judged unfit for duty home. (See Table 16-3.)
- Make a written record of your observations and follow up each incident. In addition, inform workers of the number of warnings the company will tolerate before requiring termination.
- Refer troubled employees to the company's employee assistance program.

The "Know Your Employment Law" feature explains some legal matters to consider.

Stress, Burnout, and Depression

Problems such as alcoholism and drug abuse sometimes reflect underlying psychological causes such as stress and depression. For example, factors such as overwork and problems with supervisors or customers may eventually put the person under so much stress that a pathological reaction such as drug abuse occurs.

A variety of external factors can lead to job stress. These include work schedule, pace of work, job security, route to and from work, and the number and nature of customers or clients. Even noise, including people talking and telephones ringing, contributes to stress.

However, personal factors also influence stress. For example, Type A personalities—people who are workaholics and who feel driven to always be on time and meet deadlines—normally place themselves under greater stress than do others. Add to job stress the stress caused by nonjob problems like divorce and, as you might imagine, many workers are problems waiting to happen.

Job stress has serious consequences for both employer and employee. The human consequences include anxiety, depression, anger, and various physical consequences, such as cardiovascular disease, headaches, and accidents. For the organization, consequences

Know Your Employment LAW | Workplace Substance Abuse

The federal Drug-Free Workplace Act requires employers with federal government contracts or grants to ensure a drug-free workplace by taking (and certifying that they have taken) a number of steps. For example, employers must agree to:

- Publish a policy prohibiting the unlawful manufacture, distribution, dispensing, possession, or use of controlled substances in the workplace.
- Establish a drug-free awareness program that informs employees about the dangers of workplace drug abuse.
- Inform employees that they are required, as a condition of employment, not only to abide by the employer's policy but also to report any criminal convictions for drug-related activities in the workplace.[103]

The U.S. Department of Transportation also has its own rules regarding drug testing in the transportation industry.[104] These rules require random breath alcohol tests as well as preemployment, postaccident, reasonable suspicion, and return-to-duty testing for workers in safety-sensitive jobs in transportation industries including aviation, interstate motor carrier, railroad, pipeline, and commercial marine.

Legal Risks

Dealing with alcoholism and drugs at work does entail legal risks. Employees have sued for invasion of privacy, wrongful discharge, defamation, and illegal searches. Therefore, before implementing any drug control program,

- Use employee handbooks, bulletin board postings, pay inserts, and the like to publicize your substance abuse plans.
- Explain the conditions under which testing may occur and the procedures for handling employees who refuse to be tested.
- Explain what accommodations you make for employees who voluntarily seek treatment. Substance abuse is a physical handicap under federal and some state laws. You may be required to make reasonable accommodations for employees who enter alcohol or drug treatment programs.

include reductions in the quantity and quality of performance, and increased absenteeism and turnover. A study of 46,000 employees concluded that high-stress workers' health care costs were 46% higher than those of their less-stressed co-workers.[105]

Reducing Job Stress   There are a number of ways to alleviate dysfunctional stress. These range from commonsense remedies (such as getting more sleep and eating better) to more exotic remedies like biofeedback and meditation. Finding a more suitable job, getting counseling, and planning and organizing each day's activities are other sensible responses. In his book *Stress and the Manager*, Dr. Karl Albrecht suggests the following ways for a person to reduce job stress:

- Build rewarding, pleasant, cooperative relationships with colleagues and employees.
- Don't bite off more than you can chew.
- Build an especially effective and supportive relationship with your boss.
- Negotiate with your boss for realistic deadlines on important projects.
- Learn as much as you can about upcoming events and get as much lead time as you can to prepare for them.
- Find time every day for detachment and relaxation.
- Take a walk around the office to keep your body refreshed and alert.

- Find ways to reduce unnecessary noise.
- Reduce the amount of trivia in your job; delegate routine work whenever possible.
- Limit interruptions.
- Don't put off dealing with distasteful problems.
- Make a constructive "worry list" that includes solutions for each problem.[106]

Meditation is another possible solution. Choose a quiet place with soft light and sit comfortably. Then meditate by focusing your thoughts, for instance by counting breaths, or by visualizing a calming location such as a beach. When your mind wanders, bring it back to focusing your thoughts back on your breathing, or the beach.[107]

The employer and its human resource team and supervisors also play a role in reducing stress. Supportive supervisors and fair treatment are two obvious steps. Other steps include reducing personal conflicts on the job, and encouraging open communication between management and employees. Huntington hospital in Pasadena California recently introduced an on-site concierge service to help its employees reduce work-related stress. It takes care of tasks like mailing bills and making vacation plans for them.[108]

One British firm follows a three-tiered employee stress-reduction approach.[109] First is *primary prevention*, and focuses on ensuring that things like job designs and workflows are correct. Second involves *intervention*, including individual employee assessment, attitude surveys to find sources of stress at work and personal conflicts on the job, and supervisory intervention. Third is *rehabilitation*, through employee assistance programs and counseling.

burnout

The total depletion of physical and mental resources caused by excessive striving to reach an unrealistic work-related goal.

Burnout **Burnout** is a phenomenon closely associated with job stress. Experts define burnout as the total depletion of physical and mental resources caused by excessive striving to reach an unrealistic work-related goal. Burnout doesn't just spontaneously appear. Instead, it builds gradually, manifesting itself in symptoms such as irritability, discouragement, entrapment, and resentment.[110]

What can a burnout candidate do? Here are some suggestions:

- *Break your patterns.* First, are you doing a variety of things or the same one repeatedly? The more well rounded your life is, the better protected you are against burnout.
- *Get away from it all periodically.* Schedule occasional periods of introspection during which you can get away from your usual routine.
- *Reassess your goals in terms of their intrinsic worth.* Are the goals you've set for yourself attainable? Are they really worth the sacrifices?
- *Think about your work.* Could you do as good a job without being so intense?

Research Insight   If you're thinking of taking a vacation to eliminate your burnout, you might as well save your money, according to one study.[111] In this study, 76 clerks in an administrative department in the headquarters of an electronics firm in central Israel completed questionnaires measuring job stress and burnout twice before a vacation, once during the vacation, and twice after the vacation.

The clerks' burnout certainly did decline during the vacation. The problem was the burnout quickly returned to pre-vacation levels by the time of the second post-vacation survey. At least for these 76 clerks, burnout moved partway back toward its pre-vacation level by three days after the vacation, and all the way by three weeks after they returned to work.[112] One implication, as these researchers point out, is that mini vacations during the workday—"such as time off for physical exercise, meditation, power naps, and reflective thinking"—might help reduce stress and burnout. A later, separate study concluded that the quality of a vacation—for instance, in terms of relaxation and nonwork hassles—affected the vacation's fade-out effects.[113]

Employee Depression   *Employee depression* is a serious problem at work. Experts estimate that depression results in more than 200 million lost workdays in the United States annually, and may cost U.S. businesses $24 billion or more per year just in absenteeism and lost productivity.[114] Depressed people also tend to have worse safety records.[115]

Employers apparently need to work harder to ensure that depressed employees utilize available support services. One survey found that while about two thirds of large firms offered employee assistance programs covering depression, only about 14% of employees with depression said they ever used one.[116]

Employers therefore need to train supervisors to identify warning signs of depression, and to counsel those who may need such services to use the firm's employee assistance program.[117] Depression is a disease, and it does no more good to tell a depressed person to "snap out of it" than it would to tell someone with a heart condition to stop acting tired. Typical warning signs of depression (if they last for more than two weeks) include: persistent sad, anxious, or "empty" moods, sleeping too little, reduced appetite, loss of interest in activities once enjoyed, restlessness or irritability, and difficulty concentrating.[118]

Computer-Related Health Problems

Even with advances in computer screen technology, there's still a risk of monitor-related health problems at work. Problems include short-term eye burning, itching, and tearing, as well as eyestrain and eye soreness. Backaches and neckaches are also widespread. These often occur because employees try to compensate for monitor problems (such as glare) by maneuvering into awkward body positions. There may also be a tendency for computer users to suffer from cumulative motion disorders, such as carpal tunnel syndrome, caused by repetitive use of the hands and arms at uncomfortable angles.[119] OSHA has no specific standards that apply to computer workstations. It does have general standards that might apply, regarding, for instance, radiation, noise, and electrical hazards.[120]

NIOSH (the National Institute of Occupational Safety and Health) provided general recommendations regarding the use of computer screens. These include:

1. Give employees rest breaks. Employees should take a 3–5 minute break from working at the computer every 20–40 minutes, and use the time for other tasks, like making copies.
2. Design maximum flexibility into the work station so it can be adapted to the individual operator. For example, use adjustable chairs with midback supports. Don't stay in one position for long periods of time.
3. Reduce glare with devices such as shades over windows, and recessed or indirect lighting.
4. Give workers a complete preplacement vision exam to ensure properly corrected vision for reduced visual strain. Special "personal glare screen" eyeglasses can lower the effect of glare.[121]
5. Allow the user to position his or her wrists at the same level as the elbow.
6. Put the screen at or just below eye level, at a distance of 18 to 30 inches from the eyes.
7. Let the wrists rest lightly on a pad for support.
8. Put the feet flat on the floor, or on a footrest.[122]

Workplace Smoking

Smoking is a serious health and cost problem for both employees and employers. For employers, these costs derive from higher health and fire insurance, as well as increased absenteeism and reduced productivity (which occurs, for instance, when a smoker takes a 10-minute break behind the store).

Furthermore, nonsmoking employees who are concerned with secondhand smoke are suing their employers. The California Environmental Protection Agency estimates that each year in the United States, secondhand smoke causes 3,000 deaths due to lung cancer and 35,000 to 62,000 illnesses due to heart problems (not all work related).[123]

What You Can and Cannot Do   Can the employer institute a smoking ban? The answer depends on several things, including the state in which you are located and whether or not your firm is unionized. For example, instituting a smoking ban in a unionized facility which formerly allowed employees to smoke may be subject to collective bargaining.[124] Many states and municipalities now ban indoor smoking in public areas (see www.smokefreeworld.com/usa.shtml for a list).

In general, you can deny a job to a smoker as long as you don't use smoking as a surrogate for some other kind of discrimination. A "no-smokers-hired" policy does not, according to one expert, violate the Americans with Disabilities Act (since smoking is not considered a disability), and in general "employers' adoption of a no-smokers-hired policy is not illegal under federal law." About 72% of the 270 human resources professionals responding to a recent SHRM online survey said their companies have designated smoking areas outside of the office; 32% offer smoking cessation programs; 27% have policies limiting the number of breaks employees can take; and 19% ban workplace smoking, both inside and outside the facility.[125]

Some firms take an extraordinarily hard-line approach. For example, WEYCO Inc., a benefits services company in Michigan, first gave employees 15 months warning and offered smoking secession assistance. Then they began firing or forcing out all its workers who smoke, including those who do so in the privacy of their homes.[126]

Violence at Work

A disgruntled employee recently walked into DaimlerChrysler's Ohio Jeep assembly plant and fatally shot one worker, after reportedly being involved in an argument with a supervisor.[127]

Violence against employees has become an enormous problem at work. Homicide is the second biggest cause of fatal workplace injuries, and surveys by NIOSH found that nonfatal workplace assaults resulted in more than 876,000 lost workdays and about $16 billion in lost wages in one recent year. While robbery was the primary motive for homicide at work, a co-worker or personal associate committed roughly one of seven workplace homicides.[128] In one survey, over half of senior human resource management or security executives surveyed reported that disgruntled employees had threatened senior managers in the past 12 months.[129]

Who Is at Risk?   Violence is more associated with some jobs than others. In one study, researchers constructed a "risk for violence scale." This listed 22 job characteristics that the researchers found correlated with violence on the job. Jobs with a high likelihood for violence include those jobs that: involve physical care of others; decisions that influence other people's lives; involve handling guns; exercise security functions; exercise physical control over others; interact with frustrated individuals; and handle weapons other than guns, for instance.[130]

While men have more fatal occupational injuries than do women, the proportion of women who are victims of assault is much higher. The Gender-Motivated Violence Act, part of the Violence Against Women Act passed by Congress in 1994, imposes significant liabilities on employers whose women employees become violence victims.[131] Most women (many working in retail establishments) murdered at work were victims of random criminal violence carried out by an assailant unknown to the victim, as might occur during a robbery. Co-workers, family members, or previous friends or acquaintances carried out the remaining homicides.

Most workplace violence incidents are predictable and avoidable. *Risk Management Magazine* estimates that about 86% of past workplace violence incidents were apparent to co-workers, who had brought them to management's attention prior to the incidents actually occurring. Yet, in most cases, management did little or nothing.[132] Employers can take several steps to reduce workplace violence. Let's look at them.

Heightened Security Measures   Heightened security measures are an employer's first line of defense against workplace violence. NIOSH suggests:[133] Improve external lighting; use drop safes to minimize cash on hand and post signs noting that only a limited amount of cash is on hand; install silent alarms and surveillance cameras; increase the number of staff on duty; provide staff training in conflict resolution and nonviolent response; and close establishments during high-risk hours late at night and early in the morning. Employers can also issue a weapons policy, for instance barring firearms and other dangerous or deadly weapons from the facility.

Because about half of workplace homicides occur in the retail industry, OSHA issued voluntary recommendations aimed at reducing homicides and injuries in such establishments. Particularly for late-night or early-morning retail workers, the suggestions include: Install mirrors and improved lighting; provide silent and personal alarms; reduce store hours during high-risk periods; install drop safes and signs that indicate little cash is kept on hand; erect bullet-resistance enclosures; and increase staffing during high-risk hours.[134]

Improved Employee Screening   That testing can screen out those prone to workplace aggression is clear. In one study researchers measured the relationship among personal characteristics such as "trait anger" (for instance, how participants feel about exhibiting a fiery temper when they do not receive recognition for doing good work) and "attitude toward revenge" (which of course measures a person's attitude toward revenge). The researchers concluded that measurable individual differences variables like trait anger "account for more than 60% of the variance in our measure of the incidence of workplace aggression."[135]

At a minimum, the employer should do a thorough background check. Obtain a detailed employment application and solicit and verify the applicant's employment history, educational background, and references. A personal interview, personnel testing, and a review and verification of all information provided should also be included. Sample interview questions to ask might include, for instance, "What frustrates you?" and "Who was your worst supervisor and why?"[136]

Certain background facts suggest the need for a more in-depth background investigation. Red flags include:[137]

- An unexplained gap in employment.
- Incomplete or false information on the résumé or application.
- A negative, unfavorable, or false reference.
- Prior insubordinate or violent behavior on the job.
- A criminal history involving harassing or violent behavior.
- A prior termination for cause with a suspicious (or no) explanation.
- A history of significant psychiatric problems.
- A history of drug or alcohol abuse.
- Strong indications of instability in the individual's work or personal life as indicated, for example, by frequent job changes or geographic moves.
- Lapsed or lost licenses or accreditations.[138]

Workplace Violence Training   Several firms offer video training programs that explain what workplace violence is, identify its causes and signs, and offer tips to supervisors on how to prevent it and what to do when it occurs. Firms should also train supervisors to identify the clues that typically precede violent incidents. These include:[139]

- *Typical profiles.* The typical perpetrator is male, between 25 and 40, and exhibits an inability to handle stress, manipulative behavior, and steady complaining. Of course, many non-violent people exhibit such traits too. However, perpetrators also tend to exhibit other behaviors, such as making verbal threats and physical or verbal outbursts, disrespecting the supervisor, and harboring grudges.
- *Verbal threats.* Individuals often talk about what they may do. An employee might say, "That propane tank in the back could blow up easily."
- *Physical actions.* Troubled employees may try to intimidate others, gain access to places where they do not belong, or flash a concealed weapon to test reactions.
- *Frustration.* Most cases involve an employee who has a frustrated sense of entitlement to a promotion, for example.
- *Obsession.* An employee may hold a grudge against a co-worker or supervisor, and some cases stem from romantic interest.[140]

Organizational Justice   Instituting safeguards to ensure that managers treat employees fairly can reduce violent behavior at work. As three researchers noted, "from the emerging empirical evidence, it appears that even though revenge can be motivated by nonjustice concerns, such as organizational politics, it typically occurs in response to a perceived injustice."[141]

These researchers asked respondents to reply to the following item: "Think back over your time as an employee in your current organization when you've been offended by another person. Please write a description of the offense below." The researchers also asked the respondents how they reacted to the injustice.

Here's what they found. First, they found that the employees were more willing to exact revenge against less powerful offenders.[142] Second, high-status victims were less likely to try to get revenge against low-status employees, possibly because of societal norms that people in positions of power should not take retaliatory action. Third, it was clear that blame was positively related to revenge; an employee who blamed another for some injustice or personal affront was more likely to try to seek revenge, and less likely to seek reconciliation. The implication is that reducing unjust actions will likely reduce the chances that employees will seek revenge.

Enhanced Attention to Employee Retention/Dismissal   Employers also need effective procedures for identifying potentially lethal employees. Circumstances to watch out for include:

- An act of violence on or off the job.
- Erratic behavior evidencing a loss of awareness of actions.
- Overly defensive, obsessive, or paranoid tendencies.
- Overly confrontational or antisocial behavior.
- Sexually aggressive behavior.
- Isolationist or loner tendencies.
- Insubordinate behavior with a suggestion of violence.
- Tendency to overreact to criticism.
- Exaggerated interest in war, guns, violence, catastrophes.
- The commission of a serious breach of security.
- Possession of weapons, guns, knives at the workplace.

- Violation of privacy rights of others such as searching desks or stalking.
- Chronic complaining and frequent, unreasonable grievances.
- A retribution-oriented or get-even attitude.[143]

Dismissing Violent Employees   The manager should use caution when firing or disciplining potentially violent employees. Consider the case of an executive suspected of sabotaging his former employer's computer system, causing up to $20 million in damage. What made this man, who'd been earning $186,000 a year, do such a thing? A note he wrote anonymously to the president provides some insight:

> "I have been loyal to the Company in good and bad times for over thirty years. . . . What is most upsetting is the manner in which you chose to end our employment. I was expecting a member of top management to come down from his ivory tower to face us directly with a layoff announcement, rather than sending the kitchen supervisor with guards to escort us off the premises like criminals. . . . We will not wait for God to punish you—we will take measures into our own hands."[144]

In dismissing potentially violent employees,

- Analyze and anticipate, based on the person's history, what kind of aggressive behavior to expect.
- Have a security guard nearby when the dismissal takes place.
- Clear away furniture and things the person might throw.
- Don't wear loose clothing that the person might grab.
- Don't make it sound as if you're accusing the employee; instead say that according to company policy, you're required to take action.
- Maintain the person's dignity and try to emphasize something good about the employee.
- Provide job counseling for terminated employees, to help get the employee over the traumatic postdismissal adjustment.[145]
- Consider obtaining restraining orders against those who have exhibited a tendency to act violently in the workplace. Human resource managers should understand what restraining orders do, and the process for obtaining them.[146]

Dealing with Angry Employees   What do you do when confronted by an angry, potentially explosive employee? Here are some suggestions:[147]

- Make eye contact.
- Stop what you are doing and give your full attention.
- Speak in a calm voice and create a relaxed environment.
- Be open and honest.
- Let the person have his or her say.
- Ask for specific examples of what the person is upset about.
- Be careful to define the problem.
- Ask open-ended questions and explore all sides of the issue.
- Listen: As one expert says, "Often, angry people simply want to be listened to. They need a supportive, empathic ear from someone they can trust."[148]

Legal Constraints on Reducing Workplace Violence   As sensible as it is to try to screen out potentially violent employees, doing so incurs the risk of lawsuits. Most states have policies that encourage the employment and rehabilitation of ex-offenders, and some states therefore limit the use of criminal records in hiring decisions.[149] For example, except in certain limited instances, Article 23-A of the New York Corrections Law makes it unlawful to discriminate against job applicants based on their prior criminal convictions. Similarly, courts have interpreted Title VII of the Civil Rights Act of 1964 as restricting employers from making employment decisions based on arrest records, since doing so may unfairly discriminate against some minority groups.

Aside from federal law, most states prohibit discrimination under any circumstances based on arrest records, and on prior convictions unless a direct relationship exists between the prior conviction and the job, or the employment of the individual presents an unreasonable risk to people or property.[150] And developing a "violent employee" profile could end up merely describing a mental impairment and thus violate the Americans with Disabilities Act.[151]

OCCUPATIONAL SECURITY AND SAFETY

A majority of employers have instituted new security arrangements since 2001.[152] Figure 16-10 illustrates steps employers took to upgrade safety and security after the Trade Center attacks. For example, about 46% of the surveyed employers issued gloves, masks, or other personnel protective equipment to at least specific employees (such as mail room workers). Forty-three percent instituted new, more stringent, building entry procedures. Those instituting identification requirements or hiring security personnel rose by 15% between December 2001 and July 2002. A SHRM survey found that about 85% of responding organizations now have some type of formal disaster plan in place.[153] Many firms have also instituted special handling procedures for suspicious mail packages, and hold regular emergency evacuation drills.

Basic Prerequisites for a Security Plan

As one corporate security summary put it, "workplace security involves more than keeping track of who comes in a window, installing an alarm system, or employing guards for an after-hours watch. Organizations that are truly security conscious plan and implement

FIGURE 16-10

Safety, Security, and Emergency Planning Initiatives Following Terrorist Incidents

Source: Adapted from "After Sept. 11th, Safety and Security Moved to the Fore," *BNA Bulletin to Management,* January 17, 2002, p. 52.

Initiatives	Percent of Employers
	(146)
Safety and Security	
Personal protective equipment	46%
New/more stringent building entry procedures	43
Restricted access to some areas	19
Closed entrances/areas	17
New/additional security personnel	12
Extended work hours for security personnel	10
New security devices (e.g., metal detectors)	10
New/more stringent applicant screening	7
Physical barriers to building entry	5
Emergency Planning and Disaster Recovery	
Review emergency/disaster recovery plan(s)	46
Revise emergency/disaster recovery plan(s)	32
New/revised evacuation drills	23
Form committee or task force to address emergency planning/disaster recovery	15
Develop emergency/disaster recovery plan(s)	14
Develop/revise procedures for data backup	14
Develop/revise procedures for tracking employee whereabouts	10

policies and programs that involve employees in protecting against identified risks and threats."[154]

Ideally, a comprehensive corporate security program should start with the following:

1. Company philosophy and policy on crime—In particular, make sure employees understand that no crime is acceptable and that the employer has a zero tolerance policy with respect to workers who commit crimes.
2. Investigations of job applicants—Conduct a full background check as part of your selection process for every position.
3. Security awareness training—Make it clear, during training and orientation programs, that the employer takes a tough approach to workplace crime.
4. Crisis management—Establish and communicate the procedures employees should follow in the event of a terrorist threat, bomb threat, fire, or other emergency.

Setting Up a Basic Security Program

In simplest terms, actually instituting a basic security program requires four steps: analyzing the current level of risk, and then installing mechanical, natural, and organizational security systems.[155]

Security programs ideally start with an analysis of the facility's *current level of risk*. The employer, preferably with the aid of security experts, should assess the company's exposure. Here, it is logical to start with the obvious. For example, what is the neighborhood like? Does your facility (such as the office building you're in) house other businesses or individuals (such as federal law enforcement agencies) that might bring unsafe activities to your doorstep? Is your facility close to major highways or railroad tracks (where, for instance, toxic fumes from the trains could present a problem)?

As part of its initial current threat assessment, the employer should also review at least these six matters:

1. *Access to the reception area,* including number of access points, and need for a "panic button" for contacting emergency personnel;
2. *Interior security,* including possible need for key cards, secure restrooms, and better identification of exits;
3. *Authorities' involvement,* in particular emergency procedures developed with local law enforcement authorities;
4. *Mail handling,* including how employees screen and open mail and where it enters the building;
5. *Evacuation,* including a full review of evacuation procedures and training; and,
6. *Backup systems* that allow the company to capture computer information at alternative locations if disaster strikes.

Having assessed the potential current level of risk, the employer then turns its attention to assessing and improving three basic sources of facility security: mechanical security, natural security, and organizational security.[156]

natural security

Taking advantage of the facility's natural or architectural features in order to minimize security problems.

mechanical security

The utilization of security systems such as locks, intrusion alarms, access control systems, and surveillance systems.

Natural Security   **Natural security** means taking advantage of the facility's natural or architectural features in order to minimize security problems. For example, Are there unlit spots in your parking lot? Does having too many entrances mean it is difficult to control facility access?

Mechanical Security   **Mechanical security** is the utilization of security systems such as locks, intrusion alarms, access control systems, and surveillance systems to reduce the need for continuous human surveillance.[157] Here, technological advances are making it

Many employers install video security cameras to monitor areas in and around their premises.

easier for employers to institute new security arrangements. Many mail rooms now use special scanners to check the safety of incoming mail. And for access security, biometric scanners that read thumb or palm prints or retina or vocal patterns make it easier to enforce plant security. However, critics say these also may undermine employee privacy, for instance, by identifying where the employee is at any point in time.[158]

organizational security
Using good management to improve security.

Organizational Security   Finally, **organizational security** means using good management to improve security. For example, it means properly training and motivating security staff and lobby attendants, and ensuring that security staff has written orders that define their duties, especially in situations such as fire, elevator entrapment, hazardous materials spills, medical emergencies, hostile intrusions, hostage situations, bomb or terrorist attacks, suspicious packages, civil disturbances, and workplace violence.[159] Other questions to ask include, Are you properly investigating the backgrounds of new hires? Are you requiring the same types of background checks for the contractors who supply security and other personnel to your facility? And, do you provide new employees with security orientations?

Evacuation Plans

The possibility of emergencies prompted by fires, explosions, chemical releases, power outages, and severe weather means that employers need facility evacuation plans.[160] Such plans should contain several elements. These include *early detection of a problem, methods for communicating the emergency externally*, and *communications plans for initiating an evacuation and for providing information to those the employer wants to evacuate*. Regarding the latter, a simple alarm often does not suffice. Ideally, an initial alarm should come first. The employer should then follow the initial alarm with an announcement providing specific information about the emergency, and letting employees know what action they should take next. Some use text messaging for this.[161]

Company Security and Employee Privacy

Security programs like these have been accompanied by a significant rise in the monitoring of employee communications and workplace activities, and this has prompted many to ask, Are employee privacy rights being violated?

As noted earlier in this book, employers must consider employee privacy when using monitoring to control or investigate possible employee security breaches. For example, the Federal Electronic Communications Privacy Act prohibits someone from intercepting oral, wire, or electronic communication. However, this act does permit employees to consent to the monitoring of business communications. Ideally, employers should get employees' express consent for such monitoring, for instance, when employees sign for receipt of company policy forms during orientation. (The employer may also use monitoring if it is clear from its policies that employees should have known that such monitoring might take place.)

However, getting express permission doesn't give employers carte blanche to monitor employee communications. Several state courts have held that monitoring phone conversations (even on company phones) invades employees' privacy once it becomes apparent that the conversation is personal.

The employer can take several steps to make it easier to investigate employees for potential security breaches. These include:[162]

1. Distribute a policy that (a) says the company reserves the right to inspect and search employees as well as their personal property, electronic media, and files; and (b) emphasizes that company-provided conveniences such as lockers and desks remain the property of the company and are subject to its control and search;
2. Train investigators to focus on the facts and avoid making accusations;
3. Make sure your investigators know that employees can request that an employee representative be present during the interview;
4. Make sure all investigations and searches are evenhanded and nondiscriminatory.

REVIEW

SUMMARY

1. Safety and accident prevention is of concern to managers at least partly because of the staggering number of deaths and accidents occurring at work. There are also legal and economic reasons for safety programs.
2. The purpose of OSHA is to ensure every working person a safe and healthful workplace. OSHA standards are very complete and detailed and are enforced through a system of workplace inspections.
3. Supervisors play a key role in monitoring workers for safety. Workers in turn have a responsibility to act safely. A commitment to safety on the part of top management is an important aspect of any safety program.
4. There are three basic causes of accidents: chance occurrences, unsafe conditions, and unsafe acts on the part of employees. In addition, three other work-related factors (the job itself, the work schedule, and the psychological climate) also contribute to accidents.
5. Most experts doubt that there are accident-prone people who have accidents regardless of the job. Instead, the consensus seems to be that the person who is accident prone in one job may not be on a different job.

6. There are several approaches to preventing accidents. One is to reduce unsafe conditions. The other approach is to reduce unsafe acts—for example, through an emphasis on safety, selection and placement, training, and positive reinforcement.

7. Alcoholism, drug addiction, stress, and emotional illness are four important and growing health problems among employees. Alcoholism is a particularly serious problem and one that can drastically lower the effectiveness of your organization. Disciplining, discharge, in-house counseling, and referrals to an outside agency are techniques used to deal with these problems.

8. Stress and burnout are other potential health problems at work. Asbestos, video display health problems, AIDS, and workplace smoking are other employee health problems discussed in this chapter.

9. Violence against employees is an enormous problem at work. Steps that can reduce workplace violence include improved security arrangements, better employee screening, and violence-reduction training.

10. Most workplace health hazards aren't obvious ones like unguarded equipment or slippery floors. Many are unseen hazards. Typical workplace exposure hazards may include chemicals and other hazardous materials, excessive noise and vibrations, temperature extremes, biohazards, ergonomic hazards, and safety-related hazards such as slippery floors. Managing exposure hazards like these comes under the category of *industrial hygiene*, and involves a process of recognition, evaluation, and control.

11. With many employees traveling to and from international destinations, monitoring and controlling infectious diseases like Ebola and SARS has become an important safety issue. Steps include: Closely monitor CDC travel alerts; provide daily medical screenings; deny access to your facility for 10 days to employees or visitors from affected areas; and tell employees to stay home if they have a fever or respiratory system symptoms.

12. Ideally, a comprehensive corporate security program should include: a company philosophy and policy, investigations of job applicants, security awareness training, and crisis management. Instituting a basic security program involves four steps: analyzing the current level of risk, and then installing mechanical, natural, and organizational security systems. Evacuation plans are important. They should include early detection of a problem, methods for communicating the emergency externally, and communications plans for initiating an evacuation.

DISCUSSION QUESTIONS

1. Explain how to reduce the occurrence of unsafe acts on the part of your employees.
2. Discuss the basic facts about OSHA—its purpose, standards, inspections, and rights and responsibilities.
3. Explain the supervisor's role in safety.
4. Explain what causes unsafe acts.
5. Describe at least five techniques for reducing accidents.
6. Analyze the legal issues concerning AIDS.
7. Explain how you would reduce stress at work.
8. Describe the steps employers can take to reduce workplace violence.

INDIVIDUAL AND GROUP ACTIVITIES

1. Working individually or in groups, answer the question, "Is there such a thing as an accident prone person?" Develop your answer using examples of actual people you know who seemed to be accident prone on some endeavor.

2. Working individually or in groups, compile a list of the factors at work or in school that create dysfunctional stress for you. What methods do you use for dealing with the stress?

3. The HRCI "Test Specifications" appendix at the end of this book (pages 726–735) lists the knowledge someone studying for the HRCI certification exam needs to have in each area of human resource management (such as in Strategic Management, Workforce Planning, and Human Resource Development). In groups of four to five students, do four things: (1) review that appendix now; (2) identify the material in this chapter that relates to the required knowledge the appendix lists; (3) write four multiple choice exam questions on this material that you believe would be suitable for inclusion in the HRCI exam; and (4) if time permits, have someone from your team post your team's questions in front of the class, so the students in other teams can take each others' exam questions.

4. A recent issue of the journal *Occupational Hazards* presented some information about what happens when OSHA refers criminal complaints about willful violations of OSHA standards to the U.S. Department of Justice (DOJ). Between 1982 and 2002, OSHA referred 119 fatal cases allegedly involving willful violations of OSHA to DOJ for criminal prosecution. The DOJ declined to pursue 57% of them, and some were dropped for other reasons. Of the remaining 51 cases, the DOJ settled 63% with pretrial settlements involving no prison time. So, counting acquittals, of the 119 cases OSHA referred to the DOJ, only nine resulted in prison time for at least one of the defendants. "The Department of Justice is a disgrace," charged the founder of an organization for family members of workers killed on the job. One possible explana-tion for this low conviction rate is that the crime in cases like these is generally a misdemeanor, not a felony, and the DOJ generally tries to focus its attention on felony cases. Given this information, what implications do you think this has for how employers and their managers should manage their safety programs, and why do you take that position?

5. Recently, a 315-foot-tall, 2-million-pound crane collapsed on a construction site in East Toledo, Ohio, killing four ironworkers. Do you think catastrophic failures like this are avoidable? If so, what steps would you suggest the general contractor take to avoid a disaster like this?

EXPERIENTIAL EXERCISE

How Safe Is My University?

Purpose: The purpose of this exercise is to give you practice in identifying unsafe conditions.

Required Understanding: You should be familiar with material covered in this chapter, particularly that on unsafe conditions and that in Figures 16-6, 16-7 and 16-11.

How to Set Up the Exercise/Instructions: Divide the class into groups of four.

GENERAL

ACTION
OK NEEDED

1. Is the required OSHA workplace poster displayed in your place of business as required where all employees are likely to see it? ☐ ☐
2. Are you aware of the requirement to report all workplace fatalities and any serious accidents (where five or more are hospitalized) to a federal or state OSHA office within 48 hours? ☐ ☐
3. Are workplace injury and illness records being kept as required by OSHA? ☐ ☐
4. Are you aware that the OSHA annual summary of workplace injuries and illnesses must be posted by February 1 and must remain posted until March 1? ☐ ☐
5. Are you aware that employers with 10 or fewer employees are exempt from the OSHA record-keeping requirements, unless they are part of an official BLS or state survey and have received specific instructions to keep records? ☐ ☐
6. Have you demonstrated an active interest in safety and health matters by defining a policy for your business and communicating it to all employees? ☐ ☐
7. Do you have a safety committee or group that allows participation of employees in safety and health activities? ☐ ☐
8. Does the safety committee or group meet regularly and report, in writing, its activities? ☐ ☐
9. Do you provide safety and health training for all employees requiring such training, and is it documented? ☐ ☐
10. Is one person clearly in charge of safety and health activities? ☐ ☐
11. Do all employees know what to do in emergencies? ☐ ☐
12. Are emergency telephone numbers posted? ☐ ☐
13. Do you have a procedure for handling employee complaints regarding safety and health? ☐ ☐

WORKPLACE
ELECTRICAL WIRING, FIXTURES, AND CONTROLS

ACTION
OK NEEDED

1. Are your workplace electricians familiar with the requirements of the National Electrical Code (NEC)? ☐ ☐
2. Do you specify compliance with the NEC for all contract electrical work? ☐ ☐
3. If you have electrical installations in hazardous dust or vapor areas, do they meet the NEC for hazardous locations? ☐ ☐
4. Are all electrical cords strung so they do not hang on pipes, nails, hooks, etc.? ☐ ☐
5. Is all conduit, BX cable, etc., properly attached to all supports and tightly connected to junction and outlet boxes? ☐ ☐
6. Is there no evidence of fraying on any electrical cords? ☐ ☐
7. Are rubber cords kept free of grease, oil, and chemicals? ☐ ☐
8. Are metallic cable and conduit systems properly grounded? ☐ ☐
9. Are portable electric tools and appliances grounded or double insulated? ☐ ☐

Develop your own checklist.

10. Are all ground connections clean and tight? ☐ ☐
11. Are fuses and circuit breakers the right type and size for the load on each circuit? ☐ ☐
12. Are all fuses free of "jumping" with pennies or metal strips? ☐ ☐
13. Do switches show evidence of overheating? ☐ ☐

These are only sample questions.

14. Are switches mounted in clean, tightly closed metal boxes? ☐ ☐
15. Are all electrical switches marked to show their purpose? ☐ ☐
16. Are motors clean and kept free of excessive grease and oil? ☐ ☐
17. Are motors properly maintained and provided with adequate overcurrent protection? ☐ ☐
18. Are bearings in good condition? ☐ ☐
19. Are portable lights equipped with proper guards? ☐ ☐
20. Are all lamps kept free of combustible material? ☐ ☐
21. Is your electrical system checked periodically by someone competent in the NEC? ☐ ☐

FIGURE 16-11

Self-Inspection Safety and Health Checklist

		OK	ACTION NEEDED	Develop your own checklist.

EXITS AND ACCESS

1. Are all exits visible and unobstructed? ☐ ☐
2. Are all exits marked with a readily visible sign that is properly illuminated? ☐ ☐
3. Are there sufficient exits to ensure prompt escape in case of emergency? ☐ ☐
4. Are areas with limited occupancy posted and is access/egress controlled by persons specifically authorized to be in those areas? ☐ ☐
5. Do you take special precautions to protect employees during construction and repair operations? ☐ ☐

These are only sample questions.

FIRE PROTECTION

1. Are portable fire extinguishers provided in adequate number and type? ☐ ☐
2. Are fire extinguishers inspected monthly for general condition and operability and noted on the inspection tag? ☐ ☐
3. Are fire extinguishers recharged regularly and properly noted on the inspection tag? ☐ ☐
4. Are fire extinguishers mounted in readily accessible locations? ☐ ☐
5. If you have interior standpipes and valves, are these inspected regularly? ☐ ☐
6. If you have a fire alarm system, is it tested at least annually? ☐ ☐
7. Are plant employees periodically instructed in the use of extinguishers and fire protection procedures? ☐ ☐
8. If you have outside private fire hydrants, were they flushed within the last year and placed on a regular maintenance schedule? ☐ ☐
9. Are fire doors and shutters in good operating condition? ☐ ☐
   Are they unobstructed and protected against obstruction? ☐ ☐
10. Are fusible links in place? ☐ ☐
11. Is your local fire department well acquainted with your plant, location, and specific hazards? ☐ ☐
12. Automatic sprinklers:
   Are water control valves, air, and water pressures checked weekly? ☐ ☐
   Are control valves locked open? ☐ ☐
   Is maintenance of the system assigned to responsible persons or a sprinkler contractor? ☐ ☐
   Are sprinkler heads protected by metal guards where exposed to mechanical damage? ☐ ☐
   Is proper minimum clearance maintained around sprinkler heads? ☐ ☐

HOUSEKEEPING AND GENERAL WORK ENVIRONMENT

1. Is smoking permitted in designated "safe areas" only? ☐ ☐
2. Are NO SMOKING signs prominently posted in areas containing combustibles and flammables? ☐ ☐
3. Are covered metal waste cans used for oily and paint-soaked waste? ☐ ☐
   Are they emptied at least daily? ☐ ☐
4. Are paint spray booths, dip tanks, etc., and their exhaust ducts cleaned regularly? ☐ ☐
5. Are stand mats, platforms, or similar protection provided to protect employees from wet floors in wet processes? ☐ ☐
6. Are waste receptacles provided and are they emptied regularly? ☐ ☐
7. Do your toilet facilities meet the requirements of applicable sanitary codes? ☐ ☐
8. Are washing facilities provided? ☐ ☐
9. Are all areas of your business adequately illuminated? ☐ ☐
10. Are floor load capacities posted in second floors, lofts, storage areas, etc.? ☐ ☐
11. Are floor openings provided with toe boards and railings on a floor hole cover? ☐ ☐
12. Are stairways in good condition with standard railings provided for every flight having four or more risers? ☐ ☐

FIGURE 16-11

(continued)

13. Are portable wood ladders and metal ladders adequate for their purpose, in good condition, and provided with secure footing? **OK** ☐ **ACTION NEEDED** ☐

14. If you have fixed ladders, are they adequate, and are they in good condition and equipped with side rails or cages or special safety climbing devices, if required? ☐ ☐

15. For loading docks:

Are dockplates kept in serviceable condition and secured to prevent slipping? ☐ ☐

Do you have means to prevent car or truck movement when dockplates are in place? ☐ ☐

MACHINES AND EQUIPMENT **OK** **ACTION NEEDED**

1. Are all machines or operations that expose operators or other employees to rotating parts, pinch points, flying chips, particles, or sparks adequately guarded? ☐ ☐

2. Are mechanical power transmission belts and pinch points guarded? ☐ ☐

3. Is exposed power shafting less than 7 feet from the floor guarded? ☐ ☐

4. Are hand tools and other equipment regularly inspected for safe condition? ☐ ☐

5. Is compressed air used for cleaning reduced to less than 30 psi? ☐ ☐

6. Are power saws and similar equipment provided with safety guards? ☐ ☐

7. Are grinding wheel tool rests set to within $1/8$ inch or less of the wheel? ☐ ☐

8. Is there any system for inspecting small hand tools for burred ends, cracked handles, etc.? ☐ ☐

9. Are compressed gas cylinders examined regularly for obvious signs of defects, deep rusting, or leakage? ☐ ☐

10. Is care used in handling and storing cylinders and valves to prevent damage? ☐ ☐

11. Are all air receivers periodically examined, including the safety valves? ☐ ☐

12. Are safety valves tested regularly and frequently? ☐ ☐

13. Is there sufficient clearance from stoves, furnaces, etc., for stock, woodwork, or other combustible materials? ☐ ☐

14. Is there clearance of at least 4 feet in front of heating equipment involving open flames, such as gas radiant heaters, and fronts of firing doors of stoves, furnaces, etc.? ☐ ☐

15. Are all oil and gas fired devices equipped with flame failure controls that will prevent flow of fuel if pilots or main burners are not working? ☐ ☐

16. Is there at least a 2-inch clearance between chimney brickwork and all woodwork or other combustible materials? ☐ ☐

17. For welding or flame cutting operations:

Are only authorized, trained personnel permitted to use such equipment? ☐ ☐

Have operators been given a copy of operating instructions and asked to follow them? ☐ ☐

Are welding gas cylinders stored so they are not subjected to damage? ☐ ☐

Are valve protection caps in place on all cylinders not connected for use? ☐ ☐

Are all combustible materials near the operator covered with protective shields or otherwise protected? ☐ ☐

Is a fire extinguisher provided at the welding site? ☐ ☐

Do operators have the proper protective clothing and equipment? ☐ ☐

Develop your own checklist.

These are only sample questions.

MATERIALS **OK** **ACTION NEEDED**

1. Are approved safety cans or other acceptable containers used for handling and dispensing flammable liquids? ☐ ☐

2. Are all flammable liquids that are kept inside buildings stored in proper storage containers or cabinets? ☐ ☐

3. Do you meet OSHA standards for all spray painting or dip tank operations using combustible liquids? ☐ ☐

4. Are oxidizing chemicals stored in areas separate from all organic material except shipping bags? ☐ ☐

5. Do you have an enforced NO SMOKING rule in areas for storage and use of hazardous materials? ☐ ☐

6. Are NO SMOKING signs posted where needed? ☐ ☐

FIGURE 16-11

(continued)

		OK	ACTION NEEDED
7.	Is ventilation equipment provided for removal of air contaminants from operations such as production grinding, buffing, spray painting and/or vapor degreasing, and is it operating properly?	☐	☐
8.	Are protective measures in effect for operations involved with x-rays or other radiation?	☐	☐
9.	For lift truck operations:		
	Are only trained personnel allowed to operate forklift trucks?	☐	☐
	Is overhead protection provided on high lift rider trucks?	☐	☐
10.	For toxic materials:		
	Are all materials used in your plant checked for toxic qualities?	☐	☐
	Have appropriate control procedures such as ventilation systems, enclosed operations, safe handling practices, proper personal protective equipment (such as respirators, glasses or goggles, gloves, etc.) been instituted for toxic materials?	☐	☐

EMPLOYEE PROTECTION

		OK	ACTION NEEDED
1.	Is there a hospital, clinic, or infirmary for medical care near your business?	☐	☐
2.	If medical and first-aid facilities are not nearby, do you have one or more employees trained in first aid?	☐	☐
3.	Are your first-aid supplies adequate for the type of potential injuries in your workplace?	☐	☐
4.	Are there quick water flush facilities available where employees are exposed to corrosive materials?	☐	☐
5.	Are hard hats provided and worn where any danger of falling objects exists?	☐	☐
6.	Are protective goggles or glasses provided and worn where there is any danger of flying particles or splashing of corrosive materials?	☐	☐
7.	Are protective gloves, aprons, shields, or other means provided for protection from sharp, hot, or corrosive materials?	☐	☐
8.	Are approved respirators provided for regular or emergency use where needed?	☐	☐
9.	Is all protective equipment maintained in a sanitary condition and readily available for use?	☐	☐
10.	Where special equipment is needed for electrical workers, is it available?	☐	☐
11.	When lunches are eaten on the premises, are they eaten in areas where there is no exposure to toxic materials, and not in toilet facility areas?	☐	☐
12.	Is protection against the effect of occupational noise exposure provided when the sound levels exceed those shown in Table G-16 of the OSHA noise standard?	☐	☐

Develop your own checklist.

These are only sample questions.

FIGURE 16-11

(*continued*)

Assume that each group is a safety committee retained by your college or university's safety engineer to identify and report on any possible unsafe conditions in and around the school building. Each group will spend about 45 minutes in and around the building you are now in for the purpose of identifying and listing possible unsafe conditions. (Make use of the checklists in Figures 16-6, 16-7, and 16-11.)

Return to the class in about 45 minutes. A spokesperson for each group should list on the board the unsafe conditions you think you have identified. How many were there? Do you think these also violate OSHA standards? How would you go about checking?

APPLICATION CASE

The New Safety and Health Program

At first glance, a dot-com company is one of the last places you'd expect to find potential safety and health hazards—or so the owners of LearnInMotion. com thought. There's no danger of moving machinery, no high-pressure lines, no cutting or heavy lifting, and certainly no forklift trucks. However, there are safety and health problems.

In terms of accident-causing conditions, for instance, the one thing dot-com companies have lots of is cables and wires. There are cables connecting the computers to each other and to the servers, and in many cases separate cables running from some computers to separate printers. There are 10 telephones in this particular office, all on 15-foot phone lines that always seem to be snaking around chairs and tables. There is, in fact, an astonishing amount of cable considering this is an office with less than 10 employees. When the installation specialists wired the office (for electricity, high-speed DSL, phone lines, burglar alarms, and computers), they estimated they used well over five miles of cables of one sort or another. Most of these are hidden in the walls or ceilings, but many of them snake their way from desk to desk, and under and over doorways. Several employees have tried to reduce the nuisance of having to trip over wires whenever they get up by putting their plastic chair pads over the wires closest to them. However, that still leaves many wires unprotected. In other cases, they brought in their own packing tape, and tried to tape down the wires in those spaces where they're particularly troublesome, such as across doorways.

The cables and wires are only one of the more obvious potential accident-causing conditions. The firm's programmer, before he left the firm, had tried to repair the main server while the unit was still electrically alive. To this day, they're not sure exactly where he stuck the screwdriver, but the result was that he was "blown across the room," as one manager put it. He was all right, but it was still a scare. And while they haven't received any claims yet, every employee spends hours at his or her computer, so carpal tunnel syndrome is a risk, as are a variety of other problems such as eye strain and strained backs.

One recent accident particularly scared the owners. The firm uses independent contractors to deliver the firm's book- and DVD-based courses in New York and two other cities. A delivery person was riding his bike east at the intersection of Second Avenue and East 64th Street in New York when he was struck by a car going south on Second Avenue. Luckily he was not hurt, but the bike's front wheel was wrecked, and the close call got the firm's two owners, Mel and Jennifer, thinking about their lack of a safety program.

It's not just the physical conditions that concern the company's two owners. They also have some concerns about potential health problems such as job stress and burnout. While the business may be (relatively) safe with respect to physical conditions, it is also relatively stressful in terms of the demands it makes in hours and deadlines. It is not at all unusual for employees to get to work by 7:30 or 8 o'clock in the morning and to work through until 11 or 12 o'clock at night, at least five and sometimes six or seven days per week. Just getting the company's new online calendar fine-tuned and operational required 70-hour workweeks for three weeks from five of LearnInMotion.com's employees.

The bottom line is that both Jennifer and Mel feel quite strongly that they need to do something about implementing a health and safety plan. Now, they want you, their management consultants, to help them actually do it. Here's what they want you to do for them.

Questions

1. Based upon your knowledge of health and safety matters and your actual observations of operations that are similar to theirs, make a list of the potential hazardous conditions employees and others face at LearnInMotion.com. What should they do to reduce the potential severity of the top five hazards?

2. Would it be advisable for them to set up a procedure for screening out stress-prone or accident-prone individuals? Why or why not? If so, how should they screen them?

3. Write a short position paper on the subject, "What should we do to get all our employees to behave more safely at work?"

4. Based on what you know and on what other dot-coms are doing, write a short position paper on the subject, "What can we do to reduce the potential problems of stress and burnout in our company?"

CONTINUING CASE

Carter Cleaning Company

The New Safety Program

Employees' safety and health are very important matters in the laundry and cleaning business. Each facility is a small production plant in which machines, powered by high-pressure steam and compressed air, work at high temperatures washing, cleaning, and pressing garments, often under very hot, slippery conditions. Chemical vapors are continually produced, and caustic chemicals are used in the cleaning process. High-temperature stills are almost continually "cooking down" cleaning solvents in order to remove impurities so that the solvents can be reused. If a mistake is made in this process—like injecting too much steam into the still—a boilover occurs, in which boiling chemical solvent erupts out of the still and over the floor, and on anyone who happens to be standing in its way.

As a result of these hazards and the fact that chemically hazardous waste is continually produced in these stores, several government agencies (including OSHA and the EPA) have instituted strict guidelines regarding the management of these plants. For example, posters have to be placed in each store notifying employees of their right to be told what hazardous chemicals they are dealing with and what the proper method for handling each chemical is. Special waste-management firms must be used to pick up and properly dispose of the hazardous waste.

A chronic problem the Carters (and most other laundry owners) have is the unwillingness on the part of the cleaning–spotting workers to wear safety goggles. Not all the chemicals they use require safety goggles, but some—like the hydrofluorous acid used to remove rust stains from garments—are very dangerous. The latter is kept in special plastic containers, since it dissolves glass. The problem is that wearing safety goggles can be troublesome. They are somewhat uncomfortable, and they also become smudged easily and thus cut down on visibility. As a result, Jack has always found it almost impossible to get these employees to wear their goggles.

Questions

1. How should the firm go about identifying hazardous conditions that should be rectified? Use checklists such as Figures 16-6 and 16-11 to list at least 10 possible dry cleaning store hazardous conditions.

2. Would it be advisable for the firm to set up a procedure for screening out accident-prone individuals? How should they do so?

3. How would you suggest the Carters get all employees to behave more safely at work? Also how would you advise them to get those who should be wearing goggles to do so?

The New Safety and Health Program

The Hotel Paris's competitive strategy is "To use superior guest service to differentiate the Hotel Paris properties, and to thereby increase the length of stay and return rate of guests, and thus boost revenues and profitability." HR manager Lisa Cruz must now formulate functional policies and activities that support this competitive strategy, by eliciting the required employee behaviors and competencies.

While "hazardous conditions" might not be the first thing that comes to mind when you think of hotels, Lisa Cruz knew that hazards and safety were in fact serious issues for the Hotel Paris. Indeed, everywhere you look— from the valets leaving car doors open on the driveways to slippery areas around the pools, to tens of thousands of pounds of ammonia, chlorine, and other caustic chemicals that the hotels use each year for cleaning and laundry, hotels provide a fertile environment for accidents. Obviously, hazardous conditions are bad for the Hotel Paris. They are inhumane for the workers. High accident rates probably reduce employee morale and thus service. And accidents raise the company's costs and reduce its profitability, for instance in terms of workers' compensation claims and absences. Lisa knew that she had to clean up her firm's occupational safety and health systems.

Lisa and the CFO reviewed their company's safety records, and what they found disturbed them deeply. In terms of every safety-related metric they could find, including accident costs per year, lost time due to accidents, workers' compensation per employee, and number of safety training programs per year, the Hotel Paris compared unfavorably with most other hotel chains and service firms. "Why, just in terms of extra workers' compensation costs, the Hotel Paris must be spending $500,000 a year more than we should be," said the CFO. And that didn't include lost time due to accidents, or the likely negative effect accidents had on employee morale, or the cost of litigation (as when, for instance, one guest accidentally burned himself with chlorine that a pool attendant had left unprotected). The CFO authorized Lisa to develop a new safety and health program.

Questions

1. Based on what you read in this chapter, what's the first step the Hotel Paris should take as part of its new safety and health program, and why?
2. List 10 specific high-risk areas in a typical hotel you believe Lisa and her team should look at first, including examples of the safety or health hazards they should look for there.
3. Give three specific examples of how Hotel Paris can use HR practices to improve its safety efforts.
4. Write a one page summary addressing the topic, "How improving safety and health at the Hotel Paris will contribute to us achieving our strategic goals."

KEY TERMS

Occupational Safety and Health Act, 639
Occupational Safety and Health Administration (OSHA), 639
occupational illness, 639
citation, 642
unsafe conditions, 648

behavior-based safety, 657
material safety data sheets (MSDS), 662
burnout, 667
natural security, 674
mechanical security, 674
organizational security, 675

ENDNOTES

1. Don Williamson and Jon Kauffman, "From Tragedy to Triumph: Safety Grows Wings at Golden Eagle," *Occupational Hazards*, February 2006, pp. 17–25.
2. Data refers to 2003. See www.OSHA.gov, downloaded May 28, 2005.
3. "BLS Likely Underestimating Injury and Illness Estimates," *Occupational Hazards*, May 2006, p. 16.

4. Greg Hom, "Protecting Eyes from High-Tech Hazards," *Occupational Hazards*, March 1999, pp. 53–55; "Workplace Injuries by Industry, 2002," *Safety Compliance Letter*, February 2004, issue 2438, p. 12; Leigh Strope, "Deaths at Work Rise Slightly to 5,559 in 2003, with Most Occurring in Construction, Transportation," AP News, September 22, 2004, 11:45 P.M. GMT, downloaded September 23, 2004. See also, Katherine Torres, "Stepping into the Kitchen: Protection for Food Workers," *Occupational Hazards*, January 2007, pp. 29–30.

5. "Blame New Computers for Sick Buildings," *USA Today* 129, no. 2672 (May 2001), p. 8.

6. Michael Pinto, "Why Are Indoor Air Quality Problems So Prevalent Today?" *Occupational Hazards*, January 2001, pp. 37–39.

7. Sandy Moretz, "Safe Havens?" *Occupational Hazards*, November 2000, pp. 45–46.

8. David Ayers, "Mapping Support for an E. H. S. Management System," *Occupational Hazards*, June 2006, pp. 53–54.

9. Todd Nighswonger, "Rouge Settlement Sparks Safety Initiative at Ford," *Occupational Hazards*, October 1999, pp. 101–102. Karen Gaspers, "It's Painful for the Bottom Line, Too," *Safety and Health*, October 2003, vol. 168, issue 14, p. 323.

10. James Nash, "OSHA Targets Recalcitrant Employers," *Occupational Hazards*, May 2003, p. 12. See also, "Judge Sentences Man to Prison For Scaffolding Deaths," *Occupational Hazards*, February 2004, p. 14.

11. David Barstow and Lowell Bergman, "A Family's Profits, Wrung from Blood and Sweat," *New York Times*, January 9, 2003, p. 81.

12. Much of this is based on "All about OSHA" (revised), U.S. Department of Labor, Occupational Safety and Health Administration (Washington, DC), and www.OSHA.gov, accessed May 27, 2005.

13. "Safety Rule on Respiratory Protection Issues," *BNA Bulletin to Management*, January 8, 1998, p. 1. See also, "Staying on Top of OSHA Terms Helps Measure Safety," *Safety and Health*, July 2004, vol. 170, issue 1, p. 44.

14. "OSHA Hazard Communication Standard Enforcement," *BNA Bulletin to Management*, February 23, 1989, p. 13. See also William Kincaid, "OSHA vs. Excellence in Safety Management," *Occupational Hazards*, December 2002, pp. 34–36.

15. "What Every Employer Needs to Know About OSHA Record Keeping," U.S. Department of Labor, Bureau of Labor Statistics (Washington, DC), report 412–3, p. 3.

16. Arthur Sapper and Robert Gombar, "Nagging Problems Under OSHA's New Record-Keeping Rules," *Occupational Hazards*, March 2002, p. 58.

17. Brian Jackson and Jeffrey Myers, "Just When You Thought You Were Safe: OSHA Record-Keeping Violations," *Management Review*, May 1994, pp. 62–63.

18. "Supreme Court Says OSHA Inspectors Need Warrants," *Engineering News Record*, June 1, 1978, pp. 9–10; W. Scott Railton, "OSHA Gets Tough on Business," *Management Review* 80, no. 12 (December 1991), pp. 28–29. Steve Hollingsworth, "How to Survive an OSHA Inspection," *Occupational Hazards*, March 2004, pp. 31–33.

19. Steven Hollingsworth, "How to Survive an OSHA Inspection: Knowing What is Likely to Trigger an OSHA Inspection and How to Prepare for One Can Make This Process Much Less Painful," *Occupational Hazards* 66, no. 3, March 2004, pp. 31–35. See also http://www.osha.gov/as/opa/osha-faq.html, accessed May 26, 2007.

20. www.OSHA.gov, downloaded May 28, 2005.

21. This section is based on "All About OSHA," pp. 23–25. See also, Robert Sand, "OSHA Access to Privileged Materials: Criminal Prosecutions; Damages for Fear of Cancer," *Employee Relations Law Journal* 19, no. 1 (Summer 1993), pp. 151–157; "OSHA Final Rule Expands Employees' Role in Consultations, Protects Employer Records," *BNA Bulletin to Management*, November 2, 2000, p. 345.

22. Diane Hatch and James Hall, "A Flurry of New Federal Regulations," *Workforce*, February 2001, p. 98.

23. "Settling Safety Violations Has Benefits," *BNA Bulletin to Management*, July 31, 1997, p. 248. See also http://209.85.165.104/custom?q=cache:hMRIJ6ppbkoJ:osha.gov/SLTC/pptpresentations/armourswift_1297/december31997.ppt+OSHA+pre-citation+settlements&h1=en&ct=clnk&cd=1&gl=us, accessed May 26, 2007.

24. "Enforcement Activity Increased in 1997," *BNA Bulletin to Management*, January 29, 1998, p. 28. See also http://www.osha.gov/as/opa/osha-faq.html, accessed May 26, 2007.

25. Ibid., p. 28.

26. Sean Smith, "OSHA Resources Can Help Small Businesses with Hazards," *Westchester County Business Journal*, August 4, 2003, p. 4. See also http://www.osha.gov/as/opa/osha-faq.html, accessed May 26, 2007.

27. Lisa Finnegan, "Industry Partners with OSHA," *Occupational Hazards*, February 1999, pp. 43–45.

28. Robert Grossman, "Handling Inspections: Tips from Insiders," *HR Magazine*, October 1999, pp. 41–50, and "OSHA Inspections," OSHA, http://www.osha.gov/Publications/osha2098.pdf, accessed May 26, 2007.

29. Charles Chadd, "Managing OSHA Compliance: The Human Resources Issues," *Employee Relations Law Journal* 20, no. 1 (Summer 1994), p. 106.

30. These are based on Roger Jacobs, "Employee Resistance to OSHA Standards: Toward a More Reasonable Approach," *Labor Law Journal*, April 1979, pp. 227–230. See also, "Half of All Working Americans Feel Immune to Workplace Injuries, Nationally Workplace Deaths Up by 6% in 2001," *Internet Wire*, June 13, 2003, p. 100816442584.

31. Arthur Sapper, "The Oft-Missed Step: Documentation of Safety Discipline," *Occupational Hazards*, January 2006, p. 59.

32. These are based on James Nash, "The Top Ten Ways to Get into Trouble with OSHA," *Occupational Hazards*, December 2003, pp. 27–30.

33. Willie Hammer, *Occupational Safety Management and Engineering* (Upper Saddle River, NJ: Prentice Hall, 1985) pp. 62–63. See also, "DuPont's 'STOP' Helps Prevent Workplace Injuries and Incidents," *Asia Africa Intelligence Wire*, May 17, 2004.

34. F. David Pierce, "Safety in the Emerging Leadership Paradigm," *Occupational Hazards*, June 2000, pp. 63–66.

35. "Safety Program Results at ABB Business Services Missouri Plant," *Occupational Hazards*, July 2000, p. 23.

36. Donald Hantula et al., "The Value of Workplace Safety: A Time Based Utility Analysis Model," *Journal of Organizational Behavior Management* 21, no. 2 (2001), pp. 79–98.

37. "A Safety Committee Man's Guide," Aetna Life and Casualty Insurance Company, Catalog 87684. See also Dan Petersen, "The Barriers to Safety Excellence," *Occupational Hazards*, December 2000, pp. 37–39.

38. "Did This Supervisor Do Enough to Protect Trench Workers?" *Safety Compliance Letter*, October 2003, p. 9.

39. Ibid.

40. "A Safety Committee Man's Guide," pp. 17–21.

41. Julian Barling et al., "High-Quality Work, Job Satisfaction, and Occupational Injuries," *Journal of Applied Psychology* 88, no. 2 (2003), pp. 276–283.

42. For a discussion of this, see David Hofmann and Adam Stetzer, "A Cross-Level Investigation of Factors Influencing Unsafe Behaviors and Accidents," *Personnel Psychology* 49 (1996), pp. 307–308. See also, David Hoffman and Barbara Mark, "An Investigation of the Relationship between Safety Climate and Medication Errors as well as Other Nurse and Patient Outcomes," *Personnel Psychology* 50, no. 9, 2006, pp. 847–869.

43. Duane Schultz and Sydney Schultz, *Psychology and Work Today* (Upper Saddle River, NJ: Prentice Hall, 1998), p. 351.

44. Robert Pater and Robert Russel, "Drop That Accident Prone Tag: Look for Causes Beyond Personal Issues," *Industrial Safety and Hygiene News* 38, no. 1, (January 2004): 50, downloaded May 28, 2005.

45. Discussed in Douglas Haaland, "Who is the Safest Bet for the Job? Find Out Why the Guy in the Next Cubicle May Be the Next Accident Waiting to Happen," *Security Management* 49, no. 2, (February 2005): 51–57.

46. "Thai Research Points to Role of Personality in Road Accidents," *Asia and Africa Intelligence Wire*, February 23, 2005, downloaded May 28, 2005; Donald Bashline, et al., "Bad Behavior: Personality Tests Can Help Underwriters Identify High-Risk Drivers." *Best's Review* 105, no. 12, (April 2005): 63–64.

47. Todd Nighswonger, "Threat of Terror Impacts Workplace Safety," *Occupational Hazards*, July 2002, pp. 24–26.

48. Michael Blotzer, "Safety by Design," *Occupational Hazards*, May 1999, pp. 39–40, and http://www.designsafe.com/dsesoftware.php, accessed May 26, 2007.

49. Susannah Figura, "Don't Slip Up on Safety," *Occupational Hazards*, November 1996, pp. 29–31. See also Russ Wood, "Defining the Boundaries of Safety," *Occupational Hazards*, January 2001, pp. 41–43.

50. James Zeigler, "Protective Clothing: Exploring the Wearability Issue," *Occupational Hazards*, September 2000, pp. 81–82.

51. Tom Andrews, "Getting Employees Comfortable with PPE," *Occupational Hazards*, January 2000, pp. 35–38. Note that personal protective equipment can backfire. As one expert says, ". . . making a job safer with machine guards or PPE lowers people's risk perceptions and thus can lead to an increase in at risk behavior." Therefore, also train employees not to let their guards down. E. Scott Geller, "The Thinking and Seeing Components of People-Based Safety," *Occupational Hazards*, December 2006, pp. 38–40.

52. "The Complete Guide to Personal Protective Equipment," *Occupational Hazards*, January 1999, pp. 49–60. See also Edwin Zalewski, "Noise Control: It's More than Just Earplugs: OSHA Requires Employers to Evaluate Engineering and Administrative Controls Before Using Personal Protective Equipment," *Occupational Hazards*, September 2006, v68 i9 p. 48(3).

53. Sandy Smith, "Protecting Vulnerable Workers," *Occupational Hazards*, April 2004, pp. 25–28.

54. Katherine Torres, "Challenges in Protecting a Young Workforce," *Occupational Hazards*, May 2006, pp. 24–27.

55. Linda Tapp, "We Can Do It: Protecting Women," *Occupational Hazards*, October 2003, pp. 26–28.

56. Robert Pater, "Boosting Safety with an Aging Workforce," *Occupational Hazards*, March 2006, p. 24.

57. Cynthia Ross, "How to Protect the Aging Workforce," *Occupational Hazards*, January 2005, pp. 38–42, and Cynthia Ross, "How to Protect the Aging Workforce," *Occupational Hazards*, February 2005, pp. 52–54.

58. Elizabeth Rogers and William Wiatrowski, "Injuries, Illnesses, and Fatalities among Older Workers," *Monthly Labor Review* 128, no. 10, October 2005, pp. 24–30.

59. William Kincaid, "10 Habits of Effective Safety Managers," *Occupational Hazards*, November 1996, pp. 41–43. See also, Sandy Smith, "Breakthrough Safety Management," *Occupational Hazards*, June 2004, p. 43.

60. Dov Zohar, "A Group Level Model of Safety Climate: Testing the Effect of a Group Climate on Microaccidents in Manufacturing Jobs," *Journal of Applied Psychology* 85, no. 4 (2000), pp. 587–596. See also Judith Erickson, "Corporate Culture: The Key to Safety Performance," *Occupational Hazards*, April 2000, p. 45.

61. Gerald Borofsky, Michelle Bielema, and James Hoffman, "Accidents, Turnover, and Use of a Pre-Employment Screening Interview," *Psychological Reports*, 1993, pp. 1067–1076.

62. Ibid., p. 1072. See also Keith Rosenblum, "The Companion Solution to Ergonomics: Pretesting for the Job" *Risk Management*, November 2003, v50 i11 p. 26(6).

63. Dan Hartshorn, "The Safety Interview," *Occupational Hazards*, October 1999, pp. 107–111.

64. *Workers' Compensation Manual for Managers and Supervisors*, pp. 22–23.

65. John Rekus, "Is Your Safety Training Program Effective?" *Occupational Hazards*, August 1999, pp. 37–39.

66. See for example, Josh Cable, "Seven Suggestions for a Successful Safety Incentive Program," *Occupational Hazards*, March 2005, vol. 67, issue 3, pp. 39–43.

67. Don Williamson and Jon Kauffman, "From Tragedy to Triumph: Safety Grows Wings at Golden Eagle," *Occupational Hazards*, February 2006, pp. 17–25.

68. See for example, Josh Cable, "Safety Incentives Strategies," *Occupational Hazards* 67, no. 4, April 2005, p. 37. E. Scott Geller, December 2006, op.cit.

69. James Nash, "Construction Safety: Best Practices in Training Hispanic Workers," *Occupational Hazards*, February 2004, pp. 35–38.

70. Ibid., p. 37.

71. James Nash, "Rewarding the Safety Process," *Occupational Hazards*, March 2000, pp. 29–34.

72. Quoted in Josh Cable, "Seven Suggestions for a Successful Safety Incentives Program," *Occupational Hazards* 67, no. 3, March 2005, pp. 39–43.

73. Judi Komaki, Kenneth Barwick, and Lawrence Scott, "A Behavioral Approach to Occupational Safety: Pinpointing and Reinforcing Safe Performance in a Food Manufacturing Plant," *Journal of Applied Psychology* 63 (August 1978), pp. 434–445. See also Anat Arkin, "Incentives to Work Safely," *Personnel Management* 26, no. 9 (September 1994), pp. 48–52; Peter Making and Valerie Sutherland, "Reducing Accidents Using a Behavioral Approach," *Leadership and Organizational Development Journal* 15, no. 5 (1994), pp. 5–10. Sandy Smith, "Why Cash Isn't King," *Occupational Hazards*, March 2004, pp. 37–38.

74. Stan Hudson and Tim Gordon, "Tenneco's Drive to Become Injury Free," *Occupational Hazards*, May 2000, pp. 85–87. For another example, see Terry Mathis, "Lean Behavior-Based Safety," *Occupational Hazards*, May 2005, pp. 33–34.

75. Kim McDaniel, "Employee Participation: A Vehicle for Safety by Designing," *Occupational Hazards*, May 2002, pp. 71–76.

76. For another good example, see Christopher Chapman, "Using Kaizen to Improve Safety and Ergonomics," *Occupational Hazards*, February 2006, pp. 27–29.

77. Linda Johnson, "Preventing Injuries: The Big Payoff," *Personnel Journal*, April 1994, pp. 61–64; David Webb, "The Bathtub Effect: Why Safety Programs Fail," *Management Review*, February 1994, pp. 51–54. See also http://www.osha.gov/Publications/osha2098.pdf, accessed May 26, 2007.

78. Lisa Cullen, "Safety Committees: A Smart Business Decision," *Occupational Hazards*, May 1999, pp. 99–104. See also http://www.osha.gov/Publications/osha2098.pdf, accessed May 26, 2007.

79. Michael Blotzer, "PDA Software Offers Auditing Advances," *Occupational Hazards*, December 2001, p. 11.

80. Anthea Zacharatos et al., "High-Performance Work Systems and Occupational Safety," *Journal of Applied Psychology* 90, no. 1, 2005, pp. 77–93.

81. Ibid., p. 89.

82. Note that the vast majority of workers' injury related deaths occur not at work, but when the employees are off the job, often at home. More employers, including Johnson & Johnson, are therefore implementing safety campaigns encouraging employees to apply safe practices at home, as well as at work. Katherine Torres, "Safety Hits Home," *Occupational Hazards*, July 2006, pp. 19–23.

83. Michelle Campolieti and Douglas Hyatt, "Further Evidence on the 'Monday Effect' in Workers' Compensation," *Industrial and Labor Relations Review* 59, no. 3, April 2006, pp. 438–450.

84. See for example, Rob Wilson, "Five Ways to Reduce Workers' Compensation Claims," *Occupational Hazards*, December 2005, pp. 43–46.

85. "Strict Policies Mean Big Cuts in Premiums," *Occupational Hazards*, May 2000, p. 51.

86. See for example, *Workers' Compensation Manual for Managers and Supervisors*, pp. 36–39.

87. "Study: No Warm Welcome After Comp Leave," *Occupational Hazards*, February 2001, p. 57.

88. Ibid., p. 51.

89. Donna Clendenning, "Taking a Bite Out of Workers' Comp Costs," *Occupational Hazards*, September 2000, pp. 85–86.

90. This is based on Paul Puncochar, "The Science and Art to Identifying Workplace Hazards," *Occupational Hazards*, September 2003, pp. 50–54.

91. Ibid., p. 52.

92. Marco Wysong, "A Prescription for Managing Chemicals: Use These Strategies for Successful Electronic MSDS," *Industrial Safety and Hygiene News* 37, no. 1 (January 2003), p. 42.

93. Michael Blotzer, "PDA Software Offers Auditing Advances," p. 11.

94. Sandy Smith, "SARS: What Employers Need to Know," *Occupational Hazards*, July 2003, pp. 33–35.

95. "15% of Workers Drinking, Drunk, or Hungover while at Work, According to New University Study," *BNA Bulletin to Management*, January 24, 2006, p. 27.

96. Todd Nighswonger, "Just Say Yes to Preventing Substance Abuse," *Occupational Hazards*, April 2000, pp. 39–41.

97. "Facing Facts About Workplace Substance Abuse," *Rough Notes* 144, no. 5 (May 2001), pp. 114–118.

98. See, for example, Kathryn Tyler, "Happiness from a Bottle?" *HR Magazine*, May 2002, pp. 30–37.

99. William Corinth, "Pre-Employment Drug Testing," *Occupational Hazards*, July 2002, p. 56.

100. Diane Cadrain, "Are Your Employees' Drug Tests Accurate?" *HR Magazine*, January 2003, pp. 41–45.

101. Brenda Sunoo, "Positive Drug Test Results: Terminate or Rehabilitate?" *Personnel Journal*, December 1996, p. 94.

102. Ibid., p. 94. See also Carrie Printz, "No Practice Is Immune," *American Medical News*, January 16, 2006, v49 i2 p. 21(2).

103. This is quoted from "Drug-Free Workplace: New Federal Requirements," *BNA Bulletin to Management*, February 9, 1989, pp. 1–4. Note that the Drug-Free Workplace Act does not mandate or mention testing employees for illegal drug use. See also http://www.dol.gov/elaws/drugfree.htm, and http://www.dot.gov/ost/dapc/ (this site contains detailed guidelines on urine sampling, who's covered, etc.) both accessed May 26, 2007.

104. "Alcohol Misuse Prevention Programs: Department of Transportation Final Rules," *BNA Bulletin to Management*, March 24, 1994, pp. 1–8. See also http://www.dol.gov/elaws/drugfree.htm and http://www.dot.gov/ost/dapc/, both accessed May 26, 2007.

105. "Stress, Depression Cost Employers," *Occupational Hazards*, December 1998, p. 24. See also Charlene Solomon, "Stressed to the Limit," *Workforce*, September 1999, pp. 48–54, and "To Slash Health-Care Costs, Look to the Company Culture," *Managing Benefits Plans*, December 2004, p. 1(5).

106. Karl Albrecht, *Stress and the Manager* (Englewood Cliffs, NJ: Spectrum, 1979). For a discussion of the related symptoms of depression, see James Krohe Jr., "An Epidemic of Depression?" *Across-the-Board*, September 1994, pp. 23–27, and Todd Nighswonger, "Stress Management," *Occupational Hazards*, September 1999, p. 100.

107. Catalina Dolar, "Meditation Gives Your Mind Permanent Working Holiday; Relaxation can Improve Your Business Decisions and Your Overall Health," *Investors Business Daily*, March 24, 2004, p. 89. See also, "Meditation Helps Employees Focus, Relieve Stress," *BNA Bulletin to Management*, February 20, 2007, p. 63.

108. Kathryn Tyler, "Stress Management," *HR magazine*, September 2006, pp. 79–82.

109. "Going Head to Head with Stress," *Personnel Today*, April 26, 2005, p. 1.

110. Madan Mohan Tripathy, "Burnout Stress Syndrome in Managers," *Management and Labor Studies* 27, no. 2 (April 2002), pp. 89–111.

111. Mina Westman and Dov Eden, "Effects of a Respite from Work on Burnout: Vacation Relief and Fade-Out," *Journal of Applied Psychology* 82, no. 4 (1997), pp. 516–527.

112. Ibid., p. 516.

113. Ibid., p. 526. See also Charlotte Fritz and Sabine Sonnentag, "Recovery, Well-being, And Performance-Related Outcomes: The Role of Workload and Vacation Experiences," *Journal of Applied Psychology*, July 2006, v91 i4 p. 936(10).

114. Todd Nighswonger, "Depression: The Unseen Safety Risk," *Occupational Hazards*, April 2002, pp. 38–42.

115. Ibid., p. 40.

116. "Employers Must Move From Awareness to Action in Dealing with Worker Depression," *BNA Bulletin to Management*, April 29, 2004, p. 137.

117. See for example Felix Chima, "Depression and the Workplace: Occupational Social Work Development and Intervention," *Employee Assistance Quarterly* 19, no. 4, 2004, pp. 1–20.

118. Ibid.

119. "Risk of Carpal Tunnel Syndrome Not Linked to Heavy Computer Work, Study Says," *BNA Bulletin to Management*, June 28, 2001, p. 203.

120. www.OSHA.gov, downloaded May 28, 2005.

121. Anne Chambers, "Computervision Syndrome: Relief Is in Sight," *Occupational Hazards*, October 1999, pp. 179–184, and www.OSHA.gov/ETOOLS/computerworkstations/index.html, downloaded May 28, 2005.

122. Sondra Lotz Fisher, "Are Your Employees Working Ergosmart?" *Personnel Journal*, December 1996, pp. 91–92. See also http://www.cdc.gov/od/ohs/Ergonomics/compergo.htm, accessed May 26, 2007.

123. Ronald Davis, "Exposure to Environmental Tobacco Smoke: Identifying and Protecting Those at Risk," *Journal of the American Medical Association*, December 9, 1998, pp. 147–148; see also Al Karr, "Lighting Up," *Safety and Health* 162, no. 3 (September 2000), pp. 62–66.

124. Kenneth Sovereign, *Personnel Law* (Upper Saddle River, NJ: Prentice Hall, 1999), pp. 76–79.

125. Daniel Warner, "We Do Not Hire Smokers," p. 138. See also "Workplace Smoking: How Far Should You Go?," *Managing Benefits Plans*, June 2005, i05-06 p. 2(2).

126. Stephen Bates, "Where There Is Smoke, There are Terminations: Smokers Fired to Save Health Costs," *HR Magazine* 50, no. 3, March 2005, pp. 28–29.

127. "Worker Opens Fire at Ohio Jeep Plant," *Occupational Hazards*, March 2005, p. 16.

128. Gus Toscano and Janaice Windau, "The Changing Character of Fatal Work Injuries," *Monthly Labor Review*, October 1994, p. 17. See also Robert Grossman, "Bulletproof Practices," *HR Magazine*, November 2002, pp. 34–42.

129. Kelly Gurchiek, "Workplace Violence on the Upswing," *HR Magazine*, July 2005, p. 27.

130. Manon Mireille LeBlanc and E. Kevin Kelloway, "Predictors and Outcomes of Workplace Violence and Aggression," *Journal of Applied Psychology* 87, no. 3 (2002), pp. 444–453.

131. Kenneth Diamond, "The Gender-Motivated Violence Act: What Employers Should Know," *Employee Relations Law Journal* 25, no. 4 (Spring 2000), pp. 29–41.

132. Paul Viollis and Doug Kane, "At Risk Terminations: Protecting Employees, Preventing Disaster," *Risk Management Magazine* 52, no. 5, (May 2005): 28–33.

133. "Workplace Violence: Sources and Solutions," *BNA Bulletin to Management*, November 4, 1993, p. 345. See also, "Creating a Safer Workplace: Simple Steps Bring Results," *Safety Now*, (September 2002): 1–2, and J. W. Elphonestone, "Better Safe Than Sorry: Hotels, Malls Balance Security Measures with Public Accessibility," *Commercial Property News* 19, no. 10, (May 16, 2005): 30.

134. "OSHA Addresses Top Homicide Risk," *BNA Bulletin to Management*, May 14, 1998, p. 148. See also http://www.osha.gov/Publications/osha3148.pdf, accessed May 26, 2007.

135. Scott Douglas and Mark Martinko, "Exploring the Role of Individual Differences in the Prediction of Workplace Aggression," *Journal of Applied Psychology* 86, no. 4 (2001), p. 554.

136. Dawn Anfuso, "Workplace Violence," *Personnel Journal*, October 1994, pp. 66–77.

137. Feliu, "Workplace Violence and the Duty of Care," p. 395.

138. Quoted from ibid., p. 395.

139. "Preventing Workplace Violence," *BNA Bulletin to Management*, June 10, 1993, p. 177. See also Paul Viollis and Doug Kane, "At-risk Terminations: Protecting Employees, Preventing Disaster," *Risk Management*, May 2005, v52 i5 p. 28(5).

140. Quoted or paraphrased from Younger, "Violence Against Women in the Workplace," p. 177, and based on recommendations from Chris Hatcher. See also Paul Viollis and Doug Kane, "At-risk Terminations: Protecting Employees, Preventing Disaster," op. cit.

141. Karl Acquino et al., "How Employees Respond to Personal Offense: The Effect of the Blame Attribution, Victim Status, and Offender Status on Revenge and Reconciliation in the Workplace," *Journal of Applied Psychology* 86, no. 1 (2001), pp. 52–59.

142. Ibid. p. 57.

143. Feliu, "Workplace Violence," pp. 401–402.

144. Eve Tahmincioglu, "Vigilance in the Face of Layoff Rage," *New York Times*, August 1, 2001, pp. C1, C6.

145. Shari Caudron, "Target HR," *Workforce*, August 1998, pp. 44–52.

146. Diane Cadrain, "And Stay Out! Using Restraining Orders Can Be an Effective and Proactive Way of Preventing Workplace Violence," *HR Magazine*, August 2002, pp. 83–86.

147. Donna Rosato, "New Industry Helps Managers Fight Violence," *USA Today*, August 8, 1995, p. 1.

148. Helen Frank Bensimon, "What to Do About Anger in the Workplace," *Training and Development* 51, no. 9 (September 1997), pp. 28–32. See also Paul Viollis and Doug Kane, "At-risk Terminations: Protecting Employees, Preventing Disaster," *Risk Management*, May 2005, v52 i5 p. 28(5).

149. DiLorenzo and Carroll, "The Growing Menace," p. 25.

150. Quoted from Feliu, "Workplace Violence," p. 393.

151. DiLorenzo and Carroll, "The Growing Menace," p. 27.

152. This is based on "New Challenges for Health and Safety in the Workplace," Society for Human Resource Management, *Workplace Vision*, no. 3 (2003), pp. 2–4. See also, "Protecting Chemical Plants From Terrorists: Opposing Views," *Occupational Hazards*, February 2004, pp. 18–20.

153. "Survey Finds Reaction to September 11 Attacks Spurred Companies to Prepare for Disasters," *BNA Bulletin to Management*, November 29, 2005, p. 377.

154. "Focus on Corporate Security," BNA HR Executive Series, Fall 2001, p. 4.

155. Unless otherwise noted, following based on Richard Maurer, "Keeping Your Security Program Active," *Occupational Hazards*, March 2003, pp. 49–52.

156. Ibid., p. 50.

157. Ibid., p. 50.

158. Della Roberts, "Are Your Ready for Biometrics?" *HR Magazine*, March 2003, pp. 95–99.

159. Maurer, "Keeping Your Security Program Alive," p. 52.

160. Craig Schroll, "Are Your Employees Ready to Leave the Building? Evacuation Planning: A Matter of Life-and-Death," *Occupational Hazards*, June 2002, pp. 49–51.

161. Ibid., p. 52, and Li Yuan, et al, "Texting When There's Trouble," The Wall Street Journal, April 18, 2007, p. B.1.

162. Louis Obdyke, "Investigating Security Breaches, Workplace Theft, and Employee Fraud," *Society for Human Resource Management Legal Report*, January–February 2003, pp. 1–2.

17 Managing Global Human Resources

Wal-Mart, a company famously resistant to unions in America, recently had a surprise. Opening stores in China at a fast clip, it attempted to dissuade local unions there from organizing Wal-Mart's employees. However, the All China Federation of Trade Unions (ACFTU), with strong government backing, quickly established itself in several Wal-Mart stores, and it seems likely that it will succeed in unionizing many Wal-Mart China workers. •

After studying this chapter, you should be able to:

1 List the HR challenges of international business.
2 Illustrate how intercountry differences affect HRM.
3 Discuss the global differences and similiarities in HR practices.
4 Explain five ways to improve international assignments through selection.
5 Discuss how to train and maintain international employees.

To this point, we've discussed human resource management's functional areas, including job analysis, recruitment, selection, training, appraisal, compensation, and labor relations and safety. The purpose of this final chapter is to improve your effectiveness at applying your human resources knowledge and skills in an international arena. The topics we'll discuss include the internationalization of business, intercountry differences affecting HR, improving international assignments through selection, and training and maintaining international employees.

① List the HR challenges of international business.

HR AND THE INTERNATIONALIZATION OF BUSINESS

Most companies do business abroad. Huge firms like Procter & Gamble and IBM have long had extensive overseas operations, of course. But with the globalization of the world economy, even small firms are finding that success depends on marketing and managing overseas.

The Global Challenges

Doing so presents firms with various management challenges. Plans for marketing and producing goods abroad are required. And, the employer needs to install all those management systems it will require to manage its overseas activities. These management systems include organization structures, managerial controls, worldwide banking relationships, and, of course, human resource management systems for recruiting, selecting, training, and appraising and compensating its workers abroad.

Managing human resources internationally creates questions and challenges all its own. For example, "Should we staff the local offices abroad with local or U.S. managers?" "How should we appraise and pay our local employees?" "How should we deal with the unions in our offices abroad?" and, "How will cultural differences abroad impact the sorts of employee selection, appraisal, and compensation policies we use?"

Several years ago, researchers asked senior international human resource managers, "What are the key global pressures affecting human resource management practices in your firm?" The three that emerged were:[1]

- *Deployment.* Easily getting the right skills to where we need them, regardless of geographic location.
- ***Knowledge and innovation dissemination.*** Spreading state-of-the-art knowledge and practices throughout the organization regardless of where they originate.
- ***Identifying and developing talent on a global basis.***[2]

Dealing with global staffing challenges like these is quite complex. In China, for instance, special insurance should cover emergency evacuations for serious health problems, and medical facilities in Russia may not meet international standards. So, the challenge of international human resource management doesn't just come from the vast distances involved (though this is important). Perhaps the bigger challenge is in coping with the cultural, political, legal, and economic differences among countries and their peoples. These are the sorts of issues we'll address in this chapter. We'll start with intercountry differences.

② Illustrate how intercountry differences affect HRM.

How Intercountry Differences Affect HRM

Companies operating only within the borders of the United States generally have the luxury of dealing with a relatively limited set of economic, cultural, and legal variables. The United States is a capitalist, competitive society. And while the U.S. workforce reflects a multitude of cultural and ethnic backgrounds, shared values (such as an appreciation for democracy) help to blur potentially sharp cultural differences. Although the different states and municipalities certainly have their own employment laws, a basic federal framework helps produce a fairly predictable set of legal guidelines regarding matters such as employment discrimination, labor relations, and safety and health.

A company operating multiple units abroad isn't blessed with such homogeneity. For example, minimum legally mandated holidays range from none in the United Kingdom to five weeks per year in Luxembourg. And while Italy has no formal requirements for employee representatives on boards of directors, they're required in Denmark for companies with more than 30 employees. The point is that managers have to be cognizant of and generally adapt their human resource policies and practices to the countries in which they're operating. Consider some examples.

Cultural Factors   Countries differ widely in their *cultures*—in other words, in the basic values their citizens adhere to, and in the ways these values manifest themselves in the nation's arts, social programs, politics, and ways of doing things. For example, in a study of about 330 managers from Hong Kong, the People's Republic of China, and the United States, the U.S. managers tended to be most concerned with getting the job done. Chinese managers were most concerned with maintaining a harmonious environment, and Hong Kong managers fell between these extremes.[3]

A classic study by Professor Geert Hofstede identified other international cultural differences. For example, Hofstede says societies differ in *power distance*—in other words, the extent to which the less powerful members of institutions accept and expect an unequal distribution of power.[4] He concluded that acceptance of such inequality was higher in some countries (such as Mexico) than in others (such as Sweden).

Similarly, compared to U.S. employees, "Mexican workers expect managers to keep their distance rather than to be close, and to be formal rather than informal."[5] In Germany, you should never arrive even a few minutes late and should always address senior people formally, with their titles.[6] Such cultural differences are a two-way street.[7] For example, in the Intel booklet "Things You Need to Know About Working in the U.S.A.," topics for incoming workers from abroad include sexual harassment, recognition of gay and lesbian rights, and Intel's expectations about behavior.[8] (Visitors abroad will also notice that globalization is blurring national differences in cultures, as people come to share common cultural experiences like McDonalds).[9]

In any case, cultural differences do influence human resource policies and practices. For example, American's emphasis on individuality may help to explain why European managers have more employment-related constraints, for instance with regard to laying off workers.[10] As another example, local cultural norms can undermine employers' attempts to institute uniform codes of conduct. Thus in countries with a history of fascist rule, employees often had to divulge information about their coworkers. Here, whistleblowing rules, popular in America, are frowned upon.[11]

Economic Systems   Differences in *economic systems* also translate into differences in human resource management policies. For one thing, some countries are more wedded to the ideals of free enterprise than are others. For instance, France—though a capitalist society—imposed tight restrictions on employers' rights to discharge workers, and limited the number of hours an employee could legally work each week.

Employers need to adapt their HR practices to the cultures of the countries where they do business.

Differences in labor costs are also substantial. Hourly compensation costs in U.S. dollars for production workers range from $2.38 in Mexico to $5.41 in Taiwan, $17.47 in the United Kingdom, $21.33 in the United States, and $25.08 in Germany, for instance.[12]

As another example, there are wide gaps in hours worked. Portuguese workers average about 1,980 hours of work annually, while German workers average 1,648 hours. Several European countries, including the United Kingdom and Germany, require substantial severance pay to departing employees, usually equal to at least one years' service in Germany. Compared to the usual two or three weeks of U.S. vacation, workers in France can expect two and a half days of paid holiday per full month of service per year, and Germans get about 18 vacation days per year after six months of service.

Legal and Industrial Relations Factors   Legal as well as industrial relations (the relationships among the worker, the union, and the employer) factors also vary from country to country. For example, the U.S. practice of employment at will does not exist in Europe, where firing or laying off workers are usually expensive. And in many European countries, *work councils* replace the informal or union-centric worker–management mediations typical in U.S. firms. Work councils are formal, employee-elected groups of worker representatives that meet monthly with managers to discuss topics ranging from no-smoking policies to layoffs.[13]

codetermination

Employees have the legal right to a voice in setting company policies.

Codetermination is the rule in Germany and several other countries. **Codetermination** means employees have the legal right to a voice in setting company policies. Workers elect their own representatives to the supervisory board of the employer, and there is a vice president for labor at the top management level.[14] In the United States, HR policies on most matters such as wages and benefits are set by the employer, or by the employer in negotiations with its labor unions. The codetermination laws, including the Works Constitution Act, largely mold human resource policies in German firms.

HR Abroad: The European Union   Over the past two decades, the separate countries of the former European Community (EC) were unified into a common market for goods, services, capital, and even labor called the European Union (EU). Tariffs for goods moving across borders from one EU country to another generally disappeared, and employees (with some exceptions) now find it easy to move freely between jobs in the EU countries. The introduction of a single currency—the euro—has further blurred many of these differences.

Companies doing business in Europe must adjust their human resource policies and practices to both European Union (EU) directives as well as to country-specific employment laws. The directives are basically EU laws, the objectives of which are binding on all member countries (although each member country can implement the directives as they so choose). For example, the EU directive on confirmation of employment requires employers to provide employees with written terms and conditions of their employment, but these terms vary from country to country.[15] In England, a detailed written statement is required, including things like rate of pay, date employment began, and hours of work. Germany doesn't require a written contract, but it's still customary to have one specifying most particulars about the job and conditions of work.

The interplay of directives and country laws means that human resource practices must vary from country to country. For example:[16]

- ***Minimum EU wages.*** Most EU countries have minimum wage systems in place. Some set national limits. Others allow employers and unions to work out their own minimum wages.

- *Working hours.* The EU sets the workweek at 48 hours, but most countries set it at 40 hours a week, and some, like France, implemented a 35 hour workweek.
- *Employee representation.* Europe has many levels of employee representation. In France, for instance employers with 50 or more employers must consult with their employees' representatives on matters including working conditions, training, and profit-sharing plans and layoffs. In Italy, all employers with 15 or more employees must consult with their work councils on internal work rules and the working environment. By 2008, most companies—including all those with 50 or more employees in the EU—must "inform and consult" employees about employee-related actions, even if the firms don't operate outside their own countries' borders. And the consultation will then be "ongoing" rather than just for major, strategic decisions.[17]
- *Termination of employment.* There are a wide range of required notice periods when dismissing employees in Europe. They range from none in Spain to two months in Italy.

HR Abroad: China   All firms in China must deal with national issues including relatively scarce employment services and an increasingly active union movement. However, how they deal with these issues depends to a large extent on the ownership of the firm. State-owned enterprises use fewer modern human resource management tools than do giant Chinese multinationals like Lenova, for instance. There are therefore wide variations in HR management practices among companies in China, and between Chinese and Western firms. For example:

Recruiting   Because of governmental migration and other constraints, it is surprisingly difficult to recruit, hire, and retain good employees. Sporadic labor shortages are fairly widespread.

   In recruiting in China, employers should know that recruiting effectiveness depends to a great extent on nonrecruitment human resource management issues. Employees are highly career oriented, and gravitate toward employers that can provide the best career advancement training and opportunities. Firms like Siemens China, with impressive training and development programs, have the least difficulty attracting good candidates. Poaching employees is a serious matter in China. The employer must verify that the applicant is free to sign a new employment agreement.

Selection   The dominant employee selection method involves analyzing the applicant's résumé and then interviewing him or her.

   Unfortunately, as we saw in Chapter 6, employment interviews are not particularly useful for distinguishing among candidates who will or will not succeed on the job. When the interview is just one selection tool of many, this may not be a big concern. However, where it is the predominant and, often, sole selection tool, as in China, employers need to ensure that their interviews are effective. The ideal way to do this is to institute a structured interview process, as several of the largest foreign firms in China have done.

Appraising   Employee appraisal is particularly sensitive to the cultural realities in China. The challenge comes from the Chinese emphasis on harmony, face, and nonconfrontation. The appraisal therefore needs to follow the formalities of saving face and avoiding confrontational, tension-producing situations. In general, it's best to talk in terms of objective work data (as opposed to personal comments like "you're too slow").

Compensation   Although many managers endorse performance-based pay in China, many employers, to preserve group harmony, make incentive pay a small part of the pay package. And, as in other parts of Asia, team incentives are advisable.[18]

❸ Discuss the global differences and similiarities in HR practices.

GLOBAL DIFFERENCES AND SIMILARITIES IN HUMAN RESOURCE PRACTICES

As these examples show, human resource management practices tend to differ from country to country. One long-term study helps to illustrate this. Beginning in the 1990s, human resource management scholars from 13 countries and regions used the *Best International Human Resource Management Practices Survey* to assess human resource management practices around the world.[19] The results provide a snapshot of the differences and similarities in a wide range of countries. We'll look at some of these next.

Personnel Selection Procedures

Employers around the world tend to use similar criteria and methods for selecting employees. As in the United States, employers around the world usually rank "personal interviews," "the person's ability to perform the technical requirements of the job," and "proven work experiences in a similar job" at or near the top of the criteria or methods they use. The top rankings were the same or similar in the United States, Australia, and Latin America, for instance. Cultural differences did have some impact across countries, however. In Mexico, "having the right connections" was a top consideration in being hired. "Employee tests" were one of the three top selection practices in the People's Republic of China, Indonesia, and Korea, but not in the United States. And, "the person's ability to get along well with others already working here" was one of the three personnel selection criteria in Japan and Taiwan, but not in other countries.

The Purpose of the Performance Appraisal

There tends to be more variation in how employers in different countries use performance appraisals.[20] For example, employers in Taiwan, the United States, and Canada rank "to determine pay" as one of the top three reasons for appraising performance, while that purpose is of relatively little significance in Korea and Mexico. Employers in the United States, Taiwan, and Australia emphasize using the appraisal to "document the employee's performance," while in Mexico and the People's Republic of China this purpose is far down the list. "To recognize subordinate" was a main purpose for appraisals in Japan and Mexico, but nowhere else.

Training and Development Practices

The amount of training firms provide varies substantially from country to country.[21] For example, training expenditures per employee range from a low of $241 per employee in Asia (outside Japan) to $359 in Japan and $724 in the United States. Similarly, the total hours of training per eligible employees per year ranges from 26 total training hours in Asia up to just over 49 total hours of training per year in Europe.

However, when it comes to the purposes of training, there are usually more similarities than differences across countries.[22] Employers just about everywhere rank "to improve technical abilities" as the main reason for providing employees with training.

The Use of Pay Incentives

Findings regarding the use of financial incentives were somewhat counterintuitive. Given the People's Republic of China's communist roots, and the traditional U.S. emphasis on pay for performance, one might have expected U.S. managers to stress incentives more heavily than their Chinese peers. However, that was not the case. Based on this survey, in terms of their use, incentives play an only "moderate" role in U.S. pay

Comparing Small Businesses, HR Practices in the United States and China

Intercountry differences like these tend to manifest themselves in small businesses around the world, too. One study compared compensation practices in 248 small (less than 500 employees) U.S. companies with those in 148 small Chinese companies.[23]

The researchers found several differences. First, in terms of *job analysis*, jobs in small Chinese companies tend to be more narrowly defined and set in stone than those in small U.S. businesses. Work in small Chinese firms appears to be more structured than in comparably sized U.S. firms. The small Chinese firms have more up-to-date job descriptions, their employees deviate from their assigned job duties less frequently, their job descriptions tend to cover all the job's duties, and in general the Chinese job descriptions shape the job's duties, rather than the employee.

Second, the researchers found significant differences between U.S. and Chinese firms in *performance appraisal practices*. In Chinese firms, compared to the United States, performance appraisals more often focus on the bottom line; appraisal feedback is evaluative rather than developmental; the appraisal focuses on objective, quantifiable results; and the main objective is to improve performance (rather than to develop the employee). So, perhaps surprisingly, performance appraisals in small Chinese companies tend to be more hard-nosed than are those in small U.S. firms.

These differences extend to the firms' *actual pay practices*. Again (perhaps surprisingly given China's communist roots), there's significantly more emphasis on incentive pay than guaranteed salaries in China's small businesses. Employees in the Chinese firms are more likely to receive bonuses based on the company's profits, to receive bonuses based on companywide gainsharing plans, to get stock or stock options as incentives, and to be paid based mostly on an incentive plan rather than on a guaranteed income plan. On the other hand, there tends to be less variation among Chinese employees in pay, and more emphasis than in U.S. firms on seniority.

packages. In the People's Republic of China, Japan, and Taiwan incentives play a relatively important role.[24]

Owners of small businesses are not immune to global differences like these. The "When You're on Your Own" feature illustrates this.

HOW TO IMPLEMENT A GLOBAL HR SYSTEM

Given such cross-cultural differences in human resource management practices, one could reasonably ask, "Is it realistic for a company to try to institute a standardized human resource management system in all or most of its facilities around the world?" A study suggests that the answer is "yes." In brief, the study's results show that employers may have to defer to local managers on some specific human resource management policy issues. However, in general, the findings also suggest that big intercountry policy differences are often not necessary or even advisable. The important thing is that the employer needs to understand how to install its preferred human resource policies and practices globally.

In this study, the researchers interviewed human resource personnel from six global companies—Agilent, Dow, IBM, Motorola, Procter & Gamble, and Shell Oil Co.—as well as international human resources consultants.[25] The study's overall conclusion was that employers who successfully implement global HR systems do so by applying various best practices. Doing so enables them to implement more or less uniform global human resource systems around the world. The basic idea is to devise systems that are *acceptable* to employees in units around the world, and ones that the employers can *develop* and *implement* more effectively. We'll look at each of these three requirements' best practices.

Making the Global HR System More *Acceptable*

First, employers engage in three best practices so that the global human resource systems they eventually develop will be *acceptable* to their local managers around the world. These best practices include:

1. *Remember that global systems are more accepted in truly global organizations.* These companies and all their managers think of themselves as global in scope and perspective, and all or most functions and business units operate on a truly global basis. For example, truly global organizations require their managers to work on global teams, and identify and recruit and place the employees they hire globally. As one Shell manager put it, "If you're truly global, then you are hiring here [the United States] people who are going to immediately go and work in the Hague, and vice versa."[26] This makes it easier for managers everywhere to accept the global imperative for having a more standardized human resource management system.

2. *Investigate pressures to differentiate and determine their legitimacy.* Human resource managers seeking to standardize selection, training, appraisal, compensation, or other HR practices worldwide will always meet resistance from local managers who insist, "you can't do that here, because we are different culturally and in other ways." Based on their research, these investigators found that these "differences" are usually not persuasive. For example, when Dow wanted to implement an online employee recruitment and selection tool in a particular region abroad, the hiring managers there told Dow that there was no way their managers would use it. After investigating the supposed cultural roadblocks and then implementing the new system, "what we found is that the number of applicants went through the roof when we went online, and the quality of the applicants also increased."[27]

   However, the operative word here is "investigate"—do not try ramming through a change without ascertaining whether there may in fact be some reason for using a more locally appropriate system. Carefully assess whether the local culture or other differences might in fact undermine the new system. Be knowledgeable about local legal issues, and be willing to differentiate where necessary. Then, market test the new method.

3. *Try to work within the context of a strong corporate culture.* Companies that create a strong corporate culture find it easier to obtain agreement among far-flung employees when it comes time to implement standardized practices worldwide. For example, Procter & Gamble has a strong corporate culture. Because of how P&G recruits, selects, trains, and rewards them, its managers have a strong sense of shared values. For instance, Procter & Gamble emphasizes orderly growth, and its culture therefore encourages a relatively high degree of conformity among managers. New recruits quickly learn to think in terms of "we" instead of "I." They learn to value thoroughness, consistency, self-discipline, and a methodical approach. Because all P&G managers worldwide tend to share these values, they are in a sense more similar to each other than they are geographically different. Having such global unanimity makes it easier to develop and implement standardized human resource practices worldwide.

Developing a More Effective Global HR System

Similarly, the researchers found that these companies engaged in several best practices in *developing* effective worldwide human resource management systems.

1. ***Form global HR networks.*** The firm's human resource managers around the world should feel that they're not merely local HR managers, but are part of a greater whole, namely, the firm's global human resource management network. These six firms did this in various ways. For instance, they formed global teams, to help develop the new human resources systems. The researchers found that in developing global HR systems, the most critical factor for success is "creating an infrastructure of partners around the world that you use for support, for buy-in, for organization of local activities, and to help you better understand their own systems and their own challenges."[28] Treat the local human resource managers as equal partners, not just implementers.

2. ***Remember that it's more important to standardize ends and competencies than specific methods.*** For example, (with regard to screening applicants) the researchers concluded that "while companies may strive to standardize tools globally, the critical point is [actually] to standardize what is assessed but to be flexible in how it is assessed."[29] Thus, IBM uses a more or less standardized recruitment and selection process worldwide, but "details such as who conducts the interview (hiring manager vs. recruiter) or whether the prescreen is by phone or in person, differ by country."[30]

Implementing the Global HR System

Finally, in actually *implementing* the global HR systems, several best practices can help ensure a more effective implementation.

1. ***Remember, "You can't communicate enough."*** For example, "There's a need for constant contact with the decision makers in each country, as well as the people who will be implementing and using the system."[31]

2. ***Dedicate adequate resources for the global HR effort.*** For example, do not expect local HR offices to suddenly start implementing the new job analysis procedures unless the head office provides adequate resources for these additional activities. Table 17-1 below summarizes these best practices for instituting global HR systems.

STAFFING THE GLOBAL ORGANIZATION

Explain five ways to improve international assignments through selection.

Staffing the employer's global organization is the heart of international human resource management. The process involves identifying and selecting the people who will fill your positions abroad, and then placing them in those positions.

International Staffing: Home or Local?

expatriates (expats)
Noncitizens of the countries in which they are working.

home-country nationals
Citizens of the country in which the multinational company has its headquarters.

third-country nationals
Citizens of a country other than the parent or the host country.

Multinational companies (MNCs) employ several types of international managers. *Locals* are citizens of the countries where they are working. **Expatriates ("expats")** are noncitizens of the countries in which they are working (an American working in France is an expat).[32] **Home-country nationals** are citizens of the country in which the multinational company has its headquarters (so an American working for America-based GM's subsidiary in China is a home-country national, as well as an expat). **Third-country nationals** are citizens of a country other than the parent or the host country—for example, a British executive working in the Tokyo branch of a U.S. multinational bank.[33] Expatriates still represent a minority of multinationals' managers. "Most managerial positions are filled by locals rather than expatriates in both headquarters or foreign subsidiary operations."[34]

TABLE 17-1 Summary of Best Global HR Practices

Do . . .	Don't . . .
• Work within existing local systems—integrate global tools into local systems	• Try to do everything the same way everywhere
• Create a strong corporate culture	• Yield to every claim that "we're different"—make them prove it
• Create a global network for system development—global input is critical	• Force a global system on local people
• Treat local people as equal partners in system development	• Use local people just for implementation
• Assess common elements across geographies	• Use the same tools globally, unless you can show that they really work and are culturally appropriate
• Focus on what to measure and allow flexibility in how to measure	• Ignore cultural differences
• Allow for local additions beyond core elements	• Let technology drive your system design—you can't assume every location has the same level of technology investment and access
• Differentiate when necessary	• Assume that "if we build it they will come"—you need to market your tools or system and put change management strategies in place
• Train local people to make good decisions about which tools to use and how to do so	
• Communicate, communicate, communicate!	
• Dedicate resources for global HR efforts	
• Know, or have access to someone who knows, the legal requirements in each country	

Source: Ann Marie Ryan et al., "Designing and Implementing Global Staffing Systems: Part 2—Best Practices," *Human Resource Management* 42, no. 1 (Spring 2003), p. 93. Reproduced with permission of Society for Human Resource Management in the Format Textbook via Copyright Clearance Center.

Using Locals   There are several reasons employers rely more on local managers to fill their foreign subsidiary's management ranks. Many people don't want to work in a foreign country, and the cost of using expatriates is usually far greater than the cost of using local workers.[35] In one survey, employers reported a 21% attrition rate for expatriate employees, compared with an average of 10% for their general employee populations.[36] Local people may view the multinational as a "better citizen" if it uses local management talent, and some governments even press for the "nativization" of local management.[37] There may also be a fear that expatriates, knowing they're posted to the foreign subsidiary for only a few years, may overemphasize short-term results rather than more necessary long-term tasks.[38] Some companies don't realize what it actually costs to send an expatriate abroad. Agilent Technologies routinely estimated that it cost about three times the expatriate's annual salary to keep the person abroad for one year. When Agilent outsourced is expatriate program, it discovered that the costs were much higher. The firm then dramatically reduced the number of expats it sent abroad, from about 1000 to 300 per year.[39]

It's also become more difficult to bring workers into the United States from abroad. Under new rules in effect since 2005, U.S. employers must now try to recruit U.S. workers before filing foreign labor certification requests with the Department of Labor. In particular, employers must now first post open positions in the Department of Labor's job bank, and run two Sunday newspaper advertisements before filing such requests.[40]

Using Expats Yet there are also reasons for using expatriates—either home-country or third-country nationals—for staffing subsidiaries. The main reason is usually technical competence. In other words, employers often can't find local candidates with the required technical qualifications. Multinationals also view a successful stint abroad as a required step in developing top managers. (For instance, after a term abroad, the head of General Electric's Asia-Pacific region was transferred back to a top executive position as vice chairman at GE.) Control is another important reason to use expatriates. The assumption here is that home-country managers are already steeped in the firm's policies and culture, and thus more likely to apply headquarters' ways of doing things.

Other Solutions Today, the choice is not just between expatriate versus local employees; there are other solutions. Many employers have switched to more flexible expatriate assignments. Some dub these "short-term," "commuter," or "frequent-flier" assignments. They basically involve much travel but no formal relocation.[41] Other firms use Internet-based video technologies and group decision-making software to enable global virtual teams to do business without either travel or relocation.[42]

One survey found that about 78% of employers had some form of "localization" policy. This is a policy of transferring a home-country national employee to a foreign subsidiary as a "permanent transferee." The assumption here is that the employee would not be an expatriate but instead would become and be treated as, say, a French local hire.[43]

Offshoring

offshoring
Having local employees abroad do jobs that the firm's domestic employees previously did in-house.

Offshoring is an important international staffing issue. **Offshoring** means having local employees abroad do jobs that the firm's domestic employees previously did in-house. Offshoring is increasingly popular. Forrester Research projects that about 1.5 million jobs will move offshore by 2010, 2.5 million jobs will go by 2013, and over three million jobs will go by 2015.[44] Put another way, a report from the McKinsey Global Institute says that the total value of offshoring (also called outsourcing) will grow from about $33 billion in 2002, to over $100 billion in 2008.

Offshoring is very controversial. In the 1990s, it was mostly manufacturing jobs that employers shipped overseas. Between 2000 and 2015, the U.S. Labor Department and

IBM staffer leaves the offices of IBM Argentina. HR plays a big role in offshoring: recruiting and hiring the best people; providing information on local wage rates, working conditions, and productivity; making sure there is a supervisory and management structure in place; and seeing that required screening and training is done.

Forrester Research estimate that about 288,000 management jobs will go offshore, 472,000 computer jobs, 184,000 architecture jobs, almost 75,000 legal jobs, and about 1.7 million office jobs. Proponents contend that employers must offshore jobs to remain globally competitive, and that the money employers thereby save boosts research and development and, eventually, create even more domestic jobs for U.S. workers. Opponents naturally worry that this "jobs drain" will mean millions fewer jobs for American workers.

Offshoring and HR   The pros and cons notwithstanding, offshoring is a matter that human resource managers will have to deal with. For one thing, offshoring tends to be a uniquely HR-dependent activity. The traditional reason firms went abroad was to develop new markets or to open up new manufacturing facilities to serve local markets. In such cases, marketing, sales, and production executives naturally played the pivotal roles. Offshoring, on the other hand, mostly involves human resource management. Employers seeking to gain a cost advantage by offshoring, say, a call center, look to their human resource managers to help identify high-quality, low-cost talent abroad and to provide the necessary information on things like foreign wage rates, working conditions, and productivity.

Finding a city abroad that provides a wealth of low-paid, high-quality technically competent workers is only part of the task of making offshoring succeed. Among other things, the human resource manager also needs to make sure that there is an effective supervisory and management structure in place to manage these workers, and that all the employees receive the screening and training that they require. In staffing its local facilities, it may be advisable to retain local legal counsel, both to navigate local laws and for advice regarding cultural hiring practices.[45] Furthermore, particularly given the vast distances involved, the HR manager also needs to ensure that the compensation policies and working conditions are satisfactory. Offshoring, after all, is a fast-growing industry, and these local employees are just the sorts of mobile talent who can easily move to new employers.

Management Values and International Staffing Policy

What determines whether firms use locals or expats? Ideally, rational reasons like cost and competency will prevail. However, the company's top executives' values will also undoubtedly play a role. For example, experts often classify top executives' values as *ethnocentric, polycentric,* or *geocentric.* In an ethnocentrically run corporation, "the prevailing attitude is that home-country attitudes, management style, knowledge, evaluation criteria, and managers are superior to anything the host country might have to offer."[46] In the polycentric corporation, "there is a conscious belief that only host-country managers can ever really understand the culture and behavior of the host-country market; therefore, the foreign subsidiary should be managed by local people."[47] Geocentric executives believe they must scour the firm's whole management staff on a global basis, on the assumption that the best manager for a specific position anywhere may be in any of the countries in which the firm operates.

ethnocentric
The notion that home-country attitudes, management style, knowledge, evaluation criteria, and managers are superior to anything the host country has to offer.

Ethnocentric   These values translate into three broad international staffing policies. With an **ethnocentric** staffing policy, the firm fills key management jobs with parent-country nationals.[48] At Royal Dutch Shell, for instance, most financial officers around the world are Dutch nationals. Reasons given for ethnocentric staffing policies include lack of qualified host-country senior management talent, a desire to maintain a unified corporate culture and tighter control, and the desire to transfer the parent firm's core competencies (for instance, a specialized manufacturing skill) to a foreign subsidiary more expeditiously.[49]

polycentric
A conscious belief that only the host-country managers can ever really understand the culture and behavior of the host-country market.

Polycentric   A **polycentric**-oriented firm would staff its foreign subsidiaries with host-country nationals, and its home office with parent-country nationals. This may reduce the local cultural misunderstandings that might occur if it used expatriate managers. It will also almost undoubtedly be less expensive. One expert estimates that an expatriate executive can cost a firm up to three times as much as a domestic executive because of relocation expenses and other expenses such as schooling for children, annual home leave, and the need to pay income taxes in two countries.[50]

geocentric

The belief that the firm's whole management staff must be scoured on a global basis, on the assumption that the best manager of a specific position anywhere may be in any of the countries in which the firm operates.

Geocentric   A **geocentric** staffing policy "seeks the best people for key jobs throughout the organization, regardless of nationality."[51] This may let the global firm use its human resources more efficiently by transferring the best person to the open job, wherever he or she may be. It can also help build a stronger and more consistent culture and set of values among the entire global management team.

Why Expatriate Assignments Fail

Because international assignments are the heart of international human resource management, it's disconcerting to see how often such assignments fail. The exact number of failures is hard to quantify, in part because "failure" means different things to different people. For example, some expatriates may fail less conspicuously, quietly running up the hidden costs of reduced productivity and poisoned customer and staff relations.[52] However, there is some evidence that the rate of early departures, at least, is declining. This appears to be because more employers are taking steps to reduce expats' problems abroad. For example, they are selecting expats more carefully, helping spouses to get jobs abroad, and providing more ongoing support to the expat and his or her family.[53] As another example, some companies have formal "global buddy" programs. Here local managers assist new expatriates with advice on things such as office politics, norms of behavior, and where to receive emergency medical assistance.[54]

Traits of Successful Expats   Discovering why expatriate assignments fail is an important research task, and experts have made considerable progress. *Personality* is one factor. For example, in a study of 143 expatriate employees, extroverted, agreeable, and emotionally stable individuals were less likely to want to leave early.[55] Furthermore, the person's *intentions* are important. For example, people who want expatriate careers try harder to adjust to such a life.[56] Nonwork factors like *family pressures* usually loom large in expatriate failures. In one study, U.S. managers listed, in descending order of importance for leaving early: inability of spouse to adjust, managers' inability to adjust, other family problems, managers' personal or emotional immaturity, and inability to cope with larger overseas responsibility.[57] Managers of European firms emphasized only the inability of the manager's spouse to adjust as an explanation for the expatriate's failed assignment. Other studies similarly emphasize dissatisfied spouses' effects on the international assignment.[58]

These findings underscore a truism regarding international assignee selection: It's usually not incompetence, but family and personal problems that undermine the international assignee. Yet, employers still tend to select expatriates based on technical competence rather than interpersonal skills or domestic situations.[59] As one expert puts it:

> The selection process is fundamentally flawed. . . . Expatriate assignments rarely fail because the person cannot accommodate to the technical demands of the job. The expatriate selections are made by line managers based on technical competence. They fail because of family and personal issues and lack of cultural skills that haven't been part of the process.[60]

Family Pressures   Given the role of family problems in expat failures, it's important that the employer understand just how unhappy and cut off the expat manager's spouse can feel in a foreign environment. One study involved analyzing questionnaire data from 221 international assignee couples working in 37 countries.[61] Perhaps the most poignant finding concerned the degree to which many spouses often felt cut off and adrift; consider this quote:

> It's difficult to make close friends. So many expats have their guard up, not wanting to become too close. Too many have been hurt, too many times already, becoming emotionally dependent on a friend only to have the inevitable happen—one or the other gets transferred. It's also difficult to watch your children get hurt when their best friend gets transferred. Although I have many acquaintances, I have nowhere near the close friends I had in the States. My spouse therefore has become my rock.[62]

One study identified three things that helped make it easier for the spouse to adjust. First is *language fluency*. Since spouses will obviously feel even more cut off from their new surroundings if they can't make themselves understood, the employer should provide the spouse—not just the employee—with language training. Second, having *preschool-age children* (rather than school-age children or no children) seemed to make it easier for the spouse to adjust. "This suggests that younger children, perhaps because of their increased dependency, help spouses retain that part of their social identities: as parents, their responsibilities for these children remain the same."[63] Third, it also clearly helps that there be a *strong bond of closeness* and mutual sharing between spouse and expat partner, to provide the continuing emotional and social support many spouses find lacking abroad.

What Employers Can Do   There are other useful steps the employer can take. Providing realistic previews of what to expect, careful screening, improved orientation, and improved benefits packages are some obvious solutions. A less obvious solution is to institute procedures that ensure your firm treats its employees fairly—treating them with respect, providing an appeal process, and so on.[64] In one study of international assignees, nonwork problems were "significantly less pronounced when the organization's procedures were judged to be more fair."[65]

Another way to reduce expat problems is simply to shorten the length of the assignment, something employers are doing. About 23% of employers' overseas assignments last over three years, down from 32% in 1996.[66] Person–job match is also important, insofar as expatriates who are more satisfied with their jobs are more likely to adapt to the foreign assignment.[67]

Selecting Expatriate Managers

The processes firms use to select managers for their domestic and foreign positions obviously have many similarities. For either assignment, candidates need the technical knowledge and skills to do the job, and the intelligence and people skills to be successful managers.[68] Testing, interviewing, and background checks are as applicable for selecting expatriates as for domestic assignments.

However, foreign assignments are also different. There is the need to cope with colleagues whose culture may be drastically different from one's own, and the stress that being alone in a foreign land can put on the single manager. And if spouse and children will share the assignment, there are the complexities and pressures that the family will have to confront, from learning a new language to finding new friends and attending new schools. Furthermore, it's not how different culturally the host country is from the person's home country, it's the person's ability to adapt that's important. Some people do fine anywhere; others fail to adapt anywhere.[69]

Selecting managers for assignments abroad therefore means testing them for traits that predict success in adapting to new environments. One study asked 338 international assignees

FIGURE 17-1

Five Factors Important in International Assignee Success, and Their Components

Source: Adapted from Arthur Winfred Jr., and Winston Bennett Jr., "The International Assignee: The Relative Importance of Factors Perceived to Contribute to Success," *Personnel Psychology* 18 (1995), pp. 106–107.

I. Job Knowledge and Motivation

Managerial ability
Organizational ability
Imagination
Creativity
Administrative skills
Alertness
Responsibility
Industriousness
Initiative and energy
High motivation
Frankness
Belief in mission and job
Perseverance

II. Relational Skills

Respect
Courtesy and fact
Display of respect
Kindness
Empathy
Nonjudgmentalness
Integrity
Confidence

III. Flexibility/Adaptability

Resourcefulness
Ability to deal with stress
Flexibility
Emotional stability
Willingness to change
Tolerance for ambiguity
Adaptability
Independence
Dependability
Political sensitivity
Positive self-image

IV. Extracultural Openness

Variety of outside interests
Interest in foreign cultures
Openness
Knowledge of local language(s)
Outgoingness and extroversion
Overseas experience

V. Family Situation

Adaptability of spouse and family
Spouse's positive opinion
Willingness of spouse to live abroad
Stable marriage

---

from various countries and organizations to specify which traits were important for the success of managers on foreign assignment. The researchers identified five factors that contribute to success in such assignments: job knowledge and motivation, relational skills, flexibility/adaptability, extracultural openness, and family situation (spouse's positive opinion, willingness of spouse to live abroad, and so on). Figure 17-1 shows some of the specific items that make up each of the five factors. The five factors were not equally important in the foreign assignees' success, according to the assignees. "Family situation was generally found to be the most important factor, a finding consistent with other research on international assignments and transfers." A recent review of the research reports "strong support" for the importance of factors like interpersonal skills and family adjustment for expatriate adjustment.[70]

Adaptability Screening   With flexibility and adaptability often appearing high in studies like these, adaptability screening is sometimes part of the expatriate screening process. Often conducted by a psychologist or psychiatrist, **adaptability screening** aims to assess the assignee's (and spouse's) probable success in handling the foreign transfer, and to alert them to issues (such as the impact on children) the move may involve.[71] Here, experience is often the best predictor of future success. Companies like Colgate-Palmolive therefore look for overseas candidates whose work and nonwork experience, education, and language skills already demonstrate a commitment to and facility for living and working with different cultures.[72] Even several successful summers spent traveling overseas or participating in foreign student programs might provide some basis to believe that the potential transferee can adjust when he or she arrives overseas.

Many firms also use paper-and-pencil tests such as the Overseas Assignment Inventory. This test reportedly identifies the characteristics and attitudes international assignment candidates should have. Realistic previews about the problems to expect in the new

adaptability screening
A process that aims to assess the assignee's (and spouse's) probable success in handling a foreign transfer.

job (such as mandatory private schooling for the children) as well as about the cultural benefits, problems, and idiosyncrasies of the country are another important part of the screening process. The rule, say some experts, should always be to "spell it all out" ahead of time, as many multinationals do for their international transferees.[73]

Unfortunately, theory doesn't always translate into practice. As noted above, the importance of adaptability screening notwithstanding, 70% of respondents in one survey listed "skills or competencies" as the most important selection criteria when choosing candidates for international assignments. They ranked "job performance" second. The ability to adapt to new cultural conditions—as measured by items like "prior international living experience or assignment," and "familiarity with assignment country"—were rarely ranked as most important or second most important.[74] One study found that selection for positions abroad is so informal that the researchers called it "the coffee machine system": Two colleagues meet at the office coffee machine, strike up a conversation about the possibility of a position abroad, and based on that and little more a selection decision is made.[75] Perhaps this helps explain the high failure rate of foreign assignees.

"The New Workforce" feature provides a perspective on how such informality can affect women managers.

The NEW Workforce   Sending Women Managers Abroad

Women are underrepresented as management expatriates. For example, while women represent about 50% of the middle management talent in U.S. companies, they represent only 14% of expat managers sent abroad. What accounts for this? Line managers make most of these assignments, and many of these managers suffer from misperceptions that hinder them from recommending women to work abroad. Consider the results of one survey, by the International Personnel Association.[76] It found that many managers assume that women don't want to work abroad, or are reluctant to move their families abroad, or can't get their spouses to move because the husband is the main breadwinner. In fact, this survey found, women do want international assignments, they are not less inclined than male managers to move their families abroad, and their male spouses are not necessarily the families' main breadwinners.

What other perceptions (or misperceptions) inhibit managers from recommending women to work abroad? Safety is often an issue. Employers tend to assume that women posted abroad are more likely to become crime victims. However, most surveyed women expats said that safety was no more an issue with women than it was with men. As one said, "It doesn't matter if you're a man or woman. If it's a dangerous city, it's dangerous for whomever."[77]

Fear of cultural prejudices against women is another common issue. Here, there's no doubt that in some cultures women have to follow different rules than do their male counterparts, for instance, in terms of their attire. But even here, as one expat said, "Even in the more harsh cultures, once they recognize that the women can do the job, once your competence has been demonstrated, it becomes less of a problem."[78]

There are several steps employers can take to short-circuit misperceptions like these, and to identify more women to assign abroad. For example, *formalize a process* for identifying employees who are willing to take assignments abroad. (At Gillette, for instance, supervisors use the performance review interview to identify the subordinate's career interests, including the possibility of assigning the person abroad.) *Train managers* to understand how employees really feel about going abroad, and what the real safety and cultural issues are. Let successful female expats *help recruit* prospective female expats, and discuss with them the pros and cons of assignments abroad. Provide the expat's spouse with employment assistance.[79]

⑤ Discuss how to train and maintain international employees.

TRAINING AND MAINTAINING EXPATRIATE EMPLOYEES

Careful screening is just the first step in ensuring the foreign assignee's success. The employee may then require special training, and the firm will also need special international human resource management policies for compensating the firm's overseas employees and for maintaining healthy labor relations.

Orienting and Training Employees on International Assignment

When it comes to providing the orientation and training required for success overseas, the practices of most U.S. firms reflect more form than substance. Despite many companies' claims, there seems to be relatively little or no systematic selection and training for assignments overseas. Company executives tend to agree that international business requires that employees be firmly grounded in the economics and practices of foreign countries. However, too few companies actually provide such training.

Required Training   What sort of special training do overseas candidates need? One firm specializing in such programs prescribes a four-step approach.[80]

- Level 1 training focuses on the impact of cultural differences, and on raising trainees' awareness of such differences and their impact on business outcomes.
- Level 2 aims at getting participants to understand how attitudes (both negative and positive) are formed and how they influence behavior. (For example, unfavorable stereotypes may subconsciously influence how a new manager responds to and treats his or her new foreign subordinates.)
- Level 3 training provides factual knowledge about the target country, and
- Level 4 provides skill building in areas like language and adjustment and adaptation skills.

Beyond these special training needs, managers abroad continue to need traditional skills-oriented training and development. At many firms, including IBM, such development includes rotating assignments that permit overseas managers to grow professionally. IBM and other firms also have management development centers around the world where executives can hone their skills. And classroom programs (such as those at the London Business School, or at INSEAD in France) provide overseas executives the sorts of educational opportunities (to acquire MBAs, for instance) that similar stateside programs do for their U.S.-based colleagues.

In addition to honing these managers' skills, international management development activities hopefully have other less tangible effects on the managers and their firms. For example, rotating assignments can help managers form bonds with colleagues around the world, and these can help the managers make cross-border decisions more expeditiously. Activities such as periodic seminars (in which the firm brings together managers from its global subsidiaries and steeps them for a week or two in the firm's values, strategy, and policies) are also useful. They can help provide consistency of purpose and thereby improve control, by building a unifying set of values, standards, and corporate culture.

Trends in Expatriate Training   There are several trends in expatriate training and development. First, rather than providing only predeparture cross-cultural training, more firms are providing continuing, in-country cross-cultural training during the early stages of an overseas assignment. Second, employers are using returning managers as resources to cultivate the "global mind-sets" of their home-office staff. For example, automotive

Many global employers bring their international managers together periodically for training seminars

equipment producer Bosch holds regular seminars. Here newly arrived returnees pass on their knowledge and experience to relocating managers and their families.

There's also increased use of software and the Internet for cross-cultural training. For example, *Bridging Cultures* is a self-training multimedia package for people who will be traveling and/or living overseas. It uses short video clips to introduce case study intercultural problems, and then guides users to selecting the strategy to best handle the situation. Cross-cultural training firms' Web sites include: www.livingabroad.com, and www.globaldynamics.com.[81]

Compensating Expatriates

The whole area of international compensation presents some tricky problems. On the one hand, there is logic in maintaining companywide pay scales and policies so that, for instance, divisional marketing directors throughout the world are paid within the same narrow range. This reduces the risk of perceived inequities, and dramatically simplifies the job of keeping track of disparate, country-by-country wage rates.

Yet not adapting pay scales to local markets can produce more problems than it solves. The fact is, it can be enormously more expensive to live in some countries (like Japan) than others (like Spain); if these cost-of-living differences aren't considered, it may be almost impossible to get managers to take "high-cost" assignments. However, the answer is usually not just to pay, say, marketing directors more in one country than in another. For one thing, you could get resistance when you tell a marketing director in Tokyo who's earning $4,000 per week to move to your division in Spain, where his or her pay for the same job will drop by half (cost of living notwithstanding). One way to handle the problem is to pay a similar base salary companywide, and then add on various allowances according to individual market conditions.[82]

Determining equitable wage rates in many countries is no simple matter. There is a wealth of "packaged" compensation survey data available in the United States, but such data are not so easy to come by overseas. As a result, one of the greatest difficulties in managing multinational compensation is establishing consistent compensation measures between countries.

Some multinational companies conduct their own local annual compensation surveys. For example, Kraft conducts an annual study of total compensation in Belgium, Germany, Italy, Spain, and the United Kingdom. It focuses on the total compensation paid to each of 10 senior management positions held by local nationals in these firms. The survey covers all forms of compensation including cash and short- and long-term incentives. The employers then use this information for things like annual salary increases and proposed changes in benefits.

The Balance Sheet Approach The most common approach to formulating expatriate pay is to equalize purchasing power across countries, a technique known as the balance sheet approach.[83] More than 85% of North American companies reportedly use this approach.

The basic idea is that each expatriate should enjoy the same standard of living he or she would have had at home. With the balance sheet approach, four groups of expenses—income taxes, housing, goods and services, and discretionary expenses (child support, car payments, and the like)—are the focus of attention. The employer estimates what each of these four expenses is in the expatriate's home country, and what each will be in the host country. The employer then pays any differences—such as additional income taxes or housing expenses.

In practice, this usually boils down to building the expatriate's total compensation package around five or six components. For example, base salary will normally be in the same range as the manager's home-country salary. In addition, however, there might be an overseas or foreign service premium. The executive receives this as a percentage of his or her base salary, in part to compensate for the cultural and physical adjustments he or she will have to make.[84] There may also be several allowances, including a housing allowance and an education allowance for the expatriate's children. Income taxes represent another area of concern. A U.S. manager posted abroad must often pay not just U.S. taxes but also income taxes in the host country.

Table 17-2 illustrates the balance sheet approach. In this case, the manager's annual earnings are $80,000, and she faces a U.S. income tax rate of 28%, and a Belgium income tax rate of 70%. The other costs are based on the index of living costs abroad published in the "U.S. Department of State Indexes of Living Costs Abroad, Quarters Allowances, and Hardship Differentials," available at http://www.state.gov.

Incentives While the situation is changing, employers still tend to use performance-based incentives less abroad. In Europe, firms traditionally emphasized a guaranteed annual salary and companywide bonus.[85] European firms tend to be moving toward more incentive pay, but

TABLE 17-2 The Balance Sheet Approach (Assumes Base Salary of $80,000)

Annual Expense	Chicago, U.S.	Brussels, Belgium (U.S.$ Equivalent)	Allowance
Housing & utilities	$35,000	$67,600	$32,600
Goods & services	6,000	9,500	3,500
Taxes	22,400	56,000	33,600
Discretionary income	10,000	10,000	0
Total	$73,400	$143,100	$69,700

Source: Joseph Martocchio, *Strategic Compensation: A Human Resource Management Approach*, 2nd edition (Upper Saddle River, NJ: Prentice Hall, 2001), Table 12-15, p. 294.

foreign service premiums
Financial payments over and above regular base pay, typically ranging between 10% and 30% of base pay.

hardship allowances
Compensate expatriates for exceptionally hard living and working conditions at certain locations.

mobility premiums
Typically, lump-sum payments to reward employees for moving from one assignment to another.

still have to overcome several problems—including the public relations aspects of such a move (such as selling the idea of more emphasis on performance-based pay). U.S. firms that offer overseas managers long-term incentives use overall corporate performance criteria (like worldwide profits) when awarding incentive pay—although, ironically, a manager's local performance may have little or no effect on how the company as a whole performs.

U.S. companies do offer various incentives to get expatriates to accept and stay on international assignment. **Foreign service premiums** are financial payments over and above regular base pay. These typically range from 10% to 30% of base pay, and appear as weekly or monthly salary supplements. **Hardship allowances** compensate expatriates for exceptionally hard living and working conditions at certain foreign locations. Employers also usually pay these incrementally (with each paycheck), so it's important to make it clear that this is not a permanent raise. **Mobility premiums** are typically lump-sum payments to reward employees for moving from one assignment to another.

In general, executive compensation systems around the world are becoming more similar: "The structures have common broadband base salary ranges, flexible annual incentive targets/maximums, and internationally established share option guideline awards."[86] And, as in the United States, more multinational employers are granting more stock options to a broader group of their employees overseas, a step that requires even more attention to complying with local tax laws.[87]

The accompanying "When You're on Your Own" feature outlines how to set up a global pay system.

When You're on Your OWN   Establishing a Global Pay System
HR for Line Managers and Entrepreneurs

Balancing global consistency in compensation with local considerations is never easy, but doing so best starts with establishing a more centralized global rewards program. This means providing "a global rewards philosophy supported by guidelines, tools, and technological support to enable compensation management and decision making on a global basis."[88] In practice, this involves a five-phase, multi-year program:[89]

Phase I: Global philosophy framework. Here the employer (1) defines its global rewards philosophy (in terms of how the rewards will help the employer achieve its strategic goals), (2) reviews and inventories its existing rewards programs around the world, (3) assesses the "gap" or differences between these existing programs and the firm's rewards philosophy, and (4) creates a compensation plan for each location.

Phase II: Job structure framework. The aim of this second phase is to systematize job descriptions and performance expectations around the world. For example, it involves creating more consistent performance assessment practices, establishing

consistent job requirements and performance expectations for similar worldwide jobs, and planning personnel requirements and recruitment needs worldwide.

Phase III: Rewards framework. The main aim of this phase is to formulate specific pay policies that are both globally consistent and locally competitive. Among other things, the employer here will conduct surveys and analyses to assess local competitive pay practices. It will then fine tune specific pay policies for each location that make sense in terms of the firm's global compensation philosophy.

Phase IV: Talent management framework. Here, the employer institutes career development practices, in recognition of the fact that promotional opportunities and career progress are necessary supplements to the company's compensation programs.

Phase V: Ongoing program assessment. Here, the employer periodically reevaluates its global pay policies, given the fact that its own strategic needs and its competitors' pay practices may change.

Appraising Expatriate Managers

Several things complicate the task of appraising an expatriate's performance. For one thing, the question of who actually appraises the expatriate is crucial.[90] Obviously, local management must have some input, but cultural differences here may distort the appraisals. Thus, host-country bosses might evaluate a U.S. expatriate manager in India somewhat negatively if they find his or her use of participative decision making culturally inappropriate. On the other hand, home-office managers may be so out of touch that they can't provide valid appraisals, since they're not fully aware of the situation the manager faces locally. Similarly, the procedure may be to measure the expatriate by objective criteria such as profits and market share, but local events (such as political instability) may affect the manager's performance while remaining "invisible" to home-office staff.

Suggestions for improving the expatriate appraisals follow. The Employment Law Feature presents related issues.

1. Stipulate the assignment's difficulty level, and adapt the performance criteria to the situation.
2. Weigh the evaluation more toward the on-site manager's appraisal than toward the home-site manager's.
3. If the home-office manager does the actual written appraisal, have him or her use a former expatriate from the same overseas location for advice.

Know Your Employment LAW

The Equal Employment Opportunity Responsibilities of Multinational Employers

American equal employment opportunity laws, including Title VII, the ADEA, and the ADA, impact U.S. employers doing business abroad, and foreign firms doing business in the United States or its territories.[91] For example, *foreign multinational employers* that operate in the United States or its territories (American Samoa, Guam, the Commonwealth of the Northern Mariana Islands, Puerto Rico, and the U.S. Virgin Islands) must abide by EEO laws to the same extent as U.S. employers, unless the employer is covered by a treaty or other binding international agreement that limits the full applicability of U.S. antidiscrimination laws. Similarly, *U.S. employers*—those that are incorporated or based in the United States or are controlled by U.S. companies—that employ U.S. citizens outside the United States or its territories are subject to Title VII, the ADEA, and the ADA with respect to those U.S. citizen employees. U.S. EEO laws do not apply to *non*-U.S. citizens working for U.S. (or foreign) firms *outside* the United States or its territories.

If equal employment opportunity laws conflict with the laws of the country in which the U.S. employer is operating, the laws of the local country generally take precedence. In particular, U.S. employers are not required to comply with requirements of Title VII, the ADEA, or the ADA if adherence to that law would violate the law of the country where the workplace is located. For example, an employer would have a "Foreign Laws Defense" for a mandatory retirement policy if the law in the country in which the company is located requires mandatory requirement. However, a U.S. employer may not transfer an employee to another country in order to put that person at disadvantage because of his or her race, color, sex, religion, national origin, age, or disability. For example, an employer may not transfer an older worker to a country with a mandatory retirement age for the purpose of forcing the worker's retirement.

International Labor Relations

Firms opening subsidiaries abroad will find substantial differences in labor relations practices among countries and regions. This is important, because, while union membership is dropping in the United States, it is still relatively high abroad, and unions abroad therefore tend to be more influential. Wal-Mart, for instance has successfully neutralized attempts to organize its U.S. employees, but in 2006 had to accept unions in many of its stores in China.

Consider, for example, Europe.

Unions in Europe are influential, and labor–management bargaining and relations reflect this fact. In general European labor relations are characterized by:

- *Centralization* Collective bargaining in Western Europe tends to be industrywide, whereas in the United States it generally occurs at the enterprise or plant level.
- *Employer organization* Due to the prevalence of industrywide bargaining in Europe, employers tend to bargain via employer associations, rather than as individual employers.
- *Union recognition* Union recognition is less formal than in the United States. For example, even if a union represents 80% of an employer's workers, another union can try to organize the other 20%.
- *Content and scope of bargaining* U.S. labor–management agreements tend to focus on wages, hours, and working conditions. European agreements tend to be brief and to leave individual employers free to institute more generous terms.

Terrorism, Safety, and Global HR

The increased threat of terrorism is affecting human resource activities both domestically and abroad. Domestically, for instance, anecdotal evidence suggests that the new federal antiterrorism laws and procedures are affecting employers' ability to import and export workers.[92] For example, getting working papers for foreign workers now takes weeks or months instead of days. This is because in most cases, the prospective employee must have an interview at his or her local U.S. Embassy, and scheduling these is a relatively time-consuming process.

Employers are also facing more resistance from prospective expats. More are reluctant to accept foreign postings and take their families abroad, and those that do are demanding more compensation.[93] And for their employees and facilities abroad, employers have had to institute more comprehensive safety plans, including, for instance, evacuation plans to get employees to safety, if that becomes necessary. Even before 2001, the threats facing expat employees were on the rise. For example, the number of overseas kidnappings more than doubled from 830 to 1,728 during the mid- to late 1990s.[94] Developments like these had already prompted employers to take steps to better protect their expat employees.

Taking Protective Measures   Employers are doing so in a variety of ways. Many employers retain crisis management teams' services. They then call on these crisis management teams, for instance, when they receive notice that criminal elements have kidnapped one of their expats, or threatened the person with harm unless a ransom is paid. As one insurance executive puts it, "When you have a specialist, there's a better chance to get the person back. You want a specialist in there because you don't want the employee coming home in a body bag."[95]

Kidnapping and Ransom (K&R) Insurance   Hiring crisis teams and paying ransoms can be prohibitively expensive for all but the largest firms, so many employers buy kidnapping and ransom (K&R) insurance. Any one or more of several events may trigger payments under such policies. The obvious ones are kidnapping (for instance, the employee is a hostage until the employer pays a ransom), extortion (threatening bodily harm), and detention (holding an employee without any ransom demand). Other triggering events include threats to property or products unless the employer makes a payment.

The insurance itself typically covers several costs associated with kidnappings, abductions, or extortion attempts. These costs might include, for instance, hiring a crisis team, the actual cost of the ransom payment to the kidnappers or extortionists, ensuring the ransom money in case it's lost in transit, legal expenses, and employee death or dismemberment.[96]

Keeping business travelers out of crime's way is a specialty all its own, but suggestions here include:[97]

- Provide expatriates with general training about traveling, living abroad, and the place they're going to, so they're more oriented when they get there.
- Tell them not to draw attention to the fact that they're Americans—by wearing flag emblems or by using American cars, for instance.
- Have travelers arrive at airports as close to departure time as possible and wait in areas away from the main flow of traffic where they're not as easily observed.
- Equip the expatriate's car and home with adequate security systems.
- Tell employees to vary their departure and arrival times and take different routes to and from work.
- Keep employees current on crime and other problems by regularly checking, for example, the State Department's travel advisory service and consular information sheets (http://travel.state.gov/travel_warnings.html).
- Advise employees to remain confident at all times: Body language can attract perpetrators, and those who look like victims often become victimized.[98]

Repatriation: Problems and Solutions

One of the most confounding and worrisome facts about sending employees abroad is that 40% to 60% of them will probably quit within three years of returning home. One study suggests that a three-year assignment abroad for one employee with a base salary of about $100,000 costs the employer $1 million, once extra living costs, transportation, and family benefits are included.[99] Given the investment the employer makes in training and sending these often high-potential people abroad, it obviously makes sense to do everything possible to make sure they stay with the firm. For this, formal repatriation programs can be quite useful.[100] One study found that about 5% of returning employees resigned if their firms had formal repatriation programs, while about 22% of those left if their firms had no such programs.[101]

The heart and guiding principle for any repatriation program is this: Make sure that the expatriate and his or her family don't feel that the company has left them adrift. For example, AT&T has an effective three-part repatriation program, one that actually starts before the employee leaves for the assignment abroad.[102] First, AT&T *matches the expat and his or her family with a psychologist* trained in repatriation issues. The psychologist meets with the family before they go abroad. The psychologist discusses the challenges they will face abroad, assesses with them how well he or she think they will adapt to their new culture, and stays in touch with them throughout their assignment. (Other firms, like Dow, also provide written repatriation agreements. These guarantee in writing that the company won't keep the expat abroad for more than some period, such as three years, and that on return he or she will receive a mutually acceptable job.)

Second, AT&T makes sure that *the employee always feels that he or she is still "in the loop"* with what's happening back at the home office. For example, AT&T assigns the expat a mentor, and brings the expat back to the home office periodically for meetings and to socialize with his or her colleagues.

Third, once it's time for the expat employee and his or her family to return home, AT&T *provides formal repatriation services.* About six months before the overseas assignment ends, the psychologist and an HR representative meet with the expat and the family, to start preparing them for the return. For example, they help plan the employee's next career move, help the person update his or her résumé, and begin putting the person in contact with supervisors back home. They work with the person's family on the logistics of the move back home. Then, about a month after returning home, the expat and family attend a "welcome home" seminar, where they discuss matters like the stress of repatriation.[103]

Improving Productivity Through HRIS: *Taking the HRIS Global*

As a company grows, relying on manual HR systems to manage activities like worldwide safety, benefits administration, payroll, and succession planning becomes unwieldy. As we've seen, more firms are therefore automating and integrating their HR systems into human resource information systems (HRIS).

For global firms, it makes particular sense to expand the firm's human resource information systems to include the firm's operations abroad. For example, electrical components manufacturer Thomas & Betts once needed 83 faxes to get a head count of its 26,000 employees in 24 countries; it can now do so with the push of a button, thanks to its global HRIS system.[104] Most global HRIS uses are more sophisticated. Without a database of a firm's worldwide management talent, for instance, selecting employees for assignments abroad and keeping track of each unit's compensation plans, benefits, and personnel practices and policies can be overwhelming.

When Buildnet, Inc., decided to automate and integrate its separate systems for things like applicant tracking, training, and compensation, it chose a Web-based software package called MyHRIS, from NuView, Inc. (www.nuviewinc.com). This is an Internet-based system that includes human resource and benefits administration, applicant tracking and résumé scanning, training administration, and succession planning and development.[105] With MyHRIS, managers at any of the firm's locations around the world can access and update more than 200 built-in reports such as "termination summary" or "open positions."[106] And the firm's home-office managers can access data on and monitor global human resource activities on a real-time basis.

Employers are also increasingly taking their employee self-service HR portals international. For example, Time Warner's "Employee Connection" portal lets its 80,000 worldwide employees self-manage much of their benefits, compensation planning, merit review, and personal information updating online.[107]

REVIEW

SUMMARY

1. International business is important to almost every business today, and so firms must increasingly be managed globally. This presents managers with many new challenges, including coordinating production, sales, and financial operations on a worldwide basis. As a result, companies today have pressing international HR needs with respect to selecting, training, paying, and repatriating global employees.

2. Intercountry differences affect a company's HR management processes. Cultural factors suggest differences in values, attitudes, and therefore behaviors and reactions of people from country to country. Economic and labor cost factors help determine local compensation issues. Industrial relations and specifically the relationship between the worker, the union, and the employer influence the nature of a company's specific HR policies from country to country.

3. Countries differ in cultures, legal/political systems, and economies, and so HR practices tend to differ from country to country. For example, "to determine pay" is one of the top reasons for appraising performance in Taiwan, the United States, and Canada but not in Mexico. Similarly, training expenditures for employees range from $241 per employee in Asia to $724 in the United States. In the People's Republic of China, pay incentives play a relatively important role, compared with U.S. pay packages.

4. Research shows that employers engage in three "best practices" to help make their global HR systems acceptable to their local managers around the world. These are: Remember that global systems are more accepted in truly global organizations; investigate pressures to differentiate and determine their legitimacy; and, try to work within the context of a strong corporate culture. To develop effective worldwide HR systems: form global HR networks; remember that it's more important to standardize ends and competencies than specific methods; remember, "you can't communicate enough," and, dedicate adequate resources for the global HR effort.

5. A large percentage of expatriate assignments fail, but the average can be improved through careful selection. There are various sources HR can use to staff domestic and foreign subsidiaries. Often managerial positions are filled by locals rather than expatriates, but this is not always the case.

6. Selecting managers for expatriate assignments means screening them for traits that predict success in adapting to dramatically new environments. Such traits include adaptability and flexibility, cultural toughness, self-orientation, job knowledge and motivation, relational skills, extracultural openness, and family situation. Adaptability screening focusing on the family's probable success in handling the foreign assignment can be an especially important step in the selection process.

7. Training for overseas managers typically focuses on cultural differences, on how attitudes influence behavior, and on factual knowledge about the target country. The most common approach to formulating expatriate pay is to equalize purchasing power across countries, a technique known as the balance sheet approach. The employer estimates expenses for income taxes, housing, goods and services, and discretionary costs, and pays supplements to the expatriate in such a way as to maintain the same standard of living he or she would have had at home.

8. The expatriate appraisal process can be complicated by the need to have both local and home-office supervisors provide input into the performance review. Suggestions for improving the process include stipulating difficulty level, weighing the on-site manager's appraisal more heavily, and having the home-site manager get background advice from managers familiar with the location abroad before completing the expatriate's appraisal.

9. Repatriation problems are common but you can minimize them. They include the often well-founded fear that the expatriate is "out of sight, out of mind," and difficulties in reassimilating the expatriate's family back into the home-country culture. Suggestions for avoiding these problems include using repatriation agreements, assigning a sponsor, offering career counseling, keeping the expatriate plugged in to home-office business, and offering reorientation programs to the expatriate and his or her family.

DISCUSSION QUESTIONS

1. You are the president of a small business. What are some of the ways you expect "going international" will affect HR activities in your business?
2. What are some of the specific, uniquely international activities an international HR manager typically engages in?
3. What intercountry differences affect HRM? Give several examples of how each may specifically affect HRM.
4. You are the HR manager of a firm that is about to send its first employees overseas to staff a new subsidiary. Your boss, the president, asks you why such assignments often fail, and what you plan to do to avoid such failures. How do you respond?
5. What special training do overseas candidates need? In what ways is such training similar to and different from traditional diversity training?
6. How does appraising an expatriate's performance differ from appraising that of a home-office manager? How would you avoid some of the unique problems of appraising the expatriate's performance?
7. As an HR manager, what program would you establish to reduce repatriation problems of returning expatriates and their families?

INDIVIDUAL AND GROUP ACTIVITIES

1. Working individually or in groups, write an expatriation and repatriation plan for your professor, whom your school is sending to Bulgaria to teach HR for the next three years.
2. Give three specific examples of multinational corporations in your area. Check on the Internet or with each firm to determine in what countries these firms have operations. Explain the nature of some of their operations, and summarize whatever you can find out about their international employee selection and training HR policies.
3. Choose three traits useful for selecting international assignees, and create a straightforward test to screen candidates for these traits.
4. Use a library or Internet source to determine the relative cost of living in five countries as of this year, and explain the implications of such differences for drafting a pay plan for managers being sent to each country.
5. The HRCI "Test Specifications" appendix at the end of this book (pages 726–735) lists the knowledge someone studying for the HRCI certification exam needs to have in each area of human resource management (such as in Strategic Management, Workforce Planning, and Human Resource Development). In groups of four to five students, do four things: (1) review that appendix now; (2) identify the material in this chapter that relates to the required knowledge the appendix lists; (3) write four multiple choice exam questions on this material that you believe would be suitable for inclusion in the HRCI exam; and (4) if time permits, have someone from your team post your team's questions in front of the class, so the students in other teams can take each others' exam questions.
6. A recent issue of *HR Magazine* contained an article titled "Aftershocks of War," which said that soldiers returning to their jobs from Iraq would likely require HR's assistance in coping with "delayed emotional trauma." The term *delayed emotional trauma* refers to the personality changes such as anger, anxiety, or irritability and associated problems such as tardiness or absenteeism that exposure to the traumatic events of war sometimes triggers in returning veterans. Assume you are the HR manager for the

employer of John Smith, who is returning to work next week after one year in Iraq. Based on what you read in this chapter, what steps would you take to help ensure that John's reintegration into your workforce goes as smoothly as possible?

EXPERIENTIAL EXERCISE

A Taxing Problem for Expatriate Employees

Purpose: The purpose of this exercise is to give you practice identifying and analyzing some of the factors that influence expatriates' pay.

Required Understanding: You should be thoroughly familiar with this chapter and with the Web site, www.irs.gov.

How to Set Up the Exercise/Instructions: Divide the class into teams of four or five students. Each team member should read the following: One of the trickiest aspects of calculating expatriates' pay relates to the question of the expatriate's U.S. federal income tax liabilities. Go to the Internal Revenue Service's Web site, www.irs.gov. Scroll down to Individuals, and go to Overseas Taxpayers. Your team is the expatriate-employee compensation task force for your company, and your firm is about to send several managers and engineers to Japan, England, and Hong Kong. What information did you find on this site that will help your team formulate expat tax and compensation policies? Based on that, what are the three most important things your firm should keep in mind in formulating a compensation policy for the employees you're about to send to Japan, England, and Hong Kong?

APPLICATION CASE

"Boss, I Think We Have a Problem"

Central Steel Door Corporation has been in business for about 20 years, successfully selling a line of steel industrial-grade doors, as well as the hardware and fittings required for them. Focusing mostly in the United States and Canada, the company had gradually increased its presence from the New York City area, first into New England and then down the Atlantic Coast, then through the Midwest and West, and finally into Canada. The company's basic expansion strategy was always the same: Choose an area, open a distribution center, hire a regional sales manager, then let that regional sales manager help staff the distribution center and hire local sales reps.

Unfortunately, the company's traditional success in finding sales help has not extended to its overseas operations. With the introduction of the new European currency in 2002, Mel Fisher, president of Central Steel Door, decided to expand his company abroad, into Europe. However, the expansion has not gone smoothly at all. He tried for three weeks to find a sales manager by advertising in the *International Herald Tribune*, which is read by businesspeople in Europe and by American expatriates living and working in Europe. Although the ads placed in the *Tribune* also run for about a month on the *Tribune*'s Web site, Mr. Fisher so far has received only five applications. One came from a possibly viable candidate, whereas four came from candidates whom Mr. Fisher refers to as "lost souls"—people who seem to have spent most of their time traveling aimlessly from country to country sipping espresso in sidewalk cafés. When asked what he had done for the last three years, one told Mr. Fisher he'd been on a "walkabout."

Other aspects of his international HR activities have been equally problematic. Fisher alienated two of his U.S. sales managers by sending them to Europe to temporarily run the European operations, but neglecting to work out a compensation package that would cover their relatively high living expenses in Germany and Belgium. One ended up staying the better part of the year, and Mr. Fisher was rudely surprised to be informed by the Belgian government that his sales manager owed thousands of dollars in local taxes. The managers had hired about 10 local people to staff each of the two distribution centers. However, without full-time local European sales managers, the level of sales was disappointing, so Fisher decided to fire about half the distribution center employees. That's when he got an emergency phone call from his temporary sales manager in Germany: "I've just been told that all these employees should have had written employment agreements and that in any case we can't fire anyone without at least one year's notice, and the local authorities here are really up in arms. Boss, I think we have a problem."

Questions

1. Based on this chapter and the case incident, compile a list of 10 international HR mistakes Mr. Fisher has made so far.
2. How would you have gone about hiring a European sales manager? Why?
3. What would you do now if you were Mr. Fisher?

CONTINUING CASE

Carter Cleaning Company Going Abroad

With Jennifer gradually taking the reins of Carter Cleaning Company, Jack decided to take his first long vacation in years and go to Mexico for a month in January 2004. What he found surprised him: While he spent much of the time basking in the sun in Acapulco, he also spent considerable time in Mexico City and was surprised at the dearth of cleaning stores, particularly considering the amount of air pollution in the area. Traveling north he passed through Juarez, Mexico, and was similarly surprised at the relatively few cleaning stores he found there. As he drove back into Texas, and back toward home, he began to think about whether it is advisable to consider expanding his chain of stores into Mexico.

Quite aside from the possible economic benefits, he had liked what he saw in the lifestyle in Mexico and was also attracted by the idea of possibly facing the sort of exciting challenge he faced 20 years ago when he started Carter Cleaning in the United States: "I guess entrepreneurship is in my blood," is the way he put it.

As he drove home to have dinner with Jennifer, he began to formulate the questions he would have to ask before deciding whether or not to expand abroad.

Questions

1. Assuming they began by opening just one or two stores in Mexico, what do you see as the main HR-related challenges he and Jennifer would have to address?
2. How would you go about choosing a manager for a new Mexican store if you were Jack or Jennifer? For instance, would you hire someone locally or send someone from one of your existing stores? Why?
3. The cost of living in Mexico is substantially below that of where Carter is now located: How would you go about developing a pay plan for your new manager if you decided to send an expatriate to Mexico?
4. Present a detailed explanation of the factors you would look for in your candidate for expatriate manager to run the stores in Mexico.

TRANSLATING STRATEGY INTO HR POLICIES AND PRACTICES CASE:
THE HOTEL PARIS

Managing Global Human Resources

The Hotel Paris's competitive strategy is, "To use superior guest service to differentiate the Hotel Paris properties, and to thereby increase the length of stay and return rate of guests, and thus boost revenues and profitability." HR manager Lisa Cruz must now formulate functional policies and activities that support this competitive strategy, by eliciting the required employee behaviors and competencies.

With hotels in 11 cities in Europe and the United States, Lisa knew that the company had to do a better job of managing its global human resources. For example, there was no formal means of identifying or training management employees for duties abroad (either for those going to the United States or to Europe). As another example, recently, after spending upwards of $600,000 sending a U.S. manager and her family abroad, they had to return her abruptly when the family complained bitterly of missing their friends back home. Lisa knew this was no way to run a multinational business. She turned her attention to developing the HR practices her company required to do business more effectively internationally.

On reviewing the data, it was apparent to Lisa and the CFO that the company's global human resource practices were probably inhibiting the Hotel Paris from being the world-class guest services company that it sought to be. For example, high-performing service and hotel firms had formal departure training programs for at least 90% of the employees they sent abroad; the Hotel Paris had no such programs. Similarly, with each city's hotel operating its own local hotel HR information system, there was no easy way for Lisa, the CFO, or the company's CEO to obtain reports on metrics like turnover, absences, or workers' compensation costs across all the different hotels. As the CFO summed it up, "If we can't measure how each hotel is doing in terms of human resource metrics like these, there's really no way to manage these activities, so there's no telling how much lost profits and wasted efforts are dragging down each hotel's performance." Lisa received approval to institute new global human resources programs and practices.

Questions

1. Provide a one page summary of what individual hotel managers should know in order to make it more likely incoming employees from abroad, like those in the Hotel Paris's management development program, will adapt to their new surroundings.

2. In previous chapters you recommended various human resource practices Hotel Paris should use. Choose one of these, and explain why you believe they could take this program abroad, and how you suggest they do so.

3. Choose one Hotel Paris human resources practice that you believe is essential to the company achieving its high-quality-service goal, and explain how you would implement that practice in the firm's various hotels worldwide.

KEY TERMS

codetermination, 696
expatriates (expats), 701
home-country nationals, 701
third-country nationals, 701
offshoring, 703
ethnocentric, 704

polycentric, 704
geocentric, 705
adaptability screening, 707
foreign service premiums, 712
hardship allowances, 712
mobility premiums, 712

ENDNOTES

1. Karen Roberts, Ellen Kossek, and Cynthia Ozeki, "Managing the Global Workforce: Challenges and Strategies," *Academy of Management Executive* 12, no. 4 (1998), pp. 93–106.
2. Ibid., p. 94.
3. David Ralston, Priscilla Elsass, David Gustafson, Fannie Cheung, and Robert Terpstra, "Eastern Values: A Comparison of Managers in the United States, Hong Kong, and the People's Republic

of China," *Journal of Applied Psychology* 71, no. 5 (1992), pp. 664–671. See also, P. Christopher Early and Elayne Mosakowski, "Cultural Intelligence," *Harvard Business Review*, (October 2004): 139–146.

4. Geert Hofstede, "Cultural Dimensions in People Management," in Vladimir Pucik, Noel Tishy, and Carole Barnett (eds.), *Globalizing Management* (New York: John Wiley & Sons, 1992), p. 143.

5. Randall Schuler, Susan Jackson, Ellen Jackofsky, and John Slocum Jr., "Managing Human Resources in Mexico: A Cultural Understanding," *Business Horizons*, May–June 1996, pp. 55–61.

6. Valerie Frazee, "Establishing Relations in Germany," *Global Workforce*, April 1997, p. 17.

7. Charlene Solomon, "Destination U.S.A.," *Global Workforce*, April 1997, pp. 19–23.

8. Ibid., p. 21.

9. Tyler Cowen, "Creative Destruction: How Globalization Is Changing the World's Cultures," *Princeton University Press*, Princeton, New Jersey, 2002.

10. Chris Brewster, "European Perspectives on Human Resource Management," *Human Resource Management Review* 14, (2004): 365–382.

11. "SOX Compliance, Corporate Codes of Conduct Can Create Challenges for U.S. Multinationals," *BNA Bulletin to Management*, March 28, 2006, p. 97.

12. Annual 2002 figures, www.bls.gov/news.release/ichcc.hr0.htm.

13. Carolyn Hirschman, "When Operating Abroad, Companies Must Adopt European Style HR Plan," *HR News* 20, no. 3 (March 2001), pp. 1, 6.

14. This is discussed in Eduard Gaugler, "HR Management: An International Comparison," *Personnel*, 1988, p. 28. See also Carlos Castillo, "Collective Labor Rights in Latin America and Mexico," *Relations Industrielles/Industrial Relations* 55, no. 1 (Winter 2000), p. 59.

15. Frances Taft and Cliff Powell, "The European Pensions and Benefits Environment: A Complex Ecology," *Compensation and Benefits Review*, January/February 2005, pp. 37–50.

16. Ibid.

17. "Inform, Consult, Impose: Workers' Rights in the EU," *Economist*, June 16, 2001, p. 3.

18. Gary Dessler, "Expanding into China? What Foreign Employers Entering China Should Know About Human Resource Management Today," *SAM Advanced Management Journal*, August 2006.

19. Y. Paul Yo et al., "Divergence or Convergence: A Cross National Comparison of Personnel Selection Procedures," *Human Resource Management* 41, no. 1 (Spring 2002), pp. 31–44.

20. John Milliman et al., "An Exploratory Assessment of the Purposes of Performance Appraisals in North and Central America and the Pacific Rim," *Human Resource Management* 41, no. 1 (Spring 2002), pp. 87–102.

21. Martin Van Buren and Stephen King, "The 2000 ASTD International Comparisons Report," American Society for Training and Development (2000); this training survey reflects usable responses from 501 U.S. organizations plus over 400 organizations from 47 countries outside the United States.

22. Ellen Drost et al., "Benchmarking Training and Development Practices: A Multicountry Comparative Analysis," *Human Resource Management* 41, no. 1 (Spring 2002), pp. 67–86.

23. Robert Heneman et al., "Compensation Practices in Small Entrepreneurial and High-Growth Companies in the United States and China," *Compensation and Benefits Review*, July/August 2002, pp. 15–16.

24. Kevin Lowe et al., "International Compensation Practices: A Ten Country Comparative Analysis," *Human Resource Management* 41, no. 1 (Spring 2002), pp. 45–66.

25. Ann Marie Ryan et al., "Designing and Implementing Global Staffing Systems: Part 2—Best Practices," *Human Resource Management* 42, no. 1 (Spring 2003), pp. 85–94.

26. Ibid., p. 86.

27. Ibid., p. 87.

28. Ibid., p. 89.

29. Ibid., p. 90.

30. Ibid., p. 90.

31. Ibid., p. 92.

32. Daniels and Radebaugh, *International Business*, p. 767. See also Castillo, "Collective Labor Rights in Latin America and Mexico," p. 59.

33. Arvind Phatak, *International Dimensions of Management* (Boston: PWS Kent, 1989), p. 106. See also, Charles Hill, *International Business: Competing in the Global Marketplace* (Burr Ridge, IL: Irwin McGraw-Hill, 2001), pp. 564–566.

34. Daniels and Radebaugh, *International Business*, p. 767.

35. Ibid., p. 769; Phatak, *International Dimensions of Management*, p. 106.

36. "Survey Says Expatriates Twice as Likely to Leave Employer as Home-Based Workers," *BNA Bulletin to Management*, May 9, 2006, p. 147.

37. Phatak, *International Dimensions of Management*, p. 108.

38. Daniels and Radebaugh, *International Business*, p. 769.

39. Leslie Klass, "Fed Up with High Costs, Companies Winnow the Ranks of Career Expats," *Workforce Management*, (October 2004): 84–88.

40. "DOL Releases Final Rule Amending Filing, Processing of Foreign Labor Certifications," *BNA Bulletin to Management*, (January 11, 2005): 11.

41. Helene Mayerhofer, et al., "Flexpatriate Assignments: A Neglected Issue in Global Staffing," *International Journal of Human Resource Management* 15, no. 8, December 2004, pp. 1371–1389, and Martha Frase, "International Commuters," *HR Magazine*, March 2007, pp. 91–96.

42. Michael Harvey et al., "Global Virtual Teams: A Human Resource Capital Architecture," *International Journal of Human Resource Management* 16, no. 9, September 2005, pp. 1583–1599.

43. Timothy Dwyer, "Localization's Hidden Costs," *HR Magazine*, (June 2004): 135–144.

44. Based on Pamela Babcock, "America's Newest Export: White Collar Jobs," *HR Magazine*, April 2004, pp. 50–57.

45. Mary Medland, "Setting Up Overseas," *HR Magazine*, January 2004, p. 71.

46. Phatak, *International Dimensions of Management*, p. 129.

47. Ibid.

48. Charles Hill, *International Business: Competing in the Global Marketplace*, (Burr Ridge, IL: Irwin, 1994), p. 507.

49. Ibid., pp. 507–510.

50. Ibid., p. 509.

51. Ibid. See also Michael Harvey et al., "An Innovative Global Management Staffing System: A Competency-Based Perspective," *Human Resource Management* 39, no. 4 (Winter 2000), pp. 381–394.

52. Margaret Shaffer and David Harrison, "Expatriates' Psychological Withdrawal from International Assignments: Work, Nonwork, and Family Influences," *Personnel Psychology* 51 (1998), p. 88. See also, Jan Selmer, "Psychological Barriers to Adjustment of Western Business Expatriates in China: Newcomers vs. Long Stayers," *International Journal of Human Resource Management*, June–August 2004, vol. 15, issue 4–5, p. 794 (21).

53. Gary Insch and John Daniels, "Causes and Consequences of Declining Early Departures from Foreign Assignments," *Business Horizons* 46, no. 6 (November–December 2002), pp. 39–48.

54. Eric Krell, "Budding Relationships," *HR Magazine* 50, no. 6, June 2005, pp. 114–118.

55. Paula Caliguri, "The Big Five Personality Characteristics as Predictors of Expatriates' Desire to Terminate the Assignment and Supervisor-Rated Performance," *Personnel Psychology* 53, no. 1 (Spring 2000), pp. 67–88.

56. Jan Selmer, "Expatriation: Corporate Policy, Personal Intentions and International Adjustment," *International Journal of Human Resource Management* 9, no. 6 (December 1998), pp. 997–1007.

57. Discussed in Charles Hill, *International Business*, pp. 511–515.

58. Charlene Solomon, "One Assignment, Two Lives," *Personnel Journal*, May 1996, pp. 36–47; Michael Harvey, "Dual-Career Couples During International Relocation: The Trailing Spouse," *International Journal of Human Resource Management* 9, no. 2 (April 1998), pp. 309–330.

59. Barbara Anderson, "Expatriate Selection: A Good Management Are Good Luck?" *International Journal of Human Resource Management* 16, no. 4, April 2005, pp. 567–583.

60. Michael Schell, quoted in Charlene Marmer Solomon, "Success Abroad Depends on More Than Job Skills," p. 52.

61. Mark Shaffer and David Harrison, "Forgotten Partners of International Assignments: Development and Test of a Model of Spouse Adjustment," *Journal of Applied Psychology* 86, no. 2 (2001), pp. 238–254.

62. Ibid., p. 251.
63. Ibid., p. 250.
64. For example, see Stephen Maurer and Shaomin Li, "Understanding Expatriate Manager Performance: Effects of Governance Environments on Work Relationships in Relation-Based Economies," *Human Resource Management Review* 16, no. 1, March 2006, pp. 29–46.
65. Ron Garonzik, Joel Brockner, and Phyllis Siegel, "Identifying International Assignees at Risk for Premature Departure: The Interactive Effect of Outcome Favorability and Procedural Fairness," *Journal of Applied Psychology* 85, no. 1 (2000), pp. 13–20. For a discussion of the importance of organizational support in expatriate adjustment, see, for example, Maria Kraimer et al., "Sources of Support and Expatriate Performance: Mediating Role of Expatriate Adjustment," *Personnel Psychology* 54 (2001), pp. 71–99.
66. Carla Joinson, "Cutting Down the Days," *HR Magazine*, April 2000, pp. 90–97; "Employers Shortened Assignments of Workers Abroad," *BNA Bulletin to Management*, January 4, 2001, p. 7.
67. Hung-Wen Lee and Ching Hsing, "Determinants of the Adjustment of Expatriate Managers to Foreign Countries: An Empirical Study," *International Journal of Management* 23, no. 2, 2006, pp. 302–311.
68. Mason Carpenter et al., "International Assignment Experience at the Top Can Make a Bottom-Line Difference," *Human Resource Management* 30, no. 223 (Summer–Fall 2000), pp. 277–285. See also Gunter Stahl and Paula Caligiuri, "The Effectiveness of Expatriate Coping Strategies: The Moderating Role of Cultural Distance, Position Level, and Time on the International Assignment," *Journal of Applied Psychology* 90, no. 4, 2005, pp. 603–615.
69. Sunkyu Jun and James Gentry, "An Exploratory Investigation of the Relative Importance of Cultural Similarity and Personal Fit in the Selection and Performance of Expatriates," *Journal of World Business* 40, no. 1, February 2005, pp. 1–8. See also, Jan Selmer "Cultural Novelty and Adjustment: Western Business Expatriates in China," *International Journal of Human Resource Management* 17, no. 7, 2006, pp. 1211–1222.
70. Winfred Arthur Jr. and Winston Bennett Jr., "The International Assignee: The Relative Importance of Factors Perceived to Contribute to Success," *Personnel Psychology*, 48 (1995), p. 110; Gretchen Spreitzer, Morgan McCall Jr., and Joan Mahoney, "Early Identification of International Executive Potential," *Journal of Applied Psychology* 82, no. 1 (1997), pp. 62–69. For recent, similar conclusions, see for example, Handan Kepir Sinangil, and Deniz Ones, "Expatriate Management," in Neil Anderson, (Ed); Deniz Ones, (Ed); Handan Kepir Sinangil, (Ed); Chockalingam Viswesvaran, (Ed.). *Handbook of Industrial, Work and Organizational Psychology*, vol. 1: *Personnel Psychology*, (Thousand Oaks, CA: Sage Publications Ltd, 2002), pp. 424–443, Regina Hechanova, Terry Beehr, and Neil Christiansen, "Antecedents and Consequences of Employees' Adjustment to Overseas Assignment: A Meta-Analytic Review," *Applied Psychology: An International Review*, vol. 52(2), April 2003, pp. 213–236, and Raymond Edward Branton, "A Multifaceted Assessment Protocol for Successful International Assignees," *Dissertation Abstracts International: Section B: The Sciences and Engineering*, vol. 64(8B), 2004, p. 4024.
71. Phatak, *International Dimensions of Management*, p. 119. See also Arno Haslberger, "The Complexities of Expatriate Adaptation," *Human Resource Management Review* 15, no. 2, June 2005, pp. 160–180.
72. See for example, Blocklyn, "Developing the International Executive," p. 45.
73. Blocklyn, "Developing the International Executive," p. 45. See also Eric Krell, "Evaluating the Returns on Expatriates," *HR Magazine* 50, no. 3, March 2005, pp. 61–65.
74. "International Assignment Policies and Practices," *BNA Bulletin to Management*, May 1, 1997, pp. 140–141, based on a survey by Organization Resources Counselors, Inc., New York City. See also, Michael Stevens et al., "HR Factors Affecting Repatriate Job Satisfaction and Job Attachment for Japanese Managers," *International Journal of Human Resource Management* 17, no. 5, 2006, pp. 831–841.
75. Hilary Harris and Chris Brewster, "The Coffee Machine System: How International Selection Really Works," *International Journal of Human Resource Management* 10, no. 3 (June 1999), pp. 488–500.
76. Kathryn Tyler, "Don't Fence Her In," *HR Magazine* 46, no. 3 (March 2001), pp. 69–77.
77. Ibid.

78. Ibid.

79. See Nancy Napier and Sully Taylor, "Experiences of Women Professionals Abroad," *International Journal of Human Resource Management* 13, no. 5 (August 2002), pp. 837–851; Iris Fischlmayr, "Female Self-Perception as a Barrier to International Careers?" *International Journal of Human Resource Management* 13, no. 5 (August 2002), pp. 773–783; and Wolfgang Mayrhofer and Hugh Scullion, "Female Expatriates in International Business: Evidence from the German Clothing Industry," *International Journal of Human Resource Management* 13, no. 5 (August 2002), pp. 815–836.

80. This is based on ibid., p. 30. See also Rita Bennett et al., "Cross-Cultural Training: A Critical Step in Ensuring the Success of National Assignments," *Human Resource Management* 39, nos. 2–3 (Summer–Fall 2000), pp. 239–250, and Jill Elswick, "Worldly Wisdom: Companies Refine Their Approach to Overseas Assignments, Emphasizing Cost-Cutting and Work-Life Support for Expatriates," *Employee Benefit News*, June 15, 2004, pITEM0416600B.

81. Mark Mendenhall and Gunther Stahl, "Expatriate Training and Development: Where Do We Go from Here?" *Human Resource Management* 39, no. 223 (Summer–Fall 2000), pp. 251–265.

82. See, for example, Victor Infante, "Three Ways to Design International Pay: Headquarters, Home Country, Host," *Workforce*, January 2001, pp. 22–24; and Gary Parker and Erwin Janush, "Developing Expatriate Remuneration Packages," *Employee Benefits Journal* 26, no. 2 (June 2001), pp. 3–51.

83. Hill, *International Business*, pp. 519–520; Valerie Frazee, "Is the Balance Sheet Right for Your Expats?" *Global Workforce*, September 1998, pp. 19–26; Stephenie Overman, "Focus on International HR," *HR Magazine*, March 2000, pp. 87–92. See also Sheila Burns, "Flexible International Assignee Compensation Plans," *Compensation and Benefits Review*, May/June 2003, pp. 35–44.

84. Phatak, *International Dimensions of Management*, p. 134. See also, "China to Levy Income Tax on Expatriates," *Asia Africa Intelligence Wire*, August 3, 2004, p. NA. Elec. Coll.: A120140119.

85. Except as noted, this section is based on Martocchio, *Strategic Compensation*, pp. 280–283. See also, Gary Parker, "Establishing Remuneration Practices Across Culturally Diverse Environments," *Compensation and Benefits Review*, Spring 2001, vol. 17, issue 2, p. 23.

86. J. E. Richard, "Global Executive Compensation: A Look at the Future," *Compensation and Benefits Review*, May/June 2000, pp. 35–38.

87. Stan Veliotis, "Offshore Equity Compensation Plans," *Compensation and Benefits Review*, July/August 2000, pp. 39–45.

88. Robin White, "A Strategic Approach to Building a Consistent Global Rewards Program," *Compensation and Benefits Review*, July/August 2005, p. 25.

89. Ibid., pp. 23–40.

90. See for example, Jie Shen, "Effective International Performance Appraisals: Easily Said, Hard to Do," *Compensation and Benefits Review*, July/August 2005, pp. 70–78.

91. The following is quoted from or adapted from "The Equal Employment Opportunity Responsibilities of Multinational Employers," The U.S. Equal Employment Opportunity Commission: www.EEOC.gov/facts/multi-employers.html, downloaded February 9, 2004.

92. "Terrorism Impact Ability to Import, Export Workers," *BNA Bulletin to Management*, April 3, 2002, p. 111.

93. Ibid.

94. Frank Jossi, "Buying Protection from Terrorism," *HR Magazine*, June 2001, pp. 155–160.

95. Ibid.

96. Ibid.

97. These are based on or quoted from Samuel Greengard, "Mission Possible: Protecting Employees Abroad," *Workforce*, August 1997, pp. 30–32.

98. Ibid., p. 32.

99. Carla Joinson, "Save Thousands Per Expatriate," *HR Magazine*, July 2002, p. 77.

100. Kathryn Tyler, "Retaining Repatriates," *HR Magazine*, March 2006, pp. 97–102.

101. Quoted in Leslie Klaff, "The Right Way to Bring Expats Home," *Workforce*, July 2002, p. 43.

102. Ibid., p. 43.

103. Ibid., p. 43.

104. Bill Roberts, "Going Global," *HR Magazine*, August 2000, pp. 123–128.

105. Diane Turner, "NuView Brings Web-Based HRIS to Buildnet," *Workforce*, December 2000, p. 90.

106. Jim Meade, "Web-Based HRIS Meets Multiple Needs," *HR Magazine*, August 2000, pp. 129–133.

107. Drew Robb, "Unifying Your Enterprise with a Global HR Portal," *HR Magazine*, March 2006, pp. 119–120.

APPENDIX FOR CHAPTER 17

HRCI Appendix

This appendix contains the complete test specifications for the Human Resource Certification Institutes certification exams. Note the specific areas of *knowledge* ("knowledge of") listed for each HR functional area. (Note that HRCI numbers all *knowledge* questions sequentially, with, for instance, the last Strategic Management question numbered 6, and the first Workforce Planning knowledge question numbered 7.)

Appendix A: HRCI Test Specifications

The percentages that follow each functional area heading are the PHR and SPHR percentages, respectively.

1. Strategic Management (12%, 26%) The processes and activities used to formulate HR objectives, practices, and policies to meet the short- and long-range organizational needs and opportunities, to guide and lead the change process, and to evaluate HR's contributions to organizational effectiveness.

Responsibilities

1. Interpret information related to the organization's operations from internal sources, including financial/accounting, marketing, operations, information technology, and individual employees, in order to participate in strategic planning and policy making.

2. Interpret information related to the general business environment, industry practices and developments, and technological developments from external sources (for example, publications, government documents, media and trade organizations) in order to participate in strategic planning and policy making.

3. Participate as a partner in the organization's strategic planning process.

4. Establish strategic relationships with individuals in the organization, to influence organizational decision making.

5. Establish relationships/alliances with key individuals in the community and in professional capacities to assist in meeting the organization's strategic needs.

6. Evaluate HR's contribution to organizational effectiveness, including assessment, design, implementation and evaluation of activities with respect to strategic and organizational measurement in HR objectives.

7. Provide direction and guidance during changes in organizational processes, operations, planning, intervention, leadership training, and culture that balances the expectations and needs of the organization, its employees, and other stakeholders (including customers).

8. Develop and shape organizational policy related to the organization's management of its human resources.

9. Cultivate leadership and ethical values in self and others through modeling and teaching.

10. Provide information for the organizational budgeting process, including budget development and review.

11. Monitor legislative environment for proposed changes in law and take appropriate action to support, modify, or stop the proposed action (for example, write to a member of Congress, provide expert testimony at a public hearing, lobby legislators).

Knowledge of

1. Lawmaking and administrative regulatory processes.
2. Internal and external environmental scanning techniques.
3. Strategic planning process and implementation.
4. Organizational social responsibility (for example, welfare to work, philanthropy, alliances with community-based organizations).
5. Management functions, including planning, organizing, directing, and controlling.
6. Techniques to sustain creativity and innovation.

2. Workforce Planning and Employment (26%, 16%)   The processes of planning, developing, implementing, administering, and performing ongoing evaluation of recruiting, hiring, orientation, and organizational exit to ensure that the workforce will meet the organization's goals and objectives.

Responsibilities

1. Identify staffing requirements to meet the goals and objectives of the organization.
2. Conduct job analyses to write job descriptions and develop job competencies.
3. Identify and document the essential job functions for positions.
4. Establish hiring criteria based on the competencies needed.
5. Assess internal workforce, labor market, and recruitment agencies to determine the availability of qualified applicants.
6. Identify internal and external recruitment methods and implement them within the context of the organization's goals and objectives.
7. Develop strategies to market the organization to potential applicants.
8. Establish selection procedures, including interviewing, testing, and reference and background checking.
9. Implement selection procedures, including interviewing, testing, and reference and background checking.
10. Develop and/or extend employment offers.
11. Perform or administer post-offer employment activities (for example, employment agreements, completion of I-9 verification form, relocation agreements, and medical exams).
12. Facilitate and/or administer the process by which non-U.S. citizens can legally work in the United States.
13. Design, facilitate, and/or conduct the orientation process, including review of performance standards for new hires and transfers.
14. Evaluate selection and employment processes for effectiveness and implement changes if indicated (for example, employee retention).
15. Develop a succession planning process.
16. Develop and implement the organizational exit process, including unemployment insurance claim responses.
17. Develop, implement, manage, and evaluate affirmative action program(s), as may be required.

Knowledge of

1. Federal/state/local employment-related laws (for example, Title VII, ADA, ADEA, Vietnam Veterans, WARN) and regulations (for example, EEOC Uniform Guidelines on Employee Selection Procedures).

2. Immigration law (for example, visas, I-9).
3. Quantitative analyses required to assess past and future staffing (for example, cost-benefit analysis, costs per hire, selection ratios, adverse impact).
4. Recruitment methods and sources.
5. Staffing alternatives (for example, telecommuting, outsourcing).
6. Planning techniques (for example, succession planning, forecasting).
7. Reliability and validity of selection tests/tools/methods.
8. Use an interpretation of selection tests (for example, psychological/personality, cognitive and motor/physical assessments).
9. Interviewing techniques.
10. Relocation practices.
11. Impact of compensation and benefits plans on recruitment and retention.
12. International HR and implications of international workforce for workforce planning and employment.
13. Downsizing and outplacement.
14. Internal workforce planning and employment policies, practices, and procedures.

3. Human Resource Development (15%, 13%)   The processes of ensuring that the skills, knowledge, abilities, and performance of the workforce meet the current and future organizational and individual needs through developing, implementing, and evaluating activities and programs addressing employee training and development, change and performance management, and the unique needs of particular employee groups.

Responsibilities

1. Conduct needs analyses to identify and establish priorities regarding human resource development activities.
2. Develop training programs.
3. Implement training programs.
4. Evaluate training programs.
5. Develop programs to assess employees' potential for growth and development in the organization.
6. Implement programs to assess employees' potential for growth and development in the organization.
7. Evaluate programs to assess employees' potential for growth and development in the organization.
8. Develop change management programs and activities.
9. Implement change management programs and activities.
10. Evaluate change management programs and activities.
11. Develop performance management programs and procedures.
12. Implement performance management programs and procedures.
13. Evaluate performance management programs and procedures.
14. Develop programs to meet the unique needs of particular employees (for example, work/family programs, diversity programs, outplacement programs, repatriation programs, and fast-track programs).
15. Implement programs to meet the unique needs of particular employees (for example, work/family programs, diversity programs, outplacement programs, repatriation programs, and fast-track programs).
16. Evaluate programs to meet the unique needs of particular employees (for example, work/family programs, diversity programs, outplacement programs, repatriation programs, and fast-track programs).

Knowledge of

1. Applicable international, federal, state, and local laws and regulations regarding copyrights and patents.
2. Human resource development theories and applications (including career development and leadership development).
3. Organizational development theories and applications.
4. Training methods, programs, and techniques (design, objectives, methods, etc.).
5. Employee involvement strategies.
6. Task/process analysis.
7. Performance appraisal and performance management methods.
8. Applicable international issues (for example, culture, local management approaches/ practices, societal norms).
9. Instructional methods and program delivery (content, building modules of program, selection of presentation/delivery mechanism).
10. Techniques to assess HRD program effectiveness (for example, satisfaction, learning, and job performance of program participants, and organizational outcomes such as turnover and productivity).

4. Compensation and Benefits (20%, 16%) The processes of analyzing, developing, implementing, administering, and performing ongoing evaluation of a total compensation and benefits system for all employee groups consistent with human resource management goals.

Responsibilities

1. Ensure the compliance of compensation and benefits with applicable federal, state, and local laws.
2. Analyze, develop, implement, and maintain compensation policies and a pay structure consistent with the organization's strategic objectives.
3. Analyze and evaluate pay rates based on internal worth and external market conditions.
4. Develop/select and implement a payroll system.
5. Administer payroll functions.
6. Evaluate compensation policies to ensure that they are positioning the organization internally and externally according to the organization's strategic objectives.
7. Conduct a benefit plan needs assessment and determine/select the plans to be offered, considering the organization's strategic objectives.
8. Implement and administer benefit plans.
9. Evaluate benefits program to ensure that it is positioning the organization internally and externally according to the organization's strategic objectives.
10. Analyze, select, implement, maintain, and administer executive compensation, stock purchase, stock options and incentive, and bonus programs.
11. Analyze, develop, select, maintain, and implement expatriate and foreign national compensation and benefit programs.
12. Communicate the compensation and benefits plan and policies to the workforce.

Knowledge of

1. Federal, state, and local compensation and benefit laws (for example, FLSA, ERISA, COBRA).
2. Accounting practices related to compensation and benefits (for example, excess group term life, compensatory time).
3. Job evaluation methods.

4. Job pricing and pay structures.
5. Incentive and variable pay methods.
6. Executive compensation.
7. Noncash compensation methods (for example, stock option plans).
8. Benefit needs analysis.
9. Benefit plans (for example, health insurance, life insurance, pension, education, health club).
10. International compensation laws and practices (for example, expatriate compensation, socialized medicine, mandated retirement).

5. Employee and Labor Relations (21%, 24%)   The processes of analyzing, developing, implementing, administering, and performing ongoing evaluation of the workplace relationship between employer and employee (including the collective bargaining process and union relations), in order to maintain effective relationships and working conditions that balance the employer's needs with the employees' rights in support of the organization's strategic objectives.

Responsibilities

1. Ensure compliance with all applicable federal, state, and local laws and regulations.
2. Develop and implement employee relations programs that will create a positive organizational culture.
3. Promote, monitor, and measure the effectiveness of employee relations activities.
4. Assist in establishing work rules and monitor their application and enforcement to ensure fairness and consistency (for union and nonunion environments).
5. Communicate and ensure understanding by employees of laws, regulations, and organizational policies.
6. Resolve employee complaints filed with federal, state, and local agencies involving employment practices.
7. Develop grievance and disciplinary policies and procedures to ensure fairness and consistency.
8. Implement and monitor grievance and disciplinary policies and procedures to ensure fairness and consistency.
9. Respond to union organizing activity.
10. Participate in collective bargaining activities, including contract negotiation and administration.

Knowledge of

1. Applicable federal, state, and local laws affecting employment in union and nonunion environments, such as antidiscrimination laws, sexual harassment, labor relations, and privacy.
2. Techniques for facilitating positive employee relations (for example, small group facilitation, dispute resolution, and labor/management cooperative strategies and programs).
3. Employee involvement strategies (for example, alternate work schedules, work teams).
4. Individual employment rights issues and practices (for example, employment at will, negligent hiring, defamation, employees' rights to bargain collectively).
5. Workplace behavior issues/practices (for example, absenteeism and discipline).
6. Methods for assessment of employee attitudes, opinions, and satisfaction (for example, opinion surveys, attitude surveys, focus panels).
7. Unfair labor practices.

8. The collective bargaining process, strategies, and concepts.
9. Public-sector labor relations issues and practices.
10. Expatriation and repatriation issues and practices.
11. Employee and labor relations for local nationals (i.e., labor relations in other countries).

6. Occupational Health, Safety, and Security (6%, 5%)   The processes of analyzing, developing, implementing, administering, and performing ongoing evaluation of programs, practices, and services to promote the physical and mental well-being of individuals in the workplace, and to protect individuals and the workplace from unsafe acts, unsafe working conditions, and violence.

Responsibilities

1. Ensure compliance with all applicable federal, state, and local workplace health and safety laws and regulations.
2. Determine safety programs needed for the organization.
3. Develop and/or select injury/occupational illness prevention programs.
4. Implement injury/occupational illness prevention programs.
5. Develop and/or select safety training and incentive programs.
6. Implement safety training and incentive programs.
7. Evaluate the effectiveness of safety prevention, training, and incentive programs.
8. Implement workplace injury/occupational illness procedures (for example, workers' compensation, OSHA).
9. Determine health and wellness programs needed for the organization.
10. Develop/select, implement, and evaluate (or make available) health and wellness programs.
11. Develop/select, implement, and evaluate security plans to protect the company from liability.
12. Develop/select, implement, and evaluate security plans to protect employees (for example, injuries resulting from workplace violence).
13. Develop/select, implement, and evaluate incident and emergency response plans (for example, natural disasters, workplace safety threats, evacuation).

Knowledge of

1. Federal, state, and local workplace health and safety laws and regulations (for example, OSHA, Drug-Free Workplace Act, ADA).
2. Workplace injury and occupational illness compensation laws and programs (for example, workers' compensation).
3. Investigation procedures of workplace safety, health, and security enforcement agencies (for example, OSHA).
4. Workplace safety risks.
5. Workplace security risks (for example, theft, corporate espionage, information systems/technology, and vandalism).
6. Potential violent behavior and workplace violence conditions.
7. General health and safety practices (for example, fire evacuation, HAZCOM, ergonomic evaluations).
8. Incident and emergency response plans.
9. Internal investigation and surveillance techniques.
10. Employee assistance programs.
11. Employee wellness programs.
12. Issues related to chemical use and dependency (for example, identification of symptoms, drug testing, discipline).

CORE Knowledge Required by HR Professionals

13. Needs assessment and analysis.
14. Third-party contract management, including development of requests for proposals (RFPs).
15. Communication strategies.
16. Documentation requirements.
17. Adult learning processes.
18. Motivation concepts and applications.
19. Training methods.
20. Leadership concepts and applications.
21. Project management concepts and applications.
22. Diversity concepts and applications.
23. Human relations concepts and applications (for example, interpersonal and organizational behavior).
24. HR ethics and professional standards.
25. Technology and human resource information systems (HRIS) to support HR activities.
26. Qualitative and quantitative methods and tools for analysis, interpretation, and decision-making purposes.
27. Change management.
28. Liability and risk management.
29. Job analysis and job description methods.
30. Employee records management (for example, retention, disposal).
31. The interrelationships among HR activities and programs across functional areas.

Appendix B: Certification Handbook Recertification Guide

Introduction

What Is Certification?   Certification is a voluntary action by a professional group to establish a system to grant recognition to professionals who have met a stated level of training and work experience. Certified individuals are usually issued a certificate attesting that they have met the standards of the credentialing organization and are entitled to make the public aware of their credentialed status, usually through the use of acronyms (i.e., PHR, SPHR, or GPHR) after their names.

Certifications differ from certificate programs because certifications, by definition, include a work experience component. Certificate programs, on the other hand, award certificates once a course of study has been completed and do not require previous work experience.

Why Is Certification Desirable?   Certification sets those with the credential apart—or above—those without it. There are a number of advantages to seeking certification. Certification becomes a public recognition of professional achievement—both within and outside of the profession. For many, achieving certification becomes a personal professional goal—a way to test knowledge and to measure it against one's peers. Others see certification as an aid to career advancement.

Purpose and Use of Certification   PHR and SPHR certifications show that the holder has demonstrated mastery of the HR body of knowledge and, through recertification, has accepted the challenge to stay informed of new developments in the HR field.

The PHR and SPHR exams are completely voluntary. Organizations or individuals incorporating PHR or SPHR certification as a condition of employment or advancement do so of their own volition. Individuals should determine for themselves whether the use of this process, including its eligibility and recertification requirements, when coupled with any other requirements imposed by individuals or organizations, meets their needs and complies with any applicable laws.

The PHR and SPHR designations are a visible reminder to peers and co-workers of the holder's significant professional achievement. PHR and SPHR certified professionals should proudly display their certificates and use the credentials on business correspondence.

Certification Denial and Revocation Certification may be denied or revoked for any of the following reasons:

- Falsification of work experience or other information on the exam application.
- Misrepresentation of work experience or other information on the exam application.
- Violation of testing procedures.
- Failure to pass the certification exam.
- Failure to meet recertification requirements.

Candidates whose certifications are denied or revoked should contact HRCI for more information about how to appeal the denial or revocation. There is no appeal based on failure to pass the exam or to recertify.

Exam Overview

- 225 multiple choice questions.
- Four hours to complete.
- Administered by computer.
- Administered only in English.

Are You Ready?

- Take the HRCI Online Assessment Exam (www.hrci.org).

There are two levels of certification, the Professional in Human Resources (PHR®) and the Senior Professional in Human Resources (SPHR®). Both exams are generalist (i.e., they assess all the functional areas of the HR field) but differ in terms of focus and the cognitive level of questions. PHR questions tend to be at an operational/technical level. SPHR questions tend to be more at the strategic and/or policy level. HRCI exams are offered only in English.

Test questions on both exams reflect the most recently published test specifications (see Appendix A). The exams are multiple choice and consist of 200 scored questions plus 25 pretest questions randomly distributed throughout the exam (a total of 225 questions). Each question lists four possible answers, only one of which is the correct or "best possible answer." The answer to each question can be derived independently of the answer to any other question. Four hours are allotted to complete the exam. All exams are administered by computer at more than 250 Prometric testing centers. There are no paper-and-pencil exam administrations.

Pretest questions are not counted in scoring. They are, however, essential in building the PHR and SPHR item (or test question) banks and are on the exam to statistically assess their difficulty level and effectiveness at discriminating between candidates who meet the passing standard and those who do not. The information gathered in the pretest process determines whether or not the question will be included on a future exam.

On test day, answer questions that are easy first and mark the more difficult ones to return to later. There is no penalty for guessing, so try to answer all the questions. Unanswered questions are counted as incorrect.

There are survey questions at the end of the exam that candidates are encouraged to answer if time allows. These questions are optional. Responses are confidential. The information collected is used for statistical purposes only.

Exam questions represent the following functional areas in HR. The percentages indicate the extent to which each functional area is emphasized at either exam level.

Exams reflect the percentages listed above and are reviewed by a panel of certified professionals with subject matter expertise to ensure that the questions are up to date and reflect the published test specifications.

PHR and SPHR Exam Functional Areas

	PHR	SPHR
Strategic Management	12%	26%
Workforce Planning and Employment	26%	16%
Human Resource Development	15%	13%
Compensation and Benefits	20%	16%
Employee and Labor Relations	21%	24%
Occupational Health, Safety, and Security	6%	5%

Passing Score The passing score for both exams (based on a scaled score) is 500. The minimum possible score is 100. The maximum possible score is 700.

For more information about scaled scoring, please see "Understanding the Score Report" and "How the Passing Score Was Set" in the separate HRCI handbook.

HRCI Online Assessment Exam HRCI offers an online assessment exam comprised of actual exam questions that have appeared on previous exams but were removed from the item bank to develop the assessment exam. Before registering for the exam, consider taking this online assessment exam. The assessment exam exposes candidates to the types of questions that are on the actual exam. For more information about the assessment exam (including fees), visit the HRCI Web site at www.hrci.org.

About Computer-Based Testing (CBT) Starting in 2004, HRCI has delivered all PHR and SPHR exams by computer at Prometric test centers. Here's what you need to know about this exciting development:

Advantages to Computer-Based Exam Delivery

- Exams will be administered exclusively by computer. Exams will no longer be available in paper-and-pencil format.
- The exams will be administered at more than 250 test centers across the United States, U.S. territories, and Canada. Exams will also be offered internationally wherever a Prometric test center is located. See HRCI's separate Appendix D for more information about taking the exam outside the United States, U.S. territories, or Canada.
- There are two annual testing windows—May 1–June 30, 2007 and November 15, 2007–January 15, 2008 for 2007–2008.
- Exams will no longer be offered at SHRM conferences.
- Candidates can schedule their exams Monday through Friday and take their exams Monday through Saturday, during the testing windows.
- Candidates will have access to a built-in clock and calculator.
- Individual testing stations will allow for more privacy and test security.

- Immediate (preliminary) pass/fail score results will be provided to candidates before they leave the testing center. Official score reports will be mailed within two to three weeks of testing.
- There are more testing dates.
- There are more test center locations.
- There will be consistent exam administration and test-taking environments.
- Candidates are able to mark more difficult questions to return to later.
- Computer-based testing provides ease of use (no computer experience necessary).
- A self-paced tutorial shows you how to take the test (including how to mark questions to return to later) to ensure that you are comfortable with the exam administration process.
- Prometric, the leading provider of computer-based testing, will deliver the exams.

What Will Stay the Same

- Exam content, number of questions (225), and duration (4 hours).
- Eligibility requirements.
- Strict deadline dates.
- Official score reports will be mailed to candidates.
- PES will review exam applications, process payments, score the exams, and mail score reports.

For more information about CBT, visit the HRCI homepage at www.hrci.org.

PART IV VIDEO CASES APPENDIX

Video 9: Ethics and Fair Treatment in Human Resource Management

Video Title: Global Business and Ethics

This video suggests, among other things, that there is no absolute statement on what constitutes ethical behavior. Instead, ethics tends to be determined by social, cultural, and other value-laden factors, such as religion. Similarly, as the video points out, the degree of enforcement (for instance, regarding ethical lapses like bribery of customers) tends to vary with social, cultural, and other factors, so what is considered ethical or unethical in one society might not be in another.

This video also discusses the interplay between ethics and management practices. For example, the video points out that "most people look first at how a company treats its employees when viewing its ethics." Focus primarily on the introductory material in the video, the part on ethics and management practices.

Discussion Questions

1. What is the meaning of ethics, and how does the social and cultural context of the business affect what it means to be "ethical" as we move from country to country and society to society?
2. What does the video say about how the company's social and cultural context (in particular, the country in which it does business) affects how you might define what is, or is not, ethical treatment of employees?
3. Based on what you saw in this video, assume for a moment that child labor (as defined by the U.S. Fair Labor Standards Act) is acceptable behavior in some country. How, based on this video, should American companies deal with child labor issues in their own plants in these countries? Why?

Video 10: Managing Labor Relations and Collective Bargaining

Video Title: Labor Relations

In this video, Sarah has just accepted a position in HotJobs' computer programming department as a full-time programmer. She has come to the HR department a bit nervously, to ask whether she has the option of joining the union there. As Sarah says, "I had a lot of benefits with my previous job and there was a union there." HotJobs does not offer union membership. The human resource representative goes on to explain that HotJobs is committed to its employees, and grievances are dealt with on a case-by-case basis. Therefore there is no need for a third party to intercede between the union and the employee, she says. This video also explains the importance of union membership in specific industries and the benefits that union membership provides to employees.

Discussion Questions

1. If you were the company's human resource representative, would you be at all concerned that Sarah might become a leader in a unionization movement at HotJobs, and if so what if anything would you suggest the human resource representative do about it? Why?
2. Do you think human resources provided as comprehensive an answer to Sarah about why she does not need a union as HR could have? If not, what else would you have told Sarah?
3. Do you believe, based on what you read in this part of the book and saw in the video, that union membership may be more important in some industries than others, and if so why?
4. If you were Sarah, would you have even brought a question like this to HR? Why or why not?

Video 11: Protecting Safety and Health

Video Title: Stress

As Chapter 16 explains, stress is an ever-present and potentially debilitating factor at work. In this video, the sources of stress include the employees' own dedication and sense of responsibility, changes in job scope and workload that resulted from the company's rapid growth, and the pressure to make the company a success. At Student Advantage, the stressors appear to be counterbalanced somewhat by most employees' feeling that it's fun to work at the company, and that the atmosphere is collegial and the challenges are worthwhile.

The fun and psychic rewards notwithstanding, it's apparent from the video that stress at this company is a fact of life. For example, Vinny mentions that one source of stress is when someone comes to him and says something needs to be done "an hour ago." Another source of stress here is that employees have to do a sort of balancing act, balancing the needs of their workplace and job with outside interests and family. Sympathy from co-workers helps, but employers still need to be able to refresh themselves and keep stress at tolerable levels.

Discussion Questions

1. What other sources of stress are articulated by the people in this video, and do you think any of the employees seem to be candidates for burnout? Why?
2. What prescriptions for reducing or dealing with stress did the employees in this video mention?
3. What additional methods of dealing with stress would you suggest based upon what you read in Chapter 16?
4. How many potential safety hazards can you identify at this company by watching the video? What are they?

APPENDIX A

Applying HR Content, Personal Competencies, and Business Knowledge

SUPPLEMENTARY STUDY AND DISCUSSION ASSIGNMENTS*

I INTRODUCTION: SHRM'S HUMAN RESOURCE CURRICULUM GUIDEBOOK

SHRM, the Society for Human Resource Management, recently distributed its new *SHRM Human Resource Curriculum Guidebook and Templates for Undergraduate and Graduate Programs*. It contains SHRM's recommended curriculum templates or guides "to assist university faculty, deans, program directors, and other stakeholders in the dissemination of HR knowledge that will better prepare students and the organizations they support. . . ."

In a nutshell, the *Guidebook* advocates building human resource management programs and courses around twenty-four major and minor "HR Learning Modules." Each module contains three interrelated components—*HR Content* (such as "employment law"), *Personal Competencies* (such as "ethical decision-making"), and *Business or Policy Knowledge Applications* (such as "business law, public policy, and corporate social responsibility"). SHRM's stated aims are to systematize and standardize the knowledge and skills HR students leave the classroom with, and to make sure that they learn, not just human resource management skills, but also how to apply personal skills (like communicating) as well as business knowledge to the human resource problems at hand. SHRM wants schools to use the modules to build multi-course programs in human resource management.

II THE PURPOSES OF THIS APPENDIX

The exercises in the following sections III, IV, and V serve two purposes. *First*, they provide an opportunity to learn more about SHRM recommended HR Content Areas, Personal Competencies, and Business/Policy Areas. For example, section III just below lets you practice applying some of what you learned in the book about most of SHRM's main HR Content Areas. *Second* (since not all adopters will cover the new SHRM guidelines in detail), we also prepared this appendix so that all adopters and readers can use these exercises to supplement the behavioral objectives and case questions now in each chapter and case, simply as supplementary exercises.

*© Gary Dessler, Ph.D. 2007.

III ASSESSING WHAT YOU KNOW ABOUT MAJOR SHRM *HR CONTENT AREAS*

List of SHRM Recommended *HR Content Areas*	Supplementary Discussion Questions for Assessing Your Knowledge and Skills with Respect to SHRM HR Content Areas
History of HR and Its Role (we covered in Ch. 1)	**1.** Briefly discuss the evolution of the personnel/HR field in the United States over the last 100 years to its current role in modern globally competitive societies. **2.** Describe HR's role in developing human capital. **3.** Describe HR's impact on firm success. **4.** Discuss the partnership of line managers and HR managers and departments.
Employment Law (Ch. 2)	**1.** List and discuss the major equal employment laws, and give examples of how they influence the various HR functions such as recruiting and training employees. **2.** Describe the basic equal employment law enforcement procedure, from complaint to conclusion.
Managing a Diverse Workforce (Ch. 2)	**1.** List and discuss several important strategies for successfully increasing workforce diversity. **2.** Explain with examples how diversity management can improve business results. **3.** Give some examples of how creating a diverse workforce can enhance employee perceptions of fairness and equity throughout the organization.
HR and Organizational Strategy (Ch. 3)	**1.** List and explain with examples the basic types of corporate, competitive, and functional strategies. **2.** Define Strategic Human Resource Management and explain with examples how managers devise HR practices to support their companies' strategies. **3.** Answer the question, "How do firms gain sustainable competitive advantage through effective human resource management strategies and practices?"
HR and Mergers and Acquisitions (Ch. 3)	**1.** Give several examples of how HR practices can contribute to the success of corporate mergers and acquisitions.
Measuring HR Outcomes and the Bottom-Line (Ch. 3)	**1.** Explain and provide examples of at least 5 HR metrics. **2.** Discuss how you as a manager could use HR and broader business metrics to link HR practices to achieving bottom-line business results.
Job Analysis (Ch. 4)	**1.** List and describe the methods and procedure you would use to conduct a job analysis. **2.** Briefly discuss the main factors that must be taken into account in designing a job. **3.** List and briefly describe the main sections in a job description.
Workforce Planning and Talent Management (Ch. 5)	**1.** Describe the basic process and methods of human resource planning, and explain, in doing so, how they relate to corporate strategy. **2.** Show how you would create a simple staffing plan.

(continued)

List of SHRM Recommended *HR Content Areas*	Supplementary Discussion Questions for Assessing Your Knowledge and Skills with Respect to SHRM HR Content Areas
Outsourcing (Chs. 5, 13)	**1.** Explain the difference between employee leasing and outsourcing. **2.** Discuss the pros and cons of outsourcing.
Recruiting and Selection (Ch. 5)	**1.** Describe the various methods of locating qualified job candidates and the advantages and disadvantages of each. **2.** Briefly discuss what you believe would illustrate a successful strategy for developing a diverse talent pool of qualified candidates.
Recruiting and Selection (Chs. 6, 7)	**1.** List and compare and contrast the main assessment methods an employer can use for identifying a candidate's suitability for employment. **2.** Discuss the main legal implications associated with employment selection techniques, including interviewing.
Organizational Entry and Socialization (Ch. 8)	**1.** Answer the question, "Why is it important to familiarize new employees with the organization, and with their new jobs and work units?"
Training and Development (Ch. 8)	**1.** Explain how you would link training objectives to organizational goals. **2.** List and discuss the principles of learning, and describe how they facilitate training. **3.** Explain how you would create a training program. **4.** List and briefly describe five important training methods. **5.** Why is it important to assess training effectiveness, and how would you go about doing so?
Performance Appraisal and Feedback (Ch. 9)	**1.** Explain what you would consider to be the main *purposes, characteristics, methods* and *communication techniques* of an effective performance appraisal program. **2.** Answer the question, "How would you use performance management techniques to develop a clear 'line of sight' connecting the employees' performance and the company's goals?"
Career Planning (Ch. 10)	**1.** Answer the question, "How would you use HR management functions to better match individual and organizational needs?" **2.** List and describe the basic stages of one's career development. **3.** Describe five methods employers can use to support their employees' career development needs.
Compensation Benefits and Total Rewards (Ch. 11)	**1.** Discuss the major federal laws affecting compensation. **2.** What role does "equity" play in devising a compensation plan? **3.** Define "strategic compensation" and explain how you would go about linking pay, employee performance, and organizational objectives.
Compensation Benefits and Total Rewards (Ch. 12)	**1.** What is meant by "variable pay"? **2.** List and explain the nature and pros and cons of at least one individual, group, and companywide incentive plan.

(continued)

List of SHRM Recommended *HR Content Areas*	Supplementary Discussion Questions for Assessing Your Knowledge and Skills with Respect to SHRM HR Content Areas
Employee Benefits (Ch. 13)	**1.** List the employee benefits required by law. **2.** What are the trends with respect to employee benefits costs and what strategies are employers using to control these costs? **3.** What are the major trends in retirement policies and pension plans? **4.** What strategic considerations should guide the design of benefits programs?
Employee and Labor Relations (Ch. 14, 2)	**1.** Explain the concepts of employment at will, wrongful discharge, implied contract, and constructive discharge. **2.** What is "discipline" and what are the characteristics of a defensible discipline system? **3.** Answer the question, "How can effective employee relations policies and practices create a positive organizational culture and improved employee commitment and performance?" **4.** With respect to fair and equitable treatment, what are employees' rights and responsibilities?
HR and Downsizing (Ch. 14)	**1.** Identify the legal issues associated with organizational downsizings and layoffs. **2.** What are some other, business and people, issues to consider when making downsizing and/or layoff decisions?
Employee and Labor Relations (Ch. 15)	**1.** List and discuss each of the principal federal laws that provide a framework for labor relations. **2.** Briefly define collective bargaining, union representation, union organizing, and bargaining and negotiation. **3.** Discuss the main types of alternative dispute resolution procedures.
Occupational Health, Safety, and Security (Ch. 16)	**1.** Explain the general provisions of the Occupational Safety and Health Act of 1970. **2.** Answer the question, "How would you go about creating a safe work environment?"
HR and Globalization (Ch. 17)	**1.** For the manager, HR manager, and employer, what are the main challenges that influence designing HR policies and practices when managing across borders?
HR Information Systems (Chs. 1–17)	**1.** In general, how can employers use technology to improve the efficiency and effectiveness of their human resource management operations? **2.** Explain how HR information systems can lessen time spent on transactional HR activities and thereby allow HR professionals to focus more on strategic activities. **3.** Give specific examples of how employers use HR information systems to improve HR practices in each of the main HR functions such as recruiting and training. **4.** Answer the question, "How can technology help HR and other managers to make better short and long term decisions?"

(continued)

IV APPLYING YOUR KNOWLEDGE OF SHRM *PERSONAL COMPETENCIES* TO SOLVE HR ISSUES

List of SHRM Recommended *Personal Competencies* Needed for Effectively Carrying Out the Manager's Various HR Activities	Supplementary Discussion Questions for Assessing Your Ability to Apply SHRM Personal Competencies in Solving HR Issues
Change Management: Demonstrate an ability to develop a planned approach to help employees adjust to changes within the organization.	**1.** Bandag Automotive case (Appendix B, pp. 745–747): Assuming Jim Bandag's father decides to step back in and implement the required changes, what issues might he encounter, and how exactly would you suggest he plan and execute the changes (using guidelines like those in chapter 8)? **2.** BP Texas City case (Appendix B, pp. 756–760): In 2007 Lord Browne stepped down as BP's CEO, and the firm's president took charge. Based on the case, what organizational changes should BP make now and how would you suggest the new CEO go about executing them? **3.** Jack Nelson case (ch. 1, pp. 25–26): Assuming the bank decides to set up a central HR office, what employee resistance issues would you expect them to face and how (in outline form) do you suggest they implement the change?
Communication Skills: Demonstrate an ability to effectively convey information both verbally and in writing.	**1.** Video case 3: Recruitment and Placement (ch. 7, p. 289): In this video, Paul and BMG's vice president have a heated and not particularly productive exchange regarding the firm's hiring practices. What did each of these two people do right and wrong with respect to communicating, and what do you think they each should have done to make the discussion more useful? **2.** "Helping 'The Donald'" experiential exercise (ch. 1, p. 25): Would you consider Mr. Trump's communication style in the evaluation sessions entirely effective or not, and if not how would you suggest he improve his style?
Conflict Management: Demonstrate an ability to develop strategies to help productively resolve disagreements between individuals or groups within the organization.	**1.** Disciplinary Action case (ch. 15, p. 631): The parties' actions in this case, which may merely reflect misunderstandings, have the potential to turn into a more serious union–management conflict. If you were the supervisor in this case, what would you have done at this point to reduce the potential for conflict? If you are the firm's HR manager, what if anything would you do to reduce the potential that the conflict will escalate? **2.** Video case 5: Training and Development (ch. 10, p. 419): In this video the training director handles a fairly confrontational meeting with the firm's marketing director. What was the source of the conflict, how well do you think the parties managed the conflict, and what would you have done differently?

(continued)

List of SHRM Recommended *Personal Competencies* Needed for Effectively Carrying Out the Manager's Various HR Activities	Supplementary Discussion Questions for Assessing Your Ability to Apply SHRM Personal Competencies in Solving HR Issues
Cross-Cultural Effectiveness: Demonstrate an ability to successfully recognize and deal with cultural differences that may affect behavior in the workplace.	1. Google case (Appendix B, pp. 750–753): What sorts of factors will Google have to take into consideration as it tries transferring its culture and reward systems and way of doing business to its operations abroad? 2. Carter Cleaning Company Going Abroad case (ch. 17, p. 720): What do you see as the two or three main cultural challenges Carter would face in opening a store in Mexico? How (in terms of specific HR policies and practices) would you suggest the Carters deal with these challenges?
Ethical Decision-Making: Demonstrate an ability to make decisions that reflect a high standard of professional behavior.	1. BP Texas City case (Appendix B, pp. 756–760): The textbook defines ethics as "the principles of conduct governing an individual or a group," and specifically as the standards one uses to decide what their conduct should be. To what extent do you believe that what happened at BP is as much a breakdown in the company's ethical systems as it is in its safety systems, and how would you defend your conclusion? What would you have done differently, ethically? What should the new CEO do now? 2. Fire My Best Salesperson case (ch. 14, p. 588): In this case, Greg, the sales manager, faces what is probably (and unfortunately) an ethical dilemma. Focusing on the ethical issues, what would you do now if you were Greg, and why?
Leadership: Demonstrate the ability to direct, lead, and inspire others toward a shared vision.	1. Carter Cleaning Company Guaranteeing Fair Treatment case (ch. 14, p. 589): "To change her employees' behavior in this matter, Jennifer will have to exhibit effective leadership." Explain why you do (or do not) agree with that statement, and (if you do agree) explain exactly what you would do now if you were Jennifer with respect to exercising effective leadership to improve the situation. 2. Reinventing the Wheel at Apex Door Company case (ch. 8, pp. 326–327): In what ways is Apex's current problem a failure of leadership, what leadership mistakes has president Jim Delaney made, and what leadership steps would you take now if you were in his shoes?
Managing Organizational Culture: Demonstrate an ability to recognize and influence organizational norms and values.	1. BP Texas City case (Appendix B, pp. 750–756): Based on the case, how would you characterize the organizational culture at BP companywide and at its refineries, and what exactly would you do to change that culture (assuming it needs changing)? 2. Honesty Testing at Carter Cleaning Company case (ch. 6, pp. 245–246): Often, the best way to reduce problems like the one now facing the Carters is to create an organizational culture that strongly supports ethical behavior. How exactly could the Carters have fostered such a culture, and what exactly should they do now to do so?

(continued)

List of SHRM Recommended *Personal Competencies* Needed for Effectively Carrying Out the Manager's Various HR Activities	Supplementary Discussion Questions for Assessing Your Ability to Apply SHRM Personal Competencies in Solving HR Issues
Negotiation Skills: Demonstrate an ability to communicate, discuss, and agree on something among people with differing objectives.	**1.** Video case 7: Compensation (ch. 13, p. 550): In this case Angelo is negotiating a pay raise with Cheryl and Gina. How would you rate each person's negotiating skills? Why? What would you advise Cheryl and Gina to do with respect to their negotiating technique? **2.** Salary Inequities at Acme Manufacturing case (ch. 11, pp. 454–455): Joe Black may well now find himself negotiating with the female supervisors in order to reach an equitable salary arrangement with them. What negotiating strategy (for instance, "take it or leave it" vs. "collaboration") would you suggest he use in this situation, and why?
Quantitative Analysis: Demonstrate an ability to ascertain quantitatively, for example, the attributes, behavior, or opinions of the entity you are measuring.	**1.** Muffler Magic case (Appendix B, pp. 753–756): Create a spreadsheet showing the titles of the main measurable factors owner Ron Brown should take into consideration in analyzing whether to take the professor's pay plan advice. **2.** Carter Cleaning Company Incentive Plan case (ch. 12, p. 502): What measurable factors should the Carters take into consideration in costing out and deciding on the new incentive plan?
Teambuilding: Demonstrate an ability to engage in a planned effort to improve the working relationships within a group of people in an organizational setting.	**1.** Angelo's Pizza case (Appendix B, pp. 747–750): If Angelo wants to open more stores, he will have to take steps to make sure that teamwork prevails in each store—that employees in each store work together collaboratively, supportively, and in support of each store's goals. What concrete steps can Angelo take to make sure that teamwork prevails in each store? **2.** Video case 8: Nova Soft Information Technology (ch. 13, p. 550): What specifically can Neal do to use incentives to encourage teamwork among Nova Soft's employees?

V SHRM'S *BUSINESS/POLICY AREAS:* WHY MANAGERS APPLYING HR PRACTICES NEED A BROAD-BASED BUSINESS BACKGROUND

SHRM's Recommended List of *Business or Policy Area* Knowledge and Skills Managers Require for Executing HR Activities	*Assignment: Give specific examples of how dealing with the following HR activities depends on your knowledge and skills in the business or policy areas listed in the left column.*
Accounting	Ch. 3, Strategic HR—computing costs and benefits of various HR activities
Business Law	Chs. 2, 11, 15, 16, HR's Legal Framework—understanding the context of equal employment, safety, compensation, labor relations law.

(continued)

SHRM's Recommended List of *Business or Policy Area* Knowledge and Skills Managers Require for Executing HR Activities	**Assignment:** *Give specific examples of how dealing with the following HR activities depends on your knowledge and skills in the business or policy areas listed in the left column.*
Corporate Social Responsibility	Ch. 13, Fair treatment—excersing fairness in downsizings
Economics	Ch. 5, Personnel planning—labor supply and demand forecasting
Entrepreneurship	Chs. 1–17, When You're on Your Own—How does understanding the entrepreneur's unique challenges make it possible to formulate HR policies and practices that are appropriate for the small business's needs?
Finance	Chs. 11–13, Compensation—formulating possible pay plans
General Management	Ch. 3, Strategic HR—How does understanding how interplay of various business functions influences company strategy, and how HR can support various departments' (sales, production, etc.) strategic aims?
Information Technology	Ch. 5, Recruitment—using technology-based services such as applications service providers to support the recruitment function
International Business	Ch. 17, Managing global human resources—creating international HR services (such as testing and compensation) that make sense in terms of the company's global sales, production, and finance operations
Managing Information Systems	Chs. 1–17, HRIS—instituting companywide human resource information systems
Organizational Behavior	Chs. 9, 12, 14, Applying your knowledge of human behavior in counseling, motivating, and disciplining employees
Statistics	Ch. 6, Testing and selection—assessing the effectiveness of various selection tools
Strategic Management	Ch. 3, Strategic HR—being able to formulate an HR strategy that supports the company's broader strategic aims
Supply-Chain Management	Chs. 11–13, Compensation—creating a compensation plan that motivates employees to work cooperatively with supply chain partners such as vendors, distributors, and customers.

APPENDIX B

Comprehensive Cases

BANDAG AUTOMOTIVE*

Jim Bandag took over his family's auto supply business in 2005, after helping his father, who founded the business, run it for about 10 years. Based in Illinois, Bandag employs about 300 people, and distributes auto supplies (replacement mufflers, bulbs, engine parts, and so on) through two divisions, one that supplies service stations and repair shops, and a second that sells retail auto supplies through five "Bandag Automotive" auto supply stores.

Jim's father, and now Jim, have always endeavored to keep Bandag's organization chart as simple as possible. The company has a full-time controller, managers for each of the five stores, a manager that oversees the distribution division, and Jim Bandag's executive assistant. Jim (and his father, working part-time) handles marketing and sales.

Jim's executive assistant administers the firm's day-to-day human resource management tasks, but they outsource most HR activities to others, including an employment agency that does their recruiting and screening, a benefits firm that administers their 401(k) plan, and a payroll service that handles their paychecks. Bandag's human resource management systems consist almost entirely of standardized HR forms they purchase from an HR supplies company. It supplies HR tools including forms such as application forms, performance appraisal forms, and an "honesty" test Bandag uses to screen the staff that works in the five stores. The company performs informal salary surveys to see what other companies in the area are paying for similar positions, and use these results for awarding annual merit increases (which in fact are more accurately cost-of-living adjustments).

Jim's father took a fairly paternal approach to the business. He often walked around speaking with his employees, finding out what their problems were, and even helping them out with an occasional loan—for instance when he discovered that one of their children were sick, or for part of a new home down payment. Jim, on the other hand, tends to be more abrupt, and does not enjoy the same warm relationship with the employees as did his father. Jim is not unfair or dictatorial. He's just very focused on improving Bandag's financial performance, and so all his decisions, including his HR-related decisions, generally come down to cutting costs. For example, his knee-jerk reaction is usually to offer fewer days off rather than more, fewer benefits rather than more, and to be less flexible when an employee needs, for instance, a few extra days off because a child is sick.

It's therefore perhaps not surprising that over the past few years Bandag's sales and profits have increased markedly, but that the firm has found itself increasingly enmeshed in HR/equal employment type issues. Indeed, Jim now finds himself spending a day or two a week addressing HR problems. For example, Henry Jaques, an employee of one of their stores, came to Jim's executive assistant and told her he was "irate" about his recent firing

*© Gary Dessler, Ph.D.

and was probably going to sue. On Henry's last performance appraisal, his store manager had said Henry did the technical aspects of his job well, but that he had "serious problems interacting with his coworkers." He was continually arguing with them, and complaining to the store manager about working conditions. The store manager had told Jim that he had to fire Henry because he was making "the whole place poisonous," and that (although he felt sorry because he'd heard rumors that Henry suffered from some mental illness) he felt he had to go. Jim approved the dismissal.

Gavin was another problem. Gavin worked for Bandag for 10 years, the last two as manager of one of the company's five stores. Right after Jim Bandag took over, Gavin told him he had to take a Family and Medical Leave Act medical leave to have hip surgery, and Jim approved the leave. So far so good, but when Gavin returned from leave, Jim told him that his position had been eliminated. They had decided to close his store and open a new, larger store across from a shopping center about a mile away, and appointed a new manager in Gavin's absence. However, the company did give Gavin a (non-managerial) position in the new store as a counter salesperson, at the same salary and with the same benefits as he had before. Even so, "this job is not similar to my old one" Gavin insisted, "it doesn't have nearly as much prestige." His contention is that FMLA requires that the company bring him back in the same or equivalent position, and that this means a supervisory position, similar to what he had before he went on leave. Jim said no, and they seem to be heading toward litigation.

In another sign of the times at Bandag, the company's controller, Miriam, who had been with the company for about six years, went on pregnancy leave for 12 weeks in 2005, (also under the FMLA), and then received an additional three weeks' leave under Bandag's extended illness days program. Four weeks after she came back, she asked Jim Bandag if she could arrange to work fewer hours per week, and spend about a day per week working out of her home. He refused, and about two months later fired her. Jim Bandag said, "I'm sorry, it's not anything to do with your pregnancy-related requests, but we've got ample reasons to discharge you—your monthly budgets have been several days late, and we've got proof you may have forged documents." She replied, "I don't care what you say your reasons are, you're really firing me because of my pregnancy, and that's illegal."

Jim felt he was on safe ground as far as defending the company for these actions, although he didn't look forward to spending the time and money that he knew it would take to fight each. However, what he learned over lunch from a colleague undermined his confidence about another case that Jim had been sure would be a "slam dunk" for his company. Jim was explaining to his friend that one of Bandag's truck maintenance service people had applied for a job driving one of Bandag's distribution department trucks, and that Jim had turned him down because the worker was deaf. Jim, (whose wife has occasionally said of him, "No one has ever accused Jim of being politically correct.") was mentioning to his friend the apparent absurdity of a deaf person asking to be a truck delivery person. His friend, who happens to work for UPS, pointed out that the U.S. Court of Appeals for the Ninth Circuit had recently decided that UPS violated the Americans with Disabilities Act by refusing to consider deaf workers for jobs driving the company's smaller vehicles.

Although Jim's father is semi-retired, the sudden uptick in the frequency of such EEO-type issues troubled him, particularly after so many years of labor peace. However, he's not sure what to do about it. Having handed over the reins of the company to his son Jim, he was loath to inject himself back into the company's operational decision-making. On the other hand, he was afraid that in the short run, these issues were going to drain a great deal of Jim's time and resources, and that in the long run they might be a sign of things to come, with problems like these eventually overwhelming Bandag Auto. He comes to you, who he knows consults in human resource management, and asks you the following questions.

Questions

1. Given Bandag Auto's size, and anything else you know about it, should we reorganize the human resource management function, and if so why and how?

2. What, if anything, would you do to change and/or improve upon the current HR systems, forms, and practices that we now use?

3. Do you think that the employee that Jim fired for creating what the manager called a poisonous relationship has a legitimate claim against us, and if so why and what should we do about it?

4. Is it true that we really had to put Gavin back into an equivalent position, or was it adequate to just bring him back into a job at the same salary, bonuses, and benefits as he had before his leave?

5. Miriam, the controller, is basically claiming that the company is retaliating against her for being pregnant, and that the fact that we raised performance issues was just a smokescreen. Do you think the EEOC and/or courts would agree with her, and, in any case, what should we do now?

6. An employee who is deaf has asked us to be one of our delivery people and we turned him down. He's now threatening to sue. What should we do, and why?

7. In the previous 10 years we only had one equal employment complaint, and now in the last few years we had four or five. What should I do about it? Why?

Based generally on actual facts, but Bandag is a fictitious company. Bandag source notes: "The Problem Employee: Discipline or Accommodation?" Monday Business Briefing, March 8, 2005, p. n/a; "Employee Says Change in Duties after Leave Violates FMLA," *BNA Bulletin to Management*, January 16, 2007, p. 24; "Manager Fired Days after Announcing Pregnancy," *BNA Bulletin to Management*, January 2, 2007, p. 8; "Ninth Circuit Rules UPS Violated ADA by Barring Deaf Workers from Driving Jobs," *BNA Bulletin to Management*, p. 329, October 17, 2006.

ANGELO'S PIZZA[*]

Angelo Camero was brought up in the Bronx, New York and basically always wanted to be in the pizza store business. As a youngster, he would sometimes spend hours at the local pizza store, watching the owner knead the pizza dough, flatten it into a large circular crust, fling it up, and then spread on tomato sauce in larger and larger loops. After graduating from college as a marketing major, he made a beeline back to the Bronx, where he opened his first Angelo's Pizza store, emphasizing its clean, bright interior, its crisp green, red, and white sign, and his all-natural, fresh ingredients. Within five years, Angelo's store was a success, and he had opened three other stores and was considering franchising his concept.

Anxious as he was to expand, his four years in business school had taught him the difference between being an entrepreneur and being a manager. As an entrepreneur/small-business owner, he knew he had the distinct advantage of being able to personally run the whole operation himself. With just one store and a handful of employees, he could make every decision and watch the cash register, check in the new supplies, oversee the takeout, and personally supervise the service.

When he expanded to three stores, things started getting challenging. He hired managers for the two new stores (both of whom had worked for him at his first store for several years) and gave them only minimal "how to run a store"-type training, on the assumption that, having worked with him for several years, they already knew pretty much everything they needed to know about running a store. However, he was already experiencing human resource management problems, and he knew there was no way he could expand the number of stores he owned, or (certainly) contemplate franchising his

[*]© Gary Dessler, Ph.D.

idea, unless he had a system in place that he could clone in each new store, to provide the manager (or the franchisee) with the necessary management knowledge and expertise to run their stores. Angelo had no training program in place for teaching his store managers how to run their stores. He simply, (erroneously, as it turned out) assumed that by working with him they would learn how to do things on the job. Since Angelo really had no system in place, the new managers were, in a way, starting off below zero when it came to how to manage a store.

There were several issues that particularly concern Angelo. Finding and hiring good employees was number one. He'd read the new National Small Business Poll from the National Federation of Independent Business Education Foundation. It found that 71% of small-business owners believed that finding qualified employees was "hard." Furthermore, "the search for qualified employees will grow more difficult as demographic and education factors" continue to make it more difficult to find employees. Similarly, reading the Kiplinger Letter one day, he noticed that just about every type of business couldn't find enough good employees to hire. Small firms were particularly in jeopardy; the Letter said: Giant firms can outsource many (particularly entry-level) jobs abroad, and larger companies can also afford to pay better benefits and to train their employees. Small firms rarely have the resources or the economies of scale to allow outsourcing or to install the big training programs that would enable them to take untrained new employees and turned them into skilled ones.

While finding enough employees was his biggest problem, finding enough honest ones scared him even more. Angelo recalled from one of his business school courses that companies in the United States are losing a total of well over $400 billion a year in employee theft annually. As a rough approximation, that works out to about $9 per employee per day and about $12,000 a year lost annually for a typical company. Furthermore, it was small companies like Angelo's that were particularly in the cross hairs, because companies with fewer than 100 employees are particularly prone to employee theft. Why are small firms particularly vulnerable? Perhaps they lack experience dealing with the problem. More importantly: Small firms are more likely to have a single person doing several jobs, such as ordering supplies and paying the delivery person. This undercuts the checks and balances managers often strive for to control theft. Furthermore, the risk of stealing goes up dramatically when the business is largely based on cash. In a pizza store, many people come in and just buy one or two slices and a cola for lunch, and almost all pay with cash, not credit cards.

And, Angelo was not just worried about someone stealing cash. They can steal your whole business idea, something he learned from painful experience. He had been planning to open a store in what he thought would be a particularly good location, and was thinking of having one of his current employees manage the store. Instead, it turned out that this employee was, in a matter of speaking, stealing Angelo's brain—what Angelo knew about customers, suppliers, where to buy pizza dough, where to buy tomato sauce, how much everything should cost, how to furnish the store, where to buy ovens, store layout—everything. This employee soon quit and opened up his own pizza store, not far from where Angelo had planned to open his new store.

That he was having trouble hiring good employees, there was no doubt. The restaurant business is particularly brutal when it comes to turnover. Many restaurants turn over their employees at a rate of 200% to 300% per year—so every year, each position might have a series of two to three employees filling it. As Angelo said, "I was losing two to three employees a month." As he said, "We're a high-volume store, and while we should have [to fill all the hours in a week] about six employees per store, we were down to only three or four, so my managers and I were really under the gun."

The problem was bad at the hourly employee level: "We were churning a lot at the hourly level," said Angelo. "Applicants would come in, my managers or I would hire them and not spend much time training them, and the good ones would leave in frustration after a few weeks, while often it was the bad ones who'd stay behind." But in the last two years, Angelo's three company-owned stores also went through a total of three store managers—"They were just blowing through the door" as Angelo put it, in part because, without good employees, their workday was brutal. As a rule, when a small-business owner or manager can't find enough employees (or an employee doesn't show up for work), about 80% of the time the owner or manager does the job him or herself. So, these managers often ended up working seven days a week, 10 to 12 hours a day, and many just burned out in the end. One night, working three jobs himself with customers leaving in anger, Angelo decided he'd never just hire someone because he was desperate again, but would start doing his hiring more rationally.

Angelo knew he should have a more formal screening process. As he said, "If there's been a lesson learned, it's much better to spend time up-front screening out candidates that don't fit than to hire them and have to put up with their ineffectiveness." He also knew that he could identify many of the traits that his employees needed. For example, he knew that not everyone has the temperament to be a waiter a waitress (he has a small pizza/Italian restaurant in the back of his main store). As Angelo said, "I've seen personalities that were off the charts in assertiveness or overly introverted, traits that obviously don't make a good fit for a waiter a waitress."

As a local business, Angelo recruits by placing help-wanted ads in two local newspapers, and he's been "shocked" at some of the responses and experiences he's had in response to his help-wanted ads. Many of the applicants left voice mail messages (Angelo or the other workers in the store were too busy to answer) and some applicants Angelo "just axed" on the assumption that people without good telephone manners wouldn't have very good manners in the store either. He also quickly learned that he had to throw out a very wide net, even if only hiring one or two people. Many people, as noted, he just deleted because of the messages they left, and about half the people he scheduled to come in for interviews didn't show up. He'd taken courses in human resource management, so (as he said) "I should know better," but he hired people based almost exclusively on a single interview (he occasionally made a feeble attempt to check references). In total, his HR approach was obviously not working. It wasn't producing enough good recruits, and the people he did hire were often problematical.

What was he looking for? Service-oriented courteous people, for one. For example, he'd hired one employee who used profanity several times, including once in front of a customer. On that employee's third day, Angelo had to tell her, "I think Angelo's isn't the right place for you," and he fired her. As Angelo said, "I felt bad," but also knew that everything I have is on the line for this business, so I wasn't going to let anyone run this business down." Angelo wants reliable people (who'll show up on time), honest people, and people who are flexible about switching jobs and hours as required.

Angelo's Pizza business has only the most rudimentary human resource management system. Angelo bought several application forms at a local Office Depot, and rarely uses other forms of any sort. He uses his personal accountant for reviewing the company's books, and Angelo himself computes each employee's paycheck at the end of the week and writes the checks. Training is entirely on-the-job. Angelo personally trained each of his employees. For those employees who go on to be store managers, he assumes that they are training their own employees the way to Angelo trained them (for better or worse, as it turns out). Angelo pays "a bit above" prevailing wage rates (judging by other help wanted ads) but probably not enough to make a significant difference in the quality of employees that he attracts. If you asked Angelo what his reputation is as an employer, Angelo, being a candid and forthright person, would probably tell you that he is a supportive but hard-nosed employer who treats people fairly, but whose business reputation may suffer from disorganization stemming from inadequate organization and training. He approaches you to ask you several questions.

Questions

1. My strategy is to (hopefully) expand the number of stores and eventually franchise, while focusing on serving only high-quality fresh ingredients. What are three specific human resource management implications of my strategy (including specific policies and practices).

2. Identify and briefly discuss five specific human resource management errors that I'm currently making.

3. Develop a structured interview form that we can use for hiring (1) store managers, (2) waiters and waitresses, and (3) counter people/pizza makers.

4. Based on what you know about Angelo's, and what you know from having visited pizza restaurants, write a one-page outline showing specifically how you think Angelo's should go about selecting employees.

Based generally on actual facts, but Angelo's Pizza is a fictitious company. Angelo's Pizza source notes: Dino Berta, "People Problems: Keep Hiring from Becoming a Crying Game," *Nation's Business News*, May 20, 2002, vol. 36, issue 20, pp. 72–74; Ellen Lyon, "Hiring, Personnel Problems can Challenge Entrepreneurs," *Patriot-News*, October 12, 2004, p. n/a; Rose Robin Pedone, "Businesses' $400 Billion Theft Problem," *Long Island Business News*, July 6, 1998, no. 27, pp. 1B–2B; "Survey Shows Small-Business Problems with Hiring, Internet," *Providence Business News*, September 10, 2001, vol. 16, pp. 1B; "Finding Good Workers is Posing a Big Problem as Hiring Picks Up," *the Kiplinger Letter*, February 13, 2004, vol. 81, p. n/a.

GOOGLE[*]

Fortune magazine recently named Google the best of the 100 best companies to work for, and there is little doubt why. Among the benefits they offer are free shuttles equipped with Wi-Fi to pick up and drop-off employees from San Francisco Bay area locations, unlimited sick days, annual all-expense-paid ski trips, free gourmet meals, five on-site free doctors, $2000 bonuses for referring a new hire, free flu shots, a giant lap pool, on-site oil changes, on-site car washes, volleyball courts, TGIF parties, free on-site washers and dryers (with free detergent), Ping-Pong and foosball tables, and free famous people lectures. For many people, it's the gourmet meals and snacks that make Google stand out. For example, human resources director Stacey Sullivan loves the Irish oatmeal with fresh berries at the company's Plymouth Rock Cafe, near Google's "people operations" group. "I sometimes dream about it," she says. Engineer Jan Fitzpatrick loves the raw bar at Google's Tapis restaurant, down the road on the Google campus. Then, of course there are the stock options—each new employee gets about 1200 options to buy Google shares (recently worth about $480 per share). In fact, dozens of early Google employees ("Googlers") are already multimillionaires thanks to Google stock.

For their part, Googlers share certain traits. They tend to be brilliant, team oriented (teamwork is the norm, especially for big projects), and driven. *Fortune* describes them as people who "almost universally" see themselves as the most interesting people on the planet, and who are happy-go-lucky on the outside, but type A—highly intense and goal directed—on the inside. They're also super-hardworking, (which makes sense, since it's not unusual for engineers to be in the hallways at 3 A.M. debating some new mathematical solution to a Google search problem). They're so team oriented that when working on projects, it's not unusual for a Google team to give up its larger, more spacious offices and to crowd into a small conference room, where they can "get things done." Historically, Googlers generally graduate with great grades from the best universities, including Stanford, Harvard, and MIT. For many years, Google wouldn't even consider hiring someone with less than a 3.7 average—while also probing deeply into the why behind any B grades. Google also doesn't hire lone wolves, but wants people who work together and people who also have diverse interests (narrow interests or skills are a turnoff at Google).

[*]© Gary Dessler, Ph.D.

Google also wants people with growth potential. The company is expanding so fast that they need to hire people who are capable of being promoted five or six times—it's only, they say, by hiring such overqualified people that they can be sure that the employees will be able to keep up as Google and their own departments expand.

The starting salaries are highly competitive. Experienced engineers start at about $130,000 a year (plus about 1200 shares of stock options, as noted), and new MBAs can expect between $80,000 and $120,000 per year (with smaller option grants). Most recently, Google had about 10,000 staff members, up from its start a few years ago with just three employees in a rented garage.

Of course, in a company that's grown from three employees to 10,000 and from zero value to hundreds of billions of dollars in about five years, it may be quibbling to talk about "problems," but there's no doubt that such rapid growth does confront Google's management, and particularly its "people operations" group, with some big challenges. Let's look at these.

For one, Google, as noted above, is a 24-hour operation, and with engineers and others frequently pulling all-nighters to complete their projects, the company needs to provide a package of services and financial benefits that supports that kind of lifestyle, and that helps its employees maintain an acceptable work–life balance.

As another challenge, Google's enormous financial success is a two-edged sword. While Google usually wins the recruitment race when it comes to competing for new employees against competitors like Microsoft or Yahoo, Google does need some way to stem a rising tide of retirements. Most Googlers are still in their late twenties and early thirties, but many have become so wealthy from their Google stock options that they can afford to retire. One 27-year-old engineer received a million-dollar founder's award for her work on the program for searching desktop computers, and wouldn't think of leaving "except to start her own company." Similarly a former engineering vice president retired (with his Google stock profits) to pursue his love of astronomy. The engineer who dreamed up Gmail recently retired (at the age of 30).

Another challenge is that the work not only involves long hours but can also be very tense. Google is a very numbers-oriented environment. For example, consider a typical weekly Google user interface design meeting. Marisa Meyer, the company's vice president of search products and user experience runs the meeting, where her employees work out the look and feel of Google's products. Seated around a conference table are about a dozen Googlers, tapping on laptops. During the two hour meeting, Meyer needs to evaluate various design proposals, ranging from minor tweaks to a new product's entire layout. She's previously given each presentation an allotted amount of time, and a large digital clock on the wall ticks off the seconds. The presenters must quickly present their ideas, but also handle questions such as "what users do if the tab is moved from the side of the page to the top?" Furthermore, it's all about the numbers—no one at Google would ever say, for instance "the tab looks better in red"—you need to prove your point. Presenters must come armed with usability experiment results, showing, for instance, that a certain percent preferred red or some other color, for instance. While the presenters are answering these questions as quickly as possible, the digital clock is ticking, and when it hits the allotted time, the presentation must end, and the next team steps up to present. It is a tough and tense environment, and Googlers must have done their homework.

Growth can also undermine the "outlaw band that's changing the world" culture that fostered the services that made Google famous. Even cofounder Sergi Brin agrees that Google risks becoming less "zany" as it grows. To paraphrase one of its top managers, the hard part of any business is keeping that original innovative, small-business feel even as the company grows.

Creating the right culture is especially challenging now that Google is truly global. For example, Google works hard to provide the same financial and service benefits every place it does business around the world, but it can't exactly match its benefits in every country because of international laws and international taxation issues. Offering the same benefits everywhere is more important than it might initially appear. All those benefits make life easier for Google staff, and help them achieve a work–life balance. Achieving the right work–life balance is the centerpiece of Google's culture, but also becomes more challenging as the company grows. On the one hand, Google does expect all of its employees to work super hard; on the other hand, it realizes that it needs to help them maintain some sort of balance. As one manager says, Google acknowledges "that we work hard but that work is not everything."

Recruitment is another challenge. While Google certainly doesn't lack applicants, attracting the right applicants is crucial if Google is to continue to grow successfully. Working at Google requires a special set of traits, and screening employees is easier if they recruit the right people to begin with. For instance, they need to attract people who are super-bright, love to work, have fun, can handle the stress, and who also have outside interests and flexibility.

As the company grows internationally, it also faces the considerable challenge of recruiting and building staff overseas. For example, Google now is introducing a new vertical market-based structure across Europe, to attract more business advertisers to its search engine. (By vertical market-based structure, Google means focusing on key vertical industry sectors such as travel, retail, automotive, and technology). To build these industry groupings abroad from scratch, Google promoted its former head of its U.S. financial services group to be the vertical markets director for Europe; he moved there recently. Google is thus looking for heads for each of its vertical industry groups for all of its key European territories. Each of these vertical market heads will have to educate their market sectors (retailing, travel, and so on) so Google can attract new advertisers. Most recently, Google already had about 12 offices across Europe, and its London office had tripled in size to 100 staff in just two years.

However, probably the biggest challenge Google faces is gearing up its employee selection system, now that the company must hire thousands of people per year. When Google started in business, job candidates typically suffered through a dozen or more in-person interviews, and the standards were so high that even applicants with years of great work experience often got turned down if they had just average college grades. But recently, even Google's cofounders have acknowledged to security analysts that setting such an extraordinarily high bar for hiring was holding back Google's expansion. For Google's first few years, one of the company's cofounder's interviewed nearly every job candidate before he or she was hired, and even today one of them still reviews the qualifications of everyone before he or she gets a final offer.

The experience of one candidate illustrates what Google is up against. They interviewed a 24-year-old for a corporate communications job at Google. Google first made contact with the candidate in May, and then, after two phone interviews, invited him to headquarters. There he had separate interviews with about six people and was treated to lunch in a Google cafeteria. They also had him turn in several "homework" assignments, including a personal statement and a marketing plan. In August, Google invited the candidate back for a second round, which they said would involve another four or five interviews. In the meantime, he decided he'd rather work at a start-up, and accepted another job at a new Web-based instant messaging provider.

Google's new head of human resources, a former GE executive, says that Google is trying to strike the right balance between letting Google and the candidate get to know each other while also moving quickly. To that end, Google recently administered a survey to all Google's current employees, in an effort to identify the traits that correlate with success at Google. In the survey, employees had to respond to questions relating to about 300 variables, including their performance on standardized tests, how old they were when they first used a computer, and how many foreign languages they speak. The Google survey team that went back and compared the answers against the 30 or 40 job performance factors they keep for each employee. They thereby identified clusters of traits that Google might better focus on during the hiring process. Google is also trying to move from the free-form interviews they've had in the past to a more structured process.

Questions

1. What do you think of the idea of Google correlating personal traits from the employee's answers on the survey to their performance, and then using that as the basis for screening job candidates? In other words, is it or is it not a good idea and please explain your answer.
2. The benefits that Google pays obviously represent an enormous expense. Based on what you know about Google and on what you read in this book, how would you defend all these benefits if you're making a presentation to the security analysts who were analyzing Google's performance?
3. If you wanted to hire the brightest people around, how would you go about recruiting and selecting them?
4. To support its growth and expansion strategy, Google wants (among other traits) people who are super-bright, and who work hard, often round-the-clock and who are flexible and maintain a decent work–life balance. List five specific HR policies or practices that you think Google has implemented or should implement to support its strategy, and explain your answer.
5. What sorts of factors do you think Google will have to take into consideration as it tries transferring its culture and reward systems and way of doing business to its operations abroad?
6. Given the sorts of values and culture Google cherishes, briefly describe four specific activities you suggest they pursue during new-employee orientation.

Source notes for Google: "Google Brings Vertical Structure to Europe," *New Media Age*, August 4, 2005, p. 2; Debbie Lovewell, "Employer Profile—Google: Searching for Talent," *Employee Benefits*, October 10, 2005, p. 66; "Google Looking for Gourmet Chefs," *Internet Week*, August 4, 2005, p. n/a; Douglas Merrill, "Google's 'Googley' Culture Kept Alive by Tech," *eWeek*, April 11, 2006, p. n/a; Robert Hof, "Google Gives Employees Another Option," *BusinessWeek Online*, December 13, 2005, p. n/a; Kevin Delaney, "Google Adjusts Hiring Process as Needs Grow," the *Wall Street Journal*, October 23, 2006, pp. B1, B8; Adam Lishinsky, "Search and Enjoy." *Fortune*, January 22, 2007, pp. 70–82.

MUFFLER MAGIC*

Muffler Magic is a fast-growing chain of 25 automobile service centers in Nevada. Originally started 20 years ago as a muffler repair shop by Ronald Brown, the chain expanded rapidly to new locations, and as it did so Muffler Magic also expanded the services it provided, from muffler replacement to oil changes, brake jobs, and engine repair. Today, one can bring an automobile to a Muffler Magic shop for basically any type of service, from tires to mufflers to engine repair.

Auto service is a tough business. The shop owner is basically dependent upon the quality of the service people he or she hires and retains, and the most qualified mechanics find it easy to pick up and leave for a job paying a bit more at a competitor down the road. It's also a business in which productivity is very important. The single largest expense is usually the cost of labor. Auto service dealers generally don't just make up the prices that

*© Gary Dessler, Ph.D.

they charge customers for various repairs, instead, they charge based on standardized industry rates for jobs like changing spark plugs, or repairing a leaky radiator. Therefore, if, for instance, someone brings a car in for a new alternator, and the standard number of hours for changing the alternator is an hour, but it takes the mechanic two hours, the service center's owner may end up making less profit on the transaction.

Quality is a persistent problem as well. For example, "rework" has recently been a problem at Muffler Magic. A customer recently brought her car to a Muffler Magic to have the car's brake pads replaced, which the store did for her. Unfortunately, when she drove off, she only got about two blocks before she discovered that she had no brake power at all. It was simply fortuitous that she was going so slowly she was able to stop her car by slowly rolling up against a parking bumper. It subsequently turned out that the mechanic who replaced the brake pads had failed to properly tighten a fitting on the hydraulic brake tubes, and the brake fluid had run out, leaving the car with no braking power. In a similar problem the month before that, a (different) mechanic replaced a fan belt, but forgot to refill the radiator with fluid; that customer's car overheated before he got four blocks away, and Muffler Magic had to replace the whole engine. Of course problems like these not only diminish the profitability of the company's profits, but, repeated many times over, have the potential for ruining Muffler Magic's word-of-mouth reputation.

Organizationally, Muffler Magic employs about 300 people total, and Ron runs his company with eight managers, including Mr. Brown as president, a controller, a purchasing director, a marketing director, and the human resource manager. He also has three regional managers to whom the eight or nine service center managers in each area of Nevada report. Over the past two years, as the company has opened new service centers, companywide profits have actually diminished, rather than gone up. In part, these diminishing profits probably reflect the fact that Ron Brown has found it increasingly difficult to manage his growing operation ("Your reach is exceeding your grasp" is how Ron's wife puts it).

The company has only the most basic HR systems in place. They use an application form that the human resource manager modified from one that she downloaded from the Web, and they use standard employee status change request forms, sign-on forms, I-9 forms, and so on that they purchased from a human resource management supply house. Training is entirely on-the-job. They expect the experienced technicians that they hire to come to the job fully trained; as noted, to that end, the service center managers generally ask candidates for these jobs basic behavioral questions that hopefully provide a window into these applicants' skills. However most of the other technicians they hire to do jobs like rotating tires, fixing brake pads, and replacing mufflers are untrained and inexperienced. They are to be trained by either the service center manager or by more experienced technicians, on-the-job.

Ron Brown faces several HR-type problems. One, as he says, is that he faces the "tyranny of the immediate" when it comes to hiring employees. While it's fine to say that he should be carefully screening each employee and checking their references and work ethic, from a practical point of view, with 25 centers to run, the centers' managers usually just hire anyone who seems to be breathing, as long as they can answer some basic interview questions about auto repair, such as, "What do you think the problem is if a 2001 Camry is overheating, and what would you do about it?"

Employee safety is also a problem. An automobile service center may not be the most dangerous type of workplace, but it is potentially dangerous. Employees are dealing with sharp tools, greasy floors, greasy tools, extremely hot temperatures (for instance on mufflers and engines), and fast-moving engine parts including fan blades. There are some basic things that a service manager can do to ensure more safety, such as insisting that all oil spills be cleaned up immediately. However, from a practical point of view, there are a few ways to get around many of the problems—such as when the technician must check out an engine while it is running.

With Muffler Magic's profits going down instead of up, Brown's human resource manager has taken the position that the main problem is financial. As he says, "You get what you pay for" when it comes to employees, and if you compensate technicians better then your competitors do, then you get better technicians, ones who do their jobs better and stay longer with the company—and then profits will rise. So, the HR manager scheduled a meeting between himself, Ron Brown, and a professor of business who teaches compensation management at a local university. The HR manager has asked this professor to spend about a week looking at each of the service centers, analyzing the situation, and coming up with a compensation plan that will address Muffler Magic's quality and productivity problems. At this meeting, the professor makes three basic recommendations for changing the company's compensation policies.

Number one, she says that she has found that Muffler Magic suffers from what she calls "presenteeism," in other words employees drag themselves into work even when they're sick, because the company does not pay them at all if they are out—there are no sick days. In just a few days the professor couldn't properly quantify how much Muffler Magic is losing to presenteeism. However, from what she could see at each shop, there are typically one or two technicians working with various maladies like the cold or flu, and it seemed to her that each of these people were probably really only working about half of the time (although they were getting paid for the whole day). So, for 25 service centers per week, Muffler Magic could well be losing 125 or 130 personnel days per week of work. The professor suggests that Muffler Magic start allowing everyone to take three paid sick days per year, a reasonable suggestion. However, as Ron Brown points out, "Right now, we're only losing about half a day's pay for each employee who comes in and who works unproductively; with your suggestion, won't we lose the whole day?" The professor says she'll ponder that one.

Second, the professor also recommends putting the technicians on a skill-for-pay plan. Basically, here's what she suggests. Give each technician a letter grade (A through E) based upon that technician's particular skill level and abilities. An "A" technician is a team leader and needs to show that he or she has excellent diagnostic troubleshooting skills, and the ability to supervise and direct other technicians. At the other extreme, an "E" technician would typically be a new apprentice with little technical training. The other technicians fall in between those two levels, based on their individual skills and abilities.

In the professor's system, the "A" technician or team leader would assign and supervise all work done within his or her area but generally not do any mechanical repairs him or herself. The team leader does the diagnostic troubleshooting, supervises and trains the other technicians, and test drives the car before it goes back to the customer. Under this plan, every technician receives a guaranteed hourly wage within a certain range, for instance:

A tech = $25–$30 an hour
B tech = $20–$25 an hour
C tech = $15–$20 an hour
D tech = $10–$15 an hour
E tech = $8–$10 an hour

Third, to directly address the productivity issue, the professor recommends that at the end of each day, each service manager calculate each technician-team's productivity for the day and then at the end of each week. She suggests posting the running productivity total conspicuously for daily viewing. Then, the technicians as a group get weekly cash bonuses based upon their productivity. To calculate productivity, the professor recommends dividing the total labor hours billed by the total labor hours paid to technicians, in other words: Total labor hours billed, *divided by* total hours paid to technicians.

Having done some homework, the professor says that the national average for labor productivity is currently about 60%, and that only the best-run service centers achieve 85% or greater. By her rough calculations, Muffler Magic was attaining about industry average, (about 60%—in other words, they were billing for (as an example) only about 60 hours for each 100 hours that they actually had to pay technicians to do the jobs. (Of course, this was not entirely the technicians' fault. Technicians get time off for breaks, and for lunch, and if a particular service center simply didn't have enough business on a particular day or during a particular week, then several technicians may well sit around idly waiting for the next car to come in.) The professor recommends setting a labor efficiency goal of 80% and posting each team's daily productivity results in the workplace to provide them with additional feedback. She recommends that if at the end of a week the team is able to boost its productivity ratio from the current 60% to 80%, then that team would get an additional 10% weekly pay bonus. After that, for every 5% boost of increased productivity above 80%, technicians would receive an additional 5% weekly bonus. (So, if a technician's normal weekly pay is $400, that employee got an extra $40 at the end of the week when his team moved from 60% productivity to 80% productivity.)

After the meeting, Ron Brown thanked the professor for her recommendations and told her he would think about it and get back to her. After the meeting, on the drive home, Ron was pondering what to do. He had to decide whether to institute the professor's sick leave policy, and whether to implement the professor's incentive and compensation plan. Before implementing anything, however, he wanted to make sure he understood the context in which he was making his decision. For example, did Muffler Magic really have an incentive pay problem, or were the problems more broad? Furthermore, how, if at all, would the professor's incentive plan impact the quality of the work that the teams were doing? And should they really start paying for sick days? Ron Brown had a lot to think about.

Questions

1. Write out a one-page summary outline listing three or four recommendations you would make with respect to each HR function (recruiting, selection, training, and so on) that you think Ron Brown should be addressing with his HR manager now.
2. Develop a 10-question structured interview form Ron Brown's service center managers can use to interview experienced technicians.
3. If you were Ron Brown, would you implement the professor's recommendation addressing the presenteeism problem, in other words start paying for sick days? Why or why not?
4. If you were advising Ron Brown, would you recommend that he implement the professor's skill-base pay and incentive pay plans as is? Why? Would you implement it with modifications? If you would modify it, please be specific about what you think those modifications should be, and why.

Based generally on actual facts, but Muffler Magic is a fictitious company. This case is based largely on information in Drew Paras', "The Pay Factor: Technicians' Salaries Can Be the Largest Expense in a Server Shop, as well as the Biggest Headache. Here's How One Shop Owner Tackled the Problem," *Motor Age*, November 2003, pp. 76–79; see also, Jennifer Pellet, "Health Care Crisis," *Chief Executive*, June 2004, pp. 56–61; "Firms Press to Quantify, Control Presenteeism," *Employee Benefits*, December 1, 2002, p. n/a.

BP TEXAS CITY[*]

In March 2005, an explosion and fire at British Petroleum's (BP) Texas City, Texas refinery killed 15 people and injured 500 people in the worst U.S. industrial accident in more than 10 years. The disaster triggered three investigations, one internal investigation by BP,

[*]© Gary Dessler, Ph.D.

one by the U.S. Chemical Safety Board, and another, independent investigation chaired by former U.S. Secretary of State James Baker and an 11 member panel, and organized at BP's request.

To put the results of these three investigations into context, it's useful to understand that under its current management, BP has pursued, for the past 10 or so years, a strategy emphasizing cost-cutting and profitability. The basic conclusion of the investigations was that cost-cutting helped compromise safety at the Texas City refinery. It's useful to consider each investigation's findings.

The Chemical Safety Board's (CSB) investigation, according to Carol Merritt, the board's chairwoman, showed that "BP's global management was aware of problems with maintenance, spending, and infrastructure well before March 2005." Apparently, faced with numerous earlier accidents, BP did make some safety improvements. However, it focused primarily on emphasizing personal employee safety behaviors and procedural compliance, and on thereby reducing safety accident rates. The problem (according to the CSB) was that "catastrophic safety risks remained." For example, according to the CSB, "unsafe and antiquated equipment designs were left in place, and unacceptable deficiencies in preventive maintenance were tolerated." Basically, the CSB found that BP's budget cuts led to a progressive deterioration of safety at the Texas City refinery. Said Ms. Merritt, "In an aging facility like Texas City, it is not responsible to cut budgets related to safety and maintenance without thoroughly examining the impact on the risk of of a catastrophic accident."

Looking at specifics, the CSB said that a 2004 internal audit of 35 BP business units, including Texas City (BP's largest refinery) found significant safety gaps they all had in common, including for instance, a lack of leadership competence, and "systemic underlying issues" such as a widespread tolerance of noncompliance with basic safety rules and poor monitoring of safety management systems and processes. Ironically, the CSB found that BP's accident prevention effort at Texas City had achieved a 70% reduction in worker injuries in the year before the explosion. Unfortunately, this simply meant that individual employees were having fewer accidents. The larger, more fundamental problem was that the potentially explosive situation inherent in the depreciating machinery remained.

The CSB found that the Texas City explosion followed a pattern of years of major accidents at the facility. In fact, there had apparently been an average of one employee death every 16 months at the plant for the last 30 years. The CSB found that the equipment directly involved in the most recent explosion was an obsolete design already phased out in most refineries and chemical plants, and that key pieces of its instrumentation were not working. There had also been previous instances where flammable vapors were released from the same unit in the 10 years prior to the explosion. In 2003, an external audit had referred to the Texas City refinery's infrastructure and assets as "poor" and found what it referred to as a "checkbook mentality," one in which budgets were not sufficient to manage all the risks. In particular, the CSB found that BP had implemented a 25% cut on fixed costs between 1998 and 2000 and that this adversely impacted maintenance expenditures and net expenditures, and refinery infrastructure. Going on, the CSB found that in 2004, there were three major accidents at the refinery that killed three workers.

BP's own internal report concluded that the problems at Texas City were not of recent origin, and instead were years in the making. It said BP was taking steps to address them. Its investigation found "no evidence of anyone consciously or intentionally taking actions or making decisions that put others at risk." Said BP's report, "The underlying reasons for the behaviors and actions displayed during the incident are complex, and the team has spent much time trying to understand them—it is evident that they were many years in the making and will require concerted and committed actions to address." BP's report concluded that there were five underlying causes for the massive explosion:

- A working environment that had eroded to one characterized by resistance to change, and a lack of trust
- Safety, performance, and risk reduction priorities had not been set and consistently reinforced by management
- Changes in the "complex organization" led to a lack of clear accountabilities and poor communication
- A poor level of hazard awareness and understanding of safety resulted in workers accepting levels of risk that were considerably higher then at comparable installations
- A lack of adequate early warning systems for problems, and no independent means of understanding the deteriorating standards at the plant.

The report from the BP-initiated but independent 11 person panel chaired by former U.S. Secretary of State James Baker contained specific conclusions and recommendations. The Baker panel looked at BP's corporate safety oversight, the corporate safety culture, and the process safety management systems at BP at the Texas City plant as well at BP's other refineries.

Basically, the Baker panel concluded that BP had not provided effective safety process leadership and had not established safety as a core value at the five refineries it looked at (including Texas City).

Like the CSB, the Baker panel found that BP had emphasized personal safety in recent years and had in fact improved personal safety performance, but had not emphasized the overall safety process, thereby mistakenly interpreting "improving personal injury rates as an indication of acceptable process safety performance at its U.S. refineries." In fact, the Baker panel went on, by focusing on these somewhat misleading improving personal injury rates, BP created a false sense of confidence that it was properly addressing process safety risks. It also found that the safety culture at Texas City did not have the positive, trusting, open environment that a proper safety culture required. The Baker panel's other findings included:

- BP did not always ensure that adequate resources were effectively allocated to support or sustain a high level of process safety performance
- BP's refinery personnel are "overloaded" by corporate initiatives
- Operators and maintenance personnel work high rates of overtime
- BP tended to have a short-term focus and its decentralized management system and entrepreneurial culture delegated substantial discretion to refinery plant managers "without clearly defining process safety expectations, responsibilities, or accountabilities"
- There was no common, unifying process safety culture among the five refineries
- The company's corporate safety management system did not make sure there was timely compliance with internal process safety standards and programs
- BP's executive management either did not receive refinery specific information that showed that process safety deficiencies existed at some of the plants, or did not effectively respond to any information it did receive[1]

The Baker panel made several safety recommendations for BP, including these:

1. The company's corporate management must provide leadership on process safety.
2. The company should establish a process safety management system that identifies, reduces, and manages the process safety risks of the refineries.

3. The company should make sure its employees have an appropriate level of process safety knowledge and expertise.

4. The company should involve "relevant stakeholders" in developing a positive, trusting, and open process safety culture at each refinery.

5. BP should clearly define expectations and strengthen accountability for process safety performance.

6. BP should better coordinate its process safety support for the refining line organization.

7. BP should develop an integrated set of leading and lagging performance indicators for effectively monitoring process safety performance.

8. BP should establish and implement an effective system to audit process safety performance.

9. The company's board should monitor the implementation of the panel's recommendations and the ongoing process safety performance of the refineries.

10. BP should transform into a recognized industry leader in process safety management.

In making its recommendations, the panel singled out the company's chief executive at the time, Lord Browne, by saying, "In hindsight, the panel believes if Browne had demonstrated comparable leadership on and commitment to process safety [as he did for responding to climate change] that would have resulted in a higher level of safety at refineries."

Overall, the Baker panel found that BP's top management had not provided "effective leadership" on safety. It found that the failings went to the very top of the organization, to the company's chief executive, and to several of his top lieutenants. The Baker panel emphasized the importance of top management commitment, saying, for instance that "it is imperative that BP leadership set the process safety tone at the top of the organization and establish appropriate expectations regarding process safety performance." It also said BP "has not provided effective leadership in making certain its management and U.S. refining workforce understand what is expected of them regarding process safety performance."

Lord Browne, the chief executive, stepped down about a year after the explosion. About the same time, some BP shareholders were calling for the company's executives and board directors to have their bonuses more closely tied to the company's safety and environmental performance in the wake of Texas City.

Questions

1. The textbook defines ethics as "the principles of conduct governing an individual or a group," and specifically as the standards one uses to decide what their conduct should be. To what extent do you believe that what happened at BP is as much a breakdown in the company's ethical systems as it is in its safety systems, and how would you defend your conclusion?

2. Are the Occupational Safety and Health Administration's standards, policies, and rules aimed at addressing problems like the ones that apparently existed at the Texas City plant? If so, how would you explain the fact that problems like these could have continued for so many years?

3. Since there were apparently at least three deaths in the year prior to the major explosion, and an average of about one employee death per 16 months for the previous 10 years, how would you account for the fact that mandatory OSHA inspections missed these glaring sources of potential catastrophic events?

4. The textbook lists numerous suggestions for "how to prevent accidents." Based on what you know about the Texas City explosion, what do you say Texas City tells you about the most important three steps an employer can take to prevent accidents?

5. Based on what you learned in this chapter, would you make any additional recommendations to BP over and above those recommendations made by the Baker panel and the CSB? If so, what would those recommendations be?

6. Explain specifically how strategic human resource management at BP seems to have supported the company's broader strategic aims. What does this say about the advisability of always linking human resource strategy to a company's strategic aims?

Source notes for BP Texas City: Sheila McNulty, "BP Knew of Safety Problems, Says Report," *the Financial Times*, October 31, 2006, p. 1; "CBS: Documents Show BP Was Aware of Texas City Safety Problems," *World Refining & Fuels Today*, October 30, 2006, p. n/a; "BP Safety Report Finds Company's Process Safety Culture Ineffective," *Global Refining & Fuels Report*, January 17, 2007, p. n/a; "BP Safety Record under Attack," *Europe Intelligence Wire*, January 17, 2007, p. n/a; Mark Hofmann, "BP Slammed for Poor Leadership on Safety, Oil Firm Agrees to Act on Review Panel's Recommendations," *Business Intelligence*, January 22, 2007, p. 3; "Call for Bonuses to Include Link with Safety Performance," *The Guardian*, January 18, 2007, p. 24.

1. These findings and the following suggestions based on "BP Safety Report Finds Company's Process Safety Culture Ineffective," *Global Refining & Fuels Report*, January 17, 2007, p. n/a.

GLOSSARY

action learning A training technique by which management trainees are allowed to work full-time analyzing and solving problems in other departments.

adaptability screening A process that aims to assess the assignee's (and spouse's) probable success in handling a foreign transfer.

adverse impact The overall impact of employer practices that result in significantly higher percentages of members of minorities and other protected groups being rejected for employment, placement, or promotion.

affirmative action Making an extra effort to hire and promote those in protected groups, particularly when those groups are under-represented.

Age Discrimination in Employment Act of 1967 (ADEA) The act prohibiting arbitrary age discrimination and specifically protecting individuals over 40 years old.

agency shop A form of union security in which employees who do not belong to the union must still pay union dues on the assumption that union efforts benefit all workers.

alternation ranking method Ranking employees from best to worst on a particular trait, choosing highest, then lowest, until all are ranked.

alternative dispute resolution or ADR program Grievance procedure that provides for binding arbitration as the last step.

alternative staffing The use of nontraditional recruitment sources.

Americans with Disabilities Act (ADA) The act requiring employers to make reasonable accommodations for disabled employees; it prohibits discrimination against disabled persons.

annual bonus Plans that are designed to motivate short-term performance of managers and are tied to company-profitability.

applicant tracking systems Online systems that help employers attract, gather, screen, compile, and manage applicants.

application form The form that provides information on education, prior work record, and skills.

appraisal interview An interview in which the supervisor and subordinate review the appraisal and make plans to remedy deficiencies and reinforce strengths.

apprenticeship training A structured process by which people become skilled workers through a combination of classroom instruction and on-the-job training.

arbitration The most definitive type of third-party intervention, in which the arbitrator usually has the power to determine and dictate the settlement terms.

at-risk variable pay plans Plans that put some portion of the employee's weekly pay at risk, subject to the firm's meeting its financial goals.

authority The right to make decisions, direct others' work, and give orders.

authorization cards In order to petition for a union election, the union must show that at least 30% of employees may be interested in being unionized. Employees indicate this interest by signing authorization cards.

bargaining unit The group of employees the union will be authorized to represent.

behavior modeling A training technique in which trainees are first shown good management techniques in a film, are asked to play roles in a simulated situation, and are then given feedback and praise by their supervisor.

behavior modification Using contingent rewards or punishment to change behavior.

behavioral interviews A series of job-related questions that focus on how the candidate reacted to actual situations in the past.

behaviorally anchored rating scale (BARS) An appraisal method that aims at combining the benefits of narrative critical incidents and quantified ratings by anchoring a quantified scale with specific narrative examples of good and poor performance.

behavior-based safety Identifying the worker behaviors that contribute to accidents and then training workers to avoid these behaviors.

benchmark job A job that is used to anchor the employer's pay scale and around which other jobs are arranged in order of relative worth.

benefits Indirect financial and non-financial payments employees receive for continuing their employment with the company.

bias The tendency to allow individual differences such as age, race, and sex to affect the appraisal ratings employees receive.

bona fide occupational qualification (BFOQ) Requirement that an employee be of a certain religion, sex, or national origin where that is reasonably necessary to the organization's normal operation. Specified by the 1964 Civil Rights Act.

boycott The combined refusal by employees and other interested parties to buy or use the employer's products.

broadbanding Consolidating salary grades and ranges into just a few wide levels or "bands," each of which contains a relatively wide range of jobs and salary levels.

bumping/layoff procedures Detailed procedures that determine who will be laid off if no work is available; generally allow employees to use their seniority to remain on the job.

burnout The total depletion of physical and mental resources caused by excessive striving to reach an unrealistic work-related goal.

candidate-order error An error of judgment on the part of the interviewer due to interviewing one or more very good or very bad candidates just before the interview in question.

career The occupational positions a person has had over many years.

career anchors Pivots around which a person's career swings; require self-awareness of talents and abilities, motives and needs, and attitudes and values.

career cycle The various stages a person's career goes through.

career development The lifelong series of activities that contribute to a person's career exploration, establishment, success, and fulfillment.

career management The process for enabling employees to better understand and develop their career skills and interests, and to use these skills and interests most effectively.

career planning The deliberate process through which someone becomes aware of personal skills, interests, knowledge, motivations, and other characteristics; and establishes action plans to attain specific goals.

career planning and development The deliberate process through which a person becomes aware of personal career-related attributes and the lifelong series of steps that contribute to his or her career fulfillment.

case management Treating injured workers on a case-by-case basis using an assigned case manager, who coordinates the employee's treatments.

case study method A development method in which the manager is presented with a written description of an organizational problem to diagnose and solve.

cash balance plans Defined benefit plans under which the employer contributes a percentage of employees' current pay to employees' pension plans every year, and employees earn interest on this amount.

central tendency A tendency to rate all employees the same way, such as rating them all average.

changed requirements of the job Employee's inability to do job after the employer changed the nature of the job.

citation Summons informing employers and employees of the regulations and standards that have been violated in the workplace.

Civil Rights Act of 1991 (CRA 1991) It places burden of proof back on employers and permits compensatory and punitive damages.

classes Grouping jobs based on a set of rules for each group or class, such as amount of independent judgment, skill, physical effort, and so forth, required. Classes usually contain similar jobs.

closed shop A form of union security in which the company can hire only union members. This was outlawed in 1947 but still exists in some industries (such as printing).

codetermination Employees have the legal right to a voice in setting company policies.

collective bargaining The process through which representatives of management and the union meet to negotiate a labor agreement.

college recruiting Sending an employer's representatives to college campuses to prescreen applicants and create an applicant pool from the graduating class.

comparable worth The concept by which women who are usually paid less than men can claim that men in comparable rather than in strictly equal jobs are paid more.

compensable factor A fundamental, compensable element of a job, such as skills, effort, responsibility, and working conditions.

competencies Demonstrable characteristics of a person, including knowledge, skills, and behaviors, that enable performance.

competency-based job analysis Describing a job in terms of the measurable, observable, behavioral competencies an employee must exhibit to do a job well.

competency-based pay Where the company pays for the employee's range, depth, and types of skills and knowledge, rather than for the job title he or she holds.

competitive advantage Any factors that allow an organization to differentiate its product or service from those of its competitors to increase market share.

compressed workweek Schedule in which employee works fewer but longer days each week.

computerized forecast Determination of future staff needs by projecting sales, volume of production, and personnel required to maintain this volume of output, using software packages.

content validity A test that is content valid is one that contains a fair sample of the tasks and skills actually needed for the job in question.

controlled experimentation Formal methods for testing the effectiveness of a training program, preferably with before-and-after tests and a control group.

corporate campaign An organized effort by the union that exerts pressure on the corporation by pressuring the company's other unions, shareholders, directors, customers, creditors, and government agencies, often directly.

criterion validity A type of validity based on showing that scores on the test (predictors) are related to job performance (criterion).

critical incident method Keeping a record of uncommonly good or undesirable examples of an employee's work-related behavior and reviewing it with the employee at predetermined times.

Davis-Bacon Act (1931) A law that sets wage rates for laborers employed by contractors working for the federal government.

decertification Legal process for employees to terminate a union's right to represent them.

decline stage Period where many people face having to accept reduced levels of power and responsibility, and must learn to develop new roles as mentors or confidantes for younger people.

deferred profit-sharing plan A plan in which a certain amount of profits is credited to each employee's account, payable at retirement, termination, or death.

defined benefit pension plan A plan that contains a formula for determining retirement benefits.

defined contribution pension plan A plan in which the employer's contribution to employees' retirement savings funds is specified.

dejobbing Broadening the responsibilities of the company's jobs, and encouraging employees not to limit themselves to what's on their job descriptions.

diary/log Daily listings made by workers of every activity in which they engage along with the time each activity takes.

direct financial payments Pay in the form of wages, salaries, incentives, commissions, and bonuses.

dismissal Involuntary termination of an employee's employment with the firm.

disparate rejection rates A test for adverse impact in which it can be demonstrated that there is a discrepancy between rates of rejection of members of a protected group and of others.

distributive justice The fairness and justice of a decision's result.

diversity The variety or multiplicity of demographic features that characterize a company's workforce, particularly in terms of race, sex, culture, national origin, handicap, age, and religion.

downsizing The process of reducing, usually dramatically, the number of people employed by a firm.

early retirement window A type of offering by which employees are encouraged to retire early, the incentive being liberal pension benefits plus perhaps a cash payment.

Economic Growth and Tax Relief Reconciliation Act (2001) (EGTRRA) An act that improves the attractiveness of retirement benefits like 401(k) plans by boosting individual employees' elective deferred limits to $15,000, effective in 2006.

economic strike A strike that results from a failure to agree on the terms of a contract that involve wages, benefits, and other conditions of employment.

Electronic Communications Privacy Act (ECPA) Intended in part to restrict interception and monitoring of oral and wire communications, but with two exceptions: employers who can show a legitimate business reason for doing so, and employers who have employees' consent to do so.

electronic performance monitoring (EPM) Having supervisors electronically monitor the amount of computerized data an employee is processing per day, and thereby his or her performance.

electronic performance support systems (EPSS) Sets of computerized tools and displays that automate training, documentation, and phone support, integrate this automation into applications, and provide support that's faster, cheaper, and more effective than traditional methods.

employee advocacy HR must take responsibility for clearly defining how management should be treating employees, make sure employees have the mechanisms required to contest unfair practices, and represent the interests of employees within the framework of its primary obligation to senior management.

employee assistance program (EAP) A formal employer program for providing employees with counseling and/or treatment programs for problems such as alcoholism, gambling, or stress.

employee compensation All forms of pay or rewards going to employees and arising from their employment.

employee orientation A procedure for providing new employees with basic background information about the firm.

employee recruiting Finding and/or attracting applicants for the employer's open positions.

Employee Retirement Income Security Act (ERISA) Signed into law by President Ford in 1974 to require that pension rights be vested and protected by a government agency, the PBGC.

employee stock ownership plan (ESOP) A qualified, tax-deductible stock bonus plan in which employers contribute stock to a trust for eventual use by employees.

employment or personnel planning The process of deciding what positions the firm will have to fill, and how to fill them.

Equal Employment Opportunity Commission (EEOC) The commission, created by Title VII, is empowered to investigate job discrimination complaints and sue on behalf of complainants.

Equal Pay Act of 1963 The act requiring equal pay for equal work, regardless of sex.

establishment stage Spans roughly ages 24 to 44 and is the heart of most people's work lives.

ethics The principles of conduct governing an individual or a group; specifically, the standards you use to decide what your conduct should be.

ethics code Memorializes the standards to which the employer expects its employees to adhere.

ethnocentric The notion that home-country attitudes, management style, knowledge, evaluation criteria, and managers are superior to anything the host country has to offer.

executive coach An outside consultant who questions the executive's boss, peers, subordinates, and (sometimes) family in order to identify the executive's strengths and weaknesses, and to counsel the executive so he or she can capitalize on those strengths and overcome the weaknesses.

exit interviews Interviews with employees who are leaving the firm, conducted for the purpose of obtaining information about the job or related matters, to give the employer insight about the company.

expatriates (expats) Noncitizens of the countries in which they are working.

expectancy A person's expectation that his or her effort will lead to performance.

expectancy chart A graph showing the relationship between test scores and job performance for a group of people.

exploration stage The period (roughly from ages 15 to 24) during which a person seriously explores various occupational alternatives.

fact finder A neutral party who studies the issues in a dispute and makes a public recommendation for a reasonable settlement.

factor comparison method A widely used method of ranking jobs according to a variety of skill and difficulty factors, then adding up these rankings to arrive at an overall numerical rating for each given job.

fair day's work Standards of output which employers should devise for each job based on careful, scientific analysis.

Fair Labor Standards Act (1938) This act provides for minimum wages, maximum hours, overtime pay, and child labor protection. The law has been amended many times and covers most employees.

family-friendly benefits Benefits such as child care and fitness facilities that make it easier for employees to balance their work and family responsibilities.

Federal Violence Against Women Act of 1994 Provides that a person who commits a crime of violence motivated by gender shall be liable to the party injured.

financial incentives Financial rewards paid to workers whose production exceeds some predetermined standard.

flexible benefits plan/cafeteria benefits plan Individualized plans allowed by employers to accommodate employee preferences for benefits.

flextime A plan whereby employees' workdays are built around a core of mid-day hours, such as 11:00 A.M. to 2:00 P.M.

forced distribution method Similar to grading on a curve; predetermined percentages of ratees are placed in various performance categories.

foreign service premiums Financial payments over and above regular base pay, typically ranging between 10% and 30% of base pay.

4/5ths rule Federal agency rule that minority selection rate less than 80% (4/5ths) that of group with highest rate evidences adverse impact.

401(k) plan A defined contribution plan based on section 401(k) of the Internal Revenue Code.

functional authority (or functional control) The authority exerted by an HR manager as coordinator of personnel activities.

functional job analysis A method for classifying jobs similar to the DOL method, but additionally taking into account the extent to which instructions, reasoning, judgment, and mathematical and verbal ability are necessary for performing job tasks.

gainsharing plan An incentive plan that engages employees in a common effort to achieve productivity objectives and share the gains.

geocentric The belief that the firm's whole management staff must be scoured on a global basis, on the assumption that the best manager of a specific position anywhere may be in any of the countries in which the firm operates.

globalization The tendency of firms to extend their sales, ownership, and/or manufacturing to new markets abroad.

golden parachutes Payments companies make in connection with a change in ownership or control of a company.

good faith bargaining Both parties are making every reasonable effort to arrive at agreement; proposals are being matched with counterproposals.

good faith effort strategy Employment strategy aimed at changing practices that have contributed in the past to excluding or underutilizing protected groups.

grade definition Written descriptions of the level of, say, responsibility and knowledge required by jobs in each grade. Similar jobs can then be combined into grades or classes.

grades A job classification system like the class system, although grades often contain dissimilar jobs, such as secretaries, mechanics, and firefighters. Grade descriptions are written based on compensable factors listed in classification systems.

graphic rating scale A scale that lists a number of traits and a range of performance for each. The employee is then rated by identifying the score that best describes his or her level of performance for each trait.

grievance Any factor involving wages, hours, or conditions of employment that is used as a complaint against the employer.

group life insurance Provides lower rates for the employer or employee and includes all employees, including new employees, regardless of health or physical condition.

growth stage The period from birth to age 14 during which a person develops a self-concept by identifying with and interacting with other people.

halo effect In performance appraisal, the problem that occurs when a supervisor's rating of a subordinate on one trait biases the rating of that person on other traits.

hardship allowances Compensate expatriates for exceptionally hard living and working conditions at certain locations.

health maintenance organization (HMO) A prepaid health care system that generally provides routine round-the-clock medical services as well as preventive medicine in a clinic-type arrangement for employees, who pay a nominal fee in addition to the fixed annual fee the employer pays.

high-performance work system An integrated set of human resources policies and practices that together produce superior employee performance.

home-country nationals Citizens of the country in which the multinational company has its headquarters.

HR Scorecard Measures the HR function's effectiveness and efficiency in producing employee behaviors needed to achieve the company's strategic goals.

human capital The knowledge, education, training, skills, and expertise of a firm's workers.

human resource management (HRM) The policies and practices involved in carrying out the "people" or human resource aspects of a management position, including recruiting, screening, training, rewarding, and appraising.

illegal bargaining items Items in collective bargaining that are forbidden by law; for example, a clause agreeing to hire "union members exclusively" would be illegal in a right-to-work state.

impasse Collective bargaining situation that occurs when the parties are not able to move further toward settlement, usually because one party is demanding more than the other will offer.

implied authority The authority exerted by an HR manager by virtue of others' knowledge that he or she has access to top management (in areas like testing and affirmative action).

indirect financial payments Pay in the form of financial benefits such as insurance.

indirect payments Pay in the form of financial benefits such as insurance.

in-house development center A company-based method for exposing prospective managers to realistic exercises to develop improved management skills.

injunction A court order compelling a party or parties either to resume or to desist from a certain action.

inside games Union efforts to convince employees to impede or to disrupt production—for example, by slowing the work pace.

instrumentality The perceived relationships between successful performance and obtaining the reward.

insubordination Willful disregard or disobedience of the boss's authority or legitimate orders; criticizing the boss in public.

interactional (interpersonal) justice The manner in which managers conduct their interpersonal dealings with employees.

interest inventory A personal development and selection device that compares the person's current interests with those of others now in various occupations so as to determine the preferred occupation for the individual.

job aid Is a set of instructions, diagrams, or similar methods available at the job site to guide the worker.

job analysis The procedure for determining the duties and skill requirements of a job and the kind of person who should be hired for it.

job classification (or grading) method A method for categorizing jobs into groups.

job description A list of a job's duties, responsibilities, reporting relationships, working conditions, and supervisory responsibilities—one product of a job analysis.

job enlargement Assigning workers additional same-level activities, thus increasing the number of activities they perform.

job enrichment Redesigning jobs in a way that increases the opportunities for the worker to experience feelings of responsibility, achievement, growth, and recognition.

job evaluation A systematic comparison done in order to determine the worth of one job relative to another.

job instruction training (JIT) Listing each job's basic tasks, along with key points, in order to provide step-by-step training for employees.

job posting Publicizing an open job to employees (often by literally posting it on bulletin boards) and listing its attributes, like qualifications, supervisor, working schedule, and pay rate.

job rotation Systematically moving workers from one job to another to enhance work team performance and/or to broaden his or her experience and identify strong and weak points to prepare the person for an enhanced role with the company.

job sharing Allows two or more people to share a single full-time job.

job specifications A list of a job's "human requirements," that is, the requisite education, skills, personality, and so on—another product of a job analysis.

job-related interview A series of job-related questions that focus on relevant past job-related behaviors.

lack of qualifications Employee's inability to do the assigned work although he or she is diligent.

Landrum-Griffin Act (1959) The law aimed at protecting union members from possible wrongdoing on the part of their unions.

law of individual differences The fact that people differ in personality, abilities, values, and needs.

leveraging Supplementing what you have and doing more with what you have.

line authority The authority exerted by an HR manager by directing the activities of the people in his or her own department and in service areas (like the plant cafeteria).

line manager A manager who is authorized to direct the work of subordinates and is responsible for accomplishing the organization's tasks.

lockout A refusal by the employer to provide opportunities to work.

maintenance stage Period between ages 45 and 65 when many people slide from the stabilization substage into an established position and focus on maintaining that place.

management assessment center A simulation in which management candidates are asked to perform realistic tasks in hypothetical situations and are scored on their performance. It usually also involves testing and the use of management games.

management by objectives (MBO) Involves setting specific measurable goals with each employee and then periodically reviewing the progress made.

management development Any attempt to improve current or future management performance by imparting knowledge, changing attitudes, or increasing skills.

management game A development technique in which teams of managers compete by making computerized decisions regarding realistic but simulated situations.

management process The five basic functions of planning, organizing, staffing, leading, and controlling.

managing diversity Maximizing diversity's potential benefits while minimizing the potential barriers that can undermine the company's performance.

mandatory bargaining items Items in collective bargaining that a party must bargain over if they are introduced by the other party—for example, pay.

mass interview A panel interviews several candidates simultaneously.

material safety data sheets (MSDS) Sheets that describe the precautions required by OSHA that employees are to take when dealing with hazardous chemicals, and what to do if problems arise.

mechanical security The utilization of security systems such as locks, intrusion alarms, access control systems, and surveillance systems.

mediation Intervention in which a neutral third party tries to assist the principals in reaching agreement.

mentoring Formal or informal programs in which mid- and senior-level managers help less experienced employees—for instance, by giving them career advice and helping them navigate political pitfalls.

merit pay (merit raise) Any salary increase awarded to an employee based on his or her individual performance.

metrics A set of quantitative performance measures HR managers use to assess their operations.

midcareer crisis substage Period during which people often make major reassessments of their progress relative to original ambitions and goals.

miniature job training and evaluation Training candidates to perform several of the job's tasks, and then evaluating the candidates' performance prior to hire.

misconduct Deliberate and willful violation of the employer's rules.

mission Spells out who the company is, what it does, and where it's headed.

mixed motive case A discrimination allegation case in which the employer argues that the employment action taken was motivated, not by discrimination, but by some non-discriminatory reason such as ineffective performance.

mobility premiums Typically, lump-sum payments to reward employees for moving from one assignment to another.

national emergency strikes Strikes that might "imperil the national health and safety."

National Labor Relations (or Wagner) Act This law banned certain types of unfair practices and provided for secret-ballot elections and majority rule for determining whether or not a firm's employees want to unionize.

National Labor Relations Board (NLRB) The agency created by the Wagner Act to investigate unfair labor practice charges and to provide for secret-ballot elections and majority rule in determining whether or not a firm's employees want a union.

natural security Taking advantage of the facility's natural or architectural features in order to minimize security problems.

negligent hiring Hiring workers with questionable backgrounds without proper safeguards.

negligent training A situation where an employer fails to train adequately, and the employee subsequently harms a third party.

nonpunitive discipline Discipline without punishment, usually involving a system of oral warnings and paid "decision-making leaves" in lieu of more traditional punishment.

Norris-LaGuardia Act (1932) This law marked the beginning of the era of strong encouragement of unions and guaranteed to each employee the right to bargain collectively "free from interference, restraint, or coercion."

occupational illness Any abnormal condition or disorder caused by exposure to environmental factors associated with employment.

Occupational Safety and Health Act The law passed by Congress in 1970 "to assure so far as possible every working man and woman in the nation safe and healthful working conditions and to preserve our human resources."

Occupational Safety and Health Administration (OSHA) The agency created within the Department of Labor to set safety and health standards for almost all workers in the United States.

Office of Federal Contract Compliance Programs (OFCCP) This office is responsible for implementing the executive orders and ensuring compliance of federal contractors.

offshoring Having local employees abroad do jobs that the firm's domestic employees previously did in-house.

on demand recruiting services (ODRS) A service that provides short-term specialized recruiting to support specific projects without the expense of retaining traditional search firms.

one-on-one interview Two people meet alone and one interviews the other by seeking oral responses to oral inquiries.

on-the-job training Training a person to learn a job while working on it.

open shop Perhaps the least attractive type of union security from the union's point of view, the workers decide whether or not to join the union; and those who join must pay dues.

organization chart A chart that shows the organizationwide distribution of work, with titles of each position and interconnecting lines that show who reports to and communicates to whom.

organizational culture The characteristic values, traditions, and behaviors a company's employees share.

organizational development A special approach to organizational change in which employees themselves formulate and implement the change that's required.

organizational security Using good management to improve security.

organizationwide incentive plans Plans in which all or most employees can participate, and which generally tie the reward to some measure of companywide performance.

outplacement counseling A systematic process by which a terminated person is trained and counseled in the techniques of self-appraisal and securing a new position.

outsourced learning The outsourcing of companies' learning functions to major consulting firms.

outsourcing Letting outside vendors provide services.

paired comparison method Ranking employees by making a chart of all possible pairs of the employees for each trait and indicating which is the better employee of the pair.

panel interview An interview in which a group of interviewers questions the applicant.

pay grade A pay grade is comprised of jobs of approximately equal difficulty.

pay ranges A series of steps or levels within a pay grade, usually based upon years of service.

Pension Benefits Guarantee Corporation (PBGC) Established under ERISA to ensure that pensions meet vesting obligations; also insures pensions should a plan terminate without sufficient funds to meet its vested obligations.

pension plans Plans that provide a fixed sum when employees reach a predetermined retirement age or when they can no longer work due to disability.

performance analysis Verifying that there is a performance deficiency and determining whether that deficiency should be corrected through training or through some other means (such as transferring the employee).

performance appraisal Evaluating an employee's current and/or past performance relative to his or her performance standards.

performance management Taking an integrated, goal-oriented approach to assigning, training, assessing, and rewarding employees' performance.

personnel replacement charts Company records showing present performance and promotability of inside candidates for the most important positions.

picketing Having employees carry signs announcing their concerns near the employer's place of business.

piecework A system of pay based on the number of items processed by each individual worker in a unit of time, such as items per hour or items per day.

point method The job evaluation method in which a number of compensable factors are identified and then the degree to which each of these factors is present on the job is determined.

polycentric A conscious belief that only the host-country managers can ever really understand the culture and behavior of the host-country market.

portability Making it easier for employees who leave the firm prior to retirement to take their accumulated pension funds with them.

position analysis questionnaire (PAQ) A questionnaire used to collect quantifiable data concerning the duties and responsibilities of various jobs.

position replacement card A card prepared for each position in a company to show possible replacement candidates and their qualifications.

preferred provider organizations (PPOs) Groups of health care providers that contract with employers, insurance companies, or third-party payers to provide medical care services at a reduced fee.

Pregnancy Discrimination Act (PDA) An amendment to Title VII of the Civil Rights Act that prohibits sex discrimination based on "pregnancy, childbirth, or related medical conditions."

preretirement counseling Counseling provided to employees who are about to retire, which covers matters such as benefits advice, second careers, and so on.

procedural justice The fairness of the process.

process chart A work flow chart that shows the flow of inputs to and outputs from a particular job.

profit-sharing plan A plan whereby employees share in the company's profits.

programmed learning A systematic method for teaching job skills involving presenting questions or facts, allowing the person to respond, and giving the learner immediate feedback on the accuracy of his or her answers.

promotions Advancements to positions of increased responsibility.

protected class Persons such as minorities and women protected by equal opportunity laws, including Title VII.

qualifications inventories Manual or computerized records listing employees' education, career and development interests, languages, special skills, and so on, to be used in selecting inside candidates for promotion.

qualified individuals Under ADA, those who can carry out the essential functions of the job.

ranking method The simplest method of job evaluation that involves ranking each job relative to all other jobs, usually based on overall difficulty.

ratio analysis A forecasting technique for determining future staff needs by using ratios between, for example, sales volume and number of employees needed.

reality shock Results of a period that may occur at the initial career entry when the new employee's high job expectations confront the reality of a boring, unchallenging job.

recruiting yield pyramid The historical arithmetic relationships between recruitment leads and invitees, invitees and interviews, interviews and offers made, and offers made and offers accepted.

reengineering The fundamental rethinking and radical redesign of business processes to achieve dramatic improvements in critical, contemporary measures of performance, such as cost, quality, service, and speed.

reliability The consistency of scores obtained by the same person when retested with the identical tests or with alternate forms of the same test.

restricted policy Another test for adverse impact, involving demonstration that an employer's hiring practices exclude a protected group, whether intentionally or not.

retirement The point at which one gives up one's work, usually between the ages of 60 and 65.

reverse discrimination Claim that due to affirmative action quota systems, white males are discriminated against.

right to work A term used to describe state statutory or constitutional provisions banning the requirement of union membership as a condition of employment.

role playing A training technique in which trainees act out parts in a realistic management situation.

salary compression A salary inequity problem, generally caused by inflation, resulting in longer-term employees in a position earning less than workers entering the firm today.

salary survey A survey aimed at determining prevailing wage rates. A good salary survey provides specific wage rates for specific jobs. Formal written questionnaire surveys are the most comprehensive, but telephone surveys and newspaper ads are also sources of information.

savings and thrift plan Plan in which employees contribute a portion of their earnings to a fund; the employer usually matches this contribution in whole or in part.

Scanlon plan An incentive plan developed in 1937 by Joseph Scanlon and designed to encourage cooperation, involvement, and sharing of benefits.

scatter plot A graphical method used to help identify the relationship between two variables.

scientific management movement Management approach that emphasizes improving work methods through observation and analysis.

scientific management Management approach based on improving work methods through observation and analysis.

sequential (or serial) interview Several persons interview the applicant, in sequence, one-on-one, before a decision is made.

severance pay A one-time payment some employers provide when terminating an employee.

sexual harassment Harassment on the basis of sex that has the purpose or effect of substantially interfering with a person's work performance or creating an intimidating, hostile, or offensive work environment.

sick leave Provides pay to an employee when he or she is out of work because of illness.

simulated training Training employees on special off-the-job equipment, as in airplane pilot training, so training costs and hazards can be reduced.

situational interview A series of job-related questions that focus on how the candidate would behave in a given situation.

situational tests Examinees respond to situations representative of the job.

Social Security Federal program that provides three types of benefits: retirement income at the age of 62 and thereafter; survivor's or death benefits payable to the employee's dependents regardless of age at time of death; and disability benefits payable to disabled employees and their dependents. These benefits are payable only if the employee is insured under the Social Security Act.

stabilization substage Firm occupational goals are set and the person does more explicit career planning.

staff authority Gives the manager the right (authority) to advise other managers or employees.

staff manager A manager who assists and advises line managers.

standard hour plan A plan by which a worker is paid a basic hourly rate but is paid an extra percentage of his or her rate for production exceeding the standard per hour or per day. Similar to piecework payment but based on a percent premium.

Standard Occupational Classification (SOC) Classifies all workers into one of 23 major groups of jobs which are subdivided into minor groups of jobs and detailed occupations.

stock option The right to purchase a stated number of shares of a company stock at today's price at some time in the future.

straight piecework An incentive plan in which a person is paid a sum for each item he or she makes or sells, with a strict proportionality between results and rewards.

strategic control The process of assessing progress toward strategic goals and taking corrective action as needed.

strategic human resource management Formulating and executing human resource policies and practices that produce the employee competencies and behaviors the company needs to achieve its strategic aims.

strategic management The process of identifying and executing the organization's mission by matching its capabilities with the demands of its environment.

strategic plan The company's plan for how it will match its internal strengths and weaknesses with external opportunities and threats in order to maintain a competitive advantage.

strategic planning Manager formulates specific strategies to take the company from where it is now to where he or she wants it to be.

strategy The company's long-term plan for how it will balance its internal strengths and weaknesses with its external opportunities and threats to maintain a competitive advantage.

strategy map Diagram that summarizes the chain of major activities that contribute to a company's success.

stress interview Interviewer seeks to make the applicant uncomfortable with occasionally rude questions.

strictness/leniency The problem that occurs when a supervisor has a tendency to rate all subordinates either high or low.

strike A withdrawal of labor.

structured or directive interview An interview following a set sequence of questions.

structured sequential interview An interview in which the applicant is interviewed sequentially by several persons; each rates the applicant on a standard form.

structured situational interview A series of job-oriented questions with predetermined answers that interviewers ask of all applicants for the job.

succession planning The ongoing process of systematically identifying, assessing, and developing organizational leadership to enhance performance.

supplemental pay benefits Benefits for time not worked such as unemployment insurance, vacation and holiday pay, and sick pay.

supplemental unemployment benefits Provide for a "guaranteed annual income" in certain industries where employers must shut down to change machinery or due to reduced work. These benefits are paid by the company and supplement unemployment benefits.

SWOT analysis The use of a SWOT chart to compile and organize the process of identifying company **S**trengths, **W**eaknesses, **O**pportunities, and **T**hreats.

sympathy strike A strike that takes place when one union strikes in support of the strike of another.

Taft-Hartley Act (1947) Also known as the Labor Management Relations Act, this law prohibited unfair union labor practices and enumerated the rights of employees as union members. It also enumerated the rights of employers.

task analysis A detailed study of a job to identify the specific skills required.

team or group incentive plan A plan in which a production standard is set for a specific work group, and its members are paid incentives if the group exceeds the production standard.

telecommuting Where employees work at home, usually with computers, and use phones and the Internet to transmit letters, data, and completed work to the home office.

termination at will Without a contract, either the employer or the employee could *terminate at will* the employment relationship.

termination interview The interview in which an employee is informed of the fact that he or she has been dismissed.

test validity The accuracy with which a test, interview, and so on measures what it purports to measure or fulfills the function it was designed to fill.

third-country nationals Citizens of a country other than the parent or the host country.

Title VII of the 1964 Civil Rights Act The section of the act that says an employer cannot discriminate on the basis of race, color, religion, sex, or national origin with respect to employment.

training The process of teaching new employees the basic skills they need to perform their jobs.

transfers Reassignments to similar positions in other parts of the firm.

trend analysis Study of a firm's past employment needs over a period of years to predict future needs.

trial substage Period that lasts from about ages 25 to 30 during which the person determines whether or not the chosen field is suitable; if not, changes may be attempted.

U.S. Department of Labor (DOL) job analysis procedure A standardized method by which different jobs can be quantitatively rated, classified, and compared based on data, people, and things scored.

unclear standards An appraisal that is too open to interpretation.

unemployment insurance Provides benefits if a person is unable to work through some fault other than his or her own.

unfair labor practice strike A strike aimed at protesting illegal conduct by the employer.

uniform guidelines Guidelines issued by federal agencies charged with ensuring compliance with equal employment federal legislation explaining recommended employer procedures in detail.

union salting A union organizing tactic by which workers who are in fact employed full-time by a union as undercover organizers are hired by unwitting employers.

union shop A form of union security in which the company can hire nonunion people, but they must join the union after a prescribed period of time and pay dues. (If they do not, they can be fired.)

unsafe conditions The mechanical and physical conditions that cause accidents.

unsatisfactory performance Persistent failure to perform assigned duties or to meet prescribed standards on the job.

unstructured or nondirective interview An unstructured conversational-style interview in which the interviewer pursues points of interest as they come up in response to questions.

unstructured sequential interview An interview in which each interviewer forms an independent opinion after asking different questions.

valence The perceived value a person attaches to the reward.

value chain Identifies the primary activities that create value for customers and the related support activities.

value chain analysis Identifying the primary activities that create value for customers and the related support activities.

variable pay Any plan that ties pay to productivity or profitability, usually as one-time lump payments.

vested funds Money placed in a pension fund that cannot be forfeited for any reason.

video-based simulation A situational test in which examinees respond to video simulations of realistic job situations.

virtual classroom Special collaboration software used to enable multiple remote learners, using their PCs or laptops, to participate in live audio and visual discussions, communicate via written text, and learn via content such as PowerPoint slides.

vision A general statement of its intended direction that evokes emotional feelings in organization members.

Vocational Rehabilitation Act of 1973 The act requiring certain federal contractors to take affirmative action for disabled persons.

voluntary bargaining items Items in collective bargaining over which collective bargaining is neither illegal nor mandatory—neither party can be compelled against its wishes to negotiate over those items.

wage curve Shows the relationship between the value of the job and the average wage paid for this job.

Walsh-Healey Public Contract Act (1936) A law that requires minimum wage and working conditions for employees working on any government contract amounting to more than $10,000.

wildcat strike An unauthorized strike occurring during the term of a contract.

work samples Actual job tasks used in testing applicants' performance.

work sampling technique A testing method based on measuring performance on actual basic job tasks.

work sharing Refers to a temporary reduction in work hours by a group of employees during economic downturns as a way to prevent layoffs.

workers' compensation Provides income and medical benefits to work-related accident victims or their dependents regardless of fault.

wrongful discharge An employee dismissal that does not comply with the law or does not comply with the contractual arrangement stated or implied by the firm via its employment application forms, employee manuals, or other promises.

PHOTO CREDITS

NAME AND ORGANIZATION INDEX

London, Manuel, 375*n*44

London Business School, 709

London House, Inc., 236

Longo Toyota, 62, 85, 86

Lopez, Tara Burnthorne, 505*n*43

Losey, Michael, 27*n*2

Lowe, Kevin, 720*n*24

Lowe, Linda, 161

Lowry, Phillip, 283*n*73

Lucas, James M., 101*n*4

Lucky Stores, 585

Lundell, Michael, 163*n*5

Luo, Sonjun, 505*n*41

Luthans, Fred, 505*n*28, 508*n*95

Lutz, Terry, 12, 294

Lyeness, Karen, 375*n*40

Lyndaker, Marie, 251*n*102

Lyness, Karen, 401*n*35

M

Mabey, Christopher, 376*n*63

Macaler, Bill, 122*n*2, 205*n*2, 205*n*4

Macan, Therese, 283*n*82

MacDonald, J. Randal, 95, 102*n*31

MacDonald, Scott, 251*n*102, 251*n*106, 251*n*108, 548*n*77

Madigan, John, 379

Mael, Fred, 208*n*117

Magliochetti, Joseph, 444

Maher, Kris, 634*n*11, 634*n*25, 636*n*74

Mahoney, Douglas, 208*n*115

Maier, Ayesha, 332*n*79

Maier, Norman R. F., 313, 332*n*79

Mann, Everett, 74*n*99

Mann, Phil, 161

Manolopoulos, Dimitris, 459*n*54

Manus, Bert, 80, 101*n*4

Mariani, Matthew, 164*n*18, 164*n*25

Marion, Craig, 331*n*47

Markham, Steven, 507*n*66

Markoff, John, 205*n*8

Markowich, M. Michael, 546*n*16

Marks, Susan, 459*n*45, 508*n*100

Marlowe, Cynthia, 282*n*52

Marquardt, Michael, 332*n*75

Marquez, Jessica, 205*n*21, 458*n*17

Marriott International, 384, 391

Martin, Christopher, 281*n*28

Martin, David, 375*n*53

Martineau, Jennifer, 330*n*34

Martinez, Michelle, 205*n*19, 207*n*74, 207*n*82

Martinko, Mark, 691*n*135

Martocchio, Joseph, 460*n*61, 545*n*9, 711

Massachusetts Institute of Technology (MIT), 408

Masterson, Suzanne, 592*n*46

Materna, Jessica, 636*n*63

Matthews, Mike, 330*n*39

Matusewitch, Eric, 73*n*80

Mauborgne, Rene, 592*n*43, 592*n*54

Maurer, Steven, 283*n*73

Maurer, Todd, 283*n*73

Mayer, Mary, 250*n*72

Mayerhofer, Helene, 723*n*41

Mayfield, Jacqueline, 71*n*6

Mayfield, Milton, 71*n*6

Maynard, Chris, 284*n*93

Maynard, Micheline, 636*n*60

Mayo Clinic, 292

McCarthy, Julie, 283*n*85

McCormick, Ernest J., 164*n*26

McCullough, Winston, 75*n*121

McCunney, R. J., 251*n*107

McDaniel, Ann, 75*n*116

McDaniel, Kim, 689*n*75

McDaniel, Michael A., 252*n*114, 280*n*2, 280*n*7, 280*n*12, 281*n*33, 281*n*35

McDonald, James Jr., 72*n*29

McDonalds, 315, 695

McFarland, Linda, 282*n*47

McFarland, Lynn, 249*n*60

McGann, Anthony, 374*n*24

McGovern, T. V., 282*n*43

McGregor, Jena, 373*n*19

McIntire, Lauren, 164*n*14

McIntyre, Nina, 505*n*37

MCI-WorldCom, 20

McKay, Jim, 207*n*68

McKay, Patrick, 205*n*13

McKinsey Global Institute, 703

McLarney, William, 330*n*32

McNabb, Robert, 102*n*26, 460*n*62

Meade, Jim, 123*n*29, 401*n*25, 548*n*74, 726*n*106

Medland, F. F., 375*n*50

Medland, Mary, 723*n*45

Meisler, Andy, 636*n*76, 636*n*81

Meltzer, Mark, 459*n*43, 507*n*71, 507*n*74, 507*n*75, 508*n*83

Melymuka, Kathleen, 402*n*39

Mendelsohn, Susan, 247*n*22, 248*n*23

Mendenhall, Mark, 725*n*81

Men's Warehouse, 300

Mercedes-Benz, 8, 83, 125

Mercer Human Resource Consulting, 472

Merck, 119

Meredith, Robyn, 207*n*68

Merrill Lynch, 625

Meyer, Gary, 374*n*30

Miami Herald, 433

Miceli, Michael, 282*n*58

Michalak, Donald, 330*n*36

Michaluk, Dan, 331*n*52

Michigan State University, 308

Microsoft, 170, 186, 259, 478, 493

Microsoft Windows, 658

Middendorf, Catherine, 283*n*82

Middlemist, Dennis, 548*n*88

Midvale Steel Company, 472

Miklas, Donald, 330*n*32

Miklaue, Matthew, 73*n*80

Milkovich, George, 546*n*37

Miller, Jospeh, 330*n*37

Miller, Marc, 122*n*16

Miller, Rockley, 331*n*45

Milliman, John, 722*n*20

Mills, Amy, 249*n*60

Mink, Mary, 123*n*22

Minnesota Department of Natural Resources, 479

Minorities Job Bank, 64

Mirabile, Richard, 164*n*35

Mitchell, Kristin, 164*n*23

Moberg, Dennis, 590*n*1

Moen, Phyllis, 400*n*1

Mohr, Erica, 331*n*46

Mohrman, Susan, 332*n*90

Mollica, Kelly, 592*n*53

Moncarz, Roger, 28*n*11, 28*n*15

Mone, Edward, 375*n*44

Monies, Paul, 634*n*8

Monthly Labor Review, 172

Montier, Richard, 330*n*29

Moore, Brian, 507*n*65

Moore, Celia, 73*n*56

Moore, Linda, 208*n*110, 208*n*113

Moore, Sarah, 594*n*96

Moran, John, 73*n*59, 73*n*62

Morath, Ray, 208*n*117

Moravec, Milan, 164*n*37

Moretz, Sandy, 686*n*7

Morfopoulos, Richard, 164*n*23

Morgan, Hal, 28*n*21

Morgeson, Frederick P., 163*n*6, 164*n*15, 164*n*30, 280*n*5, 280*n*9, 282*n*49, 282*n*51, 283*n*68

Morris, David, 401*n*29

Morris, Sara, 591*n*15

Morrisey, George, 101*n*5

Morrison, Clenn, 664

Morrison, Katheryn, 247*n*22, 248*n*23

Morrow, Charlie, 333*n*104

Mosakowski, Elayne, 721*n*3

Moskowitz, Rachel, 72*n*44

Motorola, 699

Motowidlio, Stephen, 282*n*44

moving.com, 433

SUBJECT INDEX